Card Cross and Jones

Criminal Law

Twelfth edition

Richard Card, LL.B., LL.M.
Professor of Law and Head of the School of Law at
Leicester Polytechnic

Butterworths
London, Dublin, Edinburgh
1992

United Kingdom	Butterworth & Co (Publishers) Ltd, 88 Kingsway, LONDON WC2B 6AB and 4 Hill Street, EDINBURGH EH2 3JZ
Australia	Butterworths Pty Ltd, SYDNEY, MELBOURNE, BRISBANE, ADELAIDE, PERTH, CANBERRA and HOBART
Canada	Butterworths Canada Ltd, TORONTO, VANCOUVER
Ireland	Butterworth (Ireland) Ltd, DUBLIN
Malaysia	Malayan Law Journal Sdn Bdh, KUALA LUMPUR
New Zealand	Butterworths of New Zealand Ltd, WELLINGTON and AUCKLAND
Puerto Rico	Equity de Puerto Rico, Inc, HATO REY
Singapore	Malayan Law Journal Pte Ltd, SINGAPORE
USA	Butterworth Legal Publishers, AUSTIN, Texas; BOSTON, Masssachusetts; CLEARWATER, Floridas (D & S Publishers); ORFORD, New Hampshire (Equity Publishing); ST PAUL, Minnesota; and SEATTLE, Washington

A CIP Catalogue record for this book is available from the British Library.

ISBN 0 406 00086 7

Printed by Billing & Sons Ltd, Worcester

Preface

As in the past, this continues to be essentially a first book on criminal law. I have had in mind the syllabuses for degree courses, for Common Professional Examination courses and for other courses for professional examinations. Most of the work is devoted to the substantive criminal law of England and Wales, but Chapters 1 to 5 provide an outline of the legal system and court procedure to the extent required to understand the substantive law. Readers of this book who are ignorant of the legal system and of criminal procedure should read these chapters before embarking on the others; readers who are cognisant with these matters may safely skip the first five chapters, with the exception of Chapter 3 (most of which may be new to them). Changes in the substantive law resulting from judicial decisions and from legislation have meant that this edition is substantially longer than its predecessor. The greatest expansion has been in the chapters on capacity, offences against property, road traffic offences, inchoate offences, general defences and participation in crime.

Since the publication of the last edition in 1988, Parliament has been particularly active in the sphere of the criminal law. Mention may be made, in particular, of the Criminal Justice Acts 1988 and 1991, the Road Traffic Acts 1988 and 1991, the Road Traffic Offenders Act 1988, the Firearms (Amendment) Act 1988, the Computer Misuse Act 1990 and the Criminal Procedure (Insanity and Unfitness to Plead) Act 1991. These and other pieces of statute law are referred to at the relevant points in this book. At the time of writing the provisions in the Road Traffic Act 1991 and the Criminal Justice Act 1991 described in this book have not been brought into force. However, it is understood that they will be brought into force in the Summer or early Autumn of 1992 and this book is written on the assumption that they are in force.

I wish to thank all those who have assisted me in various ways. In particular, I would like to thank my wife for the many hours which she spent in assisting in the preparation of the manuscript and in reading the proofs, and the publishers for compiling the tables of cases and statutes and the index.

I have tried to summarise and explain the law as it was on 1 October 1991, although I have been able to insert in proof some changes up to 1 March 1992.

Richard Card   1 March 1992

Contents

Preface   v
Table of Statutes   xi
List of Cases   xxi

Chapter 1   The characteristics of criminal offences   1
   Definition   1
   The initiative of the State   3

Chapter 2   Courts of criminal jurisdiction   5
   Magistrates' courts   5
   The Crown Court   6
   Appellate courts   7

Chapter 3   The sources and classifications of the criminal law   9
   Sources   9
   Common law   9
   Legislation   15
   Codification   17
   Social morality and the proper scope of the criminal law   17
   The classification of offences   20

Chapter 4   Elements of criminal procedure: before trial   22
   Prosecutions   22
   Jurisdiction   24
   Institution of proceedings   25
   Committal proceedings   28

Chapter 5   Elements of criminal procedure: trial and appeal   34
   Trial on indictment   34
   Summary trial (other than young offenders)   39
   The trial of young offenders   41
   Appeal   42

Chapter 6   Criminal liability   48
   Actus reus and mens rea   48
   Actus reus   50
   Mens rea   57
   Jurisdiction   86

Chapter 7   Proof   89
   The two burdens   89
   Presumptions   94

Proof of a state of mind 95
The negation of mens rea 96
Mistake 97
Mistake negativing mens rea 97
Mistakes relating to a matter of defence etc 100

Chapter 8 Strict liability 105
Strict liability at common law 106
Strict liability in statutory offences 107

Chapter 9 Capacity 121
Children 121
Mental disability 123
Unfitness to be tried 123
Defence of insanity 126
Diminished responsibility 138
Automatism and other involuntary conduct 142
Intoxication 148
Corporations 165
Unincorporated associations 172

Chapter 10 Non-fatal offences against the person 173
Consent 173
Assault and battery 177
Aggravated assaults 182
Wounding and grievous bodily harm 184

Chapter 11 Homicide and related offences 190
Homicide generally 190
Murder 201
Manslaughter 206
Voluntary manslaughter 207
Involuntary manslaughter 215
Infanticide 229
Abortion and child destruction 230

Chapter 12 Sexual offences 236
Rape 237
Other offences involving sexual intercourse 240
Indecency 243
Abduction 247
Buggery 249
Gross indecency 251
Homosexual offences: restrictions on prosecutions 252

Chapter 13 Offences against property 1: Theft 253
The elements 253
Actus reus 253
Mens rea 278

Chapter 14 Offences against property 2: Offences under the Theft Acts
other than theft 289
Robbery 289
Burglary and aggravated burglary 291

Temporary deprivation   297
Deception offences   301
Obtaining property by deception   301
Theft and obtaining property by deception   308
Obtaining a pecuniary advantage by deception   311
Obtaining services by deception   314
Evasion of liability by deception   316
Making off without payment   320
Falsification   323
Liability of controlling officer for deception or falsification offence by
   corporation   324
Blackmail   324
Handling   327
Section 23   336
Going equipped for stealing etc   336

Chapter 15   Offences against property 3: Offences other than under the
            Theft Acts   339
Criminal damage   339
Threats to destroy or damage property   347
Possessing anything with intent to destroy or damage property   347
Criminal Damage: Draft Criminal Code   348
Entering and remaining on property   349
Aggravated trespass   354
Forgery and related offences   356
Forgery   357
Copying a false instrument   362
Using a false instrument or a copy of a false instrument   362
Offences relating to money orders, share certificates, passports etc   363
Counterfeiting   364
Computer misuse   364

Chapter 16   Offences against the administration of justice   368
Assisting offenders   368
Concealing   370
Causing wasteful employment of the police   371
Perjury   371
Contempt of court   373
Attempting to pervert the course of justice   384
Offences relating to bail   386

Chapter 17   Political offences   388
Treason   388
Terrorism   391
Sedition   391
Official secrets   392

Chapter 18   Offences against public order   398
Riot   398
Violent disorder   402
Affray   403
Threatening, abusive, insulting or disorderly conduct   405

Fear or provocation of violence 405
Harassment, alarm or distress 409
Racial hatred 413
Public processions and assemblies 418
Obstructing the police 424
Firearms 429
Offensive weapons 433
Ancillary offence 435
Other offensive weapon offences 436

Chapter 19 Offences against public morals 437
Bigamy 437
Obscenity 439
Outraging public decency 444
Misuse of drugs 446

Chapter 20 Road traffic offences 452
Some general matters 452
Dangerous driving 455
Careless driving 457
Drinking and driving 458
Uninsured use 473

Chapter 21 Inchoate offences 475
Incitement 475
Conspiracy: General 479
Statutory conspiracy 482
Common law conspiracy 493
Attempt 500

Chapter 22 General defences and justifications 513
Public or private defence 513
Duress by threats 519
Marital coercion 527
Necessity 528
Superior orders 534

Chapter 23 Participation 536
Perpetrators 536
Accomplices 537
Liability for criminal conduct of another brought about by one's own act
    or default 554
Liability for the unauthorised criminal acts of another 554

Index 559

Table of statutes

References in this Table to *Statutes* are to Halsbury's Statutes of England (Fourth Edition) showing the volume and page at which the annotated text of the Act may be found.

PARA

Abortion Act 1967 (12 *Statutes* 380): 11.81, 22.33
  s 1 .... 22.32
    (1)–(4) 11.79, 11.80
    4 (2) 11.80
    5 (1) 11.82
    (2) 11.78, 11.79, 11.80
Accessories and Abettors Act 1861 (12 *Statutes* 80)
  s 8 .... 23.3
Administration of Justice Act 1960 (12 *Statutes* 302) 1.6
  s 1 .... 5.35
    10 .... 16.28
    12 .... 16.28
    (1), (2) 16.28
Administration of Justice (Miscellaneous Provisions) Act 1933 (12 *Statutes* 206)
  s 2 .... 5.1, 5.2
Anatomy Act 1984 (28 *Statutes* 238)
  s 11 .... 8.22
Antarctic Treaty Act 1967 (2 *Statutes* 309)
  s 2 (2) 22.32
Aviation Security Act 1982 (4 *Statutes* 269)
  s 1, 2 .... 6.81
Bail Act 1976 (12 *Statutes* 661)
  s 3 (1) 4.29
    (2) 4.27
    (3) 4.27, 4.28
    (4), (5) 4.27
    (6) 4.28
    4 .... 4.26
    6 .... 16.36
    (1)–(7) 16.35
    7 (1)–(3) 4.29
    9 .... 16.36
    (3)–(5) 16.36
  Sch 1 .... 4.26, 4.28
Banking Act 1987 (4 *Statutes* 527)
  s 96 .... 8.22
Bankruptcy Act 1914
  s 157 (1) 8.2

PARA

British Nationality Act 1948 (31 *Statutes* 10)
  s 3 .... 11.1, 17.5, 19.8
British Nationality Act 1981 (31 *Statutes* 112)
  s 51 .... 17.5
British Telecommunications Act 1981
  s 48 .... 13.23
Broadcasting Act 1990
  s 162 .... 19.11
  Sch 15 .... 19.14, 19.15, 19.16, 19.26
Building Societies Act 1986 (5 *Statutes* 433)
  s 112 .... 8.22
Children Act 1989 .... 16.28
  s 31 (1), (2) 5.24
    78 .... 3.23
    103 .... 9.90
Children and Young Persons Act 1933 (6 *Statutes* 17)
  s 1 .... 8.10, 11.60
    (1) 6.8
    46 .... 5.21
    47 .... 5.23
    49 .... 5.23, 16.20
    50 .... 9.1
    107 (1) 5.21
Children and Young Persons Act 1963 (6 *Statutes* 17)
  s 16 .... 9.1
Civil Aviation Act 1982 (4 *Statutes* 114)
  s 92 .... 6.80
Coinage Offences Act 1936 .... 15.41
Computer Misuse Act 1990 .... 15.59
  s 1 .... 13.21, 15.44, 15.61, 15.63
    (1)–(3) 15.60
    2 .... 15.63
    (1) 15.61, 15.62
    (3)–(5) 15.61
    3 .... 15.62, 15.63
    (1)–(3) 15.62
    (6) 15.8
    (7) 15.62

PARA

Computer Misuse Act 1990—*contd*
s 4 (1), (4), (6) 15.63
5 .... 15.63
    (5) 15.62
8 (1) 15.63
17 (2), (3), (5) 15.60
    (6) 15.16, 15.62
    (7), (8) 15.62
Consular Relations Act 1968 (10 Statutes 570) 4.9
Consumer Credit Act 1974 (11 Statutes 15) 23.4
Consumer Protection Act 1987 (39 Statutes 188)
s 39 .... 8.22
40 .... 9.90, 23.35
Consumer Safety Act 1978 (39 Statutes 82)
s 2 .... 8.22
Contempt of Court Act 1981 (11 Statutes 185) 16.12
s 1 .... 16.13, 16.18
2 .... 16.13
    (1) 16.14
    (2) 16.15
    (3) 16.16
3 .... 16.13, 16.18, 16.19
    (1)–(3) 16.19
4 .... 16.13, 16.18
    (1) 16.20, 16.21, 16.22
    (2) 16.20, 16.21
    (3) 16.20
5 .... 16.13, 16.18, 16.22
6 .... 16.13
7 .... 16.30, 16.31
8 (1), (2) 16.30
10 .... 16.24, 16.25
11 .... 16.29, 16.31
12 .... 16.31, 16.32
14 (1) 16.12
19 .... 16.16
Sch 1 .... 16.16
Control of Pollution (Amendment) Act 1989
s 1 (1) 22.42
    (4) 22.32, 22.42
Controlled Drugs (Penalties) Act 1985 (28 Statutes 568) 19.29, 19.30
Copyright Act 1956 (11 Statutes 261): 21.38
County Courts Act 1984 (11 Statutes 603)
s 118 .... 16.31, 16.32
Courts Act 1971 (11 Statutes 833) 2.5
s 13 .... 4.25
24 .... 2.6
Criminal Appeal Act 1968 (12 Statutes 385)
s 1 .... 5.28
2 .... 5.30
    (1) 5.12, 5.30
3, 7 .... 5.30
9, 10 .... 5.31
11 .... 5.31

PARA

Criminal Appeal Act 1968—*contd*
s 11 (3) 5.31
12 .... 9.25
13 .... 9.10, 9.25
15 .... 9.10
17 .... 5.32
    (1) 5.32
23 (1), (2) 5.29
33 .... 5.35
Criminal Attempts Act 1981 (12 Statutes 776) 21.16, 21.81
s 1 .... 21.52, 21.53, 21.54,
                21.63, 21.74, 21.75,
                21.76, 21.77
    (1) 21.52, 21.64, 21.66,
                21.67, 21.72
    (2) 21.67, 21.69, 21.70,
                21.73
    (3) 6.20, 21.67, 21.69,
                21.70, 21.72, 21.73
    (4) 16.10, 21.53, 21.54
2 .... 21.74
3 .... 20.17, 21.77
    (3)–(5) 21.77
4 (1) 21.75, 21.77
    (3) 21.66
    (4) 21.77
    (5) 21.76
5 (1) 21.15
6 (1) 21.52
8 .... 14.18
Sch 1 .... 16.10
Criminal Damage Act 1971 (12 Statutes 526) 3.17, 3.18, 6.53,
                13.13, 15.34
s 1 .... 6.44, 6.46
    (1) 6.12, 6.56, 9.64, 15.1,
                15.2, 15.5, 15.10,
                15.11, 15.12, 15.15,
                15.17
    (2) 9.63, 9.64, 9.76,
                15.5, 15.13, 15.14,
                15.15, 15.16
    (3) 6.12, 15.1, 15.13,
                15.16
2 .... 15.17, 15.19
3 .... 15.12, 15.18, 15.19
5 .... 7.27, 15.12, 15.17,
                22.32, 22.41
    (1) 15.17, 15.18
    (2) 9.68, 15.12, 15.18,
                15.20
    (3) 9.68, 15.12
    (5) 15.12
10 (1), (2) 15.9
Criminal Justice Act 1925 (27 Statutes 27) 22.28
s 47 .... 22.28, 22.29
Criminal Justice Act 1967 (12 Statutes 357)
s 4 (2) 21.79
6 (3) 21.79
    (4) 21.78, 21.79

PARA

Criminal Justice Act 1967—*contd*
s 8 . . . . 7.14, 7.20, 9.53,
             9.54, 9.55, 11.34,
                     11.67
  22 . . . . 4.25
  25 . . . . 19.17
Criminal Justice Act 1972 (12 *Statutes*
  536)
s 36 . . . . 5.34
Criminal Justice Act 1982 (27 *Statutes*
  321)
  s 37 . . . . 5.20
Criminal Justice Act 1987 (12 *Statutes*
  1069)
  s 1 . . . . 4.3
  4 . . . . 4.21
  12 . . . . 21.44, 21.51
Criminal Justice Act 1988 (12 *Statutes*
  1154) 15.4
  s 3 . . . . 10.16
  13 . . . . 18.89
  33 (3) 18.79
  36 . . . . 5.31
  37 (1) 14.18
  39 . . . . 10.16
  40 . . . . 15.5
  41 . . . . 10.16, 14.18
  44 . . . . 18.76
  122 . . . . 5.7
  139 (1)–(5) 18.89
  159 . . . . 16.21, 16.29
  160 (4) 19.21
  161 . . . . 19.20
Criminal Justice Act 1991
  s 17 . . . . 5.20
  25 . . . . 5.21
  26 . . . . 13.2, 14.6
  53 . . . . 4.21
Criminal Law Act 1967 (12 *Statutes*
  328) 3.32, 22.2, 23.4
  s 1 . . . . 3.32, 21.55
  3 . . . . 4.17, 22.8
    (1) 22.2, 22.3, 22.7
    (2) 22.2
  4 . . . . 16.2
    (1) 16.1, 21.54
    (1A) 16.2
    (2) 21.80
    (3) 16.3
    (4) 16.1
  5 . . . . 16.2
    (1) 16.4, 16.5, 21.54
    (2) 16.6
    (3) 16.4
    (5) 16.5
  6 (3) 12.8, 21.80
    (4) 21.79, 21.80
  Sch 2 . . . . 12.8
Criminal Law Act 1977 (12 *Statutes*
  690) 15.21, 21.11
  s 1 . . . . 21.15, 21.28, 21.48,
                       21.57
    (1) 21.15, 21.16, 21.18,
            21.25, 21.27, 21.28,
                21.57, 21.61

PARA

Criminal Law Act 1977—*contd*
  s 1 (2) 21.23
    (3) 21.21, 21.61
    (4) 21.21
  2 . . . . 21.15, 21.48, 21.73
    (1) 21.30
    (2) 21.13, 21.30
    (3) 21.30
  3 . . . . 21.33, 21.48
  4 . . . . 21.48
    (1), (2) 21.31
    (3) 21.31
    (4) 21.31
  5 . . . . 21.48
    (1) 21.11
    (2) 21.37, 21.47
    (3) 21.47, 21.48, 21.49
    (6) 21.15
    (7) 21.2
    (8) 21.14
  6 . . . . 4.15, 15.27, 15.37
    (1) 15.22, 15.25
    (2) 15.26
    (3) 15.27
    (4) 15.23
  7 . . . . 4.15, 15.24, 15.27,
                      15.37
    (1) 15.28
    (2)–(5) 15.29
    (6)–(8) 15.31
    (9) 15.28, 15.29
    (11) 15.28
  8 . . . . 4.15, 18.90
    (2) 18.90
  9 . . . . 4.15, 15.32
    (3), (5), (6) 15.32
  10 . . . . 4.15, 18.73
  12 (1), (2) 15.21
    (3)–(5) 15.27
  52 . . . . 19.28
  53 . . . . 19.11
    (3) 21.49
  54 . . . . 12.22, 12.23, 21.6
  Sch 1 . . . . 2.3
  Sch 6 . . . . 16.6
  Sch 12 . . . . 23.3
Criminal Lunatics Act 1880 . . . . 9.24
Criminal Procedure (Insanity) Act
  1964 (12 *Statutes* 317)
  s 1 . . . . 9.24
  4 . . . . 9.9, 9.11
    (2) 9.9
  4A 9.9, 9.11
  5 . . . . 9.9, 9.11, 9.24,
                      9.45
  6 . . . . 9.28, 9.34
  Sch 1, 2 . . . . 9.24
Criminal Procedure (Insanity and
  Unfitness to Plead) Act 1991 . . . . . 9.10,
                 9.24, 9.26, 9.27
  s 1 . . . . 9.22
  2 . . . . 9.25
  Sch 1 . . . . 9.24
  Sch 3 . . . . 9.10

PARA

Criminal Procedure (Right of Reply)
Act 1964 (17 *Statutes* 153) 5.10
Customs and Excise Management Act
1979 (13 *Statutes* 273)
s 147 (3) 5.25
170 (2) 6.61, 6.75, 21.23,
21.28
Deer Act 1991
s 1 ....13.26
Defamation Act 1952 (24 *Statutes* 108)
s 4 ....8.3
Diplomatic and other Privileges Act
1971 (10 *Statutes* 615) 4.9
Diplomatic Privileges Act 1964 (10
Statutes 559) 4.9
Education (No 2) Act 1986 (15 *Statutes*
328)
s 47 ....10.13
Electricity Act 1989 (15 *Statutes* 1088)
s 59 (1) 6.60
European Communities Act 1972 (10
Statutes 617)
s 11 ....16.8
Explosive Substances Act 1883
s 4 ....7.7
Family Allowances Act 1945 ....21.4
Fire Services Act 1947 (18 *Statutes* 6)
s 30 ....22.32
31 ....16.6
Firearms Act 1968 (12 *Statutes* 424):   18.74,
18.87
s 1 ....18.75, 18.80, 18.81
(1) 18.75
2 ....18.80, 18.81
(1) 18.76
5 ....18.78
(1) 18.78
16 ....18.80
17 ....18.82
(1) 18.81, 18.82
(2) 18.82
(4) 18.82
18 (1) 18.82, 18.86
19 ....18.85
20 (1), (2) 18.90
25 ....6.65
57 (1) 18.74, 18.78
58 (2) 18.74
Sch 1 ....18.82
Sch 6 ....18.74
Firearms Act 1982 (12 *Statutes* 788)
s 1 ....18.75
(5) 18.77
Firearms (Amendment) Act 1988 (12
Statutes 1255)
s 1 ....18.78
2 ....18.75
5 ....18.76
Food Act 1984 (27 *Statutes* 401)
s 94 ....9.90
Food Safety Act 1990 (18 *Statutes* 478)
s 20 ....23.35
21 ....8.22
36 ....9.90

PARA

Football Spectators Act 1989
s 5 (7) 6.60
Forgery Act 1913 ......15.41, 15.44, 15.55
Forgery and Counterfeiting Act 1981
(12 *Statutes* 753) 15.41, 15.58,
21.44
s 1 ....15.42, 15.44, 15.51
2 ....15.49
3 ....15.51, 15.52
4 ....15.52
5 ....15.53
(1) 15.54
(2) 15.55
(3) 15.56
(4) 15.57
6 (1)–(3) 15.41
(4) 15.55, 15.57
8 (1)–(4) 15.44
9 (1) 15.45, 15.46
(2) 15.43
10 (1)–(5) 15.47
Gas Act 1986 (19 *Statutes* 278)
s 38 (2) 6.8
Health and Safety at Work etc Act
1974 (19 *Statutes* 620)
s 36 ....23.35
Highway Act 1835 (20 *Statutes* 9) 20.1
Homicide Act 1957 (12 *Statutes* 281) ..9.26,
11.22, 11.26
s 1 ....11.23, 11.26
2 ....9.33, 9.38, 9.40
(1) 9.32, 9.33, 9.34
(2) 9.34
(3) 9.32
(4) 23.26
3 ....11.34, 11.35, 11.36,
11.37, 11.38, 11.40,
11.42, 11.43, 11.46,
11.47
4 ....11.33
(1), (2) 11.32
Housing Act 1988
s 29 ....8.6
Human Fertilisation and Embryology
Act 1990
s 1 ....11.79
37 ....11.79, 11.80, 11.82
Indecency with Children Act 1960 (12
Statutes 300) 12.21, 12.22, 12.23,
19.26
s 1 (1) 12.21
Indecent Displays (Control) Act 1981
(12 *Statutes* 874)
s 1 (1)–(5) 19.22
3, 4 ....19.22
5 (2) 19.22
Schedule 19.22
Infant Life (Preservation) Act 1929
(12 *Statutes* 203)
s 1 ....11.82, 22.32
(2) 11.82
2 (2), (3) 11.83
Infanticide Act 1922 ....11.73

PARA

Infanticide Act 1938 (12 *Statutes* 220)
  s 1 ....11.72
    (2) 11.72
Insolvency Act 1985 (4 *Statutes* 699)
  Sch 10 ....8.2
Insolvency Act 1986 (4 *Statutes* 717) ..3.18
  s 432 ....9.90
International Organisations Act 1981
  (10 *Statutes* 697) 4.9
Interpretation Act 1978 (41 *Statutes*
  899)
  Sch 1 ....5.20
Intoxicating Substances (Supply) Act
  1985 (12 *Statutes* 967)
  s 1 ....7.7
Judicial Proceedings (Regulation of
  Reports) Act 1926 (12 *Statutes* 201)
  s 1 ....16.20
Juries Act 1974 (22 *Statutes* 409) 5.8
  s 12 (1) 5.9
  17 ....5.14
Juries (Disqualification) Act 1984 (22
  Statutes 428) 5.8
Larceny Act 1861 ....13.26
  s 23 ....8.10
  Sch 1 ....13.26
Libel Act 1792 [Fox's Act] (24 *Statutes*
  80) 17.8
Libel Act 1843 [Lord Campbell's Act]
  (24 *Statutes* 95)
  s 7 ....23.37
Licensing Act 1872 (24 *Statutes* 87)
  s 12 ....6.15, 8.18
  13 ....8.12
  16 (1), (2) 8.12
Licensing Act 1964 (24 *Statutes* 303) ..3.18
  s 59 ....23.37
  160 (1) 7.8
  161 (1) 23.40
  163 ....23.37
  172 (3) 8.12
  178 (b) 8.12
Magistrates' Courts Act 1980 (27 *Statutes* 157) 2.2
  s 1 ....6.79
    (3) 4.11
    (4) 4.12
  2 ....6.79
  3 ....5.21
  4, 5 ....4.19
  6 ....4.19
    (2) 4.22
    (4) 4.25
  7 ....4.19
  8 ....4.19, 4.24, 16.21
    (3) 16.20
  12 ....5.16
  17 (1) 10.17, 10.19, 12.13,
                12.15, 12.30, 12.32,
                13.2, 14.1, 15.2,
                15.19, 16.1, 16.4,
                16.11, 19.2, 21.9
  19 ....4.20
    (4) 4.20

PARA

Magistrates' Courts Act 1980—*contd*
  s 19 (5) 4.20
  20 ....4.20
  21 ....4.20
  22 ....15.2, 15.4
    (1), (2) 15.2, 15.5
    (11) 15.4
  23 ....15.2
  24 (1) 5.21
  31 ....5.20
  32 (1) 21.9
  44 ....23.3
  45 (1), (3) 21.9
  101 ....7.8
  102 ....4.22
  108 (1) 5.25
  111 ....5.26
    (4) 5.26
  127 (1), (2) 4.7
  133 ....5.20
  143 ....5.20
  Sch 1 ....2.3, 10.17, 10.19,
                12.13, 12.15, 12.30,
                12.32, 13.2, 14.1,
                15.2, 15.19, 16.1,
                16.4, 16.11, 19.2,
                21.2, 21.9
  Sch 2 ....15.2
Malicious Communications Act 1988
  (12 *Statutes* 1152)
  s 1 ....6.38
Marriage Act 1949 ....19.10
Medicines Act 1968 (28 *Statutes* 344)
  s 58 (2) (a) 8.12
Mental Health Act 1983 (28 *Statutes*
  632)
  s 36 ....9.7
  37 (3) 9.11, 9.30, 9.32
  48 ....9.6
Mental Health (Amendment) Act
  1982 (28 *Statutes* 626)
  Sch 3 ....12.12
Merchant Shipping Act 1894 (39 *Statutes* 424)
  s 686, 687 ....6.80
Misuse of Drugs Act 1971 (28 *Statutes*
  500) 8.5, 19.28
  s 1 ....19.28
  4 ....19.29
  5 ....2.3
    (1), (2) 7.8, 19.30
    (3) 19.30
    (4) 19.33
  7 ....7.8
  8 ....19.34
  21 ....19.35
  28 ....8.22, 9.67, 19.31,
                                  19.32
  37 (1) 19.28
    (3) 19.31
  Sch 4 ....19.29, 19.30
Murder (Abolition of Death Penalty)
  Act 1965 (12 *Statutes* 327) 3.3

PARA

Obscene Publications Act 1959 (12
    Statutes 291) 19.11, 19.21, 19.22
  s 1 .... 19.12
    (2) 19.12
    (3) 19.11, 19.12
    (4), (5) 19.12
  2 (1) 19.12, 19.15
    (3A) 19.16
    (4) 19.11, 19.26
    (4A) 21.49
    (5) 19.14
  3 .... 19.17
  4 (1), (1A), (2) 19.14
Obscene Publications Act 1964 (12
    Statutes 314) 19.11
  s 1 (2) 19.15
Offences against the Person Act 1861
    (12 *Statutes* 88) 3.17, 10.1, 11.1
  s 4 .... 21.9
  5 .... 3.3, 11.30
  18 .... 6.30, 9.48, 9.62,
                      10.18, 10.23, 10.24,
                      10.25, 10.26, 10.27,
                      11.7, 11.26, 23.26
  20 .... 2.3, 6.54, 9.48,
                      10.18, 10.19, 10.20,
                      10.21, 10.24, 10.25,
                      10.26, 10.27, 11.7,
                      23.23, 23.26
  21 .... 6.55, 10.17
  24 .... 10.11
  35 .... 20.1
  38 .... 10.17
  44, 45 .... 1.5
  47 .... 10.12, 10.17, 10.27
  55 .... 7.17, 8.2
  56 .... 23.13
  57 .... 7.32, 19.2, 19.5,
                                  19.8
  58 .... 11.75, 11.76, 11.77,
                      11.78, 11.79, 11.80,
                      11.81, 11.82, 11.83,
                                  22.33
Official Secrets Act 1911 (12 *Statutes*
    176) 4.4
  s 1 .... 6.38, 17.9, 17.10
  2 .... 17.12
  3, 8, 11 .... 17.10
Official Secrets Act 1920 (12 *Statutes*
    191) 17.9
Official Secrets Act 1989 (12 *Statutes*
    1345) 4.4, 17.12
  s 1 .... 17.17
    (1) 17.13, 17.19
    (3)–(5) 17.13
  2 .... 17.17
    (1), (3), (4) 17.14
  3 .... 17.17
    (1), (4), (5) 17.15
  4 .... 17.16, 17.17
    (1) 17.16
    (2) 17.16, 17.20
    (3)–(5) 17.16
  5 .... 17.17

PARA

Official Secrets Act 1989—*contd*
  s 5 (2) 6.65, 6.74, 17.17
    (3), (4) 17.17
    (6) 17.10, 17.19, 17.21
  6 (2), (3) 17.18
  7 (1)–(4) 17.19
  9 .... 17.10, 17.20
  10 .... 17.20
  15 .... 17.21
Perjury Act 1911 (12 *Statutes* 165) ... 16.11
  s 1 (1) 16.7
    (2), (3) 16.8
    (4) 16.9
    (6) 16.8
  1A 16.9
  2 .... 16.11
  3 .... 16.11, 19.10
    (1) 16.11
  4 .... 4.7, 16.11
    (1) 16.11
  5, 6 .... 16.11
  7 (1) 16.10
  15 .... 16.8
Police Act 1964 (33 *Statutes* 597)
  s 51 .... 18.69
    (1) 10.17
    (3) 18.68
Police and Criminal Evidence Act
    1984 (12 *Statutes* 842)
  s 17 .... 4.14, 15.28
  24 (1), (2) 4.14
    (4)–(7) 4.14
  25 .... 4.15
  28 (3) 18.69
  46 (2) 4.18
  78 .... 20.28, 23.30
  79 .... 5.10
Post Office Act 1953 (34 *Statutes* 395)
  s 11 .... 19.13
Prevention of Crime Act 1953 (12 *Stat-
    utes* 237)
  s 1 .... 2.3, 7.7, 18.85
    (4) 18.86
Prevention of Terrorism (Temporary
    Provisions) Act 1989 (12 *Statutes*
    1279)
  s 1 .... 17.6
  2 .... 17.6
    (3) 17.6
  3, 9, 10, 18 .... 17.7
Prohibition of Female Circumcision
    Act 1985 (12 *Statutes* 969) 10.4
Prosecution of Offences Act 1985 (12
    Statutes 933) 4.2
  s 6 .... 4.3
  10 .... 21.45
  11 .... 4.5
  15 (2) 4.2
  22 .... 4.23, 5.4
  25 .... 4.4
Protection from Eviction Act 1977 (23
    Statutes 302)
  s 1 (3) 6.30, 6.40, 8.6

PARA

Protection of Children Act 1978 (12
 Statutes 729)
  s 1 ....19.19
   (3) 19.21
  3 ....19.21
  7 (2), (5) 19.21
Public Meeting Act 1908 (12 *Statutes*
 164)
  s 1 (1), (2) 18.67
Public Order Act 1936 (12 *Statutes*
 215)
  s 2 ....17.7
  5 ....18.20, 18.23
Public Order Act 1986 (12 *Statutes*
 1030) 4.4, 18.1
  s 1 ....18.11, 18.28
   (1) 18.2
   (2) 18.7
   (4) 18.9
   (5) 18.3
   (6) 18.2
  2 ....18.28
   (1) 18.12, 18.13
   (3), (4) 18.13
   (5) 18.12
  3 ....18.28
   (1) 18.15
   (2) 18.18
   (3) 18.17
   (4) 18.18
   (5) 18.16
   (7) 18.15
  4 ....10.10, 18.20, 18.21,
              18.22, 18.24, 18.25,
              18.26, 18.28, 18.30,
              18.31, 18.32, 18.34,
              18.35, 18.37, 18.38,
              18.41, 18.45, 18.46,
                     18.55, 18.67
   (1) 18.21, 18.28
   (2) 18.26
   (4) 18.21
  5 ....18.13, 18.20, 18.24,
              18.25, 18.32, 18.34,
              18.35, 18.37, 18.38,
              18.39, 18.41, 18.45,
              18.46, 18.47, 18.55,
                            18.67
   (1) 18.33, 18.35
   (2) 18.38
   (3) 18.40
   (6) 18.33
  6 ....18.11
   (1) 18.6, 18.10
   (2) 18.14, 18.19
   (3) 18.27
   (4) 18.39
   (5) 9.79, 18.10, 18.14,
            18.19, 18.27, 18.39
   (6) 18.10
   (7) 18.6
  7 (1) 18.2
  8 ....18.5, 18.13, 18.26,
                            18.29
Pt II (ss 11–16) 18.56

PARA

Public Order Act 1986—*contd*
  s 11 ....18.59, 19.86
   (1), (2) 18.58
   (5), (6) 18.58
   (7)–(10) 18.59
  12 ....18.59, 18.60, 18.61,
              18.62, 18.63, 18.64,
                     18.66, 18.86
   (1)–(3) 18.60
   (4)–(6) 18.61
   (8)–(10) 18.61
  13 ....18.59, 18.62, 18.63,
                     18.66, 18.86
   (1)–(4) 18.62
   (7)–(9) 18.63
   (11)–(13) 18.63
  14 ....18.59, 18.64, 18.66
   (1)–(3) 18.64
   (4)–(6) 18.65
   (8)–(10) 18.65
  15 ....18.66
  16 ....18.57, 18.64
  Pt III (ss 17–29) 18.42
  s 17 ....18.43
  18 ....18.13, 18.46, 18.47
   (1), (2), (4) 18.46
   (5) 18.47
   (6) 18.46
  19 (1) 18.48, 18.51
   (2) 18.49
   (3) 18.48
  20 ....18.52
  21 ....18.46, 18.52
  22 ....18.52
  23 ....18.51
   (1) 18.50
   (3) 18.51
  26 (1), (2) 18.54
  27 (1), (3) 18.55
  28 ....9.90, 18.53
  29 ....18.46, 18.50
  39 ....15.21, 15.34, 15.39
   (1) 15.33, 15.34, 15.35
   (2) 15.33, 15.34, 15.36,
                            15.37
   (3) 15.40
   (4) 15.39
   (5) 15.34
  40 (2) 18.86
  Sch 2 ....18.86
Punishment of Incest Act 1908 ....3.15
Race Relations Act 1965 ....18.43
Rivers (Prevention of Pollution) Act
 1951 (49 *Statutes* 229) 8.14
Road Traffic Act 1972
  s 25 ....8.12
Road Traffic Act 1988 (38 *Statutes*
 823) 18.70, 20.1
  s 1 ....20.13, 20.24
  2 ....20.10, 20.15, 20.24
  2A 20.24
   (1)–(4) 20.11
  3 ....20.10, 20.14, 20.22,
                     20.24, 21.76

PARA

Road Traffic Act 1988—contd
s 3A 20.16, 20.22, 20.24,
                    20.28, 20.30, 20.31
  (2) 20.22
4 .... 6.15, 20.16, 20.24,
                    20.28, 20.30
  (1) 20.17, 21.77
  (2)–(4) 20.18
  (5) 20.20
  (6), (7) 20.19
5 .... 20.16, 20.28
  (1) 20.19, 20.23, 21.77
  (2) 20.19, 20.24
6 .... 20.16, 20.34, 20.35
  (1) 20.24, 20.25
  (2) 20.25, 20.26
  (3) 20.26
  (4) 20.34
  (5), (6) 20.27
  (8) 20.25
7 .... 20.16, 20.20, 20.22,
                 20.27, 20.29, 20.30,
                 20.34, 20.35, 20.36
  (1) 20.28
  (2) 20.27, 20.29
  (3), (4) 20.30
  (5) 20.30, 20.35
  (6) 20.29, 20.34, 20.35
  (7) 20.30
8 .... 20.16
  (1), (2) 20.29
9 .... 20.16, 20.30
  (1), (2) 20.26
10 .... 20.16
11 (1) 20.35
  (2) 20.17, 20.26
  (3) 20.35
28 .... 20.12
30 .... 20.21
38 (7) 20.14
51–89 .... 20.5
143 (1) 20.37
  (3) 20.38
163 .... 20.25
170 .... 8.12, 20.3
185, 189 .... 20.7
192 .... 20.8
Road Traffic Act 1991 ... 11.54, 20.1, 22.34
s 1 .... 20.10, 20.13, 20.14
2 .... 20.13
3 .... 20.22
4 .... 20.16
7 .... 20.12
Road Traffic Offenders Act 1988 (38
  Statutes 1056) 20.1
s 1 .... 20.2
2 .... 20.2, 20.4
  (3) 20.2
6, 7 .... 20.32
15 (2) 20.30, 20.31, 20.32
  (3) 20.31, 20.33
  (4), (5) 20.30, 20.32
35, 44 .... 20.4
Sch 2 .... 20.4, 20.9

PARA

Road Traffic Regulation Act 1984 (38
  Statutes 507)
s 25 (5) 6.8
  35A 14.54
87 .... 22.32
Sale of Goods Act 1979 (39 *Statutes*
  106)
s 17, 18 .... 13.28
Sexual Offences Act 1956 (12 *Statutes*
  245) 10.1, 12.1, 12.10
s 1 .... 12.3
2, 3 .... 12.8, 12.11
4 .... 12.8
5 .... 12.13
6 .... 12.13
  (2), (3) 12.13
7, 9 .... 12.12
10, 11 .... 12.14
12 .... 12.27
13 .... 12.32
14 .... 12.15
  (2) 12.17
  (3) 12.19
  (4) 12.17, 12.19
15 .... 12.15
  (2) 12.17
  (3) 12.17, 12.19
16 .... 12.30
17 .... 10.17, 12.25
19 .... 12.25, 12.26
  (2) 12.26
20 .... 7.17, 8.2, 12.25,
                    12.26, 21.23
21 .... 12.25, 12.26
  (2) 12.26
37 .... 12.1, 12.14, 21.76
44, 45 .... 12.2
Sch 2 .... 12.1, 12.8, 12.14,
                  12.29, 12.35, 21.76
Sexual Offences Act 1967 (12 *Statutes*
  351) 12.28, 12.34
s 1 (2), (6) 12.28
3 .... 12.29, 12.35
4 (3) 12.34
8 .... 12.36
Sexual Offences Act 1985 (12 *Statutes*
  972)
s 4 (3) 12.15
Sexual Offences (Amendment) Act
  1976 (12 *Statutes* 682)
s 1 .... 6.53, 12.3
  (1) 12.4, 12.7
  (2) 9.56, 12.7
7 (2) 12.4
Shops Act 1912 .... 9.82
Stamp Duties Management Act 1891
  (41 *Statutes* 131)
s 27 .... 15.44
Statutory Instruments Act 1946 (41
  Statutes 717)
s 3 .... 6.74

PARA

Suicide Act 1961 (12 *Statutes* 311)
s 2 ....11.33
  (1), (2) 11.33
Summary Jurisdiction Act 1875 (27 *Statutes* 15)
s 6 ....5.26
Supreme Court Act 1981 (11 *Statutes* 966) 2.5
s 8 (1) 2.6
  9 ....2.6
   (4) 2.6
  18 (1) 1.6
  28 ....5.27
  29 ....5.36
   (3) 5.36
  31 ....5.36
  45 (4) 16.31
Tattooing of Minors Act 1969 (6 *Statutes* 212) 10.4
Territorial Waters Jurisdiction Act 1878 (12 *Statutes* 145)
s 2 ....6.79
Theft Act 1968 (12 *Statutes* 484) 2.3, 3.17, 3.18, 6.76, 13.1, 14.1, 14.68, 15.44
s 1 ....13.1, 13.51, 14.78
  (1) 13.2, 13.5, 13.7
  (2) 13.51
  2 ....13.1
  (1) 6.74, 13.52, 13.53, 13.54, 13.57, 13.58, 13.59, 14.3
  (2) 13.59
  3 ....13.1, 13.3
  (1) 13.3, 13.4, 13.14, 13.17, 13.18, 14.88
  (2) 13.17, 13.52, 14.29, 14.88
  4 ....13.1, 13.22, 13.23, 14.34, 15.9
  (1) 13.21, 14.34
  (2), (3) 13.23, 13.24, 14.34
  (4) 13.25, 14.34
  5 ....13.1
  (1) 13.27, 13.28, 13.32, 13.34, 13.35, 13.37, 13.38, 13.41, 13.44, 13.45, 13.47, 13.48, 13.49, 14.34, 14.46, 15.10
  (2) 13.38, 13.41, 13.50
  (3) 13.39, 13.40, 13.41, 13.42, 13.43, 13.45, 13.48, 13.50
  (4) 13.45, 13.46, 13.47, 13.48, 13.49, 13.50, 14.46
  (5) 13.50
  6 ....13.1, 13.66, 14.42
  (1) 13.62, 13.63
  (2) 13.64

PARA

Theft Act 1968—*contd*
s 7 ....13.1, 13.2
  8 ....6.40, 10.17, 14.2
  9 ....14.6, 14.8
  (1) 14.7, 14.11, 14.13, 14.14
  (2) 14.7, 14.12
  (3) 14.10, 14.11
  10 ....14.15
  (1) 14.15
  (2)–(4) 15.10
  11 (1)–(4) 14.17
  12 ....14.18, 14.19, 14.20, 14.22, 14.24
  (1) 14.18, 14.25, 14.92
  (2), (4) 14.18
  (5) 14.25
  (6) 14.24
  (7) 14.19, 14.22
  13 ....13.21, 13.22, 15.59
  15 ....13.17, 14.34, 14.49, 14.50, 14.69, 14.70, 14.72, 14.98
  (1) 14.27
  (2) 14.34
  (3) 14.42
  (4) 14.28, 14.51
  16 ....14.48, 14.49, 14.50, 14.52, 14.70
  (1) 14.48
  (2) 14.50, 14.52
  (3) 14.49, 14.51
  17 ....14.69, 14.70, 15.59
  18 ....9.90, 14.69, 14.70
  19 ....14.69
  20 ....14.69
  (3) 14.69
  21 ....14.71, 14.78
  (1) 14.75
  (2) 14.72, 14.73
  22 ....14.76
  (1) 14.81
  23 ....14.91
  24 ....14.78
  (1) 14.78
  (2) 14.80
  (3) 14.79
  (4) 14.78
  25 ....6.15
  (1), (2), (5) 14.92
  27 (3) 14.89
  30 ....13.36, 15.6
  34 (1) 14.34
  (2) 14.74, 14.78
Theft Act 1978 (12 *Statutes* 725) 6.53, 6.76, 13.1, 14.1, 15.44
s 1 ....13.21, 14.48, 14.54, 14.68, 14.70
  (1) 14.53
  2 ....14.48, 14.56, 14.60, 14.61, 14.62, 14.70

PARA

Theft Act 1978—*contd*
s 2 (1) 14.56, 14.57, 14.60,
                14.61, 14.62, 14.63,
                14.64, 14.66, 14.67,
                14.78
  (2) 14.54, 14.56
  (3) 14.60
  (4) 14.63
 3 .... 14.65, 14.66, 14.78
  (1) 14.65
  (2), (3) 14.66
 4 .... 14.53, 14.56, 14.65
  (1) 14.1
 5 (1) 14.54, 14.55, 14.56,
              14.58, 14.61, 14.64
  (2) 14.70
  (5) 14.52
Town and Country Planning Act 1990
  (46 *Statutes* 514)
 s 179 (1) 1.7
Trade Descriptions Act 1968 (39 *Statutes* 41)
 s 14 (1) 8.6, 23.38
 20 .... 9.90
 23 .... 23.35
 24 .... 23.44

PARA

Trade Union and Labour Relations
  Act 1974 (16 *Statutes* 127) 21.21
 s 11 .... 9.91
Treason Act 1351 (12 *Statutes* 17) 17.1
Treason Act 1795 (12 *Statutes* 34) 17.2
Treason Felony Act 1848 (12 *Statutes*
 71) 17.1, 17.2
Trial of Lunatics Act 1883 (12 *Statutes*
 155) 9.24
Vagrancy Act 1824 (12 *Statutes* 50)
 s 4 .... 12.24
Video Recordings Act 1984 (45 *Stat-
utes* 536)
 s 10–14 .... 8.22
War Crimes Act 1991 .... 4.21
 s 1 .... 11.1
 Sch 1 .... 4.21
Water Industry Act 1991
 s 73 .... 6.64
Weights and Measures Act 1985 (50
 Statutes 9)
 s 32 .... 23.35
 34 .... 8.22, 23.44
Wildlife and Countryside Act 1981 (32
 Statutes 186)
 s 13 .... 13.25

List of cases

Cases are listed under the name of the accused whenever the usual method of citation would cause them to be preceded by the abbreviation "R v" signifying that the prosecution was undertaken by the Crown.

A

	PARA
A v DPP (1992)	9.2
A (a juvenile) v R (1978)	15.8
AB (1941)	4.9
AMK (Property Management) Ltd (1985)	6.30
Abbott v R (1977)	22.17, 22.23
Abraham (1973)	6.20, 7.9, 22.7
Abramovitch (1914)	14.89
Adams (1980)	19.17
Ahlers (1915)	6.39
Ahmad (1986)	6.9, 6.12
Air-India v Wiggins (1980)	6.78
Albert v Lavin (1981); affd (1982)	7.20, 7.30, 22.12
Alcock v Read (1980)	20.36
Ali (1989)	11.43
Allamby (1974)	18.86
Allan (1963)	23.9
Allen (1872)	19.6
Allen (1985)	14.67
Allen (1988)	9.51
Allen v Ireland (1984)	23.9
Allen v Metropolitan Police Comr (1980)	22.8
Allen v Whitehead (1930)	23.39, 23.41
Allsop (1976)	21.38, 21.39
Alphacell Ltd v Woodward (1972)	8.6, 8.11, 8.14, 8.19
Amand v Home Secretary and Minister of Defence of Royal Netherlands Government (1943)	1.6
Ambard v A-G for Trinidad and Tobago (1936)	16.27
Ambler (1979)	14.22
Anderson (1966)	23.23, 23.24
Anderson (1972)	19.13
Anderson (1986)	21.23, 21.27
Anderton v Burnside (1984)	13.3
Anderton v Goodfellow (1980)	20.36
Anderton v Lythgoe (1985)	20.29
Anderton v Rodgers (1981)	23.38, 23.41
Anderton v Ryan (1985)	3.8, 21.70
Anderton v Waring (1985)	20.36

	PARA
Andrews (1962)	16.2
Andrews (1973)	16.33
Andrews v DPP (1937)	11.53, 11.60
Andrews and Hedges (1981)	14.60
Andrews Weatherfoil Ltd (1972)	9.84
Anon (1702) 12 Mod Rep 559	9.81
Anon (circa 1634) Kel 53	23.2
Ansell v Thomas (1974)	10.10
Anthony (1965)	21.14
Antoniou (1989)	14.95
Appleyard (1985)	15.12
Archbold v Jones (1986)	20.29
Ardalan (1972)	21.12
Armstrong v Clark (1957)	20.16
Arobieke (1988)	11.60, 11.62
Arrowsmith (1975)	6.73
Arundel Justices, ex p Westminster Press Ltd (1985)	16.29
Asbury (1986)	7.21
Ashman (1858)	10.20
Ashton-Rickardt (1978)	19.31, 19.32
Aston and Mason (1991)	23.33
Atkin v DPP (1989)	18.25
Atkinson (1985)	9.38
Attewell-Hughes (1991)	14.61
A-G v Able (1984)	11.33, 23.17
A-G v BBC (1981); revsd (1981)	16.15, 16.31
A-G v Butterworth (1963)	16.25
A-G v English (1982)	16.15, 16.22
A-G v Leveller Magazines Ltd (1979)	16.29
A-G v Lockwood (1842)	8.14
A-G v News Group Newspapers Ltd (1987)	16.15, 16.23
A-G v News Group Newspapers plc (1989)	16.23
A-G v Newspaper Publishing plc (1987)	16.12, 16.23
A-G v Sport Newspapers Ltd (1992)	16.23
A-G v Times Newspapers Ltd (1973); revsd (1974)	16.15, 16.23
A-G v Times Newspapers Ltd (1991)	16.23

PARA

A-G for Northern Ireland v
  Gallagher (1963)   .   . 9.51, 9.63, 9.69,
                              9.70, 9.72
A-G for State of South Australia v
  Brown (1960) 9.21
A-G of Ceylon v Perera (1953)   .   11.34
A-G of Hong Kong v Chan
  Nai-Keung (1987)   .   .   . 13.6, 13.20
A-G of Hong Kong v Tse Hung-Lit
  (1986) 8.11
A-G's Reference (No 1 of 1974)
  (1974) 14.79
A-G's Reference (No 2 of 1974)
  (1975) 20.35
A-G's Reference (No 1 of 1975)
  (1975)   .   . 5.34, 12.10, 23.6, 23.12,
                              23.17
A-G's Reference (No 1 of 1977)
  (1978) 19.28
A-G's Reference (No 3 of 1977)
  (1978) 19.14
A-G's Reference (No 1 of 1978)
  (1978) 20.35
A-G's Reference (No 5 of 1980)
  (1980) 19.12
A-G's Reference (No 4 of 1979)
  (1981) 5.34, 14.80
A-G's Reference (No 4 of 1980)
  (1981) 11.28
A-G's Reference (No 6 of 1980)
  (1981) 10.3, 10.6
A-G's Reference (No 1 of 1982)
  (1983)   .   .   . 21.38, 21.39, 21.43
A-G's Reference (No 2 of 1982)
  (1984) 13.53
A-G's Reference (No 2 of 1983)
  (1984) 22.4, 22.14
A-G's Reference (No 1 of 1983)
  (1985) 13.46
A-G's Reference (No 3 of 1983)
  (1985) 18.18
A-G's Reference (No 1 of 1985)
  (1986) 13.34, 13.39
A-G's Reference (No 4 of 1989)
  (1989) 5.31
A-G's Reference for Northern
  Ireland (No 1 of 1975) (1977)   .   . 22.8,
                              22.11
A-G's References (Nos 1 and 2 of
  1979) (1980)   .   .   . 14.12, 21.63
Atwal v Massey (1971)   .   .   .   14.88
Austin (1981) 23.13
Aves (1950) 14.89

B

B (1979) 9.2
B (1984) 21.30
B v R (1958) 9.2
B and S v Leathley (1979)   .   .   14.10
Badkin v DPP (1988)   .   .   .   20.30
Badry v DPP of Mauritius (1983)   .   16.27
Bailey (1800) 6.73

PARA

Bailey (1961) 9.38
Bailey (1983) 9.48, 9.77
Bainbridge (1960) 23.20
Bains (1981) 16.33
Baker (1962) 18.82
Bale v Rosier (1977)   .   .   .   14.48
Ball (1983) 14.89
Ball (1989) 11.59, 11.66
Balogh v Crown Court at St Albans
  (1975) 16.31
Barker v Levinson (1951)   .   .   23.41
Barr (1986) 23.19
Barratt (1873) 12.5
Barrett and Barrett (1980)   .   .   7.21
Bashir (1982) 12.7
Bastable v Little (1907)   .   .   18.70
Bateman (1925) 11.53
Bates v Bulman (1979)   .   .   .   18.86
Baugh v Crago (1976)   .   .   .   20.38
Bayley and Easterbrook (1980)   .   21.63
Beal v Kelley (1951)   .   .   .   12.16
Beasley (1981) 10.21
Beatty v Gillbanks (1882)   .   .   18.30
Beauchamp-Thompson v DPP
  (1989) 20.32
Becerra (1975)   .   .   . 23.31, 23.32
Beck (1985) 12.10, 23.6
Beck v Sager (1979)   .   .   .   20.36
Beckford v R (1987)   . 6.20, 7.21, 11.24,
                              22.4, 22.8
Bedder v DPP (1954)   .   .   .   11.43
Bell (1984) 6.48, 9.12, 9.42
Bello (1978) 6.62
Benge (1865) 11.11
Bennett (1978) 23.32
Bennett v Brown (1980)   .   .   .   18.74
Bennett v Richardson (1980)   .   .   23.38
Bensley v Smith (1972)   .   .   .   20.14
Bentham (1973) 18.80
Bentley v Brudzinski (1982)   .   .   18.69
Bentley v Dickinson (1982)   .   .   20.2
Bentley v Mullen (1986)   .   .   .   23.6
Beresford (1971) 5.29
Berry (1977) 9.8
Berry (1985) 6.16, 6.78
Betts v Stevens (1910)   .   .   .   18.70
Betts and Ridley (1930)   .   . 23.8, 23.24
Betty (1963) 23.25
Bevens (1987) 14.74
Bickley (1909) 23.28
Bilbie v Lumley (1802)   .   .   .   6.73
Bingham (1991) 9.15, 9.46
Bird (1985) 22.3
Birmingham and Gloucester Rly Co
  (1842) 9.82, 9.87
Bishop (1880) 8.14
Blades v Higgs (1865)   .   .   .   13.25
Blakely and Sutton v DPP (1991)   .   23.17
Bland (1988)   .   .   . 19.31, 23.9, 23.11
Blaue (1975) 11.15, 11.19
Bloxham (1983) 14.81, 14.84
Board of Trade v Owen (1957)   .   21.40

PARA

Board of Visitors of Hull Prison, ex
  p St Germain (1979) 1.6
Bochin and Bodin (1979) 21.2
Bodden v Metropolitan Police Comr
  (1990) 16.31
Bogacki (1973) 14.20
Bohrmann's Estate, Re, Caesar and
  Watmough v Bohrmann (1938) . 9.29
Bolton v Crawley (1972) 9.64
Bolton (H L) (Engineering) Co Ltd v
  T J Graham & Sons Ltd (1957) . 9.85
Bonalumi v Secretary of State for the
  Home Department (1985) . . . 1.6
Bone (1968) 7.4, 22.28
Bonner (1970) 13.35
Boucher v R (1951) 17.8
Bourne (1939) . . . 11.82, 22.33, 22.38
Bourne (1952) . . . 5.13, 22.16, 23.14
Bow (1976) 14.21
Boyesen (1982) 19.30
Boyle (1986) 21.67
Braden (1987) 15.4
Bradford v Wilson (1983) 20.16
Bradish (1990) 8.16, 18.78
Bradley (1979) 14.89
Brain (1834) 11.3
Brannan v Peek (1948) 23.28
Bratty v A-G for Northern Ireland
  (1963) . . 7.4, 9.13, 9.16, 9.28, 9.41,
              9.42, 9.45, 9.46, 9.47,
                                9.64
Bravery v Bravery (1954) 10.4
Brazil v Chief Constable of Surrey
  (1983) 18.69
Breckenridge (1983) . . . 6.53, 12.7
Brend v Wood (1946) 6.2
Briggs (1977) 6.44
Briggs (1987) 7.8, 14.24
Brindley (1971) 16.2
Britton (1967) 18.48
Britton (1973) 16.33, 20.33
Broadfoot (1976) 12.10
Brookes v Retail Credit Card Ltd
  (1985) 23.4
Brooks v Mason (1902) 8.4
Brooks and Brooks (1982) . . . 14.66
Broom v Crowther (1984) . . . 13.18
Broome v Perkins (1987) . . . 9.42
Broomhead (1975) 20.35
Brown (1899) 21.7
Brown (1970) 14.85
Brown (1972) 11.46
Brown (1984) 7.22, 21.61
Brown (1985) 14.8
Brown (1992) 10.3
Brown v Ridge (1979) 20.35
Browne (1970) 3.9
Browne (1973) 22.9
Browning v J W H Watson
  (Rochester) Ltd (1953) 6.65
Brutus v Cozens (1973) . . 15.23, 18.5,
                                18.23

PARA

Bruzas (1972) 11.34, 21.55
Bryan v Mott (1975) . . . 18.86, 18.88
Bryson (1985) . . . 6.30, 6.37, 10.25
Buck and Buck (1960) 23.23
Buckingham (1976) 15.18
Bullard v R (1957) 7.9
Bullock (1955) 23.8
Bullock v Turnbull (1952) . . . 8.10
Bundy (1977) 14.93
Burden v Rigler (1911) 18.68
Burgess (1991) . 9.15, 9.18, 9.29, 9.42, 9.46,
                                     9.47
Burgoyne v Phillips (1983) . . . 20.6
Burke (1987) 11.43
Burles (1970) 9.9
Burns (1886) 17.8
Burns (1973) 9.64
Burns v Bidder (1967) 9.43
Burns v Currell (1963) 20.7
Burrell v Harmer (1967) 10.7
Burrows (1952) 12.21
Bush v Green (1985) 16.31
Buswell (1972) 19.31
Buzalek and Schiffer (1991) . . . 14.41
Byrne (1960) 9.33, 9.35, 9.38

C

C v S (1988); affd (1988) . . 11.3, 11.82
Calder (John) (Publications) Ltd v
  Powell (1965) 19.13
Caldwell (1982) . 6.43, 6.44, 6.45, 6.46,
                   6.49, 6.51, 9.54, 9.58,
                      9.63, 9.64, 10.14,
                     14.40, 15.11, 15.14,
                                21.61
Calhaem (1985) . . 23.6, 23.12, 23.23
Callow v Tillstone (1900) . . . 23.22
Campbell (1985) . . . 15.47, 15.48
Campbell (1986) 9.34
Campbell (1991) 21.65, 21.66
Camplin (1845) 12.5
Canterbury and St Augustine
  Justices, ex p Klisiak (1982) . . 15.3
Carmichael & Sons (Worcester) Ltd
  v Cottle (1971) 23.4
Carr v Atkins (1987) 1.6
Carr-Briant (1943) 7.5
Carter v Richardson (1974) . . . 23.18
Cartledge v Allen (1973) . . . 10.21
Cascoe (1970) 11.47
Case (1850) 12.17
Casement (1917) 17.4
Cash (1985) 14.87
Cassady v Reg Morris (Transport)
  Ltd (1975) 23.10
Cassidy v Daily Mirror Newspapers
  Ltd (1929) 8.3
Cato (1976) . 11.9, 11.62, 11.66, 11.77
Champ (1981) 8.6
Chan Man-sin v A-G of Hong Kong
  (or R) (1988) 13.3, 13.62
Chan Wing-Siu v R (1985) . 23.19, 23.24

PARA

Chandler v DPP (1964)   .   .   6.38, 17.10
Chapman (1959) 12.9, 12.26
Chapman v Honig (1963) 16.25
Chappell v DPP (1988) 18.34
Chard (1984) 5.32
Charles (1977)   .   .   14.29, 14.37, 14.50
Charlson (1955)   .   .   .   9.13, 9.42, 9.46
Charman (F E) v Clow (1974)   .   .   23.38
Charnock's Case (1696) 17.2
Chase Manhattan Bank NA v
   Israel-British Bank (London) Ltd
   (1981) 13.44
Cheshire (1991)   .   .   11.9, 11.11, 11.18
Cheshire County Council v Alan
   Helliwell & Sons (Bolton) Ltd
   (1990) 8.9
Chief Constable of Avon and
   Somerset v Kelliher (1987)   .   .   .   20.30
Chief Constable of Avon and
   Somerset Constabulary v Creech
   (1986) 20.32
Chief Constable of Avon and
   Somerset Constabulary v O'Brien
   (1987) 20.35
Chief Constable of Avon and
   Somerset Constabulary v Shimmen
   (1986) 6.52
Chief Constable of Avon and
   Somerset Constabulary v Singh
   (1988) 20.35, 20.36
Chief Constable of Gwent v Dash
   (1986) 20.25
Chief Constable of Hampshire v
   Mace (1986) 21.54
Chief Constable of West Midlands
   Police v Billingham (1979) .   .   .   20.25
Chief Metropolitan Stipendiary
   Magistrate, ex p Choudhury
   (1991) 8.3
Chilvers v Rayner (1984) 8.14
Chisam (1963) 7.29, 18.11
Choraria (1989) 14.74
Chrastny (1992)   .   .   .   21.12, 21.13
Christian (1913) 12.10
Christie (1977) 19.34
Church (1966) 11.27, 11.67
Churchill v Walton (1967)   .   .   .   21.28
Clarence (1888)   .   10.7, 10.12, 10.21
Clarke (1949) 12.6
Clarke (1972) 9.18
Clarke (1984) 23.28
Clarke (1986) 18.78
Clarke (1990) 6.49, 9.58
Clarke (1991) 11.46
Clarkson (1971)   .   .   23.8, 23.9, 23.17
Clayton v Chief Constable of
   Norfolk (1983) 21.80
Clear (1968) 14.73
Cleary v Booth (1893) 10.13
Clegg (1977) 14.36
Clerk to Croydon Justices, ex p
   Chief Constable of Kent (1989)   .   9.91

PARA

Clode v Barnes (1974) 23.38
Closs (1857) 15.44
Clouden (1987) 14.4
Clow (1963) 20.14
Clow (1978) 14.38
Clowser v Chaplin (1981); affd
   (1981) 4.17, 20.27
Cocker (1989) 11.40
Cocks (1976) 13.61
Codere (1916) 9.20
Coffey (1987) 13.61
Coffin v Smith (1980) 18.69
Cogan (1976) 9.57, 23.14
Cole v Turner (1704)   .   .   .   10.8, 10.12
Coleman (1985) 14.85
Collins (1973)   .   .   .   14.8, 14.9, 14.11
Collins (1990) 23.19
Collins v Wilcock (1984)   .   .   10.7, 10.8,
                                  10.15, 18.69
Collinson (1931) 20.8
Collis-Smith (1971) 14.38
Collister (1955) 14.72
Commission for Racial Equality v
   Dutton (1989) 18.43
Coney (1882)   .   .   10.4, 10.5, 23.9
Congdon (1990) 23.27
Conway (1988) 22.35, 22.38
Cook v Atchison (1968) 9.47
Cooke (1826) 21.14
Cooke (1986) 13.39, 14.95
Cooper v Motor Insurers' Bureau
   (1985) 20.37
Coppen v Moore (No 2) (1898)   .   23.38,
                                     23.41
Corbett v Corbett (otherwise Ashley)
   (1971) 10.4
Corcoran v Anderton (1980)   .   .   .   13.11
Cory Bros & Co (1927) 9.87
Cotterill v Penn (1936) 8.10
Couglan (1976) 21.14
Coupe v Guyett (1973) 23.38
Court (1989)   .   12.16, 12.17, 12.18, 12.20
Courtie (1984)   .   6.1, 6.61, 12.29, 12.35,
                     14.6, 15.1, 19.28,
                     21.23
Cousins (1982) 22.3
Cox (1968) 9.39
Cox v Riley (1986) 15.8
Craig (1962) 16.2
Cramp (1880); affd (1880)   .   .   .   11.77
Crawley Justices, ex p DPP (1991)   .   4.7
Creamer (1966) 23.23
Cribben (1980) 21.14
Croft (1944) 23.31
Cronin (1940) 5.33
Crown Court at Ipswich, ex p
   Baldwin (1981) 5.36
Crown Court at Winchester, ex p
   Lewington (1982) 5.26
Crown Suppliers (Property Services
   Agency) v Dawkins (1991) .   .   .   18.43
Crunden (1809) 19.23

PARA

Cuddy (1843) 10.2
Cugullere (1961) 6.58, 18.87
Cullen (1974) 13.40
Cullum (1873) 13.39
Cundy v Le Cocq (1884) . . . 8.12
Cundy v Lindsay (1878) . . . 13.44
Cunningham (1957) . . 6.45, 10.22
Cunningham (1959) 11.34
Cunningham (1982) . . 3.8, 11.23, 11.26
Curphey (1957) 20.13
Curr (1968) 21.2, 21.4
Curtis (1885) 6.11

D

D (1984) 16.12
Dadson (1850) 6.20
Dalby (1982) 11.63
Damaree (1709) 17.3
Davenport (1954) 13.20
Davey v Towle (1973) 9.43
Davies (1906) 16.31
Davies (1975) 11.36
Davies (1982) 13.44
Davies (1983) 9.73
Davies (1991) 9.53, 11.14
Davies v DPP (1989) 20.30
Davies v Flackett (1972) . . . 14.28
Davies v Harvey (1874) . . . 8.14
Davis (1881) 9.69
Davis (1988) 13.45
Davis v DPP (1988) 20.30
Davis v Lisle (1936) 18.69
Dawes v Taylor (1986) . . . 20.36
Dawson (1976) 14.4
Dawson, Nolan and Walmsley
  (1985) 11.68, 11.69
Day (1841) 10.7
Delgado (1984) 19.29
Dempsey and Dempsey (1985) . 19.29
Denham v Scott (1983) . . . 14.91
Denton (1982) 15.12, 22.41
Derby Magistrates' Court, ex p
  Brooks (1984) 4.7
Devlin v Armstrong (1971) . . 22.3
Dibble v Ingleton (1972) . 18.70, 20.33
Dickie (1984) 9.13, 9.28
Diggin (1981) 14.25
Dilks v Bowman-Shaw (1981) . 20.14
Dino Services Ltd v Prudential
  Assurance Co Ltd (1989) . 15.23, 18.5
DPP v A and BC Chewing Gum Ltd
  (1968) 19.13
DPP v Beard (1920) . 9.51, 9.52, 9.63,
                      9.69, 9.70
DPP v Billington (1988) . 20.35, 20.36
DPP v Byrne (1990) 20.29
DPP v Camplin (1978) . . 7.9, 11.38,
                      11.42, 11.43
DPP v Carey (1970) 20.35
DPP v Daley (1980) 11.63
DPP v Doot (1973) 21.12
DPP v Eddowes (1991) . . . 20.36

PARA

DPP v Fisher (1991) 20.38
DPP v Frost (1989) 20.24
DPP v Goodchild (1978) . . . 19.28
DPP v Gordon (1990) 20.30
DPP v Huskinson (1988) . . . 13.39
DPP v Jones (1990) 22.37
DPP v Jordan (1977) 19.14
DPP v K (a minor) (1990) . 10.11, 10.12,
                          10.14
DPP v Kent and Sussex Contractors
  Ltd (1944) 9.82, 9.86
DPP v Little (1992) . . 10.9, 10.16
DPP v McGladrigan (1991) . . 20.28
DPP v Magill (1988) 20.29
DPP v Majewski (1977) . 6.41, 9.51, 9.52,
                      9.53, 9.63, 9.64, 9.73,
                      18.10
DPP v Morgan (1976) . 6.42, 7.20, 7.29,
                      9.57, 12.3, 19.7
DPP v Newbury (1977) . 11.63, 11.67
DPP v Nock (1978); revsd (1978) . 21.8,
                      21.50
DPP v Orum (1988) 18.36
DPP v Parmenter (1991) . 6.53, 6.55,
                      10.17, 10.21, 10.22
DPP v Pidhajeckyj (1990) . . . 20.2
DPP v Ray (1974) . 14.28, 14.33, 14.37
DPP v Schildkamp (1971) . . 14.94
DPP v Shannon (1975) . . . 21.14
DPP v Singh (1988) 20.33
DPP v Smith (1961) . 10.20, 11.23, 11.26
DPP v Stonehouse (1978) . 5.12, 6.81,
                      13.57, 21.1, 21.66
DPP v Taylor (1992) . . 10.9, 10.16
DPP v Turner (1974) 14.50
DPP v Watkins (1989) . . . 20.18
DPP v Webb (1988) . . 20.18, 20.35
DPP v Whalley (1991) . . . 20.36
DPP v Whyte (1972) 19.13
DPP v Withers (1974) . . . 21.40
DPP for Northern Ireland v Lynch
  (1975) . . 3.8, 22.16, 22.17, 22.23,
          22.28, 23.6, 23.17
DPP for Northern Ireland v Maxwell
  (1978) . . . 23.3, 23.18, 23.20
Ditta, Hussain and Kara (1988) . 7.32,
                      22.28
Dix (1982) 9.38
Dobinson (1977) . 6.11, 6.13, 11.51, 11.52
Dobson v General Accident Fire and
  Life Assurance Corpn plc (1990) . 13.7,
                      14.45
Dodge (1972) 15.46
Dolan (1975) 14.77
Donald (1986) 16.2
Donnelly (1984) 15.46
Donnelly v Jackman (1970) . . 18.69
Donovan (1934) . . 10.3, 10.6, 10.13
Doughty (1986) 11.35
Doukas (1978) 14.95
Downes (1984) 19.30
Downey (1970) 20.36

PARA

Du Cros v Lambourne (1907) . . 23.10
Dudley (1989) 15.13
Dudley and Stephens (1884) . . . 22.37
Duffy (1949) . . . 11.37, 11.40, 11.46
Duke (1961) 9.25
Duke v Reliance Systems Ltd
   (1987) 3.9
Dunbar (1958) 9.34
Dunbar (1982) 19.30
Dunbar (1988) 23.24, 23.25
Duncan v Jones (1936) 18.69
Dunnington (1984) . . . 21.54, 23.4
Durante (1972) 9.63, 9.64
Durkin (1973) 14.17
Duru (1973) 13.63, 14.34
Dyson (1908) 11.7, 11.8
Dytham (1979) 6.11

E

Ealing Justices, ex p Dixon (1990) . 4.2
Easom (1971) 13.65
Eaton v Cobb (1950) 8.10
Eddy v Niman (1981) 13.12
Edmonds (1963) 18.86
Edwards (1975) 7.8
Edwards (1991) 21.27
Edwards (alias Murray) v R (1973) . 11.38
El-Hakkaoui (1975) 6.78
Eldershaw (1828) . . . 12.2, 23.14
Elkins v Cartlidge (1947) . . . 20.8
Ellames (1974) 14.94
Ellerton (1977) 22.17, 22.19
Elliott v C (a minor) (1983) . 6.43, 6.47,
                                6.48, 6.49
Ellis (1899) 6.78
Ellis v Burton (1975) 1.5
Ellis and Street (1986) . . . 6.61
Enoch (1833) 11.3
Esop (1836) 6.73
Evans (1986) 21.2
Evans v Ewels (1972) 12.24
Evans v Hughes (1972) . . . 18.88
Evening Standard Co Ltd (1954) . 16.17

F

F (a minor), Re (1977) 16.28
F v West Berkshire Health Authority
   (Mental Health Act Commission
   intervening) (1989) . 10.7, 10.8, 10.15,
                                22.33
Fagan v Metropolitan Police Comr
   (1969) . . . 6.71, 10.9, 10.10, 10.11
Fairclough v Whipp (1951) . 10.10, 12.21
Farrell v Secretary of State for
   Defence (1980) 22.8
Faulkner v Talbot (1981) . . . 12.17
Feely (1973) 13.54
Feeney (1991) 14.41
Felstead v R (1914) 9.25
Fennell (1971) 10.17, 22.12
Fenton (1975) 9.36, 9.38

PARA

Ferguson v Weaving (1951) . . 8.9, 23.6,
                                23.43
Ferrymasters Ltd v Adams (1980) . 8.9
Finch and Jardine (1983) 22.4
Finney (1874) 11.53
Firetto (1991) 16.32
Firth (1990) . . . 14.33, 14.62, 14.63
Fisher (1865) 15.8
Fisher (1987) 7.21
Fitzmaurice (1983) 21.8
Fitzpatrick v Kelly (1873) . . . 8.14
Flack v Hunt (1980) 10.22
Fleming (David Michael) (1989) . . 18.86
Forbes and Webb (1865) 10.17
Forde (1923) 5.30
Formosa (1991) 18.78
Fotheringham (1988) . 9.56, 9.62, 9.63,
                                9.64
Fowler (1987) 14.89
Fowler v Padget (1798) 6.70
Fox v Chief Constable of Gwent
   (1985); affd (1986) . 20.27, 20.28, 20.32,
                                20.35
Francis (1982) 12.7, 14.15
Francis (Colin Leslie) (1988) . . . 12.21
Franklin (1883) 11.60
Fransman v Sexton (1965) . . . 8.9
Fretwell (1862) 23.17
Fritschy (1985) . . . 13.5, 13.6, 13.12

G

Galbraith (1981) 5.10
Gammon (Hong Kong) Ltd v A-G of
   Hong Kong (1985) 8.5, 8.7
Gannon (1988) 9.68, 14.24
Garcia (1987) 15.47
Gardner v Akeroyd (1952) . 23.43, 23.45
Gardner v DPP (1988) . . 20.16, 20.18,
                                20.23
Garlick (1980) 9.53
Garrett v Arthur Churchill (Glass)
   Ltd (1969) 23.8
Garwood (1987) 14.73
Gaston (1981) 12.4
Gateshead Justices, ex p Usher
   (1981) 16.35
Gatland v Metropolitan Police Comr
   (1968) 7.8
Gauthier (1943) 11.46
Gayford v Chouler (1898) . . . 15.8
Georgiades (1989) . . . 18.80, 22.14
Getty v Antrim County Council
   (1950) 15.8
Ghosh (1982) . 13.54, 13.55, 14.41, 21.41
Gibbins and Proctor (1918) . 6.11, 11.6
Gibson (1991) . 8.3, 19.23, 19.25, 19.26
Gibson and Gibson (1984) . . . 23.10
Gilbert (1977) 11.47
Gilks (1972) 13.45, 13.47
Gill (1963) 7.4, 22.19, 22.28
Gill and Henry (1818) 21.12
Gill and Ranuana (1989) . . . 23.30

PARA

Gillick v West Norfolk and Wisbech
 Area Health Authority (1986);
 revsd (1986) . . . 6.26, 22.33, 23.17
Gilmartin (1983) 14.29
Giscombe (1985) 16.23
Gittens (1984) 9.38
Gittins (1982) 8.10
Godfrey (1923) 23.4
Gold (1988) 15.44
Gold Star Publications Ltd v DPP
 (1981) 19.18
Golechha (1989) 14.74
Gomez (1964) 9.33
Gomez (1991) . 13.8, 13.9, 13.10, 13.15,
 14.45, 14.47
Goodfellow (1986) . . 11.55, 11.59, 11.60,
 11.63, 11.66
Goodfellow v Johnson (1966) . . 23.38
Gorrie (1918) 9.2
Gott v Measures (1948) . . . 15.12
Gotts (1991) 22.22, 22.24
Gould (1968) . . . 3.9, 7.32, 19.7
Goult (1982) 16.31
Governor of Pentonville Prison, ex p
 Chinoy (1992) 23.30
Governor of Pentonville Prison, ex p
 Osman (1989) 3.7, 13.4
Grady v Pollard (1988) . . . 20.36
Graham (1982) . . 7.29, 22.18, 22.23
Graham-Kerr (1988) . . 19.19, 19.21
Grahme (1691) 17.3
Grainge (1974) 14.88
Grant (1960) 9.28, 9.34
Grant v Borg (1982) 6.74
Gray (1900) 16.27
Gray v Barr (1971) . 7.16, 11.51, 11.52
Gray's Haulage Co Ltd v Arnold
 (1966) 6.65, 8.9
Greater Manchester Coroner, ex p
 Tal (1985) 3.10
Green v Burnett (1955) . 23.38, 23.42
Green v DPP (1991) 18.71
Green v Moore (1982) 18.70
Greenberg (1919) 16.33
Greenfield (1983) 19.30
Greenstein (1976) 14.41
Gregory (1981) 11.40
Gregory (1982) 14.4
Griffin (1869) 10.13
Griffin (1988) 16.31
Griffith v Jenkins (1991); on appeal
 (1992) 5.26
Griffiths (1974) 14.88
Griffiths (1990) 9.58
Griffiths v Freeman (1970) . . 14.81
Griffiths v Studebakers Ltd (1924) . 23.42
Grimes (1968) 16.33
Gross (1913) 11.36
Grundy (1977) 23.31
Gull v Scarborough (1987) . . 20.28
Gullefer (1990) . . 21.65, 21.66, 21.67
Gumbley v Cunningham (1989) . . 20.32

PARA

H

Haider (1985) 14.82
Halai (1983) 14.54
Hale (1978) 14.4
Hall (1961) 11.67
Hall (1973) 13.42
Hall (1985) 14.88
Hall (1987) 12.12
Hall (1988) 5.12, 15.12
Hall v Cotton (1987) 18.77
Halliday (1889) 10.21
Hamilton (1987) 23.21
Hamilton (1990) 14.29
Hammond (1941) 5.10
Hammond (1982) 14.66
Hampton v US (1976) 23.29
Hancock (1986) . . 6.28, 6.33, 6.41
Handley (1874) 11.3
Handyside (circa 1750) 13.22
Harbax Singh (1979) 16.35
Harden (1963) 6.78
Hardie (1984) . 6.48, 6.54, 9.54, 9.76,
 15.14
Harding (1974) 20.36
Harding v Price (1948) 8.12
Hargreaves (1985) 14.94
Harrington (1866) 11.37
Harris (1972) 15.46
Harris (1986) 14.88
Hartland v Alden (1987) . . . 20.35
Harvey, Uylett and Plummer (1981) . 14.75
Harwood (1989) 23.30
Haughton v Smith (1975) . 21.8, 21.50,
 21.68, 21.78
Havant Justices, ex p Palmer
 (1985) 16.31
Hayes (1976) 13.42, 13.51
Hayles (1989) . 6.25, 6.29, 6.30, 6.35,
 21.60
Haynes v Swain (1975) . . . 20.14
Hayward (1908) 11.13
Head (1978) 16.36
Hehl (1976) 13.13, 14.87
Hendrickson and Tichner (1977) . . 21.3
Hennah (1877) 11.77
Hennessey (1978) 6.61
Hennessy (1989) . . 9.15, 9.17, 9.46
Hennigan (1971) . . . 11.9, 20.13
Hensey (1758) 17.2
Henshall (John) (Quarries) Ltd v
 Harvey (1965) 9.86
Hensler (1870) 14.37
Herbert (1960) 13.21
Hibbert (1869) . . . 7.17, 8.2, 12.26
Higgins (1801) 21.2
Hill (1851) 9.29
Hill (1986) 16.31
Hill (1988) 5.12, 15.12
Hill v Baxter (1958) . . . 7.9, 9.42
Hills v Ellis (1983) 18.71
Hinchcliffe v Sheldon (1955) . . 18.70
Hircock (1978) . . . 13.15, 14.45

PARA

Hirst and Agu v Chief Constable of
  West Yorkshire (1987) 7.8
Hobbs v Clark (1988) 20.29
Hobson v Impett (1957) . . .   14.82
Hodge v Higgins (1980) 23.36
Hodgson (1973) 12.8
Hogdon (1962) 14.22
Holden (1991) 13.52
Holland (1841) 11.15
Holling v DPP (1991) 20.31
Hollinshead (1985); revsd (1985) .   21.16,
                                    21.38
Holmes (1953) 9.21
Holmes v DPP (1946) 11.35
Holt (1981) 14.56
Hoof (1980) 15.14
Hopley (1860) 10.13, 11.62
Hornigold v Chief Constable of
  Lancashire (1985) 3.10
Horseferry Road Metropolitan
  Stipendiary Magistrate, ex p
  Siadatan (1991) 18.28
Horsey v Hutchings (1984) . . .   15.48
Horsham Justices, ex p Farquharson
  (1982); affd (1982) . . .   4.24, 16.21
Horton v Gwynne (1921) . . .   7.16
Houghton (1982) 18.83
Houghton v Chief Constable of
  Greater Manchester (1987) . .   18.86
Howard (1965) 10.7, 12.5
Howard v G T Jones & Co Ltd
  (1975) 23.38
Howard v Hallett (1984) . . .   20.32
Howe (1986); affd (1987) .   3.8, 3.9, 7.29,
                   22.16, 22.18, 22.22,
                   22.23, 22.24, 22.37,
                   23.17, 23.26
Howell (1982) 4.16
Howells (1977) .   8.15, 8.16, 12.33, 18.77
Howker v Robinson (1973) . . .   23.39
Huckerby v Elliott (1970) . . .   9.90
Huddersfield Police Authority v
  Watson (1947) 3.10
Hudson (1966) 6.65, 12.12
Hudson (1971) . . .   22.17, 22.20, 22.22
Huggins (1730) 23.36
Hughes (1841) 12.2
Hui Chi-ming v R (1992) .   23.24, 23.26
Humphreys (1977) 18.86
Humphreys and Turner (1965) .   23.15
Humphries (1987) 18.86
Hunt (1977) 15.12
Hunt (1987) 7.8, 19.29, 19.30
Hurley and Murray (1967) . .   22.17
Hussain (1969) 6.61
Hussain (1981) 8.16, 18.77
Hussey (1924) 22.13
Hyam v DPP (1975) .   6.26, 11.22, 11.23,
                                    11.26
Hyde (1990) 23.19, 23.24

PARA

I

ICR Haulage Ltd (1944) .   9.82, 9.83, 9.87
IPH v Chief Constable of South
  Wales (1987) 9.2
Ibrams (1981) 11.40
Inner West London Coroner, ex p
  De Luca (1989) . . .   11.7, 11.33
Inseal (1992) 9.36
Invicta Plastics Ltd v Clare (1975) .   21.3
Isitt (1978) 9.42
Ives (1970) 11.34

J

JBH and JH (minors) v O'Connell
  (1981) 9.2
JJC (a minor) v Eisenhower (1983) .   10.20
JM (a minor) v Runeckles (1984) .   9.2
Jackson (1985) 7.21
Jackson, Golding and Jackson
  (1985) 21.20
Jaggard v Dickinson (1981) .   7.8, 9.68,
                            13.52, 15.12
Jakeman (1983) 6.70
James (1837) 22.41
James (1844) 10.10
James (1976) 14.4
James & Son Ltd v Smee (1955) .   6.59, 8.9
Janaway v Salford Area Health
  Authority (1989); affd (1989) .   11.80
Jarvis (1903) 12.25
Jarvis v Williams (1979) . .   20.14
Jenkins (1983); revsd (1984) .   3.9, 14.13
Jennings (1990) .   11.62, 11.63, 11.64
Jennion (1962) 9.38
Jervis (1833) 11.41
Johnson (1964) 12.10
Johnson (1989) 7.9
Johnson, Re (1887) 16.26
Johnson v Phillips (1975) . . .   22.33
Johnson v West Yorkshire
  Metropolitan Police (1986) . .   20.32
Johnson v Youden (1950) .   23.18, 23.22
Johnson and Jones (1841) . .   23.32
Johnstone, Comerford and Jalil
  (1982) 13.62
Jones (1832) 21.12
Jones (1861) 12.5
Jones (1973) 12.25, 12.26
Jones (1976) 14.9, 14.11
Jones (1977) 23.9
Jones (1986) . . .   7.21, 10.3, 10.22
Jones (1990) 21.65, 21.67
Jones v Pratt (1983) 20.6
Jones v Sherwood (1942) . . .   10.9
Jordan (1956) 11.18
Jordan v Burgoyne (1963) . .   18.28
Josephs (1977) 19.34
Joyce v DPP (1946) 17.5
Julien (1969) 22.3
Jura (1954) 18.88

PARA

Justice of the Peace for
Peterborough, ex p Hicks (1978) . 15.55

K

Kaitamaki (1980); affd (1985) . . 6.12,
6.71, 12.7
Kanwar (1982) 14.85
Kavanagh v Hiscock (1974) . . . 18.71
Kay v Butterworth (1945) . . . 9.49
Kay v Hibbert (1977) 18.69
Kellett (1976) 16.33
Kelt (1977) 18.83
Kemp (1957) . . 9.13, 9.15, 9.42, 9.46
Kemp v Liebherr - GB Ltd (1987) . 4.7
Kenlin v Gardiner (1967) . . 10.17, 18.69,
22.12
Kewal (1985) 6.53
Khan (1990) . . 9.62, 9.63, 12.7, 21.55,
21.59, 21.61
Kilbride v Lake (1962) 9.41
Kimber (1983) . . 6.20, 7.21, 10.9, 10.14,
12.16
Kindon (1957) 9.64
King (1964) 7.32, 19.7
King (1987) 14.38, 14.50
King v Hodges (1974) 18.69
Kirkland v Robinson (1986) . . . 8.12
Kiszko (1978) 9.38
Knightley (1971) 20.36
Knott (1973) 14.89
Knowles Transport Ltd v Russell
(1975) 8.9
Knuller (Publishing, Printing and
Promotions) Ltd v DPP (1973) . 3.8,
3.12, 19.13, 19.23,
19.24, 21.46
Kohn (1979) 13.20
Kong Cheuk Kwan v R (1985) . . 11.55,
11.56
Kooken (1981) 9.34
Krause (1902) 21.3
Krebbs (1977) 20.4
Krumpa and Anderson v DPP
(1989) 15.35
Kwaku Mensah v R (1946) . . . 10.10

L

L v K (1985) 9.3
Lamb (1967) 11.60, 11.63
Lambie (1982) 14.29, 14.37
Landy (1981) 21.41
Lane and Lane (1985) 23.33
Lang (1975) 12.5
Lankford (1959) 21.78
Large v Mainprize (1989) . . . 6.53
Larkin (1943) 11.51, 11.67
Larsonneur (1933) 8.18
Latimer (1886) 6.56
Lattimore (1975) 5.29
Laverty (1970) 14.38
Law v Stephens (1971) . . 20.35, 20.36

PARA

Lawrence (1971) 14.73, 14.75
Lawrence (1982) . 6.43, 6.49, 6.51, 6.68,
11.54, 11.58, 20.13
Lawrence v Metropolitan Police
Comr (1972) . . . 13.5, 14.43, 14.45
Lawrence v Same (1968) 5.19
Le Brun (1991) 11.27
Lee Chun-Chuen (alias Lee
Wing-Cheuk) v R (1963) . 7.9, 11.34
Lefroy (1873) 16.31
Leicester v Pearson (1952) . . . 9.43
Lemon (1979) 8.1, 8.3
Lennard (1973) 20.36
Lennard's Carrying Co Ltd v Asiatic
Petroleum Co Ltd (1915) . . . 9.86
Lester (1938) 5.12
Letenock (1917) 9.66, 11.48
Leung Kam Kwok v R (1984) . . 11.22
Lewin v Bland (1985) 9.90
Lewis (1970) 10.21
Lewis (1975) 13.54
Lewis (1988) 19.31
Lewis v Cox (1985) . 6.71, 18.70, 18.71
Lewis v Dickson (1976) 22.40
Lewis v James (1887) 16.23
Lewis v Lethbridge (1987) . . . 13.43
Liangsiriprasert v United States
Government (1990) . . . 6.81, 21.1
Licensing Authority for Goods
Vehicles in Metropolitan Traffic
Area v Coggins (1985) . . . 8.9
Lim Chin Aik v R (1963) . 8.12, 8.17
Lincolnshire (Kesteven) Justices, ex
p O'Connor (1983) 9.11
Lines (1844) 12.2
Linnett v Metropolitan Police Comr
(1946) 23.39
Lipman (1970) . 9.51, 9.64, 11.63, 11.67
Lloyd (1887) 16.8
Lloyd (1967) 9.37
Lloyd (1985) . . . 13.61, 13.62, 13.63
Loade v DPP (1990) 18.28
Lobell (1957) 7.4, 22.7
Lockwood (1986) 13.55
Lockyer v Gibb (1967) 19.31
Lodge v DPP (1988) 18.35
Logdon v DPP (1976) 10.10
Lomas (1913) 23.8
London and Globe Finance Corpn
Ltd, Re (1903) . . . 14.28, 14.37
Long (1971) 16.2
Longbottom (1849) 11.12
Longhorn (1679) 17.2
Longman (1980) 21.14
Lonrho plc, Re (1990) . . 16.15, 16.31
Lord George Gordon (1781) . . . 17.3
Lord Kylsant (1932) 14.33
Lovelace v DPP (1954) 8.11
Lovesey (1970) 23.24
Low v Blease (1975) 13.22
Lowe (1973) 11.60
Ludlow v Burgess (1971) . . . 18.69

PARA

Lynch (1903) 17.4
Lyons v May (1948) . . . 8.9, 20.38

M

McBean v Parker (1983) . . . 18.69
McBride v Turnock (1964) . . . 10.17
McCalla (1988) . . 6.70, 18.87, 18.88,
                                    19.31
McCann (1971) 23.28
McCarthy (1954) 11.46
McCarthy (1967) 9.8
McConnell v Chief Constable of the
   Greater Manchester Police (1990) . 4.16
McCormack (1969) 12.17
McCrone v Riding (1938) . . 20.14
McCullum (1973) 6.61
McDavitt (1981) 14.66
MacDonagh (1974) 20.6
McDonnell (1966) 21.13
McDonough (1962) 21.8
McEvilly (1973) 23.29
McGill (1970) 14.20, 14.22
McGrath v Vipas (1983) . . . 20.36
McGregor (1962) 11.44
M'Growther's Case (1746) . . 22.25
Machent v Quinn (1970) . . 13.19
Machin (1980) 16.32
McHugh (1988) . . . 13.5, 13.6
McInnes (1971) . . . 22.3, 22.11
Mackie (1973); affd (1973) . 10.13, 11.14,
                                    11.67
Macklin and Murphy's Case (1838) . 23.1
McKnight v Davies (1974) . . 14.20
McKoen y Ellis (1986) . . . 20.6
Maclane (1797) 17.2
McLeod v St Aubyn (1899) . . 16.27
M'Loughlin (1838) 10.20
McMillan (1984) 10.20
McNaghten's Case (1843) . . 7.6, 9.12,
                                    9.23
McNamara (1988) . . . 19.31, 19.32
McNiff (1986) 14.50
McPherson (1957) . . . 7.4, 11.47
MacPherson (1973) . . . 9.64, 14.24
McQuaid v Anderton (1980) . . 20.6
McShane (1977) 21.54
McVey (1988) 13.57
Madan (1961) 4.9
Madden (1975) 8.3
Maddy (1671) 11.35
Madigan (1983) 6.49
Maginnis (1987) 19.29
Magna Plant v Mitchell (1966) . 9.86
Maguire (1991) 5.32
Maidstone Borough Council v
   Mortimer (1980) 8.10
Mainwaring (1981) 13.39
Malcherek (1981) . 11.4, 11.9, 11.18, 11.19
Mallows v Harris (1979) . . 7.8, 20.36
Manchester Crown Court, Re, ex p
   Hill (1985) 21.80
Mancini v DPP (1942) . . 7.9, 11.46

PARA

Mandla v Dowell Lee (1983); revsd
   (1983) 18.43
Manktelow (1853) 12.25
Manley (1844) 23.2
Mansfield (1975) 14.94
Marchant (1985) 14.21
Marcus (1981) 11.77
Maria v Hall (1807) 11.5
Marlow (1964) 11.77
Marsh v Arscott (1982) . . . 18.23
Martin (1827) 11.12
Martin (1848) 16.25
Martin (1867) 14.38
Martin (1881) 10.12
Martin (1989) . 7.29, 22.17, 22.36, 22.38
Martindale (1966) 11.34
Martindale (1986) . . . 18.87, 19.31
Matheson (1958) . . 9.33, 9.34, 9.38
Matto v DPP (or Crown Court at
   Wolverhampton) (1987) . . . 20.28
Maughan (1934) 12.19
Mawji v R (1957) 21.13
Maxwell and Clanchy (1909) . . 10.17
May (1990) 19.26
Mayers (1872) 12.5
Mayling (1963) . . 19.23, 19.24, 19.26
Meade and Belt (1823) . . . 10.10
Mealey (1974) 23.29
Medford (1974) 18.86
Meech (1974) 13.19, 13.40
Meli v R (1954) 11.27
Melik (1985) 21.38
Melwani (1989) 14.41
Metropolitan Police Comr, ex p
   Blackburn (No 2) (1968) . 16.27, 16.31
Metropolitan Stipendiary Magistrate
   Tower Bridge, ex p Aniifowosi
   (1985) 9.11
Meyrick (1929) 21.12
Mickleborough v BRS (Contracts)
   Ltd (1977) 23.38
Middleton (1873) 13.47
Midland Bank Trust Co Ltd v Green
   (No 3) (1982) 21.13
Millard v DPP (1990) 20.32
Millard and Vernon (1987) . . 21.60
Miller (1954) 10.3, 10.17
Miller (1976) 14.25
Miller (1983) . . . 6.1, 6.12, 6.49, 6.71
Miller v Minister of Pensions
   (1947) 7.5
Millward (1985) 16.8
Minor v DPP (1988) 14.94
Mirrless (1977) 23.9
Mitchell (1983) . . . 6.56, 11.66
Mitchell (1990) 13.55
Modupe (1991) 14.57
Mogul SS Co v McGregor Gow &
   Co (1888); affd (1892) . 21.12, 23.32
Mohan (1976) . 6.25, 6.41, 9.64, 21.57
Moloney (1985) . 6.24, 6.28, 6.41, 11.22,
                                    11.25

PARA

Moore (1975) 9.53
Moore (1986) 7.9
Moore v Clerk of Assize, Bristol
  (1970) 16.25
Moore v Gooderham (1960) . . . 18.74
Moore v Green (1983) 18.71
Moore v I Bresler Ltd (1944) . 9.82, 9.86
Moore and Dorn (1975) 11.27
Morais (1988) 5.2
Moran (1985) 16.31
Morden v Porter (1860) . . . 8.14
More (1987) 15.46
Moreton (1913) 14.38
Morgan (1972) 16.2
Morphitis v Salmon (1990) . . . 15.8
Morris (1951) 3.3, 3.4
Morris (1966) 23.23, 23.24
Morris (1972) 20.25
Morris (1984) . 13.4, 13.12, 13.60, 14.45
Morris v Beardmore (1981) . 20.27, 20.35
Morris v Tolman (1923) . . . 23.13
Morrison (1938) 19.4
Morrison (1988) 10.26
Morry (1946) 4.22
Moses v Winder (1981) . . 9.47, 9.49
Moses and Ansbro (1991) . . . 21.40
Most (1881) 21.3
Mousell Bros Ltd v London and
  North-Western Rly Co (1917) . . 9.82,
                                    23.38
Mowatt (1968) 10.22, 10.26
Moys (1984) 14.88
Mullins (1848) 23.28
Murphy v DPP (1990) . . . 16.35
Murphy and Douglas (1837) . . 21.12
Murray (1982) 16.32, 16.33
Murtagh and Kennedy (1955) . . 23.26

N

National Coal Board v Gamble
  (1959) 23.6, 23.8, 23.17
Navvabi (1986) . . . 13.13, 13.19
Neal v Evans (1976) . . 18.70, 20.33
Neal v Gribble (1978) 14.19
Nedrick (1986) 6.29, 6.34
Neville v Mavroghenis (1984) . . 8.12
New Statesman (Editor), ex p DPP
  (1928) 16.27
Newberry v Simmonds (1961) . . 20.7
Newbury v Davis (1974) . . . 20.38
Newell (1980) 11.44
Newell (1989) 11.47
Newsome (1970) 3.9
Newton and Stungo (1958) . . 11.82
Newton (G) Ltd v Smith (1962) . 23.38
Nicholls (1874) 6.11
Nicholls v Brentwood Justices
  (1991) 4.20
Nichols (1745) 21.14
Nicholson v Tapp (1972) . . . 20.2
Nicklin (1977) 14.81

PARA

Norfolk Constabulary v Seekings and
  Gould (1986) 14.10
Northumberland Compensation
  Appeal Tribunal, ex p Shaw
  (1952) 3.10
Norton (1977) 18.80
Nugent (1987) 22.8

O

Oakwell (1978) 18.23
O'Boyle (1973) 20.36
O'Brien (1974) 12.6
O'Connell (1991) . . . 9.60, 13.57
O'Driscoll (1977) . . . 9.64, 11.63
O'Grady (1987) 9.59
Ohlson v Hylton (1975) . . . 18.86
Oldcastle's Case (1419) . . . 22.25
Olugboja (1982) 12.5
Orpin (1975) 2.6
Ortiz (1986) 22.17, 22.18
Osborn (1919) 21.67
Ostler v Elliott (1980) . . . 18.71
O'Sullivan and Lewis (1989) . . 13.57
O'Toole (1987) 21.60
Owen (1830) 9.2
Owen (1976) 16.31, 16.34
Owen (1988) 19.21
Oxford v Moss (1978) 13.21

P

P & O European Ferries (Dover) Ltd
  (1987) 9.87
Page (1954) 11.5
Pagett (1983) . . . 11.9, 11.17, 11.19
Palmer v R (1971) 22.8, 22.11
Panayiotou (1973) 16.33
Pannell (1982) 18.78
Park (1987) 14.86
Parkes (1973) 14.74
Parkin v Norman (1983) . 18.23, 18.28
Parmenter (1991) . . . 10.17, 10.21
Parnell (1881) 21.12
Parrott (1913) 17.9
Partington v Williams (1975) . . 21.69
Patel (1991) 21.23
Paterson v DPP (1990) . . . 20.30
Paul (1952) 20.7
Pawley v Wharldall (1966) . . 20.14
Peace (1976) 5.33
Peacock v London Weekend
  Television (1985) 16.31
Pearce (1973) 14.21
Pearce (1980) 21.31
Pearman (1985) 21.57
Peart (1970) 14.22
Peaston (1978) 19.31
Peck (1975) 11.34, 21.55
Pedro v Diss (1981) . 10.17, 18.69, 22.12
Pembliton (1874) 6.56
Pender v Smith (1959) . . . 21.80
Perry v McGovern (1986) . . 20.30

PARA

Peterson (1970) 23.24
Pettigrew v Northumbria Police
　Authority (1976) 20.35
Pharmaceutical Society of Great
　Britain v Storkwain Ltd (1986) . 8.12
Phekoo (1981) 7.21, 8.6, 8.16
Philip Reid (1973) 20.36
Philippou (1989) 13.7
Philips (1839) 9.3
Phillips (1983) 16.31
Phillips v R (1969) 11.46
Phipps (1970) 14.20, 14.22
Phipps v Hoffman (1976) 23.38
Pickering v Liverpool Daily Post and
　Echo Newspapers plc (1991) . . 16.28,
　　　　　　　　　　　　　16.31
Piddington v Bates (1960) . . . 18.69
Pierre (1963) 18.81
Pigg (1983); revsd (1983) . . 5.14, 12.7
Pike (1961) 11.52
Pilgram v Rice-Smith (1977) . 13.14, 13.19
Pitchley (1972) 14.84, 14.85
Pitham (1976) 13.13, 14.87
Pittard v Mahoney (1977) . . . 18.88
Pitts (1842) 11.14
Pittwood (1902) 6.11, 11.53
Plummer (1902) 21.14
Plunkett v Matchell (1958) . . . 10.11
Podola (1960) 9.8
Poole v Lockwood (1981) . . . 20.35
Pordage (1975) 9.53, 9.62
Porritt (1961) 11.37
Porter (1910) 16.36
Poulterers' Case (1610) 21.12
Poulton (1832) 11.3
Poultry World Ltd v Conder (1957) . 23.18
Powell v MacRae (1977) . . 13.34, 13.39
Practice Direction [1967] 3 All ER
　137 . . . . 5.14
Practice Direction [1970] 1 WLR
　916. See Practice Note [1970] 2 All
　ER 215
Practice Direction [1981] 2 All ER
　831 . . . . 5.19
Practice Direction [1983] 1 WLR
　1292. See Practice Note [1983] 3
　All ER 608
Practice Note [1966] 3 All ER 77,
　sub nom Practice Statement [1966]
　1 WLR 1234 . . . . . . 3.8
Practice Note [1970] 2 All ER 215,
　sub nom Practice Direction [1970]
　1 WLR 916 . . . . . . 5.14
Practice Note [1977] 2 All ER 540 . 21.34
Practice Note [1983] 1 All ER 64 . 16.21,
　　　　　　　　　　　　　16.29
Practice Note [1983] 3 All ER 608,
　sub nom Practice Direction [1983]
　1 WLR 1292 . . . . . . 5.31
Practice Note [1987] 1 All ER 128,
　sub nom [1987] 1 WLR 79 . . 16.35
Practice Note [1987] 3 All ER 1064 . 2.6

PARA

Practice Note [1988] 3 All ER 1086 . 5.9
Practice Note [1990] 3 All ER 320,
　CA 4.21
Practice Note [1990] 3 All ER 979 . 4.20
Practice Note [1991] 1 All ER 288 . 5.1
Practice Statement [1966] 1 WLR
　1234. See Practice Note [1966] 3
　All ER 77
Preece (1977) 12.33
Prescott, Re (1979) 15.4
Preston (1986) 20.4
Preston Justices, ex p Lyons (1982) . 20.14
Price (1838) 22.23
Price (1989) 14.41
Price v Cromack (1975) 8.11
Pridige v Gant (1985) 20.4
Prince (1875) . . 7.17, 8.2, 12.26, 12.29,
　　　　　　　　　　　　　22.32
Pritchard (1836) 9.8
Proprietary Articles Trade
　Association v A-G for Canada
　(1931) 1.6, 3.23
Pugsley v Hunter (1973) 20.4
Pullen (1991) 9.47
Purcell (1986) 10.25
Purdy (1946) 22.25
Purdy (1975) 10.17
Pursell v Horn (1838) 10.11

Q

Quality Dairies (York) Ltd v Pedley
　(1952) 23.38
Quelch v Phipps (1955) 20.25
Quick (1973) . 9.15, 9.16, 9.42, 9.45, 9.48,
　　　　　　　　　　　　　9.69

R

R— (1991) . . 3.12, 12.4, 12.6, 12.9
Rabey (1977) 9.17
Rabjohns v Burgar (1971) . . . 20.14
Race Relations Board v Applin
　(1973) 21.3
Rakhit v Carty (1990) 3.9
Ram and Ram (1893) 23.14
Ramsgate Justices, ex p Kazmarek
　(1984) 9.11
Rance v Mid-Downs Health
　Authority (1991) . . 11.2, 11.3, 11.82
Ransford (1874) 21.3, 21.54
Rapier (1979) 18.86
Raven (1982) 11.45
Raymond v A-G (1982) 4.3
Rayner v Hampshire Chief
　Constable (1971) 20.35
Reader (1977) 14.88
Reakes (1974) 12.28
Redhead Freight Ltd v Shulman
　(1989) 8.11, 9.86
Reed (1982) 21.19
Reeves (1839) 11.3
Reid (1975) 23.25

PARA

Reid (1990) . . . 6.47, 6.52, 11.58
Reigate Justices, ex p Counsell
  (1983) 10.17
Renouf (1986) 22.5
Reynolds v G H Austin & Sons Ltd
  (1951) 8.17, 23.45
Ribuffi (1929) 21.12
Rice v Connolly (1966) . 18.69, 18.70,
  18.71
Richards v Curwen (1977) . . 18.74
Richman (1982) 22.29
Richmond upon Thames London
  Borough Council v Pinn &
  Wheeler Ltd (1989) 9.82
Rickards v Rickards (1990) . . 3.9
Ricketts v Cox (1981) 18.71
Rider (1954) 12.13
Rivett (1950) 9.19, 9.22
Robbins (1988) 12.28
Robert Millar (Contractors) Ltd
  (1970) 9.87, 23.4
Roberts (1971) 10.17, 11.14
Roberts (1983) 21.14
Roberts (1986) . . 12.6, 13.57, 14.41
Roberts (1990) 11.43
Roberts v Egerton (1874) . . . 8.14
Robertson (1968) 9.8, 9.28
Robins (1844) 12.25
Robinson (1975) 5.7
Robinson (1977) . . . 13.53, 14.3
Robinson v DPP (1989) . . . 20.4
Robson v Hallett (1967) . . 18.69
Roe v Kingerlee (1986) . . . 15.8
Rogers (1984) 6.47, 6.49
Rolfe (1952) 10.9, 12.16
Rolle v R (1965) 7.9
Roney v Matthews (1975) . . 20.30
Roper v Knott (1898) 15.8
Roper v Sullivan (1978) . . . 20.3
Roper v Taylor's Central Garages
  (Exeter) Ltd (1951) . 6.58, 6.59, 8.12
Rose (1884) 7.29
Rose (1961) 16.2
Rose (1982) 5.33
Rose v R (1961) 9.33
Ross v Moss (1965) 6.59
Ross Hillman Ltd v Bond (1974) . 8.11
Rowell (1978) 16.32, 16.33
Rowley (1991) 19.24
Royal College of Nursing of the
  United Kingdom v Department of
  Health and Social Security (1981) . 11.80
Ruse v Read (1949) 9.64
Russell (1984) 18.87
Russell and Russell (1987) . 23.10, 23.33
Ryan v R (1967) 9.41
Rynsard v Spalding (1986) . . 20.31

S

Sagoo (1975) 19.4
St George (1840) 10.10

PARA

St Helens Justices, ex p McClorie
  (1983) 15.4
St Margaret's Trust Ltd (1958) . . 8.15
Sainthouse (1980) 14.77
Salisbury (1976) 10.21
Salisbury Magistrates' Court, ex p
  Mastin (1986) 15.3
Salter (1968) 8.2
Sampson v Crown Court at Croydon
  (1987) 5.36
Sanders (1982) 14.85
Sanders (1991) 9.38
Sang (1980) . . . 20.28, 23.28, 23.29
Sangha (1988) 6.49
Sansom (1991) 6.81, 21.1
Satnam (1985) 6.53
Saunders (1985) 10.20, 11.26
Saunders and Archer (1573) . . . 23.21
Savage (1991) . 6.53, 6.55, 10.17, 10.21,
  10.22
Sawyer (1989) 11.47
Saycell v Bool (1948) 20.6
Schama (1914) 14.89
Schiavo v Anderton (1986) . . 16.35
Schifreen (1988) 15.44
Scott (1978) 21.12
Scott v Baker (1969) 20.35
Scott v Metropolitan Police Comr
  (1975) 21.38
Scudder v Barrett (1980) . . . 21.63
Searle v Randolph (1972) . . . 19.31
Secretary of State for the Home
  Department, ex p Garner (1991) . 1.6
Secretary of State for Trade v
  Markus (1976) 6.78
Secretary of State for Trade and
  Industry v Hart (1982) . . . 6.74
Seers (1984) 9.33
Selby v Chief Constable of Avon and
  Somerset (1988) 8.12, 20.3
Selvage (1982) 16.32
Senior (1832) 11.3
Senior (1899) 11.60
Seymour (1983) . 6.53, 11.51, 11.54,
  11.59, 20.13
Shadrokh-Cigari (1988) . 13.34, 13.44,
  13.48
Shah v Swallow (1984) . . . 4.11
Shankland (1986) . . 6.28, 6.33, 6.41
Shannon (1980) 22.8
Sharp (1987) 22.26
Sharpe (1857) 6.71
Shaw v DPP (1962) . 3.8, 21.46, 21.47
Sheehan (1975) 9.53, 9.63
Shelton (1986) 14.77
Shephard (1919) 21.5
Shepherd (1987) 22.26
Sheppard (1981) . 8.5, 8.6, 8.10, 11.60
Sheridan (1974) 23.29
Sherras v De Rutzen (1895) . 6.22, 8.12,
  8.14
Sherriff (1969) 10.11, 18.72

PARA

Shivpuri (1987) . . 3.8, 6.1, 6.61, 21.70
Sibartie (1983) 14.63
Silverman (1987) 14.29
Simcock v Rhodes (1977) 18.23
Simcox (1964) 9.37, 9.38
Simmonds (1969) 21.12
Simpson (1915) 11.36
Simpson (1983) 18.86
Simpson v Peat (1952) 20.14
Singh (1973) 22.17
Singh v Rathour (Northern Star
  Insurance Co Ltd, third party)
  (1988) 14.20
Siracusa (1989) . 21.24, 21.25, 21.27, 21.28
Sirat (1985) 21.2
Sivalingham v DPP (1975) . . . 5.26
Skipp (1975) 13.15, 14.45
Skivington (1968) 14.3
Slack (1989) 23.24
Sleep (1861) 6.58, 6.59
Smails (1985) 3.9
Smalley (1959) 16.33
Smalley, Re (1985) 5.36
Smith (1855) 14.82
Smith (1858) 15.44
Smith (1900) 22.40
Smith (1959) . . . 11.9, 11.11, 11.18
Smith (1960) 6.71, 23.28
Smith (1974) . . 6.55, 6.74, 7.20, 11.80,
                                    15.11
Smith (1976) . . . 14.9, 14.11, 14.88
Smith (1985) 10.13
Smith (1986) 6.61
Smith, Re (1858) 23.6
Smith v Chief Superintendent,
  Woking Police Station (1983) . 10.10
Smith v Dear (1903) 1.4
Smith v Hand (1986) 20.35
Smith v Mellors and Soar (1987) . 23.33
Smith v Reynolds (1986) . . . 23.9
Smith and Smith (1986) . . . 21.63
Smythe (1980) 14.82
Soanes (1948) 11.73
Socialist Worker Printers and
  Publishers Ltd, ex p A-G (1975) . 16.29
Sockett (1908) 23.27
Sodeman v R (1936) 7.5
Solesbury v Pugh (1969) . 20.35, 20.36
Somerset v Hart (1884) . . . 9.90
Somerset v Wade (1894) . . . 8.9
Sopp v Long (1970) 8.11
Sorrells v US (1932) 23.29
Souter (1971) 8.9
Southwark London Borough Council
  v Williams (1971) 22.33
Southwell v Chadwick (1986) . 18.86
Spalding v Paine (1985) . . . 20.36
Spanner, Poulter and Ward (1973) . 18.88
Sparks v Worthington (1986) . . 9.43
Speck (1977) 12.21
Spencer (1985) 3.9
Spencer (1989) 13.57

PARA

Spicer (1955) 11.77
Spicer (1988) 13.57
Spight (1986) 12.28
Spratt (1991) . . . 6.53, 10.14, 10.17
Spriggs (1958) 9.33
Spring Hill Prison Governor, ex p
  Sohi (1988) 5.4
Spurge (1961) 20.14
Squire (1990) 21.41
Stafford Justices, ex p Customs and
  Excise Comrs (1991) 4.2
Staines (1970) 14.40
Standen v Robertson (1975) . . 20.30
Stapleton v R (1952) 9.21
Steane (1947) . . 6.26, 22.17, 22.25
Steel v Goacher (1983) . . . 20.25
Steele (1976) 12.6
Steer (1986); affd (1988) . . 6.16, 15.13
Stephens (1866) 8.3, 23.37
Stephens v Myers (1830) . . . 10.10
Stephenson (1979) 6.44
Stevens (1981) 19.28
Stockwell (1987) . . . 14.38, 14.50
Stokes (1983) 14.21
Stokes v Sayers (1988) . . . 20.30
Stone (1977) . 6.11, 6.13, 11.51, 11.52
Stones (1989) 14.15
Stratton (1779) . . 22.21, 22.25, 22.33
Stringer and Banks (1991) . . 23.2
Stripp (1978) . . . 7.4, 9.47, 9.48
Studer (1915) 14.72
Sullivan (1981) . . 9.62, 9.64, 10.22
Sullivan (1984) . . 9.15, 9.20, 9.27, 9.29
Sullivan v Earl of Caithness (1976) . 18.77
Surrey County Council v Battersby
  (1965) 6.73
Surrey Justices, ex p Witherick
  (1932) 20.14
Sussex (1991) 23.19
Swallow v LCC (1916) . . . 18.73
Swaysland (1987) 7.5
Sweet v Parsley (1970) . 6.22, 6.58, 8.5,
                                   8.7, 8.16
Sweetland (1957) 21.12
Swindall and Osborne (1846) . 11.12, 23.33
Sykes v White (1983) 20.36
Syme (1972) 14.81

T

T (1990) 9.17
T v DPP (1989) 9.2
T v T (1988) 10.8
Taaffe (1984) 6.75
Tait (1989) 11.3
Tan (1983) 3.12
Tandy (1989) 9.36
Tao (1977) 19.34
Tatam (1921) 9.3
Taylor (1869) 10.21
Taylor (1950) 3.9
Taylor (1971) . . 22.17, 22.20, 22.22
Taylor (1983) 10.13

PARA

Taylor (1984) 12.7
Taylor (1987) 14.14
Taylor v Rajan (1974) 20.4
Taylor v Rogers (1960) . . . 20.14
Tegerdine (1982) 12.26
Telford Justices, ex p Badhan
  (1991) 4.7
Teong Sun Chuah (1991) . . . 14.54
Teong Tatt Chuah (1991) . . . 14.54
Terry (1961) 9.33
Tesco Supermarkets Ltd v Nattrass
  (1972) . . . 9.84, 9.85, 9.89, 9.90,
                                  23.45
Thambiah v R (1966) . . . 23.6, 23.8
Thistlewood (1820) 17.3
Thomas (1976) 8.9
Thomas (1979) 16.33
Thomas (1982) 12.7
Thomas v DPP (1989) . . . 20.36
Thomas v Lindop (1950) . . . 23.22
Thomas v Sawkins (1935) . . 18.69
Thompson (1984) 6.78
Thompson v Lodwick (1983) . . 20.38
Thompson v Thynne (1986) . . 20.30
Thomson (1976) 8.9
Thorne (1977) 5.3
Thorne v Motor Trade Association
  (1937) 14.73
Thornton (1992) 11.40
Thornton v Mitchell (1940) . . 23.13
Thorpe (1987) 18.74
Titus (1971) 18.78
Tobierre (1986) 15.52
Tolley v Giddings (1964) . . . 14.25
Tolson (1889) . . . 6.2, 7.32, 19.7
Tomsett (1985) 13.4, 21.21
Toor (1986) 14.88
Trainer (1864) 22.41
Treacy v DPP (1971) . 6.16, 6.78, 14.72
Trim (1943) 11.78
Tringhamm (1988) . . . 13.5, 13.6
Troughton v Metropolitan Police
  (1987) 14.66
Tuck v Robson (1970) . . . 23.10
Turnbull (1977) 9.38
Turner (1975) 11.41
Turner (1989) 13.57
Turner (No 2) (1971) 13.35
Tweney v Tweney (1946) . . . 19.4
Tyler (1838) 22.23
Tyler v Whatmore (1976) . . 20.6, 23.1
Tynan v Balmer (1967) . . . 18.70
Tyrrell (1894) 21.3, 23.27

U

United States of America
  Government v Jennings (1983) . 11.54
Upton (1991) 18.78
Utting (1987) 15.47

PARA
V

Valderrama-Vega (1985) . . . 22.18
Vane v Yiannopoullos (1965) . 23.38, 23.39
Vantandillo (1815) 22.33
Velumyl (1989) 13.60
Venna (1976) 10.9, 10.14
Vernege (1982) 9.38
Verrier v DPP (1967) . . . 3.4, 21.34
Vickers (1957) 11.23, 11.26
Vinagre (1979) 9.39
Vreones (1891) 16.32, 16.33

W

Wai Yu-tsang v R (1991) . . . 21.39
Waite (1892) 9.3
Waites (1982) 14.50
Wakeley v Hyams (1987) . . 20.29, 20.32
Wakely (1990) 23.24
Wakeman v Farrar (1974) . . 13.39
Walden (1959) 9.33
Walkden (1845) 10.11
Walker (1989) . . 6.25, 6.29, 6.30, 6.35,
                                  21.60
Walker v Tolhurst (1976) . . . 20.14
Walkington (1979) . . . 14.10, 14.12
Wall (1802) 11.15
Walters v W H Smith & Son Ltd
  (1914) 4.14
Walton v R (1978) 9.38
Ward (1986) 23.19, 23.24
Warner (1970) 13.61
Warner v Metropolitan Police Comr
  (1969) . . . 8.12, 8.16, 19.31
Waterfield (1964) 18.69
Watkins (1976) 14.50
Watson (1989) 11.68
Webb (1969) 9.9
Webley v Buxton (1977) . . . 21.79
Wells Street Metropolitan
  Stipendiary Magistrate, ex p
  Westminster City Council (1986) . 8.7
Welsh (1974) 13.21
West (1848) 11.3
West London Coroner, ex p Gray
  (1987) 11.59
West Yorkshire Coroner, ex p Smith
  (No 2) (1985) 16.31
Westminster City Council v
  Croyalgrange Ltd (1986) . . 6.59, 8.4
Weston v Central Criminal Court
  Courts Administrator (1976) . 16.26
Whale and Lockton (1991) . . 4.4
Wheeler (1967) 6.20
White (1910) 6.18, 11.8
Whitefield (1984) 23.31
Whitehouse (1852) 21.13
Whitehouse (1977) . 5.30, 12.22, 21.6, 23.27
Whitely (1991) 15.8
Whiteside (1989) 14.95
Whitfield (1976) 11.47
Whiting (1987) 14.14

	PARA
Whittaker v Campbell (1984)	14.22
Whittall v Kirby (1947)	20.4
Whybrow (1951)	21.60
Whyte (1987)	22.8
Wibberley (1966)	14.20
Widdowson (1986)	14.54
Wilcox v Jeffery (1951)	23.8
Willer (1987)	22.34
Williams (1893)	9.3
Williams (1898)	12.11
Williams (1923)	12.5, 12.11
Williams (1980)	14.29
Williams (1987)	6.20, 7.29, 7.30, 9.60, 10.14, 11.24, 22.8
Williams (1990)	16.32
Williams (1991)	11.14
Williams v Critchley (1979)	20.36
Williams v Fawcett (1986)	3.9
Williams v Johns (1773)	16.26
Williams v Phillips (1957)	13.29
Williams and Blackwood (1973)	23.21
Williamson (1977)	18.86, 22.17, 22.19
Willis (1972)	14.81
Willshire (1881)	19.4
Wilson (1856)	11.76
Wilson (1955)	10.10
Wilson (1983)	10.12, 10.21
Wilson v Pringle (1986)	10.15
Windle (1952)	9.21
Windsor, Re (1865)	15.46
Wings Ltd v Ellis (1985)	8.6, 8.7, 23.38
Winson (1969)	23.38, 23.39
Winter v Hinkley and District Industrial Co-operative Society Ltd (1959)	23.38

	PARA
Winzar v Chief Constable of Kent (1983)	8.18
Wood (1987)	14.89
Wood (or Woods) v Richards (1977)	20.14, 22.33
Woodley v Woodley (1978)	13.36
Woodman (1974)	13.33
Woodrow (1846)	8.14
Woods (1921)	11.62
Woods (1981)	9.56, 9.62, 9.63, 9.64
Woolmington v DPP (1935)	7.3, 9.41
Wootton and Peake (1990)	13.58
Worthy v Gordon Plant (Services) Ltd (1989)	9.85, 9.86
Wright (1841)	11.3
Wright v Brobyn (1971)	20.35
Wright v Wenlock (1971)	20.14
Wuyts (1969)	15.55

Y

	PARA
Yates (1986)	20.4
Young (1838)	10.2
Young (1984)	6.65, 9.67, 19.32
Young v Bristol Aeroplane Co Ltd (1944)	3.9
Younghusband v Luftig (1949)	6.1

Z

	PARA
Zecevic v DPP (Victoria) (1987)	22.11
Zemmel (1985)	21.38

1 The characteristics of criminal offences

Definition

1.1 A crime or offence is an illegal act, omission or event, whether or not it is also a tort, a breach of contract or a breach of trust, the principal consequence of which is that the offender, if he is detected and it is decided to prosecute, is prosecuted by or in the name of the State, and if he is found guilty is liable to be punished whether or not he is also ordered to compensate his victim.

1.2 A wrong is a breach of a rule; it may be moral or legal according to whether the rule is one of morality or law. The relations between these two types of rule are considered in Chapter 3.[1] Legal wrongs may be civil or criminal, and this distinction depends upon that between civil and criminal law. The civil law is primarily concerned with the rights and duties of individuals among themselves, whereas the criminal law defines the duties which a person owes to society, but a legal wrong may be both civil and criminal.

1 Paras 3.22–3.28.

1.3 Civil law is not exclusively concerned with the definition of wrongs, for it embraces the law of property, which largely consists of the rules governing the methods whereby property may be transferred from one person to another, and the law of succession, which concerns the devolution of property on death. There are, however, several branches of the civil law which exist in whole or in part to provide redress for wrongs; the most important of these are contract, tort and trusts.

One purpose of the law of contract is to provide redress for breaches of legally binding agreements. The aggrieved party may claim damages as plaintiff in civil proceedings, and the amount which he recovers is assessed on the basis of the loss he has sustained in consequence of the non-fulfilment of the contract.

The object of the law of tort is to provide redress for breaches of duties which are owed to persons generally and do not depend on an agreement between parties. If B assaults A, or publishes a libel concerning him, or causes him personal injuries by the negligent driving of a motor car, he commits a tort and is liable to be sued by A in civil proceedings. In these, as in those for breach of contract, the plaintiff's damages will be assessed on the basis of the loss sustained in consequence of the tort, although the detailed rules of assessment may not be the same in each case.

One purpose of the law of trusts is to provide redress for breaches of trust. A breach of trust occurs where someone who holds property as trustee for another fails to carry out the duties of his office, for example by making an improper investment or wrongfully converting the trust property to his own use. He is then civilly liable to make good the loss occasioned to those on whose behalf the property was held.

1.4 The foregoing account of civil wrongs should be sufficient to indicate the two important respects in which they differ from crimes. In each instance the wrongdoer's liability is based on the loss which he has occasioned, and in each the law is brought into play at the option of the injured party. Generally speaking, no one can be obliged to sue for damages for a breach of contract or a tort, and a beneficiary cannot be forced to claim restitution of the trust property. On the other hand, where an offence has been committed, the wrongdoer is liable to punishment, which is a very different thing from being ordered to compensate the victim of the wrong,[1] and as a general rule a criminal prosecution may proceed although the victim has been fully compensated and desires it to be discontinued.[2]

1 If a convicted person is ordered to pay a fine, this is paid to the State and not to the victim. However, the criminal courts do have power to order, in addition to the punishment imposed, that a convicted person pay compensation to the victim.
2 *Smith v Dear* (1903) 88 LT 664.

1.5 The same conduct may be both a civil wrong and a crime. There are many cases in which one who commits a tort is also guilty of a crime. Assaults and collisions between vehicles are two out of numerous examples. Where a crime is also a civil wrong, criminal and civil proceedings may usually take place concurrently and the one is normally no bar to the other.[1]

The only exception to this rule of any general importance is that, where criminal proceedings are taken in a magistrates' court in respect of a common assault or a common battery by or on behalf of the party aggrieved, the defendant is released from all other proceedings, civil or criminal, for the same cause, if he obtains the magistrates' certificate of the dismissal of the complaint or undergoes the punishment inflicted upon him.[2] A certificate of dismissal must be issued if the magistrates decide that the offence is not proved, or if proved is so trifling as not to merit any punishment. The power to dismiss a case even though the offence is proved, which is peculiar to the above offences, depends on there having been a hearing 'on the merits' and this will not have occurred if the accused pleaded guilty.[3]

1 In many cases the exercise of the power of a court in criminal proceedings (which normally take place more speedily than civil ones) to order a convicted person to compensate his victim renders separate civil proceedings unnecessary.
2 Offences against the Person Act 1861, ss 44, 45; North 'Civil and Criminal Proceedings for Assault' (1966) 29 MLR 16. In its Fourteenth Report: Offences against the Person, Cmnd 7844 (1980), the Criminal Law Revision Committee recommended the repeal of ss 44 and 45.
3 *Ellis v Burton* [1975] 1 All ER 395, DC.

1.6 The principal criticism of the definition of a crime set out at the start of this chapter is that it fails to indicate what types of conduct are included in the category of crimes. The answer is that a definition is not the same thing as a description; its aim is simply to draw attention to the features which distinguish that which is being defined from other things of the same kind. In any event, it is impossible to find a concise formula which will cover every kind of criminal conduct. As Lord Atkin said in 1931,[1] 'The criminal quality of an act cannot be discerned by intuition; nor can it be discovered by reference to any standard but one: is the act prohibited with penal consequences?'

It has not been necessary for Parliament to formulate a definition of a crime, but the judges have been called upon from time to time to distinguish between civil and criminal proceedings. In the former the rules of evidence and procedure may be waived by the parties, and a pardon may be granted by the Crown in the latter. Furthermore, under the provisions of s 18(1)(a) of the Supreme Court Act 1981, no appeal lies to the Court of Appeal (Civil Division), except as provided by the Administration of Justice Act 1960, from any judgment of the High Court in any criminal cause or matter. Whether or not a judgment is in a criminal cause or matter depends on the nature of the proceedings to which that judgment relates.[2] The authorities on the subsection and its predecessor show that, if the direct outcome of the proceedings may be the trial and punishment of a person by a court for a breach of the public law, they are a 'criminal cause or matter'.[3]

1 *Proprietary Articles Trade Association v A-G for Canada* [1931] AC 310 at 324.
2 Or of the underlying proceedings or decision if the judgment is in judicial review proceedings (para 5.36): *Carr v Atkins* [1987] QB 963, [1987] All ER 684, CA; *Secretary of State for the Home Department, ex p Garner* (1991) 3 Admin LR 33, CA.
3 *Amand v Home Secretary and Minister of Defence of Royal Netherlands Government* [1943] AC 147, [1942] 2 All ER 381, HL; *Hull Prison Board of Visitors, ex p St Germain* [1979] QB 425, [1979] 1 All ER 701, CA; *DPP, ex p Raymond* (1979) 70 Cr App Rep 233, CA; *Bonalumi v Secretary of State for the Home Dept* [1985] QB 675, [1985] 1 All ER 797, CA.

The initiative of the State

1.7 All criminal proceedings are in theory[1] instituted and conducted on behalf of the Crown. It is not sufficient to leave the remedy for certain wrongs in the hands of private persons for various reasons:

a) Many wrongs are so serious, not only for the persons injured but for the public as a whole, that a claim for compensation would be quite inadequate to restrain the offender or to deter others. It is obviously in the interests of the public at large that burglars should be liable to imprisonment and not simply liable to be sued in the civil courts.

b) Many wrongful acts do no particular harm to particular individuals so that no one is sufficiently interested to institute proceedings, even if he were able to do so. Within this category come most of the offences against public order in its widest sense and certain offences against public morals, such as incest and bigamy, where the parties concerned do not necessarily regard themselves as injured.

c) Many offences have been created which might be dealt with as civil matters but to do so would expose private persons to considerable trouble and expense. A good example is afforded by s 179(1) of the Town and Country Planning Act 1990, under which an owner of land who contravenes an enforcement notice issued by a local authority commits an offence. Before the modern town planning legislation the use of land was unregulated except by private contract and restrictive covenants. The enforcement of these contracts and covenants was

3

always a matter of some difficulty and so the new and simpler process is now gradually replacing the older and more complicated, and the type of restriction which may be imposed has been extended.

1 See paras 4.1–4.6.

2 Courts of criminal jurisdiction

2.1 There are two methods of trying persons accused of criminal offences. One is by judge and jury in the Crown Court after committal for trial on a written accusation of crime called an indictment; the other is summary by a magistrates' court without a jury. Over 97 per cent of all offences are tried summarily, which means that formality is reduced. The chart following p 6 shows the outline of the English court structure and the following paragraphs explain this, beginning at the bottom.

Magistrates' courts[1]

2.2 *Composition* A magistrates' court must normally be composed of at least two, and not more than seven, magistrates when trying a case summarily. One magistrate can:

a) determine whether summary trial or trial on indictment is more suitable where a person is charged with an offence triable either way; and
b) conduct committal proceedings in his capacity of examining magistrate.

The terms 'justice of the peace' and 'magistrate' are synonymous and henceforth to avoid confusion the word 'magistrate' will be used.

Almost all magistrates are lay magistrates. Lay magistrates are not required to possess any legal qualifications: for legal advice they rely on their clerk, who is a solicitor or barrister, but even though the clerk to the magistrates is legally qualified, an individual court may be served by an unadmitted assistant.

In the inner London area and in an increasing number of places outside, jurisdiction is exercised both by legally qualified stipendiary magistrates and by lay magistrates. Stipendiary magistrates sit alone and have all the powers of two lay magistrates in a magistrates' court.

1 The principal statute governing the constitution and functions of magistrates' courts is the Magistrates' Courts Act 1980.

2.3 *Functions* Magistrates' courts have two functions in criminal matters:

The first is that of a court of summary jurisdiction, which determines cases without a jury. Leaving aside the special provisions relating to the trial of young offenders, magistrates' courts deal with two types of offence under this jurisdiction:

5

a) *Summary offences* These are offences which, if committed by an adult, are triable only summarily. They comprise a large number of relatively minor offences, which can be summarised as follows:

   i) offences defined by the statute creating them as summary offences;

   ii) offences listed in Sch 1 of the Criminal Law Act 1977;

   iii) any offences consisting in the incitement to commit one of the above two types of offence.

b) *Offences triable either way* These are offences which, if committed by an adult, are triable either on indictment or summarily. Such offences may only be tried summarily with the accused's consent. They comprise the following types of offence:

   i) offences listed in Sch 1 of the Magistrates' Courts Act 1980. Examples are: unlawfully and maliciously wounding or inflicting grievous bodily harm on another, contrary to s 20 of the Offences against the Person Act 1861, and most offences under the Theft Act 1968.

   ii) offences which are triable either way by virtue of any other statute, such as having an offensive weapon in a public place without lawful authority or reasonable excuse, contrary to s 1 of the Prevention of Crime Act 1953, and unauthorised possession of a controlled drug, contrary to s 5 of the Misuse of Drugs Act 1971.

2.4   The second function of a magistrates' court is that of examining magistrates, by whom committal proceedings are held as a necessary preliminary in almost all cases to a trial by jury. The function of examining magistrates is different from that when magistrates sit to determine a case. All they have to decide is whether there is evidence upon which a reasonable jury properly directed could convict. The system has two principal justifications. It should act as a filter so that those against whom there is no evidence on which a reasonable jury could convict are spared the anxiety and expense of a trial. It also enables the accused to learn the evidence for the prosecution and thus he has time to consider the weight of the case against him in advance of the trial.

The Crown Court[1]

2.5 *Functions* The Crown Court has exclusive jurisdiction over all offences tried by jury on indictment, together with jurisdiction:

a) to deal with persons committed for sentence by magistrates' courts; and

b) to hear appeals from magistrates' courts, including youth courts.[1]

1 The principal statutes concerning the composition and functions of the Crown Court are the Courts Act 1971 and the Supreme Court Act 1981.

2.6 *Judges of the Crown Court* The jurisdiction and powers of the Crown Court are exercised by:

a) any judge of the High Court;

b) any Circuit judge;

c) any Recorder;

THE CRIMINAL COURTS IN ENGLAND AND WALES

HOUSE OF LORDS

DIVISIONAL COURT OF THE QUEEN'S BENCH DIVISION

COURT OF APPEAL CRIMINAL DIVISION

CROWN COURT

TRIAL ON INDICTMENT JURY

SENTENCE NO JURY

APPEAL BY REHEARING NO JURY

VOLUNTARY BILL OF INDICTMENT

COMMITTAL PROCEEDINGS

SUMMARY TRIAL

MAGISTRATES' COURT NO JURY

Case-stated

Case-stated

Committal for Sentence

Committal for Trial

Appeals

Committals

d) in some circumstances, any judge of the High Court, Circuit judge or Recorder sitting with lay magistrates.

All such persons when exercising the jurisdiction and powers of the Crown Court (including lay magistrates) are judges of the Crown Court.[1]

Judges of the High Court and Circuit judges are full-time judges, whereas Recorders are part-time judges.

In order to reduce so far as possible any delay in the administration of justice in the Crown Court which is due to the shortage of judges, the Lord Chancellor has wide powers to appoint as a temporary measure deputy Circuit judges.[2]

Lay magistrates can sit as judges of the Crown Court only with a High Court or Circuit judge or a Recorder and not by themselves. They must form part of the Crown Court when it hears appeals from magistrates' courts and also when it is sentencing persons who have been committed for sentence by magistrates' courts.[3] On the other hand, they may not sit in trials in the Crown Court (ie where a person charged on indictment has pleaded not guilty).[4] When they sit in the Crown Court, the number of magistrates must be not less than two nor more than four. Rulings on questions of law are matters for the judge but decisions on other questions, e g sentence, are the product of all the members of the court.[5]

1 Supreme Court Act 1981, ss 8(1) and 9.
2 Courts Act 1971, s 24 (as substituted by s 146 of the Supreme Court Act 1981); Supreme Court Act 1981, s 9(4).
3 Supreme Court Act 1981, s 74(1).
4 *Practice Note (Crown Court: distribution of court business)* [1987] 3 All ER 1064.
5 *Orpin* [1975] QB 283, [1974] 2 All ER 1121, CA.

Appellate Courts[1]

2.7 *Divisional Court of the Queen's Bench Division of the High Court* This court consists of two or more judges, almost invariably two, of whom one will be a Lord Justice of Appeal. It has these two functions in the administration of the criminal law:

a) To be a court of appeal only on points of law or jurisdiction from magistrates' courts and from the Crown Court when that court has heard an appeal from a magistrates' court.
b) In relation to the jurisdiction of the Crown Court other than its jurisdiction in matters relating to trials on indictment, and in relation to magistrates' courts, to hear applications for judicial review.

1 The jurisdiction of these courts is discussed in more detail in Chap 5.

2.8 *Criminal Division of the Court of Appeal* This hears appeals against conviction and sentence from the Crown Court. The Criminal Division usually sits in at least two courts; one composed of the Lord Chief Justice and two judges of the Queen's Bench Division, and the other of a Lord Justice of Appeal and two Queen's Bench judges. By way of exception to the general requirement that criminal appeals must be heard by not less than three judges, a two-judge court may hear appeals against sentence.[1]

1 Supreme Court Act 1981, s 55.

2.9 *House of Lords* Further appeal may be made from the appellate courts just mentioned to the House of Lords in its judicial capacity which, subject to the exception in the next paragraph, is the supreme court of appeal in criminal cases. Appeals to the House of Lords are normally heard by five Lords of Appeal in Ordinary (commonly called 'law lords').

2.10 *European Court* For the sake of completeness mention must be made of the Court of Justice of the European Communities. The impact on our criminal law of the law of the European Economic Communities is extremely limited and is confined to matters with a 'European' element, such as controls over aliens and customs legislation. If, at a trial or on appeal, a question is raised as to the interpretation of a piece of Community law the matter can be referred to the European Court, and if the question is raised on appeal in the House of Lords it must be so referred, for a 'preliminary ruling' on the interpretation of the Community law in issue. In the event of a referral the English proceedings will be postponed to await the ruling on the point of *interpretation*, which must be *applied* by the English court when it is given. To the limited extent that the European Court is the ultimate court on the interpretation of Community law, it is no longer true to say that the House of Lords is the supreme court of appeal in criminal cases.

3 The sources and classifications of the criminal law

Sources

3.1 There are two sources of English criminal law: common law and legislation.

Common law

3.2 Common law is that part of English law which is not the result of legislation, ie it is the law which originated in the custom of the people and was justified and developed by the decisions and rulings of the judges.

COMMON LAW OFFENCES

3.3 From the twelfth to the fourteenth centuries, the judges of the Court of King's Bench elaborated the rules relating to the more serious offences which came to be known as 'felonies'. In the fourteenth century, less serious offences known later as 'misdemeanours' were similarly evolved. A few misdemeanours were subsequently created by the rulings of the judges in particular cases and by the Court of Star Chamber.[1] After the Restoration, some of the latter were developed by the common law judges, who 'always claimed the right of defining given acts as misdemeanours, although they never attempted to do so in the case of felonies',[2] but in modern times statute has played a preponderant part in the criminal law.

There are still a number of offences which exist at common law only. This means that their definition cannot be found in an Act of Parliament, but must be sought in the rulings of the judges. Prima facie, not only the definition of the offence itself but also the punishment to be awarded is contained in the common law, but several statutes prescribe specific punishments for certain common law offences. For example, murder is an offence at common law; in no statute is there to be found a definition of it, but by reason of the wealth of judicial pronouncements it is possible to construct a comprehensive definition of the offence. The punishment for murder is, however, governed by statute.[3] Manslaughter also remains an offence at common law; imprisonment for life is laid down as the maximum punishment by s5 of the Offences against the Person Act 1861 but, by way of contrast with the case of murder, a lesser sentence of imprisonment, a fine, or even a conditional or absolute discharge is possible. The relevant statutes

9

content themselves with naming the offences of murder and manslaughter and assume the existence of these offences without giving any definition. Another example of a common law offence is incitement to commit an offence, for which the punishment on conviction on indictment is generally still prescribed by the common law.

1 Jackson *Modern Approach to Criminal Law* pp 292–300.
2 *Morris* [1951] 1 KB 394 at 395, [1950] 2 All ER 965, per Lord Goddard CJ.
3 Murder (Abolition of Death Penalty) Act 1965.

3.4 In *Morris*[1] the Court of Criminal Appeal affirmed the rule that, where the punishment for a common law offence is not laid down by statute, the judge may sentence the accused to be imprisoned for a period or fined an amount, or both, to be fixed at his discretion. It follows that, in theory, the decision in *Morris* could lead to some very anomalous results.[2] This is because, in the case of a common law offence for which no maximum punishment is provided by statute, the court could impose a longer sentence than it could in the case of a more serious offence, the punishment of which is dealt with by statute. There is, however, an overriding requirement that the punishment should not be excessive, and there is no reason to suppose that the decision in *Morris* gives rise to any injustice in practice.

1 [1951] 1 KB 394, [1950] 2 All ER 965, CCA, approved by the House of Lords in *Verrier v DPP* [1967] 2 AC 195, [1966] 3 All ER 568.
2 Williams 'Common Law Misdemeanours' (1952) 68 LQR 500.

GENERAL PRINCIPLES OF CRIMINAL LIABILITY

3.5 The common law remains the source of virtually all the general principles of criminal liability. Examples of such principles are the defence of insanity and the rules concerning participation in crime.

THE DOCTRINE OF PRECEDENT

3.6 The common law has been built up on the basis of the doctrine of precedent, under which the reported decisions of certain courts are more than just authoritative legal statements whose effect is persuasive since they can be binding (i e must be applied) in subsequent cases.

So far as the operation of the doctrine of precedent in relation to the criminal law is concerned, trial on indictment involves trial by jury in the Crown Court, and, subject to the accused's right of appeal,[1] their verdict is final. The jury are subject to the trial judge who sums up the evidence and explains the law.[2] The trial judge's explanations do not constitute a binding precedent for the future, but are merely of persuasive authority.[3] It must be emphasised that the principles enunciated by the judge must be ascertained solely by reference to his words and without reference to the verdict of the jury, which may have been unexpected by the judge, or even contrary to his direction on the law. If the case goes to appeal, the comments made by the appellate court which directly relate to the judge's direction on the law constitute a binding precedent (subject to what is said in para 3.7). Other statements on the law by the appellate court, obiter dicta (statements not necessary to the decision) as they are called, can never constitute a binding precedent, although they may be of persuasive authority for subsequent cases, their strength depending on the eminence of the court.

In cases tried summarily,[4] the decision of the magistrates or, on appeal, of the Crown Court[5] does not constitute a binding precedent. Doubtful points of law may, however, be dealt with on appeal or further appeal, as the case may be, by the Divisional Court of the Queen's Bench Division, when the decision, which will constitute a binding precedent, will be reached on the basis of the facts which the magistrates or Crown Court find to be proved. Accordingly, account may have to be taken of the court's conclusion of guilty or not guilty as based on those facts in order to ascertain the principle of the case.

1 Paras 5.28–5.31 and 5.35.
2 Para 5.12.
3 Ashworth 'The Binding Effect of Crown Court Decisions' [1980] Crim LR 402.
4 Chapter 2.
5 Cross *Precedent in English Law* (3rd edn) p 7. The appellate decisions or rulings of the Crown Court are of persuasive authority: Ashworth, loc cit.

3.7 *Operation of doctrine of precedent* The doctrine of precedent depends on the principle that the courts form a hierarchy which, in the case of courts with criminal jurisdiction, is in the following descending order: House of Lords; Court of Appeal (Criminal Division); Divisional Court of the Queen's Bench Division; Crown Court, and magistrates' courts.[1] The basic rule is that a decision by an appellate court binds those courts below that in which it was given and will normally be followed by a court of equal status.[2]

1 In the limited areas of its jurisdiction, the decisions of the Court of Justice of the European Communities bind all English courts.
2 A 'decision' made by a court on a point which counsel has declined to argue is not capable of being a binding precedent, since the point is regarded as having been undecided for the purposes of the doctrine of precedent: *Governor of Pentonville Prison, ex p Osman* [1989] 3 All ER 701, 90 Cr App Rep 281, DC.

3.8 In 1966 the House of Lords declared (reversing its former practice) that it would not be bound by its own decisions but, when announcing this, the Lord Chancellor emphasised the need for maintaining certainty in the criminal law.[1] This emphasis was repeated in *Knuller Ltd v DPP*[2] where the House of Lords refused to overrule its decision in *Shaw v DPP*.[3] It stated that because of the need for certainty as to the content of the criminal law the House must be sure that there is a very good reason before it departed from one of its own earlier criminal decisions. Their Lordships' speeches indicate that the House will be very slow to overrule such a decision, particularly if many convictions have been secured on the basis of it, an attitude which appears to prefer consistency to justice but one which impressed members of the House of Lords in the subsequent case of *Cunningham*.[4] More recently the House of Lords has overruled two of its previous decisions. In *Shivpuri*[5] it overruled its decision of the previous year in *Anderton v Ryan*[6] concerning impossibility in attempts, and in *Howe*[7] it overruled its decision made 12 years before in *Director of Public Prosecutions for Northern Ireland v Lynch* [8] that the defence of duress by threats was available to an accomplice to murder. Considerations which weighed with the House in *Shivpuri* were that its decision in *Anderton v Ryan* was recent, and that (in the nature of the case before it) no one could have acted in reliance on that decision in the belief that he was acting innocently only to find out that that he had after all committed an offence if the decision was overruled. However, neither of these considerations can be regarded as essential ones, since the absence of both of them did not prevent the House of Lords in *Howe* overruling its decision in *Lynch*.[9]

1 *Practice Note* [1966] 3 All ER 77, [1966] 1 WLR 1234.

2 [1973] AC 435, [1972] 2 All ER 898, HL. See Brazier 'Overruling House of Lords Criminal Cases' [1973] Crim LR 98.
3 [1962] AC 220, [1961] 2 All ER 446, HL.
4 [1982] AC 566, [1981] 2 All ER 863, HL.
5 [1987] AC 1, [1986] 2 All ER 334, HL.
6 [1985] AC 560, [1985] 2 All ER 355, HL.
7 [1987] AC 417, [1987] 1 All ER 771, HL.
8 [1975] AC 653, [1975] 1 All ER 913, HL.
9 See articles by Canton and Gearty (1987) 137 NLJ 491 and 707 respectively on the House of Lords' power to overrule one of its decisions.

3.9   The Court of Appeal (Criminal Division) is bound not only by the decisions of the House of Lords but also by its own decisions and those of its predecessor, the Court of Criminal Appeal. However, in the case of its own decisions and those of the Court of Criminal Appeal, there are exceptions:

a) Like the Court of Appeal (Civil Division) the Criminal Division is not bound, under the rule in *Young v Bristol Aeroplane Co Ltd*,[1] in three situations:

   ii) The court must refuse to follow a previous decision of its own which, though not expressly overruled, cannot stand with a later House of Lords decision.

   i) Where two of its previous decisions conflict, in which case the decision not followed will be overruled.[2] It has been held by the Court of Appeal that if one of the previous decisions is favourable to the accused, and the other not, it must follow the former one.[3]

   iii) The court is not bound to follow its previous decision if that decision was given *per incuriam*. A decision is given *per incuriam* if some relevant statute or binding precedent, which would have affected the decision, was not brought to the attention of the court. Only in very rare instances can a case not strictly within this formulation be held to have been decided *per incuriam*, since such a case must involve a *manifest* slip or error and it must be an exceptional case in some way.[4]

   The Court of Appeal is also not obliged to follow another of its decisions if, although not itself *per incuriam*, that decision was based solely on another Court of Appeal decision which, unknown to the Court of Appeal in the former case, was *per incuriam*.[5]

b) The Court of Appeal (Criminal Division) has power to overrule a previous decision of its own on the ground that the law has been 'misapplied or misunderstood',[6] but only if this is necessary in the interests of the appellant.[7] In practice, this power has only been exercised by a 'full court' of five or more judges (as opposed to the usual three), but there is no statutory requirement to this effect.

1 [1944] KB 718, [1944] 2 All ER 293, CA.
2 E g *Gould (No 2)* [1968] 2 QB 65, [1968] 1 All ER 849, CA.
3 *Jenkins* [1983] 1 All ER 1000, CA.
4 *Williams v Fawcett* [1986] QB 604, [1985] 1 All ER 787, CA; *Rickards v Rickards* [1989] 3 All ER 193, [1989] 3 WLR 748, CA. Cf *Duke v Reliance Systems Ltd* [1987] 2 All ER 858, CA, for an even stricter view.
5 *Rakhit v Carty* [1990] 2 All ER 202, CA
6 *Taylor* [1950] 2 KB 368, [1950] 2 All ER 170, CA; *Newsome and Browne* [1970] 2 QB 711, [1970] 3 All ER 455, CA. See also Cross *Precedent in English Law* (3rd edn) pp 145–146.
7 *Spencer and Smails* [1985] QB 771, [1985] 1 All ER 673, CA; *Howe* [1986] QB 626, [1986] 1 All ER 833, CA. For arguments against the power to overrule in b), see Pattenden 'The Power of the Criminal Division of the Court of Appeal to Depart from its own Precedents'

[1984] Crim LR 592. On the question of precedent in the Criminal Division generally, see Zellick 'Precedent in the Court of Appeal, Criminal Division' [1974] Crim LR 222.

3.10 The Divisional Court of the Queen's Bench Division is bound by decisions of the House of Lords. It is also bound by decisions of the Court of Appeal or Court of Criminal Appeal, except, apparently, if such a decision was *per incuriam* in that a relevant decision of the House of Lords was not cited[1]. A Divisional Court hearing an appeal (or exercising the High Court's supervisory jurisdiction) in criminal matters is bound by a previous Divisional Court decision unless the *Young v Bristol Aeroplane* principles apply[2] or the former decision was clearly wrong.[3]

1 *Northumberland Compensation Appeal Tribunal, ex p Shaw* [1952] 1 KB 338, [1952] 1 All ER 122, CA.
2 *Huddersfield Police Authority v Watson* [1947] KB 842, [1947] 2 All ER 193, DC.
3 *Greater Manchester Coroner, ex p Tal* [1985] QB 67, [1984] 3 All ER 240, DC; *Hornigold v Chief Constable of Lancashire* [1985] Crim LR 792, DC.

3.11 Reference will occasionally be made to decisions of the Judicial Committee of the Privy Council, which is the final court of appeal from the colonies and certain Commonwealth countries. Decisions of the Judicial Committee do not bind English courts but are of very strong persuasive authority.

3.12 *Theoretical basis* The theory underlying the development of the common law is that new cases simply illustrate the application of old doctrine to varying facts. Until fairly recently this theory was strained because the courts on occasion reserved the right to create new offences, which is open to the following objections:

a) In a democratic society the creation of new offences should be done by the legislature.
b) There is a danger that the creation of new offences under the guise of developing old law promotes uncertainty concerning the extent of the legal rule.
c) The existence of a judicial power to create new offences contravenes the principle that no one should be punished for acts which were not criminal when they were performed. The principle is embodied in the Latin maxim *nulla poena sine lege*, and is sometimes spoken of as the principle of legality. It is even more important from the point of view of the liberty of the subject than other principles, such as those embodied in the doctrine that an accused's conduct must be voluntary or in the rule that guilt must be proved beyond reasonable doubt, which tend to receive a greater depth of discussion in books on criminal law.

Fortunately, the judicial creation of offences is no longer permissible since, in 1972, the House of Lords in *Knuller Ltd v DPP*[1] unanimously rejected the existence of a residual power vested in the courts to create new offences. It also rejected a residual power so to widen existing offences as to make punishable conduct of a type not hitherto subject to punishment. There is, however, a fine line between this and the application of established offences to new circumstances within their scope, which the House of Lords recognised was permissible. For example, the recent decision of the House of Lords in *R*,[2] that a husband could be convicted of raping his wife if he had sexual intercourse with her without her consent, involved the abolition of the previous proposition of law, formulated in the eighteenth century, whereby a husband could not be so convicted. That proposition, which had been subjected to a number of limited exceptions in modern times, was based on the notion – prevalent in the eighteenth century – that a wife was a subservient chattel of her husband and by marriage gave her irrevocable consent to sexual intercourse with him. The House of Lords held that, since that notion was now clearly unacceptable, the proposition should be held no longer to be applicable. There is a strong case for saying that this decision involved an impermissible widening of the offence so as to make punishable conduct of a type not hitherto punishable, rather than simply being an application of the offence to new circumstances (the changed social position of wives) within its scope.[3]

1 [1973] AC 435, [1972] 2 All ER 898, HL.
2 [1991] 4 All ER 481, HL; para 12.6. For another example, see *Tan* [1983] QB 1053, [1983] 2 All ER 12, CA.
3 If the decision does involve an impermissible widening of the offence, it is nevertheless binding.

TEXTWRITERS

3.13 In criminal law, as in other branches of English law, statements in text books have no binding force. This means that the judge is not bound to apply them in the same way as he must follow the directions contained in a statute or the principle to be inferred from a decided case. Nevertheless, some mention should be made of certain works which are treated with great respect by the judges. To go back only so far as the seventeenth century, the writings of Sir Edward Coke (d 1634) are as important in the sphere of crime, which is dealt with in his *Third Institute*, as in other branches of the law. There is also the statement of the criminal law of a slightly later period in the unfinished *History of the Pleas of the Crown* by Sir Matthew Hale (d 1676).

In the eighteenth century, Sir Michael Foster (d 1763) left a valuable set of reports with notes and appendices entitled *Crown Law*, while Hawkins (d 1746) wrote a treatise on *Pleas of the Crown* which was used by Sir William Blackstone (d 1780) in the compilation of the fourth book of his *Commentaries*, which deals with criminal law. Finally, Sir Edward Hyde East (d 1847) published a general treatise on criminal law, known as *Pleas of the Crown*, in 1803; this book is regarded as the successor to the treatises of Coke, Hale and Foster.

All these works are regarded as of persuasive authority on the law as it stood when they were written. Several of the standard works of the nineteenth century have been re-edited and, although they are not authoritative in any strict sense of the word, some of them are still relied on. They include *Stephen's Digest of the Criminal Law* and, in particular, *Archbold's Pleading, Evidence and Practice in Criminal Cases*. Modern works which are frequently quoted are *Smith and Hogan's Criminal Law*, *Smith's Law of Theft* and *Griew's Theft Acts 1968 and 1978*. *Stone's Justices' Manual* is the standard work on summary procedure. The work of Sir James Stephen is of great importance because he was responsible for a three-volume *History of the Criminal Law* in addition to his *Digest*, and for the draft Criminal Code prepared in the 1870's which is mentioned below.

Legislation

STATUTE

3.14 The majority of offences are defined and regulated by statutes, ie Acts of Parliament which have been duly passed through both Houses and received the Royal Assent.

3.15 Statute may create an entirely new offence. For example, before the passing of the Punishment of Incest Act 1908, it was not an offence for a man to have sexual intercourse with an adult female whom he knew to be his grand-daughter, daughter, sister or mother, although such incestuous intercourse had generally been regarded as morally abhorrent. The Act made such conduct criminal. This is an instance of a serious offence which has been created by statute and there are many others, since, from time to time in the history of the criminal law, Parliament has found it necessary to punish acts which were not punished by the common law. It is in the sphere of the less morally reprehensible offences, however, that Parliament has been most active and it is true to say at the present day that the vast majority of offences have been created by statute.

3.16 Apart from the creation of new offences by statute, it is also necessary to bear in mind, in order to have a full and proper understanding of the criminal law, that many offences which now exist by virtue of statute were originally common law offences. Many statutes have replaced common law offences and in so doing have changed the common law very considerably.

3.17 It follows from what has been said that in England we have no single criminal code such as exists in many countries. The result is that, with the exception of common law offences and those created by subordinate legislation,[1] the criminal law of England is contained in a number of statutes. The Offences against the Person Act 1861, for example, covers a variety of offences which are broadly defined as being committed against the person and, besides prescribing the punishment for murder and manslaughter, includes such crimes as wounding with intent to do grievous bodily harm, administering poison, using explosives, assaults, bigamy and abortion. The Theft Act 1968 covers most offences against property, and replaces the common law with regard to them. Another important statute covering offences against property is the Criminal Damage Act 1971, which deals with damaging a person's property as distinct from depriving him of it. The two last mentioned statutes are a vast improvement on, and simplification of, earlier enactments dealing with the same subject matter.

1 Para 3.19.

3.18 In addition to Acts of the kind mentioned in the last paragraph, there is a large number whose main object is to set up public services of some description, or to control certain activities such as road traffic, but which contain offences for which punishments are prescribed. They are not entirely concerned with the criminal law, but they certainly create offences and as far as they do so must be regarded as one of the sources of the criminal law. This already large category is increasing because in modern times the State has assumed the responsibility for controlling and curtailing a range of activities which previously anyone was free to undertake.

Thus the field which is covered by criminal offences created by statute at the present day is very wide indeed. A glance at the Table of Statutes in *Stone's Justices' Manual* is a clear demonstration of the fact that, to comprehend the extent of the criminal law, the student must not confine himself merely to those statutes which appear to be immediately concerned with it. As well as being aware of the Theft Act 1968 and the Criminal Damage Act 1971, he must remember that there are penal provisions in the Insolvency Act 1986, the Licensing Act 1964 and a host of others.

SUBORDINATE LEGISLATION

3.19 A statute may give power to some body such as the Queen in Council, a Minister or a local authority to make regulations and prescribe for their breach.

This method of creating criminal offences is of increasing importance at the present day, although it is not new. A good example is the power of the Secretary of State for Transport under the Road Traffic Acts to make regulations. Acting under this power, he has made regulations which cover a very large number of different subjects and prosecutions are regularly instituted for breach of them. Such matters as the efficiency of brakes and the use of car horns are to be found not in the Acts themselves, but in the regulations.

Subordinate legislation is of two kinds. The more important kind are Orders in Council made by the Queen in Council and regulations made by Ministers. Generally, these must be made by statutory instrument and are subject to the rules governing publication and procedure contained in the Statutory Instruments Act 1946. The other kind of subordinate legislation, byelaws, are made by local authorities, nationalised industries and certain other bodies authorised by statute. Although general in operation, they are restricted to the locality or undertaking to which they apply.

All forms of subordinate legislation are invalid if they exceed the powers conferred by the enabling statute on the rule-making body or if they are made in breach of a mandatory part of the procedure prescribed by the enabling statute. A byelaw, but not any other form of subordinate legislation, is also invalid if it is unreasonable or excessively uncertain or repugnant to the general law.

LEGISLATION OF THE EUROPEAN COMMUNITIES

3.20 This legislation is to be found in the Treaties of the Communities and in regulations, directives and decisions of their organs. It is largely concerned with economic matters, such as fair competition and traffic regulation, but it also deals with other matters, such as immigration. As already stated, and as just implied, the impact of Community law on our criminal law is limited. Such impact as it has is in the area of the regulatory criminal law, such as offences relating to shop opening hours and to the use of tachographs in goods vehicles and long distance coaches.

In discussing the types of legislation of the Communities, a fundamental point must be emphasised at the outset: some rules of Community law are 'directly applicable' in the sense that they confer rights and duties on individuals and institutions which are enforceable in the courts of member states without being re-enacted by legislation in those states.

Certain provisions of the Treaties are directly applicable, but in the main directly applicable rules are contained in 'regulations', which have general application and are made by the Council of Ministers or by the Commission (a supranational body composed of the highest officials) under the treaties. It is inconceivable that the other two types of Community legislation, decisions and directives (both of which can be made by the Council or the Commission), could have any direct effect in the unlikely event that they impacted on the criminal law.

Codification

3.21 Reference has already been made to the fact that English law does not contain a Criminal Code. A draft Code was brought before Parliament in 1878, 1879 and 1880, but it was never given statutory effect.

It is the aim of the Law Commission that there should be a Criminal Code, which would include general principles of liability, specific offences, rules of criminal procedure and evidence, and provisions relating to the disposal of offenders. At the request of the Commission, a group of distinguished academic lawyers prepared a report, published in 1985,[1] formulating the general principles of liability which should be contained in a Code, including a standard terminology to be used in it, together with a draft Criminal Code Bill which stated those general principles and included some specific offences against the person and of damage to property for the purpose of illustrating how those principles would function. The draft Code Bill was subject to substantial and detailed scrutiny and debate. In the light of the support shown for the principle of codification of the criminal law, the Law Commission decided to present to the public and to the Government a more comprehensive draft Criminal Code Bill, which would be a revised and expanded version of the previous one, covering offences against the person, offences against property, sexual offences and public order offences, as well as the general principles of liability.[2] In this work the Commission was greatly assisted by the group which had produced the 1985 report, who acted as advisers and draftsmen. In 1989 the Commission published a report,[3] including the revised and expanded version of the draft Criminal Code Bill, which was laid before Parliament. Much of this draft Code simply restates in the standard terminology of the existing law, but parts of it resolve matters of inconsistency or uncertainty under the present law, while other parts incorporate various proposals for reform made in modern times. The provisions of the draft Criminal Code Bill of 1989 are referred to at appropriate points in this book.

1 Codification of the Criminal Law: A Report to the Law Commission (1985) Law Com No 143.
2 It is intended that provisions relating to evidence and procedure and to the disposal of offenders should be added to the Code when they are drafted.
3 Law Commission: Criminal Code for England and Wales (1989): Law Com No 177.

Social morality and the proper scope of the criminal law[1]

3.22 Although common law, statute and subordinate legislation are the only direct sources of the criminal law, allowance must be made for the very important indirect source of morality. Much of our criminal law inherited from the past has undoubtedly been influenced by Christian beliefs, but at the present day these beliefs are not the only basis of the morals of our society.

1 Devlin *The Enforcement of Morals*; Hart *Law, Liberty and Morality*.

3.23 The spheres of social morals and the criminal law are co-extensive up to a point, but many of the rules enforced by the criminal have nothing to do with social morality, and many rules of social morality are not enforced by the criminal law.

For the purposes of the present discussion, a rule may be said to be one of social morality when it is accepted by the bulk of a given society as laying down a standard of behaviour to which its members ought to conform and as justifying severe censure for those who break it. Many rules of current social morality are enforced by the criminal law, the person who breaks them thus being liable to punishment by the State as well as the censure of his fellows; obvious instances are the prohibition of all forms of deliberate violence, theft and damage to property. No doubt it was rules of this nature which Lord Coleridge CJ had in mind when he said that 'A legal common law duty is nothing else than the enforcing by law of that which is a moral obligation without legal enforcement.'[1]

The restriction of the observation to common law duties is, however, of the utmost importance. Most, if not all, of the common law duties enforced by the criminal law are recognised by current social morality, but over the last century at least our criminal law has had added to it by statute a vast number of offences which carry no moral blame at all. We have already seen that an owner of land who uses it for a purpose which is contrary to the requirements of a local authority commits an offence, and a person who, without reasonable excuse, provides day care at premises for children under eight without being registered with the local authority also commits an offence and is liable to a fine not exceeding level 5 on the standard scale (£5,000).[2] These are not exceptional cases; there are many hundreds like them. To complete the quotation from Lord Atkin's speech in *Proprietary Articles Trade Association v A-G for Canada*,[3] cited in para 1.6, 'Morality and criminality are far from co-extensive, nor is the sphere of criminality necessarily part of a more extensive field covered by morality – unless the moral code necessarily disapproves of all acts prohibited by the State, in which case the argument moves in a circle.'

1 *Instan* [1893] 1 QB 450.
2 Children Act 1989, s 78.
3 [1931] AC 310 at 324.

3.24 Many rules of social morality are not enforced by the criminal law. The man who seduces his friend's wife and ruins his home, the stranger who watches a child drown in a shallow pool, or the man who breaks a contract and thereby causes thousands of pounds worth of damage, is free from any kind of criminal responsibility. It is not difficult to give reasons for the reluctance of the criminal law to enforce all the rules of social morality. The type of seduction which anyone would wish to make criminal is difficult to define, difficult to prove and something of which proof would frequently involve gross infringement of individual privacy. The enforcement by the criminal law of a general duty to take active steps to save life would give rise to problems concerning the point at which it is proper to punish people for failing to act like the Good Samaritan; these problems are far from being susceptible of a clear answer. A similar observation may be made with regard to the question of whether there should be criminal liability when the civil remedy for breach of contract is an inadequate protection for the victims of broken promises. So drastic is the criminal sanction that its imposition is something which must be justified to the hilt.

3.25 Reflections of the kind mentioned in the last paragraph prompt the question whether the fact that conduct is prohibited by a rule of social morality can ever, without something more, justify its punishment by the criminal law. This is a matter upon which there has been, and no doubt will continue to be, a deep cleavage of opinion. Although it is possible to adopt a number of intermediate positions, two diametrically opposed answers to the question have been given; they may respectively be described as the 'libertarian' and 'authoritarian' answers.

3.26 The libertarian answer was given in the nineteenth century by John Stuart Mill in his essay *On Liberty* and, in the twentieth century, by the Report of the Committee on Homosexual Offences and Prostitution (the Wolfenden Committee) published in 1957.[1] Mill stated the principle underlying his essay as follows:

'The principle is, that the sole end for which mankind are warranted, individually or collectively, in interfering with the liberty of action of any of their number is self-protection. That the only purpose for which power can be rightfully exercised over any member of a civilised community against his will is to prevent harm to others.'

According to the Wolfenden Committee, the function of the criminal law is:

'to preserve public order and decency, to protect the citizen from what is offensive or injurious and to provide sufficient safeguards against exploitation or corruption of others, particularly those who are specially vulnerable because they are young, weak in body or mind or inexperienced or in a state of special physical, official or economic dependence. . . .
    Unless a deliberate attempt is to be made by society, acting through the agency of the law, to equate the sphere of crime with that of sin, there must remain a realm of private morality and immorality which is, in brief and crude terms, not the law's business.'

The Wolfenden Committee recommended the legalisation of acts of homosexuality performed in private between consenting males of and above the age of 21, in spite of the fact that such acts may well be condemned by contemporary social morality.

1 Cmnd 247.

3.27 The authoritarian answer to the question whether the fact that conduct is prohibited by a rule of social morality can ever, without something more, such as harm to others, justify its punishment by the criminal law was given in the nineteenth century by Stephen in his book *Liberty, Equality, Fraternity* and, in the twentieth century, by Lord Devlin in his Maccabaean lecture to the British Academy in 1959 on the enforcement of morals. According to Stephen, the criminal law affirms in a singularly emphatic manner a principle which is absolutely inconsistent with and contradictory to Mill's, namely, the principle that 'there are acts of wickedness so gross and outrageous that, self-protection apart, they must be prevented as far as possible at any cost to the offender, and punished, if they occur, with exemplary severity'.

According to Lord Devlin,

'The suppression of vice is as much the law's business as the suppression of subversive activities.'

He was criticising the Wolfenden Committee's view that there is a realm of private morality. Lord Devlin expressed no opinion with regard to the propriety of the Wolfenden Committee's recommendations, but he said that no society can do without 'intolerance, indignation and disgust', and suggested that people should ask themselves whether, looking at the matter calmly and dispassionately, they regarded homosexuality as 'a vice so abominable that its mere presence is an offence'. If that turned out to be the genuine feeling of society, he did not see how society could be denied the right to try to eradicate homosexuality.

3.28   The difficulty about the libertarian view, when stated without qualification, is the inability to justify such commonly accepted prohibitions of the criminal law as those on the possession of dangerous drugs for consumption, the keeping of a brothel and cruelty to animals. The difficulty about the authoritarian view is its apparent acquiescence in the suggestion that it may sometimes be right to punish conduct simply because it is highly distasteful to a large number of people.

THE PROPER SCOPE OF THE CRIMINAL LAW

3.29   Whatever view be taken about the enforcement of social morality as such, it must be recognised that it is something which, like the concept of crime, varies from country to country and from time to time. Under the conditions prevailing in contemporary England, a case can be made out for the abolition of such crimes as incest between adults[1] and bigamy; but it by no means follows that the case should be accepted. In the case of incest, it may be urged that the criminal sanction is necessary for the protection of women in a vulnerable position, and it is possible that the decision to cease to regard bigamy as a crime would undermine the institution of marriage. A case can also be made out for the legalisation of voluntary euthanasia, but here again it by no means follows that the case should be accepted because well nigh insuperable difficulties can be raised with regard to the method of determining that the deceased really was a consenting party to his death. A case can also be made out for the legalisation of the possession for sale or consumption of cannabis but many people think that the case is met by our ignorance of the long-term effects of this substance.

1 For a compromise proposal for reform, see para 12.14.

The classification of offences

3.30   Offences may be classified according to:

   a) their source, into statutory and common law offences;
   b) their effect on the law of arrest, into arrestable and other offences; or
   c) the method by which they are tried, into offences triable only on

indictment, offences triable only summarily and offences 'triable either way'.

The sources of the criminal law have already been discussed and nothing more need be said about the first division. The second division is explained in para 4.14.

CLASSIFICATION BY METHOD OF TRIAL

3.31 This method of classifying crimes is essentially procedural. An offence triable on indictment is known as an indictable offence, whether or not it is only so triable. Trial on indictment takes place in the Crown Court.[1] An offence triable only summarily is known as a summary offence, and is tried before a magistrates' court.[2] Offences triable either way may be tried on indictment in the Crown Court or summarily in a magistrates' court.

1 Paras 5.1–5.15.
2 Paras 5.16–5.21.

FELONIES AND MISDEMEANOURS

3.32 Until the Criminal Law Act 1967, there were distinctions between offences classified as felonies and offences classified as misdemeanours.

We have already seen in para 3.3 that the serious offences created by the judges from the twelfth to the fourteenth century were called felonies, and the less serious came to be known as misdemeanours. The same distinction was subsequently drawn by Parliament in enacting statutory offences. The principal original felonies were homicide, rape, theft, robbery, burglary and arson. Important consequences flowed from the characterisation of an offence as a felony or a misdemeanour. For instance, only in the case of a felony was there a general power of arrest without warrant; similarly, it was an offence to conceal a felony (misprision of felony) but not to conceal a misdemeanour. At one time, there was a further important difference between the two categories of offence due to the fact that felonies were more serious offences. This had ceased to be so long before the abolition of the distinctions between felonies and misdemeanours by s 1 of the Criminal Law Act 1967, which provides that, on all matters on which a distinction between felonies and misdemeanours had previously been made, the law applicable at the commencement of the Act to misdemeanours applies.

4 Elements of criminal procedure: before trial

Prosecutions

4.1 The statement in the last paragraph of Chapter 1 that all criminal proceedings are in theory instituted and conducted by the Crown did not indicate who can perform the tasks of instituting and conducting such proceedings. This omission will now be rectified.

4.2 Although the police may institute criminal proceedings, the responsibility for the conduct thereafter of proceedings instituted by them lies with the Director of Public Prosecutions. The one exception is in the case of various minor traffic offences, and even then only where the 'pleading guilty by post'[1] procedure is adopted.

The Director of Public Prosecutions is the head of the Crown Prosecution Service. The Director is under the general supervision of the Attorney-General. The Director's functions are discharged on his behalf and under his direction by Crown Prosecutors working in the Crown Prosecution Service.[2]

The Director's principal function is to take over the conduct of criminal proceedings instituted[3] on behalf of the police[4] (with the road traffic offences exception mentioned above); once those proceedings are instituted the Director takes over. In addition, he may actually institute criminal proceedings where this is appropriate, e g because of the difficulty or importance of the case.

1 Para 5.16.
2 The relevant legislation is contained in Part I of the Prosecution of Offences Act 1985.
3 Proceedings are instituted:
   a) where a summons or arrest warrant is issued, when the information for the offence is laid before a magistrate;
   b) where a person is arrested without warrant, when he is informed of the particulars of the charge; or
   c) where a voluntary bill of indictment is preferred, when that bill is preferred before the court: Prosecution of Offences Act 1985, s 15(2).
   For an explanation of these terms, see paras 4.11–4.18 and 5.2.
4 See *Stafford Justices, ex p Customs and Excise Comrs* [1990] Crim LR 742, DC; cf *Ealing JJ, ex p Dixon* [1989] Crim LR 656, DC.

4.3 There is generally nothing to prevent a private individual instituting and conducting criminal proceedings, and such private prosecutions are occasionally instituted. In addition, criminal proceedings for various types of minor offences are instituted and conducted by officials of local authorities or other public bodies, and criminal proceedings for cases of serious or complex fraud may be instituted and conducted by the Director of the Serious Fraud Office.[1] However, the Director of Public Prosecutions may intervene at any time and undertake the conduct of proceedings by a private individual or such an official,[2] even if his purpose is to offer no evidence against the accused in the public interest and thereby to abort those proceedings.[3]

1 Criminal Justice Act 1987, s 1.
2 Prosecution of Offences Act 1985, s 6.
3 *Raymond v A–G* [1982] QB 839, [1982] 2 All ER 487, CA. The Director's decision to do so can only be impugned if it is manifestly unreasonable: *Raymond v A–G* ibid.

4.4　An exception to the general rule that a police officer, private individual or public official may institute criminal proceedings is that there are numerous offences where the leave of the Attorney-General or of the Director of Public Prosecutions is required.[1] For example, proceedings for all but one of the offences under the Official Secrets Acts 1911 and 1989 or for one of the offences relating to racial hatred under the Public Order Act 1986 may only be instituted by or with the consent of the Attorney-General, and proceedings for over 50 offences may only be instituted by or with the consent of the Director.[2] In the latter case, the Director's functions can, of course, be exercised by a Crown Prosecutor on his behalf. Where proceedings for an offence may only be instituted by or with the consent of the Attorney-General or of the Director, this is indicated at the appropriate point in this book.

1 Such a requirement does not prevent the arrest of a person for an offence subject to the requirement, nor does it prevent the remand in custody or on bail of an accused pending committal proceedings: Prosecution of Offences Act 1985, s 25. See also *Whale and Lockton* [1991] Crim LR 692, CA.
2 Such a provision in relation to the Director of Public Prosecutions does not, however, prevent the Director of the Serious Fraud Office instituting criminal proceedings.

4.5　Any person in whose hands the decision lies to institute or continue proceedings has a discretion whether or not to do so. The existence of the discretion to prosecute, which is much wider than in most continental countries, has not only been acknowledged but encouraged by the courts.

In relation to the exercise of discretion at various stages of the prosecution process, Crown Prosecutors are subject to the Code for Crown Prosecutors issued by the Director of Public Prosecutions pursuant to s 11 of the Prosecution of Offences Act 1985.[1] This provides that, when considering the institution or continuation of proceedings, the first question to be determined is the sufficiency of the evidence. A prosecution should not be started or continued unless the Crown Prosecutor is satisfied that there is admissible, substantial and reliable evidence against an identifiable person and that there is on that evidence a realistic prospect of a conviction. The Code goes on to provide that, if the evidence itself can justify proceedings, the Crown Prosecutor must then consider whether the public interest requires a prosecution. The factors which can lead to a decision not to prosecute will, of course, vary from case to case. Broadly, the graver the offence, the less likely it is that the public interest will not require a prosecution. The Code lists various instances which, if the offence is not so serious as plainly to require a prosecution, indicate that proceedings may not be required; examples are the likelihood that the penalty will be nominal (which is particularly significant where the proceedings are likely to be long and costly); the youth, old age or infirmity of the offender, and the wish of the complainant that no action be taken. The Code then goes on to provide that, if, after this process, the Crown Prosecutor is in doubt, the scale will normally be tipped in favour of prosecution.

1 The Code is set out as an Appendix to the DPP's annual report to the Attorney-General.

4.6   The interest of the State in the prosecution of crime is reflected in the way in which indictments are headed, e g *The Queen v Titus Oates*, and by the way in which cases tried on indictment are named in the law reports, e g *R v Brown* . 'R' stands for 'Rex' or 'Regina' (King or Queen), as the case may be. This title is retained on appeals to the Court of Appeal. In this book, following the modern practice, cases tried on indictment are cited under the name of the accused, e g 'Brown', as are appeals to the Court of Appeal or its predecessors. It used to be the practice, if an appeal was taken from the Court of Appeal to the House of Lords, for the name of the Director of Public Prosecutions or other official conducting the appeal on behalf of the Crown to appear in the title, but now the case is given the same title as in the Court of Appeal. In appeals to the Judicial Committee of the Privy Council it is the custom to place the letters 'v R' after the appellant's name.

The name of the Director of Public Prosecutions, or of the actual prosecutor if the prosecution is not undertaken by the Crown Prosecution Service, appears in the title of cases tried summarily or heard on appeal after summary conviction.

Jurisdiction

TIME

4.7   At common law a prosecution for an offence can be begun at any time after its commission, although any court may refuse to deal with the case if it considers that there has been such a lapse of time that it would be an abuse of process to do so (because a fair trial is no longer possible as a result of unjustifiable delay by the prosecution). Therefore, subject to this qualification,[1] a person may be prosecuted for an offence committed by him many years previously. For certain offences, however, statute expressly provides that a prosecution must be brought within a limited time after their alleged commission. For example, s 4 of the Perjury Act 1911[2] provides that a prosecution for the making of a false statement in registering a birth or death must be brought within three years. Most important of all, s 127(1) of the Magistrates' Courts Act 1980 lays down the general rule, which is subject to relatively few exceptions, that informations relating to summary offences must be laid within six months of their commission. This limitation does not apply to the summary trial with the accused's consent of offences triable either way.[3]

1 *Derby Magistrates Court, ex p Brooks* (1984) 80 Cr App Rep 164, DC; *Telford JJ, ex p Badham* [1991] 2 QB 78, [1991] 2 All ER 854, DC; *Crawley JJ, ex p DPP* (1991) Times, 5 April, DC.
2 Para 16.11.
3 Magistrates' Courts Act 1980, s 127(2); *Kemp v Liebherr-GB Ltd* [1987] 1 All ER 885, DC.

PLACE

4.8   The courts of England and Wales are only concerned with conduct which is an offence against English Law, or, to put it another way, with offences over which they have jurisdiction. With certain exceptions, mentioned in paras 6.80 and 6.81, to be an offence against English law an offence must be committed in England or Wales. This requirement is explained in para 6.78.

SOVEREIGN AND DIPLOMATIC IMMUNITY

4.9 The Queen and foreign sovereigns and Heads of State[1] are immune from the criminal as well as the civil jurisdiction of the English courts. Foreign diplomats and the like[2] enjoy a similar privilege but it is that of the government which they represent; therefore it may be waived by or on behalf of the foreign government, as it usually is in serious cases,[3] but it cannot be waived by an accused person himself unless he does so as an agent on behalf of the foreign government concerned.[4]

1 State Immunity Act 1978.
2 See, for instance, Diplomatic Privileges Act 1964; Consular Relations Act 1968; Diplomatic and Other Privileges Act 1971; International Organisations Act 1981.
3 *AB* [1941] 1 KB 454, 110 LJKB 268, CCA.
4 *Kanhya Lal Madan* [1961] 2 QB 1, [1961] 1 All ER 588, CCA.

Institution of proceedings

4.10 Except in the cases of contempt of court and absconding from bail, where special provisions[1] often apply, criminal proceedings are instituted in one of two ways:

   a) by laying an information and then securing the accused's presence before a magistrates' court by an arrest under a warrant or by a summons; or
   b) by an arrest without warrant, followed by a charge; or
   c) exceptionally, by the preferring of a voluntary bill of indictment.[2]

1 Paras 16.31 and 16.35.
2 In relation to voluntary bills of indictment, see para 5.1.

LAYING THE INFORMATION

4.11 An information, addressed to a magistrate or clerk to the magistrates, may be laid by the prosecutor, or by his counsel or solicitor, or by a person authorised on his behalf.[1] It need not be in writing or on oath,[2] unless a warrant of arrest is sought.[3]

The information must contain such particulars as are necessary to give the accused reasonable information of the nature of the charge, including the statutory provision alleged to have been infringed.[4] Not more than one offence may be alleged in each information, although several informations may be set out in one document.[5]

1 Magistrates' Courts Rules 1981, r 4(1).
2 Ibid, r 4(2).
3 Magistrates' Courts Act 1980, s 1(3).
4 Magistrates' Courts Rules 1981, r 100.
5 Ibid, r 12. See *Shah v Swallow* [1984] 2 All ER 528, [1984] 1 WLR 886, HL.

WARRANT OF ARREST

4.12 A warrant of arrest must be signed by a magistrate.[1] It is normally directed to all the police officers of the police area. It must state shortly the offence on which it is founded, and name or otherwise describe the offender, and order the officers to arrest the offender and bring him before the magistrates.[2] The warrant may be endorsed with a direction that the person to be arrested shall on arrest be released on bail, with or without sureties. This is known as 'backing for bail'.

Section 1(4) of the Magistrates' Courts Act 1980 provides that a warrant must not be issued in the first instance unless the offence to which it relates is either indictable or punishable with imprisonment, or the address of the accused is not sufficiently established for a summons to be served on him.

1 Magistrates' Courts Rules 1981, r 95.
2 Magistrates' Courts Rules 1981, r 96.

SUMMONS

4.13 A summons must be issued and signed by a magistrate or the clerk to the magistrates.[1] A summons is addressed to the accused. It must state shortly the offence or offences alleged together with such reasonable particulars as to enable the accused to know what facts are alleged to constitute the offence, and must require the accused to appear at a certain time and place before the magistrates.

The summons must be served on the accused:

a) personally; or
b) by leaving it for him with some person at his last known or usual place of abode or by sending it to that place by post.[2]

Service on a corporation is effected by delivering the summons at, or sending it to, its registered office.[3]

1 Justices' Clerks Rules 1970.
2 Magistrates' Courts Rules 1981, r 99(1).
3 Ibid, r 99(3).

ARREST WITHOUT WARRANT

4.14 *Arrestable offences* The only general powers of arrest without warrant relate to arrestable offences. These are defined as offences for which the sentence is fixed by law or for which a person (not previously convicted) may be sentenced to imprisonment for a term of five years, and certain other offences whose maximum punishment is less than five years' imprisonment such as taking a conveyance or going equipped for stealing.[1] The sentences for treason (death) and murder (life imprisonment) are fixed by law. In other cases maximum terms of imprisonment are generally prescribed by statute. Most serious offences are punishable with five years' imprisonment or more. For example, manslaughter (life), theft (seven years) and unlawful wounding (five years) are all arrestable offences along with many others.

Any person may arrest without warrant anyone who is (or whom he, with reasonable cause, suspects to be) in the act of committing an arrestable offence. Where an arrestable offence has been committed, *any person* may arrest without warrant anyone who is (or whom he, with reasonable cause, suspects to be) guilty of the offence.

Additionally, a *constable* may arrest without warrant:

a) where he suspects, with reasonable cause, that an arrestable offence has been committed, any person whom he suspects, with reasonable cause, to be guilty of it; or

 b) any person who is (or whom he suspects, with reasonable cause, to be) about to commit an arrestable offence.[2]

To effect an arrest under these powers a constable may enter, if need be by force, and search any place where the person to be arrested is, or is with reasonable cause suspected by the constable to be.[3] An important distinction, based on the common law,[4] between the powers of a constable and those of a private individual to arrest without warrant is that an arrest on reasonable suspicion is permissible in the case of the constable, even though the offence has not been committed, whereas to justify an arrest on reasonable suspicion in the case of a private individual it is essential that the offence should actually have been committed, though not necessarily by the person arrested.

1 Police and Criminal Evidence Act 1984, s 24(1) and (2). Criminal damage where the value of the property destroyed, or of the alleged damage, as the case may be, is less than £2,000 is an arrestable offence, despite the fact that in such a case the maximum punishment is normally less than five years' imprisonment: ibid, s 24(1).
2 The various powers of arrest are set out in the Police and Criminal Evidence Act 1984, s 24(4)–(7).
3 Ibid, s 17.
4 *Walters v WH Smith & Son Ltd* [1914] 1 KB 595, 83 LJKB 335.

4.15 *Offences which are not arrestable offences* Sometimes legislation provides a police officer with power to arrest without warrant in relation to a particular offence on specified conditions. Such special provisions do not make the offence an 'arrestable offence' in its technical sense and the powers of arrest thereunder are more limited than for an arrestable offence. Examples are the offence of affray; offences relating to entering and remaining on property, contrary to ss 6 to 10 of the Criminal Law Act 1977; and offences relating to drink and driving.

In addition, a constable, who reasonably suspects that *any* offence which is not an arrestable offence has been, or is being, committed or attempted, may arrest without warrant any person whom he reasonably suspects of having committed or attempted, or of being in the course of committing or attempting, that offence. However, this power is only exercisable if it appears to the constable that service of a summons is impracticable or inappropriate because any of the 'general arrest conditions' is satisfied. These are:

 a) that the name of the suspect is unknown to the constable and cannot be ascertained by him;
 b) that the constable has reasonable grounds for doubting whether the name furnished is the person's real name; or
 c) that the person has failed to furnish a satisfactory address, or that the constable has reasonable grounds for doubting whether the address furnished is a satisfactory address; or
 d) that the constable has reasonable grounds for believing that the arrest is necessary to prevent the suspect:
  i) causing physical harm to himself or another;
  ii) suffering physical injury;
  iii) causing loss of or damage to property;
  iv) causing an obstruction of the highway; or

v) committing an offence to public decency (provided members of the public going about their normal business cannot readily avoid the person to be arrested); or

e) that there are reasonable grounds for believing that arrest is necessary to protect a child or other vulnerable person from the person to be arrested.[1]

1 Police and Criminal Evidence Act 1984, s 25.

4.16 *Arrest for breach of the peace* At common law, a police officer or any one else may arrest without warrant a person who commits a breach of the peace in his presence, or a person who has been guilty of such a breach (provided there is a reasonable belief that a renewal of it is threatened), or a person whom he reasonably believes will commit a breach of the peace in the immediate future (although that person has not yet committed a breach).[1] A mere disturbance is not a breach of the peace; a breach of the peace requires that harm is actually done or is likely to be done to a person, or in his presence to his property, or that a person is in fear of being so harmed by an assault, riot or other disturbance.[1] A breach of the peace may occur on private premises even if the only persons likely to be affected by the conduct are on those premises.[2]

1 *Howell* [1982] QB 416, [1981] 3 All ER 383, CA.
2 *McConnell v Chief Constable of Greater Manchester Police* [1990] 1 All ER 423, CA.

4.17 *Unlawful arrest* Unless authorised by statute or the common law, an arrest without warrant is unlawful and may be the basis for proceedings for false imprisonment at the suit of the person arrested. An arrest is also unlawful if the force used to effect it is unreasonable in the circumstances,[1] or if the person making the arrest is trespassing at the time.[2]

1 Criminal Law Act 1967, s 3.
2 *Clowser v Chaplin* [1981] 2 All ER 267, [1981] 1 WLR 837, HL.

4.18 The arrest without warrant of a person is followed by his being charged. If he is kept in police detention thereafter, he must be brought before a magistrates' court as soon as practicable after being arrested, and in any event not later than the first sitting after he is charged.[1]

1 Police and Criminal Evidence Act 1984, s 46(2). There are special rules where the accused is to appear in a court in some other area than that in which he was arrested.

Committal proceedings

4.19 A person who is summoned or arrested for an offence triable only on indictment, ie triable only in the Crown Court by a jury, must, subject to rare exceptions,[1] appear before a magistrate or magistrates whose duty is not to try the case but to decide whether there is enough evidence on which a reasonable jury if properly directed could find him guilty and, if so, to commit him for trial to the Crown Court. These are committal proceedings and the magistrates who conduct them are called examining magistrates.[2]

1 Paras 4.21 and 5.1.
2 Magistrates' Courts Act 1980, ss 4–8.

4.20 Where a person who is summoned or arrested for an offence triable either way first appears before a magistrates' court, the magistrates must consider initially whether summary trial is more suitable, and they must decide this before any evidence is called. In doing so, they must have regard to any relevant circumstances, including:

a) the nature of the case;
b) whether the circumstances make the offence one of a serious character; and
c) whether the punishment which a magistrates' court would have power to inflict for it would be adequate.

The court must also give the prosecutor and then the accused an opportunity to make representations as to which mode of trial would be more suitable. Before the court considers which mode of trial is more suitable, the accused is entitled to request and receive advance information of the case against him; he must be informed as soon as practicable after the institution of proceedings against him of his right to make this request.[1] When considering which mode of trial is more appropriate, the magistrates should bear in mind guidelines laid down in a *Practice Note* in 1990. The effect of these is that in general, except where otherwise stated, either way offences should be tried summarily unless the magistrates consider that the particular case has one or more of a list of aggravating features and that their sentencing powers are insufficient.[2]

Where it appears to the court that the offence is more suitable for trial on indictment, the court proceeds to hold committal proceedings in the same way as if the offence was triable only on indictment.

On the other hand, where it appears that the offence is more suitable for summary trial, the court must explain this to the accused and explain that he can either consent to be tried summarily in the magistrates' court or, if he wishes, be tried on indictment in the Crown Court by a jury. The court must also explain that if he is tried summarily and convicted it is nevertheless possible for him to be committed to the Crown Court for sentence if the court forms the opinion on one of the grounds stated in para 5.21 that a greater punishment should be imposed than is within its power. The court must then ask the accused where he wants to be tried. Where the accused consents to summary trial, the magistrates' court will then proceed to summary trial of the information, but where he does not so consent the magistrates' court will proceed to inquire into the information as examining magistrates, in the same way as if it had decided that trial on indictment was more suitable.[3] If more than one accused are jointly charged with an offence, each of them individually has the right of election for trial on indictment. Consequently, the fact that one co-accused elects for trial on indictment does not mean that the other co-accused who have elected for summary trial must also be committed for trial.[4]

The above procedure does not apply if the prosecution is being carried on by the Attorney-General or Solicitor-General and he applies for the offence to be tried on indictment. In such a case, the magistrates' court must proceed to inquire into the information as examining magistrates; it has no discretion.[5] The same is true if the prosecution is being carried on by the Director of Public Prosecutions (or a Crown Prosecutor on his behalf) provided that the application for trial on indictment is made with the Attorney-General's consent.[6]

1 Magistrates' Courts (Advance Information) Rules 1985.
2 *Practice Note* [1990] 3 All ER 979.
3 Magistrates' Courts Act 1980, ss 19–21.

4 *Nicholls v Brentwood JJ,* [1991] 3 All ER 359, HL.
5 Magistrates' Courts Act 1980, s 19(4).
6 Ibid, s 19(5).

4.21   In certain cases, a 'designated authority' may issue a 'notice of transfer' whose effect is to transfer a case for trial in the Crown Court without the
need for committal proceedings. A 'notice of transfer' may be issued:

a) by the Director of Public Prosecutions, the Director of the Serious Fraud
Office or certain other designated authorities, in the case of a serious or
complex fraud case;[1]

b) by the Director of Public Prosecutions, in the case of a sexual offence or
an offence of violence or cruelty involving a child-victim or child-witness,
if the Director considers that (for the purpose of the child's welfare) the
case should be proceeded with in the Crown Court without delay;[2]

c) by the Attorney-General, in the case of a complex offence under the War
Crimes Act 1991.[3]

In all three cases the designated authority must consider that there is
sufficient evidence for the accused to be committed for trial.

1 Criminal Justice Act 1987, s 4. The case will be transferred to one of the Crown Court centres
specified for serious and complex fraud cases: *Practice Note* [1990] 3 All ER 320, CA.
2 Criminal Justice Act 1991, s 53.
3 War Crimes Act 1991, Sch 1.

4.22   If the court embarks on committal proceedings, the accused is told
what he is charged with but is not asked to plead. The court has two courses
open to it, depending on the circumstances:

a) If the prosecution informs the court that all the evidence consists of
written statements which have been served on the accused, and provided:
i)   the accused has (or all have) a solicitor acting for him in the case;
ii) no solicitor or counsel for the accused objects to the use of the
written statements or requests the court to consider a submission
that the written statements disclose insufficient evidence to commit the accused for trial; and
iii) the accused does not wish to give evidence,
the court may commit the accused for trial without looking at the
statements.
    The safeguard for the accused is that this procedure cannot be used
unless he is legally represented and he can object without giving
reasons to any of the evidence being given by means of a written
statement. This procedure is called committal without consideration of
the evidence and cannot take place without written statements.[1]

b) If the foregoing procedure is not used, the prosecuting advocate opens
his case by giving a summary of the facts and then calls the witnesses
for the prosecution; they are examined in chief and may be cross-
examined by the accused or his advocate and then re-examined. The
whole of the evidence of each witness must be taken down as nearly as
possible in his own words. It must then be read over to him and signed
by him; this becomes his deposition and the statements are collectively
known as the depositions. It is possible to shorten the proceedings by
using s 102 of the Magistrates' Courts Act 1980, which enables written
statements to be used instead of oral evidence on certain

conditions. In practice they are read aloud or summarised. The statements take the place of depositions.

When all the evidence for the prosecution has been given the court must consider whether a prima facie case has been made out. The accused's counsel or solicitor may submit that there is no case for his client to answer. If the court decides that there is a case to answer, the accused must be asked whether he has anything to say and, if he is not represented, he must be told that he need not say anything and that he has the right to give evidence and call witnesses.[2]

Whatever the accused may say in answer to the charge must be taken down, unless it amounts to an oration,[3] read over to him and (if the accused wishes) signed by him and transmitted to the court of trial with the depositions or written statements or both.

1 Magistrates' Courts Act 1980, s 6(2); Magistrates' Courts Rules 1981, r 6.
2 Magistrates' Courts Rules 1981, r 7.
3 *Morry* [1946] KB 153, [1945] 2 All ER 632, CCA.

4.23 *Custody time limits* There is a limit on the time that a person can be detained in custody pending his committal for trial or summary trial. Unless the examining magistrates extend the custody time limit on the ground that there is good and sufficient cause for doing so and that the prosecution has acted with all due expedition, the maximum period for an accused's remand in custody between his first appearance in the magistrates'court and the time when the court decides whether or not to commit him for trial[1] is generally 70 days; it is 56 days from first appearance if the magistrates decide on summary trial, unless a decision so to proceed has not been made within that period, in which case the limit is 70 days.[2] If he has not been committed or tried by the end of the appropriate period, the accused must be released on bail unless the period has already been extended.

1 Somewhat surprisingly, this time is deemed by the Prosecution of Offences Regulations 1987, reg 4(5), to be the time when the examining magistrates begin to hear the evidence for the prosecution.
2 Prosecution of Offences Act 1985, s 22; Prosecution of Offences (Custody Time Limits) Regulations 1987, reg 7.

REPORTING

4.24 In order to prevent cases being tried by jurors with pre-conceived ideas, s 8 of the Magistrates' Courts Act 1980 contains stringent restrictions on the reporting of committal proceedings. Under s 8, the general rule is that it is an offence to publish, or to broadcast, in Great Britain a report of committal proceedings in England and Wales, other than purely nominal matters such as the identity of the court and magistrates, the names of the parties and the nature of the charges. There are two exceptions:

a) Reporting must be authorised by the magistrates on the application of the accused or any of the accused (if more than one), provided in the latter case that if one of the accused objects to such authorisation an order can only be made if it is in the interests of justice to do so, and this means the interests of justice as they affect the accused persons.[1]
b) Reporting is permitted after the magistrates have decided not to commit, or after the trial where there has been a committal.

1 *Horsham Justices, ex p Farquharson* [1982] QB 762 at 797, [1982] 2 All ER 269, per Shaw LJ.

BAIL

4.25 Examining magistrates have the power to grant bail to persons who are committed for trial. It is very unusual to grant bail in murder cases. Those who are not granted bail by examining magistrates may re-apply[1] or apply either to a judge of the Crown Court in chambers[2] or to a judge of the High Court in chambers,[3] or to both.

1 Magistrates' Courts Act 1980, s 6(4).
2 Courts Act 1971, s 13 and Crown Court Rules 1982, rr 19–21.
3 Criminal Justice Act 1967, s 22.

4.26 By s 4 of the Bail Act 1976, the accused must be granted bail except in the cases specified in Sch 1 of that Act. One example of these exceptions is that the offence is imprisonable and the court is satisfied that there are substantial grounds for believing that, if released on bail, the accused would:

a) fail to surrender to custody; or
b) commit an offence while on bail; or
c) interfere with witnesses or otherwise obstruct the course of justice.

Another exception is that, in the case of any type of offence, the accused need not be granted bail if:

a) he should be kept in custody for his own protection or, if under 17, for his own welfare; or
b) he is already in custody pursuant to the sentence of a court; or
c) having already been released on bail in proceedings for the offence in question, he has been arrested for absconding or breaking conditions of bail.

These exceptions do not apply where a custody time limit has expired.[1]

1 Prosecution of Offences (Custody Time Limits) Regulations 1987, reg 8.

4.27 Unless he has been released on the expiry of a custody time limit,[1] the court may require the accused to provide other acceptable persons to act as sureties, ie to enter into recognizances for a stated sum which may be forfeited, in whole or in part, if he does not surrender into custody. No recognizance may be taken from the accused. Nor may a security for his surrender to custody be required to be given by him or on his behalf, unless it seems unlikely that he will remain in Great Britain;[2] such a security can never be required if the accused has been released on expiry of a custody time limit.[1]

1 Prosecution of Offences (Custody Time Limits) Regulations1987, reg 8.
2 Bail Act 1976, s 3(2)–(5).

4.28 The court may require the accused to comply with such conditions as appear necessary to it to secure that:

a) he surrenders to custody;
b) he does not commit an offence on bail;
c) he does not interfere with witnesses or otherwise obstruct the course of justice;
d) he makes himself available for enabling inquiries or a report to be made to assist the court in dealing with him for the offence.

Conditions may not be imposed for any purposes other than those specified.[1]

1 Bail Act 1976, s 3(3) and (6) and Sch 1.

4.29 If an accused person is granted bail, he is under a duty to surrender himself into custody at the time and place appointed for him to do so.[1] Failure to do so without reasonable cause, the onus of proving which is on him, is an offence.[2] In addition, the accused may be arrested on a warrant.[3]

A police officer may arrest without a warrant a person who has been released on bail if the police officer has reasonable grounds for believing that that person is unlikely to surrender to custody, or has broken or will break any condition of his bail, or if a surety gives him written notice that the person is unlikely to surrender to custody and for that reason the surety wishes to be relieved from his obligations.[4]

1 Bail Act 1976, s 3(1).
2 Ibid, s 6. See, further, para 16.35.
3 Ibid, s 7(1) and (2).
4 Ibid, s 7(3).

5 Elements of criminal procedure: trial and appeal

Trial on indictment

5.1 The normal practice is for an accused person to be tried on indictment in the Crown Court after being committed for trial by examining magistrates. However, a person can be tried on indictment without having been committed by examining magistrates in two types of case. First, where a 'notice of transfer' has been issued, as explained in para 4.21. Second, where an application has been made successfully to a High Court judge for a voluntary bill of indictment. An application for a voluntary bill may be necessary, for example, where magistrates have refused to commit for trial, or where it is desired to add a further count charging an offence not disclosed by the facts made known to the accused by the documents founding his committal.[1] A voluntary bill should only be granted where good reason to depart from the normal practice has clearly been shown, and even then only where the interests of justice (rather than administrative convenience) require it.[2]

1 Administration of Justice (Miscellaneous Provisions) Act 1933, s 2.
2 *Practice Direction (Crime: Voluntary Bills)* [1991] 1 All ER 288.

5.2 Before a person can be tried in the Crown Court, an indictment must be prepared. Generally, the Crown Prosecution Service is responsible for drafting the indictment. The draft indictment is known as the 'bill of indictment'. The bill of indictment must be 'preferred' by delivering it to the appropriate officer of the court of trial. Once the bill has been preferred, the appropriate officer signs and dates it. If the bill of indictment is not signed there is not only no valid indictment but also no valid trial, no valid verdict and no valid sentence.[1]

1 *Morais* [1988] 3 All ER 161, CA.

PRE-TRIAL REVIEW

5.3 After the indictment has been signed, the trial may be preceded by a 'pre-trial review'. At such a review, the court is informed of the pleas to be tendered, the prosecution witnesses required as shown on the committal documents, any additional witnesses who may be called by the prosecution, the evidence which is agreed, the probable length of the trial, any points of law or question as to the admissibility of evidence which may arise at the trial, and various other matters which may affect the proper and convenient trial of the case. In complex cases such a review should always be held.[1]

1 *Thorne* (1977) 66 Cr App Rep 6, CA.

TIME LIMITS

5.4 Although statute provides that the trial must take place not more than eight weeks after committal this period may be (and invariably is) extended by the Crown Court.[1] Even if it is not, a trial begun after its expiry is not a nullity.[2]

There is a maximum period during which a person may be kept in custody pending trial. It is a period of 112 days from committal. Unless this period is extended by the Crown Court, a person must be released on bail on its expiry.[3] The grounds for an extension are the same as apply to the corresponding period in a magistrates' court and which were described in para 4.23.

1 Supreme Court Act 1981, s 77; Crown Court Rules 1982, r 24.
2 *Spring Hill Prison Governor, ex p Sohi* [1988] 1 All ER 424, [1988] 1 WLR 596, DC.
3 Prosecution of Offences Act 1985, s 22; Prosecution of Offences (Custody Time Limits) Regulations 1987, rr 5–7.

ARRAIGNMENT

5.5 Provided that there has been no successful motion to quash the indictment, the next step in the trial is the arraignment of the accused which means that he is called to the bar (i e the front of the dock) by name and, after each count of the indictment has been read out, asked by the clerk of the court whether he pleads guilty or not guilty.

5.6 If, in answer to the clerk's question, the accused pleads 'guilty', the court hears a statement of the circumstances of the offence and evidence of his character and circumstances.

The following reports on the offender may be provided for the court:

a) A police officer gives an account of the previous convictions and general character and history of the offender, which are called 'the antecedents'.
b) There may be a report from the governor of the prison where the offender has been awaiting trial.
c) Medical or psychiatric reports may have been prepared between conviction and sentence on the direction of the judge.
d) There may be a pre-sentence report, often prepared before trial with the consent of the offender, by a probation officer. Such a report may be required by the judge in any case, and in many cases he is obliged to obtain one.

These reports are followed possibly by witnesses as to character on behalf of the offender; the court then hears the offender or his counsel in mitigation and proceeds to sentence him.

5.7 If the accused denies the charge, he pleads not guilty, and the case proceeds.

The accused is not limited to pleading guilty or not guilty. If he has already been tried for the same offence and convicted or acquitted, he may plead 'autrefois convict' or 'autrefois acquit', as the case may be. These pleas are available only if the accused has previously been at risk of a valid conviction on a charge for the same or substantially the same offence, and he must show that on a former occasion there has been an adjudication of the case, whether or not there has been a trial on the merits.[1] Where an accused leads autrefois convict or autrefois acquit it is for the judge, without the presence of the jury, to decide the issue.[2]

An accused may plead not guilty to the offence specifically charged in the indictment but guilty of another offence of which he might be found guilty on that indictment.

1 *Robinson* [1975] QB 508, [1975] 1 All ER 360, CA.
2 Criminal Justice Act 1988, s 122.

THE JURY

5.8 If the accused pleads not guilty, jurors are selected by ballot from the panel, which is the name given to the list of persons summoned to serve as jurors.

Most registered electors are eligible for jury service but there are many categories of people who are ineligible or disqualified, for example barristers, solicitors and police officers and certain ex-prisoners. In addition, the court has a discretion to excuse a juror from service.[1]

1 See, generally, the Juries Act 1974 and the Juries (Disqualification) Act 1984.

5.9 The prosecution or the accused has the right to challenge for cause. Such a challenge may be in respect of the whole jury ('to the array'), which is virtually unknown, or be confined to an individual or individuals ('to the polls'). A challenge for cause of an individual juror may be on the ground of ineligibility or disqualification, but a more frequent cause is that the juror is related to the accused or may be suspected of being prejudiced for some reason either in his favour or against him. Any challenge for cause is tried by the judge.[1] The prosecution has the right to challenge without cause to an unlimited extent by saying 'Stand by for the Crown', but it may only be exercised in certain exceptional circumstances (and generally only with the Attorney-General's authorisation).[2] These jurors stand by and can be called upon again if the panel is exhausted, whereupon the prosecution must show cause.

Provided that there is no successful challenge, each member of the jury is sworn or affirms individually, and the accused is then given in charge to the jury. If after this he wishes to change his plea to one of guilty, the verdict of the jury must be taken.

1 Juries Act 1974, s 12(1)(b).
2 *Practice Note* [1988] 3 All ER 1086.

THE CONDUCT OF THE CASE

5.10 As soon as the accused has been given in charge to the jury, the prosecution makes its opening speech. The witnesses for the prosecution are then each called, examined in chief, cross-examined and re-examined. If the defence intends to object to the admissibility of a piece of evidence, it should inform the prosecution beforehand (at the pre-trial review, if there is one); if this is done it is the duty of the prosecution not to refer to that evidence in its opening speech, in order that there shall be no disclosure to the jury of matters which it may not be possible to prove.[1] After this opening speech is concluded, each witness for the prosecution is called.

At the end of the case for the prosecution, the defence may submit that there is no case for him to answer on the prosecution's evidence, whether

1 For the procedure which must be adopted before a majority verdict may be accepted, see *Practice Direction* [1967] 3 All ER 137, [1967] 1 WLR 1198, CA and *Practice Note* [1970] 2 All ER 215, [1970] 1 WLR 916, CA. Also see *Pigg* [1983] 1 All ER 56, [1983] 1 WLR 6, HL.

5.15   After a verdict of guilty has been given, accepted and recorded, evidence is given of previous convictions and of the general character etc of the accused, and any plea in mitigation, in the same way as in a plea of guilty,[1] in order to enable the court to determine the appropriate sentence. The court will also take into consideration any offences for which the accused has not yet been tried but which he admits, unless it declines to do so.

1 Para 5.6.

Summary trial (other than young offenders)

5.16   A summary trial in a magistrates' court will take place if the offence with which the accused is charged is:

a) a summary offence; or
b) an offence which is triable either way, and the magistrates have decided, with the accused's consent, to try it summarily.[1]

In a summary trial the accused usually appears in answer to a summons, although he may have been arrested. The first step is for the clerk to the magistrates to read out the offence with which the accused is charged.

Although the accused frequently appears, s 12 of the Magistrates' Courts Act 1980 enables the accused to plead guilty in many cases without attending and without the need to call evidence. Provided that the offence is not one which carries a sentence of more than three months' imprisonment, there may be served with the summons a notice stating the effect of s 12 of the Magistrates' Courts Act 1980, together with a concise statement of such facts relating to the alleged offence as will be placed before the court by or on behalf of the prosecution if the accused pleads guilty without appearing in court. If the clerk of the court has received written notification from the accused or his solicitor that the accused desires to plead guilty without appearing, the court may hear and dispose of the case in the absence of the accused. If the case is dealt with in this way the prosecution is limited to the concise statement served on the accused who may send to the court a statement in mitigation.

1 Paras 2.3 and 4.20.

5.17   If the offence is one which is triable either way, i e summarily or on indictment, it is necessary to ascertain which is to be the form of trial, a matter discussed in para 4.20.

5.18   Where a case is to be tried summarily, the clerk asks the accused if he pleads guilty or not guilty. Generally, the same rules apply as in a trial on indictment.

5.19   At the end of the evidence and speeches the magistrates may retire in order to consider their decision. The clerk is responsible for advising the magistrates on questions of law, and as to matters of procedure. In addition, the clerk has the responsibility to refresh the magistrates' memories as to the evidence and to advise them on sentence. The clerk is not required to give his advice in open court, except in the case of refreshing the magistrates' memories.[1]

The magistrates' decision is reached by a majority, and chairman has no casting vote. Where there is an equality of voting, the case may be adjourned to be re-heard before another court.

There is generally no power on summary trial to return an alternative verdict.[2]

If the accused pleads guilty or is convicted, the court enquires into his record, hears the defence in mitigation and, where appropriate, considers the accused's mental condition at the time of conviction and other reports in the same way as in a trial on indictment.

1 *Practice Direction* [1981] 2 All ER 831, [1981] 1 WLR 1163.
2 *Lawrence v Same* [1968] 2 QB 93, [1968] 2 All ER 1191, DC.

5.20 The maximum sentences for summary offences and for offences triable either way which are tried summarily are laid down by the relevant statutes. However, unless it is expressly excluded, s 31 of the Magistrates' Courts Act 1980 prevents a magistrates' court imposing more than six months' imprisonment for any offence. Consecutive sentences of imprisonment must not normally exceed six months in aggregate in the case of summary offences nor 12 months in the case of offences triable either way.[1]

There are also limits on the fines which magistrates may impose. The maximum fine which they may impose on conviction of most offences triable either way is a standard sum, known as the 'prescribed sum' or 'statutory maximum'. At the time of writing that sum is £2,000 but after October 1992 it will be £5,000; the Home Secretary has power to amend the prescribed sum in the light of a change in the value of money.[2] In the case of summary offences, the maximum fine is governed by the level (on the standard scale of fines) assigned to the offence in question. The amounts specified for the various levels is to be raised in October 1992 and all references in this book to these amounts will be to them as so raised. The standard scale is as follows the amounts in brackets being those prevailing at the time of writing:[3]

Level on scale	Amount of fine
1	£200 (£50)
2	£500 (£100)
3	£1,000 (£400)
4	£2,500 (£1,000)
5	£5,000 (£2,500)

The Home Secretary has power to amend the amounts specified in the light of a change in the value of money.[4]

1 Magistrates' Courts Act 1980, s 133.
2 Ibid, ss 32 and 143; Interpretation Act 1978, Sch 1. The sum applicable from October 1992 is prescribed by the Criminal Justice Act 1991, s 17.
3 Criminal Justice Act 1982, s 37; Interpretation Act 1978, Sch 1. The amounts applicable from October 1992 are prescribed by the Criminal Justice Act 1991, s 17.
4 Magistrates' Courts Act 1980, s 143.

5.21 If a person has been tried summarily and convicted of an offence triable either way and the court is of the opinion:

a) that the offence or the combination of the offence and associated offences was so serious that some greater punishment should be imposed than it has power to impose; or

b) in the case of a violent or sexual offence, that a longer sentence of imprisonment than it has power to impose is necessary to protect the public,

it may commit him in custody or on bail to the Crown Court for sentence. The accused then appears before the higher court and is dealt with as if he had been convicted on indictment.[1]

1 Magistrates' Courts Act 1980, s 38 (as substituted by the Criminal Justice Act 1991, s 25).

The trial of young offenders

5.22 For the purposes of criminal proceedings, a child is any person under the age of 14; a young person is any person who has attained 14 and is under 18.[1] A magistrates' court before which a person under 18 appears charged with an offence which, in the case of an adult, is triable only on indictment or triable either way must deal with it summarily unless:

a) the charge is one of homicide; or

b) he is a young person and the offence is so grave that under specific statutory powers he, if found guilty, may be sentenced to be detained for a long period; or

c) he is charged jointly with a person who has attained 18 and the court considers it necessary in the interests of justice to commit them both for trial.[2]

Subject to a few exceptions, all charges against a person under 18 which are dealt with summarily must be heard by a youth court.[3]

1 Children and Young Persons Act 1933, s 107(1).
2 Magistrates' Courts Act 1980, s 24(1).
3 Children and Young Persons Act 1933, s 46.

5.23 A youth court is composed of magistrates specially appointed for the purpose. Normally, the court must consist of at least one man and one woman, and of not more than three persons in all. The only persons who are permitted to be present in court are members and officers of the court, parties in the case and their solicitors and counsel, witnesses, newspaper reporters and other persons specifically authorised to be present.[1]

No newspaper report of any proceedings in a youth court may reveal the name, address or school, or include any particulars calculated to lead to the identification, of any child or young person who is accused or is a witness. The only exception is where there is a direction to the contrary by the court or the Home Secretary.[2]

1 Children and Young Persons Act 1933, s 47.
2 Ibid, s 49.

5.24 *Care or supervision proceedings* Apart from its powers in criminal proceedings, a magistrates' court, sitting as a family proceedings court, also has powers in civil proceedings (known as 'care or supervision proceedings') to make orders in relation to persons under 17 who are in need of care or control. The provisions relating to care or supervision proceedings do not distinguish between a child and a young person in the way that is done by the provisions relating to criminal proceedings; consequently, the reference to a 'child' in what follows is not limited to someone under 14.

An order cannot be made in care or supervision proceedings unless the child is suffering, or likely to suffer, significant harm *and* that harm, or likelihood of harm, is attributable to the care given to the child, or likely to be given to him, not being what it would be reasonable to expect a parent to give to him or attributable to the child's being beyond parental control.[1]

At the end of the proceedings the family proceedings court, if satisfied that the application has been substantiated, may make an order placing the child in the care of a local authority or putting him under the supervision of a local authority or of a probation officer.[2]

1 Children Act 1989, ss 31(2) .
2 Ibid, s 31(1).

Appeal

FROM A MAGISTRATES' COURT TO THE CROWN COURT

5.25 a) If he did not plead guilty, a person convicted by a magistrates' court may appeal to the Crown Court against conviction, or against sentence, or against both.

      b) A person convicted by a magistrates' court after a plead of guilty may appeal to the Crown Court against sentence only.[1]

An appeal to the Crown Court against conviction takes the form of a re-hearing of the case, ie the case is tried all over again, witnesses being called etc, without any reference to the proceedings in the magistrates' court (except that the Crown Court may have regard to inconsistencies in the evidence given in the magistrates' court compared with that given in the Crown Court). Where the appeal is founded upon a question of law alone, it is usually thought preferable to ask the magistrates to state a case for the opinion of the Divisional Court, as described in para 5.26. In the case of an appeal against sentence alone, the proceedings will be similar to proceedings in the Crown Court after a finding of guilt (see paras 5.6 and 5.15).

On hearing an appeal the Crown Court has the same sentencing powers as a magistrates' court, and this means that it can (if it thinks appropriate) increase the severity of a sentence up to the maximum that the magistrates could have awarded.

Normally only a convicted person may appeal to the Crown Court, but an exception is the power of a customs and excise officer[2] to appeal against a dismissal of an information laid by him.

1 Magistrates' Courts Act 1980, s 108(1).
2 Customs and Excise Management 1979, s 147(3).

FROM A MAGISTRATES' COURT TO THE QUEEN'S BENCH DIVISION

5.26 Either the prosecution or the defence, or any other party to a proceeding before a magistrates' court, if aggrieved by a conviction, order, determination or other proceeding of that court on the ground that it is wrong in law or is in excess of jurisdiction, may apply to that court to state a case for the opinion of the Divisional Court of the Queen's Bench Division.[1] Unless it involves an issue of law, an appeal against sentence is more appropriately brought in the Crown Court than by case stated in the Divisional Court.

The magistrates' court may refuse to state a case if it is of the opinion that the application is frivolous, but in any event a court which refuses to state a case may be compelled to do so by an order of mandamus issued by the Divisional Court.[2] If this method of appeal is chosen, an appeal to the Crown Court against the decision in question is excluded.[3] Consequently, a person who applies to appeal to the Divisional Court against conviction loses the right to appeal to the Crown Court in relation to the decision to convict but not in relation to the decision as to sentence;[4] if he applies to appeal to the Divisional Court against conviction and sentence he loses the right to appeal to the Crown Court against both decisions.[5] The case stated by the magistrates must state the facts found by them and the question or questions of law or jurisdiction on which the opinion of the Divisional Court is sought.

After hearing argument by counsel, the Divisional Court may reverse, affirm or amend the magistrates' decision, or remit the case to them with its opinion thereon, or remit the case for re-trial[6].

1 Magistrates' Courts Act 1980, s 111.
2 Para 5.36.
3 Magistrates' Courts Act 1980, s 111(4).
4 *Sivalingham v DPP* (1975) unreported.
5 *Winchester Crown Court, ex p Lewington* [1982] 1 WLR 1277, DC.
6 Summary Jurisdiction Act 1875, s 6; *Griffiths v Jenkins* [1992] 1 All ER 65, HL.

FROM THE CROWN COURT TO THE QUEEN'S BENCH DIVISION

5.27 When the Crown Court has decided an appeal against conviction or sentence from a magistrates' court, either the prosecution or the defence may, if dissatisfied with the determination of the Crown Court as being wrong in law or in excess of jurisdiction, apply to the court to state a case for the opinion of the Divisional Court of the Queen's Bench Division.[1] The procedure is similar to that described in para 5.26.[2]

1 Supreme Court Act 1981, s 28.
2 Crown Court Rules, 1982, r 26 and RSC Ord 56, rr 1 and 4.

FROM THE CROWN COURT TO THE COURT OF APPEAL

5.28 *Appeal against conviction* A person convicted on indictment before the Crown Court may appeal to the Court of Appeal against conviction:

a) without any leave, on a question of law alone;
b) with leave of the Court of Appeal or of the trial judge
  i) on a question of fact alone, or
  ii) on a question of mixed law and fact;
c) with leave of the Court of Appeal, on any other ground which appears to the Court to be sufficient.[1]

1 Criminal Appeal Act 1968, s 1.

5.29 Under s 23(2) of the Criminal Appeal Act 1968, where fresh evidence is tendered to it, the Court of Appeal *must*, unless satisfied that the evidence would not afford any ground for allowing the appeal, receive it if it is likely to be credible, would have been admissible below, and the Court is satisfied that there is a reasonable explanation for the failure to adduce it. In general, the Court must be satisfied that the evidence could not with reasonable diligence have been obtained for use at the trial.[1]

Even though the conditions of s 23(2) are not met, the Court may, under s 23(1), receive admissible[2] fresh evidence if it thinks it necessary or expedient in the interests of justice.

1 *Beresford* (1971) 56 Cr App Rep 143, CA.
2 *Lattimore* (1975) 62 Cr App Rep 53, CA.

5.30   After hearing the appeal, the Court of Appeal may do one of the following:

a) It may allow the appeal on the following grounds:
   i)   that the conviction should be set aside on the ground that under all the circumstances of the case it is unsafe or unsatisfactory;
   ii) that the trial judge made a wrong decision on any question of law; or
   iii) that there was a material irregularity in the course of the trial.[1]
   Because of the constitutional primacy of the jury in trials on indictment and the fact that it is the function of the jury not only to find the facts but also to apply the law as directed by the trial judge, the Court of Appeal's function is limited to a power of review, rather than a full appellate function of determining appeals on the facts of the case. It cannot upset the verdict of a jury on a question of fact unless it thinks the conviction unsafe or unsatisfactory.[2]

   The most common allegations upon which an appeal is founded are misdirections on a point of law by the judge, and the wrongful admission of evidence. A person who pleaded guilty may appeal against conviction, but usually he will not satisfy one of the above three grounds. Three cases where he will are where he did not appreciate the nature of the charge or did not intend to admit that he was guilty of it (conviction unsafe or unsatisfactory),[3] or where there is fresh evidence putting in doubt the safety or satisfactory nature of the conviction, or where on the admitted facts the accused could not in law have been convicted of the offence charged (judge's acceptance of guilty plea will involve a wrong decision on a point of law).[4]

   Where the Court of Appeal allows an appeal against conviction, it will normally quash the conviction. However, where it appears to the Court that it is in the interest of justice to do so, it may instead order the appellant to be retried.[5]

b) It may dismiss the appeal. A proviso to s 2(1) of the Criminal Appeal Act 1968 states that, even though the Court is of opinion that the ground of appeal is good, it may dismiss the appeal if no miscarriage of justice has occurred. The test is whether the Court is satisfied that the only verdict which a reasonable jury could have returned after a proper summing up would have been one of guilty.[6] This is sometimes called 'applying the proviso'.

c) Instead of allowing or dismissing the appeal, it may substitute for a conviction for one offence a conviction for another offence if it was open to the jury at the trial to find the accused guilty of the latter offence, and if the Court considers that the jury must have been satisfied of the facts which were necessary to prove the accused guilty of that latter offence.[7]

1 Criminal Appeal Act 1968, s 2.
2 *McIlkenny* (1991) 141 NLJ 456, CA.
3 *Forde* [1923] 2 KB 400, 92 LJKB 501, CA.

4 *Whitehouse* [1977] QB 868, [1977] 3 All ER 737, CA.
5 Criminal Appeal Act 1968, s 7.
6 *Stirland v DPP* [1944] AC 315, [1944] 2 All ER 13, HL.
7 Criminal Appeal Act 1968, s 3.

5.31 *Appeal against sentence* A person convicted on indictment before the Crown Court may appeal to the Court of Appeal against sentence, unless it is one fixed by law.[1] In most cases, a person committed to the Crown Court for sentence after summary conviction may also appeal to the Court of Appeal against the sentence imposed by the Crown Court.[2] An appeal against sentence may only be brought with the leave of the Court of Appeal or (if there is a 'particular and cogent ground of appeal') with a certificate granted by the Crown Court judge involved.[3]

On appeal against sentence, the Court may quash that sentence and substitute another. However, the Court must so exercise its power of substitution that, taking the case as a whole, the appellant is not dealt with more severely than he was dealt with by the Crown Court.[4]

Although the prosecution has no right of appeal against a sentence imposed by the Crown Court, the Attorney-General may in certain cases refer such a sentence to the Court of Appeal with its leave if it appears to him to be unduly lenient.[5] On such a reference the Court of Appeal may increase the severity of the sentence. Somewhat surprisingly, it also has power to substitute a more lenient sentence, should it think it appropriate.[6] The cases in which the Attorney-General may refer a sentence are those where the sentence passed was for an offence triable only on indictment or for an offence triable either way specified by the Home Secretary.

1 Criminal Appeal Act 1968, s 9.
2 Ibid, s 10.
3 Ibid, s 11. *Practice Note* [1983] 3 All ER 608, [1983] 1 WLR 1292, CA.
4 Criminal Appeal Act 1968, s 11(3).
5 Criminal Justice Act 1988, s 36.
6 *A-G's Reference (No 4 of 1989)* [1990] 1 WLR 41, CA.

5.32 *Reference by the Home Secretary* By s 17 of the Criminal Appeal Act 1968, the Home Secretary may, at any time after a conviction on indictment, refer either the whole case or a particular point to the Court of Appeal. The Home Secretary exercises the power to refer only in exceptional cases, such as where fresh evidence suitable for judicial inquiry emerges or the conviction of a co-accused is quashed. Matters of sentence are very rarely referred.

Where the Home Secretary has referred the whole case to the Court of Appeal, the case is treated for all purposes (including disposal) as an appeal by the person concerned,[1] and that person can raise any ground of appeal which he could have raised if he had been the appellant, whether or not it was mentioned in the Home Secretary's letter setting out his reasons for the reference[2]. On the other hand, if a particular point is referred, the Court of Appeal is confined to that point and must give the Home Secretary its opinion on it.[3]

The Home Secretary may refer a case even though the person concerned has died.[4]

1 Criminal Appeal Act 1968, s 17(1)(a).
2 *Chard* [1984] AC 279, [1983] 3 All ER 637, HL.
3 Criminal Appeal Act 1968, s 17(1)(b).
4 *Maguire* (1991) Times, 28 June, CA.

5.33 *Venire de novo* The Court of Appeal has jurisdiction to order a new trial by the writ of *venire de novo*. The writ can only be issued if there has been an irregularity of procedure which has prevented the trial from ever having been validly commenced or if, although validly commenced, the trial has not validly been concluded by a properly constituted jury returning an unequivocal verdict followed by sentence or discharge.[1] Examples of the first of these two cases are that the judge was not qualified for appointment as such,[2] or that a plea of guilty was made by an accused who had lost his power to make a voluntary and deliberate choice (with the result that the plea was a nullity and the trial invalid from the start).[3]

1 *Rose* [1982] AC 822, [1982] 2 All ER 731, HL.
2 *Cronin* [1940] 1 All ER 618, 162 LT 423, CCA.
3 *Peace* [1976] Crim LR 119, CA.

5.34 *Reference on a point of law* By s 36 of the Criminal Justice Act 1972, the Attorney-General may refer to the Court of Appeal a point of law arising at a trial on indictment where the person tried has been acquitted. The opinion of the Court does not affect the acquittal but provides authoritative guidance for the future. This procedure is not confined to heavy questions of law. It may also be used for short but important points which require a quick ruling before a potentially false decision has too wide a circulation.[1] The procedure is limited to points of law which have actually arisen in a real case; the Attorney-General has no power to refer a hypothetical question of law, however interesting or difficult.[2]

1 *A-G's Reference (No 1 of 1975)* [1975] QB 773, [1975] 2 All ER 684, CA.
2 *A-G's Reference (No 4 of 1979)* [1981] 1 All ER 1193, [1981] 1 WLR 667, CA.

FROM THE COURT OF APPEAL OR THE DIVISIONAL COURT TO THE
HOUSE OF LORDS

5.35 After the determination of an appeal by the Court of Appeal or by the Divisional Court of the Queen's Bench Division, either the prosecution or the defence may appeal to the House of Lords provided that the necessary conditions are fulfilled and leave is granted either by the court below (ie the Court of Appeal or the Divisional Court) or by the House of Lords. The necessary conditions which must be fulfilled are:

a) The court below must certify that a point of law of general public importance is involved.
b) Either the court below or the House of Lords must be satisfied that the point of law is one which ought to be considered by the House of Lords.[1]

A point of law referred to the Court of Appeal by the Attorney-General may be further referred to the House of Lords, and so may a point of law involved in a sentence referred to the Court of Appeal by him.

1 Administration of Justice Act 1960, s 1; Criminal Appeal Act 1968, s 33.

OTHER PROCEEDINGS IN THE NATURE OF APPEALS

5.36 Independently of any right of appeal proper, all inferior courts of criminal jurisdiction are subject to control by the Divisional Court of the

Queen's Bench Division by means of the prerogative orders of mandamus, prohibition, or certiorari.[1] As the orders issue only to inferior courts, the Crown Court is not subject to them in relation to its jurisdiction in matters relating to trial on indictment (ie matters which affect the conduct of such a trial or are an integral part of the trial process, such as sentence or certain other orders dealing with an offender after verdict), but it is in respect of other matters (such as appeals from magistrates' courts).[2]

The order of mandamus is used to compel an inferior court to carry out a definite duty imposed on it by law. The order cannot be used to compel the court to exercise its discretion in a particular way, but it may be used to compel it to hear and determine a case, or to state a case for the opinion of the Divisional Court.

The order of certiorari is used to quash the decision of an inferior court on the ground that there has been an excess (or lack) of jurisdiction, or clear evidence of fraud, collusion, perjury or the like, or that the the decision involves such an unreasonable exercise of discretion that no reasonable body could have come to it, or that there has been a denial of natural justice. Natural justice will be denied, for instance, if a party is not given a chance to state his case, or if there is a real risk of bias on the part of a member of the court.

The order of prohibition is used to prevent an inferior court from doing something improper, and covers much the same ground as an order of certiorari, but before, and not after, the damage is done.

Applications for any of the above orders must be made by a procedure known as application for judicial review.[3]

In cases where the facts are involved and in issue the appropriate course is to appeal to the Divisional Court by case stated, and not to apply for judicial review.[4]

1 Supreme Court Act 1981, s 29.
2 Supreme Court Act 1981, s 29(3); *Re Smalley* [1985] AC 622, [1985] 1 All ER 769, HL; *Sampson v Crown Court at Croydon* [1987] 1 All ER 609, [1987] 1 WLR 194, HL.
3 Supreme Court Act 1981, s 31.
4 *Ipswich Crown Court, ex p Baldwin* [1981] 1 All ER 596, 72 Cr App Rep 131, DC.

6　Criminal liability

Actus reus and mens rea

6.1　A cardinal principle of criminal law is embodied in the maxim *actus non facit reum, nisi mens sit rea* – an act does not make a person legally guilty unless the mind is legally blameworthy.[1] In this chapter it is proposed to deal generally with what must be proved in order to secure a conviction although it may be that the accused person can avoid conviction by relying on a defence. Two points are involved – first the outward conduct which must be proved against the accused (which is customarily known as the actus reus), and secondly the state of mind which he must be proved to have had at the time of the relevant conduct (customarily known as the mens rea). Although the opinion has been expressed by at least two members of the House of Lords[2] that it would be conducive to clarity of analysis of the ingredients of an offence to avoid these Latin tags and to replace them with the terms 'prohibited conduct' and 'state of mind', their use is so firmly established that they are unlikely to be abandoned before the codification of the criminal law. If the draft Criminal Code Bill[3] is enacted, the two tags would be replaced by 'external elements' and 'fault element' respectively.

1 *Younghusband v Luftig* [1949] 2 KB 354 at 370.
2 *Miller* [1983] 2 AC 161, [1983] 1 All ER 978 at 979–80, per Lord Diplock; *Courtie* [1984] 1 All ER 740 at 741, per Lord Diplock. Also see *Shivpuri* [1986] 2 All ER 334 at 336, per Lord Hailsham LC.
3 Law Commission: A Criminal Code for England and Wales (1989): Law Com No 177; see para 3.21 above.

6.2　It is convenient to begin with a few general observations before analysing the expressions actus reus and mens rea. The maxim *actus non facit reum, nisi mens sit rea* has not escaped criticism. When commenting on a similar phrase *non est reus nisi mens sit rea*, Stephen J said 'though this phrase is in common use, I think it most unfortunate, and not only likely to mislead, but actually misleading, on the following grounds. It naturally suggests that, apart from all particular definitions of crimes, such a thing exists as a "mens rea", or "guilty mind", which is always expressly or by implication involved in every definition. This is obviously not the case, for the mental elements of different crimes differ widely.'[1] This remains true today. Mens rea means in murder an intention unlawfully to kill or cause grievous bodily harm; in theft that the accused acted 'dishonestly' and with the intention of permanently depriving another of the property; and in criminal damage an intention to damage property belonging to another, or recklessness as to whether any such property would be damaged. In some cases, such as criminal damage or manslaughter, mens rea can denote mere blameworthy inattention.

The maxim can also be criticised in that mens rea is not always required for criminal liability; in some offences a person can be convicted despite the fact of his blameless inattention.

Notwithstanding these strictures, the significance of the maxim has been stressed in a number of judgments. In *Brend v Wood*,[2] for example, Lord Goddard CJ said 'It is of the utmost importance for the protection of the liberty of the subject that a court should always bear in mind that, unless a statute either clearly or by necessary implication rules out mens rea as a constituent part of a crime, the court should not find a man guilty of an offence against the criminal law unless he has a guilty mind.'

1 *Tolson* (1889) 23 QBD 168 at 187.
2 (1946) 175 LT 306, DC.

6.3 Most people would agree that, as a general rule, the infliction of punishment is only justified when the accused was at fault.

The requirement of mens rea is thus designed to give effect to the idea of just punishment. For those who believe that everyone who does an act prohibited by the criminal law should be liable to therapeutic treatment rather than punishment, the state of mind with which the act was performed is a relevant consideration only when the method of treatment falls to be determined,[1] but the holders of these beliefs have not supplied a blueprint of the practical means of giving effect to their views.

Nonetheless, these views at least have the merit of emphasising the fact that the requirement that an actus reus should always be proved is even more important than the requirement of mens rea. The Christian moral code may condemn evil intentions just as much as evil deeds, but it is unnecessary for the law to go to such lengths. Evil intentions only become sufficiently dangerous to society to merit punishment when the agent has gone a considerable distance towards carrying them out. Even the most diehard believers in punishment concede that a system of law according to which wishes were equivalent to deeds would be even less satisfactory than one which punished deeds without considering the mental state of the doer. 'The reasons for imposing this great leading restriction upon the law are obvious. If it were not so restricted it would be utterly intolerable; all mankind would be criminals and most of their lives would be passed in trying and punishing each other for offences which could never be proved'.[2]

1 Wootton *Crime and the Criminal Law* (2nd edn).
2 Stephen *History of the Criminal Law* vol II, p 78.

6.4 Not only does the maxim *actus non facit reum, nisi mens sit rea* serve the important purpose of stressing two basic requirements of criminal liability but it also suggests a useful framework for the analysis of the definition of specific offences. This task is undertaken in chapters 10 to 21 and the discussion is generally divided into a consideration of the actus reus and mens rea required in each case. It is, however, most important that the maxim should not be allowed to become the master rather than the tool of the criminal lawyer. A perfectly coherent account of the criminal law could be given without it, and time is sometimes wasted by the consideration of pointless questions concerning the heading under which certain undeniable requisites of criminal liability should be discussed. Thus, there is no doubt that, even when the accused is sane, automatism is generally a defence. This means that, if there is sufficient evidence that because of non-insane automatism the accused did not know what he was doing at the material time, the prosecution will fail unless it can satisfy the jury that the accused did know what he was doing. No useful purpose is served by considering whether the requirement that the accused must generally have acted voluntarily, i e when not in a state of automatism, relates to actus reus or mens rea or to neither.

Actus reus

6.5 It is necessary to refer to the definition of the offence charged in order to ascertain the precise nature of the prohibited conduct, and even the most cursory consideration of the different offences makes it plain that, if the phrase actus reus is to be used as a description of the requisite external conduct, it must be given a far wider meaning than 'criminal act'. One reason is that an omission to act or the mere occurrence of an event may suffice, no act on the accused's part being required. Another reason is that rarely, if ever, is a mere act sufficient for criminal liability for a substantive offence. The definitions of offences often specify surrounding circumstances, such as time or place, which are essential to render the act criminal. Sometimes the definition requires a consequence to result from the act, such as the consequence of the death of another human being in murder.

The expression actus reus can be summarised as meaning an act (or sometimes an omission or other event) indicated in the definition of the offence charged *together with*:

    a) any surrounding *circumstances* (other than references to the accused's mens rea[1] or any defence[2]); and

    b) any *consequences* of that act which are indicated by that definition.

1 But see Lynch 'The Mental Element in The Actus Reus' (1982) 98 LQR 109.
2 See further, paras 6.19–6.21.

ACTS, OMISSIONS AND EVENTS

6.6 *Acts* An act is the most common basis of the actus reus. Of course, the nature of the requisite act varies from offence to offence. The definitions of some offences indicate the requisite act precisely, so that in rape an act of sexual intercourse is required and in causing death by dangerous driving an act of driving. However, the relevant act is specified less precisely in the definitions of other offences, particularly where they use words which comprise two concepts, that of an act and that of a consequence flowing from it. For example, the common law definitions of murder and manslaughter simply require the 'killing' of another. Where the act is left undefined in this way, any act which results in the death of another will suffice. Thus, murder can be committed by an act of shooting or hitting or strangling or planting a bomb or poisoning or by any other of the many ways which men and women have devised for killing each other. Likewise, there are a number of statutory offences involving the 'obstruction' of various types of public officer; such an offence can be committed by any act which results in the 'obstruction' of an officer of the appropriate type.

6.7 *Omissions*[1] An omission to act is a less common basis of criminal liability than a positive act. Historically, the criminal law has been concerned essentially with prohibiting (and punishing) positive actions rather than with imposing duties to act (and punishing failure to do so). In recent times, however, it has increasingly concerned itself with failures to act.

1 Smith 'Liability for omissions in the criminal law' (1984) *4 Legal Studies* 88; Gross 'A note on omissions' ibid 308; Hogan 'Omissions and the duty myth' *Criminal Law: Essays in Honour of JC Smith* 85; Ashworth 'The Scope of Criminal Liability for Omissions' (1989) 105 LQR 424; Williams 'Criminal Omissions: The Conventional View' (1991) 107 LQR 86.

6.8 *Express offences of omission* An obvious instance where an omission to act can give rise to liability is where the definition of an offence actually specifies an omission to act. Examples are the offence of wilful neglect, by a person with responsibility for it, of a child in a manner likely to cause it unnecessary suffering or injury to health,[1] the offence of failing without reasonable excuse to provide information required under the Gas Act 1986,[2] and the offence of failing to accord precedence to a pedestrian on a 'zebra' pedestrian crossing.[3]

Apart from the common law offence of misprision of treason (a failure to report a treason), all offences of this type are statutory. Such offences are increasingly common in modern statutes; generally they are minor in nature. Normally, the statute in such a case is drafted in terms of imposing on a specified type of person a duty to do a particular thing and then providing that it is an offence not to do it. Even if the statute is not drafted in this way, it will be clear from its wording who is under a duty to do the particular thing, and therefore liable for failure to do it.

1 Contrary to the Children and Young Persons Act 1933, s 1(1).
2 Contrary to the Gas Act 1986, s 38(2).
3 Contrary to the 'Zebra' Pedestrian Crossings Regulations 1971, reg 8, and Road Traffic Regulation Act 1984, s 25(5). For another example in the sphere of road traffic, see para 20.3.

6.9 *Other offences* Leaving aside offences which by their express definition are committed by an omission, the issue of when an omission to act can give rise to criminal liability can be explained as follows. The starting point is to note that the issue relates to offences whose definition employs an active verb (otherwise the offence would expressly be an omission offence or an event offence, described later) and that the determination of the issue involves in part the construction of that verb.

In the case of some offences it is impossible to imagine their commission by an omission; examples are the various offences involving sexual intercourse by a male accused, offences involving driving, and the offences of robbery and burglary. In addition, the words used in the definition of an offence may indicate clearly that it may only be committed by an act; for example, if an offence requires an accused to 'do an act with intent' to bring about a specified consequence, criminal liability cannot be imposed on an accused who has simply failed to act with the requisite intent.[1]

1 *Ahmad* (1986) 84 Cr App Rep 64, CA.

6.10 Apart from these offences, and any others which may have been held incapable of commission by an omission, the situation is that while an offence may ordinarily require an act on the part of the accused it can also in principle be committed by an omission to act, *provided the accused was under a duty to act recognised by the criminal law* but failed to fulfil it. 'In principle' is used deliberately since there is nothing to stop a court, when an offence is first construed authoritatively, from giving the active verb in the definition a narrow construction so as to require an act on the accused's part.

Whereas some continental Codes provide a general duty on all persons to assist others in peril according to their abilities, our criminal law does not impose a general duty to act to save other people or property from harm, even if this could be done without any risk or inconvenience. For example, a stranger who stands by and watches a child drown in a shallow pool when he could easily rescue it commits no offence because he is not under a duty to rescue it. Duties to act recognised by the criminal law may arise under statute but more commonly in the present type of case they arise under the common law. The common law has developed particularly in this respect in relation to a duty to act to save another from physical harm, and it is this duty on which we shall concentrate.

6.11 The following examples of a common law duty to act *to save another from physical harm* can be derived from the cases, most of which were concerned with the offence of manslaughter:

a) A duty to act may arise under a contract, at least where the failure to fulfil a contractual obligation is likely to endanger the lives of others, and maybe in other cases. Although a contractual obligation can only be owed to other parties to the contract, a duty recognised by the criminal law which arises from it can also be owed to persons who are not parties to the contract. In *Pittwood*,[1] for example, D, a level-crossing keeper, failed in breach of his contract of employment to close the gate when a train was approaching with the result that someone was killed on the crossing. D was convicted of manslaughter after Wright J had held that a person might incur criminal liability from failure to perform a duty arising out of a contract and that that duty could be owed to road users even though the contractual obligation was only owed to the railway company.

b) A person is under a duty to care for others if he holds a public office which requires him to do so. For example, in *Curtis*[2] a relieving officer of a local authority was held liable for manslaughter when he had failed to provide medical assistance for a destitute person. Likewise, in *Dytham*,[3] where a uniformed police officer had failed to intervene when he saw a man being kicked to death some 30 yards away, it was held that he could be convicted of the common law offence of misconduct in a public office.

c) A parent is under a duty to his young child to save it from physical harm. Consequently, a mother who fails to feed her young child with the result that it dies can be convicted of murder or manslaughter, depending on her state of mind.[4] Presumably, a child over the age of criminal responsibility (ie 10) owes a corresponding duty to his parents, and other close relationships (eg husband and wife) may possibly involve a similar duty.[5]

d) A person who voluntarily undertakes the care of another who is unable to care for himself owes a duty to that person. The undertaking of care may be done by some express (or overt) act, as in *Nicholls*,[6] where D received into her home her young grandchild after the death of its mother. On an indictment for manslaughter by neglect, Brett J directed the jury that if a person chooses to undertake the care of a person who is helpless either from infancy, mental illness or other infirmity, he is bound to execute that responsibility and if (with the necessary mens rea) he allows him to die he is guilty of manslaughter.

Following the Court of Appeal's decision in *Stone and Dobinson* ,[7] it is now clear that a voluntary undertaking of care may be *implied* from the accused's conduct generally towards the victim of his neglect, in which case a duty to act will arise. The importance of this is that it is possible for a duty to a helpless person to arise where the accused and the victim of the neglect were initially in a relationship, for example as members of the same household, where each was able to look after him or herself but where the victim has subsequently become helpless through mental or physical illness and become dependent on the accused for care. In such a case it cannot be said that the accused has undertaken the care of the victim by any express (or overt) act, such as the act of receiving the grandchild into the home in *Nicholls*. In *Stone and Dobinson* D1's sister came to live with D1 and his mistress (D2) in 1972. At the time she was able to look after herself but later, being morbidly anxious about putting on weight, she denied herself proper meals and by July 1975 became unable or unwilling to leave her bed. D1 and D2 made ineffectual efforts to get a doctor and D2 undertook the task of trying to wash the sister and of taking such food to her as she required, but they made no effort to contact the social services or similar agencies. The sister was found dead in bed in an emaciated and filthy condition in August 1975. The Court of Appeal dismissed appeals by D1 and D2 against convictions for manslaughter. On the question of whether D1 and D2 had been under a duty to care for the sister it held that there was evidence on which the jury could conclude that by mid-July 1975, when the sister had become helplessly infirm, D1 and D2 were under a legal duty to summon help or care for her themselves. This evidence was that D1 and D2 were aware of the sister's poor condition and had attempted to get a doctor, and (in D1's case) that the victim was his sister and occupied a room in his house, and (in D2's case) that she had tried to wash her and provide food. From this the undertaking of a duty of care could be inferred. Clearly, very little is needed for such an undertaking.

1 (1902) 19 TLR 37.
2 (1885) 15 Cox CC 746.
3 [1979] QB 722, [1979] 3 All ER 641, CA.
4 *Gibbins and Proctor* (1918) 82 JP 287, 13 Cr App Rep 134, CCA (father). There can be no doubt that a guardian is likewise under a duty.
5 Smith and Hogan *Criminal Law* (6th edn) 50. If such a duty exists a boy of 14 would, for example, owe a duty to take steps to save his mother if he found her drowning in a shallow pool: ibid.
6 (1874) 13 Cox CC 75.
7 [1977] QB 354, [1977] 2 All ER 341, CA. Also see *Gibbins and Proctor* (1918) 82 JP 287, 13 Cr App Rep 134, CCA (common law wife of father failed to feed his children with fatal consequences and with mens rea for murder; held guilty of murder).

6.12 *A special situation* In one situation liability may be based on an omission to act even if the offence is one which is generally incapable by judicial construction of commission by an omission,[1] although not where the express terms of the offence require an act.[2] This is the situation where the accused inadvertently and without the appropriate mens rea does an act which puts a person or property in danger but before the resulting harm is complete he becomes aware of the train of events caused by his act. In such a situation the accused is under a duty to take such steps as lie within his power to try to prevent or reduce the risk of harm. Consequently if, before the harm resulting from the accused's act is complete, he realises what he has done and fails to take such steps to prevent or reduce the risk, and provided he then has the relevant mens rea, he will be criminally liable.

The leading authority for the principle is the decision of the House of Lords in *Miller*.[3] At his trial for arson (contrary to s 1(1) and (3) of the Criminal Damage Act 1971) in relation to P's house, D claimed that he had started the fire accidentally, having fallen asleep while smoking a cigarette. On his own admission he had woken up before the house was damaged and discovered that he had set his mattress on fire but had simply gone to another room to resume his slumbers. Dismissing D's appeal against conviction, the House of Lords held that a person would commit the actus reus of the offence in question if, having accidentally started a fire which created a risk of damage to property, he became aware of what he had done before the resultant damage was complete but failed to take steps within his power to prevent or reduce the damage to the property at risk. The reason was that he would be in breach of a duty (or 'responsibility', as Lord Diplock, with whose speech the other Lords agreed, preferred) to take such steps, which resulted from his accidental act. For further discussion on this point, see para 6.71.

1 *Kaitamaki* [1980] 1 NZLR 59 (New Zealand CA), affirmed [1985] AC 147, [1984] 2 All ER 435, PC.
2 *Ahmad* (1986) 84 Cr App Rep 64, CA.
3 [1983] 2 AC 161, [1983] 1 All ER 978, HL.

6.13 *Extent of duty to act* A general point which may be made about the extent of a duty arising under the common law is that its extent varies depending on the circumstances and the nature of the duty. For example, a person who owes a duty of care towards a person who is helpless must take steps to care for him, such as summoning medical help or providing food.[1] Someone like *Miller* must take such steps as lie within his power to counteract the danger he has accidentally created, either himself or by calling out the fire brigade. As yet there is no clear authority on how much of a risk a person under a duty to act can be expected to run in order to perform that duty, but there can be little doubt that a common law duty requires reasonable steps to be taken to perform it (reasonableness being assessed in the light of all the circumstances, including the accused's age and other relevant characteristics, and any risks to the accused or others involved).

1 *Stone and Dobinson* [1977] QB 354, [1977] 2 All ER 341, CA.

6.14 It must be emphasised that, even if the actus reus of an offence is constituted by an accused's failure to fulfil a duty to act, he cannot be criminally liable unless his omission was accompanied by the relevant mens rea.

6.15 *Events* Sometimes the definition of an offence simply requires the occurrence of an event in which the accused is involved, no act or omission on his part being required. All offences where a mere event is sufficient are statutory. One example is provided by s 25 of the Theft Act 1968, whereby a person is guilty of an offence if, when not at his place of abode, he has with him any article for use in the course of or in connection with any burglary, theft or cheat; another is provided by s 12 of the Licensing Act 1872, whereby it is an offence to be found drunk in a public place. A third example is provided by s 4 of the Road Traffic Act 1988, whereby it is an offence to be in charge of a mechanically propelled vehicle on a road or other public place when unfit to drive through drink or drugs.

CIRCUMSTANCES AND CONSEQUENCES

6.16 *Consequences* The accused's act or omission may be required to cause a particular consequence. In murder and manslaughter it must be proved that the accused's act or omission resulted in the unlawful killing of a human being, and in obtaining property by deception it must be proved that property belonging to another was obtained as the result of the accused's deception. The rules relating to the issue of causation are dealt with later at appropriate points, especially in relation to offences of homicide where most of the issues seem to have arisen.

There is an increasing tendency to refer to offences requiring a consequence to result from the accused's act or omission as 'result crimes' and to refer to other offences as 'conduct crimes'.[1]

1 See, for example, *Treacey v DPP* [1971] AC 537 at 560, per Lord Diplock; *Berry* [1984] 3 All ER 1008 at 1012, per Lord Roskill; *Steer* [1986] 3 All ER 611, [1986] 1 WLR 1286, CA. 'Conduct crime' would seem to be an inappropriate term to describe offences based on an omission or an event.

6.17 *Circumstances* The circumstances in which the act, omission or external event must occur vary widely from offence to offence. The sexual intercourse in rape must be with a woman who does not consent; the act of entry in burglary must be by a trespasser, and bigamy can be perpetrated only by a person who is already married.

6.18 *Whole of actus reus must be proved* There can be no criminal liability unless the whole actus reus is proved. In *White*,[1] for instance, the accused put potassium cyanide in his mother's drink, intending to kill her. Shortly afterwards the mother was found dead with the glass, partly full, beside her. The medical evidence was that she had died from a heart attack, and not from poisoning, and that the quantity of potassium cyanide administered was insufficient to cause her death. The accused was acquitted of murder (but convicted of attempted murder) because although the intended consequence – death – had occurred it had not been caused by his conduct and thus an element of the actus reus of murder was missing. Similarly, one who handles goods, mistakenly believing that they are stolen goods, cannot be convicted of handling stolen goods (but only of attempted handling)[2] since the necessary circumstance that the goods are stolen is absent.

1 [1910] 2 KB 124.
2 Para 21.69.

6.19 *Are elements of justification or defences part of the actus reus?* The definitions of many offences refer to elements of justification or to defences. Sometimes, the reference is to an element of justification or defence specifically provided for the offence charged, which may be defined in detail. In other definitions, reference is made to a number of general justifications or defences and is made by one word or phrase.

6.20 An element of *justification* differs from a defence in that it renders the accused's conduct lawful whereas a defence simply excuses an accused from liability for conduct which is nevertheless unlawful.

Examples of elements of justification are the 'defences' of self-defence, prevention of crime and related 'defences'.[1] 'Defences' has been placed in inverted commas because, as has been indicated in the Court of Appeal,[2] none of these elements of justification is properly to be regarded as a defence; instead, they are matters which the prosecution must disprove as an *essential part* of the prosecution case before a guilty verdict is possible. In the definitions of murder and other offences against the person[3] there appear the words 'unlawful' or 'unlawfully' which indicate that no offence is committed, the accused's conduct being lawful, if one of these elements of justification exists, as where D kills P in lawful self-defence. This being so, it would certainly be odd to say that, for example, a person who kills another in lawful self-defence has committed the actus reus of murder, and it is clear from modern cases, particularly *Williams*[4] and *Beckford v R*,[5] that references to these and other elements of justification in the definition of an offence are an element of its actus reus, being part of its prescribed consequence. An oddity about this is that, while an accused does not have to prove an element of justification, he does have an evidential burden in relation to it and only if he shifts this does the prosecution have to disprove it (and thereby prove the element of unlawfulness).[6] This is an exceptional situation where an accused has even an evidential burden in relation to an element of the actus reus of an offence.

A question which arises from the principle that a reference to elements of justification in the definition of an offence is part of its actus reus is this. Does the principle mean that a person does not commit the actus reus of such an offence if he acts in circumstances which justify his conduct, but without realising that those circumstances exist? Such a situation is, of course, extremely unlikely to arise. The answer to the question is that the principle does not necessarily mean that the person concerned does not commit the actus reus of such an offence. The reason is that all that 'unlawfully' or some other word in the definition referring to elements of justification does is to make it clear that the offence is not committed if a relevant element of justification applies on the facts. Such a word says nothing about the nature of the element of justification, and it may be that the element is only available if the accused knew of the facts which justified his use of force (or believed that they existed). Authority that this is the position in law is provided by the decision in the old case of *Dadson*[7], where D, a constable, was employed to guard a copse from which wood had been stolen. He saw P come out carrying wood, which he was stealing. P refused to stop and D shot him in the leg. At the time, it was assumed that it was lawful to shoot an escaping felon. The theft of the wood was not itself a felony but P was committing a felony because (unknown to D) he had repeatedly been convicted of stealing wood. It was held that D had rightly been convicted of unlawfully wounding P with intent to do him grievous bodily harm since there was no justification for it, D being ignorant of the facts making P a felon.

In practice, the point is not a particularly important one. The reason is that, if (contrary to *Dadson*) a person who acts under circumstances of justification of which he is ignorant does not commit the actus reus of an offence requiring him by its definition to act 'unlawfully' or otherwise without justification, he may nevertheless be guilty of an attempt to commit that offence. This is because s 1(3) of the Criminal Attempts Act 1981[8] provides that, on a charge of attempt, the accused is to be treated as if the facts were as he believed them to be. Consequently, a person, who commits what would otherwise be an offence in ignorance of circumstances of justification, can be convicted of attempting to commit the full offence, even if (contrary to *Dadson*) he cannot be convicted of the full offence.[9]

1 These are described in detail in paras 22.1–22.15. For other examples, see para 10.13.
2 *Wheeler* [1967] 3 All ER 829 at 830; *Abraham* [1973] 3 All ER 694 at 696.
3 For present purposes, sexual offences are not included within this category.
4 (1987) 78 Cr App Rep 276, CA; para 7.21.
5 [1987] 3 WLR 611, PC; para 7.21. Also see *Kimber* [1983] 3 All ER 316, [1983] 1 WLR 1118, CA; para 7.21.
6 Para 7.9.
7 (1850) 3 Car & Kir 148; affd 2 Den 35.
8 Para 21.68.
9 Hogan 'The *Dadson* Principle' [1989] Crim LR 684.

6.21 There are far more defences (ie legal rules which excuse an accused from liability for conduct which is nevertheless unlawful) than there are elements of justification.

It is a matter of dispute[1] whether or not a defence is part of the actus reus of the offence. The arguments on both sides are fairly evenly balanced but the view taken in this book is that under the law as it now stands, particularly in relation to the issue of mistake,[2] matters of defence referred to in the definition of an offence are not part of its actus reus. That is why it was stated in para 6.5 that the circumstances of an actus reus do not include defences to which the definition of an offence refers.

A fortiori, it follows from this view that the general defences of duress by threats, duress of circumstances and marital coercion, which apply to most offences, even though not referred to in their definitions, are not in a negative form (eg 'otherwise than under duress...') part of the actus reus of an offence.

1 For a different view to that adopted in this book, see Smith 'On Actus Reus and Mens Rea' *Reshaping the Criminal Law* (1978) 95; Williams 'Offences and Defences' (1982) 2 *Legal Studies* 233.
2 Paras 7.18–7.33.

Mens rea

6.22 Despite occasional judicial utterances to the contrary,[1] it is clear from the application of mens rea in the courts that it has nothing necessarily to do with notions of an evil mind or knowledge of the wrongfulness of the act. The accused's ignorance of the criminal law is no defence, nor generally is the fact that the accused did not personally consider his conduct to be immoral or know that it was regarded as immoral by the bulk of society. Moreover, it is generally irrelevant to liability whether the accused acted with a 'good' or 'bad' motive.

The expression mens rea refers to the state of mind expressly or impliedly required by the definition of the offence charged. This varies from offence to offence but typical instances are intention, recklessness and knowledge. In the course of our examination of typical states of mind it will be necessary to refer to so-called *Caldwell*-type recklessness and to negligence, although these can hardly be said to be states of mind. The mens rea required for an offence normally relates to the consequences or circumstances, or both, required for the actus reus of the offence charged.

1 See, for example, *Sherras v de Rutzen* [1895] 1 QB 918 at 921, per Wright J; *Sweet v Parsley* [1970] AC 132 at 152, per Lord Morris of Borth-y-Gest.

INTENTION[1]

6.23 Where the definition of the actus reus of the offence charged requires the accused's conduct to produce a particular consequence he has a sufficient mental state as to that consequence if he intended it to occur. In many offences where the accused's conduct is required to produce a particular consequence liability can be based either on his intention or his recklessness as to that consequence. However, in the definitions of some offences liability can be based only on intention and it is in these that the question of what is meant in law by intention is of crucial importance.

1 See Buxton 'Some Simple Thoughts on Intention' [1988] Crim LR 484.

6.24 Like the other concepts of mens rea referred to in this chapter, 'intention' is not defined by any statute and its meaning must therefore be derived from judicial decisions. Unfortunately, the courts, and in particular the House of Lords, have been remarkably reluctant to tell us what the current legal meaning of 'intention' is. On the other hand, the House of Lords in 1985 in the leading case of *Moloney*,[1] while refraining from defining what 'intention' is in law, was prepared to describe things which do not constitute intention. For example, it held that intention is something quite distinct from motive (ie a person's reason for acting as he did) or desire; if D kills P with great regret (but seeing no other way) in order to take P's money, his intention is to kill P but his motive is to take the money, and it is irrelevant that D did not desire P's death. Generally speaking, however, as we shall see, recent judicial pronouncements have served not to clarify the law on 'intention' but to obscure it. Nevertheless, it is possible to make some concrete statements, and we shall start with these.

1 [1985] AC 905, [1985] 1 All ER 1025, HL.

6.25 *Something which is 'intention'* Intention was defined by the Court of Appeal in *Mohan*[1] as: 'a decision to bring about, insofar as it lies within the accused's power, [a particular consequence], no matter whether the accused desired that consequence of his act or not'. As the court recognised,[2] this can be described more briefly as the 'aim'. Alternatively, it can be described as the accused's 'purpose'. The definition in *Mohan* could be described as a common-sense definition, since it probably accords with most people's idea of what constitutes intention, as well as being the relevant meaning given by the dictionaries.[3] As Lloyd LJ said in *Walker and Hayles*,[4] 'It has never been suggested that a man does not intend what he is trying to achieve'. Provided that he has decided to bring about a particular consequence, insofar as it lies within his power, a person acts with intention in relation to it even though he believes he is unlikely to succeed in bringing it about. For example, a person has an intention to kill if he fires at someone whom he believes to be outside the normal range of his gun in an endeavour to kill him.

Although the House of Lords in *Moloney* did not expressly confirm the *Mohan* definition of 'intention', it did not include it among the things which did not constitute intention, and there can be no doubt that this definition still holds good.

1 [1976] QB 1, [1975] 2 All ER 193 at 200.

2 [1976] QB 1, [1975] 2 All ER at 198.
3 See, e g, Shorter Oxford English Dictionary; Chambers Twentieth Century Dictionary.
4 (1989) 90 Cr App Rep 226 at 230.

6.26 It follows, from the reference in the definition in *Mohan* to the fact that it is irrelevant that the accused did not desire a consequence which he had decided to bring about, that a person can be said to act with an intention to cause a particular consequence, even though it is not desired in itself, if it is the means (ie a condition precedent) to the achievement of a desired objective and he decides to cause that consequence, insofar as it lies within his power. Not only is this implicit in that definition, but also support for it can be found in the speech of Lord Hailsham in *Hyam v DPP*,[1] decided by the House of Lords a year before *Mohan*. Lord Hailsham, adopting a definition of intention very similar to that in *Mohan*, stated that it should be held to include 'the means as well as the end' (ie that a person who has decided to bring about a consequence as a means to a desired end or objective falls within the definition in relation to that consequence). Suppose that a person is charged with an offence which requires him to intend to cause economic loss to another, and that the accused admittedly acted to make a gain for himself by depriving another of something. It is no defence for him to say that, since his desired objective was to make a gain for himself, he did not intend to cause economic loss.

The case law, however, is not wholly in accord with the principle just stated. In *Steane*[2] D made broadcasts in Germany during the war in order to save his family from a concentration camp. It was held on appeal that the broadcasts were not made 'with intent to assist the enemy' even though D knew full well that his purpose of saving his family could only be achieved by doing acts assisting the enemy. This decision perverted the concept of intention so as to excuse an accused who was deserving. As we shall see in Chapter 22, there may have been a more acceptable basis (the defence of duress by threats) for Steane not being guilty. Hard cases can make bad law and it is submitted that *Steane* should not be allowed to cast doubt on the statements concerning intention in the previous paragraph. It is inconceivable that the court would have reached the same conclusion if Steane had broadcast in order to obtain a packet of cigarettes.

1 [1975] AC 55 at 74, [1974] 2 All ER 41 at 52.
2 [1947] KB 997, [1947] 1 All ER 813, CCA. Also see *Gillick v West Norfolk & Wisbech Area Health Authority* [1986] AC 112, [1985] 3 All ER 402, HL, para 23.17, in relation to which, to the extent that it may relate to the present point, the comments in the text concerning *Steane* are equally applicable.

6.27 *Foresight not intention* Before the House of Lords' decision in *Moloney*, the general understanding from the cases was that, for the purposes of most offences, a person would intend a consequence of his conduct if he foresaw that that consequence was virtually certain to result from his act, although he did not aim to produce it. Thus, if F, who wished to collect the insurance money on an air cargo, put a time bomb on an aircraft to blow it up in flight, realising that it was inevitable that those on board would be killed by the explosion, he was regarded as having intended those deaths, even though he wished those on board no harm and would have been delighted if they had survived.

Indeed, before *Moloney*, the balance of judicial statements also supported the view that, for the purpose of murder and some other offences, a person who foresaw a consequence as a highly probable (or, perhaps, even probable) consequence of his act intended it, although he did not aim to produce it.

Foresight of the type described in this paragraph was described as oblique intention, to distinguish it from purposive intention (often described as direct intention).

6.28 The House of Lords in *Moloney*[1] decided, and affirmed in *Hancock and Shankland*,[2] that foresight, even of virtual certainty, is not intention in a legal sense nor the equivalent of it. As a result the authority to the contrary was impliedly overruled.

In *Moloney* D and his stepfather, P, drank heavily at the ruby wedding anniversary of the D's maternal grandparents. D and P stayed up late into the night and were heard laughing and talking. At about 4 am a shot was heard. D telephoned the police and said: 'I've just murdered my father'. D stated that he and P had a disagreement as to who was the quicker at loading and firing a shotgun, that (at P's request) he got two shotguns and cartridges, that he had easily beaten P in loading his shotgun and had pulled the trigger of the empty barrel, whereupon P had taunted him by saying that he knew D would not have the nerve to pull the trigger of the loaded barrel, and that he had pulled it and killed P. He said: 'I didn't aim the gun. I just pulled the trigger and he was dead.'

The trial judge directed the jury that murder required D to intend to kill P or to cause him some really serious harm and that a person intended the consequences of his voluntary act a) when he desired it to happen and b) when he foresaw that it would probably happen, whether he desired it or not.

The jury convicted D of murder and his appeal was dismissed by the Court of Appeal. He then appealed to the House of Lords, the question certified by the Court of Appeal was whether the mens rea for murder was established by proof that the accused either:

a) intended to kill or do serious harm; or
b) foresaw that death or serious harm would probably occur, whether or not he desired either of those consequences.

The House of Lords answered 'no' to this question. It held that the mens rea for murder was an intention to kill or do serious harm, and that foresight of the probability (or even high probability) of death or serious bodily harm was neither intention as to such a consequence nor the equivalent of intention.

1 [1985] AC 905, [1985] 1 All ER 1025, HL.
2 [1986] AC 455, [1986] 1 All ER 641, HL.

6.29 Although the House of Lords' answer to the certified question was necessarily in terms of foresight of probability, it seems clear from the statements overall in that case and from the subsequent decision of the House of Lords in *Hancock and Shankland* that they must be interpreted as also applying to foresight of certainty.[1] Any doubts on this score were settled by the Court of Appeal in *Nedrick*,[2] where it was stated that foresight of a consequence as 'for all practical purposes inevitable' could give rise to an irresistible inference of intention (as opposed to being intention in itself), and in *Walker and Hayles*,[3] where the Court agreed that foresight of the virtual certainty of a consequence was not intention.

1 Cf Norrie 'Oblique Intention and Legal Politics' [1989] Crim LR 793, especially at 802-803.
2 [1986] 3 All ER 1, CA.
3 (1989) 90 Cr App Rep 226, CA.

6.30 *Moloney, Hancock and Shankland* and *Nedrick* concentrated on intention in murder. However, the statements in those cases are not limited to that offence, and they have subsequently been applied by the courts to the concept of intention in other offences.[1]

1 *AMK (Property Management) Ltd* [1985] Crim LR 600, CA (doing acts likely to interfere with the peace or comfort of a residential occupier with intent to cause him to give up occupation, contrary to the Protection from Eviction Act 1977, s 1(3)); *Bryson* [1985] Crim LR 669, CA (wounding with intent to do grievous bodily harm, contrary to the Offences Against the Person Act 1861, s 18); *Walker and Hayles* (1989) 90 Cr App Rep 226, CA (attempted murder).

6.31 *Inference of intention where achieving prohibited consequences is not proved to be accused's purpose* As is explained in Chapter 7, proof of an intention on the accused's part depends on inferences which the jury (in their discretion) draw from all the evidence, including any evidence of foresight on his part of the consequence as certain or probable to result which the accused admits or the jury infers. For example, if D points a gun at P and fires it at P who is killed, and D's foresight of the risk of death is established, it is normally easily inferable from that foresight coupled with any other evidence, such as evidence of motive, that D's purpose (and therefore his intention) was to kill P. This 'ordinary' type of case presents no difficulty and in such a case the meaning of 'intention' will not normally have to be spelt out to the jury, because there will be no doubt that – if it is proved that D's purpose was to kill – the jury will find that D intended the death.

6.32 In contrast, a problem may arise where the evidence suggests that achieving the prohibited consequence was not the accused's purpose, because he had some other purpose, although he may have foreseen that that consequence was certain or probable to result from his conduct, as in the case of F, the planter of the bomb, referred to in para 6.27. In such a case, the judge will have to direct the jury. What is the relevant law? This is the issue dealt with between this point and the end of para 6.35.

The starting point in such a case is *Moloney* where Lord Bridge (with whom the rest of their Lordships agreed) said that the jury should be told that, if it is proved that the accused foresaw a consequence of his act, they are entitled (but not obliged) to infer that the accused intended it. Thus, although foresight is not itself intention, intention can be inferred from it. This raises the question of the degree of risk of the consequence which must have been foreseen before it can be inferred that the accused intended it.

6.33 *Inferring intention from foresight: what degree of risk must be foreseen?* In *Moloney* it seems on balance that Lord Bridge was of the view that foresight of virtual certainty was required before intention could be inferred from it. A more liberal view, that intention could be inferred from foresight of the probability of a consequence, seemed to be taken soon afterwards by the House of Lords in *Hancock and Shankland*.[1] P, a taxi-driver, was killed when two lumps of concrete hit his car as it passed under a bridge during the 1984-85 miners' strike. P's passenger was a miner going to work. The accused were miners on strike and they objected to P's passenger going to work. They had placed the lumps of concrete on the parapet of the bridge and projected them into the path of the taxi as it approached. P died as the result of the wrecking of the taxi by the two lumps of concrete.

At their trial for murder, the accused said that they had intended simply to block the road and stop the passenger going to work but not to kill or do serious harm to anyone. The accused were convicted of murder but appealed successfully to the Court of Appeal. Rejecting an appeal by the prosecution, the House of Lords held that the trial judge had misdirected the jury by failing to explain to them accurately the degree of risk which must be foreseen before an intention to kill or cause grievous bodily harm (the mens rea for murder) could be inferred.

Lord Scarman (with whom the rest of their Lordships agreed) said:[2]

'In a murder case where it is necessary to direct a jury on the issue of intent by reference to foresight of consequences the probability of death or serious injury resulting from the act done may be critically important. Its importance will depend on the degree of probability: if the likelihood that death or serious injury will result is high, the probability of that result may . . . be seen as overwhelming evidence of the existence of the intent to kill or injure. . . . [T]he greater the probability of a consequence the more likely it is that the consequence was foreseen and that if that consequence was foreseen the greater the probability is that that consequence was also intended.'

1 [1986] AC 455, [1986] 1 All ER 641, HL.
2 [1986] 1 All ER at 650–1.

6.34 The statements in *Moloney* and *Hancock and Shankland* were repeated by the Court of Appeal in *Nedrick*. In the latter part of the following quotation from the Court of Appeal's judgment, there is a statement that (at least in murder cases) the inference of intention may only be drawn in a case of foresight of virtual certainty. The Court of Appeal, purporting to crystallise *Moloney* and *Hancock and Shankland*, said this about the situation where achieving the prohibited purpose may not have been the accused's purpose:

'When determining whether the defendant had the necessary intent, it may be helpful for a jury to ask themselves two questions. (1) How probable was the consequence which resulted from the defendant's voluntary act? (2) Did he foresee that consequence?

If he did not appreciate that death or serious harm was likely to result from his act, he cannot have intended to bring it about. If he did, but thought that the risk to which he was exposing the person killed was only slight, then it may be easy for the jury to conclude that he did not intend to bring about that result. On the other hand, if the jury are satisfied that at the material time the defendant recognised that death or serious harm would be virtually certain (barring some unforeseen intervention) to result from his voluntary act, then that is a fact from which they may find it easy to infer that he intended to kill or do serious bodily harm, even though he may not have had any desire to achieve that result.

As Lord Bridge said in *Moloney*:

". . . the probability of the consequence taken to have been foreseen must be little short of overwhelming before it will suffice to establish the necessary intent."

Later he uses the expression moral certainty and says, "will lead to a certain consequence unless something unexpected supervenes to prevent it".

Where the charge is murder and in the rare case where the simple direction is not enough, the jury should be directed that they are not entitled to infer the necessary intention unless they feel sure that death or serious bodily harm was a virtual certainty (barring some unforeseen intervention) as a result of the defendant's actions and that the defendant appreciated that such was the case.

Where a man realises that it is for all practical purposes inevitable that his actions will result in death or serious harm, the inference *may* be irresistible that he intended that result, however little he may have desired or wished it to happen. The decision is one for the jury to be reached on a consideration of all the evidence.'[1]

1 [1986] 3 All ER 1 at 3–4.

6.35 It appears from these words that the Court of Appeal ultimately endorsed the view that it is only where a consequence is foreseen as virtually certain that intention may be inferred, although the earlier parts of the statement indicate a lack of firmness of view (especially outside murder) in relation to foresight of degrees of risk between mere probability and virtual certainty.

The question of the degree of risk which must be foreseen was subsequently considered in *Walker and Hayles*,[1] a case of attempted murder where the judge had directed the jury that they could infer the necessary intent to kill from foresight of a very high degree of probability of death. The Court of Appeal considered that a direction in terms of virtual certainty would have been better. However, it did not accept that the reference to foresight of a very high degree of probability was a misdirection because it did not regard the difference of degree, 'if there was one',[2] between 'virtual certainty' and 'very high degree of probability' as sufficient to render the direction a misdirection. It is submitted that there is a difference of degree between the two terms. If a consequence is virtually certain it is almost inevitable[3] that it will occur, whereas a consequence which is very highly probable is not almost inevitable but merely one which is very likely to occur.

The above paragraphs can be summarised as follows. Where it was not the accused's aim or purpose to bring about a particular consequence, but it is established that he acted with foresight that that consequence was *virtually certain* to result from his conduct, the jury may infer from that degree of foresight that the accused intended that consequence. All the cases from *Moloney* on described above support this. However, *Walker and Hayles* is authority that, while it is preferable for juries to be directed in terms of foresight of virtual certainty, it is not a misdirection to direct them that intention may be inferred from foresight of the very high degree of probability of the consequence resulting. On the other hand, despite some indication to the contrary in *Hancock and Shankland*, the clear balance of the case law from *Moloney* on indicates that the inference of intention cannot be drawn from foresight of a lower degree of probability than very high probability.

1 (1989) 90 Cr App Rep 226, CA.
2 Ibid, at 232.
3 Leaving aside the ultimate death of a person, nothing is absolutely certain since something, however unexpected, may intervene to prevent what seems inevitable occurring.

6.36 Where the jury are not satisfied that the achievement of the prohibited consequences was the accused's aim or purpose, the inference of intention from foresight postulated in *Moloney* and the other cases referred to above is *nonsense*. If foresight in itself is not intention, and the accused did not act with what is established in law as intention (ie he had not decided to bring about, insofar as it lay within his power, the particular consequence), how can it be inferred from foresight of a consequence on his part that he intended it when any additional type of 'intention' is left undefined by the law? The courts have not stated what the mystery ingredient is that can be inferred from foresight and which converts foresight (which is not intention) into intention. The only obvious ingredients are:

a) aim or purpose on the accused's part but that, of course, will have been ruled out – otherwise one would not be concerned with the present point;

b) motive or desire on the accused's part, but in *Moloney* the House of Lords has said that intention is something quite distinct from motive or desire.

Until the courts tell us what the mystery ingredient is, the present proposition must be regarded with scepticism as a matter of principle.

That said, there can be no doubt that in practice juries will not often be bothered by these problems of principle, and where they find that the accused foresaw the virtual certainty of the requisite consequence will generally have no problems in inferring that he intended it. In practice such foresight will almost invariably be equated with intention in the minds of a jury.

6.37 *Uncertainty* The statements in *Moloney* and *Hancock and Shankland* about the inference of intention were clearly not limited to proof of intention in murder.[1] Whether taken alone, or taken together with the subsequent cases, they have left the law in a state of uncertainty. It is unacceptable that, in addition to the clearly established definition of intention in the sense of aim or purpose, the law should permit 'intention' to have some other, undefined meaning. Legal concepts must be certain in advance if the principle of legality, referred to in Chapter 3, is not to be infringed seriously.

This defect is aggravated by the different approaches taken in the recent cases as to when intention may be inferred where a direction in terms of foresight is necessary. The recent performance of the superior courts suggest that they are incapable of resolving the present uncertainty. Legislation along the lines of the draft Criminal Code Bill (see para 6.68) is urgently required as the only sound way out of the existing confusion.

1 See those cases and *Bryson* [1985] Crim LR 669, CA.

6.38 *Offences where the inference of intention may not be drawn* In some offences, the inference of intention may not be drawn where the jury are not satisfied that the prohibited consequence was the accused's aim or purpose. Among these are a few offences which expressly require the accused to act with a specified purpose. Clearly, only intention in the purposive sense defined in *Mohan* will suffice for such offences. The best examples are offences under s 1 of the Official Secrets Act 1911,[1] which require the accused to have entered a prohibited place (or done certain other acts) 'for a purpose prejudicial to the safety or interests of the state'.[2]

1 Lord Devlin's statement in *Chandler v DPP* [1964] AC 763, [1962] 3 All ER 142, HL, that in its ordinary sense in the criminal law in general, and in this statute in particular, 'purpose' designates those objects which a person knows will probably be achieved by his act was not echoed by the other law lords in that case, and it is inconceivable that it would now be followed in the light of the way that the law on 'intention' in general has developed.

2 Other examples are the offence of violence for securing entry (see para 15.25), and the
  offence of sending a malicious communication with intent to cause distress or anxiety
  (contrary to the Malicious Communications Act 1988, s 1).

6.39 In addition, in the case of some other offences requiring 'intention',
their nature may be such that only a 'purposive' intention can meaningfully
be required, in which case the inference of some other (non-purposive) type
of intention would be inappropriate. Alternatively, they may have been held
to require such an intent. An offence which has been held to require a
purposive intention is the common law offence of treason (at least in the
form of treason by adhering to the Queen's enemies).[1]

Sometimes, the use of the words 'with intent to. . .' in a statutory
definition of an offence is in a context where only a purposive intention can
meaningfully be said to be possible. In such a case it would appear proper to
say that the offence requires such an intention; examples of such offences
appear in para 6.40.

1 *Ahlers* [1915] 1 KB 616, 84 LJ KB 901, CCA.

FURTHER INTENTION

6.40 This type of intention is alternatively known as 'ulterior intention'.
These terms are used to describe an intention on the part of the accused
which does not relate to a consequence of his conduct required by the
definition of the actus reus of the offence charged but relates instead to
something ulterior to it. Where the definition of an offence requires a
further intent as to a particular thing, the offence cannot be committed
unless that thing was intended; recklessness, as opposed to intention, as to
the further thing occurring is insufficient. The important point is that, since
the further thing is not a requisite of the actus reus, it is irrelevant that it
never occurs.

Certain acts which would not otherwise be criminal are made criminal if
they are performed with intent to do some further act. For example, it is
normally not an offence to enter a building as a trespasser, but, by s 8 of the
Theft Act 1968, a person who does so with intent to steal anything in the
building is guilty of burglary. Sometimes the criminal law punishes what
would otherwise be a comparatively minor offence with much greater severity if it was committed with the further intent of perpetrating a more serious
offence. For example, the offence of common assault is punishable with a
very modest period of imprisonment, but the offence of assault with intent to
rob is punishable with imprisonment for life. In these and the fairly numerous similar cases, it must be proved that, when he did the prohibited act, the
accused had decided to do all that he could towards the performance of the
subsequent act. Talk of anything other than a purposive intention would
generally be quite out of place.

Sometimes the further intent relates to an intended consequence of the
prohibited act committed by the accused. An example is the offence of
harassment of a residential occupier. By s 1(3) of the Protection from
Eviction Act 1977, it is an offence for a landlord to do any act likely to
interfere with the peace or comfort of a residential occupier if he does so
with intent to cause the residential occupier to give up the occupation of the
premises. In such a case, the necessary intention is not necessarily limited to
a purposive intention.

65

SPECIFIC INTENT AND BASIC INTENT

6.41   'Specific intent' is used frequently in the reports and should be treated with caution since, although it does not connote an additional species of intention, it can bear four different meanings:

a) the intention which must be proved to secure a conviction for a particular offence for which intention is the only state of mind specified in relation to an element;[1]
b) a purposive intention;[2]
c) a further intention; and
d) a state of mind, required for particular offences only, in relation to which the accused may successfully plead its absence by relying on evidence of voluntary intoxication.[3]

1 *Mohan* [1976] QB 1, [1975] 2 All ER 193, CA; *Moloney* [1985] AC 905, [1985] 1 All ER 1025, HL; *Hancock and Shankland* [1986] AC 455, [1986] 1 All ER 641, HL.
2 *Makewski v DPP* [1977] AC 443 at 479-480, per Lord Simon.
3 Paras 9.50–9.65.

6.42   Some judges have added to the confusion by introducing the term 'basic intent'. A 'basic intent' is not another type of intent and, surprisingly, it is not limited to intention at all. 'Basic intent' bears at least two meanings:[1]

a) In the words of Lord Simon in *DPP v Morgan*:[2] 'By "crimes of basic intent" I mean those crimes whose definition expresses (or, more often, implies) a mens rea [whether intention, or recklessness or knowledge which are discussed later] which does not go beyond the actus reus.'
b) A state of mind whose absence is no excuse if the evidence indicates that this was due to the accused's voluntary intoxication.[3]

The variety of meanings of 'specific intent' and 'basic intent' means that the reader must, when confronted with one of these terms, stop and consider what meaning it bears in the particular context.

1 For a third possible meaning, see para 11.63.
2 [1976] AC 182 at 192, [1975] 2 All ER 347 at 363.
3 Para 9.54.

RECKLESSNESS

6.43   In many offences 'recklessness', either as to the consequence required for the actus reus or as to a requisite circumstance of it or as to some other risk, suffices for criminal liability as an alternative to some other mental state such as intention or knowledge.

Following the House of Lords' decision in *Caldwell*[1] in 1981, 'recklessness' must now be understood as bearing two different legal meanings,

a) subjective recklessness; and
b) *Caldwell*-type recklessness,

which have in common the fact that they are both concerned with the taking of an unjustified risk.

Before explaining these two types of recklessness, something must be said about the terms 'objective' and 'subjective', which are used both in this chapter and the rest of this book, although their use in relation to questions of criminal liability was criticised by Lord Diplock in *Caldwell* and in

Lawrence[2] and by Lord Hailsham in the latter case.[3] Despite this criticism, the courts continue to use these terms in such a context[4] and they are used throughout this book as a convenient way of distinguishing between two well-established notions. A fault element is 'objective' when it involves judging the accused by the standards or mental state of a reasonable person, and not those of the accused; it is 'subjective' when it is the accused's actual standards or mental state by which he is judged.

1 [1982] AC 341, [1981] 1 All ER 961, HL.
2 [1981] 1 All ER at 966 and [1981] 1 All ER at 982–983 respectively.
3 [1982] AC 510, [1981] 1 All ER 974 at 978.
4 Eg *Elliott v C* [1983] 2 All ER 1005, [1983] 1 WLR 939, DC.

SUBJECTIVE RECKLESSNESS

6.44 Subjective recklessness means the *conscious* taking of an unjustified risk. A person acts with subjective recklessness as to a consequence of a deliberate act of his if, when he carries out that act, he actually foresees that there is a risk that that consequence may possibly result from his act and in all the circumstances it is unreasonable for him to take the risk of it occurring.[1] Provided that this is proved, it is irrelevant that for some reason, such as bad temper, he chooses to disregard the risk or to put it to the back of his mind, not caring whether the risk materialises or not.[2] Indeed, although it is normally the case that a person who consciously takes an unjustified risk does not care whether or not it materialises, it is not necessary that this should be so. A person who consciously takes an unjustified risk which he hopes will not materialise is generally[3] also subjectively reckless. The risk which must be foreseen for subjective recklessness need merely be a possible risk. If the degree of risk foreseen is that of virtual certainty or very high probability, it may be inferred that the accused intended the consequence in question, as shown in paras 6.31 to 6.37; if the inference is drawn there will be to that extent an overlap between intention and subjective recklessness.

Foresight of the risk that a particular consequence may result from an act is not of itself sufficient to constitute subjective recklessness as to that consequence. As with *Caldwell*-type recklessness the risk must have been unjustified (or unreasonable). All that can be said by way of generalisation with regard to this point is that it has to be judged objectively – so that even subjective recklessness contains an objective element – and that it raises a variety of questions. How great was the risk?[4] How beneficial to society or to the victim was the object which the accused was seeking to achieve? Every surgeon foresees the risk of the death of the patient upon whom he is operating but, unless he takes an unjustified risk, he cannot be regarded as being reckless as to the patient's death.

A person acts with subjective recklessness to a circumstance of his act if, when he carries out that act, he actually realises that the circumstance may possibly exist, provided it was unjustifiable for him to take the risk of its existence.

As we shall see shortly, recklessness in its subjective sense is narrower than in its other sense. We shall also see, however, that in some offences where recklessness suffices for liability that term is limited to its subjective sense.

1 *Briggs* [1977] 1 All ER 475, [1977] 1 WLR 605, CA; *Stephenson* [1979] QB 695, [1979] 2 All ER 1198, CA. In *Caldwell* [1982] AC 341, [1981] 1 All ER 961 the House of Lords overruled these cases insofar as they stated that 'recklessness' in s 1 of the Criminal Damage Act 1971

was limited to subjective recklessness, but the formulation of subjective recklessness in these cases was not overruled.

2 *Stephenson* [1979] QB 695, [1979] 2 All ER 1198, CA.
3 Recklessness in rape, for example, is an exception: para 12.7.
4 If the risk was so slight that an ordinary reasonable person, having considered the matter, would have taken it, the accused would not be reckless: *Caldwell* [1981] 1 All ER 961 at 966, per Lord Diplock.

CALDWELL-TYPE RECKLESSNESS[1]

6.45 Before the House of Lords' decision in *Caldwell*[2] the prevailing approach of the courts had been to limit recklessness, where it sufficed for an offence, to recklessness in its subjective sense. An example is provided by the meaning given to the adverb 'maliciously' which appeared in a large number of offences enacted in Victorian times and which has been judicially defined to refer to intention or recklessness. In *Cunningham*[3] the Court of Criminal Appeal approved the following principle which was expounded by Professor Kenny in 1902:

'... in any statutory definition of a crime, "malice" must be taken not in the old vague sense of "wickedness" in general but as requiring either (1) an actual intention to do the particular kind of harm that in fact was done; or (2) recklessness as to whether such harm should occur or not (i e the accused has foreseen that the particular kind of harm might be done and yet has gone on to take the risk of it).'

The words in brackets at the end of the quotation make it clear that recklessness was being used in a subjective sense.

1 Lynn ' "Obvious" and "serious" difficulties' (1986) 37 NILQ 237.
2 [1982] AC 341, [1981] 1 All ER 961, HL.
3 [1957] 2 QB 396, [1957] 2 All ER 412, CCA.

6.46 The limitation of recklessness to subjective recklessness appeared to have been confirmed by the Law Commission in 1978,[1] when its proposed standard test of recklessness was framed in subjective terms, and by the Criminal Law Revision Committee in 1980, whose Fourteenth Report: Offences against the Person[2] adopted the same meaning.

Nevertheless, the prevailing subjective approach received a rude rebuff from the majority[3] of the House of Lords in *Caldwell*[3] in 1981, a case concerned with offences of arson (i e criminal damage by fire) under s 1 of the Criminal Damage Act 1971, the mens rea for which is framed expressly in terms of intention or recklessness. Lord Diplock, with whose speech Lords Keith of Kinkel and Roskill agreed, saw no reason to assume that 'reckless' in the Criminal Damage Act 1971 was intended by Parliament to be understood only in the sense in which it was used in *Cunningham*. 'Reckless' as used in s 1 of the Criminal Damage Act 1971, he said, was an ordinary English word. It had not by 1971 become a legal term of art with a more limited meaning than its ordinary meaning, which included not only deciding to ignore a risk of harmful consequences from one's act which one has recognised as existing, but also failing to give any thought to whether or not there was any such risk in circumstances where, if any thought had been given to the matter, it would be obvious that there was.

Lord Diplock gave the following model direction to a jury:

'A person ... is "reckless" as to whether or not any property would be destroyed or damaged if (1) he does an act which creates an obvious risk that property will be destroyed or damaged and (2) when he does the act he either has not given any thought to the possibility of there being any such risk or has recognised that there was some risk involved and has none the less gone on to do it'.[4]

Although this was stated in relation to offences of criminal damage, it is clear that Lord Diplock did not intend to limit the general tenor of the statement to those offences but intended it to apply generally when the adjective 'reckless' was used in a criminal statute. We shall return later to the application of the ruling.[5]

1 *Report on the Mental Element in Crime*, Law Com No 89.
2 Cmnd 7844, para 11.
3 [1982] AC 341, [1981] 1 All ER 961, HL.
4 [1981] 1 All ER 961 at 967.
5 Para 6.53.

6.47 The type of recklessness recognised by the majority of the House of Lords in *Caldwell* (hereafter referred to as *Caldwell*-type recklessness) can be expressed in general terms as follows:

A person is *Caldwell*-type reckless as to a particular risk which attends his conduct if that risk is obvious *and* either:

a) he has not given any thought to the possibility of there being any *such* risk; *or*

b) he has recognised that there is *some* risk involved and has nevertheless persisted in his conduct.

Part b), of course, refers to subjective recklessness. The reference to '*some*' risk suggests that the accused need not recognise the risk in question as an obvious one, so that it is enough that he thinks it is a remote one (provided, of course, that the risk was in reality an obvious one). However, in *Reid*[1] the Court of Appeal was inclined, without deciding the point, to a different view, that there was no difference between 'some risk' in part b) and 'such risk' in part a) (which clearly refers to 'obvious risk'). This view seems to strain the words used by Lord Diplock, and it is submitted should not be adopted.

As is explained shortly, part a) is a purely objective formulation, and it is this formulation which has given rise to criticism, not least because failure to think about a risk can hardly be described as mens rea, a state of mind, with regard to it; it is quite the contrary – the absence of a state of mind. The effect of part a) is that if there was an obvious risk, e g of damage to property, the accused can be convicted despite the absence of any realisation or thought on his part that that risk might exist. It is not easy to see how this can be reconciled with Lord Diplock's statement that 'mens rea is a state of mind of the accused himself. .., it cannot be the state of mind of some non-existent, hypothetical person'. Quite apart from this, the decision is open to the criticism that the interpretation which it gives to 'reckless' in the Criminal Damage Act is contrary to the clearly expressed views of the Law Commission, who drafted the Act, to the effect that 'recklessness' in the Act should be understood in its subjective sense only. It is noteworthy that Lord Diplock did not advert to the Law Commission's views in his speech in *Caldwell*.

Caldwell-type recklessness has not met with unqualified judicial approval. For example, Robert Goff LJ in *Elliott v C*[2] stated that, although bound to apply the rule in *Caldwell*, he regarded the conclusion to which it forced him as unjust and inappropriate.

1 (1990) 91 Cr App Rep 263 at 270.
2 [1983] 2 All ER 1005, [1983] 1 WLR 939, DC. Similar reluctance was expressed by the Court of Appeal in *Rogers* (1984) 149 JP 89, 79 Cr App Rep 334, CA.

6.48 *Why the accused gave no thought* If the accused did not give any thought to the possibility of there being any risk of the relevant kind, it is irrelevant why he did not give such thought. In *Bell*,[1] for example, where the accused, a schizophrenic[2] who subsequently claimed that he was driven on by God, used a van as a battering ram against other vehicles and property, the Court of Appeal (refusing leave to appeal against conviction for reckless driving) held that, if the jury concluded that the accused had not given any thought to the possibility of there being any risk of the relevant kind, his explanation that he was driven on by God was irrelevant. The reason was that it would merely explain how it came about that part a) of the formulation from *Caldwell* given above was satisfied.

In the following limited cases, however, the reason why no thought was given will be relevant:

a) if the explanation gives rise to the defence of insanity or the defence of automatism or other involuntary conduct;[3]

b) if the failure to give thought was due to the accused being intoxicated through taking a prescribed drug in a way which does not comply with medical instructions or through taking a non-dangerous drug, like valium, provided in either case that the accused was not reckless in becoming so intoxicated.[4] This exception, which is discussed further in paras 9.76 to 9.78, is surprising; why should the explanation of intoxication through a non-dangerous drug be treated differently from other explanations for not thinking (such as mental handicap or youth) which are irrelevant? No answer has been given by the judges.

1 [1984] 3 All ER 842, CA. Also see *Elliott v C* [1983] 2 All ER 1005, [1983] 1 WLR 939, DC.
2 The accused was not proved to be legally insane.
3 Paras 9.12–9.30 and 9.41–9.49 respectively.
4 *Hardie* [1984] 3 All ER 848, [1985] 1 WLR 65, CA.

6.49 *Obvious to whom?* A question which is of great importance where the accused has not thought about the matter is whether the 'obvious risk' in *Caldwell*-type recklessness must have been one which would have been obvious to an ordinary reasonable person who gave thought to the matter (ie a purely objective test) or one which would have been obvious to the accused if he had given any thought to the matter.

In *Caldwell* Lord Diplock's speech is ambiguous on the point. At one stage it appears that he chose the second alternative. For example, he said that 'recklessness' 'presupposes that if thought were given to the matter by the doer before the act was done, it would have been apparent to him that there was a real risk of its having the relevant harmful consequences'.[1] However, later in his speech his Lordship said:

'...to decide whether someone has been "reckless" whether harmful consequences of a particular kind will result from his act, does call for some consideration of how the mind of the ordinary prudent individual would have reacted to a similar situation. If there were nothing in the circumstances that ought to have drawn the attention of the ordinary prudent individual to the possibility of that kind of harmful consequence, the accused would not be described as "reckless" in the natural meaning of the word for failing to address his mind to the possibility...'[2]

In *Lawrence*,[3] another decision of the House of Lords given on the same day as *Caldwell* but in relation to the subsequently repealed offences of reckless driving, both Lords Hailsham and Diplock (with whose speeches the other three Lords agreed) clearly indicated that the question was whether the relevant risk would have been obvious to the ordinary, prudent motorist. Moreover, in *Miller*,[4] another House of Lords case concerning arson (ie criminal damage by fire), which has already been discussed in relation to omissions to act, Lord Diplock (with whose speech the remainder of their Lordships agreed) seems to have preferred the 'obvious to an ordinary reasonable person' approach since he spoke of happenings which 'would make it obvious to anyone who troubled to give his mind to them that they present a risk . . .'

Other decisions, such as those of the Court of Appeal in *Madigan*[5] (a reckless driving case) and of the Divisional Court in *Elliott v C*[6] (another arson case), have made it clear that, for the purposes of *Caldwell*-type recklessness, 'obvious risk' means a risk which would have been obvious to an ordinary reasonable (or prudent) person who gave thought to the matter, whether or not it would have been obvious to the accused if he had thought about the matter. In *Elliott v C*, where the accused was aged 14 years four months at the time of the offence, the Divisional Court held that the test of *Caldwell*-type recklessness was whether the risk would have been obvious to an ordinary adult, and not whether it would have been obvious to an ordinary 14-year-old. Evidence of the girl's age, that she was tired and exhausted at the time and had little knowledge and experience of inflammable liquids (which she had ignited and thereby caused the damage) was therefore held not admissible because it was not relevant to the test of liability.

In *Rogers*[7] the Court of Appeal rejected the possibility of softening the objective nature of the test along lines which have been adopted in relation to the defence to murder of provocation.[8] In dismissing an appeal against a conviction for arson by an accused who had been 15 at the time of the offence, it held that the ordinary person in the present context was a person with ordinary characteristics rather than sharing the accused's age, sex and other characteristics (eg limited intelligence) which would affect his recognition of the risk and forethought as to its possibility. The fact that the risk must have been obvious to an ordinary reasonable person must be stressed, and so must the fact that the ordinary reasonable person is not deemed to have expert knowledge and is not endowed with hindsight.[9]

1 [1981] 1 All ER 961 at 964.
2 Ibid, at 966.
3 [1982] AC 510, [1981] 1 All ER 974, HL. In this case it was held in relation to the subsequently repealed offences of reckless driving that there must be an obvious and *serious* risk of injury to another road user or of doing substantial damage to property. A requirement of serious risk has not been made in relation to *Caldwell*-type recklessness where it applies in other offences, except in the case of involuntary manslaughter. For meaning of 'serious' in this context, see para 11.58.
4 [1983] 2 AC 161, [1983] 1 All ER 978, HL.
5 (1982) 75 Cr App Rep 145, [1982] Crim LR 692, CA. Also see *Clarke* (1990) 91 Cr App Rep 69, CA.
6 [1983] 2 All ER 1005, [1983] 1 WLR 939, DC.
7 (1984) 149 JP 89, 79 Cr App Rep 334, CA. See [1985] Crim LR 173 (editorial) and Mitchell 'Recklessness and the *Camplin* argument' (1986) 150 JPN 388.
8 Paras 11.43–11.45.
9 *Sangha* [1988] 2 All ER 385, [1988] 1 WLR 519, CA.

6.50 It is not often that the requirement that the risk must have been one which would have been obvious to an ordinary reasonable person who gave thought to the matter, regardless of whether it would have been obvious to the accused if he had given any thought to the matter, will produce a different result from that which would have been produced by a rule that the risk had to be one which would have been obvious to the accused if he had stopped to think. The reason is that most accused, if they had stopped to think, would have realised a risk which would have been obvious to an ordinary reasonable person who gave thought to the matter. The difference is likely only to affect the result where the accused is, as appears to have been the case in *Elliott v C*, for example, of limited intelligence or young or in some other condition which would affect his thought processes had he stopped to think.

6.51 *What degree of risk must have been obvious?* This is a matter touched on by Lord Diplock in *Caldwell*,[1] although it does not appear in his model direction. His Lordship stated that a person would not be reckless if the risk of the harmful consequences was so slight that the ordinary prudent individual on due consideration of the risk would not be deterred from treating it as negligible. In other words, the risk must be of a greater degree than this before a person can be *Caldwell*-type reckless as to it.

1 [1981] 1 All ER 961 at 966. Also see *Lawrence* [1981] 1 All ER 974 at 982, per Lord Diplock.

6.52 *Where the accused has thought Caldwell*-type recklessness is negatived where a person has given thought to the obvious possibility of the risk in question and has decided (albeit wrongly) that there is *no* such risk; such a case is not one where the accused has not given any thought to the possibility of there being any such risk or has recognised that there is some risk involved. This point, the so-called 'lacuna' in the test of *Caldwell*-type recklessness, which is implicit in Lord Diplock's speech in *Caldwell*, is briefly referred to in his speech in *Lawrence*. In the latter case, his Lordship stated that, where a particular risk was obvious, the jury are entitled to infer that the accused was either aware of it or had never thought about whether it existed, but that regard must be paid to any explanation as to his state of mind which will displace that inference. In *Reid*[1] the Court of Appeal recognised obiter the existence of the lacuna in the test of *Caldwell*-type recklessness.

The situation is different where the accused is aware of the kind of risk that will attend his act if he does not take adequate precautions and he takes precautions to eliminate it as far as possible. The reason is that he *has* recognised that the risk exists and gone on to take it, albeit that he thought that he had eliminated it as far as possible, and therefore he is caught by the subjective limb of *Caldwell*-type recklessness.[2] In *Chief Constable of Avon and Somerset v Shimmen*[3] D was demonstrating his skill in Korean martial arts, in which he had a qualification. He made to kick near a shop window, misjudged his kick and broke the window. He said he had thought about the risk of breaking the window and had concluded that he had eliminated as much risk as possible by aiming his kick to miss by two inches rather than a closer margin. It was held that there had been awareness on his part of the risk and that was sufficient for conviction. Where the accused takes steps which (in his misconceived opinion) will eliminate the risk as far as possible, it is not easy to see why the law treats the situation differently from that where he concludes that no precautions are necessary since there is no risk at all.

1 (1989) 91 Cr App Rep 263 at 269.

2 *Chief Constable of Avon and Somerset Constabulary v Shimmen* (1986) 84 Cr App Rep 7, DC. See Taylor 'Recklessness – Ruling out the Risk' (1987) 137 NLJ 231; Mitchell 'Reckless-ness Could Still be a State of Mind' (1988) 51 JC 300.
3 (1986) 84 Cr App Rep 7, DC.

6.53 *When does Caldwell-type recklessness suffice?* In *Seymour*[1] Lord Roskill, with whose speech the other members of the House of Lords agreed, stated that 'reckless' should now be given the same meaning (viz *Caldwell*-type recklessness) in relation to all offences in which 'recklessness' suffices 'unless Parliament has otherwise ordained'. However, this state-ment was an obiter dictum[2] and therefore not binding, and does not cor-rectly state the position. The reasons are as follows.

In *Caldwell* Lord Diplock's remarks about *Caldwell*-type recklessness were directed towards statutory offences in whose definition the word 'reckless' appears. Any doubts about whether he intended his remarks to have a wider application appear to be resolved by his statement in *Lawrence* that 'The conclusion of the majority [in *Caldwell*] was that the adjective "reckless" when used in a criminal statute, ie the Criminal Damage Act 1971,' meant *Caldwell*-type recklessness and that 'the same must be true of the adverbial derivative "recklessly".'[3]

However, even where 'reckless' or 'recklessly' appears in the statutory definition of a statutory offence it is not an invariable rule that *Caldwell*-type recklessness suffices, since the courts have recognised exceptions to it. One concerns the offence of rape which is defined by s 1 of the Sexual Offences (Amendment) Act 1976, under which definition recklessness as to the absence of the woman's consent suffices. At one point, the Court of Appeal regarded itself as bound to hold that *Caldwell*-type recklessness sufficed for rape, but it is now clear from two decisions of the Court of Appeal[4] that s 1 must be understood as being declaratory of the common law relating to that offence, with the result that only subjective recklessness suffices for rape.

Another example of an exception is provided by *Large v Mainprize*.[5] In that case the Divisional Court applied the subjective test of recklessness to the statutory offence of recklessly furnishing false information as to a fishing catch, although it did so without reference to any of the reported decisions on the meaning of recklessness, and seemed to be influenced by the view that the meaning of recklessness was self-evident! There are many statutory offences of recklessly making a false statement and this decision provides persuasive authority in relation to the meaning of recklessness in them.

In the light of the fact that there can be exceptions to the rule that 'reckless' or 'recklessly' in the statutory definition of an offence refers to *Caldwell*-type recklesness, it is generally impossible, in the absence of an appellate decision, to be certain what meaning those terms bear in such a definition. However, it is submitted that one can be confident that they will not refer to *Caldwell*-type recklessness where the wording of the statutory provision as a whole indicates that 'reckless' is limited to its subjective sense. Clear examples are the various offences of obtaining by deception under the Theft Acts 1968 and 1978[6] which, by their statutory definition, can be committed by a reckless deception. In each offence the accused is required to have 'obtained' dishonestly and a person cannot be said to be dishonest if he never thought about the risk that he was making a deception; subjective recklessness alone suffices for these offences.

With the exception of the common law offence of involuntary man-slaughter, *Caldwell*-type recklessness has not been applied to 'reckless' or 'recklessly' in any offence other than a statutory offence in whose statutory definition one of these terms appears; and in the case of involuntary manslaughter there may be special reasons preceding *Caldwell* for the application of *Caldwell*-type recklessness to it. In some statutory offences the accused is required to have acted 'maliciously'.[7] While, as we have seen, recklessness suffices in the alternative to intention for this purpose, the subjective sense to which recklessness in this context was limited in *Cunningham* remains unaffected by *Caldwell* and subsequent cases. This was confirmed by the House of Lords in 1991 in the consolidated appeals in *Savage; Parmenter*.[8]

Caldwell-type recklessness does not suffice in the various statutory offences of assault, such as common assault or assault occasioning actual bodily harm.[9] An 'assault' is defined by the common law; it can be committed recklessly but nowhere does 'reckless' appear in any of the statutory provisions dealing with the various types of assault. It was confirmed by the Court of Appeal in 1991 in *Spratt*[10] that in the various offences of assault 'reckless' is limited to its subjective sense.

One result of all this is to demonstrate that 'recklessness' bears a wider meaning (ie *Caldwell*-type) in relation to offences of criminal damage to property than in relation to offences involving personal injury. The judges have not yet explained why, in effect, greater protection is given by the criminal law to property than to persons.

1 [1983] 2 All ER 1058 at 1064.
2 A point acknowledged in *Spratt* [1991] 2 All ER 210, [1990] 1 WLR 1073, CA.
3 [1981] 1 All ER 974 at 981.
4 *Satnam and Kewal S* (1984) 78 Cr App Rep 149, CA; *Breckenridge* (1984) 79 Cr App Rep 244, CA.
5 [1989] Crim LR 213, DC.
6 Paras 14.27–14.64.
7 See, for example, paras 10.22, 10.26.
8 [1991] 4 All ER 698, HL.
9 Paras 10.9–10.17.
10 [1991] 2 All ER 210, [1990] 1 WLR 1073, CA.

GENERAL POINTS CONCERNING INTENTION OR RECKLESSNESS
AS TO A CONSEQUENCE

6.54 Where the offence charged can be committed either intentionally or recklessly, and the prosecution relies in the alternative on these two states of mind, the alternatives should be embodied in separate counts in the indictment.[1] The reason for this is to enable the judge to know, when sentencing, on what basis the jury have convicted and to assist both him in summing up and the jury in understanding the summing up.[1]

1 *Hardie* [1984] 3 All ER 848 at 853–4. Also see para 15.14. It is uncertain whether this applies to the offences under s 20 of the Offences against the Person Act 1861 whose definition does not refer to these two types of mens rea (although they have been construed as requiring either intention or subjective recklessness).

6.55 So far, the discussion of intention and recklessness with reference to the consequences of an act has generally assumed that the accused must intend, or be reckless as to, the consequence of the actus reus of the offence in question as it is described in the definition of the offence, e g the destruction of or damage to property belonging to another in the offence of criminal damage. This is generally true,[1] but, as Lord Ackner (with whose speech the other Law Lords agreed) observed in *Savage; Parmenter*,[2] there is no hard and fast principle to this effect. There are some exceptional offences where intention or recklessness, or in some cases only intention, in relation to something less than the actual consequence required for their actus reus suffices. For example, in the offences under s 20 of the Offences against the Person Act 1861 of unlawfully and maliciously wounding another and of unlawfully and maliciously inflicting grievous bodily harm on another, the accused has sufficient mens rea if he merely intended or was subjectively reckless as to *some* unlawful physical harm to a person, albeit of a minor nature: he need not have foreseen that his act might cause physical harm of the gravity described in the statute, i e a wound or grievous bodily harm.[3] Other examples are provided by the offences of murder and involuntary manslaughter discussed in Chapter 11.

1 See, for example, *Smith* [1974] QB 354, [1974] 1 All ER 632, CA.
2 [1991] 4 All ER 698, HL.
3 Paras 10.18–10.22.

6.56 Provided the accused acted intentionally or recklessly in the way required by the definition of the offence charged, it is irrelevant that the actual object (whether person or property) was unintended or unforeseen. For example, if the accused does something intending that it should damage X's property, or being reckless as to this occurring, and quite unforeseeably P's property is damaged instead, the accused can be committed of criminal damage, contrary to s 1(1) of the Criminal Damage Act 1971, since the mens rea for that offence is intention or recklessness as to damaging property belonging to another and the accused acted with such intention or recklessness. This is a simple application of the wording of the mens rea requirement of the offence. This being so, the general practice of writers to dignify this simple application of the mens rea requirement by calling it the doctrine of 'transferred fault', 'transferred intention' or 'transferred malice' seems unnecessary[1] and, in the case of the last two terms, inaccurate (since the 'doctrine' is not limited to intention or 'malice').[2]

Latimer[3] provides an example of the operation of the above point. D aimed a blow at X which glanced off him and struck P who was standing beside X, wounding her severely. It was held that D could be convicted of maliciously wounding P because he had an intent to injure and it was irrelevant that he had not intended to injure P. Likewise, in *Mitchell*[4] the Court of Appeal upheld the conviction for manslaughter of an accused who intentionally hit X (which intention could suffice as the mens rea for manslaughter)[5] in a post office queue, causing him to fall against an 89-year-old woman who died as a result of the injuries sustained.

By way of contrast, and not surprisingly, the accused cannot be convicted if he acted with the mens rea for one offence but unexpectedly commits the actus reus of another offence, unless the offence is one where recklessness suffices and he is proved to have been reckless as to the risk of the type of harm which he actually caused. This is shown by *Pembliton*,[6] where D,who had been fighting with persons in the street, threw a stone at them, which missed but went through the window of a nearby public house. His conviction for maliciously damaging the window was quashed because he had acted with intent to injure persons and not with intent to injure property. The Court for Crown Cases Reserved pointed out that if the jury had found the accused had been reckless as to the risk of the window being broken the conviction would have been upheld, because recklessness was sufficient for the offence in question.

1 Ashworth 'Transferred Malice and Punishment for Unforeseen Consequences' *Reshaping the Criminal Law* (1978) p 77.
2 It is surprising that it has been thought necessary to insert a 'transferred fault' provision in the draft Criminal Code Bill (cl 24) (see Law Commission: A Criminal Code for England and Wales (1989): Law Com No 177; see para 3.21 above).
3 (1886) 17 QBD 359.
4 [1983] QB 741, [1983] 2 All ER 427, CA.
5 Paras 11.60–11.70.
6 (1874) LR 2 CCR 119.

6.57 It is irrelevant, as far as the question of mens rea is concerned, that the consequence in relation to which the accused acted intentionally or recklessly occurred in an unexpected manner.

KNOWLEDGE

6.58 Knowledge of the *circumstances* by virtue of which an act or omission or event is criminal (i e those specified for the actus reus) is expressly required in the case of many statutory offences on account of the inclusion of some such word as 'knowingly' in the definition. However, the use of 'knowingly' or the like is not essential since, even when no appropriate word appears in the definition, a requirement of knowledge is frequently[1] implied by the courts, as explained in Chapter 8. In *Sleep*,[2] for example, the accused was charged with being in possession of naval stores marked with the broad arrow, an offence under a statute of William III which has since been repealed. It was held that he must be acquitted as there was no proof that he knew that the stores in question were marked with the broad arrow as was in fact the case. Similarly, in *Sweet v Parsley*[3] the House of Lords held that a person could not be guilty of 'being concerned in the management of premises used for the purpose of smoking cannabis' (an offence which has subsequently been modified) in the absence of proof of knowledge of such use.

1 *Roper v Taylor's Central Garages (Exeter) Ltd* [1951] 2 TLR 284, per Devlin J.
2 (1861) Le & Ca 44; see also *Cugullere* [1961] 2 All ER 343, CCA.
3 [1970] AC 132, [1969] 1 All ER 347, HL.

6.59 *Degrees of knowledge* As Lord Devlin has indicated, there are three degrees of knowledge known to the criminal law.[1] The first is actual knowledge which may be inferred from the conduct of the accused. Where a person has actual knowledge of the circumstances in which he is acting he is said to act intentionally in relation to them.

Knowledge of the second degree consists of wilful blindness, where a person realises the risk that a surrounding circumstance may exist and deliberately refrains from making enquiries, the results of which he may not care to have. Wilful blindness is a species of subjective recklessness with reference to surrounding circumstances, and it is often called connivance.[2] It is equal in law to actual knowledge and normally[3] suffices even where the statute uses the word 'knowingly'. The first reported instance of the recognition of wilful blindness is *Sleep*[4] where several members of the Court for Crown Cases Reserved would clearly have been prepared to treat it as a basis for liability. In a more recent case, it was held that a person cannot be convicted of permitting a vehicle to be used on a road with a defective braking system unless he actually knew of this or shut his eyes to the obvious not caring whether a contravention occurred or not.[5] Even more recently the House of Lords in *Westminster City Council v Croyalgrange Ltd* [6] held that a person could be convicted of knowingly permitting the use of premises as a sex establishment without a licence if he actually knew of their use as a sex establishment without a licence or was wilfully blind as to this.

Actual knowledge and wilful blindness must be sharply distinguished from knowledge of the third degree, otherwise described as constructive knowledge, which exists where a person did not know but ought to have known that a surrounding circumstance might exist. Thus, a person has knowledge of the third degree if he fails to make the enquiries which a reasonable and prudent person would make. It is distinguishable from wilful blindness in that the failure to inquire is not deliberate; and unlike wilful blindness it is only a sufficient basis in exceptional cases,[7] being necessarily irrelevant where words such as 'knowingly' are used. Constructive knowledge is a species of negligence and will be discussed further under that head.[8]

1 *Roper v Taylor's Central Garages (Exeter) Ltd* [1951] 2 TLR 284, DC.
2 Edwards *Mens Rea in Statutory Offences* p 203; see also *Ross v Moss* [1965] 2 QB 396, [1965] 3 All ER 145, DC.
3 For an exception, see para 6.60.
4 (1861) Le & Ca 44.
5 *James & Son Ltd v Smee* [1955] 1 QB 78, [1954] 3 All ER 273, DC.
6 [1986] 2 All ER 353, [1986] 1 WLR 674, HL.
7 *Roper v Taylor's Central Garages (Exeter) Ltd* [1951] 2 TLR 284, per Devlin J.
8 Para 6.65.

6.60 Some offences require the accused to have acted 'knowing or being reckless' as to a specified circumstance or 'knowing or believing' that it exists. For example, there are a large number of statutory offences which consist of knowingly or recklessly making a statement which is false in a material particular in a specified respect,[1] and the offences of handling stolen goods and of assisting offenders require the accused to know or believe that, respectively, the goods are stolen and that the person assisted has committed an arrestable offence.[2] In offences like these 'knowing' is limited to actual knowledge.

The concept of 'recklessness' has already been discussed,[3] but that of 'belief' has not. 'Belief' is not far short of actual knowledge; it refers to the state of mind of someone who does not actually know that the particular circumstance exists but who realises that there can be no substantial doubt that it does.[4] Consequently, wilful blindness does not amount to belief.[4]

1 Recent examples are provided by the Football Spectators Act 1989, s 5(7), and the Electricity Act 1989, s 59(1).
2 See paras 14.88 and 16.2.
3 Paras 6.43–6.53.
4 Para 14.88.

6.61 *How much must be known?* For the avoidance of doubt it should be mentioned that knowledge need extend only to a circumstance as it is prescribed in the definition of the offence in question.[1] Thus, a publican is guilty of the offence of knowingly allowing a person under 18 to consume intoxicating liquor in a bar if he knows, or is wilfully blind, that he is allowing such a person to consume intoxicating liquor there, it being irrelevant, for instance, that he thinks the person is 16 when he is in fact 17 years old.

In a few offences, knowledge of something less than the specified circumstances suffices, as is shown by decisions relating to s 170(2) of the Customs and Excise Management Act 1979, under which there are various offences[2] of being knowingly concerned in the fraudulent evasion of a prohibition on the importation of various types of goods. For example, it is an offence, punishable with a maximum of life imprisonment, for a person knowingly to be concerned in the fraudulent evasion of the prohibition on the importation of a Class A controlled drug, and it is also an offence – a separate offence – to be knowingly concerned in the fraudulent evasion of the prohibition on the importation of obscene material (for which offence the maximum imprisonment is seven years). There is clear authority that, provided a person knows that the thing in question is something which is a prohibited good, he has sufficient mens rea in this respect, even if he was mistaken as to its precise nature.[3]

Thus, for example, a person who has been concerned in the evasion of the prohibition on the importation of a Class A controlled drug can be convicted of the former of the two offences just mentioned even if he thought that the article in question (which was in a sack) was obscene material, because he will have known that it was a prohibited good, and even though on his understanding of the facts he was committing the latter, less serious offence.[4]

1 *McCallum* (1973) 57 Cr App Rep 645, CA.
2 *Courtie* [1984] AC 463, [1984] 1 All ER 740, HL.
3 *Hussain* [1969] 2 QB 567, [1969] 2 All ER 1117, CA; *Hennessey* (1978) 68 Cr App Rep 419, CA; *Shivpuri* [1987] AC 1, [1986] 2 All ER 334, HL; *Ellis, Street and Smith* (1987) 84 Cr App Rep 235, CA.
4 *Hennessey*; *Shivpuri*; *Ellis, Street and Smith*.

6.62 *Forgotten knowledge* It sometimes happens that the accused has had the necessary knowledge of the circumstances but has forgotten them by the inception of the conduct in question. According to the Court of Appeal in *Bello*,[1] he is to be treated as having knowledge at that time if he then had the capacity to restore the circumstances to his mind. While this decision may be regarded as common sense, it must be recognised that it constitutes a breach of the general requirement (dealt with in para 6.70) that the accused must have the relevant mens rea at the time of the relevant conduct on his part.

1 (1978) 67 Cr App Rep 288, CA.

NEGLIGENCE[1]

6.63 A person is negligent if his conduct in relation to a reasonably intelligible risk falls below the standard which would be expected of a reasonable person in the light of that risk. For the vast majority of offences, negligence does not suffice for liability.

1 Hart 'Negligence, Mens Rea and Criminal Responsibility' *Oxford Essays in Jurisprudence* p 29.

6.64 The reasonably intelligible risk in question may concern a consequence of a person's conduct or a circumstance in relation to which it occurs. An accused is negligent as to a consequence of an act or omission on his part if the risk of it occurring would have been foreseen by a reasonable person and the accused either fails to foresee the risk and to take steps to avoid it or, having foreseen it, fails to take steps to avoid it or takes steps which fall below the standard of conduct which would be expected of a reasonable person in the light of that risk. Negligence as to a consequence very rarely suffices for criminal liability.[1]

1 For a recent example of an offence where it does, see the Water Industry Act 1991, s 73(1).

6.65 An accused is negligent as to a circumstance relevant to his conduct if he ought to have been aware of its existence because a reasonable person would have thought about the risk that it might exist and would have found out that it did. As stated previously, negligence as to a circumstance is otherwise known, rather misleadingly, as knowledge of the third degree or constructive knowledge. It suffices for liability only in exceptional cases, such as the following:

a) In statutory offences by whose definition the accused can be convicted on the ground that he had 'reasonable cause to believe', 'reason to believe' or 'reason to suspect' that a circumstance existed.[1] For example, under s 5(2) of the Official Secrets Act 1989, a person who has come into possession, in one of certain ways, of information protected against disclosure by the Act is guilty of an offence if he discloses it without lawful authority, knowing, or having reasonable cause to believe, that it is protected against disclosure by the Act and that it has come into his possession in one of those ways. Likewise, under s 25 of the Firearms Act 1968, it is an offence for a person to sell any firearm or ammunition to another person whom he knows or has reasonable cause for believing to be drunk or of unsound mind.

b) Where phrases of the above type have been introduced into the offence by judicial interpretation of its definition. There are a few modern instances where this has been done,[2] but the tendency has been deplored.[3]

1 Phrases such as these undoubtedly postulate a wholly objective test; see, for example, *Young* [1984] 2 All ER 164, [1984] 1 WLR 654 (a decision of the Courts-Martial Appeal Court, whose powers and membership correspond in general with those of the Court of Appeal (Criminal Division)). The only case apparently to the contrary, *Hudson* [1966] 1 QB 448, [1965] 1 All ER 721, CA, contains a dictum that not only must there be an objective 'reason to suspect' but also the accused himself, taking into account his mental and other capacities, ought to have suspected. However, this dictum has not been followed in any other case.
2 *Browning v JWH Watson (Rochester) Ltd* [1953] 2 All ER 775, [1953] 1 WLR 1172, DC.
3 *Gray's Haulage Co Ltd v Arnold* [1966] 1 All ER 896, [1966] 1 WLR 534, DC.

6.66 In most offences where negligence suffices for liability it only does so in relation to a particular element, normally a circumstance of the actus reus of the offence, intention, recklessness or knowledge of the first or second degree normally being required as to any other elements. In such offences the actus reus is established without reference to the accused's negligence.

However, in a very limited number of offences, of which careless driving and dangerous driving are the most obvious examples, negligence is the very essence of the offence, in that whether or not the accused's conduct constitutes the actus reus of the offence depends on whether it can be described as negligent. A person is guilty of driving without due care and attention if the standard of his driving falls below the level of care and attention which a reasonable and prudent driver would have exercised in the circumstances.[1] In this case the nature of the reasonably foreseeable risk is not specified; the matter is at large, in that the question is whether the accused driver fell below the requisite standard in the light of any foreseeable and unjustifiable risk. A person is guilty of dangerous driving if the standard of his driving falls *far* below the standard which would be expected of a reasonable and prudent driver and it would be obvious to such a driver that driving in the way in question would endanger a person or property.[2] As a comparison of the definitions of careless driving and dangerous driving shows, there can be degrees of negligence. Dangerous driving requires a higher degree of negligence, usually called gross negligence, because the accused must fall *far* below the standard of a reasonable person, and not simply below it.

1 Para 20.14.
2 Para 20.11.

6.67 Negligence is distinguishable from intention, subjective recklessness and knowledge of the first or second degree since it does not require foresight or awareness of the risk in question; it is a truly objective fault element.

There is a very marked overlap between *Caldwell*-type recklessness and negligence in that a person who takes a risk of which he ought to have been aware without realising it exists (an 'inadvertent risk-taker') is guilty of both *Caldwell*-type recklessness and of negligence. However, negligence is a wider concept because it includes the case where a person has adverted to the possibility of the risk in question but unreasonably concluded that it does not exist. Such a person will be negligent as to that risk but will not have acted with *Caldwell*-type recklessness as to it.

Of course, where negligence suffices for an offence it is no defence for the accused to claim that he was not negligent as to the risk in question but acted intentionally in relation to it. Where an offence can be committed negligently in some respect this simply means that the prosecution does not need to prove any intention or the like on the part of the accused in that respect; it does not mean that he cannot commit the offence if he actually has that state of mind.

6.68 It was stated at the start of this chapter that mens rea means the state of mind expressly or impliedly required by the definition of the offence charged. It has already been pointed out that *Caldwell*-type recklessness cannot properly be described as a state of mind since it involves the absence of a state of mind;[1] a fortiori, negligence cannot be so described.

For this reason, *Caldwell*-type recklessness and negligence cannot strictly be described as species of mens rea, despite the fact that they have on occasions been so described by judges.[2] Nevertheless, for convenience, whenever the term 'mens rea' is used in a general sense in this book the reference to it should be understood as including *Caldwell*-type recklessness and negligence, unless the context indicates the contrary. The replacement of the term 'mens rea' by that of 'fault element' in the draft Criminal Code has much to commend it.

The question of the inclusion of *Caldwell*-type recklessness and negligence under the head of mens rea also raises the question of whether they should be a sufficient fault element for criminal liability. Both concepts involve fault, but usually it is less blameworthy than the fault displayed by people who intend, or are aware of the risk of, their wrongdoing. Neither Parliament nor the courts appear so far to have considered fully the answer to the question: 'When is it proper to punish a person because he has failed to match up to the standard expected of a reasonable person?' It would be easier to accept negligence as a basis of liability if an accused could only be liable on that ground if he *could*, given his mental ability, skill and experience, have avoided being negligent. The same points can be made in relation to *Caldwell*-type recklessness.

1 Para 6.47.
2 For a recent example, see *Lawrence* [1982] AC 510, [1981] 1 All ER 974, HL.

PROVISIONS OF DRAFT CRIMINAL CODE BILL

6.69 Clause 18 of the draft Criminal Code Bill[1] provides that, for the purposes of the Code and of any offence other than a pre-Code offence, a person would act:

a) 'knowingly' with respect to a circumstance not only when he is aware that it exists or will exist, but also when he avoids taking steps that might confirm his belief that it exists or will exist;
b) 'intentionally' with respect to:
i) a circumstance when he hopes or knows that it exists or will exist;
ii) a result when he acts either in order to bring it about or being aware that it will occur in the ordinary course of events;[2]
c) 'recklessly' with respect to:
i) a circumstance when he is aware of a risk that it exists or will exist;
ii) a result when he is aware of a risk that it will occur,
and it is, in the circumstances known to him, unreasonable to take the risk.

The enactment of this provision would bring certainty to the meaning of these terms. However, it would not resolve problems and uncertainties relating to them in offences in existence before the enactment of the Code. Clause 18 does not provide a definition of a fault element corresponding to *Caldwell*-type recklessness or negligence because neither of these fault elements suffices for any offence contained in the draft Code. However, the list of terms in cl 18 is not intended to be an exhaustive list and future legislation may use fault terms other than those in the clause.

1 Law Commission: A Criminal Code for England and Wales (1989): Law Com No 177; see para 3.21 above.
2 For criticism of the definition in b) ii), see Smith 'A Note on Intention' [1990] Crim LR 85.

CONTEMPORANEITY[1]

6.70 It is a cardinal rule that the accused's mens rea must exist at the time of the relevant act, omission or event on his part.[2] Provided that the accused had the necessary mens rea at that time, he may be convicted of the offence in question even though (for example, because of repentance) he lacks that mens rea when a consequence required for the actus reus occurs.[3] In addition, in the case of conduct which is clearly continuing in nature, as is almost invariably so in the case of an event and common in the case of an omission, once that continuing conduct by a person has started and he has had the the relevant mens rea, that person can be convicted even though he has forgotten a material circumstance at the material time. For example, a person, who picks up a cosh, puts it in the locker of his car, forgets about it and is later detected with it by the police, can be convicted of having with him at that time an offensive weapon in a public place, the mens rea for which offence is knowingly having the thing with one.[4] On the other hand, a person cannot be convicted of an offence if he only acquires the relevant mens rea after the culpable act, omission or event on his part has ceased.

1 Marston 'Contemporaneity of Act and Intention' (1970) 86 LQR 208.
2 *Fowler v Padget* (1798) 7 Term Rep 509, per Lord Kenyon CJ.
3 *Jakeman* (1983) 76 Cr App Rep 223, CA.
4 *McCalla* (1988) 87 Cr App Rep 372, CA.

6.71 The requirement of contemporaneity can give rise to problems in the case of offences which are normally based on some act on the part of the accused because an act is usually momentary, as opposed to continuing, in nature, in which case the time span in which any accompanying mens rea must exist is limited. The courts have postulated two different ways in which the difficulties which this could cause can be mitigated or avoided.

The first, which is illustrated by *Fagan v Metropolitan Police Comr*,[1] is that where an act can be regarded as a continuing one it is enough if mens rea exists at some stage during its continuance and that, in deciding whether an act is continuing, a liberal approach should be taken. In *Fagan* a motorist, having been asked by a police officer to draw into the kerb, drove his car on to the officer's foot. The officer requested him to drive off his foot but the motorist refused to do so for some little time thereafter. The question was whether the motorist's conduct amounted to a battery, since it had not been proved that the original driving on to the foot had been accompanied by the relevant mens rea. The majority of the Divisional Court held that the motorist's conduct did amount to a battery because the driving of the car on to the officer's foot and allowing it to remain there could be treated as a continuing act of application of force with the result that the motorist's act was not spent and complete by the time his mens rea began, as would have been the case if the driving on to the foot had been treated as a single complete act. His mens rea could therefore be superimposed on his existing continuing act.

The type of solution adopted in *Fagan* is clearly sensible where the accused's act is truly continuing. For example, an act of sexual intercourse continues as long as the penetration lasts.[2] If X penetrates a woman, thinking she is consenting, and then becomes aware that she is not consenting but continues to penetrate her, there is no difficulty in saying that his mens rea can be superimposed on his existing but still continuing act.[2]

However, the actual application of the approach in *Fagan* in a particular case may be open to the objection that it may involve (as it did in that case) a certain degree of artificiality in finding a continuing act and that it is not easy to explain it to a jury. For these reasons the approach which was preferred and adopted by the House of Lords in *Miller*,[3] whose facts were set out in para 6.12, is to be welcomed. As was stated in para 6.12, the rule adopted by the House of Lords is that, where a person inadvertently and without the appropriate mens rea does an act which puts a person or property in danger but before the resulting harm is complete he becomes aware of the train of events caused by his act, he is under a duty to take such steps as lie within his power to try to prevent or reduce the risk of harm. Consequently if, before the harm resulting from his act is complete, he realises what he has done and fails to take such steps to prevent or reduce the risk, and provided he *then* has the relevant mens rea, he will be criminally liable because his mens rea will be contemporaneous with his culpable omission to act.

The adoption in *Miller* by the House of Lords of what may be called the 'duty theory' in preference to the theory adopted in *Fagan* means that the latter is now unlikely to be utilised, unless the act is truly of a continuing character or unless the offence is one which by its express terms can only be committed by an act.

The theories discussed above are not, of course, exceptions to the requirement of contemporaneity but are methods of satisfying it. There are, however, exceptions to the requirement of contemporaneity in three types of situation; one is the case of forgotten knowledge dealt with in para 6.62, and the other two will be dealt with later.[4]

1 [1969] 1 QB 439, [1968] 3 All ER 442, DC.
2 *Kaitamaki* [1980] 1 NZLR 59 (New Zealand CA), affirmed [1985] AC 147, [1984] 2 All ER 435, PC.
3 [1983] 2 AC 161, [1983] 1 All ER 978, HL.
4 Paras 9.72 and 11.27.

MOTIVE

6.72 A person's motive is his reason for acting as he did. Thus A's motive for killing B may be financial gain, and C's motive for stealing may be his wish to feed his starving children. The general rule is that the accused's motives, good or bad, are irrelevant to his criminal liability, although they may affect the punishment imposed. In *Sharpe,*[1] where the accused, motivated by affection for his mother and religious duty, had removed her corpse from a grave in a cemetery belonging to Protestant Dissenters in order to bury it with the body of his recently deceased father in a churchyard, it was held that his motives, however estimable they might be, did not provide a defence to a charge of removing a corpse without lawful authority. However, Sharpe's 'good' motives were reflected in the punishment awarded, a fine of one shilling being imposed.

Intention, whether relating to an element required for the actus reus or ulterior to it, must be distinguished from motive. Motive is secondary intention; the distinction between further intention and motive is difficult to draw, the former being relevant simply because it is specified in the definition of a particular offence.

An illustration of the distinction between intention and motive is provided by *Smith.*[2] D was charged with corruptly offering a gift to the mayor of a borough. He had handed an IOU to his agent with the intention that it should be given to the mayor to induce him to promote the sale of land by the borough council to D; the agent had then given the IOU to the mayor. D did not intend to go through with the transaction, his reason for causing the offer to be made being his desire to expose what he believed to be the corrupt habits of those connected with the local administration. It was held that 'corruptly' in the definition of the relevant offence meant 'with intent that the donee should enter into a corrupt bargain' and that, even though his motive was not corrupt, D was guilty of the offence since he had offered the money with that requisite further intent.

1 (1857) Dears & B 160, 26 LJMC 47. For a recent authority, see *Lewis v Cox* [1985] QB 509, [1984] 3 All ER 672, DC.
2 [1960] 2 QB 423, [1960] 1 All ER 256, CCA.

IGNORANCE OR MISTAKE OF LAW[1]

6.73 It should be clear by now that mens rea does not mean that the accused must have been aware of the illegality of his conduct. Ignorance or mistake of law is usually no defence. Various reasons have been given for this rule. First, it is said that everyone knows the law, but this is palpably untrue. Secondly, it is said that it would be difficult to prove that the accused knew the law; if this were the real reason for the rule, ignorance of the law should be a defence when it can be clearly proved. However, it has been held that a person who was on the high seas, in circumstances in which he could not have been informed of the contents of a recent statute, might be convicted of contravening it.[2] The best reason for the rule is expediency.

'Every man must be taken to be cognisant of the law, otherwise there is no knowing of the extent to which the excuse of ignorance might be carried. It would be urged in almost every case.'[3]

Even a foreigner who proves that he mistakenly believed his conduct to be lawful is not, under the rule, exempt from criminal liability in England.[4]

The rule that ignorance or mistake of law is no excuse (which is applied more strictly in England than in many other countries) is only rendered compatible with most people's idea of justice by the fact that many offences are also moral wrongs and even when this is not so the ordinary member of the public or, at least, the ordinary member of the class most affected (as motorists are affected by traffic legislation) has a rough idea of the provisions of the criminal law. The rule is liable to be particularly harsh where a person has reasonably relied on the advice of a lawyer or someone in authority that a proposed course of action is not criminal. It has been suggested that a person should have a defence to a charge concerning that action in such circumstances;[5] at present reasonable reliance on erroneous advice can only be reflected in mitigation of the sentence imposed.[6]

1 For critical appraisals of this issue, see Matthews 'Ignorance of the Law is no Excuse?'(1983) 3 *Legal Studies* 174 and Smith 'Error and Mistake of Law in Anglo-American Criminal Law' (1985) 14 Anglo-Am LR 3.
2 *Bailey* (1800) Russ & Ry 1.
3 *Bilbie v Lumley* (1802) 2 East 469.
4 *Esop* (1836) 7 C & P 456.
5 Ashworth 'Excusable Mistake of Law' [1974] Crim LR 652. See also the note by Smith [1988] Crim LR 138, and Williams 'The Draft Code and Reliance on Official Statements' (1989) 9 *Legal Studies* 177.
6 *Surrey County Council v Battersby* [1965] 2 QB 194, [1965] 1 All ER 273, DC. See also *Arrowsmith* [1975] QB 678, [1975] 1 All ER 463, CA.

6.74 *Exceptions* By way of exception to the general rule, s 3 of the Statutory Instruments Act 1946 provides that it is a defence for a person charged with an offence under a statutory instrument[1] to prove that it had not been issued by the Stationery Office at the date of the alleged offence, unless it is proved that at that date reasonable steps had been taken to bring the purport of the instrument to the notice of the public, or of persons likely to be affected by it, or of the accused.

As a further exception to the general rule, ignorance or mistake of law (normally, of the civil law) does provide a defence where it precludes the accused from having the mens rea required for the offence charged,[2] as opposed simply to causing him to be ignorant that what he knows he is doing constitutes an offence. For instance, it has been held that a person who acts as an auditor for a company, in ignorance of a statutory provision whereby he is disqualified in the circumstances in question, cannot be convicted of the statutory offence of acting as an auditor *knowing* that one is disqualified.[3] Likewise, a person, who disclosed protected information in breach of s 5(2) of the Official Secrets Act 1989,[4] under a reasonably mistaken belief that it was not protected information under the Act, would not be guilty of an offence under that subsection because he would lack the mens rea specified for that offence, knowledge or reasonable cause to believe that the information is protected against disclosure by the Act.

Some offences contain mental elements which expressly envisage the defence of mistake of law. For example, in the offence of theft, where the accused's appropriation of another's property must be proved to have been dishonest, s 2(1) of the Theft Act 1968 provides that an appropriation is not to be regarded as dishonest if the appropriator believed that he had in law the right to deprive the other of it.[5]

For another case where ignorance or mistake of law may be relevant to criminal liability, the reader is referred to para 9.21.

Of course, it is open to a piece of legislation to provide expressly that ignorance or mistake as to a matter of law is a defence, but such cases are likely to be rare.

1 Para 3.19.
2 *Smith* [1974] QB 354, [1974] 1 All ER 632, CA.
3 *Secretary of State for Trade and Industry v Hart* [1982] 1 All ER 817, [1982] 1 WLR 481, DC. Contrast *Grant v Borg* [1982] 2 All ER 257, [1982] 1 WLR 638, HL.
4 Paras 6.65 and 17.17.
5 Para 13.53.

6.75   *Mistaken belief that conduct is criminal*   A mistake of law cannot render an accused criminally liable. For example, if a man has intercourse with a girl of 17, mistakenly believing that it is an offence to have sexual intercourse with a girl under 18, he cannot be convicted of a substantive offence because, contrary to his belief, he has not committed the actus reus of an offence, nor can he be convicted of an attempt.[1]

Moreover, even if an accused has committed the actus reus of an offence, he is to be judged (in terms of any requisite mens rea) on the facts as he believed them to be, regardless of his understanding of their implications in criminal law. This was held by the House of Lords in *Taaffe*,[2] where D had mistakenly believed that he was bringing currency into the country and that such importation was prohibited. In fact, he had been bringing in cannabis resin, the importation of which was prohibited. The House of Lords held that D was not guilty of the relevant offence (under s 170(2) of the Customs and Excise Management Act 1979) of being knowingly concerned in the fraudulent evasion of the prohibition on the importation of a [Class B] controlled drug, because (although only knowledge that the importation of the article was prohibited was required) on the facts as he believed them to be the article was not prohibited goods and it was irrelevant that he thought that the currency was the subject of a prohibition on its importation. Nor would D have been guilty of an attempt to commit the above offence.

1 Para 21.72.
2 [1984] AC 539, [1984] 1 All ER 747, HL.

IGNORANCE OF MORALS

6.76   The fact that the accused did not personally consider his conduct to be immoral or know that it was regarded as immoral by the bulk of society is generally irrelevant to his criminal liability. The principal exceptional cases where it is relevant that the accused was unaware of the moral turpitude of his conduct relate to the criminal responsibility of children between the ages of 10 and 14[1] and to the various offences of dishonesty under the Theft Acts 1968 and 1978 and the offence of blackmail.[2]

1 Para 9.2.
2 Chaps 13 and 14.

Jurisdiction

6.77 The courts of England and Wales are only concerned with conduct which is an offence against English law, or, to put it another way, with offences over which they have jurisdiction. A detailed examination of this matter is outside the scope of this book but the following should be noted.

TERRITORIAL JURISDICTION

6.78 With certain exceptions which are mentioned in paras 6.79 and 6.80, it is clearly established that to be an offence against English law an offence must be committed in England (which term includes Wales in the rest of this chapter).[1] Normally, the application of this requirement is easy since either all the essential elements of an offence occur in England or they do not, and this may be true even in circumstances where there is a foreign element. In *Treacy v DPP*,[2] for instance, it was held that a person who posts in England an unwarranted demand with menaces addressed to a person abroad can be convicted of blackmail because the offence is complete when the demand is posted, with the result that the offence is wholly committed in England. Similarly, in *El-Hakkaoui*[3] it was held that a person can be convicted of possessing a firearm with intent by means thereof to endanger life, even though the intention relates to endangering life abroad, if the possession of the firearm is in England.

Difficulties arise, however, where part of the elements of an offence take place in England and others abroad (including Scotland and Northern Ireland). Where an offence requires the causing of a consequence, the offence is only regarded as committed in England if the consequence occurs here. Thus, in the case of such an offence, if an act is done in England but its consequence occurs abroad no offence against English law is committed. This can be demonstrated by contrasting *Ellis*[4] and *Harden*.[5] In *Ellis* D made false statements in Scotland as a result of which he obtained goods on credit in England. It was held that, the consequence of the offence having taken place in England, D could be convicted of what is now obtaining property by deception. In *Harden*, on the other hand, it was held that a deception made in England which resulted in property being obtained abroad did not constitute the offence of what is now obtaining property by deception under English law. In *Treacy's* case Lord Diplock thought that the decision in *Harden* depended on the particular wording of the offence in question, and that an offence might be committed against English law provided an essential element of it, whether conduct or a consequence, took effect in England although other such elements occurred abroad. However Lord Diplock's views have not yet been adopted as the basis of the decision in any reported case.

Where an offence does not require a consequence to result from proscribed conduct, for example blackmail, it appears that conduct outside England which can be regarded as continuing and which takes effect in England is an offence under English law. For example, in *Treacy* the House of Lords accepted that a person who posted an unwarranted demand with menaces abroad, which was received by a victim in England, would commit the offence of blackmail under English law.

1 In construing a statute, there is a well-established presumption that, in the absence of clear and specific words to the contrary, an 'offence-creating provision' was not intended to make conduct outside the territorial limits of England an offence triable in an English court: *Air India v Wiggins* [1980] 2 All ER 593, [1980] 1 WLR 815, HL.
2 [1971] AC 537, [1971] 1 All ER 110, HL.
3 [1975] 2 All ER 146, [1975] 1 WLR 396, CA. Also see *Berry* [1985] AC 246, [1984] 3 All ER 1008, HL.
4 [1899] 1 QB 230, 68 LJQB 103. Also see *Secretary of State for Trade v Marcus* [1976] AC 35, [1975] 1 All ER 958, HL.
5 [1963] 1 QB 8, [1962] 1 All ER 286, CCA. Also see *Thompson* [1984] 3 All ER 565, [1984] 1 WLR 962, CA.

6.79 *Territorial limits* It is obviously important, for the purposes of the above rules, to know the territorial limits of England within which English criminal law applies. For the purpose of offences triable only on indictment and offences triable either way the boundaries of England are, round the coast, the outer limit of territorial waters whether the offence is committed by a British citizen or not.[1] In the case of summary offences (ie an offence triable only in a magistrates' court), the boundaries are the low water mark[2] except where the offence may expressly be committed in territorial waters, in which case the boundary is the outer limit of those waters.

1 Territorial Waters Jurisdiction Act 1878, s 2.
2 This is implied by the Magistrates' Courts Act 1980, ss 1 and 2.

JURISDICTION OVER OFFENCES ON BOARD SHIPS AND AIRCRAFT

6.80 Section 686 of the Merchant Shipping Act 1894 gives English courts jurisdiction for the trial of offences charged as having been committed:

a) by a Commonwealth citizen on board a British ship on the high seas or in any foreign port or harbour;
b) by a Commonwealth citizen on board a foreign ship 'to which he does not belong' (ie is not a crew member);
c) by a non-Commonwealth citizen on board a British ship on the high seas,

so that in these cases the whole of our criminal law is extended as if the offence had been committed in English territory.

Further discussion of s 686 and of other ship-related provisions, such as that in s 687 of the 1894 Act, which deals with the rules to be applied to offences against property or person committed ashore or afloat by persons who at the time of the offence are, or have been during the previous three months, employed on a British ship, is beyond the scope of this book. So is discussion of s 92 of the Civil Aviation Act 1982, which extends our criminal law to conduct in British-controlled aircraft while in flight outside the United Kingdom.

EXTRA-TERRITORIAL JURISDICTION

6.81 English courts have jurisdiction over an incitement, conspiracy or attempt committed abroad provided that it was intended to result in the commission of an offence in England, even though no overt act (eg an act pursuant to a conspiracy) takes place in England.[1]

In addition, various statutes giving effect to international conventions provide that the English courts shall have jurisdiction over offences covered by the conventions by whomsoever and wheresoever they may be committed. One example is the Aviation Security Act 1982, s 1 of which punishes with a maximum of life imprisonment the unlawful seizure by force of control of an aircraft while it is in flight, whether or not the aircraft is registered in the United Kingdom. Section 2 of the 1982 Act makes similar provision concerning acts of destroying, damaging or endangering the safety of any aircraft.

Other examples of extra-territorial jurisdiction are mentioned when the relevant offences are described elsewhere in this book.[2]

1 *DPP v Stonehouse* [1978] AC 55, [1977] 2 All ER 909, HL; *Liangsiriprasert v Government of the United States of America* [1991] 1 AC 225, [1990] 2 All ER 866, PC; *Sansom* [1991] 2 QB 130, [1991] 2 All ER 145, CA.
2 Eg paras 11.1, 15.63, 17.5, 17.11 and 19.8.

7 Proof

7.1 The general rule is that the prosecution has the burden of proving beyond reasonable doubt that the accused has committed the actus reus of an offence with the mens rea required for it. Proof of the commission of an actus reus requires proof of all its elements.

In relation to elements of justification or excuse, hereafter simply referred to as defences,[1] the accused normally has the burden of adducing sufficient evidence to raise a defence; if he does so it is then for the prosecution to disprove the alleged defence. Exceptionally, the accused has the burden of proving a defence on the balance of probabilities.

The burden of proof is sometimes known as the 'persuasive burden', while the burden of adducing evidence is sometimes known as the 'evidential burden'.

1 The use of 'defence' is not strictly accurate in relation to an element of justification (see para 6.20) but is used here for convenience.

7.2 Although the great majority of criminal cases are tried before magistrates, and therefore without a jury,[1] it is convenient for the student to think in terms of a trial by judge and jury when considering the following paragraphs. All questions of fact have to be determined by the jury, but the judge exercises a considerable degree of control in two ways in particular. One concerns the judge's power to withdraw a case, or an issue in a case, from the jury on the ground that the supporting evidence is in law insufficient. This step is sometimes taken on a submission by the defence, at the close of the prosecution's evidence, that there is no case to answer; an acquittal is directed if the submission is successful. The other way is by means of his summing up.[2]

1 Paras 5.16–5.20
2 Para 5.12

The two burdens

THE BURDEN OF PROOF

7.3 The party who bears the burden of proof on a given issue will lose on that issue if, after reviewing all the evidence, the jury or magistrates entertain the appropriate degree of doubt whether the proposition in question has been established. As the prosecution bears the burden of proving most issues in a criminal case beyond reasonable doubt, it is generally true to say that the guilt of the accused must be established beyond reasonable doubt. This has been the recognised position for a long time so far as most criminal charges are concerned, but before 1935 there was believed to be an exception in the case of murder. It was thought that, if the deceased was shown to have met his death as a result of the conduct of the accused, it was incumbent on the accused to satisfy the jury of his innocence, or of the existence of a mitigating circumstance, such as provocation, which would justify a verdict of manslaughter.

There were several authorities which seemed to support this view concerning the law of murder, but they were overruled or explained on other grounds by the House of Lords in *Woolmington v DPP*.[1] Woolmington was charged with murdering his wife by shooting. He admitted that she was killed by a bullet fired from a rifle which he was handling, but said that he squeezed the trigger involuntarily while endeavouring to induce her to return to live with him by threatening to shoot himself. Woolmington was convicted after a summing up which contained the following sentences: 'The Crown has got to satisfy you that this woman . . . died at the prisoner's hands . . . If they satisfy you of that, then he has to show that there are circumstances to be found in the evidence which has been given from the witness box in this case, which alleviate the crime so that it is only manslaughter, or which excuse the homicide altogether by showing that it was a pure accident.' An appeal to the Court of Criminal Appeal was dismissed, but a further appeal to the House of Lords succeeded and Woolmington was acquitted. The following important sentences are taken from the speech of Lord Sankey.

'If it is proved that the conscious act of the prisoner killed a man and nothing else appears in the case, there is evidence upon which the jury may, not must, find him guilty of murder. It is difficult to conceive so bare and meagre a case, but that does not mean that the onus is not still on the prosecution . . . Throughout the web of the English criminal law one golden thread is always to be seen, that it is the duty of the prosecution to prove the prisoner's guilt . . . If, at the end of and on the whole of the case, there is a reasonable doubt, created by the evidence given by either the prosecution or the prisoner, as to whether the prisoner killed the deceased with a malicious intention, the prosecution has not made out the case and the prisoner is entitled to an acquittal. No matter what the charge or where the trial, the principle that the prosecution must prove the guilt of the prisoner is part of the common law of England and no attempt to whittle it down can be entertained.'

1 [1935] AC 462, HL.

7.4 The rule that the prosecution must prove the accused's guilt beyond reasonable doubt means that it is generally incumbent on the prosecution to negative any defence raised by the accused. In *Woolmington v DPP* Lord Sankey said that the prosecution bears the burden of negativing a plea that a verdict of manslaughter should be returned on a charge of murder because of provocation caused by the conduct of the deceased; and on appeal a verdict of manslaughter has been substituted for one of murder when the trial judge left it to the jury to decide whether the accused had been provoked, but failed to tell them that the burden of disproving provocation rested on the prosecution[1]. It has also been held on appeal that the burden of negativing a plea of duress,[2] or of self-defence,[3] is borne by the prosecution. In addition, it has been held by the House of Lords, as well as by the Court of Appeal, that the burden of negativing automatism, when it is not caused by insanity, is likewise borne by the prosecution.[4]

1 *Macpherson* (1957) 41 Cr App Rep 213, CCA.
2 *Gill* [1963] 2 All ER 688, CCA; *Bone* [1968] 2 All ER 644, CA.
3 *Lobell* [1957] 1 QB 547, [1957] 1 All ER 734, CCA.
4 *Bratty v A-G for Northern Ireland* [1963] AC 386, [1961] 3 All ER 523, HL; *Stripp* (1978) 69 Cr App Rep 318, CA.

BURDEN OF PROOF ON ACCUSED

7.5 In three types of case the burden of proving certain exculpating facts is placed on the accused, but when this is so the burden borne by him is lighter than that borne by the prosecution on the issues on which it has to prove guilt, for the accused has only to prove the exculpating fact on the balance of probabilities, not beyond reasonable doubt.[1] He will succeed in doing this if the jury are satisfied that it is more likely than not (or more probable than not) that the particular fact is made out.[2] These three types of case are open to the grave objection that a jury may have to convict a man although they think it as likely as not that he had a defence. The situations where the accused bears the burden of proof are shown in paras 7.6 to 7.8.

1 *Sodeman v R* [1936] 2 All ER 1138, PC; *Carr-Briant* [1943] KB 607, [1943] 2 All ER 156, CCA.
2 *Miller v Minister of Pensions* [1947] 2 All ER 372 at 373–374; *Swaysland* (1987) Times, 15 April, CA.

7.6 *Defence of insanity* It was said in *M'Naghten's Case*,[1] which contains the leading statement on the subject, that everyone is to be presumed to be sane until the contrary is proved to the satisfaction of the jury. There is therefore no doubt that under the present law an accused person who raises the defence of insanity has the burden of proving it.

1 (1843) 10 Cl & Fin 200, para 9.11.

7.7 *Express statutory provision* A statute sometimes provides that it shall be for the defence to prove certain facts. The following are examples. Section 4 of the Explosive Substances Act 1883 makes it an offence for a person to make or possess an explosive substance under suspicious circumstances, unless he proves that he made or possessed it for a lawful object. Under s 1 of the Prevention of Crime Act 1953 it is an offence for a person to have with him an offensive weapon in a public place 'without lawful authority or reasonable excuse, the proof whereof shall lie on him'. Lastly, a person charged with supplying intoxicating glue to someone under 18, contrary to s 1 of the Intoxicating Substances (Supply) Act 1985, has a defence if he proves that he was under 18 and acting otherwise than in the course or furtherance of a business.

7.8 *Implied statutory provision* Even if a statute does not expressly place on the accused the burden of proving a defence provided by it, the statutory provision may, on its true construction, place that burden on him. A statutory provision will have this effect if, on its true construction, it contains 'any exception, exemption, proviso, excuse or qualification, whether or not it accompanies the description of the offence . . . in the enactment creating the offence'. The words quoted are contained in s 101 of the Magistrates' Courts Act 1980, which goes on to provide that in relation to a case tried summarily the burden of proving the exception, exemption, proviso, excuse or qualification is borne by the accused. The law on this matter is identical where a case is tried on indictment, as the House of Lords affirmed in *Hunt*.[1] This is fortunate since many offences are triable either way and it would be anomalous if a different rule applied to the same offence depending on whether it was tried summarily or on indictment. The rule is one of statutory interpretation and has no application to common law defences.

If what might be regarded as a defence appears in a statutory provision, it is of crucial importance in terms of the burden of proof to ascertain whether it is an 'exception, exemption, proviso, excuse or qualification'. In the absence of previous authority, the court will have to construe the enactment. If the words in question appear in a provision separate from the offence-creating provision it is easier to infer that, on their true construction, they were intended to provide an exception, exemption or the like (which the accused must prove) than if they appear in the offence-creating provision itself.[2] If the linguistic construction of the statute does not clearly indicate on whom the burden should lie, the court must look to other considerations to determine Parliament's intention, such as the mischief at which the Act was aimed and practical considerations affecting the burden of proof and, in particular, the ease or difficulty that the respective parties would encounter in discharging the burden (since Parliament cannot lightly be taken to have intended to impose an onerous duty on an accused to prove his innocence).[3] As a guide to construction, a statute which prohibits the doing of an act 'save in specified circumstances or by persons of specified classes or with specified qualifications or with the licence or permission of specified authorities' is likely to be construed as providing an exception, exemption or the like which the accused must prove,[4] and a statute falling outside that formulation will rarely be construed as doing so.[5]

The application of these principles is illustrated by the House of Lords' decision in *Hunt*. Morphine is a controlled drug. Section 5(1) of the Misuse of Drugs Act 1971 provides: 'Subject to any regulations under s 7 . . . , it shall not be lawful for any person to have a controlled drug in his possession'. By s 5(2), contravention of s 5(1) is an offence. One of the regulations under s 7 provides that s 5(1) (and therefore s 5(2) as well) shall not have effect in relation to any preparation of morphine of a specified type which does not constitute a risk to health. The House of Lords held that, on the true construction of the regulation, it dealt with the definition of an essential ingredient of the offence and not with an exception to what would otherwise be unlawful. Consequently, the burden lay on the prosecution to prove not only that the substance in question contained the controlled drug, morphine, but also that it was not morphine in the form permitted by the regulation, and the Court of Appeal had been wrong to hold that the burden of proof in relation to the morphine being of the permitted form lay on the accused. A different construction was given to the provision in issue in *Edwards*[6] , where the accused was charged with selling intoxicating liquor without holding a justices' licence authorising such sale, contrary to s 160(1) of the Licensing Act 1964. The Court of Appeal, having construed the enactment, held that the offence was one which prohibited the doing of something subject to an exemption and that the onus of proving the exemption (that he was the holder of a licence) was on the accused.

The problem with the above principles is that the courts may find their application difficult and the answer which they come up with may be controversial.[7] It would be better if Parliament enacted that the only time that the accused bore a persuasive burden was where the statute enacting the offence expressly so provided. For this reason the enactment of cl 13 of the draft Criminal Code Bill[8] would be welcome. By cl 13 there would only be an evidential burden in relation to any exception, exemption or the like, unless the statute otherwise indicated. However, cl 13 would not apply to pre-Code offences, so that s 101 of the Magistrates' Courts Act 1980 and the corresponding rule for trials on indictment would continue to apply to them.

1 [1987] 1 All ER 1, HL.
2 Ibid at 10, per Lord Griffiths.
3 Ibid at 11, per Lord Griffiths, and 15 and 17, per Lord Ackner.
4 *Edwards* [1975] QB 27 at 39–40, as explained by Lord Griffiths in *Hunt* [1987] 1 All ER at 11.
5 *Hunt* [1987] 1 All ER 1 at 11, per Lord Griffiths. It is worthy of note that phrases such as 'without reasonable excuse' or 'without lawful authority or excuse' have generally not been construed as imposing on the accused the burden of proving the excuse etc: *Mallows v Harris* [1979] RTR 404, DC; *Jaggard v Dickinson* [1981] QB 527, [1980] 3 All ER 716, DC; *Briggs* [1987] Crim LR 708, CA; *Hirst and Agu v Chief Constable of West Yorkshire* (1986) 85 Cr App Rep 143, DC. Cf *Gatland v Metropolitan Police Comr* [1968] 2 QB 279, [1968] 2 All ER 100, DC.
6 [1975] QB 27, [1974] 2 All ER 1085, CA.
7 See, for example, *Alath Construction Ltd* [1990] Crim LR 516, CA, and commentary thereon.
8 Law Commission: A Criminal Code for England and Wales (1989): Law Com No 177; see para 3.21 above.

THE BURDEN OF ADDUCING EVIDENCE

7.9 The prosecution must adduce prima facie evidence of the accused's guilt, for otherwise there is no case to answer and the judge directs an acquittal; this means only that the prosecution must adduce sufficient evidence of the actus reus and mens rea mentioned in the definition of the offence charged. It is not necessary to negative every defence that might be available to the accused. In the words of Devlin J, 'It would be quite unreasonable to allow the defence to submit at the end of the prosecution's case that the Crown had not proved affirmatively and beyond reasonable doubt that the accused was at the time of the crime sober, or not sleepwalking or not in a trance or blackout.'[1] It follows that it is normally incumbent on the accused to adduce sufficient evidence to raise a particular defence and he satisfies this burden if he indicates material which could induce a reasonable doubt as to the availability of that defence or justification.[2] If the accused does this the judge must leave the issue to the jury, directing them that the defence must succeed (and the accused be acquitted) unless the Crown disproves one or more elements of it beyond reasonable doubt.[3]

For example, in murder the prosecution must dispel all reasonable doubt on the question of provocation for otherwise a verdict of manslaughter must be returned, but this duty of the prosecution only arises if there is evidence to raise the issue of provocation. If there is no such evidence, the judge need not allude to the question in his direction to the jury.[4] On the other hand, if there is such evidence the judge must leave the issue of provocation to the jury, even though the accused has not specifically raised it as a defence. This may happen, for example, at a murder trial where the accused specifically pleads self-defence, but not provocation, and there is evidence raising the issue of provocation.[5]

It is common practice to speak of the accused's burden of adducing evidence, but it should never be forgotten that the burden may have been discharged for the accused by the evidence of a witness for the prosecution or of a co-accused.[6] If a prosecution witness says that he saw the deceased aim a blow at the accused just before the fatal injury was inflicted, the judge might well leave the issue of provocation to the jury even if the accused neither gave evidence himself nor called witnesses.

1 *Hill v Baxter* [1958] 1 QB 277 at 284.
2 *Lee Chun-Chuen v R* [1963] AC 220, [1963] 1 All ER 73, PC.
3 *Abraham* [1973] 3 All ER 694 at 697–698; *Moore* [1986] Crim LR 552, CA. Statements in *Moore* that it is enough if some of the jury are satisfied beyond reasonable doubt that one element is not made out, while the rest are so satisfied that another element is not made out, must be regarded as wrong.
4 *Mancini v DPP* [1942] AC 1, [1941] 3 All ER 272, HL.
5 *Camplin* [1978] AC 705 at 716, [1978] 2 All ER 168, per Lord Diplock; *Johnson* [1989] 2 All ER 839, CA.
6 *Bullard v R* [1957] AC 635, PC; *Rolle v R* [1965] 3 All ER 582, PC.

Presumptions

7.10 Proof may be aided by certain presumptions which are classified as irrebuttable presumptions of law, rebuttable presumptions of law and presumptions of fact.

A presumption is the product of a rule according to which on proof of one fact the jury may or must find that some other fact (often called the 'presumed fact') exists. The 'may' or 'must' in the last sentence gives the clue to the classification of presumptions into presumptions of law and presumptions of fact.

PRESUMPTION OF LAW

7.11 When the jury must find that the presumed fact exists, the presumption is a presumption of law. There are two kinds of presumption of law, rebuttable and irrebuttable. When the presumption is irrebuttable, no evidence can be received to contradict the presumed fact. Examples of irrebuttable presumptions of law are provided by the rules[1] that a child under 10 is incapable of committing an offence and that a boy under 14 is incapable of rape or any other form of unlawful intercourse. Irrebuttable presumptions of law are sometimes called conclusive presumptions.

Where there is a rebuttable presumption of law, the jury must find that the presumed fact exists unless sufficient evidence to the contrary is adduced. The amount of evidence required in rebuttal varies somewhat in different presumptions. An example of a rebuttable presumption of law is provided by the presumption that a marriage ceremony constitutes a valid union. When a marriage ceremony has been proved, the jury must assume that it constituted a valid marriage until sufficient evidence to the contrary is adduced.

1 Paras 9.1 and 9.3.

PRESUMPTIONS OF FACT

7.12 When the jury may find that the presumed fact exists on proof of some other fact, the presumption is one of fact. Presumptions of fact are sometimes called provisional presumptions, and they play a very important part in the administration of the criminal law because they are frequently the only means by which the state of the accused's mind can be proved. The judge will tell the jury that they are entitled to infer knowledge, foresight or intent from the fact that the prohibited act was done by the accused, and if the accused offers no explanation the inference will usually be drawn. This is a matter of common sense, because people generally are aware of the circumstances in which they act, and they generally do foresee that what does result from their conduct will result from it. If a credible explanation is offered, the jury must consider the evidence as a whole and, if they entertain any reasonable doubt, the general rule that the prosecution has the burden of proof obliges them to give the accused the benefit of that doubt.

Proof of a state of mind

7.13 The extent to which it is possible to prove the past state of the accused's mind is apt to trouble the student. Regard must be had to the statements of the accused at the time, or at a later date, or in the course of his testimony. If the statements out of court amount to admissions, great weight is attached to them on the assumption that what people say adverse to their case is probably true. Regard must also be had to the conduct and circumstances of the accused. The mere doing by him of the prohibited act can justify an inference that he did it voluntarily, with knowledge of the surrounding circumstances, and, where relevant, with foresight of its normal consequences, although it must never be forgotten that this is only an inference, and the jury may well conclude that it is not warranted on the particular facts of the case. The presence or absence of motive is another important consideration.

7.14 Certain acts are known to be likely to produce certain consequences which are frequently spoken of as the 'natural and probable' consequences of those acts. This fact, coupled with the fact that people usually do foresee the normal consequences of their conduct, has led people to talk of a presumption (or inference) that everyone intends or foresees the natural and probable consequences of his conscious acts. Such talk is harmless provided it is always remembered that the presumption is one of fact. If this point is forgotten, it is fatally easy to suggest that, once a particular act is proved against him, it is incumbent on the accused as a matter of law to adduce evidence to disprove that he intended or foresaw the natural and probable consequences of that act; it may even come to be suggested that the accused bears the burden of disproving such an intention or foresight.

That the presumption is one of fact is made clear by s 8 of the Criminal Justice Act 1967, which states:

'A court or jury in determining whether a person has committed an offence (a) shall not be bound in law to infer that he intended or foresaw a result of his actions by reason only of its being a natural and probable consequence of those actions, but (b) shall decide whether he did intend or foresee that result by reference to all the evidence, drawing such inferences from the evidence as appear proper in the circumstances.'

It must be borne in mind constantly that this provision is not concerned with when intention or foresight is required for criminal liability but with how it is proved if required.[1]

1 See, for example, the speeches of Lords Diplock, Dilhorne and Edmund-Davies in *Lemon* [1979] 1 All ER at 904, 908 and 920.

The negation of mens rea

7.15 In this and the following paragraphs we deal with cases in which there is no doubt that the conscious conduct of the accused satisfied the requirements of the actus reus of an offence. The question at issue is whether he had the necessary mens rea, something which he denies on account of accident, ignorance or mistake. For convenience, the situation where the accused had the necessary mens rea but mistakenly believed that he was acting in circumstances which would provide him with a defence will also be discussed. These are not matters on which the accused bears the burden of proof. Indeed, except in certain contexts where a mistake is alleged, he does not even bear the burden of adducing sufficient evidence.

ACCIDENT

7.16 'Accident' is a word which has several shades of meaning but, when we speak of an alleged accident in a case in which the conscious conduct of the accused constitutes the actus reus of the crime charged, the allegation always is that the accused did not intend to produce the prohibited consequence.

The typical instance is one in which someone, who was conscious of, and in control of, his bodily movements and aware of all relevant circumstances, did not foresee that his conduct would have the prohibited consequence. The accused aims a bullet at a crow, but owing to the presence of a high wind or the fact that his is a poor shot he hits a house pigeon. In either event, he is said to have killed the bird accidentally.[1]

The accused cannot be said to bear the burden of adducing evidence of accident because, however weak his evidence may be, the issue of his intention must be left to the jury as it is raised by the prosecution.

When the prohibited consequence occurs in a way which would be described as an 'accident' because it was unintended,[2] an accused can be convicted of an offence in which liability may be based on negligence or recklessness if he has been negligent or reckless (in the appropriate sense) as to the risk of that consequence; an accident caused by negligent or reckless conduct cannot constitute a defence to a charge of such an offence.

1 *Horton v Gwynne* [1921] 2 KB 661, DC.
2 *Gray v Barr* [1971] 2 QB 554, [1971] 2 All ER 949, CA.

IGNORANCE

7.17 The accused's ignorance of fact or law prevents him being criminally liable if it results in him lacking the intention, subjective recklessness, knowledge or other subjective mental element which is expressly or impliedly required by the definition of the offence charged. It is most exceptional for ignorance of law to have this effect, as opposed simply to causing the accused to be unaware that what he is doing is criminal (which is not an excuse, as explained in para 6.73).

A case where ignorance of fact resulted in the accused lacking the required mental element is *Hibbert*[1]. There a man was charged with an offence against s 55 of the Offences against the Person Act 1861 (substantially re-enacted by s 20 of the Sexual Offences Act 1956), which provided that 'whosoever shall unlawfully take ... any unmarried girl, being under the age of 16 years, out of the possession and against the will of her father or mother, or of any other person having lawful care or charge of her, shall be guilty of a misdemeanour .. .'. The accused met a girl of 14 in the street, took her to another place where he seduced her, and left her where he had found her. The girl was in the custody of her father, but it was held that, in the absence of a finding by the jury that the prisoner was aware of this fact, he must be acquitted. This case is of special interest because of the problem of reconciling it with *Prince*,[2] discussed later.[3] To avoid possible confusion, it should be pointed out that having intercourse with a girl under 16 has since been made an offence, as it was an offence in 1869 to have intercourse with a girl under 12, but the crime with which the section quoted above is concerned may be committed by a person who abducts a girl without any improper intention.

Where the prosecution has to prove a subjective mental element, the accused does not bear the burden of adducing evidence with regard to his lack of it because the issue of mens rea must be left to the jury as it is part of the prosecution's case. In most cases the accused will adduce evidence of ignorance but its sufficiency is no concern of the judge at a trial with a jury.

Lack of intention, subjective recklessness or knowledge etc caused by simple ignorance (ie where the accused's mind is a complete blank as to a particular matter) is comparatively rare because lack of a subjective mental element is normally connected with a mistake, in that the accused has thought about the possible existence of the matter but wrongly concluded that it does not exist.

1 (1869) LR 1 CCR 184.
2 (1875) LR 2 CCR 154.
3 Para 8.2.

Mistake

7.18 As will be seen, where an accused pleads that he acted under a mistake of fact or of law it is of vital importance to classify the matter to which the mistake relates. In particular, it is vital to determine whether the alleged mistake negatives the mens rea required for the offence charged or whether (although it does not have that effect) it relates to facts which, if true, would have given rise to a particular defence or would have prevented an element of the actus reus being established. If the alleged mistake has neither effect it is immaterial and cannot affect the accused's liability. A mistake of law will rarely have either effect because usually its sole effect is to cause the accused to be unaware that he is committing an offence (which is not an excuse, as explained in para 6.73).

Mistake negativing mens rea

MISTAKES NEGATIVING MENS REA (OTHER THAN *CALDWELL*-TYPE RECKLESSNESS OR NEGLIGENCE)

7.19 An accused cannot be convicted of an offence if, because of a mistake, he lacked the intention, subjective recklessness, knowledge or other state of mind which the prosecution is required to prove. The law does not require the mistake to be reasonable.

Clearly, the judge is not going to leave the mistake to the jury unless it is raised at the trial. However, with the exception indicated shortly, the accused does not bear the normal evidential burden,[1] so that he does not have to adduce evidence capable of inducing a reasonable doubt that he might have been mistaken. Instead, the judge must leave the mistake to the jury, however weak the evidence is. The exception is that the normal evidential burden applies where the alleged mistake relates to a matter in relation to which the accused bears the normal evidential burden, for example a mistaken belief in the need to act in self-defence or the prevention of crime. Here, the judge may only leave the mistake to the jury if there is evidence capable of raising a reasonable doubt that the accused might have been mistaken.[2]

When a judge leaves evidence of mistake to a jury, the jury must acquit the accused unless the prosecution prove beyond reasonable doubt that the accused was not mistaken in the alleged way and that he had the state of mind required for the offence.

1 Williams 'The Evidential Burden' (1977) 127 NLJ 156.
2 Para 7.9.

7.20 The rule that a mistake negativing a state of mind which the prosecution must prove need not be reasonable was clearly implied in relation to mistakes negativing intention or subjective recklessness as to consequences by s 8 of the Criminal Justice Act 1967 and it was affirmed in relation to mistakes negativing the requisite state of mind, whatever its description, by the majority of the House of Lords in *DPP v Morgan*.[1]

In *Morgan*, which was concerned with the common law offence of rape, the majority held that, since he would lack the mens rea which had to be proved by the prosecution, an accused could not be convicted if he believed (albeit unreasonably) that the woman was consenting. As Lord Hailsham said:

'Once one has accepted . . . that the prohibited act in rape is non-consensual sexual intercourse, and that the guilty state of mind is an intention to commit it, it seems to me to follow as a matter of inexorable logic that there is no room either for a 'defence' of honest[2] belief or mistake, or of a defence of honest and reasonable belief or mistake. Either the prosecution proves that the accused had the requisite intention, or it does not. In the former case it succeeds, and in the latter it fails.'[3]

1 [1976] AC 182, [1975] 2 All ER 347, HL. See also *Smith* [1974] QB 354, [1974] 1 All ER 632, CA.
2 The word 'honest' may be useful emphasis but in fact adds nothing: *Albert v Lavin* [1981] 1 All ER 628 at 633, per Hodgson J.
3 [1976] AC at 214.

7.21 In some subsequent cases, there were obiter dicta to the effect that the decision in *Morgan* was confined (and intended to be confined) to the common law offence of rape,[1] but this view was not accepted by the Court of Appeal in *Kimber*[2] nor in *Williams*,[3] where the principle endorsed in *Morgan* was applied to two different offences of assault, and there can now be no doubt that that principle is of general application.

In *Kimber,* which was concerned with the statutory offence of indecent assault on a woman, the accused had alleged that the woman had consented to his actions. The Court of Appeal held that, since the mens rea required for the offence of indecent assault on a woman was intentionally causing the woman to apprehend immediate, or to sustain, *unlawful* personal violence,[4] and since violence would not be unlawful if the woman had consented to it, an accused was entitled to be acquitted if because of his mistaken belief in consent he did not intend to lay hands on the woman without her consent, whether or not his mistake was reasonable.

Williams was concerned with the statutory offence of assault occasioning actual bodily harm. P saw a youth seizing a woman's handbag. P chased and caught the youth and knocked him to the ground. D, who had only seen the later stages of the incident, was told by P that he was arresting the youth for mugging and that he was a policeman (which he was not). D asked P for his warrant card. When P could not produce it, a struggle ensued, during which D punched P and injured P's face. P was entitled to arrest the youth[5] and therefore his use of reasonable force against the youth was lawful. Although it is lawful to use reasonable force in self-defence or the prevention of crime, a person is not entitled to use force against someone using lawful force and therefore D's use of force was unlawful. At his trial for assault occasioning actual bodily harm D said that he had acted under the honest but mistaken belief that P was unlawfully attacking the youth and that he must use force against P in order to protect the youth. The trial judge directed the jury that D could have an excuse if he had a belief based on reasonable grounds that P was acting unlawfully. The Court of Appeal held that that direction was wrong. It said that a person who mistakenly believed that he had to act in self-defence or in the prevention of crime had to be judged on the facts as he believed them to be. Consequently, if, on the facts as he mistakenly believed them to be, he was entitled to use reasonable force in self-defence or the prevention of crime, he would lack the necessary mens rea for the offence charged. The reason was that mens rea was not simply an intent to apply force to another; instead, it was an intention to apply *unlawful* force to another[6] (and, on the facts as D understood them, the force which he intended to apply would not be unlawful).

The statement of law in *Williams* may have been an obiter dictum, since the conviction had to be quashed because of a misdirection concerning the onus of proof, but it has been applied or referred to with approval in a number of cases.[7] In particular, it was followed by the Privy Council in *Beckford v R,*[8] where it was held that an essential element of the offence of murder was that the violence used by the accused was unlawful and that a mistaken belief (albeit unreasonable) in facts which – if true – would justify self-defence would negative the mens rea for murder (provided that the force was reasonable on the facts believed to exist) because it would negative the intent *unlawfully* to kill or cause grievous bodily harm.

It follows from the general application of the principle endorsed in *Morgan* and subsequent cases that, for example, on a charge of murder by shooting, the accused's evidence that he believed the gun with which he shot the deceased to be unloaded must be left to the jury, however weak that evidence may be, and that the jury must be directed to acquit the accused of murder if they are not sure that he knew it was loaded, even if they think that his alleged belief was utterly unreasonable, since the prosecution will have failed to prove that he had the mens rea for murder.

1 *Phekoo* [1981] 3 All ER 84, [1981] 1 WLR 1117, CA; *Barrett and Barrett* (1980) 72 Cr App Rep 212, CA.
2 [1983] 3 All ER 316, [1983] 1 WLR 1118, CA. Also see *Jones* (1986) 83 Cr App Rep 375, CA.
3 (1983) 78 Cr App Rep 276, CA.
4 This formulation sufficed for the purposes of the Court of Appeal's decision. For the full definition of the elements of indecent assault, see paras 12.15–12.20.
5 Para 4.14.

6 This formulation sufficed for the purposes of the Court of Appeal's decision. For the full definition of this offence see paras 10.9–10.17.
7 *Jackson* [1985] RTR 257, CA; *Fisher* [1987] Crim LR 334, CA; *Asbury* [1986] Crim LR 258, CA; *Beckford v R* [1987] 3 WLR 611, PC.
8 [1987] 3 WLR 611, PC.

7.22 The fact that in the present context the accused's mistaken belief is not required as a matter of law to be a reasonable one does not mean that the reasonableness of a mistake is entirely irrelevant. As was recognised in *Morgan* and in *Williams,* the reasonableness of the accused's alleged mistake is of considerable evidential significance because the more reasonable the mistake the more likely it is that the jury (or magistrates) will accept his story that he was acting under a mistake.[1]

1 The courts occasionally still confuse the distinction between whether the reasonableness of a mistake is relevant as a matter of law and the evidential relevance of the reasonableness of a mistake. See, for example, *Brown* [1984] 3 All ER 1013 at 1015.

7.23 Special rules apply where the accused's mistake was attended by intoxication; they are discussed in Chapter 9.

MISTAKES AND *CALDWELL*-TYPE RECKLESSNESS

7.24 A person who acts under a mistake, whether reasonable or not, which leads him to believe that there is no risk, when that risk would be obvious to a reasonable person, is not *Caldwell*-type reckless as to it. The reason is that the case is not one where where the accused has not given any thought to the possibility of there being any such risk or has recognised that there is some risk. This matter has already been dealt with in para 6.52.

MISTAKE IN OFFENCES WHERE NEGLIGENCE SUFFICES

7.25 Where, because of a mistake, the accused does not realise a risk in relation to which proof of negligence suffices, his mistake must have been a reasonable one in order to negative negligence. The reason is that a person who acts under a mistaken belief which is not based on reasonable grounds is necessarily negligent, because a reasonable person would not, by definition, have made the mistake and would have realised the risk. For example, even if he has thought about the matter but wrongly concluded that his customer is sober, a person can be convicted of the statutory offence[1] of selling a firearm to a person whom he knows or has *reasonable cause to believe* to be drunk unless his mistaken belief was based on reasonable grounds.

1 Para 6.65.

Mistake relating to a matter of defence etc

7.26 What we are concerned with under the present heading is the case where the accused acts with the requisite mens rea for the offence charged but does so under a mistake which leads to a belief in the existence of facts which, if true: *either*

    a) would constitute a defence applicable to the offence charged (whether that defence is specific to the offence charged or more general in its nature) *or*

    b) would prevent an element of the actus reus being established (*as to which element no mens rea is required to be proved* by the prosecution in the first instance).

7.27 Some specific statutory defences, particularly in recent legislation, are framed in terms of the accused's own belief in a situation. For example, under the Criminal Damage Act 1971 it is an offence intentionally or recklessly to destroy or damage another's property 'without lawful excuse'. Section 5 of the Act provides that, inter alia, a person is to be treated as having a lawful excuse if he believed that the person whom he believed to be entitled to consent to the destruction or damage had so consented to it or would have so consented if he had known of it.[1]

In the case of the present type of defence it may be for the accused to prove the relevant belief or it may be for the prosecution to disprove it once he has adduced evidence of it, depending on the terms of the defence, but in either case it is no bar to the defence succeeding that the belief was based on unreasonable grounds.

1 For other examples, see paras 14.24 and 19.8.a.

7.28 The position is different where the defence is framed in terms simply of a factual situation without reference to the accused's belief in the situation, and the accused mistakenly believes that it exists. It is also different where the accused believes in facts which, if true, would prevent an element of the actus reus being established (in relation to which element the prosecution does not have to prove mens rea). In these cases the offence may be one of strict liability as to the defence or element in question, in which case not even a reasonable mistake will excuse the accused. Whether or not an offence involves strict liability is a matter discussed in the next chapter. If the offence is not one of strict liability as to the defence or element in question, the situation is governed by a well-established rule which is discussed in the rest of this chapter.

The rule is that, as a matter of law, to excuse the accused the mistake must have been reasonable. Moreover, the accused bears the burden of adducing evidence of such a mistake, ie the judge may tell the jury that they are obliged, as a matter of law, to disregard the evidence of mistake if he considers it to be insufficient. If the issue of mistake is left to the jury, the prosecution bears the burden of disproving the accused's allegation of a reasonable mistake on the principles of *Woolmington's* case.

7.29 This well-established rule[1] was not affected by the decision in *DPP v Morgan*,[2] where the House of Lords was concerned with mistakes negativing the mens rea required as to an element of the actus reus; in fact, in their speeches their Lordships accepted the requirement of reasonableness in relation to mistaken belief in facts which, if true, would constitute a defence or would prevent the establishment of an element of the actus reus as to which mens rea was not required to be proved. Subsequently, the Court of Appeal adopted this approach in *Graham*[3] in the context of the defence of duress by threats; it held that for that defence to succeed the accused's belief that he was being subjected to duress must have been reasonable. It also stated that 'in general, if a mistake is to excuse what would otherwise be criminal, the mistake must be a reasonable one.'[4] Subsequently, the House of Lords in *Howe*[5] and the Court of Appeal in *Martin*[6] have defined the defences of duress by threats and duress of circumstances respectively in terms which endorse the approach in *Graham*.

1 See, for example, *Rose* (1884) 15 Cox CC 540; *Chisam* (1963) 47 Cr App Rep 130, CCA, which provide authority for the principle although the actual decisions in both cases would now be different, following the Court of Appeal's decision in *Williams* (1983) 78 Cr App Rep 276, CA; see para 7.21.
2 [1976] AC 182, [1975] 2 All ER 347, HL.
3 [1982] 1 All ER 801, [1982] 1 WLR 294, CA.
4 Presumably, 'what would otherwise be criminal' refers to the case where the accused has committed the actus reus of an offence with the required mens rea.
5 [1987] AC 417, [1987] 1 All ER 771, HL.
6 [1989] 1 All ER 652, CA.

7.30 The present rule does not offend the 'inexorable logic' to which Lord Hailsham referred in *Morgan* because the types of mistake covered by it do not prevent the accused having the mens rea for the offence charged. However, it cannot be denied that fine distinctions can be involved in classifying that to which an alleged mistake relates. For example, reasonable force used in self-defence is lawful force. In *Albert v Lavin*[1] the Divisional Court proceeded on the basis that the requisite mens rea for an assault was an intention to apply force to another without his consent and held that an accused who, with such a state of mind, had hit someone mistakenly believing that he was acting in self-defence could be convicted of an offence involving an assault, unless his mistaken belief was reasonable. The Court's reason was that the mistake related to a matter of defence (and therefore had to be reasonable), as opposed to a 'definitional element' of the offence in relation to which the accused had to have subjective mens rea. On the other hand, the law is now different as a result of *Williams*,[2] where the decision in *Albert v Lavin* was disapproved, simply because the element of unlawfulness was classified in *Williams* as a definitional element of the offence in relation to which an accused must have the required state of mind. Once the Court of Appeal in *Williams* had held that the mens rea for an assault was an intention to apply *unlawful* force, it would have been inconsistent (and contrary to *Morgan*) for it to have required a mistaken belief that one was acting in self-defence or the like to be reasonable, since such a mistake would negative the state of mind required. This brings us back to the point made earlier on the importance of classifying that to which an alleged mistake relates.

1 [1982] AC 546, [1981] 1 All ER 628, DC. On appeal to the House of Lords [1982] AC 546, [1981] 3 All ER 878, HL, the House did not find it necessary to discuss the present issue.
2 (1983) 78 Cr App Rep 276, CA. Also see *Beckford v R* [1988] AC 130, [1987] 3 All ER 425.

7.31 The rule that, in the two types of case specified above, a mistake must be reasonable in order to excuse seems to be based on judicial policy. Its effect is to convict a person on the grounds of his negligence,[1] a concept which usually has no place in the criminal law. So far the courts have not given any adequate explanation as to why the rule is as it is.

1 Paras 6.63–6.67.

7.32 The distinction between cases in which the mistake need not, as a matter of law, be a reasonable one, and those in which evidence of the reasonableness of the mistake must be available, may also be illustrated by bigamy.[1] The offence, which is contained in s 57 of the Offences against the Person Act 1861, is committed by a person who 'being married, shall marry any other person during the life of the former (sic) husband or wife'. The mens rea required to be proved by the prosecution is merely the intent to go through the second marriage ceremony;[2] proof of knowledge that the first spouse was still alive at the time of the second ceremony is not required. If there is evidence, accepted by the jury, that the accused mistakenly believed that the marriage ceremony was a mere betrothal, he is entitled to be acquitted, however unreasonable his belief may have been, because he would lack the intention to go through a marriage ceremony which the prosecution must prove.

Section 57 provides, inter alia, that it shall not extend to those cases in which, at the time of the accused's second marriage, the first marriage had been dissolved or annulled. The effect of this proviso is to provide a defence to a charge of bigamy. It has been held that a mistaken belief on the part of someone charged with bigamy that his first marriage had been dissolved is a defence,[3] provided that it was a reasonable mistake. Clearly, such a mistake would not prevent the accused having the mens rea for bigamy, since he intended to go through the second marriage ceremony. It would merely lead him to believe in facts which, if true, would give rise to the defence under s 57 just mentioned.

The same has been held in relation to a mistaken belief in facts which, if true, would prevent the element of 'being married' being proved, although they would not fall within the defence just mentioned. For example, if the accused alleges that he believed that the first spouse was dead, it is necessary for there to be evidence showing that the belief was based on reasonable grounds. The accused here will not be seeking to negative the mental element which the prosecution must prove, but will be raising a new issue. The availability of the defence of reasonable mistake of fact in such a case was established in *Tolson*.[4] Mrs Tolson married for a second time within less than seven years of the disappearance of her first husband from whom she had not been divorced. None of the defences provided by s 57 was available to her. Nevertheless, she was found by the jury to have believed on reasonable grounds and in good faith that he was dead, and her conviction was quashed by a majority decision of the Court for Crown Cases Reserved.

Likewise, it has subsequently been held that a mistaken belief on the part of someone charged with bigamy that his first marriage was void[5] is an excuse provided that the mistake was reasonable. In this case the judge was held to have acted rightly in refusing to allow the defence of mistake to go to the jury because there was insufficient evidence that the accused had made reasonable inquiries before concluding that his first marriage was void.

1 Paras 19.2–19.8.
2 *DPP v Morgan* [1975] 2 All ER at 383, per Lord Fraser of Tullybelton.
3 *Gould (No 2)* [1968] 2 QB 65, [1968] 1 All ER 849, CA. The statement, obiter, by the Court of Appeal in *Ditta, Hussain and Kara* [1988] Crim LR 43 that this mistake related to an essential ingredient of the offence is not supported by the clear structure of the wording of the section.
4 (1889) 23 QBD 168.
5 *King* [1964] 1 QB 285, [1963] 3 All ER 561, CCA.

7.33 The rule derived from *Tolson* (that a mistaken belief in facts which, if true, would prevent an element of the actus reus being established must be reasonable) is of limited operation because normally *either* the offence expressly requires or has been held to require mens rea to be proved as to each of the elements of an actus reus *or* (at the other extreme) the courts have held that the offence is one of strict liability as to an element so that not even a reasonable mistake as to that element can excuse the accused. Thus, the *Tolson* rule is limited to cases where mens rea is not expressly or impliedly required as to an element of the actus reus of the offence charged *and* that offence is not one of strict liability as to that element.

8 Strict liability

8.1 In some exceptional offences the accused may be convicted although his conduct was neither intentional nor reckless nor negligent with reference to the requisite consequence of the offence charged, or although he did not have knowledge or act negligently in relation to a requisite circumstance, or although he acted under a reasonably mistaken belief that he had a defence applicable to the offence charged. In such a case, he is liable to punishment in the absence of any fault on his part and is said to be under strict liability (of which there are many critics), even though, as is usually the case, mens rea is required as to the other circumstances or consequences of the actus reus.[1]

1 Cf *Lemon* [1979] 1 All ER 898 at 906, 921 and 925.

8.2 One of the earliest and most important cases on the exceptions to the application of the doctrine of mens rea in statutory offences is *Prince*.[1] The charge was one of taking an unmarried girl under the age of 16 out of the possession of her father against his will, contrary to s 55 of the Offences against the Person Act 1861[2] (re-enacted by s 20 of the Sexual Offences Act 1956). Prince knew that the girl was in the custody of her father but he believed, on reasonable grounds, that she was 18. Had this been so, the offence would not have been committed; but Prince was held to have been rightly convicted since knowledge that the girl was under 16 was not required. The decision that such knowledge was not required was based variously on the views that, even on the facts as he supposed them to be, the accused's conduct would have been immoral,[3] or a tort against the father's parental rights,[4] and he took the risk that the girl was under the statutory age, and that a requirement of knowledge as to age would render the offence nugatory.[5] The court clearly took the view that an intention to take the girl out of the possession of her father was required to be proved, proof of which intention was not disputed. Although the contrary has been maintained,[6] *Prince* is distinguishable from *Hibbert*,[7] discussed above,[8] because Hibbert did not intend to take the girl he abducted from anybody's possession. The jury appear to have found that he did not have actual or constructive knowledge that she was in anybody's guardianship.

Most cases of strict liability are ones in which it has been held that ignorance or mistake, however reasonable, in relation to a particular element of the actus reus of an offence is no excuse since no mens rea need be proved as to that element. But there have been cases of strict liability where the courts have held that a reasonable mistake as to a matter of defence is no excuse. There have also been isolated instances in which the total absence of fault has been held to be no defence. In *Salter*[9] a bankrupt trader was held guilty of having failed to give a satisfactory explanation of his losses contrary to s 157(1)(c) of the Bankruptcy Act 1914,[10] although he might have done his best to provide full accounts. It was no defence for him to show that he had acted honestly and reasonably with regard to his explanations.

There are very few common law offences of strict liability; the list only includes public nuisance, blasphemous libel (and probably blasphemy), outraging public decency, certain areas of criminal contempt of court, and possibly criminal defamatory libel. However, for the most part it is in statutory offences that strict liability in criminal cases is imposed, normally as the result of the courts' interpretation of a particular statute.

1 (1875) LR 2 CCR 154.
2 Para 12.26.
3 Judgment of Bramwell B.
4 Judgment of Denman J.
5 Judgment of Blackburn J.
6 Stallybrass (1936) 52 LQR at 64.
7 (1869) LR 1 CCR 184.
8 Para 7.17.
9 [1968] 2 QB 793, [1968] 2 All ER 951, CA.
10 Repealed by the Insolvency Act 1985, Sch 10.

Strict liability at common law

8.3 a) *Public nuisance* A person may be vicariously liable, on a criminal charge, for a nuisance committed by those under his control although he did not know of its existence.[1] A public nuisance has been defined as an act not warranted by law, or the omission to discharge a legal duty, which obstructs or causes inconvenience or damage to the public in the exercise of rights common to all Her Majesty's subjects;[2] a section of the public must be so affected.[3] Typical examples are the obstruction of the highway or the emission of noise or smells from a factory in such a way as to cause serious inconvenience to the neighbourhood.

b) *Blasphemous libel* This offence is committed if a person publishes in a permanent form any matter attacking the Christian religion or the Bible, or the doctrine of the Church of England, or God, Christ or other persons sacred to the Christian religion, provided that the material is calculated to outrage and insult a Christian's religious feelings.[4] The accused must have intended to publish the material which was in fact blasphemous. However, in *Lemon*,[5] a majority of the House of Lords held that an intention to outrage and insult Christian believers (or any other type of mens rea in this respect) is not required. Despite the denials of those in the majority, it follows that the offence is one of strict liability to this extent. It may well be that the offence of blasphemy, which is committed by speaking matter of the above type, would also be held to be one of strict liability to the same extent.

c) *Outraging public decency* This offence requires proof of conduct of such a lewd, obscene or disgusting nature as to result in an outrage to public decency. It does not have to be proved that the accused intended his conduct to have the effect of outraging public decency or was reckless as to this (or, indeed, that he had any type of mens rea as to this).[6]

d) *Criminal contempt of court* Subject to various limitations, liability for contempt in relation to publications which interfere with the course of justice in particular proceedings is strict.[7]

e) *Criminal defamatory libel* This offence consists of the publication of defamatory matter in a permanent form concerning any individual or class of individuals, subject to the defence of justification (ie the truth of the publication), which is only available where publication was in the public interest, and to the defences of absolute and qualified privilege. An absolutely privileged publication includes a fair, accurate and contemporaneous report of judicial proceedings published in a newspaper and Parliamentary papers, while a publication has qualified privilege if, for instance, it is a report of Parliamentary proceedings or a professional communication between solicitor and client. In the law of tort, a person may, subject to a special statutory defence,[8] be liable in defamation although he did not know that that which he published was defamatory of another, as where someone says that a couple are engaged, when (unknown to him) the man is in fact married to a third person who complains that her reputation has been impugned.[9] If, on such facts, a criminal prosecution would be successful, the case would undoubtedly be one of strict liability, but there is no decision conclusively answering this point.[10]

1 *Stephens* (1866) LR 1 QB 702.
2 Stephen *Digest of Criminal Law* (9th edn) p 179.
3 *Madden* [1975] 3 All ER 155, [1975] 1 WLR 1379, CA.
4 *Lemon* [1979] AC 617, [1979] 1 All ER 898, HL. The law of blasphemy does not extend to religions other than Christianity: *Bow Street Magistrates' Court, ex p Choudhury* [1991] 1 All ER 306, DC.
5 [1979] AC 617, [1979] 1 All ER 898, HL.
6 *Gibson* [1991] 1 All ER 439, CA; para 19.25.
7 Para 16.13–16.18.
8 Defamation Act 1952, s 4.
9 *Cassidy v Daily Mirror Newspapers Ltd* [1929] 2 KB 331, CA.
10 For a brief review of some of the authorities, see Law Commission Report No 84: Criminal Libel, para 3.12.

Strict liability in statutory offences

8.4 Most of the statutory offences of strict liability arise under the regulatory legislation controlling such matters as the sale of food, the conduct of licensed premises and the use of false or misleading trade descriptions. Similarly, many of the offences in statutes regulating road traffic have been held to be of strict liability, as have certain financial provisions.

Strict liability in statutory offences normally results from the courts' refusal to read into a statutory provision which does not use a word like 'intentionally', 'recklessly' or 'knowingly' in relation to an element of the actus reus of a particular offence a requirement that mens rea in relation to it must be proved by the prosecution.

Where the statutory definition of an offence expressly requires the accused to have acted 'knowingly', knowledge is normally required as to all the circumstances of the actus reus prescribed by that definition. Thus, in relation to the statutory offence of knowingly permitting the use of premises as a sex establishment without a licence, the House of Lords held in *Westminster City Council v Croyalgrange Ltd*[1] that the accused must have knowledge not only of the premises' use as a sex establishment but also that that use is without a licence. However, the judicial interpretation of a particular statutory offence has occasionally deviated from the normal rule, as happened in 1902 in *Brooks v Mason*,[2] where the Divisional Court held that a person could be convicted of the statutory offence of knowingly delivering intoxicating liquor to a child under 14 except in a vessel sealed in the prescribed manner, even though he lacked knowledge that the vessel was not so sealed. It is submitted that it is most unlikely that a court today would hold that an express requirement of knowledge does not extend to all the prescribed circumstances of the actus reus of an offence.

As explained later,[3] some statutory offences are made subject by their parent statute to a defence whereby an accused is not guilty if he proves that he neither believed, nor suspected nor had reason to suspect that one or more of the specified elements of the offence existed. Where such a defence is provided in relation to a particular offence, its effect is to make it clear that the accused can be convicted even though no mens rea as to the specified element or elements is proved by the prosecution.

1 [1986] 2 All ER 353, [1986] 1 WLR 674, HL.
2 [1902] 2 KB 743, 72 LJKB 19, DC.
3 Para 8.22.

PRESUMPTION THAT MENS REA IS REQUIRED

8.5 It was stated by Lords Diplock and Fraser in *Sheppard* [1] in 1980 that in relatively recent years the climate of judicial opinion has grown less favourable to the recognition of strict liability offences.

In particular, the decision of the House of Lords in 1969 in *Sweet v Parsley*[2] indicated a significant shift in the judicial approach to statutory offences which do not clearly require mens rea by categorically re-affirming a principle which had increasingly appeared to be of little importance. This is the principle that, in interpreting a statutory provision which is silent on the point, there is a presumption that mens rea is required to be proved, unless this is rebutted by clear evidence that Parliament intended the contrary. In *Sweet v Parsley* the House of Lords (reversing the Divisional Court and overruling previous decisions of that court) held that a person could not be convicted of the offence of 'being concerned in the management of premises used for the purpose of smoking cannabis' in the absence of knowledge of such use, the presumption that mens rea was required not having been rebutted. (Parliament subsequently made the requirement of knowledge doubly sure by inserting the word 'knowingly' in the definition of the corresponding offence in the Misuse of Drugs Act 1971, which replaced the previous provision.)

The presumption that mens rea is required was again affirmed in 1984 by the Privy Council in *Gammon (Hong Kong) Ltd v A-G of Hong Kong*.[3]

1 [1981] AC 394, [1980] 3 All ER 899, HL.
2 [1970] AC 132, [1969] 1 All ER 347, HL.
3 [1985] AC 1, [1984] 2 All ER 503, PC. For a more recent reference in the House of Lords to the presumption, see *Court* [1988] 2 All ER 221 at 228, per Lord Ackner.

8.6 Despite what was said by Lords Diplock and Fraser in *Sheppard*, it would be wrong to leave the reader with the impression that there has been a massive reduction in recent years in the number of occasions on which the courts have held that an offence is one of strict liability. *Sweet v Parsley* was concerned with a drugs offence, and the shift of approach has clearly been maintained in relation to the more serious types of offence. In *Phekoo*,[1] for instance, the Court of Appeal held that the offence of harassment of a residential occupier (contrary to s 1(3) of the Protection from Eviction Act 1977) was not one of strict liability as to the fact that the person harassed was a residential occupier, and in *Sheppard*[2] the House of Lords, overruling well-established decisions to the opposite effect, held that the offence of wilful neglect of a child in a manner likely to cause him unnecessary suffering or injury to health was not one of strict liability as to the risk of suffering or injury to health.

However, as far as regulatory offences are concerned, the change of attitude towards strict liability revealed in *Sweet v Parsley* has had less effect. On a number of subsequent occasions, appellate courts, including the House of Lords in *Alphacell Ltd v Woodward*[3] and *Wings Ltd v Ellis*,[4] have paid little or no regard to the weight of this presumption in holding that, on the true interpretation of a statutory offence, Parliament intended to rule out the need for mens rea to be proved in relation to an element of its actus reus. Indeed, in *Champ*[5] the Court of Appeal stated, obiter, that the presumption may not always apply in the case of regulatory offences. Not the least of the objections to this statement is that the term 'regulatory offence' is a loose one; the Court of Appeal regarded the offence of cultivating cannabis (which is punishable with up to 14 years' imprisonment on conviction on indictment) as regulatory. It is submitted that the term must properly be limited to offences of the type mentioned at the beginning of para 8.4.

Despite the fact that the suggestion in the decision in *Sweet v Parsley* that any further expansion of strict liability would be closely scrutinised and confined with narrow limits has not wholly borne fruit, it nevertheless remains true that the general approach re-affirmed in *Sweet v Parsley*, and equally emphatically in *Gammon (Hong Kong) Ltd v A-G of Hong Kong*, has not been overruled and remains the correct approach to the interpretation of whether a statutory provision imposes strict liability.

1 [1981] 3 All ER 84, [1981] 1 WLR 1117, CA. The terms of the offence were amended by the Housing Act 1988, s 29.
2 [1981] AC 394, [1980] 3 All ER 899, HL.
3 [1972] AC 824, [1972] 2 All ER 475, HL.
4 [1985] AC 272, [1984] 1 All ER 1046, HL. The House of Lords held that s 14(1)(a) of the Trade Descriptions Act 1968, which makes it an offence for a person 'to make a statement which he knows to be false' is an offence of strict liability as to the making of the statement (but not as to its falsity). Two reasons were given: the denial of the need for proof of mens rea as to the making of the statement was consistent with the purpose of the statute, and there was available to the accused a no-negligence defence.
5 (1981) 73 Cr App Rep 367, [1982] Crim LR 108, CA.

REBUTTING THE PRESUMPTION

8.7 In *Gammon (Hong Kong) Ltd v A-G of Hong Kong*[1] Lord Scarman, giving the opinion of the Privy Council, said:

'In their Lordships' opinion, the law relevant to this appeal may be stated in the following propositions ... : (1) there is a presumption of law that mens rea is required before a person can be held guilty of a criminal offence; (2) the presumption is particularly strong where the offence is "truly criminal" in character; (3) the presumption applies to statutory offences, and can be displaced only if this is clearly or by necessary implication the effect of the statute; (4) the only situation in which the presumption can be displaced is where the statute is concerned with an issue of social concern; public safety is such an issue; (5) even where a statute is concerned with such an issue, the presumption of mens rea stands unless it can also be shown that the creation of strict liability will be effective to promote the objects of the statute by encouraging greater vigilance to prevent the commission of the prohibited act'.[2]

In deciding whether the effect of the statutory provision is 'clearly or by necessary implication' to rebut the presumption that mens rea is required in respect of the elements of the offence, the court will be seeking to discover Parliament's intention, evidence of which is provided by the words of the statute, various extrinsic factors and whether strict liability would promote the object of the provision.[3] Of course, once an authoritative interpretation of a statutory provision has been given, it will be applicable in subsequent cases, subject to the rules of precedent.

1 [1985] AC 1, [1984] 2 All ER 503 at 508.
2 Applied in *Wings Ltd v Ellis* [1985] AC 272, [1984] 3 All ER 577, HL; *Wells Street Stipendiary Magistrate, ex p Westminster City Council* [1986] 3 All ER 4, [1986] 1 WLR 1046, DC.
3 *Sweet v Parsley* [1970] AC 132 at 163, per Lord Diplock; *Gammon (Hong Kong) Ltd v A-G of Hong Kong* [1985] AC 1, [1984] 2 All ER 503, PC; *Wings Ltd v Ellis.*

WORDS OF THE STATUTE

8.8   Certain words which commonly appear in statutory offences have been considered by appellate courts on a sufficient number of occasions as to indicate whether they are likely to be held to support or rebut the presumption that mens rea is required. Examples of such words are as follows:

8.9   *'Permitting'* or *'suffering'*   There are a substantial number of statutory offences of 'permitting' or 'suffering' (which terms have been held to be synonymous)[1] a particular thing to be done by another, and it has been said that 'It is of the very essence of the offence of permitting someone to do something that there should be knowledge'.[2] However, while it is nearly always the case that an offence of 'permitting' or 'suffering' will be interpreted as requiring mens rea as to *all* the elements of its actus reus,[3] there continue to be isolated exceptions in relation to the interpretation of particular offences.[4]

1 *Somerset v Wade* [1894] 1 QB 574, 63 LJMC 126, DC; *Ferguson v Weaving* [1951] 1 KB 814, [1951] 1 All ER 412, DC.
2 *Gray's Haulage Co Ltd v Arnold* [1966] 1 All ER 896 at 898, per Lord Parker CJ.
3 *James & Son Ltd v Smee* [1955] 1 QB 78, [1954] 3 All ER 273, DC (described in para 6.59); *Fransman v Sexton* [1965] Crim LR 556, DC; *Gray's Haulage Co Ltd v Arnold* [1966] 1 All ER 896, [1966] 1 WLR 534, DC; *Souter* [1971] 2 All ER 1151, [1971] 1 WLR 1187, CA; *Knowles Transport Ltd v Russell* [1975] RTR 87, DC; *Thomas and Thompson* (1976) 63 Cr App Rep 65, CA; *Licensing Authority for Goods Vehicles in Metropolitan Traffic Area v Coggins* (1985) Times, 28 February, DC.
4 *Lyons v May* [1948] 2 All ER 1062, DC; *Baugh v Crago* [1975] RTR 453, DC; *Ferrymasters Ltd v Adams* [1980] RTR 139, [1980] Crim LR 187, DC; *Cheshire County Council Trading Standards Dept, ex p Alan Helliwell & Sons (Bolton) Ltd* [1991] Crim LR 210, DC.

8.10   *'Wilfully'*   The appearance of the adverb 'wilfully' in a statutory offence might be thought clearly to indicate a requirement of mens rea as to all the elements of its actus reus but the courts have not always been willing to accept such an indication.[1] In *Cotterill v Penn*,[2] for example, the Divisional Court held that the offence of unlawfully and wilfully killing a house pigeon, contrary to s 23 of the Larceny Act 1861 (which has now been repealed), merely required that the accused should intend to do the act forbidden, which was that of shooting at the bird in that case, and did not also require that he should realise that what he was shooting at was a house pigeon, so that a belief that it was a wild pigeon was immaterial. However, in more recent years the prevalent, but by no means invariable,[3] judicial approach has been to interpret 'wilfully' so as to require mens rea as to all the elements of the actus reus.[4] A particularly important decision is that of the House of Lords in 1980 in *Sheppard*[5] which was concerned with s 1 of the Children and Young Persons Act 1933. This makes it an offence where someone having the responsibility for a child or young person under 16 'wilfully assaults, ill-treats, neglects, abandons or exposes him . . . in a manner likely to cause unnecessary suffering or injury to health'. By a majority of three to two, the House of Lords, overruling previous decisions to the contrary, held that in the offence of wilfully *neglecting* under s 1 there was an element of mens rea as to the relevant risk and that, where the charge involved failure to provide adequate medical aid, the requirement of wilfulness could only be satisfied where the accused was aware the child's health might be at risk if it was not provided with medical aid or where his unawareness of this fact was due to his not caring whether the child's health was at risk or not. The requirement of mens rea as to the relevant risk made in *Sheppard* was made solely in relation to 'wilfully neglects' but there can be little doubt that it will be held to apply to 'wilfully assaults, ill-treats, abandons or exposes' in s 1 of the 1933 Act.

1 Andrews 'Wilfulness: a lesson in ambiguity' (1981) 1 *Legal Studies* 303.
2 [1936] 1 KB 53, 105 LJKB 1, DC.
3 See *Maidstone Borough Council v Mortimer* [1980] 3 All ER 552, DC, for one modern example of an offence which was interpreted as one of strict liability despite the use of the word 'wilfully.' Another example is provided by the case law on the offence of perjury: paras 16.7 and 16.8.
4 See, for example, *Eaton v Cobb* [1950] 1 All ER 1016, DC; *Bullock v Turnbull* [1952] 2 Lloyd's Rep 303, DC; *Gittins* [1982] RTR 363, CA.
5 [1981] AC 394, [1980] 3 All ER 899, HL.

8.11 '*Cause*' Some statutory offences are framed in terms of causing something to happen (e g the pollution of a river) or of causing someone to do something (e g to drive a mechanically defective motor vehicle). 'Cause' requires some positive act by the accused which results in the prohibited occurrence (e g filling a holding tank with a pollutant which then leaks into a river or telling a junior employee to drive a defective vehicle).[1] A mere acquiescence in the prohibited occurrence (e g where the accused stands by and watches it occur) is not enough.[2]

Where a statutory offence is defined simply in terms of causing something to happen, the courts are very likely to interpret it as an offence of strict liability as to the occurrence of that thing. An example is provided by *Alphacell Ltd v Woodward*,[3] whose facts are set out in para 8.14. On the other hand, where the offence is defined in terms of causing someone else to do something, 'cause'[4] is likely to be interpreted as requiring mens rea as to the thing being done.[5]

1 *Price v Cromack* [1975] 2 All ER 113, [1975] 1 WLR 988, DC; *Redhead Freight Ltd v Shulman* [1989] RTR 1, DC.
2 Ibid. Often an offence of 'causing' is accompanied by an offence of 'permitting' the prohibited occurrence; mere acquiescence is, of course, 'permitting'.
3 [1972] AC 824, [1972] 2 All ER 475, HL.
4 D 'causes' someone else to do something if it is done on the actual authority, express or implied, of D or in consequence of D exerting some influence on the acts of the other person: *A-G of Hong Kong v Tse Hung-Lit* [1986] AC 876, [1986] 3 All ER 173, PC.
5 *Lovelace v DPP* [1954] 3 All ER 481, [1954] 1 WLR 1468, DC; *Ross Hillman Ltd v Bond* [1974] QB 435, [1974] 2 All ER 287, DC. Contrast *Sopp v Long* [1970] 1 QB 518, [1969] 1 All ER 855, DC.

8.12 *Wording of other offences in statute* Another way in which the wording of the statute can be important is that the appearance in the definition of other offences in the statute of words such as 'knowingly' is likely to lead to a finding that mens rea is not required in relation to an element or elements of the offence in question, although, as is shown by a comparison of *Cundy v Le Cocq*[1] (and similar cases) and *Sherras v De Rutzen*,[2] this will not necessarily be so.

The former case concerned the offence under s 13 of the Licensing Act 1872 (re-enacted by s 172(3) of the Licensing Act 1964) of sale by a publican of liquor to a drunken person. It was held that the accused licensee's belief, even if founded on reasonable grounds, in the sobriety of his customer was no defence. This conclusion was reached in the light of the general scope of the Act, which was for the repression of drunkenness, and of a comparison of the various sections in the relevant part of the Act, some of which, unlike the section in question, contained the word 'knowingly'. The same conclusion as in *Cundy v Le Cocq* was reached by the Divisional Court in *Neville v Mavroghenis*,[3] where contrasting provisions actually appeared in two limbs of the same sub-section, one limb requiring the accused to have acted 'knowingly' and the other containing no such word; it was held that the offence in the latter limb was one of strict liability. Another decision to like effect is *Pharmaceutical Society of Great Britain v Storkwain Ltd*,[4] which was concerned with the offence of supplying specified medicinal products except in accordance with a prescription by an appropriate practitioner, contrary to s 58(2)(a) of the Medicines Act 1968. The House of Lords relied principally on the fact that other offence-creating provisions in the Act expressly required mens rea in holding that the presumption that mens rea was required was rebutted in relation to s 58(2)(a), which did not make such express provision. Consequently, it upheld the conviction under s 58(2)(a) of pharmacists who had supplied drugs after being given forged prescriptions which they believed to be genuine.

In *Sherras v De Rutzen* a licensee had supplied liquor to a police officer who was on duty, contrary to s 16(2) of the Licensing Act 1872 (re-enacted by s 178(b) of the Licensing Act 1964). The licensee reasonably believed that the officer was off duty because he had removed his armlet which at that time, to the knowledge of the licensee, was worn by police officers in the locality when on duty. The licensee was convicted by the magistrates but his conviction was quashed on appeal, the Divisional Court holding that the licensee could not be convicted if he did not know that the police officer was on duty, even though the other subsection of the section in question used the word 'knowingly'.

One of the two judges in *Sherras v de Rutzen* (Day J) held that the effect of the appearance of 'knowingly' in s 16(1), and its absence in s 16(2), of the Licensing Act 1872 did have some effect, since it had the effect of shifting the burden of proof onto the accused in the latter provision. Consequently, while the prosecution had to prove the relevant knowledge on a charge under s 16(1), under s 16(2) it was for the accused to prove that he did not know that the police officer was on duty. In *Harding v Price*,[5] which was concerned with the offence of failing to report an accident, contrary to what is now s 170 of the Road Traffic Act 1988, one of the three judges (Singleton J) held that the absence of a word like 'knowingly' from the definition of the offence meant that, once it was proved that the accused had committed the actus reus of the offence, he was guilty unless he proved that he was unaware that an accident had occurred. However, this approach has been dis-approved in a number of more recent cases,[6] although in an even more recent case[7] (concerning s 170 of the Road Traffic Act 1988) it was followed.

1 (1884) 13 QBD 207, 53 LJMC 125, DC.
2 [1895] 1 QB 918, 64 LJMC 218, DC.
3 [1984] Crim LR 42, DC. Also see *Kirkland v Robinson* (1986) 151 JP 377, DC.
4 [1986] 2 All ER 635, [1986] 1 WLR 903, HL.
5 [1948] 1 KB 695, [1948] 1 All ER 283, DC.
6 *Roper v Taylor's Central Garages (Exeter) Ltd* [1951] 2 TLR 284, per Devlin J; *Lim Chin Aik v R* [1963] AC 160, [1963] 1 All ER 223, PC; *Warner v Metropolitan Police Comr* [1969] 2 AC 256 at 303, per Lord Pearce.
7 *Selby v Chief Constable of Avon and Somerset* [1988] RTR 216, DC.

EXTRINSIC FACTORS

8.13 Where no clear indication of Parliament's intention is given by the words of the statute, the courts will go outside the Act and examine all the relevant circumstances to determine whether Parliament intended to dis-place the need for mens rea. The following are among these circumstances:

8.14 *The subject-matter of the enactment* In many cases this is the only extrinsic factor referred to by the court in deciding whether the presumption is rebutted. An offence is more likely to be construed as one of strict liability if it falls within the three classes enumerated by Wright J, in *Sherras v De Rutzen*:[1]

'Apart from isolated and extreme cases [such as *Prince*], the principal classes of exceptions [to the general rule that mens rea is required] may perhaps be reduced to three. One is a class of acts which, in the language of Lush J, in *Davies v Harvey*,[2] are not criminal in any real sense, but are acts which in the public interest are prohibited under a penalty. Several such instances are to be found in the decisions on the Revenue Statutes, eg *A-G v Lockwood*,[3] where the innocent possession of liquorice by a beer retailer was held to be an offence. So under the Adulteration Acts, *Woodrow*[4] as to innocent possession of adulterated tobacco; *Fitzpatrick v Kelly*[5] and *Roberts v Egerton*[6] as to the sale of adulterated food ... to the same head may be referred *Bishop*[7] where a person was held rightly convicted of receiving lunatics in an unlicensed house, although the jury found that he honestly and on reasonable grounds believed that they were not lunatics. Another class comprehends some, and perhaps all, public nuisances ... Lastly, there may be cases in which, although the proceeding is criminal in form, it is really only a summary mode of enforcing a civil right: see per Williams and Willes JJ in *Morden v Porter*,[8] as to unintentional trespass in pursuit of game ... But except in such cases as these, there must in general be guilty knowledge on the part of the defendant ...'

This dictum was referred to by the House of Lords in *Alphacell Ltd v Woodward*,[9] where the accused company, whose settling tanks overflowed into a river, was held to have been rightly convicted of causing polluted matter to enter a river contrary to the Rivers (Prevention of Pollution) Act 1951, despite the fact that there was no evidence that it knew that pollution was taking place from its settling tanks or had been in any way negligent. In construing the offence as one of strict liability, Viscount Dilhorne and Lord Salmon regarded the statute as dealing with acts falling within the first class, ie acts which 'are not criminal in any real sense, but are acts which in the public interest are prohibited under a penalty', while Lord Pearson thought that the offence fell within the second class enumerated, saying 'mens rea is generally not a necessary ingredient in an offence of this kind which is in the nature of a public nuisance'.[10]

The first of Wright J's three classes is particularly important since it covers many statutes regulating particular activities involving potential danger to public health or safety which a person may choose to undertake, such as those relating to the sale of food and drink (including alcohol), pollution, dangerous substances and the condition and use of vehicles. The fact that an offence is not truly criminal is often given by a court as a reason (or one of the reasons) for concluding that it is one of strict liability.[11] In contrast, as Lord Scarman said in the *Gammon* case, the presumption of mens rea is particularly strong where the offence is 'truly criminal' in character.[12] All this prompts one to ask what the criteria of 'true criminality' are.

1 [1895] 1 QB 918 at 921.
2 (1874) LR 9 QB 433, 43 LJMC 121.
3 (1842) 9 M & W 378.
4 (1846) 15 M & W 404, 16 LJMC 122.
5 (1873) LR 8 QB 337, 42 LJMC 132.
6 (1874) LR 9 QB 494, 43 LJMC 135.
7 (1880) 5 QBD 259, 49 LJMC 45.
8 (1860) 7 CB NS 641, 29 LJMC 213.
9 [1972] AC 824, [1972] 2 All ER 475, HL.
10 [1972] AC at 842.
11 See, for example, *Chilvers v Rayner* [1984] 1 All ER 843 at 847, per Robert Goff LJ.
12 Para 8.7.

8.15 *The mischief of the crime* In offences which are aimed at the prevention of some particularly serious social danger, such as inflation or pollution, the need for mens rea is particularly likely to be displaced. This is illustrated by *St Margaret's Trust Ltd*[1] where the accused finance company was charged with offences against the Hire-Purchase and Credit Sales Agreements (Control) Order 1956, article 1 of which prohibited a person from disposing of any goods in pursuance of a hire-purchase agreement unless 50 per cent of the cash price had been paid. This requirement was not satisfied in the case of a number of hire-purchase transactions relating to motor cars because, although the company had acted innocently, it had been misled as to the true cash price and had been informed that the requisite 50 per cent had been paid. The Court of Criminal Appeal dismissed the company's appeal against conviction, holding that the offence was one of strict liability. Donovan J had this to say about the mischief of the offence:

'The object of the order was to help to defend the currency against the peril of inflation which, if unchecked, would bring disaster on the country. There is no need to elaborate this. The present generation has witnessed the collapse of the currency in other countries and the consequent chaos, misery and widespread ruin. It would not be at all surprising if Parliament, determined to prevent similar calamities here, enacted measures which it intended to be absolute prohibitions of acts which might increase the risk in however small a degree. Indeed, that would be the natural expectation. There would be little point in enacting that no one should breach the defences against a flood, and at the same time excusing anyone who did it innocently. For these reasons we think that art. 1 of the order should receive a literal construction [under which mens rea was not required].'[2]

1 [1958] 2 All ER 289, [1958] 1 WLR 522, CCA. Also see *Howells* [1977] QB 614, [1977] 3 All ER 417, CA.

2 [1958] 2 All ER 289 at 293.

8.16 *The maximum punishment* Not surprisingly, this is a factor to be taken into account in interpreting the statute, as was pointed out by Lord Pearce in *Sweet v Parsley*[1] and by the Court of Appeal in *Phekoo*.[2] If the offence is punishable with imprisonment, particularly if the maximum term is severe, this suggests that Parliament cannot have intended it to be one of strict liability, partly because it can hardly be said to be concerned with acts 'which are not criminal in any real sense'. Nevertheless, on occasions the courts have construed such offences as not requiring mens rea. In *Warner v Metropolitan Police Comr*[3] the offence of unauthorised possession of drugs was held not to require proof that the accused knew that what he was in possession of was a drug, despite the fact that the offence in question was punishable with a maximum of two years' imprisonment, and could, if the drug had been of a different type, have been punished with a maximum of ten years. (The law on this subject has been changed since *Warner*.)[4] Similarly, in *Howells*[5] and *Bradish*[6] the offences of possessing a firearm without a certificate (*Howells*) and of possessing a prohibited weapon (*Bradish*) were held to be ones of strict liability as to their circumstances that the article possessed was respectively a firearm and a prohibited weapon, although the maximum punishment on conviction on indictment for the former offence is three, or in some cases five, years' imprisonment, and for the latter offence five years. Again, the offence of abduction in *Prince*[7] is punishable with two years' imprisonment, as are the offences of which the accused in *Salter* and in *Pharmaceutical Society of Great Britain v Storkwain Ltd*[8] were convicted.

1 [1970] AC 132 at 156.
2 [1981] 3 All ER 84, [1981] 1 WLR 1117, CA.
3 [1969] 2 AC 256, [1968] 2 All ER 356, HL.
4 Para 8.22.
5 [1977] QB 614, [1977] 3 All ER 417, CA. See also *Hussain* [1981] 2 All ER 287, [1981] 1 WLR 416, CA.
6 [1990] 1 QB 981, [1990] 1 All ER 460, CA.
7 Para 8.2.
8 Paras 8.2 and 8.12.

WHETHER STRICT LIABILITY WOULD ASSIST THE ENFORCEMENT OF THE LAW

8.17 In *Gammon (Hong Kong) Ltd v A-G of Hong Kong*[1] Lord Scarman, giving the Privy Council's opinion, said that, even where a statute is concerned with an issue of social concern, the presumption of mens rea stands unless it can be shown that strict liability will be effective to promote the objects of the statute by encouraging greater vigilance to prevent the commission of the prohibited act. This is a point which had been previously developed by the Privy Council in *Lim Chin Aik v R*,[2] a case concerned with Singapore immigration regulations, where it was said not to be enough merely to label the statute before the court as one dealing with a grave social evil, and from that to infer that strict liability was intended. It is also necessary to inquire whether putting the accused under strict liability will assist the enforcement of the law. There must be something he could do 'directly or indirectly, by supervision or inspection, by improvement of his business methods or by exhorting those whom he may be expected to influence or control, which will promote the observance of the regulations . . . Where it can be shown that the imposition of strict liability would result in the prosecution and conviction of a class of persons whose conduct would not in any way affect the observance of the law, their Lordships consider that, even where the statute is dealing with a grave social evil, strict liability is not likely to be intended'.[3] Lim Chin Aik had been convicted under the Singapore Immigration Ordinance which makes it an offence for someone prohibited from entering Singapore to enter or remain there. He had been prohibited from entering Singapore, but the prohibition had not been published or made known to him. The Privy Council advised that his conviction should be quashed on account of the futility of imposing punishment in such a case.

1 Para 8.7.
2 [1963] AC 160, [1963] 1 All ER 223, PC.
3 [1963] AC 160 at 174–175. See also *Reynolds v G H Austin & Sons Ltd* [1951] 2 KB 135 at 150, [1951] 1 All ER 606 at 612, per Devlin J.

HOW STRICT IS STRICT LIABILITY?

8.18 Strict liability is sometimes spoken of as 'absolute liability' and the corresponding expressions of 'absolute prohibition' and 'absolute offences' are occasionally used. They are, however, like 'absolute liability' open to the suggestion that no defences are available to the accused. Certainly, the wording of some so-called 'status offences', such as that in issue in *Larsonneur*,[1] may lead to such a conclusion.

In *Larsonneur* D, an alien who had not got leave to land in the United Kingdom, was deported from Eire. She was brought to England under police custody, and was 'found', still in custody, in a cell at Holyhead. She was convicted of an offence under orders made under the Aliens Restriction Acts, according to which it was an offence for an alien, to whom leave to land in the United Kingdom had been refused, to be found in any place within the United Kingdom.[2] D appealed unsuccessfully against conviction, the Court of Criminal Appeal taking the view that she came precisely within the wording of the relevant order, and it is a matter of speculation whether she might not equally have been held guilty if she had been insane, or if she had mistakenly believed that she was not an alien, or even if she had been parachuted from an aeroplane against her will.

In *Winzar v Chief Constable of Kent*,[3] decided in 1983, the Divisional Court evinced the same attitude as in *Larsonneur*. D was taken to hospital on a stretcher. The doctor discovered that he was drunk and he was told to leave. Later, he was seen slumped on a seat in a corridor. The police were called and they removed him to their car in the highway. D's conviction of the offence, under s 12 of the Licensing Act 1872, of being found drunk in a highway was affirmed by the Divisional Court. Such cases are most exceptional, because very few offences are defined in the same way as those with which Mlle Larsonneur and Mr Winzar were charged, ie in terms of 'being found'.

However, apart from such rare offences, most of the general defences of the criminal law (some of which are discussed in the next chapter, while others are discussed later)[4] are available to a person accused of an offence of strict liability. It is very doubtful, to say the least, whether there are any offences, except those whose wording is similar to that of the offence in *Larsonneur*, to which the general defences of insanity, duress by threat or of

116

circumstances, compulsion and automatism would not apply. Not the least of the troubles about strict liability is that no one knows how strict it is.

1 (1933) 149 LT 542, CCA. For a defence of this decision, see Lanham '*Larsonneur* revisited' [1976] Crim LR 276.
2 This offence has since been repealed.
3 (1983) Times, 28 March, DC.
4 See Ch 22.

THE JUSTIFICATION FOR STRICT LIABILITY

8.19   One justification for strict liability is that the commission of many regulatory offences is very harmful to the public and, it being very difficult to prove that the accused had acted with mens rea as to all the elements of the actus reus, such offences would often go unpunished and the legislation rendered nugatory.[1] Again, it is sometimes said that too many bogus defences would succeed if excusable ignorance or mistake were always accepted as defences. It is also argued that the great pressure of work upon the minor criminal courts nowadays makes it impractical to inquire into mens rea in each prosecution for a regulatory offence.[2] Moreover, it is urged that the imposition of strict liability does something towards ensuring that the controllers of business organisations do everything possible to see that important welfare regulations are carried out.[3] Repeated convictions may discourage or oblige the incompetent to refrain from certain undertakings and ensure that the competent stay competent.

There are many who remain unconvinced by these arguments[4] and who reply that the fact that the prosecution may find proof of mens rea as to a particular element or elements of the actus reus difficult is of itself no reason for depriving the accused of his customary safeguards. They argue, in any event, that it does not follow that, even if proof of mens rea is impossible in certain types of cases, the only solution is to go to the other extreme by denying that the accused's mental state is relevant to the question of responsibility, since there are other possibilities such as a defence of no-negligence. They add that it is improper to jettison the requirement of mens rea simply to facilitate the flow of judicial business, that the courts' time is taken up anyway by considerations of mens rea in determining sentence, and that anyway it is not a satisfactory answer to say that it is always possible to subject the offender to a small fine (or even to grant him an absolute discharge). In addition, they point out that strict liability cannot make an improvement in the systems of those who infringe regulatory legislation despite taking all possible care to avoid doing so.

1 *Alphacell Ltd v Woodward* [1972] AC 824 at 839 and 848, [1972] 2 All ER 475 at 483 and 491, per Viscount Dilhorne and Lord Salmon.
2 Sayre 33 *Columbia Law Review* at 69.
3 *Alphacell Ltd v Woodward* [1972] AC 824 at 848, [1972] 2 All ER 475 at 491; Smith and Pearson 'The Value of Strict Liability' [1969] Crim LR 5.
4 For instance, Howard *Strict Responsibility* 9–28.

8.20   To those who remain unconvinced by the arguments for strict liability the following developments are particularly welcome:

  a) the re-affirmation in *Sweet v Parsley* of the presumption in construing a criminal statute that mens rea is required, although, as the subsequent cases of *Alphacell Ltd v Woodward* and *Pharmaceutical Society of Great Britain v Storkwain Ltd* show, the House of Lords is still prepared to construe a statute in such a way as to impose strict liability;

b) the increase in the number of statutes providing 'no-negligence' and other defences; and

c) the provisions in the draft Criminal Code Bill.

STATUTORY DEFENCES

8.21 Since the purpose of many offences of strict liability is to catch the person who negligently performs an activity, it is odd that the courts have interpreted as imposing strict liability statutes which catch the person who took reasonable care as well as the one who did not. The injustice involved is increasingly being mitigated in statutory offences by the provision of defences. The most common examples are 'no-negligence' defences. It must be emphasized that there is no general 'no-negligence' defence. Instead, a statutory offence is only subject to such a defence if the statute in question expressly creates it and applies it to that offence.

8.22 A 'no-negligence' defence is one whereby a burden is placed on the accused of proving that he had no knowledge of, and was not negligent as to, a particular element of the offence. An example is provided by s 28 of the Misuse of Drugs Act 1971, which applies to offences of possession of a controlled drug and certain other drugs-related offences.[1] The section provides that the accused shall be acquitted if he proves that he neither believed, nor suspected, nor had reason to suspect, that the substance he possessed was a controlled drug, although it is not generally a defence for him to show that he neither knew, nor suspected, nor had reason to suspect, that the drug was the particular controlled drug it was alleged to be.[2]

Another example of a 'no-negligence' defence is s 24(1) of the Trade Descriptions Act 1968, which provides the accused with a defence if he proves that the commission of an offence under the Act was due to a mistake, or to reliance on information supplied to him or to the act or default of another person, an accident or some other cause beyond his control, and that he exercised due diligence to avoid committing the offence in question.

A third example of a 'no-negligence' defence is provided by s 34 of the Weights and Measures Act 1985, which provides that it is a defence for a person charged with an offence under Part IV of the Act to prove that he took all reasonable precautions and exercised all due diligence to avoid the commission of the offence.[3]

Such defences solve the problems of proof of mens rea urged by the supporters of strict liability.

1 Para 19.32.
2 Para 19.25. For other similar examples, see Video Recordings Act 1984, ss 10–14, and paras 12.12, 12.13, 12.19, 12.26, 12.28, and 17.13–17.16.
3 Similar examples of this provision are provided by the Consumer Safety Act 1978, s 2; Anatomy Act 1984, s 11, Building Societies Act 1986, s 112, Banking Act 1987, s 96, Consumer Protection Act 1987, s 39, and Food Safety Act 1990, s 21.

PROPOSALS FOR REFORM

8.23 In *Sweet v Parsley* Lords Reid and Pearce suggested a 'halfway house'[1] based on their understanding[2] of the Australian solution to the problems engendered by regulatory offences, whereby statutory offences which appear at first sight to be offences of strict liability would be construed as subject to the defence that the accused acted under an honest and reasonable belief in a state of facts which, if they existed, would make his conduct innocent, the burden of proving this being on the accused. The effect of this suggestion would be to provide a general no-negligence defence. However, like the existing specific no-negligence defences mentioned above, this suggestion is open to the objection that the burden of proving his innocence is on the accused.

This objection does not apply to Lord Diplock's solution which he put forward in *Sweet v Parsley*.[3] His Lordship said:

> 'Even where the words used to describe the prohibited conduct would not in any other context connote the necessity for any particular mental element, they are nevertheless to be read as subject to the implication that a necessary element in the offence is the absence of a belief, held honestly and upon reasonable grounds, in the existence of facts which, if true, would make the act innocent.'

Lord Diplock went on to say that the accused did not bear the burden of proving such a mistake, although the burden of adducing evidence of it was borne by him. The adoption of the course taken by Lord Diplock is already open to the courts if they choose to construe a statutory offence in the way, for example, that the offence of bigamy has been construed in *Tolson*[4] and other cases, but they have not chosen it frequently. Its adoption as a general principle of construction of criminal statutes would be welcomed by opponents of strict liability.

1 [1970] AC at 150 and 158.
2 Brett 'Strict Responsibility: Possible Solutions' (1974) 37 MLR 417 argues that the Australian cases were misunderstood by their Lordships.
3 [1970] AC at 163.
4 Para 7.32.

8.24   The draft Criminal Code Bill,[1] essentially adopting recommendations made in 1978 by the Law Commission,[2] provides that, in relation to any offence in the Code (if it is ever enacted) and to any offence subsequently created, there is a presumption that liability depends on fault of the degree of recklessness (ie subjective recklessness) in relation to all the elements of the offence. The presumption would be rebuttable only if the statutory provision expressly or by necessary implication indicated the contrary. This would occur where there was expressly or by necessary implication an indication:

a)   that some other fault element was required in respect of an element of the offence; or
b)   that no fault was required in respect of such an element; or
c)   that a person would not commit the offence if in relation to such an element he had or did not have a specified state of mind or complied with a specified standard of conduct.

1 Law Commission: A Criminal Code for England and Wales (1989): Law Com No 177, cl 20 and paras 8.25–8.28.
2 Report on the Mental Element in Crime, Law Com No 89.

8.25   The enactment of provisions along the lines of the draft Code would, by giving it statutory force, strengthen further the existing common law presumption that mens rea is required as to the elements of the actus reus of an offence. It would also make it clear that the mens rea presumed to be required to be proved is a subjective one; something that the common law presumption does not do. It is, however, unfortunate that under the draft Code, the presumption that subjective recklessness was required would be rebuttable not only by an express indication in the statutory provision but also by a *necessarily implied* indication in it.

8.25 *Strict liability*

There would have been even greater certainty if the draft Code provided that, unless a statutory provision expressly opted for liability based on negligence or for strict liability, the necessary mental element as to the requirements of an offence would be a subjective one. References to 'necessary implication' can be found in formulations of the common law presumption,[1] and the ease with which the courts have on occasion found that that presumption is rebutted means that one cannot be wholly confident that the draft Code will be as effective in this respect as intended.

1 See, for example, para 8.7.

8.26 It must be emphasised again that the above provisions of the draft Criminal Code would not apply to pre-Code offences.

9 Capacity

Children

9.1 It is irrebuttably presumed that no child under the age of 10 years can be guilty of an offence.[1] Such a child is said to be *doli incapax* (not capable of crime). At common law the age of immunity from responsibility was seven. It was raised to eight by statute in 1933 and, again by statute, to 10 in 1963.

1 Children and Young Persons Act 1933, s 50, as amended by the Children and Young Persons Act 1963, s 16. The draft Criminal Code Bill, cl 32(1), expresses this rule (Law Commission: A Criminal Code for England and Wales (1989): Law Com No 177; see para 3.21 above).

9.2 The common law lays down a special rule concerning children of 10 years or over but under the age of 14. They are presumed to be incapable of committing an offence, but this presumption may be rebutted by proof of a 'mischievous discretion', ie knowledge that what was done was seriously wrong.[1] Thus, a child aged between 10 and 14 can be convicted only if the prosecution proves beyond reasonable doubt that he committed the actus reus with mens rea[2] and knew he was doing something seriously wrong.[3] In relation to this last requirement, it is not enough merely to prove that the child realised that what he was doing was naughty or mischievous.[4] On the other hand, it is not necessary to prove that the accused appreciated that he was doing something morally wrong, although that may be one way of proving that he appreciated that what he was doing was seriously wrong.[5]

In *Gorrie*[6] a boy of 13 jabbed another boy with a penknife and caused his death. He was charged with manslaughter and the jury was directed that it was not sufficient to prove the presence of such a state of mind as would suffice in the case of a person of 14 or over; it was necessary to go further and prove that, when the boy did the act, he knew he was doing what was wrong – not merely what was wrong but what was gravely wrong, seriously wrong. Another illustration is provided by *J M (a minor) v Runeckles*.[7] D, aged 13 and of apparently normal intelligence, had a discussion with another girl and then followed her home. She knocked at the door and, when the girl opened it, threw a milk bottle at her. D then hit the girl with the bottle, which had broken, and stabbed her with it. Dismissing D's appeal against a finding of guilt for assault occasioning actual bodily harm, the Divisional Court held that the juvenile court was entitled to conclude from the evidence that D had appreciated that what she was doing was seriously wrong and therefore had mischievous discretion.

The evidence in rebuttal of the presumption of incapability may consist of evidence as to the child's home background and upbringing,[8] his conduct after the offence,[9] his replies to police questioning,[10] his conduct and demeanour in court,[11] his mental capacity[11] and any previous convictions relevant to whether he knew he was doing wrong.[12]

It is open to question whether any useful purpose is served by the rebuttable presumption of incapability to commit crime in the case of children between 10 and 14,[13] but it is retained by cl 32(2) of the draft Criminal Code Bill.

1 *Owen* (1830) 4 C & P 236; *Gorrie* (1918) 83 JP 136; *J M (a minor) v Runeckles* (1984) 79 Cr App Rep 255, DC.
2 The requirement of mens rea is no different from that for adults; no allowance is made for youth (see, for example, para 6.49).
3 *Gorrie* (1918) 83 JP 136; *J M (a minor) v Runeckles* (1984) 79 Cr App Rep 255, DC.
4 *J M (a minor) v Runeckles*; *IPH v Chief Constable of South Wales* [1987] Crim LR 42, DC.
5 *J M (a minor) v Runeckles* (1984) 79 Cr App Rep 255, DC.
6 (1918) 83 JP 136.
7 (1984) 79 Cr App Rep 255, DC.
8 *B v R* (1958) 44 Cr App Rep 1, DC.
9 *T v DPP* [1989] Crim LR 498, DC. The mere fact that a child runs away after the offence cannot in itself rebut the presumption since a 'merely naughty' child would run away even if what he had done was in no way criminal but simply a breach of some school or parental rule; therefore it cannot in itself constitute proof of knowledge that he was doing something seriously wrong: *A v DPP* [1992] Crim LR 34, DC.
10 *T v DPP*.
11 *J B H and J H (minors) v O'Connell* [1981] Crim LR 632, DC; *J M (a minor) v Runeckles* (1984) 79 Cr App Rep 255, DC.
12 *B* [1979] 3 All ER 460, [1979] 1 WLR 1185, CA. Evidence of previous convictions is not normally admissible in a criminal trial and may have a considerable prejudicial effect.
13 Arguments for and against the rebuttable presumption are neatly summarised by Manchester (1986) 150 JPN 6 at 9. Also see [1985] Crim LR 173.

9.3 Boys under 14 are irrebuttably presumed incapable of sexual intercourse or buggery and thus cannot be convicted, as perpetrators, on charges of rape,[1] other offences involving sexual intercourse or buggery.[2] In *Waite*,[3] for instance, it was held that a boy under 14 could not be convicted of having sexual intercourse with a girl under 13. It has not yet been decided whether such a boy can be convicted of attempting to commit an offence involving sexual intercourse, if he succeeds in having intercourse or attempts to do so; the reported dicta are divided on the point.[4] Youthful sexual athletes should, however, be warned that in *Waite* and other similar cases[5] convictions for common assault or, more appropriately, indecent assault (which does not require sexual intercourse) have been upheld. They should also be warned that the presumption of incapacity to have sexual intercourse does not apply outside the criminal law,[6] so that, for example, a boy of under 14 can be adjudged to be the father in financial provision proceedings.

Where the evidence shows that the boy was capable of intercourse it seems indefensible that he should be irrebuttably presumed incapable. Consequently, the Criminal Law Revision Committee's recommendation,[7] adopted by the draft Criminal Code Bill,[8] that this presumption should be abolished is to be welcomed.

1 *Philips* (1839) 8 C & P 736.
2 *Tatam* (1921) 15 Cr App Rep 132, CCA.
3 [1892] 2 QB 600.
4 See *Waite* [1892] 2 QB 600, 61 LJMC 187 and *Williams* [1893] 1 QB 320, 62 LJMC 69.
5 Eg *Williams* [1893] 1 QB 320.

6 *L v K* [1985] Fam 144, [1986] 1 All ER 961, Family Division of High Ct.
7 Fifteenth Report: Sexual Offences (1984) Cmnd 9213, para 2.48.
8 Cl 87.

Mental disability

9.4 Mental disability on the part of the accused may affect the outcome of a case in three ways:

a) Mental disability at the time when the accused is committed or brought for trial may render him unfit to be tried.
b) Mental disability at the time of the alleged offence by him may give rise to the defence of insanity or (in the case or murder) of diminished responsibility.
c) Mental disability at the time of conviction may result in a hospital order or some other similar order being made, instead of one of the normal types of sentence being imposed.

The first two of these three categories will be discussed in turn, concentrating on b).

Unfitness to be tried[1]

PERSONS COMMITTED TO THE CROWN COURT

9.5 Whether or not the accused may have the defence of insanity, and therefore even though there may be no doubt that he was sane at the time of his alleged offence, his mental condition after he has been committed for trial, or when he is brought to trial, may prevent him being tried at all or may result in his trial being suspended, as opposed to being a defence at a trial.

1 Emmins 'Unfitness to Plead: Glenn Pearson's Case' [1986] Crim LR 604.

9.6 *Urgent need for treatment: transfer direction by Home Secretary* In cases where there is an urgent need for treatment, the Home Secretary may be able to exercise his powers under s 48 of the Mental Health Act 1983. Section 48 provides, inter alia, that, where a person has been committed in custody for trial, the Home Secretary may order his detention in a mental hospital for treatment without trial. The Home Secretary can only make such an order if he is satisfied by medical reports that the accused is suffering from mental illness or severe mental impairment of a nature and degree which makes it appropriate for him to be detained in a hospital for treatment and that he is in urgent need of treatment. Such an order is called a 'transfer direction'. Normally, when the accused is well enough he is either produced in court or returned to prison to await trial.[1]

1 Report of the Committee on Mentally Abnormal Offenders (Cmnd 6244), para 3.38.

9.7 *Unfit to stand trial* When an accused whose mental condition has not required the making of a transfer order or who has been returned for trial after being subject to such an order is arraigned he may be found unfit to stand trial (or, as it is often put, 'unfit to plead').

In recent years there has been a decline in the number of findings of unfitness to be tried from an average of 25 a year in the early 1980s to an average of 13 a year by the late 1980s.[1] One reason may be s 36 of the Mental Health Act 1983, which permits the Crown Court to remand certain mentally disordered accused for treatment in hospital rather than remanding them in custody, and it may be that this is being used instead of the unfitness to be tried procedure described below.[2]

1 See Mackay 'The Decline of Disability in Relation to the Trial' [1991] Crim LR 87, and Mackay *The Operation of the Criminal Procedure (Insanity) Act 1964* 1-14.
2 See Bluglass 'The Mental Health Act 1983' in *Principles and Practice of Forensic Psychiatry*, ed Bluglass and Bowden, 1179.

9.8   The issue of fitness to stand trial may be raised by the defence, the prosecution or the judge.[1] It is for a jury, normally a different one from that which tries the case if the trial proceeds, to decide on the evidence whether the accused is capable of understanding the charge, the difference between a plea of guilty and not guilty and the course of the proceedings so as to make a proper defence; of challenging a juror to whom he might wish to object; of understanding the details of the evidence; and of giving evidence.[2] As can be seen, this test covers not only some people who are mentally disordered but also others, such as deaf mutes, who are incapable of understanding the proceedings or the evidence or of communicating. On the other hand, an attack of hysterical amnesia rendering it impossible for the accused to remember what happened at the time of the events in respect of which he is charged has been held not to make him unfit to stand trial.[3] In such a case, there is no difficulty for the accused in understanding the proceedings or the evidence, or the difference between a plea of guilty and one of not guilty, or in communicating, although his lack of memory may make it difficult for him to decide whether to plead guilty or not guilty.

Where the accused has raised the issue of unfitness to be tried he has the burden of proving this, although he only has to satisfy the jury of his unfitness on the balance of probabilities.[4] However, if the issue is raised by the prosecution or, presumably, by the judge it must be established by the prosecution beyond reasonable doubt.[5]

1 *MacCarthy* [1967] 1 QB 68, [1966] 1 All ER 447, CA.
2 *Pritchard* (1836) 7 C & P 303; *Berry* (1977) 66 Cr App Rep 156, CA; *Robertson* [1968] 3 All ER 557, [1968] 1 WLR 1767, CA.
3 *Podola* [1960] 1 QB 325, [1959] 3 All ER 418, CCA.
4 Ibid.
5 *Robertson* [1968] 3 All ER 557, [1968] 1 WLR 1767, CA.

9.9   Where the issue of fitness to stand trial is raised, the procedure is governed by s 4 of the Criminal Procedure (Insanity) Act 1964.[1] Normally, the question must be determined as it is raised, i e before the trial itself. However, to prevent the accused being found unfit and deprived of his right to trial where he may be entitled to acquittal of the offence charged, s 4(2) provides that the judge has a discretion to postpone the question of fitness to be tried until any time up to the opening of the case for the defence, where he considers it expedient to do so and in the interests of the accused. In applying this provision, the judge should consider the strength or weakness of the prosecution case as disclosed in the depositions or written statements, as the case may be, and the nature and degree of the suggested disability; he should then ask himself whether postponement is expedient and in the accused's interest.[2] The prosecution case may be so strong, and the accused's condition so disabling, that postponement of the trial would be wholly inexpedient. Conversely, the prosecution case may be so thin that, whatever the degree of disability, it clearly would be expedient to postpone.[3] If there is a reasonable chance that the prosecution case will be successfully challenged, postponement will usually be in the accused's interests.[4]

If the issue of fitness to be tried is postponed and the prosecution evidence is insufficient to convict, the jury will be directed to acquit the accused and the issue of fitness will not be determined. If there is sufficient evidence to convict, the postponed issue of fitness will be determined before the defence case is opened.

A jury must not make a determination on the question of fitness to be tried except on the evidence of two or more registered medical practitioners, at least one of whom is a specialist approved by the Home Secretary.

Section 4A of the Criminal Procedure (Insanity) Act 1964[1] lays down the procedure which applies where it is determined by a jury that the accused is unfit to be tried. It provides that the trial must not proceed or further proceed but it must be determined by a jury whether they are satisfied, as respects the count or each of the counts against the accused, that he did the act or made the omission charged. If they are so satisfied in relation to that count or any of those counts, they must make a finding that the accused did the act or made the omission charged. If they are not so satisfied in respect of the count or any of those counts, they must acquit the accused on the count in question. A determination as to whether or not the accused did the act or made the omission charged is made:

a) by a different jury from that which determined the question of disability, if that question was determined on the arraignment of the accused; and

b) by the trial jury, if the question of fitness was determined at a later stage.

Section 5 of the Criminal Procedure (Insanity) Act 1964 provides that, where a jury finds that the accused is under a disability and that he did the act or made the omission charged, the judge must either:

a) make an order that the accused be admitted to a mental hospital; or

b) make a guardianship order, a supervision and treatment order, or an order of absolute discharge.

Where the finding relates to a murder charge, the judge has no choice; he must make a hospital admission order. A hospital admission order may be made with or without an additional order restricting discharge from hospital, except where the finding relates to murder (in which case a restriction order without limit of time must be made). For further detail, see para 9.24.

1 As substituted by the Criminal Procedure (Insanity and Unfitness to Plead) Act 1991.
2 *Burles* [1970] 2 QB 191, [1970] 1 All ER 642, CA.
3 Ibid.
4 *Webb* (1969) 2 QB 278, [1969] 2 All ER 626, CA.

9.10 The accused has a right of appeal to the Court of Appeal against findings that he is unfit to stand trial and that he did the act or made the omission charged. The rules relating to the necessity for leave to appeal are the same as in the case of an appeal against the special verdict of insanity[1], as are the grounds on which the court may allow the appeal.[2]

1 Para 9.25.

2 Criminal Appeal Act 1968, ss 13 and 15, as amended by the Criminal Procedure (Insanity and Unfitness to Plead) Act 1991, Sch 3..

MAGISTRATES' COURTS

9.11 Sections 4, 4A and 5 of the Criminal Procedure (Insanity) Act 1964 only applies to trials on indictment.[1] There is no procedure expressly devised for the question of fitness to plead in relation to magistrates' courts; in particular, magistrates dealing with a summary only offence have no power to commit an accused to the Crown Court for a jury to decide his fitness to plead under the procedure in s 4.[1] However, where the accused is suffering from mental illness or from severe mental impairment and appears unfit to plead, the magistrates may make use of their power under s 37(3) of the Mental Health Act 1983 to make a hospital order without proceeding to a trial or conviction, if they are satisfied that he did the act or made the omission charged.[2] Normally, the consent to this course of action of those acting on behalf of the accused is required.[3]

This power applies whether the offence charged is purely summary or triable either way, but the wording of s 37(3) seems to preclude it applying where the offence is triable only on indictment.[4] In the case of an offence triable either way, the magistrates can exercise their power under s 37(3), even though the accused's disability is such that he would be unable to give the necessary consent to summary trial, since no trial is involved.[5] For the same reason, the magistrates can exercise the power even though the accused has elected trial by jury.[6]

1 *Metropolitan Stipendiary Magistrate, ex p Aniifowosi* (1985) 149 JP 748, DC.
2 *Lincolnshire (Kesteven) Justices, ex p O'Connor* [1983] 1 All ER 901, [1983] 1 WLR 335, DC. Section 37(3) is also referred to in para 9.30.
3 *Lincolnshire (Kesteven) Justices, ex p O'Connor.*
4 In *Ramsgate Justices, ex p Kazmarek* (1984) 80 Cr App Rep 366, DC, Mann J reserved this question.
5 *Lincolnshire Justices, ex p O'Connor.*
6 *Ramsgate Justices, ex p Kazmarek.*

Defence of insanity

9.12 The defence of insanity is contained in the *M'Naghten Rules*. The defence is concerned with the accused's legal responsibility at the time of his alleged offence, and not simply with whether he was medically insane at that time. In other words, it is concerned with insanity in a legal sense, and not in a medical or psychological sense. What the law regards as insanity may be far removed from what would be regarded as insanity by a doctor or psychologist, as we shall see.

Mental illness short of insanity under the *M'Naghten Rules* cannot in itself affect the liability of the accused (although it may provide evidence in support of a plea of lack of some element of subjective mens rea); the only exception is the offence of murder where it may give rise to the qualified defence of diminished responsibility.[1] Thus, for example, it is irrelevant, in relation to an offence where *Caldwell*-type recklessness suffices, that the accused failed to give any thought to the 'obvious risk' in question because of mental illness less than insanity under the *M'Naghten Rules*.[2]

The *M'Naghten Rules* were laid down by the judges in their advice to the House of Lords in *M'Naghten's Case*.[3] Their advice was sought in consequence of the acquittal of M'Naghten, who was found to be insane on a charge of murdering Sir Robert Peel's private secretary. Although the rules are not laid down in a case decided by the House of Lords, they have been recognised again and again as representing the present law.

The *M'Naghten Rules* can be summarised thus:

a) Everyone is presumed sane until the contrary is proved.
b) It is a defence to a criminal prosecution for the accused to show that he was labouring under such a defect of reason, due to disease of the mind, as *either* not to know the nature and quality of his act *or*, if he did know this, not to know that he was doing wrong.

We have seen that when the defence of insanity is pleaded by the accused the onus of proof is exceptionally on him, but he may rebut the presumption of sanity by adducing evidence which satisfies the jury on the balance of probabilities that he was insane within the terms of the *M'Naghten Rules* when he committed the alleged offence. The same is true if the judge rules that the accused is raising the defence of insanity.

1 Para 9.32.
2 *Bell* [1984] 3 All ER 842, CA; para 6.48.
3 (1843) 10 Cl & Fin 200.

9.13 *Role of the judge* If the accused puts his state of mind in issue and there is medical evidence relating to it, it is irrelevant whether or not he expressly pleads the defence of insanity. The reason is that whether or not he has *raised* that defence is a question of law for the judge in the light of the medical evidence.[1] The medical evidence may indicate the factual nature of the accused's mental condition but it is for the judge to say whether that is evidence of a defect of reason from disease of the mind. If, but only if, the judge concludes that there is medical evidence in support of *all* the elements of the *M'Naghten Rules*, he may rule that the accused is raising the defence of insanity and leave it to the jury to decide whether or not those elements are actually satisfied. In the most recent authority on this point, *Dickie*,[2] the Court of Appeal held that the 'circumstances in which a judge will do that will be exceptional and very rare'. If the judge decides to leave the defence of insanity to the jury, he must give counsel on both sides the chance to call evidence on the point before so leaving it.[3] The judge's power to rule that evidence which is not expressly introduced in support of a defence of insanity does in fact raise that defence is of great practical importance, as explained in para 9.27.

The above power does not mean that the judge can seek out further evidence. On the other hand, if he has doubts on the evidence before him, he can seek clarification from the witnesses to enable him to reach a conclusion on that evidence.

1 *Kemp* [1957] 1 QB 399, [1956] 3 All ER 249; *Bratty v A–G for Northern Ireland* [1963] AC 386 at 411–12, [1961] 3 All ER 523; *Dickie* [1984] 3 All ER 173, [1984] 1 WLR 1031, CA. *Charlson* [1955] 1 All ER 859, [1955] 1 WLR 317, which is to the contrary (see para 9.46), must now be taken to be wrongly decided, although it has not been expressly overruled. See further, para 9.46.
2 [1984] 3 All ER at 178.
3 Ibid.

REQUIREMENTS OF THE DEFENCE

9.14 In order to succeed with his defence of insanity the accused must prove three things.

9.15 *Disease of the mind* The accused must show that he was suffering from a 'disease of the mind' (in the legal sense of that term)[1] when he did the prohibited act. The disease must be of the *mind*; it need not be of the brain.[2] The meaning of 'disease of the mind' was explained by the House of Lords in *Sullivan*,[3] where the view taken in previous cases[4] was endorsed. Lord Diplock, with whose speech the rest of their Lordships agreed, stated the law as follows.[5]

'"Mind" in the *M'Naghten Rules* is used in the ordinary sense of the mental faculties of reason, memory and understanding. If the effect of a disease is to impair these faculties. . . , it matters not whether the aetiology [ie assignment of the cause] of the impairment is organic, as in epilepsy [or arteriosclerosis], or functional, or whether the impairment itself is permanent or is transient and intermittent, provided it subsisted at the time of the commission of the act.'

To this one may add that it is irrelevant whether the condition of the mind is curable or incurable.[6]

The requirement that the mental impairment should be caused by disease must be stressed. The distinction between mental impairment due to disease and mental impairment not due to disease is now established as being between internal and external causes. For the mental impairment to be due to disease, the *immediate* cause of the impairment must be internal to the accused.[7] 'A malfunctioning of the mind of transitory effect caused by the application to the body of some external factor such as violence, drugs, including anaesthetics, alcohol and hypnotic influences cannot fairly be said to be due to disease' and does not constitute a disease of the mind.[6] The same is true where a woman suffers a state of dissociation resulting (as post traumatic stress disorder) from being raped[8] or where a diabetic who gets into a hypoglycaemic coma as a result of failing to take food after taking insulin (since the consequent effect of the insulin is due to an external factor).[9] It would be different if a diabetic failed to take his insulin and got into a hyperglycaemic coma as a result, because it would be the diabetes itself (an internal factor) which would have caused the coma.[10] The distinction which the law draws between hypoglycaemia (not a disease of the mind) and hyperglycaemia (disease of the mind) is not easy to defend. Why should a distinction be drawn between a diabetic who gets into a hypoglycaemic coma as a result of taking too much insulin or failing to eat adequately after taking the correct dose and a diabetic who gets into a hyperglycaemic coma as a result of not taking his insulin?

1 See, for instance, *Sullivan* [1983] 2 All ER 673 at 677, per Lord Diplock.
2 *Kemp* [1957] 1 QB 399, [1956] 3 All ER 249; *Burgess* [1991] 2 QB 92, [1991] 2 All ER 769, CA.
3 [1983] 2 All ER 673, [1983] 3 WLR 123, HL.
4 Eg *Kemp* [1957] 1 QB 399, [1956] 3 All ER 249; *Quick* [1973] QB 910, [1973] 3 All ER 347, CA.
5 [1983] 2 All ER 673 at 677, per Lord Diplock.
6 *Kemp* [1957] 1 QB 399 at 407.
7 *Quick* [1973] QB 910, [1973] 3 All ER 347, CA; *Sullivan* [1983] 2 All ER 673, [1983] 3 WLR 123, HL; *Burgess* [1991] 2 All ER 769, CA.
8 *T* [1991] Crim LR 256, Crown Ct.
9 *Quick* [1973] QB 910, [1973] 3 All ER 347, CA. See also *Sullivan* [1983] 2 All ER 673 at 678, per Lord Diplock; *Bingham* [1991] Crim LR 433, CA.
10 *Hennessy* [1989] 2 All ER 9, CA; para 9.46. Diabetes is a deficiency in the system of the production of the hormone, insulin, which balances the sugar metabolism. In the absence of that hormone the blood sugar rises and that results in hyperglycaemia and ultimately a hyperglycaemic coma. If a diabetic takes too much insulin to treat his hormonal deficiency, or fails to eat adequately after taking the correct dose in order to counterbalance it, the

blood sugar may fall too far and hypoglycaemia and ultimately a hypoglycaemic coma may result.

9.16   In *Bratty v A-G for Northern Ireland*[1] Lord Denning said: 'It seems to me that any mental disorder which has manifested itself in violence and is prone to recur is a disease of the mind'. However, a significant rider was placed on Lord Denning's statement in *Burgess*[2], where it was stated that, while the fact that there is a danger of recurrence may be an added reason for categorising a condition as a disease of the mind, the absence of the danger of recurrence is not a reason for saying that it cannot be a disease of the mind.

The rider in *Burgess* is one reason why Lord Denning's statement in *Bratty* should be regarded as misleading. A second reason is that, as pointed out in *Quick*,[3] the statement wrongly suggests that it would be irrelevant that the immediate cause of the mental disorder was an external one. A third reason is that the reference to 'violence' in the statement must not be read as an indication that the defence of insanity is limited to offences of violence. There is no suggestion that it is so limited in the other cases on the defence and it has long been accepted that insanity is a defence to most (if not all) offences. In the light of these comments, Lord Denning's statement seems of little value.

1 [1963] AC 386 at 412.
2 [1992] 2 QB 92, [1991] 2 All ER 769, CA.
3 [1973] QB 910, [1973] 3 All ER 347, CA.

9.17   The distinction between mental impairment due to disease (i e due to an internal cause) and mental impairment not due to disease (i e due to an external cause) is not always easy to draw, as was pointed out by the Court of Appeal in *Burgess*,[1] where D had claimed that he had been sleepwalking when he wounded a woman. There was medical evidence indicating that at the material time D was suffering an abnormality or disorder, albeit transitory, due to an internal factor, whether functional or organic, which had manifested itself in violence and might recur. The Court of Appeal held that, in the light of the medical evidence, the judge had been correct to rule that on any view of the medical evidence D had been suffering from a disease of the mind at the material time.

The difficulty in distinguishing between mental impairment due to disease (internal cause) and mental impairment not due to disease (external cause) is shown by reference to cases concerned with whether a dissociative state resulting from a psychological blow can amount to a disease of the mind. In the Canadian case of *Rabey v R*,[2] which was considered by the Court of Appeal in *Burgess*, the majority of the Supreme Court of Canada approved the view of Martin J in the Ontario Court of Appeal that the mental impairment of a person, who acted under a dissociative state consequent on the psychological blow of his rejection by a girl with whom he was infatuated, was due to an internal cause; the psychological blow was not to be equated with an external cause such as concussion. The Court of Appeal in *Burgess* referred approvingly to Martin J's statement that:

'[T]he ordinary stresses and disappointments of life which are the common lot of mankind do not constitute an external cause constituting an explanation for a malfunctioning of the mind which takes it out of the category of a disease of the mind'.

Martin J went on to say that the reason was that the exceptional effect which this *ordinary* event had on the accused had to be considered as having its source primarily in the accused's psychological make-up. Martin J did not say what would be the legal effect of an extraordinary event of such severity that it might reasonably be expected to cause a dissociative state in a reasonable person. The point was dealt with by the Crown Court in *T*,[3] where the judge held that a state of dissociation resulting (as post traumatic stress) from being raped was due to an external cause, and was therefore not due to a disease of the mind. Clearly, the cause of the dissociative state here fell outside the ordinary stresses of life; this extraordinary event could not be said to have its source in the accused's psychological make-up but, instead, its immediate cause was external to the rape.

1 [1991] 2 QB 92, [1991] 2 All ER 769, CA.
2 (1977) 37 CCC (2d) 461. Also see *Hennessy* [1989] 2 All ER 9 at 14.
3 [1990] Crim LR 256, Crown Ct.

9.18 *Defect of reason* The accused must prove that he was suffering from a 'defect of reason' due to disease of the mind. A 'defect of reason' is more than a momentary confusion or absent-mindedness; a deprivation of reasoning power is required.[1] Such a condition would usually render the accused insane for medical purposes. In *Clarke*[2] D was charged with theft by shoplifting. Her defence was that she had no intention to steal but had acted in a moment of absent-mindedness caused by a diabetic depression induced by sugar deficiency. The trial judge ruled that D's defence was one of insanity because she was pleading a defect of reason due to disease of the mind. D did not wish to be found insane and changed her plea to one of guilty. The Court of Appeal, allowing her appeal against conviction, held that D's defence was simply one of lack of mens rea and not a defence of insanity, since temporary absent-mindedness due to disease was not a defect of reason due to disease. 'Defect of reason', it held, meant the deprivation of reasoning power; it did not cover people who retain their reasoning power but in moments of confusion or absent-mindedness fail to use it fully.

1 *Clarke* [1972] 1 All ER 219, 56 Cr App Rep 225, CA.
2 [1972] 1 All ER 219, 56 Cr App Rep 225, CA.

9.19 *Ignorance of nature and quality of act or that it is wrong* The defect of reason must affect legal responsibility,[1] something to which a person's capacity to appreciate what he was doing and whether it was lawful is highly relevant, and the accused must go on to prove that because of his insanity *either* he did not know the nature and quality of his act *or*, if he did know this, he did not know he was doing wrong.

1 *Rivett* (1950) 34 Cr App Rep 87, CCA.

9.20 The words 'nature and quality' in the *M'Naghten Rules* refer to the physical nature of the act.[1] The jury must be satisfied that the accused did not know what he was doing, or did not appreciate the probable effects of his conduct, or did not realise the material circumstances in which he was acting. An insane person who was acting in a state of automatism would not know the nature and quality of his act,[2] nor would someone who stabbed another with a knife without knowing that he was using the implement at all or under the insane delusion that he was about to be killed by him. The same would be the case where a person cut a sleeper's head off because 'it would be great fun to see him looking for it when he woke up'.[3] He would know he was engaged on the act of decapitation, but would be manifestly incapable of appreciating its physical effects. Similarly, if an insane person squeezes someone's throat, thinking that he is squeezing an orange, he does not know the nature and quality of his act, but if he kills a boy, mistakenly believing the victim is a girl, he knows the nature and quality of his act since his mistake is not material.

1 *Codère* (1916) 12 Cr App Rep 21 at 28.
2 *Sullivan* [1983] 2 All ER 673, [1983] 3 WLR 123, HL.
3 Stephen *History of the Criminal Law* vol II, 166.

9.21 Turning to the alternative limb of the test of responsibility, the jury must be asked whether, assuming the accused knew what he was doing, he also knew that it was wrong. Some difficulty has been experienced with regard to the meaning of 'wrong' in this context. It is settled that a person is not able to establish a case of insanity within the *M'Naghten Rules* if he knew that his conduct was prohibited by law, ie legally wrong. This is shown by *Windle*,[1] where D induced his wife, who had frequently spoken of committing suicide, to consume 100 aspirins, because he thought it would be beneficial for her to die. On appeal, it was held that the trial judge was justified in withdrawing the case from the jury on the question of insanity. D had said that he would be hanged for what he had done, and there was no doubt that he knew it was contrary to law. The High Court of Australia has declined to follow *Windle*, being of the opinion that 'wrong' in the *M'Naghten Rules* means contrary to the moral views of the majority of the members of society.[2] According to this opinion, if Windle had believed his wife to be suffering from a painful incurable illness, and if he had also believed that euthanasia was approved by the bulk of ordinary Englishmen, he ought to have been acquitted even though he knew that mercy killing was prohibited by law.[3]

Sir James Stephen once said that the absence of the power of self-control would involve an incapacity to know right from wrong.[4] But this was at a time when it was not clear whether, according to English law, 'wrong' in the *M'Naghten Rules* meant legally wrong or morally wrong. Since it was decided that 'wrong' means legally wrong the Privy Council has held that the absence of the power of self-control is not per se evidence of incapacity to know the nature and quality of an act or that it is wrong. However, on the facts of a particular case, there may be medical evidence warranting the conclusion that a disease which impairs the accused's power of self-control also impairs his ability to distinguish right from wrong.[5]

There is a significant difference between this limb and the previous one, since a person who did not know the nature and quality of his act for reasons other than a defect of reason due to a disease of the mind will often be entitled to a complete acquittal, and the defence of insanity in such a case merely results in a different verdict being returned in the Crown Court. On the other hand, ignorance of law is normally no excuse, but it becomes an excuse if it results from a defect of reason due to disease of the mind.

1 [1952] 2 QB 826, [1952] 2 All ER 1, CCA. Also see *Holmes* [1953] 2 All ER 324, [1953] 1 WLR 686, CCA.
2 *Stapleton v R* (1952) 86 CLR 358.
3 Norval Morris ' "Wrong" in the M'Naghten Rules' (1953) 16 MLR 435.
4 *History of the Criminal Law* vol II, 171.
5 *A-G for State of South Australia v Brown* [1960] AC 432, [1960] 1 All ER 734, PC.

9.22 It is for the jury, not medical witnesses, to determine whether the requirements for the defence of insanity have been satisfied after a proper direction from the judge,[1] but they may not acquit on the ground of insanity except on the evidence of two or more registered medical practitioners, at least one of whom is a specialist approved by the Home Secretary.[2] It seems that a verdict of guilty which is contrary to unanimous medical evidence will be upset on an appeal by the accused unless there is some other evidence contradicting the medical evidence.[3]

1 *Rivett* (1950) 34 Cr App Rep 87, CCA.
2 Criminal Procedure (Insanity and Unfitness to Plead) Act 1991, s 1.
3 This is the position in the defence of diminished responsibility, see para 9.38.

9.23 In their advice in *M'Naghten's Case* the judges enunciated a third test: that, where a man commits a criminal act under an insane delusion, he is under the same degree of responsibility as he would have been if the facts had been as he imagined them to be. This test is generally regarded as redundant since it merely restates a principle provided by the two tests just mentioned. To illustrate their third test the judges said:

> 'For example, if, under the influence of his delusion, the accused supposes another man to be in the act of attempting to take away his life, and he kills that man, as he supposes in self-defence, he would be exempt from punishment. If his delusion was that the deceased had inflicted a serious injury to his character and fortune, and he killed him in revenge for such supposed injury, he would be liable to punishment.'[1]

The same answers would have been provided by the 'knowledge of wrong' or the 'nature and quality' tests. The third test can also be criticised as defective in that it suggests that if the accused kills his wife under the insane delusion that he is killing a cat he can be convicted of an offence in relation to a cat, since, said the judges, one who acts under an insane delusion is under the same degree of responsibility as he would have been if his delusion had been true. This clearly cannot be so since the accused would not have committed any actus reus in relation to a cat. A study of the directions made in insanity cases shows that the third test has fallen into desuetude and it can safely be ignored.

1 (1843) 10 Cl & Fin 200 at 211.

VERDICT AND APPEAL

9.24 Until 1800, the verdict, in cases of insanity, was simply 'not guilty'. The Criminal Lunatics Act 1800 gave the court power to detain the accused in such cases and provided that the jury should declare that the accused was acquitted on the ground of insanity. The Act of 1800 applied only to felonies, but it was extended to misdemeanours by the Trial of Lunatics Act 1883, which also provided that, in cases tried with a jury, the verdict should be 'Guilty of the act or omission charged against him but insane at the time' or, more tersely, 'guilty but insane'. This alteration was made at the wish of Queen Victoria who was distressed by the finding that one McLean who fired a pistol at her was 'not guilty' on account of his insanity. The verdict provided for by the 1883 Act was illogical, and s 1 of the Criminal Procedure (Insanity) Act 1964 provides that the verdict shall now be 'not guilty by reason of insanity'.

When the accused is found not guilty by reason of insanity he does not necessarily go free. Until very recently, he had to be ordered to be detained in a hospital indefinitely until the Home Secretary was satisfied that this was no longer required for the protection of the public. However, the law on this matter was changed by the Criminal Procedure (Insanity and Unfitness to Plead) Act 1991, which substitutes new provisions in the relevant parts (s 5 and Scheds 1 and 2) of the Criminal Procedure (Insanity) Act 1964.

Section 5 of the 1964 Act now provides that, where an accused is found not guilty by reason of insanity, the judge must either:

a) make an order that the accused be admitted to a hospital ; or

b) make a guardianship order, a supervision and treatment order, or an order of absolute discharge.

Where the special verdict relates to a murder charge, the judge has no choice; he must make a hospital admission order.

If a hospital admission order is made the accused is admitted to a hospital selected by the Home Secretary and detained there; it may be a special hospital, such as Broadmoor, or a local NHS hospital including a Regional Secure Unit. If the order is made without restrictions on release, the decision about release is one for the hospital authorities. However, if he considers it necessary in order to protect the public from serious harm, the judge can make an additional order imposing restrictions on discharge from hospital.[1] A restriction order may specify a minimum limit of time for the detention or it may be without limit of time. The Home Secretary has power to terminate either type of restriction order. The effect of the latter type of restriction order is that the accused will be detained until the Home Secretary is satisfied that this is no longer required for the protection of the public. In the case of murder, a restriction order without limit of time must be made.

1 Criminal Procedure (Insanity) Act 1991, Sch 1.

9.25 It was decided in *Felstead v R*[1] that there was no appeal against a verdict of 'guilty but insane' because it was tantamount to an acquittal. This rule, though logical, could produce hardship in a case in which the accused's defence to a charge of murder, or other offence against the person, was accident, as well as insanity,[2] or in a case in which the accused pleaded diminished responsibility in answer to a murder charge and was found to be insane. Accordingly, s 12 of the Criminal Appeal Act 1968 provides that there may be an appeal to the Court of Appeal against the special verdict of acquittal on the ground of insanity.[3] No leave is required for an appeal on a question of law alone, but the leave of the Court of Appeal or of the trial judge is required for an appeal on a question of fact alone or of mixed law and fact. The grounds for allowing the appeal are the same as those which apply on an appeal against conviction.[4]

1 [1914] AC 534, HL.
2 *Duke* [1963] 1 QB 120, [1961] 3 All ER 737, CCA.
3 This right of appeal was introduced by the Criminal Procedure (Insanity) Act 1964, s 2.
4 Criminal Appeal Act 1968, s 13.

USE OF THE M'NAGHTEN RULES

9.26 Cases in which insanity has been expressly raised as a defence have been extremely rare. Partly, this has been a reaction against the prospect of prolonged, even lifelong, detention in a hospital.[1] But it has also reflected the narrow test of legal responsibility under the *M'Naghten Rules* and the existence since the Homicide Act 1957 of the defence to murder of diminished responsibility.[2] Before that Act accused persons generally raised the defence of insanity only in murder cases, but since then a plea of the wider defence of diminished responsibility has been far more common in such cases because, if that defence succeeds, the accused may be given a determinate prison sentence (or some other 'normal' sentence).

A recent survey has indicated that, in a 14-year period commencing in 1975, the special verdict of not guilty by reason of insanity was returned only in respect of 49 accused.[3] Now that the Criminal Procedure (Insanity and Unfitness to Plead) Act 1991 has removed from judges, except in the case of murder, the obligation to commit indefinitely to hospital a person acquitted on grounds of insanity, it is likely that insanity pleas will become rather more common.

1 A recent survey has revealed that the consequences of a verdict of not guilty by reason of insanity have not been as severe in many cases as had been thought: Mackay 'Fact and Fiction about the Insanity Defence' [1990] Crim LR 247. See also Mackay *The Operation of the Criminal Procedure (Insanity) Act 1964.*
2 Para 9.32
3 Mackay, loc cit.

9.27 It is doubtless true to say today, although less so than it was before the passing of the Criminal Procedure (Insanity and Unfitness to Plead) Act 1991, that the most important thing about understanding the *M'Naghten Rules* is not how to make use of them as a defence, but how to avoid them being raised at the trial. The reason is that, although insanity is rarely expressly raised as a defence by the accused, it may be raised indirectly by him. As stated in para 9.13, whether or not a mental condition amounts to a disease of the mind is a question of law for the judge to decide, and the danger is that, if the accused pleads that he lacked the necessary mens rea (or was an automaton) and relies in support on evidence of a mental condition, he is liable to find that the judge rules that the alleged condition amounts to a disease of the mind and that, there being medical evidence in support of all elements of the *M'Naghten Rules,* he is raising the defence of insanity, which alone must be left to the jury. Thus, the accused cannot avoid the question of insanity being raised by simply describing the medical evidence as evidence of lack of mens rea (or of automatism).

An example is provided by *Sullivan,*[1] where the accused, who was charged with inflicting grievous bodily harm, pleaded that he had acted as a non-insane automaton, adducing evidence that the attack in question had happened during the last stages of a minor epileptic seizure. The trial judge, correctly in the eyes of the House of Lords, ruled that on the evidence before him the defence amounted to one of insanity, rather than non-insane automatism, and that he would only leave the defence of insanity to the jury. At this point, the accused changed his plea to guilty.

1 [1984] AC 156, [1983] 2 All ER 673, HL.

CAN THE PROSECUTION SEEK TO PROVE INSANITY?

9.28 Although the *M'Naghten Rules* are described as the defence of insanity, this is somewhat misleading since it is sometimes possible for the prosecution to call evidence and seek to prove that an accused who has not pleaded insanity is insane within the *M'Naghten Rules* and therefore not guilty by reason of insanity.

First, s 6 of the Criminal Procedure (Insanity) Act 1964 provides that, where, on a trial for murder, the accused pleads the defence of diminished responsibility, the prosecution may adduce or elicit evidence of insanity. It is for the prosecution to prove its contention beyond reasonable doubt.[1]

Second, although the Court of Appeal doubted, obiter, in *Dickie*[2] that the prosecution could raise the issue of insanity, Lord Denning had previously stated the contrary, obiter, in *Bratty v A-G for Northern Ireland*[3], which was not cited to the Court of Appeal in *Dickie* and which, it is submitted, represents the better view. According to Lord Denning, if the accused puts his state of mind in issue, e g by pleading non-insane automatism, it is open to the prosecution to show what his true state of mind was by raising the issue of insanity.[4] In principle, the prosecution must prove its contention beyond reasonable doubt;[5] Lord Denning's statement in *Bratty*[6] that the prosecution need only prove the accused's insanity on the balance of probabilities is questionable.

There is a certain paradox in the prosecution seeking an acquittal in the above types of case.

1 *Grant* [1960] Crim LR 424.
2 [1984] 3 All ER 173, [1984] 1 WLR 1031.
3 [1963] AC 386 at 411–412, [1961] 3 All ER 523, per Lord Denning.
4 According to the Court of Appeal in *Dickie,* if the prosecution possesses evidence of insanity it must simply make it available to the defence, so that in its discretion the defence may make use of it.
5 An analogy may be drawn with the rule that, where it alleges that the accused is unfit to plead, the prosecution must prove this beyond reasonable doubt: *Robertson* [1968] 3 All ER 557, [1968] 1 WLR 1767, CA.
6 [1963] AC 386 at 411–412, [1961] 3 All ER 523.

CRITICISMS OF THE M'NAGHTEN RULES

9.29 Five criticisms may be made of the *M'Naghten Rules* :

a) The rule concerning the burden of proof is anomalous. In the case of other general defences, the accused merely bears the burden of adducing evidence sufficient to raise a particular defence, and there is no reason why someone who pleads insanity should be any worse off.

b) It may be maintained that the word 'wrong' should be interpreted to mean morally wrong in accordance with the opinion of the High Court of Australia. This is a very debatable point. The decision in *Windle*[1] to the effect that 'wrong' in the *M'Naghten Rules* means legally wrong has been supported extra-judicially by Lord Devlin in the following words: 'I do not see how an accused man can be heard to say that he knew he was doing an act which he knew to be contrary to law, and yet that he is entitled to be acquitted at the hands of the law. Guilt, whether in relation to the *M'Naghten Rules*, or any other rules, means responsibility in law'.[2] In any event, the 'knowledge of wrong' test as interpreted in *Windle* provides a very narrow ground of exemption since even grossly disturbed persons generally know that murder, for instance, is a crime.[3] Consequently, it is somewhat surprising that the recent survey referred to in para 9.26 found that, of the 49 special verdicts, the 'knowledge of wrong' test was the relevant one in 23 of them and that in ten others both tests were regarded as satisfied.[4] It would appear from the survey that the test was treated by the judges more liberally in practice in directing juries than is necessary under the rules set out above and that little attempt was made in many cases to distinguish between ignorance of legal wrong and ignorance of moral wrong.

c) It is said that the *M'Naghten Rules* are based on the outmoded theory that partial insanity is possible. Lawyers cannot pronounce on the validity of this criticism, but partial insanity is regarded as a possibility in several other branches of the law in which the *M'Naghten Rules* are not applied.[5]

d) The *Rules* are limited to cognitive factors, excluding all matters concerning volition or the emotions, and thus make no allowance for so-called 'irresistible impulse'. It is said that it should be a defence for a person to show that, although he was aware of the nature and quality of his act and knew it to be wrong, he found, owing to insanity, that it was difficult, if not impossible, to prevent himself from doing what he did. Allowance is made for irresistible impulse in a number of Commonwealth and North American jurisdictions and the defence of diminished responsibility admits it on a charge of murder.

e) It is objectionable that the label of insanity should be applied, and the consequences of the special verdict should follow, in cases, such as where the accused acted during an epileptic fit or hyperglycaemic coma or while sleepwalking, where the accused would not be regarded as insane in common – let alone medical – language. It is certainly odd that such people are labelled as insane by the law when the vast majority of people who are regarded medically (and in common parlance) as mentally ill or disordered are not, The incongruity of this has been recognised in the House of Lords and the Court of Appeal but they have maintained that it does not lie within their power to alter the law in this respect.[6]

1 Para 9.21.
2 [1954] Crim LR 681–682.
3 Butler Committee on Mentally Abnormal Offenders (Cmnd 6244) para 18.8.
4 Mackay 'Fact and Fiction about the Insanity Defence' [1990] Crim LR 247. See also Mackay *The Operation of the Criminal Procedure (Insanity) Act 1964.*
5 *Hill* (1851) 2 Den 254; *Re Bohrmann, Caesar and Watmough v Bohrmann* [1938] 1 All ER 271.
6 *Sullivan* [1984] AC 156 at 173, [1983] 2 All ER 673, per Lord Diplock; *Burgess* [1991] 2 All ER 769 at 776, CA.

SUMMARY TRIALS[1]

9.30 The following variations to what has been said above apply to summary trials in magistrates' courts. The *M'Naghten Rules* apply to cases tried in magistrates' courts but the legislation concerning the special verdict of acquittal, and the results thereof, do not apply to magistrates' courts which must, as at common law, give an ordinary acquittal if the defence is made out, in which case the accused goes free. This is satisfactory if the interests of the accused or society do not require protection, but some power is clearly necessary to deal with cases tried by magistrates where the public or the accused's interests demand further action. This need is met by s 37(3) of the Mental Health Act 1983, under which, when the accused is suffering from mental illness or severe mental impairment, the magistrates may make a hospital or guardianship order without registering a conviction, if satisfied merely that the accused did the act or made the omission charged. No causal connection between the offence and the disorder need exist. Section 37(3) is not limited to insanity under the *M'Naghten Rules,* of course, but includes also a wide range of mental disorders.

1 White 'Insanity in a Magistrates' Court' (1984) 148 JPN 419, 435 and 439.

PROPOSALS FOR REFORM

9.31 The draft Criminal Code Bill[1] incorporates, with some adaptation, proposals for reform made by the Butler Committee on Mentally Abnormal Offenders,[2] which found the *M'Naghten Rules* unsatisfactory and proposed a complete re-casting of the law relating to the legal responsibility of mentally abnormal offenders.

The draft Bill provides:

a) A new special verdict, 'not guilty on evidence of mental disorder'. The power to give this verdict would be extended to magistrates' courts.
b) Two alternative grounds for the verdict of not guilty on evidence of mental disorder:
   i) By cl 35, a mental disorder verdict could be returned if the accused was proved to have committed an offence but it was proved on the balance of probabilities (whether by the prosecution or by the accused) that he was at the time suffering from severe mental illness or severe mental handicap. This would not apply if the jury or magistrates were satisfied beyond reasonable doubt that the offence was not attributable to the severe mental illness or severe mental handicap. This provision would extend the law considerably. It covers not only cases at present covered by the 'knowledge of wrong' test under the *M'Naghten Rules* but also any other case where, at the time of the act or omission charged, and proved, the accused, although able to form intentions and carry them out, was suffering from severe mental illness or severe mental handicap. This ground would be of importance where the prosecution succeeded in proving the necessary mens rea for the offence charged.
   ii) By cl 36, the mental disorder verdict could also be returned if the accused was acquitted of an offence only because, by reason of mental disorder or a combination of mental disorder and intoxication, it was found that he acted or might have acted in a state of automatism, or without the fault required for the offence, or believing that an exempting circumstance existed, and it was proved on the balance of probabilities (whether by the accused or the prosecution) that he was suffering from mental disorder at the time of the act. By cl 34, 'mental disorder' is defined as severe mental illness, arrested or incomplete development of mind, or a state of automatism (not resulting only from intoxication) which is a feature of disorder, whether organic or functional and whether continuing or recurring, that may cause a similar state on another occasion. The present ground would work as follows: if, although the prosecution had proved the actus reus, it was found that the accused acted or may have acted in a state of automatism, or without the fault required for the offence, or believing that an exempting circumstance existed, the accused would be entitled to a complete acquittal unless the jury or magistrates were satisfied

137

on the balance of probabilities that he was mentally disordered at the time of the offence.

The draft Bill does not set out provisions relating to the disposal of those subject to a mental disorder verdict, but it provides that they are to be included in one of its schedules. Doubtless, that schedule would make similar provision to that which currently applies if a verdict of not guilty by reason of insanity is returned.

1 Law Commission: A Criminal Code for England and Wales (1989): Law Com No 177; see para 3.21 above.
2 Cmnd 6244, paras 18.1–18.50. For a discussion of the Committee's proposals, see Ashworth 'The Butler Committee and Criminal Responsibility' [1975] Crim LR 687.

Diminished responsibility

9.32 The concept of diminished responsibility, which had been known to Scots law for some time, was introduced into English law by s 2 of the Homicide Act 1957, sub-s (1) of which provides:

'Where a person kills or is a party to the killing of another, he shall not be convicted of murder if he was suffering from such abnormality of mind (whether arising from a condition of arrested or retarded development of mind or any inherent causes or induced by disease or injury) as substantially impaired his mental responsibility for his acts and omissions in doing or being a party to the killing.'

The defence of diminished responsibility is quite different from that of insanity. Insanity covered by the *M'Naghten Rules* is a complete defence to most, if not all, offences and leads to an acquittal. Diminished responsibility, on the other hand, is merely a mitigating factor limited to charges of murder and, if successfully pleaded, reducing liability from murder (which carries the mandatory life sentence) to manslaughter (which simply carries a maximum punishment of life imprisonment).[1] This means that the court has a discretion in the matter of punishment which may vary from imprisonment for life to an absolute discharge; where considered appropriate, a hospital order (with or without restriction of time) or a guardianship order may be made under s 37(1) of the Mental Health Act 1983. A defence of diminished responsibility is not required for other offences because they do not carry a fixed penalty, so that the judge has a discretion as to the punishment imposed.

1 Homicide Act 1957, s 2(3).

9.33 Section 2(1) makes it plain that the accused may rely on the defence although he knew what he was doing and knew that it was wrong, and soon after the section came into force it was held that the fact that a killing was premeditated does not destroy a plea of diminished responsibility.[1]

At first, there was a tendency to direct the jury to consider whether the case came on the borderline of insanity under the *M'Naghten Rules* and to refrain from explaining the words of the statute to them,[2] but all the earlier decisions have to be read in the light of the judgment of the Court of Criminal Appeal in *Byrne*,[3] which will be discussed shortly. Since *Byrne* was decided, it has been held that it is not appropriate in every case to direct a jury that the test of diminished responsibility is partial or borderline insanity.[4] It is certainly not appropriate where the abnormality relied on cannot readily be related to any of the generally recognised types of 'insanity', as, for example, where the accused pleads diminished responsibility occasioned by a depressive illness.[4] In cases such as this no reference to partial or borderline insanity should be made by the judge.[4] Moreover, even where it is appropriate for a judge to invite a jury to take into consideration partial or borderline insanity, he should make it plain that he is not using the word 'insanity' in the narrow legal sense of the *M'Naghten Rules* but in its broad popular sense.[4]

It has also been held that it is not right for the judge merely to refer the jury to the terms of s 2 of the 1957 Act without some guidance on their meaning.[5]

1 *Matheson* [1958] 2 All ER 87, [1958] 1 WLR 474, CCA.
2 *Walden* [1959] 3 All ER 203, [1959] 1 WLR 1008, CCA; *Spriggs* [1958] 1 QB 270, [1958] 1 All ER 300, CCA.
3 [1960] 2 QB 396, [1960] 3 All ER 1, CCA.
4 *Rose v R* [1961] AC 496, [1961] 1 All ER 859, PC; *Seers* (1984) 79 Cr App Rep 261, CA.
5 *Terry* [1961] 2 QB 314, [1961] 2 All ER 569, CCA. See also *Gomez* (1964) 48 Cr App Rep 310, CCA.

9.34　The wording of s 2(1) can be broken down into three elements which by s 2(2) the accused has the burden of proving, and it has been held that the burden is discharged by proof on the balance of probabilities.[1] The Court of Appeal will quash a conviction for murder and substitute one for manslaughter where there is sufficient evidence to shift the onus of proof with regard to diminished responsibility and that evidence is not contradicted by the Crown.[2]

The Court of Appeal in *Campbell*[3] held, obiter, that the wording of s 2(2) is such that only the accused can raise the defence of diminished responsibility, with the result that, if there is prima facie evidence of the elements of diminished responsibility, the judge cannot leave that defence to the jury without the accused's consent.

There is one exception to the imposition of the burden of proof on the accused and to the obiter dictum in *Campbell*. It is provided by s 6 of the Criminal Procedure (Insanity) Act 1964, which provides that, where, at a murder trial, the accused contends that he was insane under the *M'Naghten Rules,* the prosecution may adduce or elicit evidence that he was suffering from diminished responsibility. In such a case, it is for the prosecution to prove the elements of diminished responsibility beyond reasonable doubt.[4]

1 *Dunbar* [1958] 1 QB 1, [1957] 2 All ER 737, CCA.
2 *Matheson* [1958] 2 All ER 87, [1958] 1 WLR 474, CCA.
3 (1986) 84 Cr App Rep 255, CA. Also see *Kooken* (1982) 74 Cr App Rep 30, CA.
4 *Grant* [1960] Crim LR 424.

9.35　The first of the three elements required for diminished responsibility is that the accused must have been suffering from 'abnormality of mind' at the material time. This phrase was explained by the Court of Criminal Appeal in *Byrne*.[1] D was a sexual psychopath who suffered from perverted, violent sexual desires. While under the influence of these desires he strangled a girl and mutilated her body. He was charged with murder and pleaded diminished responsibility. There was evidence that the impulse of those desires was stronger than the normal impulse of sex, so that D found it very difficult or, perhaps, impossible in some cases to resist putting the desires into practice and that the killing was done under such an impulse. The trial judge told the jury that D would not have established the defence even if he satisfied them that he found it very difficult or impossible to control his perverted sexual impulses. D was convicted, and he successfully appealed to the Court of Criminal Appeal. The Court held that it was wrong to say that these facts did not constitute evidence which would bring a case within the defence of diminished responsibility, and substituted a verdict of manslaughter on the ground of diminished responsibility. It held that 'abnormality of mind' meant a state of mind so different from that of an ordinary person that the reasonable man would term it abnormal. The term was wide enough to cover the mind's activities in all its aspects, not only the perception of physical acts and the ability to form a rational judgment as to whether the act is wrong, but also the ability to exercise will-power to control physical acts in accordance with that rational judgment. Seriously impaired self-control, though irrelevant to the *M'Naghten Rules* as construed in this country, is thus highly relevant to the question whether the accused was suffering from diminished responsibility.

1 [1960] 2 QB 396, [1960] 3 All ER 1, CCA.

9.36 The second element required for diminished responsibility is that the abnormality of mind must result from one of the specified causes, ie it must result from a condition of arrested or retarded development of mind or any inherent causes or be induced by disease or injury. Thus, abnormality of mind due to hate, jealousy or intoxication is outside the defence.[1] However, an abnormality of mind would be due to a specified cause ('disease or injury') if due to alcoholism of such a degree that *either* the brain had been injured so that there was gross impairment of judgment and emotional response *or*, where the brain had not been damaged to that extent, the drinking was involuntary in that the accused was unable to resist the impulse to take a first drink.[2] If an accused had the ability to resist the impulse to take the first drink, but thereafter found it irresistible to go on drinking, his mental abnormality would not be due to disease or injury (or either of the other specified causes).

1 *Fenton* (1975) 61 Cr App Rep 261, CA.
2 *Tandy* [1989] 1 All ER 267, CA; *Inseal* [1992] Crim LR 35, CA.

9.37 The third element is that the abnormality of mind must have substantially impaired the accused's mental responsibility for his acts and omissions in doing or being a party to the killing. In *Byrne* the Court of Criminal Appeal held that 'mental responsibility for his acts' pointed to a consideration of the extent to which the accused's mind was answerable for his physical acts. Whether there had been a substantial impairment of the accused's mental responsibility was a question of degree. Thus, while, in a case where the abnormality of mind due to a specified cause was one which affected the accused's self-control, there would clearly be substantial impairment where there was *inability* to exercise will-power to control acts, where there was *difficulty* in exercising will-power to control acts it would depend on the degree of difficulty. In this connection 'substantial' means what it says. The impairment of the accused's ability to resist the impulse under which he acts need not be 'total' but it must be more than 'trivial' or 'minimal'. 'Substantial' means something in between.[1] The difficulty which the accused had in controlling his conduct must have been substantially greater than would have been experienced by an ordinary person, without mental abnormality, in the circumstances in question.[2]

1 *Lloyd* [1967] 1 QB 175, [1966] 1 All ER 107, CCA.
2 *Simcox* [1964] Crim LR 402, CCA.

EVIDENCE

9.38 Unless there is some medical evidence to support all three elements of the defence it must not be left to the jury.[1] Assuming that there is such evidence, the position is as follows.

Whether the accused was suffering from abnormality of mind such as substantially to impair his mental responsibility is a question for the jury. The jury should approach these issues in a broad, commonsense way, taking into account all the evidence, including the acts or statements of the accused and his demeanour.[2] Of course, the medical evidence is important but the jury are not bound to accept it, even though it is unanimous, if there is other material before it which, in their opinion, conflicts with and outweighs it.[3] However, the jury must found their verdict on the evidence, and, if the medical evidence is unanimous and unchallenged and there is no other evidence which would justify the jury in rejecting the medical evidence, the jury are bound to accept the medical evidence and a verdict against the accused (ie of murder) contrary to the medical evidence will be set aside.[4] Sometimes the jury are faced with the difficult task of weighing conflicting medical evidence.[5]

The aetiology of the mental abnormality (ie whether it arose from a specified cause) is a matter to be determined solely on the medical evidence.[6]

Where the evidence is that the accused was suffering from abnormality of mind due to two or more causes, one of which is intoxication (or any other cause not specified by s 2), the jury must be told to ignore the effect of the intoxication (or other cause) and consider whether the effect of the other, admissible, causes amounted to such abnormality of mind as substantially impaired the accused's mental responsibility.[7] The Court of Appeal has approved the following way of putting the matter to the jury. They should be asked whether they are satisfied:

 a) that, if the accused had not taken drink, he would have killed as he in fact did, and
 b) whether he would have been under diminished responsibility when he did so.[8]

This seems a difficult, if not impossible, task for the jury.

1 *Dix* (1982) 74 Cr App Rep 306, CA.
2 *Simcox* [1964] Crim LR 402, CCA; *Byrne* [1960] 2 QB 396 at 403–404; *Kiszko* (1978) 68 Cr App Rep 62, CA.
3 *Byrne* [1960] 2 QB 396 at 403; *Walton v R* [1978] AC 788, [1978] 1 All ER 542, PC; *Sanders* [1991] Crim LR 781, CA.
4 *Matheson* [1958] 2 All ER 87, [1958] 1 WLR 474, CCA; *Bailey* (1961) 66 Cr App Rep 31 (note), CCA; *Vernege* [1982] 1 WLR 293, 74 Cr App Rep 232, CA. For a contrary view in relation to the question of substantial impairment of mental responsibilities, see Cohen 'Medical Evidence and Diminished Responsibility' [1981] NLJ 667.
5 *Jennion* [1962] 1 All ER 689, [1962] 1 WLR 317, CCA.
6 *Byrne* [1960] 2 QB 396, CCA.
7 *Fenton* (1975) 61 Cr App Rep 261, CA; *Turnbull* (1977) 65 Cr App Rep 242, CA; *Gittens* [1984] QB 698, [1984] 3 All ER 252, CA.
8 *Atkinson* [1985] Crim LR 314, CA.

9.39 With the prosecution's consent, the court may accept a plea of guilty of manslaughter on grounds of diminished responsibility, in which case a verdict from the jury will not be required, but this should only be done where there is clear and undisputed medical evidence of diminished responsibility.[1] The acceptance of such a plea is common.[2]

1 *Cox* [1968] 1 All ER 386, 52 Cr App Rep 130, CA; *Vinagre* (1979) 69 Cr App Rep 104, CA.
2 See Dell 'Diminished Responsibility Reconsidered' [1982] Crim LR 809.

PROPOSALS FOR REFORM

9.40   The Butler Committee[1] found s 2 of the Homicide Act 1957 unsatisfactory, particularly because of the imprecision of 'abnormality of mind' and 'mental responsibility', which has created problems for doctors, judges and juries. Clearly, the only substantial justification for the existence of the defence of diminished responsibility is the mandatory life sentence for murder. The Committee thought there was a strong case for giving the judge a discretion in passing sentence for murder, in which case the defence could be abolished. If this preferred solution was rejected, the Committee proposed that the defence should be amended.

In its Fourteenth Report: Offences against the Person, published in 1980,[2] the Criminal Law Revision Committee favoured a retention of the defence of diminished responsibility, even if the mandatory life sentence for murder was abolished, on the grounds that if the defence was not retained the offence of murder would range from killings meriting severe punishment to ones where only a small penalty was appropriate, and the judge would have no guidance from the jury to assist him in sentencing, and that juries might be reluctant to convict of murder in clear cases of diminished responsibility. In relation to these points, similar arguments could be made with regard to other offences, although they would not appear to be borne out in practice. The Committee also favoured a re-formulation of the defence.

The draft Criminal Code Bill[3] essentially incorporates the recommendations of the Criminal Law Revision Committee. Clause 56 provides that a person who, otherwise, would be guilty of murder, is guilty of manslaughter instead if, at the time of his act, he is suffering from such mental abnormality as is substantial enough reason to reduce his offence to manslaughter. 'Mental abnormality' here means mental illness, arrested or incomplete development of mind, psychopathic disorder, and any other disorder or disability of mind, except intoxication. As now, where the abnormality of mind arose from inherent causes and intoxication combined, the jury would have to be told to ignore the effect of the alcohol on the accused's mind.

With the consent of a person charged with murder, it would be open to the prosecution to have him committed for trial or indicted for manslaughter (on the ground of diminished responsibility) instead of for murder.

1 Committee on Mentally Abnormal Offenders (Cmnd 6244) paras 19.1–19.21. For a discussion of the Committee's proposals, see Ashworth [1975] Crim LR 692.
2 Cmnd 7844, paras 75, 76 and 91–98.
3 Law Commission: A Criminal Code for England and Wales (1989): Law Com No 177; see para 3.21 above.

Automatism and other involuntary conduct[1]

9.41   Generally,[2] it is a defence that the act or omission or, even, event with which the accused is charged was involuntary.[3] An act, omission to act or event on the part of the accused is involuntary where it is beyond his control;

where an act is beyond the control of that person's mind the situation is known as one of automatism. For convenience acts, omissions and events will be discussed in turn.

1 See Edwards 'Automatism and Criminal Responsibility' (1958) 21 MLR 375; Hart *Punishment and Responsibility* p 90.
2 For exceptions, see paras 9.43, 9.48 and 8.18.
3 *Woolmington v DPP* [1935] AC 462 at 482; *Bratty v A-G for Northern Ireland* [1963] AC 386 at 409, [1961] 3 All ER 523 at 532; *Kilbride v Lake* [1962] NZLR 590; *Ryan v R* (1967) 121 CLR 205.

9.42 *Involuntary act* One of the best known examples of an involuntary act is where the act is compelled by external physical force. Hale gave the following example: 'If there be an actual forcing of a man, as if A by force take the arm of B and the weapon in his hand, and therewith stabs C whereof he dies, this is murder in A, and B is not guilty.'[1] In *Hill v Baxter*[2] it was stated that a man could not be said to be driving where at the material time he was attacked by a swarm of bees and was prevented from exercising any directional control over the vehicle, any movements of his arms and legs being solely caused by the action of the bees. Another example is where a motorist is suddenly deprived of control over his vehicle by a sudden blow-out or brake-failure.[3]

However, some involuntary acts are not directly caused by external physical force or the like but are done in a state of automatism. An act is done in such a state if it is done by the muscles without any control by the mind (such as a reflex action, or a spasmodic or convulsive act)[4] *or* if it is done during a state involving a loss of consciousness, or a state of impaired consciousness such as to deprive the accused of effective control over his act.[5]

In the case of impaired consciousness the law is not clearly established. A person who is unconscious clearly lacks any control over his limbs, but a person whose consciousness is impaired may exercise some, albeit limited, control over his limbs. The balance of authority, however, indicates that a person is in law an automaton if his consciousness is impaired to such an extent that, while he exercises some control over his act, he is deprived of *effective* control over it. In cases like *Charlson*[6] and *Kemp*[7], whose facts are set out in para 9.46, and *Quick*[8], the accused's acts of violence were treated as done in a state of automatism although they were probably done in a state of impaired consciousness in which it could not be said for sure that the accused did not exercise any control over their acts. Moreover, in *Burgess*,[9] the facts of which were set out in paras 9.17, the Court of Appeal appears to have treated the accused's acts of violence as done in a state of automatism where '[h]is mind was to some extent controlling his actions which were purposive rather than the result simply of muscular spasm, but without being consciously aware of what he was doing'. On the other hand, in *Broome v Perkins*,[10] where D drove five miles home, very erratically, in a hypogly-caemic state in which he might not have been conscious of what he was doing, the Divisional Court directed a conviction of driving without due care and attention, on the ground that D's impaired consciousness, if it existed, would not have constituted automatism because he must have reacted to stimuli, made decisions (eg to brake or steer) and given direction to his limbs. To require, as *Broome v Perkins* does, a total lack of control for automatism would severely and unnecessarily limit its range. Fortunately, as stated above, the balance of authority indicates that it is enough that the accused is deprived of *effective* control over his act. If cl 33 of the draft Criminal Code Bill is ever enacted the issue would be clearly resolved. Under cl 33 an accused would be in a state of automatism if his act occurred while he was in a condition depriving him of effective control over it.

As already implied, the fact that at the material time the accused's mind was 'not working in to gear' with the result that he was not aware of moral inhibitions does not in itself bring him within the legal concept of automatism.[11]

It is clear from the cases that the phrase 'automatism and other involuntary conduct' has a meaning limited to cases of unconscious or reflex actions and other actions beyond the effective control of the accused. Thus, acts done under an irresistible impulse are not regarded as 'involuntary acts' because, although the person concerned may not be able to control the impulse which prompts his act, the doing of the act itself is not beyond his effective control.[12] The narrow meaning given to 'involuntary conduct' also prevents that phrase covering acts done under duress (where there is a threat of physical force unless an act is done),[13] although the threat may, as we shall see later,[14] provide an excuse.

1 Hale *Pleas of the Crown* vol I, p 434. Also see Hawkins *Pleas of the Crown* vol I, ch 29, s 3.
2 [1958] 1 QB 277, [1958] 1 All ER 193, DC.
3 This example was given in *Bell* [1984] 3 All ER 842 at 846.
4 *Bratty v A-G for Northern Ireland* [1963] AC 386, [1961] 3 All ER 523, HL.
5 *Charlson* [1955] 1 All ER 859, [1955] 1 WLR 317; *Kemp* [1957] 1 QB 399, [1956] 3 All ER 249; *Quick* [1973] QB 910, [1973] 3 All ER 347, CA.
6 [1955] 1 All ER 859, [1955] 1 WLR 317.
7 [1957] 1 QB 399, [1956] 3 All ER 249.
8 [1973] QB 910, [1973] 3 All ER 347, CA.
9 [1991] 2 QB 92, [1991] 2 All ER 769, CA.
10 (1987) 85 Cr App Rep 321, DC. Also see *Isitt* (1977) 67 Cr App Rep 44, CA.
11 *Isitt* (1977) 67 Cr App Rep 44, CA.
12 *Bratty v A-G for Northern Ireland* [1963] AC 386 at 409.
13 Edwards (1958) 21 MLR 375 at 381.
14 Paras 22.16–22.37.

9.43 *Involuntary omission* An omission to act is involuntary (ie beyond the accused's control) where he is physically restrained from acting or otherwise incapable of acting. Thus, in *Leicester v Pearson*,[1] which was concerned with the offence of failing to accord precedence to a pedestrian on a zebra crossing, it was held that if the failure was beyond the control of a driver (eg because he had been pushed onto the crossing by a bump from a car behind) he would not be liable.

While it is generally the case that an involuntary omission is not culpable, the wording of the offence may lead to it being construed as one in which impossibility of complying with the duty in question is no excuse. An example of such an offence is provided by *Sparks v Worthington*.[2] In that case the Divisional Court held that the statutory offence of failing to produce a driving licence for examination had been committed, even though it was physically impossible for the licence holder to produce the licence because it had been sent to the Driver and Vehicle Licensing Centre at Swansea. Likewise, it has been held that a driver can be convicted of the statutory offence of failing to produce a vehicle test certificate notwithstanding that it was impossible for him to do so because it is in the possession of the vehicle's owner who refuses to give it to the driver to produce.[3] Such an exceptional construction is likely to be limited to offences of a minor, regulatory nature.[4]

1 [1952] 2 QB 668, [1952] 2 All ER 71, DC. Also see *Burns v Bidder* [1967] 2 QB 227, [1966] 3 All ER 29, DC.
2 [1986] RTR 64, DC.
3 *Davey v Towle* [1973] RTR 328, DC.
4 The relevant provision in the draft Criminal Code Bill (cl 33) is essentially the same as the definition of involuntary omission given here, but it does not envisage any exception to the rule that an involuntary omission is not culpable (Law Commission: A Criminal Code for England and Wales (1989): Law Com No 177).

9.44 *Involuntary event* An event, eg possession of a prohibited thing, is involuntary where it is brought about by the physical compulsion of another or its occurrence is otherwise beyond the accused's control. However, as we saw in para 8.18, in status offences and the like it is liable to be held that a person can be convicted despite the fact that the relevant event was involuntary on his part.

THE DISTINCTION BETWEEN INSANE AND NON-INSANE AUTOMATISM[1]

9.45 Where the accused was suffering from non-insane automatism he must be acquitted, but if the case is one where the accused was suffering from a 'defect of reason due to disease of the mind' the *M'Naghten Rules* apply and, if the trial is on indictment, he is found not guilty by reason of insanity and an order will be made against him under s 5 of the Criminal Procedure (Insanity) Act 1964, as explained in para 9.24. This distinction was established by the House of Lords in *Bratty v A-G for Northern Ireland*.[2] D was charged with the murder of a girl. It was not disputed that he had strangled her. D said that he had had a blackout and there was some evidence that he was suffering from psychomotor epilepsy, which is undoubtedly a disease of the mind. D relied on the defences of automatism and insanity, but the trial judge only directed the jury on the issue of insanity. D was convicted, and his appeals to the Northern Irish Court of Criminal Appeal and the House of Lords were dismissed. It was held that, where the only evidence of the cause of automatism is a disease of the mind, the case is one of insane automatism and the *M'Naghten Rules* apply. If, on the other hand, the evidence is that automatism was caused not by a disease of the mind (i e not by an internal cause) but by some other (external) cause, such as a blow on the head, the case is one of non-insane automatism.[3]

1 Lederman 'Non-Insane and Insane Automatism: Reducing the Significance of a Problematic Distinction' (1983) 34 ICLQ 819.
2 [1963] AC 386, [1961] 3 All ER 523, HL. Also see *Quick* [1973] QB 910, [1973] 3 All ER 347, CA.
3 Paras 9.15–9.17.

9.46 An accused who wishes to plead automatism may well be reluctant to claim that it is of the insane variety but he cannot prevent his defence being treated as one of insanity if the medical evidence before the court, whether adduced by the defence or the prosecution, indicates that the alleged automatism arose from a disease of the mind, because it is for the judge to determine whether that evidence discloses a disease of the mind.

What has just been said was denied by Barry J in *Charlson*,[1] where D was charged with unlawfully and maliciously inflicting grievous bodily harm, having struck his small son with a mallet and thrown him out of a window. There was evidence that D had acted as an automaton as a result of a cerebral tumour. Barry J directed the jury (who subsequently acquitted D) that the case did not involve the defence of insanity, since that defence had not been raised by D who was alone competent to do so, and left the defence of non-insane automatism to them. However, in *Kemp*[2] a contrary view was taken in a similar type of case. D was charged with causing grievous bodily harm to his wife with intent to murder her, a statutory offence which has since been repealed because it was identical with the offence of attempted murder. It was not disputed that D had struck his wife with a hammer in a period of unconsciousness, caused by the effect on his brain of arteriosclerosis. The defence asked for an acquittal on the authority of *Charlson*, but Devlin J distinguished *Charlson* on the ground that in that case the doctors were apparently agreed that the accused was not suffering from a 'disease of the mind', whereas in Kemp's case they were not so agreed. Devlin J accordingly held that Kemp's defence, if any, was one of insanity and directed the jury accordingly. The old style verdict of guilty but insane was subsequently returned.

The two cases are not so easily reconciled since, as we have seen,[3] whether the alleged condition from which the accused is suffering is a 'disease of the mind' is not a medical question to be decided by medical witnesses but a question of law for the judge. *Kemp* was approved, and *Charlson* doubted, in *Bratty's* case[4] by Lord Denning, who pointed out that the old notion that only the defence can raise insanity has gone, and it is now clear that the approach in *Kemp* now represents the law.

A recent example of the approach taken in *Kemp* is *Hennessy*.[5] D, a diabetic, was charged with taking a conveyance without authority and with driving while disqualified. His defence was that he had failed to take his proper dose of insulin because of stress, anxiety and depression, and consequently was suffering from hyperglycaemia and in a state of automatism when the offences occurred. The trial judge ruled that, since D's alleged automatism was due to a disease of the mind, the defence (if any) was one of insanity. At this D changed his plea to guilty. The Court of Appeal held that the judge's ruling was correct since the hyperglycaemia caused by diabetes (a disease) not corrected by insulin was a disease of the mind and the stress, anxiety and depression were not factors of a kind to prevent automatism, if it resulted from them, being due to a disease of the mind.[6]

The development of the law relating to insanity and automatism is such that many cases of automatism are, in law, of the insane type, although they would not be so described in common or medical parlance. An extreme example is provided by *Burgess*,[7] where the Court of Appeal held that sleepwalking constituted insane automatism because it was not due to an external cause.

1 [1955] 1 All ER 859, [1955] 1 WLR 317.
2 [1957] 1 QB 399, [1956] 3 All ER 249.
3 Para 9.13.
4 [1963] AC 386 at 411.
5 [1989] 2 All ER 9, [1989] 1 WLR 287, CA. Cf *Bingham* [1991] Crim LR 433, where the Court of Appeal held that evidence that a diabetic had been suffering from *hypoglycaemia* (deficient blood sugar level caused by too much insulin or failing to eat properly after taking insulin to counteract it) was evidence of non-insane automatism.
6 See para 9.17.
7 [1991] 2 QB 92, [1991] 2 All ER 769, CA; para 9.17. Under the draft Criminal Code Bill, cl 33 sleepwalking would be classed as (non-insane) automatism.

9.47 The distinction between insane and non-insane automatism is one of great importance because, in the case of non-insane automatism, the accused simply bears the burden of adducing evidence;[1] once the issue is raised, the burden of disproving automatism is borne by the Crown in accordance with the general principles enunciated in *Woolmington's* case.[2] If, however, the case is one of insane automatism the accused bears the burden of proof as well as the burden of adducing evidence.[3]

The accused bears the burden of adducing evidence of non-insane automatism because there is a rebuttable presumption of law that everyone has sufficient mental capacity to be responsible for his crimes. If the prosecution had to adduce evidence of capacity in every case, its position would be intolerable. It is up to the accused to indicate the nature of his alleged incapacity, and since, generally speaking, the mere statement 'I had a black-out' or 'I can't remember what happened' will be totally insufficient,[4] the accused's evidence will very rarely be sufficient unless it is supported by medical evidence.[5]

The task of the judge where the defence of automatism is raised by the accused was neatly summarised by the Court of Appeal in *Burgess*.[6] The Court said two questions fell to be decided by the judge before the defence could be left (with a direction on the applicable law, including the burden of proof) to the jury:

a) Whether a proper evidential burden for the defence of automatism has been laid.

b) Whether the evidence showed the case to be one of insane automatism or of non-insane automatism.

1 *Bratty v A-G for Northern Ireland* [1963] AC 386, [1961] 3 All ER 523; *Stripp* (1978) 69 Cr App Rep 318, CA; *Pullen* [1991] Crim LR 457, CA.
2 Ibid; see para 7.3.
3 Para 9.12.
4 *Cook v Atchison* [1968] Crim LR 266, DC.
5 *Bratty v A-G for Northern Ireland* [1963] AC 386 at 414, [1961] 3 All ER 523, per Lord Denning; *Moses v Winder* [1981] RTR 37, DC.
6 [1991] 2 QB 92, [1991] 2 All ER 769, CA.

SELF-INDUCED AUTOMATISM

9.48 Sometimes, non-insane automatism can be regarded as self-induced in that it results from something done by the accused or not done by him (as where a diabetic becomes an automaton as a result of not taking his insulin or, having taken insulin, failing to eat sufficient food so that the insulin reacts adversely).

In such a case, the position is as follows:

a) As was held by the Court of Appeal in *Bailey*,[1] where the offence is one requiring proof of a 'specific intent', a term discussed in paras 9.63 and 9.64, an accused who was suffering from self-induced automatism at the material time cannot be convicted of that offence whatever the cause of the automatism. Examples of offences of specific intent are murder, wounding or causing grievous bodily harm with intent (contrary to s 18 of the Offences against the Person Act 1861) and attempt to commit an offence.

b) Where the offence is one of 'basic intent', ie an offence other than one of specific intent, such as manslaughter or unlawful wounding or infliction of grievous bodily harm (contrary to s 20 of the Offences against the Person Act 1861), then:

i) If the automatism was due to voluntary intoxication, the accused's automatism is no defence and he can be convicted[2] despite the fact that at the material time he lacked the mens rea normally required for the offence charged. This is discussed in more detail in paras 9.54 to 9.64.

ii) Where the automatism was due to some other cause, such as a failure by a diabetic to eat adequately after taking insulin, then, it was held by the Court of Appeal in *Bailey*,[3] the accused cannot, except in the case mentioned below, be convicted of an offence of basic intent. Within this category falls the situation where the accused's automatism was caused by an occurrence which was brought about by his voluntary intoxication, as where, because of his intoxication, a person falls over, bangs his head and thereby becomes concussed; the concussion, and not the intoxication, is the immediate cause of the automatism.[4]

The exceptional case just referred to is where the accused is proved to have been subjectively reckless in the following way: viz that before he became an automaton, he appreciated the risk that something which he did or failed to do was likely to make him aggressive, unpredictable or uncontrollable with the result that he might endanger others (as opposed simply to becoming unconscious) and he deliberately ran the risk or otherwise disregarded it. In such a case, as the Court of Appeal held in *Bailey*,[5] the accused can be convicted of an offence of basic intent, even though at the time of his conduct which constituted the actus reus of such an offence he lacked the mens rea normally required for it.[6]

1 [1983] 2 All ER 503, [1983] 1 WLR 760, CA.
2 This was recognised by the Court of Appeal in *Bailey* [1983] 2 All ER 503, [1983] 1 WLR 760, CA.
3 [1983] 2 All ER 503, [1983] 1 WLR 760, CA, disapproving dicta in *Quick* [1973] QB 910, [1973] 3 All ER 347, CA, on this point.
4 *Stripp* (1978) 69 Cr App Rep 318 at 323.
5 [1983] 2 All ER 503, [1983] 1 WLR 760, CA.
6 The relevant provisions of the draft Criminal Code Bill (cl 33) are essentially the same as the rules set out above (Law Commission: A Criminal Code for England and Wales (1989): Law Com No 177).

9.49 Where negligence is the very essence of an offence, as in the case of careless driving, an accused who, for example, falls asleep at the wheel or goes into a hypoglycaemic coma at the wheel can be convicted under the ordinary principles of liability, not in relation to the time when he was an automaton but in relation to the time when he realised or should have realised that he was about to become unconscious and should have stopped driving.[1]

1 *Kay v Butterworth* (1945) 173 LT 191, DC; *Moses v Winder* [1981] RTR 37, DC.

Intoxication

9.50 Alcohol is a drug which is capable of altering mood, perception or consciousness, of loosening inhibitions and self-control, of impairing movements, reactions, judgement and ability to foresee consequences. Certain other drugs and substances (including some glues) can also have such effects.

In some offences, such as driving, or being in charge of, a mechanically propelled vehicle under the influence of drink or drugs, or being drunk and disorderly in a public place, intoxication is the essence of the offence, but the matter which must be dealt with in this chapter is the extent to which intoxication may be relevant to criminal liability for an offence, such as murder, assault or theft, where it is a factor but not of the essence.

VOLUNTARY INTOXICATION

9.51 Intoxication is voluntary where it results from the accused knowingly taking alcohol or some other drug or intoxicating substance (such as glue) or a combination of these,[1] even though he does not know its precise nature or strength[2] or even though the effect of the amount taken is much greater than would have been expected. There are two exceptions. Intoxication is not voluntary *in certain cases* where it is caused a) by a drug taken under medical advice, or b) by a non- dangerous drug (ie a drug which is not normally liable to cause unpredictability or aggressiveness, such as a sedative or soporific drug). These cases of involuntary intoxication are dealt with in paras 9.73 to 9.78.

Voluntary intoxication is not, and never has been, in itself a defence. Thus, it is no excuse that the accused's power to judge between right and wrong was impaired so that he would not have acted as he did but for his intoxication, nor that his powers of self-control were relaxed so that he more readily gave way to temptation than if he were sober, nor even that, in his intoxicated condition, he found the impulse to act as he did irresistible,[3] and it is not a defence in itself that the accused's voluntary intoxication caused him to become an automaton.[4]

However, voluntary intoxication is a factor relevant to criminal liability in three cases:

a) if a specific intent is an essential element of the offence charged and the accused's intoxication affords evidence that he lacked this intent;
b) where statute expressly provides that a particular belief shall be a defence to the offence charged;
c) if it causes such a disease of the mind as to bring the *M'Naghten Rules* into play.

1 *Lipman* [1970] 1 QB 152, [1969] 3 All ER 410, CA; *DPP v Majewski* [1977] AC 443, [1976] 2 All ER 142, HL.
2 *Allen* [1988] Crim LR 698, CA.
3 *DPP v Beard* [1920] AC 479, HL; *A-G for Northern Ireland v Gallagher* [1963] AC 349, [1961] 3 All ER 299, HL.
4 *Lipman* [1970] 1 QB 152, [1969] 3 All ER 410, CA; approved in *DPP v Majewski* [1977] AC 443, [1976] 2 All ER 142, HL.

VOLUNTARY INTOXICATION AS EVIDENCE OF THE ABSENCE OF SPECIFIC INTENT

9.52 Particularly in offences involving violence, the accused may lack the necessary mens rea for the offence charged because of his intoxication, as where he kills another mistakenly believing in his drunken stupor that the other is a theatrical dummy or where because of his intoxication he is unable to appreciate that firing a gun at another is likely to harm him or he believes that the gun is unloaded and merely wants to scare the other by pretending to fire it. In such a case a simple claim of lack of mens rea is extremely unlikely to succeed unless the accused introduces evidence of intoxication to support it. There is a mass of authority that the accused may rely on voluntary intoxication as evidence that he lacked the necessary mens rea only if the offence is one requiring a specific intent (as opposed to a basic intent). This rule was affirmed by the House of Lords in 1976 in *DPP v Majewski*.[1] The House of Lords' decision in this case confirmed the view previously taken by the House in *DPP v Beard*,[2] although that decision was not free from ambiguity and some statements in it are no longer correct.

1 [1977] AC 443, [1976] 2 All ER 142, HL.
2 [1920] AC 479, 89 LJKB 437, HL.

9.53 It is important to emphasise that intoxication does not negative mens rea. All that the cases decide is that the accused may adduce evidence of intoxication if charged with an offence requiring specific intent, and this evidence may be taken into account by the magistrates or jury along with all the other evidence in deciding whether the prosecution has proved that he did have that intent.

At one time, the law was different. In *Beard* Lord Birkenhead LC, giving the judgment of the House, said that evidence of intoxication could be taken into consideration only if it rendered the accused incapable of forming the specific intent essential to constitute the offence charged. This proposition had the following arbitrary result where, through intoxication, the accused lacked the necessary specific intent: if the accused's intoxication was such that he did not have the capacity to form the specific intent, he was exculpated; whereas if his intoxication did not render him incapable of forming that intent, although because of it he did not have that intent, he was criminally liable.

Fortunately, it is clear that, following s 8 of the Criminal Justice Act 1967, Lord Birkenhead's requirement of incapacity to form the requisite specific intent exists no longer. As we have seen,[1] under s 8 a person is no longer to be presumed to intend the natural and probable consequences of his act; instead the question whether the accused had the necessary intent is to be decided by the jury or magistrates on all the evidence. Thus, the jury in deciding whether the accused had the necessary specific intent must take into account all the evidence, including that relating to intoxication, drawing such inferences from the evidence as appear proper in the circumstances.[2] The strongest evidence, of course, is that the accused was too intoxicated to be capable of forming the specific intent, but it is enough if, on all the evidence (including that relating to the accused's intoxication), the jury find that while the accused's intoxication was not such as to make him incapable of forming a specific intent, i e he could have intended, he did not in fact have that intent.[2]

A second change is that, contrary to dicta in *Beard*, it is now established that the burden is on the prosecution to establish that, despite the evidence of intoxication, the accused had the necessary specific intent.[3]

1 Para 7.14.
2 *Pordage* [1975] Crim LR 575, CA; *Sheehan and Moore* [1975] 2 All ER 960, [1975] 1 WLR 739, CA; *Garlick* (1980) 72 Cr App Rep 291, CA; *Davies* [1991] Crim LR 469, CA.
3 *Sheehan* [1975] 2 All ER 960, [1975] 1 WLR 739, CA.

9.54 *Voluntary intoxication and offences of basic intent* These amendments to the propositions of law in *Beard's* case do not remove the major limitation of the rule affirmed in *Majewski*: that, if the offence charged is one of basic intent (i e does not require a specific intent), the accused may be convicted of it if he was voluntarily intoxicated at the time of committing its actus reus, even though because of his intoxication he did not have the mens rea normally required for a conviction for that offence, and even though he was then in a state of automatism.

The rules relating to a claim by a person accused of a basic intent offence that he lacked the necessary mens rea have sometimes been explained by the courts on the ground that the intoxicated person is convicted because he was reckless as to the risk of becoming mentally impaired involved in taking the drink or drugs and recklessness is sufficient mens rea for the offence in question.[1] Even if recklessness was sufficient for all offences of basic intent (see para 9.63), it would be difficult to accept this theory. One reason is that it proceeds on the basis that one who takes drink or dangerous drugs is conclusively presumed to be reckless, which (in offences where subjective recklessness is required) conflicts with the provisions of s 8 of the Criminal Justice Act 1967.[2] Another reason is that mens rea must exist at the time of the accused's prohibited conduct and in relation to the risks specified in the definition of the offence. To convict an accused simply on the basis of recklessness at an earlier point of time (when he took the drink or drug) as to the risk involved in taking it is to base liability on a very different ground from that specified by the definition of the offence.

1 See, for example, *DPP v Majewski* [1977] AC 443, [1976] 2 All ER 142, HL, per Lord Elwyn-Jones LC, with whom Lords Diplock and Kilbrandon agreed, and Lord Edmund-Davies; *Caldwell* [1982] AC 341, [1981] 1 All ER 961, per Lord Diplock, with whom Lords Keith and Roskill agreed; *Hardie* [1984] 3 All ER 848 at 853.
2 Para 7.14.

9.55 A better explanation is that, as the House of Lords recognised in *Majewski*, there is a substantive rule of law that, if a person is charged with an offence not requiring a specific intent and relies on evidence of voluntary intoxication, the prosecution need not prove the mens rea normally required for that offence (even though it is specified in the definition of the offence), nor a voluntary act on his part, and the accused can be convicted simply on proof that he committed the actus reus. In effect, where evidence of voluntary intoxication is introduced to support a claim of lack of mens rea on a charge of an offence not requiring a specific intent but some other form of mens rea, that offence is transformed into one not requiring proof of mens rea. The fact that this rule is one of substantive law means that it is unaffected by s 8 of the Criminal Justice Act 1967,[1] which directs the court or jury to refer to all the evidence and to draw such inferences as it thinks proper in determining whether the accused had the necessary intention or foresight. As we have seen,[2] this provision is of importance where the accused pleads voluntary intoxication in relation to an offence requiring a specific intent, but, as their Lordships stated in *Majewski*, where the offence charged does not require a specific intent s 8 of the 1967 Act has no application because the effect of introducing evidence of intoxication is to remove the need for proof of mens rea, so that liability is strict, and there is therefore no mens rea to be proved to which the evidential rule in s 8 can relate. It appears that this is so even though the accused introduces other evidence, as well as that of intoxication, in support of his claim that he lacked the mens rea for the offence charged.

1 Para 7.14.
2 Para 9.53.

9.56 It must be admitted that, despite what has just been said, the Court of Appeal's decision in *Woods*[1] provides authority for the proposition that, at least in the offence of rape (which is one of basic and not specific intent),[2] where the accused introduces evidence of voluntary intoxication in support of a plea of lack of mens rea, the jury should be told to decide whether the accused had the necessary mens rea but to disregard the evidence of his intoxication in doing so. At his trial for rape, Woods pleaded that he had been so drunk that he had not realised that the girl was not consenting. Section 1(2) of the Sexual Offences (Amendment) Act 1976 provides that, if the jury has to consider whether a man believed that a woman was consenting to intercourse, it must have regard to the presence or absence of reasonable ground for such a belief 'in conjunction with any other relevant matters'. The Court of Appeal held that intoxication was not a 'legally relevant matter' in this context, but that s 1(2) required the jury to look at all the other relevant evidence before making up their minds on what the accused believed. This decision is probably limited to rape,[3] since no other offence has a provision corresponding to s 1(2), but even in the context of the offence of rape it gives rise to an absurd test (and one requiring a feat of mental gymnastics) since to ask the hypothetical question whether the accused would have known the woman was not consenting if he had not been intoxicated seems to admit of only one answer: 'yes'.

1 (1981) 74 Cr App Rep 312, CA. See Williams *Textbook of Criminal Law* (2nd edn) 474-475.
2 *Woods* (1981) 74 Cr App Rep 312, CA; *Fotheringham* (1989) 88 Cr App Rep 206, CA.
3 It was applied in *Fotheringham* (1989) 88 Cr App Rep 206, CA, another rape case.

9.57 In relation to the rule that proof of mens rea is not required when an accused who was voluntarily intoxicated at the material time is charged with an offence of basic intent, it has been argued[1] that the rule only applies to an accused who was completely intoxicated (ie in a state of severely reduced awareness through intoxication), and that the need for proof of mens rea is not removed where a person pleads partial intoxication in order to give credibility to his plea of lack of mens rea. Some implicit support for this can be found in the cases.[2] However, as the point was not argued or expressly considered in them, it would be premature to state that it represents the law, and it is not so regarded in this book.

1 Lynch 'The Scope of Intoxication' [1982] Crim LR 139 and 392.
2 *DPP v Morgan* [1976] AC 182, [1975] 2 All ER 347, HL; *Cogan* [1976] QB 217, [1975] 2 All ER 1059, CA.

9.58 The effect of the rule in *Majewski* that proof of mens rea is not required when an accused who was voluntarily intoxicated at the material time is charged with an offence of basic intent is greatly reduced when *Caldwell*-type recklessness[1] suffices for that offence. This is because, as in *Caldwell*[2] itself, an accused who was intoxicated at the material time can be convicted of such an offence if he gave no thought to the risk in question where it would have been obvious to an ordinary, reasonable person who (by definition) is not intoxicated.[3] Nevertheless, even here, *Majewski* does have some significance because an intoxicated person who *has* thought about a possible risk, which would have been obvious to an ordinary, reasonable person, and wrongly concluded that it did not exist can be convicted under *Majewski* (on the basis that he has committed the actus reus of the relevant offence), even though he falls outside the definition of *Caldwell*-type recklessness.[4]

1 Paras 6.45–6.52.

2 [1982] AC 341, [1981] 1 All ER 961, HL.
3 Evidence of voluntary intoxication may in fact strengthen the prosecution's case since, if the evidence is of intoxication to such an extent as to impair control or disinhibit the accused, it is admissible as evidence that the accused gave no thought to the risk or that he realised it and took it when he would not have if he had been sober: *Griffiths* (1989) 88 Cr App Rep 6, CA; *Clarke* (1990) 91 Cr App Rep 69, CA.
4 Para 6.50.

9.59 *Voluntary intoxication as evidence of absence of specific intent: an exception* In one situation, at least, the rule, that a person charged with an offence requiring a specific intent may rely on evidence of voluntary intoxication as evidence that he lacked the necessary mens rea, is abrogated. This is the situation where under a mistake induced by voluntary intoxication the accused mistakenly believes that he must act in self-defence or the like. Whether there are other exceptional situations is discussed in para 9.62.

We have seen that in the definitions of some offences against the person the words 'unlawful' or 'unlawfully' (which refer to the absence of elements of justification, such as self-defence and the prevention of crime) are employed. We have also seen that where they are used they are an element of the actus reus and that the accused must be proved to have mens rea in relation to that element. For example, in murder the accused must be proved to have intended *unlawfully* to kill or cause grievous bodily harm.

If a sober person kills another in the dark mistakenly believing that the other is a tailor's dummy, he is not guilty of murder because he lacks an *intent* unlawfully *to kill or cause grievous bodily harm*, and if he does so mistakenly believing that the person coming towards him is about to stab him, he is not guilty of murder because he lacks an *intent unlawfully* to kill or cause grievous bodily harm.[1] Except in two instances, the nature of the evidence adduced in support of the alleged mistake will not affect the outcome of the plea in either type of case if the alleged mistake is not disproved. The two exceptions are a) where the accused's plea is in effect one of insanity,[2] and b) where the evidence in support involves voluntary intoxication. This second exception arises as a result of the reasoning of the Court of Appeal in *O'Grady*.[3] According to that reasoning, if the accused intended to kill but acted under an intoxicated and mistaken belief that he was being attacked and had to kill to defend himself, he is guilty of murder even though he did not intend *unlawfully* to kill or cause grievous bodily harm (whereas he would not be guilty if an intoxicated mistake had prevented him having an intent to kill or do grievous bodily harm, as where he drunkenly believed his victim was a tailor's dummy). The same rule would apply on a charge of any other offence requiring a specific intent unlawfully to cause some sort of harm.

1 Paras 7.19–7.21.
2 Paras 9.12–9.30.
3 [1987] QB 995, [1987] 3 All ER 420, CA; see MacDonald (1987) 137 NLJ 914 and Milgate [1987] CLJ 381.

9.60 The facts of *O'Grady* were that D and the deceased had fallen asleep after a day's heavy drinking. D woke to find the deceased hitting him and retaliated with what he thought were blows to defend himself. The fight subsided and D fell asleep again. When he awoke he found the deceased was dead, having suffered serious wounds consistent with blows from both blunt and sharp objects. D was charged with murder but convicted of manslaughter.

D appealed, arguing that the trial judge had been right to say that he should be judged according to his intoxicated mistaken belief that he was under attack, but wrong in not stating that the reasonableness of the force used should be judged according to D's understanding of the situation (the severity of the attack), and not objectively.

The Court of Appeal dismissed D's appeal. Indeed it took an even narrower view of the law than the trial judge, since (in the absence of binding authority) it concluded that an accused 'is not entitled to rely, so far as self-defence is concerned, upon a mistaken belief that one is under attack which has been induced by voluntary intoxication' and that this rule applied to specific intent offences, such as murder, as well as to basic intent offences, such as manslaughter.

The court held that its decision in *Williams*,[1] that an accused who might have been labouring under a mistaken belief that it was necessary to use force to defend another (or in self-defence etc) must be judged according to that mistaken view, whether the mistake was reasonable or not, was irrelevant where the jury are satisfied that the mistake was caused by voluntary intoxication.

While the dismissal of D's appeal in *O'Grady* would seem correct under the present law, since after all manslaughter is an offence of basic intent, the reasoning behind it (which was probably obiter) introduces additional complication and uncertainties and contradicts the rule affirmed in *Majewski*. We know that the mens rea for murder is an intention unlawfully to kill or do grievous bodily harm and that murder is an offence requiring specific intent, but apparently only in relation to the intention to kill or do grievous bodily harm, not in relation to the element of unlawfulness. This nonsense derives from the view of the Court of Appeal that 'the question of mistake can and ought to be considered separately from the question of intent'. This view contradicts the clear statement to the contrary of the Court of Appeal in *Williams* to the effect that the element of unlawfulness is part of the actus reus of an offence against the person, in relation to which the accused must be proved to have had mens rea.

Despite these criticisms, it is clear from *O'Connor*[2] that the Court of Appeal continue to regard *O'Grady* as representing the law on this matter.

1 [1987] 3 All ER 411, 78 Cr App Rep 276, CA.
2 [1991] Crim LR 135, CA.

9.61 The decision in *O'Grady* was clearly influenced by policy considerations, just as the rule affirmed in *Majewski* was. The Court of Appeal stated:

> 'There are two competing interests. On the one hand the interest of the defendant who has only acted according to what he believed to be necessary to protect himself, and on the other hand that of the public in general and the victim in particular who, probably through no fault of his own, has been injured or perhaps killed because of the defendant's drunken mistake. Reason recoils from the conclusion that in such circumstances a defendant is entitled to leave the court without a stain on his character. We find support for that view in the decision of the House of Lords in *Majewski*.'

But here is another fallacy: the defendant would not leave court without a stain, because he could certainly be convicted of manslaughter under the normal rules applicable to basic intent offences, whereby if evidence of voluntary intoxication is adduced the offence is converted into one not requiring proof of mens rea, so that the policy of the courts of protecting the public against voluntarily intoxicated offenders would have been upheld.

9.62 *Other exceptions?* The approach taken in *O'Grady*[1] leaves open the more general possibility of the mental elements in offences of specific intent being divided into elements of specific intent and elements of mens rea which are not, so that an accused who had the specific intent element but lacked the other mental element because of voluntary intoxication could be convicted on the basis of a rule corresponding to the rule that proof of mens rea is not required where the accused is charged with an offence of basic intent. This can be explained by reference to the offence of wounding with intent to prevent the lawful apprehension of any person, contrary to s 18 of the Offences against the Person Act 1861. The mens rea for this offence is that the accused must act 'maliciously', ie with intention or subjective recklessness as to some unlawful physical harm resulting from his act, *and* with the further intent to prevent lawful apprehension of any person. The further intent is, of course, a specific intent.[2] Consequently, if the accused is charged with this offence he may rely on evidence of voluntary intoxication as evidence that he lacked the intent to prevent lawful apprehension. On the other hand, it *may* be that in the somewhat unlikely event of an accused admitting that he intended to prevent lawful apprehension but saying that in his intoxicated state he did not realise the risk that what he did to the police officer might cause physical harm, evidence of voluntary intoxication is irrelevant (just as it is in line with *O'Grady* in relation to mens rea as to the element of unlawfulness) and the accused can be convicted under s 18 without proof that he acted 'maliciously' because his intoxication evidence is not being used to deny a mental element which is a specific intent but to deny a mental element which, in other offences,[3] is not a specific intent.[4]

If this argument is ever established to be the law, another argument would be hard to resist. This would be the argument that some offences currently classed as offences of basic intent (as opposed to specific intent) do contain a specific intent element. An example of a basic intent offence which *may* contain a specific intent element is rape. The mens rea for this offence is an intention to have sexual intercourse *with a woman*,[5] knowing or being subjectively reckless that she does not consent. There is clear authority that evidence of voluntary intoxication cannot be used as evidence of the lack of mens rea as to the absence of the woman's consent, and for this reason the offence is classified as a basic intent one.[6] As yet the unlikely situation has not arisen where D claims that he acted under an intoxicated mistake as to the sex of his victim (as where D says that he meant to have non-consensual intercourse with X, a childhood friend born male but who had undergone a sex-change operation (which in law does not change a person's sex), but because of his befuddled state he had such intercourse instead with X's twin sister, P) and therefore did not have the intent to have sexual intercourse with a woman. It is arguable that the court would hold that this intent is a specific one and that the accused's voluntary intoxication may be relied on as evidence that he lacked that intent and that he would have to be acquitted unless the prosecution proved that he did have that intent, although the obiter statement of the Court of Appeal in *Fotheringham* that 'in rape self-induced intoxication is no defence, [where the issue is] intention'[7] seems to provide some authority against this.

At present, of course, the above ideas are no more than speculation. They cannot be said with confidence to be part of the law. If they do become established as part of the law, the strict division discussed in the next paragraph between specific intent offences and those not requiring such an intent would disappear, to be replaced by a distinction between specific intent mental elements and non-specific intent ones in offences.

1 Para 9.60.
2 *Pordage* [1975] Crim LR 575, CA.
3 *Sullivan* [1981] Crim LR 46, CA.
4 See White 'Offences of Basic and Specific Intent' [1989] Crim LR 271.
5 *Khan* [1990] 2 All ER 783, CA; para 12.7.
6 *Woods (1981)* 74 Cr App Rep 312, CA; *Fotheringham* (1989) 88 Cr App Rep 206, CA.
7 (1989) 88 Cr App Rep 206 at 212.

9.63 *Determining whether an offence is one of specific intent* Since the relevance of the accused's voluntary intoxication at the material time depends on whether the offence charged requires proof of a 'specific intent', a clear definition of that term is essential.[1]

Unfortunately, the judges have put forward various definitions, at least two of which are clearly incorrect. For example, in *Majewski*[2] Lord Elwyn-Jones LC, with whom Lords Diplock and Kilbrandon concurred, appears to have adopted the view that 'specific intent' was equivalent to 'further intent'. However, murder and various other offences which were recognised in *Majewski* itself and other cases to be ones of specific intent in the present context do not require a further intent. This definition must therefore be rejected. So must that of Lord Simon in *Majewski* who took the view that a further intent was only one type of 'specific intent', which term he understood simply to mean (and require) 'intention' in the purposive sense which that term can bear. This definition must also be rejected, since murder[3] and handling stolen goods[4] have both been held to be offences of specific intent, but for neither is a 'purposive' intent essential.

The best definition, which can be implied from the speeches of Lords Elwyn-Jones LC, Edmund-Davies and Russell in *Majewski*, is that if intention and nothing less is required as to at least one element of the offence the offence is one of specific intent, whereas if recklessness as to the elements of a particular offence suffices that offence is one of basic intent. A fortiori, the offence is one of basic intent – not specific intent – if something less than recklessness suffices as to the various elements. This definition seems to be the most compatible with the cases; but even it is not wholly supported. One reason is that the offence of causing criminal damage contrary to s 1(2) of the Criminal Damage Act 1971 (the mens rea for which is intention or recklessness as to destruction or damage, coupled with intention or recklessness as to endangering life) was held by the majority of the House of Lords in *Caldwell*[5] to be an offence of specific intent in the event of only an intention to endanger life being alleged. Another reason is that the offence of handling stolen goods has been held to be an offence of specific intent[6] even though the mens rea required for it is dishonesty coupled with knowledge or belief that the goods are stolen.[7] A third reason is that rape has been held to be an offence of basic intent,[8] even though intent is required as to one element of its actus reus, sexual intercourse with a woman.[9] Similar comments may no doubt be made of other offences.

1 For a recent discussion of this matter, see Ward 'Making Some Sense of Self-Induced Intoxication' [1986] CLJ 247.

2 [1977] AC 443, [1976] 2 All ER 142, HL.
3 See *DPP v Beard* [1920] AC 479, HL; *A-G for Northern Ireland v Gallagher* [1963] AC 349, [1961] 3 All ER 299, HL; *Sheehan* [1975] 2 All ER 960, CA.
4 *Durante* [1972] 3 All ER 962, [1972] 1 WLR 1612, CA.
5 [1982] AC 341, [1981] 1 All ER 961, HL.
6 *Durante* [1972] 3 All ER 962, [1972] 1 WLR 1612, CA.
7 Paras 14.88–14.90.
8 *Woods* (1982) 74 Cr App Rep 312, CA; *Fotheringham* (1989) 88 Cr App Rep 206, CA.
9 *Khan* [1990] 2 All ER 783, CA; para 12.7.

9.64 In truth, there is no completely watertight definition and, in advance of a judicial decision concerning a particular offence, it is impossible to be certain whether or not it is one of 'specific intent'. Arguably, the courts grant or withold the title of 'offence of specific intent' depending on whether or not they wish evidence of voluntary intoxication in relation to the major mental element of the offence to be relevant to the question of liability for a particular offence.

All that can be said with confidence is that, in this context, the following have been held to be offences of specific intent: murder, wounding or causing grievous bodily harm with intent,[1] criminal damage contrary to s 1(2) of the Criminal Damage Act 1971 (provided that it is only alleged that the accused intended by destroying or damaging property to endanger the life of another),[2] theft,[3] robbery, burglary with intent to steal,[4] handling stolen goods,[5] and attempt to commit an offence,[6] although the list could no doubt be extended to cover a number of other offences, especially those with statutory definitions in which the only mens rea specified as sufficient is intent.

Conversely, it is possible to draw up a list of those offences which are ones of basic intent, and not specific intent: manslaughter (subject to what is said in para 11.63),[7] maliciously wounding or inflicting grievous bodily harm,[8] assault occasioning actual bodily harm,[9] assaulting a constable in the execution of his duty,[10] indecent assault,[11] rape,[12] taking a conveyance without lawful authority,[13] and criminal damage contrary to s 1(1) of the Criminal Damage Act 1971[14] or (provided intention or recklessness as to endangering life, or only recklessness, is alleged)[15] contrary to s 1(2) of that Act, can be included in this list.

1 *Bratty v A-G for Northern Ireland* [1963] AC 386, [1961] 3 All ER 523, per Lord Denning; *Pordage* [1975] Crim LR 575, CA.
2 *Caldwell* [1982] AC 341, [1981] 2 All ER 961, HL.
3 *Ruse v Read* [1949] 1 KB 377, [1949] 1 All ER 398, DC; *Kindon* (1957) 41 Cr App Rep 208, CA.
4 Ibid.
5 *Durante* [1972] 3 All ER 962, CA.
6 *Majewski* per Lord Salmon. Also see *Mohan* [1976] QB 1, [1975] 2 All ER 193, CA.
7 *Lipman* [1970] 1 QB 152, [1969] 3 All ER 410, CA.
8 *Sullivan* [1981] Crim LR 46, CA.
9 *Bolton v Crawley* [1972] Crim LR 222, DC; *DPP v Majewski* [1977] AC 443, [1976] 2 All ER 142, HL.
10 *DPP v Majewski* [1977] AC 443, [1976] 2 All ER 142, HL.
11 *Burns* (1973) 58 Cr App Rep 364, CA.
12 *Woods* (1981) 74 Cr App Rep 312, CA; *Fotheringham* (1988) 88 Cr App Rep 206, CA.
13 *MacPherson* [1973] Crim LR 457, CA; criticised by White 'Taking the Joy out of Joy-Riding' [1980] Crim LR 609.
14 *O'Driscoll* (1977) 65 Cr App Rep 50, CA.
15 *Caldwell* [1982] AC 341, [1981] 1 All ER 961, HL.

9.65 The limited nature of the rules relating to a plea of voluntary intoxication means that the rules are not exclusively based on the negation of mens
rea, and are best explained as rules of judicial policy based on a perception
that it would not be acceptable to the public that voluntarily intoxicated
offenders should secure an absolute acquittal and aimed at maintaining law
and order, while taking account of the effects on mental responsibility of
intoxication.[1] Their consequence is that, while a man who lacked the requisite mens rea because of intoxication cannot be convicted of murder or
wounding with intent, he can be convicted of the lesser offences of manslaughter or unlawful wounding despite his lack of the mens rea normally
required. However, the application of this policy is imperfect. If it operated
uniformly one would have expected rape to be an offence of specific intent
with indecent assault as the basic intent offence of which a voluntarily
intoxicated offender could be convicted. Moreover, there are some specific
intent offences, such as theft, for which there is generally no basic intent
offence to fall back on.

Those who are drunk and dangerous should certainly be punished but the
difficulty is how this can be done while still paying attention to the requirements of the particular offence and the general principles of criminal
liability.

1 See Dashwood 'Logic and the Lords in *Majewski*' [1977] Crim LR 532, 591.

VOLUNTARILY INTOXICATED BELIEF IN MATTER OF DEFENCE

9.66 We have seen that whether an intoxicated mistaken belief negativing
the mens rea which the prosecution must normally prove affords a defence
depends on whether or not the offence charged requires a specific intent.
Another question is the effect of an intoxicated mistake as to a matter of
defence, as where the accused intoxicatedly believed that he was acting
under duress. Such a mistake must normally be reasonable to exculpate the
accused,[1] and since, a fortiori, an intoxicated mistake cannot be reasonable
it would seem that a mistake as to a matter of excuse cannot excuse.
However, it has been held, for the purposes of the defence of provocation,
that if the accused acted under a drunken mistaken belief that he was being
provoked he must be judged as if the facts were as he mistakenly believed
them to be.[2] It is thought, in the light of the current approach of the courts to
the question of intoxication, that this decision would not now be followed.

1 Paras 7.28–7.32.
2 *Letenock* (1917) 12 Cr App Rep 221, CCA.

9.67 Support for the last statement in the last paragraph is derivable in
particular from the approach of the Courts-Martial Appeal Court in *Young*[1]
in relation to the relevance of voluntary intoxication to a 'no-negligence
defence'.[2] In that case the accused had undoubtedly been in possession of a
controlled drug, namely LSD, with intent to supply it to another, and the
only defence which might have been available to him was that under s 28 of
the Misuse of Drugs Act 1971. As we saw in para 8.22, s 28 provides that the
accused shall be acquitted if he proves that he neither believed, nor suspected, nor had reason to suspect that the substance in question was a
controlled drug. There was evidence that the accused was voluntarily intoxicated at the material time. Dismissing his appeal against conviction, the
Courts-Martial Appeal Court held that, although (for the same reasons as in
the next paragraph) evidence of voluntary intoxication was relevant to the

question of belief or suspicion in s 28, it was irrelevant to the question of whether there was 'reason to suspect'. The question was not whether the accused, with his intoxication, had reason to suspect that the substance was a controlled drug, but whether there was an objective reason to suspect that (to which question the accused's intoxication was wholly irrelevant).

1 [1984] 2 All ER 164, [1984] 1 WLR 654, Courts-Martial Appeal Court. The powers of this court correspond in general with those of the Court of Appeal (Criminal Division), as does its composition.
2 Para 8.22.

9.68 There is, however, one type of case where an intoxicated belief as to a matter of defence can excuse. As was stated in para 7.27, there are some statutory defences, specific to a particular offence, which are framed in terms of the accused's belief. In such a case it is no bar to the defence succeeding that the accused's belief was unreasonable, even though the unreasonableness was due to his voluntary intoxication.

In *Jaggard v Dickinson*[1] D was convicted by magistrates of intentional or reckless criminal damage to property, by breaking two windows and damaging a curtain in P's house. The incident occurred late at night and D, due to voluntary intoxication, mistakenly but honestly believed that she was damaging the property of X, a friend, and that he would have consented to her doing so. D's defence was that she had a lawful excuse within s 5 of the Criminal Damage Act 1971. Section 5(2) provides, inter alia, that a person charged with criminal damage is treated as having a lawful excuse if, at the material time, he believed that the person whom he believed to be entitled to consent to the damage had so consented, or would have so consented to it if he had known of the damage and its circumstances. Section 5(3) adds that it is immaterial whether such a belief is justified or not if it is honestly held. The magistrates, being of the opinion that D could not rely on the defence under s 5(2) because her belief was induced by voluntary intoxication, convicted her.

Allowing D's appeal against conviction, the Divisional Court held that the fact the offence charged was not one of specific intent was irrelevant because D was not relying on her intoxication to displace an inference of intention or recklessness, but was relying on it to give credibility to her alleged belief which, if honestly held, would give her a defence under s 5(2). It was clear from s 5(3), said the court, that if the belief was honestly held it was irrelevant that it was unreasonable; no exception was made by the Act for a mistake which was unreasonable because it was caused by voluntary intoxication and therefore the magistrates had been wrong to decide that D did not have the defence under s 5(2) because she was drunk at the time.[2]

1 [1981] QB 527, [1980] 3 All ER 716, DC.
2 The accused has an evidential burden in relation to such a defence, which can pose problems for an accused who was so intoxicated that he cannot clearly remember later what his belief was: see *Gannon* (1988) 87 Cr App Rep 254, CA.

VOLUNTARY INTOXICATION CAUSING INSANITY

9.69 The last exception to the general rule that voluntary intoxication is irrelevant to criminal liability is where drinking or drug-taking produces a distinct disease of the mind so that the accused is insane within the *M'Naghten Rules*; the accused will be found not guilty by reason of insanity[1] if he proves that at the material time he was suffering from a defect of reason, due to the disease of the mind caused by intoxication, such that he did not know the nature and quality of his act or that it was wrong.[2] The defence of insanity is, of course, of general application; it is not limited to offences requiring a specific intent.

Although mere malfunctioning of the mind due to intoxication does not constitute a 'disease of the mind',[3] habitual drinking or drug-taking can sometimes lead to such permanent changes in the brain tissues as to be accounted insanity, such as delirium tremens or alcoholic dementia. A plea of insanity based on intoxication is extremely rare but an old example is *Davis*.[4] At his trial for wounding with intent to murder (an offence which no longer exists in those words), D raised the defence of insanity. There was evidence that at the time, although sober, he was suffering from delirium tremens resulting from excessive drinking. Stephen J directed the jury that 'drunkenness is one thing and the diseases to which drunkenness leads are different things'.[5] He said that if a man by drink brought on a disease of the mind which caused a defect of reason, albeit temporary, which would have relieved him from responsibility if it had been produced in any other way, he would not be criminally responsible. The jury were told to find a verdict of not guilty on the ground of insanity if they thought that D had been suffering from a distinct disease of the mind caused by drinking, but differing from drunkenness, and that by reason thereof he did not know that his act was wrong.

1 *Davis* (1881) 14 Cox CC 563; *DPP v Beard* [1920] AC 479, HL; *A-G for Northern Ireland v Gallagher* [1963] AC 349, [1961] 3 All ER 299, HL.
2 If the prosecution has raised the issue of insanity, as it may, it will be for the prosecution – not the accused – to prove these things; para 9.28.
3 *Quick* [1973] QB 910, [1973] 3 All ER 347, CA.
4 (1881) 14 Cox CC 563.
5 Ibid at 564.

9.70   Two observations may be made about this exception to the general rule. First, it is only where it applies that the accused's appreciation of the legal implications of his conduct becomes relevant; ignorance of the wrong-fulness of conduct is irrelevant in the case of those who are sane but intoxicated, as has been stated above. Secondly, the distinction between temporary insanity caused by drink or drugs and simple intoxication is not easy to make. This is unfortunate since the distinction is important where the accused alleges that because of drinking or drug-taking he did not know his conduct was wrong.

Stephen J's direction was approved by the House of Lords in both *DPP v Beard*[1] and *A-G for Northern Ireland v Gallagher*.[2] The latter case is particularly important in this context since the judgments emphasise that if the accused was suffering from a disease of the mind which was insufficient to bring him within the *M'Naghten Rules*, e g because it would never induce anything more than lack of control, the fact that the disease was exacerbated by intoxication at the material time would not make the defence of insanity available to him. When sober, D formed the intention of killing his wife. He then purchased a bottle of whisky, and he may have drunk some of it before he in fact killed his wife with a knife. At D's trial he pleaded insanity and intoxication preventing him having specific intent. There was evidence that D was a psychopath, and that his psychopathy was a disease of the mind which would be aggravated by drink in such a way as to cause him the more readily to lose his self-control. The trial judge told the jury that, in consider-ing whether the *M'Naghten Rules* applied to the case, they should have regard to D's state of mind just before he took the whisky. D was convicted. He successfully appealed to the Northern Irish Court of Criminal Appeal, but his conviction was subsequently reinstated by the House of Lords. The basis of the House of Lords' decision was that D's psychopathy was quiescent and, without the drink, could not have brought the *M'Naghten Rules* into play because it merely weakened his power of self-control, and the defence of insanity could not be made good by getting drunk on whisky. It would have been different, it was said, if D's psychopathy had been caused by drink and he had been insane within the *M'Naghten Rules*.

1 [1920] AC 479, HL.
2 [1963] AC 349, [1961] 3 All ER 299, HL.

9.71 A plea of diminished responsibility cannot be based on intoxication itself,[1] but it can be based on alcoholism of the degree described earlier in this chapter.[1]

1 Para 9.36.

DUTCH COURAGE

9.72 A restriction on the exceptions to the general rule that voluntary intoxication is no defence was postulated by Lord Denning in *A-G for Northern Ireland v Gallagher*.[1] His Lordship dealt with the issues raised in that case in a way different from that of his colleagues and introduced what may be called the 'Dutch courage' rule, which is particularly important in the case of intoxication as evidence of the lack of a necessary specific intent.

Lord Denning said that the case had to be decided on the general rule that drunkenness is no defence to a criminal charge. He recognised that there were exceptions to this rule but held that they were inapplicable, because Gallagher had deliberately made himself drunk in order to give himself Dutch courage to commit the offence.

His Lordship said:

'If a man, whilst sane and sober, forms an intention to kill and makes preparation for it, knowing it is a wrong thing to do, and then gets himself drunk so as to give himself Dutch courage to do the thing, and whilst drunk carries out his intention, he cannot rely on this self-induced drunkenness as a defence to a charge of murder, nor even as reducing it to manslaughter. He cannot say that he got himself into such a stupid state that he was incapable of an intent to kill. So, also, when he is a psychopath, he cannot by drinking rely on his self-induced defect of reason as a defence of insanity. The wickedness of his mind before he got drunk is enough to condemn him, coupled with the act which he intended to do and did do. A psychopath who goes out intending to kill, knowing it is wrong, and does kill, cannot escape the consequences by making himself drunk before doing it.'[2]

Lord Denning suggested that the case would have been different if Gallagher had resiled from his intention to kill his wife before taking the drink. In that event, the question would have been whether the drunkenness was such as to bring the case within the first exception to the general rule (intoxication as evidence of the lack of a necessary specific intent).

Although Lord Denning's formulation of the Dutch courage rule is to be welcomed as a matter of policy, it does provide an apparent exception to the rule that mens rea and conduct must be contemporaneous.[3]

1 [1963] AC 349, [1961] 3 All ER 299, HL; para 9.70.
2 [1963] AC at 382.
3 Para 6.70.

INVOLUNTARY INTOXICATION

9.73 A person who is involuntarily intoxicated cannot, unlike a voluntarily intoxicated person, be said to be responsible for his condition. Consequently, it is not surprising that, although the authority is scanty, the law takes a more liberal view in his case and provides that, where the accused was involuntarily intoxicated, evidence of his intoxication may be taken into account in deciding whether he had the necessary mens rea for the offence (whether or not a specific intent is required).[1] However, it would seem that, provided he acted voluntarily with the requisite mens rea, the fact that involuntary intoxication led the accused to commit an offence which he would not have committed when sober does not afford him a defence[2] (although it may mitigate his punishment), and this is so even though because of his intoxication he acted under an irresistible impulse.

1 This was recognised in *DPP v Majewski* [1977] AC 443, [1976] 2 All ER 142, HL.
2 See *Davies* [1983] Crim LR 741, Crown Ct.

9.74 Intoxication is involuntary where it is not self-induced, as where the accused's friends have slipped vodka into his ginger beer or where he has been drugged by his enemies.

Intoxication is also involuntary, even though it might be regarded as self-induced, in the following cases.

9.75 The first is where it results from the taking of drugs administered or prescribed by a doctor. However, in the case of prescribed drugs, if the accused has become intoxicated because he has not taken them in accordance with the doctor's instructions, as where he exceeds the prescribed dosage or where he has thereafter taken alcohol or some other drug against medical advice, his intoxication will be voluntary – not involuntary if he was reckless when taking the overdose or taking that alcohol or other drug. The comments about recklessness made below are equally applicable here.

9.76 The second case where self-induced intoxication is nevertheless involuntary (subject to the exception mentioned shortly) is where it is caused by a non-dangerous drug, even if the drug is taken in excessive quantities and is not taken under and in accordance with medical advice. A non-dangerous drug is one which is not normally liable to cause unpredictability or aggressiveness (eg a sedative or soporific drug, such as valium). However, the intoxication will be voluntary, not involuntary, if the accused was reckless when he took the non-dangerous drug.

The authority is *Hardie*.[1] D's relationship with a woman with whom he was living in a flat broke down and she insisted that he must leave. He became distressed and took several of her valium tablets to calm his nerves. Two of the tablets were taken in front of the woman, who had said 'Take as many as you like. They are old stock and will do you no harm'. Later D started a fire in the bedroom of the flat while the woman and the daughter were in the sitting room. He was charged, under s 1(2) of the Criminal Damage Act 1971, with intentionally or recklessly damaging property, intending to endanger the life of another thereby or being reckless as to whether another's life would thereby be endangered. D argued that the effect of the drug was to prevent him having the relevant mens rea (a basic intent). The judge directed the jury that, because the intoxication was self-induced, it was irrelevant as a defence and its effects could not negative mens rea. In other words, he dealt with the case under the normal rule which applies to voluntary intoxication in a basic intent offence.

D was convicted but appealed successfully to the Court of Appeal, which held that the normal rule did not apply where the intoxication was due to a non-dangerous drug, even if it had been taken in excessive quantities.[2] Instead, the jury should have been told that, if they concluded that as a result of the valium D had been unable to appreciate the risks to property and persons from his actions, they should then consider whether the taking of valium was itself reckless. Only if it was would D be guilty.

1 [1984] 3 All ER 848, [1985] 1 WLR 64, CA.
2 The Court of Appeal's view at one point ([1984] 3 All ER at 851) that the intoxication in such a case would not be self-induced cannot be correct.

9.77 The Court of Appeal left a couple of points open in *Hardie*. First, it said that self-induced intoxication through a non-dangerous drug might in certain circumstances never be an answer; it gave the subsequently repealed offence of reckless driving, which has been replaced by that of dangerous driving, as an example. Second, it did not define what it meant by a 'reckless taking' of a drug. Clearly, it meant recklessness as to the risk of becoming unpredictable or aggressive or incapable of appreciating risks to others, but is subjective recklessness as to this risk required or merely *Caldwell*-type recklessness? Comparison with *Bailey*,[1] from which the Court of Appeal derived support, suggests that subjective recklessness is required (so that the accused must have been aware when he took it that the taking of the drug might render him aggressive, unpredictable or incapable of appreciating risks to others).

1 [1983] 2 All ER 503, [1983] 1 WLR 760, CA; para 9.48.

9.78 An interesting aspect of the decision in *Hardie*, as it applies to offences where *Caldwell*-type recklessness suffices as mens rea, is that, while it is no defence to an accused who gave no thought to a risk which would have been obvious to a reasonable person that the accused was of limited intelligence or young or in some other condition which would affect his thought processes,[1] it is a defence to an accused who gave no thought to such a risk that he was involuntarily intoxicated through a non-dangerous drug (unless he was reckless as to its effects when he took it).

1 Para 6.48.

SPECIAL STATUTORY PROVISION

9.79 Section 6(5) of the Public Order Act 1986 makes special provision for cases where the awareness of a person accused of riot or affray or some other offence under Part I of the 1986 Act was impaired by intoxication. All the offences in question require an intention or awareness as to a specified factor. Section 6(5) provides that, for the purposes of an offence under Part I, an accused whose awareness is impaired by intoxication shall be taken to be aware of that of which he would be aware if not intoxicated, unless he shows that his intoxication was not self-induced or that it was caused solely by the taking or administration of a substance in the course of medical treatment.[1] The effect of this is the same as would have resulted from an application of the common law rules on voluntary and involuntary intoxication, except that the burden of proving involuntary intoxication is placed on the accused and that those who become intoxicated after taking non-dangerous drugs (otherwise than in the course of medical treatment) are dealt with differently.

1 See further, para 18.10.

DRAFT CRIMINAL CODE BILL AND INTOXICATION

9.80 Clause 22 of the draft Criminal Code,[1] which is based primarily on the recommendations of the Fourteenth Report of the Criminal Law Revision Committee,[2] provides:

'1)   Where an offence requires a fault element of [subjective] recklessness (however described), a person who was voluntarily intoxicated shall be treated–
a) as having been aware of any risk of which he would have been aware had he been sober;
b) as not having believed in the existence of an exempting circumstance (where the existence of such a belief is in issue) if he would not have so believed had he been sober.
2)   Where an offence requires a fault element of failure to comply with a standard of care, or requires no fault, a person who was voluntarily intoxicated shall be treated as not having believed in the existence of an exempting circumstance (where the existence of such a belief is in issue) if a reasonable sober person would not have so believed.
3)   Where the definition of a fault element or of a defence refers, or requires reference, to the state of mind or conduct to be expected of a reasonable person, such person shall be understood to be one who is not so intoxicated.
4)   Subsection (1) does not apply–
a) to murder [to which a special provision mentioned in para 11.71 applies]; or
b) to the case (to which [the mental disorder verdict provision mentioned in para 9.31] applies) where a person's unawareness or belief arises from a combination of mental disorder and voluntary intoxication.
5)   –
a) 'Intoxicant' means alcohol or any other thing which, when taken into the body, may impair awareness or control.
b) 'Voluntary intoxication' means the intoxication of a person by an intoxicant which he takes, otherwise than properly for a medicinal purpose, knowing that it is or may be an intoxicant.
c) For the purposes of this section, a person 'takes' an intoxicant if he permits it to be administered to him.
6)   An intoxicant, although taken for a medicinal purpose, is not properly so taken if–
a) –
i)   it is not taken on medical advice; or
ii)   it is taken on medical advice but the taker fails then or thereafter to comply with any condition forming part of the advice; and
b) the taker is aware that the taking, or the failure, as the case may be, may result in his doing an act capable of constituting an offence of the kind in question;
and accordingly intoxication resulting from such taking or failure is voluntary intoxication.'

1 Law Commission: A Criminal Code for England and Wales (1989): Law Com No 177; see para 3.21 above. The clause is critically examined by Williams (1990) 140 NLJ 1564, but see response by de Burca (1991) 141 NLJ 560.
2 Offences against the Person (1980) Cmmd 7844, paras 257–278.

Corporations[1]

9.81 The general rule is that a corporation, such as an incorporated company, a public corporation like those formed for nationalised industries, or a local authority, may be criminally liable to the same extent as a natural person, subject to two exceptions:

a) in the case of offences which from their very nature cannot be committed by corporations; and

b) where the only punishment the court can impose is physical.

In law a corporation is a separate person distinct from its members. There has never been any doubt that the members, like the employees, of a corporation cannot shelter behind the corporation and may be successfully prosecuted for criminal acts performed or authorised by them; the problem with which we are concerned is the extent to which the corporate body itself may be criminally liable. The law on this subject has been developed comparatively recently and is due to the growth in the activities of limited liability companies. The chief obstacle to the acceptance of the concept of the criminal liability of a corporation has been the combination of its artificiality with the traditional need for the proof of mens rea in crime: '. . . did you ever expect a corporation to have a conscience, when it has no soul to be damned and no body to be kicked?'[2] In 1700, a corporation was not indictable at all;[3] today the situation is as we have described it.

1 Leigh *The Criminal Responsibility of Corporations in English Law.*
2 Attributed to the second Baron Thurlow.
3 *Anon* (1702) 12 Mod Rep 559.

9.82 The courts had little difficulty in holding that a corporation can be guilty of breach of a statutory duty, such as the duty imposed on the 'occupier' of a factory to fence its machinery or on the 'keeper' of a dangerous wild animal to license it. Since the middle of the nineteenth century it has been clear that, like anyone else, a corporation is liable if it is in breach of a statutory duty imposed on it as an occupier or keeper or in some other similar capacity.[1] In *Evans & Co Ltd v LCC*[2] the defendant company was charged that, being the occupier of a shop, it did not close it on the afternoon of an early closing day in breach of the duty imposed on the occupiers of shops by the Shops Act 1912. The Divisional Court held that the company was liable for breach of this statutory duty. Unlike the other methods of imposing corporate liability, it is not necessary to find an act or omission by an employee which is imputable to the corporation.

There was equally little difficulty in holding a corporation vicariously liable for the acts of employees and others in the same way as an individual,[3] except that, if the prescribed act (for example, 'driving' as opposed to 'using' or 'selling') can only be performed by a natural person, a corporation cannot be vicariously liable for it whereas an individual can.[4]

These two grounds of liability can render a corporation criminally liable only for a relatively small number of offences, essentially statutory offences of strict liability. Much more important is that, since 1944 at the latest,[5] it has been possible to impose criminal liability on a corporation, whether as a perpetrator or as an accomplice, for virtually any offence, notwithstanding that mens rea is required, by the use of the principle of identification, which (with any amendments indicated below) has been adopted in cl 30 of the draft Criminal Code Bill.[6]

1 *Birmingham and Gloucester Rly Co* (1842) 3 QB 223.
2 [1914] 3 KB 315.
3 Paras 23.36–23.44; also see *Mousell Bros Ltd v London and North Western Rly Co* [1917] 2 KB 836 at 846.
4 *Richmond-upon-Thames London Borough Council v Pinn and Wheeler Ltd* [1989] Crim LR 510, DC.
5 Three cases in 1944 went far to establish the present law: *DPP v Kent and Sussex Contractors Ltd* [1944] KB 146, [1944] 1 All ER 119, DC; *ICR Haulage Ltd* [1944] KB 551, [1944] 1 All ER 691, CCA; *Moore v I Bresler Ltd* [1944] 2 All ER 515, DC.
6 Law Commission: A Criminal Code for England and Wales (1989): Law Com No 177; see para 3.21 above.

THE PRINCIPLE OF IDENTIFICATION

9.83 In one of the earliest cases in which this principle was applied, *ICR Haulage Ltd*,[1] a company was held indictable for a common law conspiracy to defraud, an offence which requires mens rea and to which vicarious liability cannot apply. As this case shows, whereas the other kinds of corporate liability are creatures of statute and statutory construction, the present principle is a judicial creation which depends on the fiction that the acts (or omissions) and state of mind of certain superior officers ('controlling officers') who are seen as composing the very personality of the organisation are the acts and state of mind of the corporation. In such a case liability is not vicarious, in that the corporation is not held responsible on the basis of liability for the acts of its agents; instead the corporation, as in the case of breach of a statutory duty, is regarded as having committed the offence personally. Where personal liability is imposed on a corporation on the basis that a controlling officer has perpetrated an offence, it will be liable as a perpetrator. On the other hand, if the controlling officer was an accomplice to the commission of an offence by another the corporation's personal liability will be as an accomplice. Such liability may arise either through a positive act of aiding, abetting, counselling or procuring by a controlling officer or through a failure by such an officer to exercise a right of control over another, e g a junior employee, who perpetrates the offence.[2]

1 [1944] KB 551, [1944] 1 All ER 691, CCA.
2 Para 23.10.

9.84 The nature of the principle of identification, and the clear distinction which exists between corporate liability by virtue of it and the corporation's vicarious liability as an employer, is shown in the following passage from Lord Reid's speech in *Tesco Supermarkets Ltd v Nattrass*:[1]

'A living person has a mind which can have knowledge or intention or be negligent and he has hands to carry out his intentions. A corporation has none of these: it must act through living persons, though not always one and the same person. Then the person who acts is not speaking or acting for the company. He is acting as the company and his mind which directs his acts is the mind of the company. There is no question of the company being vicariously liable. He is not acting as a servant, representative, agent or delegate. He is an embodiment of the company, or, one could say, he hears and speaks through the *persona* of the company, within his appropriate sphere, and his mind is the mind of the company. If it is a guilty mind then that guilt is the guilt of the company.'

It remains to be determined whether this principle can apply to a director or the like whose appointment is invalid;[2] it would be unfortunate if it did not.[3]

It is a question of law whether a person in doing (or failing to do) a particular thing is to be regarded as the company or merely as the company's employee or agent. It follows that the judge should tell the jury that if they find certain facts proved then they must find that the acts (or omissions) and state of mind of that person are those of the company.[4]

It is implicit in the principle of identification that it can only operate if there is a sufficient act (or omission) with sufficient mens rea on the part of an individual controlling officer to render that officer criminally liable. It is not possible to aggregate the acts and states of mind of two or more controlling officers (none of whom could be criminally liable) so as to render the corporation liable. This may seem unfortunate in the light of the fact that many corporate decisions or failures are constituted not by one individual controlling officer but by the distinct contributions of a number of them.

1 [1972] AC 153 at 170, [1971] 2 All ER 127 at 131–132.
2 There is dicta by Lord Diplock in *Tesco Supermarkets Ltd v Nattrass* [1972] AC 153 at 199–200 suggesting that it does not apply.
3 Under the draft Criminal Code Bill, cl 30(3) it would apply to such a person.
4 Ibid, and at 173 and 134 respectively. See also *Andrews Weatherfoil Ltd* [1972] 1 All ER 65, [1972] 1 WLR 118, CA.

9.85 A widely approved dictum on the question of who can be identified with the corporation is that of Lord Denning in the civil case of *H L Bolton (Engineering) Co Ltd v P J Graham & Sons Ltd*:[1]

'A company may in many ways be likened to a human body. It has a brain and nerve centre which controls what it does. It also has hands which hold the tools and act in accordance with directions from the centre. Some of the people in the company are mere servants and agents who are nothing more than hands to do the work and cannot be said to represent the mind or will. Others are directors and managers who represent the directing mind and will of the company, and control what it does. The state of mind of these managers is the state of mind of the company and is treated by the law as such.'

This dictum was approved in *Tesco Supermarkets Ltd v Nattrass*[2] by Lords Reid, Dilhorne and Pearson who held that only those who constitute the 'directing mind and will' of the corporation can be identified with it. These were people such as directors and others who manage the affairs of the corporation. In addition, they included a person to whom those responsible for the general management of the corporation had delegated some part of their functions of management, giving to that person full discretion to act independently of instructions from them. Within the scope of the delegation, the delegate could act as the corporation. In assessing whether a particular person could be identified with the corporation in this way, account should be taken of the constitution of the corporation.[3]

The fact that a person is not a director or employee of a corporation is not a bar to him being identified with it.[4]

One consequence of the above statements about who can be identified with the corporation would seem to be that the larger the corporation the less likely it is to be personally liable by virtue of the identification principle, since the larger the corporation the fewer (relatively) will be the activities and decisions of its controlling officers.

1 [1957] 1 QB 159 at 172, [1956] 3 All ER 624.
2 [1972] AC 153, [1971] 2 All ER 127, HL.
3 Ibid at 170–171 and 148 respectively per Lord Pearson. See also the speech of Lord Diplock at 199–200.

4 *Worthy v Gordon Plant (Services) Ltd* [1989] RTR 7, DC (person a self-employed traffic manager of the corporation; his conduct and mens rea were imputed to the corporation).

9.86 The corporation may on the above criteria be identified with a manager to whom the directors have delegated full power in the running of its affairs[1] or part of its affairs.[2] For example, the traffic manager of a company has been identified with it in relation to the operation of its fleet of goods vehicles under an operators' licence.[3] On the other hand, a corporation has not been identified with the branch manager of a company with a large number of branches who was required to comply with the general directions of the board of directors,[4] nor with a depot engineer,[5] nor with the operator of a weighbridge belonging to the corporation.[6]

It is important to remember that the question of identification does not depend on the title of a person's post but on whether or not the person is part of the directing mind and will of the corporation. The fact that a person with a particular title is held in one case to be part of a corporation's directing mind and will does not mean that someone with that title in another corporation will be so identified. It will depend on the constitution and organisational structure of the corporation.

The person identified with the corporation renders it liable only so long as he acts within the scope of his office,[7] ie for things done by him in his capacity as a controlling officer of the corporation, which means that the corporation is not liable for something done by him in some other capacity, such as his personal capacity. If the managing director of a company picks someone's pocket or commits manslaughter by his dangerous driving to a business meeting, his acts and state of mind are not imputed to the company. However, the present requirement does not mean that activities contrary to the corporation's interests will exclude its liability. A corporation may be convicted even though it is itself defrauded, provided that the offence was committed by a person identified with the corporation acting within the scope of his office.[8] Clause 30(6) of the draft Criminal Code Bill reverses this rule, declaring that a controlling officer does not act within the scope of his office if he acts with the intention of doing harm or of concealing harm to the corporation.

1 *Lennard's Carrying Co Ltd v Asiatic Petroleum Co Ltd* [1915] AC 705, HL.
2 *Worthy v Gordon Plant (Services) Ltd* [1985] CLY 624, DC.
3 Ibid; *Redhead Freight Ltd v Shulman* [1989] RTR 1, DC.
4 *Tesco Supermarkets Ltd v Nattrass*; para 9.85.
5 *Magna Plant Ltd v Mitchell* [1966] Crim LR 394, DC.
6 *John Henshall (Quarries) Ltd v Harvey* [1965] 2 QB 233, [1965] 1 All ER 725, DC.
7 *DPP v Kent and Sussex Contractors Ltd* [1944] KB 146, [1944] 1 All ER 119, DC.
8 *Moore v I Bresler Ltd* [1944] 2 All ER 515, DC.

OFFENCES TO WHICH THE PRINCIPLE OF IDENTIFICATION CANNOT APPLY

9.87 In the *ICR Haulage Ltd* case,[1] although it was said that a corporation was prima facie criminally liable to the same extent as a natural person, two exceptions to this general rule were mentioned and it was recognised that there might be others. The first exception was said to consist of 'cases where from its very nature, the offence cannot be committed by a corporation'.[2] The court gave perjury and bigamy as examples, and sexual offences such as rape and incest also fall within this category. It is open to question whether or not a corporation can be indicted for perjury, for the act of the corporate representative in swearing a false oath, and his guilty knowledge, could be attributed to the corporation. Therefore it has been suggested[3] that a company whose governing body authorised one of its number to swear a false affidavit could be convicted of perjury. In the case of perjury in judicial proceedings, the false statement must be made by a person who has been lawfully sworn, and the corporation cannot be so described. Nevertheless, if a governing body were to authorise the making of a false statement on oath in court, a corporation might be convicted of subornation (i e procuration) of perjury. Similarly, although a corporation cannot commit bigamy as a perpetrator, if a marriage bureau is managed by a limited company, one of whose directors knowingly negotiates a bigamous marriage, it is difficult to see why the company should not be convicted of aiding or abetting bigamy, for a natural person may be convicted of aiding or abetting an offence which he could not commit himself as a perpetrator.[4] Clearly, although a corporation cannot be convicted as a perpetrator of offences involving sexual intercourse, theoretically it could be convicted as an accomplice but it is difficult to visualise a situation where the responsible officer would be acting within the scope of his office.

The second exception to the general rule of corporate liability for crime referred to in the *ICR Haulage Ltd* case arises from the fact that 'the court will not stultify itself by embarking on a trial in which, if a verdict of guilty is returned, no effective order by way of sentence can be made'.[5] This exception is now confined to murder and treason for which the only punishment which the court can impose is imprisonment or death.

It was said obiter in several old cases that a corporation could not be indicted for a crime of violence.[6] These dicta were acted upon by Finlay J in *Cory Bros Ltd*,[7] where he held that a company could not be indicted for manslaughter or the statutory offence of setting up an engine (in this case an electric fence) calculated to destroy life with intent to injure a trespasser. This decision is no longer good law; it was questioned in *ICR Haulage Ltd* and a company has since been convicted as an accomplice to causing death by dangerous driving.[8] In addition, in 1991 in *P & O European Ferries (Dover) Ltd*,[9] a case concerned with the Zeebrugge ferry disaster, Henry J ruled that a corporation is capable of being convicted of manslaughter. While this ruling, being made in the Crown Court, is strictly only of persuasive authority, it was apparently made after very full argument from counsel and after particularly careful consideration by the judge. Consequently, the persuasive effect of the ruling is greater than is normal for a ruling in the Crown Court.

This discussion of the boundaries of corporate liability should not obscure the fact that most prosecutions for offences involving mens rea against corporations under the present principle are concerned with commercial fraud.

1 [1944] KB 551, [1944] 1 All ER 691, CCA.
2 Ibid at 594 and 693 respectively.
3 Stephen *Digest of Criminal Law* (9th edn) 4.
4 Para 23.14.
5 [1944] KB at 554, [1944] 1 All ER at 693.
6 Eg *Birmingham and Gloucester Rly Co* (1842) 3 QB 223 at 232.
7 [1927] 1 KB 810.
8 *Robert Millar (Contractors) Ltd* [1970] 2 QB 54, [1970] 1 All ER 577, CA.
9 (1987) 88 Cr App Rep 10, Crown Ct. At the subsequent trial for manslaughter the accused company and individuals were acquitted.

SOCIAL POLICY

9.88 Neither Parliament nor the courts have ever considered comprehensively the merits or otherwise of imposing criminal liability on corporations, either in principle or in its practical applications. As we have seen, the idea has developed on a pragmatic and expedient basis. Writers have demonstrated the unreality of imputing to a corporation the mind or minds of its controlling officers, the absurdity of imposing fines which are trifling when compared with the profits or losses of the body concerned and the injustice of penalising shareholders, consumers or taxpayers, who ultimately bear the burden of fines imposed on corporations, for acts or omissions of which usually they are unaware. These and others are fair points, but few people seem reluctant to accept the principle of corporate personality and it is but a short step to accept its full implications. Adverse publicity following the conviction of a corporation may have a strong deterrent effect and, where it has benefited financially from the criminal conduct, the imposition of a fine on the corporation is a means of depriving it, at least in part, of unjust enrichment. Whatever may be the intellectual arguments, the conception of corporate responsibility is by now well entrenched in the public mind. No doubt this is one of the many topics which call for systematic research and consideration but it is one of the least urgent.

IDENTIFICATION AND STATUTORY DEFENCES

9.89 The principle of identification can also excuse a corporation from liability for certain regulatory offences. Some statutes provide that it is a defence for a person, who would otherwise be vicariously liable, to show that he has exercised all due diligence and that the commission of the offence was due to the act or default of 'another person'. As far as corporations are concerned, the due diligence must have been exercised by an officer or officers who can be identified with the corporation, and 'another person' means a person other than such an officer. In *Tesco Supermarkets Ltd v Nattrass*[1] a local shop manager employed by a company running a chain of 800 supermarkets was not identified with the company. His faulty supervision had caused a shop assistant to sell goods in circumstances in which the company was prima facie guilty, under the principles of vicarious liability, of an offence under the Trade Descriptions Act 1968. The House of Lords held that the manager, though an employee, could not be identified with the company and therefore, despite his default, the company could rely on the statutory defence under s 24 of the Act that, through its officers who could be identified with it, it had taken all reasonable precautions and exercised due diligence, and that the commission of the offence was due to the default of another (the manager).

1 [1972] AC 153, [1971] 2 All ER 127, HL; paras 9.84 and 9.85.

LIABILITY OF DIRECTORS AND SIMILAR PERSONS

9.90 Where a corporation has been held criminally liable the natural persons involved may be liable, of course, as perpetrators or accomplices. In addition, many statutes now provide for the guilt of senior officers of the corporation who would not be criminally liable under ordinary principles, or whose guilt it would otherwise be hard to prove. The following is a common example of this type of provision:

'Where an offence under this Act which has been committed by a body corporate is proved to have been committed with the consent or connivance of, or to be attributable to any neglect on the part of, any director, manager [ie someone managing the affairs of the corporation],[1] secretary or other similar officer of the body corporate, or any person who was purporting to act in that capacity, he, as well as the body corporate, shall be guilty of that offence'.[2]

A person 'consents' to the commission of an offence by a corporation if he is aware of what is going on and agrees to it.[3] 'Connivance' is generally regarded as involving wilful blindness as to the commission of the offence,[4] which must no doubt be coupled in this context with acquiescence in it. A person who consents to, or connives at, an offence committed by a corporation (through another person's conduct) may be guilty of that offence as an accomplice; and this is so even in the case where he does nothing positive, if he had a right of control over that other person.[5] The importance of this part of the provision is that it makes the task of the prosecution less difficult, since it is enough for them to prove consent or connivance by a person of the specified type and they do not have to prove that it amounted to aiding, abetting, counselling or procuring.

By comparison, a person cannot be an accomplice to an offence simply because it is attributable to his neglect. Consequently, the words 'attributable to any neglect on the part of' are important since they considerably extend the ambit of the criminal law in this context, rendering a person of the specified type liable for his negligence in failing to prevent the offence committed by the corporation.[3]

In *Lewin v Bland*[6] it was held that an offence is only attributable to any neglect on the part of a director, manager or other similar officer of a corporation if he was in breach of a duty to check the conduct (which resulted in the offence) of the person who committed the offence, and that normally there is no duty to check the conduct of an experienced member of staff whom one can expect to act in accordance with his instructions unless there is something to prompt one into checking.

A similar type of provision to that just described is one whose wording is the same except that it omits any reference to 'attributable to neglect', so that a director, manager or other similar officer is only guilty (by virtue of it) of an offence committed by a corporation if he consented to it or connived at it.[7] For the reasons given above, this does not extend the bounds of criminal liability but simply makes the task of the prosecution easier.

1 *Tesco Supermarkets Ltd v Nattrass* [1972] AC 153 at 178.
2 Examples, among many, of such a provision are the Trades Description Act 1968, s 20; Food Act 1984, s 94; Insolvency Act 1986, s 432; Consumer Protection Act 1987, s 40; Children Act 1989, s 103; Food Safety Act 1990, s 36. The draft Criminal Code Bill, cl 31 provides a general provision along these lines which would apply to offences generally, other than pre-Code ones. The reference to 'attributable to neglect' would, however, only apply to such an offence if it was one of strict liability. Liability under cl 31 would be as an accomplice.
3 *Huckerby v Elliott* [1970] 1 All ER 189, DC.
4 *Somerset v Hart* (1884) 12 QBD 360, 53 LJMC 77.
5 Para 23.10.
6 [1985] RTR 171, DC.
7 Theft Act 1968, s 18 (see para 14.70); Public Order Act 1986, s 28 (see para 18.53).

Unincorporated associations

9.91 Generally, an unincorporated association, such as a partnership, trade union or members' club, cannot be convicted of an offence (although, of course, its individual members can be convicted if they are parties to an offence). By way of exception, some statutes provide that offences under them can be committed by an unincorporated association[1] and some statutory offences have been construed as capable of commission by such an association.[2] These exceptions are rare.

1 For example, a trade union or employers' association is guilty of an offence if it refuses or wilfully neglects to perform certain duties under the Trade Unions and Labour Relations Act 1974: s 11 of the 1974 Act.
2 See, for example, *Clerk to Croydon JJ, ex p Chief Constable of Kent* (1989) Times, 15 June, DC.

10 Non-fatal offences against the person

10.1 The most serious offences against the person – murder and manslaughter – are not defined by any statute. The Offences against the Person Act 1861 deals in detail with those offences against the person, such as assaults and wounding, which are not fatal. These were treated very leniently by the common law, but have been dealt with by statute for some time. The 1861 Act also covers abortion and bigamy, while sexual offences are now governed by the Sexual Offences Act 1956 and certain other statutes.

Consent

10.2 Many offences against the person, such as rape and assault, cannot be committed if the victim gives a valid consent. On the other hand, no one can lawfully consent to his own death at the hands of another.[1] Although suicide is no longer an offence, euthanasia still is. However excellent his motives may be, someone who kills another at that other's request is guilty of murder unless he acted in pursuance of a suicide pact, in which case his offence is manslaughter.[2] It is also an offence to assist or encourage another to commit suicide.[3]

1 *Young* (1838) 8 C & P 644; *Cuddy* (1843) 1 Car & Kir 210.
2 Paras 11.32.
3 Para 11.33.

10.3 *To what bodily harm, short of death, can one validly consent?* Whether consent renders lawful what would otherwise be unlawful in the case of non-fatal offences against the person depends upon the following principles.

In *A-G's Reference (No 6 of 1980)*[1] the Court of Appeal held that, subject to exceptions mentioned below, a person's consent is irrelevant and cannot prevent criminal liability for an offence if actual bodily harm was intended and/or caused. 'Actual bodily harm' means any hurt or injury calculated to interfere with the health or comfort of the victim.[2] 'Injury' in this context is not limited to physical injury since it includes a hysterical or nervous condition.[2] 'Actual bodily harm' is explained further in para 10.17.

The strict rule stated in *A-G's Reference (No 6 of 1980)* was based on the view that it is not in the public interest that people should try to cause, or should cause, each other actual bodily harm for no good reason. In some cases there may be a good reason, and the Court of Appeal was at pains to emphasise that the above rule did not affect the accepted legality of certain situations which included properly conducted games and sports, reasonable surgical interference and dangerous exhibitions. In these situations the consent of the person to whom actual bodily harm is intended and/or caused is legally relevant and renders the conduct in question lawful. The Court of Appeal explained these exceptions to the strict rule as needed in the public interest, and it is clear from its judgment that other exceptions can be recognised by the judges if they regard them as necessary in the public interest. Another exception, subsequently recognised by the Court of Appeal in *Jones*,[3] is that, if a person is caused actual bodily harm by rough and undisciplined horseplay which is not intended to cause injury, his consent is legally relevant and prevents the conduct being unlawful. Because they depend on the views of the judges as to what the public interest necessitates, and because these may change with the times, the extent of the exceptions is uncertain.

1 [1981] QB 715, [1981] 2 All ER 1057, CA. Also see *Brown* (1992) Times, 21 February, CA.
2 *Miller* [1954] 2 QB 282 at 292, [1954] 2 All ER 529.
3 (1986) 83 Cr App Rep 375, CA. Also see *Donovan* [1934] 2 KB 498 at 508.

10.4 What is a 'properly conducted game or sport' or 'reasonable surgical interference' itself turns on the public interest. For example, a prize fight (a fight with bare fists until one participant is unable to continue) is not regarded as a properly conducted sport,[1] whereas boxing and wrestling are, because the serious physical risks which attach to the former are against the public interest,[1] while the latter are 'manly diversions, they intend to give strength, skill and activity, and may fit people for defence, public as well as personal, in time of need'.[2]

The question whether a surgical operation is 'reasonable surgical interference' is answered in some cases by legislation which declares that particular types of interference, eg female circumcision and the tattooing of minors,[3] are unlawful (and therefore not reasonable surgical interference) save in specified circumstances. In other cases, the question whether a surgical operation is 'reasonable surgical interference' clearly admits only of the answer 'yes' where it is performed for therapeutic reasons. It appears, for example, that even a sex-change operation performed for genuine therapeutic reasons is not open to legal objection.[4]

On the other hand, the answer *may* be different in *some* cases where an operation is performed for non-therapeutic reasons.[5] A prime example is an operation involving the mutilation of the body in accordance with religious or tribal ritual or custom or in order to secure a discharge from military service. Another example would be a sex-change operation performed simply to enable the person to appear in a 'freaks' show' at a fair. Other operations which may not be performed for therapeutic reasons include sterilisation and cosmetic surgery. Whether a non-therapeutic operation is contrary to the public interest in this area may give rise to differences of opinion, and opinions may change with the times. For example, in *Bravery v Bravery*,[6] a civil case decided in 1954, Denning LJ held that a sterilisation operation performed on a man for non-eugenic reasons (to enable him to enjoy sexual intercourse without the risk of becoming a father) would be unlawful as being injurious to the public interest, whereas the other two Lords Justices expressly dissociated themselves from this view, saying that they were not prepared 'in the present case' to hold that such operations were injurious to the public interest. There can be no doubt that a sterilisation operation for such a purpose would now be held to be reasonable surgical interference, as would a cosmetic operation,[7] so that a valid consent could be given to them, whereas the other non-therapeutic operations mentioned in this paragraph would seem to be against the public interest, in which case a valid consent could not be given to them.

1 *Coney* (1882) 8 QBD 534, 51 LJMC 66.
2 Foster *Crown Law* (3rd edn) 259.
3 Prohibition of Female Circumcision Act 1985; Tattooing of Minors Act 1969. Contravention of these statutes is in itself an offence, quite apart from invalidating any consent on the part of the 'patient'.
4 *Corbett v Corbett* [1971] P 83 at 99, [1970] 2 All ER 33.
5 See Skegg 'Medical Procedures and the Crime of Battery' [1974] Crim LR 693.
6 [1954] 3 All ER 59, [1954] 1 WLR 1169, CA.
7 Except presumably for a cosmetic operation performed for some purpose contrary to the public interest, e g to enable a criminal to avoid detection: see Denning LJ in *Bravery v Bravery*.

10.5 If the issue of consent is raised at a trial the ambit of a consent may be important. For example, although a person who participates in a properly conducted game, such as football or boxing, consents to the risk of actual bodily harm he only consents to such harm as may be incidental to the game in question and not to any other type of harm;[1] a footballer does not consent to being deliberately punched on the nose.

1 *Coney* (1882) 8 QBD 534 at 537, per Cave J.

10.6 One consequence of the legal rules just described is that it is not unlawful to cause actual bodily harm or worse to the other participant during the ordinary course of a boxing match, whereas blows given for the purposes of sexual gratification during a flagellation session[1] or given during a fist-fight by two men who are 'settling a score' are unlawful,[2] even though the actual bodily harm intended and/or resulting may well be (and is very likely to be in the case of flagellation) less serious than in the case of the boxing match.

1 *Donovan* [1934] 2 KB 498, 103 LJKB 683, CCA.
2 *A-G's Reference (No 6 of 1980)* [1981] QB 715, [1981] 2 All ER 1057, CA.

10.7 *Apparent consent invalid* In some cases an apparent consent which would otherwise be valid is treated by the law as invalid.

a) In most sexual offences, the consent of young people under certain ages is invalid.[1]
b) An apparent consent will be treated as invalid where:
   i)   The victim is so young or mentally disordered as to be unable to comprehend the nature of the act committed.[2] However, the act will nevertheless be lawful in such a case if the physical contact is generally acceptable in the ordinary conduct of daily life.[3]
   ii) The victim's apparent consent has been procured by duress. In *Day*[4] D was charged, inter alia, with an assault on a girl of nine. The girl had not resisted his conduct and it was argued that, since she had submitted to his acts, she must be taken to have consented and that therefore D was not guilty. The jury were directed that if the girl had submitted to D's acts out of fear there would have been no real consent on her part and they would be without her consent.

iii) There is no real consent if a person, apparently consenting, is induced to do so by fraud as to the nature of the act or as to the identity of the accused, but provided that the victim knows of the nature of the act, it is irrelevant that he is mistaken about a collateral detail of it.[5] Thus, it was held that no assault had occurred in *Clarence*[6] where D had intercourse with his wife, knowing that he had venereal disease, and thereby infected her. The wife did not know of D's disease. It was argued that D's concealment of his condition amounted to a fraud which negatived his wife's consent to the intercourse and thus rendered the bodily contact an assault. It was held that even if D's conduct did amount to a fraud it would not vitiate the wife's consent because she understood the nature of the act; her ignorance of D's disease was not enough.

1 Ch 12.
2 *Burrell v Harmer* [1967] Crim LR 169, DC; *Howard* [1965] 3 All ER 684, [1966] 1 WLR 13, CCA.
3 *Collins v Wilcock* [1984] 3 All ER 374 at 378; *F v West Berkshire Health Authority* [1989] 2 All ER 545 at 563.
4 (1841) 9 C & P 722.
5 *Clarence* (1888) 22 QBD 23 at 44.
6 (1888) 22 QBD 23.

10.8 *Implied consent* Consent may be express or implied. One impliedly consents to the risk of accidental bodily contact in ordinary activities in the street, in queues or on buses, to name a few places. Likewise, one impliedly consents to a person seizing one's hand to shake it in friendship or to having one's back slapped (within reason) in congratulation or to having an emergency operation after an accident (assuming one has not regained consciousness after the accident).[1]

Of course, consent cannot be implied if it is clear, by words or conduct, that the victim is positively not consenting.

A drawback with the concept of implied consent is that consent cannot be implied if the victim is mentally incapable, on grounds of youth or mental disorder, of understanding the nature of the act and therefore incapable of giving consent. For this reason, a test put forward by Robert Goff LJ, as he then was, when giving the judgment of the Divisional Court in *Collins v Wilcock*,[2] has much to commend it. His Lordship said: 'Generally speaking, consent is a defence to battery; and most of the physical contacts of ordinary life are not actionable because they are impliedly consented to by all who move in society and expose themselves to the risk of bodily contact. So nobody can complain of the jostling which is inevitable from his presence in, for example, a supermarket, an underground station or a busy street; nor can a person who attends a party complain if his hand is seized in friendship, or even if his back is (within reason) slapped.... Although such cases are regarded as examples of implied consent, it is more common nowadays to treat them as falling within a general exception embracing all physical contact which is generally acceptable in the ordinary conduct of daily life.[3].... Among such forms of conduct,... is touching a person for the purpose of engaging his attention, though of course using no greater degree of physical contact than is reasonably necessary in the circumstances for that purpose.' Lord Goff repeated this view in *F v West Berkshire Health Authority*.[4]

1 *Cole v Turner* (1704) 6 Mod Rep 149; *Collins v Wilcock* [1984] 3 All ER 374 at 378.
2 [1984] 3 All ER 374 at 378.
3 Surgical operations and medical treatment do not fall within this phrase: *T v T* [1988] 1 All ER 613 at 624; *F v West Berkshire HA* [1989] 2 All ER 545 at 564, per Lord Goff.
4 [1989] 2 All ER 545 at 563.

Assault and battery

10.9   Assault (common assault) and battery (common battery) are separate offences, and for that reason a conviction of assault or battery will be quashed because a person cannot be convicted of alternative offences.[1] A person is guilty of an assault if he intentionally or recklessly causes another person to apprehend the application to his body of immediate, unlawful force. A person is guilty of battery if he intentionally or recklessly applies unlawful force to the body of another person.[2]

A battery generally includes an assault (and for this reason the two offences are frequently referred to generically though misleadingly as assaults or common assaults),[3] but this is not always so. Someone who hit another without having previously caused him to fear that unlawful force was about to be used against him, because, for example, he had crept up behind him, would commit battery even though no assault had been committed.

1 *Jones v Sherwood* [1942] 1 KB 127, 111 LJKB 95, DC; *DPP v Taylor; DPP v Little* [1992] 1 All ER 299, DC.
2 *Fagan v Metropolitan Police Comr* [1969] 1 QB 439, [1968] 3 All ER 442, DC; *Venna* [1976] QB 421, [1975] 3 All ER 788, CA; *Kimber* [1983] 3 All ER 316, [1983] 1 WLR 1118, CA.
3 *Rolfe* (1952) 36 Cr App Rep 4, CCA; *DPP v Taylor; DPP v Little* [1992] 1 All ER 299, DC.

ACTUS REUS OF ASSAULT[1]

10.10   The actus reus of assault is causing the victim to apprehend the immediate application of unlawful force to his body. A mere omission to act which creates such an apprehension is not enough.[2] In principle, there is no reason why a threat by words *alone* (ie unaccompanied by any act) of the immediate use of force should not suffice for an assault, even if the threat is not accompanied by instant action,[3] but such authority as there is may be against this view.[4] It would be unfortunate if threatening words should not suffice. To go up behind a person and shout 'Hit him, boys' is probably more frightening for him than to confront him with a raised fist. However, such conduct could usually be prosecuted under s 4 of the Public Order Act 1986.[5]

The requirement that the immediate application of force must be apprehended means that:

a) pointing an unloaded gun or an imitation gun at one who is unaware of its harmlessness may amount to an assault;[6]
b) inviting another to touch the invitor cannot amount to an assault on the invitee,[7] and
c) a man may be guilty of this offence if he shakes his fist at another in a threatening manner, although he thereafter was prevented from touching him.[8]

Clearly, if the circumstances are such that there cannot possibly be any fear that the threats will be carried out immediately, as where a person on a rapidly moving train shakes his fist at someone who is standing on a station platform, there is no assault. Moreover, the threatening gesture may be accompanied by words indicating that there is no intention to carry it out, as in the old case of *Tuberville v Savage*.[9] There, a man put his hand menacingly upon his sword but said 'If it were not assize time I'd run you through the body'; it was held that an assault had not been committed.

The Divisional Court has taken a generous view of what is 'immediate'. For example, in *Smith v Chief Superintendent, Woking Police Station*[10] it held that it had been open to magistrates to infer that a woman, who had been frightened (as he had intended) by seeing the accused looking at her through the window of her bed-sitting room at 11pm, had apprehended the immediate application of force.

1 Turner *Modern Approach to Criminal Law* pp 344–355.
2 *Fagan v Metropolitan Police Comr* [1969] 1 QB 439, [1968] 3 All 442, DC.
3 Williams 'Assaults and Words' [1957] Crim LR 216.
4 *Meade's and Belt's Case* (1823) 1 Lew CC 184; Hawkins *Pleas of the Crown* vol I, ch 62 (words alone cannot be an assault); but see *Wilson* [1955] 1 All ER 744, [1955] 1 WLR 493, CCA; *Ansell v Thomas* [1974] Crim LR 31 (words alone can be an assault).
5 Para 18.21.
6 *St George* (1840) 9 C & P 483; *Logdon v DPP* [1976] Crim LR 121, DC; cf *James* (1844) 1 Car & Kir 530; *Kwaku Mensah v R* [1946] AC 83, PC.
7 *Fairclough v Whipp* [1951] 2 All ER 834, 35 Cr App Rep 138, DC.
8 *Stephens v Myers* (1830) 4 C & P 349.
9 (1669) 1 Mod Rep 3.
10 (1983) 76 Cr App Rep 234, DC. Also see *Logdon v DPP* [1976] Crim LR 121, DC.

ACTUS REUS OF BATTERY

10.11 The actus reus of battery is the application of unlawful force to the body of another. The force applied does not have to be personal contact (with the result, for example, that throwing water at someone[1] or setting a dog on him[2] can be a battery), but without the application of some force there cannot be a battery. Thus, it has been held that a person who put Spanish fly (harmful irritants) into the guests' beer at a wedding reception was not guilty of a battery.[3] (Such conduct could, however, result in a conviction for the offence of administering a noxious thing with intent to injure or annoy, contrary to s 24 of the Offences against the Person Act 1861.) Similarly, the use of force merely to pull away from another does not constitute a battery.[4] In *Fagan v Metropolitan Police Comr*[5] the Divisional Court was adamant that a mere omission to act which results in force to another, eg failing to step aside so that another runs into you, will not suffice. However, the decision of the Divisional Court in *DPP v K*,[6] described in the next paragraph, appears to indicate that liability may be based on an omission (with the appropriate mens rea) to rectify a dangerous situation created by the accused himself. This is an application of the principle in *Miller*, discussed in para 6.71. In the light of the emphatic statement in *Fagan* that a *mere* omission will not suffice for a battery, it would seem that an omission to fulfil some other type of legal duty cannot constitute a battery if force to another results from it.[7]

1 *Pursell v Horn* (1838) 8 Ad & El 602.
2 *Plunkett v Matchell* [1958] Crim LR 252, DC.
3 *Walkden* (1845) 1 Cox CC 282.
4 *Sherriff* [1969] Crim LR 260, CA.
5 [1969] 1 QB 439, [1968] 3 All ER 442, DC.
6 [1990] 1 All ER 331, [1990] 1 WLR 1067, DC.
7 Contrast the view of Harrison and Bell 'Assaulting our Common Sense' (1990) 53 MLR 518 at 522–523.

10.12 The slightest degree of force, even mere touching, will suffice.[1] Blackstone justified this by saying that the law cannot distinguish between criminal and non-criminal violence and therefore prohibits the lowest degree of it.[2]

The force may be applied *directly*, for example, hitting the victim with a fist or cosh, or throwing a stone at him, or by treading or driving on to his foot,[3] or *indirectly*, as where the victim falls into a hole which the accused has dug,[4] or where the victim is hit by a bucket of water placed by the accused on top of a door as a 'booby trap', or where the accused causes a theatre audience to panic and rush down an unlighted staircase across whose exit doorway he has placed an iron bar and against which those at the front of the crowd are injured.[5]

DPP v K[6] provides recent authority that a battery can be committed by an indirect application of force. D, a schoolboy had been carrying out an experiment using concentrated sulphuric acid during a chemistry class. He was given permission to go to the toilet to wash some acid off his hand. He surreptitiously took with him a test tube of the acid to test its reaction on toilet paper. While he was in the toilet he heard some footsteps in the corridor. In a panic he poured the acid into a hot air drier to conceal it. He then returned to class, intending to remove the acid from the drier and to wash it out. Before he could do so, another pupil used the drier and had acid squirted in his face; he was permanently scarred. The Divisional Court held that D was guilty of assault occasioning actual bodily harm, contrary to s 47 of the Offences against the Person Act 1861.[7] Parker LJ, with whom the other member of the court agreed, had no doubt that, if an accused placed acid in a machine and the acid was ejected on to the next user of the machine, the accused (provided that he had the appropriate mens rea) would commit a battery on the next user just as if the accused had himself switched on the machine. The decision is also interesting in that it recognises that a battery can be committed by an omission to rectify an inadvertently created dangerous situation, which results in the application of force, since the court based its decision on D's abandonment of the drier (with the necessary mens rea) after he had poured the acid into it without the necessary mens rea. On this basis, D's liability was based on his *omission* (with the appropriate mens rea) to rectify a dangerous situation which he had created.

1 *Cole v Turner* (1704) 6 Mod Rep 149.
2 4 Bl Com (18th edn) 217, referring to 3 Bl Com (18th edn) 120.
3 *Fagan v Metropolitan Police Comr*.
4 This example was given by Stephen and Wills JJ in *Clarence* (1888) 22 QBD 23.
5 Stephen and Wills JJ in *Clarence* referring to *Martin* (1881) 8 QBD 54. Cf the view taken in *Wilson* [1983] 3 All ER 448 at 455, per Lord Roskill.
6 [1990] 1 All ER 331, [1990] 1 WLR 1067, DC. The court's assumptions concerning the nature of recklessness for this offence are no longer, if ever, good law; para 10.14.
7 Para 10.17.

UNLAWFUL FORCE

10.13 A threat or use of force cannot constitute an assault or a battery if the force threatened or used is not unlawful, and it will not be unlawful if:

a) the victim validly consents to it;[1]
b) the accused uses reasonable force in public or private defence, as where he uses reasonable force in self-defence, the defence of another

or of property, the prevention of crime or the furtherance of lawful arrest,[2]

c) the accused is acting under statutory authority; or

d) the accused is acting in the exercise of the right of corporal punishment.

Parents and other persons in loco parentis are entitled as a disciplinary measure[3] to apply a reasonable degree of force to their children or charges old enough to understand its purpose.[4] However, if the corporal punishment is given out of spite or anger,[5] or for some other non-disciplinary reason, or if the degree of force is unreasonable, it is unlawful.[6]

Teachers are no longer entitled by virtue of their position as such to apply reasonable corporal punishment as a disciplinary measure, except in relation to a pupil at an independent school which receives no public funding (and even then only if that pupil's fees are not publicly funded).[7] However, if a parent has given a teacher or teachers express permission to apply reasonable corporal punishment, a teacher who does so with this permission will act lawfully because he will have been placed in loco parentis in this respect and will not simply be acting by virtue of his position.

An accused does not have to prove that the force used or threatened was lawful. Instead, if there is evidence that it may have been the prosecution must prove beyond reasonable doubt that the force was not lawful under the relevant rules of law.[8] For example, if the accused is a parent and claims that the force was used as corporal punishment, he must be acquitted unless the prosecution proves that the force used was unreasonable (or disproves some other element relevant to the claim).

1 Paras 10.2–10.8.
2 Or in any other circumstances of justification, see para 22.1–22.15.
3 *Cleary v Booth* [1893] 1 QB 465, 62 LJMC 87; *Donovan* [1934] 2 KB 498 at 509; *Mackie* (1973) 57 Cr App Rep 453, CA.
4 *Griffin* (1869) 11 Cox CC 402.
5 *Taylor* (1983) Times, 28 December, CA.
6 *Hopley* (1860) 2 F & F 202.
7 Education (No 2) Act 1986, s 47.
8 Para 22.7; *Smith (David George)* [1985] LS Gaz R 198, CA.

MENS REA IN ASSAULT AND BATTERY

10.14 An intention to injure is not required, nor need the accused act with any sort of hostile state of mind towards his victim. Instead what must be proved is that the accused:

a) in the case of an assault, intended to cause the victim to apprehend the immediate application to his body of unlawful force, or was subjectively reckless[1] as to whether the victim might so apprehend;

b) in the case of a battery, intended to apply unlawful force, or was subjectively reckless[1] as to whether such force might be applied.[2]

It follows, for example, that if A lays hands on B, whom he wrongly believes is consenting to a piece of horseplay, A must be acquitted of committing an assault or a battery. In relation to a battery, the reason is that, while A intends to apply force to B, he does not (because of his mistake as to B's consent) intend to apply unlawful force to B, nor is he subjectively reckless as to this.[3] (Similar reasoning applies in relation to an assault.) The same would be true if G hit H, wrongly believing that he must do so in self-defence, provided his force was reasonable on the facts as he believed them.[4] On the other hand, if X, a sexual pervert, beats Y severely, wrongly believing that Y is consenting, he can be convicted because, even if Y had consented, the consent would have been invalid and therefore X would not merely have intended to apply force but would have intended to apply force which was unlawful on the facts as he understood them.

1 *Spratt* [1991] 2 All ER 210, [1990] 1 WLR 1073, CA. The wider meaning given to 'reckless-ness' in *Caldwell* [1982] AC 341, [1981] 1 All ER 961, HL, does not apply to 'recklessness' in the various offences of 'assault', i e assault, battery and the aggravated 'assaults' mentioned in para 10.17: *Spratt* (where it was held that the Divisional Court's assumption to the contrary in *DPP v K* [1990] 1 All ER 331, [1990] 1 WLR 1067, DC, was wrong) .
2 *Venna* [1976] QB 421, [1975] 3 All ER 788, CA; *Kimber* [1983] 3 All ER 316, [1983] 1 WLR 1118, CA; *Williams* [1987] 3 All ER 411, CA.
3 *Kimber.*
4 *Williams.*

10.15 *Element of hostility* We said in para 10.14 that there is no need for a hostile state of mind. An embrace by a rejected lover, or an unwanted kiss, may be a battery.[1] This is true despite its apparent contradiction in the civil case of *Wilson v Pringle*[2] where the Court of Appeal held that for a battery 'touching must be proved to be a hostile touching'. However, it seems that this does not require a hostile state of mind, since the Court of Appeal said that 'hostile'

'cannot be equated with ill-will or malevolence. It cannot be governed by the obvious intention shown in acts like punching, stabbing or shooting. It cannot be governed solely by an expressed intention, although that may be strong evidence. But the element of hostility ... must be a question of fact.'[3]

Unfortunately, having said what 'hostility' does not mean, the Court of Appeal said little about what it does mean. Indeed, it provided only one example of its meaning, stating that in *Collins v Wilcock*,[4] where a police officer touched a woman intending simply to restrain her temporarily, there was a hostile touching because the officer was acting unlawfully, having no power to restrain her.[5] Probably, the reference to hostile touching does not add anything to the law and is merely another way of saying that the use of force (touching) must be unlawful.[6]

1 Depending on the facts, it may constitute an indecent assault, para 12.15.
2 [1986] 2 All ER 440, CA.
3 Ibid, at 447–448.
4 [1984] 3 All ER 374, [1984] 1 WLR 1172, DC.
5 Para 18.69.
6 In *F v West Berkshire Health Authority* [1989] 2 All ER 545 at 563 Lord Goff doubted that it was correct that a touching be hostile for it to amount to a battery. See also *Collins v Wilcock* [1984] 3 All ER 374 at 378.

TRIAL AND PUNISHMENT

10.16 Assault and battery were originally common law offences, triable only on indictment as common assault. However, since 1861 they have been statutory offences.[1] The current position is governed by s 39 of the Criminal Justice Act 1988. By s 39, assault and battery (described by the section as 'common assault and battery' but generally simply described as 'common assault')[2] are purely summary offences. The maximum punishment is six months' imprisonment or a fine not exceeding level 5 on the standard scale (£5,000) or both. However, by s 41 of of the 1988 Act, a count charging a person with common assault or battery may be included in an indictment if the charge:

a) is founded on the same facts or evidence as a count charging an indictable offence; or

b) is part of a series of offences of the same or similar character as an indictable offence which is also charged,

but only if (in either case) the facts or evidence relating to the offence were disclosed in an examination or deposition taken before a magistrate in the presence of the accused.

If a count for common assault or battery is included in an indictment under the present provision the maximum punishment is limited to the maximum for the offence available in a magistrates' court.

1 *DPP v Taylor; DPP v Little* [1992] 1 All ER 299, DC.
2 It is so described, for example, in s 41 of the 1988 Act.

Aggravated assaults

10.17 There are several statutory offences of assault (which term includes battery) which by virtue of defined aggravating elements are subject to higher penalties. In each case it must be proved that the accused committed the actus reus of an assault or battery with the relevant mens rea for *that* offence. The most common offences of aggravated assault are:

a) *assault with intent to rob*, triable only on indictment and punishable with a maximum of life imprisonment;[1]

b) *assault with intent to resist or prevent the lawful arrest of the accused or another for any offence*; this offence is triable either way and punishable with a maximum of two years' imprisonment on conviction on indictment;[2]

c) *assault with intent to commit buggery*, triable only on indictment and punishable with a maximum of ten years' imprisonment;[3]

d) *assault occasioning actual bodily harm*, triable either way and punishable with a maximum of five years' imprisonment on conviction on indictment.[4] The actus reus consists in the actus reus of assault or battery plus a requirement that it should have caused actual bodily harm. 'Actual bodily harm' means any hurt or injury calculated to interfere with the health or comfort of the victim.[5] Such hurt or injury need not be permanent, but must be more than transient or trifling.[5] Consequently, if a victim of an assault suffers great pain immediately and for some time thereafter suffers tenderness and soreness, this can constitute actual bodily harm even though there is no physically discernible injury.[6] For the purposes of this offence, 'injury' is not limited to physical injury, since it also includes a hysterical or nervous condition.[5]

Although the accused's assault or battery must have been causally related[7] to the actual bodily harm, the mens rea required to be proved is simply that for assault or battery, as the case may be, and bodily harm to another does not have to have been intended or foreseen as a risk by the accused. Authority for this proposition of law was originally provided by the decision of the Court of Appeal in *Roberts*.[8] In that case D had tried to remove the coat of a girl in a moving car, indicating that he meant to take liberties with her against her will. The girl jumped out of the car and was injured. D appealed against conviction for assault occasioning actual bodily harm on the ground that the jury were not directed to consider whether he foresaw that she would jump and suffer injury. The Court of Appeal rejected this, saying that the only issue was one of causation; the question was whether the victim's actions were the natural result of D's conduct, in the sense that they were something that could reasonably have been foreseen as the consequence of what D was saying and doing.

The view taken by the Court of Appeal in *Roberts* was confirmed by the House of Lords in 1991 in the consolidated appeals in *Savage; Parmenter*.[9] In *Savage* D committed a battery on P, a former girlfriend of D's husband, when she threw a pint of beer over her. Not only was P soaked but she was also cut by a piece of flying glass, because D had let go of the glass and it had shattered. It was not clear whether D had deliberately thrown the glass or whether it had accidentally slipped from her grasp. D was charged with unlawfully and maliciously wounding P, contrary to s 20 of the Offences against the Person Act 1861. The jury convicted D but her conviction was quashed on appeal by the Court of Appeal because of a misdirection as to the meaning of the word 'maliciously'. The Court of Appeal, however, substituted a verdict[10] of guilty of assault occasioning actual bodily harm. Before the House of Lords it was not disputed that D had committed a battery on P and that that battery had occasioned actual bodily harm. However, the trial judge had not directed the jury that they had to find that D foresaw the risk that some bodily harm would result from what he did, and therefore it was not clear what view the jury had formed on that issue of foresight. The question for the House of Lords was whether a s 47 offence had been established on the basis that it had been proved that actual bodily harm had been occasioned by the battery or whether such an offence would only have been established if foresight as to the risk of bodily harm resulting from the battery had also been proved. The House of Lords, approving *Roberts*, answered 'yes' to the first alternative; the prosecution did not have to prove that a person charged with an offence under s 47 intended to cause some actual bodily harm or was reckless as to whether such harm would be caused.

The decision in *Savage* is also interesting in that it indicates that the question of causation is not whether the actual bodily harm was occasioned by the force proved to have been intended or foreseen by the accused (the application of beer to P's body in *Savage*) but whether it was occasioned by the act which resulted in that force. The importance of this is that, as in *Savage*, the offence can be committed where the causal link between the accused's act and the resulting actual bodily harm is via an unforeseen application of force (such as the flying fragment of glass which was not proved in *Savage* to have been foreseen by the accused).

e) *assault on a constable acting in the execution of his duty*, triable only summarily and punishable with a maximum of six months' imprisonment or a fine not exceeding level 5 on the standard scale (£5,000) or both.[11] A 'constable' is anyone holding the office of constable, whatever his rank in his force. The phrase 'in the execution of his duty' is discussed in para 18.69. It is unnecessary for the prosecution to prove that the accused knew that his victim was a constable acting in the execution of his duty; ignorance in this respect is no defence.[12]

If a constable purports to exercise some power which he does not possess or makes an improper use of one of his powers he is not acting in the execution of his duty, and the threat or use of force against him, for example to escape an unlawful detention for questioning, is not an assault on him in the execution of his duty.[13] However, if unreasonable force is used or threatened in order to escape, the person using it may be convicted of common assault, common battery, assault occasioning actual bodily harm or affray (as the circumstances warrant).[14]

If a person who is being lawfully arrested or detained uses reasonable force in order to resist or escape, his mistaken belief (even though reasonable) that the arrest or detention is unlawful affords him no defence.[15]

f) *indecent assault*, whose punishment varies depending on the victim, is discussed later.[16]

1 Theft Act 1968, s 8; para 14.3.
2 Offences against the Person Act 1861, s 38; Magistrates' Courts Act 1980, s 17(1) and Sch 1.
3 Sexual Offences Act 1956, s 16; paras 12.27–12.28.
4 Offences against the Person Act 1861, s 47; Magistrates' Courts Act 1980, s 17(1) and Sch 1.
5 *Miller* [1954] 2 QB 282 at 292, [1954] 2 All ER 529 at 534.
6 *Reigate Justices, ex p Counsell* (1984) 148 JP 193, DC.
7 The principles relating to causation set out in Chapter 11 are equally applicable to non-fatal offences against the person.
8 (1971) 56 Cr App Rep 95, CA.
9 [1991] 4 All ER 698, HL. The decision to the contrary in *Spratt* [1991] 1 All ER 210, [1990] 1 WLR 1073, CA, was overruled.
10 For the Court of Appeal's power to substitute a verdict for another offence, see para 5.30.
11 Police Act 1964, s 51(1).
12 *Forbes and Webb* (1865) 10 Cox CC 362; *Maxwell and Clanchy* (1909) 2 Cr App Rep 26; *McBride v Turnock* [1964] Crim LR 456, DC; *Kenlin v Gardiner* [1967] 2 QB 510, [1966] 3 All ER 931, DC; Howard 'Assaulting Policemen in the Execution of their Duty' (1963) 79 LQR 247.
13 *Kenlin v Gardiner* [1967] 2 QB 510, [1966] 3 All ER 931, DC; *Pedro v Diss* [1981] 2 All ER 59 at 64; see, further, para 22.27.
14 *Purdy* [1975] QB 288, [1974] 3 All ER 465, CA.
15 *Fennell* [1971] 1 QB 428, [1970] 3 All ER 215, CA. See also para 22.12.
16 Para 12.15.

Wounding and grievous bodily harm

10.18   The offences under ss 18 and 20 of the Offences against the Person Act 1861 discussed below resemble each other in various ways. One is that their definitions contain the word 'unlawfully', which is simply a reference to the fact that a person cannot be convicted of an offence under ss 18 or 20 if his conduct is legally justified, e g by the fact that he was using reasonable force in self-defence or to prevent crime or effect a lawful arrest,[1] or if the victim has given a valid consent.

1 Para 22.17.

SECTION 20

10.19   Section 20 of the Offences against the Person Act 1861 provides that it is an offence unlawfully and maliciously to wound or inflict any grievous bodily harm upon any other person, either with or without a weapon or instrument. The last phrase adds nothing to the definition but was presumably added for the avoidance of doubt. An offence under s 20 is triable either way[1] and punishable on conviction on indictment with a maximum of five years' imprisonment.

1 Magistrates' Courts Act 1980, s 17(1) and Sch 1.

10.20 *Actus reus* Section 20 creates two offences. The actus reus of one being an act resulting in the unlawful wounding of another, and of the other an act resulting in the unlawful infliction of grievous bodily harm on him. To constitute a wound, the inner and outer skin must actually be broken;[1] a bruise is not sufficient, but the wound need not be grievous. 'Grievous bodily harm' was defined by the House of Lords in *DPP v Smith*[2] as meaning really serious harm; it has since been held that 'really' adds nothing to 'serious harm' and that it is not a misdirection to direct a jury that 'grievous bodily harm' means serious harm.[3] There is no modern authority on whether a hysterical or nervous condition unaccompanied by any physical injury can (as in the case of actual bodily harm) constitute bodily harm and hence grievous bodily harm if serious,[4] but there is no reason why it should not.

1 *M'Loughlin* (1838) 8 C & P 635; *JJC (a minor) v Eisenhower* [1983] 3 All ER 230, [1983] 3 WLR 537, DC.
2 [1961] AC 290, [1960] 3 All ER 161, HL.
3 *McMillan* (1984) unreported, CA; *Saunders* [1985] Crim LR 230, CA.
4 In *Ashman* (1858) 1 F & F 88 it was held that there could be grievous bodily harm in such case, but at the time the definition of grievous bodily harm corresponded to the modern definition of actual bodily harm and therefore required a lower degree of harm than is now required for grievous bodily harm.

10.21 In a number of cases over the years, including the particularly well-known decision in *Clarence*,[1] the courts have held that grievous bodily harm is not inflicted for the purposes of s 20 unless it is caused by an 'assault'. Although the term 'assault' is normally used generically to mean assault or battery, it appears that in the present context the judges have used the term only in the sense of a battery. In *Clarence* D, as already mentioned, knowing that he had venereal disease but concealing this fact from her, had intercourse with his wife as a result of which she contracted that disease. The majority of the Court for Crown Cases Reserved held that D could not be convicted of unlawfully inflicting grievous bodily harm on his wife because 'inflict' implied the need for an assault and, since the wife had consented to the bodily contact involved, there had been no assault.

Despite this insistence on the need for an assault, the position was somewhat confused because there were a number of cases where facts were held to disclose the offence of inflicting grievous bodily harm without any inquiry being made as to whether those facts also constituted an assault. While these cases did not expressly state that an assault was not required, it was difficult, if not impossible, to discover an assault on their facts. In *Lewis*,[2] for example, D shouted at his wife through the front door of their third floor flat, which she had locked against him. He threatened her and said he would kill her, and she heard the sound of breaking glass. She was in another room but, fearing what would happen if she stayed in the flat, she jumped out of the window and broke both legs. The Court of Appeal dismissed D's appeal against conviction for inflicting grievous bodily harm, contrary to s 20, saying that it made no difference that he had not been in the same room. The events here would not seem to have amounted even to a battery of the indirect type, the unintended injury being far more remote than the examples given above.[3]

The conflict between the cases was resolved in 1983 by the House of Lords in *Wilson*,[4] where the House, approving and adopting the decision of the Supreme Court of Victoria in *Salisbury*,[5] held that there can be an infliction of grievous bodily harm contrary to s 20 without an 'assault'.

If 'inflict' does not require an assault, are there any limits on the ways in which grievous bodily harm may be inflicted? In *Salisbury*, the Supreme Court of Victoria held that such harm may be inflicted 'either where the accused has directly and violently "inflicted" it by assaulting the victim,[6] or where the accused has "inflicted" it by doing something intentionally [ie deliberately], which, though it is not itself a direct application of force to the body of the victim, does directly result in force being applied violently to the body of the victim, so that he suffers grievous bodily harm'.

Under this formula, cases where, as in *Lewis*, the accused frightens someone who injures himself seriously in trying to escape, or where the accused interferes with the braking system of a car and thereby causes the driver to be involved in an accident and suffer serious harm,[7] clearly involve the infliction of grievous bodily harm, whereas causing someone such harm by an omission or by poisoning would not because in such a case there is no assault and no force is 'applied violently to the body of the victim'. Consequently, the actual decision in *Clarence* (as opposed to its reasoning) remains unaffected by *Wilson*.

It was thought that there could not be a wounding unless the wound resulted from an assault,[8] in the sense of a battery.[9] The decision in *Wilson* did not, strictly, affect this, although it suggested that a wound could be directly inflicted in the same way as grievous bodily harm (ie even though there was no battery). In *Savage*,[10] the Court of Appeal was of the opinion that, although almost inevitably a wounding would result from a battery, it would not do so if the facts were 'quite extraordinary' (which would seem to refer to situations of the second type referred to in *Salisbury*). On appeal, Lord Ackner, with whose speech the other Law Lords agreed, was of the same opinion as the Court of Appeal.[11]

1 (1888) 22 QBD 23, 58 LJMC 10; para 10.7. Also see *Taylor* (1869) LR 1 CCR 194, 38 LJMC 106; *Beasley* (1981) 73 Cr App Rep 44, CA.
2 [1970] Crim LR 647, CA. Also see *Halliday* (1889) 61 LT 701; *Cartledge v Allen* [1973] Crim LR 530, DC.
3 Para 10.12.
4 [1983] 3 All ER 448, [1983] 3 WLR 686, HL.
5 [1976] VR 452, 76 Cr App Rep 261n. In this case an Australian offence practically identical to s 20 was considered and the English cases on s 20 examined.
6 A battery of the indirect type (see para 10.12) is covered by the second alternative.
7 *Savage; Parmenter* [1991] 4 All ER 698 at 710, per Lord Ackner.
8 *Taylor* (1869) LR 1 CCR 194, 38 LJMC 106.
9 *Beasley* (1981) 73 Cr App Rep 44, CA.
10 (1990) 91 Cr App Rep 317, CA.
11 *Savage; Parmenter* [1991] 4 All ER 698, HL.

10.22 *Mens rea* The mens rea required for both offences is comprised by the word 'maliciously', which does not connote spite or ill-will.[1] It was confirmed by the House of Lords in 1991 in *Savage; Parmenter*[2] that, in order to prove that the accused acted maliciously, it is sufficient to prove that he intended his act to result in *some* unlawful[3] bodily harm to some other person, albeit of a minor nature, or was *subjectively* reckless as to the risk that his act might result in such harm. Thus, it is not necessary to prove that the accused intended, or was subjectively reckless as to, the infliction of a wound or grievous bodily harm.[4] On the other hand, it is not enough to prove that the accused ought to have foreseen the risk of bodily harm to another; he must be proved *actually* to have foreseen the risk of such harm.[5]

Because the accused must have been aware that his act might cause some *unlawful* physical harm, an accused who mistakenly believes, for example, that he is acting in self-defence, or that his victim has consented to the horseplay which injures him accidentally, is not guilty of the present offence if he wounds or inflicts grievous bodily harm on his victim.

1 *Cunningham* [1957] 2 QB 396, [1957] 2 All ER 412, CCA.
2 [1991] 4 All ER 698, HL.
3 *Jones* (1986) 83 Cr App Rep 375, [1987] Crim LR 123, CA.
4 *Savage; Parmenter* [1991] 4 All ER 698, HL. For earlier authority, see, for example, *Mowatt* [1968] 1 QB 421, [1967] 3 All ER 47, CA; *Flack v Hunt* [1980] Crim LR 44, DC; *Sullivan* [1981] Crim LR 46, CA.
5 Confirmed in *Savage; Parmenter*.

SECTION 18

10.23   Section 18 of the Offences against the Person Act 1861 provides that it is an offence, triable only on indictment and punishable with a maximum of imprisonment for life, unlawfully and maliciously to wound or cause grievous bodily harm to any person by any means whatsoever with intent to do grievous bodily harm or with intent to resist or prevent the lawful apprehension or detainer of any person. There are two offences under s 18: wounding with intent and causing grievous bodily harm with intent.

10.24   *Actus reus* 'Wound' and 'grievous bodily harm' mean the same as in s 20. Section 18 speaks of 'causing by any means whatsoever', as opposed to 'inflicting', grievous bodily harm. Presumably this difference in terminology was deliberate. The phrase 'cause . . . by any means whatsoever' suggests that a wider range of situations is covered by it than by 'inflicts', although the only obvious examples where grievous bodily harm could be said to be 'caused', but not 'inflicted', would seem to be where a person deliberately fails to do something which he is under a legal duty to do and thereby grievous bodily harm is caused to another, and where he causes such harm by poisoning.

10.25   *Mens rea* Section 18 also differs significantly from the s 20 offences in relation to its mens rea because the prosecution must prove that the accused had the intent to do (unlawful) grievous bodily harm or to resist or prevent the lawful apprehension (i e arrest) or detainer of himself or another. 'Intention' bears its normal meaning, outlined in Chapter 6, so that it is irrelevant whether or not the accused desired to cause grievous bodily harm or to resist or prevent arrest.[1] On the other hand, while a person who causes grievous bodily harm by means of a practical joke will be guilty of an offence under s 20 if he merely foresaw the risk of some harm, he cannot be convicted of an offence under s 18 on account of the absence of an intention to do grievous bodily harm. The requirement of an intent to cause grievous bodily harm does not mean that the accused himself should regard his intended consequence as grievous bodily harm. Provided that, in the view of the jury, his intended consequence amounts to grievous bodily harm he will have an intent to cause such harm. Thus, if the jury decides that D intended to break P's wrist and that a broken wrist is serious (ie grievous) bodily harm, it is irrelevant that D did not think that a broken wrist was serious harm; the necessary intent will have been proved.

1 *Bryson* [1985] Crim LR 669, CA; *Purcell* (1986) 83 Cr App Rep 45, CA.

10.26 A debatable point is the precise import of the word 'maliciously' in s 18. If it means the same thing as 'maliciously' in s 20, it is redundant in s 18, at least where the accused has the intent to do grievous bodily harm.[1] Causing grievous bodily harm or wounding with intent to do grievous bodily harm must, given the nature of the requisite intent, include foresight of the possibility of some physical harm which, as we have seen, is the meaning to be attached to 'maliciously' in s 20; but it is possible to attach some force to the word 'maliciously' in s 18 when the alleged intent is to resist or prevent lawful apprehension or detainer. If D gently seizes a policeman's jacket, or even gently trips him up, in order to prevent him giving instant chase to X, an escaping criminal, D would undoubtedly have acted with intent to prevent X's apprehension, but, if the policeman suffered serious injury wholly unforeseen by D, D would not have acted 'maliciously', ie with foresight of the risk of some harm to the policeman. It is submitted that that meaning should be given to 'maliciously' in this context since it would seem unduly harsh to convict a person of the serious offence under s 18 where he accidentally but seriously injured another in trying to resist or prevent a lawful arrest. It was said in *Mowatt*[2] that ' "maliciously" adds nothing' in s 18, but the case was concerned with causing grievous bodily harm with intent to do so.[3]

1 See the article by Sir Bernard Mackenna [1966] Crim LR 548.
2 [1968] 1 QB 421, [1967] 3 All ER 47, CA.
3 It seems to have been assumed in *Morrison* (1988) 89 Cr App Rep 17, CA, that 'maliciously' in the context of a charge under s 18 involving an intent to resist etc arrest does bear some meaning, that given to it in relation to s 20.

DRAFT CRIMINAL CODE

10.27 Under the draft Criminal Code Bill[1] the offences discussed in this chapter would be replaced by the following provisions.

The law relating to common assault and battery would be replaced by the following provision (cl 75) which would create a single offence of assault:

'A person is guilty of assault if he intentionally or recklessly[2] –
  a) applies force to or causes an impact on the body of another; or
  b) causes another to believe that any such force or impact is imminent,
without the consent of the other or, where the act is likely or intended to cause personal harm to another, with or without his consent.'

The existing exceptions whereby a person can give a valid consent to an act likely or intended to cause personal harm, where the act is reasonable surgical interference or is done in the course of a properly conducted game or sport or of a dangerous entertainment or is otherwise justified or excused in law, would be preserved by virtue of cl 4(4). In addition, of course, the offence would not be committed if the accused was acting in self-defence etc.

In relation to the offence of assaulting a constable in the execution of his duty, cl 76 of the draft Criminal Code Bill, following the recommendations of the Criminal Law Revision Committee,[3] provides that it would have to be proved that the accused knew or was reckless as to whether his victim was a constable, although proof that the accused was or ought to have been aware that the constable was acting in the course of his duty should not be required (since anyone who assaults a constable, knowing or being reckless as to his victim's status, should do so at his peril).

By cls 77 and 78 there would continue to be offences of assault with intent to resist lawful arrest and assault with intent to rob. Indecent assault would continue to be an offence (see para 12.23) but assault with intent to commit buggery would not continue to be a separate offence (although, of course, it could be punished as an indecent assault).

Cls 70, 71 and 71 of the draft Criminal Code Bill, following the recommendations of the Criminal Law Revision Committee,[3] would replace ss 18, 20 and 47 (assault occasioning actual bodily harm) of the Offences against the Person Act 1861 with three new offences. The substance of the three offences would be:

a) intentionally[2] causing serious personal harm to another. This would cover most cases at present falling within s 18 of the 1861 Act. As in the case of the next proposed offence the distinction between wounding and grievous bodily harm would disappear;
b) recklessly[2] causing serious personal harm to another. This offence would replace s 20 of the 1861 Act, but the mental element would be stricter since the accused would have to be aware that he is taking the risk of causing *serious* personal harm and persist in taking it; and
c) intentionally or recklessly causing personal harm to another. This offence would replace s 47 of the 1861 Act.

None of these three offences would be committed if the accused was acting in self-defence etc or if his act was justified or excused by any enactment or by the common law (as where the injury is caused during a lawful sport).

The main reason why the Criminal Law Revision Committee[3] recommended separate offences of intentionally causing serious personal harm and recklessly causing serious personal harm is that there is a moral and psychological distinction between the two offences which it is appropriate for the criminal law to reflect. On the other hand, it appreciated that the moral distinction between intention and recklessness is not an easy one for the police, magistrates and juries to make, and, with regard to acts of violence amounting to injury but not serious injury, it considered that the law need not be altered to require the distinction in mental element to be made in every case (which would be necessary if there were two separate offences of causing personal harm).

1 Law Commission: A Criminal Code for England and Wales (1989): Law Com No 177; para 3.21 above.
2 For the meaning of 'intention' and 'recklessness' in the draft Code, see para 6.69.
3 Cmnd 7844, paras 149–182.

11 Homicide and related offences

Homicide generally

ACTUS REUS

11.1 Homicide may be lawful or unlawful and, if it is unlawful, it may be murder, manslaughter, infanticide, causing death by dangerous driving, or causing death by careless driving when under the influence of drink or drugs. For convenience the last two offences will be dealt with later.[1]

Murder, manslaughter and infanticide share a common actus reus. According to Coke, it is unlawfully killing a reasonable creature under the Queen's peace, death following within a year and a day of the infliction of the injury.[1] The three offences are distinguished in some instances by the state of mind which they require on the part of the accused, and in others by the availability of certain mitigating defences which are available to a person otherwise guilty of murder.

By way of exceptions to the rule that our courts only have jurisdiction over offences committed in England and Wales (or on a British ship or aircraft on or over the high seas):[3]

a) a person who commits murder or manslaughter in a foreign country is subject to the jurisdiction of our courts if he is a British citizen (or a British dependent territories citizen or a British overseas citizen);[4] and

b) proceedings for murder or manslaughter may be brought against a person irrespective of his nationality at the time of the alleged offence if it was committed as a war crime in Germany or German occupied territory during the Second World War, provided that on or after 8 March 1991 he was or has become a British citizen or resident in the United Kingdom, the Isle of Man or the Channel Islands.[5]

1 Paras 20.13 and 20.22.
2 3 Inst 47.
3 Paras 6.77–6.81.
4 This is the effect of the Offences against the Person Act 1861 and s 3 of the British Nationality Act 1948.
5 War Crimes Act 1991, s 1. A prosecution may only be instituted by or with the consent of the Attorney-General.

THE VICTIM

11.2 Before any question of a person's liability for homicide can arise, it must be established that he killed a 'reasonable creature' (ie a human being). On rare occasions the offspring of human parentage may be so deformed as to be unrecognisable as a human being, or barely so

190

recognisable. Such offspring are usually a freak of nature but they can result from radiation or the use of drugs. They may be anencephalic (i e lacking a head and brain, although they may have a brain stem) or ectocardiac. Sometimes they belong to the fish stage of development with gills, webbed arms and feet and sightless eyes. Such 'monsters' are usually still born, but some do survive for a short period ranging from minutes to days or, even, a couple of weeks. If a person kills such a being the question may arise whether he has committed an offence of homicide. The tentative view has been expressed that a 'monster' is not protected by the law,[1] but it seems probable that the courts would regard any offspring of a human mother as itself human. In *Rance v Mid-Downs Health Authority*[2] Brook J took the view, obiter, that an anencephalic child was protected by the law of homicide.

1 Williams *The Sanctity of Life and the Criminal Law* 31-35; Braham (1988) 138 NLJ 91.
2 [1991] 1 All ER 801 at 817.

11.3 The issues of when life begins and ends for the purposes of the law are clearly relevant to homicide. It is not homicide to destroy a baby who is not yet born alive or the corpse of a person already dead.

The law states that a child is born alive when two conditions are satisfied:

a) the whole body of the child must have emerged into the world,[1] and
b) thereafter the child must have had an existence independent of its mother.[2]

It is not necessary that the umbilical cord should have been severed.[3] There is no modern authority on what is required for an independent existence but earlier case law reveals that some judges favoured the test of independent breathing,[4] while others favoured that of independent circulation in addition to breathing.[5] This difference of opinion remains unresolved, although the fact that the current judicial approach to the related phrase 'capable of being born alive' in the offence of child destruction[6] is based on an understanding that independent breathing is required for live birth strongly suggests that, when the matter next comes up for decision, the test of independent breathing will be adopted. The addition of a requirement of independent circulation does not really make any difference because it is now known that within a couple of months of conception the embryonic heart is maintaining the foetal bloodstream, with no direct communication with the mother's blood. It appears that it is irrelevant to whether or not, in law, a child is born alive that it is not viable (i e incapable of survival for even a short time).

What constitutes a 'live birth' is controversial even among the medical profession, who prefer to speak of viability but it would seem that members of that profession would generally agree that the birth of a child incapable of breathing is not a live birth.

Although the destruction of an unborn child cannot amount to an offence of homicide (or, indeed, any other offence against the person, since such a child is not a 'person' in law),[7] the wilful destruction of a child capable of being born alive before it is born alive may amount to the offence of child destruction, while the intentional procuring of a miscarriage may constitute the offence of abortion.[8] If a child is born alive, and dies because of ante-natal injuries which were inflicted, the person who inflicted them is guilty of murder[9] or manslaughter[10] depending on the state of mind with which he acted.[11]

1 *Poulton* (1832) 5 C & P 329.
2 *Enoch* (1833) 5 C & P 539; *Handley* (1874) 13 Cox CC 79.
3 *Reeves* (1839) 9 C & P 25.
4 *Handley*; contrast *Brain* (1834) 6 C & P 349.
5 *Enoch* (1833) 5 C & P 539; *Wright* (1841) 9 C & P 754.
6 Such capacity has been held to require a capacity to breathe without any connection with the mother: *Rance v Mid-Downs Health Authority* [1991] 1 All ER 801. See also *C v S* [1987] 1 All ER 1230, [1987] 2 WLR 1108, High Ct and CA.
7 *Tait* [1989] 3 All ER 682, [1989] 3 WLR 891, CA.
8 Paras 11.75–11.81.
9 *West* (1848) 2 Car & Kir 784, 2 Cox CC 500.
10 *Senior* (1832) 1 Mood CC 346.
11 The law set out above is substantially repeated in the draft Criminal Code Bill, cl 53 (Law Commission: A Criminal Code For England and Wales (1989): Law Com No 177; see para 3.21 above).

11.4 The point of time at which life ends for legal purposes is obscure. Medical science recognises that death is not instantaneous but is a continuing process, since different parts of the body die at different times. At one time, the medical view was that death occurred when the heart stopped beating and breathing ended. This was not very satisfactory since these symptoms can occur in conditions like barbiturate overdosage and hypothermia, from both of which recovery is possible. The concept of 'heart death' was established before the technology was developed whereby heart beats and breathing can be artificially maintained by ventilating a body on a respirator. Because of the medical dilemma of determining when a respirator may be switched off in the case of comatose and unresponsive patients, the Conference of Royal Medical Colleges and their Faculties of the United Kingdom adopted in 1976 the concept of 'brain death' as the determinant of death.[1] This occurs where irremediable structural brain damage is diagnosed by tests establishing that none of the vital centres of the brain stem is still functioning. The concept of 'brain death' is important in relation to the transplant of hearts and livers, which are most likely to succeed if the organ is taken from the donor while his heart is still beating.

In the absence of authority,[2] and subject to any alteration in medical knowledge and opinion,[3] it is likely that 'brain death' will be adopted as the legal definition of death. If so, a surgeon who removes an organ from a person who has suffered irreversible brain damage, but whose body is being ventilated by a respirator, does not commit any offence of homicide by switching off the respirator (nor does he commit any other offence against the person) because that person is already dead in a legal sense. The legal situation where a doctor switches off the respirator of a patient who has not suffered 'brain death' but is irreversibly comatose is a matter of dispute.[4]

In its Fourteenth Report: Offences against the Person,[5] published in 1980, the Criminal Law Revision Committee recommended that there should not be a statutory definition of death, mainly because it might become outmoded and defective in the light of increased medical knowledge and thereby hinder the medical profession, for example in cases of transplants. It is submitted that this recommendation is unsatisfactory. The law should be certain, and a statute can always be amended. The legal definition of death is a more appropriate matter for Parliament than the courts and, without a statutory definition, one will eventually have to be provided by the courts; they will not be able to dodge the issue for ever.

1 [1976] 2 *British Medical Journal* 1187. Also see Pace 'Defining Human Death' (1976) 126 NLJ 1232.
2 In *Malcherek* [1981] 2 All ER 422, [1981] 1 WLR 690, CA, referred to in para 11.17, the Court of Appeal did not find it necessary to decide what constituted the legal definition of death.
3 There appears to be a mounting belief among the medical profession that death does not occur unless, in addition to irremediable structural brain stem damage, there is a cessation of breathing and heartbeats, in which case a person on a ventilator would still be alive. See Sunday Times, 7 December 1986.
4 See Kennedy 'Switching Off Life Support Machines' [1977] Crim LR 443; Williams [1977] Crim LR 635.
5 Cmnd 7844, para 37.

11.5 *Under the Queen's peace* Any human being can be the victim of homicide with the exception of persons who are not 'under the Queen's Peace', ie alien enemies killed in the actual heat and exercise of war and, perhaps, rebels who are at the time actually engaged in hostile operations against the Crown.[1] The deliberate and unjustified shooting of prisoners of war amounts to murder.[2]

1 Hale *Pleas of the Crown* vol I, 433; *Page* [1954] 1 QB 170, [1953] 2 All ER 1355, Courts-Martial Appeal Court. The powers of this court correspond in general with those of the Court of Appeal (Criminal Division), as does its composition.
2 *Maria v Hall* (1807) 1 Taunt 33 at 36.

THE KILLING

11.6 A homicide may be punishable even if it is the outcome of an omission to act, rather than a positive act, provided the omission consists of a failure to perform a duty to act recognised by the criminal law. As was explained in paras 6.7 to 6.14, duties to act can be imposed by the common law or by statute. However, up to the present, the law has been slow to impose duties to do positive acts. Almost all the prosecutions for homicide by omission have been prosecutions for manslaughter, but if a person who is under a legal duty to act, as where a parent is under a duty to provide food for his or her helpless child, omits to perform that duty intending thereby to cause death (and death does result), that person can be convicted of murder.[1] Proving the necessary intent in such a case is not easy. The possibility of infanticide by omission is expressly contemplated by the Infanticide Act 1938.

1 *Gibbins and Proctor* (1918) 13 Cr App Rep 134, CCA.

11.7 *Year and a day rule*[1] The death with which it is sought to charge the accused must be shown to have occurred within a year and a day of the infliction of the injury by which it is alleged to have been caused.[2] This rule was evolved by the common law because of the difficulty in proving that an injury outside the period did cause the death in question. It is now possible to diagnose the cause of death even though it occurred a substantial time afterwards; it is unfortunate that the rule should allow a person to escape liability for a homicide which he is scientifically shown to have caused. It also seems unfortunate that a person who severely injures another should escape any criminal liability for homicide if his victim is kept alive, say in a coma, for more than a year and a day before dying as a result of his injuries. Somewhat surprisingly, the Criminal Law Revision Committee, in its Fourteenth Report: Offences against the Person,[3] recommended in 1981 that the rule should be retained. Its reasons were that it would be wrong for a person to remain indefinitely at risk of a prosecution for homicide and that the present drawing of the line operates satisfactorily. It also recommended that, where pre-natal injury is inflicted, time should run from birth.[4] In relation to the Committee's first reason for retaining the year and a day rule, it may be objected that such a view does not prevent a person being tried and convicted for a homicide offence (where the death followed within a year and a day) many years afterwards. In relation to the second reason it may be noted that in other jurisdictions the law has operated satisfactorily without ever having the rule or has abandoned it.

The application of the year and a day rule is well illustrated by the facts of *Dyson*.[5] The victim died in March 1908, having been injured by D in November 1906, and again in December 1907. The Court of Criminal Appeal quashed a conviction for manslaughter on the ground that the jury had been directed wrongly that they could convict if they found that death had been caused wholly by the injuries inflicted in 1906. The jury should have been asked whether the death had been accelerated by the injuries in 1907, in which case they could have properly convicted D. There is, of course, no objection in a case caught by the year and a day rule to an indictment founded on some offence less than homicide, such as attempted murder or an offence under ss 18 or 20 of the Offences against the Person Act 1861.

1 Yale 'A Year and a Day in Homicide' (1989) 48 CLJ 202.
2 Coke, 3 Inst 47; *Dyson* [1908] 2 KB 454, 77 LJKB 813, CCA; *Coroner for West London, ex De Luca* [1988] 3 All ER 414, [1988] 3 WLR 286, CA.
3 Cmnd 7844, paras 39 and 40.
4 The draft Criminal Code Bill, cl 53(b), incorporates this recommendation in its restatement of the rule.
5 [1908] 2 KB 454, 77 LJKB 813, CCA.

CAUSATION

11.8   Finally, the prosecution must prove that the victim's death was caused by the accused's conduct.[1] The principles relating to causation set out below are equally applicable to non-fatal offences (subject to the substitution of the relevant non-fatal injury for 'death').

The question of causation involves two issues, since an accused can only be convicted if his conduct was both a *factual cause* of the victim's death and a *legal cause* of it. For the purposes of causation, 'cause' simply means 'accelerate'. Thus, it is no defence, in itself, that the victim was already dying from some mortal illness if the accused's conduct has accelerated death.[2]

The accused's conduct is not a *factual cause* of death unless the death would not have occurred, when and as it did, *but for* that conduct; this is often described as the 'but for' test.

Application of the 'but for' test indicates whether or not the death can be attributed to the accused's conduct as a matter of fact. If it can be, the question of whether that death can be attributed to him for the purposes of legal liability depends on whether or not his conduct is a *legal cause* of death; only if it is (and this depends on the principles set out in paras 11.9 to 11.18) can the death be attributed to it for that purpose.

All this can be illustrated as follows:

a) D stabs P. X subsequently decapitates P.
b) D administers a slow-working poison to P. Before it can take effect P dies of a heart attack induced by natural causes.

In neither of these cases is D's conduct a factual cause of death since the death occurred, when and as it did, independently of it.[3] Contrast the following:

c) D stabs P who is later stabbed by X. P dies from the effects of both wounds.

d) D stabs P who receives emergency treatment in hospital from which he dies.

In these two cases the death would not have occurred, when and as it did, but for D's conduct which is therefore a factual cause. However, whether P's death in these two cases is attributable to D for the purposes of liability (ie whether D's conduct is a legal cause of P's death) depends on the principles set out below.

1 Hart and Honoré *Causation in the Law* chs XII–XIV; Williams 'Causation in Homicide' [1957] Crim LR 429 and 510.
2 *Dyson* [1908] 2 KB 454, 77 LJKB 813, CCA.
3 For another example, see *White* [1910] KB 124; para 6.18.

PRINCIPLES OF LEGAL ATTRIBUTION

11.9 Courts have often said that death can only be attributed to the accused if he substantially caused it,[1] although such a requirement has also been denied.[2] Whether or not there is such a requirement is unimportant because it is clear that 'substantial' in this context merely means that the accused's contribution to the death must be more than a minute or negligible contribution (which would be ignored anyway under the general *de minimis* principle).[3] In some cases the courts have used the term 'significant contribution to death' rather than 'substantial cause of death',[4] but there is no difference between the effect of the two terms.

1 See, for example, *Smith* [1959] 2 QB 35, [1959] 2 All ER 193, Courts-Martial Appeal Court (see para 11.5, note 1).
2 *Malcherek* [1981] 2 All ER 422, [1981] 1 WLR 690, CA.
3 *Hennigan* [1971] 3 All ER 133; *Cato* [1976] 1 All ER 260, [1976] 1 WLR 110, CA.
4 *Pagett* (1983) 76 Cr App Rep 279 at 288; *Cheshire* [1991] 3 All ER 670, CA.

11.10 In the event of one of the circumstances outlined below being involved, principles specific to it also come into operation.

11.11 *Contributions by third parties* As already implied, the accused's conduct need not be the sole, or even the main, cause of death.[1] Thus, even though a third party has substantially contributed to the death, the accused can be convicted if his act is also a substantial cause. It is not the function of the jury to evaluate competing causes or to choose which is dominant.[2] In *Benge*[2] D, a foreman platelayer, misread the timetable so that the track was up when a train arrived. D had placed a signalman with a flag up the line but only half as far as he should have been sent under the company's rules and the engine driver, who was not keeping a very sharp lookout, did not see the signal in time to stop. The resulting accident caused several deaths. If the signalman had gone the proper distance and the driver had been keeping a proper lookout there would not have been an accident, but D was convicted of manslaughter after the judge had ruled that, if his conduct was a substantial cause of the accident, it was irrelevant that the conduct of others had contributed to it. Of course, in a case like this the other railwaymen could also be convicted of homicide in relation to the same death, and this would be possible whether or not they were acting in combination.

1 *Smith* [1959] 2 QB 35, [1959] 2 All ER 193, Courts-Martial Appeal Court (see para 11.5, note 1, in relation to this court); *Cheshire* [1991] 3 All ER 670,CA.
2 *Cheshire*.
3 (1865) 4 F & F 504.

11.12 *Contributory negligence* Unless it is so gross as to prevent the accused's act being a substantial cause,[1] the contributory negligence of the victim is no defence. In *Longbottom*[2] the victim, who was deaf, was walking in the middle of the highway and was run over by D, who was driving too fast. It was held that D could be convicted of manslaughter notwithstanding any contributory negligence on the part of the victim in walking as he had done.

1 *Martin* (1827) 3 C & P 211.
2 (1849) 13 JP 270, 3 Cox CC 439. Also see *Swindall and Osborne* (1846) 2 Car & Kir 230.

11.13 *Pre-existing conditions in the victim* The existence of a medical condition which rendered the victim more susceptible to mortal injury, e g haemophilia, does not prevent attribution of the death to the accused. In *Hayward*[1] D arrived home in a state of agitation, saying that he was 'going to give his wife something' when she came home. On her arrival there was an altercation and the wife ran into the road, closely pursued by D who was making violent threats towards her. The wife fell down in the road and was found to be dead when she was picked up. The medical evidence was that the wife was in good health apart from a persistent thyrus gland, but that in this condition death might result from a combination of fright and physical exertion. The jury were directed that the wife's susceptibility to death, whether D knew of it or not, was irrelevant if they were satisfied that her death was accelerated by his threats of violence.

1 (1908) 21 Cox CC 692.

11.14 *Where the victim dies in trying to escape* If the victim brings about his own death under a reasonable apprehension, occasioned by the accused, of immediate violence to himself, the death can be attributable legally to the accused. Thus, in *Pitts*[1] it was held that if a person drowns after throwing himself into a river in order to avoid immediate acts of violence against him, which he reasonably apprehends, the death could be attributable to his assailant. The relevant rule has sometimes been expressed differently, that if the victim's actions in trying to escape were a reasonably foreseeable reaction to the accused's threat of violence his death is attributable to the accused.[2] It would seem that either formulation produces the same result. Whichever test is applied, the way in which the victim reacted must also have been reasonable; otherwise the chain of causation will have been broken.[3] Thus, if the victim kills himself by doing something daft in trying to escape under a reasonable apprehension of immediate violence occasioned by the accused, the death cannot be legally attributable to the accused.

1 (1842) Car & M 284. Also see *Mackie* (1973) 57 Cr App Rep 453, CA.
2 E g *Roberts* (1971) 56 Cr App Rep 95, CA.
3 *Pitts* (1842) Car & M 284; *Roberts* (1971) 56 Cr App Rep 95, CA; *Williams and Davis* (1991) Times, 23 October, CA.

11.15 *Victim's neglect of treatment or maltreatment of self* In *Wall*[1] the governor of a colony was held guilty of the murder of a soldier whom he had sentenced to an illegal flogging, although it was argued that the victim might not have died if he had refrained from drinking spirits while in hospital in consequence of the blows he had received. Macdonald LCB directed the jury that:

> 'There is no apology for a man if he puts another in so dangerous and hazardous a situation by his treatment of him, that some degree of unskilfulness and mistaken treatment of himself may possibly accelerate the fatal catastrophe.'

A case involving neglect of treatment by the victim is *Holland*.[2] D deliberately inflicted some wounds on the deceased. One of these caused blood poisoning in a finger, and the deceased was advised to have it amputated. Had he done so, his surgeon stated, his life would probably have been saved. However, lockjaw set in and death ensued. The jury were directed that it made no difference whether the wound was instantly mortal of its own nature, or became the cause of death only by reason of the deceased's not having adopted the best mode of treatment. A verdict of guilty of murder was returned.

The dictum of Macdonald LCB cited above did not preclude the possibility that the victim's neglect or maltreatment of himself might provide a defence if it was unreasonable; in which case a direction given today of the type in *Holland* might have been incorrect because, medical science having advanced greatly since 1841, a refusal of an operation might now be regarded as unreasonable. However, such an argument was rejected in 1975 by the Court of Appeal in *Blaue*.[3] Giving the Court's judgment, Lawton LJ said:

> 'It has long been the policy of the law that those who use violence on other people must take their victims as they find them. This in our judgment means the whole man, not just the physical man. It does not lie in the mouth of the assailant to say that his victim's religious beliefs which inhibited him from accepting certain kinds of treatment were unreasonable. The question for decision is what caused the death. The answer is the stab wound.'[4]

In *Blaue* the deceased girl, who had been stabbed by D, was a Jehovah's Witness and consequently refused to have a blood transfusion which was required before surgery and which might have saved her life. The Court of Appeal held that a victim's refusal to have medical treatment could not provide a defence. In such a case the accused would be liable if his act was still an operative and substantial cause of death. D was liable because the physical cause of death was the bleeding in the pleural cavity arising from the penetration of the lung. This was not brought about by any decision of the girl but by the stab wound. While the decision in *Blaue* seems to be right, particularly since the adjudication of the reasonableness of religious objections to medical treatment would raise a number of difficulties, it appears to indicate that (unless the wound is not a 'substantial cause of death') the 'bloody minded' victim of a petty wound can make the wounder guilty of manslaughter by obstinately refusing medical treatment, and so bringing about his own death. It is submitted that such a result is intolerable.

1 (1802) 28 State Tr 51.
2 (1841) 2 Mood & R 351; for a full account of the facts see [1957] Crim LR 702.
3 [1975] 3 All ER 446, [1975] 1 WLR 1411, CA.
4 [1975] 3 All ER 446 at 450.

11.16 *Intervening events* An intervening event which causes death will only prevent the legal attribution of the death to the accused if its occurrence was not likely (ie not reasonably foreseeable). Thus, if D injures P and leaves him lying injured on the ground, it is immaterial that P died of exposure or from an infection caused by the wound or from a combination of the wound and the supervening event. Conversely, the death would not be attributable to D if P had been killed by an unlikely event such as an earthquake or a stroke of lightning.[1]

1 Perkins *Criminal Law* (2nd edn) 722–723.

11.17 *Intervening acts by a third party* Here we are concerned with cases where, although the death would not have occurred without the accused's act, an intervening act by another contributed to the death. Separate consideration is given below to the case of intervening medical treatment.

Where the accused's act directly contributes to the death, that result is attributable legally to him. Suppose D stabs P and shortly afterwards E stabs P. P dies from the cumulative effect of the two wounds, the second merely aggravating the effect of the first. The death can be attributed to both D and E, whether or not they were acting in combination and whether or not either wound was mortal in itself.

The position is more complicated where the accused's act does not directly cause death but does so indirectly, in that the intervening act, from which the victim's death directly results, would not have occurred but for the accused's act. Here the death is attributable to the accused as well as to the intervener, unless the intervening act was not likely to occur (i e not reasonably foreseeable) in the circumstances. Thus, if D knocks P unconscious in a busy road and leaves him lying there, P subsequently being killed by a car, P's death can be attributed to D. However, if during an altercation D knocks P down, whereupon a bystander acting independently steps up and kicks P, thereby causing his death, the death is not attributable to D since the fatal intervening act was unlikely.[1]

In *Pagett*[2] D, in order to resist arrest, held a girl in front of him as a shield and fired at armed policemen who fired back instinctively and killed the girl. Dismissing an appeal against a conviction for manslaughter, the Court of Appeal held that if a reasonable act of self-defence, or in the execution of duty, against an act by an accused causes the death of a third party the causal link between the accused's act and the third party's death is not broken. Although the court did not explain its decision on this ground, it can no doubt be explained, in accordance with what was said above, on the ground that the policemen's act of firing back was reasonably foreseeable in the circumstances.

1 Perkins *op cit* 728–729.
2 (1983) 76 Cr App Rep 279, CA.

11.18 *Intervening medical treatment* The fact that the victim subsequently receives medical treatment for his injury, which kills him, will not excuse the person who injured him if that treatment is not negligent (i e if it is given with the care and skill of a competent medical practitioner).[1] Moreover, even if the treatment is negligent it is only in the most exceptional case that it will break the chain of causation between the act which caused the injury and the death.

In *Smith*[2] a person who had been stabbed by D in a barrack room brawl was twice dropped on the way to hospital and when he got there he was given treatment which was 'thoroughly bad' and might have affected his chances of recovery. He died some two hours after being stabbed. The Courts-Martial

Appeal Court held that these events did not break the chain of causation between the stabbing and the death. Lord Parker CJ said:

> 'It seems to this court that if at the time of death the original wound is still an operating cause and a substantial cause, then the death can properly be said to be the result of the wound, albeit that some other cause of death is also operating. Only if it can be said that the original wound is merely the setting in which another cause operates can it be said that the death did not result from the wound. Putting it another way, only if the second cause is so overwhelming as to make the original wound merely part of the history can it be said that the death does not flow from the wound'.[3]

The facts in *Smith* clearly fell within the first sentence of this dictum since D's act was an operating and substantial cause of death. Similarly, if D has injured P so severely that P has suffered irreversible brain damage and is being 'kept alive' by a respirator, and his doctors discontinue the use of the respirator, thereby bringing about P's death (assuming he is not already dead), P's death can be attributed to D.[4] Here again D's act will be an operating and substantial cause of death.

The second two sentences in Lord Parker's statement are concerned with the situation where the wound or injury caused by the accused's act is not an operating cause of death because the deceased dies not from the wound or injury caused by the accused but from treatment given for it. Further explanation of the law which applies in such a situation was given by the Court of Appeal in *Cheshire*,[5] where it was emphasised that it will only be in the most extraordinary and unusual case that negligent medical treatment for wounds or injuries caused to the victim by the accused can be so independent of the acts of the accused that in law it breaks the chain of causation from his conduct. The Court held that, provided the accused's conduct is a significant contribution[6] to the death, there is in law a causal link between his conduct and the death, even if negligent treatment (however negligent) is the immediate cause of death. It held that the chain of causation would not be broken unless the negligent treatment was so independent of the accused's conduct and in itself so potent as to render the contribution to death of the accused's conduct insignificant. It is the consequences of the treatment, said the Court, rather than possible degrees of fault attached to it, which are the essential issues.

The operation of these statements can be demonstrated by reference to the facts of *Cheshire*. In the course of an argument in a fish and chip shop, D shot P in the leg and stomach, seriously wounding him. After an operation, P developed respiratory problems and a tracheotomy tube was inserted to assist his breathing. P died in hospital over two months after the shooting; the immediate cause of death was a narrowing of the windpipe where the tracheotomy tube had been inserted, such a condition being a rare but not unknown complication arising out of a tracheotomy. P had complained of further breathing difficulties and suffered a chest infection after the tracheotomy. At D's trial for murder there was evidence that P's wounds no longer threatened his life at the time of his death and that his death was caused by the negligence of the hospital staff in failing to diagnose and treat P's respiratory condition. The trial judge directed the jury to consider the degree of fault in the medical treatment (rather than its practical consequences) in deciding whether or not the death was to be legally attributed to D.

Dismissing D's appeal against conviction for murder, the Court of Appeal held that, while the judge had misdirected the jury, there had been no miscarriage of justice because, even if more experienced doctors than those who attended P would have recognised the rare complication in time to have prevented P's death, that complication was a direct consequence of D's acts which remained a significant cause of death. It was inconceivable that a jury properly directed (ie along the lines indicated in the Court's judgment above) would have found otherwise.

1 *Cheshire* [1991] 3 All ER 670 at 674.
2 [1959] 2 QB 35, [1959] 2 All ER 193, Courts-Martial Appeal Court (see para 11.5, note 1, in relation to this court). Cf *Jordan* (1956) 41 Cr App Rep 152, CCA, described as a very special case in *Smith*.
3 [1959] 2 QB at 42–43.
4 *Malcherek* [1981] 2 All ER 422, [1981] 1 WLR 690, CA.
5 [1991] 3 All ER 670, CA. Also see *McKechnie, Gibbons and Dixon* [1992] Crim LR 194, CA.
6 See para 11.9.

THE FUNCTION OF JUDGE AND JURY

11.19 This was dealt with by the Court of Appeal in *Pagett*,[1] where any uncertainty as to the position was resolved. It was held that, in line with the normal well-established principle, it is for the judge to direct the jury on the relevant principles relating to causation, and then to leave it to the jury to decide, in the light of those principles on which they are bound to act, whether or not the relevant causal link has been established. However, it was stated, it is rarely necessary to give the jury any direction on causation as such, because that issue is usually not in dispute. Where such a direction is necessary, the Court held, it is usually enough to direct the jury simply that in law the accused's act need not be the sole cause, or even the main cause, of the victim's death, it being enough that his act contributed significantly to that result. Occasionally, however, a specific issue of causation may arise, such as whether an intervening act by a third person broke the causal connection between the accused's act and the victim's death. Where such a specific issue of causation arises, the judge should also direct the jury in terms of the specific legal principles which apply to that issue. Robert Goff LJ, giving the judgment of the court in *Pagett*, continued:

'It would then fall to the jury to decide the relevant factual issues which, identified with reference to those legal principles, will lead to the conclusion whether or not the prosecution have established [the relevant causal link].'[2]

1 (1983) 76 Cr App Rep 279, CA.
2 Ibid, at 290. Contrast *Blaue* [1975] 3 All ER 446, [1975] 1 WLR 1411, CA, and *Malcherek* [1981] 2 All ER 422, [1981] 1 WLR 690, CA, where the Court of Appeal held that where there is no conflict on the evidence the judge could withdraw the question of causation, even in the case of a specific issue of the present type, from the jury by telling them that the accused's act was (or was not) a cause in law of the death.

UNLAWFUL KILLING

11.20 A killing is unlawful unless it falls within one of the following categories of lawful homicide:

  a) *Public or private defence,* as where the accused kills by using reasonable force in self-defence, in defence of another, in prevention of crime or in effecting a lawful arrest. This is explained in paras 22.1 to 22.15.
  b) *Advancement of justice* If a hangman duly carries out the lawful sen-

tence of a competent court, the homicide is lawful. If he acts contrary to his authority, by poisoning the convict, for instance, or if the sentence is not one which the court could impose, the hangman is guilty of murder, unless the facts are such that a defence of mistake or superior orders (if such a defence exists)[1] is available to him.

1 Para 22.40

Murder

11.21 Murder, an offence for which the only punishment is imprisonment for life and which is triable only on indictment, is unlawful homicide with 'malice aforethought'.

There is no exception to the mandatory life sentence for murder, even in the case of mercy killings. However, verdicts of murder are rare in such cases because legal and medical consciences are stretched so as to bring about a conviction of manslaughter by diminished responsibility.

MALICE AFORETHOUGHT

11.22 Malice aforethought consists of intention on the part of the accused:

a) unlawfully to kill another human being; or
b) unlawfully to cause grievous bodily harm to another human being.[1]

Nothing less, such as subjective recklessness as to death, suffices.[2]

Malice aforethought does not imply either premeditation or ill-will. The sudden intentional killing of one's nearest and dearest is no less murder than the cunningly contrived assassination of a deadly enemy. Malice aforethought is thus a misleading term of art and the abolition of that term would improve the precision and lucidity of the law of murder.[3]

1 For a modern authority that murder is an offence requiring intention, see *Moloney* [1985] AC 905, [1985] 1 All ER 1025, HL.
2 *Leung Kam Kwok v R* (1985) 81 Cr App Rep 83, PC.
3 Stephen *History of the Criminal Law*, vol 3, p 83; *Hyam v DPP* [1975] AC 55 at 66, per Lord Hailsham LC.

11.23 Before the Homicide Act 1957 came into force, there were three kinds of malice aforethought. It might have been 'express', 'implied' or 'constructive'. Constructive malice aforethought has been abolished, but malice aforethought may still be express or implied. Although the terms 'express malice' and 'implied malice' had not been used in any consistent sense by the courts prior to that Act coming into force, the judgment soon afterwards of the Court of Criminal Appeal in *Vickers*,[1] which has been endorsed by the House of Lords on three subsequent occasions,[2] made it clear that 'express malice' means an intention to kill and 'implied malice' an intention to cause grievous bodily harm.

There used to be two kinds of constructive malice aforethought, for it was murder to cause death in furtherance of a felony or when resisting lawful arrest, even though the accused might not have intended to kill or to cause grievous bodily harm, provided the accused had the mens rea for the felony or (as the case might have been) intended to resist lawful arrest. Consequently, the doctrine was capable of operating very harshly for it meant that someone would be technically guilty of murder if, when committing robbery or trying to resist lawful arrest, he gave his victim a slight push which happened to prove fatal through an unforeseen contingency such as a heart attack. There was much uncertainty concerning the proper formulation of the rules with regard to constructive malice, but this is no longer of practical importance on account of s 1 of the Homicide Act 1957. The marginal note reads 'Abolition of constructive malice', and the section reads:

'1) Where a person kills another in the course or furtherance of some other offence, the killing shall not amount to murder unless done with the same malice aforethought (express or implied) as is required for a killing to amount to murder when not done in the course or furtherance of another offence.

2) For the purposes of the foregoing subsection, a killing done in the course or for the purpose of resisting an officer of justice, or of resisting or avoiding or preventing a lawful arrest, or of effecting or assisting an escape or rescue from legal custody, shall be treated as a killing in the course or furtherance of an offence.'

The effect of these provisions is that, in considering whether the accused is guilty of murder, the fact that he killed the deceased in furtherance of another offence or in resisting an arrest can be ignored. The question is always did he have that which would have constituted express or implied malice aforethought if the 1957 Act had not been passed?

1 [1957] 2 QB 664, [1957] 2 All ER 741, CCA.
2 *DPP v Smith* [1961] AC 290, [1960] 3 All ER 161, HL; *Hyam v DPP* [1975] AC 55, [1974] 2 All ER 41, HL (Lords Diplock and Kilbrandon dissenting); *Cunningham* [1982] AC 566, [1981] 2 All ER 863, HL. For criticism of these terms, see *Cunningham* [1981] 2 All ER 863 at 867, per Lord Hailsham LC.

INTENTION UNLAWFULLY TO KILL OR CAUSE GRIEVOUS BODILY HARM

11.24 Little needs to be said about the requirement that the accused must have an intention unlawfully to kill or cause grievous bodily harm to another human being. In relation to what constitutes '*intention*', the reader is referred to paras 6.24–6.36. Essentially the prosecution must prove that the accused's aim or purpose was by his conduct unlawfully to bring about the death of, or grievous bodily harm to, another person. Failing that, the jury may be directed that they may, if they wish, infer the necessary intention if the prosecution proves that the accused foresaw that his conduct was virtually certain to result in the unlawful killing of another or in the unlawful causing of grievous bodily harm to another, although it would not be a misdirection to tell them that they can make such an inference if the prosecution proves that the accused foresaw as a very high degree of probability that his conduct might result in the unlawful killing of another or in the unlawful causing of grievous bodily harm to another. In relation to intent to cause grievous bodily harm, if the accused is proved to have intended to cause bodily harm and that harm is regarded as grievous by the jury, it is irrelevant that the accused did not so regard it.[1]

That the accused must intend *unlawfully*[2] to kill or cause grievous bodily harm to another human being was implicit in the Court of Appeal's decision in *Williams*[3] and put beyond doubt by the decision of the Privy Council in *Beckford v R*,[4] where the Privy Council held that a person could not be convicted of murder, even if he intentionally killed someone, if he did so in a mistaken belief in facts which if true would justify him in using reasonable force in self-defence and he had not exceeded such force, because he would not have intended *unlawfully* to kill his victim.

1 See para 10.25.

2 For the meaning of 'unlawfully', see para 11.20. Doubtless, a soldier who intentionally killed someone, mistakenly believing that his victim was a person who would be outside the Queen's peace (para 11.5), would also not intend unlawfully to kill.
3 [1987] 3 All ER 411, CA; para 7.21.
4 [1987] 3 WLR 611, PC.

11.25 *Intent unlawfully to kill* Not surprisingly there is uncontradicted authority[1] to support the proposition, that an intention unlawfully to *kill* another human being constitutes malice aforethought.

1 *Moloney* [1985] AC 905, [1985] 1 All ER 1025, HL, can now be regarded as the leading authority.

11.26 *Intention unlawfully to cause grievous bodily harm* 'Grievous bodily harm' was defined in *DPP v Smith*[1] as meaning really serious harm. It has since been held that 'really' adds nothing to 'serious harm' and that it is not a misdirection to direct a jury that grievous bodily harm means serious harm.[2]
It was only in 1981 in *Cunningham*[3] that it was finally settled by the House of Lords that an intention to cause grievous bodily harm to another constitutes malice aforethought. Prior to that decision the relevant law had been somewhat doubtful as a result of the decision of the House in *Hyam v DPP*,[4] where Lords Diplock and Kilbrandon held that an intention to do grievous bodily harm was not sufficient mens rea for murder. The reasoning of Lord Diplock, with whom Lord Kilbrandon agreed, was that an intention to cause grievous bodily harm had only become malice aforethought by virtue of the doctrine of constructive malice when the intentional causing of grievous bodily harm had been made a felony by statute in 1803, and that consequently it had ceased to constitute malice aforethought when constructive malice was abolished by the Homicide Act 1957. Both their Lordships thought that *Vickers*,[5] where the Court of Criminal Appeal had held that intention to cause grievous bodily harm had always been sufficient to imply malice aforethought independently of the constructive malice doctrine and (as implied malice) had been preserved by s 1 of the 1957 Act, had been wrongly decided. They considered that *Vickers* should be overruled along with that part of the House of Lords' decision in *DPP v Smith*[6] which, without consideration at any length, had approved *Vickers*.
Of the other three Law Lords in *Hyam*, Lord Hailsham and Viscount Dilhorne expressly approved *Vickers* but Lord Cross said that he was not prepared to decide on the validity of *Vickers* and would content himself 'with saying that on the footing that *R v Vickers* was rightly decided the answer to the question put to us should be "yes" and that this appeal should be dismissed.'[7]
The even split in *Hyam* between those Lords who wished to uphold, and those who wished to overrule, *Vickers* meant that the question of the correctness of that decision was open to doubt until the matter was resolved by the House of Lords in *Cunningham*, where *Vickers* was unanimously approved as correct, as was its indorsement in *DPP v Smith* and (to the extent that it was indorsed) *Hyam v DPP*.
Lord Hailsham LC, with whose speech the rest of their Lordships agreed, found two insuperable difficulties with Lord Diplock's argument. First, although the actual phrase 'grievous bodily harm' had not been in use before the Act of 1803, writers of authority and the courts had, even before that Act, consistently treated as murder any killing with intent to cause serious bodily harm, however described, to which the label 'grievous bodily harm'

as now defined could properly have been applied. Consequently, an intention to cause grievous bodily harm had existed as a species of malice aforethought independently of the doctrine of constructive malice. Second, even though the nineteenth century judges might in theory have employed constructive malice to apply to cases where death ensued in the course of the felony introduced by the 1803 Act, they had not been shown to have done so.

The reader may find it surprising that an accused who only intended to cause grievous bodily harm and did not foresee death even as a remote possibility, and who could only have been guilty of unlawfully wounding or causing grievous bodily harm with intent, contrary to s 18 of the Offences against the Person Act 1861, if death had not unexpectedly resulted, is guilty of murder, whereas an accused who realised there was a probability (but not a virtual certainty or very high probability) that death might result from his conduct but was indifferent to that risk cannot be so convicted. However, it must now be accepted that this type of malice aforethought can only be changed by legislative, not judicial, intervention.[8]

1 [1961] AC 290, [1960] 3 All ER 161, HL.
2 *McMillan* (1984) unreported, CA; *Saunders* [1985] Crim LR 230, CA.
3 [1982] AC 566, [1981] 2 All ER 863, HL.
4 [1975] AC 55, [1974] 2 All ER 41, HL.
5 [1957] 2 QB 664, [1957] 2 All ER 741, CCA.
6 [1961] AC 290, [1960] 3 All ER 161, HL.
7 [1975] AC 55 at 98.
8 [1985] AC 905 at 925, per Lord Bridge.

THE REQUIREMENT OF CONTEMPORANEITY: AN EXCEPTION

11.27 Generally, the intent unlawfully to kill or cause grievous bodily harm must exist at the time of the accused's act which caused death.[1] However, if death is caused by one act in a series of acts which it is impossible to divide up, e g because they formed part of a preconceived plan, it is irrelevant that the accused lacked the necessary intent for murder when that act was done if he had that intent when an earlier act in the series was done. In *Thabo Meli v R*[2] the accused planned to kill the deceased in a hut and thereafter to roll his body over a cliff so that it might appear to be a case of accidental death. The deceased was rendered unconscious in the hut and, believing him to be dead, the accused rolled him over the cliff. There was medical evidence that the deceased was not killed by the injuries received in the hut, but died from exposure where he had been left at the bottom of the cliff. It was argued that the accused were not guilty of murder because, while the first act was accompanied by mens rea, it was not the cause of death; and because the second act, while it was the cause of death, was not accompanied by mens rea, the accused believing their victim to be dead already. The Privy Council rejected this argument, holding that the two acts formed part of a series which could not be divided up. Accordingly, the accused were guilty of murder, and not of attempted murder or culpable homicide (manslaughter), as would have been the case if the rejected argument had prevailed.

The advice of the Privy Council suggests that its decision might have been different if the act done with intent to kill and the actual act which caused death had not formed part of a preconceived plan. However, *Thabo Meli* was held by the Court of Criminal Appeal in *Church*[3] also to apply on a charge of manslaughter and was applied by it to a case where the act which caused death was not part of a plan, being quite unforeseen at the time of the act done with mens rea. The accused had a sudden fight with a woman and rendered her unconscious. Then, believing that she was dead, he threw her body into a river, where she drowned. His conviction for manslaughter[1] was upheld on appeal on the basis that his conduct constituted a series of acts which culminated in the woman's death. These decisions seem to be right, although it will often be difficult to decide whether the accused's acts form a series which cannot be broken up.

It remains to be seen whether these principles apply to offences other than murder and manslaughter. Probably, they will be held to do so when the occasion arises.

1 Para 6.70.
2 [1954] 1 All ER 373, [1954] 1 WLR 228, PC.
3 [1966] 1 QB 59, [1965] 2 All ER 72, PC. Also see *Moore and Dorn* [1975] Crim LR 229, CA; *Le Brun* [1991] 4 All ER 673, CA.

11.28   What if one of two or more acts by the accused caused death but it is impossible to prove which one? It was held by the Court of Appeal in *A-G's Reference (No 4 of 1980)*,[1] which was concerned with involuntary manslaughter, that there can be a conviction for that offence if each act was accompanied by a sufficient state of mind or fault element (hereafter simply referred to as mens rea) for that offence.

Thus, to adopt the facts in that reference, if D pushes P downstairs and then, thinking that P is dead, cuts her throat preparatory to dismembering her body, and it is not proved which of these acts caused her death, D can be convicted of involuntary manslaughter if the jury are satisfied that, whichever act killed P, each of them was accompanied by a sufficient mens rea to establish involuntary manslaughter. Such a principle is equally applicable on a charge of murder if *each* act is proved to have been accompanied by malice aforethought.

The Court of Appeal held that if it was not proved that each act was accompanied by a sufficient state of mind the jury should acquit of manslaughter. This is open to doubt where the accused had the requisite mens rea when he committed the first act in a series of acts which could not be divided up; it would not matter in such a situation whether the first act caused death (in which case he would be guilty under the normal rules of liability) or not (in which case he would be caught by the principle in *Thabo Meli* and *Church*).

1 [1981] 2 All ER 617, [1981] 1 WLR 705, CA.

PROPOSALS FOR REFORM

11.29   The enactment of cl 54 of the draft Criminal Code Bill[1] would implement a recommendation concerning the mental element in murder made by the Criminal Law Revision Committee in its Fourteenth Report: Offences against the Person, published in 1980.[2] The Committee's recommendation was prompted by the belief that the present offence is too wide, particularly in the light of the special stigma of murder and the mandatory life sentence which attaches to it.

Clause 54(1) of the draft Bill provides that a person is guilty of murder if he causes the death of another:

a) intending to cause death; or

b) intending to cause serious personal harm and being aware that he may cause death.

'Intention' in this definition would bear the meaning given to it by cl 18 of the draft Bill.[3] The enactment of cl 54(1) would mean that a person would no longer be guilty of murder merely because he intended grievous bodily harm.

The enactment of cl 54(1) would not bring within the law of murder some forms of terrorist killings, for example, by those who plant bombs designed to damage property and cause fear (rather than to take life) and therefore timed to explode when it is unlikely that anyone will be around. Such people are not currently caught by the offence of murder, although some think that they should be. On balance, the Criminal Law Revision Committee did not think that such conduct should form part of the law of murder but, in case Parliament considered that it should, the Committee recommended that the appropriate way to achieve this would be on the following lines: that it should also be murder if a person causes death by an unlawful act intended to cause fear (of death or serious injury) and known to the accused to involve a risk of causing death. The Law Commission did not regard this as a satisfactory provision and did not include it in the draft Criminal Code Bill.

In the Report of the House of Lords Select Committee on Murder and Life Imprisonment[4] the Committee recommended the adoption of the definition of murder in the draft Bill.

1 Law Commission: A Criminal Code for England and Wales (1989): Law Com No 177; see para 3.21 above.
2 Cmnd 7844, para 14–30.
3 Para 6.69.
4 (1989) HL Paper No 78. For a discussion of the reform of the definition of murder, also see Goff 'The Mental Element in the Crime of Murder' (1988) 104 LQR 30, and Williams 'The Mens Rea for Murder: Leave It Alone' (1989) 105 LQR 387

Manslaughter

11.30 Generally, any unlawful homicide which is not classified as murder is manslaughter, which is triable only on indictment and whose punishment may vary from imprisonment for life[1] to an absolute discharge.

There are two generic types of manslaughter – voluntary and involuntary. A person is guilty of *voluntary manslaughter* where, although he has killed with malice aforethought, he has done so under circumstances which the law regards as mitigating the gravity of his offence. These are that the accused was suffering from diminished responsibility, was acting pursuant to a suicide pact or was provoked. The rationale behind this type of manslaughter is that it provides a way in these cases to avoid the mandatory sentence for murder. It is arguable that if the mandatory sentence for murder was abolished there would be no justification for having distinct offences of murder and manslaughter. *Involuntary manslaughter* is an unlawful killing where the accused has some blameworthy mental state less than an intention unlawfully to kill or cause grievous bodily harm.

1 Offences against the Person Act 1861, s 5.

Voluntary manslaughter

DIMINISHED RESPONSIBILITY

11.31   This was discussed in paras 9.32 to 9.39.

SUICIDE PACTS

11.32   It is murder intentionally to kill a person even though he desires to be killed. The only exception is where the killing is in pursuance of a suicide pact. A 'suicide pact' means a common agreement between two or more persons whose object is the death of all of them, whether or not each is to take his own life.

At common law, a survivor of such a pact which had been put into partial effect was guilty of murder, but s 4(1) of the Homicide Act 1957 now provides that it is manslaughter, and not murder, for a person, acting in pursuance of a suicide pact between him and another, to kill the other or be a party to the other being killed by a third person. On a charge of murder the burden of proving that he was acting pursuant to a suicide pact between him and the other is borne by the accused.[1]

1 Homicide Act 1957, s 4(2).

11.33   *Aiding and abetting suicide*   It is convenient here to describe the related offence of aiding and abetting suicide. At common law, a person who aided, abetted, counselled or procured another to kill himself was guilty of murder as an accomplice, because suicide was self-murder. Under s 4 of the Homicide Act 1957 the liability of one who aided, abetted etc the suicide of another was reduced to manslaughter, provided that he had agreed to die also. However, when the Suicide Act 1961 abolished the offences of suicide and attempted suicide, s 2(1) of that Act created a lesser offence of aiding, abetting, counselling or procuring[1] the suicide of another, or an attempt by another to commit suicide, which applies to all cases of such conduct. It will be noted that the offence is only committed if suicide is committed or attempted by the other person. However, if suicide is not committed or attempted, an attempt to commit the present offence may be charged. The 'year and a day rule' applies to the offence under s 2 of the Suicide Act 1961, just as it applies to the offence of manslaughter, so that an accused is not guilty of aiding and abetting suicide if the fatal act which he aids or abets results in death more than a year and a day later.[2]

The offence is triable only on indictment and punishable with up to 14 years' imprisonment. Should the facts warrant it, there may be a conviction for aiding and abetting suicide on a trial for murder or manslaughter.[3]

The offence under the 1961 Act covers a wide range of cases from the greedy son who urges a parent to commit suicide so that he can inherit the parent's estate to the distraught husband who urges his terminally ill wife to kill herself to end her pain and misery. The offence was thought to be necessary to plug what would otherwise be an unacceptable gap in the law resulting from the abolition of the crimes of suicide and attempted suicide, since it was thought that there might be good reasons for punishing someone who encouraged or assisted someone to commit suicide. Prosecutions under s 4 of the Homicide Act or s 2 of the Suicide Act are rare.

1 These words bear the same meaning as in relation to the liability of accomplices to crime in general. See *A-G v Able* [1984] QB 795, [1984] 1 All ER 277; discussed by Smith [1983] Crim LR 579.

2 *Coroner for Inner West London, ex p Da Luca* [1988] 3 All ER 414, [1988] 3 WLR 286, CA.
3 Suicide Act 1961, s 2(2).

PROVOCATION[1]

11.34 While evidence that the accused was provoked is a circumstance which the jury must take into account, along with all the other circumstances, in deciding whether he intended to kill or cause grievous bodily harm,[2] the *defence* of provocation is concerned with the situation where the accused did intend unlawfully to kill or cause grievous bodily harm but acted under a sudden loss of self-control.[3]

Unlike the other two types of voluntary manslaughter, the defence of provocation is a creature of the common law, although its terms have been extensively amended by s 3 of the Homicide Act 1957 (hereafter referred to as s 3), which provides:

> 'Where on a charge of murder there is evidence on which the jury can find that the person charged was provoked (whether by things done or by things said or by both together) to lose his self-control, the question whether the provocation was enough to make a reasonable man do as he did shall be left to be determined by the jury; and in determining that question the jury shall take into account everything both done and said according to the effect which, in their opinion, it would have on a reasonable man.'[4]

Provocation is not a defence to any charge other than murder,[5] not even to attempted murder.[6] The reasoning behind this is that in most offences it is possible to make allowance for provocation in sentence, but this is not possible in murder because the sentence is fixed by law.

1 Ashworth 'The Doctrine of Provocation' (1976) 35 CLJ 292.
2 Criminal Justice Act 1967, s 8; *Ives* [1970] 1 QB 208, [1969] 3 All ER 470, CA.
3 *A-G of Ceylon v Kumarasinghege Don John Perera* [1953] AC 200, [1953] 2 WLR 238, PC; *Lee Chun-Chuen v R* [1963] AC 220, [1963] 1 All ER 73, PC; *Martindale* [1966] 3 All ER 305, [1966] 1 WLR 1564, C-MAC.
4 English 'What did s 3 do to the Law of Provocation?' [1970] Crim LR 249; White 'A Note on Provocation' [1970] Crim LR 446.
5 *Cunningham* [1959] 1 QB 288, [1958] 3 All ER 711, CCA.
6 *Bruzas* [1972] Crim LR 367, Crown Ct; *Peck* (1975) Times, 5 December; see English 'Provocation and Attempted Murder' [1973] Crim LR 727.

11.35 Before the Homicide Act 1957 only limited types of conduct were sufficient to constitute provocation. Physical violence or the detection of a spouse in the act of adultery[1] was almost invariably required in order to found a case of provocation. In *Holmes v DPP*[2] the House of Lords stated that, save in circumstances of a most extreme and exceptional nature, words could not constitute provocation. The House held that a confession of adultery by one spouse to another could not constitute sufficient provocation to justify a verdict of manslaughter if the injured spouse killed his spouse or the adulterer. Section 3 removed these restrictions and, provided an element of the defence of provocation is not disproved, anything done or said (or a combination of acts and words) will suffice. For example, the crying and restlessness of a 17-day old baby can suffice.[3]

1 *Maddy* (1671) 2 Keb 829.
2 [1946] AC 588, [1946] 2 All ER 124, HL.
3 *Doughty* (1986) 83 Cr App Rep 319, [1986] Crim LR 625, CA.

11.36 *Provocation need not come from victim* The provocative words or conduct need not come from the person who is killed. Assuming that an element of the defence is not disproved, if a person accidentally kills someone other than the one who provoked him, when aiming at the latter, he is only guilty of manslaughter.[1] However, apart from this, at common law the provocation had to be by the person whom the accused killed.[2] It is now clear that this rule has been amended by s 3 and that acts or words amounting to provocation are not excluded from consideration merely because they emanate from some person other than the victim.[3]

1 *Gross* (1913) 23 Cox CC 455.
2 *Simpson* (1915) 84 LJKB 1893, CCA.
3 *Davies* [1975] QB 691, [1975] 1 All ER 890, CA.

11.37 *Must provocative conduct be directed at accused?* At common law, the provocative words or conduct normally had to be directed at the accused,[1] although there was an exception where the provocation was directed at a near relative.[2] However, it appears that s 3 has changed this rule since, if it can be interpreted as not requiring the provocation to have been done by the deceased, it is also interpretable as not requiring the provocation to be directed at the accused or a near relative.[3]

1 *Duffy* [1949] 1 All ER 932n; *Whitfield* (1976) 63 Cr App Rep 39 at 42.
2 *Harrington* (1866) 10 Cox CC 370; *Porritt* [1961] 3 All ER 463, [1961] 1 WLR 1372, CCA.
3 See *Pearson* [1992] Crim LR 193, CA.

11.38 *Does it matter if the accused induced the provocative conduct?* In *Edwards v R*[1] the Privy Council, in giving its advice on an appeal from Hong Kong where an identical provision to s 3 was in force, appeared to take the view that the fact that the accused caused a reaction in another, which in turn led him to lose his self-control, would (generally, at least) prevent the issue of provocation being left to the jury. However, despite the apparent clarity of the Privy Council's words, the Court of Appeal in *Johnson*[2] held that the Privy Council's statement could not be understood to mean what it appeared to say. It held that, in the light of the express words of s 3, as interpreted by the House of Lords[3] subsequently to *Edwards*, it was impossible to accept that the mere fact that the provocation was self-induced by the accused should prevent the issue of provocation being left to the jury. The Court of Appeal's decision is to be applauded since, if there is evidence that the accused was provoked to lose his self-control, the judge is required by s 3 to leave the defence to the jury to decide in accordance with the test of provocation. Section 3 does not permit any exception and it would seem impermissible for a court to have introduced one in respect of self-induced provocation.

1 [1973] AC 648, [1973] 1 All ER 152, PC.
2 [1989] 2 All ER 839, [1989] 1 WLR 740, CA.
3 In *Camplin* [1978] AC 703, [1978] 2 All ER 168, HL.

11.39 *Test of provocation* The test of whether the defence of provocation is entitled to succeed is a dual one: the alleged provocative words or conduct must be as such as:

a) actually causes in the accused a sudden and temporary loss of self-control as the result of which he kills the deceased, and

b) might have caused a reasonable man to suffer such a loss of self-control and, having lost self-control, to do as the accused did.

11.40 *The accused himself must have been provoked* The plea of provocation is not open to an unusually cool man confronted with words or conduct which would cause a normal person to lose control of himself. In *Duffy*[1] Devlin J said that there must be 'a sudden and temporary loss of self-control, rendering the accused so subject to passion as to make him or her for the moment not master of his mind'. It must be emphasised that the alleged provocative words or conduct must have caused a sudden loss of self-control on the part of the accused, during which he committed the fatal act; the defence of provocation is not open where a killing contains an element of deliberation or premeditation. The common law requirement of a sudden and temporary loss of self-control has not been changed by s 3 of the Homicide Act 1957.[2] The importance of this requirement can be shown by reference to the fairly common case where there has been a protracted course of cruel, insulting or violent conduct by P, which has sapped D's resilience and resolve to retain self-control and culminates in D intentionally killing P. The defence of provocation is not available in such a case unless the final occurrence caused a sudden and temporary loss of self-control which previously D had been able to exercise.[3] Of course, where there has been a protracted course of cruel, insulting or violent conduct, the whole course of that conduct must be taken into account by the jury in in considering the accused's reaction and whether or not he suffered a sudden and temporary loss of self-control as a result of the final occurrence.

1 [1949] 1 All ER 932n; cited with approval *Ibrams and Gregory* (1981) 74 Cr App Rep 154, CA. See also *Newell* [1989] Crim LR 906, CA.
2 *Thornton* [1992] 1 All ER 306, CA.
3 *Duffy* [1949] 1 All ER 932n; *Ibrams and Gregory* (1981) 74 Cr App Rep 154, CA; *Cocker* [1989] Crim LR 740, CA. See Wasik 'Cumulative Provocation and Domestic Killing' [1982] Crim LR 29; Edwards 'Battered Women who Kill' (1990) 141 NLJ 1380.

11.41 In deciding whether the accused had been provoked to lose self-control when he acted, the jury should take into account all the relevant circumstances, including the accused's nature and personality and whether a sufficient 'cooling time' had elapsed between the provocation and the fatal act. It is possible that at common law the defence of provocation necessarily failed if there had been a sufficient time between the occurrence of the provocation and the killing for the accused's 'blood to cool and for reason to resume its seat'.[1] It is probable, however, that this requirement of 'cooling time' was never anything more than a most important item of evidence on the issues of whether the accused was in fact provoked when he did the fatal act and whether the effect of the provocation at that moment was enough to cause a reasonable man to do what the accused did. Since the passing of s 3 of the Homicide Act 1957, there is no doubt that 'cooling time' is merely an evidential factor, albeit important, which the jury must weigh when deciding whether the accused had been provoked to lose self-control when he reacted.

In the case of an accused who was not suffering from mental illness, psychiatric evidence is not admissible to show that the accused was likely to have been provoked.[2]

1 *Jervis* (1833) 6 C & P 156 at 157.
2 *Turner* [1975] QB 834, [1975] 1 All ER 70, CA.

11.42 *The alleged provocative words or conduct must have been such as might have caused a reasonable man to suffer a sudden and temporary loss of self-control and, having lost self-control, to do as the accused did* This is a question to be decided according to the opinion of the jury. There are no legal rules as to what might (or might not) provoke a reasonable man to lose his self-control or as to what he might do if provoked.[1] Before the Homicide Act 1957 the judge had the power to withdraw the issue of provocation from the jury not only when he thought there was insufficient evidence that the accused was in fact provoked, but also if he thought the provocation insufficient to affect a reasonable man (or cause him to act as the accused did). It was under this latter power of withdrawal that restrictive rules grew up that words and non-violent acts would not generally suffice, that provocation must have been given by the deceased and so on. This latter power of withdrawal was thought to be excessive and has been abolished by s 3 of the Homicide Act 1957.

1 Homicide Act 1957, s 3; *DPP v Camplin* [1978] AC 705, [1978] 2 All ER 168, HL.

11.43 Another of the restrictive rules which evolved at common law was that the reasonable man was not notionally invested with the characteristics of the accused which would not be found in a reasonable or ordinary man, even though these might have made the accused particularly likely to be provoked. Thus, in *Bedder v DPP*,[1] where the accused was sexually impotent and part of the alleged provocation was that he had been taunted by a prostitute whom he stabbed to death after he had unsuccessfully attempted to have intercourse with her, the House of Lords held that the hypothetical reasonable man could not be imbued with the accused's impotence or other unusual physical characteristics, any more than he could be invested with the accused's unusual excitability or pugnacity, or his drunkenness.

The theory underlying the reasonable man test is that the rule with regard to provocation is a concession to ordinary human frailty, not to extraordinary bad temper or abnormal excitability,[2] but the rule made clear in *Bedder*, that the reasonable man was normal in body as well as in mind, was unduly harsh. It led to the unjust and nonsensical result that if D, a dwarf (or exceptionally disfigured, or of black skin), killed P after being provoked by taunts as to his lack of height (or looks, or colour), the jury had to be told to consider the effects of the taunt on a (reasonable) man who was not a dwarf (or disfigured, or black).

Fortunately, in 1978 it was held by the House of Lords unanimously in *DPP v Camplin*[3] that the proposition stated in *Bedder* had been changed by s 3 and was no longer the law. In *Camplin* P, a man in his fifties, buggered D, a boy aged 15, despite the accused's resistance, and then laughed at him. This caused D to lose self-control and he hit P over the head with a heavy pan, splitting P's skull. P died. At the trial for murder, the trial judge directed the jury that, in applying the reasonable man test, they should ignore the fact that D was only 15. The question, he said, was whether the reasonable adult man would have been provoked by P's conduct to do as D did. The Court of Appeal allowed D's appeal against this direction, distinguishing the case from *Bedder* by stating that the proposition in *Bedder* only stated that abnormal characteristics should not be taken into account and that being 15 was not an abnormal characteristic and could be taken into account in applying the reasonable man test. The House of Lords went further. Holding that the law had been changed by s 3, it stated that the fact that the accused was, for whatever reason,[4] exceptionally excitable or pugnacious should continue to be ignored, because it was not the law's policy to allow this to excuse loss of self-control, but otherwise the reasonable man should be invested with the accused's characteristics, usual or unusual, which would affect the gravity of the provocation to him. All their Lordships agreed with the following statement by Lord Diplock as to how the jury should be directed regarding the reasonable man in any future case of provocation:

> 'A proper direction to a jury on the question left to their exclusive determination by s 3 of the 1957 Act would be on the following lines:
> The judge should state what the question is, using the very terms of the section. He should then explain to them that the reasonable man referred to in the question is a person having the power of self-control of an ordinary person of the sex and age of the accused, but in other respects sharing such of the accused's characteristics as they think would affect the gravity of the provocation to him, and that the question is not merely whether such a person would in like circumstances be provoked to lose his self-control but would also react to the provocation as the accused did.'[5]

The Court of Appeal has subsequently held that it is not mandatory for the trial judge to rehearse these exact words, since they may not always be appropriate to the individual circumstances of a case, but he must give the jury fully the substance of these words[6] (although he need not refer to to the accused's sex or age as relevant to the definition of a reasonable man if no reasonable jury could consider that the accused's sex or age, as the case may be, would have affected the gravity of the provocation to the accused).[7]

Their Lordships in *Camplin* were also agreed that evidence of witnesses as to how a reasonable man might react to the provocation was not admissible, since this is a question for the opinion of the jury.

1 [1954] 2 All ER 801, [1954] 1 WLR 1119, HL.
2 *Camplin* [1978] 2 All ER 168 at 173 and 180, per Lords Diplock and Simon.
3 [1978] AC 705, [1978] 2 All ER 168, HL. See Wells 'The Death Penalty for Provocation?' [1978] Crim LR 662.
4 See *Roberts* [1990] Crim LR 123, CA.
5 [1978] 2 All ER at 175.
6 *Burke* [1987] Crim LR 336, CA.
7 *Ali* [1989] Crim LR 736, CA.

11.44 The decision in *Camplin* only extends to investing the reasonable man with those *characteristics* of the accused which would *affect the gravity of the provocation to him* (or, to put it another way, those characteristics which are directly connected with the provocation). In the subsequent case of *Newell*[1] the Court of Appeal, applying a passage from the judgment of the Court of Appeal of New Zealand in *McGregor*[2] (which it held represented the law in England as well as in New Zealand), explained what constitutes a 'characteristic' for the above purpose. A 'characteristic', it was held, is something definite and of sufficient significance to make the offender a different person from the ordinary run of mankind. In addition, it is a physical or mental quality, or some such more indeterminate attribute as colour, race or creed, which has a sufficient degree of permanence to warrant its being regarded as something constituting part of the accused's character or personality; a temporary or transitory state of mind, such as a mood of depression or irascibility or intoxication, is not a 'characteristic'.

The application of this can be demonstrated by reference to the actual decision in *Newell*, which also illustrates the requirement that the reasonable man is not invested with any characteristic of the accused which is not directly connected with the provocative words or conduct. The fact that the accused is exceptionally disfigured is of a sufficient degree of permanence to make it a characteristic, but the reasonable man will not be endowed with that characteristic if the provocation consists of calling the accused a cheat (as opposed to shouting out 'Look at beautiful!') because the provocative words would not be directly connected with the characteristic. In *Newell* D, a chronic alcoholic, killed P by hitting him 22 times over the head with a glass ashtray after they had been drinking and P had made disparaging remarks about a girlfriend who had left D after living with him for some time. At the time of the killing, D was drunk, emotionally upset and depressed by his girlfriend's action, and in a state of toxic confusion as a result of taking a drug overdose in a suicide attempt four days previously. At D's trial for murder, the judge did not invite the jury to take into account, in applying the 'reasonable man' test, these circumstances or the chronic alcoholism. The Court of Appeal held that the judge had acted properly in this respect. It held that, leaving aside the chronic alcoholism (which might be a characteristic), the other circumstances were too transitory in nature to be characteristics and therefore the reasonable man could not be invested with them. The Court of Appeal found it unnecessary to determine whether the chronic alcoholism was a characteristic because, even if it was, it had no connection with P's provocative words and therefore the reasonable man could not be invested with it.

While the Court of Appeal's interpretation of 'characteristic' in *Newell* may accord with the only possible interpretation of that term, and while there are good policy reasons for not endowing the reasonable man with the accused's intoxication or other states of mind which affected the accused's powers of self-control, there seems to be no good reason why the reasonable man should not be invested with temporary states of mind on the part of the accused which did not affect his powers of self-control but did affect the gravity of the provocation to him.

1 (1980) 71 Cr App Rep 331, CA.
2 [1962] NZLR 1069.

11.45   A further relaxation to the objective test is suggested by the ruling in *Raven*[1], a Crown Court case, that the jury, in applying the objective test, must consider the effect of the provocation not only from the perspective of someone with D's characteristics, but also from the perspective of someone who has lived the kind of life which D has had. In *Raven* the accused was physically aged 22 but had a mental age of nine and had lived in squats for two to three years. The judge ruled that the jury should be directed to consider the reasonable man as having lived the same life as the accused for 22 years but with the retarded mental development and mental age of the accused.

1 [1982] Crim LR 51, Crown Ct.

11.46   Something more must be said about the requirement that the provocation must have been enough to cause a reasonable man, if provoked,[1] to do what the accused did, which assumes that the reasonable man would act reasonably after he had lost self-control and which rests on the proposition, accepted by the Privy Council in *Phillips v R*,[2] that there are degrees of loss of self-control. At common law, the mode of resentment had to bear a reasonable relationship to the provocation.[3] 'Fists might be answered with fists, but not with a deadly weapon'.[4]

The reasonable relationship rule has been abolished as a rule of law by s 3 of the Homicide Act 1957. In *Brown*[5] the Court of Appeal stated that s 3 required the jury to decide whether the provocation was enough to make the reasonable man do as the accused did. It stated that, in answering this question, the jury should be told to take into account the proportion or relationship between the provocation and the retaliation. But it was not a rule of law that a plea of provocation would fail if there was no reasonable relationship; it should be made clear to the jury that the issue of reasonable relationship was merely a factor which they should take into account in deciding whether, if provoked, the reasonable man would have done as the accused did.

The reference in s 3 to whether the provocation was enough to make the reasonable man do as [the accused] did' seems clearly to relate to the time that the accused did the fatal act or acts. After all, the essence of the defence of provocation centres on loss of self-control (actually by the accused and hypothetically by the reasonable man) at that time. Consequently, the apparent decision of the Court of Appeal in *Clarke*,[6] to the effect that the jury may include in their consideration of whether the reasonable man would have done as the accused did the whole course of the accused's conduct, including acts done to the victim after the fatal act and, indeed, even after the the victim was dead (provided they were not too remote) is an aberration. It cannot be imagined that the Court of Appeal would follow this decision once reason has resumed its seat. It would be nonsense if the law was (as *Clarke* appears to state) that, in a case where the accused was clearly provoked to to lose his self-control at the time of his fatal act and a reasonable man would clearly have been provoked at that time to lose his self-control and do as the accused did, the defence of provocation should fail because a few minutes later the accused pushed his victim's dead body into a canal to conceal it, at which time the reasonable man would not have been provoked to do this (even if the accused was).

1 *Phillips v R* [1969] 2 AC 130 at 137.
2 [1969] 2 AC 130, [1969] 2 WLR 581, PC.
3 *Mancini v DPP* [1942] AC 1, [1941] 3 All ER 272, HL; *Gauthier* (1943) 29 Cr App Rep 113, CCA; *McCarthy* [1954] 2 QB 105, [1954] 2 All ER 262, CCA.
4 *Duffy* [1949] 1 All ER 932n.
5 [1972] 2 QB 229, [1972] 2 All ER 1328, CA.
6 [1990] Crim LR 383, CA.

11.47 *The function of judge and jury* Section 3 of the Homicide Act requires the judge to consider two questions:

a) whether there is any evidence on which the jury can find that the accused was provoked; and
b) whether there is any evidence on which the jury can find that the provocation caused him to lose his self-control.

Only if both questions are answered in the affirmative should the judge leave the defence of provocation to the jury,[1] but if they are so answered the judge must leave the defence to the jury, even if the defence has not been raised by the accused,[2] and even if in his opinion no reasonable jury could possibly conclude on the evidence that a reasonable man would have been provoked to lose his self-control so that a verdict of manslaughter would be perverse.[3]

As we have already seen,[4] if the issue of provocation is left to the jury the prosecution has the burden of negativing one or more elements of the defence, otherwise the jury must return a verdict of manslaughter.

1 *Gilbert* (1977) 66 Cr App Rep 237, CA.
2 *Cascoe* [1970] 2 All ER 833, CA. This is so even where the issue of provocation is inconsistent with the way in which the case has been conducted at the trial, as where the defence is simply 'I didn't do it' (*Newell* [1989] Crim LR 906, CA) or is self-defence (*Sawyer* [1989] Crim LR 831, CA).
3 *Whitfield* (1976) 63 Cr App Rep 39, CA; *Gilbert*; *Newell* [1989] Crim LR 906, CA.
4 Para 7.4; *Macpherson* (1957) 41 Cr App Rep 213, CCA.

11.48 *Mistaken belief and provocation* As in the case of other defences, the accused who acts under a reasonably mistaken belief that he was being provoked must be judged as if the facts were as he mistakenly believed them to be. Moreover, it has been held that if his mistake resulted from voluntary intoxication he is to be so judged,[1] even though a drunken mistake cannot be said to be reasonable. This latter rule, which would almost certainly not be followed now,[2] should not be confused with the rule that the accused's intoxication must be ignored in deciding whether the reasonable man would have been provoked.[3]

1 *Letenock* (1917) 12 Cr App Rep 221, CCA.
2 See paras 9.66 and 9.67.
3 Para 11.43.

11.49 *Reform* Clause 58 of the draft Criminal Code Bill[1] gives effect to the recommendations of the Criminal Law Revision Committee in its Fourteenth Report: Offences against the Person.[2] The clause provides, in place of the 'reasonable man' test, that provocation is a defence to a charge of murder if, on the facts as they appeared to the accused,[3] and in all the circumstances (including any of his personal characteristics that affect its gravity), the provocation is sufficient ground for the loss of self-control. The clause does does not make any requirement of proportionality between the provocation and the retaliation.

1 Law Commission: A Criminal Code for England and Wales (1989): Law Com No 177; see para 3.21 above.
2 Cmnd 7844, paras 77–90.
3 Draft Criminal Code Bill, cl 41.

Involuntary manslaughter

11.50 We now turn to those cases where the accused is not guilty of murder because he lacked an intention either to kill or to cause grievous bodily harm, but acted with some lesser degree of mens rea.

A person who causes the death of another is guilty of manslaughter if he does so by

a) a reckless act or omission; or
b) an act which is unlawful and dangerous.

KILLING BY A RECKLESS ACT OR OMISSION

11.51 For this type of involuntary manslaughter it is irrelevant whether or not the accused's act would have constituted an offence if death had not resulted.[1] Liability can be based on an omission to act only if the accused was under a duty to act recognised by the criminal law.[2]

The difficulty in defining this type of manslaughter concerns the element of recklessness. Until the House of Lords' decision in *Seymour*[3] in 1983, it appeared that a person who caused another's death by an act or omission was guilty of manslaughter if he was:

a) subjectively reckless as to death or bodily harm resulting; or
b) grossly negligent as to the risk of death or, possibly, grievous bodily harm resulting.

The extent to which this remains the case is discussed later.

1 *Larkin* [1943] 1 All ER 217 at 219; *Gray v Barr* [1971] 2 All ER 949 at 961, per Salmon LJ.
2 *Stone and Dobinson* [1977] QB 354, [1977] 2 All ER 341, CA.
3 [1983] 2 AC 493, [1983] 2 All ER 1058, HL.

11.52 *Subjective recklessness as to death or bodily harm* A person would fall within this category where he himself foresaw the risk of the death of another resulting from his conduct, or where he foresaw the risk of *some* bodily harm to another resulting, and nevertheless he took either of these risks without justification.[1] In one case the Court of Appeal held that subjective recklessness as to an injury to health and welfare sufficed.[2] It may be that such an injury inevitably involves some bodily harm, but if it does not this decision was open to the objection that the type of foreseen risk sufficient for manslaughter was too widely drawn. After all, manslaughter is a serious offence.

1 *Pike* [1961] Crim LR 547, CCA; *Gray v Barr* [1971] 2 All ER 949 at 961, per Salmon LJ.
2 *Stone and Dobinson* [1977] QB 354, [1977] 2 All ER 341, CA.

11.53 *Gross negligence as to death or, possibly, grievous bodily harm* A person would be grossly negligent in this sense if, in relation to a reasonably foreseeable risk of such harm, his failure to foresee it (or, having foreseen it, the steps he took to avoid it) fell so far below the standard of care which a reasonable person would have exercised as to go beyond a mere matter of compensation between individuals and to show such disregard for the life and safety of others as to amount to a crime against the State and be conduct deserving punishment.[1] The reader is reminded that negligence is a similar concept to the type of recklessness recognised by the House of Lords in *Caldwell* and *Lawrence*. Both apply where a person has failed to give any thought to an obvious risk; the difference is that a person is not reckless (in the sense recognised in *Caldwell* and *Lawrence*) as to a risk if he has thought about the possibility that it exists but, wrongly and unreasonably, concluded that it does not exist, whereas he will be negligent (and will be grossly negligent if his mistake was very unreasonable). However, this difference between the two concepts is small and gross negligence has often been referred to by the judges as recklessness.

1 *Pittwood* (1902) 19 TLR 37; *Finney* (1874) 12 Cox CC 625; *Bateman* (1925) 94 LJKB 791, CCA; *Andrews v DPP* [1937] AC 576 at 581, 583, per Lord Atkin.

11.54 *The decision in Seymour*[1] It appears that the above two formulations no longer represent the law, for the reasons given in para 11.59. It is unfortunate that this statement has to be so tentative, particularly in relation to so important an offence as manslaughter, but the regrettably obscure state of the law following the House of Lords' in *Seymour* leaves no alternative, even after clarification has been provided by subsequent cases.

In *Seymour* the accused's lorry had been involved in a slight collision with a car driven by B, a woman with whom he had been living and with whom he had just quarrelled. B got out of the car and approached the accused's lorry. Allegedly intending only to push the car out of the way, the accused drove his lorry violently against it, crushing B in the process. B died of the injuries received. Because of the gravity of the case the accused was charged with manslaughter and not (as was usually the charge) with the lesser offence of causing death by reckless driving, which offence has now been repealed by the Road Traffic Act 1991 and replaced by an offence of causing death by dangerous driving.[2]

In *Lawrence*[3] the House of Lords had defined what 'reckless' meant in the offence of causing death by reckless driving. It held that the accused must have been driving in such a manner as to create an obvious and serious risk of causing physical injury to some other person who might be using the road or of causing substantial damage to property, and that either the accused had not given any thought to the possibility of there being any such risk or, having recognised that there was some risk involved, had none the less gone on to take it. In other words, *Caldwell*-type recklessness as to the risk in question would suffice.

The trial judge in *Seymour* rejected a claim that a direction along these lines was inapplicable on a charge of manslaughter and directed the jury in the terms laid down in *Lawrence*, omitting only the reference to an obvious and serious risk of doing substantial damage to property. The accused was convicted of manslaughter and appealed unsuccessfully to the Court of Appeal, which held that, because of the House of Lords' ruling in *Government of the USA v Jennings*[4] that the ingredients of manslaughter and of causing death by reckless driving were identical, a *Lawrence* direction must be equally appropriate when manslaughter was charged. However, it certified the following question for the House of Lords (who granted leave to appeal):

> 'Where manslaughter is charged and the circumstances of the offence are that the victim was killed as the result of the reckless driving of the accused on a public highway; should the trial judge give the jury the direction suggested in *Lawrence* in its entirety; or should the direction be that only a recognition by the accused that some risk was involved and he had none-the-less gone on to take it would be sufficient to establish the commission of the offence?'

1 [1983] 2 AC 493, [1983] 2 All ER 1058, HL.
2 Para 20.13.
3 [1982] AC 510, [1981] 1 All ER 974, HL.
4 [1983] 1 AC 624, [1982] 3 All ER 104, HL.

11.55 The House of Lords dismissed the accused's appeal. Lord Roskill, with whom the others agreed, held that as the ingredients of manslaughter and causing death by reckless driving were identical the trial judge had been correct in giving the jury a direction along the lines of *Lawrence*. As we have seen, the judge had omitted any reference to an obvious and serious risk of doing substantial damage to property. Lord Roskill said that he had been 'entirely right not to refer to damage to property, a reference which was irrelevant in this case and might well have confused the jury'.

Lord Roskill's statement suggests that sometimes a reference to a risk of damage to property might be relevant, as where the accused's conduct was not accompanied by an obvious and serious risk of injuring anyone but was accompanied by an obvious and serious risk of substantially damaging property and someone was unexpectedly killed. To convict a person on the basis of *Caldwell*-type recklessness as to causing substantial damage to property would constitute a major extension to liability for manslaughter. Presumably, it was for this reason that the trial judge qualified the *Lawrence* direction by omitting any reference to any risk of damage to property. The overall tenor of the House of Lords' answer to the certified question (discussed in the next paragraph) seems to conflict with the suggestion contained in Lord Roskill's statement. The matter now seems to have been put beyond doubt in the two reported decisions in which *Seymour* has been applied in a manslaughter case, the decision of the Privy Council in *Kong Cheuk Kwan v R*[1] and that of the Court of Appeal in *Goodfellow*.[2] Although both decisions are to the effect that a *Lawrence* direction was applicable to manslaughter, they proceeded on the basis that the direction to be given should indicate the need for an obvious and serious risk of causing physical injury to another, and made no reference to any type of risk of damage to property sufficing in the alternative. While this must represent the law, it clearly contradicts the view expressed by the House of Lords in *Government of the USA v Jennings* and accepted by it in *Seymour* that the ingredients of manslaughter and causing death by reckless driving were identical.

1 (1985) 82 Cr App Rep 18, PC. Discussed by Brabyn 'A Sequel to Seymour, Made in Hong Kong' [1987] Crim LR 84.
2 (1986) 83 Cr App Rep 23, CA.

11.56 The House of Lords' decision that the trial judge's direction was correct appeared to be contradicted by another passage in Lord Roskill's answer (with which at least two of the other four Law Lords agreed) to the certified question. Lord Roskill said:

'Where manslaughter is charged and the circumstances are that the victim was killed as a result of the reckless driving of the defendant on a public highway, the trial judge should give the jury the direction suggested in *Lawrence* but it is appropriate also to point out that in order to constitute the offence of manslaughter *the risk of death* being caused by the manner of the defendant's driving must be *very high*'.[1]

This is very different from the formulation in *Lawrence*. There is the world of difference between a 'very high risk of death' and an 'obvious and serious risk of causing physical injury to some other person'.

This apparent contradiction was explained in *Kong Cheuk Kwan v R* where Lord Roskill, on behalf of the Privy Council, said that the statement in *Seymour* that there must be a very high risk of causing death was inserted not to indicate the risk as to which the accused must be reckless but only to point to those cases in which it still might be thought appropriate to charge manslaughter rather than the statutory offence of causing death by reckless driving.[2] This explanation is not very convincing but, in the light of it and of the fact that the Court of Appeal in *Goodfellow* made no reference to the statement that there must be a very high risk of causing death, it can safely be assumed that such a risk is not required for a conviction for the present type of manslaughter, and that what is required in terms of risk is an obvious and serious risk of causing physical injury to someone.

1 [1983] 2 All ER 1058 at 1066. Italics supplied.
2 (1985) 82 Cr App Rep 18 at 25.

11.57 So far, it has been assumed that the decision in *Seymour* applies to the law of reckless manslaughter in general. However, it could be argued that it is limited to 'motor manslaughter' cases (ie cases where a person is killed by the accused's reckless driving on a public road), in which case the pre-existing law would be otherwise unaffected.

On a number of occasions in *Seymour* Lord Roskill referred to 'motor manslaughter'. Moreover, the whole tenor of his speech is concerned with manslaughter by reckless driving and its relationship with the offence of causing death by reckless driving, and he did not refer to other types of fatal conduct. Moreover, the certified question was framed in terms of manslaughter charges where the death was caused by reckless driving. Nevertheless, there has not previously been a separate category of 'motor manslaughter'; nor did Lord Roskill say there was or expressly limit his remarks to it.

It is now clear that the decision in *Seymour* is not limited to motor manslaughter but is of general application. In *Kong Cheuk Kwan v R* it was held by the Privy Council to apply to a case where death had been caused by a collision between two hydrofoils and in *Goodfellow* the Court of Appeal held that it was applicable to a case where death was caused by the arson of a house.

11.58 *Summary* The preceding paragraphs can be summarised as follows. A person who unlawfully kills another is guilty of involuntary manslaughter if his conduct was attended by an obvious and serious risk of causing unlawful[1] physical injury to some other person *and*–

either he acted or failed to act without having given any thought to the possibility of there being any *such* risk'
or, having recognised that there was some risk involved, had nonetheless gone on to take it.

The elements of this formulation have already been explained in the discussion of *Caldwell*-type recklessness in paras 6.45 to 6.52, with one exception. This concerns the element of 'serious risk', which does not appear in Lord Diplock's model direction in *Caldwell*. The clue to the meaning of this term was given by Lord Diplock in *Lawrence*.[2] His Lordship said: 'Recklessness on the part of the doer of an act does presuppose that there is something in the circumstances that would have drawn the attention of an ordinary prudent individual to the possibility that his act was capable of causing the kind of serious harmful consequences that the section which creates the offence was intended to prevent, and that the risk of those harmful consequences occurring was not so slight that an ordinary prudent individual would feel justified in treating them as negligible. It is only when this is so that the doer of the act is acting 'recklessly' if, before doing the act, he either fails to give any thought to the possibility of there being any such risk or, having recognised that there was such risk, he nevertheless goes on to do it.' His Lordship then proceeded immediately to encapsulate in a model direction what he had said in the quotation, using the term 'serious risk' in doing so. From this it would seem that 'serious risk' does not mean 'grave risk' or the like but means no more than a risk which is not so slight that a reasonable person would feel justified in treating it as negligible.[3] On this interpretation, there is no real difference between the statement in

Lawrence, adopted in *Seymour*, and the corresponding statement in *Caldwell*, where Lord Diplock also spoke of a person not being reckless as to a risk if a reasonable person would have regarded it as so slight that he was justified in treating it as negligible.

1 By analogy with *Williams* and *Beckford v R*; para 7.21.
2 [1982] AC 510, [1981] 1 All ER 974 at 982.
3 In *Reid* (1990) 91 Cr App Rep 263 at 271 the Court of Appeal preferred the view that 'serious risk' meant non-negligible risk in this context.

11.59 *The effect of Seymour on the pre-existing law* The House of Lords in *Seymour* does not appear to have considered the effect of its decision on the two types of manslaughter set out in paras 11.52 and 11.53; certainly it did not expressly overrule any previous decisions.

Even though the first type of reckless manslaughter mentioned above (subjective recklessness as to death or bodily harm) did not require the risk of death or bodily harm to be an obvious and serious one and even though it might have included subjective recklessness as to an injury to health and welfare which did not involve bodily harm, unlike (in both instances) the test of recklessness recognised in *Seymour*, it would seem almost inevitable that the *Seymour* test has superseded it. Indeed, Lord Roskill's statement in *Seymour* that '"Reckless" should today be given the same meaning in relation to all offences which involve "recklessness" as one of the elements unless Parliament has otherwise ordained'[1] may well imply this. The subsequent decision of the Divisional Court in *West London Coroner, ex p Gray*[2] to the effect that, on a charge of manslaughter by neglect (omission to fulfil a legal duty of care), subjective recklessness as to an obvious and serious risk to the health and welfare of the deceased would have to be proved, must be regarded as wrong.

In relation to the second type mentioned above (killing by gross negligence), it appears from *Kong Cheuk Kwan v R* that it has probably ceased to exist as a separate type of manslaughter, since the Privy Council agreed with Watkins LJ in the Court of Appeal in *Seymour*, who said that 'it is no longer necessary or helpful to make reference to compensation and negligence. The *Lawrence* direction on recklessness is comprehensive and applicable to all[3] offences...'.[4] On the other hand, the Court of Appeal, obiter, in the subsequent case of *Ball*[5] clearly referred to manslaughter by gross negligence as an extant type of involuntary manslaughter. *Seymour* and its subsequent application and refinement do not appear to have been cited to the Court of Appeal (not surprisingly since only manslaughter by an unlawful and dangerous act was in issue). Consequently, it is impossible to say whether the Court of Appeal was simply unaware of these developments or was disagreeing that manslaughter by gross negligence has ceased to exist.[6]

Generally the point is of no practical importance because most people who would previously have been guilty of manslaughter on the basis of killing by gross negligence would now be guilty by virtue of the decision in *Seymour*, although (as indicated in para 11.53) it would be important where a person who had thought about the possibility of a risk of physical harm but, wrongly and very unreasonably, concluded that it did not exist would not.

Opinions may differ about whether or not such a person should be guilty of manslaughter, but it is worth remembering that no other offence against the person can be committed negligently and that, indeed, not even *Caldwell*-type recklessness suffices for any other offence, however minor, against the person.

It is submitted that the better view is that manslaughter by gross negligence has ceased to exist as a separate type of involuntary manslaughter.

1 [1983] 2 All ER 1058 at 1064. For a criticism of this statement, see para 6.53. That criticism is, however, not germane to the present point.
2 [1987] 2 All ER 129, DC.
3 The direction is not, in fact, applicable to all offences; see para 6.53.
4 (1983) 76 Cr App Rep 211 at 216. For the significance of these words, see para 11.54. In one passage in *Goodfellow* (1986) 83 Cr App Rep 23 at 26 Lord Lane CJ seems to have ignored the distinction between 'recklessness' and 'gross negligence' by equating the two terms. This provides yet another example of terminological confusion with which the cases on involuntary manslaughter are riddled.
5 [1989] Crim LR 730, CA. Also see *Adamako* [1991] 2 Med LR 277, Crown Ct.
6 Ibid, at 731 (commentary).

KILLING BY AN UNLAWFUL AND DANGEROUS ACT

11.60 This mode of committing manslaughter is commonly known as 'constructive manslaughter'. It is a narrower mode than that of killing by a reckless act or omission. While the latter's definition is wide enough to cover most cases of constructive manslaughter, it is clear from the continued application of its rules by the courts[1] that constructive manslaughter continues to exist as a separate mode of committing manslaughter.

At one time the unlawful act could consist of a tort[2] but now only a criminally unlawful act will suffice,[3] and there are these two further qualifications on the nature of the unlawful act:

a) An act which has become criminally unlawful simply because it was negligently performed, e g dangerous or careless driving, does not constitute an unlawful act for the purposes of 'constructive manslaughter'. In *Andrews v DPP*[4] the accused had killed another while committing the offence of dangerous driving and was convicted of manslaughter. On appeal to the House of Lords, Lord Atkin said that where an otherwise lawful act (e g driving) was unlawful merely because it was negligently performed this did not necessarily make the driver guilty of manslaughter if death resulted. The doctrine of 'constructive manslaughter' did not apply to such acts, although there might be liability for manslaughter on the basis of recklessness.[5]

b) As we have seen, there are a number of statutory offences which are constituted by an omission to do something, rather than a positive act. An example is the neglect of a child by its parent or guardian in a manner likely to cause it unnecessary suffering or injury to health, which, if wilful, is an offence under s 1 of the Children and Young Persons Act 1933.

It was thought that the unintentional causing of death as a result of the commission of such a statutory offence of omission could constitute constructive manslaughter. In *Senior*,[6] for instance, where owing to the religious belief of the accused his child was not provided with medical attendance and died in consequence, it was held that manslaughter had been committed. However, the Court of Appeal in *Lowe*[7] held that *Senior* was no longer good law and that an omission would not suffice for constructive manslaughter. The accused's baby died some 10 weeks after birth and at the time of her death was grossly dehydrated and emaciated. The accused was convicted of wilfully neglecting the child and of manslaughter after the judge had told the jury that a conviction for manslaughter must follow if wilful neglect had caused the child's death. His appeal against the latter conviction was allowed by the Court of Appeal who held that a finding of manslaughter did not inexorably follow from a finding of wilful neglect. There was a clear distinction between an omission likely to cause harm and an act likely to cause harm:

'. . . if I strike a child in a manner likely to cause harm it is right that if the child dies I may be charged with manslaughter. If, however, I omit to do something with the result that it suffers injury to health which results in death, we think that a charge of manslaughter should not be an inevitable consequence, even if the omission is deliberate'.[8]

It is difficult to see the distinction between the person who causes the death of his child by deliberate inaction and the one who does so by positive action.

An omission to act can suffice for liability for involuntary manslaughter under the other head of liability, discussed in paras 11.51 to 11.59.

1 See, for example, *Goodfellow* (1986) 83 Cr App Rep 23, CA; *Arobieke* [1988] Crim LR 314, CA; *Jennings* [1990] Crim LR 588, CA.
2 *Fenton* (1830) 1 Lew CC 179.
3 *Franklin* (1883) 15 Cox CC 163; *Lamb* [1967] 2 QB 981, [1967] 2 All ER 1282, CA.
4 [1937] AC 576, HL.
5 Paras 11.51–11.59.
6 [1899] 1 QB 283. Also see *Watson and Watson* (1959) 43 Cr App Rep 111, CCA.
7 [1973] QB 702, [1973] 1 All ER 805, CA. Overruled on the meaning of 'wilful neglect', but not on the present point, by the House of Lords in *Sheppard* [1981] AC 394, [1980] 3 All ER 899. For the House of Lords' definition of wilful neglect, see para 8.10.
8 [1973] 1 All ER at 809.

11.61 *Elements* To secure a conviction on the basis of constructive manslaughter, the prosecution must prove three things:

a) the commission of an unlawful act;
b) that that act was a cause of death; and
c) that that act was dangerous, in the sense that it was likely to cause harm to another.

11.62 *Commission of an unlawful act* It will be remembered that an act is never criminally unlawful in itself.One of the things which is required to render an act criminally unlawful is that it should occur in those circumstances and/or lead to those consequences prescribed by law as constituting the actus reus of an offence. For instance, an act of punching is not criminal but it may become so (as a battery) if it results in the consequence that someone is unlawfully hit. Thus, if a child unexpectedly dies as a result of corporal punishment by D, there will be no unlawful act (and consequently no manslaughter) if D is the child's parent and used reasonable force, since such force is lawful.[1] On the other hand, if unreasonable force is used,[2] or if D is not a person legally entitled to administer corporal punishment,[3] the force is unlawful and D commits a battery (and, doubtless, other offences); since D's act is unlawful, he will be guilty of constructive manslaughter if death unexpectedly results. (Of course, if D intended grievous bodily harm, he would be guilty of murder.)

Common examples of unlawful acts for the purposes of constructive manslaughter are offences involving a battery, but (provided the other requirements listed below can be satisfied) the fatal commission of the actus reus of some other offence can suffice, and this is so even if the offence is not an offence against the person. In *Cato*,[4] for instance, the Court of Appeal, upholding a conviction for manslaughter, relied on the fact that the accused, who had administered heroin to the deceased at the latter's request, had committed the actus reus of the statutory offence of unlawfully and maliciously administering a noxious thing so as thereby to endanger life or inflict grievous bodily harm. It went on to state, obiter, that if it could not rely on the commission of this actus reus it would have found that the injection of heroin which the accused had unlawfully taken into his possession for that purpose was in itself an unlawful act. Conduct so described is not an offence and, if the Court of Appeal intended to say that conduct which is not the actus reus of an offence may nevertheless be an unlawful act in the present context, its statement cannot be correct in the light of the authorities. This is emphasised by the Court of Appeal's decision in *Arobieke*,[5] where D had been convicted of the manslaughter of P who had been electrocuted while trying to cross an electrified railway line. Fearing that D was looking for him, P had gone to a railway station to escape. There was evidence that D had gone to the station and looked in the windows of carriages. Allowing D's appeal, the Court of Appeal held that, although the jury could properly conclude that D had gone to the station to injure or threaten P, there was no evidence of any criminally unlawful act by D; in particular, there was no assault since D would not have put P in fear of immediate force. Consequently, there could be no conviction on the basis of constructive manslaughter. It would have been different if D had put P in fear of immediate force, for example by chasing him.

The commission of an offence whose basis is an event, rather than an act, e g having with one an offensive weapon in a public place, can suffice as an unlawful act,[6] although it will be rare for it to satisfy the requirement of dangerousness discussed in para 11.67.

1 Para 10.13.
2 *Hopley* (1860) 2 F & F 202.
3 *Woods* (1921) 85 JP 272.
4 [1976] 1 All ER 260, [1976] 1 WLR 110, CA.
5 [1988] Crim LR 314, CA.
6 *Jennings* [1990] Crim LR 588, CA.

11.63 Of course, the fact that a person has committed the actus reus of an offence does not in itself make his act criminally unlawful; it only does so if the accused has the mens rea required for that offence. To take the example of punching given above, to punch another is only criminally unlawful (a battery) if the puncher intends that his fist should hit another or is reckless as to whether it does. This means that, as a matter of principle, the accused's fatal act cannot be an 'unlawful act' for the purposes of constructive manslaughter unless he had the requisite mens rea for an offence whose actus reus he has committed.

Until the House of Lords' decision in 1976 in *DPP v Newbury*,[1] it seemed clear that the law of constructive manslaughter corresponded to this statement of principle,[2] but that decision threw doubt on the matter. In *Newbury* two teenage boys pushed part of a paving stone off a railway bridge as a train approached. The stone came through the window of the cab and killed the guard. The House of Lords, upholding the boys' conviction for manslaughter, held that an accused is guilty of manslaughter if it is proved that he intentionally did an act which was unlawful and dangerous. Lord Salmon, with whose speech the other Law Lords concurred, held that a conviction for

constructive manslaughter required proof of mens rea but that, as manslaughter was a crime of 'basic' as opposed to 'specific' intention, the
necessary mens rea was simply 'an intention to do the acts which constitute
the crime'. In his speech, Lord Edmund-Davies stated that 'what is required
is no more than the *intentional* committing of an unlawful act of the designated type or nature'.[3]

These statements are open to two interpretations. The first, which seems
to be better supported by the actual words used in the speeches, is that the
only state of mind that must be proved on the part of the accused is that he
deliberately or consciously did the act, ie that there was a voluntary act on
his part, and that it is irrelevant whether or not the accused had the requisite
mens rea for an offence whose actus reus he has committed. As such, the use
of the word 'intention' is otiose: it merely states what is normally implied as a
defence, viz that involuntary conduct is not criminal. It is noteworthy that
Lord Salmon's definition of 'basic intent' differs from that adopted in other
contexts, where it has been defined as involving foresight of the consequences of the actus reus in question. One is prompted to ask whether this
difference in definition was deliberate. If this is the correct interpretation,
the question of the unlawfulness of an act in this context must be assessed on
a different basis to that otherwise used in the criminal law. Such an interpretation is also open to the objection that under it an accused can be convicted
of manslaughter without the mens rea required for the unlawful act
(offence) on which his liability is based. It would certainly be odd that,
whereas a person who committed the actus reus of (say) a battery could not
be convicted of that offence if he lacked the mens rea for it, he might
nevertheless be convicted of manslaughter if death unexpectedly resulted.

The second interpretation, which is preferable but somewhat strained on
the wording of the speeches in *Newbury*, is that, since an act can only be
unlawful if accompanied by the relevant mens rea, their Lordships must
have meant to imply the requirement that the accused must have the mens
rea for the unlawful act (offence) and that their reference to intention to do
the unlawful act is simply an unnecessary reference to the need for voluntary
conduct and does not purport to define exhaustively the state of mind
required on the part of the accused. If this is so, it is a great pity that their
Lordships did not make the point clear. This interpretation gains some
support from the fact that the House of Lords did not purport to change the
previous law on the present issue. It should be added that the decision in the
subsequent case of *O'Driscoll*,[4] mentioned further below, proceeds on the
basis that the mens rea of the unlawful act (offence) must be proved on a
constructive manslaughter charge, although *Newbury* was not discussed,
and can only be understood on this basis. Further support for the second
interpretation may be derived from *Goodfellow*,[5] where the Court of
Appeal distinguished between two questions, both of which had to be
answered in the affirmative:

a) Was the act intentional?
b) Was it unlawful? (which could be said to depend, inter alia, on whether
   the accused had the relevant mens rea).

Where an accused, who has killed by an unlawful act and is charged with
manslaughter, pleads voluntary intoxication as evidence that he lacked the
state of mind required for constructive manslaughter, he can nevertheless be
convicted despite the absence of that state of mind because manslaughter is

not an offence requiring specific intent.[6] There is one exception, which can only be reconciled with the mental element in constructive manslaughter if the second interpretation of the statement in *Newbury*, referred to above, is correct. This is that, as was held in *O'Driscoll*,[7] if the unlawful act (offence) relied on requires proof of a specific intent, the accused's intoxication may be introduced as evidence that he lacked that specific intent and he cannot be convicted unless that specific intent is proved. However, most offences of specific intent are supported, as a 'secondary offence', by an offence which is not of specific intent, so that this exception is of limited importance.

1 [1977] AC 500, [1976] 2 All ER 365, HL.
2 *Lamb* [1967] 2 QB 981, [1967] 2 All ER 1282, CA, was a strong authority for this view.
3 The same statement was made by the Privy Council in *DPP v Daley* (1978) 69 Cr App Rep 39 at 45.
4 (1977) 65 Cr App Rep 50, CA.
5 (1986) 83 Cr App Rep 23, CA. See also *Jennings* [1990] Crim LR 588, CA.
6 *Lipman* [1970] 1 QB 152, [1969] 3 All ER 410, CA.
7 (1977) 65 Cr App Rep 50, CA.

11.64 An act will not be an 'unlawful act' for the purposes of constructive manslaughter if the accused has available to him a legally recognised defence to the offence in question.[1]

1 See, for example, *Jennings* [1990] Crim LR 588, CA.

11.65 *The unlawful act must be a cause of death* The unlawful act need not have been the only cause, but it must have been a substantial cause of the death of another human being. There must be no intervening act or event which would break the chain of causation between the unlawful act and the death.

11.66 *Must the unlawful act be 'directed at another'?* The answer 'yes' appeared to have been given by the Court of Appeal in *Dalby*.[1]

In *Dalby* D was a drug addict who unlawfully supplied a controlled drug to a friend, P, in whose flat he was staying. D and P both injected themselves with the drug. Later that night someone else helped P to inject two quantities of an unspecified substance. P died the next day. In the Crown Court, D pleaded guilty to supplying a controlled drug, but not guilty to manslaughter. Dealing with constructive manslaughter, the judge directed the jury that D could be convicted if he had intentionally supplied the drug and that unlawful act had been a dangerous one and had caused P's death. The jury convicted D. Allowing D's appeal, the Court of Appeal held that, where a charge of manslaughter is based on an unlawful and dangerous act, that act must be directed at the victim, and the unlawful act of supplying drugs was not directed at the victim. Subsequently, in a case where D hit X, causing him to fall against P who died as a result, it was held that it was enough that an accused's act was directed at another, albeit not the actual victim on whom it unexpectedly took effect.[2]

A requirement that the accused's act be directed at another would exclude a substantial number of unlawful acts from the ambit of constructive manslaughter. It would also make a number of leading cases difficult to explain. For example, it is by no means obvious that the unlawful acts in *DPP v Newbury* and *Cato*[3] were directed at another.

In the light of the apparently categorical statements in *Dalby*, the view taken in 1986 by the Court of Appeal in *Goodfellow*[4] came as a surprise since it involved an interpretation of *Dalby* which contradicted the clear message in that case. In *Goodfellow* D lived in a council house. He was harassed by two men and wanted to move. He had no chance of exchanging his house, so he conceived the idea of setting the house on fire as if it had been caused by a fire bomb. He poured petrol over the furniture and ignited it. His wife, his girl friend and his young son were killed. Dismissing D's appeal against conviction for manslaughter, the Court of Appeal held that a person could be convicted of constructive manslaughter even though (as here) his unlawful act was not directed at another. The Court explained the relevant words in *Dalby* as not meaning what they appeared to mean but as simply meaning that there must be no intervening act or event (of a type, presumably, which would break the chain of causation between the accused's act and the death). In other words, it explained *Dalby* as a case concerned with the directness of causation, as opposed to being concerned with a requirement of directing an act at another.

Although the dismissal in *Goodfellow* of the clear meaning of the words in *Dalby* is difficult to accept, the interpretation in *Goodfellow* must at the moment be accepted as binding, particularly as the Court of Appeal would have had to allow the appeal if 'directed at another' bore its apparent, literal meaning. Nevertheless, obiter dicta in the Court of Appeal's decision in *Ball*[5] may indicate that there will be a reversal of the literal interpretation of 'directed at another' when the matter next comes before the Court of Appeal. In *Ball* the Court of Appeal took the view, obiter, in relation to a hypothetical case put by counsel, that a publican who sold intoxicating liquor to an under-age customer (an unlawful act) which, unknown to the publican, contained poison and had fatal consequences would not be guilty of constructive manslaughter because the unlawful act would not be directed at another. Likewise, it said, a person who stored goods known to be stolen but not known to contain explosives would not be guilty of constructive manslaughter if the goods exploded and killed another. It should be noted that there would not be manslaughter anyway on either of these sets of facts because the acts in question would not be dangerous, as explained in para 11.67 and 11.68.

1 [1982] 1 All ER 916, [1982] 1 WLR 425, CA.
2 *Mitchell* [1983] QB 741, [1983] 2 All ER 427, CA; para 6.56.
3 [1976] 1 All ER 260, [1976] 1 WLR 110, CA; para 11.62.
4 (1986) 83 Cr App Rep 23, CA. This case, like many others involving an unlawful fatal act, was also covered by the mode of manslaughter by a reckless act, as the Court of Appeal recognised at p 26.
5 [1989] Crim LR 730, CA.

11.67   *Unlawful act must be dangerous*   Not every unlawful act will suffice. At one time it was thought that death occasioned by any unlawful act would amount to manslaughter, although it was not likely to cause physical harm to anyone. It is now clear that the unlawful act causing death must be dangerous, in the sense that it is likely to injure someone, as well as unlawful. In *Larkin*[1] the accused produced a razor at the house of a man with whom his mistress had been associating: he did so in order to frighten him. His mistress, who was drunk, blundered against the razor and was killed. The Court of Criminal Appeal, in dismissing an appeal against conviction, held that where the act which a person is engaged in performing is unlawful, then, if at the same time it is an act likely to injure another person, and that person dies, the accused is guilty of manslaughter.

The present requirement was further explained in *Church* where the Court of Criminal Appeal said:[2]

'An unlawful act causing the death of another cannot, simply because it is an unlawful act, render a manslaughter verdict inevitable. For such a verdict inexorably to follow, the unlawful act must be such as all sober and reasonable people would inevitably recognise must subject the other person to, at least, the risk of some harm resulting therefrom, albeit not serious harm.'

This objective test is not concerned with proving a risk which the accused must foresee but with delimiting the type of unlawful act which will suffice for liability for manslaughter. Thus, the test is unaffected by s 8 of the Criminal Justice Act 1967, which is not concerned with when foresight has to be proved but with how it is to be proved when it is required.[3] The test is similar to that of obvious and serious risk in manslaughter by a reckless act or omission[4] but, unlike that test, the present test is satisfied where the accused has considered whether there was a risk of harm and wrongly concluded there was none, unless a reasonable person would also have reached that conclusion.

The validity of this objective limitation on the nature of the unlawful act was put beyond doubt by the decision of the House of Lords in *DPP v Newbury*,[5] where their Lordships held that an accused is guilty of manslaughter if it is proved that he intentionally did an act which was unlawful and dangerous and that act inadvertently caused death, and that it was unnecessary to prove that the accused knew that the act was unlawful or dangerous. It approved the objective test in *Church* that, in judging whether an act was dangerous, the test is whether all sober and reasonable people would recognise that the act must subject the other person to, at least, the risk of some harm resulting therefrom, albeit not serious harm.

1 [1943] KB 174, [1943] 1 All ER 217, CCA. Also see *Hall* (1961) 45 Cr App Rep 366, CCA.
2 [1966] 1 QB 59 at 70, [1965] 2 All ER 72 at 75. Also see *Mackie* (1973) 57 Cr App Rep 453, CA.
3 *Lipman* [1970] 1 QB 152, [1969] 3 All ER 410, CA; *DPP v Newbury* [1976] 2 All ER 365 at 370, per Lord Edmund-Davies.
4 Para 11.58.
5 [1977] AC 500, [1976] 2 All ER 365, HL.

11.68 The objective test is applied on the basis of the facts known to the accused, i e the question is whether – on the facts known to the accused at the time of his unlawful act – a reasonable person would have realised that the act must subject the other person to, at least, the risk of some harm resulting therefrom.[1] It follows that if, unknown to the accused, the victim had some special susceptibility to death in the circumstances in question, this must not be taken into account in applying the objective test. In *Dawson*[2] the Court of Appeal quashed convictions for the manslaughter of a filling station attendant who had suffered a fatal heart attack following an armed robbery by the accused in the course of which he was threatened with violence. There was no evidence that the accused knew that that the attendant suffered from a serious heart condition from which he was likely to die at any time, and the Court of Appeal quashed his convictions because the jury might have been given to understand by the judge that they could take into account that heart condition in reaching their verdict.

For the purpose of the rule that the reasonable person is endowed with such knowledge as the accused had *at the time* of his unlawful act, the duration of that act is not the time, possibly very brief, when the 'unlawful act' offence is technically committed but instead is that period in which the act can be said in common sense terms to continue. In *Watson*,[3] where D had entered a house as a trespasser with intent to steal (and thereby committed an unlawful act, a burglary) and, while in the house, had discovered that it was occupied by a frail, 87-year-old man, who died from a heart attack an hour and a half later, the Court of Appeal held that the unlawful act comprised the whole of the burglarious intrusion and did not end with D's entry. Consequently, it held, the trial judge had correctly directed the jury that D's knowledge of the victim's age and frailty, acquired during that intrusion, could be attributed to the reasonable person.

1 *Dawson* (1985) 81 Cr App Rep 150, CA.
2 (1985) 81 Cr App Rep 150, CA.
3 [1989] 2 All ER 865, CA.

11.69 The 'harm' referred to in the above definition is physical harm. This was affirmed by the Court of Appeal in *Dawson*,[1] where it was held that the risk of emotional disturbance produced by terror is not enough; but it would be if the risk of physical harm (e g a heart attack) from emotional disturbance was reasonably foreseeable.

1 (1985) 81 Cr App Rep 150, CA. See Stallworthy 'Can Death by Shock be Manslaughter?' (1986) 136 NLJ 51; Busuttil and McCall-Smith 'Fright, Stress and Homicide' (1990) 54 JCL 257.

11.70 Very often, a person who commits an unlawful act will himself realise the risk of some immediate harm to another resulting, but the important thing about the present requirement is that such a person can be convicted of constructive manslaughter even though he does not realise this risk, provided that a reasonable person would realise that it is likely to cause harm.

One result of the present requirement is that, although it is possible to commit constructive manslaughter by frightening a person (an assault) with fatal consequences, such cases will not be very common in practice because in normal circumstances a reasonable person would not realise that frightening a person is likely to cause him harm.

CONCLUSIONS ON INVOLUNTARY MANSLAUGHTER

11.71 Similar problems are raised by each of the types of involuntary manslaughter. Why should someone be liable to a maximum punishment of life imprisonment if he inadvertently causes death by a common assault for which he could not receive more than a minimal term of imprisonment if he had not caused death? Why should someone who inadvertently causes death, having (for reasons of inexperience, mental backwardness or whatever) failed to give any thought to an obvious and serious risk of causing physical injury, be liable to be convicted of manslaughter whereas, had he merely caused bodily harm, he would not have been guilty of any offence against the person and probably of no offence at all?

Clause 55 of the draft Criminal Code Bill[1] implements the recommendations of the Criminal Law Revision Committee in its Fourteenth Report: Offences against the Person.[2] Under cl 55(c) it would be involuntary manslaughter if a person caused death with intent to cause serious personal harm or being subjectively reckless whether death or serious personal harm will be caused. Under cl 55(b) a person who was not guilty of murder solely because, by virtue of involuntary intoxication, he was unaware that death might be caused or believed that an exempting circumstance existed would also be guilty of involuntary manslaughter. The enactment of these provisions would clearly restrict the scope of involuntary manslaughter considerably.

1 Law Commission: A Criminal Code for England and Wales (1989): Law Com No 177; see para 3.21 above.
2 Cmnd 7844 (1980), paras 116–123.

Infanticide[1]

11.72   Section 1 of the Infanticide Act 1938 provides that where a woman by any wilful act or omission causes the death of her child, being a child under the age of 12 months, in circumstances which prima facie amount to murder, but at the time of such act or omission the balance of her mind was disturbed by reason of her not having fully recovered from the effects of giving birth to the child, or by reason of the effect of lactation consequent upon the birth of the child, she is guilty of infanticide, an offence punishable in the same way as manslaughter. By s 1(2) of the Act, where a woman is tried for the murder of a child under the age of 12 months, it is open to the jury to return a verdict of not guilty of murder but guilty of infanticide.

1 Seaborne Davies *Modern Approach to Criminal Law* 301–343; O'Donovan 'The Medicalisation of Infanticide' [1984] Crim LR 259.

11.73   Thus, infanticide can either be charged in the first instance or serve as a defence on a murder charge. In the latter case a woman is enabled to plead as a defence mental disturbance of such a nature as would not amount to insanity under the rule in *M'Naghten's Case*,[1] although it would now often amount to diminished responsibility. Legally, infanticide is strictly limited to the conditions laid down in the Act, and the fact that the deceased child was less than 12 months old is not sufficient unless there is also evidence that the balance of the mother's mind was disturbed for one of the stated reasons.[2]

Although the mother who raises infanticide as a defence on a murder charge must adduce evidence sufficient to raise the defence, the burden of disproving it rests on the Crown; infanticide as a defence differs from the defences of insanity and diminished responsibility where the burden of proving the defence is on the accused.[3]

The offence/defence of infanticide was originally created by the Infanticide Act 1922. Its obvious purpose is to mitigate the rigours of the law relating to murder, especially the mandatory life sentence. It has no application to unborn children, but only to those who attain an existence independent of the mother.

1 Paras 9.12–9.29.
2 *Soanes* [1948] 1 All ER 289, CCA.
3 Paras 7.6 and 9.34.

11.74   The Butler Committee on Mentally Abnormal Offenders[1] recommended in 1975 that the provisions concerning infanticide should be repealed since the defence of diminished responsibility (as re-defined by it)[2] would cover all cases falling within the offence of infanticide. However, in the light of evidence received by it, the Criminal Law Revision Committee in its Fourteenth Report: Offences against the Person,[3] published in 1980, was unable to agree with this view. Assuming that the mandatory penalty for murder is not abolished, it recommended the retention of the offence of infanticide, whose definition would be amended to take account of modern medical knowledge, and which would apply to the killing of any child of the accused under the age of 12 months whether or not it was the birth of *that* child which gave rise to the mother's condition. It recommended that the maximum punishment be reduced to five years' imprisonment. The Criminal Law Revision Committee's recommendations have been incorporated in cl 64 and Sch 1 of the draft Criminal Code Bill,[4] which extends infanticide to women who would otherwise be guilty of manslaughter.

1 Cmnd 6244, paras 19.22–19.27.
2 Para 9.40.
3 Cmnd 7844, paras 100–113. Also see O'Donovan, loc cit.
4 Law Commission: A Criminal Code for England and Wales (1989): Law Com No 177; see para 3.21 above.

Abortion and child destruction[1]

ABORTION

11.75 Section 58 of the Offences against the Person Act 1861 provides the offence of attempting to procure a miscarriage, which is popularly known as abortion. The offence is triable only on indictment and is punishable with a maximum of imprisonment for life; it is committed in two cases:

a) where a woman 'being with child', with intent to procure her own miscarriage, unlawfully administers to herself any poison or noxious thing or unlawfully uses any instrument or other means; or
b) where any other person, with intent to procure the miscarriage of any woman, whether or not she is 'with child', unlawfully administers to her or causes to be taken by her any poison or noxious thing or unlawfully uses any instrument or other means.

1 See Williams *The Sanctity of Life and the Criminal Law* Ch 6.

11.76 In neither case is a miscarriage required to result from the accused's conduct. However, there are these distinctions between the woman who tries to procure her own miscarriage and any other persons who try to procure another's miscarriage:

a) A woman who administers poison etc to herself can only be guilty if she is in fact 'with child'; if she merely believes herself to be pregnant, but is not, she is not guilty under s 58. It has not yet been decided when a woman becomes 'with child'; is it when the ovum is fertilised or is it when the fertilised ovum is successfully implanted in the womb (or, in the rare case of ectopic pregnancy, in the peritoneal cavity)? If it is the former, the use of certain contraceptive devices by a woman, like the morning-after pill and the intra-uterine device, which prevent the implantation of a fertilised ovum appears to be an offence under s 58,[1] provided that a person who intends to prevent implantation can be said to intend to procure a miscarriage (which is by no means clear).[2] If another person administers etc, it is irrelevant that the woman concerned was not in fact 'with child' provided that the intent to procure a miscarriage can be proved.

b) A person other than the woman herself can commit the offence by causing to be taken by the woman any poison or noxious thing. This will occur where the woman administers the substance in question to herself on the directions of the accused (whether or not he is present at the time of administration).[3]

1 See Tunkel 'Modern Anti-Pregnancy Techniques and the Criminal Law' [1974] Crim LR 416; Brahms 'The Morning-After Pill: Contraception or Abortion?' (1983) 133 NLJ 417.
2 Keown ' "Miscarriage": A Medico-Legal Analysis' [1984] Crim LR 604 argues that there is an intent to procure a miscarriage. See para 11.78.
3 *Wilson* (1856) Dears & B 127, 26 LJMC 18.

11.77 *Means* Section 58 is concerned with the unlawful administration of poison or a noxious thing or the use of an instrument or any other means with intent to procure a miscarriage. 'Poison' has been said to mean a recognised poison, and it has been stated in the same case that if the thing administered is a recognised poison the offence may be committed, even though the quantity given is so small as to be incapable of doing harm.[1] 'Noxious thing' has been defined as something, other than a recognised poison, which is harmful in the dosage in which it was administered, even though it might be harmless in small quantities.[2] 'Any other means' is obviously a wide term, covering digital interference with a foetus and hitting a woman in the lower part of her body[3] among other things. It is irrelevant, provided one of these things is administered or used, that unknown to the accused it was incapable of procuring a miscarriage.[4] Although in most cases the woman will be a consenting party, the offence also covers non-consensual conduct.[5]

1 *Cramp* (1880) 5 QBD 307 at 309–310, per Field B. See also Stephen J, ibid, at 310. See also *Hennah* (1877) 13 Cox CC 547 at 549, per Lord Cockburn CJ.
2 *Cramp.* Also see *Marcus* [1981] 2 All ER 833, [1981] 1 WLR 774, CA. Contrast *Cato* [1976] 1 All ER 260 at 268.
3 *Spicer* (1956) 39 Cr App Rep 189.
4 *Spicer*; *Marlow* (1964) 49 Cr App Rep 49.
5 See Price [1988] Crim LR at 206.

11.78 *With intent to procure a miscarriage* In addition to what has already been said about this requirement in para 11.76, there is the issue of whether 'miscarriage' requires the expulsion of the foetus from the womb. It might be thought that it does, but in an Australian case the full court of the Supreme Court of Victoria stated that an intent to cause the gestation to fail would be an intent to procure a miscarriage, since an intent to procure an expulsion is not required.[1] If this view is adopted by our courts, the selective reduction of a multiple pregnancy (where one or more foetuses is destroyed in the womb) in early pregnancy in the interests of the remaining foetuses and the mother is caught by s 58, even though it results not in the expulsion of the foetus(es) but in its (or their) absorption by the womb.[2] It is assumed by s 5(2) of the Abortion Act 1967, referred to in para 11.80, that selective reduction of a multiple pregnancy does constitute a miscarriage for the purposes of s 58. A court is most unlikely to come to a contrary conclusion.

1 *Trim* [1943] VLR 109 at 112. Also see Williams *Textbook of Criminal Law* (2nd edn) 292.
2 Keown 'Selective Reduction of Multiple Pregnancy' (1987) 137 NLJ 1165; Price 'Selective Reduction and Feticide: The Parameters of Abortion' [1988] Crim LR 199. Also see Keown 'Miscarriage: A Medico-Legal Analysis' [1984] Crim LR 604.

11.79 *Unlawfully*[1] By s 5(2) of the Abortion Act 1967, as amended by s 37 of the Human Fertilisation and Embryology Act 1990, anything done with intent to procure a woman's miscarriage (or, in the case of a woman carrying more than one foetus, her miscarriage of any foetus) is unlawfully done unless authorised by s 1 of that Act. The effect of this is to preclude the application of the defence of duress of circumstances, even apparently in cases where it is totally impossible to comply with the procedural requirements of the Act (as where a foreign doctor who is not a registered medical practitioner performs an abortion on a train stuck in deep snow drifts in order to save the mother from immediate death).

1 Grubb 'The New Law of Abortion: Clarification or ambiguity?' [1991] Crim LR 659. For a comparative study of the law relating to the termination of pregnancy, see Freeman (1988) 138 NLJ 233.

11.80 Under s 1(1) of the 1967 Act an offence under s 58 of the 1861 Act is not committed if a pregnancy is terminated by a registered medical practitioner, provided that two such practitioners are of opinion formed in good faith:

a) that the pregnancy has not exceeded its twenty-fourth week[1] and that the continuance of the pregnancy would involve risk, greater than if the pregnancy were terminated, of injury to the physical or mental health of the pregnant woman or any existing children of her family (a question in the determination of which account may be taken of the mother's actual or reasonably foreseeable environment)[2]; or

b) that the termination is necessary to prevent *grave* permanent injury to the physical or mental health of the pregnant woman (a question in the determination of which account may be taken of the woman's actual or reasonably foreseeable environment)[2]; or

c) that the continuance of the pregnancy would involve risk to the life of the pregnant woman, greater than if the pregnancy were terminated; or

d) that there is a substantial risk that if the child were born it would suffer from such physical or mental abnormalities as to be seriously handicapped.

Whether the necessary opinions were formed in good faith is a question for the jury and the medical evidence although important is not conclusive.[3]

Section 1(1) refers to the termination of a pregnancy. As indicated in para 11.78, it has not yet been decided whether the selective reduction of a multiple pregnancy constitutes a miscarriage for the purposes of s 58 of the 1861 Act. Whether or not it does, s 5(2) of the 1967 Act[4] (which assumes that it does) provides that, in the case of a woman carrying more than one foetus, anything done with intent to procure miscarriage of any foetus is authorised by s 1 if the ground for termination of the pregnancy specified in s 1(1)(d) applies in relation to any foetus and the thing is done for the purpose of procuring the miscarriage of that foetus, or if any of the other grounds for termination of the pregnancy specified in s 1 applies. This is important because, if selective reduction is caught by s 58 of the 1861 Act, a medical practitioner who selectively reduced a pregnancy would not otherwise be protected by the Abortion Act. The reason is that generally that Act only protects medical practitioners who terminate a pregnancy and in a literal sense a woman remains pregnant after a selective reduction.

The abortion is lawful only if it is carried out in a National Health Service hospital, NHS Trust hospital or other place (or class of place) approved by the Secretary of State for Health.[5] This limitation and the requirement for the opinion of two registered medical practitioners do not apply in an emergency where a registered medical practitioner performs an abortion, having formed the opinion in good faith that this is immediately necessary to save the mother's life or to prevent grave permanent injury to her physical or mental health.[6]

The reference in s 1(1) to the termination of pregnancy was held by the House of Lords in *Royal College of Nursing of the United Kingdom v Department of Health and Social Security*[7] to mean the whole process of treatment undertaken to terminate a pregnancy. Two results follow from this. First, as their Lordships admitted, provided the various conditions are satisfied, s 1(1) applies where the thing administered or used to abort fails to procure a miscarriage or for some reason the operation is not completed. Second, provided a registered medical practitioner has prescribed the treatment for the termination of a pregnancy, remained in charge and accepted responsibility throughout, and the treatment was carried out in accordance with his directions, the 'termination' will have been by a registered medical practitioner for the purposes of the Act of 1967 and the exemption from liability provided by s 1(1) will extend to any person, such as a nurse, participating in that treatment. This is of particular importance because of a modern method of termination, known as medical induction, in which a very significant part in the treatment is played by nurses.

Section 4 provides that no-one shall be under a legal duty to participate[8] in any treatment authorised by the Act to which he has a conscientious objection, but s 4(2) provides that nothing shall affect any duty to participate in treatment which is necessary to save the life or to prevent grave permanent injury to the physical or mental health of the pregnant woman.

1 The Act does not define the point of time at which pregnancy begins.
2 Abortion Act 1967, s 1(2), as amended by the Human Fertilisation and Embryology Act 1990, s 37.
3 *Smith* [1974] 1 All ER 376, [1973] 1 WLR 1510, CA.
4 As amended by the Human Fertilisation and Embryology Act 1990. s 37.
5 Abortion Act 1967, s 1(3) and (3A).
6 Ibid, s 1(4).
7 [1981] AC 800, [1981] 1 All ER 545, HL.
8 E g actually take part in treatment in a NHS hospital, NHS trust hospital or other approved place (or class of place) for the purpose of terminating a pregnancy, as opposed to making arrangements for such treatment: *Jannaway v Salford AHA* [1988] 3 All ER 1079, HL.

11.81 *Draft Criminal Code Bill* Under cls 66 and 67 of the draft Criminal Code Bill,[1] s 58 would be replaced by two offences, both of which would be subject to the Abortion Act 1967: intentional termination of the pregnancy of a woman by another person and intentional termination by a woman of her own pregnancy. It will be noted that, unlike the present offence which simply requires an attempt to terminate a pregnancy, the proposed offences would require termination. Of course, if an attempt to do so failed, there could be liability for an attempt, except (as now) that where the woman herself was the accused there would be no liability if she was not actually pregnant. The maximum punishment would remain life imprisonment.

1 Law Commission: A Criminal Code for England and Wales (1989): Law Com No 177; see para 3.21 above.

CHILD DESTRUCTION

11.82 Section 1 of the Infant Life (Preservation) Act 1929 provides that any person who, with intent to destroy the life of a child capable of being born alive, by any wilful act causes a child to die before it has an existence independent of its mother, is guilty of child destruction, which, like the last offence, is triable only on indictment and punishable with a maximum of imprisonment for life.

Although the woman will normally be a consenting party, it appears that the offence also covers non-consensual conduct.[1] While the act in question will normally be some sort of surgical interference, any act done with the relevant intent and effect will do, e g hitting the woman.

Section 1 of the 1929 Act contains a proviso that the prosecution must prove 'that the act which caused the death of the child was not done in good faith for the purpose only of preserving the life of the mother', which has been construed as including preserving the mother's physical or mental health.[2] This construction is to be found only in directions by trial judges, and is therefore not binding on any other judge. Arguably, it ignores the word 'only' which appears in the provision.[3] In addition, s 5(1) of the Abortion Act 1967, as amended by s 37 of the Human Fertilisation and Embryology Act 1990, provides that no offence under the 1929 Act is committed by a registered medical practitioner who terminates a pregnancy in accordance with the provisions of the 1967 Act.

This offence was not originally intended to prevent late abortions. Instead, it was introduced to fill the gap between abortion and homicide by providing for the conviction of a person who destroys a child in the process of birth in circumstances where it could not be proved that the child had had an existence independent of the mother so as to be in law the object of murder.[4] However, as a result of the language used, the offence covers the termination of a pregnancy by a method which destroys a foetus capable of being born alive.

The present offence can be distinguished from that under s 58 of the Offences against the Person Act 1861 since it requires the actual destruction of the child while the latter offence is constituted by the act which attempts to procure a miscarriage. Another distinction is that child destruction can be committed only in respect of a child capable of being born alive. 'Capable of being born alive' means capable of being 'born alive' if delivered at the time when the act was done. A child is 'capable of being born alive' when it has reached such a stage of development in the womb that it is capable, if born then, of living and breathing through its lungs without any connection with its mother.[5] As with 'live birth' for the purposes of homicide, provided that this test is satisfied, it is irrelevant that the child is not viable, in the sense that it has no capacity to survive.[6]

Section 1(2) of the 1929 Act provides that the fact that the pregnancy has lasted for 28 weeks is prima facie evidence that the child was capable of being born alive within the definition of child destruction. However, if it is proved that a foetus of less than 28 weeks was nevertheless so developed as to be capable of being born alive, and this is possible in the case of a foetus of 24 weeks or more, it also is protected by the offence of child destruction.

The effect of s 1 of the 1929 Act is reproduced in cl 69 of the draft Criminal Code Bill in language appropriate to the Code.

1 See Price [1988] Crim LR at 206.

2 *Bourne* [1939] 1 KB 687, [1938] 3 All ER 615; *Newton and Stungo* [1958] Crim LR 469.
3 See Poole [1985] Crim LR 807.
4 Para 11.3
5 *Rance v Mid-Downs Health Authority* [1991] 1 All ER 801. Also see *C v S* [1987] 1 All ER 1230, [1987] 2 WLR 1108, CA.
6 Wright 'Capable of Being Born Alive?' (1981) 131 NLJ 188; Wright 'Legality of Abortion by Prostaglandin' [1984] Crim LR 347 and [1985] Crim LR 140. Cf Tunkel [1985] Crim LR 133 and Keown 'The Scope of the Offence of Child Destruction' (1988) 104 LQR 121 who argue that viability of the foetus is an essential requirement of 'being born alive', a view which can only be justified by reading words into the statute (which is not normally permissible, particularly when those words are unambiguous). For a third approach, see Price 'How Viable is the Present Scope of the Offence of Child Destruction?' (1987) 16 Anglo-American Law Review 220.

INTERRELATION OF ABORTION AND CHILD DESTRUCTION

11.83 In spite of the above distinctions, there is an obvious overlap between child destruction and abortion. A successful abortion can be charged as child destruction if it can be proved that the child was capable of being born alive, and, except when the destruction occurs while the child is being born, all child destruction can be charged as abortion.

Upon an indictment for an offence against s 58 of the Offences against the Person Act, the jury may bring in a verdict of child destruction, and vice versa.[1]

1 Infant Life (Preservation) Act 1929, s 2(2) and s 2(3).

12 Sexual offences

12.1 While most sexual offences are protective in purpose, some raise the question of the extent to which the criminal law should enforce social morality.[1] The principal statute in this area is the Sexual Offences Act 1956. Unless otherwise stated the maximum punishment and mode of trial for the offences mentioned in this chapter are provided by s 37 of, and the Second Schedule to, that Act.

The draft Criminal Code Bill[2] restates the present law on sexual offences with some substantial amendments which incorporate recommendations of the Criminal Law Revision Committee. These will be referred to at the appropriate points in this chapter.

1 Paras 3.22–3.29.
2 Law Commission: A Criminal Code for England and Wales (1989): Law Com No 177; see para 3.21 above.

12.2 The definition of many of the offences refers to 'sexual intercourse' which is defined as follows:

> 'Where, on the trial of any offence under this Act, it is necessary to prove sexual intercourse (whether natural or unnatural), it shall not be necessary to prove completion of the intercourse by the emission of seed, but the intercourse shall be deemed complete upon proof of penetration only.'[1]

Penetration is the entry of the penis into the vagina or the anus; the slightest degree is enough and where the intercourse is per vaginam the hymen need not be broken.[2]

Boys under the age of 14 are irrebuttably presumed to be incapable of sexual intercourse and therefore cannot be convicted, as perpetrators, of any offence involving intercourse, although they may be convicted of indecent assault instead (or, possibly, of attempting to commit an offence involving intercourse).[3] A boy under 14 may be convicted of aiding and abetting another of 14 or over to commit an offence involving intercourse with another person.[4] The Criminal Law Revision Committee has recommended that the presumption that a boy under 14 is incapable of sexual intercourse should be abolished.[5] Clause 87 of the draft Criminal Code Bill incorporates this recommendation.

Many sexual offences can only be committed, as perpetrators, by males but even in the other offences the offenders are predominantly male.

1 Sexual Offences Act 1956, s 44.
2 *Hughes* (1841) 9 C & P 752, 2 Mood CC 190; *Lines* (1844) 1 Car & Kir 393.
3 See, further, para 9.3.

4 *Eldershaw* (1828) 3 C & P 396; see para 23.13.
5 Fifteenth Report: Sexual Offences (Cmnd 9213), para 2.48.

Rape

12.3 It is an offence, triable only on indictment, for a man to rape a woman,[1] the maximum punishment being life imprisonment. Formerly, the definition of rape was to be found in the common law but it is now provided by s 1 of the Sexual Offences (Amendment) Act 1976, which essentially gives statutory force to the definition of rape expressed by the House of Lords in *DPP v Morgan*.[2]

1 Sexual Offences Act 1956, s 1.
2 [1976] AC 182, [1975] 2 All ER 347, HL.

ACTUS REUS

12.4 By s 1(1) of the 1976 Act, a man commits the actus reus of rape if he has unlawful sexual intercourse with a woman who at the time of the intercourse does not consent to it. The intercourse must be per vaginam.[1] The word 'unlawful' in s 1(1) of the 1976 Act has been held by the House of Lords not to mean 'extra-marital',[2] as it does where it is used in the definitions in the 1956 Act of other offences involving heterosexual intercourse. The House of Lords held that 'unlawful' added nothing in s 1(1) of the 1976 Act and was mere surplusage. It is not easy to accept that a word in a statutory provision bears no meaning, but if 'unlawful' in s 1(1) does not mean 'extra-marital', as has now been clearly established, it is difficult to know what meaning that term can bear in relation to sexual intercourse.

1 Sexual Offences (Amendment) Act 1976, s 7(2); *Gaston* (1981) 73 Cr App Rep 164, CA.
2 *R* [1991] 4 All ER 481, HL.

12.5 *Without woman's consent* The absence of the woman's consent is an essential feature of the actus reus of rape. Thus, it is rape to have intercourse with a woman who is asleep[1] or otherwise unconscious[2] and therefore unable to give or withhold consent. Moreover, an apparent consent is not a real consent, and rape is committed in the following cases:

a) Where the apparent consent is procured by personal violence or threats of personal violence.[3] The threat need not be an express one but may be implied from past or present conduct.[4] Probably, it need not be of violence to the woman herself. It would be unfortunate if it had to be, since a threat to harm someone else (e g her child) may have a greater effect on a woman than a threat of harm to herself. Clause 89 of the draft Criminal Code Bill incorporates the recommendation of the Criminal Law Revision Committee[5] that a threat of violence to another should suffice.

b) Where the apparent consent is obtained by fraud as to the nature of the act. Thus, in *Williams*[6] a conviction for rape was upheld where a singing master had had sexual intercourse with a girl pupil by pretending that it was a method of training her voice. The girl made no resistance, as she believed him and did not know he was having sexual intercourse with her.

c) Where the apparent consent is obtained by impersonating the woman's husband. [7] There is no good reason why a consent obtained by impersonating someone other than the woman's husband should not likewise be vitiated. Consequently, the Criminal Law Revision Committee's recommendation,[8] incorporated in cl 89 of the draft Criminal Code Bill, that it should seems eminently sensible.

d) Where the female is so mentally deficient[9] or young[10] or drunk[11] that her knowledge and understanding are such that she is not in a position to decide whether to consent or resist.

In *Olugboja*[12] the Court of Appeal stated that a jury should be directed that consent is to be given its ordinary meaning and that there is a difference between consent and submission, ie that a person who submits does not necessarily consent. If this is correct the range of cases in which a woman does not consent for the purposes of rape, despite apparently doing so, would not be limited to those just described. However, pending a further clarification on the matter, it would not be safe to assume that the range of cases is not so limited.

1 *Mayers* (1872) 12 Cox CC 311.
2 *Camplin* (1845) 1 Car & Kir 746, 1 Den 89; *Lang* (1975) 62 Cr App Rep 50.
3 *Jones* (1861) 4 LT 154.
4 Ibid.
5 Fifteenth Report: Sexual Offences (Cmnd 9213), paras 2.26–2.29.
6 [1923] 1 KB 340, 92 LJKB 230, CCA.
7 Sexual Offences Act 1956, s 1(2).
8 Fifteenth Report: Sexual Offences (Cmnd 9213), para 2.25.
9 *Barratt* (1873) LR 2 CCR 81, 43 LJMC 7.
10 *Howard* [1965] 3 All ER 684, [1966] 1 WLR 13, CCA.
11 *Lang* (1975) 62 Cr App Rep 50, CA.
12 [1982] QB 320, [1981] 3 All ER 443, CA.

12.6 It used to be the law that a wife was irrebuttably presumed to consent to sexual intercourse with her husband. This was because she was deemed, by marrying him, to give an irrevocable consent to sexual intercourse with him.[1] From the middle of this century onwards, the presumption was whittled away by the courts devising exceptions to it. Under these exceptions a wife was not irrebuttably presumed to consent to intercourse with her husband if they were separated by a court order[2] or by a formal separation agreement[3], or if a decree nisi of divorce had been granted,[4] or if the husband was subject to a non-cohabitation or non-molestation injunction.[5] Except in these cases, the position until recently was that a husband could not personally commit the offence of rape against his wife, even though she had not consented to intercourse with him at the material time. However, the law was changed in 1991 in *R*[6] where the House of Lords held that, just as the irrebuttable presumption had been narrowed by the exceptions mentioned above, the law could be developed further[7] in the light of the position of a wife in modern society by declaring that the irrebuttable presumption should be abandoned and that consequently a husband could be convicted of rape if he had intercourse with his wife without her consent just as could any man who had intercourse with a woman without her consent.

1 Hale *History of Pleas of the Crown* 629.
2 *Clarke* [1949] 2 All ER 448.
3 *Roberts* [1986] Crim LR 188, CA.
4 *O'Brien* [1974] 3 All ER 663, CA.
5 *Steele* (1976) 65 Cr App Rep 22, CA.

6 [1991] 4 All ER 481, HL. The draft Criminal Code Bill was published before this decision. It states the law as it was at the time, with the addition of another exception, a substantial one, to the irrebuttable presumption of the wife's consent, where they are not living with each other in the same household. Subsequently, in its report on Rape within Marriage (1991): Law Com No 205, the Law Commission recommended that the statutory definition of rape should be amended so as to give statutory force to the decision in *R*. There can be no doubt that the draft Bill will be amended so as to give a husband no exemption if it is ever enacted.
7 See para 3.29.

MENS REA

12.7 The accused must intend to have (i e know that he is having) vaginal sexual intercourse with a woman.[1] In addition, s 1(1) of the 1976 Act requires him to know that the woman does not consent to the intercourse or to be reckless as to whether she consents to it.

At one time, it seemed that 'recklessness' in this context meant *Caldwell-*type[2] recklessness.[3] However, it is clear from the more recent decisions of the Court of Appeal in *Breckenridge*[4] and *Taylor*[5] that a man cannot be guilty of 'reckless rape' unless his attitude as to whether the woman was consenting was that he 'could not care less'. A person cannot care less about something unless he has realised that there is a risk of it; he cannot be said not to care less about something which he has never thought about. Thus, a person who 'could not care less' about whether or not the woman was consenting falls within the subjective definition of recklessness; it follows that only subjective recklessness as to lack of consent suffices for rape.

For the avoidance of doubt, s 1(2) of the Act of 1976 provides that if at a trial for rape the jury has to consider whether a man believed that a woman was consenting, the presence or absence of reasonable grounds for such a belief is a matter to which the jury is to have regard, in conjunction with any other relevant matters, in considering whether he so believed.

Although the statutory definition of sexual intercourse, set out in para 12.2, states that intercourse is 'deemed complete upon proof of penetration only', the Privy Council has construed a similar provision under New Zealand law as follows. ' "Complete" is used in the statutory definition in the sense of having come into existence, but not in the sense of being at an end. Sexual intercourse is a continuing act which only ends with withdrawal.'[6] There can be no doubt that the same view would be taken by an English court. It follows that, if a man only realises that a woman is not (or may not be) consenting after he has penetrated her but continues the intercourse, he can be convicted of rape.[7]

1 *Khan* [1990] 2 All ER 783 at 788. In this case no reference was made by the Court of Appeal to the need for knowledge that the intercourse is vaginal but it would seem implicit in the ruling. See the article by White [1989] Crim LR 539 at 539-40, written before *Khan*.
2 Paras 6.45–6.53.
3 *Pigg* [1982] 2 All ER 591, [1982] 1 WLR 762, CA; *Francis and Thomas* (1982) 77 Cr App Rep 63, CA; *Bashir* (1982) 77 Cr App Rep 59, CA.
4 (1983) 79 Cr App Rep 244, CA.
5 (1985) 81 Cr App Rep 327, CA.
6 *Kaitamaki v R* [1984] 2 All ER 435 at 437.
7 As in *Kaitamaki v R*.

ALTERNATIVE VERDICTS

12.8 On an indictment for rape it is open to the jury, if rape is not proved, to bring in a verdict of attempted rape, or of an offence contrary to ss 2, 3 or 4 of the Sexual Offences Act 1956.[1] The offence under s 4 is that of administering to, or causing to be taken by, a woman any drug with intent to stupefy or overpower her so as thereby to enable any man to have unlawful intercourse with her. The other offences are discussed next.[2]

1 Sexual Offences Act 1956, Sch 2, as amended by Criminal Law Act 1967, Sch 2. Under the general provisions of s 6(3) of the Criminal Law Act 1967, the jury may also bring in an alternative verdict of indecent assault if rape is not proved since every rape includes the essential ingredients of an indecent assault: see *Hodgson* [1973] QB 565, [1973] 2 All ER 552, CA.
2 Paras 12.9–12.11.

Other offences involving sexual intercourse

12.9 Unless the contrary is stated, these other offences are triable only on indictment and punishable on conviction on indictment with up to two years' imprisonment. The intercourse must be per vaginam, and generally it is required to be 'unlawful' which simply means 'extra-marital',[1] as already indicated. 'Unlawful' is an odd word to use, at least in modern times, since extra-marital intercourse would not ordinarily be described as unlawful.[2]

1 *Chapman* [1959] 1 QB 100, [1958] 3 All ER 143, CCA.
2 As was pointed out by Lord Keith of Kinkel in *R* [1991] 4 All ER 481 at 488.

PROCURING UNLAWFUL SEXUAL INTERCOURSE

12.10 The Sexual Offences Act 1956 contains a number of offences of this type, which may be committed by a man or a woman. 'Procuring' involves producing by endeavour (ie bringing about) intercourse which the woman in question would not have embarked on spontaneously or of her own volition,[1] so if she needed no persuading the accused has not committed an offence.[2] Liability for the full offence arises only when the intercourse has taken place; if it does not occur the accused can be charged with an attempt to procure.[3]

1 *A-G's Reference (No 1 of 1975)* [1975] QB 773 at 779, [1975] 2 All ER 684; *Broadfoot* [1976] 3 All ER 753 at 756; *Beck* [1985] 1 All ER 571, [1985] 1 WLR 22, CA.
2 Ibid; *Christian* (1913) 78 JP 112.
3 *Johnson* [1964] 2 QB 404, [1963] 3 All ER 577.

12.11 Two examples of offences of procuring are those under ss 2 and 3 of the Act. These provide, respectively, that it is an offence for a person to procure by threats or intimidation, or to procure by false representations, any woman to have unlawful intercourse (whether with himself[1] or another) in any part of the world. Apart from the element of procuring, these offences are distinguishable from rape in the following ways:

a) Unlike rape, these offences are indictable even though the intercourse was committed abroad, provided the procuring was done within the jurisdiction.
b) 'False representations' are not limited to fraud which vitiates consent for the purposes of rape,[2] and no doubt 'threats or intimidation' is similarly not so limited, but there must be some limit.

The rationale of these offences would seem to be to protect women whose consent, although not vitiated for the purposes of rape, is imperfect for one of the stated reasons.

1 *Williams* (1898) 62 JP 310.
2 *Williams* [1923] 1 KB 340, 92 LJKB 230, CCA.

UNLAWFUL SEXUAL INTERCOURSE WITH A DEFECTIVE

12.12 Under s 7 of the Sexual Offences Act 1956, it is an offence for a man to have unlawful intercourse with a woman who is a defective, her consent being no defence. For the purposes of the various sexual offences where the term is relevant, a 'defective' is a person suffering from a state of arrested or incomplete development of mind which includes severe impairment of intelligence and social functioning.[1] Whether or not there is such severe impairment is to be measured against the standard of normal persons, and not against those of other mentally handicapped persons.[2] Medical evidence is not necessarily required, although it may be advisable, since it is open to a prosecutor simply to support his case on this point by inviting the jury to observe the reactions and behaviour of the alleged victim and draw what they consider to be an appropriate inference.[2] It is a defence for the man to prove that he did not know, and had no reason to suspect, the woman to be a defective. In *Hudson*[3] there is a dictum that 'reason to suspect' requires not only that there was an objective reason to suspect that the woman was a defective but also that the accused, taking into account his mental and other capacities, ought to have suspected. This dictum is out of line with the normal approach to 'reason to suspect', which is a wholly objective one. Consequently, one cannot be confident that the dictum in *Hudson* will be endorsed when it next comes before the courts.

Procuring a defective to have unlawful sexual intercourse anywhere in the world is also an offence, subject to a similar defence.[4]

The rationale of these offences is to protect women who, while they may understand the nature of the act, are easily open to persuasion and exploitation because of their mental defectiveness.

1 Sexual Offences Act 1956, s 45 (as substituted by the Mental Health (Amendment) Act 1982, Sch 3).
2 *Hall* (1987) 86 Cr App Rep 159, CA.
3 [1966] 1 QB 448; [1965] 1 All ER 721, CCA.
4 Sexual Offences Act 1956, s 9.

UNLAWFUL SEXUAL INTERCOURSE WITH GIRLS UNDER 16

12.13 This is criminal for reasons similar to those just mentioned. Section 6 of the Act of 1956 provides that it is an offence for a man to have unlawful sexual intercourse with a girl under the age of 16. This offence is triable either way.[1] Under s 5, it is an offence punishable with life imprisonment for a man to have unlawful intercourse with a girl under 13.

Neither the girl's consent nor the accused's mistake concerning her age is a defence to a charge of unlawful intercourse, but there are two statutory defences which may be available to a man charged under s 6 with unlawful intercourse with a girl who is under the age of 16. First, if a man has gone through a form of marriage with such a girl, it is a defence for him to prove that he believed, and had reasonable cause to believe, that the girl was his wife.[2] Secondly, when a man who has not attained his twenty-fourth birthday is charged with this offence for the first time,[3] it is a defence for him to prove that he believed, and had reasonable cause to believe, that the girl was 16 or over.[4] It must be emphasised that these defences are not available on a charge under s 5.

Clauses 93 and 94 of the draft Criminal Code Bill incorporate the recommendation of the Criminal Law Revision Committee that, irrespective of his age and of whether or not he has previously been charged with such an offence, it should be a defence for a man charged with unlawful intercourse with a girl under 16 or with a girl under 13 that he believed her to be aged 16 or over, whether or not he had reasonable grounds for this belief. The clauses also incorporate the Committee's recommendation that the defence, on a charge of intercourse with a girl under 16, of belief that the girl was his wife should not require a reasonable belief and that such a belief should also be a defence on a charge of intercourse with a girl under 13. The accused would not have the burden of proof in relation to these defences but merely an evidential burden.

1 Magistrates' Courts Act 1980, s 17(1) and Sch 1.
2 Sexual Offences Act 1956, s 6(2).
3 *Rider* [1954] 1 All ER 5, [1954] 1 WLR 463.
4 Sexual Offences Act 1956, s 6(3).

INCEST

12.14 A man who has sexual intercourse with a woman whom he knows to be his grand-daughter, daughter, sister or mother is guilty of incest, as is a woman of or above the age of 16 who permits her grandfather, father, brother or son to have sexual intercourse with her.[1] Incest is punishable with seven years' imprisonment. If the other party is a girl under 13, a more serious offence,[2] punishable with life imprisonment, is committed. A prosecution for incest may not be instituted except by or with the consent of the Director of Public Prosecutions.[3]

Consent is no defence to a charge of incest brought against a male; if the female did not consent, the man will be guilty of rape. The relationship of the persons having intercourse may be traced through the half-blood as well as through the whole blood, and through illegitimate as well as legitimate channels. On the other hand, incest cannot be committed between persons whose relationship is merely that of adoption. Clauses 103 and 104 of the draft Criminal Code Bill incorporate a recommendation by the Criminal Law Revision Committee[4] that the offence should be extended to that relationship.

Apart from the act of intercourse and the fact of relationship, it is essential to prove that the accused had knowledge of the relationship.

Nowadays, the primary aim of the offences of incest is seen as protecting the young and vulnerable against sexual exploitation within the family, rather than preventing any genetic risks which may attach to conception as a result of incest. Consequently, the Criminal Law Revision Committee's recommendations,[4] which are incorporated in cls 103 and 104 of the draft Criminal Code Bill, that brother-sister incest should not be an offence if both are 21 or over and that daughters, granddaughters and sons should be exempted from conviction for incest under the age of 21 seem eminently sensible.

1 Sexual Offences Act 1956, s 10 (incest by a man); s 11 (incest by a woman).
2 This is an offence under s 10 but is a separate offence because of the different sentence in such circumstances: *Courtie* [1984] 1 All ER 740 at 745, per Lord Diplock.
3 Ibid, s 37 and Sch 2.
4 Fifteenth Report: Sexual Offences (Cmnd 9213), paras 8.15–8.36.

Indecency

INDECENT ASSAULT

12.15   An indecent assault can be committed by a person of either sex. There are two separate offences of indecent assault: indecent assault on a woman (including a girl) and indecent assault on a man (including a boy).[1] However, with one exception, both offences are identical. An indecent assault is triable either way,[2] and the maximum punishment on conviction on indictment is ten years' imprisonment.[3]

1 Sexual Offences Act 1956, ss 14 (assault on a woman) and 15 (on a man).
2 Magistrates' Courts Act 1980, s 17(1) and Sch 1.
3 Sexual Offences Act 1985, s 4(3)

12.16   *Actus reus*   An indecent assault can be committed either by an assault or by a battery,[1] but to be an indecent assault the assault or battery, or the circumstances accompanying it, must be capable of being considered indecent by right-minded people.[2] Essentially, this means that it is for the jury (or magistrates) to decide whether what has occurred was so offensive to contemporary standards of modesty and privacy as to be indecent.[2] *Beal v Kelly*[3] provides an example of a case where the assault or battery was not itself indecent but was made so by the surrounding circumstances. D exposed himself to a 14-year-old boy and invited the boy to handle him. The boy refused, whereupon D grabbed his arm and pulled the boy towards him. D's reaching out and grabbing the boy constituted a battery (and no doubt an assault) but it was not in itself indecent. Nevertheless the surrounding circumstances were clearly indecent. Not surprisingly, the Divisional Court held that there had been an indecent assault.

Further consideration is given to the element of indecency in para 12.20.

1 *Rolfe* (1952) 36 Cr App Rep 4, CCA; *Kimber* [1983] 3 All ER 316, [1983] 1 WLR 1118, CA.
2 *Court* [1989] AC 29, [1988] 2 All ER 221, HL.
3 [1951] 2 All ER 763, DC.

12.17   *Without consent*   There cannot be an assault or battery if the victim gives a valid consent to the accused's conduct. The victim's consent is not valid if actual bodily harm was intended and/or caused,[1] nor if it was obtained by fraud as to the accused's identity or by fraud concerning the nature of the transaction, as when the accused pretends that he is performing a medical operation.[2]

In addition, the Act of 1956 provides that a person who is a defective[3] or a person who is under 16[4] cannot give a valid consent. In other words, where such a person has consented, the law by a fiction presumes that he or she has not; this is referred to as the 'fiction of assault'. Thus, although heterosexual sexual intercourse with a boy under 16 is not in itself an offence, if a woman has intercourse with such a boy and touches him before, during or after it in a way which would be an indecent assault if he had not consented she commits an indecent assault, even though the boy was willing and encouraged her.[5] Similarly, a person who indulges in petting with a willing and eager girl under 16 commits an indecent assault on her.[6]

These instances make it clear that in an indecent assault there is no requirement of hostility or aggression.[7]

1 Para 10.3.
2 *Case* (1850) 1 Den 580.

3 Sexual Offences Act 1956, ss 14(4) and 15(3).
4 Ibid, ss 14(2) and 15(2).
5 *Faulkner v Talbot* [1981] 3 All ER 468, [1981] 1 WLR 1528, DC.
6 *McCormack* [1969] 2 QB 442, [1969] 3 All ER 371, CA.
7 A point made in *Faulkner v Talbot* [1981] 3 All ER 468 at 471, [1981] 1 WLR 1528, DC, and approved in *Court* [1989] AC 29, [1988] 2 All ER 221 at 229 by Lord Ackner. Cf para 10.15 as to whether a common assault or a common battery requires an element of hostility.

12.18 *Mens rea* For there to be an assault or battery, the prosecution must, of course, prove that the accused had the requisite mens rea for an assault or battery, as appropriate.[1] In *Court*[2] Lord Ackner, giving the main speech for the majority of the House of Lords, said that the assault or battery had to be intentional. However, although a reckless assault or battery which is indecent is likely to be rare, there is no reason why if it occurs recklessness should not be sufficient mens rea as to the elements required for assault or battery, just as it is is for common assault or battery and for other aggravated assaults.

1 Para 10.14.
2 [1982] 2 All ER 221 at 232.

12.19 Where the other party was under 16 (and therefore unable to give a valid consent), no mens rea as to his or her age is required to be proved by the prosecution. In fact, even a reasonable mistaken belief that the other party was 16 or over is no defence.[1] It is illogical that a man under 24 should have a statutory defence based on his reasonable mistake about the girl's age if he is charged with unlawful intercourse, but no such defence either at common law or by statute if charged with an indecent assault based on exactly the same fact – the intercourse. However, the other defence available in unlawful intercourse, that the accused reasonably believed the girl was his wife because they have gone through a ceremony of marriage, also applies on a charge of indecent assault on a girl;[2] there is no corresponding defence for a woman charged with an indecent assault on a boy.

Where the other party is a defective the accused is only to be treated as guilty of indecent assault by reason of the other's incapacity to consent if he knew or had reason to suspect him or her to be a defective.[3]

1 *Maughan* (1934) 24 Cr App Rep 130, CA.
2 Sexual Offences Act 1956, s 14(3).
3 Ibid, ss 14(4) and 15(3).

12.20 In *Court*[1] the House of Lords held that the accused must also be proved to have intended to commit an assault or battery which in itself, or together with the circumstances accompanying it, is capable of being considered indecent by right-minded people. It is irrelevant whether the accused realised this capability. Although the House spoke of intention in this context, in reality *in part* it was referring to the accused's motive. This provides a rare exception to the rule that motive is irrelevant to liability.[2] Three types of case must be distinguished:

a) *Where the incident (i e the act and its surrounding circumstance) viewed objectively is incapable of being considered indecent* In such a case there cannot be an indecent assault, however indecent the accused's motive. This is illustrated by the ruling in *George*,[3] which was approved in *Court*.[1] In *George* the accused removed a shoe from a girl's foot and, as he admitted, he did so for purposes of sexual gratification. The prosecution submitted that an assault was indecent if committed to satisfy an indecent motive in the accused's mind, even though there were no overt circumstances of indecency. The judge ruled that an assault only became indecent if it was accompanied by circumstances capable of being considered indecent, and that therefore there was no indecent assault on the facts. A similar example would be where a doctor conducts a medically necessary intimate examination of a 14-year-old female patient. The doctor is not guilty of an indecent assault, even if he is also motivated by sexual gratification.

b) *Where the incident, viewed objectively, is inherently indecent* An example would be where a man removes a woman's clothing without her consent. Here, the accused's motives are generally irrelevant. In such a case there is an indecent assault whether (to adopt the example) the accused's motive is sexual gratification, embarrassment or humiliation of the woman, or whatever. The only exception would be where the accused's motive could be said to provide a *lawful* excuse. Otherwise, said the House of Lords in *Court*, there is an irresistible inference that the accused intended to assault his victim in a manner which right-minded people would clearly think indecent. This means that, in a case of the present type, unless the accused satisfactorily raises a lawful excuse, the only mens rea to be proved, apart from that for assault or battery, is knowledge of the circumstances which are indecent. An example of the present type of case would be where by a false representation a doctor obtained consent to an intimate examination of a female patient which was not necessary; the examination would be an assault and an assault which right-minded people would consider indecent, whether the doctor's false representations were motivated by desire for sexual gratification or for some other reason unconnected with the patient's medical needs (such as private research).[4]

c) *Where the asssault or battery is not unambiguously indecent but was capable of being so considered* In this type of case the accused's motive is crucial. If it was indecent there is an indecent assault; otherwise not. *Court* itself was a case in this category. Here, D (a male buttock-fetishist) had spanked a clothed 11-year-old girl who had come into his shop. Dismissing D's appeal against conviction for indecent assault, a majority of the House of Lords (4-1) held that evidence of D's buttock-fetish and hence of his indecent motive had properly been admitted. Conversely, to use an example given in *Court*, a man who accidentally rips open a woman's clothing with his umbrella when using unnecessary force to push his way out of a crowded tube train would not be guilty of an indecent assault (although he could be guilty of a common assault or battery) because what occurred is not inherently indecent, although capable of being so, and his motive was not indecent.[5] It would be different if his motive was to humiliate the woman.

1 [1989] AC 29, [1988] 2 All ER 221, HL.
2 Para 6.72.
3 [1956] Crim LR 52.
4 [1989] AC 29, [1988] 2 All ER 221 at 230-231.
5 [1989] 2 All ER 221 at 229.

INDECENCY WITH CHILDREN

12.21 Since an assault or battery is essential, an invitation to perform indecent acts is not an indecent assault unless accompanied by force or the threat of immediate force.[1] To deal with such conduct in relation to children, the Indecency with Children Act 1960 was passed. It provides two offences.[2] It makes it an offence for a person of either sex to commit an act of gross indecency with or towards a child under 14, and it makes it an offence for a person of either sex to incite a child under 14 to such an act with him or another.

'Gross indecency' must be distinguished from the 'mere' indecency required for indecent assault, and it is probably limited to activities involving indecent contact with the genitalia, including contact through clothing. A person *commits an act of gross indecency with or towards* a child if he co-operates with something grossly indecent by the child or if he does something grossly indecent directed towards the child for purposes of sexual gratification.[2] An example of the former type of case is where a man gets a child to masturbate him, or where he passively permits a child to touch his genitals in circumstances where he can be said to invite the child to continue.[3] An example of the latter type of case is where a man masturbates in the presence of a child and derives excitement from the fact that it is watching, whether or not he has deliberately attracted its attention, but not if he thought it was not observing him (because his actions will not be directed towards the child).[2] A person *incites a child to an act of gross indecency with him* if he exposes his penis and asks the child to touch it.

An offence under the 1961 Act is triable either way and punishable on conviction on indictment with a maximum of two years' imprisonment.[4]

1 *Fairclough v Whipp* [1951] 2 All ER 834, DC; *Burrows* [1952] 1 All ER 58, CCA.
2 *Francis* (1989) 88 Cr App Rep 127, CA.
3 *Speck* [1977] 2 All ER 859, CA.
4 Indecency with Children Act 1960, s 1(1).

INCITEMENT TO INCEST

12.22 By s 54 of the Criminal Law Act 1977, it is an offence, triable and punishable in the same way as that under the Indecency with Children Act 1960, for a man to incite to have sexual intercourse with him a girl under 16 whom he knows to be his grand-daughter, daughter or sister. This offence fills a gap in the law where the girl incited is 14 or 15. A man who incites a girl under 14 to have incestuous intercourse with him is, apart from this offence, guilty of an offence under the 1960 Act. If he incites a girl of 16 or over to such intercourse he is guilty of common law incitement to commit an offence, because such a girl is capable of committing incest (as was shown in para 12.14). But, until the enactment of the present offence, it was not criminal for a man to incite a girl aged 14 or 15 to have incestuous intercourse with him since she was too old for him to commit an offence under the 1960 Act and too young herself to commit incest.[1]

1 *Whitehouse* [1977] QB 868, [1977] 3 All ER 737, CA.

CRIMINAL CODE BILL

12.23 The draft Criminal Code Bill incorporates the following recommendations of the Criminal Law Revision Committee.[1] Indecent assaults on males and females would no longer be punishable as separate offences; cl 111 provides a single offence of indecent assault. Under cl 112 there would be an offence of procuring, by threats or intimidation, another person to participate in gross indecency with the procurer or another, which would punish, for example, a man who coerced a woman to have oral sex with him (in which case an indecent assault would not be committed by him). Under the draft Code the 'fiction of assault' (referred to in para 12.17) would be abolished, so that 'mere' indecency with a consenting child would no longer be an offence. However, an offence would be committed if the indecency was gross. This is because the draft Code provides two offences dealing with conduct of a type covered by the Indecency with Children Act 1960. One offence (cl 115) extends the offences covered by the 1960 Act to protect children under 16. The other (cl 114) deals with such conduct against a child under 13 and provides that the maximum punishment should be increased to five years. It would be a defence to either offence that the accused believed the child to be 16 or over or to be validly married to him or her. The extension of the 1960 Act to children under 16 would render redundant the offence under s 54 of the Criminal Law Act 1977, which does not appear in the draft Code.

Under the draft Code the fiction of assault would also be abolished in relation to defectives. However, cl 108 makes it a separate offence for a person of either sex to commit an act of heterosexual or homosexual gross indecency with a person of either sex who is severely mentally handicapped.

1 CLRC Fifteenth Report: Sexual Offences (Cmnd 9213), para 4.4-4.31, 7.7-7.28 and 9.6.

INDECENT EXPOSURE

12.24 Under s 4 of the Vagrancy Act 1824, it is an offence for a man wilfully and indecently to expose his penis,[1] whether in public or private, with intent to insult any female. This offence is triable only summarily and punishable with three months' imprisonment.

The indecent exposure of any part of the body, whether by a man or, possibly, a woman, and whether to a man or to a woman, can constitute the common law offence of outraging public decency, outlined in para 19.23, if two or more people are able to see the exposure and the exposure transgresses the recognised minimum contemporary standards of decency. Indecent exposure in a public place is sometimes also punishable under local Acts and byelaws.

1 *Evans v Ewels* [1972] 2 All ER 22, [1972] 1 WLR 671, DC.

Abduction

12.25 The abduction of women and girls is punished by ss 17 and 19-21 of the Sexual Offences Act 1956. The offences specify a 'taking' but this does not have to be without the consent of the female,[1] except in the case of the last offence mentioned below. If the girl is glad to go there will still be a 'taking' if the accused has persuaded her, or assists her, to do so.[2] The first three offences of abduction about to be discussed require a taking out of the possession and against the will of her parent or guardian, which means that there must be some conduct by the accused amounting to a substantial interference with the possessory relationship of parent and child. Thus, while permanent deprivation is not required, merely taking a girl for a short walk without her parent's permission, even though sexual misconduct occurs during the walk, does not constitute a taking out of parental possession for the purposes of these offences.[3]

1 *Mankletow* (1853) Dears CC 159, 22 LJMC 115.
2 *Robins* (1844) 1 Car & Kir 456; *Jarvis* (1903) 20 Cox CC 249.
3 *Jones* [1973] Crim LR 621, Crown Ct.

12.26 *Offences* The offences of abduction are:

a) Taking, without lawful authority or excuse, an unmarried girl under 16 out of the possession of her parent or guardian against his will (s 20). The taking need not be with intent that the girl should have intercourse or engage in any other sexual behaviour. A person clearly has lawful authority if he takes a girl out of parental possession pursuant to a court order. It is not certain what constitutes a 'lawful excuse'. It has been held that a good motive, such a religious or philanthropic one, is not a lawful excuse,[1] but it would presumably be a lawful excuse that the girl was taken to protect her from an offence of violence or from an offence such as incest, at least if there was no other reasonable way of doing so.[2] It is irrelevant that the accused reasonably believed that the girl was 16 or over,[3] but it must be proved that he knew she was in the possession of her parent or guardian.[4]

b) Taking an unmarried girl under 18 out of the possession of her parent or guardian against his will with intent that she shall have unlawful (i e extra-marital[5]) intercourse with men or a particular man (s 19). As in the first offence the accused must know that the girl is in the possession of her parent or guardian. Although knowledge that the girl was under 18 need not be proved, it is a defence for the accused to prove that he believed on reasonable grounds that the girl was 18 or over.[6]

c) Taking a woman who is a defective (ie severely mentally handicapped, as explained in para 12.12) out of the possession of her parent or guardian against his will with intent that she shall have unlawful intercourse with men or a particular man (s 21). Although the accused must know that the woman is in the possession of a parent or guardian, he need not be proved to have known that she was a defective; however, he has a defence if he proves that he neither knew nor had reason to suspect this.[7] Clause 109 of the draft Criminal Code Bill extends this offence to male victims and to a further intent in relation to buggery or gross indecency. It would be a defence if the accused did not believe that the victim was suffering from any mental handicap.

These three offences of abduction are punishable with two years' imprisonment. Besides the offence in c), there are no corresponding offences in the draft Criminal Code Bill. The Bill does, however, provide a number of offences of abduction of children under 16.

d) Taking away or detaining a woman of any age against her will with intent that she shall marry or have unlawful intercourse with the accused or another, if she is so taken or detained either by force or for the sake of her property or expectations of property (s 17). This offence is punishable with 14 years' imprisonment. There is no corresponding offence in the draft Criminal Code Bill.

All the above offences are triable only on indictment.

1 *Tegerdine* (1982) 75 Cr App Rep 298, CA.
2 See the judgment of Denman J in *Prince* (1875) LR 2 CCR 154, 44 LJMC 122.
3 *Prince* (1875) LR 2 CCR 154, 44 LJMC 122.
4 *Hibbert* (1869) LR 1 CCR 184, 38 LJMC 61.
5 *Chapman* [1959] 1 QB 100, [1958] 3 All ER 143, CCA; *Jones* [1973] Crim LR 710, Crown Ct.
6 Sexual Offences Act 1956, s 19(2).
7 Ibid, s 21(2).

Buggery

12.27 Section 12 of the Sexual Offences Act 1956 provides that it is an offence, triable only on indictment, for a person to commit buggery with another person or an animal. Buggery is defined by the common law and consists of sexual intercourse between a man and a woman or another man per anum, or between a man or woman and an animal per anum or per vaginam.[1] In the case of buggery between human beings, both parties are criminally liable as perpetrators, unless one of them is not a consenting party.

1 Hale *Pleas of the Crown* vol 1, 669; Hawkins *Pleas of the Crown* vol 1, c 4; East *Pleas of the Crown* vol 1, 480.

12.28 *Male homosexual buggery: when not an offence* Where the buggery is between two men the law has been qualified by the Sexual Offences Act 1967 which was passed in consequence of the recommendations of the Wolfenden Committee.[1] Section 1 of that Act provides that it is not an offence for a man to commit buggery with another man if three conditions are satisfied:

a) The act must be done in private. Section 1(2) states that an act is not done 'in private' if more than two persons are present, or if it is done in a lavatory to which the public have access. Apart from this, the question of privacy is one of fact and the jury must answer it by considering all the surrounding circumstances, such as the time, the nature of the place and the likelihood of third parties coming upon the scene.[2]

b) Both parties must consent. A person suffering from severe mental handicap is incapable of consenting, but the absence of knowledge or reason to suspect that the other party was suffering from severe mental handicap is a defence if it is proved by the accused. A 'severe mental handicap' means a state of arrested or incomplete development of mind which includes severe impairment of intelligence and social functioning.[3]

c) Both parties must have attained the age of 21. In the draft Criminal Code Bill the minimum age is reduced to 18.

The accused has an evidential burden to raise these three conditions,[4] but if he satisfies it the prosecution has the burden of proving that one of them did not exist.[5] The provisions of s 1 do not apply where the act takes place on a United Kingdom merchant ship between two members of the crew of such a ship or ships.

1 Cmnd 247; see para 3.26.
2 *Reakes* [1974] Crim LR 615, CA.
3 What was said about proof of severe mental handicap in para 12.12 is equally applicable in this offence: *Robbins* [1988] Crim LR 744, CA.

4 *Spight* [1986] Crim LR 817, CA.
5 Sexual Offences Act 1967, s 1(6).

12.29 *Offences and punishment* There are elaborate provisions under the 1967 Act[1] with regard to the punishment of buggery, which provide that the maximum varies with the circumstances. The House of Lords in *Courtie*[2] held that one effect of these provisions is to create a number of specific offences of buggery:

a) Buggery with a boy under 16 (or heterosexual buggery or buggery with an animal). This is punishable with life imprisonment, whether committed in public or in private and even though consensual.

b) Buggery with a male aged 16 or over without his consent. This is punishable with up to ten years' imprisonment, whether committed in public or in private.

c) Buggery with a consenting male aged 16–20 by an accused of 21 or over. This is punishable with a maximum of five years' imprisonment, whether committed in public or in private.

d) Buggery with a consenting male aged 16–20 by an accused of under 21. This is punishable with up to two years' imprisonment, whether committed in public or in private.

e) Buggery committed otherwise than in private between consenting men of 21 or over (or anywhere on a UK merchant ship between two crew-members of 21 or over). This is punishable with up to two years' imprisonment.

There can be little doubt that a reasonable but mistaken belief that the other party is over the relevant age limit is no defence to one of these offences.[3]

1 Sexual Offences Act 1956, Sch 2; Sexual Offences Act 1967, s 3.
2 [1984] AC 463, [1984] 1 All ER 740, HL.
3 See *Prince* (1875) LR 2 CCR 154, 44 LJMC 122. See para 8.2.

12.30 *Related offences* Under the general principles of the criminal law a person who procures the commission of an unlawful act of buggery is guilty of buggery as an accomplice. Where the buggery is not unlawful under the above provisions of the 1967 Act, it is nevertheless an offence, triable either way[1] and punishable with two years' imprisonment on conviction on indictment, to procure[2] another to commit it with a third person.[3]

By s 16 of the 1956 Act, assault with intent to commit buggery is always an offence, triable only on indictment and punishable with a maximum of ten years' imprisonment.

1 Magistrates' Courts Act 1980, s 17(1) and Sch 1.
2 Para 12.10.
3 Sexual Offences Act 1967, s 4(1).

12.31 *Draft Criminal Code Bill* Under the draft Bill consensual heterosexual buggery would no longer be an offence except where it is with a girl under 16 (in which case the same defences would be available as on a charge of unlawful intercourse with a girl under 16). Buggery with an animal would be renamed bestiality and would be a separate offence, triable summarily only.

Gross indecency

12.32   Section 13 of the Sexual Offences Act 1956 provides that it is an offence, which is triable either way,[1] for a man:

a) to commit an act of gross indecency with another man; or
b) to be a party to the commission of an act of gross indecency with another man; or
c) to procure[2] the commission by a man of an act of gross indecency with another man (who may be the procurer).

By way of comparison it should be noted that lesbian conduct between women is not an offence unless one of them is under 16 or one of them does not consent, in which cases an indecent assault is committed.

1 Magistrates' Courts Act 1980, s 17(1) and Sch 1.
2 Para 12.10.

12.33   *Gross indecency: definition*   Gross indecency bears the same meaning as that already outlined in relation to the offence of gross indecency with children, ie there must be some activity involving contact with the genitalia, as in the cases of mutual masturbation, masturbation of one by the other or oral sex. The gross indecency by one man must be *with* the other, and this means that it must be committed with his consent, overt or tacit, and not simply that it is committed towards him or in his presence. Thus, the offence requires the co-operation or participation of both men, both of whom may be convicted as perpetrators, but provided this is so there can be a conviction even though neither man touches the other, as where one man masturbates himself in front of another who, overtly or tacitly, consents to this act of gross indecency.[1]

1 *Preece and Howells* [1977] QB 370, [1976] 2 All ER 690, CA.

12.34   *When not an offence*   Gross indecency falling within categories a) and b) above is not an offence if the three conditions mentioned in the Sexual Offences Act 1967 are satisfied. Moreover, if these three conditions are satisfied the offence of procuring described in category c) is not committed if the indecency procured is with the procurer.[1]

1 Sexual Offences Act 1967, s 4(3).

12.35   *Offences and punishment*   As a result of the provisions relating to punishment[1] and of the interpretation of the corresponding provisions for buggery in *Courtie*,[2] there are three offences of gross indecency:

a) Gross indecency with a man of under 21 by a man of 21 or over. This is punishable with five years' imprisonment, whether it takes place in public or in private.
b) Gross indecency with a man of under 21 by a man of under 21. This is punishable with a maximum of two years' imprisonment, whether it takes place in public or in private.
c) Gross indecency committed otherwise than in private where both men are 21 or over (or anywhere in a UK merchant ship between two crew-members of 21 or over). This is punishable with a maximum of two years' imprisonment.

1 Sexual Offences Act 1956, Sch 2; Sexual Offences Act 1967, s 3.
2 [1984] AC 463, [1984] 1 All ER 740, HL; para 12.29.

Homosexual offences: restriction on prosecutions

12.36 By s 8 of the Sexual Offences Act 1967, no prosecution may be instituted, except by or with the consent of the Director of Public Prosecutions, against any man for buggery with, or gross indecency with, another man where either of them was under 21 at the time of the offence.

13   Offences against property 1: Theft

13.1   The law concerning theft and related offences, such as robbery, burglary, various offences involving deception, blackmail and handling stolen goods, is contained in the Theft Acts 1968 and 1978. Before the Theft Act 1968 came into force, the law concerning theft and related offences was extremely complicated, but it is fortunately unnecessary to say anything about it because that Act, which is based on the Eighth Report of the Criminal Law Revision Committee,[1] is an entirely new code.

As its title states, this chapter is concerned with the offence of theft, which is governed by ss 1 to 7 of the Theft Act 1968 (hereafter described in this chapter as 'the Act').

Clauses 139 to 145 of the draft Criminal Code Bill restate the existing definition of theft.[2]

1 Theft and Related Offences (Cmnd 2977) (1966).
2 Law Commission: A Criminal Code for England and Wales (1989): Law Com No 177; see para 3.21 above.

The elements

13.2   Section 1(1) of the Act provides that a person is guilty of theft if he dishonestly appropriates property belonging to another with the intention of permanently depriving the other of it. Theft is triable either way.[1] By s 7[2] of the Act, it is punishable with a maximum of seven years' imprisonment on conviction on indictment.

The actus reus of theft is the appropriation of property belonging to another. The mens rea is dishonesty coupled with the intention of permanently depriving the other of the property appropriated.

1 Magistrates' Courts Act 1980, s 17(1) and Sch 1.
2 As amended by the Criminal Justice Act 1991, s 26.

Actus reus

APPROPRIATION

13.3   Section 3(1) of the Act provides that:

'Any assumption by a person of the rights of an owner amounts to an appropriation, and this includes, where he has come by the property (innocently or not) without stealing it, any later assumption of a right to it by keeping or dealing with it as owner.'

The essence of this definition is an 'assumption. . . of the rights of an owner'. An owner of property has many rights in relation to it; they include the rights to use the property in question, to destroy it, to give it away, to sell it, and so on. However, in the consolidated appeals, *Morris* and *Anderton v Burnside*[1] (hereafter simply referred to as *Morris*), where the rest of their Lordships simply agreed with the speech of Lord Roskill, the House of Lords held that, despite the use of the words 'the rights' at the beginning of s 3(1), s 3 as a whole indicated that an appropriation does not require an assumption of all the rights of an owner and that it is enough that there has been an assumption of any of the rights of the owner. This conclusion does violence to the clear words of the section, despite the explanation given by Lord Roskill, but it must now be regarded as representing the correct interpretation of the words in question.[2] It is certainly very odd that the phrase 'assumption of *the* rights of *an* owner' should mean 'assumption of *any* of the rights of *the* owner'. We shall see later on that it is possible to steal from a person who is not the owner but to whom the property 'belongs' for the purposes of theft and that an owner can steal his own property. Presumably, *'the owner'* in the House of Lords' formulation must be read as 'the person to whom the property belongs' where the alleged theft is not from the owner.

1 [1984] AC 320, [1983] 3 All ER 288, HL.
2 This was accepted by the Privy Council in *Chan Man-sin v A-G of Hong Kong* [1988] 1 All ER 1.

13.4 In *Morris* the accused had in each case removed goods from a supermarket shelf and replaced the price labels attached to them with price labels showing a lesser price than the originals. They then took the goods to the checkout. Burnside was arrested before he had paid for the goods but Morris was arrested after he had paid the lesser prices. The House of Lords held that both accused had committed theft of the goods, the appropriation being complete when they switched the price labels (at which time they had the mens rea for theft) because they had thereby assumed one or more of the rights of the owner. It was irrelevant that they had not at that time assumed all the rights of an owner. Lord Roskill said: 'If, as I understand all of your Lordships to agree, the concept of appropriation in s 3(1) involves an element of adverse interference with or usurpation of some right of the owner, it is necessary . . . to consider whether that requirement is satisfied in either of these cases . . . [I]f a shopper with some perverted sense of humour, intending only to create confusion and nothing more, . . . switches labels, I do not think that that act of label-switching is without more an appropriation,[1] though it is not difficult to envisage some cases of label-switching which could be. In cases such as the present, it is in truth a combination of these actions, the removal from the shelf and the switching of the labels which evidences adverse interference with or usurpation of the rights of the owner. *Those acts, therefore, amount to an appropriation.*[2] . . . It is the doing of one or more acts which individually or collectively amount to such adverse interference with or usurpation of the owner's rights which constitute appropriation under s 3(1) and I do not think it matters where there is more than one such act in which order the successive acts take place, or whether there is any interval in time between them.'[3]

The importance of the interpretation given to s 3(1) in *Morris* is shown by *Governor of Pentonville Prison, ex p Osman*[4] which was concerned with the point of time at which the theft of a credit in a bank account,[5] by dishonest dealing with the account, occurred. The Divisional Court held that an appropriation, and therefore the theft, occurred when a cheque drawn on the account was presented or an instruction given to debit the account was sent to the bank. The reason was that presenting the cheque or sending the instruction is the exercise of one of the rights of the owner of the bank credit, the right to have his cheques or instructions relating to the account met.[6]

The result is, for example, that if D, in England, dishonestly sends a telex message to P's bank in the United States instructing it to pay X in Canada $1,000,000 out of P's bank account, there is an appropriation in England of P's bank credit and an offence of theft within the jurisdiction of the English courts.

It follows from the above that it is irrelevant that the assumption of a right of the owner has no effect on the owner's property or his enjoyment of it.

1 It is not immediately obvious why this is not an appropriation. Doubtless, the mischievous person is not guilty of theft, because he lacks an intention permanently to deprive the store of the property, but his conduct nevertheless seems to constitute an appropriation within the definition of *Morris*. The only possible reason why there may be no appropriation would seem to be that the accused does not intend any adverse interference with or usurpation of any of the owner's rights; see para 13.16.
2 Italics supplied.
3 [1983] 3 All ER 288 at 293.
4 [1989] 3 All ER 701, (1988) 91 Cr App Rep 281, DC.
5 In relation to the theft of bank credits, see further para 13.20.
6 Cf *Tomsett* [1985] Crim LR 369, CA, where the contrary view was taken by the Court of Appeal after prosecuting counsel had declined to argue the point. In *Governor of Penonville Prison, ex p Osman* the Divisional Court held that consequently the decision in *Tomsett* was not a binding authority on the point.

13.5 *Consent, authority and appropriation.* In *Lawrence v Metropolitan Police Comr*[1] Viscount Dilhorne, giving the judgment of the House of Lords, stated that the words 'without the consent of the owner' are not to be implied into the definition of the offence. The relevant passages from Viscount Dilhorne's speech are not entirely clear. It may be that his Lordship simply meant that those words were not to be implied into the definition of theft in s 1(1) since they were implicit in the concept of appropriation and it would be otiose to imply them into the express words of s 1(1). On the other hand, it may be that his Lordship meant that there could be an appropriation even though the owner (or other person to whom the property belonged) had consented to the accused's acts.

Whatever Viscount Dilhorne may have intended, it is clear from subsequent cases that the relevant passages are not to be understood in this sense. This is because, as was affirmed by the House of Lords in *Morris*, for there to be an assumption of the rights (or any right) of the owner, there must be an act by way of adverse interference with or usurpation of those rights (or any of them), and there will not be such an interference or usurpation if what is done with the property is expressly or impliedly authorised by the owner of it. Between the decisions in *Lawrence* and *Morris* this view was taken by the Court of Appeal in, for example, *Skipp* and *Hircock* (which are discussed in para 13.15) and *Eddy v Niman* (see para 13.12) and subsequent to *Morris* it was taken by the Court of Appeal in *Fritschy*[2] and *McHugh and Tringham*[3].

1 [1972] AC 626, [1971] 2 All ER 1253, HL; para 14.45.
2 [1985] Crim LR 745, CA.
3 (1988) 88 Cr App Rep 385, CA.

13.6 In *Fritschy*[1] P told D to collect some Krugerrands in England and take them to Switzerland. When D collected them, he dishonestly intended to deal with them as his own. However, he took them to Switzerland in accordance with his instructions. He then disposed of them for his own benefit. No doubt his unauthorised dealing with the Krugerrands in Switzerland satisfied the requirements for theft but that was outside the jurisdiction of the English courts. The question for the Court of Appeal was whether D had committed theft within the jurisdiction. Applying *Morris*, it held that D had not committed theft because everything which he had done within the jurisdiction had been authorised by P and therefore there had been no appropriation by him within the jurisdiction.

In *McHugh and Tringham*[2] D and another director of a company had unauthorisedly drawn cheques on the company's bank account in favour of subsidiary companies in the group. Dismissing D's appeal against conviction for theft of bank credits, the Court of Appeal held that an act done with the authority of the company, express or implied, could not in general amount to an appropriation but that an act done without such authority would.

A similar approach was taken by the Privy Council in *A-G of Hong Kong v Chan Nai Keung*,[3] where D, the director of a company which manufactured and exported textiles and had the general authority of the company to deal in its export quotas (which were property in law),[4] sold them dishonestly and at an undervalue in fraud of the company. The Privy Council held that, while D as an agent of the company would not have assumed any of the rights of the owner if he had acted within the scope of his authority, he had assumed such rights by acting as he had because he had no authority to sell the quotas at an undervalue in fraud of the company. Therefore, he had appropriated the quotas in question,

1 [1988] Crim LR 745, CA.
2 (1988) 88 Cr App Rep 385, CA.
3 [1987] 1 WLR 1339, (1987) 3 BCC 403, PC.
4 Para 13.20.

13.7 Subsequent to these cases a contrary view was taken by the Court of Appeal in 1988 in *Philippou*[1] and, in particular, *Dobson v General Accident, Fire and Life Assurance Corpn plc*.[2] In these cases the Court of Appeal held that the House of Lords in *Lawrence* had held that there could be an appropriation even though the owner had consented to what was done and that nothing in *Morris* contradicted this. The facts in *Dobson* were that P had parted with a watch and a ring under a contract of sale in exchange for a building society cheque which turned out to be stolen and worthless. The Court of Appeal (Civil Division) held that P had lost his watch and ring by theft within the meaning of his insurance policy and of the Act because, for the purposes of s 1(1), an appropriation could occur even if the owner consented to the property being taken.

1 (1989) 89 Cr App Rep 290, CA.
2 [1990] QB 274, [1989] 3 All ER 927, CA.

13.8 These decisions threw the law into disarray since there was a clear conflict in the authorities. This conflict has for all practical purposes, been resolved by the later decision of the Court of Appeal in *Gomez*,[1] which affirmed that the law is as laid down by *Morris* as described above (i e there must be an adverse interference with or usurpation of one or more of the owner's rights, which cannot occur if what is done is expressly or impliedly authorised by the owner).

In *Gomez* D1, an assistant manager of an electrical goods shop, induced his manager to authorise the supply of goods to D2 in exchange for two building society cheques which were worthless because they were stolen. D1 knew this but concealed it from the manager and told him that the cheques were 'as good as cash'. D1 and D2 were charged with theft of the goods. The Court of Appeal held that the judge had been wrong to rule that on these facts there had been an appropriation of the goods by D2 when he took possession of them; the Court of Appeal's reason was that D2 was entitled (i e authorised) to take possession of the goods under the voidable contract of sale. Clearly, the decision in *Dobson v General Accident* was directly applicable to the facts in *Gomez* but the Court of Appeal refused to follow it. Instead, it held itself bound to follow the statement in *Morris* that the concept of appropriation 'involves not an act expressly or impliedly author-ised by the owner but an act by way of adverse interference with or usurp-ation of [the owner's] rights'.

1 [1991] 3 All ER 394, CA.

13.9 There can be no doubt that, pending a review by the House of Lords, the courts will follow the decision in *Gomez* and not the decisions in *Philippou* and *Dobson v General Accident*.[1] In effect, those decisions have been overruled by *Gomez*.

Gomez is also important in that it clarifies a couple of other points. One will be mentioned here, and the other later.[2] In *Dobson v General Accident* Parker LJ (but not the other Lord Justice) distinguished between 'mere consent' by the owner and 'express authority' by the owner; the former, he said, would not prevent a dealing with property being an appropriation, whereas the latter would. It was decided in *Gomez* that *Morris* was not to be whittled down in this way. No dealing with property can amount to an appropriation if it is done with the owner's consent or express authority. As the Court of Appeal stated in *Gomez*: 'Guilt or innocence should not depend upon so fine a distinction, if indeed the distinction be shown to exist.'[3]

1 See *Shuck* [1992] Crim LR 209, CA.
2 Para 14.45.
3 [1991] 3 All ER 394 at 399.

13.10 As the reader will have observed, *Gomez* left open the true meaning of Viscount Dilhorne's statement in *Lawrence*. This is not of practical importance now since in *Gomez* the Court of Appeal stated that 'if there is a difference between [*Lawrence* and *Morris*], that was not the view taken by their Lordships in *Morris*, and that is the decision which we must follow'.[1]

1 [1991] 3 All ER 394 at 398.

13.11 *Examples of appropriation* The most common type of appropri-ation is one by unauthorised taking of possession of property; taking pos-session is clearly one of the rights of the owner. A pickpocket who takes someone's wallet clearly appropriates it. A shopper who removes goods from a shelf in a supermarket and conceals them in his shopping bag, intending not to pay for them, clearly appropriates the goods.[1] Obviously, the shopper's conduct amounts to an adverse interference with or usurp-ation of the rights of the owner (the supermarket company), whereas it does not where an honest shopper removes goods from a shelf and puts them in the trolley provided in order to take them to the checkout in order to pay for them; in such a case there is no adverse interference or usurpation because the shopper's acts are authorised, expressly or impliedly, by the owner.

It appears that a person can appropriate property even though he does not take possession of it in a technical sense but merely assumes unauthorised control of it, however momentary. This is shown by the decision in *Corcoran v Anderton*,[2] where it was held that a robbery (which requires a theft, and therefore an appropriation) was committed where a woman's handbag was wrested from her grasp, even though it then fell to the ground and was not made off with. It remains to be seen whether the mere taking hold of a wallet, handbag or other article by a pickpocket or the like in order to take it constitutes an appropriation; if it does not it is certainly an attempt to do so and could lead to a conviction for attempted theft.

1 *McPherson* (1972) 117 Sol Jo 13, CA.
2 (1980) 71 Cr App Rep 104, DC.

13.12 An act may be done with the owner's authority even though the accused has a secret dishonest intention with respect to the property.

Fritschy[1] provides an example of this. Another is provided by *Eddy v Niman*,[2] which was approved in *Morris*. It was held in *Eddy v Niman* that there was no appropriation of goods by a person who, intending not to pay for them, removed them from the supermarket shelf and placed them in the receptacle provided but then abandoned his scheme and left the store without the goods; what he had done with the goods was impliedly authorised by the supermarket. A fortiori, the mere removal of goods from the shelf would not have been an appropriation.[3] In *Eddy v Niman* Webster J said that some overt act inconsistent with the owner's rights was required, but in *Morris* Lord Roskill thought that the act need not be overt. What constitutes a non-overt act is far from clear, and in *Fritschy*[4] the Court of Appeal stated that it found Lord Roskill's view difficult to understand. Fortunately, Lord Roskill's view, being expressed obiter, is not binding and is likely to be ignored (whatever it may mean) in practice.

1 [1985] Crim LR 745, CA; para 13.6.
2 (1981) 73 Cr App Rep 237, DC.
3 *Morris* [1983] 3 All ER 288 at 293, per Lord Roskill.
4 This part of the Court of Appeal's judgment does not appear in [1985] Crim LR 745, but is contained in the transcript of the judgment, which is available on Lexis.

13.13 There can be an appropriation by a person even though he never possesses the property concerned, as where:

a) as in *Pitham and Hehl*,[1] D enters P's house in P's absence and offers to sell P's furniture to X, since the right to sell is one of the rights of ownership;

b) D destroys P's property without touching it, eg by throwing stones at a window or shooting domestic animals, since the right of destruction is one of the rights of the owner. However, such conduct would also constitute an offence under the Criminal Damage Act 1971 and be more appropriately charged under that Act.

On the other hand, the definition of appropriation means that if a person delivers a cheque (supported by a cheque card) drawn on an account which has inadequate funds and for which he has no overdraft facilities, he does not thereby appropriate any property belonging to another. This is because he has *not assumed any of the rights of the bank* to that part of the funds to which the amount specified in the cheque corresponds.[2] Nor, for the same reason, is there an appropriation when the bank transfers the specified amount to the payee of the cheque.[3] On the other hand, such a person can be convicted of the separate offence of obtaining a pecuniary advantage by deception described in para 14.48, and he may also be guilty of one or more other offences of deception,[4] depending on what precisely he has obtained by handing over the cheque.

We shall see in para 13.20 that, if P's account is in credit and D unauthorisedly writes a cheque on it, D is guilty of the theft of the relevant part of the bank balance belonging to P.

1 (1976) 65 Cr App Rep 45, CA. The actual decision in this case is open to criticism: see Smith *Law of Theft* (6th edn), para 28.
2 *Navvabi* [1986] 3 All ER 102, [1986] 1 WLR 1311, CA. All the use of the cheque card and delivery of the cheque does is to give the payee a contractual right against the bank to be paid the specified sum from the bank's funds on presentation of the cheque: ibid.
3 *Navvabi.*
4 Paras 14.27–14.64.

13.14 *Appropriation by a person in possession* As already indicated, a person can appropriate property even though he is already in possession or control of it. This is made clear by the latter part of s 3(1), which provides that 'appropriation' 'includes, where he [the accused] has come by property (innocently or not) without stealing it, any later assumption of a right to it by keeping or dealing with it as owner.' Thus, if D helps himself to P's umbrella in order to go out during a shower but intending to return it when he comes back, he does not steal it at that stage because, although there is an appropriation of the umbrella, it is not accompanied by an intention permanently to deprive P. However, if D subsequently decides to keep the umbrella or to sell it, and does so, he is then guilty of theft because his later assumption of a right to it, by keeping or dealing with it as owner, constitutes an appropriation which is accompanied by an intention permanently to deprive P.

In *Pilgram v Rice-Smith*[1] it was held that a supermarket assistant, who, in league with a customer, wrapped goods and understated their price on the wrapper so that the customer would be charged less than the true price at the checkout, had thereby appropriated the goods. Similarly, if D hires a television set from P and later purports to sell it as his own to X he thereby appropriates it.

In both these instances the requirements for an appropriation laid down by s 3(1), as interpreted in *Morris*, are satisfied since the conduct in question, being unauthorised by the owner, involved an adverse interference with or usurpation of one or more of his rights.

1 [1977] 2 All ER 658, [1977] 1 WLR 671, DC.

13.15 *Obtaining by deception: an appropriation?* Following the Court of Appeal's decision in *Gomez*,[1] there can be no doubt that a person who obtains ownership of property by deception does not thereby appropriate it. Moreover, a person who by deception dishonestly obtains possession of property, intending permanently to deprive the owner of it, does not appropriate the property when he receives delivery of it, because that is an authorised act, but only if he later does something unauthorised with it. In *Skipp*[2] D, by posing as a genuine haulage contractor, obtained instructions to collect two loads of oranges and one of onions in London and to deliver them in Leicester. D collected the loads but made off with them. The Court of Appeal held that, although D might have intended to deprive the owner permanently when he collected each load, he did not appropriate the goods when he collected them pursuant to his instructions but he did when he diverted them from their true destination. Similarly, in *Hircock*[3] it was held that D, who had obtained by deception possession of a car under a hire purchase agreement and later dishonestly sold it, had not appropriated the car when he received possession of it, although he did when he unauthorisedly sold it.

1 [1991] 3 All ER 394, CA.
2 [1975] Crim LR 114, CA.
3 (1978) 67 Cr App Rep 278, CA.

13.16 *Relevance of accused's state of mind* It is clear from *Morris* that whether or not the accused's conduct constitutes an appropriation may depend on his state of mind which accompanies it, the conduct in itself being neutral. Whether it constitutes an adverse interference with or usurpation of a right of the owner depends upon whether the accused intended such interference or usurpation, either immediately or ultimately, or not. For example, if D finds P's purse lying in the street, picks it up and puts it in his pocket, D's acts will constitute an appropriation if he intends to keep the purse for himself but not if he intends to return it to P.

13.17 *An exception for the bona fide purchaser* Section 3(2) excludes a particular type of case which falls within the definition of appropriation in s 3(1) from being an appropriation.

Section 3(2) of the Act provides that 'where property or a right or interest in property is or purports to be transferred for value to a person acting in good faith, no later assumption by him of rights which he believed himself to be acquiring shall, by reason of any defect in the transferor's title, amount to theft of the property'. The effect of the subsection is that, if A steals goods from B and sells them to D who acts in good faith (ie D neither knows nor suspects that they are stolen), a refusal by D to restore the goods (or his disposal of them) after his discovery of the theft by A is not theft by him from B. Although the refusal or disposal in itself would be no offence, if D, having discovered the truth, sold the goods this would amount to obtaining the purchase price by deception, contrary to s 15 of the Act, because of an implied representation that D was the owner of the goods.

It must be emphasised that the exception in s 3(2) is limited to cases where the goods were *transferred for value* to the accused who acted in *good faith*.

13.18 *Appropriation by omission?* The statements made about 'appropriation' by the House of Lords in *Morris* and statements made in other reported cases have been in terms of an act or acts. However, it appears that an appropriation can be made by a mere omission, such as a failure to restore property to its owner. This is implicit in s 3(1) which speaks of a person appropriating by 'keeping as owner' property which he has come by innocently, since 'keeping' does not necessarily involve doing any act. Whether or not a particular omission in relation to property can constitute an appropriation of it depends very much on the accused's state of mind which accompanies it, since it is this which will determine whether or not there has been any adverse interference with or usurpation of any right of the owner. This is shown by *Broom v Crowther*,[1] where D bought a stolen theodolite, suspecting that it was stolen. D later discovered that the theodolite had been stolen but simply let it remain in his bedroom for a week, until he was interviewed by the police, while he tried to make up his mind what to do with it. Allowing D's appeal against conviction, the Divisional Court held that, while there might be cases where (having regard to all the circumstances of the case and the fact that an accused had kept stolen goods for a period of time after discovering that they were stolen) the inference might properly be drawn that he was keeping them as owner, the inference could not be drawn here because that period of time was short and during it D had merely been wondering what to do with the theodolite.

1 (1984) 148 JP 592, DC.

13.19 *Other points* Once a person has appropriated property belonging to another with the appropriate mens rea he is guilty of theft, but such an appropriation, even though it may continue for a short period of time,[1] is a once and for all happening and subsequent appropriations of the property by the thief do not constitute fresh commissions of theft.[2] As an eminent writer has expressed it: 'Otherwise it would be possible, in theory, to convict a thief of theft of a silver teapot every time he uses it to make the tea'.[3]

A person cannot be convicted of theft unless it is proved that he appropriated a *specific piece of property* belonging to another with the appropriate mens rea. It is not in itself enough that D's conduct leads (as D realises) to someone else becoming indebted to another. This is shown by *Navvabi*,[4] where D, by unauthorisedly issued cheques backed by a cheque card, obtained gaming chips in a casino. Because the cheques were backed by the cheque card, the bank was bound to honour them, ie it became indebted to the casino. The Court of Appeal quashed D's conviction for theft, since there was no appropriation by him of that part of the bank's funds to which the sums specified in the cheques corresponded. Clearly, it was impossible to point to any specific property of the bank which had been appropriated.

A person charged with stealing a part of specific property can be convicted on that charge even though it emerges at the trial that he is guilty of stealing all of it,[5] and it seems that the converse is also true.[6]

1 Para 14.4.
2 This was accepted in *Meech* [1974] QB 549, [1973] 3 All ER 939, CA; para 13.40.
3 Williams 'Appropriation: A Single or Continuous Act?' [1978] Crim LR 69. See also [1978] Crim LR 313.
4 [1986] 3 All ER 102, [1986] 1 WLR 1311, CA.
5 *Pilgram v Rice-Smith* [1977] 2 All ER 658, [1977] 1 WLR 671, DC.
6 Certainly on a charge of stealing several specific items there can be a conviction of stealing some of them if theft of all of them is not proved: *Machent v Quinn* [1990] 2 All ER 255, DC.

PROPERTY

13.20 By s 4(1) of the Act, 'property' includes money and all other property, real or personal, including things in action and other intangible property. The reference to real property means that land and things forming part of it are included in the definition of 'property'. However, there are special provisions restricting the theft of land and things forming part of it, which are dealt with later.[1] Likewise there are special provisions restricting the theft of wild creatures.[2]

A 'thing in action' is a personal right of property which can only be enforced by a legal action and not by taking physical possession, and its inclusion in the definition of property means that one who dishonestly assumes a right of ownership over a thing in action, such as a debt, a copyright or a trade mark, with the intention of permanently depriving the person entitled to it is guilty of theft. Thus, if D dishonestly purports to assign to X a debt owed to D and his partner, P, in order to defeat P's rights, D is guilty of the theft of a thing in action belonging to P. Likewise, if D purports to sell the copyright owned by P in a book, this is theft by D of a thing in action belonging to P. A bank account in credit is a thing in action because it constitutes a debt owed by the bank to the customer.[3] Thus, for example, if a company accountant dishonestly draws a cheque on his employer's bank account for an unauthorised purpose, he is guilty of the theft of the thing in action (the amount of the bank balance) belonging to his employer,[4] as well as theft of the cheque form.[5]

'Other intangible property' covers such things as gas stored in pipes, which is undoubtedly capable of being owned. It also covers patents[6] and transferable export quotas. This last example was recognised in *A-G of Hong Kong v Chan Nai Keung*,[7] where the Privy Council held that export quotas, which could be freely bought and sold and which gave an expectation of an export licence to the amount of the quotas (although no enforceable right to it), were 'intangible property'.

1 Paras 13.23 and 13.24.
2 Para 13.25.
3 *Davenport* [1954] 1 All ER 601 at 603. The money represented by the account is the money of the banker and not of the customer.
4 *Kohn* (1979) 69 Cr App Rep 395, CA. The resulting reduction of the thing in action (bank balance) is the equivalent of an appropriation of tangible property by destroying it: ibid. There would also have been a theft in the above example, even if the bank account is not in credit, provided that, or to the extent that, the amount drawn is within the limits of an agreed overdraft facility, because the bank's obligation under such a facility is a thing in action: ibid. See further, Smith *The Law of Theft* (6th edn) paras 110 and 111.
5 See para 13.63.
6 These are declared not to be things in action: Patents Act 1977, s 30.
7 [1987] 1 WLR 739, (1987) 3 BCC 403, CA.

13.21 In spite of the broad definition of property in s 4(1) of the Act, there are some things which do not, or may not, come within the definition of property and hence cannot be stolen.

Traditionally a human corpse is not property,[1] since it cannot be owned, but there is no reason why not. If it was ever held to be property it would belong to the owner of the cemetery after burial: before burial it would belong to various people, such as executors and those with control of it, depending on the circumstances.[2] There is a particularly strong case for saying that human corpses, or parts of them, which have been preserved for some subsequent use, such as a mummy in a museum, or a corpse stored for research or teaching purposes in a medical school, or a part of a body intended for transplantation, should be regarded as property.

While it is clear that a live human body is not property, people have been convicted of the theft of products of the human body, such as hair or urine,[3] although these convictions have never been tested in an appellate court.

It has been held that confidential information, such as a trade secret or the contents of a future examination paper, is not property for the purposes of theft,[4] so that the mere abstraction of it (e g by photocopying it) is not theft. However, if the information is stored in a computer its abstraction will involve an offence under s 13 of the Act of abstracting electricity (which is described in the next numbered paragraph) or under s 1 of the Computer Misuse Act 1990 (which is dealt with in para 15.60).

Rides in cars, coaches or trains are not property, nor are lodgings for the night and other services, but those who obtain them dishonestly may be guilty of an offence under s 1 of the Theft Act 1978.[5]

1 *Handyside's Case* (1749) 2 East PC 652. See Smith 'Stealing the Body and its Parts' [1976] Crim LR 622. It is a common law misdemeanour to remove a corpse from a grave without lawful authority: *Lynn* (1788) 2 Term Rep 733, 1 Leach 497.
2 See paras 13.28–13.35
3 *Herbert* (1960) 25 *JCL* 163; *Welsh* [1974] RTR 478, CA.
4 *Oxford v Moss* (1978) 68 Cr App Rep 183, DC. See Tettenborn 'Stealing Information' (1979) 129 NLJ 967.
5 Para 14.53.

13.22 Electricity is not property within s 4, and cannot be stolen,[1] but under s 13 of the Act it is an offence triable either way, and punishable with a maximum of five years' imprisonment if tried on indictment, for a person dishonestly[2] to use without due authority, or dishonestly to cause to be wasted or diverted, any electricity. Although the wastage or diversion of electricity can no doubt constitute a serious offence, as where a person re-connects his electricity supply after it has been cut off for non-payment, it is possible to think of many trivial examples. If D turns on P's transistor radio without P's authority, he may be convicted of an offence under s 13, as may someone who inserts a false disc in an electrical weighing machine and weighs himself.

Someone who dishonestly uses a private phone without authority is guilty of an offence under s 13. This would also be so if the phone were public, but in that event it is more likely that the prosecution would be brought under s 48 of the British Telecommunications Act 1981 by which a person who dishonestly uses a public telecommunication system with intent to avoid payment is guilty of an offence triable either way. On conviction on indictment the maximum punishment is two years' imprisonment.

1 *Low v Blease* (1975) 119 Sol Jo 695, DC.
2 See paras 13.54-13.58. Section 1 of the Act (paras 13.52-13.53) does not apply to an offence under s 13.

13.23 *Land and things forming part of it* The soil and plants and other growing things are clearly things forming part of land, as are houses, walls and other similar permanent structures (or parts of them, such as bricks or fixtures) built into the land. At the other extreme, a workman's hut temporarily resting on the land while the workmen are there does not form part of the land, nor does a pile of gravel or other material on the land. In borderline cases, the issue is decided by looking at the degree of annexation (ie attachment or integration) and the degree of permanency of that annexation, and deciding whether these are sufficient for it to be said that the thing forms part of the land.

Severe restrictions on the theft of things forming part of land are imposed by s 4(2) and (3) of the Act, which provide:

'A person cannot steal land, or things forming part of land and severed from it by him or by his directions, except in the following cases, that is to say:

a) when he is a trustee or personal representative, or is authorised by power of attorney, or as liquidator of a company, or otherwise, to sell or dispose of land belonging to another, and he appropriates the land or anything forming part of it by dealing with it in breach of the confidence reposed in him; or

b) when he is not in possession of the land and appropriates anything forming part of the land by severing it or causing it to be severed, or after it has been severed; or

c) when, being in possession of the land under a tenancy, he appropriates the whole or part of any fixture or structure let to be used with the land' (s 4(2)).

'A person who picks mushrooms growing wild on any land, or who picks flowers, fruit or foliage from a plant growing wild on any land, does not (although not in possession of the land) steal what he picks, unless he does it for reward or for sale or other commercial purpose' (s 4(3)).

These are the words of the Act and, whereas the majority of the sections in the Act are easy to understand, s 4 is not.

13.24 It comes to this:

a) *Land as a whole* cannot be stolen except where the appropriator is of a defined class and acts in a defined way (s 4(2)(a)). The class of appropriators comprises a trustee or personal representative, or a person authorised by power of attorney, or as a liquidator of a company, or otherwise, to sell or dispose of land belonging to another. The defined mode of appropriation is dealing with the land in breach of the confidence reposed in him. The result is that a person cannot steal land as a whole by moving a boundary fence or by occupying it as a squatter: if, in moving the boundary fence, he resorts to any deception he can be prosecuted for obtaining property by deception, but as the law is at present he commits no offence merely by squatting.

b) *Things forming part of land* can only be stolen in the following cases:
   i)   As for land as a whole, by the defined persons in the defined way (s 4(2)(a)).
   ii) Where a person not in possession of the land appropriates the thing by severing it or causing it to be severed (s 4(2)(b)). If a trespasser or other person not in possession of the land digs gravel, removes tiles and bricks from a building or part of a wall, cuts turf, digs up flowers or other growing things, picks a flower from a cultivated plant or cuts down a tree or saws off one of its branches, or causes such severance to be done (e g letting loose a pig on the land where it uproots vegetables), he may be convicted of theft.

   The above provision does not apply to the picking of wild mushrooms or fungi nor to picking *from* wild plants and the like. Such conduct is governed instead by the special provisions of s 4(3), as follows. First, the picking of wild mushrooms or other fungi[1] by a person not in possession of the land is not theft (although clearly there has been a severance) unless it is done for reward or for sale or other commercial purpose. Second, where a person not in possession of the land picks flowers, fruit or foliage *from* a plant, shrub or tree, [2] growing wild, he cannot commit theft (although, again, there has clearly been a severance) unless the picking is done for reward or for sale or other commercial purpose.[3] 'Picking from' is a narrow term. It does not include uprooting a wild plant or lopping off a branch from a wild shrub; these are covered by s 4(2)(b) and are unaffected by s 4(3).

   The operation of these provisions is as follows: shortly before Christmas a florist and an electrician go out in their cars; both pick holly from a tree which is cultivated in a garden and both may be convicted of theft because the tree is not wild. They continue and both pick holly from a tree which is wild; the florist is intending to sell it in his shop and may be convicted of theft, whereas the electrician is intending to decorate his home and cannot be so convicted. Both dig up small fir trees growing wild and both may be convicted of theft, whatever their purpose, because the severance by them has gone beyond 'picking from'.

iii) Generally, a person in possession of land under a tenancy cannot steal things forming part of it; consequently, if he extracts gravel from the land and sells it, or digs up a plant on the land and gives it to a friend, or picks blackberries from a wild bush on the land and sells them, he cannot be convicted of theft. The only exception is provided by s 4(2)(c). It relates to the whole or part of any structure or fixture let to be used with the land; such is stealable by a tenant and is stealable by any means (ie a severance is not necessary). The obvious example of a 'structure' is a building, but the term also includes things such as a wall or a bridge. Basically, a 'fixture' is an object, such as a washbasin or fireplace, which is attached to land or to a building for the purpose of making a permanent improvement to the land or building; by the ordinary law of land it becomes part of the land. It follows from all this that if a tenant demolishes a coal-shed on the land of which he is a tenant, or removes an Adam fireplace there in order to sell it, or sells the Adam fireplace in situ with a promise to remove it later, he may be convicted of theft.

It is odd that these provisions do not apply to a person in possession of land under a licence, who therefore commits no offence if he dishonestly appropriates anything forming part of the land.

Of course, once a thing has been severed from land it ceases to form part of it and is no longer subject to any restriction on its being stolen.

1 By s 4(3), 'mushroom' includes a fungus.
2 By s 4(3), 'plant' includes any tree or shrub.
3 It may be noted that a person who, inter alia, gathers or plucks any part of a 'protected' wild plant without uprooting thereby commits a summary offence under s 13 of the Wildlife and Countryside Act 1981.

13.25 *Wild creatures* Section 4(4) of the Act provides that wild creatures tamed or untamed are to be regarded as property, but goes on to provide that a person cannot steal a wild creature not tamed nor ordinarily kept in captivity, or the carcase of any such creature, unless either it has been reduced into possession by or on behalf of another person and possession of it has not since been lost or abandoned, or another person is in course of reducing it into possession.

While they are alive, wild creatures which are neither tamed nor ordinarily kept in captivity are not owned by anyone, but on being killed or taken they become the property of the owner of the land on which they are killed or taken, or, if he has granted the sporting rights to someone else, the grantee of those rights.[1] Section 4(4) distinguishes two groups of wild creatures:

a) *Wild creatures which have been tamed or are ordinarily kept in captivity* can be stolen in the same ways as any other property. Thus a person may be guilty of theft by dishonestly appropriating a tamed fox or a bear from a zoo.

b) *Wild creatures neither tamed nor ordinarily kept in captivity* Such a creature or its carcase cannot normally be stolen but becomes 'stealable':

    i) if reduced into possession by or on behalf of another (in which case it remains 'stealable' so long as possession has not subsequently been lost or abandoned)[2], or

    ii) if another person is in course of reducing it into possession.

Thus, it is not theft to poach game on another's land, unless for instance the game is taken from a trap set by another, even another poacher (because another is in the course of reducing into possession), or from a sack into which another has put the product of his own shooting (because there has been a reduction into possession by another).[3] Poaching is subject to its own legislation.

The term 'reduced into possession by or on behalf of another' in b)i) covers (inter alia) the shooting and taking of game by a gamekeeper on his employer's behalf, since by doing so the gamekeeper reduces the game into possession on behalf of his employer ('another'), and the gamekeeper can be convicted of theft if he subsequently appropriates it. Deciding whether or not a wild creature has been reduced into possession may involve the drawing of fine distinctions. There can be no doubt that, if a person stocks tanks on his fish farm with trout, the trout are reduced into his possession. On the other hand, unless it is a very small pond, a person who stocks open water with trout for the purpose of fly fishing would not seem to have sufficient control over them for the trout to be in his possession.[4]

1 *Blades v Higgs* (1865) 11 HL Cas 621, 20 CBNS 214, HL.
2 Possession of a live wild creature is abandoned if the possessor allows it to escape from his possession; it is lost if the wild creature escapes of its own volition. Possession of the carcase of a wild creature is not lost by a person who mislays it: see para 13.29 and Smith *The Law of Theft* (6th edn) para 106.
3 It may be noted that, under the Wildlife and Countryside Act 1981, it is a summary offence intentionally to kill, injure or take away any wild bird (s 1) or certain wild animals (s 9).
4 Arguably, the trout in the first example are kept in captivity, but those in the second example retain far too much freedom for there to be any possibility of this.

13.26 *Other offences relating to wild creatures* The Eighth Report of the Criminal Law Revision Committee recommended that the whole law with regard to poaching should be considered by an appropriate committee.[1] In the meantime, certain provisions of the Larceny Act 1861 punishing summarily the unlawful taking or destroying of fish in private waters or in waters in which there is a private right of fishery are now contained in a modified form in Schedule 1 of the Act, as amended. Various Victorian statutes provide summary offences relating to the poaching of game (including rabbits), whose gist is trespassing in pursuit of game and which do not require any actual taking or destroying of game. Section 1 of the Deer Act 1991 provides summary offences relating to the intentional taking, killing or injuring of deer without the consent of the owner or occupier of the land or other lawful authority.

These offences relating to fish, game and deer are separate offences and are quite distinct from the offence of theft.

1 Cmnd 2977, para 53.

BELONGING TO ANOTHER

13.27 The property appropriated must belong to another at the time of its appropriation. In ordinary language property is frequently said to belong to someone only when he owns it, but under s 5(1) of the Act property is also regarded as belonging to any person who has possession or control of it, or any proprietary right or interest in it falling short of complete ownership. This raises questions of civil law.

13.28 *Ownership and possession* Before discussing s 5(1), it is necessary to say something about ownership and possession. Ownership of goods or money or other property is the ultimate right to control. It lasts longer than any other right to control, but ownership does not necessarily entail physical control. For example, A may have hired his car to B for a day and C's £10 note may have been taken by E, a pickpocket, who placed it in his wallet; A and C are still the owners of their car and £10 note respectively, although B and E have possession. Even if C's £10 note were mixed with E's other money, C would remain its owner (although he would probably not be able to identify it) but E could make someone who gave value and received the £10 note in good faith its owner. This is because money is negotiable; a thief can give a better title to it than he has got. Goods are not negotiable: hence, if G steals H's watch and sells it to J who acts in good faith, H remains the owner of the watch (and can sue J for its return).

Mention may also be made of the rule which determines when ownership passes on the sale of goods. This is that ownership passes when the parties intend it to pass; in the case of a sale in a supermarket the parties are normally attributed with the intention that ownership shall pass on payment, and in the case of a retail sale of petrol the intention is normally attributed that ownership shall pass when the petrol is put in the tank (even though payment is only made later).[1]

1 For the basic provisions, see the Sale of Goods Act 1979, ss 17 and 18.

13.29 Possession is essentially physical control, but:

a) Possession may mean something *more* than mere physical control; for example, a guest has not got possession of the cutlery with which he eats a meal in his host's house; nor has a customer who examines goods in a shop, nor an employee who uses his employer's tools. In each of these cases, the host, shopkeeper or employer, as the case may be, retains possession (as well as ownership, if he is the owner).

b) Possession may also mean *less* than physical control; for example, a householder possesses that which is in his house when he is at his office.

c) When no one has physical control, or when physical control is disputed, the person with the right to possession is usually said to have possession. For example, the owner of a vending machine is in possession of the coins inserted into it, even though he does not know at any moment how many coins are in the machine.

A person does not lose possession of a thing simply by mislaying it, but he will lose possession if (and when) someone else assumes physical control of it. Thus, if a purse falls out of a woman's bag in the street, she continues to possess it until someone else assumes control. (On the other hand, if property is abandoned by someone, and this requires that he should be completely indifferent as to what is done to or with the property by anyone else, he loses any rights to possession of the property, including ownership if he is the owner. The test of abandonment is a strict one; a person does not, for example, abandon goods which he puts in his dustbin.)[1]

1 *Williams v Phillips* (1957) 41 Cr App Rep 5, DC.

13.30 As already indicated, ownership and possession may be vested in different people. An example is provided by reference to a bailment. A bailment exists where A entrusts B with goods and B is under an obligation to return *those* goods to A (as when goods are hired or lent or left for repair), or to deliver *them* to a third party in accordance with A's instruction. B (the bailee) obtains possession but A (the bailor) retains ownership. (A loan of money, however, involves the transfer of ownership, as well as of possession, by the lender since by the nature of the thing he does not expect the very notes or coins transferred to be returned, although, of course, he expects to be repaid.)

13.31 In law, the ownership of goods is often spoken of as 'the property in the goods'. This use of the word 'property' is confusing and it is simpler to use that word only in its other sense, which is the one used earlier in this chapter, namely to cover those things which may be the *subject* of ownership. It is in the latter sense that the word 'property' is used in the Act and in the title of this chapter.

13.32 *Section 5(1)* The precise wording of s 5(1) is: 'Property shall be regarded as belonging to any person having possession or control of it, or having in it any proprietary right or interest (not being an equitable interest arising only from an agreement to transfer or grant an interest).'

13.33 'Control' covers cases where a person in physical control of property is nevertheless not in possession of it, such as the guest using his host's cutlery or the customer examining goods in a shop. It also covers cases where it is doubtful whether a person in control of property can be said to be in possession of it.

In *Woodman*[1] the accused took some scrap metal from a disused factory belonging to English China Clays. Originally there had been a substantial amount of scrap metal on the site. This had been sold to a company which removed the bulk of it but some was too inaccessible to be removed in such a way as to be attractive to the company: it was left on the site for perhaps a couple of years until the accused took it away. After the company had removed the bulk of the scrap, English China Clays erected a barbed wire fence and put up notices such as 'Private Property, Keep Out' and 'Trespassers will be prosecuted'. Dismissing an appeal against a conviction for theft of scrap from the site, the Court of Appeal held that there was ample evidence that English China Clays were in control of the site and therefore in control of articles which were on the site, in spite of the fact that they were not aware of the existence of the scrap: control of a site by excluding others is prima facie control of the articles on the site as well.

The fact that an occupier can be in control of items of property on the land even though unaware of their existence is of significance where the owner of the items has abandoned them there (and thereby lost ownership and possession of them). In such a case the fact that the items nevertheless belong to another, the occupier in control of them, means that someone else who dishonestly appropriates them can be convicted of theft of them. In other cases, such a person could be convicted of theft whether or not the items belonged to the occupier, because they would still belong to their owner and possessor.[2]

1 [1974] QB 754, [1974] 2 All ER 955, CA.
2 In this context the decision in *Hancock* [1990] 3 All ER 183, CA, is interesting because the Court of Appeal recognised that, if it could be proved that Celtic coins had been buried with the intention of being retrieved (and were therefore treasure trove), there could be theft from the Crown since the Crown is owner of treasure trove.

13.34 The best example of a 'proprietary right or interest' is complete ownership of property of it, but the phrase also covers proprietary rights or interests falling below that of complete ownership.

Whether a person other than the accused had a proprietary right or interest in the property at the time of the appropriation is not determined by the Act but depends on the complexities and niceties of the civil law. A full examination of these is outside the scope of this book, but an example of a proprietary interest less than complete ownership is the interest which a beneficiary of a trust has in the trust fund or a legatee under a will.

One type of trust is a constructive trust, which involves various complicated questions in civil law (for example, as to whether and in what circumstances the making of secret profits from the use of another's property gives rise to a constructive trust). In *A-G's Reference (No 1 of 1985)*[1] the Court of Appeal took the view that, even if an employee did hold a secret profit on constructive trust for his employer, the employer's proprietary interest under that trust was not a proprietary interest for the purposes of s 5(1). Such an interpretation involves adding words to s 5(1) and it can be contrasted with the decision of another Court of Appeal in *Shadrokh-Cigari*,[2] where it was held an equitable interest which could only have arisen under a constructive trust was a proprietary interest for the purposes of s 5(1). This decision renders doubtful that in *A-G's Reference* on the present point.

The wording of s 5(1) means that, although an employee who receives a bribe has to account in civil law to his employer for it, it does not belong to another under that provision because his employer does not have a proprietary right or interest in it; nor does it belong to another under any other provision in s 5. It follows that the employee cannot be convicted of the theft of the bribe.[3]

Section 5(1) says that 'proprietary right or interest' in the present context does not include 'an equitable interest arising only from an agreement to transfer or grant an interest'. This needs to be explained to those who have not yet encountered the rules of equity. When a person contracts to buy, for example, land or shares, he receives what is called an equitable interest in them although legally the person contracting to sell retains the legal ownership. The above words are designed to ensure that an owner who contracts to sell his property to A, and then contracts to sell it to B, does not steal it from A.

1 [1986] QB 491, [1986] 2 All ER 219, CA; see also para 13.39.
2 [1988] Crim LR 465; see also para 13.44.
3 *Powell v MacRae* [1977] Crim LR 571, DC; see further para 13.39.

13.35 The result of the definition of 'belonging to another' in s 5(1) is that property may 'belong' to more than one person. If A delivers goods to B with instructions to keep them safely for him, or to carry them to another, and D appropriates them dishonestly and with intent permanently to deprive A and B of them, he will commit theft from both A and B.

Another result is that a person to whom property 'belongs' under s 5(1) may steal the goods from someone else to whom they 'belong'. For instance, in the above example, if it is B who dishonestly appropriates the goods, he can be convicted of theft from A. Indeed, an owner may be convicted of stealing his own property.[1] If D lets a car to P for a month and the next week surreptitiously takes it away, he can be convicted of theft – even though he is still the owner of the car – because the car was in P's possession; and the same would be true if D removed his goods, without redeeming them, from G's pawnbroker's shop, or if D removed his shoes from J's cobblers' shop without paying for the repairs.

A partner may likewise be held guilty of stealing partnership property for partners are co-owners of their property and each of them has a proprietary right in it.[2]

As was said in para 13.34, a beneficiary under a trust (with the possible exception of a constructive trust) has a proprietary right or interest under s 5(1), and therefore the trust property is regarded for the purposes of the Act as belonging to the beneficiary as well as to the trustees who are the legal owners. If D holds goods, money or shares in trust for P, D as trustee has the legal ownership of the goods, money or shares, but P has an equitable interest in them. Thus, D will be guilty of stealing if he dishonestly appropriates them with the intention of defeating the trust by permanently depriving P of them.

1 For an example, see *Turner (No 2)* [1971] 2 All ER 441, [1971] 1 WLR 901, CA (although the actual decision is not wholly satisfactory).
2 *Bonner* [1970] 2 All ER 97, [1970] 1 WLR 838, CA.

13.36 Spouses may be guilty of stealing each other's property, although in many instances their possession, and in some instances their ownership, is joint; the leave of the Director of Public Prosecutions is required for the institution of proceedings for theft by one spouse of the other's property, unless, by virtue of any judicial decree or order, the parties were not obliged to cohabit at the material time.[1] The reason for requiring the leave of the DPP is that otherwise there is a danger of trivial marital quarrels coming into the criminal courts.

1 Theft Act 1968, s 30. See *Woodley v Woodley* [1978] Crim LR 629, DC.

SPECIAL CASES

13.37 Section 5 contains four subsections other than s 5(1). These deal with specific situations where either the property does not belong to another under s 5(1) or where, although it does so belong by virtue of complicated rules of civil law, the matter is simplified by a special rule. By virtue of the rules laid down by these four subsections property is deemed to belong to another in the specified situations for the purposes of the definition of theft in s 1.

TRUSTS

13.38 As we have seen, property subject to a trust is regarded under s 5(1) as belonging to the beneficiaries as well as to the trustees. However, in the case of charitable trusts there are no beneficiaries (in the legal sense of persons owning a beneficial interest in the trust property). Without special provision, a dishonest appropriation of property subject to a charitable trust by a sole trustee or all the trustees would not be theft because the property would not belong to another. For this reason, special provision is made by s 5(2), which provides that 'where property is subject to a trust, the persons to whom it belongs shall be regarded as including any person having a right to enforce the trust, and an intention to defeat the trust shall be regarded accordingly as an intention to deprive of the property any person having that right'. Therefore, if trustees hold property on trust for charitable purposes, the Attorney-General, as a person who, though not a beneficiary, has the right to enforce such a trust, is someone to whom the property 'belongs', and the trustees may be convicted of theft if they dishonestly appropriate it.

PROPERTY RECEIVED UNDER AN OBLIGATION TO RETAIN AND DEAL WITH IT IN A PARTICULAR WAY

13.39 Section 5(3) provides that 'where a person receives property from or on account of another, and is under an obligation to the other to retain and deal with that property or its proceeds in a particular way, the property or proceeds shall be regarded (as against him) as belonging to the other'.

The essence of s 5(3) is that property (usually money) or its proceeds is regarded (as against the accused) as belonging to another from or on whose account the accused has received the property if the accused is under a legal[1] obligation to the person from or on whose account he has received it to *retain and deal* with *the* property or *its* proceeds *in a particular way* . 'Proceeds' refers to money or other property representing what was originally received, e g a car which the recipient has bought with money entrusted to him for this purpose.

Section 5(3) requires that the accused should have received the property 'from or on account of' another to whom he is under a legal obligation to retain and deal with it in a particular way. This requirement is clearly satisfied where D receives money from P which he is legally obliged to P to use in a particular way. It is also satisfied where D (a shop assistant) receives money from a customer for some of his employers's goods since he has received the money on account of another (the employer) and is legally obliged to the employer to retain and deal with it in a particular way (i e to put it in the till).

On the other hand, the requirement of s 5(3) is not satisfied where an employee receives money from a customer for goods which (contrary to his terms of employment) he is selling on his own account on the employer's premises (as where the manager of a pub is selling his own beer)[2], or where an employee receives a bribe to enter his employer's premises[3], or where an employee receives money as a result of misusing his employer's property (such as out of hours use of a taxi by an employed taxi driver),[4] since in none of these cases is the money received from or on account of another to whom the employee is legally obliged to retain and deal with it in a particular way. Likewise, a person who receives and cashes a cheque for housing benefit to which he is entitled and who dishonestly uses the money for his own purposes instead of paying rent arrears does not satisfy the requirement of s 5(3) because there is no obligation on him, statutory or contractual, to retain and deal in a particular way with the money received.[5]

1 *Mainwaring* (1981) 74 Cr App Rep 99, CA. Also see *Wakeman v Farrar* [1974] Crim LR 136, DC; *DPP v Huskinson* (1988) 21 HLR 562, DC.
2 *A-G's Reference (No 1 of 1985)* [1986] QB 491, [1986] 2 All ER 219, CA; *Cooke* [1986] AC 909, [1986] 2 All ER 985, HL. If two or more agree to do this, they can be convicted of conspiracy to defraud: *Cooke*.
3 *Powell v MacRae* [1977] Crim LR 571, DC.

4 *Cullen* (1873) LR 2 CCR 28, 42 LJMC 64.
5 *DPP v Huskinson* (1988) 21 HLR 562, DC.

13.40   Because an obligation under s 5(3) must be a legal obligation, it is a matter of law for the judge whether or not such an obligation existed in particular circumstances. However, whether or not those circumstances existed cannot be known until the facts have been established. It is for the jury to establish these circumstances if the facts are in dispute and, where they are, the judge must direct the jury to make their findings on the facts and then say to them: 'If you find the facts to be such-and-such, then I direct you as a matter of law that a legal obligation arose to which s 5(3) applies.'[1]

The judges (including appellate judges) have on occasions reached surprising conclusions on whether or not a legal obligation of the type referred to in s 5(3) would arise in given circumstances. *Meech*[2] provides an example. P fraudulently obtained a cheque for £1,450 from a finance company. He asked D to cash the cheque for him. D agreed and paid it into his own bank account. Two days later, having discovered P's fraud, D withdrew £1,410 from his account. This represented the £1,450 less a debt of £40 which P owed him. D had arranged with E and F to stage a fake robbery with him as victim, so that he could give an excuse for not returning the money to P, and this was carried out. D, E and F were convicted of the theft of the £1,410 and appealed unsuccessfully to the Court of Appeal, who held that at the time of the appropriation, which was when the money was divided up after the fake robbery, the money (the proceeds of the cheque) belonged to another, P, under s 5(3) because D had initially received the cheque from P under an obligation to retain and deal with it or its proceeds in a particular way. This obligation was not affected by the fact that P, having acquired the cheque illegally, could not have enforced it in a court.

It is difficult to see how there was a legal obligation of the type specified in s 5(3). The Court of Appeal held that there was an intitial obligation owed to P by D to retain and deal with the cheque and its proceeds in a particular way and this sufficed for the purposes of s 5(3), even though that obligation became unenforceable by P on D's discovery of P's fraud. The Court based this initial obligation on the fact that on D's knowledge of the facts there was an obligation to P, but s 5(3) does not talk in terms of an obligation believed by the accused to exist but of an actual obligation. Moreover, it appears to require the existence of such an obligation at the time of the appropriation. It is certainly odd that, on the view taken by the Court of Appeal, an obligation which may never have existed and which did not exist at the time of the appropriation could be held to suffice for the purposes of s 5(3).

1 *Mainwaring* (1981) 74 Cr App Rep 99, CA.
2 [1974] QB 549 [1973] 3 All ER 939, CA. *Cullen* (1974), unreported but noted in Smith and Hogan *Cases and Materials in Criminal Law* (4th edn) 430, provides another good example.

13.41   Where the accused has received the property as a bailee or trustee, it belongs to another under s 5(1) (or under s 5(2) in the case of a charitable trustee) for reasons already explained. Consequently, although property which has been bailed or handed over subject to a trust clearly belongs to another under s 5(3), recourse to that sub-section is unnecessary.

In fact, it may be that s 5(3) is virtually otiose since, in nearly every other case covered by it, it can be established that, under the civil law, someone other than the recipient (ie the accused) had a 'proprietary right or interest' in the property or proceeds in question, so that it belonged to another under s 5(1). Even if this is so, the civil law in this area is complex and s 5(3) plays a useful role in making it quite clear that, in the circumstances fairly simply specified by it, the property or its proceeds shall be regarded as 'belonging to another' for the purposes of theft.

13.42 It cannot be overemphasised that, for property to belong to another under s 5(3), the accused must be under a specific legal obligation to the person from or on whose account he received the property to retain and deal with that property or its proceeds in a particular way; the fact that he is under some contractual obligation to that person to do something will not normally mean that he is obliged to retain and deal with the property received in a particular way. For example, if P makes a contract with D, a decorator, to have his house painted and pays to D a down-payment of £50, the £50 will belong only to D. It will not belong to P under s 5(3) because, although D is under a legal (contractual) obligation to paint the house, he is not under a legal obligation to retain and deal with the £50 (or its proceeds) in a particular way; he can do what he likes with it. It would be different if the £50 is handed over specifically to enable D to buy the necessary materials to paint the house; here D is under a legal obligation to retain and deal with *the* money or *its* proceeds (eg the paint) in a particular way; therefore they belong to P under s 5(3) and D can be convicted of theft if he dishonestly appropriates them. This distinction can be illustrated by reference to *Hall*.[1]

D, a travel agent, received money from clients as deposits and payments for air trips to America: in some instances a lump sum was paid by schoolmasters in respect of charter flights for their pupils; in other instances individuals made payments in respect of their own projected flights. In none of the seven cases covered by the charges did the flights materialise and in none was there any refund. D claimed to have paid into his firm's general trading account all sums received by him and asserted that those sums had become his own property and had been applied by him in the conduct of the firm's business; he submitted that he could not be convicted of theft just because the firm had not prospered and there was no money. D was convicted but appealed successfully to the Court of Appeal who held that, in the absence of some further arrangement, it was not established that D had been under an obligation to the clients concerned to retain and deal with the money in a particular way; therefore the money did not belong to another under s 5(3) at the material time. It would have been different if D had been required by the terms of the contracts to pay the money into a separate account and use it to purchase the tickets. In that case he would have been under a legal obligation to retain and deal with the money or its proceeds in a particular way and it would have belonged to another under s 5(3).

1 [1973] QB 126, [1972] 2 All ER 1009, CA. Also see *Hayes* (1976) 64 Cr App Rep 82, CA.

13.43 Another example of the limits and operation of s 5(3) is as follows. If D is engaged by P to collect rent from P's tenants, or football pool money, and to account to P for the money he receives (less any commission or other reward), the money collected will belong to another (P) under s 5(3) if under their arrangement the circumstances are such that D is legally obliged to hand over the actual money received or to maintain a distinct fund containing the money received or other money representing it (its proceeds) (so that if he dishonestly appropriates any of the money to which he is not entitled he is guilty of theft). However, the money or its proceeds will not belong to P under s 5(3) if the relationship between D and P is simply one of debtor and creditor (i e D is not obliged to P to hand over the actual money received or to keep the money or its proceeds in a particular fund and merely has to account in due course to P for an equivalent sum).[1] In such a case, D will not commit theft by dishonestly appropriating the money, unless in some way an obligation to the tenants or punters had arisen to keep the money or its proceeds in a particular fund (in which event the money or its proceeds will belong to them under s 5(3)).

1 *Lewis v Lethbridge* [1987] Crim LR 59, DC.

MISTAKE

13.44 In some cases in which D gets property from P in consequence of P's mistake, the property will still belong to another under s 5(1) and it is strictly unnecessary for the prosecution to invoke the aid of any other part of s 5. One case is where P merely intended to pass possession to D and to retain ownership of the property for himself, so that P continues to have a 'proprietary right' in it under s 5(1) and D can be convicted of theft if subsequently he dishonestly appropriates the property. Another case is where P does intend to transfer ownership as well as possession of the property to D but acts under a mistake, known to D, as to the identity of D or of the property transferred, or as to the quantity of money paid, since such a mistake prevents ownership passing to D[1] and P continues to have a 'proprietary right' in it under s 5(1). Thus, if D writes to P, pretending to be X, one of P's trusted regular customers, and asks P to send him a quantity of goods on credit (a transaction into which P would never have entered if he had known that he was dealing with D), D can be convicted of theft when he subsequently appropriates the goods dishonestly since the contract for the sale of goods is void for mistake of identity and, P remaining their owner, an appropriation by D will be of goods belonging to another under s 5(1).[2] The same would be true if P, intending to give D a bar of lead, picks up the wrong bar and gives him a bar of gold instead, the mistake being known by D.[3]

Although his mistake will not prevent him transferring ownership, property will still belong to the transferor under s 5(1) if the facts fall within a recently-stated rule of civil law,[4] which was applied to the law of theft in *Shadrokh-Cigari*[5]. The rule is that, where an action will lie to recover money or other property paid or transferred under a mistake of fact, the person paying or transferring it under the mistake retains an equitable proprietary (beneficial) interest in it. In *Shadrokh-Cigari* £286,001 was transferred from an American bank to the English bank account of X, a boy, instead of the £286 actually due. X's guardian, D, procured X to authorise the English bank to issue banker's drafts drawn in favour of D for most of the sum of £286,000. D then used the drafts for his own purposes. The Court of Appeal upheld D's conviction for theft of the drafts from the English bank; D had appropriated the drafts and they belonged to another (the English bank) for the purposes of s 5(1) because, having transferred them to D under a mistaken belief (of fact) that D could properly deal with the funds in the account, the bank, although it transferred ownership, retained an equitable proprietary (beneficial) interest in them.

Under the rules of equity, where the transferor (T) of money or other property under a mistake retains an equitable proprietary interest in it, then, if that money or other property is used to acquire property or is combined with other money to do so, T can 'trace'[6] his interest in that property or fund with the result that he will have a proprietary interest in those proceeds to the extent that they represent the original money or other property and they will belong to T for the purposes of s 5(1).

Too much must not be made of the decision in *Shadrokh-Cigari* since the situations in which an action will lie to recover money or other property transferred under a mistake, or, in other words, situations where the transferee is under a legal obligation to make restoration, are strictly limited. This is a point dealt with in slightly more detail in para 13.46. What is said there about an obligation to restore is equally applicable in the present context.

1 See, for instance, *Cundy v Lindsay* (1878) 3 App Cas 459, 47 LJQB 481, HL.
2 Of course, D could also be convicted of obtaining property by deception under s 15 of the Act discussed in paras 14.27–14.42.
3 For a third type of case see *Davies* [1982] 1 All ER 513, CA, discussed in [1982] Crim LR 458.
4 *Chase Manhattan Bank NA v Israel-British Bank (London) Ltd* [1981] Ch 105, [1978] 3 All ER 1025.
5 [1988] Crim LR 465, CA.
6 Subject to the normal restrictions on tracing; see Pettit *Equity and the Law of Trusts* (6th edn) 451–460.

13.45 So far we have considered the effect on the operation of s 5(1) of a transfer of property under a mistake. Section 5(1) does not make express provision for mistake. Section 5(4), on the other hand, does.

Section 5(4) provides that 'where a person gets property by another's mistake, and is under an obligation to make restoration (in whole or in part) of the property or its proceeds or of the value thereof, then to the extent of that obligation the property or proceeds shall be regarded (as against him) as belonging to the person entitled to restoration, and an intention not to make restoration shall be regarded accordingly as an intention to deprive that person of the property or proceeds'.

It must be emphasised that to bring s 5(4) into play it is not enough simply that P has acted under a mistake; in addition, the transferee, D, must be under a legal[1] obligation to make restoration (in whole or in part) of *the* property received from P or *its* proceeds or *its* value. Only then, and to the extent of that obligation, is the property regarded under s 5(4) as belonging to the person entitled to restoration. It is a matter of law for the judge whether or not an obligation to restore existed in particular circumstances, but whether or not it existed cannot be known until the facts have been established. It is for the jury to establish whether or not these circumstances existed if the facts are in dispute, and the judge should direct them in a similar way to that described in para 13.41 in relation to s 5(3).

The application of s 5(4) is illustrated by *Davis*.[2] D was entitled to housing benefit from the local authority. Because of an administrative mistake, D was sent two housing benefit cheques (which we shall call 'duplicate cheques') every month for eight months; each cheque was for the full amount due. D then ceased to be entitled to housing benefit but he still received a single housing benefit cheque each month. Instead of returning the cheques, D dishonestly endorsed them. Some of the duplicate cheques were endorsed to his landlord for rent. The Court of Appeal quashed his conviction of theft of *money*[3] in relation to this conduct because D had not thereby received, and therefore could not appropriate, money.

In relation to one set of duplicate cheques and some of the single cheques, D had endorsed these to shopkeepers for cash. The Court of Appeal upheld his conviction of theft of money in relation to these. Dealing with the single cheques, it held that, since the cheques (i e the cheque forms as opposed to the thing in action which they represented) had been got by mistake in circumstances where D was under a legal obligation to make restoration of them and since the cash into which D converted the cheques was the 'proceeds' of that property (the cheques) which D had received under a mistake, D was under a legal obligation to make restoration of those proceeds and therefore they belonged to another (the local authority) under s 5(4). In the case of the set of duplicate cheques which had been cashed, it could not be proved which was the one to which D was entitled and which one had been sent under a mistake. The Court of Appeal dealt with this by holding that they were to be treated together as 'got' by another's mistake in the same way as if the excessive payment had been made in a single cheque, and that D was under a legal obligation to make restoration to the local authority *in part* of them or their proceeds *to the extent of that obligation, and that therefore the proceeds to that extent belonged to another (the local authority) under s 5(4).*

1 *Gilks* [1972] 3 All ER 280, [1972] 1 WLR 1341, CA.
2 (1988) 88 Cr App Rep 347, CA.
3 D could have been convicted of the theft of these *cheques*, since they would have belonged to another under s 5(4) for the reasons set out in the rest of the paragraph in the text.

13.46 When does a legal obligation to make restoration arise for the purposes of s 5(4)? The answer to this is by no means clear-cut and could only be exhaustively attempted by a lengthy discussion of the civil law of restitution, which would not be appropriate for a book such as this. Suffice it to say that the most obvious case where an obligation to make restoration arises in a case where the mistake has not prevented ownership passing is where P transfers money under a mistake which leads him to believe that D is legally entitled to the money, and it is this type of case which s 5(4) was principally intended to cover. For example, if P, an employer, pays D, an employee, a week's wages of £180, forgetting that he has already paid D £60 as an advance against wages, this mistake is not as to identity and does not prevent ownership of the £180, which P intended to pay, passing to D, but D is under an obligation in civil law to make restoration to P of the £60 excess and, to the extent of that obligation, the money is regarded as belonging to P. If D spends the excess on becoming aware of the mistake, he can be convicted of the theft of £60 since it belongs to another (to P) under s 5(4).

Another example is provided by *A-G's Reference (No 1 of 1983).*[1] The accused was a woman police officer. She was paid by her employer by direct debit. Once she was overpaid by £74. When she realised this, she decided to do nothing about it, although she did not withdraw any of this money. At the accused's trial for theft, the judge directed an acquittal. On a reference by the Attorney-General, the Court of Appeal held that, to the extent of the overpayment, the debt due to the accused from her bank (a thing in action) was property which belonged to another under s 5(4). This was because the accused had got that property under another's (the employer's) mistake as to her legal entitlement and was under an obligation in civil law to make restoration. This obligation to make restoration did not relate to the property (the debt), since it was not something which could be restored, or its proceeds, since there were no proceeds to restore; instead, it related to the value of the property – £74. Therefore, as against the accused, the debt was regarded as belonging to another, the person (the employer) entitled to restoration, under s 5(4).[2]

1 [1985] QB 182, [1984] 3 All ER 369, CA.
2 The Court of Appeal did not deal with whether, and-if so-how, the property had been appropriated by the accused. For a discussion of 'appropriation' in such a case, see Griew *Theft Acts 1968 and 1978* (6th edn), para 2.40.

13.47 The limits of s 5(4) are shown by *Gilks*[1] where D placed a bet with one of Ladbrokes' betting shops on a horse called *Fighting Scot*. This animal was unsuccessful but the relief manager of the betting shop made a mistake and paid D as if *Fighting Scot* had won. D knew that a mistake had been made but kept the money, his attitude being that it was Ladbrokes' hard lines. At first sight, the case came within s 5(4). However, as it was a gaming debt, there was no legal obligation to make restoration and, as the Court of Appeal held that obligation means legal obligation, s 5(4) did not apply. Nevertheless, D did not escape criminal liability, because the Court of Appeal held that when the manager paid the money the ownership was not affected and that it remained with Ladbrokes, so that the money had belonged to another under s 5(1) at the material time. It based this decision on *Middleton*,[2] an old case on the law of larceny, where money had been paid by a post office clerk under a mistake of identity, but the decision in that case was strictly inapplicable to the facts in *Gilks* since there was no mistake of identity of any kind on the part of the relief manager, and it seems that the decision that ownership of the money never passed must be wrong.

1 [1972] 3 All ER 280, [1972] 1 WLR 1341, CA.
2 (1873) LR 2 CCR 38, 42 LJMC 73.

13.48 As we have seen,[1] in *Shadrokh-Cigari*[2] the Court of Appeal applied to the law of theft the rule of civil law that, where an action will lie to recover money or other property transferred under a mistake of fact, the transferor retains a proprietary (beneficial) interest in it which can be 'traced' into things into which it is converted.[3] Consequently, the original money or other property or its proceeds will belong to another (the transferor) for the purposes of s 5(1). In the light of the application of this principle, it is not apparent what situation covered by s 5(4) is not also covered by s 5(1). A similar point was made in para 13.41 about s 5(3) and a similar comment can be made here as there. This is that s 5(4) makes clear in fairly simple terms that in the circumstances specified by it property is regarded as belonging to another and avoids the need for the criminal courts to get involved in esoteric points of law relating to proprietary interests. Since, as the Court of Appeal admitted in *Shadrokh-Cigari*, s 5(4) was an alternative route to a finding in that case that the property in question belonged to another, it seems an unnecessary complication for it to have based its decision primarily on that point primarily on s 5(1) by an application of such esoteric points of law.

1 Para 13.44.
2 [1988] Crim LR 465, CA.
3 Pettit *Equity and the Law of Trusts* (6th edn) 451–460.

13.49 There are many cases in which a person gets property by another's mistake but is under no obligation to make restoration of the property or its proceeds or its value. If P were to make a gift of a book to D, mistakenly believing that it was of little value when it was in fact a valuable first edition,

D would be guilty of no offence by appropriating the book even if he were aware of P's mistake from the outset. The reason that D would not be guilty of theft is that P's mistake, not being as to the identity of the book or of D, would not prevent ownership passing to D and, since P's mistake did not relate to D's legal entitlement, neither would P retain a proprietary interest in the book nor would D be under any legal obligation to make restoration of it at the time of the appropriation, with the result that the book would not belong to another under s 5(1) or s 5(4) at that time.

If D induces P to sell him goods on credit by dishonestly saying that he is a very rich man and P hands the goods to D, there is a sense in which D gets the goods by P's mistake. However, the goods will not belong to another under s 5(1) or (4). They will not belong to another (P) under s 5(1) because the mistake is not of a type which prevents the transfer of ownership or which leaves P with an equitable proprietary interest, and they will not belong to another under s 5(4) because, although D is under a legal obligation to pay the price, D is not under a legal obligation to make restoration of the property or its proceeds or value. Of course, D is guilty of obtaining the goods by deception, but he is not guilty of the theft of the goods *at this stage*.[1] If P subsequently avoids the contract of sale on account of D's fraud, the ownership of the goods will revert to P and they will then clearly belong to him under s 5(1), and D will be guilty of theft if he thereafter appropriates the goods, e g by retaining or disposing of them, with the requisite mens rea.

Because of the complexities of the law relating to mistake and its effects on the operation of the law of theft, there can be no doubt that where property is transferred under a mistake induced by deception it is preferable to charge the offence of obtaining property by deception.

1 See further, paras 14.43–14.46.

CORPORATION SOLE

13.50 Section 5(5) deals with a different kind of special case from those covered by s 5(2) to (4). It provides that the property of a corporation sole, examples of which are a bishop and the Treasury Solicitor, shall be regarded as belonging to the corporation notwithstanding a vacancy in the corporation. This is simply to guard against the possibility that, for example, the property of a bishopric might be regarded as belonging to no one, and therefore incapable of being stolen, during a vacancy in the see.

Mens rea

13.51 Section 1(2) of the Act states that it is immaterial that the appropriation is not made with a view to gain or is not made for the thief's own benefit (so that D can be convicted of theft if he throws P's ring into a river or tears to pieces P's clothing, although a charge of criminal damage would be more appropriate in the latter case). The mens rea required for theft by s 1(1) is that the appropriation must have been made dishonestly and with the intention of permanently depriving another person to whom the property belongs.[1]

The width of the requirement of 'appropriation' means that these requirements of mens rea, particularly that of dishonesty, play a crucial role in the offence, since not every appropriation of property belonging to another constitutes theft; whether it does so or not depends on the appropriator's state of mind.

1 The accused must, of course, have this mens rea at the time of the appropriation alleged; see *Hayes* (1976) 64 Cr App Rep 82, CA.

'DISHONESTLY'

13.52 *Section 2(1)* The question of dishonesty is one of fact for the jury and not of law for the judge, subject to the provisions of s 2(1) of the Act which expressly and as a matter of law excludes some states of mind from being dishonest.

Section 2(1) provides:

'A person's appropriation of property belonging to another is not to be regarded as dishonest:
a) if he appropriates the property in the belief that he has in law the right to deprive the other of it, on behalf of himself or of a third person; or
b) if he appropriates the property in the belief that he would have the other's consent if the other knew of the appropriation and the circumstances of it; or
c) (except where the property came to him as trustee or personal representative) if he appropriates the property in the belief that the person to whom the property belongs cannot be discovered by taking reasonable steps.'

Where one of these beliefs is alleged, it is irrelevant that it was unreasonable,[1] or even a drunken belief,[2] although, of course, the reasonableness of an alleged belief is of evidential importance when the issue of its genuineness is being considered.

1 *Holden* [1991] Crim LR 478, CA.
2 Cf *Jaggard v Dickinson* [1981] QB 527, [1980] 3 All ER 716, DC.

13.53 Section s 2(1)(a) makes a claim of right (i e a belief in a legal right to deprive) a defence to theft, which means that a mistake of law may excuse, as where a creditor seizes property belonging to his debtor, intending to recoup himself thereby, under the erroneous belief that the law permits debts to be recovered in this way. The concluding words of s 2(1)(a) make it plain that someone who appropriates property in the belief that he is entitled to do so on behalf of, for example, the company by which he is employed is not guilty of theft. If the accused genuinely believes that he has the right in law to deprive another of the property, he cannot be convicted of theft even though he knows that he has no legal right to appropriate it in the way, e g by the use of force, which he does.[1]

Section s 2(1)(a) is limited to beliefs in a *legal* right to deprive another of property, as opposed to beliefs in a moral right to do so (such as Robin Hood had when he stole from the rich to feed the poor). Where the accused believes that he has a moral right to deprive, the question of his dishonesty depends on the tests outlined in paras 13.54–13.58.

Section s 2(1)(b) (belief that the person to whom the property belongs would have consented if he had known of the appropriation and its circumstances) would clearly cover the case of an undergraduate who takes a bottle of beer from a friend's room, leaving the price behind him and believing that his friend would have consented had he known of all the circumstances. An accused's belief that he would have had the other's consent must be a belief that he would have had a 'true consent, honestly obtained'.[2]

Section 2(1)(c) (belief that the person to whom the property belongs cannot be discovered by taking reasonable steps) does not apply where the property came to the accused as trustee or personal representative. It aims principally at protecting the honest finder as long as he remains honest. There is no dishonesty, and therefore no theft, if, believing that the owner of goods or money found by him cannot be discovered by taking reasonable steps, the finder appropriates the goods or money during the currency of that belief.

It is important to appreciate the extremely limited nature of the immunity conferred on the honest finder. In the first place property may, as we have seen, belong to more than one person for the purpose of the Act. Although someone who finds goods on or embedded in another's land may well believe that their owner, the loser, cannot be discovered by taking reasonable steps, the goods would probably be held to belong also to the landowner on the ground that he has possession or control of them.[3] Appropriation with knowledge of the landowner's rights would be theft. Secondly, if, while he is in possession of the goods, the finder becomes aware of the person to whom they belong, he may be guilty of theft in consequence of any subsequent appropriation by keeping or disposing of the goods with the intention of permanently depriving that person. There is no equivalent to the protection of honest purchasers from thieves conferred by s 3(2) of the Act.[4]

Section 2(1)(c) is not limited to honest finders. For example, it also protects a cobbler who, believing that he cannot find the owner of some uncollected shoes, appropriates them.

1 *Robinson* [1977] Crim LR 173, CA; para 14.3.
2 *A-G's Reference (No 2 of 1982)* [1984] QB 624 at 641.
3 Paras 13.27–13.35.
4 Para 13.17.

13.54 *Cases not covered by s 2(1)* The negative definition of dishonesty in s 2(1) is only a partial definition. Consequently an accused's appropriation may not have been made dishonestly even though the case falls outside s 2(1). This was held by the Court of Appeal in 1973 in *Feely*.[1] Moreover, as the court made clear in that case, in situations other than those referred to in s 2(1) the meaning of dishonesty is not a matter of law for the judge to decide but a matter of fact for the jury. This means that in such situations it is not for the judge to tell the jury whether or not the accused's appropriation, assuming his version of the facts is not disproved, was made dishonestly but for the jury to decide this.

In *Feely* D was employed by a firm of bookmakers as a manager of one of their branches. D's employers sent a circular to all their managers stating that the practice of borrowing from tills was to stop and after receiving that circular D knew that he had no right of any kind to take money from a till or safe for his own purposes. Subsequently, D took about £30 from a safe at his branch in order to give it to his father. When the deficiency was discovered, D gave an IOU to his successor as branch manager and said that he intended to repay the sum, taking it out of money due to him by his employers, who owed him about twice that amount. The judge in his summing up told the jury '... as a matter of law ... I am bound to direct you, even if he were prepared to pay back the following day and even if he were a millionaire, it makes no defence in law to this offence'. The Court of Appeal held that this was wrong: it may happen that an employee is acting dishonestly when he removes money from a till but it is for the jury to decide. 'We do not agree', said Lawton LJ, 'that judges should define what "dishonestly" means'. Instead the question of whether the accused's appropriation was dishonest should be left to the jury to decide and the jury should apply to that question the current standards of ordinary decent people.

'Dishonestly' is not intended to characterise a course of conduct but to describe a state of mind.[2] What this means, for the purpose of the above test, is that the jury (or magistrates), having determined the accused's state of mind at the time of the appropriation, must ask themselves whether, given that state of mind (e g an intention to repay coupled with a belief, whether reasonable or not,[3] that he will be able to do so), the accused was acting dishonestly according to the current standards of ordinary decent people.

1 [1973] QB 530, [1973] 1 All ER 341, CA. For a criticism of this decision, see Elliott 'Law and Fact in Theft Act Cases' [1976] Crim LR 707.
2 *Ghosh* [1982] 2 All ER 689 at 696.
3 *Lewis* (1975) 62 Cr App Rep 206, CA.

13.55 In *Ghosh*,[1] a case concerned with other offences of dishonesty under the Act but the decision in which is expressly applicable to theft, the Court of Appeal added a second test to that laid down in *Feely*. It held that, to determine whether the prosecution had established dishonesty, the jury (or magistrates) must first see whether, as explained above, the accused's actions were dishonest according to the ordinary standards of reasonable and honest people. If his actions were not dishonest according to those standards, the matter ends there and the prosecution fails. However, second, and this is the additional test, if the accused's actions were dishonest according to those standards, the jury (or magistrates) must go on to decide whether the accused must have realised that what he was doing would be considered dishonest according to the ordinary standards of reasonable and honest people. If he did not realise this, then, however irrational or bigoted his state of mind may be,[2] his appropriation will not have been dishonest; if he did it will have been. The second test comes to this: it is dishonest for a person to act in a way which he knows ordinary people would consider to be dishonest, even if he believed that his actions were morally justified. In most cases where, given his state of mind, the accused's actions are obviously dishonest by ordinary standards, there will be no doubt that he himself knew he was acting dishonestly by the ordinary standards of reasonable and honest people.

It must be emphasised that the second test is not whether the accused believed that his behaviour was not dishonest by *his* standards. It is no defence for him to say: 'I knew that what I was doing is generally regarded as dishonest, but I did not regard it as dishonest myself'.[3] On the other hand, it is a defence to say – unless disproved: 'I did not know that ordinary people would regard what I was doing as dishonest'. In other words, under this test 'dishonestly' is not governed by the accused's own moral standards but by his understanding of the moral standards of ordinary, decent people. Of course, the more outrageous his alleged understanding of them is the less likely he is to be believed.

In *Ghosh* the Court of Appeal stated that Robin Hood would act dishonestly because he would know that ordinary people would consider his actions to be dishonest. However, assuming that the jury did consider that Robin Hood's actions were dishonest by the current standards of ordinary decent people, it is by no means certain that a claim by Robin Hood that he thought an ordinary person would not regard his actions as dishonest would easily be disproved.[4]

1 [1982] 2 All ER 689, CA. The definition of 'dishonesty' in this case has been held to be of general application, even outside the Theft Acts: *Lockwood* [1986] Crim LR 244, CA.
2 *Mitchell* (1990) unreported, CA.
3 *Ghosh* [1982] 2 All ER 689 at 696.
4 For a critical evaluation of the position after *Ghosh*, see Elliott 'Dishonesty in Theft' [1982] Crim LR 395. Also see Williams 'The Standard of Honesty' (1983) 133 NLJ 636. For suggestions for reform, see Elliott, loc cit; Smith *Law of Theft* (5th edn) para 124; Williams (1985) 5 *Legal Studies* 183.

13.56 The approach laid down in *Ghosh* is liable to create an additional ground for contested trials, to complicate the judge's direction, and to lead to arbitrary and inconsistent verdicts by different juries or benches of magistrates as to what is dishonest.[1] It would be much better if statute laid down as a matter of law a full definition of what is (or what is not) dishonesty.

1 These and other objections are neatly summarised by Griew 'Dishonesty: Objections to *Feely* and *Ghosh*' [1985] Crim LR 341.

13.57 *General* Although the judge in his summing up should inform the jury that dishonesty is one of the ingredients of theft, he is not required to give the jury a direction on the meaning of that term[1] unless there is evidence that D appropriated the property with one of the beliefs specified in s 2(1) or that he appropriated the property in circumstances which may cause a jury to find that he was not dishonest on the basis of the answers to the *Ghosh* questions (as where the accused claims that he intended to repay or that he thought that what he was doing was not dishonest).[2] To adopt the language of civil proceedings, a direction on dishonesty is relevant where the accused confesses and avoids, ie accepts that certain facts alleged against him are true but then goes on to allege a state of mind which may cause a jury to find that he was not dishonest.[3]

The fact that the judge need not direct the jury on the *Ghosh* questions if there is no evidence (as determined by the judge) of a state of mind which might cause a jury to find that the accused was not dishonest represents an inconsistency with the view taken by the House of Lords in *DPP v Stonehouse*[4] that, where a question of fact is involved (as in the case of dishonesty, outside the situations governed by s 2(1)), the judge should leave the issue to the jury even though on the evidence there can only be one answer, one adverse to the accused.

1 *McVey* [1988] Crim LR 127, CA, as explained in *O'Sullivan* [1989] Crim LR 506, CA.
2 See, for example, *Roberts* (1987) 84 Cr App Rep 117, CA; *Price* (1990) 91 Cr App Rep 409, CA; *O'Connell* [1991] Crim LR 781, CA. Where it is admitted that D's appropriation was dishonest from an objective point of view (i e under the first of the two questions in *Ghosh*), the judge need only direct the jury about the second question in *Ghosh*: *Thompson, Schwab and Spicer* (1988) unreported, CA.
3 *Spencer and Turner* (1989) unreported, CA.
4 [1978] AC 55, [1977] 2 All ER 909,HL; para 21.66.

13.58 The interrelation of the partial definition of dishonesty in s 2(1) with the tests of dishonesty which originated in *Feely* and were developed in *Ghosh* can be summarised as follows.

If there is evidence of a belief which is covered by s 2(1), the judge must tell the jury that as a matter of law they must acquit the accused unless the prosecution disproves his alleged belief beyond reasonable doubt.[1]

If there is evidence of a state of mind (other than a s 2(1) belief) that may cause a jury to find that the accused was not dishonest on the basis of answers to the *Ghosh* questions, the judge must leave the issue to the jury. He must not direct them that that the accused's appropriation, assuming the accused's version of the facts is not disproved, was or was not dishonest. Instead, he must tell them to determine what the accused's state of mind actually was (ie what his beliefs and intentions were); unless the accused's alleged state of mind is disproved by the prosecution the jury will, of course, have to find that it existed. The judge must then go on to tell the jury that, having determined the accused's actual state of mind, the jury must determine whether the accused's actions were dishonest according to the ordinary standards of reasonable and honest people, and that if they were not dishonest according to those standards the prosecution fails.[2] The judge should then go on to say that, if the accused's actions were dishonest according to the ordinary standards of reasonable and honest people, the jury must decide whether the accused must have realised that what he was doing was dishonest according to those standards and that if he did not realise this his appropriation will not have been dishonest, whereas if he did it will have been.

1 See *Wootton and Peake* [1990] Crim LR 201, CA, where this point is made, albeit rather weakly.
2 Note para 13.57, footnote 2.

13.59 For the sake of completeness it should be noted that s 2(2) expressly says what has already been implied: 'A person's appropriation of property belonging to another may be dishonest notwithstanding that he is willing to pay for the property'. Someone who knows that the owner of a picture does not wish to sell it might well be held guilty of theft if he took the picture, intending to deprive the owner permanently of it but leaving the price behind. On the other hand, an undergraduate who takes a bottle of beer from a friend's room, leaving the price, might not be held to have acted dishonestly, even if he did not believe that the owner would have consented to the appropriation (so that the case would not be covered by the provisions of s 2(1)).

INTENTION OF PERMANENTLY DEPRIVING

13.60 Actual permanent deprivation is not required for theft but the accused must be proved to have intended at the time he appropriated property belonging to another to deprive the other permanently of it. If D dishonestly takes P's watch, intending to deprive P permanently of it, D is guilty of theft, even though he is arrested almost immediately afterwards and the watch is returned to P. The intention permanently to deprive relates to the actual thing appropriated, so that an appropriator of money who intends to spend it but to repay it with other notes nevertheless has an intention permanently to deprive (although he may be found not to have acted dishonestly).[1] The same is, of course, true where other property, such as a pint of milk, is appropriated with the intention of consuming it and of replacing it with its equivalent.

Normally, D will intend permanently to deprive P by the act of appropriating P's property itself, but this is not necessary. Provided that it exists at the time of the appropriation, an intent to deprive P in the future by some subsequent act will do.[2]

The question of whether or not there was an intention permanently to deprive the person to whom the property belongs gives rise to no difficulty in the ordinary case because the accused's conduct with the property will often provide a clear inference as to his intention. For example, if D takes P's pork pie and eats it, or if D takes P's bricks and builds them into a wall on his property, or if D takes P's money and spends it in a pub, the inference of an intention permanently to deprive is very strong indeed (although it would be a misdirection for a judge to tell a jury that they must draw it). On the other hand, if D picks up P's copy of this book in the student work room and takes it over to his desk and reads it, or if D takes P's squash racquet and, after using it, leaves it elsewhere at the squash club, it is unimaginable that an inference could be drawn on these facts that D appropriated the property with an intention permanently to deprive.

It appears that in one case a person can intend permanently to deprive even though he only intends a purely temporary borrowing. This is where a victim of an appropriation has a limited interest in the property. For example, if P hires a power tool for a week from X and during that week D, knowing these facts, takes the tool, intending to return it to X ten days later, D can be convicted of the theft of the tool from P (since he intended permanently to deprive P of the whole of his interest in the property) but not of the theft of it from X (because he did not so intend in relation to X).

1 *Velumyl* [1989] Crim LR 299, DC.
2 This follows from the decision in *Morris* [1984] AC 320, [1983] 3 All ER 288, HL, where the appropriation consisted of label-swapping but the intended deprivation would only have occurred through an act of buying at the checkout.

13.61 *Section 6* In certain exceptional cases a person can be convicted of theft even though he did not mean permanently to deprive, and even though he positively intended to return the actual property at some future date (or did actually return it). A conviction in such a case is possible if the case falls within s 6 of the Act, which extends the meaning of 'intention of permanently depriving'.

It cannot be emphasised too much that s 6 does not provide a complete definition of 'intention of permanently depriving'; instead it simply extends or clarifies that phrase.[1] In the vast majority of cases it need not be referred to at all, and it certainly should not be referred to if the issue of whether or not the accused had the intention of permanently depriving can be determined without reference to it. The Court of Appeal in *Lloyd*[1] said that reference to s 6 should be made in exceptional cases only, and these are cases where the accused does not mean the other person permanently to lose the thing but has acted in a way which may fall within s 6.

1 [1985] QB 829 at 834–6. Also see *Warner* (1970) 55 Cr App Rep 93, CA; *Cocks* (1976) 63 Cr App Rep 79, CA; *Coffey* [1987] Crim LR 498, CA.

13.62 *Section 6(1): Part 1* Section 6(1) provides that a person appropriating property belonging to another without meaning the other permanently to lose the thing itself is nevertheless to be regarded as having the intention of permanently depriving the other of it if his *intention is to treat the thing as his own to dispose of regardless of the other's rights*. The following are examples of cases which are caught by the above words of s 6(1), even though the accused does not mean the other permanently to lose the thing in question.

D takes P's Ming vase, intending to sell it back to P (or to hold it to ransom) and to return it to P only if P pays the asking price or ransom. D clearly intends to treat the thing as his own to dispose of regardless of the rights of the other (P), since he intends that P should only get back what he is already entitled to[1] by paying for it, even though he does not mean P to be permanently deprived because he hopes that P will pay the asking price (or ransom).[2] Similarly, D would intend to treat the vase as his own to dispose of if he intends to pledge it and send the pawn receipt to P, even though he hopes that P will redeem the vase.

Another type of case which can fall within the above words of s 6(1) is where the accused abandons the property and he is indifferent as to whether it is recovered by the person to whom it belongs (or he may even hope that it is). If, by the circumstances of the abandonment and/or the nature of the property, it is (to the accused's knowledge) extremely unlikely that the property will be recovered, he can be said to intend to dispose of it regardless of the rights of the other. An obvious example of a case which would be caught by s 6(1) would be where D takes P's watch in Leicester and abandons it in Newcastle. At the other extreme D, who took and used P's squash racquet and then left it elsewhere at the squash club, would not be caught by s 6(1), and neither, generally speaking, would a person who takes another's car and then abandons it because it is a well known fact that cars which are abandoned are almost invariably returned to their owners.

If D appropriates P's piano by pretending to be its owner and purporting to sell it to X, knowing that P's imminent return will prevent the removal of the piano, he can be convicted of its theft since he intends to treat it as his own to dispose of regardless of P's rights and is therefore deemed by s 6(1) to intend permanently to deprive P of it. (However, it would be more appropriate to charge D with obtaining by deception any money received from X.) The decision of the Privy Council in *Chan Man-sin v A-G of Hong Kong*[3] provides an interesting example of the fact that the requirements of s 6(1) can be satisfied even where D knows that the person to whom the property belongs will not lose anything. A company accountant drew and presented forged cheques in his favour on the company's account. The Privy Council held that there was evidence from which it could be inferred that his appropriations of a thing in action (the credit in the company's bank account) had been accompanied by an intention permanently to deprive the company of that thing because he intended to treat the bank credit as his own to dispose of regardless of the company's rights, and it would not matter if he had realised that the fraud would be discovered and that the company's credit balance would be unaffected.

1 Section 6(1) would not apply if P was not entitled to the property without paying for it: *Johnstone, Comerford and Jalil* [1982] Crim LR 454 and 607, Crown Ct.
2 Such an example was given in *Lloyd* [1985] QB 829, [1985] 2 All ER 661, CA.
3 [1988] 1 All ER 1, [1988] 1 WLR 196, PC.

13.63 *Section 6(1): Part 2* Section 6(1) goes on to provide that a borrowing or lending of property may amount to treating it as the accused's own to dispose of regardless of the rights of the other if, but only if, the borrowing or lending is for a period and in circumstances making it equivalent to an outright taking or disposal. In *Lloyd* [1] the Court of Appeal held that this part of s 6(1) 'is intended to make clear that a mere borrowing is never enough to constitute the necessary [mens rea] unless the intention is to return the "thing" in such a changed state that it can truly be said that all its goodness or virtue has gone'. It is clear from the example given in *Lloyd* and set out below that 'changed state' does not mean that the thing's physical state must have changed.

An example of a case covered by the second part of s 6(1), which was given by the Court of Appeal in *Lloyd*, is where someone takes railway tickets intending that they should be returned to the railways board only after the journeys have been completed. Clearly, the borrowing here is for a period and in circumstances equivalent to an outright taking or disposal because, if the tickets are returned as intended, all their goodness and virtue will have gone. The same can be said if D takes P's football season ticket, intending to return it at the end of the season. D's borrowing is clearly for a period and in circumstances making it equivalent to an outright taking since, when it is returned as he intends, the season ticket will be a virtually worthless piece of paper. His intention to borrow the season ticket in this way amounts to the intention to treat the thing as his own to dispose of regardless of P's rights and is thereby deemed by s 6(1) to be an intention permanently to deprive P of it.

The same analysis would apply if D unauthorisedly took from P a cheque drawn in his favour by P, which was only to be handed over when D had delivered some goods, intending to pay it into his bank account. If it is paid in and honoured by P's bank, the cheque, which will have become a worthless piece of paper, will eventually return to P (or be available at his bank). Clearly, the intended borrowing of the cheque is for a period and in circumstances making it equivalent to an outright taking and, even if he realises the cheque will eventually be returned, D is deemed to intend permanently to deprive P of it. [2] Likewise, if D took a battery from P's shop for his torch, intending to return it when the battery was exhausted, he would be deemed to intend permanently to deprive P of the battery. (He could, of course, also be convicted of the offence of abstracting electricity, which might be a more appropriate charge.) Lastly, we saw in para 13.21, that confidential information in an examination paper is not property and cannot be stolen. However, if a student surreptitiously borrows a college examination paper a week before the examination, intending to copy it and then to return it, his appropriation of the piece of paper will be done with the intention of permanently depriving the college authorities of it (the paper) because the borrowing is for a period and in circumstances making it equivalent to an outright taking or disposal (since, if the paper is returned as intended, all its goodness and virtue will have gone).

In these cases the property would be virtually worthless at the time of the intended return. It remains uncertain what the position would be if the property at the time of its intended return would have some value, but a greatly reduced value (as where the season ticket had one match's unexpired use). Can it really be said that all the goodness or virtue of the ticket has gone; is the borrowing really for a period and in circumstances equivalent to an outright taking? It is submitted that the answer must be 'no'.

The above examples may be contrasted with the facts of *Lloyd* itself. The accused removed films from a cinema, for a few hours on each occasion, in order to make 'pirate' copies of them. The Court of Appeal held that this did not constitute theft of the films because, although great financial harm would be caused to the copyright owner and others, the goodness and virtue of the films would not have gone out of them on their return; they could still be projected to cinema audiences. Therefore, the borrowing was not for a period, or in circumstances, making it equivalent to an outright taking or disposal.

So far, we have been concerned with 'borrowings'; an example of a lending falling within s 6(1) would be where D, the bailee of P's can of fly spray, lends it to X, telling X that he can keep it and use it for as long as he likes. If D realises that the can may never be returned or may be returned empty, the intended lending is for a period and in circumstances equivalent to an outright disposal and he is deemed by s 6(1) to intend permanently to deprive P of the can, even though he may not mean P to be so deprived.

1 [1985] QB 829, [1985] 2 All ER 661, CA.
2 *Duru* [1973] 3 All ER 715, [1974] 1 WLR 2, CA. For another explanation of this case, see Smith *The Law of Theft* (6th edn), para 139.

13.64 *Section 6(2)* Section 6(2) provides a further explanation of 'treating as one's own to dispose of regardless of the other's rights'. It provides that where a person parts with property belonging to another under a condition as to its return which he may not be able to perform, this (if done for purposes of his own and without the other's authority) amounts to treating the property as his own to dispose of regardless of the other's rights. Thus, where D takes P's property and then pawns it, intending to redeem it and return it if he wins a bet, this amounts to 'treating as his own to dispose of . . .' and his intention to do so is regarded as an intention permanently to deprive P of it.

13.65 *Conditional intention* This rather misleading term is commonly used to describe the accused's state of mind in the type of case where he looks for something to steal, as where he rifles through P's handbag, intending to keep anything worth keeping but finds nothing worthwhile. In such a case the accused cannot be convicted of the theft of the handbag or any of its contents,[1] although he may be convicted of attempted theft on a suitably framed charge.[2] The true reason why D cannot be convicted of theft in such a case, and the reason why 'conditional intention' is a misleading description of the accused's state of mind, is that, even if his conduct can be described as an appropriation, the accused has *no* intention permanently to deprive P of the handbag or its contents. On the other hand, if D finds something which may, on further examination be worth keeping and he retains it for further examination, it is arguable, at least where he expects that the thing will be worth keeping, that he does commit theft of it because his appropriation at that stage is accompanied by an intention permanently to deprive P of the thing.[3]

1 *Easom* [1971] 2 QB 315, [1971] 2 All ER 945, CA.
2 Para 21.63.
3 See Griew *Theft Acts 1968 and 1978* (6th edn), para 2.113-2.117.

13.66 *Comment* Except to the extent that s 6 applies, the requirement of an intention of permanent deprival excludes from the law of theft unauthorised borrowing, which many think should be included, but this is a question of the proper sphere of the criminal law. Are people to be punished for simply being a nuisance to others? Is it wise to have prohibitory laws (and there are plenty of them as it is) which work only provided that there are no prosecutions in venial cases?[1] Such offences of unauthorised borrowing as exist are covered in paras 14.16 to 14.25.

1 For argument in favour of abolishing the requirement of intention permanently to deprive, see Williams 'Temporary Appropriation Should be Theft' [1981] Crim LR 129.

14 Offences against property 2: Offences under the Theft Acts other than theft

14.1 In the last chapter we described the basic law of theft and the definitions necessary to it. In this chapter we have to deal with a variety of other offences under the Theft Acts 1968 and 1978, some of which are related to theft in some way but which differ from it in one or more vital respects. Clauses 146 to 150, 152 to 163 and 172 to 175 of the draft Criminal Code Bill[1] restate these offences with some amendments; most of these are designed simply to make the relevant provisions simpler or clearer, but two amendments which are identified at appropriate points in this chapter make minor changes to the substance of some offences.

Unless otherwise indicated the offences discussed in this chapter are triable either way,[2] the maximum punishments stated relating to convictions on indictment.

1 Law Commission: A Criminal Code for England and Wales (1989): Law Com No 177; see para 3.21 above.
2 Magistrates' Courts Act 1980, s 17(1) and Sch 1; Theft Act 1978, s 4(1).

Robbery

14.2 Section 8 of the Theft Act 1968 provides that a person is guilty of robbery if he steals and, immediately before or at the time of doing so, and in order to do so, he uses force on any person or puts or seeks to put any person in fear of being then and there subjected to force. Robbery is triable only on indictment; the maximum punishment is life imprisonment.

14.3 *Need for a theft* Robbery is theft aggravated by the use of force or the threat of force. It follows that the necessary ingredients of theft must be proved, so that a person who forces another to hand over money, believing that he has a legal right to it, is not guilty of robbery since, not being dishonest,[1] he is not guilty of theft, and this is so even though he does not believe he was entitled to use force to get the money.[2] In *Robinson*,[3] for example, it was alleged that D, who was owed £7 by P's wife, approached P, brandishing a knife. A fight followed, during which P dropped a £5 note. D picked it up and demanded the remaining £2 owed to him. Allowing D's appeal against conviction for robbery, the Court of Appeal held that the prosecution had to prove that D was guilty of theft, and that he would not be (under s 2(1)(a) of the 1968 Act) if he honestly believed that he had a right in law to deprive P of the money, even though he knew he was not entitled to use the knife to get it. Therefore the trial judge had been wrong to tell the jury that D must have believed he had the legal right to take the money in the way he did.

Where the accused has used force on another (or put another person in fear of force) in order to steal but has not achieved the appropriation of any property, and is therefore not guilty of robbery, he can be convicted of assault with intent to rob, which is triable only on indictment and punishable with life imprisonment.

1 Para 13.52.
2 *Skivington* [1968] 1 QB 166, [1967] 1 All ER 483, CA; *Robinson* [1977] Crim LR 173, CA.
3 [1977] Crim LR 173, CA.

14.4 *Additional elements* To constitute robbery, the force must be used or threatened immediately before or at the time of the theft. It need not be used against the owner or possessor of the property stolen, so that if a gang uses force against a signalman only in order to stop and steal from a train, its members are guilty of robbery. Difficult questions of degree can arise. If the signalman were bound and gagged by force an hour before the stealing from the train, the gang having operated the signals in the meantime, it could be argued that the force was used immediately before the theft, but there must be some limit unless the word 'immediately' becomes meaningless. Questions of degree are, however, difficult to avoid if the definition of robbery is not to be unduly wide.

It is clear that there is no robbery if the force is used or threatened after 'the time' of the theft. The thief who uses force to defend his possession after he has taken the goods is guilty of robbery only if it can be established that he is doing so at 'the time' of the theft. This is not limited to the period (possibly a split second of time) during which the initial appropriation with the mens rea for theft occurs, since an act of appropriation may be a continuing one.[1] It is for the jury to decide when it is over,[2] although they should presumably be given some direction on this. It may be that 'the time' of the theft lasts as long as the theft can be said to be still in progress in common sense terms, although here again there must be a limit.

Where force is used, it must be used 'on' a person. In *Clouden*[3] the Court of Appeal held that this does not require that force be used on the actual person to overpower his resistance, and that force used only to get possession of property can be used 'on' a person. In this case a man who had wrenched a shopping basket from the hands of a woman was held to have been rightly convicted of robbery. The Court of Appeal's view was consciously different from that of the Criminal Law Revision Committee, who did not regard the mere snatching of property, such as a handbag, from an unresisting woman as using force for the purpose of the definition of robbery, though they thought that it might be so if the owner resisted.[4] In the case of a threat of force, a threat of future force is insufficient; the threat must be 'then and there' to subject another to force. Whether what the accused has done or threatened is 'force' is a question of fact for the jury.[5]

The force must be used or threatened in order to steal; a man who knocks a woman to the ground to rape her, but then changes his mind and instead takes her handbag which she has dropped, is not guilty of robbery or assault with intent to rob, although he may be convicted of theft and of attempted rape. The force need not be used against the person from whom the property is stolen.

The use or threat of force for the purpose of types of theft other than by direct taking suffices to render the person using or threatening it guilty of robbery. For example, if D finds P's watch and, having intended to return it to P, changes his mind when P discovers the whereabouts of his watch and calls upon D to return it, D is guilty of robbery if he accompanies his refusal to return the watch with force aimed at P. On the other hand, if D appropriates the watch before P asks for it, he has already stolen it and so his use of force in order to keep it does not make him guilty of robbery.

1 *Hale* (1978) 68 Cr App Rep 415, CA. Cf *Gregory* (1982) 77 Cr App Rep 41, CA.
2 *Hale* (1978) 68 Cr App Rep 415, CA.
3 [1987] Crim LR 56, CA.
4 Eighth Report of the Criminal Law Revision Committee, para 65.
5 *Dawson and James* (1976) 64 Cr App Rep 170, CA; *Clouden* [1987] Crim LR 56, CA.

14.5 Clearly, the fact that robbery requires the use of force to be for the purpose of theft is restrictive of the scope of the offence, although some of the restrictions are perhaps of more theoretical than practical interest. A uses force against B for the purpose of temporarily taking B's car; C uses force against D who is seeking to prevent him from uttering deceitful words whereby he hopes to obtain the remission of a debt owed to a gullible old lady; E uses force against F who is preventing him from executing a fraudulent conveyance of the land of which he is trustee. Assuming that A, C and E accomplish their purposes, E alone is guilty of robbery. If their purposes are not accomplished, E alone is guilty of an assault with intent to rob, but it does not follow that those who for one reason or another escape a conviction for robbery avoid criminal liability altogether. Obviously, if force is used or threatened there is the possibility of a conviction for assault or one of the more serious offences against the person. In some cases there is the possibility of a conviction for blackmail. The man who demands the temporary possession of a car coupled with a threat of force is not guilty of robbery, because there is no theft, but he is guilty of blackmail.

Burglary and aggravated burglary

14.6 There are two separate types of offence of burglary. Both are governed by s 9 of the Theft Act 1968 and are punishable with a maximum of 14 years' imprisonment if committed in respect of a building or part of a building which is a dwelling but otherwise with a maximum of ten years'.[1] Because the maximum punishment for each type of burglary depends on whether or not a dwelling is involved, each type consists of two distinct offences: burglary in a dwelling and burglary in any other type of building.[2]

1 Criminal Justice Act 1991, s 26.
2 This is the effect of *Courtie* [1984] AC 463, [1984] 1 All ER 740, HL; para 15.2.

THE FIRST TYPE OF OFFENCE

14.7 This is defined by s 9(1)(a), whose effect is that a person is guilty of burglary if he enters any building or part of a building as a trespasser and with intent to commit one of the offences specified in s 9(2), viz: stealing anything in the building or part of the building, inflicting on any person therein any grievous bodily harm or raping any woman therein, and doing unlawful damage to the building or anything therein.

14.8 *Entry* It remains to be clearly decided what constitutes an 'entry' into a building (or part) for the purposes of s 9. However, some guidance is provided in *Brown*[1], where the Court of Appeal held that there could be an entry for the purpose of s9 by a person whose whole body had not been inside the building (or part) and that consequently there had been an entry by an accused who had been seen half inside a shop window, rummaging inside it. In fact, the Court of Appeal held that it would be astounding if it was held that there was not an entry by a smash-and-grab raider who inserted a hand through a shop window to grab goods.

In *Brown* the Court of Appeal held that whether or not an intrusion constitutes an 'entry' is a question of fact for the jury. In terms of guidance for the jury, the Court, adapting a dictum in *Collins*,[2] postulated a test of 'effective entry'. While the meaning of the word 'effective' in this context is unclear, minimal intrusions, as where the accused's fingers are inserted through a gap between a window and its frame in order to open the window, would be very unlikely to be held to be effective entries by a jury.

Under the old law an entry could be effected merely by the insertion of an *instrument* without the intrusion of any part of the body *provided it was inserted to commit a relevant further offence* (eg a hook to extract (steal) a ring), but not if it was inserted merely to facilitate access by a person's body.[3] It remains to be decided to what extent, if any, such an insertion, even if effective, can be an entry, but it would seem that, at least, an insertion to facilitate entry cannot be.

1 [1985] Crim LR 611, CA. This report does not contain all the points contained in the transcript of the Court of Appeal's judgment, which is available on Lexis.
2 [1973] QB 100, [1972] 2 All ER 1105, CA.
3 *Anon* (1584) 1 and 117.

14.9 *As a trespasser* Trespass is a concept of the civil law. A person enters a building or part of a building as a trespasser if it is in the possession of another and he enters without a right by law or permission to do so.

Rights of entry are granted by statute to certain people for certain purposes. For instance, a police officer entering premises with a search warrant authorised under some statute is not a trespasser if he enters with the intention of searching pursuant to such a warrant, but he is if he enters with the intention of raping some woman inside the premises.

Permission to enter for a particular purpose or purposes may be given only by the occupier or someone acting with his authority or, in the present context, by a member of the occupier's household acting without his authority[1] (although this probably does not apply where the invitation is for the express purpose of committing theft or one of the other further offences in the building). Permission may be express or implied. For instance, in the case of shops there is an implied permission for members of the public to enter for the purposes of inspecting goods on display or making purchases. A person who enters a building with permission, intending to commit a relevant offence, enters in excess of his permission and is a trespasser. In *Jones and Smith*[2] it was held that a man who had permission to enter his father's home entered it as a trespasser when he entered it to steal his father's television set because he entered in excess of his permission.

A permission to enter may not necessarily extend to every part of the building. Thus, a person may lawfully enter a building, such as an hotel, shop or railway station, but trespass in the manager's office, stockroom or booking office; equally he may be a lawful guest at a meal in a private house but trespass in a bedroom. In both of these cases the trespass will be in 'part of a building'.

In certain circumstances a person may enter as a trespasser despite the fact that he has apparent permission, e g where permission was given under a mistake as to his identity, which normally will have been induced by fraud.

1 *Collins* [1973] QB 100 at 107. This goes beyond the civil law rules concerning trespass.
2 [1976] 3 All ER 54, [1976] 1 WLR 672, CA. See, further, Pace 'Burglarious Trespass' [1985] Crim LR 716.

14.10 *Buildings or part of a building* The requirement that the accused must enter as a trespasser a 'building or part of a building' raises the question of what constitutes a building. Section 9(3) states that references to a building also apply to an inhabited vehicle or vessel (whether or not the person having a habitation in it is there at the time).[1] Clearly, a caravan or houseboat which is someone's permanent home is an 'inhabited vehicle or vessel', even though he is not there at the time; so is a caravan or houseboat which is used as a holiday home during the summer during those weeks or weekends in which it is being so used, but whether it is inhabited during the rest of the summer is open to doubt. Certainly, a 'holiday home' caravan or boat is not inhabited when it is closed up for the winter.

Apart from s 9(3), the Act is silent. However, it seems that a substantial portable structure with most of the attributes normally found in buildings can be a 'building' for the purpose of burglary, provided there is an element of permanence in the site which it occupies. In *B and S v Leathley*,[2] a decision by the Crown Court in its appellate capacity, it was held that a freezer container measuring 25ft by 7ft by 7ft and weighing three tons, which had occupied the same position for three years and was likely to remain there for the foreseeable future, had doors and was connected to mains electricity, was a 'building' for the purposes of burglary. This decision can usefully be contrasted with *Norfolk Constabulary v Seekings and Gould*,[3] where articulated trailers being used as temporary stores, which had electric power, steps and lockable shutters and had been so used for about a year, were held by the Crown Court in its appellate capacity not to be 'buildings' for the purposes of burglary.

A 'part of a building' does not necessarily mean a separate room; it also includes a physically marked out area in a room, such as the area behind a counter in a shop, from which the accused is plainly excluded, whether expressly or impliedly.[4]

1 Theft Act 1968, s 9(3).
2 [1979] Crim LR 314, Crown Ct.
3 [1986] Crim LR 167, Crown Ct.
4 *Walkington* [1979] 2 All ER 716, [1979] 1 WLR 1169, CA.

14.11 *Mens rea* Part of the mens rea required for an offence of burglary under s 9(1)(a) is that the accused must know that he is entering as a trespasser (i e he must know he is entering without a right by law or permission to do so) or be reckless as to this fact. This was established by the Court of Appeal in *Collins*.[1] About two o'clock early one morning in June a young lady of 18 went to bed. She wore no night apparel and the bed was very near the open lattice-type window of her room. She awoke about two hours later and saw in the moonlight a vague form crouched in the open window. She leapt to the conclusion that her boyfriend was paying her an ardent nocturnal visit; she sat up in bed, and (according to Collins, who had arrived to have intercourse with her, by force if necessary) helped him to enter the room, after which they had full intercourse; then she realised that he was not her boyfriend but Collins, who was later convicted of burglary. The Court of Appeal, allowing Collins' appeal, held that the prosecution had to prove that Collins entered as a trespasser and knew it or was reckless as to this, and that, on the basis that Collins had not entered the room before he was helped in by the young lady, the trial judge had not directed the jury adequately on the need for Collins' entry to have been accompanied by knowledge on his part that he was entering as a trespasser, or recklessness as to this. It appears that the court was using recklessness in its subjective sense, so as to require a realisation on the part of the accused that he might be entering as a trespasser. In a case such as *Jones and Smith*,[2] the accused must know that he is entering in excess of the permission given to him or be reckless as to this.

1 [1973] QB 100, [1972] 2 All ER 1105, CA.
2 [1976] 3 All ER 54, [1976] 1 WLR 672, CA; para 14.9. In *Collins* [1973] QB 100, [1972] 2 All ER 1105, CA, the Court of Appeal did not discuss whether Collins knew or was reckless as to whether he was entering in excess of the supposed permission. The case is not easy to reconcile with *Jones and Smith*.

14.12 In addition to knowledge or subjective recklessness that he enters a building as a trespasser, the accused's entry must be accompanied by the further intent to commit one of the offences specified in s 9(2), viz:

a) to steal anything in *the* building or, as the case may be, *the* part of the building trespassed in; or

b) to inflict grievous bodily harm on any person in *the* building or, as the case may be, *the* part of the building trespassed in; or

c) to rape any woman in *the* building or, as the case may be, *the* part of the building trespassed in; or

d) to do unlawful (i e criminal) damage to *the* building or anything therein (whether or not the accused has trespassed in the part in which the damage is intended to occur).

Although the wording of the provision is not entirely free from doubt, it would seem that the accused's intention at the time of entry must relate to property or a person then in the building (or part) entered as a trespasser;[1] for example, to steal property then in the building trespassed in or to rape a woman who is then there. Consequently, it is not burglary to enter a bank as trespasser, intending to steal some bullion when it is delivered to the bank, nor is it burglary to enter a building as a trespasser, intending to rape therein a woman whom one's accomplice is dragging in behind one. On the other hand, it would be burglary to enter a house, intending to drag out its female occupant and rape her elsewhere, since the wording of the provision does not seem to require the intended offence to be intended to be committed in the building (or part) entered as a trespasser.

The requisite intent will exist only if the accused's intended conduct would, if carried out in accordance with his intentions, amount to the offence allegedly intended. Thus, a person who trespasses in a building to take something to which he believes he has a legal right lacks an intent to steal and does not commit burglary.

Where a person is charged with entry into a building or part of a building with intent to steal, and the indictment does not aver an intention to steal a specific or identified object, the accused can be convicted if at the time of entry he had the necessary intent to steal something therein, even though he did not intend to steal a specific thing but merely intended to steal anything that he might find worth stealing, or even though there was in fact nothing there worth his while to steal.[2] Thus, a person who enters part of a department store, intending to steal from the till, can be convicted of burglary even though the till is empty.

The punishment of burglary by entry with intent is a branch of preventive justice, like the punishment of attempts to commit crime. A further illustration of this kind of preventive justice is contained in s 25 which is discussed in paras 14.92 to 14.95.

1 For a discussion of this point, see White 'Lurkers, Draggers and Kidnappers: The further offence in Burglary' (1986) 150 JPN 37 and 56.
2 *Walkington* [1979] 2 All ER 716, [1979] 1 WLR 1169, CA; *Re A-G's References (Nos 1 and 2 of 1979)* [1980] QB 180, [1979] 3 All ER 143, CA.

THE SECOND TYPE OF OFFENCE

14.13 The second type of offence of burglary is defined by s 9(1)(b): 'A person is guilty of burglary if having entered any building or part of a building as a trespasser he steals or attempts to steal anything in the building or that part of it or inflicts or attempts to inflict on any person therein any grievous bodily harm.' 'Trespasser' and 'building' have the same meanings as in the other offence of burglary. The important distinction is that this type of offence requires the accused, having entered the building or part as a trespasser, actually to have committed or attempted the offence of theft or the offence of inflicting grievous bodily harm (in terms both of the actus reus and mens rea of the relevant offence)[1]; on the other hand he is not required to have had the intent to commit such an offence when he entered. The accused must know or be reckless that he has entered as a trespasser when he commits or attempts one of the two offences. It is irrelevant whether or not he realised at the time of entry that he was entering as a trespasser. Thus, if a person enters a building, thinking that he has permission, and later realises that he has not and then steals something inside or inflicts grievous bodily harm on someone inside (eg the occupier who is trying to eject him) he is guilty of burglary of the present type.

1 The suggestion in an unanswered question by the Court of Appeal in *Jenkins* [1984] AC 242, [1983] 3 All ER 448, that the infliction of grievous bodily harm need not amount to an offence (so that a trespasser could be guilty of burglary if his entry caused quite unforeseen serious harm to an occupant, such as a heart attack through shock) was not commented on by the House of Lords on appeal ([1984] AC 242, [1983] 3 All ER 448). It would be unfortunate if it ever became the law, since it would extend a serious offence to cover something which is not in itself an offence. The corresponding provision in the draft Criminal Code Bill (cl 147) expressly requires an offence to be committed or attempted in relation to serious harm caused or attempted to be caused by a trespasser: Law Commission: A Criminal Code for England and Wales (1989): Law Com No 177.

GENERAL

14.14 Both types of offence require a trespassory entry into a building or part of a building. To be guilty of the first (s 9(1)(a)) type of offence, it must be proved that, at the time of his trespassory entry, the accused intended to commit one of the specified offences. Someone who enters a building as a trespasser with the intention of going to sleep inside is not guilty of burglary of the first type if he subsequently forms the intention of stealing something from the premises, but if he actually steals or attempts to steal the thing in question, he is then guilty of burglary of the second (s 9(1)(b)) type by virtue of the commission or attempted commission of theft. Where a person enters a building, or part, as a trespasser with intent to steal or inflict grievous bodily harm, and commits the intended offence or attempts to do so, he can be charged with either type of offence, since the two types are not mutually exclusive;[1] in practice he will normally be charged with the second type of offence in such a case.

Where a person is tried in the Crown Court for the second type of offence of burglary (but not the first as well), and the jury find him not guilty of that offence, the jury may return an alternative verdict of guilty of the first type if they find its requirements proved,[2] but not vice versa.

Burglary comprising the commission of, or an intention to commit, an offence triable only on indictment is itself triable only on indictment, as is burglary in a dwelling if a person there was subjected to violence or the threat of violence.

1 *Taylor* [1979] Crim LR 649, CA.
2 *Whiting* (1987) 85 Cr App Rep 78, [1987] Crim LR 473, CA.

AGGRAVATED BURGLARY

14.15 By s 10 of the Theft Act 1968 a person is guilty of aggravated burglary if he commits any burglary and at the time has with him any firearm or imitation firearm, any weapon of offence, or any explosive.

A 'weapon of offence' means any article made or adapted for use for causing injury to or incapacitating a person, or intended by the person having it with him for such use.[1] Handcuffs are an example of an article made for incapacitation, and rope is an example of one intended for such if it is intended to use it to tie up someone in the building. For further discussion of a similar definition to the present one, the reader is referred to para 18.86.

It is not necessary that the accused intended to use the article to injure or incapacitate someone in the course of the burglary itself. It suffices that he had it with him for such use on another occasion.[2]

Reference to other similarly worded offences relating to firearms and offensive weapons[3] suggests that, in order for a burglar to have with him a firearm etc, there must be a close physical link between him and the article and it must have been immediately available to him, and that 'has with him' means 'knowingly has with him' (so that a burglar who is ignorant that there is a dagger in his swag-bag is not guilty of aggravated burglary).

To commit aggravated burglary, a person must have with him a relevant article *at the time* he commits burglary. Where the burglary alleged is entry as a trespasser with intent to steal etc, this means the time of the entry into a building, or part, as a trespasser with an appropriate further intent; where the burglary alleged is that, having entered as a trespasser, the accused stole etc, it means the time when, having entered a building or part as a trespasser, a person actually steals or inflicts grievous bodily harm, or attempts such, whether or not he had with him the article when he entered.[4]

Aggravated burglary is punishable with a maximum of imprisonment for life, and is triable only on indictment.

1 Theft Act 1968, s 10(1)(b).

2 *Stones* [1989] 1 WLR 156, (1989) 89 Cr App Rep 26, CA. For a criticism of this decision, see Reville 'Mischief of Aggravated Burglary' (1989) 139 NLJ 835.
3 Para 18.83.
4 *Francis* [1982] Crim LR 363, CA.

Temporary deprivation

14.16   So far, we have considered offences in which, if property is appropriated, an intention of permanently depriving the owner must be proved. At this stage we deviate in order to consider those offences where an intention of temporarily depriving is enough.

REMOVAL OF AN ARTICLE FROM A PLACE OPEN TO PUBLIC

14.17   Section 11(1) of the Theft Act 1968 provides that 'where the public have access to a building in order to view the building or part of it, or a collection or part of a collection housed in it, any person who without lawful authority removes from the building or its grounds the whole or part of any article displayed or kept for display to the public in the building or that part of it or in its grounds is guilty of an offence.' Such an offence is punishable with a maximum of five years' imprisonment.[1]

In recommending the creation of this offence, the Criminal Law Revision Committee had in mind such eccentric behaviour as the removal of Goya's portrait of the Duke of Wellington from the National Gallery in which it was not clear beyond reasonable doubt that the taker intended to deprive the person to whom the property belonged permanently of it.

The offence under consideration covers removals only from non-commercial collections, but if the thing removed is there otherwise than as forming part of, or being on loan for exhibition with, a collection intended for permanent exhibition,[2] it must be removed on a day when the public has access to the building or grounds.[3] Thus, the offence is not committed if a painting is removed from a wholly temporary art exhibition in a church hall on a day when the hall is closed.

The accused's belief that he had lawful authority for the removal of the thing in question or that he would have it if the person entitled to give it knew of the removal and its circumstances is a defence.[4] The belief does not have to have been a reasonable one as a matter of law, and the burden of proving it is not borne by the accused.[5]

1 Theft Act 1968, s 11(4).
2 See *Durkin* [1973] QB 786, [1973] 2 All ER 872, CA.
3 Theft Act 1968, s 11(2).
4 Ibid, s 11(3).
5 Ch 7.

TAKING CONVEYANCES WITHOUT AUTHORITY

14.18   Section 12(1) of the Theft Act 1968 provides that a person is guilty of an offence triable only summarily and punishable with imprisonment for up to six months or a fine not exceeding level 5 on the standard scale (£5,000) or both[1] if, without having the consent of the owner or other lawful authority, he takes any conveyance for his own or another's use.

Although the offence under s 12(1) is a summary one, s 41 of the Criminal Justice Act 1988 provides that a count charging a person with it may be included in an indictment if the charge:

a) is founded on the same facts or evidence as a count charging an indictable offence; or

b) is part of a series of offences of the same or similar character as an indictable offence which is also charged,

but only if (in either case) the facts or evidence relating to the offence were disclosed in an examination or deposition taken before a magistrate.

When a jury acquits an accused of theft of a conveyance it may convict him of an uncharged offence under s 12(1) if satisfied that he is guilty of it.[2]

If convicted on indictment for an offence under s 12(1) an offender is punishable in the same way as he could have been on summary conviction.[3]

Where a conveyance has been taken and driven away there can be a charge of stealing the fuel consumed but usually the prosecution rely simply on a charge under s 12(1).

As an offence under s 12(1) is a summary one, an attempt to commit it is not an offence.[4] However, s 8 of the Criminal Attempts Act 1981 provides a separate offence of interference with a *motor vehicle* with the intention that an offence under s 12 shall be committed. There is no corresponding offence in relation to other types of conveyance, such as boats and aircraft.

1 Theft Act 1968, s 12(2), as amended by the Criminal Justice Act 1988, s 37(1).
2 Theft Act 1968, s 12(4), as amended by the Criminal Justice Act 1988, s 37(1).
3 Theft Act 1968, s 12(2) and (4), as amended.
4 Para 21.53.

14.19 *Conveyance* Although a dictionary definition of a conveyance confines it to a vehicle or carriage, there is no such limitation for the purposes of s 12 which defines it as 'any conveyance constructed or adapted for the carriage of a person or persons whether by land, water or air, except that it does not include a conveyance constructed or adapted for use only under the control of a person not carried in or on it'.[1] There is no need for it to have either wheels or engine, but it has been held that a horse is not a conveyance for this purpose and that s 12 is directed towards artefacts rather than towards animals.[2] It is clear that a conveyance cannot include either a handcart or a trailer because, although passengers can be carried in them, they are not constructed or adapted for this purpose and anyway, even if they are, they are constructed for use only under the control of a person not carried in or on them. For this latter reason, perambulators, pedestrian-controlled milkfloats and most lawnmowers are not conveyances. However, a conveyance would undoubtedly include a lawnmower constructed or adapted for use under the control of a person carried on it; it would also include an invalid carriage, whether powered or not, constructed or adapted for use under the control of the occupant. There seems no reason why the definition should not include skates and skis but the extension to a pair of shoes might be resisted.

1 Theft Act 1968, s 12(7)(a).
2 *Neal v Gribble* [1978] RTR 409, DC.

14.20 *Taking* The mere unauthorised assumption of possession of a conveyance was held in *Bogacki*[1] not to be enough to constitute a taking; some movement, however small, must take place.

Unauthorised use of a conveyance by a person already in lawful possession or control of a conveyance may amount to a taking. An employee who uses his employer's lorry for his own purposes after the expiry of the period for which he is authorised to use it, usually the working day, thereby takes it.[2] So does an employee who, during the period for which he is authorised to use it, appropriates the employer's lorry to his own use in a manner which is inconsistent with the rights of the employer and shows that he has assumed control of it for his own purposes. Consequently, a serious deviation from the employee's proper route may be a taking. In *McKnight v Davies*[3] D crashed his employer's lorry while driving back to the depot after making some deliveries. Scared by this, he drove to a public house for a drink, then took three men to their houses, then drove to another public house for another drink, parked the lorry near his house and only on the following day returned it to the depot. The Divisional Court, upholding D's conviction under s 12, said that not every brief unauthorised diversion from his proper route by an employed driver during the working day would necessarily involve taking; however, it would if he appropriated the vehicle to his own use in a manner which repudiated the rights of the true owner and showed that he had assumed control of the vehicle for his own purposes, which D had done on leaving the first public house.

A similar principle applies to a bailee. A bailee of a conveyance takes it if he uses it for a purpose other than that for which he has been given permission or after the end of the bailment. In *Phipps and McGill*[4] D asked the owner of a car if he could borrow it to take his D's wife to a London station. The owner agreed on the express condition that D returned the car immediately after dropping his wife, but apparently D brought his wife back because she had missed the train. Instead of returning the car, D drove it to Hastings and did not return it until two days later; the Court of Appeal held that D had taken the car as soon as he drove it outside the purpose or condition of the bailment.

1 [1973] QB 832, [1973] 2 All ER 864, CA.
2 See, for instance, *Wibberley* [1966] 2 QB 214, [1965] 3 All ER 718, CA.
3 [1974] RTR 4, DC.
4 (1970) 54 Cr App Rep 300, CA. Also see *Singh v Rathour* [1988] 2 All ER 16, [1988] 1 WLR 422, CA.

14.21 *For the accused or another's use* The taking must be for the accused's use or that of another. In *Bow*[1] the Court of Appeal held that this required that the conveyance should actually be used as a conveyance, as it will be if the accused drives a car, or coasts downhill in it, or is carried away in a boat as it drifts with the tide. It is now clear from the Court of Appeal's decision in *Marchant*[2] that, despite what was said in *Bow*, a conveyance is also taken for the accused's use or that of another where, even though it is not used as a conveyance, it is taken for later use as a conveyance. Thus, as in *Pearce*,[3] a person who puts another's dinghy on a trailer and tows it away for later use as a conveyance thereby takes it for his own use, as does someone who pushes a car a few feet, intending to use it later as a conveyance.[4] Provided someone acts in one of the two ways referred to in this paragraph, his motive is irrelevant; thus, a person who drives another's vehicle a few yards to remove it as an obstruction may be convicted of the present offence.[5]

Examples of cases where there is no taking for the use of the accused or another are where the accused releases the handbrake of a car so that it runs downhill empty, where he cuts adrift a boat so that it drifts away empty, or where he pushes an obstructing vehicle out of the way or pushes a car round a corner as a joke on its owner.

1 (1976) 64 Cr App Rep 54, [1977] RTR 6, CA. Also see *Stokes* [1983] RTR 59, CA.
2 (1985) 80 Cr App Rep 361, CA.
3 [1973] Crim LR 321, CA; applied in *Marchant* (1985) 80 Cr App Rep 361, CA, where it was assumed that the accused in *Pearce* intended to make later use of the dinghy.
4 See *Marchant*.
5 *Bow*; *Stokes*.

14.22 *Without consent or other lawful authority* The taking must be without the consent of the owner or other lawful authority. The offence will not be committed if the owner has actually consented to the taking; if there is no actual consent at the time of the taking, the fact that the owner would have consented if he had been asked does not prevent the taking being without consent.[1]

A consent obtained by means of a deception is nevertheless valid and prevents the offence being committed, however fundamental (eg as to the identity of the deceiver) the mistake which is induced.[2] In *Whittaker v Campbell*[3] D found a driving licence belonging to X, and used it to hire from P a motor vehicle, representing that he was X. The Divisional Court held that, even if P had made a mistake of identity which would have rendered void the contract of hire between him and D, this did not render invalid his consent to D's taking of the conveyance for the purposes of s 12. *Peart*[4] provides another example. D in Newcastle obtained the owner's consent to the loan of a van by falsely saying that if he were not in Alnwick by 2.30 pm he would lose an important contract, whereas his actual intention was to drive to Burnley which is much further away. It was held that the initial taking was with the consent of the owner. Of course, as *Phipps and McGill*[5] shows, once the accused used the vehicle outside the terms of the bailment the taking became without consent.

It remains to be decided whether a consent obtained by force or the threat of force is nevertheless valid so as to prevent an offence under s 12 being committed, but the better view is that it would not be valid.[6]

Section 12(7)(b) provides that, in relation to a conveyance which is subject to a hiring agreement or a hire-purchase agreement, 'owner' means the person in possession of it under that agreement. It follows that during the currency of the agreement such a person cannot commit the present offence since he can hardly be said to act without the consent of the owner.

1 *Ambler* [1979] RTR 217, CA.
2 *Peart* [1970] 2 QB 672, [1970] 2 All ER 823, CA; *Whittaker v Campbell* [1984] QB 318, [1983] 3 All ER 582, DC.
3 [1984] QB 318, [1983] 3 All ER 582, DC.
4 [1970] 2 QB 672, [1970] 2 All ER 823, CA.
5 (1970) 54 Cr App Rep 300, CA.
6 Smith *The Law of Theft* (6th edn), para 289; *Hogdon* [1962] Crim LR 563, CCA.

14.23 A taking is not without lawful authority where it is by police or local authority officers in the exercise of statutory powers to remove vehicles which constitute obstructions or are dangerous, or where bailors of conveyances recover them under a term in the bailment.

14.24 *Another defence* Not only is the actual consent of the owner or other lawful authority a defence, but under s 12(6) a person does not commit an offence under s 12 by anything done in the belief that he has lawful authority or that he would have the owner's consent if the owner knew of his doing it and of the circumstances. Such a belief does not have to be reasonable; the burden of proving it is not borne by the accused but he does have an evidential burden in relation to it.[1] One case where an accused will believe that he has lawful authority is where he believes the conveyance is his.[2]

1 *Gannon* [1988] RTR 49, CA.
2 *MacPherson* [1973] RTR 157, CA; *Briggs* [1987] Crim LR 708, CA; *Gannon* [1988] RTR 49, CA.

OTHER OFFENCES UNDER SECTION 12

14.25 Section 12(1) contains an ancillary offence which is committed where the accused, 'knowing that any conveyance has been taken without [the owner's consent or other lawful authority], drives[1] it or allows himself to be carried in or on it'. This offence is triable and punishable in the same way as the 'taking' offence. In order to be 'carried in or on' a conveyance there must be some movement of it; it is not enough merely to be in or on it.[2] The requisite knowledge may probably be constituted by wilful blindness[3] (as well as by actual knowledge), as in other statutes. A person may be guilty of the present offence if the conveyance has, to his knowledge, been stolen and not merely taken temporarily.[4]

Although a pedal cycle falls within the definition of 'conveyance', referred to in para 14.19, the above offences under s 12(1) do not apply to them. Instead, two similar offences, triable only summarily and punishable with a fine not exceeding level 3 on the standard scale (£1,000), apply to pedal cycles.[5] Under the draft Criminal Code Bill, pedal cycles are excluded from the definition of a 'conveyance', but this is only for the sake of simplification since the two pedal cycle offences would continue under the Code.[6]

1 For the meaning of 'drive' in relation to a motor vehicle, see para 20.6.
2 *Miller* [1976] Crim LR 147, CA; *Diggin* (1980) 72 Cr App Rep 204, CA.
3 See para 6.59.
4 *Tolley v Giddings* [1964] 2 QB 354, [1964] 1 All ER 201, DC.
5 Theft Act 1968, s 12(5).
6 Clause 150(2) and (3). See Law Commission: A Criminal Code for England and Wales (1989): Law Com No 177.

Deception offences

14.26 In the following 19 pages we shall consider a number of offences involving deception (and various other common elements):

a) obtaining property by deception;
b) obtaining a pecuniary advantage by deception;
c) obtaining services by deception;
d) evading liability by deception.

Obtaining property by deception

14.27 Section 15(1) of the Theft Act 1968 provides that a person who by any deception dishonestly obtains property belonging to another, with the intention of permanently depriving the other of it, is guilty of an offence punishable with a maximum of ten years' imprisonment.[1]

1 For a special provision for the liability of its officers when this offence is committed by a corporation, see para 14.70.

14.28 The basic element of the actus reus is a deception by the accused. 'Deception' means, for the purposes of this and later offences, 'any deception (whether deliberate or reckless) by words or conduct as to fact or as to law, including a deception as to the present intentions of the person using the deception or any other person'.[1] There can be no deception unless a person is induced to believe that a thing is true which is in fact false.[2] Consequently there is no deception if a false coin is inserted into a vending machine or the like,[3] so that there cannot be a conviction for the present offence if property is obtained as a result (although there can be a conviction for theft on the ground that the accused has dishonestly appropriated that property, provided he had the necessary intent permanently to deprive).

1 Theft Act 1968, s 15(4).
2 *Re London and Globe Finance Corpn Ltd* [1903] 1 Ch 728 at 732; *DPP v Ray* [1974] AC 370 at 379, 384, [1973] 3 All ER 131, per Lords Reid and Morris; see further para 14.37.
3 This point was reserved in *Davies v Flackett* [1973] RTR 8, DC.

14.29 *Deception by conduct* The inclusion of deception by conduct covers not only express misrepresentation by conduct, as where a rogue dresses up in a security guard's uniform in order to convey the impression that he is a security guard, but also implied representations, such as the implied representation made by someone who sells property that he has a right to do so. That is why it was stated in the last chapter[1] that the disposal of stolen goods by way of sale by someone protected from a charge of theft by s 3(2) of the Act would amount to obtaining the price by deception. Similarly, a person who proffers an obsolete foreign banknote for exchange at a bureau de change impliedly represents that it is valid as currency in its country of origin, and if it is not he makes an implied deception as to that fact.[2] Whether or not there is a deception by conduct must be judged in the light of the circumstances existing at the time of the conduct or preceding it. For example, in *Silverman*,[3] where a jobbing builder, who had built up a relationship of mutual trust with two sisters so that they would expect him to act fairly towards them, obtained money from them for work which he had quoted and charged a grossly excessive price, it was held that in the circumstances of the relationship of mutual trust he implied by quoting and charging an amount that it was a fair and reasonable one; since it was not he had made a deception.

A common example of an implied deception by conduct concerns bouncing cheques. The giver of a cheque impliedly represents that the state of facts existing at the date of the delivery of the cheque is such that the cheque will be honoured in the ordinary course of events on presentation for payment on or after the date specified in the cheque.[4]

If a cheque is supported by a cheque card, then, provided the conditions on the cheque card are complied with, the bank is legally obliged to honour the cheque because a contract to this effect is brought into being between the payee and the bank, and it is irrelevant that the drawer's authority to use the cheque card has been withdrawn or that he is exceeding it. In such a case, there will not be a deception of the type mentioned in the last paragraph. However, it was held by the House of Lords in *Charles*[5] that a person who draws a cheque backed by a cheque card impliedly represents by his conduct that he has actual authority from the bank to use the card to make a contract with the payee on behalf of the bank that it will honour the cheque on presentment for payment, and that if he has no such authority (eg because he is in excess of the amount which he is allowed to overdraw) a deception is made.

The use of a credit card to finance a transaction also gives rise to a contractual relationship between the retailer or the like and the credit card company whereby the latter must honour the relevant sales voucher on presentation, provided the conditions on the credit card are complied with. Adopting its reasoning in *Charles*, the House of Lords held in *Lambie*[6] that, if a person uses a credit card, he thereby impliedly represents by his conduct that he has actual authority from the credit card company to use the card to make a contract with the retailer or the like on behalf of the credit card company that the latter will honour the voucher on presentation, and if he has no such authority (eg because he is in excess of his credit limit) a deception is made.

1 Para 13.17.
2 *Williams* [1980] Crim LR 589, CA. Also see *Hamilton* (1990) Times, 24 August, CA.
3 (1988) 86 Cr App Rep 213, (1987) 151 JP 657, CA.
4 *Gilmartin* [1983] QB 953, [1983] 1 All ER 829, CA.
5 [1977] AC 177, [1976] 3 All ER 112, HL.
6 [1982] AC 449, [1981] 2 All ER 776, HL.

14.30 *Deception as to fact* The requirement that the deception must be as to fact or law means that a statement which merely expresses an opinion does not constitute a deception if the opinion turns out to be unjustified, but if the person making the statement is aware that the opinion is unjustified he will at the same time by his conduct make a deception of fact, viz the fact that he does not honestly hold the opinion.

14.31 *Deception as to law* Assuming that the other ingredients of the offence are present, it seems right that deception about the law should be enough, although it is not clear that a misrepresentation of law will always found civil liability in the tort of deceit.[1]

1 *Winfield and Jolowicz on Tort* (13th edn) 264–265.

14.32 *Deception as to intention* Greatly to the detriment of the criminal law, it used to be held in the context of the old offence of obtaining property by false pretences that a false statement of intention was not a false pretence. This meant that someone who made a promise with the intention of breaking it was not guilty of making a false pretence. The definition of deception makes it clear that the making of a false statement of the present intentions of the person making the statement or another person (eg a false promise) can amount to deception. Thus, if the accused falsely states that he, or his employer, X, intends to do something in the future he makes a deception. The promise may, of course, be implied from the nature of the transaction in which the accused engages. A request for a loan of money implies an intention to repay, and a purchase of goods implies a representation that the representor (or, possibly, another) intends to pay for them.

14.33 *Deception by omission* The statutory definition of deception does not deal with whether a failure to state the truth can constitute a deception, but in three types of case it can.

a) A statement which is a half-truth because, although it is literally true, it omits a material matter is a well-established type of deception.[1] For example, it would be a deception to say that one had a clean driving licence if one was awaiting sentence for a driving offence for which endorsement was mandatory.

b) A statement which is true when made but which, to the knowledge of its maker has become untrue before it is acted on by its addressee, is a deception if its maker fails to tell the addressee of the change. As we have seen, a person who orders a meal in a restaurant impliedly represents that he intends to pay for it. If this representation is true when made there is, of course, no deception at that stage, but what if he subsequently changes his mind before the meal is served but does not tell the waiter? In *DPP v Ray*[2] the House of Lords held that there would be a deception in such a case, either because the initial representation is a continuing one which remains alive and operative and has become false,[3] or (and this has more support in the decision) because by remaining at the table after the change of mind the diner continues to make from moment to moment, but now falsely, the representation that he intends to pay.[4] Between these two reasons there may be no real difference because the former appears to involve some conduct after the change of mind (continuing to sit at the table in *Ray*) from which, in conjunction with his silence, it may be inferred that the customer was making the now false representation. The decision in *Ray* is equally applicable to any situation where an initially true representation of fact, law or intention has become untrue.

c) In both the above instances there is some statement by the accused which is or becomes false. In *Firth*,[5] whose facts are given in para 14.63, the Court of Appeal held that there could be a deception, even though there was no statement by the accused, if he refrained from stating something which it was his legal duty to disclose to the person deceived. This seems to stretch the concept of deception but it must be accepted until overruled. The problem, which remains to be fully resolved, is when a person is under a legal duty to disclose information. It is submitted, by analogy with the civil law, that a person is not under a legal duty to say something, and therefore there is no deception, if he merely fails to correct an erroneous belief on the part of another which he has not induced by his words or conduct, as where D fails to point out to P that the painting which he is offering to sell to P (who clearly thinks it is very valuable) is of very little value.

1 *Kylsant* [1932] 1 KB 442, CCA.
2 [1974] AC 370, [1973] 3 All ER 131, HL. See White 'Continuing Representations in the Criminal Law' (1986) 37 NILQ 255.
3 [1974] AC at 382, per Lord MacDermott.
4 Ibid, at 385–6 and 391, per Lords Morris and Pearson.
5 [1990] Crim LR 328, CA. Arguably, there was a deception by conduct in that case but the Court of Appeal did not deal with it on that basis.

14.34 *The consequence of the deception* In addition to proving deception, the prosecution must prove that it resulted in the accused obtaining property belonging to another. For this purpose a person is treated as obtaining property if he obtains ownership, possession or control of it.[1]

The offence is not limited to cases where the accused obtains for himself; by s 15(2) 'obtaining' also includes:

a) obtaining for another, as where D gets money sent to a third party by telling lies;[2]
b) enabling another to obtain or retain, as where D by deception persuades P to enter into a contract with X under which X receives money from P (enabling another to obtain) or by deception persuades P to allow X to remain in possession of property (enabling another to retain).

'Obtaining' must hereafter be understood in this wide sense.

'Property' includes money and all other property, real or personal, including things in action and other intangible property.[3]

The provisions of s 4(2) to (4) limiting the occasions when land, things forming part of it and wild creatures may be stolen do not apply to an offence under s 15.[3] Thus, land may be the subject of this offence, although generally it cannot be stolen.

At the time that ownership, possession or control of it is obtained the property must 'belong to another' within s 5(1) of the 1968 Act, ie another person must then have possession or control of it, or a proprietary right or interest in it.[4] If P has lent his bicycle to D, thereby transferring possession but not ownership to D, and D by deception persuades P to make a gift to him of the bicycle, D obtains ownership of property belonging to another because at the time of the obtaining P is owner of (and therefore has a proprietary right in) it.

1 Theft Act 1968, s 15(2).
2 See *Duru* [1973] 3 All ER 715, [1974] 1 WLR 2, CA.
3 Theft Act 1968, s 34(1), applies s 4(1) (but not the other subsections of s 4) to s 15.
4 Theft Act 1968, s 34(1), applies s 5(1) (but not the other subsections of s 5) to s 15.

14.35 What is said hereafter about the requirement that the property must have been obtained as a result of the deception is equally applicable to the issue of deception and the requisite causal link in the other offences of deception mentioned in this chapter, such as obtaining a pecuniary advantage by deception or obtaining services by deception.

14.36 For the requirement to be satisfied:

a) someone must have been deceived, since as already indicated there cannot be a deception unless someone is deceived; and
b) the deception must operate on the mind of the victim (the person deceived) and be a cause of the thing in question being obtained.

Provided that these two conditions are satisfied, the deception need not be the only cause of the obtaining, nor need the person deceived be the person from whom the property (or pecuniary advantage etc) is obtained. Thus, if D, an insurance agent, dishonestly deceives someone into entering into an insurance contract with an insurance company, as a result of which the company pays D commission, D can be convicted of obtaining the commission by deception.[1]

1 *Clegg* [1977] CLY 619, Crown Ct.

14.37 It was said by Buckley J in *Re London and Globe Finance Corpn Ltd*[1] that: 'To deceive is ... to induce a man to believe that a thing is true which is false ...' Clearly, the condition that a person must be deceived is not satisfied if a person to whom a false representation is addressed sees through it or already knows the truth. It follows that if, nevertheless, he transfers property to the misrepresentor (as the misrepresentor intended), there cannot be a conviction for obtaining property by deception, although there can be a conviction for attempting to commit that offence.[2]

The terms of Buckley J's statement are not, at first sight, satisfied in a case where the person to whom a false representation is addressed is not induced positively to believe the truth of what is contained in it, although he does not believe it is untrue. However, it appears from the decisions of the House of Lords in *Charles*[3] and *Lambie*[4] that it will suffice that the addressee is ignorant of the truth *and* relies on the representation in question. This is particularly important where a cheque card or credit card is used by the accused without authority.

As we have seen, where a person uses a cheque card or credit card to obtain something and he has no authority to use it for the transaction concerned (e g because he has been told not to make further use of it by the bank), there is an implied misrepresentation from his conduct that he has authority to use the card. However, provided the conditions on the back of the card attaching to its use are satisfied, the bank will be obliged to pay, and will pay, the amount involved in the transaction. Consequently, since the victim of the misrepresentation will not suffer if the implied representation of authority turns out to be untrue, he may well have acted without any positive belief that that representation was true.

Nevertheless, in *Charles* and *Lambie* the House of Lords, upholding convictions for obtaining a pecuniary advantage by deception, held that victims of such a misrepresentation had been deceived. In *Charles* D had a bank account and a cheque card. He had an overdraft with a limit of £100 and was already overdrawn in excess of that amount. One night he went to a gaming club and used all the cheques in a new cheque book to buy chips for gaming, each cheque being supported by his cheque card. Because D was already overdrawn over the permitted limit he had no authority from the bank to use the cheque card. The cheques were accepted by the manager of the club; it was clear from his evidence that he did so only because they were supported by the cheque card and that he would not have done so if he had known that D had no authority to use the card. On the other hand, it was clear from his evidence that the manager did not positively believe that D was authorised to use the card; the most that could be said was that he had no belief one way or the other about D's authority. Nevertheless, the House of Lords asserted that the manager had accepted the cheques only because he had been deceived by D into believing that he had authority to use the card. The only way in which there could be said to be such a 'belief' on the manager's part is if belief in the present context means ignorance of the truth plus reliance on the representation of authority.[5]

In *Lambie* D was the holder of a credit card (a Barclaycard) with a £200 credit limit. Knowing that she was over that limit, D produced it to a departmental manager in a shop to pay for some goods. There was no evidence from the departmental manager that she would not have completed the transaction if she had known that D was acting dishonestly and had no authority from the bank. However, the House of Lords held that the only answer possible was that she would not have done so if she had had such knowledge, and therefore, *Charles* being indistinguishable, D's conviction was confirmed.

1 [1903] 1 Ch 728 at 732; *DPP v Ray* [1974] AC 370 at 379, 384, [1973] 3 All ER 131, per Lords Reid and Morris.
2 *Hensler* (1870) 22 LT 691, 11 Cox CC 570.
3 [1977] AC 177, [1976] 3 All ER 112, HL.
4 [1982] AC 449, [1981] 2 All ER 776, HL.
5 Griew *Theft Acts 1968 and 1978* (6th edn), para 7-41.

14.38 We now turn from the condition that someone must have been deceived to the other condition, that the deception must operate on that person's mind and be a cause of the obtaining. Whether or not this condition is satisfied is a question of fact for the jury, applying their common sense.[1] However, it is obvious that it is not satisfied if the deception occurs after the obtaining.[2] Similarly, it is not satisfied if the person deceived is completely indifferent as to the matter to which the deception relates; it cannot be said that the deception is a cause of any subsequent obtaining if the person deceived would have acted in the same way if he had known the truth.[3] In *Laverty*[4] P bought a second-hand car from D, ignorant of the fact that the car had been stolen and that its number plates had been changed. The deception alleged was that the car did not bear its original number plates. However, there was no evidence that P had bought the car in reliance on that deception nor that he would have minded at all that the car did not bear its original plates. Consequently, it was held that D's conviction for obtaining the purchase price by deception must be quashed. It would have been different if the deception alleged had been that D was entitled to sell the car, because there was evidence that P had bought the car because he thought D was the owner.

In many cases a deception by the accused will result in a contract between him and the person deceived, property subsequently being transferred to the accused under the contract. The fact that there is the intervention of a contract does not prevent the deception being a cause of the accused obtaining the property. The crucial question, as always, is whether the deception was operating on the mind of the victim when he transferred the property.[5]

1 *King and Stockwell* [1987] QB 547, [1987] 1 All ER 547, CA.
2 *Collis-Smith* [1971] Crim LR 716, CA.
3 *Clow* (1978) Times, 9 August, CA.
4 [1970] 3 All ER 432, CA.
5 *Martin* (1867) LR 1 CCR 56, 36 LJMC 20; *Moreton* (1913) 8 Cr App Rep 214, CCA.

MENS REA

14.39 The accused must have:

a) made his deception deliberately or recklessly;
b) obtained the property dishonestly; and
c) intended permanently to deprive the other of the property obtained.

14.40 In this context 'reckless' is limited to its subjective meaning of the state of mind of someone who knows that there is a risk that his statement is false, but nonetheless makes it without caring whether it is true or false.[1] This statement is unaffected by the decision in *Caldwell*,[2] in which the House of Lords held that the word 'reckless' in a criminal statute normally includes failing to give any thought to the existence of an obvious risk (otherwise known as *Caldwell* -type recklessness), since the requirement of dishonesty clearly indicates that recklessness can only bear its subjective meaning here. Consequently, a person who makes a statement which is false, without realising this and without giving any thought to whether it is false, in circumstances where there is an obvious risk that it is, does not make it recklessly.

1 *Staines* (1970) 61 Cr App Rep 160, CA.
2 [1982] AC 341, [1981] 1 All ER 961, HL; para 6.46.

14.41   The question of whether or not the accused has dishonestly obtained the property is separate from that of whether or not he made the deception deliberately or recklessly.[1] A person may well make a deliberate or reckless deception, and obtain property thereby, without being found by the jury to have obtained it dishonestly; an example might be where he believed that he had a legal right to property obtained by the deception. The question of dishonesty is one of fact for the jury in each case,[2] and the judge must never rule that any deceptive obtaining is dishonest. The partial definition of dishonesty in s 2 of the 1968 Act, discussed in para 13.52, some of which is inappropriate anyway to deception offences, is limited to theft and does not extend to the various offences of deception. Whenever it is in issue, the question of dishonesty must be determined by answering the questions set out in *Ghosh*,[3] in the same way as in a trial for theft; in relation to this the statements made in paras 13.54 to 13.58 apply equally here. As in the case of theft, the judge is not required to direct the jury on those questions unless there is evidence that the accused obtained the property in circumstances which may cause the jury to find that he was not dishonest.[4]

1 *Feeney* [1991] Crim LR 561, CA.
2 *Greenstein* [1976] 1 All ER 1, [1975] 1 WLR 1353, CA; *Ghosh* [1982] QB 1053, [1982] 2 All ER 689, CA; *Melwani* [1989] Crim LR 566, CA. Of course, in a summary trial the magistrates perform the task of the jury.
3 [1982] QB 1053, [1982] 2 All ER 689, CA.
4 See, for example, *Roberts* (1987) 84 Cr App Rep 117, CA; *Price* (1990) 91 Cr App Rep 409, CA; *Buzalek and Schiffer* [1991] Crim LR 130, CA. See comment in para 13.57.

14.42   The extended meaning of 'intention of permanently depriving' provided by s 6 of the 1968 Act in relation to the definition of theft, mentioned in para 13.61 to 13.64, is applied to the present offence by s 15(3).

Theft and obtaining property by deception

14.43   There is some overlap of theft and obtaining property by deception in the sense that a person may commit both offences in relation to the same property. Of course, a very large number of cases of theft cannot have anything to do with obtaining property by deception for the simple reason that no deception was practised by the accused; within this category come all cases of theft by direct taking and all cases of theft of property the original receipt of which was entirely innocent, for example by a bailee or trustee. In addition, it is clear from the wording of the 1968 Act that there are a very few cases where a person who can be convicted of obtaining property by deception cannot be convicted of theft in relation to it because the property cannot be stolen; land and things forming part of it may be obtained by deception but they cannot generally be stolen.[1] Apart from this, whether a person who can be convicted of obtaining property by deception may also be convicted of theft depends on whether he can be said to have appropriated property belonging to another at the time of appropriation,[2] and this in turn depends partly on the interpretation given to that requirement by the courts. Two situations must be distinguished.

1 *Lawrence v Metropolitan Police Comr* [1971] 2 All ER 1253 at 1255, per Viscount Dilhorne.
2 Paras 13.3–13.50.

14.44 *Where, by deception, the accused has obtained possession or control of property from another, but ownership remains in that other person or someone else* Since the property still belongs to another under s 5(1) of the 1968 Act, an appropriation of it by the accused will constitute theft, assuming that he has the necessary mens rea. However, because of the meaning given to 'appropriation' by the courts, the accused will not steal the property when he obtains possession of it (because taking possession is an authorised act), but he will steal the property if he later does something unauthorised with it, such as selling it.[1] Thus, if D hires a television by deception or induces P to sell the television to him under a contract which is void for mistake as to D's identity (a very rare happening) so that ownership does not pass to D,[2] D does not appropriate the television by taking possession of it, although he will if he does something unauthorised with it thereafter.

1 Paras 13.3–13.19, especially para 13.15.
2 Para 13.44.

14.45 *Where, by deception, the accused has obtained ownership, possession and control of the property to the exclusion of any other person* The type of case with which we are concerned here is exemplified as follows. Suppose that D offers to buy goods on credit from P without intending to pay for them. Deceived into believing that D intends to pay, P accepts the offer and the goods instantly come into D's hands. Can D be said to have appropriated the goods while they still belonged to P simultaneously with the obtaining by him of ownership, possession and control of them?

There can be no doubt that if the earliest time at which an appropriation can be said to occur is some time after the property has come into the accused's sole ownership, possession and control, there cannot be a conviction for theft. However, there is authority that simply obtaining ownership, possession and control of property by deception constitutes an appropriation of property which at that time belongs to another. This view was taken by the Court of Appeal in *Dobson v General Accident Fire and Life Assurance Corpn*,[1] and it may have been taken by the House of Lords in *Lawrence v Metropolitan Police Comr*.[2] One cannot be certain since the basis of the House of Lords' decision is not easy to discern.

In *Lawrence v Metropolitan Police Comr* P, an Italian student who spoke little English, wanted to take a taxi from Victoria Station to Ladbroke Grove. D, a taxi driver, said it was a long way and very expensive, although the correct fare was in the region of 50p. P, holding open his wallet, gave a pound to D, and D took a further £6 from the wallet. P did not resist this. D was charged with stealing this sum. He was convicted and appealed unsuccessfully to the Court of Appeal and the House of Lords. The House of Lords, held that 'without the consent of the owner' could not be read into s 1 and that obtaining property by deception and theft were not mutually exclusive although they did not overlap completely, but it did not explain this further. Viscount Dilhorne, giving the judgment of the House, said that the money in the wallet which D appropriated belonged to another, P, at that time.

The decision of the House is open to the interpretation that, where a person is deceived into parting with ownership, possession and control of property and it instantly comes into the accused's hands, the accused's simultaneous taking or receipt of the property is an appropriation of property belonging to another, so that he can be convicted of theft. However, it is far more likely that this is not the correct interpretation of the decision. This is because it appears that the House held that D appropriated the £6 when, without P's authority, he took it from the wallet, at which point of time the money was owned, possessed and controlled by P and therefore 'belonged to another', even if P, who was clearly taken by surprise, had subsequently consented to the £6 being taken[3] and thereby transferred ownership of it to D.

The Court of Appeal's decision in *Dobson v General Accident* cannot be explained away in this way. In this case, P sold a a watch and ring to D who purported to pay by means of a stolen and worthless cheque (a deception). As a result, P consented to D taking the articles away. The question before the Court of Appeal (Civil Division) was whether P could claim under an insurance policy for 'loss or damage caused by theft'. That court answered 'Yes'. It held that, when (as in the case in question) ownership in goods was intended to pass on delivery of them (and not before) under a contract of sale which was voidable because of D (the buyer's) deception, theft and obtaining property by deception coincided. This decision is irreconcileable with other decisions, in particular those mentioned below.

In *Gomez*,[4] where the facts were indistinguishable from *Dobson*, the Court of Appeal, relying on the House of Lords' decision in *Morris*[5] as authority, held that when a person by deception induced the owner to transfer his entire proprietary interest, there was no appropriation when he took possession of the goods because he would be authorised to do so under the contract of sale, a contract which though voidable had not been avoided at the time the goods were handed over, and there could be no appropriation if a dealing with property was done with the consent or authority of its owner.

The fact that the Court of Appeal in *Gomez* refused to follow *Dobson* and relied on the House of Lords' decision in *Morris* means that there can be no real doubt that a future Court of Appeal will follow *Gomez*. In effect, although it did not do so expressly, the Court of Appeal in *Gomez* overruled *Dobson*.

To return to the House of Lords' decision in *Lawrence*, we have seen that there are at least two possible interpretations of it; the first in line with the decision in *Dobson*, and the second with *Morris*. Again, *Gomez* is instructive since the Court of Appeal held that, if there was a difference between *Lawrence* and *Morris*, *Morris* was the decision which it had to follow. Thus, if in reality the first interpretation of *Lawrence* is the correct one it would, according to *Gomez*, have been impliedly overruled by *Morris*.

The clarity which the decision in *Gomez* has brought to the law in this area is welcome, not least because it removes any conflict (as there otherwise would be) with the Court of Appeal's decisions in *Skipp*[6] and *Hircock*[7]. As we have seen, in *Skipp* and *Hircock* it was held that a person who deceives another into parting with possession of property does not appropriate it when he receives it because his receipt is authorised (albeit the authority was obtained by deception). It would be extremely odd if a different rule applied where the deceiver has also obtained ownership of the property.

1 [1990] QB 274, [1989] 3 All ER 927, CA.
2 [1972] AC 626, [1971] 2 All ER 1253, HL.
3 Viscount Dilhorne made an obscure statement which may have been intended to mean that absence of consent had been established, in which case there would be no difficulty in convicting D of theft.
4 [1991] 3 All ER 394, CA.
5 [1984] AC 320, [1983] 3 All ER 288, HL.
6 [1975] Crim LR 114, CA.
7 (1978) 67 Cr App Rep 278, CA.

14.46   In one case a subsequent appropriation of property, the ownership, possession and control of which have been obtained by deception, is clearly theft. This is where the accused has by deception induced a mistake which is of such a type as to place him under an immediate obligation to make restoration of the property. This is because in such a case the transferor retains an equitable proprietary interest in the property, so that it will still belong to him under s 5(1) of the 1968 Act. An alternative reason is that s 5(4) of the 1968 Act expressly provides that, to the extent of the obligation to make restoration, the property is regarded, as against the accused, as belonging to the person entitled to restoration. An employee who falsely informs his employer that he has not received an advance of £80 on his weekly wage of £160 is guilty both of obtaining £80 by deception when he receives the £160 wages and of stealing that sum when he spends it or does some other unauthorised thing with it – the employer cannot have authorised him to spend money to which he is not entitled – even though he became the owner of it on receiving it. However, as indicated in paras 13.44 and 13.46, these rules are confined to a limited class of cases of which the most obvious example is a mistake of fact as to the legal entitlement of the person to whom money is paid, and do not cover most other mistakes induced by deception in consequence of which property is obtained.

14.47   It is regrettable that the relationship between theft and obtaining property by deception has had to be discussed at some length. It would not have been necessary if the prosecution always adopted the obvious and sensible course where the accused has caused someone to part with property by deception, and that is to charge him with obtaining property by deception, and not with theft. As the Court of Appeal said in *Gomez*,[1] if the accused there had been charged with obtaining property by deception he would have had no defence.

1 [1991] 3 All ER 394, CA.

Obtaining a pecuniary advantage by deception

14.48   Section 16(1) of the Theft Act 1968 provides that a person who by any deception dishonestly obtains for himself or another any pecuniary advantage commits an offence punishable with a maximum of five years' imprisonment.[1]

The section, like ss 1 and 2 of the Theft Act 1978 which are discussed shortly, is designed to cover a range of situations where the accused has made a deception but *either* he has not thereby obtained any property, although he has gained some advantage which can be expressed in pecuniary terms, *or*, if he has obtained property thereby, he did not make the deception with intent permanently to deprive the other of it. Although s 16 is concerned with a number of different types of pecuniary advantage it only creates one offence which can be committed in different ways.[2]

1 For a special provision for the liability of its officers when this offence is committed by a corporation, see para 14.70.
2 *Bale v Rosier* [1977] 2 All ER 160, DC.

ACTUS REUS

14.49 Nothing need be said about the requirement that there must be a deception, since s 16(3) provides that for the purposes of s 16 'deception' has the same meaning as in s 15, and the reader should refer to paras 14.28 to 14.33 concerning this. Similarly, nothing more need be said about the necessity that the accused's deception should be a cause of him or another obtaining a pecuniary advantage, except to point out that it is not an offence under s 16 to enable another to obtain or retain such an advantage. However, something must be said about the meaning of 'pecuniary advantage'.

14.50 By s 16(2)(b) and (c) a pecuniary advantage within the meaning of the section is regarded as obtained for a person where, but *only where*:[1]

a) *He is allowed to borrow by way of overdraft, or to take out any policy of insurance or annuity contract, or obtains an improvement of the terms on which he is allowed to do so* (s 16(2)(b)).

A person who obtains an overdraft facility for himself or another by deception (eg as to his assets) falls within this category even though he never draws on it,[2] and so does a person who obtains motor insurance by falsely stating that he has not been disqualified from driving or who obtains improved terms of insurance by faking a 'no-claims' discount.

A striking example of the width of this provision is *Charles*.[3] As we have seen, the House of Lords held that, by using his cheque card in support of cheques used to pay for gaming chips, D had by that conduct made a deception as to his authority from his bank to use the cheque card to oblige his bank to honour the cheques, and that this had operated on the mind of the gaming club manager and caused him to accept the cheques. As a result of the cheque card being used his bank was obliged to honour the cheques and D's overdraft rose by £750. The House of Lords upheld D's conviction for obtaining a pecuniary advantage by deception, namely increased borrowing by way of overdraft, on the ground that, as a result of the manager being misled into accepting the cheques, the bank had had to honour the cheques and D's overdraft had increased. As this case indicates, the person deceived need not suffer financial loss, nor need the pecuniary advantage emanate from him.

A point which was not raised in *Charles* is that s 16(2)(b) speaks of a person being 'allowed' to borrow by way of overdraft. However, this point was argued in *Waites*,[4] where D, who had not made any arrangements to overdraw her bank account, created an overdraft of £850 by means of cheques backed by her cheque card. The Court of Appeal held that she had been 'allowed' to borrow by way of overdraft, despite the fact that in reality the bank, far from permitting her so to borrow, would have been doing all in its power to stop her doing so.

b) *He is given the opportunity to earn remuneration or greater remuneration in an office or employment, or to win money by betting* (s 16(2) (c)).

A person who obtains paid employment by deception commits an offence under s 16, even if he is never paid anything. (If he does receive his wages, he can be convicted under s 15 of obtaining them by deception provided that his deception was an operative cause of them being obtained, but not if he is paid *solely* because of the work which he has done.)[5] By way of a further example, a person who gains promotion by falsely stating that he has just passed some examinations commits an offence under s 16 because thereby he is given the opportunity to earn greater remuneration. The limitation of this provision to the opportunity to earn remuneration or greater remuneration in an 'office or employment' means that a person who, by deception, is engaged to work as an independent contractor does not obtain a pecuniary advantage by deception, since, although he obtains the opportunity to earn remuneration, it will not be earned as an officer or employee. A fortiori, a person who, by deception, obtains from a brewery the tenancy of a public house does not obtain the opportunity to earn remuneration in an office or employment.[6]

The reference to the opportunity to win money by betting appears to have been inserted purely in order to make it an offence to deceive someone into accepting a bet. (If the bet is successful and the deceiver is paid his winnings, he can be convicted of obtaining them by deception provided that his deception was an operative cause of them being obtained. In *Clucas*[7] it was held that the accused, who had deceived bookmakers into accepting bets on horses which won, could not be convicted of what is now the offence of obtaining property by deception because the winnings were paid to the accused as the result of the horses winning and not because of the deception. However, this case must not be viewed as laying down a general rule of law on the point, since whether or not a deception is an operative cause of the winnings being obtained is a question of fact depending on the facts of each case.)[8]

If a pecuniary advantage is to be regarded as obtained under one of the above provisions, it is *deemed* to have been obtained by the accused or another (as the case may be), and it is irrelevant that in fact no actual pecuniary advantage was obtained by the accused or anyone else.[9]

1 *DPP v Turner* [1974] AC 357 at 365, [1973] 3 All ER 124, per Lord Reid.
2 *Watkins* [1976] 1 All ER 578, CA.
3 [1977] AC 177, [1976] 3 All ER 112, HL.
4 [1982] Crim LR 369, CA. Followed in *Bevan* (1986) 84 Cr App Rep 143, [1987] Crim LR 129, CA.
5 *King and Stockwell* [1987] QB 547, [1987] 1 All ER 547, CA.
6 *McNiff* [1986] Crim LR 57, CA.
7 [1949] 2 KB 226, [1949] 2 All ER 40, CCA.
8 *King and Stockwell* [1987] QB 547, [1987] 1 All ER 547, CA.
9 *DPP v Turner* [1974] AC 357 at 365, [1973] 3 All ER 124, per Lord Reid.

MENS REA

14.51 The accused must:

a) have made his deception deliberately or recklessly;[1] and

b) obtained for himself or another the pecuniary advantage dishonestly.[2]

As in obtaining property by deception, the effect of the requirement of dishonesty is to limit 'reckless' deception to cases of recklessness in its subjective sense.

1 Theft Act 1968, s 16(3) applies s 15(4) to this offence. See para 14.40.
2 See paras 13.54–13.58 and 14.41. The statements in para 14.41 are equally applicable to the present offence.

REPEAL OF THIRD TYPE OF ADVANTAGE

14.52 Section 16(2)(a) of the Theft Act 1968 laid down a third type of pecuniary advantage, whereby it was an offence dishonestly by deception to obtain the reduction or (in whole or in part) the deferment or evasion of a debt or charge for which a person made himself liable or was or might become liable. This form of offence under s 16 became the subject of criticism, partly because its wording was obscure and not always easy to apply, partly because it did not cover some clear cases of dishonesty deserving punishment, and partly because it did cover some other cases of dishonesty which did not deserve punishment.

Consequently, the Criminal Law Revision Committee proposed that s 16(2)(a) of the 1968 Act should be repealed, and drafted a number of offences to be created in its stead.[1] The Theft Act 1978 repealed s 16(2)(a)[2] and, with substantial amendments to the Committee's proposals, introduced the following offences:

a) obtaining services by deception;
b) evasion of liability by deception;
c) making off without payment.[3]

1 Thirteenth Report of the Criminal Law Revision Committee: Section 16 of the Theft Act 1968 (Cmnd 6733) (1977).
2 Theft Act 1978, s 5(5).
3 For a discussion of the 1978 Act, see Spencer [1979] Crim LR 24.

Obtaining services by deception

14.53 Section 1(1) of the Theft Act 1978 provides that a person who by any deception dishonestly obtains services from another is guilty of an offence.[1] The maximum punishment is five years' imprisonment.[2]

1 For a special provision for the liability of its officers when this offence is committed by a corporation, see para 14.70.
2 Theft Act 1978, s 4.

ACTUS REUS

14.54 The services in question must be obtained by deception. No offence is committed where D creeps into a hotel unobserved and spends the night in an empty bedroom because, even if he could be said to have obtained a service, he has not done so by deception.

'Deception' in this context has the same meaning as in obtaining property by deception,[1] and it must be a cause of the services being obtained. Consequently, since a machine cannot be deceived, there cannot be a conviction for obtaining services by deception if a false coin is inserted in a machine, such as the barrier-machine at the entrance to a car park, if services, such as entry to the car park, are obtained as a result.[2]

Section 1 does not say that the services must be obtained for the accused himself; the offence is committed by a person who dishonestly by deception obtains services for another, as where D induces P to clean X's windows by falsely telling P that he, D, will pay.

What constitutes an obtaining of services is defined by s 1(2), which provides that it is an obtaining of services where the other is induced to confer a benefit by doing some act, or causing or permitting some act to be done, on the understanding that the benefit has been or will be paid for. Only if this definition is satisfied is there an obtaining of services for the purposes of s 1. Two conditions must be satisfied:

a) The accused's deception must induce the other *actually* to confer a benefit by doing some act, or causing some act to be done by another, or permitting some act to be done by the accused or another. Examples are where by deception D induces the other to repair his car (or X's car), or to give him (or X) a taxi ride, or to give him (or X) a hair-cut (because he induces the other to confer a benefit by doing an act); where by deception the accused induces the other to tell one of his employees to repair the accused's car (or X's car), or to give him (or X) a taxi ride and so on (because he induces the other to confer a benefit by causing an act to be done); and where by deception the accused induces the other, who runs a sauna bath, to let him (or X) use his sauna, or induces the other to let him (or X) enter a theatre without a ticket (because he induces the other to confer a benefit by permitting some act to be done). In *Halai*,[3] where the accused by deception (a 'bouncing' cheque in payment for it) had caused a building society to have a survey done, it was held that he had obtained a service by deception because there was a benefit to him from the survey (as well as to the society) since the survey was an essential step in obtaining a mortgage.

It was also held in *Halai* that a mortgage advance is not a service, apparently because it is a lending of money for property. While obtaining a mortgage advance is no doubt an obtaining of property, there is no reason why it should not also be regarded as an obtaining of services. A person who obtains it by deception will have caused the building society to do an act which confers a benefit on him and is done on the understanding that it will be paid for. *Halai* was distinguished on the present point in *Widdowson*,[4] where the Court of Appeal stated that obtaining goods on hire-purchase was an obtaining of services. There is no relevant distinction in principle between a mortgage advance and obtaining goods under a hire-purchase agreement, and it is submitted that this part of *Halai* was wrongly decided. In *Teong Sun Chuah; Teong Tatt Chuah*[5] the Court of Appeal said that the present aspect of *Halai* had 'all the hallmarks of being per incuriam'.

b) The benefit conferred in one of the above three ways must be conferred on the understanding that it has been or will be paid for. This is an important limitation: it is not an offence to obtain a free service by deception. If D by deception gets P, a taxi driver, to drive him to the station he will obtain services by deception because the benefit conferred is conferred on the understanding that it will be paid for. But if D by deception gets P, his neighbour, to drive him to the station free of charge he will not obtain services by deception because the benefit was not conferred on the understanding that it would be paid for. Of course, although the benefit must be conferred on the understanding that it has been or will be paid for, the accused's deception need not relate to the question of payment and, subject to the question of dishonesty, the offence can be committed even though the service is paid for. An example would be where, by pretending to be a member and by paying the admission price, the accused attends a members-only performance at a theatre club.

It does not matter that the transaction under which the benefit is conferred involves a contract which is illegal or otherwise unenforceable. Thus, a man who, by deception (e g as to his intention to pay), induces a prostitute to provide him with her professional services may be convicted of the present offence, despite the fact that the contract with her is illegal and unenforceable.

1 Theft Act 1978, s 5(1); paras 14.28–14.33.
2 Where a false coin or card is used to operate or attempt to operate a barrier in certain car parks an offence is committed under the Road Traffic Regulation Act 1984, s 35A.
3 [1983] Crim LR 624, CA.
4 (1985) 81 Cr App Rep 314, CA
5 [1991] Crim LR 463, CA

MENS REA

14.55 The prosecution must prove that the accused:

a) made his deception deliberately or recklessly;[1] and
b) obtained the services dishonestly. [2]

As in obtaining property by deception, the effect of the requirement of dishonesty is to limit 'reckless' deception to cases of recklessness in its subjective sense.[3]

1 Theft Act 1978, s 5(1).
2 Paras 13.54–13.58 and 14.41. The statements in para 14.41 are equally applicable to the present offence.
3 See para 14.40.

Evasion of liability by deception

14.56 Section 2(1) of the Theft Act 1978 provides:

'Subject to subsection (2) below, where a person by any deception—

a) dishonestly secures the remission of the whole or part of any existing liability to make a payment, whether his own liability or another's; or
b) with intent to make permanent default in whole or in part on any existing liability to make a payment, or with intent to let another do so, dishonestly induces the creditor or any person claiming payment on behalf of the creditor to wait for payment (whether or not the due date for payment is deferred) or to forgo payment; or
c) dishonestly obtains any exemption from or abatement of liability to make a payment;
he shall be guilty of an offence.'[1]

A person convicted of an offence under s 2(1) is punishable with a maximum of five years' imprisonment.[2]

Section 2(1) lays down three separate offences.[3] Although there is overlap between them, there are substantial differences in their elements; nevertheless, they do have the following common elements:

a) There must be a *deception* on the part of the accused. 'Deception' in s 2 bears the same meaning as in obtaining property by deception;[4] one consequence is that the deception must be deliberate or reckless.

b) The deception must result in[5] the 'evasion' (in one of the prescribed ways) of a *liability to make a payment*. Section 2(2) provides that, for the purposes of the section, 'liability' means legally enforceable liability, such as a liability to pay money under a valid and enforceable contract or a liability to pay money, e g income tax, under a statute. However, s 2(2) goes on to provide that the provisions in s 2(1) do not apply in relation to a legally enforceable liability that has not been accepted or established to pay compensation for a wrongful act or omission. This means that if D has negligently injured P or P's property, thereby becoming legally liable to pay P compensation, and he evades this liability (in whole or in part) by deception in one of the ways specified in s 2(1), he does not commit an offence under s 2 unless previously he has accepted his liability to pay compensation or this has been established in a court. Another general point is that the liability to pay evaded by the accused's deception may be the liability of another.

c) The accused must have 'evaded' the liability *dishonestly*.[6] As in obtaining property by deception, the effect of the requirement of dishonesty is to limit 'reckless' deception to cases of recklessness in its subjective sense.[7]

1 For a special provision for the liability of its officers when this offence is committed by a corporation, see para 14.70.
2 Theft Act 1978, s 4.
3 *Holt* [1981] 2 All ER 854, [1981] 1 WLR 1000, CA.
4 Theft Act 1978, s 5(1); paras 14.28–14.33.
5 Paras 14.35–14.38.
6 Paras 13.54–13.58 and 14.41. The statements in para 14.41 are equally applicable to the present offences.
7 Para 14.40.

SECTION 2(1)(A)

14.57 *Actus reus* A person commits the actus reus of an offence under this provision if by any deception he secures the remission of the whole or part of any *existing* liability to make a payment, whether his own liability or another's. A liability to make a payment can be an existing one even though payment is only due in the future, provided the obligation to pay already *actually* exists. Moreover, there can be an existing liabilty to pay even though, as in the case of a liability under an improperly executed consumer credit agreement, it can only be enforced by an order of the court.[1]

A person secures remission of the whole or part of a liability to pay if he gets the person to whom the money is payable (the creditor) to agree to extinguish the debt in whole or in part, whether or not the creditor's agreement is binding on him because it was obtained by deception.[2] An example is where D persuades P, who has lent him money, to agree that the loan need never be repaid (or a lesser sum be repaid), by telling him a false

317

hard-luck story. Similarly, D secures remission of part of the liability to pay of another (X) if he tells P (to whom X owes £50) that X has lost his job and thereby induces P to agree to accept £25 in full discharge of X's debt. On the other hand, if D deceives P into believing that a debt has already been paid (or is less than it actually is), D will not have secured the remission of a liability to pay because a creditor cannot be said to agree to extinguish a debt (in whole or in part) when he is simply led to believe that it no longer exists (or that it is less than it actually is). Section 2(1)(b) is the relevant offence.

1 *Modupe* [1991] Crim LR 530, CA (a case concerning 'existing liability' in s 2(1)(b)).
2 Contrast the view of Smith *The Law of Theft* (6th edn), paras 240–243.

14.58 *Mens rea* Apart from the fact that the accused's securing of the remission should be dishonest, the other element of mens rea is that his deception should be deliberate or reckless.[1]

1 Theft Act 1978, s 5(1). See paras 14.40 and 14.41.

SECTION 2(1)(B)

14.59 This is a more involved provision. Essentially, it covers dishonestly, by deception, inducing a creditor to wait for or forgo payment of an existing liability to make payment, with intent to make permanent default in whole or in part in payment.

14.60 *Actus reus* The actus reus requires that the accused's deception should induce the creditor, or any other person claiming payment on the creditor's behalf (such as the creditor's employee or debt-collector), to wait for payment, or to forgo payment, of an *existing* liability to pay, whether the accused's own or another's. The comments about 'existing liability' in para 14.57 are equally applicable here.

Unlike the other parts of s 2, this provision does not require that the creditor or person claiming payment on his behalf agrees to forgo or wait for payment. A creditor etc is induced by deception to forgo payment if a deception by the debtor or another causes him to give up waiting for payment and (although he does not necessarily agree to extinguish it) to write off the debt, or if the creditor is convinced by the debtor or another that there is no liability to pay. Thus, if D writes on an envelope containing a bill to him from P: 'No longer at this address', or 'Paid last week', and sends it back to P, thereby inducing P to write off the debt, D has committed the present actus reus.

A creditor etc is induced by deception to wait for payment if, by deception, the debtor or another induces him not to enforce payment for the time being (whether or not the due date for payment is deferred), and in this context s 2(3) is of great importance. It provides that a person induced to take a cheque or other security for money by way of conditional satisfaction of an existing liability is to be treated not as being paid but as being induced to wait for payment. It follows that a person, who owes another money and gives him a cheque which is not honoured in due course by his bank, commits the actus reus under s 2(1)(b), even though the recipient of the cheque thinks he is being paid and does not agree to give time to pay. This is because, according to s 2(3), by his deception concerning the cheque[1] he has induced his creditor to wait for payment. It has been held in the Crown Court[2] that s 2(1)(b) only applies in the case of a dud cheque where the creditor has been induced to accept it instead of cash, because only then does s 2(3) operate to deem the creditor as having been induced to wait for payment. Consequently, if the payment by cheque is in the course of dealings on the basis of previously agreed credit terms where payment by cheque would be accepted in the ordinary course of the dealings, there is no inducement to wait for payment.[2]

1 Para 14.29.
2 *Andrews and Hedges* [1981] Crim LR 106, Crown Ct. See also, ibid, 276.

14.61 *Mens rea* The mens rea required under s 2(1)(b) is that the accused must:

a) make his deception deliberately or recklessly;[1]
b) dishonestly[2] induce the creditor etc to wait for or forgo payment; and
c) make his deception with intent to make permanent default in whole or in part on any existing liability to make a payment of his own[3], or with intent to let another do so. A person who merely intends to 'stall', e g not to pay now but to pay in two weeks' time, does not commit an offence under s 2 or any other offence. It remains to be seen whether the phrase 'with intent to let another do so [i e make permanent default on an existing liability to pay]' is satisfied by an intent that another's debt is permanently unpaid or whether it must be intended that the other person should be involved in making permanent default with the assistance or encouragement of the accused.

1 Theft Act 1978, s 5(1). See para 14.40.
2 Para 14.41.
3 *Attewell-Hughes* [1991] 4 All ER 810.

SECTION 2(1)(c)

14.62 This provides that dishonestly obtaining by deception any exemption from or abatement of liability to make a payment is an offence. Unlike the provisions in s 2 already mentioned, s 2(1)(c) is not limited to the evasion of an existing liability to pay since it also covers evasion of a liability to pay which does not yet exist,[1] and which may never exist. Where an exemption or abatement of liability to pay obtained by deception relates to an existing liability the offence overlaps with that of 'remission' in s 2(1)(a) and (in the case of exemption) with 'forgoing' in s 2(1)(b).

1 This was confirmed in *Firth* [1990] Crim LR 320, CA; para 14.63.

14.63 *Actus reus* The prosecution must prove that the accused committed a deception and thereby obtained an exemption from or abatement of liability to make a payment. Like 'remission' in s 2(1)(a), 'exemption' and 'abatement' imply the need for the creditor or potential creditor to agree to let the accused or another off the liability to pay (exemption) or to reduce the amount which must be paid (abatement). Although s 2(1)(c) could be read strictly so as to require that the agreement should be legally operative to affect the liability to pay, it is submitted that this cannot be the proper interpretation since such a requirement would rarely be satisfied under the law of contract and would render s 2(1)(c) virtually useless.[1]

It follows from what was said in the last paragraph that, if D, a taxpayer, by deception obtains a lower tax assessment than should have been made, he obtains the abatement of a future liability to pay money; and if D, knowing that old-age pensioners are allowed to travel free on Corporation buses, falsely states that he is an old-age pensioner and gets a free bus pass he has by deception obtained exemption from a liability to pay bus fares in the future. Likewise, if D induces a taxi-driver into giving him a ride at a reduced price, he will obtain an abatement of liability and can be convicted of the present offence (although it would be more appropriate to charge obtaining services by deception). Another example is provided by *Firth*.[2] D, a consultant at a NHS hospital, obtained exemptions from liability for charges for various services for his *private* patients by failing to notify the hospital that they were private patients (which was held to be a deception that they were NHS patients).[3] D was held to have obtained by deception an exemption from a liability to make a payment.

It was held in *Sibartie*[4] that a person, who 'flashes' an inapplicable season ticket in order to evade paying for a train journey, obtains an exemption from liability to pay the fare if his ruse succeeds (and of an attempt if it does not). This is hard to accept because, if deceived, the ticket collector will be induced to believe that there is no liability to pay, as opposed to agreeing to exempt the person from liability. The appropriate charge in such a case is one of 'forgoing payment' under s 2(1)(b). Any suggestion that 'exemption' or 'abatement' do not require agreement by the creditor, which suggestion would seem equally applicable to 'remission' under s 2(1)(a), should be resisted. Not only would it be contrary to the natural meaning of the provisions in question, but it would also deprive s 2(1)(b) of any utility in the case of 'forgoing payment' because this would also be covered by s 2(1)(a) and (c) without the need for proof of an intention to make permanent default.

It is not necessary that the accused should obtain the exemption or abatement for himself; he is also caught not only if he obtains such for another but also if he enables another to obtain an exemption or abatement.[5]

1 Contrast the view of Smith *The Law of Theft* (6th edn), para 246.
2 [1990] Crim LR 320, CA.
3 The Court of Appeal dealt with the deception as one by omission; see para 14.33. Arguably, the deception could have been regarded as one by conduct; see para 14.29.
4 [1983] Crim LR 470, CA.
5 Theft Act 1978, s 2(4).

14.64 *Mens rea* The mens rea required under s 2(1)(c) is that the accused must make his deception deliberately or recklessly[1] and dishonestly[1] obtain etc the exemption or abatement.

1 Theft Act 1978, s 5(1). See para 14.40.
2 See para 14.41.

Making off without payment

14.65 Section 3 of the Theft Act 1978 provides yet another offence to deal with those who dishonestly gain some sort of financial advantage. This offence, which is aimed at what are commonly described as 'bilkers', is different from the other offences discussed on the previous ten pages in that deception is not one of its elements (although in a particular case a deception may have facilitated the 'making off') and the maximum punishment is only two years' imprisonment.[1]

The definition of the offence is set out in s 3(1), which provides that a person who, knowing that payment on the spot for any goods supplied or service done is required or expected from him, dishonestly makes off without having paid as required or expected and with intent to avoid payment of the amount due is guilty of an offence.

1 Theft Act 1978, s 4.

ACTUS REUS

14.66 The accused must make off without paying as required or expected, in circumstances where payment on the spot for any goods supplied or service done is required or expected.

'Makes off' refers to making off from the spot where payment is required or expected; what is the 'spot' depends on the circumstances of each case. It is clear that the following are examples of this offence: walking out of a hotel or restaurant without paying the bill, driving out of a car park without paying the fee and jumping out of a taxi and running off without paying the fare. On the other hand, walking towards the exit of the hotel or restaurant, driving towards the exit of the car park or moving towards the door of the taxi, with intent to leave and avoid payment, will not suffice for an offence under s 3 (although it may constitute an attempt to commit that offence).[1]

A moot point is whether a person 'makes off' if he leaves without payment with the consent of the creditor (albeit that it is procured by deception). We are not concerned here with the type of case where a taxi driver allows a passenger to leave his taxi in order to go into a house to collect the fare and the passenger never returns, because the driver has not consented to the passenger leaving without payment and there is no difficulty in saying he makes off without payment. The difficulty is where someone leaves without payment, having deceived the creditor into believing that payment has been made, as where X walks out of a hotel with his suitcases, having told the proprietor that he has paid the receptionist. A Circuit judge appears to have held that one cannot make off if the creditor consents to one's leaving,[2] but this interpretation is not warranted by the wording of the section and, it is submitted, is not the correct view. However, a charge of evading liability by deception contrary to s 2(1)(b) of the 1978 Act would be more appropriate in such a case.

The accused must make off 'without having paid as required or expected'. This raises another moot point, which is whether a person who purports to pay but does so with a cheque which 'bounces' or with a forged cheque makes off without payment when he leaves the spot where payment is required. Assuming that a person who leaves with the creditor's consent can nevertheless be said to 'make off', the better view is that in the case of a bouncing cheque the person will not make off *without payment* (because by giving the cheque he conditionally discharges his liability to pay), whereas in the case of a forged cheque he will (because a forged cheque is void and, just like payment with counterfeit money or forged notes, does not operate as a conditional discharge of the obligation to pay).[3] The point, however, is somewhat academic since the appropriate offence to charge in such a case is generally that of evading liability by deception contrary to s 2(1)(b).

Making off without payment is only an offence if payment on the spot is required or expected of the accused for any goods supplied or services done, as in the above examples. 'Payment on the spot' includes cases where payment is expected or required at the time of collecting goods on which work has been done or in respect of which service has been provided.[4] The present requirement does not mean that payment by cash must be required or expected; cases where the common understanding is that payment on the spot will be by cheque or credit card are therefore covered.

An offence is not committed under s 3 if the payment avoided relates to the supply of goods or the doing of services which is contrary to law, or where the service done is such that payment is not legally enforceable.[5] For example, as has been stated already, a contract with a prostitute for her services is illegal and unenforceable in civil law; in consequence a man who has intercourse with a prostitute and then leaves, having refused to pay her the agreed fee, does not commit an offence under s 3. It may be noted that if, instead he had deceived her into letting him off paying, he would not be guilty of evading liability by deception because, as we have seen, that offence only relates to legally enforceable liability. However, as we saw in para 14.54, if from the start he had not intended to pay (and by his conduct had deceived her as to this), he may be convicted of obtaining services by deception, since that offence is not limited to the case where the expectation of payment refers to a legally enforceable liability to pay.

Lastly, an offence is not committed under s 3 if the payment required or expected is not legally due; for example the offence is not committed by a passenger who refuses to pay anything to a taxi-driver, and makes off, after the driver has in breach of contract abandoned the journey before reaching its destination.[6]

1 *McDavitt* [1981] Crim LR 843, Crown Ct; *Brooks* (1982) 76 Cr App Rep 66, CA.
2 *Hammond* [1982] Crim LR 611, Crown Ct. See also [1983] Crim LR 205 and 573.
3 Syrota 'Are Cheque Frauds Covered by Section 3 of the Theft Act 1978?' [1981] Crim LR 412. Also see *Hammond* [1982] Crim LR 611, Crown Ct.
4 Theft Act 1978, s 3(2).
5 Ibid, s 3(3).
6 *Troughton v Metropolitan Police* [1987] Crim LR 138, DC.

MENS REA

14.67 The mens rea required of a person charged with making off without payment is that, knowing[1] that payment on the spot was required or expected, he made off dishonestly[2] and with intent to avoid payment of the amount due. In *Allen*[3] the House of Lords held that an intent permanently to avoid payment is required; an intent to defer or delay payment is not sufficient. In this case, the accused left a hotel without paying. At his trial for making off without payment, he put forward the defence that he had been prevented from paying the bill by temporary financial difficulties but had expected to be able to do so subsequently. The House of Lords held that the trial judge had been wrong to tell the jury that an intent not to pay on the spot would suffice, since the accused could only be convicted if he was proved to have intended never to pay. The decision is surprising – but, of course, binding – given the appearance of 'permanent' in the further intent to make permanent default in s 2(1)(b) and its absence in the present further intent.

1 No doubt 'knowing' includes being wilfully blind; para 6.59.
2 See paras 13.54–13.58 and 14.41 which apply equally to the present offence.
3 [1985] AC 1029, [1985] 2 All ER 641, HL.

14.68 There is considerable overlap between the various offences under the 1978 Act inter se and also between them and the offences of deception under the Theft Act 1968, as is shown by the following examples.

D induces P to give him a taxi ride by falsely saying or implying that he will pay at his destination. When the taxi reaches the destination D runs off without paying. Assuming that he has the necessary mens rea, D is guilty of obtaining services by deception (as to his present intentions), contrary to s 1 of the 1978 Act, and of making off without payment, contrary to s 3.

D goes into a garage and asks the attendant to put four gallons of petrol into his car's tank. After this is done D drives off without paying. If D never intended to pay he is guilty of obtaining property by deception (as to his present intentions), and, in any case, he is guilty of making off without payment.

If, instead of suddenly driving off, D had induced the garage owner to take a cheque which was subsequently dishonoured as D knew it would be, D would still be guilty of obtaining property by deception if he never intended to pay, and, in any case, guilty of inducing the garage owner to wait for payment by his deception as to the cheque, contrary to s 2(1)(b) of the 1978 Act. It remains to be authoritatively decided whether he can be said to have 'made off without payment' contrary to s 3 (although the better view is that he does not).

Falsification

14.69 Sections 17 to 20 of the Theft Act 1968 define several offences dealing with false accounting, false statements by officers of corporations or unincorporated associations, the destruction, defacement or concealment of a valuable security, will or court or government document, and procuring the execution or destruction of a valuable security. All these offences are punishable with a maximum of seven years' imprisonment on conviction on indictment. They do not call for detailed discussion.

Section 17 punishes the dishonest destruction, defacement, concealment or falsification of any account 'or any record or document made or required for any accounting purpose' with a view to gain for oneself or another or with intent to cause loss to another. Section 17 also punishes a person who, with such a view or intent, dishonestly in furnishing information for any purpose produces or makes use of any account, or any such 'record or document', which to his knowledge is or may be misleading, false or deceptive in a material particular. This is a very convenient section to use where there has been an elaborate and complicated system of fraud in which it is not easy to identify the particular sums of money and other property of which the owner has been deprived, although it is certainly not limited to this. This is one of those sections in which the definitions of gain and loss in s 34, which are discussed in para 14.74, are incorporated, so that it suffices that merely a temporary gain or loss is intended.

Section 19 punishes the publishing of a written statement known to be (or possibly to be) misleading, false or deceptive in a material particular by an officer of a body corporate or unincorporated association (or person purporting to act as such), with intent to deceive its members or creditors about its affairs.

Section 20 makes it an offence for a person:

a) to destroy, deface or conceal any valuable security, any will or any original document of or belonging to, or filed or deposited in, any court or any government department; or

b) by any *deception* to procure the execution of a valuable security,

provided, in each instance, that the accused acted dishonestly and with a view to gain for himself or another or with intent to cause loss to another.

'Deception' bears the same meaning as in s 15.[1] A 'valuable security' means any document creating, transferring, surrendering or releasing any right to, in or over property, or authorising the payment of money or delivery of any property, or evidencing such creation etc, or such payment etc, or the satisfaction of any obligation.[1]

1 Theft Act 1968, s 20(3); see para 14.28 for the definition of deception.

Liability of controlling officer for deception or falsification offence by corporation

14.70 Under s 18 of the 1968 Act,[1] a director or other controlling officer of a body corporate is liable for offences under ss 15, 16 or 17 of the 1968 Act or ss 1 or 2 of the Theft Act 1978 which have been committed[2] by the body corporate with his connivance or consent.[3]

1 Section 5(2) of the 1978 Act extends s 18 to offences under ss 1 and 2 of the 1978 Act.
2 Paras 9.83–9.86.
3 See, further, para 9.90.

Blackmail

14.71 By s 21 of the Theft Act 1968, a person is guilty of blackmail, an offence triable only on indictment and punishable with imprisonment for a maximum of 14 years, if, with a view to gain for himself or another or with intent to cause loss to another, he makes any unwarranted demand with menaces; and for this purpose a demand with menaces is unwarranted unless the person making it does so in the belief that he has reasonable grounds for making the demand, and that the use of the menaces is a proper means of reinforcing the demand.

DEMAND WITH MENACES

14.72 *Demand* The essence of the offence is a demand, so that a person may be guilty of blackmail if the other ingredients are present, and not merely of an attempt, if he obtains nothing. The demand need not be express, since (taken together with the menaces) it may be implied by a request or suggestion[1] or other conduct. The nature of the act or omission demanded is immaterial;[2] the offence is not limited to a demand for the transfer of property, although this represents the usual type of blackmail. It is irrelevant whether or not the demand is complied with. In *Treacy v DPP*[3] the House of Lords held by a majority that a demand by letter is made when the letter is posted; it is therefore irrelevant that the letter is never delivered (or that its recipient is illiterate). A similar rule probably applies to an oral demand, so that it is irrelevant that the addressee is, for instance, deaf or cannot understand what is said (at least, if an ordinary person would have understood).

1 As in the pre-Act cases of *Studer* (1915) 11 Cr App Rep 307, CA, and *Collister* (1955) 39 Cr App Rep 100, CA.
2 Theft Act 1968, s 21(2).
3 [1971] AC 537, [1971] 1 All ER 110, HL.

14.73 *Menaces* When the word was first used in this branch of the law, 'menaces' was limited to threats of violence, but it has long since come to include 'threats of action detrimental to or unpleasant to the person addressed'.[1] It is immaterial whether the menaces do or do not relate to action to be taken by the person making the demand.[2] The thug who says 'Give me money or the boys will beat you up', and the man who says 'Give up your claim to my Picasso or my daughter will tell the world that you seduced her', are both as guilty of blackmail as the man who reinforces his demands with threats of action by himself.

It was held by the Court of Appeal in *Lawrence*[3] that the word 'menaces' is an ordinary word which a jury can be expected to understand and that consequently it is only rarely that a judge will need to enter on a definition of that word. However, there are two occasions[4] when a judge must give a definition:

a) If, on the facts known to the accused, his threats might have affected the mind of an ordinary person of normal stability, although they did not affect the addressee, the jury should be told that they would amount to menaces.[5]

b) If, although they would not have affected the mind of a person of normal stability, the threats affected the mind of the victim, the jury should be told that the menaces would be proved if the accused was aware of the likely effect of his actions on the victim, e g because he knew of some unusual susceptibility on the victim's part.

1 *Thorne v Motor Trade Association* [1937] AC 797 at 817, per Lord Wright.
2 Theft Act 1968, s 21(2).
3 (1971) 57 Cr App Rep 64, CA.
4 *Garwood* [1987] 1 All ER 1032, [1987] 1 WLR 319, CA.
5 Also see *Clear* [1968] 1 QB 670, [1968] 1 All ER 74, CA.

WITH A VIEW TO GAIN OR INTENT TO CAUSE LOSS

14.74 The demand with menaces must be made by the accused with a view to gain for himself or another, or with intent to cause loss to another. Under s 34(2) of the 1968 Act 'gain' and 'loss' are confined to money or other property. Consequently, it is not blackmail to demand with menaces that a person should cease committing adultery or should commit adultery or should surrender the custody of a child. On the other hand, it is not necessary that the accused should be motivated by the desire to achieve economic gain or to cause economic loss. In *Bevans*,[1] for example, a man in severe pain, who threatened to shoot a doctor if he did not give him an injection of morphine, was held guilty of blackmail. The drug was property, the man had demanded it (and thereby acted with a view to gaining it for himself) and the requirements of blackmail were satisfied; it was irrelevant that his motive had been relief from pain rather than economic gain.

The gain in view or loss intended need not be permanent, which differentiates blackmail from some other offences under the Act. Hence, girl D, who tells girl P that D will reveal details of P's sexual aberrations to her fiancé unless P lends her a dress for a dance, is guilty of blackmail.

Under s 34(2) of the 1968 Act, 'gain' includes a gain by keeping what one has, as well as getting what one has not; 'loss' includes a loss by not getting what one might get, as well as losing what one has. The width of these terms means that blackmail extends to a wide variety of demands with menaces which do not involve a demand for the transfer of property. For example, a demand that the victim should abandon a claim against the accused to specific property can constitute blackmail if it is accompanied by menaces, because the accused has a view to gain by keeping what he has; of course, he also has an intent to cause loss to the victim by the victim not getting what he might get. Thus, a person who demands with menaces that compromising letters be destroyed acts with an intent to cause loss to another (by the latter losing what he has) and therefore he can be convicted of blackmail. However, it has been held that, where the abandonment of a claim to property is demanded, the particular property must be specific and identifiable; consequently, where the demand is that the victim should forebear to sue to enforce a financial obligation it is not made with a view to gain or with intent to cause loss.[2] This is not a necessary, or even obvious, interpretation of the words of the subsection.

A person who demands with menaces a job can be convicted of blackmail since he acts with a view to gain for himself. A person acts with a view to gain if he seeks to recover a debt, for he is endeavouring to get money which he has not got although it is legally due to him,[3] but so long as the menaces go no further than the threat of legal proceedings no offence is committed since, as we shall see in the next paragraph, it is inconceivable that the demand with menaces would be found to be unwarranted.

1 (1988) 87 Cr App Rep 64, CA.
2 *Goleccha and Choraria* [1989] 3 All ER 908, [1989] 1 WLR 1050, CA.
3 *Parkes* [1973] Crim LR 358, Crown Ct.

UNWARRANTED

14.75 As was stated above, the demand with menaces must be unwarranted. For this purpose s 21(1) provides that a demand with menaces is unwarranted unless the person making it does so in the *belief* that he has reasonable grounds for making the demand *and* that the use of the menaces is a proper means of reinforcing the demand. Legally, it is irrelevant whether or not the accused's beliefs are unreasonable; the question is whether *he* had such beliefs, but, of course, the reasonableness of his alleged belief is evidentially important in relation to his credibility. The accused does not have to prove these beliefs, but this does not mean that the prosecution must negative the existence of a belief for which there is no evidence. Instead, the accused has an evidential burden and, unless he adduces evidence (or there is evidence from another source) which raises the issue that he had the beliefs required, the jury will be obliged to find that the demand with menaces was unwarranted.[1]

Assuming the issue is raised, the prosecution must negative either the accused's alleged belief that he had reasonable grounds for making the demand, *or* his alleged belief that the use of the menaces was a proper means of reinforcing it. Normally, it will be easier to negative the second of these alleged beliefs, since a person who makes a demand with menaces may well believe he has reasonable grounds for making the demand but realise that the use of the menaces in question was not a proper means of reinforcing the demand. For example, a bookmaker may well believe that he has reasonable grounds for demanding payment of a bet by a customer (although he knows the bet is not legally enforceable), but realise that his threat to have the customer beaten up otherwise is not a proper means of reinforcing the demand.

It seems clear that the accused is to be judged according to his own understanding of general moral standards. It follows that the person whose understanding of general moral standards is of standards which are low may succeed in a defence in a case where another person whose understanding of general moral standards is of higher standards may not, even though the jury thinks that he acted reasonably.

It was held by the Court of Appeal in *Harvey*[2] that no act known by the accused to be unlawful could be believed by him to be proper, even though he might regard it as justified. This seems incontrovertible where the act is a serious crime since D cannot credibly say that he believed that a threat of murder or rape, as in *Harvey*, was proper according to general moral standards. On the other hand, it is less acceptable where the threatened act involves a minor illegality since D may well believe that to threaten a minor offence is proper according to his understanding of general moral standards.

The following provides an example of the operation of the provisions relating to 'unwarrantedness'. Suppose that the unmarried mother of a child by a rich and distinguished man demands a settlement of a large sum of money in excess of her legal rights for the benefit of herself and the child against a threat to publish the facts in the press. If the issue is raised that the demand with menaces was not unwarranted, the woman must be acquitted unless the jury are satisfied that *she* did not believe there were reasonable grounds for her demand or did not believe her means of enforcing it were proper.

1 *Lawrence* (1971) 57 Cr App Rep 64, CA.
2 (1981) 72 Cr App Rep 139, CA.

Handling

14.76   By s 22 of the Theft Act 1968, a person handles stolen goods if (otherwise than in the course of the stealing) knowing or believing them to be stolen goods he dishonestly receives the goods, or dishonestly undertakes or assists in their retention, removal, disposal or realisation by or for the benefit of another person, or if he arranges to do so. Handling stolen goods is punishable with imprisonment for a maximum of 14 years.

14.77   There is a considerable overlap between handling and theft. In many instances, a person who 'handles' stolen goods is thereby appropriating property belonging to another and is also guilty of theft if he has the necessary mens rea.[1] Nevertheless, there are two reasons for having the separate offence of handling. One is that sometimes handling stolen goods does not involve the appropriation of property belonging to another – either because the dealing with them does not constitute an appropriation (as in the case of handling by 'arranging' to do something with them, which is discussed below) or because, the original 'thief' having obtained ownership of them, a person who subsequently handles them may not appropriate property belonging to another. The other reason is that professional receivers or disposers of stolen property (otherwise known as 'fences' and 'placers', respectively) are a serious nuisance and it is widely believed that without them there would be fewer thieves[2] since many 'professional' thieves would be deterred from their activities if they could not pass on to others the task of disposing of stolen goods at a profit. The existence of the separate offence of handling, which is more severely punishable than theft, ensures that large-scale fences and placers can be punished more severely than the thieves for whom they act.

1 *Dolan* (1975) 62 Cr App Rep 36, CA; *Sainthouse* [1980] Crim LR 506, CA.
2 A point made by the Court of Appeal in *Shelton* (1986) 83 Cr App Rep 379, [1986] Crim LR 637, CA.

ACTUS REUS

14.78   *Stolen goods* The seemingly straightforward actus reus, handling stolen goods, in fact involves a good deal of complexity, and the meaning of 'stolen goods' is an example of this.

Section 34(2)(b) of the Act states that 'goods' includes money and every other description of property, except land, and includes things severed from the land by stealing.

By s 24, 'stolen goods' means goods which have been stolen (contrary to s 1 of the Act) or obtained by deception (contrary to s 15) or by blackmail (contrary to s 21),[1] and hereafter 'steal', 'stolen', 'theft' and 'thief' must be understood in this extended sense. Goods 'stolen' in a foreign country (including Scotland and Northern Ireland) are stolen goods if they were appropriated or obtained abroad in such a way as to satisfy the requirements of ss 1, 15 or 21 *and* the 'stealing' was criminal by the law of the foreign country in question.[2]

1 Theft Act 1968, s 24(4).
2 Ibid, s 24(1).

14.79   For the offence of handling to be committed the goods must not only have been stolen, but *remain* stolen at the time of their handling. In this context s 24(3) is important. It provides that no goods which have been stolen are to be regarded as having continued to be stolen after one of the following events has occurred:

a) *After they have been restored to the person from whom they were stolen or to other lawful possession or custody.*

It is often difficult to decide whether goods have been restored to lawful possession or custody, particularly when the police have traced the goods. The crucial question here is whether the police officer has reduced the stolen goods into his possession, and this depends upon the intention with which he has acted. In *A-G's Reference (No 1 of 1974)*[1] it was held that a police officer, who had removed the rotor arm of a car containing goods about which the officer wished to question the driver, would have reduced them into his possession, if he had acted with intent to take charge of them so that they could not be removed and so that he could have the disposal of them; but, if he had retained an open mind as to whether he should take possession and merely removed the rotor arm in order that the driver should not get away without interrogation, he would not have reduced them into his possession.

b) *After the person from whom they were stolen and any other person claiming through him have otherwise ceased as regards those goods to have any right to restitution in respect of the theft.*

An illustration of this provision is where A obtains goods from B under a contract which is voidable because of A's deception. If B, on realising the deception, affirms the contract he thereby ceases to have any right to restitution of the goods and they therefore cease to be stolen goods at that point of time.

1 [1974] QB 744, [1974] 2 All ER 899, CA.

14.80 For the purpose of the present offence, references to 'stolen goods' include the proceeds of dealings with such goods by the thief or a handler. This is provided by s 24(2) of the 1968 Act, which states that references to stolen goods:

'include, in addition to the goods originally stolen and parts of them (whether in their original state or not),—

a) any other goods which directly or indirectly represent or have at any time represented the stolen goods in the hands of the thief as being the proceeds of any disposal or realisation of the whole or part of the goods stolen or of goods so representing the stolen goods; and

b) any other goods which directly or indirectly represent or have at any time represented the stolen goods in the hands of a handler of the stolen goods or any part of them as being the proceeds of any disposal or realisation of the whole or part of the stolen goods handled by him or of goods so representing them.'

'The thief' means the person by whose conduct, with the appropriate mens rea, the goods were originally stolen or obtained by deception or blackmail. 'A handler' means any person who has committed the actus reus of handling with the appropriate mens rea.

The operation of s 24(2) can be illustrated as follows. A steals a car (or obtains it by deception or blackmail). He sells it to B for £1,000 and receives that sum in cash. The car and cash are now both stolen goods, the latter because it directly represents the original stolen goods (the car) in the hands of the thief (A) as the proceeds of the car's realisation or disposal. Therefore, if A then gives £500 of the £1,000 to C, who receives the money knowing that it has represented part of the original stolen goods, C can be convicted of handling. If C buys a camera with the £500, the camera becomes stolen goods once it is in his hands because it indirectly represents the original stolen goods in the hands of a handler as the proceeds of the realisation or disposal of part of goods representing the original stolen goods. Consequently, if E receives the camera from C, knowing that it has represented part of the stolen goods in the hands of C, E can be convicted of handling stolen goods. However, if F receives the camera from E, unaware that it represents the original stolen goods, and then sells it for cash, the cash which F receives will not become stolen goods because, lacking mens rea, F is not a handler and therefore *that* cash does *not* represent the original stolen goods in the hands of a handler as proceeds of their realisation or disposal.[1] Consequently, if G receives that cash from F, G cannot be convicted of receiving stolen goods, even though he knows all the material facts.

1 For an extreme example of the application of s 24(2), see *A-G's Reference (No 4 of 1979)* [1981] 1 All ER 1193, [1981] 1 WLR 667, CA.

14.81 *Forms of handling* Section 22(1) states that handling consists of receiving stolen goods, or undertaking or assisting in their retention, removal, disposal or realisation by or for the benefit of another, or arranging to do one of these things. As will be shown later, this definition comprises 18 different forms of handling.[1] However, although Lord Bridge stated, obiter, in *Bloxham*[2] that s 22(1) creates two distinct offences (one of receiving, and the other capable of being committed in the other ways specified in s 22(1)), the weight of authority[3] is in favour of the view that the provision creates only one offence, which can be committed by receiving or by any of the other ways specified.

If Lord Bridge's view was correct, an indictment alleging an unparticularised offence of handling would be bad for duplicity, but it has been held by the Court of Appeal[4] and by the Divisional Court[5] that such an indictment is not defective, although the better practice is to particularise the form of handling relied on, and, if there is any uncertainty about the form of handling in question, it will be advisable to have more than one count in the indictment. In the case of uncertainty, only two counts should generally be inserted since they will normally cover every form: one count for receiving, and the other either for the other forms of handling or for one or two of those forms (e g assisting in the removal or disposal of stolen goods by another).[6] Similar principles apply to informations laid before a magistrates' court.[7] If the accused is charged solely with receiving, he may not be convicted on that count of some other form of handling.[8]

The various forms of handling are set out below (paras 14.82 to 14.86).

1 *Nicklin* [1977] 2 All ER 444, [1977] 1 WLR 403, CA.
2 [1982] 1 All ER 582 at 584.
3 *Nicklin* [1977] 2 All ER 444, [1977] 1 WLR 403, CA; *Griffiths v Freeman* [1970] 1 All ER 1117, [1970] 1 WLR 659, DC.
4 *Nicklin* [1977] 2 All ER 444, [1977] 1 WLR 403, CA.
5 *Griffiths v Freeman* [1970] 1 All ER 1117, [1970] 1 WLR 659, DC.
6 *Nicklin*; *Willis and Syme* [1972] 3 All ER 797, [1972] 1 WLR 1605, CA.
7 *Griffiths v Freeman*.
8 *Nicklin*.

14.82 *Receiving* Receiving consists of a 'single finite act' whereby 'the accused came into possession' of the goods.[1] 'Possession' here means exclusive control. 'Receiving' also involves a receipt from someone else, so that a person who finds stolen goods and helps himself to them does not receive them.[2] It is possible for a receiver to be in joint possession with the thief or another receiver if he shares exclusive control with such a person.

It follows from the requirement of possession that a person who holds goods while he inspects them during negotiations with the thief does not receive them, nor does someone who helps the thief to unload the goods from a lorry.[3] In order to be in possession (and therefore to be a receiver), a person need not have physical contact with the goods so long as he takes them under his exclusive control or an agent or employee does so acting under his orders, in which case the agent or employee is also a receiver if he has the necessary mens rea.[4] Of course, the accused can only be convicted of handling if at the relevant time, here the time of the receiving, he had the requisite mens rea. If he did not, but later discovers that the goods are stolen, any subsequent dealing with them by him may constitute a handling of the types outlined in paras 14.84 to 14.86.

1 *Smythe* (1980) 72 Cr App Rep 8 at 13.
2 *Haider* (1985) unreported; available on Lexis.
3 *Hobson v Impett* (1957) 41 Cr App Rep 138, DC.
4 *Smith* (1855) Dears CC 559, 25 LJMC 29.

14.83 *Arranging to receive* What is required here is a concluded agreement between the accused and another (eg the thief) for the receiving of stolen goods by the accused. A mere offer to receive stolen goods, or the participation in negotiations for their receipt by him (as where the accused offers to purchase, or negotiates to purchase, stolen goods), will not suffice. However, certainly in the case of an offer, it may amount to an attempt to handle (in that it is an attempt to arrange to receive).

The other forms of handling set out below differ in one vital respect from receiving or arranging to receive in that all must be done 'by or for the benefit of' a person other than the alleged handler.

14.84 *Undertaking the retention, removal, disposal or realisation of stolen goods for the benefit of another* These four forms of handling are appropriate to cover the case where it is the accused, either alone or with another, who retains, removes, disposes or realises the stolen goods for the benefit of another. A person who undertakes one of the four activities *solely* for his own benefit cannot be convicted of handling, unless he has received the goods with the relevant mens rea. Thus, if C who has innocently received stolen goods simply retains them for his own benefit, he cannot be convicted of handling, although (unless he paid for them) he may be guilty of theft.

The four activities can be explained as follows.

'Retention' means 'keeping possession of, not losing, continuing to have'.[1]

'Removal' clearly refers to the movement of stolen goods from one place to another. Thus, a person undertakes the removal of stolen goods for the benefit of another if he transports the goods to a hideout for the benefit of the thief or some other person. However, a very slight movement of goods probably does not suffice.

'Disposal' covers not only the dumping or giving away of stolen goods but also their destruction, as where the accused melts down stolen candlesticks for the benefit of the thief or another.[2]

'Realisation' means the exchange of stolen goods for money or some other property. A person who sells stolen goods as agent for a third party (eg the thief) undertakes their realisation for the benefit of another. However, as was held by the House of Lords in *Bloxham*,[3] a person who sells stolen goods on his own behalf does not undertake their realisation for the benefit of another because the buyer benefits from the purchase and *not* from the realisation (which benefits the seller only). In such a case, the seller can only be convicted of handling if he has received the stolen goods with the relevant mens rea.

1 *Pitchley* (1972) 57 Cr App Rep 30, CA.
2 Griew *Theft Acts 1968 and 1978* (6th edn) para 14-26; contrast Williams *Textbook of Criminal Law* (2nd edn) 687 ('disposal' limited to alienation).
3 [1983] 1 AC 109, [1982] 1 All ER 582, HL.

14.85 *Assisting in the retention, removal, disposal or realisation of stolen goods by another* These four forms of handling are appropriate to cover cases where the accused provides assistance to another person who is undertaking or going to undertake the retention, removal, disposal or realisation of stolen goods.

'Assist' was construed in a wide way by the Court of Appeal in *Kanwar*.[1] Here, D was charged with assisting in the retention of stolen goods but the Court's statement would seem to apply to the other three forms of assistance. 'Assistance', the Court held, requires that something be done by the accused for the purpose of enabling the goods to be retained etc; it is not limited to physical acts since verbal representations, whether oral or written, for the purpose of enabling stolen goods to be retained etc can suffice. The requisite assistance, the Court stated, need not be successful in its object. Further elucidation of 'assist' was provided by the Court of Appeal in *Coleman*,[2] where it was held that the term includes helping or encouraging.

Although the decision in *Kanwar* does not refer to the possibility of assisting by failing to do something, there is authority (as will be seen shortly) that in one case a person can assist in the *retention* of stolen goods by an omission to act.

There is some overlap with cases of 'undertaking'. For example, a person who joins with another in removing stolen goods for the latter's benefit not only undertakes their removal for the benefit of another but also assists in that removal by another.

'Retention', 'removal', 'disposal' and 'realisation' have already been defined but the following are examples of these terms in the context of assistance.

A person assists in the retention of stolen goods by another if he puts the thief in touch with a warehouse keeper, or provides tarpaulins to cover the goods (or himself covers them) in order to conceal stolen goods in the possession of the thief or a handler, or tells lies so as to make it more difficult for the police to find or identify stolen goods retained by the thief or a handler. On the other hand, a refusal to answer questions put by the police as to the whereabouts of stolen goods does not amount to handling,[3] even though it may well assist in their retention by another. However, if the goods have been left on his premises by the thief or a handler such a refusal may be evidence that the accused has permitted them to remain there, which does constitute assisting in their retention.[3] Where the permission has not been communicated to the other but the accused passively allows the goods to remain under his control, there is only an omission to get rid of the goods on his part. Nevertheless, it has been held that this is a sufficient act of assistance in their retention.[4] This is the exceptional case where an omission can constitute 'assistance'. Merely to use stolen goods does not suffice, since it does not in itself amount to assistance in their retention.[5] Likewise, merely to accept the benefit of a disposal by another does not in itself suffice, since it does not amount to assistance in the disposal,[6] although if the benefit consists of the proceeds[7] of the original stolen goods and they are received by the accused he may be convicted of handling by receiving.

There will be assistance in the removal of stolen goods by another if the accused lends a lorry for their removal. An example of assistance in the disposal of stolen goods by another occurs where the accused advises the thief as to how to get rid of stolen goods.

A person assists in the realisation of stolen goods by another if he puts a fence in touch with a thief.

1 [1982] 2 All ER 528, [1982] 1 WLR 845, CA.
2 (1985) 150 JP 175, [1986] Crim LR 56, CA.
3 *Brown* [1970] 1 QB 105, [1969] 3 All ER 198, CA.
4 Ibid; *Pitchley* (1972) 57 Cr App Rep 30, CA.
5 *Sanders* (1982) 75 Cr App Rep 84, [1982] Crim LR 695, CA.
6 *Coleman* (1985) 150 JP 175, [1986] Crim LR 56, CA.
7 Para 14.80.

14.86 *Arranging to undertake or assist in the retention, removal, disposal or realisation of stolen goods by or for the benefit of another* These eight forms of handling require no explanation in the light of what has been said in paras 14.83 to 14.85. An example covered by these forms is agreeing to send a van to collect the thief and the stolen goods, which constitutes arranging to assist in the removal of stolen goods by another.

The reader is reminded that the offence of handling can only be committed if the goods are already stolen at the time of the alleged act of handling. Any arrangement, including an arrangement to receive, made before goods are stolen will therefore not constitute handling stolen goods,[1] although it may constitute the separate offence of conspiracy to handle.[2]

1 *Park* (1987) 87 Cr App Rep 164, CA.
2 Ibid, at 173. For conspiracy, see Ch 21.

14.87 *Limitation* The requirement that the handling must have been 'otherwise than in the course of the stealing' (ie the stealing by which the goods originally became stolen goods) means that the original thief is not guilty of handling so long as the stealing continues, nor is one of joint thieves, even in respect of the assistance he gives to the other or others. It is difficult to define exactly when the course of the stealing finishes, but clearly, as in the case of the 'time' of stealing in robbery, it is not limited to the initial act of appropriation with mens rea whereby the goods were stolen. Arguably, 'the course of the stealing' lasts as long as the stealing can be said to be still in progress in common sense terms.[1] If so, any handling of goods which have been stolen by a person removing them from a cupboard will be done in the course of the stealing if it is done at the scene of the crime or while he is leaving the immediate vicinity of the theft with the goods; on the other hand, handling of the goods four hours later after they have been driven 200 miles from the scene of the crime is clearly not done in the course of the stealing. The difficulty, of course, comes in drawing the line in between; this may be more difficult, however, in the abstract than in a concrete case.

It must be emphasised that, once the course of the stealing has ended, even the original thief of the goods can be convicted of handling them. An example would be if, after the course of the stealing, he helps a fence to whom he has sold them to move them from one hiding place to another since he dishonestly assists in their removal by another.

Unless there is an issue on the evidence that the accused was the thief or that the handling was in the course of the stealing, the prosecution does not have to prove that the handling was 'otherwise than in the course of the stealing'; indeed, the judge should not even tell the jury about these words.[2]

1 See further the comments in para 14.4, which would seem to be equally applicable here. Depending on the facts, the 'course of the stealing' may be very brief, as in *Pitham and Hehl* (1976) 65 Cr App Rep 45, CA.
2 *Cash* [1985] QB 801, [1985] 2 All ER 128, CA.

MENS REA

14.88 *Knowledge or belief* None of the actions described above is enough to amount to handling unless the accused either knows or believes that the goods are stolen (in the extended meaning) when they are handled.[1] It follows that, goods being received at the moment when they come into possession, subsequent knowledge by the person that they are stolen does not of itself make him a handler, although if he then goes on to commit some other act of handling, such as undertaking their disposal for *the benefit of another*, he can be convicted of handling. 'Undertaking' and 'assisting' can be continuing forms of conduct, and where this occurs it is enough that the accused only discovers that the goods are stolen after he began to handle them in one of these ways, provided he has not yet ceased to do so.

It must be remembered that if a person, who has innocently received as a gift stolen goods, subsequently decides to keep them when he discovers that they are stolen, he commits theft, since his keeping them as owner amounts to an appropriation under s 3(1) of the 1968 Act. It would be different if the goods were transferred to him for value in good faith because s 3(2) would prevent him being guilty of theft (see para 13.17).

A person 'knows' that goods are stolen if he has actual knowledge of this, or if he is told of this by someone with first-hand knowledge (for example, by the thief himself).[2] The Court of Appeal held in *Hall*[3] that 'belief' was something short of 'knowledge', and might be said to be the state of mind of a person who said to himself: 'I cannot say I know for certain that those goods are stolen, but there can be no other reasonable conclusion in the light of all the circumstances, in the light of all that I have heard and seen'. On the other hand, suspicion – even a very strong one – that goods are stolen is not enough,[4] nor is wilful blindness[5] (although it normally constitutes knowledge in other contexts). However, it has been held that knowledge or belief *may* be inferred from wilful blindness, which is somewhat difficult to understand if the suspicion involved in wilful blindness is not enough for 'belief'.[6] Clearly, there is little, if any, difference between 'knowing' and 'believing' in this context. It has been held that 'knowledge or belief' are words in ordinary usage in English and that it is not necessary in every case for the jury to be given any definition of them,[7] which is rather surprising in the light of what has just been said about these terms. However, it has also been held that in cases 'where much reference is made to suspicion, it will be prudent to give [a direction]'.[8]

The answer to the question, 'How much must the accused know or believe?' is this. The accused must know or believe enough facts about the way in which the goods have been acquired or dealt with as to indicate that, in law (*whether or not he realises this*), they have been stolen or obtained by deception or blackmail. Where the charge relates to the proceeds of the original stolen goods the accused must know the relevant history of those goods.

1 For an analysis of the position of the innocent receiver with subsequent mens rea, see Tunkel (1983) 133 NLJ 844.
2 *Hall* (1985) 81 Cr App Rep 260, CA. The test of 'knowledge or belief' being subjective, it is not enough that a person ought to have known the goods were stolen: *Atwal v Massey* [1971] 3 All ER 881, DC.
3 (1985) 81 Cr App Rep 260, CA.
4 *Moys* (1984) 79 Cr App Rep 72, CA.
5 *Grainge* [1974] 1 All ER 928, [1974] 1 WLR 619, CA; *Griffiths* (1974) 60 Cr App Rep 14, CA; *Reader* (1977) 66 Cr App Rep 33, CA.
6 The problem is similar to that of inferring intention from foresight, when foresight is not intention; see para 6.36.
7 *Smith* (1976) 64 Cr App Rep 217, CA; *Harris* (1986) 84 Cr App Rep 75, CA; *Reader*.
8 *Toor* (1986) 85 Cr App Rep 116, [1987] Crim LR 122, CA.

14.89 *Proof of knowledge or belief* This may be assisted by the so-called 'doctrine of recent possession'. This common law 'doctrine' applies where the accused received or otherwise handled[1] recently stolen goods. Under the 'doctrine' the judge may direct the jury that they *may*, if they think fit, in the absence of an explanation by the accused or if they are satisfied beyond reasonable doubt that any explanation given is untrue, infer that he knew or believed that they were stolen.[2] Of course, the jury are not obliged to draw the inference, and the onus of proving knowledge or belief remains on the prosecution throughout.[2]

The 'doctrine of recent possession' is misnamed,[3] since it has nothing to do with goods recently possessed but concerns the possession or handling of recently stolen goods; moreover, it is not even a doctrine since it is merely an application of the ordinary rules of circumstantial evidence.

Quite apart from the common law 'doctrine', s 27(3) of the 1968 Act[4] lays down a special rule to assist in the proof of knowledge or belief, which applies[5] where the accused is being prosecuted at the trial in question[5] only for handling stolen goods *and* evidence has been given of his having committed an act of handling in relation to the goods in question. In such a case s 27(3) provides that the following evidence (which would not otherwise be admissible under the law of evidence) is admissible[6] for the purpose of proving that the accused knew or believed the goods to be stolen goods:

a) evidence that he has had in his possession, or has undertaken or assisted in the retention, removal, disposal or realisation of, stolen goods from any theft taking place not earlier than 12 months before the offence charged; and

b) provided seven days' written notice has been given to him of the intention to prove the conviction, evidence that he has within the five years preceding the date of the offence been convicted of theft or handling stolen goods.

Section 27(3) does not authorise the introduction of evidence which goes beyond what it specifically describes.[7] Thus, evidence given under para a) is limited to the fact that the accused has had in his possession, or has undertaken or assisted in the retention etc of, stolen goods from any theft taking place not earlier than 12 months before the offence of handling charged (with the result that evidence may not be given that the accused knew or believed those goods to be stolen).[8] Likewise, evidence given under para b) is limited to a bare recital of the conviction and when and where it occurred (with the result that evidence of other details, such as a description of the goods, may not be given under that paragraph).[9]

1 *Ball* [1983] 2 All ER 1089, [1983] 1 WLR 801, CA.
2 *Schama and Abramovitch* (1914) 11 Cr App Rep 45, CCA; *Aves* [1950] 2 All ER 330, 34 Cr App Rep 159, CA.
3 *Ball* [1983] 2 All ER 1089 at 1092.
4 For a discussion of this provision, see Munday 'Handling the Evidential Exception' [1988] Crim LR 345.
5 *Bradley* (1979) 70 Cr App Rep 200, CA.
6 Subject to the judge's discretion to exclude it if this is necessary to ensure a fair trial: *Knott* [1973] Crim LR 36, CA. See, further, Griew *Theft Acts 1968 and 1978* (6th edn) para 14–41.
7 *Bradley* (1979) 70 Cr App Rep 200, CA.
8 Ibid; *Wood* [1987] 1 WLR 779, (1987) 85 Cr App Rep 287, CA.
9 *Fowler* (1987) 86 Crim App Rep 219, CA. Providing a description of the goods seems unavoidable under para a): *Fowler*

14.90 *Dishonesty* Knowledge or belief that the goods were stolen is not enough. The prosecution must also prove that, when he handled the goods, the accused was dishonest.[1] No doubt, on the ground that he was not dishonest a person would not be guilty of handling stolen goods, even if he knew them to be stolen, if he acquired them in order to return them to the owner, or to hand them over to the police. Likewise, it would be most unlikely for a person to be found to have dishonestiy handled stolen goods if he induced a thief to hand a stolen gun over to him in order to prevent the thief committing suicide by shooting himself.

1 Paras 13.54–13.58 and 14.41.

Section 23

14.91 Section 23 of the Theft Act 1968 punishes as a summary offence public advertisements of a reward for the return of stolen or lost goods with statements to the effect that no questions will be asked, or that the person returning them will be safe from inquiry, or that money paid or loaned for the goods will be returned. The printers and publishers (including an employee who can be identified with a newspaper company as part of its controlling mind)[1] are liable as well as the advertiser.

It was held by the Divisional Court in *Denham v Scott*[2] that the offence is one of strict liability in relation to the publication of such an advertisement, so that someone who publishes such an advertisement in a newspaper without knowledge of its inclusion can be convicted of the offence.

1 *Denham v Scott* (1983) 77 Cr App Rep 210, DC.
2 (1983) 77 Cr App Rep 210, DC.

Going equipped for stealing etc

14.92 Section 25(1) and (2) of the Theft Act 1968 provides that a person is guilty of an offence punishable with a maximum of three years' imprisonment if, when not at his place of abode, he has with him any article for use in the course of or in connection with any burglary, theft, or cheat. For this purpose, 'theft' includes an offence under s 12(1) of the Act of 1968 (ie taking a conveyance other than a pedal cycle) and 'cheat' means obtaining property by deception contrary to s 15 of that Act.[1]

1 Theft Act 1968, s 25(5).

14.93 It is not an offence for a person to have at his place of abode articles which are for use in the course of any offence mentioned in s 25, but if he is away from his place of abode he commits an offence if he has with him any such article. Where a person lives, and drives around, in a car in which he keeps his tools for burglary, the car is his place of abode for the present purpose only when it is on a site where he intends to abide.[1] The phrase 'has with him' would seem to bear the same meaning as in aggravated burglary, which has been discussed in para 14.15.

Some articles are specifically and clearly *made* or *adapted* for use in committing a burglary or one of the other offences mentioned in para 14.92, and possession of these is rebuttable evidence that they were intended for such use,[2] but there must be very few of them. Most articles have both innocent and criminal uses and the prosecution must prove that such articles were intended for criminal use.

1 *Bundy* [1977] 2 All ER 382, [1977] 1 WLR 914, CA.
2 Theft Act 1968, s 25(3). Under the draft Criminal Code Bill, this provision is not repeated on the ground that it is merely an example of a wider general proposition that the jury or magistrates may draw a reasonable inference in the absence of evidence raising a doubt about the safety of the inference: Law Commission: A Criminal Code for England and Wales (1989): Law Com No 177, para 16.17.

14.94 It is not necessary to prove that the accused intended the article to be used in the course of or in connection with any particular burglary, theft or cheat; it is enough to prove a general intention that it should be used for some burglary, theft or cheat if the opportunity arises. [1] On the other hand, the offence is not committed if the accused does not have a firm intention to use the thing for a burglary, theft or cheat, given the opportunity.[2] It is not necessary to prove that the accused intended to use the article himself, but it is not enough to prove that the article had been used before the accused came into possession of it.[3] Nor is it enough to prove that the articles were used to get a job which would give the opportunity to steal.[4] The phrase 'for use . . . in connection with' extends the scope of the offence, since it covers the case where the article is intended for use while making preparations for a burglary, theft or cheat, or while making an escape after it has been committed.[5] The Divisional Court has held that a person who has embarked on the commission of a theft, burglary or cheat and, for the first time, comes into possession of, and decides to make immediate use of, some implement to help him do so (e g something which he has just found) can be convicted of the present offence.[6] This is surprising since it cannot be said in common sense terms that he has the thing with him,[7] nor that he was 'going equipped for stealing etc' (which is the description of the offence given by the marginal note[8] to the section).

1 *Ellames* [1974] 3 All ER 130, [1974] 1 WLR 1391, CA.
2 *Hargreaves* [1985] Crim LR 243, CA.
3 *Ellames*.
4 *Mansfield* [1975] Crim LR 101, CA.
5 *Ellames*.
6 *Minor v DPP* (1988) 86 Crim App Rep 378, DC.
7 Cf the interpretation given to the similar offence described in para 18.86.
8 The marginal note is not technically part of the statute and cannot normally affect its interpretation: *DPP v Schildkamp* [1971] AC 1 at 28, [1969] 3 All ER 1640.

14.95 There can only be a conviction on a charge of going equipped with an article for use in the course of or in connection with any cheat if it is proved that the intended deception would be a cause of the intended obtaining of property. The question (which is one for the jury in the Crown Court) is not whether anyone was actually deceived.[1] Instead, the question is concerned with the effect of the intended deception on a hypothetical person, who is reasonably honest and intelligent. Only if he would not have parted with property if he had known the truth can there be a conviction; there cannot be a conviction if he would nevertheless have parted with the property if he had been told the truth.[2] For example, if a restaurant car steward on a train has with him food of his own, intending to sell it as his employer's and to pocket the proceeds, he will only be guilty of the present offence if the jury are sure that hypothetical passengers would not have bought the food if they had known the truth.[2]

1 *Whiteside and Antoniou* [1989] Crim LR 436, CA.
2 *Doukas* [1978] 1 All ER 1061, [1978] 1 WLR 372, CA; *Cooke* [1986] AC 909, [1986] 2 All ER 985, HL. For criticism, see Smith [1989] Crim LR at 438.

15 Offences against property 3: Offences other than under the Theft Acts

Criminal damage[1]

15.1 Section 1(1) of the Criminal Damage Act 1971 provides that a person who without lawful excuse destroys or damages any property belonging to another, intending to destroy or damage such property, or being reckless as to whether any such property would be destroyed or damaged, is guilty of an offence punishable on conviction on indictment with imprisonment for a maximum of 10 years.

By s 1(3), if the destruction or damage contrary to s 1(1) is by fire, the offence is charged as arson and is punishable with a maximum of imprisonment for life. The higher maximum penalty for arson may be justified by the exceptional danger to life and property involved in the use of fire for the destruction or damaging of property.

According to the House of Lords in *Courtie*,[2] there is a principle that, where a greater maximum punishment can be imposed if a particular factual ingredient is established than if it is not, two distinct offences exist. On this principle there are two simple offences:

a) an offence under s 1(1) committed otherwise than by fire; and
b) an offence under s 1(1) committed by fire (arson).

Save for the ingredient of fire, the two offences are identical and will be discussed together.

1 See Elliott 'Criminal Damage' [1988] Crim LR 403.
2 [1984] AC 463, [1984] 1 All ER 740, HL.

15.2 *How triable* Both offences under s 1(1) are triable either way.[1] This is subject to the following important qualification in the case of an offence under s 1(1) committed otherwise than by fire. The qualification, provided by s 22(1) and (2) of the Magistrates' Courts Act 1980, is that, where the value of the property destroyed or of the alleged damage does not exceed £2,000, a magistrates' court must proceed *as if the offence was triable only summarily*,[2] in which case the maximum punishment is three months' imprisonment or a fine not exceeding level 4 on the standard scale (£2,500) or both.[3] The same applies where a person is an accomplice to such an offence or has incited or attempted its commission.

1 Magistrates' Courts Act 1980, s 17(1) and Sch 1.
2 Ibid, s 22 and Sch 2.
3 Ibid, s 23.

15.3 Where an accused has caused damage of more than £2,000 in value, which can be itemised into various sums, the prosecution is entitled to charge only sums of damage up to £2,000 in value and thereby ensure that the accused must be tried summarily for criminal damage.[1]

Where the prosecution is unable to prove the total amount of damage done by an individual accused, as where a number of other people have also damaged the property in question, but it can prove the minimum amount of the damage done by that accused (being an amount less than £2,000) then, unless there is material before the magistrates which gives them any real doubts as to the accuracy of the calculation, the prosecution is entitled to prove only that minimum, and thereby ensure that the accused is tried summarily.[2]

1 *Canterbury and St Augustine's Justices, ex p Klisiak* [1982] QB 398, [1981] 2 All ER 129, DC.
2 *Salisbury Magistrates' Court, ex p Mastin* (1986) 84 Cr App Rep 248, [1986] Crim LR 545, DC.

15.4 Section 22(11) of the Magistrates' Courts Act 1980, which was added by the Criminal Justice Act 1988, provides that where–

  a) an accused is charged on the same occasion with two or more offences of criminal damage under £2,000 which form part of a series of two or more offences of the same or a similar character, or
  b) the offence charged consists in the incitement to commit two or more such offences,

the qualification under s 22 is to have effect as if any reference in it to the values involved were a reference to the aggregate values involved. Thus, if D is charged with two offences of criminal damage to the value of £100 and £1,000 respectively, which form part of a series of offences of the same or a similar character, he is caught by the qualification, since the aggregate value of the damage is less than £2,000, and D cannot elect trial on indictment. On the other hand, if the value of the damage involved in the two offences had been £400 and £1,800 respectively, D would not be caught by the qualification and could elect trial on indictment.

Whether or not offences form part of a *series* depends on there being a sufficient separation in time between them. This is very much a matter of degree.[1] One thing is obvious: where the only offences in question occur simultaneously they do not form part of a series,[2] and the qualification is not ousted.

  1 *St Helen's JJ, ex p McLorie* (1984) 78 Cr App Rep 1, DC (the actual decision in this case would now be different because of the Magistrates' Courts Act 1980, s 22(11)); *Braden* (1988) 87 Cr App Rep 289, CA.
  2 *Re Prescott* (1979) 70 Cr App Rep 244, CA.

15.5 The effect of the qualification under s 22(1) and (2) of the Magistrates' Courts Act is not to make the offence triable only summarily in the circumstances outlined but to prevent a magistrates' court committing an accused for trial in the Crown Court for such an offence. The offence, nevertheless, may be tried on indictment if the requirements of s 40 of the Criminal Justice Act 1988 are satisfied. Section 40 provides that a count charging a person with criminal damage where the value is below £2,000 (or with being a party to such an offence or with attempting or inciting it) may be included in an indictment if the charge–

a) is founded on the same facts or evidence as a count charging an
indictable offence; or

b) is part of a series of offences of the same or similar character as an
indictable offence which is also charged;

but only if (in either case) the facts or evidence relating to the offence were
disclosed in an examination or deposition taken before a magistrate in the
presence of the accused.

If a count is included in an indictment under the present provision the
maximum punishment is limited to the maximum for the offence available in
a magistrates' court.

15.6 *A limit on prosecutions* Where one spouse destroys or damages the
other's property, proceedings for criminal damage contrary to s 1(1) of the
1971 Act or s 1(2), which is mentioned later, may not be instituted without
the consent of the Director of Public Prosecutions. The only exception is
where, by virtue of any judicial decision or order, the spouses were not
obliged to cohabit at the material time.[1]

1 Theft Act 1968, s 30.

15.7 *Actus reus* The requirement that the accused must destroy or damage
property belonging to another is not as simple as may at first appear, because
the terms used involve fairly complex definitions. The definitions which
follow are equally applicable to the other provisions of the Act.

15.8 Property is *damaged* if it suffers permanent or temporary physical
harm or permanent or temporary impairment of its use or value.[1] If part of a
machine is removed, without which it cannot work, the machine (but not the
part) is damaged[2] because its use is impaired; likewise if the horizontal bars
of scaffolding are removed from the vertical parts, the scaffolding (but not
the parts removed) is damaged.[3] A wall is damaged if slogans are painted on
it, as is beer if water is poured into it,[4] because its value is impaired. Grass
can be damaged by trampling on it;[5] such conduct goes beyond normally
incidental harm and impairs the utility and value of the grass.

The test of physical harm or impairment of the property's use or value
does not conclude the matter since, if the harm or impairment is minimal,
there is no 'damage' for the purposes of the Act. Nor is there such 'damage'
in the case of physical harm which is a normal incident of the type of property
in question, e g the chipping or scratching of a firedoor on a corridor.[3] In *Roe
v Kingerlee*[6] the Divisional Court held that whether what has occurred
constitutes 'damage' is a question of fact and degree for the jury (or magistrates) applying their common sense. Since it is not necessary that the effect
of what has been done should be permanent, the fact that it is rectifiable
does not prevent the property being damaged. However, where it is rectifiable the amount (and any cost) of rectification are relevant factors in
determining the question of fact and degree;[7] if these are minimal it may be
found that what has occurred is not 'damage'. In *Roe v Kingerlee* the
Divisional Court held that graffiti smeared in mud could be damage, even
though it could be washed off. A case where it might be found as a matter of
fact and degree that there was no damage might be spitting on someone's
raincoat.[8]

By s 3(6) of the Computer Misuse Act 1990, any alteration or erasure of,
or addition to, a program or data held in a computer, which is made by the

operation of any function of a computer, is not regarded as damaging any computer or computer storage medium (such as a hard or floppy disk) unless its effect in that computer or medium impairs its *physical* condition.

The *destruction* of property requires something more than damage, such as the demolition of a machine, the pulling down of a wall or other structure, or the killing of an animal.

For completeness it must be added that, if the offence of criminal damage by fire (arson) is charged, the prosecution must prove that the destruction or damage was caused by fire.

1 *Morphitis v Salmon* [1990] Crim LR 48, DC; *Whiteley* [1991] Crim LR 436,CA.
2 *Fisher* (1865) LR 1 CCR 7, 35 LJMC 57; *Getty v Antrim County Council* [1950] NI 114.
3 *Morphitis v Salmon* [1990] Crim LR 48, DC.
4 *Roper v Knott* [1898] 1 QB 868, 67 LJQB 574, DC.
5 *Gayford v Chouler* [1898] 1 QB 316, 67 LJQB 404, DC.
6 [1986] Crim LR 735, DC.
7 See *Cox v Riley* (1986) 83 Cr App Rep 54, DC, for an example of this; note that the actual decision in this case would now be different because of the Computer Misuse Act 1990, s 3(6).
8 *A (a juvenile) v R* [1978] Crim LR 689, Crown Ct. (Crown Court held on appeal, acquitting the accused, that such spitting was not damage on facts before it.)

15.9 For the purposes of the 1971 Act, '*property*' is defined by s 10(1) as:

'Property of a tangible nature, whether real or personal, including money and—

    a) including wild creatures which have been tamed or are ordinarily kept in captivity, and any other wild creatures or their carcases *if* , but only if, they have been reduced into possession which has not been lost or abandoned or are in the course of being reduced into possession; but

    b) *not* including mushrooms growing wild on any land or flowers, fruit or foliage of a plant growing wild on any land.'[1]

This definition is very similar to the definition in s 4 of the Theft Act 1968 of property which can be stolen; but there are three differences. Land itself cannot generally be stolen, but there are no limits on when it can be the subject of criminal damage. Second, although intangible property can be stolen, it is not property for the purposes of criminal damage. Third, unlike theft (where they can be stolen if picked for sale, reward or other commercial purpose) wild mushrooms and the flowers, fruit or foliage of any wild plant cannot be the subject of criminal damage.

1 'Mushroom' includes any fungus and 'plant' includes any shrub or tree: s 10(2). In relation to various terms in the quotation, see paras 13.20–13.25.

15.10 The property destroyed or damaged must '*belong to another*'. This phrase is defined by s 10(2) to (4). Section 10(2) provides:

'Property shall be treated for the purposes of this Act as belonging to any person—

    a) having the custody or control of it;

    b) having in it any proprietary right or interest (not being an equitable interest arising only from an agreement to grant or transfer an interest); or

    c) having a charge on it.'

This definition is very similar to that of 'belonging to another' in s 5(1) of the Theft Act 1968, and for further explanation the reader is referred to the relevant part of Chapter 13.

There are only two divergences from the Theft Act provision. First, s 10(2)(a) speaks of 'custody or control', as opposed to 'possession or control'. These terms are not defined by the Act but it seems that 'custody' is intended to mean 'physical custody' and 'control' to impart the notion of the power to direct what shall be done with the thing in question. Second, s 10(2)(c) states that property belongs to a person who has a charge on it; such a person will have a proprietary right or interest in the property and it is not obvious why special provision was made for charges by the Act.

Section 10(3) and (4) provides that, as in the case of theft, where property is subject to a trust, the person to whom it belongs shall include any person having the right to enforce the trust; and that property belonging to a corporation sole is to be treated as belonging to the corporation notwithstanding a vacancy in the corporation.

The requirement that the property destroyed or damaged must belong to another means that a person to whom alone the property belongs cannot be convicted under s 1(1) if he destroys or damages it, however dishonest his motive (e g to defraud an insurance company). On the other hand, as in the case of theft, an owner (or someone else to whom the property belongs) can be convicted under s 1(1) if the property also belongs to another.

15.11 *Mens rea* Section 1(1) of the 1971 Act requires that the accused should intend, or be reckless as to, the destruction or damage of property belonging to another.[1] As was stated in Chapter 6, *Caldwell*-type recklessness suffices for this offence. *Caldwell*[2] itself was concerned, inter alia, with a charge under s 1(1) and Lord Diplock, giving the majority opinion of the House of Lords, stated that a proper direction to a jury as to recklessness in s 1(1) is as follows:

> 'a person charged with an offence under s 1(1) of the 1971 Act is "reckless as to whether or not any property would be destroyed or damaged" if (1) he does an act which in fact creates an obvious risk that property will be destroyed or damaged and (2) when he does the act he either has not given any thought to the possibility of there being any such risk or has recognised that there was some risk involved and has none the less gone on to do it'.[3]

For a discussion of this statement, the reader is referred to paras 6.45 to 6.52.

1 *Smith (DR)* [1974] QB 354, [1974] 1 All ER 632, CA.
2 [1982] AC 341, [1981] 1 All ER 961, HL.
3 [1982] AC at 354. Strictly 'belonging to another' should have been included after each reference to 'property'.

15.12 *'Without lawful excuse'* In order to commit an offence under s 1(1) of the 1971 Act, including arson, the accused must destroy or damage another's property 'without lawful excuse'. Section 5(2) provides that a person is to be treated as having a lawful excuse, whether or not he would be so treated apart from its provisions:

a) if at the time of the act or acts alleged to constitute the offence he believed that the person or persons whom he believed to be entitled to consent to the destruction of or damage to the property had so consented, or would have so consented to it if he or they had known of the destruction or damage and its circumstances; or
b) if he destroyed or damaged the property in question in order to protect property belonging to himself or another or a right or interest in property which was or which he believed to be vested in himself or

another, and at the time of the act or acts alleged to constitute the
offence he believed–
  i) that the property, right or interest was in immediate need of
  protection; and
  ii) that the means of protection adopted were reasonable in the
  circumstances.

For these purposes, it is immaterial whether the belief was justified or not,
provided it was genuinely held.[1] In both situations the accused has the
burden of adducing evidence to raise the issue;[2] once he has done this the
judge must direct the jury about the defence and the prosecution must prove
beyond reasonable doubt that the accused was acting without lawful excuse.
If the accused does not adduce sufficient evidence of lawful excuse, the
judge will not leave the issue to the jury.[3]

In relation to b), the property intended to be protected, unlike that
damaged, need not be tangible; it can consist of a right or interest in, for
example, land. The test in b) is partly subjective (in that it is applied on the
basis of what was going on in the accused's mind) and partly objective (in
that it is a question of law for the judge whether, on the facts as believed by
the accused, what was done could be said to be done to protect property).[4]
This can be explained by adapting the facts of *Hill and Hall*,[5] where the
charge was one of possession of an article with intent to damage property
without lawful excuse, contrary to s 3 of the 1971 Act. If D cuts the perimeter
fence of a nuclear base and pleads as a defence to a charge of simple criminal
damage that he acted with the purpose of forcing the government to abandon its nuclear weapons policy and thereby of saving property near the bases
(which would be primary targets in war) from a nuclear strike by an enemy,
the judge in deciding whether to leave 'lawful excuse' to the jury must decide
whether, assuming that D's evidence of what was going on in his mind is
true, it can be said on those facts that cutting the fence can amount to
something done to protect property. The judge must also decide whether,
on the facts stated by D, there is evidence on which it could be said that D
believed that that property was in *immediate* need of protection. It is clear
from *Hill and Hall* that a judge would be correct in concluding that D would
not have acted to protect property (since his aim would be too remote from
the acts in question) and that there was no evidence of a belief that the
property was in immediate need of protection.

The operation of s 5(2) can be exemplified as follows. In *Denton*[6] D set
fire to some machinery on his employer's premises and thereby damaged the
premises and their contents. D gave evidence that he had so acted at his
employer's request, so that the latter could make a fraudulent insurance
claim. The Court of Appeal held that the accused's belief (which was
conceded), at the time of his act, that the person (his employer) whom he
honestly believed to be entitled to consent to the damage had so consented
provided him with lawful excuse under s 5(2)(a), despite the employer's
dishonest motive.

As another example, suppose that D has the shooting rights over a piece
of land. He shoots and kills P's dog which is chasing a hare on the land. D has
a defence under s 5(2) to a charge under s 1(1) of the Criminal Damage Act if
he believes that the hare belongs to him, although it does not in law,
provided he also believes that the hare is in immediate danger and that the

shooting of the dog is a reasonable means of preserving the hare. This is the effect of s 5 of the 1971 Act, which may have varied the previous law.[7]

Section 5(5) provides that the provisions in s 5 are not to be construed as casting doubt on any defence recognised by law as a defence to a criminal charge, eg duress by threats or of circumstances and (although they are more accurately described as 'justifications') self-defence and the defence of another.[8]

1 Criminal Damage Act 1971, s 5(3). Even a drunken belief will suffice: *Jaggard v Dickinson* [1981] QB 527, [1980] 3 All ER 716, DC; para 9.68.
2 *Hill and Hall* (1989) 89 Cr App Rep 74, CA.
3 Ibid.
4 *Hunt* (1977) 66 Cr App Rep 105, CA; *Hill and Hall.*
5 (1989) 89 Cr App Rep 74, CA.
6 [1982] 1 All ER 65, [1981] 1 WLR 1446, CA. Other aspects of this decision were criticised in *Appleyard* (1985) 81 Cr App Rep 319, CA.
7 See *Gott v Measures* [1948] 1 KB 234, [1947] 2 All ER 609, DC.
8 Chap. 22.

THE AGGRAVATED OFFENCE

15.13 By s 1(2) of the Act of 1971, a person who without lawful excuse destroys or damages any property, whether belonging to himself or another,

 a) intending to destroy or damage any property or being reckless as to whether any property would be destroyed or damaged; *and*
 b) intending by the destruction or damage to endanger the life of another or being reckless whether the life of another would be thereby endangered,

is guilty of an offence triable only on indictment[1] and punishable with a maximum of imprisonment for life. By s 1(3), an offence committed under this subsection by destroying or damaging property by fire is charged as arson.[2]

A typical example of an offence under s 1(2) is where the accused sets fire to his own house, in order to make an insurance claim, despite being aware that someone is asleep inside it. An offence under s 1(2) would also be committed, even though he was not aware of the sleeping occupant, if there was an obvious risk that another's life would be endangered and he had given no thought to it.

In *Steer*[3] the House of Lords held, in relation to b), that the accused must have intended to endanger life, or been reckless as to whether life would be endangered, *by the destruction or damaging* of property which he intentionally or recklessly caused, and that it was not enough merely that he intended to endanger life, or was reckless as to whether life would be endangered, by the act which caused the destruction or damage. Accordingly, as was held in *Steer*, a person who fires a gun from outside a house at a person standing behind a window in it cannot be convicted under s 1(2), even though he may have intended to endanger the life of that person, if he did not intend the damaging of the window (as opposed to the bullet) to endanger life (and was not reckless as to the damage endangering life).

It is irrelevant that no one's life was endangered if it was D's intention by the destruction or damage to endanger life or he was reckless as to this occurring. For example, in *Dudley*[4] D set fire to P's house with a fire bomb but P was able to extinguish the fire. Only trivial damage was caused and life was not endangered. Nevertheless, the Court of Appeal upheld D's conviction for arson being reckless as to endangering life. When D threw the fire bomb he had clearly been reckless as to life being endangered by the damage which the bomb might cause.

1 But see the correspondence in [1979] Crim LR 266 and 607 and [1980] Crim LR 69.
2 Criminal Damage Act 1971, s 1(3). For the definition of various terms in s 1(2), see paras 15.8, 15.9 and 15.11.
3 [1987] 2 All ER 833, [1987] 3 WLR 205, HL.
4 [1989] Crim LR 57, CA

15.14 In *Hoof*[1] the Court of Appeal stated that, where the offence charged under s 1(2) is by arson, there should be two counts, one alleging arson with intent to endanger life and the other arson committed recklessly as to whether life might or might not be endangered, so that the jury's verdict can be understood for the purposes of sentencing (since these two types of mens rea involve very different degrees of fault). This approach was also recommended by the Court of Appeal in *Hardie*[2] (another s 1(2) case) as being desirable whenever there is reliance in the alternative on intention or recklessness.

1 (1980) 72 Cr App Rep 126, CA.
2 [1984] 3 All ER 848 at 853–854.

15.15 It was held by a majority of the House of Lords in *Caldwell*[1] that 'recklessness' in s 1(2) is used in the same sense as in s 1(1), and that this is so not only in relation to the risk of property being destroyed or damaged but also in relation to the risk that another's life may be thereby endangered. Lord Diplock, giving the majority opinion, said[2] that, on a charge under s 1(2), the question of the accused's mens rea must be approached as follows. First, the jury must be satisfied that he intended to destroy or damage the property or was reckless (in the sense outlined in para 15.11) whether it might be destroyed or damaged. Only if they are so satisfied must the jury consider whether the accused also either intended that the destruction or damage should endanger someone's life or was reckless whether a human life might thereby be endangered. The accused will be reckless as to this if (1) he does an act which creates an obvious risk that the life of another will be endangered, and (2) when he does the act he either has not given any thought to the possibility of there being any such risk or has recognised that there was some risk involved and has nonetheless gone on to do it.

In the event of a charge under s 1(2) being framed so as to charge the accused only with *intending* by the destruction or damage to endanger the life of another, evidence of voluntary intoxication can be relevant as evidence that he lacked that intention, because that intention is a specific intent. However, if the charge is, or includes, a reference to the accused being reckless as to whether another's life would be endangered thereby, evidence of voluntary intoxication is irrelevant, just as it is on a charge under s 1(1), since the offence charged is one of basic intent.[3]

1 [1982] AC 341, [1981] 1 All ER 961, HL.
2 [1982] AC at 354.
3 [1982] AC at 354–5.

15.16 The inclusion in the 1971 Act of the offence of destruction of, or damage to, property with the intention of endangering life or with recklessness as to whether life is endangered has been criticised on the ground that such conduct should be dealt with in a statute dealing with offences against the person. Under the Criminal Damage Act 1971 a sharp distinction is drawn between offences involving an intention to endanger life or reckless-ness as to whether life is in danger and other offences. In the first place, it is only in the case of the former offences that the destruction by the accused of his own property renders him liable. Secondly, the question whether the accused had a lawful excuse for acting as he did is dependent on the general law where the charge is based on the accused's intention or recklessness that he was endangering the life of another, whereas, as we have seen, there is by virtue of s 5 of the Act of 1971 an additional statutory defence of lawful excuse where the charge is simply based on intention or recklessness with regard to the destruction of, or damage to, property.

An illustration of the operation of s 1(2) may be helpful. D sets fire to his empty house with the intention of making a false claim in respect of its destruction against his insurance company. The house is remote from other houses, so there can be no question of D's having been reckless as to whether the lives of others would be endangered. The house being D's property, he has committed no offence under the 1971 Act, and it is doubtful whether he has committed any offence at all for it would probably be found that D's conduct was merely preparatory to the commission of the main offence and therefore did not constitute an attempt to obtain money by deception. Let it be assumed that the facts were as set out above, except that D's child was asleep in the house and D acted with reckless disregard for the life of the child. D would be guilty of arson under s 1(2) and (3), even if the child miraculously escaped unharmed.

Threats to destroy or damage property

15.17 Section 2 of the Criminal Damage Act 1971 punishes with a maxi-mum of ten years' imprisonment a person who makes to another a threat without lawful excuse, *intending* the other to fear it would be carried out,

a) to destroy or damage property belonging to that other or to a third person, or
b) to destroy or damage his (ie the accused's) own property in a way which he knows is likely to endanger the life of that other or a third person.

Where the threat is of the type outlined in a) 'without lawful excuse' is subject to s 5 in the same way as the offence under s 1(1), but in the case of a threat falling within b) 'without lawful excuse' is not.[1]

It does not matter how the threat is conveyed; a letter, a telephone call or any other method of communication will do. Nor does it matter that the person making the threat does not intend to carry it out, provided that he intends that the addressee should fear that he would. It is irrelevant whether or not the addressee is actually put in such fear.

1 Criminal Damage Act 1971, s 5(1).

Possessing anything with intent to destroy or damage property

15.18 Section 3 of the 1971 Act punishes with a maximum of ten years' imprisonment those who have anything in their custody or under their control, *intending* without lawful excuse to use it or cause or permit another to use it –

a) to destroy or damage any property belonging to some other person; or
b) to destroy or damage his own or the user's property in a way which he knows is likely to endanger the life of some other person.

Provided that such an intention exists it is immaterial that there is no immediate intention to use the thing; a so-called conditional intent, ie an intention to use the thing to cause damage should it prove necessary, will suffice.[1]

It would appear that the offence is committed if the thing, e g a stone, is picked up on the spur of the moment with the intention of using it immediately to cause damage.

Where the offence involves an intent falling within a) 'without lawful excuse' is subject to s 5,[2] but in the case of an intent falling within b) 'without lawful excuse' is not.[3]

1 *Buckingham* (1976) 63 Cr App Rep 159, CA.
2 In para b) of the definition in s 5(2) set out above, the question in s 3 is whether the accused intended to use or cause or permit the use of something to destroy or damage property in order to protect property etc.
3 Criminal Damage Act 1971, s 5(1).

15.19   Offences under ss 2 and 3 are triable either way;[1] the maximum punishments referred to are, of course, only applicable on a conviction on indictment.

1 Magistrates' Courts Act 1980, s 17(1) and Sch 1.

Criminal Damage: Draft Criminal Code

15.20   Clauses 178 to 186 of the draft Criminal Code Bill[1] contain provisions which are essentially the same as those under the 1971 Act. However, since recklessness in the draft Code is limited to subjective recklessness, the substance of those offences would be changed in that respect if ever the Code becomes law. The only other changes of substance in the relevant provisions in the draft Code relate to those corresponding to s 5(2) (partial explanation of 'without lawful excuse') in the 1971 Act. Under the draft Code, which does not use the phrase 'without lawful excuse' in its definition of the various criminal damage offences, the special defences in s 5(2) are replaced by the following special defences which would apply to the same offences as s 5(2):

a) that the accused –
i) knew or believed that the person whom he believed to be entitled to consent to the destruction or damage had so consented; or
ii) believed that that person would so consent if he knew of the destruction or damage and its circumstances;
b) that (in the circumstances which existed or were believed by the accused to exist) the accused's act was immediately necessary and reasonable –
i) to protect himself or any other person from unlawful force or injury;
ii) to prevent or terminate the unlawful imprisonment of himself or another; or

iii) to protect property from unlawful appropriation, destruction or damage.

a) would replace s 5(2)(a); (b) would replace s 5(2)(b) with significant amendments necessitated by the need to achieve consistency with other parts of the Code relating to self-defence and the like.

1 Law Commission: A Criminal Code for England and Wales (1989): Law Com No 177; see para 3.21 above.

Entering and remaining on property

15.21 Part II of the Criminal Law Act 1977 contains a number of offences relating to entering and remaining on property, which are supplemented by the offence of aggravated trespass under s 39 of the Public Order Act 1986. Corresponding provisions are contained in cls 187 to 194 of the draft Criminal Code Bill.[1]

The two major offences in Part II of the 1977 Act are using or threatening violence for securing entry to any premises, and adverse occupation of residential premises. Both offences are triable only summarily and are punishable with a maximum of six months' imprisonment or a fine not exceeding level 5 on the standard scale (£5,000) or both.

The definitions of the various offences in Part II refer to 'premises', which are defined as meaning any building, any part of a building under separate occupation (such as a flat), any land ancillary to a building, and the site comprising any building or buildings together with any land ancillary thereto.[2] 'Building' in this context includes any immoveable structure, and any moveable structure, vehicle or vessel designed or adapted for residential purposes.[3] A caravan or a houseboat is an obvious example of the latter. As the definition shows, land may be 'premises' but only if it is 'ancillary to a building', which it is if it is adjacent to it and used (or intended for use) in connection with the occupation of that building or any part of it.[3] The two major offences refer to 'access' to premises, and this means any part of any site or building within which those premises are situated which constitutes an ordinary means of access to those premises (whether or not that is its sole or primary use),[4] such as a communal hallway or staircase in a block of flats.

1 Law Commission: A Criminal Code for England and Wales (1989): Law Com No 177; see para 3.21 above.
2 Criminal Law Act 1977, s 12(1)(a).
3 Ibid, s 12(2).
4 Ibid, s 12(1)(b).

VIOLENCE FOR SECURING ENTRY

15.22 Section 6(1) of the 1977 Act provides that any person who, without lawful authority, uses or threatens violence for the purposes of securing entry into any premises for himself or any other person is guilty of an offence, provided that:

a) there is someone on those premises at the time who is opposed to the entry which the violence is intended to secure, and
b) the person using or threatening the violence knows that that is the case.

15.23 *Actus reus* The crux of this offence is the use or threat of violence for the purpose of securing entry into premises on which a person opposed to the entry is present: actual entry is not required. It is immaterial whether the entry which the violence is intended to secure is for the purpose of acquiring possession of the premises or for some other purpose.[1] Thus, while the use or threat of violence in order to conduct a 'sit-in' in premises is an obvious example of the present offence, so is the use or threat of violence in an unsuccessful attempt to gate-crash a party. The violence used or threatened may be directed against a person or property,[1] and the offence can be committed even though the violence is not directed towards a person or thing on the premises but towards someone or some thing outside them, provided always that it is done for the purpose of securing entry to them.

'Violence' is a word with an every day meaning. Consequently, whether or not violence occurs is a question of fact and the term should not be subjected to legal definition by the courts.[2] While magistrates are likely to find that the use of force on a person or smashing a door or window constitutes violence, they are unlikely to find that forcing a window catch or Yale lock with a piece of wire does.

1 Criminal Law Act 1977, s 6(4).
2 *Brutus v Cozens* [1973] AC 854, [1972] 2 All ER 1297, HL. See also *Dino Services Ltd v Prudential Assurance Co Ltd* [1989] 1 All ER 422, CA.

15.24 The requirement that someone must be present on the premises at the time of the use or threat of violence who is opposed to the entry which the violence is intended to secure means that if D breaks into P's house, in order to squat in it, while P and his family are on holiday, D does not commit the present offence, although he may well be guilty of criminal damage and will commit an offence under s 7 of the 1977 Act if he fails to leave when P requests him to on his return. Even if a person is present on the premises at the time, no offence is committed unless he (or at least one of a number of persons on the premises) is opposed to the intended entry. In order for a person to be opposed to the intended entry, it must be against his will but he need not offer opposition to it. It is uncertain whether he must know of it in order that the offence be committed by the accused. This is a matter of obvious importance where the only person present on the premises is asleep at the time or, as in the case of a large factory, the premises are large and the night watchman is unaware of the intended entry.

15.25 *Mens rea* The mens rea required for this offence is as follows. It is implicit that the accused must intentionally or recklessly (in the subjective sense of that term) use or threaten violence. In addition, s 6(1) requires that this be done for the purpose of securing entry into any premises for the accused or any other person. Section 6(1) also requires that the accused should know[1] that there is a person present on the premises at the time of the use or threat of violence and that that person is opposed to the entry which the violence is intended to secure.

1 'Knowledge' includes wilful blindness, see para 6.59.

15.26 *Without lawful authority* No offence is committed if the accused has 'lawful authority' to use or threaten violence for securing entry into the premises. A number of statutes give constables power to enter premises (by force, if need be) to arrest someone and/or search them. The threat or use of violence pursuant to such a power would clearly be with lawful authority. The same would be true in relation to any other person, such as a court officer, who has power to use force to enter premises for a particular purpose, provided he was acting pursuant to that power.

On the other hand, s 6(2) provides that the fact that a person has any interest in or right to possession or occupation of any premises does not constitute lawful authority for the use or threat of violence by him or anyone else for the purpose of securing entry into them. It follows that, if the landlord of rented premises or the occupier of a lock-up shop uses violence to re-enter his premises and evict squatters, he will have no lawful authority for his action. This means that, unless it is possible to effect a peaceful re-entry, landlords and non-residential occupiers must seek to recover possession in the civil courts.

15.27 *Displaced residential occupier* Special provision is made for persons falling within the definition of a 'displaced residential occupier' of premises or any access to them. Any person who was occupying the premises in question as a residence immediately before being excluded from occupation by anyone who entered those premises, or any access to those premises, as a trespasser, is a 'displaced residential occupier' of them or any access to them,[1] except that the term does not cover a person who was himself occupying the premises as a trespasser before being excluded from occupation.[2] Obviously, a householder who discovers squatters in his house when he returns from work or from holiday is a displaced residential occupier. Since the definition does not talk in terms of 'principal' residence, a person displaced from his weekend cottage in the country while he is living in his flat in town would also seem to be a displaced residential occupier.

Even a displaced residential occupier does not have lawful authority to use or threaten violence to secure entry to his home. However, if he, or someone acting on his behalf, but no one else, does resort to such tactics a defence is afforded by s 6(3), which provides that it is a defence for an accused to prove:

a) that at the time of the alleged offence he, or any person on whose behalf he was acting, was a displaced residential occupier of the premises in question; *or*

b) that part of the premises in question constitutes premises of which he, or any other person on whose behalf he was acting, was a displaced residential occupier and that the part of the premises to which he was seeking to secure entry constitutes an access of which he or, as the case may be, that other person is also a displaced residential occupier.

The defence of being a displaced residential occupier applies only to a charge under s 6. However, if such an occupier is charged with assault or some other offence he may have the general defence of using reasonable force in the prevention of crime (if he has unsuccessfully asked the trespasser to leave, since the latter's failure to do so will be an offence under s 7 (below)) or in the defence of property.[3]

1 Criminal Law Act 1977, s 12(3) and (5).
2 Ibid, s 12(4).
3 Paras 22.1–22.11.

ADVERSE OCCUPATION OF RESIDENTIAL PREMISES

15.28 Section 7(1) of the 1977 Act provides that any person who is on any premises (including any access to them)[1] as a trespasser after having entered

351

as such[2] is guilty of an offence if he fails to leave those premises on being required to do so by or on behalf of –

a) a 'displaced residential occupier' of them; or
b) an individual who is a 'protected intending occupier' of them.

The main purpose of this offence is to give a residential occupier or an intending residential occupier of premises who has been excluded from them by trespassers, such as squatters, a swifter remedy for recovering possession of them than the available civil remedy. He can request them to leave, and, if they do not, may call on a uniformed constable, who may, as in the case of the other offences in Part II of the Act, arrest without warrant those who are, or whom he with reasonable cause suspects are, *guilty* of[3] the offence.[4] For this purpose the constable may enter (by force, if need be) and search any premises where the person to be arrested is or where he, with reasonable cause, suspects him to be. If violence is used to secure entry to the premises by a constable or a displaced residential occupier, neither will commit an offence under s 6, but a protected intending occupier who so acts may well do so.[5]

1 Criminal Law Act 1977, s 7(9).
2 What is said in para 14.9 about entry as a trespasser seems to be equally applicable here.
3 In the case of offences under ss 8 and 9 the words 'in the act of committing' are used instead of 'guilty of'.
4 Criminal Law Act 1977, s 7(11); Police and Criminal Evidence Act 1984, s 17(1).
5 Paras 15.21–15.27.

15.29 *Actus reus* What is required is a failure to leave premises (or access to them) by a person who is on those premises (or access) as a trespasser, having entered as such, and who has been required to leave by or on behalf of a person of the specified type. The requirement that the accused must have entered the premises as a trespasser means that a person who remains on premises after the termination of a tenancy or licence does not commit the present offence, since his original entry on them (to which the requirement must refer) was not as a trespasser.

The offence does not simply consist of failure by a trespasser to leave premises, since such failure only constitutes the offence if a request to leave has been made by, or on behalf of, a 'displaced residential occupier' or a 'protected intending occupier' of the premises. Failure to leave premises despite a request by the landlord of them or any other type of occupier is not an offence. The main source of complication is the involved definition of a 'protected intending occupier', of whom there are two types.

The first type is an individual who, at the time of the request to leave:

a) has in the premises in question a freehold interest or a leasehold interest with not less than 21 years still to run, which he acquired as a purchaser for money or money's worth (rather than, for instance, by inheritance); and
b) requires the premises for his own occupation as a residence; and
c) is excluded from occupation of them by a person who entered them, or any access to them, as a trespasser; and
d) holds, or a person acting on his behalf holds, a written statement, signed by him and witnessed by a magistrate or a commissioner for oaths, which –

   i) specifies his interest in the premises; and
  ii) states that he requires the premises for occupation as a residence for himself.[1]

The purpose of the statement is to enable the police to identify the protected intending occupier and thereby prevent abuse of these provisions.

The second type of protected intending occupier is an individual who, at the time of the request to leave:

a) has been authorised to occupy the premises in question as a residence by a local authority, the Housing Corporation, or a registered housing association; and
b) is excluded from occupation of them by a person who entered them, or any access to them, as a trespasser; and
c) there has been issued to him by the authority, Corporation or association a certificate stating that the authority etc is one to which these provisions apply and that he has been authorised to occupy the premises as a residence.[2]

It is worthy of note that, unlike a protected intending occupier of the first type, a person can be a protected intending occupier of the second type even if he does not require the premises for his own occupation as a residence.

In this way, protection is afforded by the criminal law to certain people, such as buyers of houses and council tenants, who have not taken up residential occupation of the premises before being excluded by a trespasser. There is no apparent reason why this protection was not extended to intending residential occupiers who have a lease with less than 21 years to run or a monthly tenancy granted by a private landlord, and who therefore fall outside the definition of a protected intending occupier. Like a displaced residential occupier, a protected intending occupier of premises is also a protected intending occupier of any access to them.[3]

1 Criminal Law Act 1977, s 7(2) and (3).
2 Ibid, s 7(4) and (5).
3 Ibid, s 7(9).

15.30 *Men rea* Presumably, at the time of committing the offence, ie when he fails to leave on being required to do so, the accused must know that he is a trespasser and entered as such, or be subjectively reckless as to this.

15.31 *Defences* Three defences are provided by s 7, the burden of proof in each case being on the accused:

a) It is a defence that the accused believed that the person requiring him to leave was not a displaced residential occupier or a protected intending occupier of the premises, or someone acting on his behalf.[1] This plea will rarely succeed, particularly in the light of the requirement in the case of a protected intending occupier of a written statement or certificate to this effect.
b) Where the request to leave was made by or on behalf of a person claiming to be a protected intending occupier, the accused has a defence if the person requesting him to leave failed at that time to produce a written statement or certificate complying with the Act although he had been asked to do so by the accused.[2]
c) It is a defence that the premises in question are or form part of

premises used mainly for non-residential purposes, and that the accused was not on any part of the premises used wholly or mainly for residential purposes.[3] This means, for instance, that people involved in a factory sit-in do not commit the present offence if they fail to leave when required by a resident caretaker, so long as they are not in his flat or in part of the premises used wholly or mainly for access to, or in connection with, the flat.

1 Criminal Law Act 1977, s 7(6).
2 Ibid, s 7(8).
3 Ibid, s 7(7).

OTHER OFFENCES

15.32 In order to fulfil this country's international obligations to protect the inviolability of diplomatic and similar premises, s 9(1) of the 1977 Act makes it an offence simply to enter as a trespasser premises which are or form part of an embassy, consulate, the private residence of a foreign diplomatic agent, or other similar premises. Alternatively, it is an offence under s 9(1) to be on such premises as a trespasser even though the initial entry was lawful. It is a defence in either case for the accused to prove that he believed that the premises in question were not premises to which s 9 applies.[1] An offence under s 9(1) is only triable summarily; the maximum punishment is six months' imprisonment or a fine not exceeding level 5 on the standard scale (£5,000) or both.[2] A prosecution under s 9 requires the Attorney-General's consent.[3]

The other two offences under Part II of the 1977 Act, resisting or obstructing court officers executing process for possession against unauthorised occupiers, and trespass with an offensive weapon, are dealt with later.[4]

1 Criminal Law Act 1977, s 9(3).
2 Ibid, s 9(5).
3 Ibid, s 9(6).
4 Paras 18.73 and 18.90.

Aggravated trespass[1]

15.33 Section 39(2) of the Public Order Act 1986 makes it an offence for a person to fail to leave land, or to return to it, knowing that a direction to leave has been given under s 39(1) which applied to him. To describe this offence as aggravated trespass is clearly not strictly accurate, but is undoubtedly convenient. The enactment of s 39 was prompted by various mass invasions which occurred in the mid-1980s, particularly in relation to the celebration of the midsummer solstice.

1 See Card *Public Order – The New Law* Ch 7.

DIRECTION TO LEAVE

15.34 The offence under s 39(2), and its related power of arrest, depend on a direction to leave having been given under s 39(1).

Such a direction to leave can only be given under s 39(1) by 'the senior police officer', i e the most senior in rank of the police officers present at the scene,[1] who need not be in uniform. In order to give a direction to leave, that officer must reasonably believe that four conditions are satisfied.

First he must reasonably believe that two or more persons have entered land as trespassers.[2] 'Land' does not include buildings, other than 'agricultural buildings'[1] and scheduled ancient monuments (such as the ruined Kenilworth Castle or Whitby Abbey),[1] with the result that the present provision does not apply where the reasonable belief is merely that persons have entered a terrace house, or a farmhouse, straight off the street.

Second, he must reasonably believe that those present have the common purpose of residing on the land for any period. If follows that a direction cannot be made against those who are simply ramblers, birdwatchers or sit-down demonstrators, nor against most other types of trespassers.

Third, he must reasonably believe that reasonable steps have been taken by or on behalf of the occupier to ask the trespassers to leave.

Fourth, the senior police officer must reasonably believe that the following condition is satisfied:

a) that any of the trespassers has caused damage[3] to property[4] on the land *or* used threatening, abusive or insulting words or behaviour towards the occupier of the land, a member of his family or an employee or agent of his; *or*

b) that the trespassers have between them brought 12 or more vehicles on to the land.

The reference to 12 or more vehicles is surprising given that the minimum number of persons who need be reasonably believed to be involved is two, but it apparently results from a desire on the part of the Government to exclude gypsy camps generally from s 39.

1 Public Order Act 1986, s 39(5).
2 Para 14.9.
3 Para 15.8.
4 This term is given the same definition as under the Criminal Damage Act 1971 by the Public Order Act 1986, s 39(5); see para 15.9.

15.35 If, but only if, the senior police officer reasonably believes that the four conditions are satisfied, he may direct any or all of the trespassers to leave the land.[1] He does not have power to make a direction simply because he reasonably believes that two or more persons are *about* to enter land as trespassers and fulfil the other conditions set out above. A direction to leave includes a direction to remove any vehicles which have been brought onto the land.[2]

1 Public Order Act 1986, s 39(1).
2 *Krumpa and Anderson v DPP* [1989] Crim LR 295, DC.

CRIMINAL LIABILITY

15.36 If a trespasser directed to leave complies with that direction, he commits no offence. On the other hand, he commits an offence under s 39(2) if, knowing that a direction has been given which applied to him:

a) he fails to leave the land (with any vehicles) as soon as reasonably practicable; or

b) having left, he again enters the land as a trespasser within a three-month period beginning on the day on which the direction was given.

It is thought likely that a) and b) constitute separate offences.

An offence under s 39(2) is a purely summary one. The maximum punishment is three months' imprisonment or a fine not exceeding level 4 on the standard scale (£2,500) or both.

15.37 *Actus reus* A person commits the actus reus of an offence under s 39(2) if, after a direction has been given under s 39(1) which applies to him, he fails to leave or again enters the land in the respective circumstances outlined in a) and b) above.

Because the offence in s 39(2)(a) consists of failing to leave 'land', which (as defined in the Act) does not include buildings other than agricultural buildings or ancient monuments, a member of a group of persons reasonably believed to have entered land (e g a field) as trespassers with the necessary common purpose etc does not commit an offence under s 39(2) if, having then entered the farmhouse and set up home there, he refuses to leave the farmhouse. The reason is that a farmhouse is not an 'agricultural building' and therefore not 'land' for the purposes of the offence; consequently there is no failure to leave 'land'. On the other hand, he may commit an offence if the building in question is a barn, henhouse or an ancient monument like Kenilworth Castle.

The exclusion of buildings other than agricultural buildings from s 39 is not as serious as it may seem, because (as we have seen)[1] s 6 of the Criminal Law Act 1977 prohibits the use of force in gaining entry to *any* premises, and s 7 provides redress against those who refuse to leave *residential* premises including land attached to a house.

1 Paras 15.22–15.31.

15.38 *Mens rea* When he fails to leave (or enters again), an accused must know that a direction to leave has been given which applies to him, which he will if he actually knows of this or is wilfully blind as to whether such a direction has been given.[1]

1 Para 6.59.

15.39 *Defences* It is a defence for the accused to prove:

a) that his original entry was not as a trespasser; or
b) that he had a reasonable excuse for failing to leave the land as soon as reasonably practicable or, as the case may be, for again entering the land as a trespasser.[1]

1 Public Order Act 1986, s 39(4).

15.40 *Arrest* The purpose of s 39 of the 1986 Act is to give the occupier of the land a swifter remedy for recovering possession of it than the available (and possibly costly) civil remedy. Consequently, s 39(3) is of crucial importance since it provides that a uniformed constable who reasonably suspects that a person *is* committing the above offence may arrest him without warrant.

Forgery and related offences

15.41 Forgery and its related offences are complementary to the offences of deception dealt with in the previous chapter in that they penalise overt preparation for deception involving false documents or other instruments. Generally, the law does not penalise *mere* preparation for crime but forgery and related offences are isolated exceptions. The reason seems to be the social and commercial necessity that documents and other instruments which are relied on are authentic.

The law relating to forgery and related offences is governed by the Forgery and Counterfeiting Act 1981. This is a codifying Act based largely on the Law Commission's Report on Forgery and Counterfeit Currency,[1] which was published in 1973. The Act repealed the whole of the Forgery Act 1913, the whole of the Coinage Offences Act 1936, and a number of other statutory provisions, and abolished the common law offence of forgery. All the offences under the 1981 Act mentioned hereafter are triable either way, the maximum punishment on conviction on indictment being ten years' imprisonment (unless otherwise stated).[2] Part I of the 1981 Act deals with forgery and related offences, and Part II with counterfeiting.

The provisions of Part I of the 1981 Act are incorporated in clauses 164 to 171 of the draft Criminal Code Bill.[3] On the other hand, those in Part II are not incorporated in the draft Bill, so that if that Bill is ever enacted they will continue to exist outside it.

1 Law Com No 55.
2 Forgery and Counterfeiting Act 1981, s 6(1)–(3).
3 Law Commission: A Criminal Code for England and Wales (1989): Law Com No 177; see para 3.21 above.

Forgery

15.42 This offence is defined by s 1 of the 1981 Act, which states that a person is guilty of forgery if he makes a false instrument, with the intention that he or another shall use it to induce somebody to accept it as genuine, and by reason of so accepting it to do or not to do some act to his own or any other person's prejudice.

ACTUS REUS

15.43 The actus reus of this offence is 'making a false instrument', and by s 9(2) this includes altering an instrument so as to make it false in any respect.

15.44 *Instrument* For the purposes of s 1 and other sections in the Act, an 'instrument' is defined by s 8(1) of the Act as –

a) any document, whether of a formal or informal character (other than a currency note);[1]
b) any stamp issued or sold by the Post Office (or a metered postage mark);[2]
c) any Inland Revenue stamp;[3]
d) any disc, tape, sound track or other device on or in which information is *recorded* or *stored* by mechanical, electronic or other means. To be 'recorded' or 'stored' the information must be preserved for an appreciable time with the object of subsequent retrieval.[4] Examples of items covered are microfilm records of bank accounts and transactions, and information on computer tapes or discs, but not electronic

impulses in a computer or its 'user segment' (which retains or stores information momentarily while the computer searches its memory, e g to check a password).[4] Unauthorised manipulation of such electronic impulses (i e computer hacking) is covered by s 1 of the Computer Misuse Act 1990, which is dealt with in para 15.60

Until recently, a difficulty with this definition related to the word 'document' in a). The Forgery Act 1913 and its predecessor dealt with the forgery of documents but did not define what constituted a 'document' for its purposes. However, judicial decisions suggested that if a thing was intended to have utility apart from the fact that it conveyed information or recorded a promise it was not a document;[5] a document for the purpose of the law of forgery was, it was thought, a writing which was only intended to convey information or record a promise. This view was based on a rationalisation of the difficult decisions in *Closs*[6] (where a picture falsely bearing the signature of a well-known artist was held not to be a document) and *Smith*[7] (where two of the judges held that wrappers made in the same distinctive form as those in which Borwick's baking powder was sold were not documents).

In their report, the Law Commission concluded that only things which conveyed two messages: a message about the thing itself (e g that it is a cheque) *and* a message to be found in its words or other symbols that is to be accepted and acted on (e g the message in a cheque to the banker to pay a specified sum), needed to be protected by the law of forgery. Thus, they sought to make clear that things, such as a painting purporting to bear the signature of the artist, a false autograph, and any writing on manufactured goods falsely indicating the name of the maker or the country of origin, were excluded from forgery by limiting the forgery of documents to 'instruments', which were defined as 'any *instrument* in writing whether of a formal or informal character'. In the view of the Commission, 'instrument' was the appropriate term to convey this meaning. However, although the new offence of forgery is concerned with making a false instrument, Parliament, in its wisdom, chose to change the proposed definition of 'instrument' and that is why the Act defines an instrument as 'any *document*, whether formal or informal'. This left open the question of the extent of the offence of forgery and left unanswered the difficulties attached to *Closs* and *Smith*.

In 1987 in *Gold and Schifreen*[8] the Court of Appeal adopted the Law Commission's view that only instruments containing both types of message needed to be protected by the law of forgery, a view which Lord Brandon, delivering the opinion of the House of Lords on appeal, referred to, obiter, with apparent approval.[9]

Applying the two-messages concept, it is now clear that paintings (even if purporting to bear the signature of an artist), a false autograph, and any writing on manufactured articles indicating the name of the manufacturer or country of origin, are not documents and therefore not 'instruments', whereas, for example, letters, wills, title deeds and cheques are.

Of course, paintings and other things which are not 'instruments' are not necessarily beyond the reach of the criminal law if they are falsified since their use (or attempted use) to deceive will invariably involve an offence of deception under the Theft Acts 1968 or 1978 or an attempt to commit such an offence.

1 Forgery and Counterfeiting Act 1981, s 8(2). For the definition of a 'currency note', see s 27.
2 Ibid, s 8(3).

3 As defined by the Stamp Duties Management Act 1891, s 27; Forgery and Counterfeiting Act 1981, s 8(4).
4 *Gold and Schifreen* [1988] AC 1063, [1988] 2 All ER 186, HL.
5 Williams (1948) 11 MLR 150 at 160.
6 (1857) Dears & B 460, 27 LJMC 54.
7 (1858) Dears & B 566, 27 LJMC 225.
8 [1987] 3 All ER 618,[1987] 3 WLR 803, CA.
9 [1988] 2 All ER 186 at 191.

15.45 *False instrument* Section 9(1) provides an exhaustive definition of the word 'false' for the purpose of forgery and related offences. It states that an instrument is false for the purposes of forgery *if it purports*:

a) to have been *made* in the *form* or *terms* in which it is made by a person who did not in fact make it in that form or in those terms; or

b) to have been *made* in the *form* or *terms* in which it is made *on the authority* of a person who did not in fact authorise its making in that form or in those terms; or

c) to have been *altered* in any respect by a person who did not in fact alter it in that respect; or

d) to have been *altered* in any respect *on the authority* of a person who did not in fact authorise the alteration in that respect; or

e) if it purports to have been *made* or *altered* on a *date* on which, or at a *place* at which, or *otherwise* in circumstances in which, it was not in fact made or altered; or

f) to have been *made* or *altered* by *an existing person* but he did not in fact exist.

Although it is irrelevant, for the purposes of the above definition, whether the falsity in question is or is not material, the nature of the requisite further intent to prejudice is such that an immaterial falsity will not normally suffice.

15.46 A crucial element in this definition is that, to be false, an instrument must *purport* to have been made or altered in a way (specified in a) to f) above) in which it was not made or altered. An instrument is not false merely because it tells a lie (ie contains a false statement); it must tell a lie about itself by purporting to have been made or altered by (or on the authority of) a person who did not make or alter it (or authorise its making or alteration), or by otherwise purporting to be made or altered in circumstances in which it was not made or altered. This requirement, sometimes described as the requirement of automendacity, was made by the old law relating to forgery.[1] The wording of s 9(1) of the 1981 Act indicates that this continues to be a requirement of the law, and it was affirmed by the House of Lords in 1987 in *More*[2] that it does. In *More* D intercepted a cheque for X. He opened a building society account in a false name and paid in the cheque. Later, he presented a withdrawal form for most of the amount paid in and was paid by the building society. The withdrawal form was, of course, completed in the assumed name of X. D was convicted of the forgery of the withdrawal form. He appealed unsuccessfully to the Court of Appeal, which held that the form was a false instrument within f) above, since it purported to have been made by an existing person who did not exist, notwithstanding that it did not tell a lie about itself because it was completed by the account holder (albeit he had chosen to be known by a false name). Allowing D's appeal, the House of Lords held that the form was not a false instrument because D was a real person. It was he who was the holder of the account and in that capacity he had signed the withdrawal form. That form clearly purported to be signed by the person who originally opened the account and in this respect it was wholly accurate. Consequently, the House of Lords held, the withdrawal form did not tell a lie about itself and was therefore not a false instrument.

Despite the affirmation in *More* of the requirement of automendacity, the decision of the Court of Appeal in *Donnelly*[3] (which was not referred to by the House of Lords in *More*) is liable to remove much of its force. This is because that decision suggests that any instrument which tells a lie about a past fact tells a lie about itself and is false within the above definition.

In *Donnelly*, D was the manager of a jeweller's shop. He completed and signed what purported to be a written valuation of jewellery for insurance purposes. The certificate stated that D had examined the items in question. In fact, the items of jewellery did not exist and the valuation was intended to be used to defraud the insurance company. D was convicted of forgery and appealed to the Court of Appeal, which dismissed his appeal. The Court of Appeal's reasoning was that the valuation certificate, the instrument in question, did tell a lie about itself because (within e) above) it 'purported to be made in circumstances in which it was not made'. However, that phrase must have been intended by Parliament to be read in the context of the rest of e) (which refers to the date on which, or the place at which, the instrument was made); consequently, it must have been intended to refer to other circumstances directly related to the making of the instrument, eg the presence of witnesses. To give the phrase an unlimited meaning would render redundant all the other provisions set out in a) to f) above, since instruments covered by them and many other instruments telling lies would also be covered by it. In particular, any instrument telling a lie about a past fact would be a forgery because it would purport to be made after the fact occurred.

1 *Re Windsor* (1856) 10 Cox CC 118 at 123, per Blackburn J; *Dodge and Harris* [1972] 1 QB 416, [1971] 2 All ER 1523, CA.
2 [1987] 3 All ER 825, [1987] 1 WLR 1578, HL. For criticism of this decision, see Arnheim (1988) 131 Sol Jo 351 and Leng 'Falsity in Forgery' [1989] Crim LR 679.
3 [1984] 1 WLR 1017, CA. This decision has been criticised by Smith [1984] Crim LR 490, but supported by Leng loc cit.

MENS REA

15.47 Presumably, the accused must know of the falsity (in one of the above senses) of the instrument. In addition, s 1 states that he must have the further intent that he or another shall use it to induce somebody to accept it as genuine, *and* the further intent to induce that person by reason of so accepting it to do or not to do some act to the prejudice of himself or anyone else[1] (besides the accused)[2]. It is therefore not enough simply to intend to induce a person to believe that an instrument is genuine. Thus, making a false birth certificate solely to induce the belief that one comes from a noble family is not forgery. The accused need not intend to induce another human being; it suffices that he intends to induce a machine to respond to the instrument as if it were genuine.[3]

The act or omission intended to be induced must be to the prejudice of the person induced or anyone else besides the accused.[2] 'Prejudice' is exhaustively defined by s 10 of the Act. Section 10(1) states that an act or omission intended to be induced is *only* to a person's prejudice if it is one which, if it occurs:

a) *will*[4] result –
   i) in his temporary or permanent loss of property (including a loss by not getting what one might get as well as a loss by parting with what one has)[5], as where a false cheque or will is made to cause another either to part with property or not to get property he might have got; or
   ii) in his being deprived of the opportunity to earn remuneration or greater remuneration; or
   iii) in his being deprived of an opportunity to gain a financial advantage otherwise than by way of remuneration, as where a false testimonial is made to obtain a contract for which a number of different tenders have been made and a genuine tenderer is deprived of what would have been his contract if it had not been for the false statement; or
b) *will*[4] result in somebody being given an opportunity –
   i) to earn remuneration or greater remuneration from him, as where a false testimonial or degree certificate is made in order to obtain a job or better pay in a job; or
   ii) to gain a financial advantage from him otherwise than by way of remuneration, as where a false aeroplane or theatre ticket is made in order to gain a flight or admission; or
c) *will*[4] be the result of his having accepted a false instrument as genuine in connection with his performance of any duty. An example would be where a cheque is falsely endorsed to induce a bank to accept it as genuine in connection with its performance of its duty to pay out only on a valid cheque.[6] Another example would be where a false pass is made to induce a doorkeeper to admit an unauthorised person to premises. This last definition shows that the prejudice intended need not have any financial connotation at all.

An act which a person has an enforceable duty to do and an omission to an act which a person is not entitled to do are to be disregarded.[7] Consequently, it is not forgery to make a false document to induce another to do what he is obliged to do, e g to pay a debt, or to refrain from doing what he is not entitled to do. Where the intended inducement is of a machine (e g a cash dispenser at a bank), the act or omission intended to be induced by the machine responding to the instrument is treated as an act or omission to a person's prejudice.[8]

1 It was accepted by the Court of Appeal in *Campbell* (1984) 80 Cr App Rep 47 that a further intention is required as to both elements.
2 *Utting* [1987] 1 WLR 1375, CA.
3 Forgery and Counterfeiting Act 1981, s 10(3).
4 I e 'must' and not merely 'may potentially': *Garcia* (1987) 87 Cr App Rep 175, CA.
5 Forgery and Counterfeiting Act 1981, s 10(5).
6 *Campbell* (1984) 80 Cr App Rep 47, CA.
7 Forgery and Counterfeiting Act 1981, s 10(2).
8 Ibid, s 10(4).

15.48 The above definition of the mens rea for forgery is an exclusive one. Dishonesty is not an element of the offence.[1] It follows, for example, that it is irrelevant that the accused believed that he was legally entitled to a gain which he intended to make as a result of falsifying the instrument.

1 *Campbell* (1984) 80 Cr App Rep 47, CA; *Horsey v Hutchings* (1984) Times, 8 November, DC.

Copying a false instrument

15.49 Section 2 of the 1981 Act makes it an offence for a person to make a copy of an instrument which is, and which he knows or believes to be, a *false instrument*, with the intention that he or another shall use it to induce somebody to accept it as a copy of a genuine instrument, and by reason of so accepting it to do or not to do some act to his own or any other person's prejudice.

ACTUS REUS

15.50 The actus reus of this offence is making a copy of a 'false instrument'; the definition of these two words is the same as for the offence of forgery.[1] The fact that the instrument must be false but need not be forged means that a person who, with the necessary intent, *copies* a false instrument will be liable, even though the instrument may have been *made* innocently.

1 Paras 15.44–15.46.

MENS REA

15.51 The mens rea required is that:

a) The accused must know or believe that the instrument copied is false. In relation to this requirement, the reader is referred to the discussion of 'know or believe' in the offence of handling stolen goods.
b) The accused must have the further intent that he or another shall use the copy of the false instrument to induce somebody to accept it as a copy of a genuine instrument, *and* the further intent to induce that person by reason of so accepting it to do or not to do some act to his own or any other person's prejudice.[1] The elements of these further intents have already been discussed in relation to forgery,[2] and what is said there applies equally here except that references to 'false instrument' and 'genuine instrument' should be read as 'copy of a false instrument' and 'copy of a genuine instrument'.

1 By anology with ss 1 and 3 (see paras 15.47 and 15.52), it is clear that a further intention is required as to both parts of this formulation.
2 Para 15.47.

Using a false instrument or a copy of a false instrument

15.52 Section 3 of the 1981 Act makes it an offence for a person to use an instrument which is, and which he knows or believes to be, false, with the intention of inducing somebody to accept it as genuine, *and* with the further intention[1] of inducing that person by reason of so accepting it to do or not to do some act to his own or any other person's prejudice. Section 4 provides an identically worded offence of using a copy of a false instrument. In the light of the explanations already given, no more need be said about these offences except to point out that 'use' is a wide term and covers (inter alia) a person who offers, delivers, tenders in payment or exchange, or exposes for sale or exchange, an instrument.

1 It was explained in *Tobierre* [1986] 1 All ER 346, [1986] 1 WLR 125, CA, that this offence requires further intentions as to both parts of this formulation.

Offences relating to money orders, share certificates, passports etc

15.53 Section 5 of the 1981 Act provides a number of offences relating to the following instruments:

a) money orders or postal orders;
b) United Kingdom postage stamps;
c) Inland Revenue stamps;
d) share certificates;
e) passports and documents which can be used instead of passports;
f) cheques or travellers' cheques;
g) credit cards;
h) birth, adoption, marriage or death certificates or officially certified copies thereof.

Any such instrument is hereafter referred to as a 'specified instrument'.

15.54 Section 5(1) of the Act makes it an offence for a person to have in his custody or under his control a specified instrument which is, and which he knows or believes to be, false, with the intention that he or another shall use it to induce somebody to accept it as genuine, and by reason of so accepting it to do or not to do some act to his own or any other person's prejudice.

'Custody' and 'control' are not explained by the Act but it appears that 'custody' is intended to mean 'physical custody' and 'control' to import the notion of the power to direct what shall be done with the things in question. These terms conveniently avoid the technicalities connected with the concept of possession. The other elements of the offence are the same as those discussed above.

15.55 By s 5(2), it is an offence for a person merely to have in his custody or control, without lawful authority or excuse, a specified instrument which is, and which he knows or believes to be, false. The maximum punishment on conviction on indictment is two years' imprisonment.[1] The only part of this offence which requires further elaboration is 'without lawful authority or excuse'. The accused does not have the burden of proving this but merely has an evidential burden. In the case of similar offences under the Forgery Act 1913, it was held that a person who intends to take a false document to the police has a lawful excuse, even if he does not hand the document over at the earliest opportunity;[2] on the other hand, a solicitor in possession of a false document on behalf of a client in order to prepare his client's defence to a criminal charge was held not to have a lawful authority or excuse.[3] Presumably, these decisions would be applied to the present offence.

1 Forgery and Counterfeiting Act 1981, s 6(4).
2 *Wuyts* [1969] 2 QB 474, [1969] 2 All ER 799, CA.
3 *Peterborough Justices, ex p Hicks* [1978] 1 All ER 225, [1977] 1 WLR 1371, DC.

15.56 Section 5(3) makes it an offence for a person to have in his custody or under his control a machine or implement, or paper or any other material, which to his knowledge is or has been specially designed or adapted for the making of a specified instrument, with the intention that he or another shall make a specified instrument which is false and that he or another shall induce somebody to accept it as genuine, and by reason of so accepting it to do or not to do some act to his own or another's prejudice.

15.57 Finally, s 5(4) makes it an offence, punishable with a maximum of two years' imprisonment on conviction on indictment,[1] for a person merely to have in his custody or under his control any such machine, implement, paper or material, without lawful authority or excuse.

1 Forgery and Counterfeiting Act 1981, s 6(4).

Counterfeiting

15.58 Part II of the Forgery and Counterfeiting Act 1981 provides a number of offences relating (inter alia) to the counterfeiting of currency notes and coins, the passing, custody or control of counterfeit notes and coins, and the making, custody or control of counterfeiting implements and materials.

Computer misuse

15.59 The misuse of computer hardware or software may involve one or more of the offences described elsewhere in this book. For example, a person who dishonestly gains access to a program or data held in a computer can be convicted of dishonestly abstracting electricity, contrary to s 13 of the Theft Act 1968, and a person who interferes with computerised records of accounts can be convicted of false accounting, contrary to s 17 of that Act.

In addition, the misuse of computer hardware or software may involve one or more of three offences under the Computer Misuse Act 1990:[1]

a) unauthorised access to computer material;
b) unauthorised access with intent to commit or facilitate commission of a further offence;
c) unauthorised modification of computer material.

1 Wasik 'The Computer Misuse Act 1990' [1990] Crim LR 767.

UNAUTHORISED ACCESS TO COMPUTER MATERIAL

15.60 By s 1(1) of the 1990 Act a person commits a summary offence, punishable with up to six months' imprisonment or a fine not exceeding level 5 on the standard scale (£5,000) or both,[1] if:

a) he causes a computer to perform any function with intent to secure access to any program or data held in any computer;
b) the access he intends to secure is unauthorised; and
c) he knows at the time when he causes the computer to perform the function that that is the case.

The intended access need not relate to any particular program or data, nor to a program or data held in any particular computer.[2]

The scope of this offence is wide, since it covers all forms of computer hacking. The title of the offence, unauthorised access to computer material, is misleading since actual access to any program or data held in a computer is not required, since it is enough that the accused merely causes a computer to perform a function (e g by causing it to respond by offering a log-on menu) with intent to secure access to a program or data held in a computer, that intended access being unauthorised to his knowledge. 'Knowledge' in this context would seem to include wilful blindness.[3] Despite its wording, the offence does not cover computer eavesdropping; mere surveillance of data displayed on a VDU screen is not enough since the accused must cause the computer to perform a function if he is to be guilty.

In relation to the requirement that the accused must intend to secure access to a program or data, it should be noted that, for the purposes of the Act, such access is secured by a person if, by causing a computer to perform any function, he:

a) alters or erases the program or data; or
b) copies or moves it to any storage medium other than that in which it is held or to a different location in the storage medium in which it is held; or
c) uses it;[4] or
d) has it output from the computer in which it is held (whether by having it displayed or in any other manner).[5]

References to any program or data held in a computer include references to any program or data held in a disk or other removable storage medium for the time being in the computer.[6]

Section 1 requires that the intended access must be unauthorised. Access of any kind by a person is unauthorised if he is not entitled to control access of the kind in question to the program or data *and* he does not have consent to such access from any person who is so entitled.[7] Thus *all* computer hackers are caught, including those 'computer enthusiasts' who seek access merely because of the challenge of breaking through a security system designed to restrict access. The fact that access by a person is unauthorised unless he has the appropriate entitlement or consent to access *of the kind in question* means that, for example, an employee authorised to obtain access to certain computer data for a particular purpose will commit the present offence if he logs into the computer with the intention of gaining access to that data for an unauthorised purpose.

1 Computer Misuse Act 1990, s 1(3).
2 Ibid, s 1(2).
3 Para 6.59.
4 A person uses a program if the function he causes the computer to perform causes the program to be executed or is itself a function of the program: ibid, s 17(3).
5 Computer Misuse Act 1990, s 17(2).
6 Ibid, s 17(6).
7 Ibid, s 17(5).

UNAUTHORISED ACCESS WITH INTENT

15.61 By s 2(1) of the 1990 Act, a person commits an offence triable either way, and punishable with up to five years' imprisonment or a fine or both on conviction on indictment,[1] if he commits the unauthorised access offence under s 1 with the further intent:

a) to commit an offence to which s 2 applies; or
b) to facilitate the commission of such an offence (whether by himself or another).

The intended further offence need not involve the use of a computer although often it will, as where a hacker is enabled to direct the computer system to transfer funds from X's bank account to his own.

Section 2 applies to any offence whose sentence is fixed by law, such as murder, or for which an offender of 21 or over may be sentenced to imprisonment for five years or more, such as the various deception offences under the Theft Acts, theft and forgery.

It is immaterial whether the further offence is to be committed on the same occasion as the unauthorised access offence (under s 1) or on any future occasion,[2] and it is also immaterial that the facts are such that the commission of the further offence is impossible.[3]

1 Computer Misuse Act 1990, s 2(5).
2 Ibid, s 2(3).
3 Ibid, s 2(4).

UNAUTHORISED MODIFICATION OF COMPUTER MATERIAL

15.62 By s 3(1) of the 1990 Act, a person is guilty of an offence, triable and punishable in the same way as an offence under s 2(1),[1] if:

a) he does any act which causes an unauthorised modification of the contents of any computer; and
b) at the time when he does the act he has the requisite intent and the requisite knowledge.

A modification of the contents of a computer takes place if, by the operation of any function of the computer concerned or any other computer, any program or data held in the computer is altered or erased, or any program or data is added to its contents.[2] Thus, the offence under s 3 can be committed in a variety of ways; for example, by the addition or deletion of material or software in a computer or by interfering with a computer or software in it by introducing a computer virus by means of an infected disk. Any act which contributes towards causing a modification is regarded as causing it.[3]

A modification is unauthorised if the person whose act causes it is not entitled to determine whether it should be made and he does not have consent to the modification from anyone who is so entitled.[4]

The 'requisite intent' is an intent to cause a modification of the contents of a computer and by so doing to impair its operation, or to prevent or hinder access to any program or data held in it, or to impair the operation of any such program or the reliability of any such data.[5] The intention need not be directed at any particular computer, program or data, or at any particular kind of program or data, or at any particular modification or kind of modification.[6]

The 'requisite knowledge' is knowledge (which would seem to include wilful blindness)[7] that any modification which the accused intends to cause is unauthorised.

It is immaterial whether an unauthorised modification or any intended effect of it is, or is intended to be, permanent or merely temporary.[8]

1 Computer Misuse Act 1990, s 3(7).
2 Computer Misuse Act 1990, s 3(7). For the meaning of 'program or data held in the computer', see the Computer Misuse Act 1990, s 17(6), para 15.60.
3 Computer Misuse Act 1990, s 17(7).
4 Ibid, s 17(8).
5 Ibid, s 3(2).
6 Ibid, s 3(3).
7 Para 6.59.
8 Computer Misuse Act 1990, s 3(5).

JURISDICTION

15.63 It is immaterial for the purposes of the offence of unauthorised access (s 1) or the offence of unauthorised modification (s 3):

a) whether any act or other element of the offence occurred in England and Wales; or
b) whether the accused was in England and Wales at the time of any such act or element occurring.

However, at least one 'significant link'[1] with domestic jurisdiction must exist for the offence to be committed,[2] except where an offence under s 1 has to be established in proceedings for an offence under s 2 of unauthorised access with intent to commit a further offence in England and Wales.

Provided that there is a 'significant link' in relation to an offence under s 1 which is alleged to have been committed with intent to commit (or facilitate) outside England and Wales an offence to which s 2 applies, there will be an offence under s 2 if the thing which the accused intended to do (or facilitate) outside England and Wales would be an offence to which s 2 applies if it took place in England and Wales and what the accused intended to do (or facilitate) would involve the commission of an offence under the law of the country where it was intended to take place.[3]

1 Computer Misuse Act 1990, s 4(1) and (6).
2 Ie that the accused was in England and Wales when he did the act which caused the computer to perform the function (s 1) or which caused the modification (s 3) *or* that any computer in question was in England or Wales (s 1) or that the unauthorised modification took place there (s 3): ibid, s 5.
3 Ibid, ss 4(4) and 8(1).

16 Offences against the administration of justice

Assisting offenders[1]

16.1 Section 4(1) of the Criminal Law Act 1967 provides that, where a person has committed an arrestable offence, any other person who, knowing or believing him to be guilty of the offence, or of some other arrestable offence, does without lawful authority or reasonable excuse any act with intent to impede his apprehension or prosecution is guilty of an offence, which is triable either way.[2] The consent of the Director of Public Prosecutions is required before a prosecution can be instituted for assisting an offender.[3] This offence replaced that of accessory after the fact to felony. It is limited to cases where the person assisted was guilty of an arrestable offence, although a person who assists someone guilty of a non-arrestable offence may be convicted of attempting to pervert the course of justice or, in some cases, obstructing a constable in the execution of his duty.[4]

1 Williams 'Evading Justice' [1975] Crim LR 430, 479, 608.
2 Magistrates' Courts Act 1980, s 17(1) and Sch 1.
3 Criminal Law Act 1967, s 4(4).
4 Paras 16.33, 16.34 and 18.68–18.71.

ELEMENTS

16.2 In order to succeed on a charge of assisting an offender, the prosecution must prove four things:

a) *The commission of an arrestable offence* In this section, and s 5 below, 'arrestable offence' has the meaning given in para 4.14.[1] In both this section and s 5, reference is made to a person who 'has committed an arrestable offence'. There seems no reason why this should not cover an accomplice to the actual perpetration of an offence, as well as the perpetrator himself, and in the following account of ss 4 and 5 it should be remembered that the person 'who has committed an arrestable offence' may have done so either as a perpetrator or an accomplice.

Although the commission of the principal arrestable offence must be proved, no one need have been convicted of it,[2] and presumably even if there has been an acquittal that would not prevent a conviction for assisting the person acquitted at a separate trial on different evidence. The arrestable offence alleged to have been committed must be specified in the indictment for assisting an offender. However, if the principal offender is not proved to be guilty of the specified offence, the accused may still be convicted if the principal offender is proved guilty of another arrestable offence of which he could be convicted on the indictment.[3]

b) *The accused's knowledge or belief that the actual arrestable offence, or some other arrestable offence, was committed by the principal offender* It is not necessary for the prosecution to prove that the accused knew or believed the particular offence to be arrestable, or that he was aware of the identity of the person who committed it.[4] Presumably, 'belief ' in this context bears the same meaning as in the offence of handling stolen goods.[5]

c) *An act done by the accused with the intention of impeding the apprehension or prosecution of the principal offender* The principal offender need not actually be assisted (the definition of this offence as assisting offenders is somewhat inaccurate) but the accused must have done some act with intent to impede the prosecution or apprehension of the principal offender. An omission to act, even if accompanied by such intent, will not suffice. Thus, failure to report the principal offender to the police or to arrest him does not constitute assisting an offender. Authorities on prosecutions of accessories after the fact suggest that the requisite intent is a purposive one.[6] Mere foresight that the offender will be assisted is insufficient, if the only purposive intent of the accused was the acquisition of money for himself or the protection of himself from prosecution.[7] The mere provision of accommodation in the ordinary way by the principal offender's family or landlord will not suffice, nor will mere efforts at persuasion not to prosecute. On the other hand, driving the principal offender away after the crime, hiding him from the police, destroying fingerprints or other evidence of the crime,[8] or telling the police lies in order to put them off the scent, do fall within the scope of the offence.[9]

d) *The absence of lawful authority or reasonable excuse for the act of assistance* There would be lawful authority for impeding the prosecution if action were taken in consequence of an executive decision not to prosecute. An example of a case in which, notwithstanding the intent to impede prosecution, there would be a lawful excuse would be one in which a forged cheque was destroyed in pursuance of a lawful agreement[10] not to prosecute in consideration of the making good of the loss caused by the forgery.[11]

1 Criminal Law Act 1967, s 4(1A).
2 *Donald* (1986) 83 Cr App Rep 49, [1986] Crim LR 535, CA.
3 *Morgan* [1972] 1 QB 436, [1972] 1 All ER 348, CA.
4 *Brindley and Long* [1971] 2 QB 300, [1971] 2 All ER 698, CA.
5 Para 14.88.
6 This view was also taken by the Criminal Law Revision Committee who drafted the offence. See its Seventh Report: Felonies and Misdemeanours (Cmnd 2659) para 30.
7 *Rose* (1962) 46 Cr App Rep 103, CCA; *Andrews and Craig* [1962] 3 All ER 961n, [1962] 1 WLR 1474, CCA.
8 *Morgan* [1972] 1 QB 436, [1972] 1 All ER 348, CA.
9 *Brindley and Long* [1971] 2 QB 300, [1971] 2 All ER 698, CA.
10 Para 16.4.
11 Seventh Report of the Criminal Law Revision Committee (Cmnd 2659) para 28.

PUNISHMENT

16.3 Punishment varies according to the nature of the principal offence which has been committed. If the punishment for that crime is fixed by law, the maximum punishment for acting with intent to impede its prosecution or the apprehension of the offender is ten years' imprisonment; it is seven years' imprisonment if the maximum punishment for the principal offence is fourteen years' imprisonment, five years' when the maximum punishment for the principal offence is ten years' imprisonment, and three years' imprisonment in all other cases.[1]

1 Criminal Law Act 1967, s 4(3).

Concealing

16.4 Section 5(1) of the Criminal Law Act 1967 provides that, where a person has committed an arrestable offence, any other person who, knowing or believing that the offence or some other arrestable offence has been committed, and that he has information which might be of assistance in securing the prosecution or conviction of an offender for it, accepts or agrees to accept for not disclosing that information any consideration other than the making good of loss or injury caused by the offence, or the making of reasonable compensation for that loss or injury, is guilty of an offence, which is triable either way.[1]

The consent of the Director of Public Prosecutions is required before a prosecution can be instituted for this offence.[2] It is far less serious than assisting offenders, the maximum punishment being two years' imprisonment.[3]

1 Magistrates' Courts Act 1980, s 17(1) and Sch 1.
2 Criminal Law Act 1967, s 5(3).
3 Criminal Law Act 1967, s 5(1).

ELEMENTS

16.5 The prosecution must prove three things:

a) The commission of an arrestable offence.
b) The accused's knowledge or belief that it, or some other arrestable offence, has been committed and that he has information which might assist the prosecution.
c) The acceptance by the accused of, or agreement by him to accept, some consideration (e g money or goods), other than the making good of loss or injury caused by the offence, in return for not disclosing that information.

It follows from the above that the acceptance of any consideration for not reporting or prosecuting a *non-arrestable* offence is not an offence under s 5(1), nor does it constitute any other offence.[1] The same is true, with one exception, in the case of merely failing to inform the police of an arrestable offence. The sole exception is failure to report a treason which still survives as the common law offence of misprision of treason, with a maximum punishment of life imprisonment.

The related offence of advertising rewards for the return of stolen or lost goods with the promise that no questions will be asked etc has already been described.[2]

1 This is the effect of the Criminal Law Act 1967, s 5(5).
2 Para 14.91.

Causing wasteful employment of the police

16.6 It is a summary offence to cause wasteful employment of the police by knowingly making a false report tending to show that an offence has been committed or that the informant has information material to any police inquiry, or giving rise to apprehension for the safety of persons or property.[1] It may be noted that it is similarly a summary offence to give a false fire alarm to any public fire brigade or member of it,[2] but there is no corresponding statutory provision concerning the wasteful employment of ambulance and similar services.

1 Criminal Law Act 1967, s 5(2). The maximum sentence is six months' imprisonment or a fine not exceeding level 4 on the standard scale (£2,500) or both.
2 Fire Services Act 1947, s 31, as amended by the Criminal Law Act 1977, Sch 6.

Perjury

16.7 Section 1(1) of the Perjury Act 1911 provides that perjury, which is triable only on indictment, is committed by a person who, lawfully sworn as a witness or interpreter in a judicial proceeding, wilfully makes a statement material in that proceeding which he knows to be false or does not believe to be true. The maximum punishment is seven years' imprisonment.

16.8 The following matters require further explanation:

a) *Lawfully sworn in a judicial proceeding* A person is 'lawfully sworn' within the meaning of the Act if he gives his evidence on oath, affirmation or solemn declaration.[1] The term 'judicial proceeding' includes a proceeding before any court, tribunal or person having by law power to hear, receive and examine evidence on oath, and a statement made for the purposes of a judicial proceeding before a person authorised to administer oaths is treated as made in a judicial proceeding.[2] A person may therefore be guilty of perjury if he wilfully makes a false statement in an affidavit in support of a summons.

   If the accused is charged with having made a false statement in a judicial proceeding it must have been made before the relevant tribunal. Therefore, in *Lloyd*,[3] when, after a person had been duly sworn in bankruptcy proceedings, the registrar left the court, it was held that no charge of perjury could be made in respect of false answers given to questions put to the witness in the registrar's absence.

b) *Material statement* It is the *statement* which must have been material to the judicial proceedings in the sense that it might have affected the outcome of the case; the question is not whether the truth, if told, would have been material in the sense that it would have affected the outcome. This was held by the Court of Appeal in *Millward*,[4] where a police officer had lied about enlisting the help of a colleague to assist him in identifying in the courtroom a person charged with driving offences. The Court held that the officer's false statement was material because it brought to a halt a line of cross-examination, which went to the heart of the case (namely his expressed belief that the person charged was the driver of the car in question), and the stopping of the cross-examination might very well have affected the outcome of the case. Whether or not the statement was material to the judicial proceedings is a question of law for the judge.[5]

c) *Mens rea* The material statement must have been made wilfully and with knowledge of its falsity or without belief in its truth. Mere inadvertence as to the falsity is not enough. Therefore, if the deponent to an affidavit made in a judicial proceeding is told, and believes, that everything is in order and proceeds to swear it without due consideration he cannot be convicted of perjury. 'Wilfully' simply means that the statement must have been made deliberately, and not inadvertently or by mistake;[6] it does not require knowledge or belief that the statement is material (nor is a mistaken belief that it is not material a defence).[6]

Because the definition of the offence includes statements which are made wilfully and which are not believed to be true, a person can be convicted of perjury even though the statement which he makes is true.[7]

Section 11 of the European Communities Act 1972 provides that any person who, in sworn evidence before the European Court, makes any statement which he knows to be false or does not believe to be true commits an indictable offence punishable in the same way as perjury.[8]

1 Perjury Act 1911, s 15.
2 Ibid, s 1(2) and (3).
3 (1887) 19 QBD 213.
4 [1985] QB 519, [1985] 1 All ER 859, CA.
5 Perjury Act 1911, s 1(6).
6 *Millward* [1985] QB 519, [1985] 1 All ER 859, CA. Cf Perjury Act 1911, s 1A; para 16.9.
7 A statement made, obiter, in *Millward* [1985] QB 519, [1985] 1 All ER 859 at 863 that it must be proved that the statement was false is contradicted by the clear words of s 1. In practice, however, prosecutions for perjury are not brought if the statement was true.
8 For proposals concerning the reform of the offence of perjury, see the Law Commission's Report, Offences relating to Interference with the Course of Justice (1975), Law Com No 96.

FALSE UNSWORN STATEMENT UNDER EVIDENCE (PROCEEDINGS IN OTHER JURISDICTIONS) ACT 1975

16.9 If a person within the jurisdiction makes a sworn statement which is false for the purpose of proceedings in another jurisdiction he may be convicted of perjury.[1] Section 1A of the Perjury Act 1911, which was inserted by the 1975 Act goes further. It makes it an offence triable either way, and punishable with a maximum of two years' imprisonment, for a person, in giving any *unsworn* testimony (whether oral or written) within the jurisdiction, where required to do so under the 1975 Act for the purpose of civil proceedings outside the jurisdiction, to make a statement which he knows to be false in a material particular, or which is so false and which he does not believe to be true.

1 Perjury Act 1911, s 1(4).

SUBORNATION OF PERJURY

16.10 Section 7(1) of the Perjury Act 1911, provides that a person who 'aids, abets, counsels, procures or suborns [ie procures by bribery or other corrupt means]' another to commit perjury is liable for perjury 'as if he were a principal offender'. This provision is redundant since it adds nothing to the criminal liability which would otherwise be imposed under the principles of aiding, abetting, counselling or procuring an offence.[1] It is no longer an offence to attempt to procure or suborn perjury.[2]

1 Paras 23.3–23.33.
2 Criminal Attempts Act 1981, s 1(4)(b) and Sch 1.

OTHER OFFENCES UNDER THE PERJURY ACT

16.11 Under the Perjury Act 1911, certain offences are punishable in the same way as perjury. These are the making of false statements on oath when required by law, otherwise than in a judicial proceeding;[1] the use of a false affidavit for the purposes of the Bills of Sale Acts;[1] the making of a false statement in relation to the registration of a marriage;[2] and the making of false statements in relation to the registration of births or deaths.[3]

The making of a false statutory declaration, or of a false statement in a document required by any public general Act of Parliament, or of a false statement in an oral answer required to be made to any question in pursuance of such an Act of Parliament, is punishable with imprisonment for two years.[4]

Lastly, the making of a false statement to procure a certificate in relation to a professional calling is punishable with imprisonment for one year.[5]

1 Perjury Act 1911, s 2.
2 Ibid, s 3.
3 Ibid, s 4.
4 Ibid, s 5.
5 Ibid, s 6. The offences under ss 3–6 are triable either way: Perjury Act 1911, ss 3(1) and 4(1) and Magistrates' Courts Act 1980, s 17(1) and Sch 1.

Contempt of Court[1]

16.12 Contempt of court, the maximum punishment for which is two years' imprisonment in the case of committal by a superior court,[2] may be of two types: criminal and civil.[3] Civil contempt of court, which consists of the disobedience of a court order (such as an injunction restraining some act or a direction to one parent to allow the other access to their child) or of the breach of an undertaking to a court, is outside the scope of this book and nothing more will be said about it.[4]

Criminal contempt involves other conduct which tends to obstruct, prejudice or bring into disrepute the administration of justice by the courts either in relation to a particular case (whether criminal or civil) or generally.

Criminal contempt of court is a common law offence. Following the report of the Phillimore Committee,[5] amendments were made to it by the Contempt of Court Act 1981.

The principal categories of criminal contempt are set out in the following paragraphs. The first two categories, described in paras 16.13 to 16.23, are concerned with conduct which gives rise to the risk that the outcome of particular legal proceedings may be prejudiced; the other categories, described in paras 16.24 to 16.30, are concerned with conduct which interferes with the administration of justice as a continuing process.

1 See Borrie and Lowe *Law of Contempt*.

2 Contempt of Court Act 1981, s 14(1).
3 With regard to the utility of this distinction, see *A-G v Newspaper Publishing plc* [1987] 3 All ER 276 at 294 and 306, per Donaldson MR and Lloyd LJ.
4 Disobedience to a court order occasionally constitutes criminal contempt. For examples, see paras 16.21 and 16.29. Another example is disobedience to an order making a child a ward of court: *D* [1984] 2 All ER 449 at 458, per Lord Brandon.
5 Report of the Committee on Contempt of Court (1974) Cmnd 5794.

PUBLICATIONS TENDING TO INTERFERE WITH THE COURSE OF JUSTICE IN
PARTICULAR PROCEEDINGS: THE 'STRICT LIABILITY RULE'[1]

16.13 Contempt of this type is now subject to ss 1 to 7 of the Contempt of Court Act 1981, whose effect is that, provided certain conditions are fulfilled and subject to certain defences and limitations, a publication potentially prejudicial to particular legal proceedings may be treated as a contempt of court regardless of an intention to prejudice them.

1 Lowe 'The Strict Liability Rule' (1981) 131 NLJ 1167; Miller 'The Contempt of Court Act 1981' [1982] Crim LR 71.

16.14 *Publication* This type of contempt usually takes the form of comments or statements in a newspaper or broadcast which tend to interfere with the course of justice in particular legal proceedings, but it is not limited to such channels of communication since 'publication' includes any speech, writing, broadcast or other communication in whatever form, which is addressed to the public at large or any section of the public.[1] While public speakers are included in this definition, they are likely to be exonerated by the provision next-mentioned unless their speeches are reported by the media. Presumably, unless they know that their speeches will be reported by the media, speakers at private meetings cannot commit the present type of contempt since their speeches can hardly be said to be addressed to the public at large or to any section of the public.

1 Contempt of Court Act 1981, s 2(1).

16.15 *Substantial risk of serious impediment or prejudice to course of justice in legal proceedings* A publication of the present type only constitutes a contempt if it creates a *substantial* risk that the course of justice in the legal proceedings in question will be *seriously* impeded or prejudiced,[1] as may occur where a publication suggests that an accused is or is not guilty or where it refers to the character of a party or of a witness. The risk which has to be assessed is that which was created by the publication of the allegedly offending matter at the time when it was published, taking into account the nature and circulation of the publication, the place of trial and the likely period of time which will elapse between the publication and the trial.[2] It is irrelevant that the risk created by the publication when it was published does not ultimately affect the outcome of the proceedings.[3] 'Substantial' does not add very much to 'risk' but the two words together are intended to exclude a risk which is only remote.[4] It is not enough that there is a substantial risk that the course of justice in the proceedings in question will be impeded or prejudiced; what is required is the substantial risk that they will seriously be impeded or prejudiced. If, for instance, it is the outcome of the trial or the need to discharge the jury without proceeding to a verdict that is put at risk, there can be no doubt that this requirement is satisfied.[5]

In relation to proceedings other than criminal proceedings, and to appellate proceedings generally, a contempt of the present type is likely to be committed only in the most exceptional circumstances. This is because a jury is extremely rarely employed in non-criminal proceedings (and never in appellate ones) and it is generally accepted that a judge is capable of remaining uninfluenced by prejudicial matter in deciding a case.[6] Nevertheless, a contempt will be committed in relation to such proceedings if a publication gives rise to a substantial risk that they will be seriously impeded or prejudiced by influencing the parties or witnesses, as where a newspaper holds a party up to public obloquy or disparagement for taking a case to court.[7]

1 Contempt of Court Act 1981, s 2(2).
2 *A-G v News Group Newspapers Ltd* [1987] QB 1, [1986] 2 All ER 833, CA.
3 *A-G v English* [1982] 2 All ER 903 at 918, per Lord Diplock.
4 Ibid, at 919, per Lord Diplock.
5 Ibid.
6 This view was taken, for example, by Lord Salmon in *A-G v BBC* [1981] AC 303 at 343, [1980] 3 All ER 161 (but cf the view of Viscount Dilhorne [1981] AC at 336) and by the House of Lords in *In re Lonrho* [1990] 2 AC 154, [1989] 2 All ER 1100.
7 *A-G v Times Newspapers Ltd* [1974] AC 273, [1973] 3 All ER 54, HL.

16.16 *Active legal proceedings* The proceedings liable to be impeded or prejudiced must be 'active' at the time of publication.[1] Schedule 1 of the 1981 Act defines the times when proceedings are 'active' for this purpose.

Criminal proceedings become active from the relevant initial step:

a) arrest without warrant;
b) the issue of a warrant for arrest;
c) the issue of a summons;
d) the service of an indictment or other document specifying the charge;
e) oral charge.

They remain active until concluded:

a) by acquittal or, as the case may be, by sentence;
b) by any other verdict, finding, order or decision which ends the proceedings;
c) by discontinuance by operation of law.

Proceedings commenced by the issue of a warrant for arrest cease to be active 12 months after the date of the warrant unless the person has been arrested within that period, but become active again if he is subsequently arrested.

Other legal proceedings, whether in a court of law, or in a tribunal or other body exercising the judicial power of the State,[2] are active from the time when arrangements for the hearing are made or, if no such arrangements are previously made, from the time the hearing begins; they do not become active simply on the issue of a writ or summons or the like. They remain active until the proceedings are disposed of or discontinued or withdrawn.

Of course, appellate proceedings are also legal proceedings in this context. They become active from the time when they are commenced:

a) by application for leave to appeal or apply for review, or by notice of such application;
b) by notice of appeal or of application for review;
c) by other originating process,

and remain active until disposed of, abandoned, discontinued or withdrawn. Where the appellate court remits the case to the court below, any further or new proceedings which result are treated as active from the conclusion of the appellate proceedings.

1 Contempt of Court Act 1981, s 2(3).
2 Section 19 of the Contempt of Court Act 1981 provides that in the Act 'court' includes these bodies and that 'legal proceedings' must be construed accordingly.

16.17 *Who can commit the contempt?* Where a publication satisfies the various requirements just mentioned, a contempt of court may be committed by any person responsible for that publication, such as the editor, the newspaper or broadcasting company, and a distributor. Despite one case to the contrary,[1] it would seem that such liability is a personal one, and not a vicarious liability[2] for the reporter or the like who originated the material contained in the publication. The reporter may, however, be liable to conviction for contempt as an accomplice, provided the requirements for such liability are satisfied.[3]

1 *Evening Standard Co Ltd* [1954] 1 QB 578, [1954] 1 All ER 1026, DC.
2 Para 23.36.
3 Paras 23.3–23.33.

16.18 *Strict Liability* Section 1 of the Contempt of Court Act 1981 provides that publications which satisfy the above requirements are subject to the 'strict liability rule'. The section defines this as 'the rule whereby conduct may be treated as a contempt of court as tending to interfere with the course of justice in particular proceedings regardless of intent to do so'. This means that a person can be convicted of the present type of contempt despite the absence of an intention to interfere with the course of justice in particular legal proceedings. Moreover, the prosecution does not have to prove that he knew of the contents of the publication or that the proceedings were active. However, liability for contempt under the strict liability rule is subject to the defences provided by s 3 of the 1981 Act and to the limitations provided by ss 4 and 5, to which we now turn.

16.19 *Defences* Section 3 provides defences of innocent publication and of innocent distribution. Under the former, set out in s 3(1), a person is not guilty of contempt under the strict liability rule as the publisher of any matter to which that rule applies if at the time of publication (having taken all reasonable care) he did not know and had no reason to suspect that relevant proceedings were active. This defence is of limited effect; it does not protect a publisher who knew that proceedings were active but took reasonable steps to exclude the prejudicial matter or was unaware of a factor which made the matter prejudicial.

The defence of innocent distribution is contained in s 3(2), which provides that a person is not guilty of contempt under the strict liability rule as the distributor of a publication containing any matter to which that rule applies if at the time of distribution (having taken all reasonable care) he did not know that it contained such matter and had no reason to suspect that it was likely to do so.

The burden of proof in relation to these two defences is on the accused.[1]

1 Contempt of Court Act 1981, s 3(3).

16.20 *A limitation: Reports of public legal proceedings* Section 4(1) of the 1981 Act provides that a person is not guilty of contempt under the strict liability rule in respect of a fair and accurate report of legal proceedings held in public, published contemporaneously and in good faith. It should, however, be noted that certain statutes[1] prohibit the publication of certain details of legal proceedings and that s 4(1) does not prevent criminal liability being incurred under these statutes.

For s 4(1) to apply the proceedings reported must be held in public; the provision does not extend to reports of proceedings in private (i e in camera or in chambers). (In fact, in certain cases the reporting of proceedings in private is itself a special type of contempt, which is dealt with in para 16.28, regardless of whether there is any risk of prejudice.) Parts of proceedings held in open court in the absence of the jury are held in public. This means that unless a postponement order is made under s 4(2), discussed below, a report that the accused has pleaded guilty to some of the counts in an indictment or that certain evidence has been ruled inadmissible, both of which will have occurred in the jury's absence, can fall within the protection of s 4(1).

The requirement of contemporaneity of publication in s 4(1) seems to exclude books published later which are liable to prejudice proceedings then active. Section 4(3) provides that a report of proceedings is deemed to be published contemporaneously:

a) in the case of a report whose publication is postponed by an order under s 4(2), if published as soon as practicable after that order expires;

b) in the case of a report of committal proceedings of which publication is permitted only by virtue of s 8(3) of the Magistrates' Courts Act 1980,[2] if published as soon as practicable after publication is so permitted.

It remains to be seen exactly what the requirement in s 4(1) of 'good faith' means.

1 E g Judicial Proceedings (Regulation of Reports) Act 1926, s 1; Children and Young Persons Act 1933, s 49 (see para 5.23).
2 Para 4.24.

16.21 Section 4(1) of the 1981 Act is subject to s 4(2), which empowers a court to postpone publication of reports of proceedings before it. Section 4(2) provides that in legal proceedings held in public the court may order that the publication of a report of them (or part of them) be postponed for such period as it thinks necessary where it appears to be necessary in order to avoid a substantial risk of prejudice to the administration of justice in those proceedings, or in any other proceedings pending or imminent.

In the case of the Crown Court, this power to order postponement of publication is particularly likely to be exercised in relation to matters occurring in the absence of the jury.

An order postponing publication can be made even though the prejudice, of which there must be a substantial risk, would not be serious, and even though the risk relates to other proceedings than those in question (providing they are pending or imminent). Thus, where magistrates in committal proceedings[1] have lifted reporting restrictions under s 8 of the Magistrates' Courts Act 1980,[2] they may make an order under s 4(2) in relation to all or part of those proceedings where it appears necessary to avoid a substantial risk of prejudice to the accused at his trial in the Crown Court (since the trial is an imminent proceeding).[3] Similarly, a court may make an order at the trial of B to avoid prejudice to C, who is not a co-accused of B but who obviously could shortly be involved in separate legal proceedings.[3]

For s 4(2) to operate an order to postpone publication must be made; a mere request or suggestion will not do. Orders under s 4(2) must be formulated in precise terms, stating their precise scope, duration and purpose, and must be committed to writing (so that a permanent record is kept for later reference). The court will normally give notice of the order to the press.[4] There is a right of appeal to the Court of Appeal, with its leave, against an order made in relation to a trial on indictment.[5]. Otherwise there is no right of appeal against an order but an order of an inferior court can be challenged by an application for judicial review.[6]

Knowingly to disregard an order under s 4(2) amounts to a contempt of court in itself, regardless of whether the publication in question is attended by any risk of prejudice to current, pending or imminent proceedings, since s 4(2) creates a new head of contempt.[7]

1 Para 4.19.
2 Para 4.24.
3 *Horsham Justices, ex p Farquharson* [1982] QB 762, [1982] 2 All ER 269, CA.
4 *Practice Note* [1983] 1 All ER 64, [1983] 1 WLR 1475.
5 Criminal Justice Act 1988, s 159.
6 *Horsham Justices, ex p Farquharson* [1982] QB 762, [1982] 2 All ER 269, CA. For judicial review, see para 5.35.
7 Ibid, per Shaw and Ackner LJJ; cf Lord Denning MR.

16.22 *Another limitation* Section 5 of the 1981 Act provides that a publication made as or as part of a discussion in good faith of public affairs or other matters of general public interest is not to be treated as a contempt under the strict liability rule if the risk of impediment or prejudice to particular legal proceedings is merely incidental to the discussion. The accused does not bear the burden of proof; once there is sufficient evidence of the issue covered by it the onus is on the prosecution to prove that it does not apply.[1] (The same appears to be the case in the case of the limitation under s 4(1).)

It must be emphasised that the test under s 5 is not whether the publication (eg of an article) could be written as effectively without the offending passages or whether some other wording might have been substituted for them that could have reduced the risk of prejudice.[1] Instead, it is whether the risk created by the words actually used was 'merely incidental to the discussion', which means no more than an incidental consequence of expounding its main theme.[1] 'Discussion' is not confined to the airing of views and the propounding of arguments but can include accusations made in good faith which are part of the basis of the discussion.[1]

The effect of s 5 is that bona fide discussion in the media of controversial matters of general public importance is not gagged merely because there are active legal proceedings in which some particular instance of those controversial matters may be in issue. On the other hand, s 5 does not protect from being treated as contempt the discussion of the specific facts of an active case.

The Contempt of Court Act 1981 does not provide a wider 'public interest' limitation or defence. Thus, a contempt may be committed if, after a dangerous person has escaped from pre-trial custody, a newspaper publishes the fact that he is dangerous in order to protect the public.

1 *A-G v English* [1983] 1 AC 116, [1982] 2 All ER 903, HL.

CONDUCT INTENDED TO IMPEDE OR PREJUDICE THE COURSE OF JUSTICE IN
PARTICULAR LEGAL PROCEEDINGS

16.23   This category of contempt covers offering bribes or threats to witnesses or jurors to distort or suppress their evidence or to reach a corrupt verdict, as the case may be.[1] The test for this category of contempt is whether the accused did an act which was intended to impede or prejudice the course of justice and was capable of having that effect.[2]

This category also covers the use of improper pressure to induce a party to compromise or discontinue an action,[3] as well as publications which interfere, and are intended to interfere, with the course of justice in particular proceedings, whether actual or potential.[4]

In the present category of case, the prosecution must prove not only the intention to interfere with the course of justice in particular proceedings but also that the accused's conduct gave rise to a real risk of such interference occurring.[5] On the other hand, it is irrelevant whether or not that risk would be of serious interference, and the proceedings need not be 'active' or even imminent.[6]

The provisions of the Contempt of Court Act 1981 relating to contemporary reports of legal proceedings and to the discussion of public affairs do not apply to publications which are proved to have been intended to interfere with the course of justice in particular proceedings.[7]

1 See, for example, *Lewis v James* (1887) 3 TLR 527.
2 *Giscombe* (1985) 79 Cr App Rep 79, CA; *A-G v Newspaper Publishing plc* [1988] Ch 333 [1987] 3 All ER 276, CA; *A-G v News Group Newspapers Ltd* [1988] Ch 365, CA; *Runting* (1989) 89 Cr App Rep 243, CA.
3 *A-G v Times Newspapers Ltd* [1973] 3 All ER 54 at 76, per Lord Diplock.
4 *A-G v Newspaper Publishing plc* [1987] 3 All ER 276, CA; *A-G v News Group Newspapers Ltd* [1988] Ch 365, CA; and *A-G v Times Newspapers Ltd* [1991] 2 All ER 398, HL, provide interesting examples. For comment, see Stone 'Intentional Contempt and Press Freedom' (1988) 138 NLJ 423.
5 *A-G v Times Newspapers Ltd* [1974] AC 273, [1973] 3 All ER 54, HL.
6 Ibid; *A-G v News Group Newspapers Ltd* [1989] QB 110, [1988] 2 All ER 906, DC; *A-G v Sports Newspapers Ltd* (1991) Times, June 6, per Bingham LJ (cf Hodgson J).
7 Contempt of Court Act 1981, s 6.

CONTEMPT IN THE FACE OF THE COURT

16.24   This is concerned with words or actions in the presence of the court which interfere, or are liable to do so, with the course of justice in a case being, or about to be, tried. Examples are throwing a tomato at the judge, threatening a witness,[1] breaking up the trial (as where students, striving to preserve its use, chanted the Welsh language in court),[2] and the refusal of a witness to be sworn or to answer a lawful question[3] or to leave court when ordered to do so.[4]

1 *Moore v Clerk of Assize, Bristol* [1972] 1 All ER 58, [1971] 1 WLR 1669, CA.
2 *Morris v Crown Office* [1970] 2 QB 114, [1970] 1 All ER 1079, CA.
3 *Ex p Fernandez* (1861) 10 CBNS 3. Refusal to disclose the source of information contained in a publication for which he is responsible does not render a witness guilty of contempt, unless that disclosure is necessary in the interest of justice or national security or for the prevention of disorder or crime: Contempt of Court Act 1981, s 10.
4 *Chandler v Horne* (1842) 2 Mood & R 423.

REPRISALS AGAINST JURORS AND WITNESSES

16.25 It has long been established that it is a contempt to threaten or punish a juror in relation to his part in legal proceedings which have ended.[1]

In modern times, in *Re A-G's Application, A-G v Butterworth*,[2] the Court of Appeal has held that it was contempt to take reprisals against a witness who has given evidence in legal proceedings. In this case a man who had appeared as a witness in proceedings involving his trade union was deprived of office as treasurer and as a delegate of a branch of the union because his colleagues thought that in giving evidence he had acted against the interests of the union. The Court of Appeal held that, although clearly the proceedings themselves were no longer capable of being affected, there was no doubt that reprisals of this kind could interfere with the administration of justice since a witness might be deterred from giving evidence by the fear of reprisals even if he had not been threatened before the proceedings, and since other witnesses in future cases might be deterred if reprisals were not punishable. It stressed that in this type of contempt the accused's purpose of punishing was important in determining whether his conduct tended to interfere with the administration of justice.

1 *Martin* (1848) 5 Cox CC 356.
2 [1963] 1 QB 696, [1962] 3 All 326, CA. See also *Chapman v Honig* [1963] 2 QB 502, [1963] 2 All ER 513, CA; *Moore v Clerk of Assize, Bristol* [1972] 1 All ER 58, [1971] 1 WLR 1669, CA.

OBSTRUCTING OFFICERS OF THE COURT

16.26 It is a contempt knowingly to obstruct such an officer when he is carrying out his duties.[1] But gross discourtesy to an officer of the court does not constitute contempt;[2] nor does failure by a legal representative to co-operate with an officer of the court unless he intends to delay or hinder the course of justice, or it is actually hindered or delayed and he has no just cause.[3]

1 *Williams v Johns* (1773) 1 Mer 303n. See also *Re Johnson* (1887) 20 QBD 68, 57 LJQB 1.
2 *Weston v Courts Administrator of Central Criminal Court* [1976] QB 32, [1976] 2 All ER 875, CA.
3 Ibid.

SCANDALISING THE JUDGE OR A COURT

16.27 'Judges and courts are alike open to criticism, and if reasonable argument or expostulation is offered against any judicial act as contrary to law or the public good no court could or would treat that as a contempt of court.'[1] Broadly speaking what is prohibited is scurrilous abuse of a judge (in his capacity as a judge) or of a court,[2] or attacks upon the impartiality of a judge (in his capacity as a judge) or of a court.[3] Thus, an allegation that a fair trial of someone who held certain views could not be obtained from a named judge constitutes contempt.[4] Proceedings for scandalising the court are rare. It appears that it would not be a defence to show that the allegations were true and that publication was for the public benefit.

1 *Gray* [1900] 2 QB 36 at 40; *Ambard v A-G for Trinidad and Tobago* [1936] AC 322, [1936] 1 All ER 704, PC; *Metropolitan Police Comr, ex p Blackburn (No 2)* [1968] 2 QB 150, [1968] 2 All ER 319, CA.
2 *McLeod v St Aubyn* [1899] AC 549 at 561, per Lord Morris.
3 *Badry v DPP of Mauritius* [1983] 2 AC 297, [1982] 3 All ER 973, PC.
4 *New Statesman (Editor), ex p DPP* (1928) 44 TLR 301, DC.

PUBLICATION OF INFORMATION RELATING TO PROCEEDINGS IN PRIVATE

16.28 Section 12 of the Administration of Justice Act 1960, as amended, provides that the publication of information relating to proceedings before any court sitting in private (ie in camera or in chambers) is not of itself contempt of court except in certain cases, such as the following:

- a) where the proceedings relate to the exercise of the inherent jurisdiction of the High Court with respect to minors, or are brought under the Children Act 1989, or otherwise relate wholly or mainly to the maintenance or upbringing of a minor;
- b) where the court sits in private for reasons of national security;
- c) where the information relates to a secret process, discovery or invention which is in issue in the proceedings;
- d) where the court, acting under a statutory or inherent power, expressly prohibits the publication of all information relating to the proceedings or of information of the description which is published.[1]

Even in these cases a publisher of information relating to such proceedings is only guilty of contempt if he knew, or was reckless, that he was giving information about such proceedings in private.[2]

The publication of the text of an order, or a summary of it, made by a court sitting in private is not of itself contempt of court, except where the court validly and expressly prohibits this.[3]

It must be emphasised that, in those cases where a publication can be a contempt under s 12, it is only the publication of 'information relating to [the] proceedings before the court sitting in private' which is caught. This phrase covers matters such as evidence and reports and any part of the recorded reasons for the court's order or judgment which discloses the evidential and other material on which it is based, but it does not cover (and does not prevent the publication of) facts such as the date, time or place of the proceedings nor (unless the court has validly prohibited publication) the name of a party to the proceedings.[4]

1 Administration of Justice Act 1960, s 12(1).
2 *Re F (a minor)* [1977] Fam 58, [1977] 1 All ER 114, CA.
3 Administration of Justice Act 1960, s 12(2).
4 *Pickering v Liverpool Daily Post and Echo Newspapers plc* [1991] 1 All ER 622, HL.

DISCLOSURE OF MATTERS EXEMPTED FROM DISCLOSURE IN COURT OR OF A JURY'S DELIBERATIONS

16.29 In some rare situations,[1] a court has power to permit a name or some other matter to be withheld from the public. Section 11 of the Contempt of Court Act 1981 provides that, where such a power is exercised, the court may give directions prohibiting the publication of the matter in question. A direction cannot be made under s 11 if the matter (e g a witness's identity) has been openly disclosed in court.[2] A direction must be committed to writing and state its precise scope, its duration (if it is not indefinite) and its specific purpose.[3] If a court validly makes a clear direction as to what information may not be published, a person who, knowing of the direction, attempts to frustrate the court's object by publishing the information as to the matter is guilty of contempt.[4]

Some courts have demonstrated a regrettable preparedness to make directions under s 11.

A person aggrieved by a direction under s 11 in relation to a trial on indictment may appeal to the Court of Appeal, with its leave.[5] Where a direction is made by a magistrates' court it may only be challenged by an application for judicial review.

1 See, for example, *Evesham Justices, ex p Evans* [1987] NLJ Rep 757, DC.
2 *Arundel Justices, ex p Westminster Press* [1985] 2 All ER 390, [1985] 1 WLR 780, DC.
3 *Practice Note* [1983] 1 All ER 64.
4 *A-G v Leveller Magazine Ltd* [1979] AC 440, [1979] 1 All ER 745, HL. Also see *Socialist Worker Printers and Publishers Ltd, ex p A-G* [1975] QB 637, [1975] 1 All ER 142, DC.
5 Criminal Justice Act 1988, s 159.

16.30 Section 8(1) of the Contempt of Court Act 1981 provides that it is a contempt to obtain, disclose or solicit any particulars of the views or votes of members of a jury in the course of their deliberations. The only exceptions are provided by s 8(2), which states that s 8(1) does not apply to any disclosure in the proceedings in question to enable the jury to reach their verdict (or in connection with its delivery) or to any disclosure in evidence in later proceedings for an alleged offence in relation to the jury, or to the publication of anything so disclosed.

The policy behind s 8 is to preserve the finality of jury verdicts and to ensure that jurors are not constrained in their deliberations by having their views bandied about by the press. However, s 8 has the unfortunate effect of preventing legitimate and controlled research into the jury system if this involves the revelation of details of the views and votes of jurors, despite safeguards as to the anonymity of all concerned.[1]

1 See Enright 'Unlocking the Jury Room' (1989) 139 NLJ 655.

TRIAL

16.31 Criminal contempt of court is triable at common law on indictment but this procedure has fallen into disuse, and the usual method of dealing with criminal contempt is by summary process without a jury. This summary power to commit to prison, being arbitrary, should be exercised with great caution.[1] A number of limits on this process should be noted:

a) County courts and magistrates' courts have no common law powers to punish for a contempt in relation to their proceedings.[2] However, s 118 of the County Courts Act 1984 empowers a county court judge of his own motion (ie an information or charge is not required, nor is any other notice of formal institution of proceedings by another) to imprison for a maximum of one month, or fine, any person who wilfully insults him or any juror, witness or officer of the court during his attendance in court, or in going to or returning from the court, or who wilfully interrupts the proceedings of the court or otherwise misbehaves in court. 'Insult' bears its ordinary English meaning,[3] and it has been held that this does not include threatening one of the persons mentioned above.[3] It is irrelevant whether or not the interruption results from an act done inside or outside the court,[4] but for it to have been wilful the interruptor must have known that there was a risk that his acts would interrupt the proceedings but nevertheless have gone on and deliberately done those acts.[4]

Section 12 of the Contempt of Court Act 1981 gives to a magistrates' court a similar power to commit to custody of its own motion, but it extends it to cases where a solicitor or barrister having business in the court is wilfully insulted.

b) A judge of the Crown Court or of the High Court or Court of Appeal has jurisdiction to punish a person of his own motion[5] whenever there has been a gross interference with the course of justice in a case being, or about to be, tried or, possibly, just over.[6] This power is normally confined to contempts in the face of the court but can be used in a proper case where the contempt is reported to the judge.[7] It should only be exercised where the matter in issue is recent and clear and it is imperative for the judge to act without delay to prevent justice being obstructed or undermined.[8] However, instead of immediately acting, the judge should normally give the contemnor and himself time to reflect, possibly overnight, and give the contemnor the opportunity of being legally advised.[9]

c) A High Court judge may punish for a contempt committed in connection with any civil proceedings in the High Court. The Court of Appeal (Civil Division) has similar powers over contempts relating to civil proceedings in that court.[10] Proceedings are instituted by the Attorney-General or a private person.

d) The House of Lords normally has sole jurisdiction of its own motion over contempts relating to proceedings, civil or criminal, before it.[11]

e) A Divisional Court of the Queen's Bench Division has *sole* jurisdiction to punish:
   i) a contempt in connection with any proceedings before it;
   ii) a contempt in connection with criminal proceedings (subject to certain exceptions such as those mentioned in b) above);
   iii) a contempt in connection with proceedings in an inferior court (subject in the case of a magistrates' court or a county court to the exceptions mentioned in a) above,[12] and to the power of a coroner's court to punish a contempt committed in the face of the court).[13] In this context 'court' means a body established by law to exercise, either generally or subject to defined limits, the judicial power of the State;[14] it does not include bodies, such as administrative courts or tribunals, whose functions are exclusively legislative or essentially executive (even though they must act judicially in discharging them);[15]
   iv) a contempt committed otherwise than in connection with any proceedings (viz scandalising any court other than the Court of Appeal, which itself has jurisdiction if either of its Divisions is scandalised);[16]
   v) a contempt, other than scandalising, of the Court of Appeal (Criminal Division).[17]

   Proceedings are normally instituted by the Attorney-General.

Proceeding for a contempt which has been committed[18] under the strict liability rule (publications unintentionally interfering with the course of justice in a particular case) can only be instituted by or with the consent of the Attorney-General or on the motion of a court of competent jurisdiction.[19]

---

1 *Davies* [1906] 1 KB 32, 75 LJKB 104.
2 *Lefroy* (1873) LR 8 QB 134; *Bush v Green* [1985] 3 All ER 721, [1985] 1 WLR 1143, CA.
3 *Havant Justices, ex p Palmer* (1985) 149 JP 609, DC.
4 *Bodden v Metropolitan Police Comr* [1990] 2 QB 397, [1989] 3 All ER 833, CA.
5 RSC Ord 52, r 5; Supreme Court Act 1981, s 45(4).
6 *Balogh v Crown Court at St Albans* [1975] QB 73, [1974] 3 All ER 283, CA.
7 Ibid.
8 Ibid. Also see *Owen* [1976] 3 All ER 239, CA; *Goult* (1983) 76 Cr App Rep 140, [1983] Crim LR 103; and *Griffin* (1989) 88 Cr App Rep 63, CA.

9 *Phillips* (1983) 78 Cr App Rep 88, CA; *Moran* (1985) 81 Cr App Rep 51, CA; *Hill* [1986] Crim LR 457, CA.
10 RSC Ord 52, r 1.
11 *In re Lonrho plc* [1990] AC 154, [1989] 2 All ER 1100, HL.
12 *Bush v Green* [1985] 3 All ER 721, [1985] 1 WLR 1143, CA.
13 *West Yorkshire Coroner, ex p Smith (No 2)* [1985] QB 1096, [1985] 1 All ER 100, DC.
14 The Mental Health Review Tribunal has been held to be a 'court' in this context: *Pickering v Liverpool Daily Post and Echo Newspapers Ltd* [1991] 2 AC 370, [1991] 1 All ER 622, HL.
15 *A-G v BBC* [1981] AC 303, [1980] 3 All ER 161, HL (Local Valuation Court not a 'court' in this context).
16 *Metropolitan Police Comr, ex p Blackburn (No 2)* [1968] 2 QB 150, [1968] 2 All ER 319, CA.
17 RSC Ord 52, r 1.
18 Where a contempt under the strict liability rule is merely apprehended, the statement in this paragraph does not apply, so that anyone with a sufficient interest may apply for an injunction to restrain the contempt: *Peacock v London Weekend Television* (1985) 150 JP 71, CA.
19 Contempt of Court Act 1981, s 7.

Attempting to pervert the course of justice[1]

16.32 This offence, which is also known by other titles, such as obstructing the administration of justice, is a common law offence triable only on indictment and punishable at the discretion of the court. The use of the word 'attempt' in the name of this offence is misleading because the attempt is itself the substantive offence,[2] which is more accurately, if less neatly, described as doing an act or series of acts which has a tendency to, and is intended to, pervert the course of justice.[3] Like contempt of court, this offence has a more general application than offences such as perjury. Broadly speaking, the offence penalises any conduct which has a tendency wrongly to interfere, directly or indirectly, with the initiation, progress or outcome of any criminal or civil proceedings, including arbitration proceedings,[4] accompanied by an intention so to interfere.

The accused's conduct will have a tendency to pervert the course of justice if he has done enough for there to be a possibility, without further action on his part, that a perversion of the course of justice may result;[5] it is irrelevant that that possibility does not materialise.[6] With regard to the requirement that an intention to interfere with the course of justice must be proved,[7] it would seem that proof of a purposive intention is necessary.

The offence is not limited to matters directly concerning proceedings already in being; but a course of justice must have been embarked on, in the sense that proceedings of some kind in a court or judicial tribunal are in being or imminent or that investigations which could or might bring proceedings about are in progress, in order that the act complained of can constitute the offence.[8]

1 Williams 'Evading Justice' [1975] Crim LR 430, 479, 608.
2 *Vreones* [1891] 1 QB 360 at 367; *Rowell* [1978] 1 All ER 665 at 671; *Machin* [1980] 3 All ER 151 at 153–4; *Williams* (1990) 92 Cr App Rep 158, CA.
3 *Vreones* [1981] 1 QB 361 at 367; *Rowell* (1977) 65 Cr App Rep 174 at 671; *Williams* (1990) 92 Cr App Rep 158, CA.
4 *Vreones*.
5 *Murray* [1982] 2 All ER 225, [1982] 1 WLR 475, CA. Cf *Firetto* [1991] Crim LR 208, CA, where a passage suggests that an offence may be committed even though there is no risk that a perversion of the course of justice may result unless D does some further act, provided that that act is one he is likely to do. If this suggestion was ever adopted the offence would be

widened significantly because, for example, a person who fabricated an item of false evidence but who had not got as far as using or tendering it, although it was likely he would, could be convicted.

6 *Murray.*
7 *Vreones; Machin; Selvage* [1982] QB 372, [1982] 1 All ER 96, CA.
8 *Selvage.*

16.33 The following types of conduct are among those which have been held to constitute attempting to pervert the course of justice:

a) Interference with witnesses. A person who threatens or seeks to persuade a witness or potential witness[1] not to give evidence,[2] or to give evidence of a particular character,[3] is guilty of attempted perversion of the course of justice, whether or not the proceedings in question have been instituted at the time.[4] The offence can be committed in relation to the complainant or a co-defendant in the proceedings in question, if he is a witness or 'potential witness' in them;[5] a 'potential witness' is anyone who (although not actually called at the time to testify) is capable of giving relevant admissible evidence.[6] It is irrelevant that the threat is to do an otherwise lawful act, such as to sue for damages or to expose misconduct.[7] The offence is not committed by a person who seeks by reasoned argument to persuade a witness to tell the truth.[7]

b) Making or using false statements to the police or other officers of justice with a view to perverting the course of, or preventing, judicial proceedings constitutes attempting to pervert the course of justice,[8] and so does knowingly making to the police a false allegation against another of criminal conduct.[9]

c) Fabrication of false evidence for the purpose of misleading a judicial body constitutes attempting to pervert the course of justice, even though the evidence is never tendered.[10]

d) Doing an act tending to, and with intent to, assist another (or, presumably, oneself) to evade lawful arrest with knowledge that the other (or oneself) is wanted by the police constitutes attempting to pervert the course of justice. This is so even though there could be no conviction for the statutory offence of assisting offenders discussed in paras 16.1 and 16.2[11] because the necessary knowledge or belief that the person assisted was guilty of an arrestable offence could not be proved. Similarly, it has been held that intentionally frustrating the 'screening' breath test procedure on which a constable has embarked under the 'drink and drive' legislation constitutes attempting to pervert the course of justice.[12]

1 *Grimes* [1968] 3 All ER 179n; *Panayiotou* [1973] 3 All ER 112, CA.
2 *Panayiotou; Kellett* [1976] QB 372, [1975] 3 All ER 468, CA.
3 *Greenberg* (1919) 26 Cox CC 466, CCA.
4 *Panayiotou.*
5 *Panayiotou; Bains* [1981] Crim LR 569, Crown Ct.
6 *Bains.*
7 *Kellett.*
8 *Andrews* [1973] 1 QB 422, [1973] 1 All ER 857, CA.
9 *Rowell* [1978] 1 All ER 665, [1978] 1 WLR 132, CA.
10 *Vreones* [1891] 1 QB 360, 60 LJMC 62. Also see *Smalley* [1959] Crim LR 587; *Murray* [1982] 2 All ER 225, [1982] 1 WLR 475, CA.
11 *Thomas* [1979] QB 326, [1979] 1 All ER 577, CA.
12 *Britton* [1973] RTR 502, CA.

16.34 Various types of conduct which fall within the broad offence of attempting to pervert the course of justice also fall within the definitions of other offences. For instance, making or using false statements to officers of justice with a view to perverting, or preventing, judicial proceedings may also amount to the statutory offences of obstructing a constable in the execution of his duty[1] or of assisting offenders,[2] and making a false allegation to the police of criminal conduct against another will also amount to the statutory offence of causing wasteful employment of the police.[3] Similarly, an attempt to influence jurors constitutes the offences of embracery (an indictable common law offence) and contempt of court. In the judgment of the Court of Appeal, embracery is an obsolescent offence because in modern times the likely charge for such conduct is contempt of court, which should be dealt with summarily by the trial judge, if only one person was involved, or conspiracy to pervert the course of justice if more than one person was involved.[4]

1 Paras 18.68–18.71.
2 Paras 16.1–16.3.
3 Para 16.6.
4 *Owen* [1976] 3 All ER 239, [1976] 1 WLR 840, CA.

Offences relating to bail

ABSCONDING

16.35 Section 6(1) of the Bail Act 1976 provides that, if a person who has been released on bail in criminal proceedings fails without reasonable cause to surrender to custody, he is guilty of an offence. 'Surrender to custody' means 'surrender at the time and place being appointed for him to do so'.[1] 'The time ... appointed' is not to be literally interpreted; the Divisional Court has held that a person who, without reasonable cause, surrendered seven minutes late had not committed an offence under s 6(1).[2]

Section 6(2) deals with the case of a person who has been released on bail but has been unable to surrender to custody because of some reasonable cause, by providing that it is an offence to fail to surrender to custody at the appointed place as soon after the appointed time as is reasonably practicable.

The accused has the burden of proving reasonable cause,[3] and it is expressly provided that failure to give him a copy of the record of the bail decision is not a reasonable cause.[4]

These offences are not triable on indictment or either way. Instead, they are only triable as follows. Where the failure to surrender is a failure to surrender to a magistrates' court, and the bail was granted by that court, the appropriate way for the court to proceed is by the initiation (at the invitation of the prosecution) of proceedings of the court's own motion,[5] ie as in the case of the jurisdiction of a magistrates' court over contempt an information or charge is not required. The prosecution will, of course, conduct the proceedings and call any evidence.[6] On the other hand, in the case of a failure to surrender to a police station or to a magistrates' court, where bail was granted by the police, an offence under s 6 must be dealt with as a summary offence and any proceedings should be instituted by charging the accused or laying an information within six months of the offence.[7] If an offence under s 6 is tried by a magistrates' court, the maximum punishment which it can impose is three months'[8] imprisonment or a fine not exceeding level 5 on the standard scale (£5,000) or both. However, if the magistrates consider that a greater punishment should be awarded, or if they commit the person for trial for another offence, they may commit him for sentence to the Crown Court. In such a case the Crown Court may impose up to 12 months' imprisonment or an unlimited fine or both.[9]

Where an offence under s 6(1) or (2) is committed by a failure to surrender to the Crown Court, the Crown Court deals with the offence as if it was a contempt of court, ie summarily and without the need for an indictment being preferred.[10] The maximum punishment is 12 months' imprisonment or an unlimited fine or both.

1 Bail Act 1976, s 2(2).
2 *Gateshead Justices, ex p Usher* [1981] Crim LR 491, DC.
3 Bail Act 1976, s 6(3).
4 Ibid, s 6(4).
5 Ibid. *Practice Note* [1987] 1 All ER 128, [1987] 1 WLR 79.
6 Ibid.
7 Ibid; *Murphy v DPP* [1990] 2 All ER 390, DC.
8 It may be that the maximum is six months where the bail was granted by a magistrates' court: see the discussion of this matter, obiter, in *Murphy v DPP*.
9 Bail Act 1976, s 6(5)–(7).
10 Ibid, s 6(5) and (7). In *Harbax Singh* [1979] QB 319 at 325, [1979] 1 All ER 524 at 527 Roskill LJ canvassed the possibility that the Crown Court might direct that summary proceedings be begun before a magistrates' court. This possibility was rejected, obiter, by Watkins LJ in *Schiavo v Anderton* [1986] 3 All ER 10 at 15.

AGREEMENT TO INDEMNIFY SURETIES

16.36 Section 9 of the Bail Act 1976 provides that, where a person agrees with a person who is or may become a surety for bail[1] to indemnify him in money or money's worth against any liability which he may incur as a surety, he and the surety commit an offence. Proceedings for the offence may only be instituted with the consent of the Director of Public Prosecutions.[2] On summary conviction the offence is punishable with a maximum of three months' imprisonment or a fine not exceeding level 5 on the standard scale or both. On conviction on indictment the maximum punishment is 12 months' imprisonment or a fine or both, and the same is the case if a magistrates' court commits a person for sentence for this offence which it may do in the same cases as for the offence under s 6.[3]

For the sake of completeness it should be noted that an agreement to indemnify a surety may also constitute a conspiracy to pervert the course of justice.[4]

1 Para 4.25.
2 Bail Act 1976, s 9(5).
3 Ibid, s 9(3) and (4).
4 *Porter* [1910] 1 KB 369, 79 LJKB 241, CCA; *Head and Head* [1978] Crim LR 427, CA.

17 Political offences

Treason

17.1 Under the Treason Act 1351, the following acts among others constitute the offence of treason, for which the only punishment is death:

a) Compassing the death of the King, the Queen, or their eldest son and heir.
b) Levying war against the King in his realm.
c) Adhering to the King's enemies in his realm, giving them aid and comfort in the realm, or elsewhere. This head of treason depends on the existence of a state of war.[1]

The Treason Act 1351, which wholly superseded the previous common law, was originally intended to apply to breach of the feudal and personal duty of loyalty to the reigning monarch. Although treason remains a breach of the duty of allegiance, the tie is now political, being to a system of government under a constitutional monarch, rather than to a particular individual.

During the seventeenth and eighteenth centuries, the judges by a process of judicial construction succeeded in adapting the wording of the 1351 Act to the altered needs of a later age. The acts which came to be held by judicial construction to be treasons under the statute are described as 'constructive treasons'. Because of the mandatory death sentence for treason, juries became unwilling to convict of such offences. Therefore, a Treason Act was passed in 1795 enacting that such constructive treasons were definitely treasons, but by the Treason Felony Act 1848 all but one of them were made felonies, usually known as 'treason felonies', punishable with imprisonment for life; the exception is referred to at the end of para 17.2. In such cases, however, it is still theoretically possible to prosecute the accused for treason under the 1351 Act.

1 Kenny *Outlines of Criminal Law* (19th edn) 339.

17.2 Although the wording of the first head of the definition of treason appears to cover mere thoughts, it has been held, on account of a subsequent clause in the statute, that an overt act manifesting the criminal intention and tending towards the accomplishment of the criminal object is necessary to render the accused guilty. Words spoken in the course of conspiring or inciting to kill the Sovereign will suffice,[1] but not loose words spoken without reference to any act or project, such as saying that the Sovereign is no more fit to be King than an ignorant shepherd.[2] In *Lord Preston*[3] it was held that hiring a ship for the conveyance of treasonable papers to an enemy government was a sufficient overt act of compassing the King's death although the project was not fulfilled.

By judicial construction, 'compassing the King's death' came to include compassing the end of his political existence. It might, therefore, be committed by someone who promoted a revolt in a colony,[4] or by inciting friendly aliens to invade the kingdom.[5] These acts would not always be covered by the second and third heads, because the levying of war must be within the realm, and the enemies adhered to must already be at war with the sovereign.

Compassing the bodily harm or restraint of the sovereign, originally constructive treason and confirmed as treason by the Treason Act 1795, was not covered by the Treason Felony Act 1848.

1 *Longhorn* (1679) 7 State Tr 417 at 463.
2 *Charnock's Case* (1694) 2 Salk 633.
3 (1691) Fost 196, 12 State Tr 645.
4 *Maclane* (1797) 26 State Tr 721.
5 *Hensey* (1758) 1 Burr 642, 19 State Tr 1341.

17.3 In relation to the second head the doctrine of constructive treason was most fully developed. 'Levying war against the King in his realm' has been held to include a riot or insurrection for some general public purpose, such as changing government policy, effecting an alteration in the law, opening all prisons or pulling down all meeting houses.[1] A rising for a limited or local purpose, or directed against a private person, does not amount to levying war.[2]

Levying war against the Sovereign or attempting to intimidate Parliament for such general political purposes was made a treason felony by the 1848 Act. A riot or plot to assassinate ministers of the Crown which does not have the general object of effecting a change of Government policy is neither treason nor treason felony.

1 *Damaree* (1709) Foster 213; *Lord George Gordon* (1781) 21 State Tr 485; *Thistlewood* (1820) 33 State Tr 681.
2 Hale *Pleas of the Crown* vol I, pp 131, 133, 143 and 149.

17.4 Almost any aid and comfort to the enemy may amount to adherence for the purposes of the third head of treason. In *Lynch*[1] it was held that there was an adherence to the enemy within the 1351 Act when a British subject became a naturalised subject of an enemy state in time of war. Both the adherence, and the giving of aid and comfort to the enemy, may take place outside the realm. In *Casement*[2] a British subject was held guilty of treason when he incited British prisoners of war to join the enemy forces and to participate in an expedition in a submarine which had as its object the landing of arms in Ireland.

1 [1903] 1 KB 444, 72 LJKB 167.
2 [1917] 1 KB 98, 86 LJKB 467, CCA.

WHO CAN COMMIT TREASON?

17.5 Anyone who owes allegiance to the Crown may commit treason. Thus, British citizens, British Dependent Territories citizens and British Overseas citizens may commit treason in any part of the world, because they owe allegiance wherever they may be. On the other hand, a Commonwealth citizen or a citizen of the Republic of Ireland who is not also a British citizen (or a British Dependent Territories citizen or a British Overseas citizen) may generally commit treason only if the act is done in the United Kingdom or in a non-self-governing part of the Commonwealth. The reason is that, by s 3 of the British Nationality Act 1948 (as amended by s 51 of the British Nationality Act 1981), a Commonwealth citizen (or an Irish citizen) who is not also a British citizen (or a British Dependent Territories citizen or a British Overseas citizen) cannot be convicted of an offence under English law in respect of anything done or omitted in a foreign country (which expression includes the Republic of Ireland and self-governing Commonwealth countries), unless his conduct would have been an offence if he had been an alien acting in a foreign country. Generally, an alien may not commit treason unless at the time he is voluntarily on British territory, in which case he owes allegiance to the Crown.

However, a person who is not a British citizen (or a British Dependent Territories citizen or a British Overseas citizen), whether he is an alien or a Commonwealth citizen, and who is not caught by the above rule may commit treason if at the time of his conduct he owed allegiance to the Crown, either on the principle of *Joyce v DPP*,[1] or by virtue of the resolution of 1707, each of which is mentioned in the next paragraph.

Joyce, an American citizen, obtained a British passport by falsely representing that he was a British subject (which term has now been replaced by 'Commonwealth citizen'), and he caused this to be renewed shortly before the outbreak of the 1939–45 war, when he went to Germany where after hostilities had begun he broadcast for, and thus adhered to, the enemy. He was convicted of treason because he owed allegiance to the Crown on account of his continuing use of a British passport which enabled him to obtain in a foreign country the protection of the Crown. There never has been any doubt that an alien owes local allegiance, and is therefore subject to the law of treason, so long as he voluntarily resides in Her Majesty's Dominions. Moreover, a resolution of the judges in 1707[2] declared that an alien, who had once settled here under the protection of the Crown, could be dealt with as a traitor if he returned to his native country and adhered to the enemy leaving his family and effects behind him, for they would still enjoy the protection of the Crown. It is not clear how far this extends. Would it cover a case in which the alien left only effects behind him? In any event, the decision under discussion is a considerable extension of the principle underlying the resolution, for Joyce did not leave either family or effects in this country. The decision in *Joyce* is open to criticism, not least because Joyce (like any British passport holder) had no legal entitlement to the protection of the Crown while abroad and, indeed, had no intention of availing himself of such protection.

Apart from cases in wartime, there have been no prosecutions for treason in English courts in modern times, and only one prosecution for treason felony – which was not proceeded with.

1 [1946] AC 347, [1946] 1 All ER 186, HL.
2 Foster *Crown Law* 183.

Terrorism

17.6 The Prevention of Terrorism (Temporary Provisions) Act 1989, most of which has to be kept in annual force by subordinate legislation, contains a number of offences, as well as other provisions relating to matters such as arrest, detention and interrogation, necessitated by the situation in Northern Ireland.

Section 2 of the 1989 Act provides that if any person:

a) belongs or professes to belong to a proscribed organisation;
b) solicits or invites support for a proscribed organisation other than support with money or other property; or
c) arranges or assists in the arrangement or management of, or addresses, any meeting of three or more persons, knowing that the meeting is to support or to further the activities of such an organisation, or is to be addressed by a person belonging or professing to belong to it;

he commits an offence triable either way and punishable on conviction on indictment with up to ten years' imprisonment or a fine or both. At present the only organisations which are proscribed are the Irish Republican Army and the Irish National Liberation Army.

Section 2(3) of the 1989 Act provides that a person belonging to a proscribed organisation organisation is not guilty of an offence under s 1 by reason of belonging to the organisation if he proves that he became a member when it was not proscribed and has not since becoming a member taken part in any of its activities while it was proscribed.

By s 19 of the 1989 Act, a prosecution for an offence under s 1 can only be brought by or with the consent of the Attorney-General.

17.7 The 1989 Act provides a number of other offences including the following: wearing any item of dress or article, or carrying or displaying any article, so as to arouse reasonable apprehension of membership of, or support for, a proscribed organisation;[1] failing to comply with an order under the Act providing for exclusion from Great Britain; soliciting, inviting or receiving a contribution in money or other property towards acts of terrorism connected with Northern Irish affairs or the affairs of the United Kingdom or any part of it other than Northern Ireland; soliciting or inviting a contribution in money or other property to a proscribed organisation, or making or receiving any such a contribution to its resources; and failing without reasonable excuse to disclose information, knowing or believing that it may be of material assistance either in preventing an act of terrorism connected with Northern Irish affairs or in securing the arrest, prosecution or conviction of a person for an offence involving such an act of terrorism.[2]

A prosecution for one of these offences may only be brought by or with the consent of the Attorney-General.

1 Also see a similar offence under the Public Order Act 1936, s 2.
2 Prevention of Terrorism (Temporary Provisions) Act 1989, ss 3, 9, 10 and 18.

Sedition

17.8 Strictly, there is no offence of sedition in English law. Instead, there are two offences: seditious libel, which consists of a written publication of words with a seditious intention, and seditious words, i e an oral publication with seditious intention. Both are common law offences, triable only on indictment and punishable with a fine and imprisonment at the discretion of the court.

Under the provisions of Fox's Libel Act 1792, the judge has to determine whether the words of the accused are capable of bearing a seditious meaning, leaving the jury to decide, after a proper direction, whether the accused was guilty of seditious libel, and the same is no doubt true on a charge of seditious words.

Proof of sedition involves proof of an intention to promote feelings of ill-will and hostility between different classes of the Queen's subjects[1] and also proof of an intention to incite to violence or to public resistance or defiance for the purpose of disturbing constituted authority (i e the Queen or the institutions of government or some person or body discharging a public function of the State).[2]

It follows from this that reasonable criticism is perfectly lawful, and that it is entirely a question of degree to distinguish such reasonable criticism from seditious utterances.

1 *Burns* (1886) 16 Cox CC 355.
2 *Boucher v R* [1951] 2 DLR 369, approved in *Bow Street Magistrates' Court, ex p Choudhury* [1990] Crim LR 711, DC. These statements were made in relation to seditious libel but are doubtless equally applicable to seditious words. Cf the approach taken in relation to blasphemy: para 8.3.

Official secrets

ESPIONAGE AND OTHER ACTS PREJUDICIAL TO THE SAFETY OR INTERESTS OF
THE STATE

17.9   Section 1 of the Official Secrets Act 1911[1] provides that a person who for any purpose prejudicial to the safety or interests of the State:

  a) approaches, inspects, passes over, or is in the neighbourhood of, or enters any prohibited place; or
  b) makes any sketch, plan, model or note which is calculated to be or might be or is intended to be directly or indirectly useful to any enemy (including a potential enemy)[2]; or
  c) obtains, collects, records, or publishes or communicates to any other person any secret code word, or pass word, or any sketch, plan, model, article or note, or other document or information which is calculated to be or might be or is intended to be directly or indirectly useful to an enemy;

is guilty of an offence triable only on indictment and punishable by imprisonment for a maximum of 14 years.

1 As amended by the Official Secrets Act 1920.
2 *Parrott* (1913) 8 Cr App Rep 186, CCA.

17.10   A 'prohibited place' includes defence works, arsenals, dockyards and many other places occupied by or on behalf of Her Majesty and any other place which is declared to be a prohibited place.[1]

The above offences are not confined to espionage, but the accused must have acted with a purpose prejudicial to the safety or interests of the State, for example sabotage in a naval dockyard or copying the plans of RAF radar equipment. Whether or not the accused's purpose was prejudicial in this way is an objective question (to be determined according to the policies of the Government of the day), and the accused's opinion as to whether or not it is prejudicial is irrelevant.[2]

By s 5(6) of the Official Secrets Act 1989, it is an offence, triable either way and punishable with up to two years' imprisonment or a fine or both on conviction on indictment, to disclose without lawful authority any information, document or article which one knows, or has reasonable cause to believe, has come into one's possession as a result of a breach of the 1911 Act.

1 Official Secrets Act 1911, s 3.
2 *Chandler v DPP* [1964] AC 763, [1962] 3 All ER 142, HL.

17.11   No prosecution may be instituted under s 1 of the 1911 Act or s 5(6) of the 1989 Act except by or with the consent of the Attorney-General.[1]

The 1911 Act extends to acts committed in any part of the Queen's dominions, and to acts elsewhere by a British officer or any type of British citizen.[2]

1 Official Secrets Act 1911, s 8; Official Secrets Act 1989, s 9.
2 Official Secrets Act 1911, s 11.

UNAUTHORISED DISCLOSURE

17.12   The Official Secrets Act 1989 replaces s 2 of the 1911 Act, a notoriously wide and ambiguous provision, with a number of offences relating to the unauthorised disclosure of any information, document or other article relating to defined types of official matter. Although the Act commonly refers to the disclosure of 'any information, document or other article', these items will, for convenience, simply be referred to as 'information' in the rest of this chapter.

17.13   *Security and intelligence* By s 1(1) of the 1989 Act, a person who is or has been:

a) a member of the security and intelligence services; or
b) a person notified in writing by a Minister of the Crown that he is subject to s 1(1),

is guilty of an offence if without lawful authority he discloses any information relating to security or intelligence which is or has been in his possession by virtue of his position as a member of any of those services or in the course of his work while subject to the notification. The disclosure need not be a damaging one.

Section 1(3) provides a second offence dealing with certain cases falling outside s 1(1), whereby a person who is or has been a Crown servant or government contractor is guilty of an offence if without lawful authority he makes a *damaging* disclosure of any information relating to security or intelligence which is or has been in his possession by virtue of his position as such a servant or contractor. A disclosure is damaging if it causes damage to the work of the security and intelligence services or if it is information which is (or which is of a type) such that its unauthorised disclosure would be likely to cause such damage.[1]

By s 1(5), a person charged with an offence under s 1(1) or s 1(3) has a defence if he proves that at the time of the alleged offence he did not know, and had no reasonable cause to believe, that the information related to security or intelligence or, in the case of an offence under s 1(3), that the disclosure would be damaging.

1 Official Secrets Act 1989, s 1(4).

17.14 *Defence* Section 2(1) of the 1989 Act provides that a person who is or has been a Crown servant or government contractor is guilty of an offence if without lawful authority he makes a *damaging* disclosure of any information relation to defence[1] which is or has been in his possession by virtue of his position as such. For the purposes of this offence, a disclosure is damaging if:

a) it damages the capability of, or of any part of, the armed forces of the Crown to carry out their task or leads to loss of life or injury to members of those forces or serious damage to the equipment or installations of those forces; or

b) it otherwise endangers the interests of the United Kingdom abroad, seriously obstructs the promotion or protection by the United Kingdom of those interests or endangers the safety of British citizens abroad; or

c) it is of information which is such that its unauthorised disclosure would be likely to have one of those effects.

By s 2(3), it is a defence for a person charged with an offence under s 2(1) to prove that he did not know, and had no reasonable cause to believe, that the information related to defence or that its disclosure would be damaging.

1 'Defence' is defined by s 2(4). It includes the size and organisation of the forces of the Crown, their weapons and equipment and their policy, planning and plans.

17.15 *International relations*[1] Section 3(1)of the 1989 Act provides that a person who is or has been a Crown servant or government contractor is guilty of an offence if without lawful authority he makes a *damaging* disclosure of:

a) any information relating to international relations; or

b) any confidential information which was obtained from a foreign State or an international organisation, being information which is or has been in his possession as a Crown servant or government contractor.

A disclosure is damaging if:

a) it endangers the interests of the United Kingdom abroad, seriously obstructs the promotion or protection by the United Kingdom of those interests or endangers the safety of British citizens abroad; or

b) it is of information which is such that its unauthorised disclosure would be likely to have any of those effects.

By s 3(4), it is a defence for a person charged with an offence under s 3(1) to prove that he did not know, and had no reasonable cause to believe, that the information was of a type covered by s 3(1) or that its disclosure would be damaging.

1 'International relations' is defined by s 3(5). It means the relations between States, between international organisations or between one or more States and one or more international organisations, and includes any matter relating to a State other than the United Kingdom or to an international organisation which is capable of affecting the relations of the United Kingdom with another State or with an international organisation.

17.16 *Crime and special investigation powers* Section 4(1) of the 1989 Act provides that a person who is or has been a Crown servant or government contractor is guilty of an offence if without lawful authority he discloses any information to which s 4 applies and which is or has been in his possession by virtue of his position as a Crown servant or government contractor.

Section 4 applies to any information of a type described in s 4(2), i e information:

a) whose disclosure results in the commission of an offence, or facilitates an escape from legal custody, or impedes the prevention or detection of offences or the arrest or prosecution of suspected offenders; or
b) which is such that its unauthorised disclosure would be likely to have any of those effects.

By s 4(3), s 4 also applies to any information[1] obtained by lawful interception of the post or telecommunication or to any information[1] relating to or obtained by any action undertaken under the Security Services Act 1989.

Section 4(4) provides that a person charged with an offence under s 4 in relation to information falling within a) above has a defence if he proves that he did not know, and had no reason to believe, that the disclosure would have any of the effects mentioned there. A person charged under s 4 in respect of any other disclosure has, by s 4(5), a defence if he proves that he did not know, and had no reason to believe, that the information in question was information to which s 4 applies.

1 In this context 'information' does not include a document or other article.

17.17 *Information resulting from unauthorised disclosures or entrusted in confidence* Section 5(2) of the 1989 Act makes it an offence for someone who is not a Crown servant or government contractor to disclose without lawful authority any information protected under ss 1 to 4 of the Act where that information has come into his possession as a result of having been:

a) unauthorisedly disclosed by a Crown servant or government contract-or;[1] or
b) entrusted to him by such a servant or contractor in confidence; or
c) unauthorisedly disclosed by a person to whom it was entrusted as mentioned in b).

The prosecution has the burden of proving that the accused knew, or had reasonable cause to believe, that the information was protected against disclosure by the Act and that it has been entrusted to him in confidence or has come into his possession by an unauthorised disclosure.[2]

In the case of information protected against disclosure by ss 1 to 3, a person does not commit an offence under s 5 unless the disclosure by him is damaging and he makes it knowing or having reasonable cause to believe it is damaging.[3]

A person does not commit an offence in relation to information unauthorisedly disclosed to him unless that disclosure was by a British citizen or took place in the United Kingdom, the Channel Islands, the Isle of Man or a colony.[4]

1 As opposed to a former Crown servant or government contractor.
2 Contrast the other offences under the 1989 Act already mentioned.

3 Official Secrets Act 1989, s 5(3).
4 Ibid, s 5(4).

17.18 *Information entrusted in confidence to other states or international organisations* Section 6(2) of the 1989 Act provides that it is an offence to make a *damaging* disclosure of any security-related information communicated in confidence by the United Kingdom to another State or to an international organisation which has unauthorisedly been disclosed to the accused. The prosecution must prove that the accused knew, or had reasonable cause to believe, that the information is of a type covered by this offence, that it has unauthorisedly come into his possession and that its disclosure would be damaging. A person does not commit an offence under s 6(2) if the information is disclosed by him with lawful authority or has previously been made available to the public with the authority of the State or organisation concerned.[1] Nor does a person commit an offence under s 6(2) if the disclosure is an offence under any of the other provisions of the 1989 Act described above.[2]

1 Official Secrets Act 1989, s 6(3).
2 Ibid, s 6(2).

17.19 *Authorised disclosure* It will have been noted that the above offences under the 1989 Act are concerned with disclosures without lawful authority.

A disclosure by a Crown servant, or by a person (not being a Crown servant or government contractor) in whose case a notification under s 1(1) is in force, is made with lawful authority *only* if it is made in accordance with his official duty.[1]

A disclosure by a government contractor is made with lawful authority *only* if it is made in accordance with an official authorisation or for the purposes of the functions by virtue of which he is a government contractor and without contravening an official restriction.[2]

A disclosure by any other person is *only* made with lawful authority if it is made to a Crown servant for the purposes of his function as such or in accordance with an official instruction.[3]

It is a defence for a person charged with any of the above offences under the 1989 Act to prove that he believed that he had lawful authority to make the disclosure in question and had no reason to believe otherwise.[4]

These provisions also apply to an offence under s 5(6), described in para 17.10.

1 Official Secrets Act 1989, s 7(1).
2 Ibid, s 7(2).
3 Ibid, s 7(3).
4 Ibid, s 7(4).

17.20 *Prosecution, trial and punishment* No prosecution for one of the above offences under the 1989 Act may be instituted except by or with the consent of the Attorney-General.[1] There is one exception: a prosecution for an offence of disclosure in respect of information mentioned in s 4(2)[2] may be instituted by or with the consent of the Director of Public Prosecutions.

All the above offences under the 1989 Act are triable either way. They are punishable with a maximum of two years' imprisonment or a fine or both on conviction on indictment.[3]

1 Official Secrets Act 1989, s 9.

2 Para 17.16.
3 Official Secrets Act 1989, s 10.

17.21 The above offences under the 1989 Act extend to acts committed abroad by a British citizen or Crown servant, or done by any person in the United Kingdom, Channel Islands, the Isle of Man or any colony.[1] This is also the case in relation to an offence under s 5(6), described in para 17.10.

1 Official Secrets Act 1989, s 15.

18   Offences against public order

18.1   Many offences against public order are now provided by the Public Order Act 1986,[1] which replaced the four common law offences of riot, rout, affray and unlawful assembly with three statutory offences: riot, violent disorder and affray. The 1986 Act also makes extensive provision relating to threatening, abusive, insulting or disorderly conduct, to public processions and meetings, to incitement to racial hatred and to aggravated trespass. The last matter has already been dealt with; the rest will be dealt with in this chapter, which also deals with offences relating to obstructing the police, to firearms and to offensive weapons (all of which have a clear connection with public order).

Unless otherwise indicated, the offences in this chapter are re-stated in cls 193, 197 to 211 and 214 to 216 of the draft Criminal Code Bill[2] and the only changes proposed in the draft are those required for consistency with the style and terminology of the Code as a whole.

1 For a detailed discussion of the Act, see Card *Public Order – The New Law.*
2 Law Commission: A Criminal Code for England and Wales (1989) : Law Com No 177; see para 3.21 above.

Riot

18.2   Section 1(1) of the Public Order Act 1986 provides that, where 12 or more persons who are present together use or threaten unlawful violence for a common purpose and the conduct of them (taken together) is such as would cause a person of reasonable firmness present at the scene to fear for his personal safety, each of the persons using unlawful violence for the common purpose is guilty of riot. The offence is triable only on indictment, the maximum punishment being ten years' imprisonment.[1] A prosecution may not be instituted for riot except by or with the consent of the Director of Public Prosecutions.[2]

1 Public Order Act 1986, s 1(6).
2 Ibid, s 7(1).

ACTUS REUS

18.3   Basically, what is required is that an accused uses violence in the following circumstances:

    a) that 12 or more persons (including the accused) who are present together use or threaten unlawful violence for a common purpose; and

b) that the conduct of them (taken together) is such as would cause a person of reasonable firmness present at the scene to fear for his personal safety; and

c) that the accused's use of unlawful violence was for the common purpose.

Riot may be committed in private as well as in public places.[1] Thus, a riot can take place at factory premises, in a club, in a college, at a tickets-only dance at a dance hall or – even – in someone's home.

1 Public Order Act 1986, s 1(5).

18.4 *Use of unlawful violence* A person does not perpetrate the offence of riot merely by threatening unlawful violence; he must actually use violence in the prescribed circumstances. If 12 or more people simply threaten violence for a common purpose in a frightening way, but none of them uses violence, riot is not committed.

On the other hand, provided one of 12 or more people actually uses violence for the common purpose, the offence of riot is perpetrated by him (or by all those who so use violence if more than one does). Those who merely threaten violence for the common purpose can, however, be convicted as accomplices to riot if, with the appropriate mens rea,[1] they aid, abet, counsel or procure the use of violence by another, but, of course, that other person (the perpetrator of riot) must have used violence for the common purpose.

1 Para 23.16.

18.5 *Unlawful violence* 'Violence' is defined by s 8 of the 1986 Act as meaning 'any violent conduct'. 'Violent' is not defined by the Act. Since it is a word with an everyday meaning whether or not conduct is violent is a question of fact for the jury and the word should not be subjected to definition by the judge.[1] Section 8 goes on to say that the term is not limited to violent conduct towards a person or persons since it includes violent conduct towards property (for example, smashing shop windows or over-turning cars). Nor, says s 8, is the term limited to conduct causing or intended to cause personal injury or damage to property, since it 'includes any other violent conduct (for example, throwing at or towards a person a missile of a kind capable of causing injury which does not hit or falls short)'. Consequently, swinging a knife at someone or firing a gun in his direction is violence under the definition in s 8, even though he is not hit.

The requirement that the violence be unlawful excludes from riot violence which is justified by law (for example, under the common law rules relating to the use of reasonable force in self-defence or under the statutory provisions relating to the use of such force in the prevention of crime or the effecting of an arrest.)

1 *Brutus v Cozens* [1973] AC 854, [1972] 2 All ER 1297, HL. See also *Dino Services Ltd v Prudential Assurance Co Ltd* [1989] 1 All ER 422, CA.

18.6 *Twelve or more persons* While the 12 or more persons must be using or threatening unlawful violence for a purpose common to them, it is not necessary that they should each be criminally responsible. Consequently, it is irrelevant that some (or even all but one) are under the age of criminal responsibility or criminally insane or acting under duress. In addition, it is irrelevant that some (or even all but one) lack the mental state (viz an intent to use violence or awareness that conduct may be violent) required by s 6(1) of a perpetrator of riot.[1] The one or more who is not lacking in criminal responsibility or the relevant mental state can nevertheless be convicted of riot if he *uses* violence for the common purpose and those who lack criminal responsibility or the relevant mens rea can be counted in determining whether or not there are '12 or more persons using or threatening violence for a common purpose', although they cannot be convicted as accomplices. This is of obvious importance when not all the participants are apprehended or before the court, so that their age (in the case of mobs including children) or state of mind cannot be proved.

Since the violence used or threatened must be unlawful, riot will not be committed if some of 12 people present together using or threatening violence for a common purpose are acting in self-defence or under some other circumstance legally justifying[2] the violence.

The phrase 'present together' does not mean that the 12 or more people should form a cohesive group. Nor need they be present pursuant to an agreement to come together; consequently, they may be 'present together' by accident. The nature of the phrase is limited by the word 'together' and by the requirement of common purpose.[3] It is submitted that what is required is some element of the people being in contact with each other or being in reasonably close proximity with each other in a particular place

1 Public Order Act 1986, s 6(7).
2 Paras 6.20 and 22.2–22.14.
3 Para 18.8.

18.7 *Use or threaten unlawful violence* The same comments apply to 'use' and 'unlawful violence' as were made above.

In relation to threats, they may be by gesture alone (e g the brandishing of a weapon) or be by words alone or be by a combination of both (e g waving a car-jack accompanied by words such as 'I'll get you with this'). Although, in the case of words, they will normally be spoken, there seems no reason why it will not do if the threat is communicated by words on placards or banners or leaflets or badges if the other conditions for riot are satisfied.

Section 1(2) provides that it is immaterial whether or not the 12 or more use or threaten violence simultaneously. Equally, it is immaterial whether or not *any* of the others used or threatened violence at the time of the use of violence by the accused which is in issue. Provided that 12 or more persons who use or threaten violence are present *together* throughout and that the violence is used or threatened by 12 or more for a common purpose, the offence of riot can be committed. Thus, it covers the situation where violence is used or threatened in one part of a crowd, then dies away, only to break out in another part at a later time.

The width of 'use or threaten violence' means that hostility or a commotion is not required for a riot (although it may colour conduct which would not otherwise be threatening), nor is any noise or disturbance to the neighbourhood or even to neighbours. A good humoured and quiet crowd of 12 or more can, therefore, commit a riot if the various requirements are fulfilled.

18.8 *In pursuance of a common purpose* It must be proved that the use or threat of violence by the 12 or more present together was for a purpose common to them (or at least to 12 of them). The question is not whether the

12 or more were present for a common purpose but whether they threatened or used violence for a common purpose. The common purpose need not be violence and it need not be an unlawful purpose (although no doubt it will normally be so).

18.9 *Conduct such as would cause fear* The question is not whether the conduct of an individual accused would cause fear but whether the conduct of the '12 or more present together...' is such as would, *taken together*, cause *fear* (ie alarm or apprehension). As with the common law offence of riot, the conduct of the 12 or more must be such as *would* cause a person (ie a third party bystander) of reasonable firmness present at the scene to fear for his *personal* safety; not whether it actually caused fear to a person present at the scene. Presumably, the fear in question must be fear for *immediate* personal safety.

No person of reasonable firmness need actually be, or be likely to be, present at the scene[1]; in fact, no one else (besides the 12 or more) need be present or likely to be present at the scene. No doubt the case where there are no bystanders will be exceptional; where it occurs proof of the riot may be particularly difficult.

What constitutes 'a person of reasonable firmness' is not elucidated by the Act, but it will be a question for the jury to determine, as will the question of the reaction of a person of reasonable firmness.

1 Public Order Act 1986, s 1(4).

MENS REA

18.10 This is specified by s 6(1) of the 1986 Act: a person is guilty of riot only if he intends to use violence or is aware that his conduct may be violent. The word 'aware' imports a concept similar to subjective recklessness, except that it does not include any requirement that there be an unreasonable risk of violence resulting.

Since the mental element for riot includes a concept akin to subjective recklessness, the accused may be convicted of it if he was suffering from *self-induced* intoxication at the time of committing the prohibited conduct, even though because of his intoxication he did not intend to use violence and was not aware that his conduct might be violent.[1] However, lest the concept of 'awareness' should be construed by a court as meaning that the offence was one of specific intent (in which case evidence of self-induced intoxication would generally be relevant),[1] s 6(5) of the 1986 Act makes the matter clear by providing that, for the purposes of the offence of riot, a person whose awareness is impaired by intoxication[2] shall be taken to be aware of that of which he would be aware if not intoxicated, unless he proves either that his intoxication was not self-induced (as where his drink has been 'laced') or that it was caused solely by the taking or administration of a substance in the course of medical treatment.[3] If one or other of these things is proved, this does not mean that the accused is not guilty of riot, but merely that he is not guilty unless it is proved that *he* actually intended to use violence or was aware that his conduct might be violent.

1 *DPP v Majewski* [1977] AC 443, [1976] 2 All ER 142, HL; para 9.52.
2 'Intoxication' here means any intoxication, whether caused by drink, drugs or other means (eg glue), or by a combination of means: Public Order Act 1986, s 6(6).
3 This provision does not appear in the draft Criminal Code Bill on the ground that to place on the accused the burden of proof in this respect would be inconsistent with the general

principles relating to intoxication set out in the draft Code (which are described at para 9.80 above).

18.11   The Act does not expressly require that an accused should have any mental element as to the unlawfulness of the violence used by him or used or threatened by the others, nor as to the element that the violence used by him or used or threatened by others is such as would cause a person of reasonable firmness present at the scene to fear for his personal safety. Given the express provisions in s 6 relating to the mental element of riot, it may be unlikely that a court would be prepared to imply mental element requirements to deal with these points. If they are not implied, the result will be that a group of 12 or more, who intentionally use violence in the circumstances outlined in s 1 in the mistaken belief that they must do so to save another's life or property, will be guilty of riot unless their mistake is a reasonable one.[1] Likewise, if 12 or more use violence to demolish a fence for a bonfire to celebrate England's victory in the World Cup, being unaware that this would cause a person of reasonable firmness present at the scene to fear for his personal safety, they are guilty of riot, unless a mental element requirement in this respect is implied by the courts.

1 See, for example, *Chisam* (1963) 47 Cr App Rep 130, CCA.

Violent disorder

18.12   Section 2(1) of the Public Order Act 1986 provides that, where three or more people who are present together use or threaten unlawful violence and their conduct (taken together) is such as would cause a person of reasonable firmness present at the scene to fear for his personal safety, each of the persons using or threatening unlawful violence is guilty of violent disorder. The offence is triable either way, the maximum punishment on conviction on indictment being five years' imprisonment.[1]

1 Public Order Act 1986, s 2(5).

ACTUS REUS

18.13   Section 2(1) of the 1986 Act requires an individual accused to use or threaten unlawful violence in the following circumstances:

a) that three or more people (including the accused) together use or threaten unlawful violence (whether towards persons or towards property)[1];
b) that the conduct of them (taken together) is such as would cause a person (ie a third party bystander) of reasonable firmness present at the scene to fear for his personal safety. No person of reasonable firmness need actually be, or be likely to be, present at the scene.[2]

As in the case of riot and affray, violent disorder may be committed in private as well as in public places.[3]

The prohibited conduct for this offence is substantially the same as that of riot (and the comments made when discussing the identical elements in riot are equally applicable here) with the exceptions that:

a) an individual accused is guilty if he uses or *threatens* unlawful violence;
b) only three persons (including the accused) who are present together are required to use or threaten unlawful violence;

c) neither the accused nor the other participants are required to use or threaten unlawful violence for a common purpose.

The operation of the above can be illustrated as follows: If a racist march or static demonstration takes place in the centre of an immigrant community, accompanied by threats of immediate violence which would make a person of reasonable firmness fear for his personal safety, the offence is committed, but not if the taunts are merely (if that word may be used) of a racist nature highly offensive to the local inhabitants, although they may give rise to an offence under s 5 or s 18 of the 1986 Act.[4]

1 Public Order Act 1986, s 8.
2 Ibid, s 2(3).
3 Ibid, s 2(4).
4 Paras 18.33 and 18.46.

MENS REA

18.14 A person is guilty of violent disorder only if he intends to use or threaten violence or is aware that his conduct may be violent or threaten violence.[1] The same comments apply to this as apply to the mens rea for riot.[2]

As in the case of riot, a person whose awareness is impaired by intoxication is to be taken to be aware of that of which he would be aware if not intoxicated, unless he shows either that his intoxication was not self-induced or that it was caused solely by the taking or administration of a substance in the course of medical treatment.[3]

1 Public Order Act 1986, s 6(2).
2 Paras 18.10 and 18.11.
3 Public Order Act 1986, s 6(5). See para 18.10.

Affray

18.15 Section 3(1) of the Public Order Act 1986 provides that a person is guilty of affray if he uses or threatens unlawful violence towards another and his conduct is such as would cause a person of reasonable firmness present at the scene to fear for his personal safety. The offence is triable either way, the maximum punishment on conviction on indictment being three years' imprisonment.[1]

1 Public Order Act 1986, s 3(7).

ACTUS REUS

18.16 The prohibited conduct is that:

a) the accused must use or threaten violence towards another; and
b) his conduct must be such as would cause a person of reasonable firmness present at the scene to fear for his personal safety.

Like riot and violent disorder, affray may be committed in private as well as in public places.[1] One result is that, if a fight breaks out at a party in someone's home or at a private function at a discotheque, those who participate in it can be guilty of affray if the terms of the offence are satisfied. In fact any assault – even a domestic one – wherever committed accompanied by the use or threat of violence is an affray if it would cause a person of reasonable firmness present at the scene to fear for his personal safety. This prompts the question whether affray should be classified as a public order offence at all. *Most* of the elements of the actus reus are common to riot and violent disorder but a fundamental difference is that there is no requirement of the participation of others.

1 Public Order Act 1986, s 3(5).

18.17 *Use or threat of violence towards another* Unlike the position in riot and violent disorder, 'violence' here does not include violent conduct towards property.[1]

Another important difference between affray and riot and violent disorder is that a threat of violence cannot be made by the use of words alone, whether the words are uttered orally or displayed or distributed in writing.[2] Of course, an affray can be committed where a threat of violence is made by a combination of words and gestures (such as shouting out 'I'll get you for that', while brandishing a weapon or even shaking a fist) as well as by gestures alone.

An affray, like riot and violent disorder, can only be committed if the violence is unlawful.[3] Thus, a person who fights another in self-defence (or in effecting a lawful arrest) cannot be guilty of an affray, although his assailant (or the person being arrested) can be if his use of violence would make a person of reasonable firmness fear for his personal safety.

1 Public Order Act 1986, s 8.
2 Ibid, s 3(3).
3 Para 18.5.

18.18 *Conduct such as would cause a person of reasonable firmness present at the scene to fear for his personal safety* Presumably, as at common law, the reference to the hypothetical person 'present at the scene' is to an 'innocent member of the public within sight or earshot' of the violence.[1]

Where two or more people use or threaten the unlawful violence, it is the conduct of them taken together that must be considered for this purpose.[2]

As in the case of riot and violent disorder, no one besides the participants (ie no bystander) need be present, or be likely to be present, at the scene; it is expressly provided by s 3(4) that no person of reasonable firmness need actually be, or be likely to be, present at the scene.

1 *A-G's Reference (No 3 of 1983)* [1985] QB 242, [1985] 1 All ER 501, CA.
2 Public Order Act 1986, s 3(2).

MENS REA

18.19 A person is guilty of affray only if he intends to use or threaten violence or is aware that his violence may be violent or threaten violence.[1] The same comments apply to this as apply to the mens rea for riot.[2]

As in the case of riot, a person whose awareness is impaired by intoxication must be taken to be aware of what he would have been aware of if not intoxicated, unless he proves that his intoxication was not self-induced or that it was caused solely by the taking or administration of a substance in the course of medical treatment.[3]

1 Public Order Act 1986, s 6(2).

2 Paras 18.10 and 18.11.
3 Public Order Act 1986, s 6(5); see para 18.10.

Threatening, abusive, insulting or disorderly conduct

18.20 Of course, the offences discussed so far in this chapter could be said to fall within this heading, but we are concerned here with two less serious offences provided by ss 4 and 5 of the Public Order Act 1986. These replace a number of statutory offences, the most important of which was the offence of threatening, abusive or insulting words or behaviour under s 5 of the Public Order Act 1936. The offences under ss 4 and 5 of the 1986 Act, which are of great practical importance, are described by their respective marginal notes as: 'fear or provocation of violence' and 'harassment, alarm or distress'.

Fear or provocation of violence

18.21 Section 4(1) of the Public Order Act 1986 provides that a person is guilty of an offence if he:

  a) uses towards another person threatening, abusive or insulting words or behaviour, or
  b) distributes or displays to another person any writing, sign or other visible representation which is threatening, abusive or insulting,

with intent to cause that person to believe that immediate unlawful violence will be used against him or another by any person, or to provoke the immediate use of unlawful violence by that person or another, or whereby that person is likely to believe that such violence will be used or it is likely that such violence will be provoked.

An offence under s 4 is triable summarily only, the maximum punishment being six months' imprisonment or a fine not exceeding level 5 on the standard scale (£5,000) or both.[1]

1 Public Order Act 1986, s 4(4).

ACTUS REUS

18.22 Section 4 of the 1986 Act requires that the accused:

  a) uses towards another person threatening, abusive or insulting words or behaviour, or
  b) distributes or displays to another person any writing, sign or other visible representation which is threatening, abusive or insulting.

18.23 *Threatening, abusive or insulting* There can be no doubt that the courts will continue to approach these words in the same way as under s 5 of the Public Order Act 1936. As a result, the words 'threatening, abusive or insulting' do not bear an unusual legal meaning. Instead, the magistrates must decide as a question of fact whether the accused's conduct was threatening, abusive or insulting in the ordinary meaning of those terms, and this is to be judged according to the impact which the conduct would have on a reasonable member of the public.[1] Behaviour is not threatening, abusive or

405

insulting merely because it gives rise to a risk that immediate violence will be feared or provoked,[2] nor simply because it gives rise to anger, disgust or distress.[3] This is demonstrated by *Brutus v Cozens*,[4] where D's activities in disrupting a tennis match at Wimbledon (by running on to No 2 court and distributing leaflets) caused anger among spectators, some of whom tried to hit him as he was removed. The House of Lords did not disturb the magistrates' finding that, albeit annoying and irritating, the D's behaviour was not threatening, abusive or insulting.

If the conduct is threatening,[5] abusive or insulting, it does not matter whether or not anyone who witnessed it felt himself to be threatened, abused or insulted.[6]

1 *Brutus v Cozens* [1973] AC 854, [1972] 2 All ER 1297, HL. See also *Simcock v Rhodes* (1977) 66 Cr App Rep 192, CA.
2 *Brutus v Cozens* [1973] AC 854, [1972] 2 All ER 1297, HL.
3 Ibid; *Parkin v Norman* [1983] QB 92 at 100.
4 [1973] AC 854, [1972] 2 All ER 1297, HL.
5 This word is not limited to threats of violence, since an actual act of fighting can be 'threatening': *Oakwell* [1978] 1 All ER 1223, CA.
6 *Parkin v Norman* [1983] QB 92, [1982] 2 All ER 583, DC; *Marsh v Arscott* (1982) 75 Cr App Rep 211, DC.

18.24 *Distribution or display of any writing etc* The distribution or display of any writing, sign or other visible representation which is threatening, abusive or insulting covers handing out leaflets (distribution) or writing graffiti on a wall, holding up a banner or placard, or even wearing a badge (which are all examples of 'display'). However, as we shall see, there may be other reasons why an offence under s 4 of the 1986 Act (as opposed to s 5) may not be committed in the case of graffiti and badges.

18.25 *Towards another ... or to another* Section 4 requires that threatening, abusive or insulting words or behaviour must be *used towards another person* or that threatening etc written material be distributed or displayed *to another*. In relation to the use of threatening, abusive or insulting words or behaviour, 'used towards another' means that the words or behaviour in question must be used in the physical presence of and in the direction of another person directly;[1] if they are not one must fall back on the lesser offence under s 5 of the 1986 Act if it is applicable on the facts. In *Atkin v DPP*[2] Customs officers accompanied by a bailiff went to D's farm to recover outstanding VAT. The bailiff remained outside in a car while the officers entered the farmhouse. When they told D that the bailiff would have to enter to distrain his goods, he said that that if the bailiff got out of the car he was a 'dead un'. An officer went out and told the bailiff of the threat and that there was a gun in the farmhouse. The Divisional Court held that an offence under s 4 had not been committed because D had not used the threatening words towards the bailiff since they had not been used in the presence of and in the direction of the bailiff directly.

The insertion of 'to another' after 'distributes or displays' would equally seem to require that the written material be distributed or displayed directly to another, rather than simply being distributed (eg by leaflets being left lying around in a shopping centre) or displayed (eg by sticking a poster on a wall in the middle of the night). If this is correct, it means that writing graffiti on a wall or wearing a badge is unlikely, however threatening, abusive or insulting it may be, to result in a conviction for an offence under s 4; generally, the written material displayed will not be displayed *to* another in the sense outlined above. By contrast, handing out abusive leaflets to people in the street or carrying an insulting banner during a demonstration clearly involves distributing or displaying written material to another.

1 *Atkin v DPP* (1989) 89 Cr App Rep 199, DC.
2 (1989) 89 Cr App Rep 199, DC.

18.26 *Public or private place* With one exception, an offence under s 4 can be committed in private places,[1] such as factory premises, clubs or college premises, as well as in public places,[1] such as football grounds, dance halls, public car parks and shopping precincts. Thus, an offence can be committed by pickets who threaten working colleagues, whether the pickets are inside or outside factory premises, or by protesters who invade a military base.

The *exception* is that, in order to exclude domestic disputes, s 4(2) has the effect of providing that the use of words or behaviour inside a dwelling is only an offence under s 4 if 'the other person' (ie another person towards whom the words or behaviour are used or the writing etc is displayed) is not inside that dwelling or any other dwelling. Thus, to use threatening, abusive or insulting words towards someone else in the same house cannot be an offence under s 4, and the same is true if such words are shouted to someone in the house next door or displayed so as to be visible only to him. In *Atkin v DPP*, referred to in para 18.25, it could have been said that that D's threatening words had been used towards the Customs officers but, since they were in the farmhouse at the time, there was no offence under s 4 in respect of them. On the other hand, if threatening, abusive or insulting words are shouted in a house at a next-door neighbour who is in his back garden, an offence under s 4 will be committed, provided that the other elements of the offence are satisfied.

For the above purpose, 'dwelling' means any structure or part of a structure occupied as a person's home or as other living accommodation (whether the occupation is separate or shared with others) but does not include any part not so occupied, such as a garage, a shop with accommodation over it or the communal parts of a block of flats.[2] Thus, if threatening words are shouted from a flat to a shop below, an offence under s 4 may be committed, and so may it if the words are shouted from the shop to the flat upstairs. 'Structure' here includes a tent, caravan, vehicle, vessel or other temporary or moveable structure.[2]

1 Public Order Act 1986, s 4(2).
2 Ibid, s 8.

MENS REA

18.27 It is submitted that the accused must intend to use the words or behaviour towards another (or to distribute or display the writing etc to another). In addition, he must either intend the words, behaviour or writing etc to be threatening, abusive or insulting or be aware that they or it may be.[1] The result of this requirement is that a person, who uses words which on their face are innocuous but which are addressed to, or heard by, persons to whom (unknown to him) they are highly insulting, is not guilty of the present offence. Likewise, an accused is not guilty if he wrongly but positively believes that his audience is made of stern stuff and will not feel threatened, abused or insulted.

A person whose awareness is impaired by intoxication must be taken to be aware of that of which he would be aware if not intoxicated, unless he proves either that his intoxication was not self-induced or that it was caused solely by the taking or administration of a substance in the course of medical treatment.[2]

1 Public Order Act 1986, s 6(3).
2 Public Order Act 1986, s 6(5). See further para 18.10.

18.28 Section 4(1) of the 1986 Act also requires that the accused's use of the words or behaviour towards another (hereafter described as 'an addressee'), or the accused's distribution or display to another ('an addressee') of the writing etc, must be intended by the accused or be likely (whether or not the accused realises this) either:

a) to provoke the immediate use of unlawful violence *by an addressee or another*; or
b) to cause *an addressee*[1] to believe that immediate unlawful violence will be used against him or another.[2]

It will be noted, under para a), that it is not necessarily an addressee who must be intended or likely to be provoked to immediate violence. It is sufficient that someone else present, towards whom the threatening etc behaviour etc was not directed, was intended or likely to be provoked. Thus, if D shouts at a coloured person whom he knows cannot speak English, 'Paki bastard, go home', intending that this should provoke immediate violence on the part of a group of skinheads who are in the near vicinity, the present offence is committed. On the other hand, for the purposes of para b), fear of immediate violence intended or likely, the fear must be on the part of an addressee (although it need not be fear of violence against himself, nor of violence by the accused).

Under para b) the intended or likely fear instilled in the addressee must be of *immediate* unlawful violence. 'Immediate' does not mean 'instantaneous'; a relatively short period of time may elapse between the conduct which is threatening, abusive or insulting and the unlawful violence. 'Immediate' connotes proximity in time and in causation; that it is likely that violence will result within a relatively short period of time and without any other intervening occurrence.[3]

It is important to note that the offence under s 4, unlike those under ss 1–3, is not concerned with the reactions of a hypothetical person of reasonable firmness. It has been held that, since constables are under a common law duty to preserve the peace, they are unlikely to respond to threatening, abusive or insulting conduct by using violence.[4] Nevertheless, such conduct directed towards a constable will constitute an offence under s 4 if it is intended or likely to put him in fear of immediate unlawful violence or is intended to provoke him to such violence. If the conduct is so serious as to amount to a breach of the peace and make it likely that a constable to whom it is addressed will have to use violence in the exercise of his common law power to arrest for a breach of the peace, an offence under s 4 will not be committed on that account because the violence likely to be provoked will not be unlawful.

A speaker must take his audience as he finds it. If he uses insulting words at a meeting, he is guilty of the present offence if they are likely to provoke the immediate use of violence by the particular audience he is addressing, even though he does not intend to provoke this and even though his words would not be likely to cause a reasonable person so to react,[5] provided that he intended his words to be insulting or was aware that they might be.[6]

1 *Loade v DPP* [1990] 1 QB 1052, [1990] 1 All ER 36, DC.
2 See *Horseferry Road Stipendiary Magistrate, ex p Siadatan* [1991] 1 All ER 324, DC.
3 *Horseferry Road Stipendiary Magistrate, ex p Siadatan* [1991] 1 All ER 324, DC.
4 *Parkin v Norman* [1983] QB 92, [1982] 2 All ER 583, DC.
5 *Jordan v Burgoyne* [1963] 2 QB 744, [1963] 2 All ER 225, DC.
6 Para 18.27.

18.29 In the reference to an intention to cause, or the likelihood of causing, the apprehension of immediate unlawful violence or the provocation of it, 'violence' means any violent conduct.[1] It includes fear or provocation of violent conduct towards property as well as violent conduct towards persons, and it is not restricted to conduct causing or intended to cause injury or damage but includes any other violent conduct (such as throwing at or towards a person a missile of a kind capable of causing injury which does not hit or falls short).[1]

1 Public Order Act 1986, s 8.

GENERAL

18.30 Section 4 of the 1986 Act does not directly deal with the principle established in *Beatty v Gillbanks*,[1] a case on the old offence of unlawful assembly (which has been partly replaced by the present offence), viz that a person commits no wrong when his conduct causes others to react with unlawful violence, provided that that reaction is not a natural and probable consequence of his conduct. However, it would seem that the essence of that principle is encapsulated by the requirement of threatening, abusive or insulting conduct; if the provocation of immediate unlawful violence is intended or likely it can hardly be argued that it is not a natural and probable consequence.

1 (1882) 9 QBD 308, 51 LJMC 117.

18.31 Acts constituting an offence under s 4 will also sometimes constitute some other offence, such as the graver offences of violent disorder, of sedition (in the case of words) or of affray (in the case of a fight), but this overlap does not prevent an offence under s 4 being charged where summary trial and the limited penalties available are appropriate.

Harassment, alarm or distress

18.32 Section 4 of the Public Order Act 1986 does not deal with many minor acts of hooliganism or other anti-social behaviour which are prevalent, particularly in inner city areas. Such conduct is a particular cause for concern when it is directed at members of especially vulnerable groups, such as the elderly and members of ethnic minority communities, who may feel unable to act themselves to remove the nuisance or who may be deterred from participating in everyday activities or even from leaving their homes, and it is at problems such as these in particular that s 5 of the 1986 Act is aimed.

18.33 Section 5(1) of the 1986 Act provides that a person is guilty of an offence if he:

a) uses threatening, abusive or insulting words or behaviour or disorderly behaviour, or

b) displays any writing, sign or other visible representation which is threatening, abusive or insulting,

within the hearing or sight of a person likely to be caused harassment, alarm or distress thereby.

An offence under s 5 is triable summarily only.[1] The maximum punishment is a fine not exceeding level 3 on the standard scale (£1,000); punishment with imprisonment is not possible.[1]

1 Public Order Act 1986, s 5(6).

ACTUS REUS

18.34 *Threatening, abusive, insulting or disorderly* The central element of the offence is that a person must use threatening, abusive, insulting or disorderly words or behaviour, or display any writing, sign or other visible representation which is threatening, abusive or insulting.

The words 'threatening, abusive or insulting' have already been discussed in para 18.23, and what is said there is equally applicable here. No doubt a similar approach applies to 'disorderly', a term with which magistrates are already familiar via the offence of being drunk and disorderly. On this basis, it is a question of fact for the magistrates whether the accused's conduct was disorderly in the ordinary meaning of the term.

In relation to any threatening, abusive or insulting writing, sign or other visible representation, the offence is limited to displaying it and cannot (unlike an offence under s 4) also be committed by distribution. One result is that handing out threatening, abusive or insulting leaflets is not caught by s 5, unless the leaflets are so printed, and so held, that their contents can be said to be displayed in the sight of another. Another result is that a person who distributes threatening, abusive or insulting literature by simply delivering it through the letter boxes of intended recipients does not commit an offence under s 5, since he does not display (and nor does he use) the threatening words.[1] An important application of s 5 will be the display of graffiti or slogans likely to cause racial harassment.

1 *Chappell v DPP* (1988) Times, 16 November, DC

18.35 *Need for a victim* Another distinction between this offence and that under s 4 is that the words or behaviour need not be used *towards* another person (nor need writing etc be displayed *to* another). It follows that words or behaviour need not be directed towards another, nor need written material be deliberately brought to the attention of another. Consequently, wearing a threatening, abusive or insulting badge is far more capable of being an offence under s 5 than under s 4, and the same is true if a T-shirt is worn bearing a slogan or picture which is threatening, abusive or insulting.

While the accused's conduct need not be directed towards another (and written material need not be displayed by him to another), there must be a victim in the sense that what the accused does must be within the hearing or sight of a person likely to be caused harassment, alarm or distress thereby,[1] although no likelihood of violence being provoked or feared is required. Where threatening etc conduct is directed at a person who is not likely to be caused harassment, alarm or distress, the offence is nevertheless capable of commission if the conduct is in the hearing or sight of someone else who is likely to be caused harassment, alarm or distress thereby. In addition, it is not necessary, in a case where it is alleged that a person was likely to be caused alarm, that it was likely that that person would be caused alarm as to harm to himself. It is enough that he would be likely to be alarmed for the safety of an unconnected third party.[2]

1 Public Order Act 1986, s 5(1).
2 *Lodge v DPP* (1988) Times, 26 October, DC.

18.36 *Harassment, alarm or distress* 'Harassment, alarm or distress' is what must be likely to be caused to a person in whose hearing or sight the accused's conduct occurs, not merely 'annoyance' or 'disturbance'. 'Harassment, alarm or distress' are not defined by the Act. They are somewhat vague terms and 'distress' in particular is capable of wide interpretation by magistrates' courts; presumably, they involve a question of fact, like 'threatening' etc. It would not, for example, be surprising to find magistrates convicting a person who in an abusive way has misused the Union Flag as some public protest, on the basis that this was likely to distress a person in whose sight it occurred.[1]

Although the Divisional Court has held that, as a matter of law, a police officer can be caused harassment, alarm or distress by conduct to which s 5 applies, it has also held that an individual officer may be less likely to suffer such a reaction than other members of society.[2]

1 Smith [1985] Public Law at 537–38.
2 *DPP v Orum* [1988] 3 All ER 449, [1989] 1 WLR 88, DC.

18.37 Because s 4 requires that the violence intended or likely to be feared or provoked must be *immediate* violence, threats etc issued against persons or property some distance away fall outside the offence under that section (save where they are likely to provoke immediate violence on the part of those to whom the threats etc are directed or others then present). On the other hand, an offence under s 5 may well be committed in such circumstances. For example, if a gang in one part of a town were to utter in the presence of an innocent bystander threats directed at members of an ethnic group resident in another part, and those threats were likely to alarm or distress him, an offence under s 5 would be committed.

18.38 *Public or private places* An offence under s 5 may be committed in a public or a private place, except that no offence is committed where the words or behaviour are used, or the writing, sign or other visible representation is displayed, by a person inside a dwelling and the other person, within whose sight or hearing it occurs and who is likely to be harassed, alarmed or distressed thereby, is also inside that or another building.[1] Consequently, displaying an abusive poster in the front window of a house adjacent to the street is capable of being an offence under s 5, whereas if the poster was displayed in a place where it could only be seen by a person in the house or by a person in the first floor flat of the house next door a s 5 offence would not be committed. It will be remembered that there is a corresponding provision in relation to an offence under s 4, and the reader is referred to para 18.26 for an explanation of it.

1 Public Order Act 1986, s 5(2).

MENS REA

18.39 The accused must either intend his words or behaviour, or the writing etc, to be threatening, abusive or insulating or be aware that it may be threatening, abusive, or insulting, or (as the case may be) intend his conduct to be disorderly or be aware that it may be.[1] Consequently, a person who gives no thought to the nature of his conduct, or who honestly believes that there is no risk of it being threatening etc, does not commit this offence. The provisions in s 6(5) concerning intoxication, referred to in para 18.27, apply equally to an offence under s 5.

1 Public Order Act 1986, s 6(4).

DEFENCES

18.40 An accused need not be proved to have intended or been aware that his conduct should be within the hearing or sight of a person likely to be caused harassment, alarm or distress thereby. On the other hand, s 5(3)(a) provides that it is a defence for the accused to prove that he had no reason to believe that there was any person within hearing or sight who was likely to be caused harassment, alarm or distress. Section 5(3)(b) provides a further related defence for an accused who alleges that he was inside a dwelling at the material time. It states that it is a defence for him to prove that he was inside a dwelling and had no reason to believe that the words or behaviour used, or the writing, sign or other visible representation displayed, would be heard or seen by a person outside that or any other dwelling.

Section 5(3)(c) provides that it is a defence for an accused to prove that his conduct was reasonable. This is an exceptionally vague escape clause. It may not, however, be easy to prove the reasonableness of one's conduct. The mind boggles at the thought that abusive, insulting or disorderly conduct can ever be reasonable.

CONCLUSIONS

18.41 Section 5 of the 1986 Act has some useful potential. For example, it can operate as a curb on racial harassment or to protect other vulnerable sectors of the public against serious hooliganism. However, conduct of the type covered by s 5 is generally covered by s 4 if it is intended, or likely, to cause fear of immediate violence or to provoke immediate violence, and the question may be asked whether it is really necessary or desirable that there should be such a broad criminal offence. There is a danger that such an offence could pose a very real threat to the freedom of the individual. By going beyond violence or threatened violence to a person or property and extending to anti-social behaviour likely to cause harassment, alarm or distress, the offence may go too far in criminalising behaviour. There is a danger that it is likely to be applied by the police and magistrates to cases where 'mere' annoyance or disturbance (as opposed to harassment, alarm or distress) is likely.

Racial hatred

18.42 Part III (ss 17 to 29) of the Public Order Act 1986, which replaced and extended provisions dating back to 1965, provides six offences relating to racial hatred.

COMMON FEATURES

18.43 *Racial hatred* These offences have a number of common features. One is that they each require an intent that 'racial hatred' be stirred up or that 'racial hatred' be likely to be stirred up. Section 17 of the 1986 Act provides that racial hatred means hatred against a group of persons in Great Britain defined by reference to colour, race, nationality (including citizenship) or ethnic or national origins. Hereafter, such a group is described for convenience as a 'racial group'.

As can be seen, a group of persons defined by reference to religion is not a racial group and therefore falls outside the protection of Part III of the Act. However, an attack on a religion may be open to the interpretation that it is likely also to stir up hatred against a racial group identified with it, e g as Jews are associated with the Jewish religion.

Most of the terms used in the definition of 'racial group' have a fairly clear meaning, but the following does need to be made clear.

First, the group of persons must be defined by reference to colour, race, nationality or ethnic or national origins. Sikhs, for example, are not a group defined by reference to colour or race or nationality, but (as we shall see) they are a group defined by reference to their ethnic origins.

Second, the term 'ethnic' is construed relatively widely and, although a cultural or religious group is not per se defined by reference to its ethnic origins, 'ethnic' is used in a sense wider than the strictly racial or biological. This was held by the House of Lords in *Mandla v Dowell Lee*,[1] where Lord Fraser of Tullybelton, with whose speech the other Law Lords agreed, said this about the above definition:

> 'For a group to constitute an ethnic group in the sense of the Race Relations Act 1976, it must, in my opinion, regard itself, and be regarded by others, as a distinct community by virtue of certain characteristics. Some of these characteristics are essential; others are not essential but one or more of them will commonly be found and will help to distinguish the group from the surrounding community. The conditions which appear to me to be essential are these: (1) a long shared history, of which the group is conscious as distinguishing it from other groups, and the memory of which it keeps alive; (2) a cultural tradition of its own, including family and social customs and manners, often but not necessarily associated with religious observance. In addition, to these two essential characteristics the following characteristics are, in my opinion, relevant: (3) either a common geographical origin, or descent from a small number of common ancestors; (4) a common language, not necessarily peculiar to the group; (5) a common literature peculiar to the group; (6) a common religion different from that of neighbouring groups or from the general community surrounding it; (7) being a minority or being an oppressed or a dominant group within a larger community, for example a conquered people . . . and their conquerors might both be ethnic groups.
>
> 'A group defined by reference to enough of these characteristics would be capable of including converts, for example, persons who marry into the group, and of excluding apostates. Provided a person who joins the group feels himself or herself to be a member of it, and is accepted by other members, then he is . . . a member.'[2]

413

Pursuant to the above dictum, it is clear that Jews are a group defined by reference to their ethnic origins, and so are Sikhs (as the House held in *Mandla's* case) and Romany gypsies.[3] On the other hand, members of the 61-year-old Rastafarian movement are not,[4] and neither are tinkers or travellers.[3]

1 [1983] 2 AC 548, [1983] 1 All ER 1062, HL.
2 Ibid, at 562 and 1066–67 respectively.
3 *Commission for Racial Equality v Dutton* [1989] QB 783, [1989] 1 All ER 306, CA.
4 *Crown Suppliers (PSA) v Dawkins* (1991) Times, 29 April.

18.44 *Racial hatred intended or likely* None of the offences under Part III of the 1986 Act requires an intent to provoke a breach of the peace, or the likelihood of such a breach (let alone that public disorder resulted), nor that it be proved that racial hatred was actually stirred up. Instead, it is 'merely' required that the accused should intend to stir up racial *hatred* by his conduct, or that such *hatred* is likely, having regard to all the circumstances, to be stirred up thereby (whether or not the accused realised this would be likely).

It is not enough simply that racial hatred in the abstract is intended or likely; it must be against a racial group. Moreover, the hatred against a racial group which is intended, or likely, to be stirred up must be in relation to a group in Great Britain, which is not surprising in an Act dealing with public order. Nevertheless, the 'Great Britain requirement' does not impose a major limitation because, given the multiracial nature of our society, it is hard to envisage racialist abuse in this country concerning a racial group abroad (including Northern Ireland) which would not be likely to stir up hatred against the same racial group in Great Britain.

18.45 *Threatening, abusive or insulting* All offences under Part III of the 1986 Act require that the material, words or behaviour in question are 'threatening, abusive or insulting'. These words do not bear an unusual legal meaning. Instead, as with offences under ss 4 and 5, the magistrates or jury must decide as a question of fact whether the material etc was threatening, abusive or insulting in the ordinary meaning of those terms, and this is to be judged according to the impact which it would have on a reasonable member of the public.

USE OF WORDS OR BEHAVIOUR OR DISPLAY OF WRITTEN MATERIAL

18.46 Section 18(1) of the 1986 Act provides that a person who uses threatening, abusive or insulting words or behaviour, or displays any written material which is threatening, abusive or insulting, is guilty of an offence if:

a) he intends thereby to stir up racial hatred, or
b) having regard to all the circumstances, racial hatred is likely to be stirred up thereby.

Section 18 does not apply to words or behaviour used, or written material displayed, *solely* for the purpose of being included in a programme service.[1] In such a case, however, an offence may be committed under s 22 when the programme is transmitted.

As in the case of an offence under ss 4 or 5 of the 1986 Act, this offence may be committed in a public place (for example, a football ground) or a private place.[2] There is one limit in relation to private places. As in the case of an offence under ss 4 or 5,[3] an offence is not committed by the use of words or behaviour, or the display of written material, by a person inside a dwelling which are not heard or seen except by other persons in that or another dwelling. Thus, racialist taunts shouted from a house to people in the street or displayed on a poster on a window visible in the street are caught, but not racialist abuse shouted inside a house or flat (and only audible within it or another house or flat) or a racialist poster displayed in an inner room of a house.

It is a defence for the accused to prove that he was inside a dwelling and had no reason to believe that his words or behaviour, or the written material displayed, would be heard or seen by a person outside that or any other dwelling.[4]

1 Public Order Act 1986, s 18(6). A 'programme service' refers with limited exceptions to a television or sound broadcasting or cable service: Public Order Act 1986, s 29, as amended.
2 Ibid, s 18(2).
3 Paras 18.26 and 18.38.
4 Public Order Act 1986, s 18(4).

18.47 *Mens rea* We have already seen that the prosecution must prove that the accused intended to stir up racial hatred by his words, behaviour or display or that such hatred was likely to be stirred up thereby.

Section 18(5) resolves an uncertainty which existed before the Act, viz whether it had to be proved that the speaker etc had mens rea as to the fact that his words or gestures were threatening, abusive or insulting or whether the offence was one of strict liability in this respect (in which case his unawareness of the effect of his speech, however reasonable, would not excuse him). It provides that a person who is not shown to have intended to stir up racial hatred is not guilty of an offence under s 18 if he did not intend his words or behaviour or the written material to be, and was not aware that it might be, threatening, abusive or insulting. Unlike comparable provisions in other offences in Part III of the 1986 Act, the accused does not have the burden of proving this lack of intent or awareness.

Racial abuse or harassment not intended or likely to stir up racial hatred may, nevertheless, result in liability for an offence under s 5 of the 1986 Act.

PUBLISHING OR DISTRIBUTING

18.48 Section 19(1) of the Public Order Act 1986 provides that a person who publishes or distributes written material which is threatening, abusive or insulting is guilty of an offence if:

a) he intends thereby to stir up racial hatred, or
b) having regard to all the circumstances, racial hatred is likely to be stirred up thereby.

There must be a publication or distribution to the public or to a section of the public.[1] 'The public' and 'section of the public' are not defined by the Act. In the only reported case which referred to the point under the previous legislation, *Britton*,[2] the Court of Appeal held that a distribution of racialist pamphlets to members of a family living together in one house was not a distribution to 'the public at large'. There appears to be no minimum number of persons to whom publication or distribution must be made in order for it to be 'the public' but to publish or distribute to one person alone cannot be to do so to 'the public', nor (it is submitted) to two or three.

Ultimately, the question must be solved by common sense, the question being whether the publication or distribution has been on a scale and on a basis such as to be describable as being to 'the public'.

A publication or distribution only to members of a club or association is not a distribution to 'the public' but to a 'section of the public', as will be seen. Again, *Britton* is the only reported case to have dealt with the phrase. The Court of Appeal held that the family was not a 'section of the public'. The Court's interpretation has been criticised on the ground that, in the light of the object of the offence, viz to punish those who attempt to stir up racial hatred, it is arguable that the section of the public to whom publication is in fact made is not a matter of concern. Nevertheless, it is submitted that the decision was sensible; a family group would not normally be described as a section of the public (and doubtless the same is true of other small, domestic groups). In *Britton*, Lord Parker CJ said, obiter, that 'section of the public' refers to some identifiable group, 'in other words members of a club or association'. It is submitted that the term is not limited to this but covers any identifiable group of people whose connection is *not* a private relationship (i e not a familial or domestic one), provided that that group is identifiable by some common interest or characteristic. If this is so, the employees of X Ltd are a section of the public, as are the inhabitants of houses in Y street, Members of Parliament, teachers, a football crowd and persons of West Indian descent.

1 Public Order Act 1986, s 19(3).
2 [1967] 2 QB 51, [1967] 1 All ER 486, CA.

18.49 *Mens rea* Although the prosecution must prove that the accused intended to stir up racial hatred by the publication or distribution or that such hatred was likely to be stirred up thereby, it does not have to prove any mens rea on the part of the accused in relation to the content of the written matter which he has published or distributed, although he will almost inevitably have had such mens rea if he is proved to have intended to stir up racial hatred. However, under s 19(2) of the 1986 Act, it is a defence for an accused who is not proved to have intended to stir up racial hatred to prove that he was not aware of the content of the matter and neither suspected nor had reason to suspect it of being threatening, abusive or insulting. The defence under s 19(2) is of obvious importance to innocent publishers or distributors, like newsagents.

POSSESSION OF RACIALLY INFLAMMATORY MATERIAL

18.50 Section 23(1) of the Public Order Act 1986, as amended, provides that a person who has in his possession written material which is threatening, abusive or insulting, with a view to its being displayed, published, distributed, or included in a 'programme service',[1] whether or not by himself, is guilty of an offence if:

a) he intends racial hatred to be stirred up thereby, or
b) having regard to all the circumstances racial hatred is likely to be stirred up thereby.

Section 23(1) also provides that a person who has in his possession a recording of visual images or sounds (e g a film or sound or video-tape) which are threatening, abusive or insulting with a view to its being distributed, shown, played, or included in a programme service, whether by himself or another, is guilty of an offence if:

a) he intends racial hatred to be stirred up thereby, or

b) having regard to all the circumstances, racial hatred is likely to be stirred up thereby.

1 'Programme service' refers with limited exceptions to a television or sound broadcasting or cable service: Public Order Act 1986, s 29, as amended.

18.51 *Mens rea* As with s 19 of the 1986 Act, the prosecution does not have to prove any mens rea on the part of a person charged with possession contrary to s 23 in relation to the content of the written matter possessed by him. Likewise, it need not necessarily be proved that the accused intended racial hatred to be stirred up by the publication or distribution, since it is enough that, if the matter were published or distributed, racial hatred would be likely (having regard to all the circumstances) to be stirred up as a result of the publication or distribution. However, under s 23(3), it is a defence for an accused who is not proved to have intended to stir up racial hatred to prove that he was not aware of the content of the written material or recording, and neither suspected nor had reason to suspect it of being threatening, abusive or insulting. This is of obvious importance to 'innocent' possessors of racialist material, such as warehousemen.

The person in possession of the material must have been in possession with a view to its publication or distribution. If there is a dispute about this, the magistrates or jury will have to draw such inferences as seem reasonable from the quantity and nature of the material possessed.

OTHER OFFENCES

18.52 Sections 20, 21 and 22 of the Public Order Act 1986 respectively provide offences relating to public plays, visual or sound recordings, and programme services, which are intended or likely to stir up racial hatred. A detailed explanation of these offences is outside the scope of this book.

GENERAL

18.53 *Offences by corporations* Under s 28 of the Public Order Act 1986, the directors, secretaries and similar officers of bodies corporate are liable for offences under Part III of the Act which have been committed by the body corporate with their consent or connivance.[1]

1 See para 9.90 for an explanation of this type of provision.

18.54 *Parliamentary and court reports* None of the above offences applies to a *fair* and *accurate* report of:

a) proceedings in Parliament;[1] or

b) proceedings publicly heard before a court or tribunal exercising judicial authority.[2]

However, in the case of a report of the proceedings of a court or tribunal, the exemption *only* applies if the report is published *contemporaneously* with those proceedings or, if it is not reasonably practicable or would be unlawful to publish a report of them contemporaneously (because of the law of contempt of court), is published *as soon as publication is reasonably practicable and lawful.*[2] This limitation is designed to prevent racists from avoiding criminal liability by subsequently simply publishing, distributing or the like, a verbatim report (including the offending material) of a criminal trial for an offence under Part III which had been proved to have been committed. If racial hatred is intended or likely to be stirred up thereby an offence is committed.

1 Public Order Act 1986, s 26(1).
2 Ibid, s 26(2).

18.55 *Prosecution, trial and punishment* No proscution for an offence under Part III of the Public Order Act 1986 may be instituted except by or with the consent of the Attorney-General.[1]

The offences under Part III are triable either way and punishable on conviction on indictment with up to two years' imprisonment.[2] In comparison, the offences involving threatening, abusive or insulting words or behaviour under ss 4 and 5 of the Act, which have elements in common with a number of offences under Part III, are only triable summarily and carry a much lower maximum punishment. This provides a clear indication of the gravity attached to offences of racial hatred by Parliament.

1 Public Order Act 1986, s 27(1).
2 Ibid, s 27(3).

Public processions and assemblies

18.56 Part II of the Public Order Act 1986 (ss 11–16) provides various controls over the holding and conduct of public processions and public assemblies, which are reinforced by a number of offences set out below.

There are no corresponding provisions in the draft Criminal Code Bill. Consequently, if that Bill is ever enacted the current provisions would continue to exist outside it.

PUBLIC PROCESSIONS

18.57 For the purposes of the 1986 Act, a 'public procession' is defined by s 16 as a procession in a 'public place' (which is defined as meaning any highway or any place to which at the material time the public or any section of the public has access, on payment or otherwise, as of right or by virtue of express or implied permission). Obvious examples of a public place are all roads, footpaths, subways and bridges (including toll bridges or tunnels), other public rights of way and municipal parks.

ADVANCE NOTICE

18.58 Section 11(1) of the Public Order Act 1986 requires written notice of a proposal to hold a public procession to be given to the police where the procession is intended:

a) to demonstrate support for or opposition to the views or action of any person or body of persons;

b) to publicise a cause or campaign (such as a 'fun run' in aid of Cancer Relief); or

c) to mark or commemorate an event.

It follows that organisers of processions which are of no interest to the police, such as crocodiles of school children, tourists following a guide, or a party of ramblers, are not required to give advance notice.

In addition, s 11(1) provides that the obligation to give advance notice does not apply where it is not reasonably practicable to give *any* advance notice of the procession. It is hard to visualise cases where this will be so. Lastly, s 11(2) provides that advance notice does not have to be given of a funeral procession organised by a funeral director in the normal course of his business, nor of a procession which is *commonly* or *customarily* held in the police area in which it is intended to be held.

A notice may be delivered by post[1] but only if the recorded delivery service is used; otherwise it must be delivered by hand.[1] A posted notice must be actually delivered at least six clear days before the date when the procession is intended to be held.[2] So must a notice delivered by hand, except that, if that is not reasonably practicable, a notice delivered by hand will be validly delivered if delivered as soon as delivery is reasonably practicable.[3] All this means that, normally, if it is proposed to hold a march at 3 pm on 8 August, notice must be delivered before midnight on 1 August.

1 Public Order Act 1986, s 11(5) and (6).
2 Ibid, s 11(5).
3 Ibid, s 11(6).

18.59 *Offences* Where a public procession is *actually* held, *each* of the persons organising it is guilty of a summary offence if the requirements of s 11 as to notice have not been satisfied; no offence is committed if the procession is never held.

Likewise, *each* of the organisers is guilty of a summary offence if the date when it is held, the time when it starts, or its route, differs from the date, time or route specified in the notice.[1] The deviation is not required to be substantial.

A person guilty of one of these offences is liable to a fine not exceeding level 3 on the standard scale (£1,000).[2]

If the prosecution proves the prohibited conduct in one or other of the two above ways beyond reasonable doubt, the accused must be convicted, since no mental element need be proved by the prosecution, unless the accused can prove that he has the defence provided by s 11(8) of the 1986 Act or the defence provided by s 11(9). It is by no means obvious why a mental element does not have to be proved by the prosecution, particularly since such a requirement is made in relation to similar offences under ss 12 to 14.

Section 11(8) provides that it is a defence for the accused to prove that he did not know of, and neither suspected nor had reason to suspect, the failure to satisfy the requirements or (as the case may be) the difference of date, time or route.

The defence under s 11(9) is limited to the second variant of the offence. The subsection provides that, to the extent that an alleged offence turns on a difference of date, time or route, it is a defence for the accused to prove that the difference arose from something beyond his control (e g because a road on the notified route has been closed to repair a burst water main) or from something done with the agreement of a police officer or by his direction.

1 Public Order Act 1986, s 11(7) and (10).
2 Ibid, s 11(10).

IMPOSING CONDITIONS

18.60 Conditions may be imposed under s 12 of the Public Order Act 1986 on any public procession (including one exempt from the need for advance notice) not only beforehand but also when the procession is assembling or, even, during it.

The power to impose conditions on public processions is conferred on a person called 'the senior police officer'. By s 12(2) of the 1986 Act, this term means:

    a) in relation to a procession *being held*, or to a procession *intended to be held in a case where persons are assembling with a view to taking part in it*, the most senior in rank of the police officers present at the scene; and

    b) in relation to a procession intended to be held in a case where a) does not apply, the chief constable (or, in the case of the City of London or Metropolitan Police, the respective Commissioner of Police).

The senior police officer only has power to impose conditions if, having regard to the time or place at which and the circumstances in which any public procession is being held or is intended to be held and to its route or proposed route, he *reasonably believes* that:

    a) it may result in serious public disorder, serious damage to property or serious disruption to the life of the community; it is not necessary that it should be apprehended that the disorder, damage or disruption will be caused by those in the procession, with the result that it is enough that there is a risk of disorder etc being caused by opponents of those in the procession; or

    b) the purpose, whether express or not, of the persons organising it is the intimidation of others with a view to compelling them not to do an act they have a right to do, or to do an act they have a right not to do.[1]

In a case falling within these provisions, the senior police officer may give directions imposing on those organising or taking part in the procession any conditions which appear to him necessary to prevent such disorder, damage, disruption or intimidation, including conditions prescribing the route of the procession or prohibiting it from entering any public place specified in the direction.[1]

Section 12 does not limit the types of condition which may be imposed. Other examples are the number of those in the procession, its starting time and duration, and the prohibition of the wearing of uniforms or masks or of the carrying of flags or banners.

Where a direction is given by a chief police officer in advance of the procession or its assembly, it must be given in writing.[2] On the other hand, a direction given during the procession or when it is assembling, need not be given in writing; clearly written notice will normally be impracticable in such a case.

1 Public Order Act 1986, s 12(1).
2 Ibid, s 12(3).

18.61 *Offences* A person who organises a public procession and knowingly[1] fails to comply with a condition imposed under s 12 commits a summary offence, whose maximum punishment is three months' imprisonment or a fine not exceeding level 4 on the standard scale (£2,500) or both.[2] It must be emphasised that an 'organiser' is not guilty of the present offence merely because the procession does not comply with a condition; he himself must have failed to comply. Thus, an organiser does not commit an offence where the breach of condition is caused by a bunch of anarchists who had not been officially invited to join in the procession or who were otherwise beyond any effective control by the organisers. An organiser who fails to comply has a defence if he proves that the failure arose from circumstances beyond his control.[3]

A person who takes part in a public procession and knowingly fails to comply with a condition imposed under s 12 is guilty of a summary offence punishable with a fine not exceeding level 3 on the standard scale (£1,000), except that it is a defence to prove that the failure arose from circumstances beyond his control.[4] It is questionable whether this defence will be proved if it is merely proved that there has been a breakdown of organisation or communication. On the other hand, the defence would be proved if a marcher proved that he was being inescapably borne along by the pressure of other marchers when the condition was broken.

A person who incites another to commit the 'participants' offence' is also guilty of a summary offence but is liable to a greater penalty (viz three months' imprisonment or a fine not exceeding level 4 on the standard scale or both).[5] Thus, if A, who knows that a march is going to involve a breach of a condition, persuades B to march with him and B does so, knowing of the breach, A commits a more serious offence than B.

1 Para 6.59.
2 Public Order Act 1986, s 12(4) and (8).
3 Ibid, s 12(4).
4 Ibid, s 12(5) and (9).
5 Ibid, s 12(6) and (10).

PROHIBITION OF PROCESSIONS

18.62 Section 13 of the Public Order Act 1986 provides for the prohibition of public processions. There are separate procedures for the provinces and for the City of London Police area and Metropolitan Police district. However, both procedures depend on the relevant chief officer of police reasonably believing that, because of the particular circumstances existing in any district (in the provinces) or in his police area (in London) or part of it, the power under s 12 to impose conditions will be insufficient to prevent the holding of public processions in that district/area or part resulting in serious public disorder.[1]

Where a chief constable has such a reasonable belief,[1] he must apply for an order prohibiting the holding of all public processions (or of any class of them) in the district or part concerned.[2] The chief constable is not required to give the grounds for his belief. His application must specify the period (up to three months) for which a ban is sought and, if a prohibition limited to a class of processions is sought (as opposed to all of them), it must specify that class.

The application for an order must be made to the council of the district (ie the district or borough council). On receiving such an application, a council may with the consent of the Home Secretary make an order either in the terms of the application or with such modifications as may be approved by the Home Secretary.[3]

Under s 13(4), essentially the same provisions apply where the Commissioner of the City of London Police or the Commissioner of the Metropolitan Police has the reasonable belief referred to above. The important difference is that a Commissioner himself makes a banning order (subject to the consent of the Home Secretary); he does not have to apply to a council for it to make an order.

1 Public Order Act 1986, s 13(1) and (3).
2 Ibid, s 13(1).
3 Ibid, s 13(2).

18.63 *Offences* A person who organises a public procession, knowing[1] that its holding is prohibited by virtue of an order under s 13, is guilty of a summary offence, for which the maximum penalty is three months' imprisonment or a fine not exceeding level 4 on the standard scale or both.[2]

A person who takes part in a public procession, knowing that its holding is prohibited by virtue of an order under s 13, is also guilty of a summary offence,[3] as is someone who incites another to commit this offence.[4] A person who commits the former offence is liable to a fine not exceeding level 3 on the standard scale.[5] A person convicted of the latter (incitement) offence is punishable in the same way as an organiser.[6]

Unlike the corresponding offences under s 12, the offences committed by an organiser or participant are not provided with a defence of 'beyond his control'.

1 Para 6.59.
2 Public Order Act 1986, s 13(7) and (11).
3 Ibid, s 13(8).
4 Ibid, s 13(9).
5 Ibid, s 13(12).
6 Ibid, s 13(13).

PUBLIC ASSEMBLIES

18.64 Section 14 of the Public Order Act 1986 provides for conditions to be imposed on a 'public assembly', a term which is defined as an assembly of 20 or more people in a 'public place' which is wholly or partly in the open air.[1] Unlike a public procession, advance notice does not have to be given of a public assembly nor can it be banned.

Conditions may only be imposed if the 'senior police officer', having regard to the time and place at which and the circumstances in which a public assembly is being held or is intended to be held, reasonably believes that one of the specified grounds are satisfied. These grounds, which are the same as apply to the imposition of conditions on a public procession, are that:

a) the assembly may result in serious public disorder, serious damage to property or serious disruption to the life of the community; or
b) the purpose of the persons organising it is the intimidation of others with a view to compelling them not to do an act they have a right to do, or to do an act they have a right not to do.[2]

'Senior police officer' bears a similar meaning as in the case of the imposition of conditions on public processions. Where an assembly is being held, the term means the most senior in rank of the police officers present at the scene; where an assembly is intended to be held it means the chief constable or (in London) the relevant Commissioner.[3] Unlike the corresponding provision in s 12, this definition does not specifically deal with where the participants are assembling; its wording suggests that conditions may only be imposed by the chief constable or Commissioner since the assembly is still at the 'intended' as opposed to 'being held' stage.

Conditions may be imposed by the senior police officer on the persons organising or taking part in the assembly. They may be imposed either in writing or orally, unless they are imposed in relation to an assembly intended to be held (in which case the chief constable or Commissioner must give them in writing.)[4]

Like conditions relating to public processions, the conditions must appear to the senior police officer necessary to prevent disorder, damage, disruption or intimidation of the type described above. However, the provision is more restrictive since, unlike s 12, it limits conditions to those which prescribe the place at which the assembly may be (or continue to be) held, its maximum duration, or the maximum number of persons who may constitute it.[5]

1 Public Order Act 1986, s 16.
2 Ibid, s 14(1).
3 Ibid, s 14(2).
4 Ibid, s 14(3).
5 Ibid, s 14(1).

18.65 *Offences* Section 14(4) to (6) provides offences dealing with those who organise or participate in a public assembly, knowing[1] of non-compliance with a condition, or who incite another so to participate, which correspond to those relating to public processions, and the same comments apply as in relation to them. Likewise, an organiser or participant has a defence if he proves that the non-compliance was due to circumstances beyond his control. By s 14(8) to (10), the maximum punishment is the same as for the corresponding offences relating to processions.[2]

1 Para 6.59.
2 Para 18.61.

DELEGATION OF CHIEF OFFICER'S POWERS

18.66 The size and complexity of modern police forces, particularly the Metropolitan Police, means that it will not always be possible or practicable for a chief officer of police to exercise his exclusive functions in relation to the imposition of conditions in advance and the prohibition of public processions. This is recognised by s 15 of the Public Order Act 1986, which provides:

a) that a chief constable may delegate any of his functions under ss 12 to 14 to a deputy or assistant chief constable; and
b) that, in the City of London and the Metropolitan Police district, the respective Commissioners may delegate any of the functions to an Assistant Commissioner of Police.

DISORDERLY CONDUCT AT MEETINGS

18.67 Disorderly conduct at a meeting, public or private, may result in criminal liability. For particularly grave cases of disorder, there are the serious offences against public order, such as riot; in less grave cases charges of offences, such as the offences under ss 4 or 5 of the Public Order Act 1986 or the offence of wilfully obstructing a constable in the execution of his duty (dealt with below), would suffice. In addition, special provision is made for disorderly behaviour at *public* meetings by the Public Meeting Act 1908. Section 1(1) of that Act provides that any person who at a lawful public meeting acts in a disorderly manner for the purpose of preventing the transaction of the business for which the meeting was called together is guilty of a summary offence. Merely asking questions or making points which the chairman of the meeting does not like is not enough. On the other hand, violence or a threat of violence is not required, so that boisterous heckling may suffice. The maximum punishment is six months' imprisonment or a fine not exceeding level 5 on the standard scale (£5,000) or both. It is also an offence under s 1(2) of the 1908 Act to incite others to act in the way described.[1]

The term 'public meeting' is not defined but appears to be used in the sense that the meeting is open to the public or a section of the public and not restricted to members of a particular organisation or club. Meetings which are open to the public but held on private premises are therefore public meetings. The Act only applies to lawful meetings, but the fact that a meeting is held on a highway does not render it unlawful merely because it is so held.[2] However, the circumstances in which the meeting is held may make participants liable for the offence of obstructing the highway, in which case the meeting will be unlawful.

1 The offence under s 1(2) is not reproduced in the draft Criminal Code Bill because its effect is preserved by cl 47 of the Bill (the general offence of incitement): Law Commission: A Criminal Code for England and Wales (1989): Law Com No 177, para 18.9.
2 *Burden v Rigler* [1911] 1 KB 337, DC.

Obstructing the police[1]

18.68 Under s 51(3) of the Police Act 1964, a person who resists or wilfully obstructs a constable in the execution of his duty, or a person assisting a constable in the execution of his duty, is guilty of an offence which is triable only summarily and punishable by a maximum of one month's imprisonment or a fine not exceeding level 3 on the standard scale (£1,000) or both. A 'constable' is anyone holding the office of constable, whatever his rank.

These offences are not reproduced in the draft Criminal Code Bill. Consequently, if the Bill is ever enacted they will continue to exist outside it.

1 See Lidstone 'A Policeman's Duty not to Take Liberties' [1975] Crim LR 617; Ross 'Two Cases on Obstructing a Constable' [1977] Crim LR 187; Gibbons 'The Offence of Obstruction' [1983] Crim LR 21, and Lidstone 'The Offence of Obstruction' ibid, 29.

IN THE EXECUTION OF HIS DUTY

18.69 We have already seen that it is an aggravated assault to assault a constable in the execution of his duty[1] and what is now said about 'in the execution of his duty' is equally applicable to that offence.

To be acting in the execution of his duty a constable need not be doing something which he is compelled by law to do,[2] but his conduct must fall within the general scope of a duty imposed on him by law (such as his duties to protect life and property, to keep the peace, to prevent and investigate crime and to prevent obstruction of the highway) and he must not be acting unlawfully at the time.[3]

The question of lawful action can give rise to fine distinctions. It has been held that a constable, like any other member of the public, has an implied licence to enter the front gate of private premises and knock on the door if on lawful business,[4] and the same is true of the 'public' part of business premises when it is open for business. A constable entering premises in this way for the purpose of inquiring about an offence is acting in the execution of his duty until he has been told to leave and a reasonable time has been allowed for him to go:[4] if a constable remains on the premises after an implied licence has been revoked his presence is unlawful and he is not acting in the execution of his duty.[5]

It frequently happens that a constable performing one of his duties does something to a person or his property, such as detaining him or entering his house without consent to search it, which would be unlawful unless authorised by a positive legal power. In such a case, the question arises whether he has such a power (either at common law or under a statute) and, if he has, whether he has exercised it correctly and without exceeding it; if his conduct does not fall within the proper execution of a power he is not acting in the execution of his duty.[6] For example, as a constable has no power physically to detain a person for questioning without making an arrest, he will be acting unlawfully and therefore not in the execution of his duty if he does so.[7] By way of exception, if he merely taps a person on the shoulder to stop him in order to speak to him his conduct does not take him outside the execution of his duty because his act is not unlawful.[8] This exception is very narrow indeed since only the most trivial touching falls within it; stopping a person, in order to speak to him, by placing a hand on his shoulder has been held not to fall within it.[9] Turning to cases where a constable does have a relevant power but fails to exercise it correctly, an arrest without warrant in circumstances where the constable has such a power is nevertheless unlawful, generally speaking, if he does not inform the person of his reasons,[10] and the same is true if he exercises a power of search without giving his reasons.[11]

On many occasions an offence under s 51 is committed against a constable who is exercising a power of arrest or search. On others he may be exercising his power, where he has reasonable grounds to apprehend a breach of the peace:

a) to forbid a meeting,[12] or
b) to remain on premises on which he has been a trespasser,[13] or
c) to enter premises (whether public or private) and remain there despite a request to leave,[14] or
d) to use reasonable force to prevent the breach of the peace.[15]

In cases of this sort it is essential that the court should find that there were reasonable grounds for the apprehension on the part of the police of a real possibility, not just a remote possibility, of a breach of the peace; an officer's statement that he expected such a breach will not suffice.[16]

1 Para 10.17.e.
2 *Coffin v Smith* (1980) 71 Cr App Rep 221, DC.
3 *Waterfield* [1964] 1 QB 164, [1963] 3 All ER 659, CA; *Rice v Connolly* [1966] 2 All ER 649 at 651; *Ludlow v Burgess* [1971] Crim LR 238, DC; *Pedro v Diss* [1981] 2 All ER 59, DC.
4 *Robson v Hallett* [1967] 2 QB 939, [1967] 2 All ER 407, DC. Also see *Kay v Hibbert* [1977] Crim LR 226, DC.
5 *Davis v Lisle* [1936] 2 KB 434, [1936] 2 All ER 213, DC.

6 *Waterfield.*
7 *Kenlin v Gardiner* [1967] 2 QB 510, [1966] 3 All ER 931, DC; *Collins v Wilcock* [1984] 3 All ER 374, [1984] 1 WLR 1172, DC.
8 *Donnelly v Jackman* [1970] 1 All ER 987, [1970] 1 WLR 562, DC. See also *Collins v Wilcock*, and paras 10.8, 10.13 and 10.14.
9 *Bentley v Brudzinski* [1982] Crim LR 825, DC.
10 Police and Criminal Evidence Act 1984, s 28(3).
11 *McBean v Parker* [1983] Crim LR 399, DC; *Brazil v Chief Constable of Surrey* [1983] 3 All ER 537, [1983] 1 WLR 1155, DC.
12 *Duncan v Jones* [1936] 1 KB 218, 105 LJKB 71, DC.
13 *Lamb v DPP* (1990) 154 JPR 172, DC.
14 *Thomas v Sawkins* [1935] 2 KB 249, 104 LJKB 572.
15 *King v Hodges* [1974] Crim LR 424, DC.
16 *Piddington v Bates* [1960] 3 All ER 660, [1961] 1 WLR 162, DC.

WILFUL OBSTRUCTION

18.70 *Obstruction* The offence of obstructing a constable may be committed without anything in the nature of an assault. In general, any conduct which actually prevents a constable from carrying out his duty or makes it more difficult for him to do so amounts to obstructing him.[1] Where a positive act has this effect it constitutes an obstruction, even though it is not unlawful independently of its operation as an obstruction. Thus, a person who consumes alcohol in order to frustrate a breath test under the Road Traffic Act 1988 may be convicted of the present offence,[2] and, curiously, it has been held that this is so even though a constable has not yet arrived to request a breath test.[3] Other examples of obstruction are hampering a constable in making an arrest or in interviewing a witness or suspect, facilitating the escape of a suspected offender and refusing to remove an obstruction from the highway when requested to do so by a constable.[4]

It amounts to an obstruction to give a warning to someone who is already committing an offence in order that the commission of the offence may be suspended while there is a danger of detection,[5] and the same is the case where a warning is given to someone who is about to commit an offence in order that its commission may be postponed until after the danger of detention has passed.[6] On the other hand, it is not an obstruction where a warning is given to a person who has not committed an offence and in order to discourage him from ever doing so.[7]

1 *Hinchliffe v Sheldon* [1955] 3 All ER 406, [1955] 1 WLR 1207, DC; *Rice v Connolly* [1966] 2 QB 414, [1966] 2 All ER 649, DC; *Lewis v Cox* [1985] QB 509, [1984] 3 All ER 672, DC.
2 *Dibble v Ingleton* [1972] 1 QB 480, [1972] 1 All ER 275, DC.
3 *Neal v Evans* [1976] RTR 333, DC.
4 See *Tynan v Balmer* [1967] 1 QB 91, [1966] 2 All ER 133, DC.
5 *Betts v Stevens* [1910] 1 KB 1, 79 LJKB 17, DC.
6 *Green v Moore* [1982] QB 1044, [1982] 1 All ER 428, DC.
7 *Bastable v Little* [1907] 1 KB 59, 76 LJKB 77, DC.

18.71 *Wilful* The obstruction must be 'wilful', which in this context has the following meaning:

a) The accused's conduct which resulted in the obstruction must have been deliberate and intended by him to bring about a state of affairs which, regarded objectively, prevented or made it more difficult for the constable to carry out his duty, whether or not the accused appreciated that that state of affairs would have that effect or that it would in law amount to an obstruction.[1] Thus, to do something deliberately which in fact makes it more difficult for a constable to carry out his duties is not enough; there must be an intention that the deliberate conduct should result in that state of affairs. There is no need for any hostility towards the constable,[2] nor need the conduct be 'aimed at' him.[3]

The above is well illustrated by *Hills v Ellis*[4] where D intervened in a lawful arrest by a constable in order to draw his attention to the fact that, as D believed, he was arresting the wrong man. The Divisional Court held that as D's deliberate conduct had resulted in a state of affairs which made it more difficult for the constable to carry out his duty, and as D had intended that state of affairs, D was guilty of wilful obstruction, despite the fact that he was actuated by good motives and not by hostility towards the constable.

It has not yet been decided whether the accused must have known that the person obstructed is a constable, but it has been held that there could not be a conviction for wilful obstruction in a case where the accused reasonably believed that that person was not a constable.[5]

b) In *Rice v Connolly*[6] it was held that 'wilfully' meant not only 'intentionally' but also 'without lawful excuse'. This is rather surprising since 'wilfully' seems to refer to the accused's state of mind, whereas the question of 'lawful excuse' generally relates to factual matters surrounding conduct which excuse it.

The requirement that the obstruction must be without lawful excuse means that, unless a constable has a legal right to require a person to do something (and thereby to impose a legal duty on him to do it), a failure by that person to do the thing when requested by the constable cannot constitute a wilful obstruction because, although it makes it more difficult for the constable to carry out his duties, there will be a lawful excuse for that failure. Thus, as there is no general legal duty to answer questions put by a constable (or, to put it another way, there is a right not to do so), a mere refusal to answer such questions is not a wilful obstruction[7] (unless a special duty to answer exists in the circumstances). Nor, according to the Divisional Court in *Green v DPP*,[7] is it a wilful obstruction to advise someone else not to answer police questions, even if that advice is given in an abusive way. A case which seems very much on the borderline is *Ricketts v Cox*,[8] where it was held by the Divisional Court that a refusal to answer his questions which is accompanied by an abusive and hostile attitude, including threats, was a wilful obstruction. In the light of the decision in *Green v DPP*, it would seem that, but for the threats (to which, admittedly, the court did not give much attention in *Ricketts v Cox*), there would not have been an obstruction because, threats apart, the person would only be exercising his right not to answer police questions. It is, of course, a wilful obstruction deliberately to give a constable false information if this makes it more difficult for him to carry out his duty,[9] and it may be a wilful obstruction to *prevent* the police asking a third party questions.

An example of a constable's power to require a person to do something is his power to order persons obstructing the highway to remove themselves;[10] consequently, failure to do so is a wilful obstruction.

1 *Hills v Ellis* [1983] QB 680, [1983] 1 All ER 667, DC; *Moore v Green* [1983] 1 All ER 663, DC.
2 *Hills v Ellis*. Also see *Moore v Green*.

3 *Lewis v Cox* [1985] QB 509, [1984] 3 All ER 672, DC (not following a statement to the contrary by Griffiths LJ in *Hills v Ellis* [1983] QB 680 at 685).
4 [1983] QB 680, [1983] 1 All ER 667, DC. Also see *Lewis v Cox.*
5 *Ostler v Elliott* [1980] Crim LR 584, DC.
6 [1966] 2 QB 414, [1966] 2 All ER 649, DC.
7 [1991] Crim LR 782,DC.
8 (1981) 74 Cr App Rep 298, DC.
9 *Rice v Connolly* [1966] 2 QB 414, [1966] 2 All ER 649, DC.
10 *Kavanagh v Hiscock* [1974] QB 600, [1974] 2 All ER 177, DC.

RESISTANCE

18.72 Like obstruction, resistance does not require an assault. The wide meaning given to 'obstruction' probably renders 'resistance' otiose, since anyone who resists seems to obstruct (although the converse is not true). However, 'resisting' is a more appropriate word in certain cases, such as where a person arrested by a constable tears himself away.[1]

The resistance is not required to be wilful. There can be no doubt that an intent to resist must be proved but it remains to be seen what intent, if any, is required as to the fact that the person resisted is a constable. Analogy with the offence of assaulting a constable in the execution of his duty,[2] suggests that it is irrelevant that the accused was ignorant (even though reasonably) that the person resisted was a constable. However, analogy with the offence of obstructing a constable suggests that a person cannot be convicted if he reasonably believed that the person resisted was not a constable.[3]

1 *Sherriff* [1969] Crim LR 260, CA.
2 Para 10.17.e.
3 Para 18.71.

RELATED OFFENCES

18.73 To deal with particular mischiefs, a number of statutes provide offences relating to the obstructing or resisting of public officials, other than constables, while they are executing particular functions.

An example is provided by s 10 of the Criminal Law Act 1977, whereby it is an offence triable only summarily, and punishable with a maximum of six months' imprisonment or a fine not exceeding level 5 on the standard scale (£5,000) or both, to resist or obstruct an officer of the High Court or of a county court in the enforcement of an order for possession under Order 113 of the Rules of the Supreme Court or Order 24 of the County Court Rules. These Orders provide a summary procedure for obtaining orders for possession of premises or any other place against squatters, including any whom the plaintiff cannot identify. It is a defence for the accused to prove that he believed that the person he was resisting or obstructing was not an officer of the court. Although the provision speaks of 'intentionally', as opposed to 'wilfully', obstructs, it is unlikely that a refusal to answer a question asked by an officer of the court for the execution of his order constitutes an offence,[1] since there is no legal duty to answer and thus there seems to be no culpable omission.

1 *Swallow v LCC* [1916] 1 KB 224, DC.

Firearms

18.74 The Firearms Act 1968 contains a wide range of provisions regulating the possession, handling and distribution of firearms and ammunition for them.

The draft Criminal Code Bill[1] does not contain firearms offences.

Section 57(1) of the 1968 Act defines a 'firearm'. Its effect is that any lethal[2] barrelled weapon of any description from which a shot, bullet or other missile can be discharged is a firearm, as is any weapon designed or adapted to discharge any noxious liquid, gas or other thing, or any component part of such weapons, or any accessory to such weapons designed or adapted to diminish their noise or flash. Nothing in the Act relating to firearms applies to an antique firearm which is sold, transferred, purchased, acquired or possessed as a curiosity or ornament.[3]

Unless otherwise stated, references in this part to sections are to sections in the Firearms Act 1968. It is not possible to go into all the detailed provisions of the Act but those of most general importance are set out below. The maximum punishments referred to are laid down by Schedule 6, as amended.

1 Law Commission: A Criminal Code for England and Wales (1989): Law Com No 177; para 3.21 above.
2 A 'lethal weapon' is one which, when misused, is capable of causing injury from which death may result: *Moore v Gooderham* [1960] 3 All ER 575, [1960] 1 WLR 1308, DC; *Thorpe* [1987] 2 All ER 108, [1987] 1 WLR 383, CA.
3 Firearms Act 1968, s 58(2). As to whether a firearm is an 'antique firearm', see *Richards v Curwen* [1977] 3 All ER 426, [1977] 1 WLR 747, DC, and *Bennett v Brown* (1980) 71 Cr App Rep 109, DC.

POSSESSION, PURCHASE OR ACQUISITION

18.75 Subject to any exemption under the Act, it is an offence under s 1(1) for a person to have in his possession, or to purchase or acquire, a firearm (or any ammunition) to which s 1 applies without holding a firearms certificate (or otherwise than as authorised by such a certificate). Section 1[1] applies to every firearm *except*

a) a 'shotgun', ie a smooth-bore gun (not being an air weapon) which:
   i) has a barrel not less than 24 inches in length and does not have a barrel with a bore which exceeds two inches in diameter;
   ii) either has no magazine or has a non-detachable magazine incapable of holding more than two cartridges; and
   iii) is not a revolver gun; or
b) an 'air weapon', ie an air rifle, air gun or air pistol not of a type declared by the Secretary of State under the Act to be dangerous.

Section 1 applies to any ammunition for a firearm, *except* the normal type of shotgun cartridge or blank cartridge and ammunition for an air weapon.

Under s 1 of the Firearms Act 1982, the provisions of the 1968 Act relating to a firearm to which s 1 of the 1968 Act applies are to apply (with limited exceptions) to an imitation firearm which has the appearance of being such a firearm and is so constructed or adapted as to be readily convertible into such a firearm.

The offence under s 1(1) is triable either way and punishable on conviction on indictment with a maximum of three years' imprisonment (or, in certain aggravated cases, five years').

1 As amended by the Firearms (Amendment) Act 1988, s 2.

18.76 Subject to any exemptions under the Act, s 2(1)[1] provides that it is an offence triable either way for a person to have in his possession, or to purchase or acquire, a shotgun (as defined above) without holding a shotgun certificate. The maximum punishment on conviction on indictment is three years' imprisonment or a fine or both.

The possession, purchase or acquisition of an air weapon or of ammunition for an air weapon or of the normal type of shotgun cartridge or blank cartridge does not require a certificate.[2]

1 As amended by the Criminal Justice Act 1988, s 44.
2 But the seller of a shotgun cartridge may commit an offence if the buyer does not hold a shotgun certificate: Firearms (Amendment) Act 1988, s 5.

18.77 A person can be in possession of a firearm or ammunition even though he does not have physical custody of it nor keeps it in his home; it is enough that he has control of it (as where he keeps a firearm at the home of a relative for safe keeping).[1] This does not mean that a person with whom a firearm is deposited cannot also be in possession of it. He will also be in possession, unless he has the barest custody (as where there is a temporary delivery to him in an emergency or for inspection, or he is entrusted with it for temporary safekeeping).[2]

The prosecution must prove that the accused was knowingly in possession of an article which, on the evidence, was a firearm or ammunition within the relevant meaning of those terms, so that the accused is not liable if a firearm is slipped into his pocket or left in his house unknown to him. It does not have to prove that the accused knew that the article possessed was a firearm or ammunition within the relevant meaning of those terms.[3] The offence is one of strict liability as to the nature of the article possessed;[3] consequently, for example, an honest and reasonable mistaken belief that the article was an antique firearm is no defence.[4] There is one exception: where the alleged offence involves an imitation firearm which is readily convertible into a firearm to which s 1 applies, it is a defence for the accused to prove that he did not know and had no reason to suspect that it was readily convertible.[5]

1 *Sullivan v Earl of Caithness* [1976] QB 966, [1976] 1 All ER 844, DC.
2 *Hall v Cotton* [1987] QB 504, [1986] 3 All ER 332, DC.
3 *Hussain* [1982] 2 All ER 287, [1981] 1 WLR 416, CA.
4 *Howells* [1977] QB 614, [1977] 3 All ER 417, CA.
5 Firearms Act 1982, s 1(5).

POSSESSION, PURCHASE OR ACQUISITION OF PROHIBITED WEAPON

18.78 Certain weapons or ammunition, known as 'prohibited weapons or ammunition', are such that they will not normally be put to legitimate use, except by the armed forces. For this reason, they are subject to the special provisions of s 5, as amended by s 1 of the Firearms (Amendment) Act 1988. Section 5(1) provides that a person commits an offence if, without the written authority of the Secretary of State, he has in his possession, or purchases or acquires, a 'prohibited weapon or ammunition'. 'Possession' bears the same meaning as in the offences just mentioned. The offence is one of strict liability as to the fact that the weapon or ammunition possessed is prohibited, so that it is no defence that its possessor is reasonably unaware of the characteristic which makes it prohibited.[1]

A prohibited weapon is:

a) any firearm so designed or adapted that two or more missiles can be successively discharged without repeated pressure on the trigger, e g a machine gun;[2]
b) any self-loading or pump-action rifle other than one which is chambered for .22 inch rim-fire cartridges;
c) any self-loading or pump-action smooth-bore gun which is not chambered for .22 inch rim-fired cartridges and either has a barrel of less than 24 inches in length or (excluding any detachable, folding, retractable or other movable butt-stock) is less than 40 inches in length overall;
d) any smooth-bore revolver gun other than one which is chambered for 8 mm rim-fire cartridges or loaded at the muzzle end of each chamber;
e) any rocket launcher, or any mortar, for projecting a stabilised missile, other than a launcher or mortar designed for line-throwing or pyrotechnic purposes or as signalling apparatus;
f) any weapon designed or adapted for the discharge of any noxious liquid, gas or other thing.

A water pistol containing a noxious liquid is not covered by the definition in f) because it is neither designed nor adapted for the discharge of such liquid,[3] and the same is the case if a Fairy liquid bottle has been filled with a noxious liquid.[4] However, if D has such a thing with him in a public place he may be liable under the Prevention of Crime Act 1953 (see para 18.86).

An offence under s 5(1) can be committed even though the firearm or weapon has been dismantled.[5] In fact, any component part of a firearm or weapon which is a prohibited weapon is itself a prohibited weapon for the purposes of the offence.[6]

Prohibited ammunition is:

a) any ammunition containing or designed or adapted to contain any noxious liquid, gas or other thing;
b) any cartridge with a bullet designed to explode on or immediately before impact, e g a 'dum-dum bullet';
c) if capable of being used with a firearm of any description, any grenade, bomb (or other like missile), or rocket or shell designed to explode on or immediately before impact.

An offence under s 5(1) is triable either way and punishable with up to five years' imprisonment on conviction on indictment.

1 *Bradish* (1990) 154 JP 21, CA.
2 An automatic weapon does not cease to satisfy this test simply by being modified so that only single shots can possibly be fired, nor does it cease to satisfy this test if it is altered by the removal of components (unless so many components are removed that it can no longer fairly be described as a weapon): *Pannell* (1982) 76 Cr App Rep 53, [1982] Crim LR 752, CA; *Clarke* [1986] 1 All ER 846, [1986] 1 WLR 209, CA.
3 *Titus* [1971] Crim LR 279.
4 *Formosa; Upton* [1991] 2 QB 1, [1991] 1 All ER 131, CA.
5 *Pannell* (1982) 76 Cr App Rep 53, [1982] Crim LR 752, CA.
6 Firearms Act 1968, s 57(1); *Clarke* [1986] 1 All ER 846, [1986] 1 WLR 209, CA.

USE OR POSSESSION FOR AN UNLAWFUL PURPOSE

18.79 The Firearms Act 1968 provides a number of serious offences of this type. Those described here are triable only on indictment. The maximum punishment for each of them is life imprisonment.[1]

1 Amendments were made to the original provisions in the 1968 Act relating to the maximum punishment for the third and fourth offences referred to below by the Criminal Justice Act 1988, s 33(3).

18.80 *Possession with intent to endanger life* Under s 16 (as amended), it is an offence to be in possession of any firearm or ammunition with intent by means thereof to endanger life or to enable another person by means thereof to endanger life, whether any injury has been caused or not.

'Possession' bears the same meaning as in offences under ss 1 and 2. As in the case of the next offence, it would seem that this offence is one of strict liability in relation to the circumstance that the thing possessed was a firearm (or ammunition) within the meaning of the Act.

The requisite intent to endanger life must relate to the life of another: if the accused merely intended to endanger his own life, as where he intended to use the firearm to commit suicide, he is not guilty of the present offence.[1] Nor is he guilty if he intended to endanger life for a lawful purpose, as where D who is being attacked by an armed gang threatens them with his firearm in lawful self-defence.[2] Presumably, where the accused intends to enable another to endanger life, the offence is not committed if the life which it is intended to endanger is only that of the accused or that other. The prosecution are not required to prove an immediate or unconditional intent to endanger life: it is enough to prove that the accused possessed a firearm ready for use, if and when the occasion arises, in a manner which would endanger life.[3]

1 *Norton* [1977] Crim LR 478, Crown Ct.
2 *Georgiades* [1989] 1 WLR 759, (1989) 89 Crim App Rep 206, CA. For self-defence, see para 22.3.
3 *Bentham* [1973] QB 357, [1972] 3 All ER 271, CA.

18.81 *Use of firearm to resist arrest* Section 17(1) provides that a person who makes or attempts to make any use whatsoever of a firearm or imitation firearm, with intent to resist or prevent the lawful arrest or detention of himself or any other person, commits an offence.

Like an offence under ss 1 and 2, this offence has been held to be one of strict liability in relation to the circumstance that the thing possessed was a firearm within the meaning of the Act.[1]

1 *Pierre* [1963] Crim LR 513.

18.82 *Possession of firearm at time of certain offences or of arrest* Under s 17(2), a person who, at the time of committing or being arrested for any of the offences specified in Schedule 1 to the Act, has in his possession a firearm or imitation firearm commits an offence, unless he shows that his possession of the firearm was for a lawful purpose. The offences mentioned in the Schedule 1 to the Act include unlawful wounding or infliction of grievous bodily harm, theft, burglary and blackmail. Where the case is one of possession *at the time of arrest*, it must be proved that the accused had actually committed an offence specified in Schedule 1.[1] A 'firearm' for the purposes of both subsections of s 17 does not include a component part or accessory.[2]

'Possession' bears the same meaning as in the offences under ss 1 or 2. Presumably, like those offences (and that under s 17(1)) this offence is one of strict liability in relation to the fact that the thing possessed was a firearm within the meaning of the Act.

1 *Baker* [1962] 2 QB 530, [1961] 3 All ER 703, CCA.
2 Firearms Act 1968, s 17(4).

18.83 *Having firearm with intent* Under s 18(1), it is an offence for a person to have with him a firearm or imitation firearm with intent to commit an indictable offence, or to resist his own or another's arrest, in either case while he has a firearm with him.

A person may have a firearm with him even though he is not carrying it, but he must have a close physical link with it and it must have been immediately available to him.[1] Thus, 'have with him' is a narrower concept than possession. The extent to which the accused must have knowledge is the same as for the corresponding offence relating to offensive weapons; see para 18.87.

It has been held that a person can be convicted of the present offence where, with intent to commit an indictable offence, he used a firearm which he had with him, even though he did not have that intent before the actual use.[2] This is somewhat surprising in the light of the wording of s 18(1).

1 *Kelt* [1977] 3 All ER 1099, [1977] 1 WLR 1365, CA.
2 *Houghton* [1982] Crim LR 112, CA.

18.84 Other offences relating to firearms are mentioned in paras 18.85 and 18.90.

Offensive weapons

18.85 Section 1 of the Prevention of Crime Act 1953 provides that any person who without lawful authority or reasonable excuse, the proof whereof shall lie on him, has with him in any public place any offensive weapon is guilty of an offence triable either way and punishable on conviction on indictment with up to two years' imprisonment.[1] (Section 19 of the Firearms Act 1968 provides an identical offence, triable either way and punishable with a maximum of five years' imprisonment on conviction on indictment, where a person has with him a firearm and ammunition for it in a public place.)

1 For a general discussion, see Ashworth 'Liability for Carrying Offensive Weapons' [1976] Crim LR 725.

ACTUS REUS

18.86 'Has with him' has the same meaning as in s 18(1) of the Firearms Act 1968, discussed in para 18.83.

A 'public place' is any highway, or other premises or place to which at the material time the public have or are permitted to have access, whether on payment or otherwise.[1] This definition is similar to that which applies to ss 11 to 13 of the Public Order Act 1986, and the same comment applies to it as was made in para 18.57.

An 'offensive weapon' is any article either made or adapted for use for causing injury to the person, or intended by the person having it with him for such use by him or by some other person.[2] There are thus two classes of offensive weapons – those which may be described as offensive per se (ie those made or adapted for use for causing injury to the person), such as a flick knife,[3] a truncheon[4] or a potato with a razor blade inserted in it,[5] and those which are per se inoffensive, such as a sheath knife, a machete, a catapult,[6] a water pistol or Fairy liquid bottle filled with acid, a hammer or a rounders bat,[7] but are rendered offensive by the accused's intention to use them for causing injury to the person. In relation to a weapon which is per se inoffensive, the better view is that the intention must be to injure another person; an article per se inoffensive does not become an offensive weapon if the accused simply intends to use it to injure himself, as where a mentally ill person walks round with a carving knife, threatening to kill himself,[8] Whether an accused, who had with him an article which is per se inoffensive, had the necessary intention is a question of fact.[9] It is not enough that he intended to frighten people with the article unless he intended to cause injury by shock.[10] Where a person has an inoffensive article on him without intending to use it to cause injury but suddenly, when attacked or in the heat of the moment, forms this intention and then and there injures someone with it, he is not guilty of the present offence.[11] Similarly, a person who picks up an inoffensive article and immediately uses it as a weapon does not commit the offence.[12] The reason is the same in each case: there is no intention to use the weapon offensively before any occasion for its actual use has arisen.[13]

1 Prevention of Crime Act 1953, s 1(4).
2 Ibid, as amended by the Public Order Act 1986, s 40(2) and Sch 2.
3 *Simpson* [1983] 3 All ER 789, [1983] 1 WLR 1494, CA.
4 *Houghton v Chief Constable of Greater Manchester* (1987) 84 Cr App Rep 319, CA.
5 *Williamson* (1977) 67 Cr App Rep 35 at 38, per Geoffrey Lane LJ.
6 *Southwell v Chadwick* (1987) 85 Cr App Rep 235, CA.
7 *Humphries* (1987) Independent, 13 April, CA.
8 *Fleming* [1989] Crim LR 71, Crown Ct. Cf *Bryan v Mott* (1975) 61 Cr App Rep 71, DC, where the contrary view taken in the Crown Court was not discussed on appeal in the Divisional Court. It is submitted that an article per se inoffensive which is intended by its carrier only to be used to injure him cannot properly be regarded as an offensive weapon and that the view in *Fleming* is preferable.
9 *Williamson* (1977) 67 Cr App Rep 35, CA.
10 *Edmonds* [1963] 2 QB 142, [1963] 1 All ER 828, CCA; *Allamby and Medford* [1974] 3 All ER 126, [1974] 1 WLR 1494, CA; *Rapier* (1979) 70 Cr App Rep 17, CA.
11 *Ohlson v Hylton* [1975] 2 All ER 490, [1975] 1 WLR 724, DC; *Humphreys* [1977] Crim LR 225, CA.
12 *Ohlson v Hylton*; *Bates v Bulman* [1979] 3 All ER 170, [1979] 1 WLR 1190, DC.
13 Ibid.

MENS REA

18.87 The Act does not expressly require proof of knowledge against the accused, but it has been held that the word 'knowingly' must be read into it; accordingly, someone who is unaware that a flick knife has been slipped into his pocket by a stranger, or who is not aware of the presence of a cosh in the van he has hired, would not be guilty of an offence under the Act.[1] However, once a person has knowingly had something with him he continues to have it with him until he or another does something to rid him of it; a person who merely forgets that he has the thing with him does not cease to have it with him.[2] Thus, where a person has forgotten that he had put a cosh in the glove compartment of his car by the time that he is stopped by the police a month later, he can be convicted of the present offence.

It has not yet been decided whether the accused must know of the facts which render the article an offensive weapon within the meaning of the Act; analogy with offences under the Firearms Act 1968 suggests that the offence is one of strict liability in this respect.

1 *Cugullere* [1961] 2 All ER 343, [1961] 1 WLR 858, CCA.
2 *Martindale* [1986] 3 All ER 25, CA, [1986] 1 WLR 1042, CA; *McCalla* (1988) 87 Cr App Rep 372, CA. The decision of the Court of Appeal to the contrary in *Russell* (1984) 81 Cr App Rep 315, [1985] Crim LR 231, was not followed in *Russell* on the ground that it was per incuriam.

WITHOUT LAWFUL AUTHORITY OR REASONABLE EXCUSE

18.88 A person does not commit the offence if he proves that he had lawful authority or a reasonable excuse for having with him an offensive weapon in a public place. The reference to 'lawful authority' is to persons such as a soldier with a rifle or a policeman with a truncheon, who carry such weapons as a matter of duty,[1] but does not extend to private security guards carrying truncheons or the like.[2] Whether there is a reasonable excuse depends on whether a reasonable man would think it excusable in the circumstances to carry the weapon in question,[3] but as a matter of law limitations have been imposed by the courts on what a reasonable man might think in this context. It appears that he would not think it reasonable for a person to have with him an offensive weapon for self-defence unless there is an imminent, particular threat to him (as opposed to a constant or enduring threat or risk)[4] which he does not deliberately bring about by creating a situation in which violence is liable to occur.[5] It would also appear that he would not think it reasonable for a person to have with him a per se offensive weapon in order to commit suicide with it[6] or for a security guard at a dance hall to carry a truncheon as a matter of routine 'as a deterrent' and 'as part of his uniform'.[7] Nor would he think it reasonable that a person had forgotten that he had the weapon with him[8] (except that if that person had it with him with a reasonable excuse, as where he had retrieved a police truncheon from the gutter in order to return it to the nearest police station, but then forgotten about it and retained it, there would – in this type of case at least – continue to be a reasonable excuse).[9]

The fact that a weapon was used for an unlawful purpose does not necessarily bring its possessor within the statute. A man may have a reasonable excuse for possessing a weapon, such as an air rifle handed to him in a shooting gallery so that he could fire it at the proper target, although he unlawfully fires it at his companion.[10]

1 *Bryan v Mott* (1975) 62 Cr App Rep 71, DC.
2 *Spanner, Poulter and Ward* [1973] Crim LR 704, CA.
3 *Bryan v Mott* (1975) 62 Cr App Rep 71, DC.
4 *Evans v Hughes* [1972] 3 All ER 412, [1972] 1 WLR 1452, DC; *Pittard v Mahoney* [1977] Crim LR 169, DC.
5 *Malnik v DPP* [1989] Crim LR 451, DC.
6 *Bryan v Mott* (1975) 62 Cr App Rep 71, DC.
7 *Spanner, Poulter and Ward* [1973] Crim LR 704, CA.
8 *McCalla* (1988) 87 Cr App Rep 372, CA.
9 Ibid. The Court of Appeal gave the example referred to in the text.
10 *Jura* [1954] 1 QB 503, [1954] 1 All ER 696, CCA.

ANCILLARY OFFENCE

18.89 Section 139 of the Criminal Justice Act 1988 provides an offence ancillary to that under the 1953 Act, which is useful where a knife or the like cannot be proved to have been made, adapted or intended to cause injury to a person. Section 139(1) makes it a summary offence, punishable with a fine not exceeding level 3 on the standard scale (£1,000), for a person to have with him in a public place an article to which the section applies. 'Have with him' and 'public place' bear essentially the same meanings as described above. Section 139 applies to any article which has a blade or is sharply pointed, except a folding pocket-knife (unless the cutting edge of its blade exceeds three inches).[1] An accused has a defence if he proves:

a) that he had good reason or lawful authority for having the article with him in a public place;[2] or
b) that he had the article with him for use at work, or for religious reasons, or as part of any national costume.[3]

1 Criminal Justice Act 1988, s 139(2) and (3).
2 Ibid, s 139(4).
3 Ibid, s 139(5).

Other offensive weapon offences

18.90 By s 8 of the Criminal Law Act 1977, it is an offence for a person who is on any premises as a trespasser, after having entered as such, to have with him any weapon of offence, without lawful authority or reasonable excuse. A weapon of offence is defined by s 8(2) as any article made or adapted for use for causing injury to *or incapacitating* a person, or intended by the person having it with him for such use. The offence is triable only summarily and is punishable with a maximum of three months' imprisonment or a fine not exceeding level 5 on the standard scale (£5,000) or both. (It may also be noted that it is an offence, triable either way, under s 20(1) of the Firearms Act 1968, for a person, while he has a firearm with him, to enter or be in any building or part thereof as a trespasser and without reasonable excuse (the proof whereof lies on him);[1] under s 20(2) there is a similar offence in relation to land.)[2]

Another offence punishing those who have with them offensive weapons is aggravated burglary, which is described in para 14.15

1 The mode of trial and maximum punishment is the same as for the offence of having a firearm in a public place. See para 18.85.
2 This offence is triable only summarily and the maximum punishment is three months' imprisonment or a fine not exceeding level 4 on the standard scale (£2,500) or both.

19 Offences against public morals

19.1 Many offences which could be placed in this chapter are discussed elsewhere in this book. For example, sexual offences have been dealt with in Chapter 12. This chapter concentrates on offences relating to bigamy, to obscenity and to drugs.

Bigamy

19.2 The effect of s 57 of the Offences against the Person Act 1861 is that whoever, being married, goes through a ceremony of marriage with any other person during the life of his or her spouse is guilty of bigamy (wherever, in the case of a Commonwealth citizen who is a British citizen or British dependent territories citizen or British overseas citizen, the second ceremony takes place), subject to the statutory and other defences which are discussed below. Bigamy is triable either way[1] and punishable by a maximum of seven years' imprisonment on indictment.

1 Magistrates' Courts Act 1980, s 17(1) and Sch 1.

ACTUS REUS

19.3 What is required is that a person who has already been married to one person (X) should go through a ceremony of marriage with any other person during the life of X. If the first marriage is invalid and one of the parties goes through a second ceremony with a third person, no offence is committed, assuming that no false declaration was made in connection with the second ceremony.

19.4 *The first marriage* The prosecution must prove that the accused went through a valid marriage ceremony with the first spouse. In the case of ceremonies celebrated in England, this is usually done by production of the marriage certificate and calling someone who was present at the ceremony to identify the parties.

Once the parties are proved to have gone through a ceremony of marriage, there is a rebuttable presumption of law that it is valid, but if the defence can raise a doubt as to its validity, the accused is entitled to the benefit of that doubt.[1]

A polygamous or potentially polygamous marriage is not a valid first marriage for the purposes of the offence of bigamy.[2] However, a potentially polygamous marriage will become monogamous if the party entitled to marry again loses his entitlement, e g because he becomes domiciled in a country which only permits monogamy, in which case the marriage will thereafter be a first marriage for the purposes of bigamy.[2]

1 *Willshire* (1881) 6 QBD 366, 50 LJMC 57; *Morrison* [1938] 3 All ER 787, CCA; cf *Tweney v Tweney* [1946] P 180, [1946] 1 All ER 564.
2 *Sagoo* [1975] QB 885, [1975] 2 All ER 926, CA.

19.5 *First spouse alive at time of second ceremony* Although s 57 speaks of the accused '*being* married' at the time of the second ceremony, this is somewhat misleading because all that need be proved in the first instance by the prosecution is that the first spouse was still alive at the time of the second marriage ceremony, and not that there has been no annulment of the marriage or a divorce (although it will have to do so if the accused adduces evidence in support of the defence of annulment or divorce, mentioned in para 19.8). Evidence that the first spouse was alive and well at an earlier date which is not too remote may suffice when no better evidence is available that that spouse was alive at the time of the second ceremony.

19.6 *The second ceremony* If the celebration of a second ceremony 'known to and recognised by the law' as being capable of producing a valid marriage is proved, it does not matter that the second ceremony would have been invalid for reasons other than that one of the parties was already married. Thus, if D, being married, goes through a form of marriage with a person within the prohibited degrees of relationship, he is guilty of bigamy, although that marriage would have been null and void in any case.[1] It would be different if the second ceremony was celebrated by a layman without a licence in a private house because the ceremony could hardly be said to have been 'known and recognised by the law' as capable apart from its bigamous nature of producing a valid marriage.

1 *Allen* (1872) LR 1 CCR 367, 41 LJMC 97.

MENS REA

19.7 The only mens rea which the prosecution must prove in the first instance is that the accused intended to go through the second ceremony of marriage.[1] It does not have to prove in the first instance that the accused knew that he was still married to his first spouse. On the other hand, as we shall see, a mistaken belief that he was not may provide a defence.

1 *DPP v Morgan* [1975] 2 All ER 347 at 382, per Lord Fraser of Tullybelton.

DEFENCES

19.8 There are several defences open to a person charged with bigamy:

a) If a person who 'marries' a second time can adduce evidence to show that his, or her, spouse had been continuously absent from him or her for seven years at the time of the second marriage and had not been known by him or her to be living during that time, there is a complete defence.[1] But such absence for seven years merely provides a defence to a charge of bigamy and does not dissolve the first marriage so that, if the first spouse is alive, the second 'marriage' is a complete nullity.

b) It is a good defence that the first marriage had been annulled by a court of competent jurisdiction or that, at the time the second marriage took place, the first had been dissolved.[1]

c) It is a defence that, at the time of the second marriage, the accused believed on reasonable grounds that his or her spouse was dead, although there has not been absence for seven years,[2] or that the first marriage was void,[3] or that the first marriage had been dissolved or annulled.[4]

d) If the accused is not a Commonwealth citizen who is also a British citizen or British Dependent Territories citizen or British Overseas citizen, he has a defence if the second ceremony took place abroad. The only exception is where the second ceremony took place in a part of the Commonwealth which is not a self-governing country, in which case *any* Commonwealth citizen may be convicted of bigamy if he is accused of that offence.[5]

1 Offences against the Person Act 1861, s 57 proviso.
2 *Tolson* (1889) 23 QBD 168, 58 LJMC 97.
3 *King* [1964] 1 QB 285, [1963] 3 All ER 561, CCA.
4 *Gould* [1968] 2 QB 65, [1968] 1 All ER 849, CA.
5 This is the apparent effect of the British Nationality Act 1948, s 3.

19.9   Bigamy is sometimes committed as a cloak for seduction or the obtaining of property and when this is so the propriety of severe punishment is not disputed. When this is not so the justification for punishing bigamy is that it endangers the sanctity of marriage by profaning the ceremony. Some people consider that the offence should not be heavily punishable, or even punishable at all, when considered in this light; in practice sentences are often very lenient.

RELATED OFFENCES

19.10   Under s 3 of the Perjury Act 1911, it is an offence, triable either way and punishable with imprisonment for seven years on conviction on indictment, wilfully to make false statements in order to procure a marriage or a certificate of marriage.

Various penalties are imposed by the Marriage Act 1949 on those who knowingly officiate at irregular marriage ceremonies.

Obscenity

19.11   Obscene publications, including obscene films, broadcasts and cable programmes, are governed by the Obscene Publications Act 1959,[1] which has superseded the common law offence of obscene libel.[2] The performance of obscene plays is not dealt with by the Act.[3] Instead, special statutory provisions, outside the scope of this book, apply to theatres. Obscene or indecent performances, such as 'live sex shows', fall outside these special provisions, but such conduct may be dealt with by a prosecution for the common law offence of outraging public decency.[4]

1 The 1959 Act has been supplemented by the Obscene Publications Act 1964, and amended by the Criminal Law Act 1977, s 53, and the Broadcasting Act 1990, s 162.
2 Obscene Publications Act 1959, s 2(4). In relation to the effect of s 2(4) on the offence of outraging public decency, see para 19.26. The reasoning referred to there could be used to support the continued existence of the common law offence of obscene libel where the item is obscene at common law but not under the test of obscenity in the 1959 Act; but this pre-supposes that the common law definition of obscenity is wider than the statutory one, which is probably not the case (see *Hicklin* (1868) LR QB 360).

3 Obscene Publications Act 1959, s 1(3).
4 Para 19.23.

PUBLICATION OF AN OBSCENE ARTICLE

19.12   Section 2(1) of the 1959 Act provides that a person who publishes, whether for gain or not, an obscene article is, subject to the defences of excusable ignorance and public good, guilty of an offence triable either way and punishable on conviction on indictment with a maximum of three years' imprisonment. The terms 'article', 'publish' and 'obscene' are defined in s 1.

'Article' means any article containing or embodying matter to be read or looked at or both, any sound record, and any film or other record of a picture or pictures[1] (such as a video cassette);[2] it also includes any matter included in a television or sound broadcast or in a cable programme service.[3]

Publishing means distributing, circulating, selling, lending, giving, hiring or offering for sale or hire. Additionally, in the case of a record or film etc it includes showing it, playing it or projecting it,[4] and in the case of television and sound broadcasting or of a cable programme service it includes matter broadcast or transmitted.[5]

1 Obscene Publications Act 1959, s 1(2).
2 *A-G's Reference (No 5 of 1980)* [1980] 3 All ER 816, [1981] 1 WLR 88, CA.
3 Obscene Publications Act 1959, s 1(4).
4 Obscene Publications Act 1959, s 1(3). The words 'play or project' cover what happens when a video cassette is used to produce pictures: *A-G's Reference (No 5 of 1980)*.
5 Obscene Publications Act 1959, s 1(5).

19.13   *Meaning of 'obscene'*   An article is deemed to be obscene if its effect, or the effect of any one of its items, is, taken as a whole, such as to tend to deprave and corrupt persons who are likely, having regard to all the circumstances, to read, see or hear the matter contained in it. Though a novel may be considered as a whole, a magazine must be considered item by item and, if any one of the items is obscene, the accused is guilty. 'A novelist who writes a complete novel and who cannot cut out particular passages without destroying the theme of the novel is entitled to have his work judged as a whole, but a magazine publisher who has a far wider discretion as to what he will and will not insert by way of items is to be judged under the 1959 Act on what we call the item to item basis.'[1]

Obscenity is not confined to that which has a tendency to corrupt sexual morals; the Act has been applied to a book depicting the career of a drug addict.[2]

'Deprave and corrupt' are strong words; to lead morally astray is not necessarily to deprave and corrupt.[3] An article may be obscene even though it is directed only to persons who are already depraved; it is sufficient that it increases or maintains a state of corruption.[4] 'Deprave and corrupt' refer to the effect of the article on the mind, including the emotions, and it is not necessary that any overt activity, such as sexual activity, should result.[4] Expert evidence is inadmissible on the issue of whether an article tends to deprave and corrupt persons likely to read, see or hear the matter in question.[5] The sole exception is where the likely readers are of a special class, such as very young children, in which case expert evidence is admissible on the issue of tendency to deprave and corrupt members of that class.[6]

The meaning of 'obscene' in the 1959 Act is specialised. The word is used in other statutes without any definition. For example, s 11 of the Post Office

Act 1953 punishes the posting of an 'obscene' article. In these contexts the word bears its ordinary meaning of 'filthy, loathsome or lewd'.[7]

1 *Anderson* [1972] 1 QB 304 at 313, [1971] 3 All ER 1152 at 1158.
2 *John Calder (Publications) Ltd v Powell* [1965] 1 QB 509, [1965] 1 All ER 159, DC.
3 *Knuller Ltd v DPP* [1973] AC 435 at 456–457 and 491, per Lords Reid and Simon.
4 *DPP v Whyte* [1972] AC 849, [1972] 3 All ER 12, HL.
5 *Anderson* [1972] 1 QB 304, [1971] 3 All ER 1152, CA.
6 Ibid; *DPP v A and BC Chewing Gum Ltd* [1968] 1 QB 159, [1967] 2 All ER 504, DC.
7 *Anderson.*

19.14 *Defences* Section 2(5) gives the accused a defence if he proves that he had not examined the article in question, and had no reasonable cause to suspect that it was obscene. In the case of obscene matter included in a broadcast or cable programme the defence requires, instead, proof by the accused that he did not know and had no reason to suspect that the programme would include obscene matter.[1]

Under s 4(1), it is a defence for a person accused of publishing an obscene article, other than a moving picture film or soundtrack or matter included in a broadcast or cable programme, to show that the publication was for the public good, on the ground that it was in the interests of science, literature, or other objects of general concern. 'Learning' in this context means the product of scholarship, something with inherent excellence gained by the work of a scholar: it does not mean education, sexual or otherwise.[2] 'Other objects of general concern' are other matters involving intellectual or aesthetic values.[3] Under s 4(2), the opinion of experts is admissible on the issue of the scientific or other merits of the article. Expert evidence is not permitted to show that the obscene article is for the public good because it is psychologically beneficial to persons with certain sexual tendencies in that it relieves their sexual tensions and may divert them from antisocial activities, since this is not within the bounds of the defence.[3] If the defence under s 4 is raised the jury should be directed first to consider whether, ignoring at this stage expert evidence in relation to the defence, they are satisfied beyond reasonable doubt that the article complained of was published by the accused and is obscene and that only if they are so satisfied should they go on to consider whether, on the balance of probabilities, the defence of public good has been made out by the accused.[4]

The public good defence is differently worded in the case of a moving picture film or soundtrack. Here, the accused has a defence if he proves that publication of the film or soundtrack was for the public good on the ground that it is in the interests of drama, opera, ballet or any other art, or of literature or learning.[5] Likewise, in the case of a broadcast or cable programme, the accused has a defence if he proves that the inclusion of the matter in question was for the public good on one of these grounds or on the ground that it is in the interests of any objects of general concern.[6]

1 Broadcasting Act 1990, Sch 15.
2 *A-G's Reference (No 3 of 1977)* [1978] 3 All ER 1166, [1978] 1 WLR 1123, CA.
3 *DPP v Jordan* [1977] AC 699, [1976] 3 All ER 775, HL.
4 Ibid; *A-G's Reference (No 3 of 1977)*.
5 Obscene Publications Act 1959, s 4(1A).
6 Broadcasting Act 1990, Sch 15.

POSSESSION OF AN OBSCENE ARTICLE

19.15 Section 2(1) of the 1959 Act provides that it is an offence for a person to have an obscene article for publication for gain (whether gain to himself or to another). A person is deemed to have an article for publication for gain if with a view to such publication he has the article in his ownership, possession or control.[1] Where a person has an obscene article in his ownership, possession or control with a view to the matter recorded on it being included in a broadcast or cable programme, the article is deemed to be had or kept by him for publication for gain.[2] The maximum punishment is the same as for the offence of publication, and 'publication', 'article' and 'obscene' bear the same meaning as in that offence. The defences of excusable ignorance and public good are available.

1 Obscene Publications Act 1964, s 1(2).
2 Broadcasting Act 1990, Sch 15.

PROSECUTIONS RELATING TO FILMS, BROADCASTS AND CABLE PROGRAMMES

19.16 Where an allegedly obscene article is a moving picture film of not less than 16mm and the publication took place or (as the case may be) was to take place in the course of a film show, a prosecution for publishing it or having it for publication for gain must not be instituted except by or with the consent of the Director of Public Prosecutions.[1]

There is a similar provision in relation to matters broadcast by television or sound or contained in a cable programme service.[2]

1 Obscene Publications Act 1959, s 2(3A).
2 Broadcasting Act 1990, Sch 15.

FORFEITURE[1]

19.17 'Obscene articles' kept on premises for 'publication for gain' may be seized under a search warrant issued by a magistrate; a warrant may only be issued on an information laid by or on behalf of the Director of Public Prosecutions or a constable.[2] A warrant may be issued not only if a magistrate is satisfied that obscene articles 'are kept' on the premises but also if he is satisfied that they 'are from time to time kept there'.[3] The user of such premises may be summoned to show cause why the articles should not be forfeited and the owner, author or maker of the article, or anyone who dealt with it before seizure, may also show cause why it should not be forfeited. The defence of public good is available in forfeiture proceedings.

1 Obscene Publications Act 1959, s 3.
2 Criminal Justice Act 1967, s 25.
3 *Adams* [1980] QB 575, [1980] 1 All ER 473, CA.

ARTICLES INTENDED FOR EXPORT

19.18 In *Gold Star Publications Ltd v DPP*[1] the House of Lords (Lord Simon of Glaisdale dissenting) held that the provisions relating to forfeiture of obscene articles kept for publication for gain apply even where the intended publication was to occur outside the jurisdiction of the English courts. Presumably, the offence of possession for publication for gain can also be committed where the intended publication was to occur outside the jurisdiction.

Where the articles are intended for export it will sometimes be very difficult (if not impossible) to decide whether they are obscene (ie whether they would tend to deprave and corrupt likely readers in the country of destination) since standards of morality vary immensely from country to country. If it is determined that the articles are obscene there may also be difficulty in dealing with the defence of public good, if it is raised.[2]

1 [1981] 2 All ER 257, [1981] 1 WLR 732, HL.
2 These difficulties were acknowledged in *Gold Star Publications Ltd v DPP*.

Indecent photographs of children

19.19   Under s 1 of the Protection of Children Act 1978, it is an offence, triable either way and punishable on conviction on indictment with a maximum of three years' imprisonment, for a person to *take*[1] an indecent photograph of a person under 16, or to *distribute or show* such a photograph, or to *possess it with a view to distributing or showing it* (whether or not for gain). A person charged with distributing or showing or with possession with a view to distribution or show has a defence if he proves:

a) that he had a legitimate reason for distributing or showing the photographs or (as the case may be) having them in his possession, or
b) that he had not himself seen the photographs and did not know, nor had any reason to suspect, them to be indecent.

1 It must be proved that the photograph was 'deliberately and intentionally' taken: *Graham-Kerr* [1988] 1 WLR 1098, (1988) 88 Cr App Rep 302, CA.

19.20   Section 161 of the Criminal Justice Act 1988 makes it a summary offence, punishable with a fine not exceeding level 5 on the standard scale (£5,000), for a person to *possess* any indecent photograph of a person under 16. This offence deals with those who possess such a photograph against whom an intent to distribute or show it cannot be proved, so that they are not guilty under the 1978 Act.
A person charged under s 161 has a defence if he proves:

a) that he had a legitimate reason for having the photograph in his possession; or
b) that he had not himself seen the photograph and did not know, nor had any reason to suspect, it to be indecent; or
c) that the photograph was sent to him without any prior request made by him or on his behalf and that he did not keep it for an unreasonable time.

19.21   In the above offences, 'photograph' includes a film or video recording,[1] and 'indecent' means offending against the recognised standards of propriety.[2] A photograph can be indecent even though it is not obscene. The child's age is a relevant factor as to whether or not the photograph is indecent,[3] but the circumstances in which it was taken or the motivation of the photographer is not.[4] There is no defence of public good, as there is in the Obscene Publications Act 1959.
Proceedings for either offence may only be instituted by or with the consent of the Director of Public Prosecutions.[5]
A director, secretary or other similar officer of a corporation is liable for either of the above offences if it was committed by the corporation with his consent or connivance or if its commission by the corporation was attributable to any neglect on his part.[6]

1 Protection of Children Act 1978, s 7(2) and (5); Criminal Justice Act 1988, s 160(4).
2 *Graham-Kerr* [1988] 1 WLR 1098, (1988) 88 Cr App Rep 302, CA.
3 *Owen* [1988] 1 WLR 134, (1988) 87 Cr App Rep 291, CA.
4 *Graham-Kerr*.
5 Protection of Children Act 1978, s 1(3); Criminal Justice Act 1988, s 160(4).
6 Protection of Children Act 1978, s 3; Criminal Justice Act 1988, s 160(4). See para 9.90.

Indecent Displays (Control) Act 1981

19.22 Section 1(1) of this Act, which repealed the previous outdated legislation on indecent displays,[1] makes it a statutory offence for a person to make a public display of indecent matter (or to cause or permit such a display).[2] The offence is triable either way and punishable with a maximum of two years' imprisonment on conviction on indictment.[3]

By s 1(2), matter is deemed to be publicly displayed if it is displayed in, or so as to be visible from, a public place. Thus, indecent matter displayed on private property is caught if it can be seen from a public place. For the purposes of s 1(2), a 'public place' means any place to which the public have, or are permitted to have, access (whether on payment or otherwise) while the indecent matter is displayed. However, the Act does not apply to displays in a place to which the public are permitted to have access only on payment which is or includes payment for the indecent display, nor to displays in a shop or part of a shop, which the public can enter only by passing beyond an adequate warning notice,[4] provided in both cases that persons under 18 are not permitted to enter while the display continues;[4] the reason is that, subject to this proviso, these are not public places for the purposes of the Act. Window displays in such places, visible from a public place outside, are, of course, subject to the Act.

The term 'indecent' is not defined by the Act and will therefore fall to be interpreted by the courts; there is no defence of public good as in the Obscene Publications Act 1959. The term 'matter' is defined by s 1(5) as including anything capable of being displayed, except an actual human body or any part of it (so that 'strip shows' are not covered by the Act). Section 1(5) also provides that matter which is not actually exposed to view is to be disregarded in determining whether any displayed matter is indecent. Thus, where a closed magazine forms part of a public display, only the cover, and not its contents, can be taken into account.

Section 1(4) states that an offence under the Act is not committed in relation to any matter included in a television broadcast, cable programme service, play or film show, or in an art gallery or museum display (provided it is only visible from within the gallery or museum). The subsection also provides that an offence is not committed in relation to any matter displayed by or with the authority of, and visible only from within a building occupied by, the Crown or a local authority.

A director, secretary or other similar officer of a corporation is liable for the above offence if it was committed by the corporation with his consent or connivance or if its commission by the corporation was attributable to any neglect on his part.[5]

1 Indecent Displays (Control) Act 1981, s 5(2) and Schedule.
2 Ibid, s 1(1).
3 Ibid, s 4.
4 Ibid, s 1(3).
5 Ibid, s 3. See para 9.90.

Outraging public decency

19.23 In 1971 in *Knuller v DPP*[1] the majority of the House of Lords held, obiter, that outraging public decency was a common law offence, examples of which are indecent exposure, acts of sexual indecency in public and mounting an indecent exhibition.[2] A modern case in which the existence of the offence had previously been recognised by the Court of Criminal Appeal in 1963 in *Mayling*.[3] Any doubt as to the existence of the offence was removed by the decision of the Court of Appeal in 1991 in *Gibson*,[4] where the Court agreed with the majority of the House of Lords in *Knuller*.[5]

1 [1973] AC 435, [1972] 2 All ER 898, HL.
2 See *Crunden* (1809) 2 Camp 89; *Mayling* [1963] 2 QB 717, [1963] 1 All ER 687, CCA; *Gibson* [1991] 1 All ER 439, [1990] 3 WLR 595, CA.
3 [1963] 2 QB 717, [1963] 1 All ER 687, CCA.
4 [1991] 1 All ER 439, [1990] 3 WLR 595, CA.
5 The Law Commission recommended that the offence should be abolished in its Report on Conspiracy and Criminal Law Reform: Law Com No 76 (1976), para 3.143.

19.24 The actus reus requires an act of such a lewd, obscene or disgusting nature as to result in an outrage to public decency.[1] The conduct or matter need not occur in a public place, ie one to which the public have access, but it must be 'public' in the sense that it *could have been seen* by more than one person, although not necessarily simultaneously.[2] Thus, it is not a defence that indecent matter is contained in a book or newspaper.

'Outrage' like 'corrupt' is a strong word. 'Outraging public decency' goes beyond offending the susceptibilities of, or even shocking, reasonable people. The offence is concerned with protecting the recognised minimum contemporary standards of decency; whether there is an 'outrage' of such standards is a question for the jury.[3]. It is not necessary to prove that the accused's act in fact disgusted and annoyed anyone.[4] It is enough that the conduct would be likely to disgust and annoy ordinary members of the public if they saw it. whether or not any actual spectators were disgusted or annoyed.

If the accused's conduct does not in itself result in an outrage to public decency the present offence is not committed, regardless of his motive or ultimate intent.[5]

1 *Mayling* [1963] 2 QB 717, [1963] 1 All ER 687, CCA.
2 Ibid; *Knuller v DPP* [1973] AC 435 at 494, [1972] 2 All ER 898, per Lord Simon with whom Lord Kilbrandon agreed.
3 *Knuller v DPP* [1973] AC 435 at 495, [1972] 2 All ER 898, per Lord Simon with whom Lord Kilbrandon agreed.
4 *Mayling* [1963] 2 QB 717, [1963] 1 All ER 687, CCA.
5 *Rowley* [1991] Crim LR 785, CA.

19.25 The mens rea required is an intention to do the physical thing complained of which is found to have outraged public decency. It is not necessary for the prosecution also to prove that the accused had an intention to outrage public decency or that he was subjectively reckless (or, indeed, that he had any mens rea) as to the risk of such an outrage occurring. In other words the offence is one of strict liability as to this element.[1]

1 *Gibson* [1991] 1 All ER 439, [1990] 3 WLR 595, CA.

19.26 A person can be convicted of outraging public decency even though his conduct also constitutes another offence, such as an offence of indecent exposure contrary to the Vagrancy Act 1824 or an offence under the Indecency with Children Act 1960, unless a statute otherwise provides.[1] Such a contrary provision is made by s 2(4) of the Obscene Publications Act 1959, whereby any liability for a common law offence (including the present one) was abolished where it is of the essence of the offence that the thing published is obscene within the meaning of that Act (which requires a tendency to deprave and corrupt).[2] However, s 2(4) does not apply to an article which is indecent or obscene in a sense not within the meaning of the 1959 Act. It was for this reason that the Court of Appeal in *Gibson*[3] upheld the convictions of the curator of an art gallery, and of the artist concerned, in which were displayed earrings made from freeze-dried human foetuses. While the exhibition of the earrings might well have seriously offended recognised standards of propriety or decency, it had not been suggested that anyone was likely to be depraved or corrupted by them.

Another contrary provision is made by Sch 15 of the Broadcasting Act 1990. This provides that a person shall not be prosecuted for a common law offence (including the present one) in respect of a broadcast or cable programme where it is of the essence of the common law offence that the programme or anything done or said in it was obscene, indecent, offensive, disgusting or injurious to morality. The effect of this provision is to remove broadcast or cable programmes from the scope of the present offence.

Unlike offences under the Obscene Publications Act 1959, the common law offence of outraging public decency is not subject to a defence of public good or the like. It is rather paradoxical that publishing something which is statutorily obscene is not an offence if it is shown to be for the public good, whereas publishing something indecent or offensive which is not so 'bad' as to fall within the statutory definition of obscenity (but which falls within the common law offence) does not.

1 *Mayling* [1963] 2 QB 717, [1963] 1 All ER 687, CCA; *May* [1990] Crim LR 415, CA.
2 Para 19.13.
3 [1991] 1 All ER 439, [1990] 3 WLR 595, CA.

19.27 As a common law misdemeanour, the offence of outraging public decency is triable only on indictment and is punishable with imprisonment fixed for a period at the discretion of the judge.[1]

1 Para 3.4.

Misuse of drugs[1]

19.28 The Misuse of Drugs Act 1971 seeks to achieve the two broad objectives of the control of dangerous or otherwise harmful drugs and the prevention of their abuse. Provision is made for the supervision of the problem of drug misuse by the Advisory Council on the Misuse of Drugs, which has been established under s 1 of the Act. The Council consists of members of the medical and allied professions and of persons experienced in the social problems to which the misuse of drugs can give rise. Its functions are to advise the Home Secretary or other Ministers on measures to prevent drug misuse and measures to deal with the social problems of misuse. It must also be consulted before the Home Secretary makes any regulations under the Act, e g regulations concerning the possession and supply of drugs by doctors and pharmacists or requiring the notification of addicts to a central authority. The bulk of the regulations made so far are contained in the Misuse of Drugs Regulations 1985.

The drugs subject to the Act (the 'controlled drugs') are specified in its second schedule. There are three classes: Class A includes cocaine, LSD, heroin, mescaline and opium; Class B includes amphetamine, cannabis, cannabis resin and codeine: Class C includes benzphetamine and pemoline.[2]

Variations in the list of controlled drugs can be made by Order in Council, as can variations of the classification.

One of the points of the classification is that it affects the maximum punishment of some of the offences under the Act. As a result, applying the reasoning of the House of Lords in *Courtie*,[3] what may appear to be one offence (e g unauthorised supply) is in law divisible into distinct offences depending on the maximum penalty provided for the drug in question.

1 See Card 'The Misuse of Drugs Act 1971' [1972] Crim LR 744.
2 For the meaning of some of these terms, see in particular the Misuse of Drugs Act 1971, s 37(1), as substituted by the Criminal Law Act 1977, s 52; *A-G's Reference (No 1 of 1977)* [1978] 1 All ER 649, [1977] 1 WLR 1213, CA; *DPP v Goodchild* [1978] 2 All ER 161, [1978] 1 WLR 578, HL; *Stevens* [1981] Crim LR 568, CA.
3 [1984] AC 463, [1984] 1 All ER 740, HL; para 12.29.

PRODUCTION AND SUPPLY

19.29 The Act provides a number of offences involving controlled drugs, several of which provide that an activity is unlawful unless authorised by regulations. Under these,[1] for example, the offences of producing, supplying or offering to supply a controlled drug, or being concerned in such, are not committed by a person who is licensed for this purpose by the Home Secretary, nor by a doctor, pharmacist, public analyst or a person in certain other occupations, acting in his capacity as such, provided in the case of supply that the recipient is a person who may lawfully possess that drug.[2] The accused bears the burden of proving that he falls within one of these exemptions.[3]

These offences are triable either way and punishable on conviction on indictment with up to life imprisonment in the case of Class A drugs, 14 years' imprisonment in the case of Class B drugs and five years' in the case of Class C drugs.[4]

'Supply' connotes more than the mere transfer of physical control from one person to another;[5] it means to furnish to another the drug for the purpose of enabling the other to use it for his own purposes.[5] Consequently, the return of a drug to someone who already owns it constitutes supplying it, as does handing over a cannabis cigarette to someone so that he can take a puff.[6] On the other hand, a person who hands drugs to another for safekeeping does not supply them to him.[7]

1 Misuse of Drugs Act 1971, s 4.
2 Misuse of Drugs Regulations 1985, regs 5–9.
3 *Hunt* [1987] 1 All ER 1 at 12 and 18, per Lords Griffiths and Ackner.
4 Misuse of Drugs Act 1971, Sch 4, as amended by the Controlled Drugs (Penalties) Act 1985.
5 *Maginnis* [1987] AC 303, [1987] 1 All ER 907, HL.
6 Ibid; *Delgado* [1984] 1 All ER 449, [1984] 1 WLR 89, CA.
7 *Dempsey* (1985) 82 Cr App Rep 291, CA.

POSSESSION

19.30 There are two sets of offences involving possession of a controlled drug:

a) *Offences of unauthorised possession*,[1] which are triable and punishable on conviction on indictment with imprisonment for up to seven, five or two years according to whether the drug belongs to Class A, B or C.[2]

Those persons, such as doctors, acting in their capacity as such, who have authority to produce or supply controlled drugs are also authorised to possess them; a doctor who is in possession of a drug for the purpose of bona fide treating himself is acting in his capacity as such, but not if his purpose is an illegitimate one (eg to use the drug to commit suicide).[3] In addition certain persons, eg constables acting in the course of their duty and persons engaged in the business of a carrier when acting in the course of it, have a general authority to possess any controlled drug. Lastly, a person in possession of a controlled drug for medical, dental or veterinary purposes in accordance with the direction of a doctor, dentist or 'vet' is not in unauthorised possession unless, in the case of supply by or on behalf of a doctor, that person has failed to disclose to him that he was then being supplied with a controlled drug by another doctor or a statement false in a material particular has been made by him or on his behalf by another.[4] The accused bears the burden of proving that he falls within one of these exemptions.[5]

If the quantity of the drug possessed by a person is so minute as in the light of common sense to amount to nothing, there can be no conviction for possession of a controlled drug. However, if the quantity of the drug is visible, tangible and measurable it will amount to something, however small, and there can be a conviction for its possession, even though the quantity is too small to be usable.[6]

b) *Offences of possession (whether authorised or not) with intent to supply the drug unlawfully to another.*[7] These are also triable either way but are punishable more severely than those in a), the maximum imprisonment on conviction on indictment being life imprisonment in the case of a Class A drug and 14 years' and five years' in the case of Class B and C drugs respectively,[8] and are aimed at those who peddle drugs. Where a person is in joint possession of a drug but does not intend personally to supply it, he can be convicted of the present offence only if he knows that his co-possessor intends to supply *and* he and his co-possessor were engaged in a joint venture of supplying it to others.[9]

1 Misuse of Drugs Act 1971, s 5(1) and (2).
2 Ibid, Sch 4.
3 *Dunbar* [1982] 1 All ER 188, [1981] 1 WLR 1536, CA.
4 Misuse of Drugs Regulations 1985, regs 5, 6 and 10.
5 *Hunt* [1987] 1 All ER 1 at 12 and 18, per Lords Griffiths and Ackner.
6 *Boyesen* [1982] AC 768, [1982] 2 All ER 161, HL.
7 Misuse of Drugs Act 1971, s 5(3).
8 Ibid, Sch 4, as amended by the Controlled Drugs (Penalties) Act 1985.
9 *Downes* [1984] LS Gaz R 2216, CA. Also see *Greenfield* (1983) 78 Cr App Rep 179n, [1983] Crim LR 397, CA.

19.31 *Meaning of 'possession'* The concept of 'possession' is an elusive one and in relation to the offences of possession of drugs the courts have not always spoken clearly or consistently. Consequently, the following account must not be viewed as necessarily the only interpretation of the cases.

Physical custody of the drug is not necessary for possession but physical control over it is.[1] It follows that a person who has bought a controlled drug is not in possession of it if it is still hidden in the seller's car or stored in the seller's car; on the other hand, a person who leaves a drug in his car or at home while he is away remains in possession of the drug since he retains physical control over it.

Possession cannot begin until the person with control is aware that the thing is under his control:[2] if a drug is slipped into a person's pocket, or left in his room, and he does not have the vaguest idea that it is there he is not in possession of it. (As an exception, a person is in possession of a drug delivered to his residence, even though he is unaware that it has arrived, provided it is delivered in response to a request by him.[3])

Knowledge of a thing's quality is not required. It follows that a mere mistake by D as to the quality of a thing under his control is not enough to prevent him being in possession.[4] For example, in *Warner v Metropolitan Police Comr*[5] Lord Pearce stated that, if D knows that he is in control of some tablets which he believes to be aspirin (or, even, sweets) but which are, in fact, heroin, he is in possession of the heroin tablets. Likewise, the Divisional Court has held that, if D picks up a cigarette containing cannabis and puts it in his pocket, believing that it only contains tobacco, he is in possession of the cannabis.[6] The law distinguishes in this context between knowledge of a thing's quality and knowledge of its nature. If a person mistakenly believes that the thing in his control is something of a wholly different nature, he is not in possession of it.[7] The distinction between quality and nature is one of degree. As indicated by the fact that drugs and sweets have not been regarded as different in nature, only if there is an extreme difference between the qualities of the actual thing and the supposed thing will there be a difference in nature. An example might be where a tablet of a controlled drug was handed to D in the dark and D thought that it was a 5p coin or a button. Clearly the distinction between a thing's quality and nature is not an easy one to draw.

In the case of drugs in a parcel, packet or other container in a person's physical control, he is in possession of those drugs if he knows that he is in control of that container and that it contains something (unless, of course, he is mistaken as to the nature – as opposed to the quality – of the contents).[8]

Possession once begun continues as long as the thing is in the person's control, even though he has forgotten about it or mistakenly believes it has been destroyed or disposed of.[9]

A person can be in joint possession of drugs in another's possession, but only if he has the knowledge and control over them normally required for possession. Consequently, for example, a person who is merely proved to have been living with a person who possesses drugs in a locked trunk in the house is not in joint possession of them.[10]

1 *Lockyer v Gibb* [1967] 2 QB 243, [1966] 2 All ER 653, DC; Misuse of Drugs Act 1971, s 37(3).
2 See, for instance, *Ashton-Rickardt* [1978] 1 All ER 173, [1978] 1 WLR 37, CA. Cf *Lewis* (1988) 87 Cr App Rep 270, CA, where the Court stated that it was not necessary that D should have had actual knowledge that the substance was under his control, since it was enough that he ought to have imputed to him knowledge that it was.
3 *Peaston* (1978) 69 Cr App Rep 203, [1979] Crim LR 183, CA.
4 *Warner v Metropolitan Police Comr* [1969] 2 AC 256, [1968] 2 All ER 356; *Searle v Randolph* [1972] Crim LR 779, DC; *McNamara* (1988) 87 Cr App Rep 246, CA. However, a mistake as to quality may afford the accused a defence under s 28 of the 1971 Act.
5 [1969] 2 AC 256 at 305, [1968] 2 All ER 356, per Lord Pearce.
6 *Searle v Randolph* [1972] Crim LR 779, DC.
7 *Warner v Metropolitan Police Comr* [1969] 2 AC 256 at 305, [1968] 2 All ER 356, per Lord Pearce.
8 *McNamara* (1987) 87 Cr App Rep 246, CA.
9 *Buswell* [1972] 1 All ER 75, [1972] 1 WLR 64, CA; *Martindale* [1986] 3 All ER 25, [1986] 1 WLR 1042, CA; *McCalla* (1988) 87 Cr App Rep 372, CA.

10 *Bland* [1988] Crim LR 41, CA. Nor, on such proof, would that person be an accomplice to the other's possession; para 23.11.

DEFENCES

19.32 Assuming that the prosecution has proved that the accused supplied etc or possessed[1] a controlled drug, he can be convicted of the relevant offence mentioned above, even though it is not proved that he knew that what he was supplying etc or possessing was a controlled drug. However, s 28 of the 1971 Act provides the accused with a defence if he can prove that he did not believe that the substance in question was any kind of controlled drug and that he neither suspected nor had reason to suspect that this was so. It is not a defence that the accused mistakenly believed the substance was a different kind of controlled drug unless he mistakenly believed that the drug was one which he was authorised to produce, supply or possess as the case may be; even so he must have had no reason to suspect that it was a controlled drug of the type alleged. Of course, ignorance of the criminal law being no defence,[2] it is no defence for the accused to prove that while he knew etc that he was in possession of LSD he did not believe or have reason to suspect that LSD was a controlled drug. In deciding whether the accused had 'no reason to suspect', voluntary intoxication on his part must be ignored.[3]

1 It has been argued that s 28 alters the burden of proof in relation to the knowledge required for *possession* and places it on the accused to prove absence of such knowledge: Mathias [1983] Crim LR 689 (also see Ribeiro and Perry [1979] Crim LR 90), but this was rejected in *Ashton-Rickardt* [1978] 1 All ER 173, [1978] 1 WLR 37, CA, and in *McNamara* (1988) 87 Cr App Rep 246, CA.
2 Para 6.73.
3 *Young* [1984] 2 All ER 164, [1984] 1 WLR 654, CA; para 9.67.

19.33 Additional defences are provided by s 5(4) of the 1971 Act for the offences of unauthorised possession, viz, that the accused took possession of the controlled drug in order to prevent the commission of an offence in connection with it by another and that as soon as possible thereafter he took reasonable steps to destroy it or to deliver it into lawful custody, or that he took possession of it for the purpose of delivering it into lawful custody and that as soon as possible afterwards he took reasonable steps to do so. The accused has the onus of proving these defences.

MISUSE ON PREMISES

19.34 The last offences to be described here are those of, being the occupier or a person concerned in the management of any premises, knowingly permitting or suffering the unauthorised production or supply of a controlled drug, or the preparation of opium for smoking, or the smoking of cannabis, cannabis resin or prepared opium, to take place on those premises.[1] These offences are triable either way and punishable on conviction on indictment with a maximum of 14 years' imprisonment where a Class A or B drug is involved and 5 years' if a Class C drug.

'The occupier' is not limited to tenants and other people with a legal estate in the premises. A person is 'the occupier' of premises if he is entitled to the exclusive possession of them, in the sense that he has the requisite degree of control over them to exclude from them those who might otherwise intend to carry on one of the forbidden activities.[2] Thus, a student who had a study bedroom in a college hostel was held in *Tao*[3] to be the occupier of it because his contractual licence gave him such exclusivity of possession, whether or not he was entitled to exclude the college authorities. A person 'concerned in the management of premises' includes someone who, though not 'the occupier' or having any legal interest in them and even though he is on them unlawfully, is concerned in exercising control over the premises or in running or organising them.[4]

Unlike the offences of production, supply and possession, these offences require proof of full mens rea since the word 'knowingly'[5] is used in their definition.

1 Misuse of Drugs Act 1971, s 8.
2 *Tao* [1977] QB 141, [1976] 3 All ER 65, CA.
3 [1977] QB 141, [1976] 3 All ER 65, CA.
4 *Josephs and Christie* (1977) 65 Cr App Rep 253, CA.
5 Para 6.59.

OFFENCES BY CORPORATIONS

19.35 A director, secretary or other similar officer of a corporation which has committed an offence under the 1971 Act is also liable for it, if it is committed with his consent or connivance or if its commission is attributable to any neglect on his part.[1]

1 Misuse of Drugs Act 1971, s 21. See para 9.90.

20   Road traffic offences

20.1   Offences connected with vehicles are not entirely a product of motor vehicles. For example, the Highway Act 1835 contains several provisions relating to vehicles, and under s 35 of the Offences against the Person Act 1861 it is an offence punishable with imprisonment for two years to cause bodily harm by the wanton or furious driving of a vehicle (whether motor or otherwise, eg a horse-drawn cart). However, in modern times the overwhelming majority of prosecutions in this field have been brought under a series of Road Traffic Acts and regulations made under them. The Road Traffic Act 1988 is currently the principal Act, although it is supplemented by a number of other statutes, in particular the Road Traffic Offenders Act 1988 (which deals with matters relating to trial, sentence and fixed penalties among other things) and the Road Traffic Act 1991 (which introduced a number of new offences and provisions relating to road traffic). The Road Traffic Act 1988 and the Road Traffic Offenders Act 1988 consolidated much of the previous road traffic legislation.

A very large number of road traffic offences are purely regulatory and involve no moral blame, but some can fairly be regarded as coming within the ambit of criminal law in its strict and traditional sense: it is difficult to know where to draw the line and standards vary. It is only possible in a book such as this to deal with those road traffic offences which are clearly the most serious.

Road traffic offences are not contained in the draft Criminal Code Bill referred to in para 3.21.

Some general matters

20.2   *Warning etc of prosecution*   Sections 1 and 2 of the Road Traffic Offenders Act 1988 provide that before a person can be convicted of several offences, notably those of dangerous driving, careless driving and speeding, one important condition must be fulfilled unless, at the time of the offence or immediately thereafter, an accident occurs owing to the presence on a road of the vehicle in respect of which the offence is committed.[1] The condition is that *either* the accused must have been warned, at the time the offence was committed,[2] that the question of prosecuting him would be taken into consideration, *or* within 14 days after the offence a summons must have been served on the accused or a notice of intended prosecution must have been served on him or the vehicle's registered owner. If this condition is not fulfilled, the court may nevertheless convict if satisfied that the name and address of the accused or registered owner could not have been ascertained in time with reasonable diligence, or that the accused himself contributed to the failure.[3]

1 This exception does not apply if the accident was so trivial that the driver was unaware of it: *Bentley v Dickinson* (1982) 147 JP 526, [1983] RTR 356, DC; cf *DPP v Pidhajecki* [1991] Crim LR 471, DC, where it was held that the exception did apply in the case of a serious accident, despite the fact that the driver had no recollection of it because of amnesia, since he would be aware of it through other sources.
2 It is often impossible to give such a warning at the 'time' of the offence in its literal sense, but the 'time' of the offence is understood in a wider sense and whether a warning was given in time is a question of fact and degree: see *Okike* [1978] RTR 489, CA. To be effective, a warning must be heard and understood by the person to whom it is addressed: *Gibson v Dalton* [1980] RTR 410, DC.
3 Road Traffic Offenders Act 1988, s 2(3). See *Nicholson v Tapp* [1972] 3 All ER 245, [1972] 1 WLR 1044, DC.

20.3 *Reporting of accidents* If personal injury or damage is caused in a motor accident to any other person, or to another vehicle (including a bicycle), or to an animal (ie any horse, cattle, sheep, pig, goat or dog), or to any property constructed on, fixed to, growing in or otherwise forming part of the road or land adjacent thereto, such as a lamp-post or bollard, the driver of the vehicle or vehicles concerned must stop and give his name and address to any person reasonably requiring it. Failure to do so is an offence.[1] If for any reason the driver does not give his name and address, he must report the accident as soon as possible at a police station or to a police constable and in any case within 24 hours, and it is a separate offence to fail to do so.[2] It has been held to be a defence if the accused proves that he was ignorant of the fact that there had been an accident.[3]

1 Road Traffic Act 1988, s 170.
2 Ibid; *Roper v Sullivan* [1978] RTR 181, DC.
3 *Selby v Chief Constable for Avon and Somerset* [1988] RTR 216, DC.

20.4 *Disqualification and endorsement* The court has the power, and in some cases the obligation (unless there are special reasons for not doing so), to order a convicted person to be disqualified from driving.[1] Unless there are special reasons for not doing so, disqualification for not less than two years must be ordered on a conviction for manslaughter, causing death by dangerous driving or causing death by careless driving when unfit through drink or drugs, or for not less than 12 months on a conviction for driving with excess alcohol in the body and in a few other cases.

'Special reasons' are reasons special to the offence and not to the offender;[2] consequently, for example, the fact that the offender is a professional driver is not a reason for not disqualifying him. The existence of a special reason does not automatically mean that disqualification will not be ordered; the court has a discretion. An example of what may be a special reason on a conviction for driving with excess alcohol (and one where the court's discretion is likely to be exercised in favour of the offender) is the fact that the offender was faced with an emergency which he alone had to deal with and had no alternative but to drive, provided his alcohol content was not far in excess of the statutory limit.[3] Another example of what may be a special reason is that, unknown to the offender and without any reason to suspect on his part, his drink was laced and that thereby his blood contained excess alcohol, which facts he must prove.[4]

If a person is convicted of an offence involving obligatory endorsement, the endorsement must include the appropriate penalty points for that offence. There are two exceptions to this requirement: where the court orders the person to be disqualified from driving, and where for special reasons it decides not to order endorsement.[5]

Under the penalty points system, an offender must with the exception mentioned below be disqualified for at least six months (or, in some cases, one or two years) if the penalty points which have been endorsed in the last three years total 12 or more.[6] Such a 'totting-up' disqualification is not mandatory. The court may not disqualify the offender at all or may order a shorter disqualification if, having regard to all the circumstances, including those relating to the offender as well as those relating to the offence,[7] but excluding hardship (unless exceptional) or the fact that the offence is not a serious one, it is satisfied that there are grounds for not doing so.[8]

1 Road Traffic Offenders Act 1988, Sch 2.
2 *Whittall v Kirby* [1947] KB 194, [1946] 2 All ER 552, DC.
3 *Taylor v Rajan* [1974] QB 424, [1974] 1 All ER 1087, DC; *Robinson v DPP* [1989] RTR 42, DC.
4 *Pugsley v Hunter* [1973] 2 All ER 10, [1973] 1 WLR 578, DC; *Pridige v Gant* [1985] RTR 196, DC. Also see *Krebbs* [1977] RTR 406, CA.
5 Road Traffic Offenders Act 1988, ss 29 and 44.
6 Road Traffic Offenders Act 1988, s 35; *Yates* [1986] RTR 68, CA.
7 *Preston* [1986] RTR 136, CA.
8 Road Traffic Offenders Act 1988, s 35.

20.5 *Fixed penalties* In relation to many minor road traffic offences, such as speeding, failure to comply with a road sign or breach of the regulations relating to the construction and equipment of motor vehicles, a fixed penalty system applies. The system is that, in relation to these offences and provided certain conditions are satisfied, a uniformed constable has a discretion to impose on the offender a fixed penalty rather than report him with a view to consideration being given to his being prosecuted. If a fixed penalty is imposed in relation to an endorseable offence, the offender's licence will be endorsed with the appropriate penalty points.[1] The fixed penalty system does not apply to the road traffic offences discussed in this chapter, which are clearly all serious ones.

1 Road Traffic Act 1988, ss 51-89.

20.6 *Driving* Most of the offences below refer to driving a mechanically propelled vehicle or a motor vehicle on a road or other public place. The essence of 'driving' is the use of the driver's controls (or, at least, one of them) in order to control the movement of the vehicle, however that movement is produced,[1] provided that what occurs can in any sense of the word be regarded as 'driving'.[2] Thus, a person who releases the handbrake and 'coasts' downhill in a car is 'driving' it (and this is so even though the steering is locked),[3] and so is a person in the driver's seat of a vehicle which is being towed if he has the ability to control its movements by means of the brakes or steering,[4] but a person who is pushing a car and steering it with his hand through the window is not.[5] As indicated in para 9.82, a corporation cannot be convicted (through the acts of an employee or agent) of an offence involving 'driving'.

1 *Macdonagh* [1974] QB 448, [1974] 2 All ER 257, CA; *Burgoyne v Phillips* (1983) 147 JP 375, [1983] RTR 49, DC; *McKoen v Ellis* (1986) 151 JP 60, [1987] Crim LR 54, DC. Also see *Tyler v Whatmore* [1976] RTR 83, DC; para 23.1.

2 *Jones v Pratt* [1983] RTR 54, DC; *McKoen v Ellis.*
3 *Burgoyne v Phillips.* Also see *Saycell v Bool* [1948] 2 All ER 83, DC.
4 *McQuaid v Anderton* [1980] 3 All ER 540, [1981] 1 WLR 154, [1980] RTR 371, DC.
5 *Macdonagh* [1974] QB 448, [1974] 2 All ER 257, CA.

20.7 *Mechanically propelled vehicle and motor vehicle* A 'mechanically propelled vehicle' is not specifically defined by the legislation but it has been held to include a vehicle whose engine has been removed, where there is a possibility that it may soon be replaced,[1] and a vehicle which has broken down because of mechanical failure.[2]

'Motor vehicle' has a more limited meaning. It is defined by s 185 of the Road Traffic Act 1988 as a mechanically propelled vehicle intended or adapted for use on roads but by s 189 of that Act certain mechanically propelled vehicles controlled by a pedestrian and certain electrically assisted pedal cycles (eg the Sinclair C5) are deemed not to be motor vehicles. Moreover, a go-kart has been held not to be a motor vehicle (since it is not designed or adapted for use on roads),[3] although it is undoubtedly a mechanically propelled vehicle.

1 *Newberry v Simmonds* [1961] 2 QB 345, [1961] 2 All ER 318, DC.
2 *Paul* [1952] NI 61.
3 *Burns v Currell* [1963] 2 QB 433, [1963] 2 All ER 297, DC.

20.8 *Road or other public place* A 'road' is defined by s 192 of the Road Traffic Act 1988 as any highway and any other road to which the public has access, including bridges over which a road passes.

A 'public place' means a place, such as a car park or sportsfield, to which the public are admitted or have access at the material time.[1]

1 *Collinson* (1931) 23 Cr App Rep 49, CCA; *Elkins v Cartlidge* [1947] 1 All ER 829, 177 LT 519, DC.

20.9 *Trial and punishment* The mode of trial and the maximum punishments for the offences described below are provided by Sch 2 of the Road Traffic Offenders Act 1988 .

Dangerous driving

20.10 Section 2 of the 1988 Act, as substituted by s 1 of the Road Traffic Act 1991, provides that a person who drives a mechanically propelled vehicle dangerously on a road or other public place commits an offence which is triable either way, and punishable with a maximum of two years' imprisonment on conviction on indictment. Unless there are special reasons, disqualification from driving for not less than 12 months must be ordered. In addition, the offender must be ordered to take an appropriate driving test and will remain disqualified after the period of disqualification has been served until he has passed the test. The offence of dangerous driving replaces that of reckless driving.

20.11 Dangerous driving is defined by s 2A(1) of the 1988 Act (which was introduced by the 1991 Act). Section 2A(1) provides that a person is to be regarded as driving dangerously if:

a) the way he drives falls far below what would be expected of a competent and careful driver; and

b) it would be obvious to a competent and careful driver that driving in that way would be dangerous.

The test in a) is a purely objective one; it would be no defence that the accused was doing his incompetent best.

The test in s 2A(1) is concerned with the *manner* of the accused's driving. However, driving may also be rendered dangerous by virtue of the *state* of the vehicle, since s 2A(2) provides that a person is also to be regarded as driving dangerously if it would be obvious to a competent and careful driver that driving the vehicle in its current state would be dangerous. In determining the state of the vehicle, regard may be had to anything attached to or carried on or in it, and to the manner in which it is attached or carried.[1]

For the purposes of both types of dangerous driving, 'dangerous' is defined by s 2A(3). It refers to danger either of injury to any person or of serious damage to property. Section 2A(3) adds that, in determining what would be expected of, or obvious to, a competent and careful driver, regard must be had not only to the circumstances of which he could be expected to be aware but also to any circumstances shown to have been within the accused's knowledge.

Since the definition of dangerous driving is concerned with the manner of the driving or the state of the vehicle, driving is not dangerous simply because the driver is in a dangerous state through drink or drugs. The appropriate offence in such a case is one of the drink/driving offences described in paras 20.17 to 20.33.

1 Road Traffic Act 1988, s 2A(4).

20.12 *Dangerous cycling* By s 28 of the Road Traffic Act 1988, as substituted by s 7 of the Road Traffic Act 1991, a person who rides a bicycle or tricycle dangerously on a *road* commits an offence which is triable only summarily and punishable with a maximum fine not exceeding level 4 on the standard scale (£2,500). This offence is limited to cycling in a dangerous *manner* and cannot be committed simply by cycling on a bicycle or tricycle whose state is dangerous.

CAUSING DEATH BY DANGEROUS DRIVING

20.13 Section 1 of the 1988 Act, as substituted by s 1 of the Road Traffic Act 1991, provides that a person who causes the death of another person by driving a mechanically propelled vehicle dangerously on a road or other public place is guilty of an offence which is punishable with up to five years' imprisonment and is triable only on indictment. Unless there are special reasons, disqualification for a minimum of two years is obligatory. In addition, the driver must also be ordered to take an appropriate driving test and he will remain disqualified after the period of disqualification until he has passed the test. The offence replaces the offence of causing death by reckless driving. In appropriate cases where the manner of the driving or the state of the vehicle gave rise to an obvious and serious risk of injuring someone, a charge of involuntary manslaughter can be brought successfully.[1]

'Dangerous driving' bears the same meaning as in s 2. Consequently, an offence is not committed under s 1 simply because the driver is in a dangerous condition and kills someone as a result of his driving in that condition, if the manner of his driving or the state of his vehicle is not dangerous.

However, if his dangerous condition is due to drink or drugs he may be guilty of the offence of causing death by careless driving while under the influence of drink or drugs, which is described in para 20.22.

The prosecution must prove a causal link between the accused's dangerous driving and the death of the other person.[2] What was said in Chapter 11 about the victim of an offence of homicide and of the requirement of causation applies to the present offence. In particular, it should be noted that the accused's dangerous driving need not be the sole cause of death; it is enough that it is a substantial (ie more than minimal) contribution to the death.[3]

No mens rea need be proved as to the risk of death resulting from the dangerous driving; it follows that it is irrelevant that that risk was unforeseen or even unforeseeable.[4]

1 Paras 11.51–11.59.
2 Paras 11.7–11.18.
3 *Curphey*(1957) 41 Cr App Rep 78; *Hennigan* [1971] 3 All ER 133, CA.
4 This was the position under the previous offence of causing death by reckless driving:*Lawrence* [1982] AC 510, [1981] 1 All ER 974, HL; *Seymour* [1983] 2 AC 493, [1983] 2 All ER 1058, HL. There is no reason to doubt that the rule is the same under the present offence.

Careless driving

20.14 This offence is governed by s 3 of the Road Traffic Act 1988, as substituted by s 2 of the Road Traffic Act 1991. Section 3 provides that, if any person drives a mechanically propelled vehicle on a road or other public place without due care and attention, or without reasonable consideration for other persons using the road or other public place, he is guilty of an offence triable only summarily and punishable with a fine not exceeding level 4 on the standard scale (£2,500). The court has a discretion to disqualify an offender from driving.

Section 3 creates two separate offences. An information which charges a person with driving 'a motor car without due care and attention or without reasonable consideration for other persons using the road' is therefore bad for duplicity.[1]

In relation to the first offence, the standard of due care and attention is an objective one, fixed and impersonal, so that it is the same for a learner driver as it is for a qualified one,[2] and there is no special standard for people like police officers who are driving to an emergency.[3] When someone is charged with driving without due care and attention, the question is whether he was exercising that degree of care and attention which a reasonable and prudent driver would have exercised in the circumstances; if he has failed to do so, however slightly, he can be convicted of careless driving, whether his failure to do so was a deliberate act or was due to an error of judgment or any other cause.[4] The present offence can be committed either by driving in a manner which falls below the standard of due care and attention or by driving a vehicle whose condition is such that to drive it in the circumstances in question is to fall below the standard of due care and attention.[5] However, an accused will have a defence if the vehicle developed a mechanical defect of which he did not know and which he could not reasonably be expected to know.[6]

It is a question of fact in every case whether an accused driver has fallen below the objective standard of care.[7] Failure to observe a provision of the

Highway Code does not of itself establish driving without due care and attention, but any such failure may be relied on as evidence of it.[8] In some cases, however, the facts are such that, unless the accused driver offers some other explanation consistent with his having taken due care which is not disproved, the only proper inference is careless driving, in which case the magistrates must convict him (and if they do not the Divisional Court will order them to do so).[9]

In any case, if the magistrates decide that there are several possible causes of what has happened, one of which is careless driving, they must convict the accused, unless he puts forward evidence in support of another possible cause.[10]

A person can drive without reasonable consideration for other persons using the road or other public place even where his lack of consideration is to his own passenger.[11]

A person who causes death by careless driving when under the influence of drink or drugs commits a more serious offence, which is dealt with in para 20.22.

1 *Surrey Justices, ex p Witherick* [1932] 1 KB 450, DC; cf *Clow* [1965] 1 QB 598, [1963] 2 All ER 216, CCA.
2 *McCrone v Riding* [1938] 1 All ER 157, DC; *Preston Justices, ex p Lyons* [1982] RTR 173, DC. See Wasik 'A Learner's Careless Driving' [1982] Crim LR 411 (and 546).
3 *Wood v Richards* [1977] RTR 201, DC.
4 *Simpson v Peat* [1952] 2 QB 24, [1952] 1 All ER 447, DC; *Taylor v Rogers* [1960] Crim LR 271, DC.
5 *Haynes v Swain* [1975] RTR 40, DC.
6 *Spurge* [1961] 2 QB 205, [1961] 2 All ER 688, CCA.
7 *Simpson v Peat*; *Walker v Tolhurst* [1976] RTR 513, DC; *Dilks v Bowman-Shaw* [1981] RTR 4, DC.
8 Road Traffic Act 1988, s 38(7).
9 *Wright v Wenlock* [1971] RTR 228, DC; *Rabjohns v Burgar* [1971] RTR 234, DC; *Jarvis v Williams* [1979] RTR 497, DC.
10 *Bensley v Smith* [1972] RTR 221, DC.
11 *Pawley v Wharldall* [1966] 1 QB 373, [1965] 2 All ER 757, DC.

20.15 *Careless cycling* By s 29 of the 1988 Act, a person who rides a bicycle or tricycle on a road without due care and attention, or without reasonable consideration for other persons using the road, is guilty of an offence triable only summarily and punishable with a fine not exceeding level 3 on the standard scale (£1,000).

Drinking and driving

20.16 Sections 3A to 11 of the Road Traffic Act 1988 contain provisions concerning various offences relating to drinking and driving. These provisions have attracted a mass of case law, but it is not appropriate in this book to do more than give a fairly simple account of them and of how they have been interpreted.

The three principal offences are driving or attempting to drive a motor vehicle when unfit to drive through drink or drugs (s 4),[1] driving or attempting to drive a motor vehicle with an alcohol concentration in excess of the prescribed limit (s 5), and causing death by careless driving when under the influence of drink or drugs (s 3A).

Clearly, many intoxicated drivers could be prosecuted under s 4 or s 5. However, apart from cases where the accused is unfit through drugs or he is below the excess limit, it is the almost invariable practice to prosecute for the latter offence rather than the former. This is because s 5 lays down an objective test; whereas under s 4 it is necessary for the prosecution to prove that the accused's ability to drive properly was for the time being impaired by drink or drugs, which is a question of fact for the magistrates.

1 As amended by the Road Traffic Act 1991, s 4.

DRIVING, ATTEMPTING TO DRIVE OR BEING IN CHARGE WHILE UNFIT

20.17 *Driving or attempting to drive when unfit* By s 4(1) of the Road Traffic Act 1988, a person who, when driving or attempting to drive a mechanically propelled vehicle on a road or other public place, is unfit to drive through drink or drugs commits an offence. The offence is triable summarily only and is punishable with a maximum of six months' imprisonment or a fine not exceeding level 5 on the standard scale (£5,000) or both. Unless there are special reasons, disqualification from driving for not less than 12 months must be ordered.

The driving or attempted driving while unfit must occur on a road or public place.[1] What constitutes 'driving' has already been explained.[2] In relation to 'attempting to drive', the reader is referred to s 3 of the Criminal Attempts Act 1981,[3] which may apply to the present offence. 'Drink' means alcoholic drink and 'drug' means any intoxicant other than alcohol,[4] and includes medicines[5] and glue.[6]

1 Para 20.8.
2 Para 20.6.
3 Para 21.77.
4 Road Traffic Act 1988, s 11(2).
5 *Armstrong v Clark* [1957] 2 QB 391, [1957] 1 All ER 433, DC.
6 *Bradford v Wilson* (1983) 147 JP 573, [1983] Crim LR 482, DC.

20.18 *In charge when unfit* Under s 4(2) of the Road Traffic Act 1988, it is an offence, separate from that of driving or attempting to drive,[1] for a person to be in charge of a mechanically propelled vehicle on a road or other public place when unfit to drive through drink or drugs. It is triable summarily only and is punishable with a maximum of three months' imprisonment or a fine not exceeding level 4 on the standard scale (£2,500) or both; disqualification is discretionary.

In *DPP v Watkins*[2] the Divisional Court held that, in order to be found to have been in charge of a vehicle, it must be proved that there was some connection between the accused and the vehicle on a road or other public place. It held that there are two distinct types of case:

a) *If the accused is the owner or lawful possessor of the vehicle or has recently driven it,* he will have been in charge of it and he will remain in charge of it unless he has put the vehicle in someone else's charge or if in all the circumstances he has ceased to be in actual control and there is no reasonable possibility of his resuming actual control while unfit (as where he is at home in bed for the night, or where he is at a great distance from the vehicle, or where the vehicle is taken by another).

b) *If the accused is not the owner, lawful possessor or recent driver,* but is sitting in the vehicle or is otherwise involved with it, the question for the court is whether he has assumed charge of it. He will have if he is voluntarily in control of it or if, in the circumstances (including his position, intention and actions), he may be expected imminently to assume control. Usually, this will involve the accused having entered the vehicle and evinced an intention to drive it. However, this may not be necessary if he has shown in some other way an intent to drive the vehicle (for example, by stealing its keys in circumstances which show that he means presently to drive it).

Although proof that a person was in charge of a vehicle does not require proof of any likelihood that he would have driven it while unfit, s 4(3) provides that a person is deemed not to have been in charge, and therefore has a defence, if he proves that at the material time the circumstances were such that there was no likelihood of his driving as long as he remained unfit to drive through drink or drugs, but in determining whether there was such a likelihood the court may disregard any injury to him or damage to property.[3]

A person can be in charge of a vehicle on a road or other public place even though he himself is somewhere other than a road or other public place at the material time.[4]

1 *Gardner v DPP* (1988) Times, 24 December, DC.
2 [1989] 1 All ER 1126, DC.
3 Road Traffic Act 1988, s 4(4).
4 *DPP v Webb* [1988] RTR 374, DC.

20.19 *Power of arrest* Whether or not he is in uniform, a constable[1] may arrest a person without a warrant if he has reasonable cause to suspect that that person is or has been committing an offence under s 5(1) or s 5(2).[2] For the purpose of effecting an arrest under *this* power, a constable may enter (if need be by force) any place where that person is or where the constable, with reasonable cause, suspects him to be.[3]

1 A 'constable' is anyone holding the office of constable, whatever his rank.
2 Road Traffic Act 1988, s 4(6).
3 Ibid, s 4(7).

20.20 *Evidence* Section 4(5) of the Road Traffic Act 1988 provides that a person is to be taken to be unfit to drive if his ability to drive properly is for the time being impaired. As already said, it is a question of fact whether a person's ability was so impaired. The evidence before the court on this point will normally include the report of a medical examination by a police surgeon, and may include the result of the analysis of a specimen of breath, blood or urine which has been required under s 7 of the Act. The procedure relating to such specimens, and the rules relating to the use of their analysis as evidence, are essentially the same as for the offences of driving, attempting to drive or being in charge with excess alcohol and are discussed in paras 20.28 to 20.33.

20.21 *Cycling when unfit* It is an offence under s 30 of the Road Traffic Act 1988 to ride a bicycle or tricycle on a road or other public place when unfit to ride through drink or drugs to such an extent as to be incapable of having proper control of the cycle. The offence is triable only summarily. It is punishable with a fine not exceeding level 3 on the standard scale (£1,000).

CAUSING DEATH BY CARELESS DRIVING WHEN UNDER THE INFLUENCE OF DRINK OR DRUGS

20.22 Section 3A of the 1988 Act, which was inserted by s 3 of the Road Traffic Act 1991, provides that, if a person causes the death of another person by driving a mechanically propelled vehicle on a road or other public place without due care and attention, or without reasonable consideration for other persons using the road or place, and:

a) he is, at the time when he is driving, unfit to drive through drink or drugs, or
b) he has consumed so much alcohol that the proportion of it in his breath, blood or urine at that time exceeds the prescribed limit, or
c) he is, within 18 hours after that time, required to provide a specimen in pursuance of s 7 of the Act but without reasonable excuse fails to provide it,

he is guilty of an offence. An offence under s 3A is triable only on indictment and is punishable with a maximum of five years' imprisonment. Unless there are special reasons, disqualification for a minimum of two years is mandatory.

The elements of an offence under s 3A have largely been explained already. The prosecution must prove that the accused drove a mechanically propelled vehicle on a road or other public place[1] and that he did so without due care and attention, or without reasonable consideration for other users of the road or other public place, depending on which type of offence is charged.[2] The test for such driving is the same as that for careless driving.[3] The prosecution must also prove that the careless driving caused the death of another[4] and that the accused falls within one of three categories of case:

The first is that, at the time that he was driving, he was unfit to drive through drink or drugs. As in the case of an offence under s 4 of the Act, 'drink' means alcoholic drink and 'drug' means any other intoxicant, including medicine or glue, and a person is taken to be unfit to drive if his ability to drive is for the time being impaired.[5]

The second and third categories only operate in relation to a person driving a motor vehicle,[6] as opposed to any other type of mechanically propelled vehicle. The second category of case is where the driver has consumed so much alcohol that the proportion of it in his blood, breath or urine, at the time when he is driving, exceeds the prescribed limit. The provisions relating to that limit, to the taking of specimens for analysis and so on mentioned below in relation to the other drink/driving offences are equally applicable to the present offence.[7]

The third category of case is where the driver of the motor vehicle, within 18 hours of the time when his careless driving resulted in death, was required to provide an evidential specimen in pursuance of s 7[8] of the Act but without reasonable excuse failed[9] to do so.

1 Paras 20.6–20.8.
2 By analogy with s 3, it seems that there are two separate offences under s 3A based on the two methods of careless driving; see para 20.14.
3 Para 20.14.
4 See para 20.13 in relation to causation.
5 Road Traffic Act 1988, s 3A(2).
6 Para 20.7.
7 Paras 20.24 and 20.28–20.33.
8 Para 20.28.
9 Paras 20.35 and 20.36.

DRIVING, ATTEMPTING TO DRIVE OR BEING IN CHARGE WITH EXCESS ALCOHOL

20.23 Under s 5(1) of the Road Traffic Act 1988, it is an offence, triable only summarily, for a person:

a) to drive or attempt to drive a motor vehicle on a road or other public place (s 5(1)(a)); or
b) to be in charge of a motor vehicle on a road or other public place (s 5(1)(b)),

after consuming so much alcohol that the proportion of it in his breath, blood or urine exceeds the relevant prescribed limit. Driving or attempting to drive with excess alcohol is a separate offence from being in charge with excess alcohol.[1]

In relation to an offence of driving or attempting to drive, the maximum punishment is six months' imprisonment or a fine not exceeding level 5 on the standard scale (£5,000) or both. Unless there are special reasons, disqualification for not less than 12 months must be ordered. The maximum punishment for the offence of being in charge is three months' imprisonment or a fine not exceeding level 4 on the standard scale (£2,500) or both; disqualification is discretionary.

1 *Gardner v DPP* (1988) Times, 24 December, DC.

20.24 *Elements and evidence* Most of the elements of these offences have already been explained.[1] It should be noted that, unlike the offences under ss 1 to 4 dealt with above, offences under s 5 are confined to motor vehicles and do not extend to mechanically propelled vehicles in general.

The prescribed limits mentioned above are at present 35 microgrammes of alcohol in 100 millilitres of breath; 80 milligrammes of alcohol in 100 millilitres of blood; or 107 milligrammes of alcohol in 100 millilitres of urine.

In relation to the offence of being in charge, a similar defence applies as in the case of being in charge when unfit through drink or drugs, the accused has a defence if he proves that at the material time the circumstances were such that there was no likelihood of his driving whilst the proportion of alcohol in his breath, blood or urine remained likely to exceed the prescribed limit; but in determining whether there was such a likelihood the court may disregard any injury to him and any damage to the vehicle.[2] Unless the case is so obvious that a layperson would reliably and confidently say that the accused's alcohol level would have fallen below the limit by the time he intended to drive (or was likely to drive), there must be expert evidence as to the rate of alcohol destruction by the body to prove that that level would be below the limit by that time.[3]

The evidence of the element of excess alcohol in the offences under s 5(1) will, except in exceptional cases, be derived solely from the analysis of a specimen of breath, blood or urine. However, a 'screening' breath test and an arrest (whether as a result of a positive screening test or of a failure to provide a breath specimen for it) will normally precede the taking of the specimen of breath, blood or urine on which the prosecution relies. In the following paragraphs the normal procedure will be dealt with in its chronological order.

1 See, especially, para 20.17.
2 Road Traffic Act 1988, s 5(2).
3 *DPP v Frost* [1989] RTR 11, DC.

20.25 *The 'screening' breath test* This is a preliminary test for the purpose of obtaining an indication whether the proportion of alcohol in a person's breath or blood is *likely* to exceed the prescribed limit. The power to require a breath test arises in three cases.

Section 6(1)(a) empowers a constable who is in uniform to require any person driving, attempting to drive or in charge of a motor vehicle on a road or other public place to provide a specimen of breath for a breath test where he has reasonable cause to suspect that that person:

a) has alcohol in his body; or
b) has committed a 'traffic offence' (which includes most offences under the Road Traffic Act 1988, as well as offences under certain other Road Traffic Acts)[1] while the vehicle was in motion.

In either case, the suspicion need not arise while the vehicle is in motion. Indeed, a uniformed constable may stop motorists, under his common law or statutory power[2] to do so, in order to see whether there is a reasonable suspicion that they have consumed alcohol and, if a reasonable suspicion then emerges of such consumption, go on to require a screening breath test.[3] Thus, *random stopping* of motorists is *not prohibited*, although *random breath tests are*.[3]

Second, s 6(1)(b) and (c) empowers a constable in uniform to require a person to provide a specimen of breath for a breath test where he has reasonable cause to suspect that that person *has* been driving or attempting to drive or been in charge of a motor vehicle on a road or other public place and:

a) has done so with alcohol in his body (*and that that person still has alcohol in his body*); or
b) has committed a traffic offence while the vehicle was in motion.

Third, a power to require a breath test is provided by s 6(2), whereby, if an accident occurs owing to the presence of a motor vehicle on a road or other public place, a constable (whether or not in uniform)[4] may require any person whom he has reasonable cause to believe was driving or attempting to drive or in charge of the vehicle at the time of the accident to provide a specimen of breath for a breath test. 'Accident' in this provision bears its ordinary meaning,[5] and it has been held that a crash which is deliberately caused falls within that meaning.[6] The person's car need not have been physically involved but there must have been a direct causal connection between his car being on the road and the accident occurring.[7]

1 Road Traffic Act 1988, s 6(8).
2 See *Steel v Goacher* [1983] RTR 98, [1983] Crim LR 689, DC, and Road Traffic Act 1988, s 163, respectively.
3 *Chief Constable of Gwent v Dash* [1986] RTR 41, DC.
4 The omission of a stipulation that the constable should be in uniform appears to be a drafting error.
5 *Morris* [1972] 1 All ER 384, [1972] 1 WLR 228, CA.
6 *Chief Constable of West Midlands Police v Billingham* [1979] 2 All ER 182, [1979] 1 WLR 747, DC.
7 *Quelch v Phipps* [1955] 2 QB 107, [1955] 2 All ER 302, DC.

20.26 The following general rules apply to a requirement for a screening breath test.

The requirement must be to provide a specimen of breath 'at or near' the place where the requirement is made,[1] except that:

a) where the requirement is made under s 6(2) (ie after an accident involving the person's vehicle), it may instead be required to be provided at a police station specified by the constable;

b) where the requirement is made of a person who is a patient at a hospital, it must be required to be provided at the hospital.[2]

A person who is a patient at a hospital must not be required to provide a specimen of breath unless the medical practitioner in immediate charge of his case has been notified of the proposal to make the requirement. If the medical practitioner objects on the ground that the requirement or the breath test itself would be prejudicial to the proper care and treatment of the patient the requirement must not be made.[3]

A screening breath test must be conducted by means of a device of an approved type.[4] Two types of hand-held device have been approved for this purpose: the first type combines a tube and bag, the crystals in which change colour with the alcohol content of the breath or blood; the second type, which is more commonly used, is a battery operated electronic device which indicates the alcohol content of the breath or blood by means of a display of lights. Neither type of device is intended to give a precise indication of the alcohol content, but merely to indicate whether the alcohol content is likely to be in excess of the prescribed limit.

1 Road Traffic Act 1988, s 6(3).
2 Ibid, s 9(1)(a).
3 Ibid, s 9(1)(b) and (2).
4 Ibid, s 11(2).

20.27 Section 6(5) of the Road Traffic Act 1988 gives a constable a power of arrest without warrant in two cases:

a) if, as a result of the breath test, he has reasonable cause to suspect that the alcohol content in a person's breath or blood exceeds the prescribed limit; or

b) if that person has failed[1] to provide the required specimen of breath and the constable has reason to suspect that he has alcohol in his body.

However, in neither case may a person be arrested when he is at a hospital as a patient.

An arrest for failing to provide a specimen will not be lawful (and will result in liability for false imprisonment) if a valid requirement for a specimen of breath has not been made or if the constable is otherwise acting unlawfully at the time, for example because he is a trespasser. We shall return to these matters shortly.

Normally, a constable will exercise his power of arrest in the above two cases but this is not a pre-condition of further steps in the procedure being adopted[2] and, strictly, is unnecessary if the person concerned is quite happy to accompany the constable to a police station for the next steps in the procedure.

Section 6(6) gives constables powers of entry (if need be by force) for two purposes related to their powers under s 7. First, for the purpose of requiring a person, whom we will call X, to provide a specimen of breath under s 7(2) *in a case where a constable has reasonable cause to suspect that the accident involved injury to someone other than X*, a constable may enter any place where X is or where the constable, with reasonable cause, suspects him to be. It remains to be seen what constitutes an 'injury' for this purpose; does a mere bruise or scratch, or nervous shock, suffice? Second, for the purpose of arresting X *in such a case* a constable may enter any place where X is or where the constable, with reasonable cause, suspects him to be.

These powers of entry are obviously very limited. In cases falling outside them, a constable can only lawfully enter private property with an express or implied licence, which can be withdrawn,[3] and if he enters without a licence (or it is withdrawn) he is (or, as the case may be, becomes) a trespasser and cannot thereafter make a valid requirement for a screening breath test[4] (and therefore failure to supply a screening breath specimen is not an offence)[5] nor a lawful arrest.[6]

1 For what constitutes a 'failure', see para 20.35.
2 *Fox* [1986] AC 281, [1985] 3 All ER 392, HL.
3 Para 18.69.
4 *Morris v Beardmore* [1981] AC 446, [1980] 2 All ER 753, HL; *Fox v Chief Constable of Gwent* [1985] 1 All ER 230, [1985] 1 WLR 33, DC (not the subject of the appeal to the House of Lords: [1986] AC 281, [1985] 3 All ER 392, HL).
5 Para 20.35.
6 *Clowser v Chaplin* [1981] 2 All ER 267, [1981] 1 WLR 837, HL.

PROVISION OF SPECIMENS FOR ANALYSIS

20.28 Section 7(1) of the Road Traffic Act 1988 provides that, in the course of an investigation whether a person has committed an offence under s 3A, s 4 or s 5 of the Act, a constable (who need not be in uniform) may require him:

a) to provide *two* specimens of breath for analysis; or
b) to provide a specimen of blood or urine for a laboratory test.

The fact that a requirement under s 7(1) can be made 'in the course of an investigation' into whether a person has committed an offence under s 3A, s 4 or s 5 indicates that it is not necessary that a screening breath test should previously have been required (although it will normally have been) and that, if there has been such a test, the fact that there has been some breach in the procedure relating to it or that the constable has acted unlawfully in some other way does not constitute a defence.[1] However, the court has a discretion under s 78 of the Police and Criminal Evidence Act 1984 to exclude the evidence obtained from a specimen provided for analysis following an unlawful arrest or other unlawful conduct if, having regard to all the circumstances (including those in which the specimen was obtained), the admission of the evidence would have such an adverse effect on the fairness of the proceedings that the court ought not to admit it.[2] If the unlawful arrest or conduct is associated with bad faith on the part of the constable (eg knowledge of the unlawfulness or trickery), the evidence of the specimens subsequently given for analysis will be particularly liable to be excluded by the court under s 78,[3] but evidence may be excluded under s 78 even if there has not been any bad faith.[4]

1 *Fox* [1986] AC 281, [1985] 3 All ER 392, HL; *Gull v Scarborough* [1987] RTR 261n, DC.
2 There is also a narrower power at common law to exclude illegally obtained evidence on the ground that its prejudicial effect outweighs its probative value: *Sang* [1980] AC 402, [1979] 7 All ER 1222, HL
3 See, for example, *Matto v DPP* [1987] RTR 332, DC.
4 *DPP v Goodwin* (1991) unreported, DC; *DPP v McGladrigan* [1991] Crim LR 851, DC.

20.29 *Evidential breath specimens* The normal method of ascertaining the proportion of alcohol in a person's body is the analysis of a specimen of his breath by means of an approved 'evidential' breath test device; two devices, both of which are electronic, have been approved for this purpose. A requirement under s 7 for the two specimens of breath for analysis can *only* be made at a police station.[1] There are no exceptions; in particular such a requirement cannot be made at a hospital, presumably because the approved evidential breath test devices are not very mobile. The Act does not, however, say that the specimens of breath must be provided at a police station.

Of any two specimens of breath provided by a person in pursuance of s 7 the one with the lower proportion of alcohol must be used as evidence and the other disregarded.[2] However, if the specimen with the lower proportion contains no more than 50 microgrammes of alcohol in 100 millilitres of breath (the prescribed limit being 35 microgrammes), the person who provided it may claim under s 8(2) that it should be replaced by a specimen of blood or urine.[3] If he does, the decision about which specimen it should be is for the constable concerned, except that if a medical practitioner is of the opinion that blood cannot or should not be taken, the specimen must be of urine. If the person then provides the blood or urine specimen requested neither specimen of breath may be used as evidence,[4] otherwise than to support the giving of the statutory option,[5] even if the blood or urine test is vitiated in some way so that its result cannot be used.[6] Although the evidential breath test devices are said to be accurate to within plus or minus five microgrammes, the right to claim a blood or urine test in the case just mentioned has been afforded so as to mitigate any fears that a person may be convicted on the evidence of such a device, whose analysis is immediate and not capable of being checked after the event. Although the Act does not require a person to be advised of his right to claim a blood or urine test in the case just mentioned, the Divisional Court has held that the results of an evidential breath test are inadmissible (otherwise than to support the giving of the statutory option) if he has not been advised of this right.[7]

Somewhat surprisingly, since the decision whether the 'replacement specimen' shall be of blood or urine is for the constable, the constable is required to inform the person that he may claim a blood *or* urine test. Simply telling him of one of the 'choices', eg a blood test, is not enough and any specimen obtained thereafter will be inadmissible.[8] The constable must also give the person the chance to indicate his preference and reasons. If he uses language which conveys that he is *requiring*, for example, a blood test without giving the person the chance to indicate his preference and reasons, any specimen obtained thereafter will be inadmissible.[9]

1 Road Traffic Act 1988, s 7(2).
2 Ibid, s 8(1).
3 Road Traffic Act 1988, s 8(2). The limits on when a blood or urine specimen can be required at a police station (see para 20.30) do not apply where a blood or urine test is claimed under the present provision: *Sivyer v Parker* [1987] RTR 169, [1986] Crim LR 410, DC. If a person provides one specimen of breath but then fails to comply with the requirement for a second specimen, the result of the specimen provided is not admissible: *Cracknell v Willis* [1987] 3 All ER 801, HL. However, he may be convicted of failing to provide a specimen of breath, contrary to the Road Traffic Act 1988, s 7(6): ibid.
4 Road Traffic Act 1988, s 8(2).
5 *Yhnell v DPP* [1989] Crim LR 384, DC.
6 *Archbold v Jones* [1986] RTR 178, DC.
7 *Anderton v Lythgoe* [1985] 1 WLR 222, [1985] RTR 395, DC; *Hobbs v Clark* [1988] RTR 36, DC; *DPP v Magill* [1988] RTR 337, DC; *Wakeley v Hyams* [1987] RTR 49, DC.
8 *Hobbs v Clark*; *DPP v Magill*.
9 *Wakeley v Hyams*; *DPP v Byrne* [1990] Times, 11 October, DC.

20.30 *Blood or urine specimen* A requirement under s 7 of the Road Traffic Act 1988 for a specimen of blood or urine can only be made at a police station or hospital, and it cannot be made at a police station unless one of three situations exists:

a) the constable making the requirement has reasonable cause to believe[1] that for medical reasons[2] a specimen of breath cannot be provided or should not be required;

b) at the time the requirement is made an evidential breath test device (or a reliable one[3]) is not available at the police station or it is otherwise impracticable to use such a device there (e g because there is no officer then present at the police station trained to use the device)[4]; or

c) the suspected offence is one under s 3A (causing death by careless driving while unfit) or s 4 (driving etc while unfit) and the constable making the requirement has been advised by a medical practioner that the condition of the person required to provide the specimen might be due to some drug (since drugs do not reveal their presence in a person's body in his breath).[5]

However, provided one of these three situations exists, a requirement for a specimen of blood or urine may[6] be made at a police station, even though a person has already provided or been required to provide two specimens of breath for analysis.[7] Consequently, for example, where a person attempts to provide such a specimen of breath but is medically incapable of doing so (and thereby has a defence to a charge of failing to provide that specimen),[8] he may be required to provide a specimen of blood or urine.

Where a specimen of blood or urine may be required under s 7 the constable concerned must inform the person that either blood or urine may be required; if he does not and simply requires blood, for example, that specimen is inadmissible. The constable must also give the person a chance to indicate his preference of these alternatives.[9] However, the decision whether the specimen in question is to be of blood or urine must be made by the constable making the requirement (so that the person required has no real choice in the matter), except that if a medical practitioner is of the opinion that for medical reasons a specimen of blood cannot, or should not, be taken the specimen must be of urine.[10]

A specimen of blood may only be taken by a medical practitioner and it must be taken with the consent of the person concerned. If it is not so taken it must be disregarded.[11]

A specimen of urine must be provided within one hour of its requirement and after the provision of a previous specimen of urine[12] (which is not subjected to a laboratory test and cannot be used as evidence). However, the fact that the relevant specimen is provided outside the prescribed time does not render the evidence of the proportion of alcohol or any drug in it inadmissible.[13]

If a person asks to be supplied with a specimen of the blood or urine which he has provided, it must be divided into two parts and one part supplied to him. Failure to fulfil this requirement makes the specimen inadmissible as evidence on behalf of the prosecution.[14] The specimen is inadmissible if the person is misled by a constable or the prosecution into believing that the specimen supplied to him is not capable of being analysed.[15]

Where it is sought to require a person who is a patient at a hospital to provide a specimen of blood or urine, the protective rules of s 9 come into play. As in the case of a requirement for a screening breath test, they provide that such a person shall not be required to provide such a specimen unless the medical practitioner in immediate charge of the case has been notified of the proposal to make the requirement. If the medical practitioner objects on the ground that the requirement or the provision of the specimen or the necessary warning, referred to below, would be prejudicial to the proper care and treatment of the patient, the requirement must not be made. If the medical practitioner does not object the requirement must be for the provision of the specimen at the hospital.

On requiring a person to provide a specimen under s 7, whether of breath, blood or urine, a constable must warn him that a failure to do so may render him liable to prosecution.[16]

1 The constable concerned need not actually believe this. The question is whether a constable with the knowledge of the constable in question would have reasonable cause to believe it: *Davis v DPP* [1988] RTR 156, DC; *Davies v DPP* [1989] RTR 391, DC.
2 'Medical reasons' are not limited to reasons relating to the person's physical or mental capacity to supply a breath specimen since they can include other medically related reasons why such a specimen should not be required, such as that the person was taking medication which would influence the analysis of his breath: *Davies v DPP* [1989] RTR 391, DC.
3 Ie one which the constable reasonably believes is reliable: *Thompson v Thynne* [1986] RTR 293, DC; *Stokes v Sayers* [1988] RTR 89, DC. If breath specimens have been provided on the unreliable machine, the prosecution cannot rely on them but only on the analysis of the blood or urine subsequently provided: *Badkin v DPP* [1988] RTR 401, DC.
4 *Chief Constable of Avon and Somerset Constabulary v Kelliher* [1987] RTR 305, DC.
5 Road Traffic Act 1988, s 7(3).
6 Even in these three situations, the constable is not obliged to require a specimen of blood or urine instead of specimens of breath.
7 Road Traffic Act 1988, s 7(3).
8 Para 20.36.
9 *DPP v Gordon* [1990] RTR 71, DC; *Paterson v DPP* [1990] RTR 329, DC; *Holling v DPP* (1991) 155 JPR 250, DC.
10 Road Traffic Act 1988, s 7(4).
11 Road Traffic Offenders Act 1988, s 15(4).
12 Road Traffic Act 1988, s 7(5).
13 *Roney v Matthews* [1975] RTR 273, 61 Cr App Rep 195, DC; *Standen v Robertson* [1975] RTR 329, DC. Also see Road Traffic Offenders Act 1988, s 15(2).
14 Road Traffic Offenders Act 1988, s 15(5).
15 *Perry v McGovern* [1986] RTR 240, DC.
16 Road Traffic Act 1988, s 7(7).

EVIDENCE IN PROCEEDINGS UNDER S 4 OR S 5

20.31 Section 15(2) of the Road Traffic Offenders Act 1988 provides that evidence of the proportion of alcohol or any drug in a specimen of breath, blood or urine provided by the accused shall, in all cases (including cases where the specimen was not provided in connection with the alleged offence), be taken into account, and it shall be assumed that the proportion of alcohol in the accused's breath, blood or urine at the time of the alleged offence was not less than in the specimen, subject to one important proviso. The proviso, which is contained in s 15(3) is that the assumption is not to be made if the accused proves:

a) that he consumed alcohol before he provided the specimen and:
    i) in relation to an offence under s 3A, after the time of the alleged offence, and

   ii) otherwise, after he had ceased to drive, attempt to drive or be in charge of (as the case may be)[1] a vehicle on a road or other public place; and

  b) that had he not done so the proportion of alcohol in his breath, blood or urine would not have been above the prescribed limit and, if it is alleged that he was unfit to drive through drink, would not have been such as to impair his ability to drive properly. This is known as the 'hip-flask defence' which is dealt with in para 20.33.

1 *Rynsard v Spalding* [1986] RTR 303, DC.

20.32 The wording of s 15(2) of the Road Traffic Offenders Act 1988 seems to indicate that evidence of the analysis of a breath specimen provided under s 7 or of the laboratory test of a blood or urine specimen is not the only admissible evidence of the proportion of alcohol in the accused's body at the time of the alleged offence. The result is that, if the analysis or test reveals a proportion below the prescribed limit, but the magistrates are sure from expert evidence that, given the lapse of time between the alleged offence and the provision of the specimen, the proportion of alcohol at the time of the alleged offence was over the prescribed limit, they may convict the accused of an offence under s 5.[1] On the other hand, since s 15(2) provides that the proportion of alcohol in the accused's breath etc *is to be assumed to be not less* than in the specimen, it is not open to the court to receive evidence that, notwithstanding that the specimen was over the limit when taken, it might have been below it when he was driving.[2] In other words, the presumption as to the minimum alcohol level made by s 15(2) is irrebuttable and it is not possible to back-track down, as opposed to up.

As indicated above, s 15(2) states that the evidence of the proportion of alcohol or any drug in a specimen provided by the accused (i e under s 7) is in all cases to be taken into account. However, as already mentioned, the Act expressly requires that evidence derived from a specimen must be disregarded where, in the case of a blood specimen, it was taken without the accused's consent and/or not by a medical practitioner,[3] or where, in the case of a blood or urine specimen, the accused's request for part of it was not properly complied with.[4] In addition, the Divisional Court on a number of occasions has held that various other breaches of the procedure laid down by s 7 will render the evidence obtained from the specimen inadmissible, because a specimen obtained in breach of that procedure cannot be said to have been obtained under the Act as s 15(2) requires.[5] Thus, since a constable has no power to require more than two specimens of breath for analysis, a third specimen required by him is invalid and must be disregarded.[6] Likewise, where a motorist provides two breath specimens one of which (at least) is no more than 50 microgrammes and is then *required* to provide a blood specimen, the evidence of the breath specimens and of the blood specimen is inadmissible.[7] The evidence of the breath specimens is inadmissible because it is part of the s 7 procedure that the motorist should be informed of his *right to claim* to provide a blood or urine specimen, and since the blood specimen is not provided after a *claim* by the accused it too is inadmissible.[7] It is uncertain whether a failure to warn a motorist that if he does not provide a specimen he may be liable to prosecution is a breach of the s 7 procedure which renders a specimen subsequently obtained inadmissible.

Breaches of the procedure relating to the taking of a screening breath test under s 6 do not in themselves render inadmissible evidence subsequently obtained from specimens required under s 7. Nor does the fact that the motorist has been unlawfully arrested, for example by a constable who was a trespasser.[8] However, even if the evidence is otherwise admissible, the court has a discretion to exclude it in such cases, as explained in para 20.27.

1 *Gumbley v Cunningham* [1989] AC 281, [1989] 1 All ER 5, HL.
2 *Beauchamp-Thompson v DPP* [1988] Crim LR 758, DC; *Millard v DPP* [1990] RTR 201, DC.
3 Road Traffic Offenders Act 1988, s 15(4).
4 Ibid, s 15(5).
5 *Howard v Hallett* [1984] RTR 353, DC; *Chief Constable of Avon and Somerset Constabulary v Creech* [1986] RTR 87, [1986] Crim LR 62, DC; *Johnson v West Yorkshire Metropolitan Police* [1986] RTR 167, DC.
6 *Chief Constable of Avon and Somerset Constabulary v Creech* [1986] RTR 87, [1986] Crim LR 62, DC. Also see *Howard v Hallett* [1984] RTR 353, DC.
7 *Wakeley v Hyams* [1987] RTR 49, DC.
8 *Fox* [1986] AC 281, [1985] 3 All ER 392, HL.

20.33 *Hip-flask defence* With regard to the proviso to s 15(3) of the Road Traffic Offenders Act 1988, often called the 'hip-flask defence', the accused must prove that he had consumed alcohol after the alleged offence and also that the level of alcohol in his body would not have exceeded the prescribed limit but for that consumption. In relation to the latter element, the accused will not normally have a chance of success unless he is supported by expert evidence[1] on the effect of the types and quantities of alcohol allegedly consumed and a 'battle of the experts' may ensue.

Accused who are able to prove the hip-flask defence may nevertheless be liable for another offence, since the deliberate consumption of alcohol after the alleged offence in order to frustrate the procedure for taking a specimen can result in a conviction for wilfully obstructing a constable in the execution of his duty[2] or for attempting to pervert the course of justice,[3] even though in the case of the former offence the accused had not then been required to provide a specimen of breath for the screening breath test.[4] In any event, such deliberate consumption is liable to be self-defeating since the accused will doubtless still be in charge of the vehicle at the time of the additional imbibing.

1 *DPP v Singh* [1988] RTR 209, DC.
2 *Dibble v Ingleton* [1972] 1 QB 480, [1972] 1 All ER 275, DC; *Neal v Evans* [1976] RTR 333, DC; para 18.70
3 *Britton* [1973] RTR 502, DC; para 16.33.d.
4 *Neal v Evans* [1976] RTR 333, DC.

FAILURE TO PROVIDE A SPECIMEN

20.34 The Road Traffic Act 1988 provides two offences relating to failure to provide a specimen, both of which are only triable summarily:

a) By s 6(4), a person who, without reasonable excuse, fails to provide a specimen of breath for a screening breath test required under s 6 commits an offence which is punishable with a fine not exceeding level 3 on the standard scale (at present £1,000); disqualification is discretionary.

b) By s 7(6), a person who, without reasonable excuse, fails to provide a specimen of breath, blood or urine required for analysis under s 7 commits an offence. The punishment depends on whether or not the specimen was required to ascertain the accused's ability to drive or the proportion of alcohol in his body at the time he was driving or attempting to drive. If it was, the offence is punishable with up to six months' imprisonment or a fine not exceeding level 5 on the standard scale (£5,000) or both; unless there are special reasons not less than 12 months' disqualification must be ordered. If it was not required for this reason, as where the specimen was required to ascertain the proportion of alcohol at the time the accused was in charge of a motor vehicle, the offence is punishable with up to three months' imprisonment or a fine not exceeding level 4 on the standard scale (£2,500) or both; disqualification is discretionary.

20.35 *Failure* A failure to provide a specimen includes a refusal to do so,[1] by words or action (such as running away). Moreover, the supply of a specimen of breath which is not sufficient to enable either type of breath test to be carried out, or which is not provided in such a way as to enable the objective of the test to be satisfactorily achieved, is stated by s 11(3) not to be the provision of such a specimen and therefore constitutes a failure to provide one.

In the case of a specimen of urine for analysis, the relevant specimen must be provided within one hour of a requirement for it being made.[2] If it is not there can be a conviction under s 7(6), except that if the accused was given an extension of time by the constable, and does provide the specimen within the extended time (but after the hour), he cannot be convicted because he has taken advantage of an extension voluntarily granted to him.[3]

A person who refuses to supply a specimen unless some condition is satisfied, such as consulting his solicitor or the taking of blood from some part of the anatomy other than that from which the medical practitioner wishes to take it in accordance with ordinary medical practice, fails to provide a specimen.[4] On the other hand, there is not a failure to provide a specimen if the accused says, in effect, 'I will but may I do so and so beforehand?'[5] or if he says 'I will but may I see a solicitor first?'[6] because he is not imposing a condition, but seeking a favour. Clearly, many cases will turn on exactly what the accused said and involve hair-splitting distinctions of a type liable to bring the law into contempt.

There cannot be a conviction of either offence of failing to provide a specimen unless it has been required under s 6 or s 7, as the case may be, and it will not have been so required if the requirement made is invalid for some reason. For example, if the constable is a trespasser at the time of requiring a screening breath test he will be behaving unlawfully and his requirement of that test will be invalid.[7] On the other hand, a requirement for an evidential specimen will not be invalidated by the fact that the constable who requested the preceding screening specimen was a trespasser, nor by the fact that the person asked to give the evidential specimen has been unlawfully arrested.[8] However, the court may decide to exercise its discretion, referred to in para 20.28, to exclude the evidence concerning the failure to provide a specimen.[9]

There cannot be a conviction of either offence if the requisite procedure for administering the test is not carried out. In terms of specimens of breath, a test is not validly administered if the device used is not an approved one, or if it is defective, or if the constable fails to comply with the manufacturer's instructions as to its *assembly*.[10] However, if the constable realises the defect or mistake he may validly require another breath test to be taken on another device,[11] and failure to comply is an offence. Provided the constable acts in good faith and not negligently, non-compliance by him with the manufacturer's instructions as to the *use* of the device does not invalidate the test unless the non-compliance is prejudicial to the accused.[12]

A person cannot be convicted of failing to provide a specimen required under s 7 unless the constable requiring it has warned him of the penal consequences of failing to provide it and he has understood the warning.[13]

1 Road Traffic Act 1988, s 11(1).
2 Road Traffic Act 1988, s 7(5).
3 *Poole v Lockwood* [1981] RTR 285, DC.
4 *Law v Stephens* [1971] RTR 358, DC; *Solesbury v Pugh* [1969] 2 All ER 1171, [1969] 1 WLR 1114, DC; *Pettigrew v Northumbria Police Authority* [1976] RTR 177, [1976] Crim LR 259, DC; cf *Brown v Ridge* [1979] RTR 136, DC; *Chief Constable of Avon and Somerset Constabulary v O'Brien* [1987] RTR 182, DC.
5 *Pettigrew v Northumbria Police Authority* [1976] RTR 177, [1976] Crim LR 259, DC.
6 *DPP v Billington* [1988] 1 All ER 435, DC. Also see *Smith v Hand* [1986] RTR 265, DC.
7 *Morris v Beardmore* [1981] AC 446, [1980] 2 All ER 753, HL; *Fox v Chief Constable of Gwent* [1985] 1 All ER 230, [1985] 1 WLR 1126, DC (not the subject of the appeal to the House of Lords: [1986] AC 281, [1985] 3 All ER 392, HL).
8 *Fox* [1986] AC 281, [1985] 3 All ER 392, HL; *Hartland v Alden* [1987] RTR 253, DC; *DPP v Webb* [1988] RTR 374, DC
9 Ibid.
10 *Scott v Baker* [1969] 1 QB 659, [1968] 2 All ER 993, DC; *Rayner v Hampshire Chief Constable* [1971] RTR 15, DC.
11 Cf *Wright v Brobyn* [1971] RTR 204, DC. Also see *Broomhead* [1975] RTR 558, CA.
12 *DPP v Carey* [1970] AC 1072, [1969] 3 All ER 1662, HL; *A-G's Reference (No 2 of 1974)* [1975] 1 All ER 658, [1975] 1 WLR 328, CA; *A-G's Reference (No 1 of 1978)* [1978] RTR 377, CA.
13 *Chief Constable of Avon and Somerset Constabulary v Singh* [1988] RTR 107, DC.

20.36 *Without reasonable excuse* A person cannot be convicted of either offence unless his failure was without reasonable excuse.

It has been stated in a number of cases that no excuse can be adjudged reasonable unless there is evidence[1] that the accused was physically or mentally unable to provide the specimen or its provision would entail a substantial risk to his health.[2] This formula covers cases such as where the accused has an invincible repugnance, amounting to a medically recognised phobia,[3] to blood being taken;[4] or where, for reasons other than self-induced intoxication,[5] he is mentally incapable of understanding that he is required to provide a specimen or what he has to do (as where he is a foreigner with little understanding of English or where he is in a hysterical state);[6] or where he was physically or mentally unable to supply a *sufficient* specimen of breath for a breath test.[7]

It follows from the formula that it is not a reasonable excuse that the accused did not think that he had consumed any alcohol,[8] nor that he mistakenly believed that the requirement made was invalid,[9] nor that he had consumed alcohol after driving,[10] nor that he had conditionally agreed to provide a specimen.[11]

A person who fails to provide a specimen required under s 7 on the ground that he has been unlawfully arrested does not have a reasonable excuse.[12]

The accused does not have the burden of proving reasonable excuse,[13] but it is not enough for him simply to allege facts which could constitute a reasonable excuse. There must be evidence, normally medical, in support of those facts; otherwise the prosecution does not have to prove that there was no reasonable excuse.[14]

1 *Anderton v Waring* [1985] RTR 74, DC; *Dawes v Taylor* [1986] RTR 81, DC.
2 *Lennard* [1973] 2 All ER 831, [1973] 1 WLR 483, CA.
3 *Harding* [1974] RTR 325, CA; *Sykes v White* [1983] RTR 419, DC.
4 *Alcock v Read* [1980] RTR 71, DC.
5 *DPP v Beech* (1991)Times, 15 July, DC.
6 *Beck v Sager* [1979] Crim LR 211, DC; *Spalding v Paine* [1985] Crim LR 673, DC; *Chief Constable of Avon and Somerset v Singh* [1988] RTR 107, DC. In *DPP v Whalley* [1991] Crim LR 211, the Divisional Court said that instances of alleged linguistic difficulty must be scrutinised very carefully.
7 *Knightley* [1971] 2 All ER 1041, [1971] 1 WLR 1073, CA; *DPP v Eddowes* [1991] RTR 35, DC.
8 *Downey* [1970] RTR 257, CA.
9 *Reid* [1973] 3 All ER 1020, [1973] 1 WLR 1283; *McGrath v Vipas* (1984) 148 JP 405, [1984] RTR 58, DC.
10 *Lennard* [1973] 2 All ER 831, [1973] 1 WLR 483, CA; *Williams v Critchley* [1979] RTR 46, DC.
11 *Solesbury v Pugh* [1969] 2 All ER 1171, [1969] 1 WLR 1114, DC; *Law v Stephens* [1971] RTR 358, DC; *DPP v Billington* [1988] 1 All ER 435, DC; *DPP v Whalley* [1991] Crim LR 211, DC.
12 *Thomas v DPP* (1989) Times, 17 October, DC.
13 *O'Boyle* [1973] RTR 445, DC.
14 *Mallows v Harris* [1978] RTR 404, DC; *Anderton v Goodfellow* [1980] RTR 302, CA; *Grady v Pollard* [1988] RTR 316, DC; *DPP v Eddowes* [1991] RTR 35, DC.

Uninsured use

20.37 Section 143(1) of the Road Traffic Act 1988 provides that a person commits an offence, triable only summarily and punishable with a fine not exceeding level 5 on the standard scale (£5,000), if he uses, or causes or permits any other person to use, a motor vehicle on a road, unless there is in force in relation to the use of the vehicle by that person or that other person, as the case may be, such a policy of insurance or such a security in respect of third party[1] risks as complies with the Act. On conviction for such an offence disqualification is discretionary.

1 A 'third party' does not include the actual driver at the time of the risk: *Cooper v Motor Insurers' Bureau* [1985] QB 575, [1984] 1 All ER 449, CA.

20.38 The prohibition against using or permitting or causing the use of an uninsured motor vehicle is strict in the sense that it is no defence that the accused reasonably believed that he, or the person allowed to drive, was covered by an insurance policy.[1] There is one exception: under s 143(3) of the Act it is a defence for a person charged with *using* an uninsured motor vehicle to prove that it did not belong to him and was not in his possession under a contract of hiring or loan, and that he was using it in the course of his employment and neither knew nor had reason to believe that it was not properly insured.

Generally, a person who permits another to have the use of his vehicle subject to the condition that use of it must be covered by insurance (for which the other is to be responsible) can nevertheless be convicted of permitting its uninsured use if this condition is not complied with.[2] It seems odd that a person can permit something which, in effect, he has forbidden.

A person cannot permit another's use if he was not in a position to forbid it.[3] Thus, D who supervises X, a learner driver, in X's own car cannot be convicted of permitting its uninsured use.[3]

1 *Lyons v May* [1948] 2 All ER 1062, DC; *Baugh v Crago* [1976] Crim LR 72, DC.
2 *DPP v Fisher* [1991] Crim LR 787, DC. Cf *Newbury v Davis* [1974] RTR 367, DC.
3 *Thompson v Lodwick* [1983] RTR 76, DC.

21 Inchoate offences

21.1 The common law offence of incitement and the statutory offences of conspiracy and attempt are known as inchoate offences since they may be committed notwithstanding that the substantive offence to which they relate is not committed. Indeed, if the substantive offence is committed, no question of attempt normally arises, and where there has been incitement the person inciting becomes a party as an accomplice to the substantive offence and is not normally proceeded against for incitement.

Conspiracy differs from the other two offences, in that even where the conspirators have committed the substantive offence there are circumstances in which a charge of conspiracy is appropriate, although appellate courts have discouraged the practice.[1]

For convenience, common law conspiracy is also discussed in this chapter although it is not strictly an inchoate offence since it includes agreements for objects which are not in themselves criminal.

The various inchoate offences are unusual in that, if they are committed abroad, they fall within the jurisdiction of the English courts provided that they were intended to result in the commission of a criminal offence in England or Wales; nothing need be done in England or Wales.[2]

1 Para 21.34.
2 *Liangsiriprasert v United States Government* [1990] 2 All ER 866, PC; *Sansom* [1991] 2 All ER 145, CA (conspiracy). *Liangsiriprasert v United States Government* [1990] 2 All ER 866 at 878 (incitement and attempt); *DPP v Stonehouse* [1978] AC 55 at 67, [1977] 2 All ER 909, per Lord Diplock (cf Lord Keith: [1978] AC 55 at 93) (attempt).

Incitement[1]

21.2 It is an offence to incite another person to commit any offence (including a summary one),[2] other than conspiracy,[3] whether or not that offence is committed. The existence of the offence of incitement was established in *Higgins*,[4] where a conviction for inciting an employee to steal his employer's property was upheld.

1 For the Law Commission's provisional proposals concerning incitement, see Law Com Working Paper No 50, Inchoate Offences: Conspiracy, Attempt and Incitement, paras 92–143.
2 *Curr* [1968] 2 QB 944, [1967] 1 All ER 478, CA.
3 Criminal Law Act 1977, s 5(7). By way of contrast, there can be a conviction for incitement to incite, although it may be that the Criminal Law Act 1977, s 5(7), prevents a charge of incitement to incite if D incites X not merely to incite another (eg by a letter not requiring a reply) but to agree with that other: *Sirat* (1985) 83 Cr App Rep 41, CA; *Evans* [1986] Crim LR

470, CA. It seems that there cannot be a conviction for incitement to aid, abet, counsel or procure the commission of an offence, or incitement to attempt. Schedule 1 of the Magistrates' Courts Act 1980 seems to assume this, and in *Bochin and Bodin* [1979] Crim LR 176 a circuit judge held that it was not an offence to incite another to aid, abet, counsel or procure the commission of an offence (a view which is also implicit in the Court of Appeal's decision in *Sirat* (1985) 83 Cr App Rep 41; see commentary in [1986] Crim LR 245). On the other hand, there can be a conviction for conspiracy to incite (para 21.16) or for attempt to incite (para 21.54.a).

It should be noted, however, that there are a few statutory offences whose actus reus is procuring or aiding and abetting something, such as aiding and abetting suicide, so that a perpetrator of them is the procurer or aider and abettor. A person who incites someone to commit such an offence can be convicted of incitement to commit such an offence.

4 (1801) 2 East 5.

ACTUS REUS

21.3 Incitement requires an element of persuasion or encouragement[1] or of threats or other pressure,[2] which may be implied as well as expressed.[3] The mere expression of a desire that someone should die, for instance, does not suffice but the encouragement or persuasion of another to kill him does.

The solicitation must come to the notice of the person intended to act on it though it need not be effective in any way,[4] but, if it is and the person incited agrees to commit an offence, he and the inciter may be guilty of conspiracy. Where the solicitation does not reach the mind of another because, for instance, the letter soliciting the commission of an offence never arrived, the person making it may be guilty of an attempt to incite.[5] The solicitation need not be directed to a particular person. In *Most* [6] it was held that the accused, who had published an article in a revolutionary newspaper exulting in the recent murder of the Emperor of Russia and commending it as an example to revolutionists throughout the world, could be convicted of incitement to murder.

A person who incites the commission of an offence of which he is the victim may be convicted of incitement, unless the offence incited is regarded as one designed to protect a person such as him from exploitation.[7] The same rule applies in relation to accomplices, and the reader is referred to the discussion in para 23.27.

1 *Hendricksen and Tichner* [1977] Crim LR 356.
2 *Race Relations Board v Applin* [1973] QB 815 at 825, [1973] 2 All ER 1190, per Lord Denning; *Invicta Plastics Ltd v Clare* [1976] RTR 251, DC.
3 *Invicta Plastics Ltd v Clare* [1976] RTR 251, DC.
4 *Krause* (1902) 18 TLR 238 at 243.
5 *Ransford* (1874) 13 Cox CC 9.
6 (1881) 7 QBD 244, 50 LJMC 113.
7 *Tyrrell* [1894] 1 QB 710, 63 LJMC 58.

MENS REA

21.4 The necessary element of encouragement or persuasion or of threats or other pressure suggests that incitement requires a purposive intention that a sufficient act for the offence incited should be committed and that any requisite consequence of that act should result. In addition, it would seem necessary under the general principles of criminal liability that the accused should know of (or be wilfully blind as to) all the circumstances which would make the act incited criminal (including 'knowing' that the person incited will act with such mens rea as is required for the offence incited). It is not necessary, of course, that the accused should know that the conduct incited constitutes an offence.[1]

In *Curr*[2] the Court of Appeal imposed an additional requirement which related to the mental element of the person incited. The accused was acquitted of inciting women to commit offences under the Family Allowances Act 1945 because the prosecution had failed to prove that the women, who had done the acts incited, had the mens rea required for such offences. It is difficult to see why the mental element of the person incited should be relevant to liability for incitement since liability for that offence does not depend on the incited offence being committed or even intended by the person incited.

1 Para 6.73.
2 [1968] 2 QB 944, [1967] 1 All ER 478, CA.

POSSIBILITY AND IMPOSSIBILITY

21.5 An incitement is criminal even if it is to commit an offence which could not be committed at the time but which is envisaged as capable of commission on the occurrence of something in the future, as when someone incites a pregnant woman to kill her child when it is born or incites another to receive goods to be stolen in the future.[1]

1 *Shephard* [1919] 2 KB 125, 88 LJKB 932, CCA.

21.6 Where the course of conduct incited would not constitute an offence by the person incited if it was carried out because that person is in law incapable of committing that offence, there is no incitement to crime and the offence of incitement is not committed.[1]

1 *Whitehouse* [1977] QB 868, [1977] 3 All ER 737, CA. Note the actual decision in this case would now be different, since the gap in the law of sexual offences which it disclosed has now been filled by the Criminal Law Act 1977, s 54; para 12.22.

21.7 If the course of conduct incited would constitute an offence by the person incited if he achieved its objective it is irrelevant that he cannot achieve it by the means suggested, as would be so if D encourages X to use a pill, which is in fact harmless, to kill P by poisoning; of course, if the inciter knows that the offence cannot be committed by the suggested means he is not guilty of incitement since he lacks the necessary mens rea.[1]

1 *Brown* (1899) 63 JP 790.

21.8 Another type of impossibility is where the course of conduct incited could *never* be achieved, whatever means were adopted, as where D incites X to steal some papers which, unknown to them, have never existed or to kill P who, unknown to them, is dead. In *McDonough*[1] it was held that in such a case a person can be convicted of incitement. There, D, believing that there were some stolen lamb carcases in a cold store, incited X to handle them. In fact there were no stolen carcases in the store but it was held nevertheless that D could be convicted of incitement. Subsequently, the House of Lords held that there could not be a conviction for the common law offences of conspiracy[2] and attempt[3] in such a case of impossibility. Although the relevant principles laid down in those decisions have been reversed by statute in relation to the statutory offences of conspiracy and attempt,[4] the

Court of Appeal in *Fitzmaurice*[5] stated, obiter, that they applied to incitement since that offence could not be treated differently *at common law* from conspiracy or attempt. If this obiter dictum is adopted, a person will not be liable for incitement in the present type of case, although he would now be liable on a charge of statutory conspiracy or attempt. The Court of Appeal, however, did not regard *McDonough* as wrongly decided. It explained it on the ground that, although there may have been no stolen goods or any goods at all in the store at the time of the incitement, it was not impossible at the relevant time in the future that the necessary goods might be there, an explanation which is not very convincing.[6]

It would also follow from the adoption of the obiter dictum in *Fitzmaurice* that a person who incites someone to a course of conduct which on the facts as he mistakenly believes them to be is criminal (as where D incites X to receive some identifiable goods, wrongly believing that they are stolen) cannot be convicted of incitement. In contrast, those who agree to commit, or attempt to commit, what on the facts as they mistakenly believe them to be is an offence, can be convicted of an offence of statutory conspiracy or attempt respectively.[7]

1 (1962) 47 Cr App Rep 37, CCA.
2 *DPP v Nock* [1978] AC 979, [1978] 2 All ER 654, HL.
3 *Haughton v Smith* [1975] AC 476, [1973] 3 All ER 1109, HL.
4 Paras 21.18 and 21.69.
5 [1983] QB 1083, [1983] 1 All ER 189, CA.
6 Cf. Cohen 'Inciting the Impossible' [1979] Crim LR 239.
7 Paras 21.18 and 21.68–21.70.

TRIAL AND PUNISHMENT

21.9 As a common law offence, incitement is punishable with imprisonment at the discretion of the court if it is prosecuted on indictment,[1] as it must be if the offence incited is triable only on indictment, but it is not likely that an incitement would be punished more severely than is possible for the offence to which the incitement relates. Incitements to commit offences which are triable either way are themselves triable either way,[2] the maximum sentence on summary conviction being the same as is available on summary conviction for the offence incited.[3] Incitement to commit a summary offence is itself triable only summarily,[4] and subject to the same maximum punishment as the offence incited.[5]

In some cases incitement to commit a particular type of offence is a statutory offence. Under s 4 of the Offences against the Person Act 1861, for instance, incitement to murder is punishable with a maximum of life imprisonment.

1 Para 3.4.
2 Magistrates' Courts Act 1980, s 17(1) and Sch 1.
3 Ibid, s 32(1).
4 Ibid, s 45(1).
5 Ibid, s 45(3).

DRAFT CRIMINAL CODE

21.10 Clauses 47 and 50 of the draft Criminal Code Bill[1] essentially make provision along the lines indicated above. The exceptions are that it would not be necessary for the person incited to have the appropriate mens rea for the offence incited, that incitement to conspire should (like incitement to incite or incitement to attempt) be an offence, that generally the maximum punishment should be the same as for the offence incited, and that the law relating to inciting an impossible offence should be brought into line with that for the offences of statutory conspiracy and of attempt, as explained in para 21.73.

1 Law Commission: A Criminal Code for England and Wales (1989): Law Com No 177; see para 3.21 above.

Conspiracy: General

21.11 There are two offences of conspiracy:

a) It is a statutory offence to agree with any other person or persons for the commission of an offence or offences.
b) It is a common law offence to agree with any person or persons to defraud or, possibly, to corrupt public morals or to outrage public decency.

Until Part I of the Criminal Law Act 1977 came into force, the common law offence of conspiracy was the only general offence of conspiracy known to the criminal law. An agreement was a common law conspiracy if it had one of five types of object:

a) To commit a criminal offence.
b) To pervert the course of justice. Generally, this did not add much to a), since normally the perversion of justice was a criminal offence.
c) To commit a tort, such as trespass, provided the execution of the agreement had as its object either
  i) the invasion of the 'public domain', e g trespass in an embassy, or
  ii) the infliction on its victim of injury or damage which was more than nominal.
d) To defraud.
e) To corrupt public morals or to outrage public decency.

The width of the non-criminal objects of a conspiracy was open to severe criticism, particularly since it was not obvious why, if a particular act was not criminal when done, an agreement to do it should be criminal. Following the recommendations of the Law Commission,[1] Part I of the Criminal Law Act 1977 introduced the statutory offence of conspiracy, which basically penalises agreements for the commission of a criminal offence, and greatly altered the extent of the common law offence of conspiracy since, except for conspiracies to defraud and, possibly, conspiracies to corrupt public morals or to outrage public decency, the offence of conspiracy at common law was abolished by s 5(1) of that Act. The rules for statutory conspiracy under the Act do not apply to common law conspiracy.

Before discussing the separate requirements of statutory conspiracy and what remains of common law conspiracy, it is proposed to deal with certain matters which are common to them.

1 Report on Conspiracy and Criminal Law Reform (1976) Law Com No 76.

AGREEMENT[1]

21.12 There cannot be a conspiracy unless there is a concluded agreement.[2] There may be any number of parties to the agreement. The offence is complete as soon as the parties agree and it is immaterial that they never begin to put it into effect[3] or that the details remain to be agreed.[4] Moreover, the repentance and withdrawal of a party after the agreement has been made cannot affect his liability for conspiracy.[5]

It is not necessary that all the parties to the agreement should have evinced their consent at the same time, nor that they should all have been in communication with each other, provided they entertained a common purpose, communicated to at least one other party, expressly or tacitly, in relation to the object of the conspiracy.[6] This would be so, for instance, with members of a society who had each worked for the same end under some common superior but had never communicated with each other.[7]

Although conspiracy is committed as soon as the agreement for the 'unlawful' object is made, it is clear that conspiracy is a continuing offence and is committed not only when agreement is first reached but also as long as the agreement to effect the unlawful object continues.[8] The most important result of this is that a number of persons may be held parties to the same conspiracy although they joined it at different times[9] and may not have been parties to the agreement at the same time as each other.[10]

1 Orchard '"Agreement" in Criminal Conspiracy' [1974] Crim LR 297, 335.
2 *Jones* (1832) 4 B & Ad 345 at 349, per Denman CJ.
3 *Poulterer's Case* (1610) 9 Co Rep 55b.
4 *Gill and Henry* (1818) 2 B & Ald 204.
5 *Mogul SS Co Ltd v McGregor, Gow & Co* (1888) 21 QBD 544 at 549, affd [1892] AC 25, HL.
6 *Ardalan* [1972] 2 All ER 257, [1972] 1 WLR 463, CA; *Scott* (1978) 68 Cr App Rep 164, CA; *Chrastny* [1992] 1 All ER 189, CA.
7 See summing up of Fitzgerald J in *Parnell* (1881) 14 Cox CC 508 at 516. See also *Meyrick and Ribuffi* (1929) 21 Cr App Rep 94, CCA.
8 *DPP v Doot* [1973] AC 807, [1973] 1 All ER 940, HL.
9 *Murphy* (1837) 8 C & P 297 at 311; *Sweetland* (1957) 42 Cr App Rep 62 at 67.
10 *Simmonds* (1967) 51 Cr App Rep 316 at 332.

21.13 The fact that there must be two or more parties to constitute an agreement produces two interesting consequences:

a) A director who is the 'one man' of a 'one man' company cannot be convicted of conspiring with the company in spite of the fact that a company can be held guilty of conspiracy and is in law a separate entity from its directors.[1] This is because, in order that there should be a conspiracy, there must be an agreement between two minds, and the director's mind is that of the company only in a purely artificial sense. A company can be convicted of conspiring with several of its directors, but presumably the rule with regard to the one man company would prevent two 'one man' companies with the same 'one man' from being convicted of conspiring together.

b) A person is not guilty of conspiracy if the only other person with whom he agrees is his or her spouse,[2] a rule which has been held by the Court of Appeal not to apply to the tort of conspiracy.[3] It remains undecided whether the rule applies to a husband and wife whose marriage is of a type which is actually or potentially polygamous.[4] It seems odd that if a husband and wife agree between themselves to commit an offence they cannot be convicted of conspiracy, whereas if the substantive offence is committed by one of them pursuant to the agreement they can both be convicted of that offence. A husband and wife can be convicted of conspiring together with a third party,[5] even if one of them does not know the identity of the third party, but a spouse (A) who agrees with his or her spouse (B) for a relevant object in ignorance of an agreement for that object between B and another person (C) cannot be so convicted since, not knowing of B's agreement with C, A cannot be said to have agreed with C but only with his or her spouse.[6]

1 *McDonnell* [1966] 1 QB 233, [1966] 1 All ER 193.
2 *Mawji v R* [1957] AC 126, [1957] 1 All ER 385, PC (common law conspiracy); Criminal Law Act 1977, s 2(2)(a) (statutory conspiracy).
3 *Midland Bank Trust Co Ltd v Green (No 3)* [1982] Ch 529, [1981] 3 All ER 744, CA.
4 This point was left open in *Mawji* in relation to the rule at common law.
5 *Whitehouse* (1852) 6 Cox CC 38.
6 *Chrastny* [1992] 1 All ER 189 at 192.

ACQUITTAL OF ALL SAVE ONE

21.14 Suppose A and B (or A, B and C) are charged with conspiracy and that B is (or B and C are) acquitted, can A nevertheless still be convicted?

In answering this question two situations must be distinguished.

The first is where a conspiracy is charged as being between two or more accused persons (eg A and B or A, B and C) and a person or persons unknown, dead or simply not charged. Here, it has long been established that the acquittal of B (or B and C) does not mean that A cannot be convicted.[1]

The second situation is where two or more persons (eg A and B or A, B and C) are charged in the same indictment with conspiracy together (but not with others), and all but one of them (eg A) are acquitted. This can happen, for example, where evidence is admissible against one conspirator but not against another. At common law, A could nevertheless be convicted if he was tried separately from B (or B and C)[2] but not if he was tried together with them.[3] However, s 5(8) of the Criminal Law Act 1977 now provides that

'The fact that the person or persons who, so far as appears from the indictment on which any person has been convicted of conspiracy, were the only other parties to the agreement on which his conviction was based have been acquitted of that conspiracy (whether after being tried with the person convicted or separately) is not a ground for quashing his conviction unless under all the circumstances of the case his conviction is inconsistent with the acquittal of the other person or persons.'

The effect of this provision was explained by the Court of Appeal in *Longman and Cribben*,[4] as follows. Where, in a case where A and B are tried together for conspiracy together but with no one else, the evidence against A and B is of equal weight or nearly equal weight, so that a verdict of guilty against A and of not guilty against B would be inexplicable and therefore inconsistent, the judge must direct the jury that the only verdicts open to them are to convict both or to acquit both. He must add that, if they are unsure about the guilt of one of them, they must acquit both. On the other hand, where the strength of the evidence against A and B in such a case is (in the view of the judge)[5] markedly different, the judge must direct the jury to consider each case separately and direct them that they may conclude that the prosecution has proved that A conspired with B but has not proved any such conspiracy against B, in which event they should convict A but acquit B.

1 For an authority, see *Anthony* [1965] 2 QB 189, [1965] 1 All ER 440, CCA. Also see *Nicolls* (1745) cited in 13 East 412n; *Cooke* (1826) 5 B & C 538, 7 Dow & Ry KB 673.
2 *DPP v Shannon* [1975] AC 717, [1974] 2 All ER 1009, HL.

Statutory conspiracy

21.15   Although a number of statutes specially provide that a particular type of conspiracy is an offence, the term 'statutory conspiracy' is used here to describe the offence of conspiracy under s 1 of the Criminal Law Act 1977. The rules laid down for statutory conspiracy by ss 1 and 2 of the Act of 1977 also apply for determining whether a person is guilty of an offence of conspiracy under any other enactment, but such an offence is excluded from being an offence under s 1.[1]

Statutory conspiracy is defined by s 1(1) of the Criminal Law Act 1977 (hereafter 'the Act'), as substituted by s 5(1) of the Criminal Attempts Act 1981. Section 1(1) provides:

'Subject to [the other provisions of Part I of the Act], if a person agrees with any other person or persons that a course of conduct shall be pursued which, if the agreement is carried out in accordance with their intentions, either—
  a) will necessarily amount to or involve the commission of any offence or offences by one or more of the parties to the agreement, or
  b) would do so but for the existence of facts which render the commission of the offence or any of the offences impossible,
he is guilty of conspiracy to commit the offence or offences in question.'

It is particularly difficult to divide the definition of statutory conspiracy into actus reus and mens rea because even the element of agreement involves a mental state on the part of the accused. Nevertheless, for the purposes of exposition some division must be made, although it is not pretended that the division made here is the only possible one.

1   Criminal Law Act 1977, s 5(6).

ACTUS REUS OF STATUTORY CONSPIRACY

21.16   There must be an agreement (as explained above) between two or more people that a course of conduct shall be pursued which, if the agreement is carried out in accordance with their intentions, either:

  a) will necessarily amount to or involve the commission of any offence or offences by one or more of the parties to the agreement, or
  b) would do so but for the existence of facts which render the commission of the offence or any of the offences impossible.

The key issue, derived from s 1(1)(a), is whether the course of conduct agreed on by the parties would necessarily amount to or involve the *commission of any offence by one or more of them* if it was '*carried out in accordance with their intentions*'.

Thus, if D1 and D2 agree to have intercourse with a woman without her consent, there is a statutory conspiracy to rape because the course of conduct agreed on – sexual intercourse – would necessarily amount to or involve the commission of rape if it was carried out in accordance with their intentions, viz to have sexual intercourse with a woman without her consent.

In *Hollinshead*[1] the Court of Appeal held that 'the commission of any offence ... by one or more of the parties to the agreement' meant commission by one or more of them as a perpetrator and not simply as an accomplice, so that there could not be a statutory conspiracy to aid and abet the commission of an offence by someone not party to the agreement. On appeal, the House of Lords did not consider it necessary to decide whether or not this view was correct but it is submitted that in the context of s 1(1)(a) the natural meaning of 'commission of any offence' must be 'commission of an offence as perpetrator' with the result that there cannot be a statutory conspiracy to aid and abet.[2] If this is correct, D1 and D2 who agree to assist X (not a party to the agreement) to rape a woman are not guilty of a statutory conspiracy to rape because the course of conduct agreed on would not amount to or involve the commission of rape by one or more of the parties (i e D1 or D2) to the agreement if it was carried out in accordance with their intentions. The same would be true if D1 and D2 agree to encourage X to commit the rape. However, in this latter case D1 and D2 could be convicted of a statutory conspiracy to commit the offence of inciting X to commit rape.[3]

What was said in the last paragraph must be qualified in the case of a few statutory offences, such as procuring an act of gross indecency or aiding and abetting suicide, whose actus reus consists of procuring or abetting something, so that the perpetrator of such an offence is the procurer or aider and abettor. People who conspire for one (or more) of them to perpetrate such an offence can be convicted of a statutory conspiracy to commit it.[4] (As to whether a person may be liable as an accomplice to a conspiracy, see para 23.4.a.)

1 [1985] AC 975, [1985] 1 All ER 850, CA; [1985] AC 975, [1985] 2 All ER 769, HL.
2 It may be noted that, under the Criminal Attempts Act 1981, an attempt to aid and abet an offence is not criminal; see para 21.54.
3 It is an offence to conspire to incite. See the decision of the Court of Appeal in *Hollinshead* [1985] 1 All ER 850 at 857–858. On appeal the House of Lords left the matter open but it is implicit in their decision that there can be conspiracy to incite: see Smith [1986] Crim LR at 146.
4 Likewise, a person can be convicted of the statutory offence of attempt in relation to such an offence: para 21.54.

21.17 It would seem that 'carried out in accordance with their intentions' refers not only to the physical course of conduct (and its surrounding circumstances) intended by the accused but also to any intended consequences of it; otherwise it would be impossible to convict a person of conspiring to commit an offence whose actus reus requires a consequence to result from conduct. Suppose that two terrorists, D1 and D2, agree that D2 should destroy an Army tank by putting inside it a time bomb to be supplied by D1. Assuming that what has just been said is correct, there is a statutory conspiracy to commit criminal damage because the course of conduct agreed on (planting the bomb) would necessarily amount to or involve the commission of criminal damage if it was carried out in accordance with their intentions of causing criminal damage.

21.18 *Impossibility* Section 1(1)(b) deals with agreements which are impossible of fulfilment. It provides that an agreement on a course of conduct which, if the agreement is carried out in accordance with the parties' intentions, would necessarily amount to or involve the commission of an offence or any offences by one or more of the parties but for the existence of facts which render the commission of the offence or any of the offences impossible is a statutory conspiracy.

If what has been said in para 21.17 is correct, s 1(1)(b) may not have been strictly necessary to deal with agreements which are impossible of fulfilment, as where D1 and D2 agree to murder P by poisoning him, not knowing that he is already dead, or where D1 and D2 agree to have intercourse with a girl of 16, thinking that she is 15. In both cases it would seem that there is a conspiracy within s 1(1)(a) because if the course of conduct agreed on is carried out in accordance with the parties' intentions this will necessarily amount to or involve the commission of an offence. Nevertheless, s 1(1)(b) is useful because it puts the matter beyond doubt. Moreover, the use of the word 'would' [necessarily amount to or involve the commission of an offence] seems more appropriate than 'will' where the existence of facts renders it impossible to commit an offence.

21.19 *Ifs and buts* Often parties to an agreement for the commission of an offence make the carrying out of their agreed course of conduct subject to a condition precedent (as where they agree to burgle a bank, provided that on arrival there it seems safe to do so). In such a case they can be convicted of statutory conspiracy since they have agreed on a course of conduct which, if it is carried out in accordance with their intentions, *will necessarily* amount to or involve the commission of an offence.[1]

It is different where carrying out the course of conduct agreed on may or may not amount to an offence. For example, if D1 and D2 agree to persuade P to lend them some money and agree that, if P is unwilling, they will take it from him by force, they cannot be convicted of conspiracy to rob because, if the agreed course of conduct is carried out in accordance with their intentions, it *will not necessarily* amount to or involve the commission of an offence.[2] Likewise, if D1 and D2 agree to commit an armed robbery on P and agree that, if necessary, e g to rob him or to escape, they will shoot to kill, they can be convicted of conspiracy to rob but not of conspiracy to murder because, if the agreed course of conduct is carried out in accordance with their intentions, it will necessarily amount to or involve robbery but not necessarily murder.

1 *Reed* [1982] Crim LR 819, CA.
2 Ibid. Contrast Williams *Textbook of Criminal Law* (2nd edn) 356.

21.20 In para 21.19, we were concerned with cases where the carrying out of the agreed course of conduct was subject to a condition *precedent*. What is the answer where the completion of the substantive offence depends on a condition *subsequent* to the carrying out of the agreed course of conduct? Such a situation is common and occurs where the parties to an agreement agree that a course of conduct be pursued which, if carried out in accordance with their intentions, will necessarily amount to or involve the commission of an offence by one or more of them *only if* some contingency occurs *after* the course of conduct has been carried out. An example is where the substantive offence is a 'result crime' since, taking conspiracy to murder as an instance, the course of conduct agreed on – e g firing a gun – will necessarily amount to or involve the offence of murder only if the bullet thereafter hits the victim and kills him. In the present type of case, there can be a conviction for conspiracy to commit the substantive offence if the parties intended that the element(s) necessary to complete that offence should occur, despite the fact that they realised that that occurrence depended on some contingency subsequent to their agreed course of conduct.[1]

1 *Jackson, Golding and Jackson* [1985] Crim LR 442, CA.

21.21 *'Offence'* The following can be said about the 'offence' which the agreed course of conduct must necessarily amount to or involve if it is carried out in accordance with the parties' intentions.

a) By s 1(4) of the Act 'offence' generally means an offence triable in England and Wales. The importance of this is that, where there is an agreement in England and Wales to pursue a course of conduct outside England and Wales, this will only constitute a conspiracy if that course of conduct outside England and Wales would necessarily amount to or involve the commission of an offence triable in England and Wales. As is shown in chapter 6, generally our courts do not have jurisdiction to try what would otherwise be an offence if it is committed abroad. For instance, an assault or theft committed in Edinburgh or Paris is not triable by our courts.[1] However, as has been shown in previous chapters, there are exceptions, e g bigamy committed abroad by a British citizen, British Dependent Territories citizen or British Overseas citizen is an offence triable in England and Wales. Thus, an agreement made in London between D1 and D2 that D1, a married man and a British citizen, should marry X bigamously in Paris will constitute a conspiracy because if the course of conduct agreed on is carried out in accordance with the parties' (D1 and D2) intentions it will necessarily amount to or involve the commission of an offence triable in England and Wales.

Section 1(4) provides an exception to the general meaning of 'offence'. A murder committed in a country other than England and Wales is only triable here if it is committed by a British citizen, British Dependent Territories citizen or British Overseas citizen. However, s 1(4) provides that 'offence' includes murder notwithstanding that the murder agreed on would not be triable in England and Wales if committed in accordance with the intention of the parties to the agreement. Thus, if D1 and D2, who are both French nationals, agree in Leicester to murder P in Rome, D1 and D2 may be convicted of conspiracy to murder, even though if the murder was actually committed our courts would lack jurisdiction to try them for murder.

b) 'Offence' includes an offence which is only triable summarily. However, where in pursuance of the agreement the acts are to be done in contemplation or furtherance of a trade dispute (within the meaning of the Trade Union and Labour Relations Act 1974) that offence is not an 'offence' for the purposes of conspiracy if it is triable only summarily and not punishable with imprisonment.[2]

1 Para 6.78. See *Tomsett* [1985] Crim LR 369, CA.
2 Criminal Law Act 1977, s 1(3).

MENS REA OF STATUTORY CONSPIRACY

21.22 As will be explained, this offence is unusual in that liability does not depend merely on the state of mind of the accused but also on the state of mind of other parties to the agreement. This is not surprising, given the nature of the offence.

21.23 *Mens rea as to circumstances of substantive offence* A person cannot be convicted of statutory conspiracy unless he and at least one other party to the agreement intend or know that any circumstance necessary for the commission of the substantive offence shall or will exist when the conduct constituting the offence is to occur.

This general rule is not stated expressly in the Act but is implied by s 1(2), which states that such a rule applies even though the substantive offence does not require knowledge as to a particular necessary circumstance, ie an offence where recklessness or negligence as to a circumstance suffices or which is of strict liability as to a circumstance. An example can be given by reference to the offence of abduction of a girl under 16, contrary to s 20 of the Sexual Offences Act 1956. As we saw in para 12.26, this offence requires a taking of an unmarried girl under 16 out of parental possession without lawful authority or excuse and against parental will, and is one of strict liability as to the girl's age so that a person can be convicted of it even though he reasonably but mistakenly believed that the girl was 16 or over. The effect of s 1(2) of the Act is that if A and B agree to abduct a girl aged 15 they can only be convicted of conspiracy to abduct her if, in addition to knowing that she is unmarried, in parental custody and that the taking is against parental will, they both know that she is under 16.

The requirement of knowledge is rather complex where the substantive offence is governed by a statutory provision which provides different maximum penalties for different forms of the same conduct, depending on the subject matter of that conduct. According to the House of Lords' decision in *Courtie*,[1] if the maximum punishment for specified conduct in one type of specified circumstances is, for instance, ten years and the maximum for that conduct in relation to another type of specified circumstances is five years, there are two separate offences. An example is provided by the offences under s 170(2) of the Customs and Excise Management Act 1979 of being knowingly concerned in the fraudulent evasion of a prohibition on the importation of various types of prohibited goods. Where, for example, the prohibited goods are a Class A controlled drug (eg heroin) an offence is committed which is distinct from the offence which is committed where the prohibited goods are a Class B controlled drug (eg cannabis); both these offences are distinct from the offence which is committed where the prohibited goods are obscene articles. The reason is that the maximum penalties in relation to these three types of subject matter are respectively life, 14 years' and seven years' imprisonment. A person charged with the offence relating to heroin can be convicted even though he did not know that the thing in question was heroin if he believed that it was some other item which constitutes prohibited goods, for example cannabis or an obscene article, whether or not he knew that such an item constituted prohibited goods.[2]

The situation is different where a person is charged with conspiracy to commit such an offence. The reason is that he is not guilty if, although he believed that the subject matter was such as would make the intended conduct criminal (whether or not he realised this), he believed that the subject matter was something which would attract a lower maximum penalty than the subject matter actually involved and which would therefore give rise to a different, less serious offence. For example, it was held by the Court of Appeal in *Siracusa*[3] that, on a charge of conspiracy to commit the offence of being knowingly concerned in the fraudulent evasion of the prohibition on the importation of a Class A controlled drug, such as heroin, a person cannot be convicted if he thought the drug was cannabis since, the illegal importation of a Class B controlled drug, such as cannabis, being a different offence from the illegal importation of a Class A drug, he will not know of the circumstance necessary for the commission of the substantive offence which is alleged to be the object of the conspiracy.

On the other hand, consistent with the normal principles relating to mens rea, provided that the accused believed that the subject matter of the conspiracy was something covered by the offence with which he is charged, it is immaterial that he is mistaken as to its precise nature. Thus, if, in the above conspiracy the accused had mistakenly believed that the drug was pethidine (another Class A controlled drug) and not heroin, he would have sufficient mens rea as to the necessary circumstance.[4] Moreover, it has also been held that, provided that the accused knows that the conspiracy relates to something falling within the overall purview of the related offences (whether or not he realised this) but without knowing the particular details, as where – in relation to the above conspiracy – he knows that it relates to drugs which (whether or not he knows this) are controlled drugs but has no idea of the precise type,[5] he can be convicted of a conspiracy to commit the offence indicated by the subject matter. It has been held that the same would be true if the accused thought that the subject matter related to a more serious type of the species of offence involved, as where – in relation to a charge of conspiracy to import Class B controlled drugs he thought that the drugs involved were heroin (ie Class A drugs) and did not realise that they were in fact cannabis (ie Class B drugs).[6]

1 [1984] AC 463, [1984] 1 All ER 740, HL.
2 Para 6.61.
3 (1989) 90 Cr App Rep 340, CA.
4 *Patel* (1991) unreported, CA.
5 Ibid.
6 Ibid.

21.24 Although generally 'knowledge' includes wilful blindness,[1] this is almost certainly not the case here. On the other hand, as already implied, in the case of impossibility due to the non-existence of a circumstance, 'knowledge' must be read as including 'belief' (ie that the accused had no substantial doubt about the matter), since one can hardly know something which does not exist. It can hardly be the case that a *correct* belief in facts making the object of the agreement criminal is insufficient until verified and turned into actual knowledge.

1 Para 6.59.

21.25 *Mens rea as to agreement being carried out and substantive offence being committed* The wording of s 1(1) seems unequivocally to indicate that, as a second element of mens rea, the accused and at least one other party to the agreement must intend that the agreement be carried out and that the substantive offence to which their agreed course of conduct will necessarily amount (or which it will involve) will be committed. Consequently, it is amazing that the House of Lords in *Anderson*[1] held that such an intention need not be proved against an individual accused. Indeed, it may be that the House of Lords thought that not even one party must have had such an intention. However, since it did not clearly indicate this, and since such an interpretation would do further violence to the wording of the Act and to the intentions of the Law Commission, it can be assumed that at least two of the parties to the agreement must have had such an intention and that otherwise there cannot be a statutory conspiracy. If this is so, there cannot be a conviction for statutory conspiracy of either D1 and D2 who are the only parties to an agreement for the commission of an offence if only D1 intends that the agreement be carried out and the substantive offence committed.

On the assumption made in the last paragraph, where the actus reus of the substantive offence requires a specific consequence to be caused, the present requirement necessitates proof of an intention on the part of two or more parties to the agreement that that consequence should result. Two points arise in relation to this. First, although an intention to cause some lesser consequence may suffice for the substantive offence, such an intention will not suffice on a charge of conspiracy.[2] Consequently, on a charge of conspiracy to murder an intention that someone be unlawfully killed must be proved, although an intention unlawfully to cause grievous bodily harm suffices for murder itself. Second, there can be little doubt that only a purposive intent will do.

It follows from the present requirement that if D1 gives D2 a parcel and tells him to deliver it to P's empty house, which D1 agrees to do, and the parcel contains a bomb with which D1 intends to cause criminal damage (an offence where recklessness suffices) to P's house, neither D1 nor D2 can be convicted of conspiracy to commit criminal damage, unless D2 also knows that the parcel contains a bomb and intends that P's property be damaged or destroyed.

1 [1986] AC 27, [1985] 2 All ER 961, HL.
2 *Siracusa* (1989) 90 Cr App Rep 340, CA

21.26 *Additional mens rea* In addition to any mens rea relating to a specified circumstance or consequence of the actus reus of the substantive offence, two or more parties to the agreement must be proved to have had any further intent or other mens rea required for that offence. For example, on a charge of conspiracy to steal the intended course of conduct must be dishonest on their part and they must intend permanently to deprive the other person to whom the property belongs.

21.27 If an individual accused need not be proved to have intended that the agreement be carried out and the substantive offence committed, must any element of intention be proved on his part? The House of Lords answered 'yes' in *Anderson*. Lord Bridge, with whose speech the other law lords agreed, stated:

> '[A]n essential ingredient of the crime of conspiring to commit a specific offence ... under s 1(1) of the 1977 Act is that the accused agreed that a course of conduct be pursued which he knows must involve the commission by one or more of the parties to the agreement of that offence ... But, beyond the mere fact of agreement, the necessary mens rea of the crime is, in my opinion, established if, and only[1] if, it is shown that the accused, when he entered into the agreement, intended to play some part in the agreed course of conduct in furtherance of the criminal purpose which the agreed course of conduct was intended to achieve. Nothing less will suffice; nothing more is required[2]'.[3]

This implication of a mens rea requirement (on the part, presumably, of each party to the agreement if he is to be guilty) was not supported by any authority[4] and is in no way warranted by s 1(1) or any other part of the Act. It is pure judicial invention. It does further violence to the unequivocal wording of s 1(1) and to the intentions of the Law Commission.

If Lord Bridge's statement represented the law, a person would not be guilty as a perpetrator of criminal conspiracy who for thoroughly bad motives entered into an agreement with others that a course of conduct be pursued which would necessarily amount to the commission of the offence if it was carried out in accordance with their intentions if he did not himself intend to play some part in the agreed course of conduct. Conversely, if a police officer or the like who joined a conspiracy in order to entrap the conspirators did intend to play a minor part in the furtherance of the agreed conduct in order to maintain his credibility as a conspirator or to obtain sufficient evidence against them, he would (according to Lord Bridge's statement) be guilty of statutory conspiracy. The application of that statement clearly gives rise to some unhappy results.

Reference to the facts and decision in *Anderson* indicates that Lord Bridge's statement in *Anderson* quoted above was not necessary to the decision in that case[4] and is merely an obiter dictum. In *Anderson* D had agreed with others to participate, in return for a fee, in a scheme to effect X's escape from prison by providing cutting wire, a rope ladder, transport and safe accommodation. According to D he had never intended the escape plan to be carried into effect and had only intended to supply the cutting wire, whereafter he was going to go abroad with the part of the fee which had been paid on account and another part he expected to have paid on account. The House of Lords held that on these facts D had correctly been convicted of statutory conspiracy to effect the escape of X, since D did not have to be proved to have intended that the substantive offence be committed and, in agreeing that a course of conduct be pursued that would, if successful, necessarily involve the offence of effecting X's escape from prison, D clearly intended, by providing the cutting wire, to play a part in the agreed course of conduct in furtherance of that criminal objective.[5] Neither the fact that D intended to play no further part in attempting to effect the escape, nor that he believed the escape to be impossible, would have afforded him any defence.

In view of the unfortunate consequences of Lord Bridge's obiter statement, it is pleasing to note that it has been explained by the Court of Appeal in *Siracusa*[6] that Lord Bridge did not mean that the prosecution must prove that the accused intended to play an active part in carrying out the agreement. The Court held that he can 'play a part' merely by continuing to concur in the criminal activity of another or others.

It is unfortunate that the other part of the House of Lords' decision, discussed in para 21.25 must be regarded as part of the ratio decidendi and therefore binding.

1 The word 'only' must be read subject to the comments in para 21.25.
2 Presumably, this means that nothing more is required against an individual accused, but not that nothing more is required against two or more other parties to the agreement.
3 [1985] 2 All ER 961 at 965.
4 See commentaries by Professor Smith in [1986] Crim LR at 54 and 247.
5 It may be that, even if the accused had been required to intend that the substantive offence be committed, he could nevertheless have been convicted as an accomplice to the conspiracy of which the others were guilty as perpetrators. See para 23.4.a.
6 (1989) 90 Cr App Rep 340, CA. Also see *Edwards* [1991] Crim LR 44, CA (commentary).

21.28 Of course, a person charged with conspiracy need not know that the course of conduct agreed on is a criminal offence. This was the position in relation to common law conspiracy to commit an offence,[1] and the wording of s 1(1) makes it clear that this continues to be the case for statutory conspiracy despite an apparently contradictory statement in *Siracusa*.[2] In that case O'Connor LJ, referring to the first sentence in Lord Bridge's dictum quoted in para 21.27, said:

> 'he plainly does not mean that the prosecution have to prove that two persons who agree to import prohibited drugs into this country know that the offence which will be committed will be a contravention of s 170(2) of the Customs and Excise Act (sic). He is not to be taken as saying that the prosecution must prove that the accused knew the nature of the crime. We are satisfied that Lord Bridge was doing no more than applying the words of s 1 of the Criminal Law Act 1977, namely, that when the accused agreed to the course of conduct, he knew that it involved the commission of an offence.'

At first sight it appears that O'Connor LJ's final words were intended to mean that an accused must positively know that what his conduct will necessarily involve is an offence (although he need not know which one), so that his ignorance of this would be a defence. This would fly in the face of the general rule that ignorance of the law is no defence, and conflict with the position at common law and with the clear wording of s 1(1). Fortunately, it would seem from the next paragraph in the judgment that O'Connor LJ, in saying that the accused must have known that the agreed course of conduct 'involved the commission of an offence' was simply condensing the statement that the accused must know that that course would involve circumstances and/or consequences which would amount to an offence if they existed or occurred.

1 *Churchill v Walton* [1967] 2 AC 224, [1967] 1 All ER 497, HL.
2 (1989) 90 Cr App Rep 340 at 349-350.

CONSPIRACY TO DO WHAT?

21.29 Liability for conspiracy relates only to those offences which would necessarily be committed if the agreement to pursue a course of conduct is carried out in accordance with the parties' intentions. If D1 and D2 agree to attack and kill P they are guilty of conspiracy to murder, even though there is a chance that P may survive the attack, since the offence of murder would necessarily be committed if the course of conduct agreed by them is carried out in accordance with their intentions. If D1 and D2 agree to do really serious harm to P they can be convicted of conspiracy to commit the offence of causing grievous bodily harm with intent, but not of conspiracy to murder, even though if they had carried out their plan and P had died of his injuries they could have been convicted of murder, since that offence is not one which would necessarily be committed if the agreement is carried out in accordance with their intentions.

EXEMPTIONS FROM LIABILITY FOR STATUTORY CONSPIRACY

21.30 a) *The intended victim* Section 2(1) of the Act provides that a person cannot be guilty of a conspiracy to commit any offence if he is the intended victim of that offence. An 'intended victim' means a person who could not be convicted (either as a perpetrator or as an accomplice) of the substantive offence itself although he participated in it, because, as the victim of the offence, he is assumed to fall outside its scope. For example, a girl under 16 cannot be convicted as an accomplice if she has unlawful intercourse with, or is abducted by, a man, even though she is a willing participant. This matter is discussed later.[1]

b) *Husband and wife conspiracies* See para 21.13.
c) *Section 2(2)(b) and (c)* These paragraphs provide that a person is not
guilty of a conspiracy to commit any offence if the only other person or
persons with whom he agrees are (both initially and at all times during
the currency of the agreement):
   i) under the age of criminal responsibility (ie under 10);[2] or
   ii) an intended victim or victims of the substantive offence.[3]

Thus, if D1 agrees with a 15-year-old girl to have intercourse with her he
cannot be convicted of conspiracy since the only other party to the agreement is an intended victim. It would, of course, be different if D1 and D2 had
agreed with the girl that they should have intercourse with her because the
exemption only applies where the only other party or parties to the agreement are under 10 or intended victims; in that case D1 and D2 could be
convicted of conspiracy, although the girl would be exempt from liability
under s 2(1).

By way of comparison, it may be noted that the fact that a party to the
agreement could not be convicted of perpetrating the substantive offence
does not mean that he or any other party to the agreement cannot be
convicted of conspiracy to commit that offence.[4] Thus, a woman cannot
perpetrate the offence of rape (although she can be convicted as an
accomplice) but, if she agrees with a man that he will rape P, they can both
be convicted of conspiracy to rape.

1 Para 23.27.
2 Criminal Law Act 1977, s 2(2)(b) and (3).
3 Ibid, s 2(2)(c).
4 *B* [1984] Crim LR 352, CA.

PROSECUTION, TRIAL AND PUNISHMENT

21.31 *Prosecution* The following restrictions on the institution of prosecutions for statutory conspiracy are provided by the Act:

a) Proceedings for conspiracy to commit any offence or offences must not
   be instituted except by or with the consent of the Director of Public
   Prosecutions if the offence or (as the case may be) each of the offences
   in question is a summary offence;[1]
b) Proceedings for conspiracy to commit an offence (other than a summary offence), for which a prosecution cannot be instituted otherwise
   than by, or on behalf of or with the consent of, the Director of Public
   Prosecutions or any other person, may only be instituted by, or on
   behalf of or with the consent of, the relevant person;[2]
c) Where an offence *has been committed* pursuant to any agreement and
   any time limit applicable to the institution of a prosecution for that
   offence has expired, the institution of a prosecution for conspiracy to
   commit that offence is also barred.[3]

1 Criminal Law Act 1977, s 4(1). Sometimes the Attorney-General's consent is required
  instead: s 4(2).
2 Ibid, s 4(3). If consent has already been given for a prosecution for the substantive offence, a
  separate consent is nevertheless necessary for a prosecution for conspiracy to commit it:
  Pearce (1980) 72 Cr App Rep 295, CA.
3 Ibid, s 4(4).

21.32 *Trial* Statutory conspiracy is triable only on indictment, even if it
relates to the commission of a summary offence (since a conspiracy charge is

thought to raise too many difficulties of substance and procedure for magistrates to try); the restriction on prosecution in such a case just mentioned is an attempt to ensure that prosecutions for conspiracy to commit summary offences are only brought in appropriate cases.

21.33 *Punishment* The penalties for statutory conspiracy are set out in a somewhat involved fashion by s 3 of the Act of 1977. Where the substantive offence, or one of them, is:

a) murder, or any other offence whose sentence is fixed by law;
b) an offence for which life imprisonment may be awarded, e g robbery; or
c) an indictable offence punishable with imprisonment but for which no maximum term is provided,

the maximum sentence is life imprisonment.

In any other case, provided the substantive offence, or one of them, is punishable with imprisonment, the maximum sentence on conviction for statutory conspiracy is the maximum for the substantive offence or the longer (or longest) maximum in the case of different substantive offences.

If none of the substantive offences is punishable with imprisonment, a person convicted of statutory conspiracy is not punishable with imprisonment, although he may be fined.

WHERE THE SUBSTANTIVE OFFENCE HAS BEEN COMMITTED

21.34 A conspiracy to commit an offence does not merge with the substantive offence when the latter is committed. However, as a general rule, where there is an effective and sufficient charge of a substantive offence, the addition of a charge for conspiracy is undesirable because it tends to prolong and complicate the trial.[1] Consequently, where an indictment contains substantive counts and a related conspiracy count, the prosecution is required to justify the joinder by satisfying the judge that the interests of justice demand it; if the judge is not satisfied, the prosecution must elect to proceed either on the substantive counts or on the conspiracy count.[2]

1 *Verrier v DPP* [1967] 2 AC 195 at 223–224, [1966] 3 All ER 568 at 575.
2 *Practice Note* [1977] 2 All ER 540.

DRAFT CRIMINAL CODE

21.35 Clauses 48 and 51 of the draft Criminal Code Bill[1] restates the relevant provisions of Part I of the 1977 Act relating to statutory conspiracy and some of the common law related to it, with some additions to amend or clarify certain matters, including

a) a provision that *the accused* and at least one other party to the agreement must intend that the substantive offences be committed;
b) a provision that, where recklessness with respect to a circumstance suffices for the substantive offence, it suffices on a charge of conspiracy;
c) a provision that a person may be guilty as an accomplice to conspiracy by others;[2]
d) a provision that there should be no liability for conspiracy to aid and abet (which would clearly resolve the point discussed in para 21.16).

Under the draft Criminal Code Bill a party to the agreement could be convicted as a conspirator even though he did not intend to play any part in the furtherance of the agreed course of conduct. The existing exemptions from liability for conspiracy for a person who agreed only with his spouse or a child under the age of criminal responsibility or an intended victim of the substantive offence involved are not contained in the Code and would cease to exist as part of the definition of statutory conspiracy if ever the draft Bill is enacted.

1 Law Commission: A Criminal Code for England and Wales (1989): Law Com No 177; see para 3.21 above.
2 See para 23.4.a.

Common law conspiracy

21.36 As was stated in para 21.11, this offence has now been reduced to conspiracy to defraud and, possibly, conspiracies to corrupt public morals or to outrage public decency.

CONSPIRACY TO DEFRAUD

21.37 This type of common law conspiracy is expressly preserved by s 5(2) of the Criminal Law Act 1977, although its preservation was intended only to be temporary since it was intended to abolish it once certain unacceptable gaps in the law relating to fraudulent conduct had been closed by legislation which was expected after the Law Commission had completed its review of the matter. The Law Commission has yet to complete this task. Once this is done and new substantive offences concerning fraud brought into force, it will be possible to deal with all types of fraudulent agreements deserving punishment by charging statutory conspiracy. In anticipation of this, the draft Criminal Code Bill does not deal with the common law offence of conspiracy to defraud, which would continue to exist if the draft Bill was enacted before its abolition.

As has been implied in the last paragraph, there can be a conspiracy to defraud even though the fraudulent object would not constitute an offence if achieved; in fact it need not even be tortious.

21.38 *Basic definition of fraud* In *Scott v Metropolitan Police Comr*[1] in 1974 the House of Lords held that there may be a conspiracy to defraud without any element of deception. D agreed with the employees of cinema owners temporarily to abstract films without the permission of the cinema owners and in return for payment to the employees, so that, without the consent of the owners of the copyright and distribution rights in such films, he could make copies and distribute them commercially. D was convicted of conspiracy to defraud and also of conspiracy to commit a relatively minor offence under the Copyright Act 1956. He appealed against conviction for conspiracy to defraud, but that conviction was upheld by the House of Lords which held that on such a charge it was not necessary for the Crown to prove an agreement to deprive the owners of their property by deception. It was sufficient to prove an agreement by dishonesty to deprive a person of something which is his or to which he is or would be or might be entitled *or* an agreement by dishonesty to injure some proprietary right of his. It is irrelevant that the execution of the agreement may not involve any actual economic loss on the part of the victim, provided his economic interests are put at risk.[2] In other words, all that is required is an agreement by dishonesty to bring about a situation which would or might deprive a person of something which is his or to which he is, or would or might be, entitled, or which would or might injure some proprietary interest of his.

It is also irrelevant that that situation is to be brought about by some perpetrator other than the parties to the agreement.[3] Thus, people who agree to supply to retailers falsely labelled bottles of whisky or to make and sell devices to by-pass electricity meters can be convicted of conspiracy to defraud, even though the perpetration of the fraud (on the purchaser of the whisky or the electricity board) will be done by the retailer of the whisky or the user of the device respectively.[3]

In the light of what was said in *Scott v Metropolitan Police Comr*, it is not easy to understand the Court of Appeal's decision in *Zemmel and Melik*[4] to the effect that an agreement dishonestly and temporarily to delay payment of a debt is not a conspiracy to defraud. Undoubtedly, such delay is not an offence but it would seem clearly to fall within the definition in *Scott*. Consequently, the decision in *Zemmel and Melik* must be regarded as wrong.

1 [1975] AC 819, [1974] 3 All ER 1032, HL.
2 *Allsop* (1976) 64 Cr App Rep 29, CA.
3 *A-G's Reference (No 1 of 1982)* [1983] QB 751, [1983] 2 All ER 721, CA; *Hollinshead* [1985] AC 975, [1985] 2 All ER 769, HL.
4 (1985) 81 Cr App Rep 279, [1985] Crim LR 213, CA.

21.39 There has been conflict in the case law on the issue of whether the causing of economic loss or prejudice must be the purpose of the parties to the agreement.[1] For practical purposes, the point has been resolved by the recent decision of the Privy Council in *Wai Yu-tsang v R*,[2] where it was held that it was enough that the alleged conspirators had dishonestly agreed to bring about a state of affairs which they realised would or might deceive the victim into so acting, or failing to act, that he would suffer economic loss or his economic interests would be put at risk. Doubtless, a similar principle applies where a deception is not involved. The decision in *Wai Yu-tsang v R* is important because, as Shaw LJ said in *Allsop*:[3] 'Generally the primary object of fraudsmen is to advantage themselves. The detriment that results to their victims is secondary to that purpose and incidental'.

1 Contrast *Attorney-General's Reference (No 1 of 1982)* [1983] QB 751, [1983] 2 All ER 721, CA (causing of economic loss or prejudice must be accused's purpose) with *Allsop* (1976) 64 Cr App Rep 29, CA (causing economic loss or prejudice need not be the accused's purpose, but he must have foreseen that economic loss or prejudice was a likely if the agreement was carried out).
2 [1991] 4 All ER 664, PC.
3 (1976) 64 Cr App Rep 29 at 31.

21.40 *Another type of fraud* Although in the vast majority of cases the agreement relates to bringing about a situation which would or might cause some sort of economic prejudice, conspiracy to defraud is not limited to this type of case. An agreement dishonestly to bring about a situation which would or might deceive a public official performing public duties (which phrase does not include bank managers and the like)[1] to act contrary to such a duty is a conspiracy to defraud, even though there is no risk of causing economic loss to anyone or of prejudicing his economic interests.[2] An example would be where D1 and D2 agree dishonestly to deceive a public official into granting a licence or into giving secret information.

As in the case of a conspiracy to defraud involving the risk of economic loss or prejudice, it need not be the aim or purpose of the parties to cause the victim to act contrary to his public duty. It is enough that they have dishonestly agreed to bring about a situation which they realised would or might deceive the victim into so acting.

1 *DPP v Withers* [1974] 3 All ER 984 at 1009, per Lord Kilbrandon; *Moses and Ansbro* [1991] Crim LR 617, CA.
2 *Board of Trade v Owen* [1957] AC 602 at 622, per Lord Tucker; *Scott v Metropolitan Police Comr* [1974] 3 All ER 1032, see especially Lord Diplock at 1040; *DPP v Withers* at 1004–1005 and 1009, per Lords Simon and Kilbrandon respectively.

21.41 The requirement that the agreement must be by dishonesty to bring about a situation which would or might cause economic loss or prejudice (or would or might cause a public official to act contrary to his public duty) refers partly to the proposed means of achieving that object and partly to the state of mind of the parties to the agreement. In *Landy*[1] statements by the Court of Appeal suggested that the accuseds' belief as to whether or not they were acting honestly was the determinant of dishonesty in conspiracy to defraud. However, subsequently in *Ghosh*[2] it held that the test of dishonesty was the same as in theft, viz whether the accuseds' proposed means were on the facts known to them dishonest according to the current standards of ordinary decent people, and whether, if they were, the accused realised that they were contrary to those standards. The extent to which the judge must leave these questions to the jury is the same as in the case of substantive offences against property,[3] and the reader is referred to the account of this earlier in this book.[4] Unless the jury give an affirmative answer to any such questions left to them, the accused will not have acted dishonestly for the purposes of conspiracy to defraud.

1 [1981] 1 All ER 1172, [1981] 1 WLR 355, CA.
2 [1982] QB 1053, [1982] 2 All ER 689, CA; para 13.55.
3 *Squire* [1990] Crim LR 341, CA.
4 Paras 13.54–13.58 and 14.41.

21.42 Of course, there cannot be a conspiracy to defraud unless there are at least two parties to an agreement who satisfy the requirements to be fulfilled on the part of the accused, which have just been explained. Even if there is a conspiracy to defraud, a person who is ostensibly a party to that agreement cannot be convicted if one of the above requirements is not satisfied in relation to him.

21.43 Where the agreement is made in this country but the intended fraud is to take effect wholly abroad the agreement is not indictable in this country as a conspiracy to defraud.[1] Thus, people who agree in London to facilitate a swindle on the New York Stock Exchange cannot be tried in this country for common law conspiracy to defraud.[2]

1 *A-G's Reference (No 1 of 1982)* [1983] QB 751, [1983] 2 All ER 721, CA; cf *Levitz, Mbele and Vowell* [1989] Crim LR 714, CA. The Law Commission has criticised this rule; see its Report on Jurisdiction over Offences of Fraud and Dishonesty with a Foreign Element (1989) Law Com No 180, para 5.5.
2 Nor can they be tried for a statutory conspiracy: para 21.23.

21.44 *Scope of conspiracy to defraud* Where the agreed fraudulent course of conduct will not, or will not necessarily, amount to or involve the commission of an offence by one or more parties to the agreement if it is carried out in accordance with the parties' intentions, as where there is an agreement temporarily to deprive a person dishonestly of a family heirloom, the agreement is only punishable as a common law conspiracy to defraud.

On the other hand, where the agreed fraudulent course of conduct will necessarily amount to or involve the commission of an offence by one or more parties to the agreement if it is carried out in accordance with the parties' intentions, the agreement is punishable either as a statutory conspiracy or as a common law conspiracy to defraud. Section 12 of the Criminal Justice Act 1987 provides that, if:

a) a person agrees with any other person or persons that a course of conduct shall be pursued; and

b) that course of conduct will necessarily amount to or involve the commission of any offence or offences by one or more of the parties to the agreement if the agreement is carried out in accordance with their intentions,

the fact that it will do so does not preclude a charge of conspiracy to defraud being brought against any of them in respect of the agreement.

As a result, there is a substantial overlap between statutory conspiracy and conspiracy to defraud. For example, any agreement to steal (or to commit most other offences under the Theft Acts or the Forgery and Counterfeiting Act 1981) or to commit a host of minor statutory offences can be prosecuted either as a statutory conspiracy or as a conspiracy to defraud. The category of offences covered by this overlap is very wide indeed. The only other category of offences approaching it in importance is that relating to offences against the person.

21.45 In order to prevent a charge of conspiracy to defraud being brought instead of, or together with, the appropriate charge for minor fraudulent criminal conduct or clear cases of theft or the like involving two or more people, which would simply serve to complicate matters, guidelines have been issued to Crown Prosecutors by the Director of Public Prosecutions under s 10 of the Prosecution of Offences Act 1985. These indicate the circumstances in which it is, and is not, appropriate to charge conspiracy to defraud. They have been commended to other prosecuting authorities, such as the Inland Revenue and the Customs and Excise, by the Attorney-General. Quite apart from these guidelines, trial judges have the power to intervene in a trial if it appears that one type of conspiracy is more appropriate on the facts or less complex than the other.

CONSPIRACY TO CORRUPT PUBLIC MORALS AND
CONSPIRACY TO OUTRAGE PUBLIC DECENCY

21.46 Whether conspiracies of this type are still common law conspiracies depends on what is said later, but they will first be defined.

a) *Conspiracy to corrupt public morals* In *Shaw v DPP*,[1] decided in 1961, the majority of the House of Lords recognised the continued existence of the offence of conspiracy to corrupt public morals. They accordingly upheld Shaw's conviction for this offence, arising out of his agreement with others for the publication of a 'Ladies' Directory', giving the names, addresses and practices of prostitutes.

   Shaw was followed by the majority of the House of Lords in 1972 in *Knuller v DPP*,[2] where further explanation was given of conspiracy to corrupt public morals. The House held that an agreement to publish advertisements soliciting homosexual acts between consenting adults in private was a conspiracy to corrupt public morals, even though such conduct is no longer an offence.[3] Lords Reid and Simon said that 'corrupt' was a strong word and that 'corrupt public morals' meant more than 'lead morally astray'. Lord Reid thought that 'corrupt' was synonymous with 'deprave',[4] while Lord Simon said that what was required was conduct which 'a jury might find to be destructive of the very fabric of society'.[5] Lord Reid thought that conspiracy to corrupt public morals was something of a misnomer. 'It really means to corrupt the morals of such members of the public as may be influenced by the matter published by the accused'.[6]

Although, of course, the judge must initially rule on whether there is evidence on which the jury can find the case proved, it is for the jury to find whether a particular object is corrupting of public morals and they should do this by applying the current standards of ordinary decent people.[7] This leads to considerable uncertainty about the conduct penalised by the criminal law.

b) *Conspiracy to outrage public decency* In *Knuller v DPP* the accused had also been convicted of conspiracy to outrage public decency. The majority of the House of Lords recognised the continued existence of this offence, although the accuseds' appeals against conviction were allowed because the jury had not been properly directed on the relevant principles.

The object of the conspiracy must be committed in public, in the sense that the circumstances must be such that the alleged outrageously indecent matter or conduct could have been seen by more than one person, although not necessarily simultaneously. Thus, it is not a defence that the indecent matter is contained in a book or newspaper sold in public.

'Outrage' like 'corrupt' is a strong word. 'Outraging public decency' goes beyond offending the susceptibilities of, or even shocking, reasonable people. The offence is concerned with protecting the recognised minimum contemporary standards of decency; whether there is an 'outrage' of such standards is a question for the jury.[8] The question is whether the matter or conduct would be likely to disgust and annoy ordinary members of the public.[9]

1 [1962] AC 220, [1961] 2 All ER 446, HL.
2 [1973] AC 435, [1972] 2 All ER 898, HL.
3 Para 12.28.
4 [1973] AC at 456.
5 Ibid at 491.
6 Ibid at 456.
7 *Shaw v DPP* [1962] AC 220, [1961] 2 All ER 446, HL; *Knuller v DPP* [1973] AC 435, [1972] 2 All ER 898, HL.
8 See, in particular, the speech of Lord Simon with whom Lord Kilbrandon agreed.
9 Para 19.24.

21.47 Section 5(3) of the Criminal Law Act 1977 preserves the offence of conspiracy at common law *if and in so far as* it may be committed by entering into an agreement to engage in conduct which:

a) tends to corrupt public morals or outrages public decency; but
b) would not amount to or involve the commission of an offence if carried out by a single person otherwise than in pursuance of an agreement.

This provision raises the questions of whether substantive common law offences of corrupting public morals and of outraging public decency exist, and (if they do) of their extent.

It was explained in Chapter 19 that there is a substantive common law offence of outraging public decency. The existence of this offence has become more clearly established since the enactment of s 5(3). The exact scope of it remains somewhat vague but it is almost indisputable that it is coterminous with outraging public decency as the object of a conspiracy, in which case a conspiracy to outrage public decency will always be a statutory conspiracy and the effect of s 5(3) is to abolish the common law offence of conspiracy to outrage public decency. However, if (as is most unlikely) outraging public decency as a substantive common law offence has a narrower ambit than outraging public decency as the object of a conspiracy, the effect of s 5(3) is that an agreement to outrage public decency will be a statutory conspiracy if, in the circumstances, the conduct agreed on would be an offence if it took place, but only a common law conspiracy if that conduct would not in itself constitute a substantive offence.

The position is even more uncertain in relation to corrupting public morals, since the only authority in favour of the existence of a substantive common law offence of corrupting public morals is *Shaw v DPP*[1] where the Court of Criminal Appeal held that there was a common law offence of conduct calculated or intended to corrupt public morals. Unfortunately, the House of Lords on appeal did not decide this point. As a result one cannot be certain that there is a common law substantive offence of corrupting public morals. If there is not it will not be a statutory conspiracy to conspire to corrupt public morals (unless the intended conduct constitutes some other substantive offence), because statutory conspiracy is limited to agreements whose object is the commission of an offence, but by s 5(3) it will be a common law conspiracy. If, on the other hand, there is a common law offence of corrupting public morals, the effect of s 5(3) is that a conspiracy to corrupt public morals will *either* only be a statutory conspiracy (if that substantive offence is coterminous with corruption of public morals as the object of a conspiracy) *or* (if the substantive offence has a narrower ambit) will be a statutory conspiracy if the conduct agreed on would amount to a substantive offence but will be a common law conspiracy if that conduct falls outside the substantive offence but within the definition of the corruption of public morals as the object of a conspiracy.

Until these issues are decided the only prudent course where conspiracy to corrupt public morals or conspiracy to outrage public decency is charged is to charge alternative counts of statutory conspiracy and common law conspiracy.

1 [1962] AC 220, [1961] 1 All ER 330, CCA; affd [1962] AC 220, [1961] 2 All ER 446, HL.

21.48 The reader may be amazed that a statute should leave the law so uncertain. In defence of the legislature it should be pointed out that, like s 5(2) of the Criminal Law Act 1977, s 5(3) was intended to be purely a temporary holding operation. The Law Commission, whose report on conspiracy was implemented with amendments by ss 1–5 of the Act, had recommended that the common law conspiracies to corrupt public morals or to outrage public decency should be abolished, along with certain common law offences concerned with morals and decency, and should be replaced by certain new statutory offences to fill the gaps in the law where desirable. However, by and large, these recommendations were not incorporated into the Bill which became the Criminal Law Act 1977, and the Government refused to accept an amendment whose effect would have been to abolish conspiracy to corrupt public morals and conspiracy to outrage public decency as forms of common law conspiracy. The Government's reason was that this should be delayed until the whole area of obscenity and indecency in publications, entertainments and the like had been reviewed. This review was completed by the Committee on Obscenity and Film Censorship, which reported in 1979,[1] but its proposals have not yet been implemented.

The draft Criminal Code Bill does not contain distinct offences of conspiracy to corrupt public morals and conspiracy to outrage public decency. Consequently, to the extent, if any, that these forms of common law conspiracy exist, they would continue to exist if ever the Bill was enacted before their abolition.

1 Cmnd 7772.

21.49 One other point must be made briefly concerning s 5(3). Its wording is such that a person cannot be convicted of common law conspiracy to corrupt public morals or to outrage public decency if the conduct agreed on would involve the commission of some other substantive offence.[1]

1 Note, there is express provision to this effect in s 2(4A) of the Obscene Publications Act 1959 (inserted by s 53(3) of the Criminal Law Act 1977) in relation to an agreement to give a cinematograph exhibition.

IMPOSSIBILITY IN COMMON LAW CONSPIRACY

21.50 This is governed by the decision of the House of Lords in *DPP v Nock*,[1] where the reasoning of the House in *Haughton v Smith*[2] concerning impossibility in relation to the common law offence of attempt was held to apply to common law conspiracy.

The position is as follows. Where the object of the agreement is at the time of the agreement capable of being achieved but cannot actually be achieved because of some supervening event or because the proposed means are insufficient, there can be a conviction for conspiracy. Thus, there can be a conviction for conspiracy to defraud in the case of an agreement to 'borrow' P's book from his locker without his consent, even though the book is subsequently destroyed before this can be done or the skeleton key which is to be used does not fit the lock. However, in any other case of impossibility, e g where the book has already been destroyed at the time of the agreement, there cannot be a conviction for common law conspiracy.

As seen in para 21.20, the law on impossibility is less strict in the case of statutory conspiracies. Consequently, where there is a conspiracy to commit an offence of fraud, which offence is impossible of commission for reasons other than inadequacy of means or a supervening event, a statutory conspiracy should be charged.

1 [1978] AC 979, [1978] 2 All ER 654, HL.
2 [1975] AC 476, [1973] 3 All ER 1109, HL.

TRIAL AND PUNISHMENT

21.51 Common law conspiracy is triable only on indictment.

The maximum punishment for a common law conspiracy to defraud is now governed by statute (s 12 of the Criminal Justice Act 1987), and is ten years' imprisonment. In the case of a common law conspiracy to corrupt public morals or to outrage public decency, to the extent that such an offence survives, statute has not intervened, with the result that these types of common law conspiracy remain punishable with imprisonment for a period fixed at the discretion of the judge.[1]

1 Para 3.4.

Attempt

21.52 The common law offence of attempt to commit an indictable offence was abolished by the Criminal Attempts Act 1981[1] (hereafter referred to as 'the Act'), and replaced by a statutory offence of attempt which is created by s 1 of the Act. The provisions relating to the statutory offence largely implement recommendations made by the Law Commission in 1980.[2]

Section 1(1) of the Act provides that, if, with intent to commit an offence to which s 1 applies, a person does an act which is more than merely preparatory to the commission of the offence, he is guilty of attempting to commit the offence.

1 Section 6(1).
2 Law Com No 102, Criminal Law: Attempts and Impossibility in relation to Attempts, Conspiracy and Incitement. For a discussion of the recommendations and of the Act, see Dennis [1980] Crim LR 758 and [1982] Crim LR 5, respectively.

THE SCOPE OF THE OFFENCE

21.53 Section 1(4) of the Act provides that s 1 applies to any substantive offence which, if it were completed, would be triable in England and Wales as an indictable offence (i e one triable only on indictment or one triable either way). This means that, contrary to the Law Commission's recommendation, it is not an offence under s 1 to attempt to commit a summary offence (i e one triable only summarily[1]). There are, however, a number of specific statutory offences of attempting to commit a particular summary offence (see para 21.77).

The reference in s 1(4) to 'any offence which, if it were completed, would be triable in England and Wales as an indictable offence' means that normally an attempt in this country to commit an indictable offence abroad is not attempt. The reason is that, as explained more fully in chapter 6, generally an offence committed abroad is not triable in England and Wales. There are, however, exceptions, such as murder committed abroad by a British citizen. Thus, if D, a British citizen, posts a letter bomb in London to P in Paris, intending to kill P, D can be convicted of attempted murder if the letter is intercepted, whereas he could not be tried in this country for attempted murder if he were an alien.

21.54 Section 1(4) goes on to provide that the offence of attempt under s 1 does not apply to the following:

a) Conspiracy (whether statutory or common law); on the other hand, attempted incitement is an offence under s 1.[1]

b) Aiding, abetting, counselling, procuring or suborning the commission of an offence; in other words, attempting to be an accomplice to an offence which is actually committed is not an offence. It should be noted, however, that there are a few statutory offences, such as procuring the commission of an act of gross indecency and aiding and abetting suicide,[2] whose actus reus consists of procuring or aiding and abetting something, so that the perpetrator of such an offence is the procurer or aider and abettor of the relevant thing. A person who attempts to perpetrate such an offence can be convicted of an attempt to commit it.[3] It is, of course, possible for a person to be liable as an accomplice to an attempt.[4]

c) Assisting an offender, or concealing an offence, contrary to ss 4(1) or 5(1), respectively, of the Criminal Law Act 1967.

1 *Ransford* (1874) 31 LT 488.
2 Para 11.33.
3 *McShane* (1977) 66 Cr App Rep 97, CA; *Chief Constable of Hampshire v Mace* (1986) 84 Cr App Rep 40, [1986] Crim LR 752, DC.
4 *Dunnington* [1984] QB 472, CA.

21.55 There are a number of other offences which, by their nature, cannot be attempted under the definition in s 1. The requirement for an act means that offences which can only be committed by an omission to act are excluded from the offence of attempt, and the requirement of an intent to commit the offence whose attempt is charged means that there cannot be a conviction for an attempt to commit involuntary manslaughter because the essence of that offence is that the killing was unintentional, and the same is true of an offence whose *essence* is recklessness or negligence (e g causing death by dangerous driving).[1] On the other hand, there is no reason in principle why a person who intends to kill, but who would have had the defence of provocation or diminished responsibility if he had killed, should not be guilty of attempted voluntary manslaughter, as opposed to attempted murder, if his attempt is unsuccessful. However, the available authorities on the point deny that this is possible.[2] If the draft Criminal Code Bill[3] was ever enacted there would be an offence of attempted manslaughter by reason of provocation or diminished responsibility,[4] and there would be an offence of attempted infanticide[5] (which the present wording of the offence of infanticide may have the effect of precluding, in which case there must be a verdict of attempted murder).[6]

1 *Khan* [1990] 3 All ER 782 at 788.
2 *Bruzas* [1972] Crim LR 367; *Peck* (1975) Times, 5 December.
3 Law Commission: A Criminal Code for England and Wales (1989): Law Com No 177; see para 3.21 above.
4 Cl 61. Under the draft Criminal Code Bill, it would also be attempted manslaughter where a person attempted to kill when using excessive force in self-defence or the like : ibid. There would also be an offence of attempting to kill in pursuance of a suicide pact: cl 62. At present it seems that the verdict in such a case must be one of attempted murder.
5 Cl 64(2).
6 Although it was held in *Smith* [1983] Crim LR 739, Crown Ct, that a conviction for attempted infanticide is possible.

MENS REA

21.56 In order that a person may be convicted of an attempt to commit an offence, he must be proved, first, to have had an intention to commit that offence, and, second, to have done an act which constituted the actus reus of an attempt (ie an act which was more than merely preparatory to the commission of the intended offence). Of these two elements, the first is particularly important because whether a particular act amounts to an attempt will often depend on the intent with which it is done. For example, to strike a match near a haystack may or may not be attempted arson of the haystack, depending on whether there is an intent to set fire to the haystack or to light a cigarette: the intent colours the act. The function of the actus reus is to regulate the point at which acts in furtherance of the accused's intention incur criminal liability. The policy of the law is that it is only when some act is done which sufficiently manifests the existence of the social danger present in the intent that authority should intervene.

21.57 The mens rea specified for the offence of attempt by s 1(1) of the Act is an 'intent to commit an offence to which this section [ie s 1] applies' and which the accused is alleged to have attempted.

'Intention' in this context bears its normal purposive meaning, ie 'a decision to bring about, insofar as it lies within the accused's power, the commission of the offence which it is alleged the accused attempted to commit, no matter whether the accused desired that consequence of his act or not',[1] although, as we shall see, to some extent it is possible for the jury to infer intention if foresight of a sufficient degree is proved.

1 *Mohan* [1976] QB 1, [1975] 2 All ER 193 at 200, CA; *Pearman* [1985] RTR 39, 80 Cr App Rep 259, CA.

21.58 The above statements require further elucidation since they involve more complexity than might at first sight appear. The reason is that an intent to commit the offence attempted may involve a number of mental elements.

21.59 *Intent to commit a sufficient act* The accused must always be proved to have intended to commit an act or to continue with a series of acts which, when completed, will amount to the offence allegedly attempted[1] (assuming any requisite consequence for that offence has resulted from the act or acts and that any requisite circumstance exists). In this context talk of anything other than a purposive intent would be meaningless.

1 *Khan* [1990] 2 All ER 783, CA.

21.60 *Mens rea as to any consequence of substantive offence* Where the definition of the offence allegedly attempted requires that some conse- quence be brought about by the accused's conduct, it must always be proved that the accused intended *that* consequence. Intention in this context can be proved by proving that the accused had a purposive intention to bring it about. However, where intention as to consequence can be inferred from foresight on a charge of the full offence, the jury may infer on a charge of attempt that the accused intended that consequence if it is proved that the accused foresaw it as a virtually certain (or very highly probable) conse- quence of his intended act, although it is not proved that his purpose was to bring that consequence about.[1]

It is not enough that the accused intended some lesser consequence, nor is it enough that he was merely reckless as to the specified consequence occurring.[2] The result is that the requirement of mens rea for attempt may be stricter on a charge of attempt than for the full offence which has been attempted. For example, a person may be convicted of murder if he kills someone when intending merely to cause unlawful grievous bodily harm, whereas on a charge of attempted murder the jury must be satisfied that he intended unlawfully to kill if he is to be convicted.[3] By way of further example, the mens rea requirement for an attempt is also stricter where recklessness as to a consequence is sufficient mens rea for the full offence (as, for example, in the case of criminal damage, since on a charge of attempted criminal damage an intent to destroy or damage another's property must be proved).[4]

1 Para 6.35.
2 *Millard and Vernon* [1987] Crim LR 393, CA.
3 *Whybrow* (1951) 35 Cr App Rep 141, CCA; *Walker and Hayles* (1990) 90 Cr App Rep 226, CA.
4 See *Millard and Vernon* [1987] Crim LR 393, CA; *O'Toole* [1987] Crim LR 759, CA.

21.61 *Mens rea as to any circumstances of the substantive offence* The accused must be proved to have had mens rea in relation to any circumstances of the actus reus of the offence allegedly attempted, and this is so even if that offence is one of strict liability as to a circumstance or circumstances. It makes no sense in this context to speak of a purposive intention as to a circumstance (ie to speak of an accused deciding to bring about, in so far as it lies within his power, a circumstance) or of foresight of it resulting from his intended act.

In the rare case where the offence allegedly attempted requires actual knowledge as to a circumstance (otherwise known as intention as to a circumstance), actual knowledge as to that circumstance is (with one qualification) required on a charge of attempting that offence. The qualification is derived from s 1(3) of the Act, which, as explained later, relates to impossibility of an attempt. Section 1(3) proceeds on the basis that an accused can be convicted of an attempt where he *mistakenly* believes in the existence of facts or circumstances which would render his intended act criminal.[1] Thus, in this case 'belief' (ie that the accused had no substantial doubt about the matter) in the existence of a circumstance suffices instead of actual knowledge. It can hardly be the case that a *correct* belief in facts or circumstances making the intended act criminal is insufficient until verified and turned into actual knowledge.[2] If belief suffices in the alternative to actual knowledge on a charge of attempting to commit an offence requiring actual knowledge, there can be no doubt that it also suffices where the offence allegedly attempted requires actual knowledge or belief as to a circumstance.

Where recklessness suffices for the offence allegedly attempted, recklessness will also suffice on a charge of attempting to commit it. In *Khan*[3] the Court of Appeal held that, since recklessness as to the absence of the woman's consent is sufficient mens rea on a charge of rape,[4] an accused could be convicted of attempted rape if if he knew that the woman was not consenting or was reckless as to the fact that she might not be. Although *Khan* is strictly an authority only in relation to attempted rape, it is inconceivable that the approach taken in it is not equally applicable to an attempt to commit any other offence for which recklessness as to a circumstance or circumstances suffices.

Two points should be noted:

a) Whether or not the recklessness which suffices in such an attempt is limited to subjective recklessness or is *Caldwell*-type recklessness depends on which type suffices for the full offence;

b) Since recklessness as to a circumstance or circumstances suffices on an attempt charge if it suffices for the full offence, recklessness will suffice on a charge of attempting to commit an offence in which negligence as to a circumstance suffices or which is one of strict liability as to a circumstance. The reason is that, although a person can be convicted of such an offence even though he is not reckless as to that circumstance, it is no defence that the accused was actually reckless as to it, so that recklessness clearly suffices in such an offence. *Caldwell*-type recklessness is enough since it suffices for the full offence. The result is, for example, that on a charge of attempted unlawful sexual intercourse with a girl under 13, an offence of strict liability in relation to age, the accused must be proved actually to have known that the girl was under 13 or been *Caldwell*-type reckless as to this.

It is submitted that recklessness as to a circumstance should not be enough on a charge of attempt. The reason is that the requirement in s 1(1) of an intention to commit the offence attempted must mean that a person who is merely reckless (particularly in the sense attributed to that term by the House of Lords in *Caldwell*)[5] as to a circumstance of the actus reus of the full offence cannot be said to have attempted it. The view taken here can be supported by reference to that of the Law Commission[6]: this was that the intent that the full offence be brought about will in practice be established by proof of the accused's intention to bring about the consequences, and of his knowledge of the factual circumstances, required by the definition of the full offence. It is interesting to compare the offence of statutory conspiracy which requires actual knowledge of the prescribed circumstances of the substantive offence.[7] The difference in this respect between the closely related statutory offences of conspiracy and attempt is surprising.

In one type of case recklessness as to a circumstance will not suffice on a charge of attempt, although it suffices on a charge of the offence allegedly attempted. This is the case of impossibility of the type covered by s 1(3) of the Act, described in para 21.68. This is because s 1(3) requires the jury or magistrates to treat the accused as if the facts were as he believed them to be, and a man who, reckless as to whether or not she consents, attempts to have intercourse with a woman who is in fact consenting, or who, reckless as to whether or not she is under 16, attempts to abduct a girl of 16, cannot be guilty of attempted rape, or of the attempted abduction of a girl under 16; on the facts as he *believed* them to be the intercourse is not non-consensual and the girl is not under 16.

1 It would be nonsensical to talk of knowledge in such a case.
2 Dennis [1981] Crim LR at 764–5. Also see *Brown* [1984] 3 All ER 1013, [1984] 1 WLR 1211, CA.
3 [1990] 2 All ER 783, CA.
4 Para 12.7.
5 [1982] AC 341, [1981] 1 All ER 961, HL.
6 Law Com No 102, para 2.15.
7 Para 21.24.

21.62 *Additional mens rea* The requirement that the accused must be proved to have intended to commit the offence allegedly attempted means that he must have any other mental element, additional to mens rea as to the consequence or circumstances of the actus reus of the offence allegedly attempted, required for that offence. Thus, a person can only be convicted of attempted theft if he acted dishonestly and with intent permanently to deprive the person to whom it belonged of the property he intended to appropriate.

21.63 *General comments* Two general comments may be made in concluding the discussion of the mens rea for an attempt:
  a) *Ignorance of law no defence* The requirement of an intent to commit an offence does not mean that the accused must be aware that what he intends to do is an offence; the Act does not derogate from the general rule[1] that ignorance of the law is no defence.
  b) *Conditional intent* A person charged with attempting to commit an offence may have acted with a so-called conditional intent, i e an intent to commit that offence if a particular condition is satisfied. Provided in such a case that the accused has formed a *firm* intention to commit the offence if the condition in question was satisfied, and that he has gone beyond mere preparation (and therefore committed the actus reus of an attempt), he can be convicted of an attempt.

A common example of a case involving a conditional intent is where the accused intends to steal whatever he might find worth stealing in his target area, as where D is arrested as he opens P's suitcase (or the door of P's car), intending to look inside it, to examine its contents and, if there is anything worth stealing, to steal that thing. Provided he is not charged with the attempted theft of specific objects but instead is merely charged with the attempted theft of some or all of the contents of the suitcase (or car), D can be convicted of attempted theft.[2] Similarly, if D is arrested as he is about to trespass in a building with the intention of stealing anything valuable therein, if he finds such a thing, D can be convicted of attempted burglary;[3] in such a case it is unnecessary for the charge to allege more than 'with intent to steal therein' since the type of offence attempted does not require anything to be stolen.

Another example of a case involving a conditional intent is where the accused intends to commit a particular offence if the circumstances are propitious or the offence proves possible of commission, as where D creeps into P's house intending to kill P if P is alone (or if P is there). Assuming that it is proved that D acted with a firm intention to commit murder and had gone beyond the stage of mere preparation, D can be convicted of attempted murder despite the condition attached to his intention.

1 Para 6.73.
2 *A-G's References (Nos 1 and 2 of 1979)* [1980] QB 180, [1979] 3 All ER 143, CA; *Scudder v Barrett* [1980] QB 195, DC; *Bayley and Easterbrook* [1980] Crim LR 503, CA; *Smith and Smith* [1986] Crim LR 166, CA.
3 *A-G's References (Nos 1 and 2 of 1979)*.

ACTUS REUS

21.64 Section 1(1) of the Criminal Attempts Act 1981 provides that the offence of attempt to commit an offence requires 'an act that is more than merely preparatory to the commission of the offence'. 'The offence' means one to which s 1 applies[1] and which the accused intends to commit.

The use of the word 'act' indicates that a mere omission to act in furtherance of a criminal intent can never suffice for an attempt.

The application of the formula 'an act that is more than merely preparatory to the commission of the offence' can be illustrated as follows. If D buys a box of matches he cannot be convicted of attempted arson, even though it may clearly be proved that he intends to set fire to a haystack at the time of the purchase. Nor can D be convicted of this offence if he approaches the stack with the matches in his pocket. However, if he bends down near the stack and lights a match which he extinguishes on seeing that he is being watched, he may be guilty of attempted arson. In the first two instances, D's acts have clearly not gone beyond the stage of mere preparation; in the third the jury (or magistrates) may find that they have.

1 Paras 21.53 and 21.54.

21.65 The formula 'an act that is more than merely preparatory to the commission of the offence' is rather vague, particularly since the Act offers no explanation of it. The formula was intended by the Law Commission to be a rationalisation of various decisions on what constituted a sufficient act for the common law offence of attempt, some of which were unsatisfactory or not easy to reconcile with others. However, the formula must not be construed according to the previous case law. The reason is that, as the long title of the Act states, it is an Act to amend the law of attempt. Consequently, the correct approach is not to refer to the previous case law and seek to fit some previous test to the words of the formula, but instead to apply the words of the formula according to their natural meaning.[1]

1 *Gullefer* [1990] 3 All ER 882, [1990] 1 WLR 1063, CA; *Jones (Kenneth)* [1990] 3 All ER 886, [1990] 1 WLR 1057, CA; *Campbell* [1991] Crim LR 268, CA.

21.66 Section 4(3) of the Act provides that, where there is evidence sufficient in law to support a finding that the accused did an act falling within s 1(1) (ie one which is more than merely preparatory to the commission of the offence allegedly attempted), the question whether or not it is proved that his act fell within s 1(1) is a question of fact. This is of particular importance in terms of the respective functions of judge and jury in relation to the actus reus of attempt. In an extremely condensed fashion, s 4(3) codifies the principles laid down in this respect by the House of Lords in *DPP v Stonehouse.*[1] It was held in that case, and s 4(3) assumes this, that whether there is evidence of an act sufficient in law to constitute an attempt (ie evidence on which a jury could reasonably conclude that the accused had gone beyond mere preparation)[2] is a question for the judge. If he decides that there is no such evidence on which the jury could properly convict of an attempt (or if he concludes that, although the matter is not as conclusive as that, it would nevertheless be unsafe to leave the evidence to the jury),[3] he must direct the jury to acquit. The effect of s 4(3) is that if, on the other hand, the judge finds that there is evidence on which a jury could properly and safely convict, he *must* leave it to the jury to decide as a question of fact whether or not the accused did an act which was more than merely preparatory to the commission of an offence, and this involves the jury in finding not only that the accused did a particular act but also that it was more than 'merely preparatory to' the commission of the intended offence. According to *Stonehouse*, the judge must not direct the jury to convict if they find a relevant act proved, even though on the evidence there can only be an affirmative answer to the question 'was it more than merely preparatory?'.

1 [1978] AC 55, [1977] 2 All ER 909, HL.
2 *Gullefer* [1990] 3 All ER 882 at 884.
3 *Campbell* [1991] Crim LR 268, CA.

21.67 It is obvious that there is sufficient evidence that an act is more than merely preparatory to the commission of an offence in a 'last act' case, ie one where the accused has done the last act towards the commission of the alleged attempted offence which, to his knowledge, it was necessary for him to do in order to commit that offence, even though something more remains to be done by another, innocent person. Thus, one who puts poison in another's drink, intending him to drink it and be killed in consequence, may be convicted of attempted murder, and so may someone who posts a parcel bomb to another, intending him to be killed when he opens it.

However, cases where there may be sufficient evidence that an act is more than merely preparatory to the commission of an offence are not restricted to 'last act' cases; otherwise the offence of attempt would hardly ever be committed and some offences, such as rape, could never be attempted. It is established that there can be sufficient evidence of a more than merely preparatory act in a case where the accused still has to take some further step or steps himself before the substantive offence can be committed[1] but, obviously, there will not always be sufficient evidence of such an act in such a case. The dividing line between acts which will or will not suffice under the formula must, of course, be drawn on the basis of its wording, and the key words are *'merely preparatory '*. Obviously, every act in furtherance of a criminal objective, can be described as preparatory to the commission of the offence but it will not always be describable as *merely* preparatory. As is indicated by common sense and by the Court of Appeal in *Gullefer*[2] and in *Jones (Kenneth)*,[3] if the accused can be said to have got as far as having embarked on the commission of the offence (ie 'on the job'),[4] as where he tries to force a door of a strongroom in order to enter it to steal or points a loaded gun at someone with intent to kill him,[5] there is sufficient evidence of an act more than merely preparatory to the commission of the intended offence. In such a case, it would be a major understatement to say that there is no sufficient evidence that his acts had gone beyond being *merely* preparatory, even though (since some further act was required of him) his acts were still at the preparatory stage.

Of course, the dividing line cannot always be easily drawn but it is submitted that in the light of the above tests many cases will be seen clearly to fall on one side or the other of the line between acts which are merely preparatory and those which go beyond mere preparation.

1 *Boyle* (1986) 84 Cr App Rep 270, [1987] Crim LR 111, CA; *Gullefer* [1990] 3 All ER 882, [1990] 1 WLR 1063, CA; *Jones (Kenneth)* [1990] 3 All ER 886, [1990] 1 WLR 1057, CA.
2 [1990] 3 All ER 882, [1990] 1 WLR 1063, CA.
3 [1990] 3 All ER 886, [1990] 1 WLR 1057, CA.
4 A phrase used in *Osborn* (1919) 84 JP 63.
5 Even if the safety catch is still on and he has yet to put his finger to the trigger: *Jones (Kenneth)* [1990] 3 All ER 886, [1990] 1 WLR 1057, CA.

ATTEMPTS TO DO THE IMPOSSIBLE

21.68 Subsections (2) and (3) of s 1 of the Act deal with attempts to do the impossible and reverse the decision in *Haughton v Smith*,[1] a House of Lords case where the actual decision and other statements of principle were to the effect that in many cases of impossibility there could not be a conviction for the common law offence of attempt.

Section 1(2) provides that a person can be convicted of an attempt to commit an offence contrary to s 1 even though the facts are such that the commission of the offence is impossible. Section 1(3) adds that in any case where:

a) apart from s 1(3) a person's intention would not be regarded as having amounted to an intention to commit an offence; but
b) if the facts of the case had been as he believed them to be, his intention would be regarded as an intention to commit an offence, then, for the purposes of s 1(1) of the Act, he is to be regarded as having had an intent to commit that offence.

1 [1975] AC 476, [1973] 3 All ER 1109, HL.

21.69 As a result of s 1(2) a person is guilty of attempted murder if, intending to kill, he places a small quantity of poison in a glass of lemonade which he expects his intended victim to drink, the quantity being insufficient to be lethal; a person is guilty of attempted burglary where, in order to burgle a house, he tries to force a window with a jemmy which is insufficient; and a person is guilty of attempting to obtain property by deception if the recipient of his fraudulent begging letter realises the falsehood.

Similarly, as a result of s 1(2), a person is guilty of attempted murder if he fires at a bolster in a bed, mistakenly believing that it is B whom he intends to kill; a person is guilty of attempted theft if he is charged with attempting to steal from a particular wallet which is in fact empty; and a person is guilty of attempting to obtain by deception if he sends a false begging letter to someone who is dead. Unlike the examples in the previous paragraph, these examples would not have constituted the common law offence of attempt as a result of the views expressed by the House of Lords in *Haughton v Smith*, which were subsequently applied as binding by the Divisional Court.[1] The rationale behind the distinction drawn in that case was not easily discernible and its reversal in this respect is therefore to be welcomed.

The effect of s 1(2), in combination with s 1(3), is that a person can be convicted of an attempt where he has achieved or could have achieved his object in physical terms, but owing to some mistake on his part his object does not after all amount to an offence. Following the decision in *Haughton v Smith* there could not have been a conviction for the common law offence of attempt. Given that the essence of the offence of attempt is to punish those who go further than mere preparation to put their 'evil intents' into practice, the reversal of that decision for the purposes of the statutory offence of attempt is clearly right. As a result of the above provisions a person who handles goods, mistakenly believing that they are stolen, can be convicted of attempting to handle stolen goods; someone who mistakenly believes that the girl with whom he has sexual intercourse is under 16 can be convicted of attempting to have unlawful sexual intercourse with a girl under 16; and a person who takes his own umbrella from a hat-stand, thinking it is another's, can be convicted of attempted theft.

1 *Partington v Williams* (1975) 62 Cr App Rep 220, DC.

21.70 The above undoubtedly reflects the current effect of the Act on attempts to do the impossible but between May 1985 and May 1986 the interpretation of the Act was different, as a result of the House of Lords' decision in May 1985 in *Anderton v Ryan*[1] that the third category of cases referred to above did not constitute an attempt under the Act. The case concerned an accused who had bought a video recorder, believing it to have been stolen. On the facts as they were assumed to be it was not stolen. The accused was charged with attempting to commit the offence of handling stolen goods. The House of Lords (Lord Edmund-Davies dissenting), allowing the appeal against conviction, held that on their true construction s 1(2) and, particularly, s 1(3) did not compel the conclusion that, where a person's acts were 'objectively innocent', although he mistakenly believed facts which if true would have made his acts a complete offence, he was guilty of attempting to commit that offence.

This decision, which was contrary to the intentions of the draftsmen of the Act, was particularly open to objection in that it introduced the concept of 'objective innocence' which rendered s 1(3) virtually redundant and which (in the view of most) it was clearly the Act's intention to exclude. Consequently, there was a general satisfaction when it was overruled in May 1986 by the House of Lords in *Shivpuri*.[2] Here, D, who had been arrested while in possession of a suitcase, had admitted that he believed that the suitcase contained either heroin or cannabis and that he had been concerned in dealing with it. When analysed the contents turned out not to be a controlled drug at all but a harmless substance. The House of Lords, overruling *Anderton v Ryan*, dismissed D's appeal against conviction for attempting to commit the statutory offence of knowingly being concerned in dealing with a drug whose importation was prohibited. Lord Bridge, with whose speech the other law lords agreed, made clear that there is no distinction between 'objectively innocent' and 'guilty' acts in the present sphere. By s 1, two things, and two things only, had always to be proved for a conviction for attempt. First, that the accused had an intention to commit the offence in question. Second, that, with that intent, the accused had done an act which was more than merely preparatory to the commission of the offence *intended* by him, which meant that the question to ask was whether the act would have been more than preparatory if the facts had been as the accused believed them to be. Applying these two tests, it was held, D was clearly guilty of the offence in question, since he had intended to deal with drugs which he believed had been illegally imported, and he had done an act which was more than merely preparatory to the commission of that *intended* offence.

1 [1985] AC 560, [1985] 2 All ER 355, HL.
2 [1987] AC 1, [1986] 2 All ER 334, HL.

21.71 Some cases of impossible attempts are hardly deserving of punishment. In such cases, assuming (and this is unlikely) that the case ever came to light, the discretion to prosecute is very likely to be exercised against the institution of a prosecution.

21.72 It must be emphasised that s 1(3) only operates where, if the facts of the case had been as the accused believed them to be, his intention would be regarded as having amounted to an intention to commit an offence. Consequently, whether or not the accused knows the true facts, if what he intends to do (and may actually do) is not an offence, although because of a mistake as to the criminal law he believes that it is, he cannot be convicted. For example, a man who has intercourse with a girl of 17, mistakenly believing that it is an offence to have intercourse with a girl under 18, cannot be convicted of an attempt contrary to s 1 because he does not intend to commit an offence to which s 1 applies.

21.73 Under cl 50 of the draft Criminal Code Bill,[1] impossibility would continue not to be a defence to a charge of attempt. Cl 50 provides that a person would be guilty of attempt to commit an offence although the commission of the offence was impossible, if it would have been possible in the circumstances which he believed or hoped existed or would exist at the relevant time. This formulation, more easily intelligible than that under s 1(2) and (3) of the Act, would also apply to the offences of incitement and conspiracy provided by the draft Bill and to offences of incitement, conspiracy or attempt created by other statutes.

1 Law Commission: A Criminal Code for England and Wales (1989): Law Com No 177; see para 3.21 above.

PROSECUTION, TRIAL AND PUNISHMENT

21.74 *Prosecution* The following restrictions on the institution of prosecutions for an offence under s 1 of attempting to commit an offence are provided by s 2 of the Act. Where the offence attempted is subject to a statutory provision whereby proceedings for it may not be instituted or carried on otherwise than by, or on behalf or with the consent of, any person (such as the Director of Public Prosecutions), such provision extends to an attempt to commit that offence, and so does any statutory time limit on the institution of proceedings for the offence attempted.

21.75 *Trial* The offence of attempt under s 1 is triable in the same way as the offence attempted. Consequently, if that offence is triable only on indictment (eg murder or rape) an attempt to commit it must be tried on indictment, whereas if the offence attempted is triable either way (eg theft or indecent assault) an attempt to commit it is triable either way. This is one of the effects of the rather obscure wording of s 4(1) of the Act of 1981.

21.76 *Punishment* Section 4(1) also specifies the penalties for a person convicted of an attempt under s 1:

a) if the offence attempted is murder or any other offence for which the sentence is fixed by law, the maximum punishment is life imprisonment;
b) in the case of any other attempt, the maximum punishment is the same as is available to the court of trial for the offence attempted.

By way of exception, s 4(5)(a) preserves the provisions of s 37 and Sch 2 of the Sexual Offences Act 1956, whereby the maximum punishments for attempts to commit certain sexual offences are lower than for the offence attempted.

SPECIFIC OFFENCES OF ATTEMPT

21.77 Quite apart from the offence of attempt to commit an indictable offence under s 1 of the Act, which has been discussed so far, there are a substantial number of specific statutory offences of attempt to commit another offence. Many of these specific offences consist of attempts to commit purely summary offences, in which cases the general offence of attempt is inapplicable.

Subject to any inconsistent provision in any other enactment, s 3 applies to specific statutory offences of attempt which are '*expressed as an offence of attempting to commit another offence*' rules which correspond to those in s 1 for the general statutory offence of attempt. Thus, s 3(3) provides that a person is guilty of an attempt under a special statutory provision if, with intent to commit the relevant full offence, he does an act which is more than merely preparatory to the commission of that offence. In addition, s 3(4) and (5) provide the same rules as in s 1 in relation to 'impossible attempts', while s 4(4) provides that the respective functions of a judge and jury are the same as in the case of an offence under s 1.

The precise meaning of the words italicised remains to be determined. Obviously, a specific statutory offence of attempt created by a separate section or subsection from the full offence is 'expressed as an offence of attempting to commit another offence', but it is by no means obvious that the same is true where the full offence and the attempt are expressed in the very same provision (as in the case of the offences under ss 4(1) and 5(1) of the Road Traffic Act 1988 of driving or attempting to drive while unfit and driving or attempting to drive with excess alcohol).[1] Thus, the precise scope of s 3 is uncertain.

1 Paras 20.17 and 20.22. In relation to the offence of attempting to drive with excess alcohol, there may be severe difficulties in proving the necessary mens rea as to the element of excess alcohol.

ABANDONMENT OF ATTEMPT[1]

21.78 Although no argument of deterrence, reformation or prevention seems to require the punishment of one who abandons his attempt before he has done any harm, being truly repentant, it was the position at common law that once the accused had committed the actus reus of an attempt with the necessary mens rea he could not escape liability by abandoning the attempt, however genuine and voluntary his repentance.[2] The Act does not change this. Of course, voluntary abandonment may mitigate the sentence imposed.

1 See Wasik 'Abandoning Criminal Intent' [1980] Crim LR 785.
2 *Lankford* [1959] Crim LR 209 at 210; *Haughton v Smith* [1975] AC 476 at 493, [1973] 3 All ER 1109 at 1115, per Lord Hailsham LC.

SUCCESSFUL ATTEMPTS

21.79 Where a person is tried on indictment for attempting to commit an offence he may, by virtue of s 6(4) of the Criminal Law Act 1967, be convicted of the attempt notwithstanding that he is shown to be guilty of the completed offence. It was held by the Divisional Court in *Webley v Buxton*[1] that the same rule applies to summary trials.

1 [1977] QB 481, [1977] 2 All ER 595, DC.

21.80 There cannot be a conviction for the completed offence on a charge of attempt to commit it.

In the converse case, where a person is charged with the completed offence but only shown to be guilty of attempting it, by virtue of s 6(3) and (4) of the Criminal Law Act 1967, there can be a conviction on indictment for an attempt on a charge of the completed offence. If the case is tried summarily, however, the magistrates may not convict of an attempt if the completed offence is charged.[1] Potential problems which may result from the magistrates' incapacity in this respect can be avoided if the prosecution lays two informations, one charging the completed offence and the other an attempt.[2]

1 *Pender v Smith* [1959] 2 QB 84 at 88, [1959] 2 All ER 360 at 360–361; *Manchester Crown Court, ex p Hill* (1985) 149 JPN 29, DC.
2 Section 4(2) of the Act provides that the magistrates may try both informations together without the accused's consent. Following the House of Lords' decision in *Clayton v Chief*

Constable of Norfolk [1983] 2 AC 473, [1983] 1 All ER 984 this express provision is strictly no longer necessary.

DRAFT CRIMINAL CODE BILL

21.81 With one or two exceptions, cl 49 of the draft Criminal Code Bill[1] restates the law set out in the Criminal Attempts Act 1981. Unlike the Act, it expressly provides that recklessness with respect to a circumstance suffices where it suffices for the offence itself; the reader is reminded that 'recklessness' in the draft code is limited to subjective recklessness. Cl 49 of the draft Bill makes the following changes to the law as it is under the Act. First, it provides that an attempt could be committed by an omission to do an act where the full offence, such as murder, can be committed by omission. Second, consistent with its provision that it should be an offence to incite to conspire, it provides that it should be an offence to attempt to conspire.

1 Law Commission: A Criminal Code for England and Wales (1989): Law Com No 177; para 3.21 above. Impossibility is dealt with by cl 50, referred to in para 21.73 above.

22 General justifications and defences

Public or private defence

22.1 The term 'public or private defence' is used to describe cases where an accused acts to prevent the commission of an offence, or to effect a lawful arrest, or to defend himself or another against an actual or imminent attack, or to defend his or another's property against such an attack. These 'defences' are different from the defences of duress by threats, duress of circumstances and marital coercion, discussed later in this chapter, because, if successfully pleaded, they render the accused's conduct lawful, as opposed simply to excusing him from liability for conduct which is nevertheless unlawful.[1] It is for this reason that inverted commas were placed round 'defences' in the last sentence.

1 Para 6.20.

22.2 Until the Criminal Law Act 1967 the legal position of any person acting in public or private defence was governed by common law rules, but s 3(1) of that Act now provides that a person may use such force as is reasonable in the circumstances in the prevention of crime, or in effecting or assisting in the lawful arrest of offenders or suspected offenders or of persons unlawfully at large. Section 3(1) permits anyone to use reasonable force for one of the specified purposes; it is not limited to police officers. In relation to the prevention of crime, the provision is not limited to serious offences (although in the case of the prevention of a minor offence it is likely that only a slight degree of force could be reasonable).

Section 3(2) of the 1967 Act provides that s 3(1) replaces the rules of the common law on when force used for the purposes mentioned in s 3(1) is justified by that purpose. Clearly, for example, s 3(1) has superseded the common law where force is used to prevent the commission of indecent exposure or to prevent a person making off without payment, but it appears that s 3(1) has not superseded the common law defences of self-defence, defence of another and defence of property.

22.3 A person acting in self-defence, defence of another or defence of property is invariably engaged in the prevention of crime, and in such a case it is arguable that s 3(1) alone now governs the situation. However, s 3(1) has not been directly applied in cases on self-defence since the 1967 Act came into force, and in *Cousins*[1] the Court of Appeal was clearly of the opinion that a person who used force to repel an attack could avail himself of the common law defence of self-defence *and* of the defence under s 3(1) of preventing the commission of the crime which such an attack would have involved, provided in both cases that the force used was reasonable in the circumstances. In such a case then (and presumably in the case of defence of others and defence of property), the common law defence survives alongside the statutory one.

In a few cases of self-defence and the like, only the common law defence will be available. These are cases where the attacker against whom the force is used is not committing a crime because, for example, he is a child under 10, or in a state of automatism, or acting under a material mistake of fact, so that force cannot be said to have been used in the prevention of crime.

Where the common law defence is pleaded, it appears that the courts will approach the question in the same way as in the case of a defence under s 3(1),[2] and that a number of restrictive rules which used to attach to the common law defence will not be applied. For example, old cases on self-defence established that the person attacked must retreat as far as he can before resorting to force. In *McInnes*,[3] decided in 1971, it was held that this is now simply a factor in deciding whether the force used was reasonable in the circumstances. (Indeed, the accused need not even demonstrate his unwillingness to fight, although this is the best evidence that he was acting reasonably and in good faith in self-defence.)[4] Similarly, it seems probable in the case of defence of property that the test of reasonableness referred to in para 22.8 will be applied by analogy to the exclusion of the old rules which can be deduced from some of the cases,[5] such as the rule that lethal force may always be used against a burglar or against someone seeking to evict a householder unlawfully and forcibly.

1 [1982] QB 526, [1982] 2 All ER 115, CA. See also *Devlin v Armstrong* [1971] NI 13 (CA of Northern Ireland).
2 *McInnes* [1971] 3 All ER 295, [1971] 1 WLR 1600, CA; *Devlin v Armstrong* [1971] NI 13 (CA of Northern Ireland).
3 [1971] 3 All ER 295, [1971] 1 WLR 1600, CA.
4 *Bird* [1985] 2 All ER 513, [1985] 1 WLR 816, CA, not following dicta in *Julien* [1969] 2 All ER 856, [1969] 1 WLR 839, CA, that a demonstration that unwillingness to fight was required.
5 Lanham 'Defence of Property in the Criminal Law' [1966] Crim LR 368, 426.

22.4 Although a person who acts in self-defence or the like is normally actually being attacked, the defences of self-defence, defence of another or defence of property are not limited to this situation since it has been recognised that there may be situations in which it will be justified to use reasonable force by way of pre-emptive action against an apprehended attack.[1] Thus, provided he uses no more than reasonable force, the law permits a person to strike first to prevent an attack which he apprehends. Of course, what is reasonable force in a pre-emptive strike may well be less than what would be reasonable force against an actual attack.

1 *Finch and Jardine* (1983) unreported. Also see *A-G's Reference (No 2 of 1983)* [1984] QB 456, [1984] 1 All ER 988, CA; *Beckford v R* [1987] 3 All ER 425 at 431.

22.5 A justification of public or private defence is normally raised by a person charged with an offence against the person, but it is not limited to such offences. For example, in *Renouf*[1] the Court of Appeal held that it is a defence to a charge of reckless driving that the act which constituted the reckless driving amounted to the use of reasonable force for the purpose of effecting the lawful arrest of an offender.

1 [1986] 2 All ER 449, [1986] 1 WLR 522, CA.

22.6 It has not yet been decided whether the defences discussed in this part can ever be pleaded successfully where the force is used against a wholly innocent person or his property, as where a policeman who is chasing a dangerous criminal knocks aside an innocent pedestrian who gets in his way or commandeers a car which he uses to ram the criminal's getaway vehicle.

THE OPERATION OF THE JUSTIFICATIONS

22.7 The accused does not have the burden of proof in relation to the defence under s 3(1) or the common law defence. However, he does have a burden of adducing sufficient evidence to raise an issue that he acted under one of these defences, and only if he shifts it (or the defence is raised by the prosecution's evidence) will the defence be left to the jury (where trial is in the Crown Court), in which case the prosecution must rebut it beyond reasonable doubt.[1]

1 *Lobell* [1957] 1 QB 547, [1957] 1 All ER 734, CCA; *Abraham* [1973] 3 All ER 694, [1973] 1 WLR 1270, CA.

22.8 If one of these defences has been raised as above, the question for the jury (or the magistrates) is whether the prosecution has proved beyond reasonable doubt that the accused did not use 'such force as is reasonable in the circumstances' in the prevention of crime, or (as the case may be) in effecting or assisting in a lawful arrest, or in defence of himself, another or property. What is reasonable force is always a question of fact for the jury, and never a point of law for the judge.[1] They should be told that if the defence is not disproved they should acquit the accused, but that if it is they should convict him; as the Privy Council held in *Palmer v R*[2] about self-defence, 'The defence of self-defence either succeeds so as to result in an acquittal or is disproved in which case as a defence it is rejected'.

The jury should be told that the test of whether reasonable force has been used in the prevention of crime or self-defence etc is an objective one. They must ask themselves whether they are satisfied that no reasonable man with knowledge of such facts as were known to the accused (or believed by him to exist)[3] could be of opinion that the prevention of a crime or of harm to himself, or another, or to property, which might otherwise be committed justified exposing the victim to the kind of harm that might result from the kind of force that the accused contemplated using.[4]

In applying this test, account should be taken of all the circumstances in which the accused was placed,[5] including in particular the nature and degree of force used on each side, the relative strength (in terms both of physical power and of numbers) on each side, the seriousness of the evil to be prevented (or of the offence for which an arrest is being made) and the possibility of preventing it by other means (because the use of force can never be reasonable if it was unnecessary)[6]. In addition, and this tempers with leniency the objectiveness of the test, there must be taken into account the time available to the accused for reflection. A direction along the lines of the following statement by Lord Morris in *Palmer v R*[7] should be given to the jury:

'If there has been an attack so that defence is reasonably necessary it will be recognised that a person defending himself cannot weigh to a nicety the exact measure of his necessary defensive action. If a jury thought that in a moment of unexpected anguish a person attacked had only done what he honestly and instinctively thought was necessary that would be most potent evidence that only reasonable defensive action had been taken.'

Although this statement was made in relation to self-defence, the principle is no doubt equally applicable to the other defences at present under discussion. It was subsequently applied by the Court of Appeal in *Shannon*,[8] where the trial judge had left the defence of self-defence to the jury with the bald question: 'Are you satisfied that the appellant used more force than was necessary in the circumstances?' The Court of Appeal held that on its own this might have precluded the jury from considering Lord Morris's qualification that if they came to the conclusion that the accused honestly thought, without having to weigh things to a nicety, that what he did was necessary to defend himself, they should regard that as 'most potent evidence' that it was actually reasonably necessary. 'In other words, if the jury concluded that the stabbing was the act of a desperate man in extreme difficulties, with his assailant dragging him down by the hair, they should consider very carefully before concluding that the stabbing was an offensive and not a defensive act, albeit it went beyond what an onlooker would regard as reasonably necessary.'[9] Consequently, the conviction for murder was quashed.

1 *Attorney-General for Northern Ireland's Reference (No 1 of 1975)* [1977] AC 105 at 137, [1976] 2 All ER 937 at 947, per Lord Diplock.
2 [1971] AC 814 at 832, [1971] 1 All ER 1077.
3 *Williams* [1987] 3 All ER 411, 78 Cr App Rep 276, CA; *Beckford v R* [1988] AC 130, [1987] 3 All ER 425, PC; para 7.21.
4 *Attorney-General for Northern Ireland's Reference (No 1 of 1975)* [1977] AC 105 at 137, [1976] 2 All ER 937 at 947, per Lord Diplock.
5 *Farrell v Secretary of State for Defence* [1980] 1 All ER 166, [1980] 1 WLR 172, HL.
6 See *Allen v Metropolitan Police Comr* [1980] Crim LR 441, DC. Also see Seventh Report of the Criminal Law Revision Committee (who proposed s 3 of the Act of 1967) (Cmnd 2659), para 23.
7 [1971] AC 814 at 832.
8 (1980) 71 Cr App Rep 192, CA. Also see *Whyte* [1987] 3 All ER 416, CA.
9 *Shannon* (1980) 71 Cr App Rep 191 at 196; *Nugent* [1987] 3 NIJB 9 (CA of N Ireland).

22.9   Although there is no binding authority on the point, it has been stated by the Lord Chief Justice of Northern Ireland that: 'The need to act must not have been created by the conduct of the accused in the immediate context of the incident which was likely or intended to give rise to that need'.[1] This can be criticised on the ground that, while it is right that a person should not be able to invoke one of these defences if he has deliberately provoked an attack with a view to using force to prevent or terminate it, it is going too far to preclude him from doing so simply because his conduct was likely to give rise to the need to act in self-defence or the like.[2]

1 *Browne* [1983] NI 96 at 107, per Lowry LCJ.
2 Smith and Hogan *Criminal Law* (6th edn), 327–328.

MISTAKE

22.10   As expressly stated in para 7.21, and implied in para 22.8, if a person acts under the mistaken belief that it is necessary for him to act in self-defence or prevention of crime or the like, the reasonableness of the force used by him is to be judged on the basis of the circumstances as he believed them to be. Thus, if P leaps out of a dark alley as a joke as D passes by late at night and D thinks that he is being attacked and hits P over the head with a heavy walking stick, the reasonableness of D's use of force must be assessed on the basis of his mistaken belief that he was being attacked by an armed and violent robber. Similarly, if D correctly believes that it is necessary to act in self-defence, prevention of crime or the like and uses force for this purpose, mistakenly believing that the assailant is armed, the reasonableness of the force used must be assessed on the basis of the facts as he believed them to be. The special rule which applies where the accused's mistake is accompanied by intoxication was dealt with in para 9.59.

EXCESSIVE FORCE

22.11 Related to the question of mistake is the situation where it is necessary for the accused (or he believes it is) to use force to prevent crime, or to effect an arrest, or to defend himself, another or property, but he uses an excessive degree of force (ie force which is unreasonable in the circumstances as he believed them to be) in order to do so. In such a case, he has no defence, although, except in the case of murder, his error of judgment may be taken into account in mitigation of sentence. It might have been expected that the fatal use of unreasonable force in public or private defence with the mens rea for murder would result in the liability of the accused being reduced from murder to manslaughter,[1] but this is not the rule in English law. In *Palmer v R*,[2] a case where the accused had been convicted of murder, the Privy Council held (as previously stated) that, 'The defence of self-defence either succeeds so as to result in an acquittal or is disproved in which case as a defence it is rejected'.[3] *Palmer's* case was followed by the Court of Appeal in England by *McInnes*.[4] Subsequently, Lord Dilhorne said in *Attorney-General for Northern Ireland's Reference (No 1 of 1975)*[5] that, where death results from the excessive use of force in the prevention of crime or in effecting an arrest, and the accused intended to kill or do grievous bodily harm (the mens rea for murder), the offence is likewise not reduced to manslaughter. There can be no doubt that the same is true where the excessive force was used in defence of another or of property.

The decisions in *Palmer v R* and *McInnes* are open to the objection that it is improper to convict of murder someone who made an error of judgment as to the amount of force which he should use. However, it must be admitted that Lord Morris's qualification in *Palmer v R*, referred to in para 22.8, is liable to limit the number of cases in which a person who uses fatal force in self-defence etc will be found to have used excessive force.

1 This used to be the position in Australian law until it was reversed by the High Court of Australia in *Zecevic v DPP (Victoria)* (1987) 162 CLR 645.
2 [1971] AC 814, [1971] 1 All ER 1077, PC.
3 Lord Morris of Borth-y-Gest. See articles by Morris [1960] Crim LR 468, Howard [1964] Crim LR 448, and Smith [1972] Crim LR 524.
4 [1971] 3 All ER 295, [1971] 1 WLR 1600, CA.
5 [1977] AC 105, [1976] 2 All ER 937 at 956.

RESISTING ARREST OR DETENTION

22.12 A person who is being lawfully arrested or detained is not entitled to use reasonable force in order to resist or escape,[1] even if he believes on reasonable grounds that the arrest or detention was unlawful[2] but a person who is being arrested or detained unlawfully is so entitled.[3] The same distinction applies where force is used to enable another person to resist or escape arrest or detention.

1 *Kenlin v Gardiner* [1967] 2 QB 510, [1966] 3 All ER 931, DC.

2 *Fennell* [1971] 1 QB 428, [1970] 3 All ER 215, CA; *Albert v Lavin* [1982] AC 546, [1981] 3 All ER 878, HL. The defence of self-defence is, however, available if the accused mistakenly believes (reasonably or not) that the 'lawful arrester' is a thug or robber who is attacking him: *Ansell v Swift* [1987] Crim LR 194, Crown Ct.
3 *Pedro v Diss* [1981] 2 All ER 59 at 64.

OTHER CASES WHERE FORCE JUSTIFIED

22.13   Although there is less authority in support, it is clearly established as a common law rule that a person may use such force as is reasonable in the circumstances to prevent or terminate a breach of the peace,[1] or the unlawful imprisonment of himself or another, or a trespass, in a case where the breach, imprisonment or trespass would not give rise to criminal liability in any event.[2] The approach in these cases is doubtless the same as where the defence of self-defence or the like is raised.

1 For the definition of 'breach of the peace', see para 4.16.
2 See, for example, *Weaver v Bush* (1798) 8 Term Rep 78; *Hussey* (1924) 18 Cr App Rep 160, CCA.

JUSTIFICATION OF CONDUCT WHERE FORCE NOT ACTUALLY USED

22.14   The defences of self-defence, prevention of crime and the like are concerned with the *use* of force but their application is not limited to offences involving the use of force, since where the definition of some other type of offence excuses a person who acts for a lawful object or purpose or refers in some other way to lawfulness or unlawfulness (as the definition of assault does by requiring a threat of immediate unlawful force) the terms of these defences can be relevant to determine the question of lawfulness or unlawfulness in issue. One authority is *Attorney-General's Reference (No 2 of 1983)*,[1] which was concerned with the offence of making or possessing an explosive substance, under such circumstances as to give rise to a reasonable suspicion that the making or possession is not for a lawful object. The Court of Appeal held that the preparation of a petrol bomb for use in self-defence or in defence of another or of property against an imminent attack would be a lawful object if the maker intended to use it in a way which was no more than reasonably necessary to meet the imminent attack. As the Court noted: 'In our judgment a defendant is not left in the paradoxical position of being able to justify acts carried out in self-defence but not acts immediately preparatory to it'.[2]

1 [1984] QB 456, [1984] 1 All ER 988, CA. See also *Georgiades* [1989] 1 WLR 759, (1989) 89 Cr App Rep 206, CA; para 18.80.
2 [1984] QB 456 at 471.

DRAFT CRIMINAL CODE BILL[1]

22.15   Under cl 44 of the draft Criminal Code Bill, a person would not commit an offence by using such force as, in the circumstances which exist or which he believes to exist, is immediately necessary and reasonable:

a) to prevent or terminate crime, or effect or assist in the lawful arrest of an offender or suspected offender or of a person unlawfully at large;
b) to prevent or terminate a breach of the peace;

c) to protect himself or another from unlawful[1] force or unlawful[2] personal harm;
d) to prevent or terminate the unlawful[2] detention of himself or another;
e) to protect property (whether belonging to himself or another) from unlawful[3] appropriation, destruction or damage; or
f) to prevent or terminate a trespass to his person or property.

For the above purpose, the use of force includes, in addition to force against a person, force against property, the threat of force against person or property, and the detention of a person without force.

A person who believed circumstances to exist which would provide a defence under the above provision would have no defence if he knew that the force was used against a constable or someone assisting a constable and the constable was acting in the execution of his duty, unless he believed the force to be immediately necessary to prevent injury to himself or another.

The defence would not apply where a person caused unlawful conduct or an unlawful state of affairs with a view to using force to resist or terminate it; but it could apply although the occasion for the use of force arose only because he did anything he might lawfully do, knowing that such an occasion might arise.

In relation to the use of excessive force in self-defence or the like by a person charged with murder, cls 55 and 59 of the draft Criminal Code Bill[3] provide that, if the accused believes the force to be necessary and reasonable to effect the self-defence or the like, he is to be convicted of manslaughter (and not murder).

1 Law Commission: A Criminal Code for England and Wales (1989): Law Com No 177. Also see the Fourteenth Report of the Criminal Law Revision Committee: Offences against the Person (1980) Cmnd 7844.
2 Force would be 'unlawful' notwithstanding that the actor was under 10 or acting under duress by threats or of circumstances, or lacked the relevant fault element, or was in a state of automatism or was suffering severe mental illness or severe mental handicap.
3 Such a defence was also recommended in the Report of a House of Lords Select Committee on Murder and Life Imprisonment (1989), HL Paper 78.

Duress by threats[1]

22.16 The defence of duress by threats, like the defence of marital coercion described later in this chapter, is concerned with the case where the accused commits the actus reus of an offence with the relevant mens rea[2] but is induced to act by a threat made by another person to the effect that unless the accused commits an offence harm will be done to him or another person. Although it has not always been recognised as such, the defence of duress by threats is a species of necessity.

If the defence of duress by threats applies, an accused who acted under it is excused from criminal liability for an offence which he has committed.[3] We have already seen that if someone is made to act by an external physical force the act is regarded as involuntary, cannot be imputed to him and cannot involve him in criminal liability.[4] Thus, if someone is made to stab another by superior physical force exerted on his arm, it is not his act which does the stabbing, but that of the person who forces him. We are now concerned with a different question the extent to which threats which do not have the effect of making the act of the accused involuntary can afford an excuse.

1 Wasik 'Duress and Criminal Responsibility' [1977] Crim LR 453; Elliott 'Duress, Necessity and Self-Defence' [1989] Crim LR 611.
2 In *Bourne* (1952) 36 Cr App Rep 125, the Court of Criminal Appeal appears to have treated duress by threats as negativing mens rea. However, such a theory was rejected by the House of Lords in *DPP for Northern Ireland v Lynch* [1975] AC 653, [1975] 1 All ER 913, according to whom the defence of duress by threats is something superimposed on the other ingredients of an offence, the actus reus and the mens rea, which by themselves would constitute the offence. See also *Howe* [1987] 1 All ER 771 at 777, 783, per Lords Hailsham LC and Bridge.
3 *DPP for Northern Ireland v Lynch* [1975] AC 653, [1975] 1 All ER 913, HL.
4 Para 9.42.

NATURE OF THREAT

22.17   Reference has been made in a number of cases[1] to the fact that the will of a person who acts under duress by threats has been 'overborne'. This simply means that the accused would not have done as he did but for the threat. However, it is not in itself enough that the accused's will has been overborne since there are certain limitations on the type of threat which can amount to duress. First, the threat, which may be express or implicit, must be of death or serious bodily harm.[2] In *Singh*[3] the Court of Appeal held that a threat to expose immorality could not give rise to the defence of duress by threats, and in *M'Growther*[4] it was ruled that the threat of harm to property was no excuse. In *Steane*[5] Lord Goddard stated that a threat of 'violence or imprisonment' could amount to duress. This statement was an obiter dictum and the reference to threats of imprisonment should be treated with reserve in view of the more restricted approach of the other cases. There are dicta in two modern cases, *DPP for Northern Ireland v Lynch*[6] and *Abbott v R*,[7] which suggest that the gravity of a threat sufficient to give rise to the defence of duress by threats varies with the gravity of the offence committed and its particular circumstances. If this became part of our law the invariable rule just mentioned would, of course, be replaced. It is not obvious why the law on duress is different from that applicable to self-defence and the like where no limit is placed on the type of threatened harm, the defence being regulated instead by a requirement of proportionality between the threatened harm and the force used in response.

It has not yet been authoritatively decided whether a threat to kill or seriously harm a person other than the accused can amount to duress, although it was assumed by the Court of Appeal in *Ortiz*[8] that a threat to injure the accused's wife and family could do so, and in duress by circumstances (which is an analogous defence) a threat of death or serious harm to a third person suffices.[9] In the Australian case of *Hurley*[10] the Supreme Court of Victoria held that threats to kill or seriously injure the accused's common law wife could amount to duress. In the light, in particular, of the rule in the defence of duress of circumstances, there can be little doubt that, when an English court is forced to decide the question, it will extend the defence of duress by threats to include threats to harm another person, whether or not he has a special relationship with him. It would be absurd if it were otherwise, since many a person who treats his own safety as of little consequence will be subjected to the most extreme mental stress if confronted with a threat to harm seriously someone else, especially someone who is dear to him.

Given the strict requirements of the defence of duress by threats, it will still remain rarely available even if the threat need not be of harm to the accused.

1 Eg *Hudson and Taylor* [1971] 2 QB 202, [1971] 2 All ER 244, CA.
2 *Hudson and Taylor*; *DPP for Northern Ireland v Lynch* [1975] AC 653, [1975] 1 All ER 913, HL; *Williamson and Ellerton* (1977) 67 Cr App Rep 63, CA.
3 [1973] 1 All ER 122, [1972] 1 WLR 1600, CA.
4 (1746) Fost 13.
5 [1947] KB 997, [1947] 1 All ER 813, CCA.
6 [1975] AC 653, [1975] 1 All ER 913, per Lord Wilberforce.
7 [1977] AC 755, [1976] 3 All ER 140, per Lords Wilberforce and Edmund-Davies.
8 (1986) 83 Cr App Rep 173, CA.
9 *Martin* [1989] 1 All ER 652, CA; para 22.36.
10 [1967] VR 526.

SUBJECTIVE AND OBJECTIVE TESTS

22.18 It is not enough simply that a threat of death or serious bodily harm has been made because, as in the case of the defence of provocation,[1] the defence of duress by threats involves both a subjective and an objective test; the law requires an accused to have the steadfastness reasonably to be expected of an ordinary citizen in his situation. If duress is raised on the evidence, the correct approach, which was laid down by the Court of Appeal in *Graham*,[2] and approved by the House of Lords in *Howe*,[3] is as follows:

a) *Subjective test* Was the accused, or may he have been, impelled to act as he did because, as a result of what he reasonably believed the person making the threat had said or done, he had good cause to fear that if he did not so act the latter would kill him or cause him serious physical injury?[4]

b) *Objective test* If so (or if this is not disproved by the prosecution), have the prosecution proved that a sober person of reasonable firmness, sharing the characteristics of the accused (ie, presumably, the accused's sex and age and any other non-transitory qualities and attributes of the accused which would affect the gravity of the threat to him), would not have responded to whatever he reasonably believed the person making the threat had said or done by acting as the accused had done? The fact that the accused's will to resist has been eroded by voluntary intoxication is, of course, irrelevant to this test.

1 Paras 11.34–11.46.
2 [1982] 1 All ER 801, [1982] 1 WLR 294, CA.
3 [1987] AC 417, [1987] 1 All ER 771, HL.
4 The accused need not have acted as he did solely because of a threat of death or serious harm. It is enough that he would not have acted as he did but for such a threat, even though he also acted for some other reason (such as an additional threat to burn down his house or to expose his immorality): *Valderrama-Vega* [1985] Crim LR 220, CA. Also see *Ortiz* (1986) 83 Cr App Rep 173, CA.

UNAVOIDABLE DILEMMA

22.19 The subjective and objective tests just mentioned are not solely concerned with the fortitude of the accused and of a reasonable person, since they also involve the question of whether, as a result of the threat, the accused was (and a reasonable person would have been) compelled to do what was in fact done. The accused has the defence of duress by threats only if, throughout the period from the making of the threat to the commission of the offence, he was faced by a dilemma between committing the offence or allowing the threatened harm to occur and had no safe third avenue of escape. In *Gill*[1] D was convicted of stealing his employer's lorry. D had raised the defence of duress by threats at his trial, in that personal violence had been threatened against him and his wife if he did not steal the lorry. The Court of Criminal Appeal stated, obiter, that it was very doubtful whether the defence of duress by threats was open to D since there was a time, after he had been left outside his employer's yard to get the lorry, when he could have raised the alarm and wrecked the whole enterprise. The Court referred approvingly to Professor Perkins' statement that: 'The excuse [of duress by threats] is not available to someone who had an obviously safe avenue of escape before committing the prohibited act.'[2]

1 [1963] 2 All ER 688, [1963] 1 WLR 841, CCA. Also see *Williamson and Ellerton* (1977) 67 Cr App Rep 63, CA.
2 Perkins *Criminal Law* (2nd edn) p 954.

22.20   The case of *Hudson and Taylor*[1] shows that a third avenue of escape must be reasonably open to the accused in order to be regarded as safe. Two girls aged 19 and 17 gave false evidence at a criminal trial after a gang had threatened to 'cut them up' if they did not do so. The girls were charged with perjury. The trial judge held that duress was no defence because the accused had not been subject to the threat of immediate physical violence when they gave the false evidence. The accused were convicted but appealed successfully to the Court of Appeal. One of the grounds on which the Crown relied in support of the conviction was that the accused should have removed the effect of the threat by seeking police protection either before or at the time of the former trial at which they had made the false statements. The Court of Appeal agreed that the defence of duress by threats could not be relied on if an accused person failed to take an opportunity which was reasonably open to him to render the threat ineffective. However, in deciding whether such an opportunity was reasonably open to the accused, the jury should have regard to his age (and, presumably, any other non-transitory qualities and attributes), and to the circumstances of the case and any risks which might be involved. Factors such as the period of time between the threat and the commission of the offence and the effectiveness of the protection which the police might be able to give would be relevant.

1 [1971] 2 QB 202, [1971] 2 All ER 244, CA.

22.21   The defence of duress by threats can only arise if the threat was operative at the time the offence was committed. Thus, the accused is not excused if the threat has ceased when he commits the offence.[1] However, it was held in *Hudson and Taylor* that, when there is no opportunity for delaying tactics and the accused must make a decision whether or not to commit the offence, the existence at that moment of a relevant threat should provide him with a defence even though the harm threatened might not follow immediately but after an interval. The Court of Appeal said that the threats of violence were likely to be no less compelling because they could not be effected in the court room when the perjury was committed, if they could be carried out in the streets the same night.

Of course, duress by threats is not a defence if the accused commits a criminal act which the compulsion does not oblige him to.[2]

1 *Stratton* (1779) 21 State Tr 1045 at 1231, per Lord Mansfield CJ; *Hudson and Taylor.*

2 *Stratton*; *Hudson and Taylor*.

EXTENT OF THE DEFENCE

22.22 The defence of duress by threats applies to offences in general,[1] except murder,[2] attempted murder[3] and, possibly, certain types of treason.[4] Since many offences have not been the subject of an authoritative decision as to the applicability of the defence, other exceptions may be established, should the occasion arise.

1 *Hudson and Taylor* [1971] 2 QB 202 at 206, [1971] 2 All ER 244. Also see *Howe* [1987] AC 417, [1987] 1 All ER 771, HL.
2 *Howe*.
3 *Gotts* [1991] 2 All ER 1, CA.
4 Para 22.25.

22.23 *Duress by threats and murder*[1] The inapplicability to murder of the defence of duress by threats was settled by the House of Lords in 1987 in *Howe*.[2] Traditionally, the view of the courts and of the writers of authority[3] has been that the defence was not available on a charge of murder. However, in *DPP for Northern Ireland v Lynch*[4] the majority (three to two) of the House of Lords held that the defence of duress was available to an accomplice to murder (such as a person who loads a rifle for someone who then fires a lethal shot or a person who drives a killer to the scene of the killing). On the other hand, in *Abbott v R*[5] a majority (three to two) of the Privy Council, while accepting the decision in *Lynch*, refused to extend it to the perpetrator of murder. The resulting distinction in the present respect between perpetrators and accomplices of a murder was open to criticism, since the contribution of an accomplice to a killing may be no less significant (and occasionally may be greater) than that of the perpetrator.

In *Howe* D1 and D2 participated with others in torturing, beating up and sexually abusing two men on different occasions. On the first occasion, D1 and D2 were accomplices to the murder of the man by O. On the second occasion, D1 and D2 had been the perpetrators of the murder by strangling the man with a shoelace. D1 and D2 said that they had acted under duress since on both occasions they had acted as they did on the directions of X, a powerful, violent and sadistic man who was participating in the events, and had been in fear that, if they disobeyed X's instructions, X would kill them or seriously injure them. In the light of *Lynch* and *Abbot*, the judge left the defence of duress by threats to the jury in relation to the first murder, but not in relation to the second. The Court of Appeal held that this was correct.

The House of Lords unanimously held that the defence of duress by threats should not have been left to the jury in relation to either murder. Among the reasons given by their lordships for denying that duress by threats could be a defence for a perpetrator of murder, the most prominent was the supreme importance which the law attaches to the protection of the life of an innocent person. This was so important, said their lordships, that a person should be required to sacrifice his own life rather than being permitted to decide who should live and who should die (but what if the threat is to kill the accused's wife, parents and six children?). Their Lordships were unimpressed by the argument that it made no sense that an accused who under duress wounded another with intent to do him grievous bodily harm, and who was therefore acquitted of that offence, should have no defence to a charge of murder on the basis of the same act committed under the same threats and with the same mens rea if the victim died within a year and a day of the original injury.

The House held that there was no valid distinction between a perpetrator of murder and an accomplice to it, and that the same rule should apply to both. Consequently, it overruled the decision to the contrary on this point in *Lynch*. Thus, duress by threats is no longer available as a defence to an accomplice to murder. (The overruling of *Lynch* on the present point does not affect the validity of statements in it on other points referred to in this and other chapters.)

The House was happy to leave questions relating to the culpability of those involved in a murder under duress to discretionary executive action after conviction and mandatory sentence to life imprisonment, viz early release on licence by the Home Secretary on the advice of the Parole Board and the exercise of the royal prerogative to grant a pardon in particularly deserving cases. These methods of mitigating the harshness of *Howe* are an unsatisfactory solution to the problem, since the outcome of the exercise of a discretion is always uncertain (whereas a person who has a defence is entitled to an acquittal) and, even if the discretion is exercised in the offender's favour, it does not remove the stigma of a guilty verdict at the trial. It is interesting to note that the availability of discretionary executive action after conviction for other offences, quite apart from the possibility of mitigation of sentence, has not prevented the development of the defence of duress by threats in relation to them. Arguably, the fact that the judge cannot mitigate the sentence for murder provides a reason for duress to be a defence to murder which is more pressing than any reason which has resulted in it being a defence to other offences where mitigating factors can be taken into account in sentencing.

The effect of *Howe* is to require a person threatened with death or serious injury unless he kills another to be a hero, something which the law does not normally do. Where the threat relates to someone else the effect of the decision is to require the accused to sacrifice that person or persons (to whom, as in the case of a parent-child relationship, he may owe a legal duty of care) in order to save another (the intended victim). An acceptable compromise solution to the problems posed in *Howe* might have been to treat duress in murder as analogous to provocation, with the result that the offence would be reduced to manslaughter in such a case, but the House of Lords rejected such an idea. This is open to criticism since, especially where the threat of death or serious harm relates to more than those killed, many people would think that the moral culpability of a person who kills under duress is less than that of one who kills under provocation. Moreover, as Lord Lane CJ said in *Graham*,[6] 'Provocation and duress are analogous. In provocation the words or actions of one person break the self-control of another. In duress the words or actions of one person break the will of another'.

The decision in *Howe* is bound to be controversial. Arguably, the decision was inevitable given the inflexibility of the defence of duress. It is easier to accept that D should not have a defence if he intentionally kills P to save his own skin than that D should not have a defence if he acted to save the life of his wife, parents and six children, particularly since the threatener can be convicted of murder.[7] The inflexible decision in *Howe* might have been avoided if the idea of proportionality between threat and response (referred to in para 22.17) had already become part of our law. As it is, the House of Lords has expressly left it to Parliament to come up with any relaxation in the law.

1 Milgate 'Duress and the Criminal Law: Another About Turn by the House of Lords' [1988] CLJ 61; Walters 'Murder, Duress and Judicial Decision-Making in the House of Lords' (1988) 8 *Legal Studies* 61.
2 [1987] AC 417, [1987] 1 All ER 771, HL.
3 *Tyler and Price* (1838) 8 C & P 616; Hale *Pleas of the Crown* vol 1, pp 51, 434; Blackstone *Commentaries* vol 4, 1809 edn, p 30.
4 [1975] AC 653, [1975] 1 All ER 913, HL.
5 [1977] AC 755, [1976] 3 All ER 140, PC.
6 [1982] 1 All ER 801, [1982] 1 WLR 294, CA
7 Para 22.30.

22.24 *Duress by threats and attempted murder* The House of Lords in *Howe* did not decide whether or not duress by threats could be a defence to a charge of attempted murder. Lord Griffiths,[1] however, was of the view, obiter, that duress was not a defence to attempted murder because the prosecution had to prove an even more evil intent (an intent unlawfully to kill)[2] than in murder (where an intent unlawfully to cause grievous bodily harm can also suffice).

The point was settled by the decision of a majority of the House of Lords in 1992 when they upheld the decision of the Court of Appeal in *Gotts*,[3] to the effect that duress is not a defence on a murder charge, whether as perpetrator or accomplice. In *Gotts* D, aged 16, attempted to kill his mother by stabbing her. His defence was that his father, a violent man, had ordered him to do so and had threatened to kill him if he did not comply. The Court of Appeal held that the trial judge had been right to rule that duress was not a defence to attempted murder. It based its decision on what it considered to be the rationale behind the exclusion of murder from the defence of duress, a rationale which had not been articulated by the House of Lords in *Howe*. The Court of Appeal considered that this rationale was that, if the defence was available, a) criminals could confer impunity on their agents (e g other members of a gang) by threats of death or serious harm if they did not kill; b) there would be a risk of collusion and bogus defences, which may be difficult to disprove, and c) even in genuine cases, the law must insist that its rules are obeyed and that the victim of the threat should not give into temptation and break them. If this rationale is a convincing one it would seem equally applicable to all offences and would bring into question the continued existence of duress by threats as a defence to any offence. It is submitted, however, that it is unconvincing. First, the 'bogus defence argument', if it has merit, could be dealt with in other ways than excluding the defence, e g by shifting the burden of proof. Second, people who belong to criminal gangs generally do not have the defence of duress by threats if they are forced by the threats of another gang member to commit an offence, as explained in para 22.26. Third, a person threatened with death or serious harm unless he kills another is unlikely to think, or know, about whether or not he would have a defence in law, and even if he realises that he would not, he is not going to be deterred by the fear of criminal liability if he has to act to save his own life or limb or that of another.

Even if the rationale of the Court of Appeal in *Gotts* is rejected, there is a risk that the denial of a defence to murder and attempted murder of duress by threats is liable to be extended to other offences since logical distinctions between offences may not be easy to draw. Now that it has been decided that duress by threats is not a defence to attempted murder, the question arises as to why it should apply to wounding with intent to do grievous bodily harm and so on.

1 [1987] 1 All ER 771 at 790. This reasoning appealed to the majority of the House of Lords in *Gotts* [1992] 1 All ER 832.
2 Para 21.60.
3 [1991] 2 All ER 1, CA; [1992] 1 All ER 832, HL.

22.25 *Duress by threats and treason* It seems that duress by threats can be a defence to some, if not all, types of treason. Lord Goddard CJ took a contrary view in *Steane*[1] but he must have overlooked cases such as *M'Growther*,[2] *Oldcastle's Case*,[3] *Stratton*[4] and *Purdy*[5] where the applicability of the defence to treason was recognised. It seems from these cases that only a threat of death will suffice, but the modern case law on the defence in general suggests that if the point arose today a threat of serious bodily injury might be held sufficient.

1 [1947] KB 997, [1974] 1 All ER 813, CCA.
2 (1746) Fost 13, 18 State Tr 391.
3 (1419) 1 Hale PC 50.
4 (1779) 1 Doug KB 239, 21 State Tr 1045.
5 (1946) 10 JCL 182.

VOLUNTARY MEMBERSHIP OF A CRIMINAL ASSOCIATION

22.26 The defence of duress by threats is not available to a person who voluntarily and with knowledge as to its nature joined a criminal organisation, gang or other conspiracy, knowing that other members might bring pressure on him to commit an offence, and who was an active member when he was put under such pressure.[1] It is, of course, for the prosecution to prove these matters.

The basis of this rule is that no excuse should be available if the risk of duress was freely undertaken.[2] It follows from the rule, for example, that the defence of duress by threats is not available to an accused who has voluntarily, and knowing its nature, joined a group dedicated to violence for a political end, and who is threatened with harm by another member or members unless he commits an offence in furtherance of that end.[2] On the other hand, the defence may be available, for example, to an accused who has voluntarily joined a criminal group or conspiracy, not knowing of any propensity to violence on the part of any member and therefore not suspecting any risk that he might be threatened with harm if he does not commit an offence, and who is unexpectedly subjected to such threats.[2] Of course, whether or not a plea of duress succeeds in such a case will depend on the various requirements of the defence set out above.

1 *Sharp* [1987] QB 853, [1987] 3 All ER 103, CA.
2 *Shepherd* [1987] Crim LR 686, CA.

PROPOSALS FOR REFORM

22.27 With a few exceptions, cl 42 of the draft Criminal Code Bill[1] follows recommendations made by the Law Commission in 1977[2] in relation to the defence of duress by threats. The defence would be defined in terms that a person does an act under duress by threats if:

'a) he does it because *he knows or believes*[3]–
    i)   that a threat has been made to kill or cause serious personal harm to himself or another if the act is not done; and

ii) that the threat will be carried out immediately if he does not do the act or, if not immediately, before he or the other can obtain official protection; and

iii) that there is no other way of preventing the threat being carried out; and

b) the threat is one which in all the circumstances (including any of his personal characteristics that affect its gravity) he cannot reasonably be expected to resist'.

The fact that the accused believed, or that it was the case, that any official protection available in the circumstances would or might be ineffective to prevent the threat being carried out would be immaterial. The defence would not apply to a person who had knowingly and without reasonable excuse exposed himself to the risk of the threat (for example, by voluntarily joining a violent association).

In its report in 1977 the Law Commission recommended that duress should be a defence to all offences, including murder and attempted murder. It is still of that view. However, since the draft Bill is a codifying Bill, the Law Commission has inserted in cl 41 a subsection providing that the defence applies to any offence, other than murder or attempted murder.

1 Law Commission: A Criminal Code for England and Wales (1989): Law Com No 177; see para 3.21 above.
2 Defences of General Application (1977) Law Com No 83.
3 Italics supplied.

Marital coercion

22.28 Before the Criminal Justice Act 1925 came into force, there was a rebuttable presumption of law that an offence, other than treason or murder or certain other offences, committed by a wife in the presence of her husband was committed under his coercion. Accordingly, the prosecution bore the burden of negativing coercion. The presumption has been abolished by s 47 of the Criminal Justice Act 1925, but this section provides that it shall be a defence on a charge of any offence, other than treason or murder, for a wife to prove that she committed the alleged offence in the presence of, and under the coercion of, her husband. It is important to note that the section places the burden of proving coercion on the wife, whereas in duress by threats the accused merely bears an evidential burden.[1] Coercion is a defence for a wife in addition to that of duress by threats, not in substitution for it.[2] Unlike duress by threats, the defence of marital coercion is available on a charge of attempted murder.

The defence is only available to a wife; it is not available to a woman who mistakenly, but reasonably, believes that she is married to the man making the threat,[3] as where that man was already married when she married him (although she had no reason to know that).

1 *Gill* [1963] 2 All ER 688, [1963] 1 WLR 841, CCA; *Bone* [1968] 2 All ER 644, [1968] 1 WLR 983, CA.
2 *DPP for Northern Ireland v Lynch* [1975] AC 653 at 684, 713, per Lords Willberforce and Edmund-Davies.
3 *Ditta, Hussain and Kara* [1988] Crim LR 43, CA.

22.29 The defence of marital coercion is rarely pleaded and, because s 47 has not yet received authoritative judicial interpretation, may give rise to difficulty in the future. One reason is that the nature of the threats covered by marital coercion is not certain, although a circuit judge has held that they are not limited to threats of personal violence since moral threats can suffice (provided in either case that the wife's will was overborne).[1] A second reason why the defence may give rise to difficulty in the future is that the word 'presence' has not yet been elucidated. It is, for instance, impossible to say whether s 47 would be held by the Court of Appeal to cover a case in which a husband induced his wife to enter a house for the purpose of stealing something, by threatening to leave her if she did not comply with his wishes, while he remained outside and kept watch.

The Law Commission has recommended the abolition of the defence of marital coercion on the grounds that it is not appropriate to modern conditions.[2] Under cl 42(6) of the draft Criminal Code, a wife would not have a separate defence of marital coercion.[3]

1 *Richman* [1982] Crim LR 507, Crown Ct.
2 Defences of General Application (1977) Law Com No 83. For a discussion of the defence and arguments in favour of its retention, see Pace [1979] Crim LR 82.
3 Law Commission: A Criminal Code for England and Wales (1989): Law Com No 177.

THE PERSON MAKING THE THREAT

22.30 Although the defences of duress by threats and marital coercion may be available to the person who actually performed the criminal act, the one who made the threats is under some form of criminal liability. There is no doubt on this point, but we shall see in the next chapter that the methods by which the result can be reached vary and have been made the subject of controversy.

Necessity

22.31 As with most of the defences referred to so far in this chapter, we are concerned here with situations in which the accused is faced with a choice between two courses, either to allow some threatened harm to occur, or to prevent that harm by committing an offence (or what would otherwise be an offence), and he chooses the second course thereby averting a greater evil. The difference between the present situations on the one hand and self-defence and the like on the other is that in the present situations the victim may be *wholly* innocent. The defence of duress by threats is a species of necessity but we are concerned here with situations where the threat is not a threat along the lines of 'Do this or else . . .'; indeed the threat need not even emanate from another person.

The subject matter will be dealt with in the following order:

a) statutory provision for situations of necessity;
b) the defence of duress of circumstances; and
c) the question of whether there is a wider defence of necessity.

STATUTORY PROVISION FOR NECESSITY

22.32 In the definition of many statutory offences allowance is made expressly or impliedly for the case where the accused has acted under the stress of necessity. One example of the express justification of what would otherwise be criminal is the offence of child destruction, contrary to s 1 of the

Infant Life Preservation Act 1929, under which the prosecution must prove that the accused was not acting in good faith in order to preserve the life of the mother.[1] Some statutes provide defences which cover necessity, as well as other circumstances. One example is s 1 of the Abortion Act 1967, which was described in para 11.80. Another example is s 87 of the Road Traffic Regulation Act 1984, which dispenses with the need for fire engines, police vehicles and ambulances to observe the speed limit if the observance of the limit would be likely to hinder the use of the vehicle for the purpose for which it is being used.[2] Likewise, the definition of 'lawful excuse' for the purposes of certain offences under the Criminal Damage Act 1971 provided by s 5 of that Act (referred to in para 15.12) clearly makes allowance for necessity, as well as other circumstances. If D destroys inflammable material belonging to another in order to prevent a fire spreading to other property, he would have the defence of lawful excuse under s 5 if he believed that that property was in immediate need of protection and that what he did was reasonable in the circumstances.

An implied allowance for necessity, as well as other circumstances, would seem to be made by the wording of some statutory offences. For example, if D in the above example was charged with theft of the material, a jury could, and no doubt would, find that he had not acted dishonestly.[3] It would presumably be a defence on a charge of abducting a girl of under sixteen 'without lawful authority or excuse' that she had been taken to protect her from an offence of violence or from an offence such as incest, at least if there was no other way of doing so.[4]

1 Para 11.82.
2 Also see the Fire Services Act 1947, s 30; the Antarctic Treaty Act 1967, s 2(2); the Traffic Signs Regulations and General Directions 1981, and the Control of Pollution (Amendment) Act 1989, s 1(4).
3 Para 13.54–13.58. For contrary view, see Griew *Theft Acts 1968 and 1978* (6th edn) para 2-135.
4 See the judgment of Denman J in *Prince* (1875) LR 2 CCR 154, 44 LJMC 122.

DURESS OF CIRCUMSTANCES

22.33 *A general defence of necessity?* A defence of necessity was recognised by many writers of authority.[1] However, until the recognition and application of the defence of duress of circumstances in the late 1980s, there were very few cases where any type of defence of necessity (apart from duress by threats) had been expressly recognised (and in all of these the recognition was obiter). One of these case was the civil case of *Southwark London Borough Council v Williams* in 1971 where the Court of Appeal stated that in a criminal case 'The plea of necessity may in certain cases afford a defence'.[2]

In addition, there were a number of cases where the decision was based on principles of necessity but without express reference to a general defence of necessity.[3] It is arguable that they provided implicit recognition of the existence of such a defence. For example, in *Vantandillo*[4] it was held that the necessity for a mother to carry her infected child through the streets to seek medical attention 'might have been given in evidence as a matter of defence' to a charge of exposing a person with a contagious disease on the public highway. Another example is provided by *Bourne*,[5] where the accused, an obstetric surgeon, performed an abortion on a 14-year-old girl who had been violently raped. He was charged with *unlawfully* using an instrument with intent to procure a miscarriage, contrary to s 58 of the Offences against the Person Act 1861. The jury acquitted the accused after MacNaghten J had told the jury that the accused would not have acted unlawfully if he had acted in good faith to save the girl's life. Although the judge dealt with the matter from the point of view of the meaning of 'unlawfully' in s 58, and did not expressly refer to a defence of necessity, the case is clearly one where principles of necessity were implied into the meaning of 'unlawful', and it has subsequently been described by the Court of Appeal in *Southwark London Borough Council v Williams*[6] as being based on necessity. As a last example, reference may be made to the opinion of Lords Fraser, Scarman and Templeman in *Gillick v W Norfolk and Wisbech Area Health Authority*.[7] Their Lordships held that a doctor, who provided a girl of under 16 with contraceptives (and thereby knowingly encouraged sexual intercourse), would not be guilty as an accomplice to an offence of unlawful intercourse committed with her by a man, if the doctor acted in a way he believed necessary for the physical, mental or emotional health of the girl. It is likely that their Lordships thought that the doctor would not be liable because he lacked the necessary intent to assit or encourage the man. However, there are problems with this approach[8] and *Gillick* is probably better explained as being based impliedly on principles of necessity.

1 Eg Hale *Pleas of the Crown* vol 1, 54.
2 [1971] Ch 734 at 743–4 and 745, [1971] 2 All ER 175. For another example, see *Wood v Richards* [1977] RTR 201, 65 Cr App Rep 300, DC.
3 *Vantandillo* (1815) 4 M & S 73; *Stratton* (1779) 1 Doug KB 239, 21 State Tr 1045; *Bourne* [1939] 1 KB 687, [1938] 3 All ER 615; *Johnson v Phillips* [1975] 3 All ER 682, [1976] 1 WLR 65, DC; *Gillick v West Norfolk and Wisbech Area Health Authority* [1986] AC 112, [1985] 3 All ER 402, HL; *F v West Berkshire Health Authority* [1989] 2 All ER 545 at 564–565, per Lord Goff.
4 (1815) 4 M & S 73.
5 [1939] 1 KB 687, [1938] 3 All ER 615. The facts of this case would now be governed by the provisions of the Abortion Act 1967; para 11.80. The decision in *Bourne* could, of course, be regarded as another example of an implied allowance for necessity by the words of the statute.
6 [1971] Ch 734 at 746.
7 [1986] AC 112, [1985] 3 All ER 402, HL; para 23.17. See Smith *Justification and Excuse in the Criminal Law* 64–70.
8 Para 6.26.

22.34 *The defence of duress of circumstances*[1] Recent decisions of the Court of Appeal make it clear that there is, at least, a limited general defence of necessity in the form of a defence of duress by circumstances.

The defence of duress by circumstances is like that of duress by threats, save that the threat need not come from a person and is not accompanied by the instruction: 'Do this or else. . . '.

The defence has its origins in *Willer*,[2] where D was charged with reckless driving[3] after he had driven over the pavement into a shopping centre in order to escape a gang who were shouting out threats to kill him and his passenger. At his trial, D pleaded a defence of necessity but the judge refused to leave any such defence to the jury. D's conviction was quashed on appeal. The Court of Appeal held that it ought to have been left to the jury to decide whether D drove 'under that form of compulsion, ie duress'. Although the Court seemed to treat the case simply as involving the defence of duress by threats, it was breaking new ground because the case did not involve a threat along the lines of 'Do this or else, . . .'. Indeed, the gang did not want D to drive onto the pavement to escape . Their wishes were quite to the contrary; they wanted him to stay to be dealt with.

1 Elliott *Necessity, Duress and Self-Defence* [1989] Crim LR 611.
2 (1986) 83 Cr App Rep 225, CA.
3 This offence was repealed by the Road Traffic Act 1991; para 20.10.

22.35 Recognition of the true nature of the defence came soon afterwards in *Conway*,[1] where *Willer* was applied. X, a passenger in D's car, had been in a vehicle a few weeks before when another man was shot and had himself been chased and narrowly escaped. On the day in question, two plain clothes police officers saw D in the driving seat of his parked car and X behind him. They knew that X was the subject of a bench warrant. They approached D's car, according to D at a run, whereupon X shouted out to D to drive off. The police officers followed in an unmarked car. It was alleged that, during the car chase, D drove recklessly. At his trial for reckless driving, D alleged that he believed throughout the the chase that the two men were out to kill X. Quashing D's conviction for reckless driving, the Court of Appeal held that the trial judge had been wrong not to direct the jury about the possibility of acquitting D on the ground of what it called 'duress of circumstances', which it distinguished from that of duress by threats and which it regarded as a species of necessity. The Court stated that, although a separate defence, duress of circumstances was like duress by threats, in that it was only available if from an objective standpoint the accused could be said to have acted in order to avoid a threat of death or serious bodily harm.

1 [1988] 3 All ER 1025, [1988] 3 WLR 1238, CA.

22.36 The development of the law in *Willer* and *Conway* was continued by the Court of Appeal in *Martin*.[1] According to D, his stepson overslept to such an extent that there was a reasonable prospect of him losing his job if D did not drive him to work. D's wife, who had suicidal tendencies, threatened suicide if D did not drive the stepson to work, and there was medical evidence that she would have carried out her threat. D, who was disqualified from driving, gave the stepson a lift. At his trial for driving while disqualified, he put forward a defence of necessity.[2] The judge ruled that necessity was not a defence to the offence charged. D's conviction was quashed by the Court of Appeal. The Court held that duress of circumstances, a species of necessity, was a defence to a charge of driving while disqualified and should have been left to the jury, however sceptically D's story might be regarded.

The Court held that the defence was only available if, from an objective standpoint, the accused could be said to be acting reasonably and proportionately in order to avoid a threat of death or serious bodily harm. Simon Brown J, giving the Court's judgment, also said this about the terms of the defence:

'[A]ssuming the defence to be open to to the accused on his account of the facts, the issue should be left to the jury who should be directed to determine these two questions: first, was the accused, or may he have been, impelled to act as he did because as a result of what he reasonably believed to be the situation he had good cause to fear that otherwise death or serious physical injury would result; second, if so, would a sober person of reasonable firmness, sharing the characteristics of the accused, have responded to that situation by acting as the accused did? If the answer to both these questions was Yes, then the jury would acquit; the defence of necessity would have been established.'[3]

1 [1989] 1 All ER 652, (1989) 88 Cr App Rep 343, CA.
2 It could be argued that duress by threats was the appropriate defence but this would raise two points not yet answered in relation to that defence: does it matter that the threat of harm is of harm to the threatener and does it matter that, as in the case of suicide, the threatened harm is not unlawful?
3 [1989] 1 All ER 652 at 653–654.

22.37 It is clear from the above that the defence of duress of circumstances is like that of duress by threats in that it is limited to cases where the accused acts to avert a threat of death or serious bodily harm and in that it involves a subjective test and an objective test along the same lines as in duress by threats.

Duress of circumstances is also like duress by threats, in that it cannot excuse the commission of an offence after the time when the threat has ceased,[1] and, almost certainly, in that it is not a defence to murder (nor presumably attempted murder).[2] In relation to murder, reference may be made to *Dudley and Stephens*,[3] a case decided long before the term 'duress by circumstances' was coined but which was a case involving a necessity situation of the duress by circumstances type. In *Dudley and Stephens* D and E were shipwrecked seamen who had been adrift in an open boat with practically no food for twenty days, after which D, abetted by E, killed the cabin boy who was with them. D and E then ate the boy's body. Four days later they were picked up, and when they got back to England they were tried and convicted of murder, although sentence of death was later commuted to six months' imprisonment. The tenor of Lord Coleridge's judgment suggests that necessity can never be a defence to a charge of murder, but the case is not conclusive on the point, because in their special verdict the jury merely found that D and E probably would not have survived to be rescued if they had not killed the boy. Thus, the decision may not deny the application of necessity to a murder charge but simply deny the application of that defence to the facts. However, analogy with the defence of duress by threats[4] suggests that, when the matter next comes up for consideration by the courts, it will be held that duress of circumstances (or any other form of necessity) can never be a defence to a charge of murder or attempted murder.[5] Indeed, in *Howe*,[6] Lord Hailsham LC was clearly of the opinion, obiter, that the court in *Dudley and Stephens* had correctly decided that necessity was never a defence to murder.

Lord Coleridge's judgment in *Dudley and Stephens* prompts similar reflection concerning the proper sphere of the criminal law[7] to that prompted by *Howe*. Is it right for the law to impose a higher standard than that to be expected of the average member of society? It can only be justified in the most exceptional cases, but *Dudley and Stephens* was just such a case.

1 *DPP v Jones* [1989] RTR 33, DC.
2 Nor presumably does it apply to those types of treason to which duress by threats is not a defence.
3 (1884) 14 QBD 273, 54 LJMC 32. For a critical review of this decision, see Williams 'A Commentary on *R v Dudley and Stephens*' (1977) 8 *Cambrian Law Review* 91. For a masterly examination of the various aspects of this case, see Simpson *Cannibalism and the Common Law* (1984).
4 Paras 22.23 and 22.24.
5 For suggestions of types of murder situation in which *Dudley and Stephens* might be distinguished, see Smith *Justification and Excuse in the Criminal Law* 77-79.
6 [1987] 1 All ER 771 at 778–779.
7 Paras 3.22–3.30.

IS THERE A WIDER DEFENCE?

22.38 Duress by threats and duress of circumstances are limited defences of necessity, being confined to cases where the evil the accused seeks to avert is death or serious bodily harm. Is necessity as a defence limited to this type of evil or is there a wider defence of necessity, over and above duress by circumstances, which may be available where an accused acts to avert some other evil, such as damage to property? We saw in para 22.33 that there was authority, none of it binding, before the cases on duress of circumstances to the effect that there is a defence of necessity. However, this is far from conclusive in favour of a wider defence since the terms of the defence envisaged by that authority is largely a matter of conjecture and the defence of necessity has not been expressly applied outside situations where death or serious bodily harm was the evil averted. In *Conway*[1] Woolf LJ, giving the judgment of the Court of Appeal, said this when admitting that duress of circumstances was a defence and a species of necessity: 'It appears that it is still not clear whether there is a general defence of necessity or, if there is, what are the circumstances in which it is available'. On the other hand, Simon Brown J, giving the judgment of the Court of Appeal in *Martin*,[2] did not think the matter in doubt. While stating that English law does recognise a defence of necessity, he added that it was only available where the accused acted to avoid a threat of death or serious bodily harm (i e where he acted under duress by threats or of circumstances). Simon Brown J's view almost certainly represents that which the Court of Appeal or House of Lords would currently take in advance of a clearly deserving case The problem in this area is that in really deserving cases a person is often not prosecuted, so that the limits of the criminal law are not put to the test. The *Gillick* case, referred to in para 22.33, was a civil case but it is submitted that should a doctor ever be prosecuted on the basis of prescribing contraceptives for an under-age girl for the health reasons referred to there, and the case be properly argued, there would be the type of case which would lead the courts to reassess fully for the first time the proper limits of the criminal law in the area of necessity.

The law is not quite as illiberal as might be thought. The reason is that in appropriate cases falling outside duress by threats or duress of circumstances a court, without saying or expressly recognising that it is doing so, may well imply principles of necessity into an offence as a matter of its construction This has been done in the past, as we saw in para 22.33. In such a case the effect may be, as in *Bourne*,[3] to justify (i e render lawful) the accused's conduct, as opposed simply to excusing him for conduct which is nevertheless unlawful, which is the effect of duress by threats or of circumstances.

1 [1988] 3 All ER 1025 at 1029.
2 [1989] 1 All ER 652 at 653.
3 [1939] 1 KB 687, [1938] 3 All ER 615; para 22.33.

REFORM

22.39 In 1977, the Law Commission recommended that the defence of necessity, if it existed at common law at all, should be abolished, and that provision should be made by statute for a defence to particular offences where appropriate.[1] It seems the height of absurdity that the Law Commission, having recommended that there should be a general defence of duress by threats, should have recommended in the same report that there should be no general defence of necessity. Fortunately, the draft Criminal Code Bill[2] does not adopt such an extreme position. Clause 43 provides a defence of duress of circumstances, which would apply if an accused acts because he knows or believes that it is immediately necessary to avoid death or serious personal harm to himself or another, and the danger that he knows or believes to exist is such that in all the circumstances (including any of his personal characteristics that affect its gravity) he cannot reasonably be expected to act otherwise. The defence would apply to any offence, except murder and attempted murder (although, as with duress by threats, the Law Commission recommend that these exceptions should be removed). The defence would not be available to a person who had voluntarily and without reasonable excuse exposed himself to the danger.

Clause 4(4) of the draft Bill has the effect of permitting the courts to recognise and develop a wider defence of necessity despite the fact that it is not contained in the Code.

1 Defences of General Application (1977) Law Com No 83. For critical discussions of those proposals, see Williams [1978] Crim LR 128, and Huxley [1978] Crim LR 141.
2 Law Commission: A Criminal Code for England and Wales (1989): Law Com No 177; see para 3.21 above.

Superior orders

22.40   Clearly, if a person acts on the lawful orders of a superior, as where a soldier is ordered by an officer to use reasonable force to resist attack, reasonable force by him to do so will be justified by the rules of public or private defence already mentioned.

The question of a separate general defence of superior orders is concerned with the situation where the superior's orders were in fact unlawful. If it is a defence in such a case that a person was acting pursuant to the orders of a superior it is probably limited to members of the armed forces.[1] Whether there is such a defence is open to doubt since there is no English decision on the point. In South Africa,[2] it has been held that: 'if a soldier honestly believes he is doing his duty in obeying the commands of his superior, and if the orders are not so manifestly illegal that he must or ought to have known that they are unlawful, the private soldier would be protected by the orders of his superior officer'. On the other hand, the *Manual of Military Law*[3] takes the opposite view as the better one, namely that a reasonable mistaken belief that the orders are lawful does not afford a defence. If it is the law that a mistaken belief, even a reasonably mistaken one, that the orders are lawful is no defence, the rule is an unrealistic one because it requires an individual soldier who is trained to obey orders instantly and whose own survival may be at risk to consider the lawfulness of orders given to him and not to carry them out if they are in fact unlawful, whether manifestly or not.[4]

1 In *Lewis v Dickson* [1976] RTR 431, DC, it was held that a civilian security officer, whose checking of vehicles in compliance with the instructions of his superior resulted in the obstruction of a road, was guilty of wilfully obstructing the highway without lawful authority or excuse.
2 *Smith* (1900) 17 SCR 561; cited in Turner and Armitage *Cases on Criminal Law* (3rd edn) p 68.
3 *Manual of Military Law* (12th edn) 156–157.
4 For arguments in favour of a defence being available where military orders are not manifestly illegal, see Brownlee 'Superior Orders: Time for a New Realism' [1989] Crim LR 396. See also Nichols 'Untying the Soldier by Refurbishing the Common Law' [1976] Crim LR 181.

22.41 The unlawful orders of a superior, whether a civilian or member of the armed forces, may bring other rules of law into play, and thus indirectly provide the accused with a defence. For example, such an order may induce in the accused a mistake which results in him lacking the mens rea for the offence.[1] Suppose that a person is ordered to use a degree of force in a situation where that degree of force is unreasonable, so that the order is unlawful, he will not be guilty of an offence against the person when he uses that force if on the facts as he believed them to be (and the order may have contributed to that belief) the force used would have been reasonable. In such a case he will lack the necessary mens rea.[2] Likewise, suppose that a farm labourer removes a horse from P's field and takes it to his employer's stables pursuant to the latter's unlawful instructions. He may well believe that the horse belongs to the employer and that he is legally entitled to deprive P of it on the employer's behalf. If so, he is not guilty of theft because a person who believes that he has a legal right to deprive another of property on behalf of a third person lacks part of the mens rea for theft, dishonesty.

Similarly, a superior order may induce in the accused a mistake which results in him having a belief which is a statutory defence.[3] For example, a person is not guilty of criminal damage if he believes that he has a legal right to do as he does, because he will have the defence provided by s 5 of the Criminal Damage Act. Consequently, if the farm labourer just referred to proceeds to dock the horse's tail pursuant to his employer's instructions, he may likewise be not guilty of criminal damage.

1 *James* (1837) 8 C & P 131; *Trainer* (1864) 4 F & F 105.
2 Para 22.10.
3 *Denton* [1982] 1 All ER 65, [1981] 1 WLR 1446, CA; para 15.12.

22.42 It is, of course, possible for a statute to make express provision for a specific defence of superior orders in relation to one or more of the offences in it. For example, s 1(4)(c) of the Control of Pollution (Amendment) Act 1989 states that, in proceedings for an offence under s 1(1) of the Act (transport of controlled waste in the course of a business or for profit by an unregistered carrier), an accused has a defence if he proves that he acted under instructions from his employer.

22.43 The draft Criminal Code Bill makes no specific reference to the question of superior orders.

23 Participation[1]

Perpetrators

23.1 Before we discuss the liability of an accomplice, we should say something about the perpetrator of an offence, otherwise known as the principal. Normally, it is clear who is the perpetrator; he is the one who, with the relevant mens rea, fires the fatal shot in murder, or has sexual intercourse in rape, or appropriates the property in theft. Of course, there can be more than one perpetrator, as where two people by their joint and aggregate violence kill another.[2] Two or more people may also be joint perpetrators where each with the relevant mens rea does distinct acts which together constitute a sufficient act for the actus reus of an offence; for example, in an offence involving driving D1 and D2 have been held both to be driving where D1 was leaning across and steering while D2 operated the foot pedals and gears.[3] Another example can be provided by reference to the offence of robbery; D1 and D2 would be joint perpetrators of that offence if, with the requisite mens rea, D1 appropriated another's property while D2 used force to enable the appropriation to occur.

1 See, generally, Smith 'Aid, Abet, Counsel or Procure' in *Reshaping the Criminal Law* (1978), p 120.
2 *Macklin and Murphy's Case* (1838) 2 Lew CC 225.
3 *Tyler v Whatmore* [1976] RTR 83, DC.

23.2 *Innocent agency* If a person makes use of an innocent agent in order to procure the commission of an offence, that person, not the innocent agent, is the perpetrator, even though he is not present at the scene of the crime and does nothing with his own hands. An innocent agent is one who commits the actus reus of an offence but is himself devoid of responsibility, either by reason of incapacity (e g infancy) or because he lacks mens rea or has a defence such as duress by threats. A striking example of innocent agency is where a daughter, acting on her mother's instructions, gave some powder to her father to relieve his cold. Unknown to the daughter it was a poison and her father died. It was held that the mother was the perpetrator of the crime of murder since the daughter, lacking mens rea, was an innocent agent by means of whom the mother had perpetrated the offence. Of course, if, as the report notes, the daughter had known that the powder was poison she would have been guilty as perpetrator and the mother as an accomplice.[1] A more modern, although more prosaic, example is provided by a case where the business manager of a company signed false invoices, intending that innocent employees would automatically pass them for payment and that the company's bank account would be debited accordingly, which duly occurred. It was held that he could be convicted of theft of the sums paid on the false invoices, having appropriated them through innocent agents.[2]

1 *Anon* (1665) Kel 53. Also see *Manley* (1844) 3 LTOS 22, 1 Cox CC 104.
2 *Stringer and Banks* [1991] Crim LR 639, CA.

Accomplices

23.3 A person who aids, abets, counsels or procures the commission of an offence (an accomplice) is liable to be tried and punished for that offence as a principal offender.[1] So that an accused may know whether he is alleged to have been a perpetrator or an accomplice, the particulars of the offence in the indictment should make it clear whether it is alleged that he was a perpetrator or accomplice.[2]

1 Accessories and Abettors Act 1861, s 8, as amended by the Criminal Law Act 1977, Sch 12 (offences triable only on indictment and offences triable either way); Magistrates' Courts Act 1980, s 44.
2 *DPP for Northern Ireland v Maxwell* [1978] 3 All ER 1140, [1978] 1 WLR 1350, HL.

23.4 Five other introductory points may be made:

a) A person can be convicted, as an accomplice, of an inchoate offence.[1] In relation to an attempt, the authority is *Dunnington*.[2] Here, the Court of Appeal held that a person who had driven would-be robbers to the scene of their intended crime could be convicted as an accomplice to attempted robbery when they were unsuccessful. There is no reason to doubt that a person can be convicted, as an accomplice, of incitement or conspiracy if he satisfies the conditions necessary for conviction as an accomplice.[3]

b) It may be that the wording of a particular offence-creating provision can have the effect of preventing a person being liable as an accomplice. In *Carmichael & Sons (Worcester) Ltd v Cottle*[4] it was stated, obiter, that when a provision uses the words 'using, causing or permitting to be used' it may be that 'there is no room for the application of the principle relating to aiders and abettors'. Terms like 'cause or permit' clearly cover many of the types of conduct encompassed by 'aid, abet, counsel or procure' but the statement in the above case remains a suggestion, and no more, at present. The statement in *Carmichael & Sons (Worcester) Ltd v Cottle* can be compared with obiter dicta in *Brookes v Retail Credit Cards Ltd*,[5] to the effect that the words 'a breach of any requirement by . . . this Act shall incur no criminal sanction . . . , except to the extent provided by this Act' in the Consumer Credit Act 1974 did not exclude the normal liability of someone who was an accomplice to an offence under the Act.

c) For the purpose of following the old cases, until the Criminal Law Act 1967 accomplices to the commission of a felony were described as 'principals in the second degree' if they were present when it was committed, or as 'accessories before the fact' if absent. In either event they were properly described as 'principals' in offences other than felonies.

d) A number of participants may also be guilty of conspiracy.

e) In relation to people who counsel or procure abroad an offence committed in England it was established in *Robert Millar (Contractors) Ltd*[6] that they may be convicted in an English court as accomplices to the principal offence, but people in England who counsel or procure the commission abroad of an offence may not.[7]

1 Inchoate offences were discussed in Ch 21.
2 [1984] QB 472, [1984] 1 All ER 676, CA.
3 Smith 'Secondary participation and inchoate offences' in *Crime, Proof and Punishment* (1982), 21.
4 [1971] RTR 11 at 14.
5 (1985) 150 JP 131, [1986] Crim LR 327, DC.
6 [1970] 2 QB 54, [1970] 1 All ER 577, CA.
7 *Godfrey* [1923] 1 KB 24, 92 LJKB 205, CCA.

23.5 In order that a person may be convicted as an accomplice, it is not necessary that the perpetrator should have been brought to trial or convicted, or even that his identity should be known, but it is necessary for the prosecution to prove:

a) that the accused aided, abetted, counselled or procured the commission of the principal offence;
b) that the principal offence was in fact committed; and
c) that he had the mens rea required for liability as an accomplice.

AIDING, ABETTING, COUNSELLING OR PROCURING

23.6 If an accused is alleged to have been an accomplice to the principal offence, the charge may allege that he aided, abetted, counselled or procured it, and he will be convicted if he is proved to have participated in one or more of these four ways.[1]

Although 'aiding' and 'abetting' have sometimes been regarded as synonymous,[2] there is a difference between them: 'aid' being used to describe the activity of a person who helps, supports or assists the perpetrator to commit the principal offence, and 'abet' to describe the activity of a person who incites, instigates or encourages the perpetrator to commit it, whether or not in either case he is present at the time of commission.[3]

'Counsel', which means 'advise', 'encourage' or the like,[4] does not add anything strictly but is used to describe encouragement before the commission of the principal offence.

A person 'procures' the commission of an offence if he causes it to be committed or brings its commission about.[5] More fully, a person procures the commission of an offence where he sets out to see that it is committed and takes appropriate steps to produce its commission. This was stated by the Court of Appeal in *A-G's Reference (No 1 of 1975)*,[6] where it was also held that, whereas aiding, abetting and counselling 'almost inevitably' involve a shared intention between the accomplice and the perpetrator that the principal offence should be committed, this is less likely to be so in the case of procuring. The importance of this decision is illustrated by the facts on which it was based. D laced the drink of E, unknown to E, who was later convicted of the offence of strict liability of driving with an excess of alcohol. In holding that D could be convicted as an accomplice to this offence, Lord Widgery CJ said: '[The principal offence] has been procured because, unknown to the driver and without his collaboration, he has been put in a position in which in fact he has committed an offence which he would never have committed otherwise.'[7]

It can be seen from the above that there are three ways of becoming an accomplice: by assisting in the commission of the principal offence, by encouraging its commission or by procuring its commission.

1 *Re Smith* (1858) 3 H & N 227, 27 LJMC 186; *Ferguson v Weaving* [1951] 1 KB 814, [1951] 1 All ER 412, DC.
2 *DPP for Northern Ireland v Lynch* [1975] AC 653, [1975] 1 All ER 913 at 924 and 941, per Lords Morris of Borth-y-Gest and Simon of Glaisdale.
3 *National Coal Board v Gamble* [1959] 1 QB 11, [1958] 3 All ER 203, DC; *Thambiah v R* [1966] AC 37, [1965] 3 All ER 661, PC; *Bentley v Mullen* [1986] RTR 7 at 10, per May LJ.
4 *Calhaem* [1985] QB 808, [1985] 2 All ER 266, CA.
5 *Beck* [1985] 1 All ER 571, [1985] 1 WLR 22, CA.
6 [1975] QB 773, [1975] 2 All ER 684, CA.
7 [1975] QB 773 at 780, [1975] 2 All ER 684

23.7 The assistance, encouragement or procuring must be given before, or at the time of, the commission of the principal offence. Someone who assists the perpetrator after the commission of the principal offence is not liable as a party to it, but one who assists the perpetrator to escape detection or arrest may be guilty of the statutory offence of assisting offenders.[1]

1 Para 16.1.

23.8 The assistance, encouragement or procuring which must be proved against an alleged accomplice may take a variety of forms. It may consist of active assistance or encouragement in the criminal act, such as holding a woman down while she is raped,[1] or keeping watch,[2] or cheering and clapping an unlawful theatrical performance.[3] Alternatively, encouragement or assistance in the preparation of an offence even at an early stage suffices, as where the accused opens a bank account with the intention of facilitating the paying in of forged cheques by the perpetrator.[4]

Supplying the instrument, materials or information for use in the commission of the principal offence constitutes assistance in its commission.[5] A thing is supplied in this context if it is given, lent or sold, or if a right of property in it is otherwise transferred.[6] A man who gives up to another for use in an offence a weapon of which the latter is owner aids in the commission of that offence as much as if he had sold or lent the weapon, but such conduct does not make him an accomplice.[7] This has been explained on the basis that, although the man who surrenders the weapon to its owner is physically performing a positive act, he is in law simply refraining from committing the civil wrong of conversion. It is unlikely that an action for the wrongful detention of a jemmy brought by a would-be burglar who owned it would succeed.[8] If E lends a gun to D, and later drags his wife before D, shouting 'Return my gun, I am going to kill this woman instantly with it', is it really the law that D incurs no liability, as accomplice, in respect of the murder of the wife if he meekly returns the gun with which she is instantly shot?

1 *Clarkson* [1971] 3 All ER 344, [1971] 1 WLR 1402, Courts-Martial Appeal Court. The powers of this court correspond in general with those of the Court of Appeal (Criminal Division), as does its composition.
2 *Betts and Ridley* (1930) 22 Cr App Rep 148, CCA.
3 *Wilcox v Jeffery* [1951] 1 All ER 464, DC.
4 *Thambiah v R* [1966] AC 37, [1965] 3 All ER 661, PC.
5 *National Coal Board v Gamble* [1959] 1 QB 11, [1958] 3 All ER 203, DC.
6 Ibid.

7 *Lomas* (1913) 110 LT 239, CCA, as explained in *Bullock* [1955] 1 All ER 15, [1955] 1 WLR 1, CCA.
8 *Garrett v Arthur Churchill (Glass) Ltd* [1969] 2 All ER 1141 at 1145, per Lord Parker CJ.

23.9   Leaving aside the types of case outlined in the next paragraph (para 23.10), it is no offence to stand by, a mere accidental spectator of the commission of an offence; failure to prevent an offence is not generally enough.[1] On the other hand, there is no problem in convicting the accused as an accomplice where he was present pursuant to a prior agreement that the principal offence be committed[2] or where the evidence clearly shows that he did a positive act of assistance or encouragement, such as shouting out 'fill him with lead' to a gunman who then fires a fatal shot.

However, the situation is more difficult where the evidence does not go so far but merely shows that the accused was present when the principal offence was committed and that his presence was not accidental (ie he was voluntarily and purposely present). In such a case, it will be more difficult for the prosecution to prove the following two elements of liability:

a) That encouragement of the perpetrator in fact occurred;[3] this requires that the perpetrator must have known he was being encouraged by the accused, although it is uncertain whether encouragement by mere presence will do or whether there must be expressions, gestures or actions intended to signify approval. In *Clarkson*[4] the Courts-Martial Appeal Court seems to have taken the former view, but statements in four cases of equal authority, *Coney*,[5] *Allan*,[6] *Jones and Mirrlees*[7] and *Allen v Ireland*[8] may be against it.

b) That the accused intended to encourage the commission of the principal offence (a general requirement dealt with in para 23.17); thus, where an accused has unwittingly encouraged another in fact by his presence, by his misinterpreted words or gestures, or by his silence or non-interference, he cannot be convicted as an accomplice,[9] nor can he be so convicted if he merely nursed a secret intention to assist a perpetrator of the principal offence if necessary.[10]

Where a person's presence at the scene of the principal offence was not accidental but there is no clear evidence of any positive assistance or encouragement, although he offered no opposition to the commission of the offence (which he might reasonably be expected to have), this can afford prima facie, but not conclusive, evidence that the two requirements outlined above are satisfied. In *Coney*,[11] where the accused had been voluntarily present at an illegal prize fight, his conviction as an accomplice to the battery of which the contestants were guilty was quashed because the direction of the judge could have been understood to mean that his voluntary presence was conclusive evidence of these requirements.

1 *Coney* (1882) 8 QBD 534, 51 LJMC 66.
2 *Smith v Reynolds* [1986] Crim LR 559, DC.
3 *Clarkson* [1971] 3 All ER 344, [1971] 1 WLR 1402, Courts-Martial Appeal Court; *Allan* [1965] 1 QB 130, [1963] 2 All ER 897, CCA; *Jones and Mirrlees* (1977) 65 Cr App Rep 250, CA; *Bland* [1988] Crim LR 41, CA .
4 [1971] 3 All ER 344, [1971] 1 WLR 1402, Courts-Martial Appeal Court.
5 (1882) 8 QBD 534, 51 LJMC 66.
6 [1965] 1 QB 130, [1963] 2 All ER 897, CCA.
7 (1977) 65 Cr App Rep 250, CA.
8 [1984] 1 WLR 903, DC.
9 *Coney* (1882) 8 QBD 534, 51 LJMC 66.

10 *Allan* [1965] 1 QB 130, [1963] 2 All ER 897, CCA.
11 (1882) 8 QBD 534, 51 LJMC 66.

23.10 Normally, an act of assistance or encouragement is required. Thus, as has already been mentioned, mere abstention from preventing an offence is generally not enough, but if D has a right of control over E and deliberately fails to prevent E committing an offence, his omission will constitute aiding or abetting. In *Tuck v Robson* [1] a publican, who deliberately made no effort to induce customers to leave his premises after closing time, was held properly convicted of aiding and abetting their consumption of liquor out of hours because of his failure to exercise his right of control. Similarly, the owner of a car, who sits in the passenger seat while another drives it dangerously, can be convicted, as an accomplice, of dangerous driving if he deliberately fails to prevent it. [2]

We saw in Chapter 6 that an omission to act can give rise to criminal liability if the accused was under a duty to do the act in question. This is applicable to the liability of an accomplice. Consequently, for example, a parent who stands by and watches someone commit an offence against his child which he could reasonably prevent may be convicted as an accomplice to that offence, [3] because he would be under a duty to take reasonable steps to intervene, whereas a stranger would not.

The definition of procuring [4] is such as to preclude an omission sufficing for liability on the basis of procuring.

1 [1970] 1 All ER 1171, [1970] 1 WLR 741, DC. Also see *Cassady v Reg Morris (Transport) Ltd* [1975] RTR 470, [1975] Crim LR 398, DC.
2 *Du Cros v Lambourne* [1907] 1 KB 40, 76 LJKB 50, DC.
3 *Gibson and Gibson* (1984) 80 Cr App Rep 24, CA; *Russell and Russell* (1987) 85 Cr App Rep 388, CA.
4 Para 23.6.

23.11 It follows from the foregoing that a person cannot be convicted as an accomplice merely because he knows that the perpetrator is committing the principal offence. This is important, for example, where one spouse knows that the other is committing an offence, or someone knows that his flatmate is committing an offence, and (in each case) does nothing about it, one way or another. *Bland* [1] provides an example. D shared a room with her lover, a drugs dealer. D was charged, as an accomplice, with the offence of being in possession of controlled drugs with intent unlawfully to supply them. It could be inferred that D knew that her lover was dealing in drugs in the room but there was no direct evidence against her that she had assisted or encouraged him in drug-dealing there. Allowing D's appeal against conviction, the Court of Appeal held that the fact that D lived in the same room with the perpetrator of offences involving the possession of drugs was not sufficient evidence from which an inference of assistance in his possession of the drugs could be drawn. As the Court of Appeal recognised, it would have been different if D had had a right of control over the perpetrator and had failed to exercise it.

1 [1988] Crim LR 41, CA. As explained in para 19.31, the accused was not a joint perpetrator of the offence because she was not in joint possession of the drugs.

THE PRINCIPAL OFFENCE

23.12 Although the commission of the principal offence must be proved, proof that the accused's assisting or encouraging was a cause of it (i e that that offence would not have occurred but for that assistance or encouragement) is generally not required,[1] but if the allegation against him is necessarily one of procuring a causal link must be established. As was said in *A-G's Reference (No 1 of 1975)*: 'You cannot procure an offence unless there is a causal link between what you do and the commission of the offence, and here we are told that in consequence of the addition of this alcohol the driver, when he drove home, drove with an excess quantity of alcohol in his body'.[2]

1 *Calhaem* [1985] QB 808, [1985] 2 All ER 266, CA. For a discussion of the question of causation in relation to complicity in an offence, see Smith 'Complicity and Causation' [1986] Crim LR 663.
2 [1975] 2 All ER 684 at 687.

23.13 The need for proof that the principal offence has been committed is shown by *Thornton v Mitchell*.[1] The driver of a bus had to reverse it. In order to do so, he relied on the signals of the conductor. The conductor gave the driver a signal to reverse, which he did, and two pedestrians were knocked down. The driver was summonsed for driving without due care and attention and the conductor for aiding and abetting him. The case against the driver was dismissed, and it was held by the Divisional Court that the conductor could not be convicted of aiding or abetting an offence which had not been committed.

It should be noted that, if the principal offence *has been committed*, there is no difficulty in convicting as an accomplice a person who assisted, encouraged or procured its commission, even though the perpetrator is exempt from *prosecution* for the offence in question. This is shown by *Austin*,[2] where D had assisted a father to snatch his young daughter from his estranged wife. The Court of Appeal held that, since the father *had committed* the offence of child stealing (contrary to s 56 of the Offences against the Person Act 1861, which has since been repealed), D could be convicted as an accomplice to that offence, even though the father could not have been prosecuted because of the proviso to the section, whereby a father was *not liable to be prosecuted* 'on account of getting possession of the child'. The proviso merely meant that the father could not be prosecuted, it did not mean that he had not committed the offence.

1 [1940] 1 All ER 339, 162 LT 296, DC. Also see *Morris v Tolman* [1923] 1 KB 166, 92 LJKB 215, DC.
2 [1981] 1 All ER 374, 72 Cr App Rep 104, CA.

23.14 Where the principal offence is proved, it is immaterial that it is one which the accomplice could not have committed as principal, so that a woman[1] or a boy under fourteen[2] may be guilty of rape as an accomplice.

Difficulties, however, arise in cases where the actus reus of an offence is performed, with another's assistance or encouragement, by someone to whom a defence is available, so that he cannot be said to have committed the offence. As we have seen,[3] normally it is possible to treat the person who does the act as the innocent agent of the other and to convict the latter as perpetrator. However, this is difficult where the offence is one which can be perpetrated personally only by a person conforming to a particular description which does not apply to the person who assists, encourages or procures, or where the offence is defined in terms implying that the act must be committed personally by a perpetrator. For example, if a bachelor exercises duress to induce a married woman to go through a ceremony of marriage with him, logic might seem to require that he should be acquitted on a charge of aiding or abetting bigamy because, the woman being entitled to an acquittal on the ground of duress by threats, she cannot be convicted of perpetrating bigamy; and that, as a bachelor, not 'being married', cannot perpetrate bigamy, he should be acquitted on a charge of perpetrating bigamy through an innocent agent. However, there is authority against both of these suppositions.

In *Bourne*[4] D compelled his wife to have intercourse with a dog. Although his wife was not charged, it was accepted that she would have had the defence of duress by threats if she had been. Nevertheless, the indictment and conviction of D as an accomplice to the buggery were upheld as proper on appeal. Thus, this case shows that a person can be convicted as an accomplice despite the fact that no one else is liable as perpetrator and despite the fact that he could not personally perpetrate the offence. However, it was held in *Cogan*,[5] as the main ground of decision in that case, that a husband, who was cohabiting with his wife and therefore could not at the time have been convicted of personally perpetrating the offence of rape against her,[6] could be convicted as the perpetrator of the rape of her through an innocent agent who lacked the necessary mens rea for rape and was acquitted.

The reasoning in *Bourne* is preferable to the main ground of decision in *Cogan* since (quite apart from difficulties inherent in the idea that a person can have sexual intercourse through an innocent agent) the latter involves convicting a man as a perpetrator for something of which he could not be convicted had he done it personally. According to the reasoning of the main ground in *Cogan*, a woman who caused a man, who was innocent for some reason, to commit a rape would be guilty of rape as a perpetrator, notwithstanding that the definition of rape says that it can only be perpetrated personally by a man.

As an alternative to its main ground of decision, the Court of Appeal in *Cogan* held that the husband could be convicted as an accomplice to rape even though the man who had intercourse lacked the necessary mens rea. This second view, together with *Bourne*, shows that if D intends that the actus reus should be performed by E and induces E to perform it but E has some defence, such as duress by threats or lack of mens rea, D's mens rea may be added to E's actus reus so as to make D liable as an accomplice when he cannot be liable as perpetrator. This assumes, of course, that the definition of the offence admits of such a solution. The problem posed by *Thornton v Mitchell* cannot be solved in this way because a bus driver who is not negligent in following his conductor's signals is not driving without due care and attention and there is thus no actus reus to which the conductor can be regarded as accomplice.

1 *Ram and Ram* (1893) 17 Cox CC 609.
2 *Eldershaw* (1828) 3 C & P 396.
3 Para 23.2.
4 (1952) 36 Cr App Rep 125, CCA.
5 [1976] QB 217, [1975] 2 All ER 1059, CA.
6 The law has been changed in this respect, see para 12.6.

23.15 As we have just seen, the acquittal of the alleged perpetrator does not mean that another person cannot be convicted as accomplice. If D is charged with aiding or abetting the commission of an offence by E, with whom he is put up for trial, it would of course be logically absurd for D to be convicted and E acquitted if the evidence against each was identical.

Nevertheless it sometimes happens that there is stronger evidence against D than against E, or that evidence which is admissible against D is inadmissible against E, and in such an event the conviction of D is not logically incompatible with the acquittal of E.[1]

1 *Humphreys and Turner* [1965] 3 All ER 689, 130 JP 45.

MENS REA

23.16 The mens rea required of an accomplice is not the same as that required of the perpetrator of the principal offence. Instead, what is required is:

a) an intent to assist, encourage or procure the commission by the perpetrator of an act which constitutes or results in the principal offence;
b) knowledge of any circumstance required for the actus reus of the principal offence; and
c) an awareness that the perpetrator is or may be acting, or that he may act, with the mens rea (if any) required for the principal offence.

23.17 *Intent to assist, encourage or procure* This may be proved by proof that it was the accused's aim or purpose to assist, encourage or procure the commission by the perpetrator of the act which constitutes or results in the commission of the principal offence by him. Alternatively, an intent to assist or encourage may be inferred from proof that the accused realised that his conduct does or will virtually certainly (or very highly probably) assist or encourage the perpetrator.[1] The definition of 'procuring', given in *A-G's Reference (No 1 of 1975)*[2] – 'producing by endeavour; setting out to see that the thing happens and taking the appropriate steps to produce that happening' means that it is meaningless to talk of inferring intention from foresight in a case where procuring is the only possible method of participation.

There is recent authority in a case decided by the Divisional Court[3] that, with the possible exceptions of a person accused only of procuring or, perhaps, only of counselling, it might be that an alleged accomplice could be convicted if he was subjectively reckless as to the risk (ie foresaw the possibility) that his conduct might bring about or assist the commission of an act which constitutes or results in the principal offence. This goes beyond the previous authorities and cannot be regarded as representing the true state of the law. If it did it would extend significantly the ambit if the law relating to participation in crime, since many people assist others realising that they may possibly be assisting them to commit an offence but without intending that they should commit it. If it was the law that recklessness as to the risk that one's conduct might bring about or assist the commission of the principal offence was sufficient for liability as an accomplice, the definition of procuring means that it is inconceivable that such recklessness could suffice in a case where procuring was the only possible method of participation. The Divisional Court's reference to the possible exception of procuring seems unduly cautious. There is no warrant for the possible distinction, suggested by the Court in the present context, between counselling and abetting.

It must be emphasised than an accomplice need not desire that the principal offence should be committed, nor (as already indicated) need he act with the purpose to assist or encourage the commission of the principal offence.[4] In *National Coal Board v Gamble*,[5] Devlin J said:

'An indifference to the result of the crime does not of itself negative abetting. If one man deliberately sells to another a gun to be used for murdering a third, he may be indifferent about whether the third lives or dies and interested only in the cash profit to be made out of the sale, but he can still be an aider and abettor.'

This approach was affirmed by the House of Lords in *DPP for Northern Ireland v Lynch*,[6] where it was held that willingness to participate in the offence did not have to be established. In consequence a person who knows of another's criminal purpose and voluntarily aids him in it can be held to have aided that offence, even though he regretted the plan or indeed was horrified by it. Of course, if he was acting under compulsion sufficient to give rise to a defence of duress he would be not guilty on that ground.

What has just been said seems inconsistent with the view taken in *Gillick v West Norfolk and Wisbech Area Health Authority*,[7] a civil case, where the House of Lords held that in certain circumstances a doctor may lawfully give contraceptive advice or treatment to a girl of under 16 without her parent's consent. Such advice or treatment could include cases where the doctor would know that it would encourage or facilitate sexual intercourse by the girl, which would be an offence by the man involved. By holding that the doctor's conduct was lawful, the decision implies that he would not be an accomplice to the man's offence. It is likely that the House of Lords thought that the doctor would not be liable because he lacked an intent to assist or encourage. However, as was stated in para 22.33, *Gillick* is probably better explained as being based impliedly on principles of necessity.

1 *National Coal Board v Gamble* [1959] 1 QB 11, [1958] 3 All ER 203, DC; *Clarkson* [1971] 3 All ER 344, [1971] 1 WLR 1402.
2 [1975] QB 773 at 777.
3 *Blakely and Sutton v DPP* [1991] Crim LR 763, DC.
4 For a contrary view, see Dennis 'The Mental Element for Accessories' in *Essays in Honour of JC Smith* (ed P Smith, 1986) 40. For a further discussion of this matter, see the articles and letters by Dennis and Sullivan in [1988] Crim LR 641 and 649 and [1989] Crim LR 166 and 168.
5 [1959] 1 QB at 23. Also see *A-G v Able* [1984] QB 795 at 811, [1984] 1 All ER 277 at 287. Cf *Fretwell* (1862) Le & Ca 161.
6 [1975] AC 653, [1975] 1 All ER 913, HL. This part of the decision was not overruled by the House of Lords in *Howe* [1987] AC 417, [1987] 1 All ER 771; para 22.23.
7 [1986] AC 112, [1985] 3 All ER 402, HL.

23.18 *Knowledge of any of the circumstances required for the actus reus of the principal offence* To be an accomplice, the accused must also have knowledge of the facts (i e circumstances) essential to constitute the offence which is being committed or is likely to be committed by the perpetrator,[1] although of course he need not know that those facts constitute an offence.[2]

'Knowledge' in this context includes wilful blindness or subjective recklessness,[3] but not *Caldwell*-type recklessness.[4] Where the assistance or encouragement is given before the time of the principal offence, it is more appropriate to speak in terms of whether the accused contemplated as a real possibility that the requisite circumstances would exist at the time of the perpetrator's act constituting or resulting in the principal offence.

1 *Johnson v Youden* [1950] 1 KB 544, [1950] 1 All ER 300, DC; *DPP for Northern Ireland v Maxwell* [1978] 3 All ER 1140, [1978] 1 WLR 1350, HL.
2 *Johnson v Youden*.
3 *Poultry World v Conder* [1957] Crim LR 803, DC; *Carter v Richardson* [1974] RTR 314, DC.
4 It was confirmed in *Blakely and Sutton v DPP* [1991] Crim LR 763, DC, that in *Carter v Richardson* recklessness was being used in its subjective sense.

23.19 *Awareness that the perpetrator is or may be acting, or may act, with the mens rea (if any) required for the principal offence¹* An example of this third element of mens rea can be given by reference to murder, where it suffices that the accused contemplated as a real possibility that the perpetrator might intend to kill or cause grievous bodily harm.² It is somewhat surprising that, while a person can only be convicted as a perpetrator of murder if he intended to kill or cause grievous bodily harm, someone who assists or encourages a person who kills with such an intention can be convicted of murder as an accomplice if he merely contemplated as a real possibility that the other might intentionally kill or cause grievous bodily harm. If a person accused as an accomplice has thought about the possibility of the perpetrator committing an offence but has dismissed it as negligible, he will not have contemplated that offence as a real possibility.³

1 *Chan Wing-siu v R* [1985] AC 168, [1984] 3 All ER 877, PC; *Ward* (1986) 85 Cr App Rep 71, CA; *Hyde, Sussex and Collins* [1990] 3 All ER 892, CA.
2 Ibid. The contrary view expressed in *Barr* (1986) 88 Cr App Rep 362, CA, and *Smith* [1988] Crim LR 616, CA, that, to be an accomplice to murder, the accused must have intended to kill or cause grievous bodily harm is inconsistent with the view taken in previous and subsequent cases which are cited in footnote 1, and cannot be regarded as representing the law.
3 *Chan Wing-siu v R* [1985] AC 168, [1984] 3 All ER 877 at 883.

23.20 *How much must be known?* The accused need not know the details of the offence; it is enough that he knows facts sufficient to indicate the particular type of offence intended and which is later committed.¹ Thus, if someone supplies another with a jemmy with knowledge that it will be used to enter a building as a trespasser in order to steal (i e knowing the particular type of offence), he is guilty of aiding such a burglary committed with the jemmy and it makes no difference that he did not know which premises were going to be burgled or when the burglary was to take place. In *Bainbridge*² D supplied thieves with oxygen cutting equipment purchased by him six weeks earlier. The equipment was used for breaking into a bank, and it was held that D was an accomplice to this offence if he knew, when supplying the equipment, that it was to be used for a 'breaking' offence. D would not have been an accomplice to the bank breaking if he had merely known that the equipment was to be used for some criminal purpose.

Bainbridge was approved and extended by the House of Lords in *DPP for Northern Ireland v Maxwell*.³ In that case it was held that, where the alleged accomplice knows that one or more of a limited range of offences may be committed by the perpetrator, and one of them is actually committed by him, the alleged accomplice can be convicted as a party to it. In this case, D in his car had guided a car containing terrorists to a public house; on arrival D had departed but shortly afterwards one of the terrorists had thrown a bomb into the building. Apparently, D did not know whether the attack would be by firing guns, planting bombs or otherwise. The House of Lords held that D had properly been convicted, as an accomplice, of the statutory offences of doing an act with intent to cause an explosion likely to endanger life and of being in possession of a bomb with the same intent, since he knew that these offences were within the range of offences which the terrorists might perpetrate.

Two questions remain unresolved:

a) Would Bainbridge have been liable, as accomplice, for a large number of breaking offences committed over a considerable period of time with the equipment?

b) What is meant by a 'particular type of offence'? Suppose A lends B a jemmy, thinking that he is going to use it to enter a building as a trespasser in order to steal (burglary), but B uses it to enter a building in order to rape a woman therein. B's conduct would constitute burglary but would A have known the particular type of offence intended? Clearly, if B raped the woman, A could not be convicted as an accomplice to rape but could he be convicted as an accomplice to burglary? This depends on the definition of 'the particular type of offence'.

1 *Bainbridge* [1960] 1 QB 129, [1959] 3 All ER 200, CCA.
2 [1960] 1 QB 129, [1959] 3 All ER 200, CCA.
3 [1978] 3 All ER 1140, [1978] 1 WLR 1350, HL. See also *Hamilton* [1987] NIJB 1, CA of Northern Ireland.

23.21 Although someone who aids, abets, counsels or procures another to commit an offence need not know the details and it generally suffices that he merely knows the type of offence, he is not liable if he has aided, abetted, counselled or procured the perpetrator to commit an offence against a *particular* person or thing and the perpetrator deliberately commits that offence against *another* person or thing. Thus, if D encourages E to assault O with his fists but E deliberately attacks P, instead of O, with his fists, D cannot be convicted as an accomplice to the assault.[1] On the other hand, the mere fact that the perpetrator carried out the offence abetted in a way different from that envisaged does not prevent a person being guilty as an accomplice.[2]

1 Nor is a person guilty as an accomplice if a perpetrator deliberately allows the intended offence to have effect on a person or property which was not the object of the unlawful enterprise: *Saunders and Archer* (1573) 2 Plowd 473, Fost 371.
2 *Williams and Blackwood* (1973) 21 WIR 329.

23.22 *Strict liability offences* The above requirements of mens rea apply even though the offence which the accused is alleged to have assisted, encouraged or procured is one of strict liability. Thus, a person charged as an accomplice to an offence of strict liability can be convicted of it only if he is proved to have known the facts essential to constitute the offence, even though such knowledge is not necessary so far as the perpetrator is concerned.[1]

1 *Thomas v Lindop* [1950] 1 All ER 966, DC; *Johnson v Youden* [1950] 1 KB 544, [1950] 1 All ER 300, DC; *Callow v Tillstone* (1900) 83 LT 411, DC.

23.23 *Unforeseen consequences* Sometimes an accomplice can be liable for the unforeseen consequences of the perpetrator's acts. When two people embark on a joint unlawful enterprise, each is liable for the other's acts done in pursuance of that enterprise to the same extent as the other, and this includes liability for a consequence which results by accident or mistake from the execution of the joint unlawful enterprise.[1] Thus, the fact that, because of a lack of skill or a mistake on the part of the perpetrator in trying to carry out the joint unlawful enterprise, the *intended offence* takes place in relation to an unintended victim or property does not prevent a person being guilty as an accomplice.[2] (Of course, if E, who has been counselled by D to kill P, accidentally kills P in a riot not knowing that he is P, D will not be an accomplice to the homicide because E will not have been involved in the execution of the joint unlawful enterprise at the time of the killing, albeit that he has done what D counselled him to do.)[3]

In many cases where the perpetrator, in trying to carry out the joint unlawful enterprise, accidentally commits the actus reus of an *offence of a different type from that intended* neither he nor the accomplice is liable for that offence because they lack the necessary mens rea in relation to it. However, the situation is different in the case of offences which do not require foresight of their necessary consequence. Particularly relevant here are manslaughter and unlawfully wounding or inflicting grievous bodily harm, contrary to s 20 of the Offences against the Person Act 1861. We have seen, for example, that a person is guilty of manslaughter if death results from the commission by him of an unlawful act likely to harm another, even though he did not foresee that death or grievous bodily harm was likely to result.[4] In the case of such an offence, the principle that both perpetrator and accomplice are liable to the same extent for an accidental consequence of their joint unlawful enterprise produces the following results. If two people agree to assault a man with fists, and he dies in consequence of blows received from one of them, they are each guilty of manslaughter.[4] Similarly, someone who arranges for a criminal abortion to be performed is, like the perpetrator, guilty of manslaughter if the operation results in death.[5]

1 *Anderson and Morris* [1966] 2 QB 110, [1966] 2 All ER 644, CCA.
2 Foster *Crown Law* pp 370–371.
3 *Calhaem* [1985] 2 All ER 266 at 269 and 272.
4 Paras 11.60–11.70.
5 *Creamer* [1966] 1 QB 72, [1965] 3 All ER 257, CCA; *Buck and Buck* (1960) 44 Cr App Rep 213.

23.24 Cases of accidental departure from the joint unlawful enterprise must be sharply distinguished from those where the perpetrator *intentionally* commits an offence (the 'incidental offence') which is not the primary object of the parties. An example would be where D has encouraged E to commit a burglary and to use his jemmy to frighten anyone who comes on him, and E, disturbed by the householder in the course of the burglary, intentionally kills him. The primary object of the parties was the commission of an offence of burglary. E is undoubtedly guilty of murder, as well as of burglary. D is clearly guilty of burglary as an accomplice but is D also guilty of murder as an accomplice?

In such a case it is well established[1] that if an accomplice to an offence has expressly or tacitly agreed to the commission of the incidental offence, as, for example, if D in the above example had tacitly agreed to E using violence to kill or injure seriously anyone who came on him while he was engaged in the burglary, the accomplice is also guilty of the incidental offence committed by the perpetrator.

It has now been established that an accomplice can also be convicted of an incidental offence, even if he has not expressly or tacitly agreed to it, provided it is proved that he contemplated as a real possibility that the perpetrator would commit it but still participated in the enterprise.[2] This is simply an application of the principle of mens rea dealt with in para 23.19. Thus, in the example given above, if it was proved that D contemplated as a real possibility that E might use his jemmy intentionally to kill or do grievous bodily harm to someone who came on him during the burglary D could be convicted as an accomplice to murder, even if it could not be proved that he had expressly or tacitly agreed to its use for that purpose. The most modern authority is *Hyde, Sussex and Collins*,[3] where statements apparently to the contrary in recent cases[4] were explained as not being so.

In *Hyde, Sussex and Collins* D, E and F kicked and punched P outside a pub. P died from a kick to the head. At the trial of D, E and F for murder, all three gave evidence denying that there was any joint enterprise or any intent to do serious harm to P. The jury were directed that if D, E and F intended to do grievous bodily harm to P then all three were guilty of murder, and that if they did not so intend but one of them decided to do it and either of the other two was proved to have foreseen the real possibility that that might be the result of the fight which he was setting in train, then he too shared responsibility for murder. D, E and F's appeals against conviction for murder were dismissed. The Court of Appeal held that, if an accomplice realised, without agreeing to such conduct being used, that a fellow assailant might intentionally kill or do grievous bodily harm, but nevertheless continued to participate with the assailant in the fight, that amounted to a sufficient mental element for the accomplice to be guilty of murder if the assailant killed with malice aforethought in the course of the fight. The reason was that in such circumstances the accomplice has lent himself to the enterprise and by so doing had given assistance and encouragement to the assailant in carrying out an enterprise which the accomplice realised might involve murder.

The rule applied in *Hyde* is as far as the law goes. An accomplice is not liable for an incidental offence if the perpetrator intentionally goes beyond the common object and does something (the incidental offence) which was neither expressly or tacitly agreed to by the accomplice nor contemplated by him as a real possibility.[5]

1 *Betts and Ridley* (1930) 21 Cr App Rep 148, CCA. This rule is recognised in *Chan Wing-siu v R* [1985] AC 168, [1984] 3 All ER 877, PC; *Ward* (1986) 85 Cr App Rep 71, CA; *Hyde, Sussex and Collins* [1990] 3 All ER 892, CA; *Hui-Chi-ming v R* [1991] 3 All ER 897, PC.
2 *Chan Wing-siu* [1985] AC 168, [1984] 3 All ER 877, PC; *Ward* (1986) 85 Cr App Rep 71, CA; *Hyde, Sussex and Collins* [1990] 3 All ER 892, [1990] 3 WLR 1115, CA.
3 [1990] 3 All ER 892, [1990] 3 WLR 1115, CA.
4 *Slack* [1989] 3 All ER 90, [1989] 3 WLR 513, CA; *Wakely* [1990] Crim LR 119, CA.
5 *Anderson and Morris* [1966] 2 QB 119, [1966] 2 All ER 644, CCA; *Lovesey and Peterson* (1969) 53 Cr App Rep 461, CA; *Dunbar* [1988] Crim LR 693, CA.

23.25   In the burglary example given above where E intentionally killed the householder, it may not be proved that the intentional killing or causing of grievous bodily harm was tacitly agreed to by D or contemplated by him as a real possibility, but it may be proved that the use of the jemmy to cause minor harm was tacitly agreed to by him or was within his contemplation as a real possibility. In such a case the better view is that (for reasons discussed in the next paragraph) D can be convicted, as an accomplice, of manslaughter, although E is guilty of murder.[1]

1 *Betty* (1963) 48 Cr App Rep 6, CCA; *Reid* (1975) 61 Cr App Rep 109, CA. Cf *Dunbar* [1988] Crim LR 693, CA.

23.26   Sometimes the perpetrator and the accomplice can be convicted of offences of a different degree:

a) A person who commits the actus reus of murder with malice aforethought, or who with the appropriate mens rea aids and abets another to do so, may have the defence of diminished responsibility which reduces his liability to manslaughter. However, s 2(4) of the Homicide Act 1957 provides that the fact that one party to the killing is not guilty of murder on account of his diminished responsibility does not affect the question whether the killing amounted to murder in the case of any other party to it. In the absence of authority, it is likely that, where the perpetrator of what would otherwise be murder is entitled to a verdict of manslaughter on the ground of provocation,[1] someone who aids or abets him without provocation would be guilty of murder as an accomplice.

b) Some offences, such as murder and manslaughter, and wounding with intent and unlawful wounding contrary to ss 18 and 20 of the Offences against the Person Act 1861, share a common actus reus but are distinguished by the fact that a different state of mind is specified for each offence. Suppose that E is encouraged by D to assault P, which he does, thereby killing P. E is guilty of murder if, knowing that P had an eggshell skull, he intended the assault to kill P; D is guilty only of manslaughter if, not knowing of P's weakness, he did not foresee the risk of death or grievous bodily harm to P.[2] Conversely, an accomplice may be convicted of a greater offence than the perpetrator if he had a greater degree of mens rea, whether or not he was present when the offence was committed.[3] Thus, if D, having decided to bring about P's death, hands a gun to E informing him that it is loaded with blank cartridges and telling him to go and scare P by firing it at him, but the cartridges are live (as D knows) and P is killed, D can be convicted of murder, even though E is guilty only of manslaughter.

1 Paras 11.34–11.46.
2 *Murtagh and Kennedy* [1955] Crim LR 315.
3 *Howe* [1987] AC 417, [1987] 1 All ER 771, HL. Also see *Hui-Chi-ming v R* [1991] 3 All ER 897, PC.

VICTIMS AS AIDERS AND ABETTORS

23.27 Where the purpose of a statutory offence is the protection of a certain class of people, it may be construed as excluding from liability as an accomplice any member of that class who is the willing victim of the offence in that he or she has assisted or encouraged its commission. So far such a construction has only been given in respect of certain sexual offences designed to protect certain classes of people, such as the young or the mentally subnormal, against exploitation to which they are peculiarly vulnerable. It was held in *Tyrrell*,[1] for example, that a girl under 16 cannot be convicted of aiding, abetting, counselling or procuring a man to have unlawful intercourse with her. More recently, a Crown Court judge has ruled that a prositute cannot be convicted of aiding, abetting, counselling or procuring a man to live off her immoral earnings, since the offence was created for the protection of prostitutes.[2] It must be emphasised that the rule acknowleged in *Tyrrell* is a rule of construction and that it does not mean that the victim of an offence can never be convicted of aiding, abetting, counselling or procuring its commission since it only applies to statutory offences designed to protect 'victims' who are peculiarly open to exploitation.[3] Thus, a woman can be convicted as an accomplice to the commission of an unlawful abortion on herself.[4] It remains to be seen how far, if at all, the rule of construction will be applied outside the realm of sexual offences.[5]

1 [1894] 1 QB 710, 63 LJMC 58. Also see *Whitehouse* [1977] QB 868, [1977] 3 All ER 737, CA.
2 *Congdon* (1990), referred to in (1990) 140 NLJ 1221.
3 See articles by Hogan and Williams respectively [1962] Crim LR 683 and [1964] Crim LR 686.

4 *Sockett* (1908) 1 Cr App Rep 101, CCA.
5 Professor Williams has argued that the 'victim rule' is only an example of a wider proposition that the courts may find that a person is excluded from liability as an accomplice to a statutory offence by implication as a matter of reasonable construction: 'Victims and other exempt parties in crime' (1990) 11 Legal Studies 245. This view is not yet supported by the available case law.

ENTRAPMENT AND AGENTS PROVOCATEURS

23.28 *Liability of agent provocateur* A law enforcement officer or some other person may participate in a criminal enterprise solely in order to entrap the other party or parties. Is such a person guilty as an accomplice if the offence is committed? The answer is that he is not liable if his participation goes no further than pretending to concur with the other parties and participating in an offence which has already been 'laid on' and which is going to be committed in any event.[1] On the other hand, it is clear that, if a private citizen, acting independently of the police, instigates an offence which might not otherwise have been committed in order to entrap a criminal, he can be convicted as a party to the offence which the other commits.[2] Some decisions[3] *may* support the view that a law enforcement officer or his agent who acts in this way is not liable as a party, but the view of Lord Salmon in *Sang*[4] to the effect that such a person would be so liable is more recent and it is submitted preferable.

1 *Mullins* (1848) 12 JP 776, 3 Cox CC 526; *McCann* (1971) 56 Cr App Rep 359, CA; *Clarke* (1984) 80 Cr App Rep 344, CA.
2 *Smith* [1960] 2 QB 423, [1960] 1 All ER 256, CCA.
3 *Bickley* (1909) 73 JP 239, 2 Cr App Rep 53, CCA; *Mullins* (1848) 3 Cox CC 526. Contrast *Brannan v Peek* [1948] 1 KB 68, [1947] 2 All ER 572, DC.
4 [1980] AC 402 at 443.

23.29 *No defence of entrapment* Whereas in the United States an accused has a defence if he commits an offence at the instigation of a law enforcement officer, or his agent, unless he was already predisposed to do so,[1] there is no such defence of entrapment in our law, although the fact of police instigation may mitigate sentence.[2] This rule was re-affirmed in 1979 by the House of Lords in *Sang*.[3]

1 *Sorrells v US* 287 US 435 (1932); *Hampton v US* 425 US 484 (1976).
2 *McEvilly* (1973) 60 Cr App Rep 150, CA; *Mealey and Sheridan* (1974) 60 Cr App Rep 59, CA; *Sang* [1980] AC 402, [1979] 2 All ER 1222, HL.
3 [1980] AC 402, [1979] 2 All ER 1222, HL.

23.30 *Admissibility of evidence obtained by entrapment* In *Sang* the House of Lords held that at common law a court has no discretion to exclude evidence of an offence obtained by entrapment, since this would in effect achieve the same result as a defence of entrapment. Subsequently, s 78 of the Police and Criminal Evidence Act 1984 has been enacted, which provides that a court may refuse to admit prosecution evidence if, having regard to all the circumstances, the admission of the evidence would have such an adverse effect on the fairness of the proceedings that the court ought not to admit it. In *Governor of Pentonville Prison, ex p Chinoy*[1] the Divisional Court held that under s 78 a court may refuse to admit evidence on the ground that it has been obtained by entrapment if the admission of the evidence would have the type of adverse effect described by the section.

1 [1992] 1 All ER 317, DC. Before this decision, the case law was divided. See *Harwood* [1989] Crim LR 285, CA (obiter, no discretion); *Gill and Renuana* [1989] Crim LR 358, CA (where reservations were expressed, obiter, on the obiter in *Harwood*).

WITHDRAWAL FROM PARTICIPATION[1]

23.31 There is no doubt that a person can excuse himself from liability for an offence which he has assisted, encouraged, counselled or procured by making an effective withdrawal from participation before it is committed. The question remains however: What is an effective withdrawal? It is clear that mere repentance is not enough, nor is a mere indication of withdrawal from the enterprise.[2] What is required depends on the nature of the accused's participation.

Where a person has merely encouraged the commission of the offence he may excuse himself from liability as an accomplice if before it is committed he expressly countermands or revokes his encouragement.[3] The communication of this must be timely and be such as will serve unequivocal notice on the perpetrator that if he proceeds he does so on his own.[4]

Where a person's participation has taken the form of assisting the commission of the principal offence by supplying an article for use in its commission, something more may be required, although exactly what depends on the circumstances of the case. If the withdrawal occurs some time before the principal offence is committed it can suffice that he communicates to the perpetrator unequivocal notice that if the perpetrator proceeds he does so on his own,[5] but if the withdrawal occurs close to the time of the commission of the offence something more is required.[6] This will vary depending on the circumstances but sometimes physical intervention in an attempt to prevent the commission of the offence will be required. In *Becerra*[7] D, E and F broke into a house to steal. D gave E a knife for use if necessary on anyone who interrupted them. P heard the noise and came downstairs. At this D said, 'There's a bloke coming. Let's go', and jumped out of the window. E then killed P with the knife. D's appeal against conviction for murder, as an accomplice, was dismissed because he had not done enough for his withdrawal from participation to be effective. It is not easy to see what more D could have done, other than to recover the knife, so that this seems to be a case where physical intervention would have been necessary for an effective withdrawal.

1 Lanham 'Accomplices and Withdrawal' (1981) 97 LQR 575.
2 *Becerra* (1975) 62 Cr App Rep 212, CA; *Whitefield* (1984) 79 Cr App Rep 36, CA.
3 *Croft* [1944] 1 KB 295, [1944] 2 All ER 483.
4 *Whitefield*.
5 *Grundy* [1977] Crim LR 543, CA; *Becerra* (1975) 62 Cr App Rep 212, CA.
6 *Becerra*.
7 (1975) 62 Cr App Rep 212, CA.

23.32 The above rules only apply where it is reasonable and practicable to communicate with the perpetrator.[1] Where this is not the case, as where the perpetrator has disappeared after receiving assistance or encouragement from the accused, it would presumably be sufficient for the accomplice to give the police timely notification of the proposed offence.

The mere fact that an accomplice is arrested before the principal offence is perpetrated does not prevent him being convicted of it.[2]

An effective withdrawal from complicity by an accomplice does not negative any possible liability for incitement or conspiracy.[3]

1 *Becerra* (1975) 62 Cr App Rep 212, CA.
2 *Johnson and Jones* (1841) Car & M 218.
3 *Mogul SS Co Ltd v McGregor, Gow & Co* (1888) 21 QBD 544 at 549. Also see *Bennett* (1978) 68 Cr App Rep 168, CA.

UNCERTAINTY[1]

23.33 The mere fact that it is not clear which of two or more people was the perpetrator does not prevent the conviction of all of them if it can be proved beyond reasonable doubt that each must have been either the perpetrator or an accomplice. Thus, it has been held that where either of two drivers, who indulged in unlawful racing in which each was encouraged by the other, might have run down the deceased, both could be convicted of manslaughter.[2] Likewise, where D1 and D2 (who were both over the blood-alcohol level) ran away from a car, were arrested and then claimed that the other had been driving, the Divisional Court held that, if it had been proved that each of the accused knew that the other was unfit to drive, both could have been convicted of driving with excess alcohol, because there would have been proof that each was either the perpetrator or the accomplice of the other.[3] On the other hand, if there is no evidence that each of the two or more possible perpetrators must either have perpetrated the offence or have assisted or encouraged the other(s) to do so, whether by positive acts or by passive assistance or encouragement by failing to exercise a right or duty to control the acts of another,[4] none of them can be convicted of the offence in question.[5]

1 See Griew 'Must have been one of them?' [1989] Crim LR 129; Williams 'Which of you did it?' (1989) 51 MLR 179.
2 *Swindall and Osborne* (1846) 2 Car & Kir 230.
3 *Smith v Mellors and Soar* (1987) 84 Cr App Rep 279 [1987] Crim LR 421, DC.
4 Para 23.10.
5 *Lane and Lane* (1985) 82 Cr App Rep 5, [1985] Crim LR 789, CA; *Russell and Russell* (1987) 85 Cr App Rep 388, CA; *Aston and Mason* [1991] Crim LR 701, CA.

REFORM OF THE LAW OF COMPLICITY

23.34 The account of the law given above discloses the technicalities involved in the law of complicity and the difficulties which it can produce.

These difficulties have led to the interesting suggestion that the law governing complicity should cease to treat the accomplice as a party to the offence which he assists or encourages, and that there should be a general and separate offence of aiding or encouraging crime. In addition to direct acts of encouragement, it should include the doing of acts known to be likely to assist the commission of an offence by another. The fact that the other would or did fail to commit an offence because of insanity, duress etc should be immaterial.[1] Anyone who has had to contend with the technicalities of the law of complicity must surely support this suggestion.

It is unfortunate, but understandable given their aim of restating the law, that in drafting the draft Criminal Code Bill[2] the Law Commission felt unable to take on board this radical suggestion. Under cls 25 to 28 of the draft Bill, the law on participation in crime would be very much as it is now, subject to the clarification or amendment of certain matters.

1 Buxton (1969) 85 LQR 252.
2 Law Commission: A Criminal Code for England and Wales (1989): Law Com No 177; see para 3.21 above.

Liability for criminal conduct of another brought about by one's own act or default

23.35 A common provision in modern consumer protection statutes and similar provisions is that, where the commission of an offence by any person (X) under the statute is due to the act or default of some other person (Y), that other person (Y) is guilty of the offence, whether or not proceedings are brought against X.[1] In such a case, Y's liability is as a perpetrator and rests simply on proof that X committed the offence due to Y's act or default. Thus, liability does not depend on the principles relating to innocent agency or to accomplices.

1 See, for example, the Trade Descriptions Act 1968, s 23; the Health and Safety at Work Act 1974, s 36; the Weights and Measures Act 1985, s 32; the Consumer Protection Act 1987, s 40, and the Food Safety Act 1990, s 20. As to whether X will have a defence of no-negligence under some of these provisions, see para 8.22.

Liability for the unauthorised criminal acts of another

23.36 As we have seen, a person can be guilty under the law of complicity for the offences of another which he has authorised or, if he has a right of control over the perpetrator, which he has deliberately failed to prevent.[1] However, it is a general rule of the criminal law that one person is not responsible for the *acts* of another which he has not authorised and of which he was ignorant, even if that other person is his employee acting in the course of his employment so that civil vicarious liability might arise. Thus, in the old case of *Huggins*[2] the warden of the Fleet prison was acquitted on a charge of murdering one of the inmates, as it appeared that death had been caused by confinement in an unhealthy cell by an employee of the accused without any direction from him and without his knowledge.

By way of contrast, where a statutory offence of strict liability consists of an *omission* to fulfil a duty imposed on the accused, he is *personally* (as opposed to vicariously) liable for that offence as perpetrator if that duty is not fulfilled, even though he has instructed an employee or subordinate of his to ensure that it was fulfilled.[3]

1 Para 23.10.
2 (1730) 1 Barn KB 358, 396, 2 Ld Raym 1574.
3 *Hodge v Higgins* [1980] 2 Lloyd's Rep 589, DC.

EXCEPTIONS TO THE GENERAL RULE

23.37 In certain limited cases a person can be criminally vicariously liable for the acts of others which he has not authorised (nor deliberately failed to prevent) and of which he was ignorant. There are only two exceptions to the general rule in common law offences, both of which are essentially civil in character:

  a) An employer is criminally liable for a public nuisance committed on his property or on the highway by his employee, even if the latter was disobeying orders.[1]
  b) An employer is criminally liable for libels published by his employee

unless he proves that he did not authorise the publication and that the publication was not due to want of due care on his part.[2]

It is, of course, possible for a statute expressly to impose vicarious liability, and this is done in the case of certain statutory offences by putting the words 'no person, himself or by his servant or agent' before the definition of the prohibited conduct.[3] However, most of the instances of vicarious liability for statutory offences have resulted not from the express wording of the statute but from judicial interpretation of it. The courts have used two principles of interpretation to impose vicarious liability for a large number of regulatory statutory offences – extensive construction and delegation.

1 *Stephens* (1866) LR 1 QB 702 at 710.
2 Libel Act 1843, s 7.
3 See, for example, the Licensing Act 1964, ss 59 and 163.

EXTENSIVE CONSTRUCTION

23.38 It has become common for the courts to give an extended construction to certain verbs used in statutory offences, such as 'sell' or 'use', so that the act of an employee is regarded as the act of his employer and thereby the employer is held to have committed the offence physically performed by his employee. Thus, an employer, as well as his driver, has been held guilty of 'using' a motor vehicle with a defective brake.[1] Similarly, an employer has been held guilty of 'exposing for sale' bags of coal containing short weight, although the short weight was due to the wrongdoing of the employee who exposed them for sale.[2] In *Coppen v Moore (No 2)*[3] D owned a number of shops in one of which an assistant, contrary to instructions, sold an American ham as a 'Scotch ham'. D was held guilty of selling goods to which a false trade description had been applied. Lastly, in *Anderton v Rodgers*[4] all 11 members of the governing committee of an unincorporated social club were held vicariously liable for illegal sales of intoxicating liquor, unknown to them and contrary to their instructions, by their bar staff, since the staff were the employees of the committee.

The extensive construction principle is not limited to the relationship of employer and employee but has also been used to impose vicarious liability on a principal for the act of his agent or independent contractor[5] and on a partner for the act of a fellow partner[6]. Moreover, the licensee of licensed premises is liable for illegal sales by bar staff who are not his employees, but like him employed by the owner of the premises, since the act of selling can only be performed by virtue of the licence.[7] On the other hand, members of a board of directors, or of a governing committee, of a body corporate are not vicariously liable for the acts of an employee of the body corporate, even though they have the exclusive power to engage or dismiss that employee[8]. (The body corporate may, of course, be vicariously liable as an employer.) Similarly, the owner of a lorry which is used in a prohibited manner cannot be vicariously liable for that use, even if it is engaged on his business, if the driver is not his employee but that of a third party, such as an employment agency.[9]

Although the matter is not entirely free from doubt, it seems that under the extensive construction principle only the act of the employee etc, and not his mens rea, can be imputed to the employer etc.[10] The result is that, unless the employer has mens rea as to all the elements of the actus reus, the principle is limited to offences of strict liability. Where, as is usually the case, a strict liability offence requires mens rea as to some of its elements, the employer (or, if the employer is a corporation, a controlling officer)[11] must have mens rea as to those elements before the employer can be vicariously liable for the offence under the extensive construction principle.[12]

1 *Green v Burnett* [1955] 1 QB 78, [1954] 3 All ER 273, DC; *Mickleborough v BRS Contracts Ltd* [1977] RTR 389, DC.
2 *Winter v Hinckley and District Co-Operative Society Ltd* [1959] 1 All ER 403, [1959] 1 WLR 182, DC.
3 [1898] 2 QB 306, 67 LJQB 689.
4 [1981] Crim LR 404, DC.
5 *Quality Dairies (York) Ltd v Pedley* [1952] 1 KB 275, [1952] 1 All ER 380, DC; *FE Charman Ltd v Clow* [1974] 3 All ER 371, [1974] 1 WLR 1384, DC.
6 *Clode v Barnes* [1974] 1 All ER 1166, [1974] 1 WLR 544, DC. Contrast *Bennett v Richardson* [1980] RTR 358, DC.
7 *Goodfellow v Johnson* [1966] 1 QB 83, [1965] 1 All ER 941, DC.
8 *Phipps v Hoffman* [1976] Crim LR 315, DC.
9 *Howard v GT Jones & Co* [1975] RTR 150, DC.
10 *Vane v Yiannopoullos* [1965] AC 486, [1964] 3 All ER 820, HL; *Winson* [1969] 1 QB 371 at 382, [1968] 1 All ER 197; *Coupe v Guyett* [1973] 2 All ER 1058, [1973] 1 WLR 669, DC; contrast *Mousell Bros v London and North Western Rly Co Ltd* [1917] 2 KB 836, 87 LJKB 82, DC; *G Newton Ltd v Smith* [1962] 2 QB 278 at 284. In *Yugotours Ltd v Wadsley* (1989) 153 JP 345, DC, the most recent reported case, the court's judgment is ambiguous on the present point. It may state that the employer (a company) could be convicted of the offence of recklessly making a false statement contrary to the Trade Descriptions Act 1968, s 14(1)(b), even though the company had not (via a controlling officer) been reckless. However, the court held that, while there was no specific evidence of recklessness on the part of any such person, there was ample evidence on which an inference of recklessness could be drawn. The better view is that it meant that there was ample evidence on which an inference could be drawn against a controlling officer (and therefore against the employer company), in which case the decision is consistent with the view taken in the text.
11 Para 9.82.
12 See *Wings Ltd v Ellis* [1985] AC 272, [1984] 3 All ER 577, HL.

DELEGATION[1]

23.39 This principle of interpretation appears to be limited to offences which can only be committed by a person of a particular status. The best examples of such offences are the various offences under the Licensing Acts and other Acts, which can only be committed by a licensee. If a licensee delegates his responsibilities as licensee to another, and the delegate acts in breach of one of the delegated responsibilities, his acts *and state of mind* are imputed to the delegator. In *Allen v Whitehead*,[2] for example, the licensee of a refreshment house delegated control of it to an employee who, in the licensee's absence and contrary to his express instructions, allowed prostitutes to enter. The licensee was convicted of 'knowingly suffering prostitutes to meet together in his house and remain therein', contrary to s 44 of the Metropolitan Police Act 1839, the acts and mens rea of the delegate employee being imputed to him.

Where the offence is one of strict liability, the extensive construction principle generally suffices to impose vicarious liability and the delegation principle normally comes into play only if the statute uses words which import a full requirement of mens rea.[3]

The delegation principle is not limited to cases where the delegate is the employee of the delegator. In *Linnett v Metropolitan Police Comr* [4] it was held that one co-licensee was vicariously liable where his co-licensee, to whom he had delegated the management of a refreshment house owned by their employer, had knowingly permitted disorderly conduct there.

1 Pace 'Delegation – A Doctrine in Search of a Definition' [1982] Crim LR 627.
2 [1930] 1 KB 211, 99 LJKB 146, DC.
3 *Winson* [1969] 1 QB 371 at 382, [1968] 1 All ER 197.
4 [1946] KB 290, [1947] 1 All ER 380, DC.

23.40 It is necessary that there should have been a complete delegation of the licensee's managerial functions and responsibilities. Thus, the House of Lords held in *Vane v Yiannopoullos*[1] that a restaurateur, who was permitted to sell intoxicants only to customers consuming a meal, and who had told a waitress to serve such customers only, and then withdrawn to the basement, was not guilty of any infringement by the waitress of what is now s 161(1) of the Licensing Act 1964 (which penalises licensees who knowingly sell intoxicants to unpermitted persons). The restaurateur had retained control of the restaurant and had not delegated this to the waitress. On the other hand, if there has been a complete delegation of managerial functions and responsibilities, it is irrelevant that this only relates to part of the licensed premises or that the delegator licensee is still on the premises.[2]

In *Vane v Yiannopoullos* Lords Morris and Donovan doubted the validity of the delegation principle, but in the light of its continued application it must still be regarded as part of the law.[3]

1 [1965] AC 486, [1964] 3 All ER 820, HL.
2 *Howker v Robinson* [1973] QB 178, [1972] 2 All ER 786, DC. Contrast Lords Reid and Hodson in *Vane v Yiannopoullos* [1965] AC 486 at 497–498 and 510.
3 See, for example, *Winson* [1969] 1 QB 371, [1968] 1 All ER 197, CA; *Howker v Robinson* [1973] QB 178, [1972] 2 All ER 786, DC.

COMMENTS ON VICARIOUS LIABILITY

23.41 *Within the scope of his employment or authority* Vicarious liability can arise only if the employee or delegate etc was acting within the scope of his employment or authority. Doing an authorised activity in an unauthorised way falls within such scope, but a wholly unauthorised activity does not. In *Coppen v Moore (No 2)*[1] an employer was held vicariously liable for a sale effected by a sales assistant in an unauthorised manner, but in *Adams v Camfoni*[2] the accused licensee was acquitted of supplying intoxicants outside permitted hours because the supply had been effected by a messenger boy who had no authority to sell anything at all.

1 [1898] 2 QB 306, 67 LJQB 689. Also see *Allen v Whitehead* [1930] 1 KB 211, 99 LJKB 146, DC; *Anderton v Rodgers* [1981] Crim LR 404, DC.
2 [1929] 1 KB 95, 98 LJKB 40, DC. Also see *Barker v Levinson* [1951] 1 KB 342, [1950] 2 All ER 825, DC.

23.42 *Liability of employee or delegate* The liability of the employee or delegate etc depends on the wording of the particular statute. If it specifies that only a person with a particular status, such as a licensee, can commit the offence, an employee or delegate who actually commits the act can be convicted only as an accomplice of that person, who is vicariously liable as perpetrator.[1] Where the statute does not specify a particular type of perpetrator, the employee etc can be convicted as perpetrator jointly with the person held vicariously liable.[2] This distinction is important because, if the offence in question is one of strict liability, the employee can be convicted in the first type of case only if he has mens rea, since a person can be convicted as an accomplice to an offence of strict liability only if he has mens rea.[3]

23.42 *Participation*

1 *Griffiths v Studebakers Ltd* [1924] 1 KB 102, 93 LJKB 50, DC.
2 *Green v Burnett* [1955] 1 QB 78, [1954] 3 All ER 273, DC.
3 Para 23.22.

23.43 *No vicarious liability as an accomplice or for attempt* A person cannot be vicariously liable for aiding or abetting[1] or for attempting to commit[2] an offence.

1 *Ferguson v Weaving* [1951] 1 KB 814, [1951] 1 All ER 412, DC.
2 *Gardner v Akeroyd* [1952] 2 QB 743, [1952] 2 All ER 306, DC.

23.44 *Statutory defences* There are several statutory defences which are open to employers and others who may be vicariously liable. The courts have refused to read into statutes, construed by them as imposing vicarious liability for offences, an exception protecting employers who show due diligence in the management of their business in cases where nothing which they could reasonably be expected to do would have prevented the commission of the offence by the employee. Accordingly, *some* statutes contain an express provision for defences of this nature in relation to offences under them, of which examples are s 34 of the Weights and Measures Act 1985 and s 24 of the Trade Descriptions Act 1968. There is much to be said for having a *general* defence of due diligence in all cases of vicarious criminal liability.[1]

1 Para 8.23.

23.45 *Justification of vicarious liability* Criminal responsibility is generally regarded as essentially personal in nature. The exceptional principles, whereby a person can be convicted of an offence of which he was ignorant and which was actually committed by another, can be justified only on the basis of the need to enforce modern regulatory legislation, such as that governing the sale of food and drugs or intoxicating liquor.[1] The courts consider that the most effective way of enforcing such legislation is to impose on the employer liability for contravention by employees in order to encourage him to prevent them infringing the legislation.[2] This justification calls for two comments. First, the assumption that the imposition of vicarious liability is the most effective method of securing compliance with the statute is unproved. Secondly, vicarious liability would be more acceptable if it were limited generally to employers who had been negligent in failing to prevent the contravention. Another justification put forward occasionally is that some offences can be committed only by a particular person, such as a licensee, and that without vicarious liability such an offence would be rendered nugatory where that person acted through others. The obvious answer is to amend the statute, not for the judges to impose vicarious liability.

1 See, for example, *Gardner v Akeroyd* [1952] 2 QB 743 at 751.
2 *Reynolds v GH Austin & Sons Ltd* [1951] 2 KB 135, [1951] 1 All ER 606, DC; *Tesco Supermarkets Ltd v Nattrass* [1971] 2 All ER 127 at 151; para 8.19.

23.46 Under cl 29 of the the draft Criminal Code Bill, vicarious liability would be as stated above, except that the delegation principle would only apply to offences existing when the Bill was enacted.[1]

1 Law Commission: A Criminal Code for England and Wales (1989): Law Com No 177; see para 3.21 above.

Index

Abduction, 12.25, 12.26
Abortion, 11.75–11.81
  child destruction, and, 11.83
  draft Criminal Code, 11.81
  intent to procure miscarriage, 11.78
  means, 11.77
  "unlawfully", 11.79, 11.80
Accident
  proof, and, 7.16
Accomplices, 23.3–23.34
  accidental departure from joint unlawful enterprise, 23.24
  acquittal of alleged perpetrator, 23.15
  agents provocateurs, 23.28–23.30. *See also* ENTRAPMENT
  awareness that perpetrator is acting with meas rea for principal offence, 23.19
  conviction of offences of different degree, 23.26
  entrapment, 23.28–23.30. *See also* ENTRAPMENT
  inchoate offence, and, 23.4
  indictment, and, 23.3
  intent to assist, encourage or procure, 23.17
  knowledge of circumstances required for actus reus of principal offence, 23.18
  mens rea, 23.16–23.26
    how much must be known, 23.20, 23.21
  offence where accomplice could not be principal, 23.14
  principal offence, 23.12–23.15
  proof in relation to, 23.5
  reform of law, 23.34
  strict liability offences, 23.22
  tacit agreement, and, 23.25
  uncertainty, 23.33
  unforeseen consequences 23.23–23.26
  withdrawal from participation, 23.31, 23.32
Actual bodily harm
  assault occasioning, 10.17
Actus non facit reum, nisi mens sit rea, 6.1, 6.2
Actus reus, 6.1 *et seq*
  acts, 6.6
  circumstances, 6.17
  consequences, 6.16
  contemporaneity with mens rea, 6.69, 6.70

Actus reus—continued
  defences, and, 6.21
  events, 6.15
  express offences of omission, 6.8
  justification, and, 6.20
  meaning, 6.5
  omissions, 6.7–6.14. *See also* OMISSIONS
  whole must be proved, 6.18
Administration of justice, offences against, 16.1–16.36
Affray, 18.15–18.19
  actus reus, 18.16–18.18
  conduct such as would cause person of reasonable firmness to fear for safety, 18.18
  mens rea, 18.19
  use or threat of violence towards another, 18.17
Agents provocateurs, 23.28–23.30. *See also* ENTRAPMENT
Aggravated burglary, 14.15
Aggravated trespass, 15.33–15.39
  actus reus, 15.37
  arrest, 15.41
  defences, 15.39
  direction to leave, 15.34, 15.35
  mens rea, 15.38
Aiding, abetting, counselling or procuring, 23.6–23.11
  abetting, 23.6
  aiding, 23.6
  counselling, 23.6
  forms of, 23.8
  knowledge, 23.11
  omission, 23.10
  positive act, 23.10
  presence, 23.9
  procuring, 23.6
  time of, 23.7
  victims as, 23.27
Aircraft
  offences on board, 6.79
Appeal, 5.25–5.36
  Court of Appeal, to. *See* COURT OF APPEAL
  Crown Court, from, 5.27–5.34
  Crown Court, to, 5.25

Appeal—*continued*
  Divisional Court, to, 5.26, 5.27
  House of Lords, to, 5.35
  insanity, and, 9.25
  magistrates' court, from, 5.25, 5.26
Appellate courts, 2.7
Appropriation
  obtaining property by deception, and, 14.44, 14.45–14.47
Arrest, 4.12, 4.14–4.18
  arrestable offences, 4.14
  breach of the peace, for, 4.16
  non-arrestable offences, 4.14
  unlawful, 4.17
  warrant of, 4.12
Assault, 10.9–10.17. *See also* BATTERY
  actual bodily harm, occasioning, 10.7
  actus reus, 10.10
  aggravated, 10.17
  element of hostility, 10.15
  indecent. *See* INDECENT ASSAULT
  mens rea, 10.14, 10.15
  prosecution, 10.16
  punishment, 10.16
  trial, 10.16
  unlawful force, 10.13
Assisting offenders, 16.1–16.3
  absence of lawful authority or reasonable excuse, 16.2
  act done by accused, 16.2
  commission of arrestable offence, 16.2
  elements, 16.2
  knowledge or belief that offence committed by principal, 16.2
  punishment, 16.3
Attempt, 21.52–21.81
  abandonment, 21.78
  actus reus, 21.64
    "act more than merely preparatory", 21.64–21.67
    "last act" case, 21.67
  draft Criminal Code, 21.81
  impossibility, and, 21.68–21.73
  mens rea, 21.56–21.63
    circumstances, as to, 21.61
    conditional intent, 21.63
    ignorance of law no defence, 21.63
    "intention", 21.57–21.63
    intention as to consequence, 21.60
    recklessness, 21.61
  "objective innocence", and, 21.70
  prosecution, 21.74
  punishment, 21.76
  scope of offence, 21.53–21.55
  specific offences, 21.77
  successful, 21.79, 21.80
  trial, 21.75
Attempted murder
  duress, and, 22.24
Attempting to pervert course of justice, 16.32–16.34
  examples, 16.33, 16.34

Automatism, 9.41–9.49
  insane and non-insane, 9.45–9.47
    burden of proof, 9.47
  involuntary act, 9.42
  involuntary event, 9.44
  involuntary omission, 9.43
  negligence, and, 9.49
  self-induced, 9.48, 9.49

Bail
  committal proceedings, and, 4.25–4.29
Bail, offences relating to, 16.35, 16.36
  absconding, 16.35
  agreement to indemnify sureties, 16.36
Basic intent, 6.42
  intoxication, and, 9.54–9.58
Battery, 10.9–10.17. *See also* ASSAULT
  actus reus, 10.11–10.12
  element of hostility, 10.15
  mens rea, 10.14, 10.15
  unlawful force, 10.13
Bigamy, 19.2–19.10
  actus reus, 19.3–19.6
  defences, 19.8
  first marriage, 19.4
  first spouse alive at time of second ceremony, 19.5
  mens rea, 19.7
  mistake, and, 7.32
  related offences, 19.10
  second ceremony, 19.6
Blackmail, 14.71–14.75
  demand with menaces, 14.72, 14.73
  menaces, 14.73
  "unwarranted", 14.75
  "with a view to gain or intent to cause loss", 14.74
Blasphemous libel
  strict liability, 8.3
Breach of the peace
  arrest for, 4.16
Breath test. *See* DRINKING AND DRIVING
Buggery, 12.27–12.31
  draft Criminal Code, 12.31
  male homosexual, 12.28
  offences, 12.29
  punishment, 12.29
  related offences, 12.30
Burden of proof, 7.3–7.9
  accused, on, 7.5–7.8
    express statutory provision, 7.7
    implied statutory provision, 7.8
  adducing evidence, 7.9
  automatism, 9.47
  defence of insanity, and, 7.6
  defences, and, 7.4
  murder, and, 7.3
Burglary, 14.7–14.15
  building or part of building, 14.10
  definition, 14.7
  entry, 14.8
  first offence, 14.7–14.12
  mens rea, 14.11, 14.12

Burglary—*continued*
second offence, 14.13
trespasser, 14.9
trespassory entry, 14.14

Capacity, 9.1–9.91
Careless cycling, 20.15
Careless driving, 20.14
Care or supervision proceedings, 5.24
Causing death by dangerous driving, 20.13
Causing wasteful employment of police, 16.6
Certiorari, 5.36
Characteristics of criminal offences, 1.1–1.7
Child destruction, 11.82, 11.83
abortion, and, 11.83
Children, 9.1–9.3
aged 10–14, 9.2
doli incapax, 9.1
indecency with, 12.21
indecent photographs of, 19.19–19.21
sexual offences, and, 9.3
Civil law
aims of, 1.3
wrongs under, 1.3–1.5
Classification of offences, 3.30–3.32
method of trial, by, 3.31
Codification, 3.21
Committal proceedings, 4.19–4.29
bail, 4.25–4.29
custody time limits, 4.23
"notice of transfer", 4.21
reporting, 4.24
Common law, 3.2–3.13
general principles of criminal liability, 3.5
offences, 3.3, 3.4
precedent, doctrine of, 3.6. *See also*
PRECEDENT, DOCTRINE OF
sentence, 3.4
theoretical basis, 3.12
Computer misuse, 15.59–15.63
jurisdiction, 15.63
unauthorised access to computer material,
15.60
unauthorised access with intent, 15.61
unauthorised modification of computer
material, 15.62
Concealing, 16.4, 16.5
elements, 16.5
Consent, 10.2–10.8
ambit of, 10.5, 10.6
apparent, 10.7
implied, 10.8
public interest, and, 10.4
valid, 10.3
Conspiracy, 21.11–21.51
acquittal of all save one, 21.14
agreement, 21.12, 21.13
common law, 21.36
impossibility, 21.50
punishment, 21.51
trial, 21.51
statutory, 21.15–21.35
actus reus, 21.16–21.21

Conspiracy—*continued*
statutory—*continued*
aim of agreement, 21.29
draft Criminal Code, 21.35
exemptions from liability, 21.30
husband and wife, 21.30
ifs and buts, 21.19
impossibility, 21.18
intended victim, 21.30
mens rea, 21.22–21.28
additional, 21.26–21.28
agreement being carried out, as to,
21.25
circumstances of substantive offence,
as to, 21.23, 21.24
substantive offence being committed,
as to, 21.25
"offence", 21.21
persons under age of criminal responsibility, 21.30
prosecution, 21.31
punishment, 21.33
substantive offence committed, where,
21.34
trial, 21.32
to corrupt public morals, 21.46–21.49
to defraud, 21.37–21.45
basic definition of fraud, 21.38
jurisdiction, 21.43
parties, 21.42
public duty, and, 21.40, 21.41
scope, 21.45
to outrage public decency, 21.46–21.49
Contempt of court, 16.12–16.31
conduct intended to impede or prejudice
course of justice, 16.23
disclosure, 16.29, 16.30
in face of court, 16.24
jurors, reprisals against, 16.25
obstructing officer of court, 16.26
publication of information relating to proceedings in private, 16.28
publications tending to interfere with
course of justice in particular proceedings, 16.13–16.22
active legal proceedings, 16.16
defences, 16.19
discussion in general public interest,
16.22
publication, 16.14
reports of public legal proceedings,
16.20–16.22
strict liability, 16.18
substantial risk of serious impediment or
prejudice to course of justice, 16.15
who can commit contempt, 16.17
scandalising judge or court, 16.27
strict liability, 8.3
trial, 16.31
witnesses, reprisals against, 16.25
Contract law
purpose of, 1.3

Conveyance
meaning, 14.19
Corporations, 9.81–9.90
directors, 9.90
false accounting, and, 14.70
general rule, 9.81
human body compared, 9.85
identification, 9.84–9.86
offences to which principle cannot apply,
9.87
statutory defences, and, 9.89
liability, 9.82
manager, 9.86
misuse of drugs, 19.35
racial hatred, and, 18.53
social policy, and, 9.88
Corporation sole
property of, 13.50
Counterfeiting, 15.58–15.63
Court of Appeal, 5.28–5.34
appeal against conviction, 5.28–5.30
appeal against sentence, 5.31
appeal to House of Lords, 5.35
Criminal Division, 2.8
reference by Home Secretary, 5.32
reference on point of law, 5.34
venire de novo, 5.33
Courts, 2.1–2.10
Crime
definition, 1.1
criticism of, 1.6
same conduct civil wrong and, 1.5
Criminal damage, 15.1–15.20
actus reus, 15.7–15.10
aggravated offence, 15.13–15.16
"recklessness", 15.15
damage, 15.8
destination, 15.8
draft Criminal Code, 15.20
how triable, 15.2–15.5
limit on prosecutions, 15.6
mens rea, 15.11, 15.12
possessing anything with intent to destroy
or damage property, 15.18, 15.19
property, 15.9
property "belonging to another", 15.10
simple offences, 15.1–15.12
threats, 15.17
"without lawful excuse", 15.12
Criminal liability, 6.1–6.80
Criminal libel
strict liability, 8.3
Criminal procedure
before trial, 4.1–4.29
Criminal proceedings, 1.5
Crown
proceedings on behalf of, 1.7
Crown Court, 2.5, 2.6
appeal from, 5.27, 5.34
appeal to, 5.25
functions, 2.5
judges, 2.6
unfitness to be tried, 9.5–9.10

Dangerous cycling, 20.12
Dangerous driving, 20.10–20.13
causing death by, 20.13
definition, 20.11
Deception offences, 14.26–14.64
Defences
actus reus, and, 6.21
mistake, and, 7.26–7.33
Diminished responsibility, 9.32
"abnormality of mind", 9.35
burden of proof, 9.34
concept of, 9.32
effect of abnormality of mind, 9.37
evidence, 9.38, 9.39
intoxication, and, 9.71
premeditated killing, and, 9.33
reform, proposals for, 9.40
specified causes, 9.36
Diplomatic immunity, 4.9
Director of Public Prosecutions, 4.2
Directors
liability, 9.90
Disease of the mind, 9.15–9.17. *See also*
INSANITY, DEFENCE OF
Disorderly conduct
meetings, at, 18.67
Divisional Court, 2.7
appeal to, 5.26, 5.27
appeal to House of Lords, 5.35
Drinking and driving, 20.16–20.36
causing death by careless driving, and,
20.22
cycling when unfit, 20.21
driving, attempting to drive or being in
charge with excess alcohol, 20.23–
20.27
elements, 20.24
evidence, 20.24
"screening" breath test, 20.25–20.27
driving or attempting to drive when unfit,
20.17
evidence, 20.20
evidence in proceedings, 20.31–20.33
hip-flask defence, 20.33
failure to provide specimen, 20.34–20.36
failure, 20.35
without reasonable excuse, 20.36
in charge when unfit, 20.18
power of arrest, 20.19
provision of specimen for analysis, 20.28
blood, 20.20
evidential breath specimens, 20.29
urine, 20.30
uninsured use, 20.37, 20.38
Duress, 22.16–22.17
attempted murder, and, 22.24
circumstances, of. *See* NECESSITY
extent of defence, 22.22
immediacy, 22.20
mistake, and, 7.29
murder, and, 22.23
nature of threat, 22.17
objective test, 22.18

Duress—*continued*
  reform, proposals for, 22.27
  subjective test, 22.18
  threats, by, 22.16–22.17
  treason, and, 22.25
  unavoidable dilemma, 22.19–22.21
  voluntary membership of criminal association, 22.26
Dutch courage, 9.72

Entering and remaining on property, 15.21–15.32
  adverse occupation of residential premises, 15.28–15.31
    actus reus, 15.29
    defences, 15.31
    mens rea, 15.30
  diplomatic premises, 15.32
  displaced residential occupier, 15.27
  violence for securing entry, 15.22–15.27
    actus reus, 15.23, 15.24
    mens rea, 15.25
    without lawful authority, 15.26
  "premises", 15.21
Entrapment, 23.28–23.30
  admissibility of evidence obtained by, 23.30
  no defence, 23.29
European Community
  legislation of, 3.20
European Court, 2.10
Evasion of liability by deception, 14.56–14.64
  section 2(1)(A), 14.57, 14.58
    actus reus, 14.57
    mens rea, 14.58
  section 2(1)(B), 14.59–14.61
    actus reus, 14.60
    mens rea, 14.61
  section 2(1)(C), 14.62–14.64
    actus reus, 14.63
    mens rea, 14.64

False accounting, 14.69, 14.70
  liability of controlling officer for offence by corporation, 14.70
False instrument, 15.49
  copying, 15.49–15.51
    actus reus, 15.50
    mens rea, 15.51
  money orders, 15.53–15.57
  passports, 15.53–15.57
  share certificates, 15.53–15.57
  using, 15.52
Felonies, 3.32
Firearms, 18.74–18.84
  acquisition, 18.75–18.78
  having with intent, 18.83
  possession, 18.75–18.78
  possession at time of arrest, 18.82
  possession at time of offences, 18.82
  possession with intent to endanger life, 18.80
  purchase, 18.75–18.78

Firearms—*continued*
  use or possession for unlawful purpose, 18.79
  use to resist arrest, 18.81
Foresight
  intention, and, 6.27–6.30
Forgery, 15.41–15.48
  actus reus, 15.43–15.46
  false instrument, 15.45, 15.46
  mens rea, 15.47, 15.48
  "instrument", 15.44

Going equipped for stealing, 14.92–14.95
  articles "made or adapted", 14.93
  causation, 14.95
  general intention, 14.94
Grievous bodily harm, 10.18–10.27
  draft Criminal Code, 10.27
  section 18, 10.23–10.26
    actus reus, 10.24
    mens rea, 10.25, 10.26
  section 20, 10.19–10.22
    actus reus, 10.20, 10.21
    mens rea, 10.22
Gross indecency, 12.32–12.35
  definition, 12.33
  offences, 12.35
  punishment, 12.35
  when not offence, 12.34

Handling, 14.76–14.91
  actus reus, 14.78–14.87
  arranging to receive, 14.83
  arranging to undertake or assist in retention, removal, disposal or realisation of stolen goods, 14.86
  assisting in retention, removal, disposal or realisation of stolen goods, 14.85
  dishonesty, and, 14.90
  forms of, 14.81–14.86
    limitation, 14.87
  knowledge or belief, 14.88
    proof of, 14.89
  meaning, 14.76
  mens rea, 14.88–14.90
  public advertisment of reward, and, 14.91
  receiving, 14.82
  stolen goods, 14.78–14.80
    "the thief", 14.80
  theft, overlap with, 14.77
  undertaking retention, removal, disposal or realisation of stolen goods, 14.84
Harassment, alarm or distress
  meaning, 18.36, 18.37
Home Secretary
  reference to Court of Appeal, 5.32
Homicide, 11.1–11.83
  actus reus, 11.1
  beginning and ending of life, 11.3, 11.4
  causation, 11.8
  contributions by third parties, 11.11
  contributory negligence, 11.12
  intervening acts by third party, 11.17

Homicide—*continued*
  intervening events, 11.16
  intervening medical treatment, 11.18
  judge and jury, function of, 11.19
  killing, 11.6, 11.7
    year and a day rule, 11.7
  pre-existing conditions in victim, 11.13
  principles of legal attribution, 11.9–11.18
  "under the Queen's peace", 11.5
  unlawful killing, 11.20
    advancement of justice, 11.20
    public or private defence, 11.20
  victim, 11.2–11.5
  victim's neglect of tratment or maltreat-
    ment of self, 11.15
  where victim dies in trying to escape, 11.14
Homosexual offences
  restriction on prosecutions, 12.36
House of Lords, 2.9
  appeal to, 5.35
  doctrine of precedent, and, 3.8–3.10

Ignorance
  proof, and, 7.17
Ignorance of law, 6.72–6.74
Ignorance of morals, 6.75
Incest, 12.14
  incitement to, 12.22
Inchoate offences, 21.1–21.81
  accomplice, and, 23.4
Incitement, 21.2–21.10
  actus reus, 21.3
  draft Criminal Code, 21.10
  impossibility, 21.5–21.8
  incest, to, 12.22
  mens rea, 21.4
  possibility, 21.5–21.8
  punishment, 21.9
  trial, 21.9
Indecency, 12.15–12.24
  Criminal Code Bill, 12.23
Indecency with children, 12.21
Indecent assault, 12.15–12.20
  actus reus, 12.16
  mens rea, 12.18–12.20
  motive, and, 12.20
  without consent, 12.17
Indecent exposure, 12.24
Indictment
  trial on. *See* TRIAL ON INDICTMENT
Infanticide, 11.72–11.74
Innocent agency, 23.2
Insanity, defence of, 9.12–9.31
  appeal, and, 9.25
  automatism, and, 9.45–9.47
  burden of proof, and, 7.6
  defect of reason, 9.18
  disease of the mind, 9.15–9.17
  hospital admission order, 9.24
  ignorance of nature and quality of act,
    9.19–9.21
  insane delusion, 9.23
  intoxication, and, 9.69–9.71

Insanity, defence of—*continued*
  judge, role of, 9.13
  jury, role of, 9.22
  M'Naghten Rules, 9.12
    criticisms, 9.29
    use of, 9.26–9.27
  prosecution, and, 9.28
  reform, proposals for, 9.31
  requirements, 9.14–9.23
  summary trials, 9.30
  verdict, 9.24–9.27
Institution of proceedings, 4.10
  laying information, 4.11
  summons, 4.13
  warrant of arrest, 4.12
Intention, 6.23–6.42
  basic, 6.42
  consequence, as to, 6.54–6.57
  degree of risk which must be foreseen,
    6.33, 6.34
  desire, and, 6.26
  foresight, and, 6.27–6.30
  further, 6.40
  inference, 6.31–6.39
    offences where may not be drawn, 6.38
  meaning, 6.24, 6.25
  proof of, 6.31
  purpose, and, 6.32
  "purposive', 6.39
  questions for jury to ask themselves, 6.35
  specific, 6.41
  ulterior, 6.40
  uncertainty, and, 6.37
Intoxication, 9.50–9.80
  basic intent, and, 9.54–9.58
    determination of, 9.63
  belief or suspicion, and, 9.67
  Caldwell-type recklessness, and, 9.58
  diminished responsibility, and, 9.71
  disease of the mind, and, 9.69, 9.70
  draft Criminal Code, and 9.80
  Dutch courage, 9.72
  insanity, causing, 9.69–9.71
  involuntary, 9.73–9.78
    non-dangerous drugs, 9.76
    not self-induced, 9.74
    prescribed drugs, 9.75
    reckless taking of drugs, 9.77, 9.78
  judicial policy, 9.65
  mistake, and, 9.59–9.61
  mistake as to defence, 9.66–9.68
  proof of mens rea, and, 9.62
  Public Order Act 1986, 9.79
  rape, and, 9.56
  self-defence, and, 9.59–9.61
  specific intent, and, 9.52, 9.53
    determination of, 9.63
    list of offences, 9.64
  statutory defences, and, 9.68
  voluntary, 9.51
Involuntary act. *See* AUTOMATISM

Judicial Committee of Privy Council
  precedent, doctrine of, 3.11
Jurisdiction, 4.7–4.9, 6.76–6.80
  extra-territorial, 6.80
  offences on board ships and aircraft, 6.79
  place, 4.8
  territorial, 6.77
    limits, 6.78
  time, 4.7
Jury, 5.8, 5.9
  proof, and, 7.2
Justification
  actus reus, and, 6.20
Juvenile court, 5.23
Juveniles
  trial of, 5.22–5.24

Knowledge, 6.58–6.62
  circumstances, of, 6.58
  degrees of, 6.59
  extent of, 6.61
  forgotten, 6.62
  specified circumstances, as to, 6.60
  wilful blindness, and, 6.59

Legal wrong
  meaning, 1.2
Legislation, 3.14–3.21
  European Communities, of, 3.20
  statute, 3.14–3.18
  subordinate, 3.19
Liability for unauthorised acts of another, 23.36–23.46. *See also* VICARIOUS LIA-
  BILITY

Magistrates' Courts, 2.2–2.4
  appeal from, 5.25, 5.26
  composition, 2.2
  examining magistrates, 2.4
  functions, 2.3, 2.4
  offences triable either way, 2.3
  summary offences, 2.3
  unfitness to be tried, 9.11
Making off without payment, 14.65–14.68
  actus reus, 14.66
  mens rea, 14.67
Mandamus, 5.36
Manslaughter, 11.30–11.71. *See also* HOMI-
  CIDE
  Caldwell-type recklessness, 11.55–11.59
  gross negligence, 11.53
  involuntary, 11.50–11.71
  killing by unlawful and dangerous act, 11.60–11.70
    commission of unlawful act, 11.62–11.64
    elements, 11.61
    legally recognised excuse, and, 11.64
    objective test, 11.68
    physical harm, 11.69
    unlawful act "directed at another", 11.66
    unlawful act must be cause of death, 11.65
    unlawful act must be dangerous, 11.67–11.70

Manslaughter—*continued*
  "motor manslaughter", 11.57
  provocation. *See* PROVOCATION
  Seymour, decision in, 11.54–11.59
    effect on pre-existing law, 11.59
  subjective recklessness as to death or bodily harm, 11.52
  suicide pacts. *See* SUICIDE PACTS
  voluntary, 11.31–11.49
Marital coercion, 22.28–22.30
  person making threat, 22.30
  proposed abolition, 22.29
Medical treatment
  homicide, and. *See* HOMICIDE
Meetings
  disorderly conduct at, 18.67
Mens rea, 6.1 *et seq*
  aim of requirement, 6.3
  contemporaneity with actus reus, 6.69, 6.70
  intention. *See* INTENTION
  meaning, 6.22
  mistake negativing, 7.19–7.23
  motive, and, 6.71
  negation of, 7.15
  negligence. *See* NEGLIGENCE
  presumption of requirement, 8.5–8.7
    rebutting, 8.7
  provisions of draft Criminal Code Bill, 6.68
  recklessness. *See* RECKLESSNESS
Mental disability, 9.4–9.40
Misdemeanours, 3.32
Mistake, 7.18–7.33
  bigamy, and, 7.32
  Caldwell-type recklessness, and, 7.24
  defence, and, 7.26–7.33
  duress, and, 7.29
  intoxication, and, 9.59–9.61, 9.66–9.68
  negativing mens rea, 7.19–7.23
  negligence, and, 7.25
  property belonging to another, and, 13.44–13.49
  provocation, and, 11.48
  reasonable, 7.28
  self-defence, and, 22.10
Mistake of law, 6.72–6.74
  exceptions, 6.73
  mistaken belief that conduct is criminal, 6.74
Misuse of drugs, 19.28–19.35
  controlled drugs, 19.28
  corporations, 19.35
  defences, 19.32, 19.33
  position, 19.30, 19.31
    meaning, 19.31
  premises, on, 19.34
  production, 19.29
  supply, 19.29
Morals
  ignorance of, 6.75
Motive, 6.71
  indecent assault, and, 12.20
Murder, 11.21–11.29. *See also* HOMICIDE
  burden of proof, and, 7.3

Murder—*continued*
contemporaneity, 11.27, 11.28
duress, and, 22.23
intent to kill, 11.24, 11.25
intention unlawfully to cause grievous
bodily harm, 11.26
malice aforethought, 11.22, 11.23
proposals for reform, 11.29

Necessity, 122.31
duress of circumstances, 22.33–22.39
limited nature of, 22.37
general defence, whether, 22.33
limited defence, as, 22.34
reasonableness test, 22.36
recognition of the nature of defence, 22.35
reform of law, 22.39
statutory provision for, 22.32
wider defence, whether, 22.38
Negligence, 6.63–6.67
automatism, and, 9.49
exceptional cases, 6.65
meaning, 6.63
mistake, and, 7.25
objective, 6.67
particular element of offence, and, 6.66
state of mind, whether, 6.67
Non-fatal offences against the person, 10.1–
10.27

Obscenity, 19.11–19.22
articles intended for export, 19.18
broadcasts, 19.16
cable programmes, 19.16
films, 19.16
forfeiture, 19.17
Indecent Displays (Control) Act 1981,
19.22
indecent photographs of children, 19.19–
19.21
possession of obscene article, 19.15
publication of obscene article, 19.12
defences, 19.14
"obscene", meaning, 19.13
Obstructing the police, 18.68–18.73
"in the execution of his duty", 18.69
obstruction, 18.70
related offences, 18.73
resistance, 18.72
wilful, 18.71
**Obtaining a pecuniary advantage by decep-
tion,** 14.48–14.52
actus reus, 14.49, 14.50
betting, 14.50
deception, meaning, 14.49
mens rea, 14.51
overdraft, 14.50
remuneration, 14.50
repeal of third type of advantage, 14.52
Obtaining property by deception, 14.27–14.47
actus reus, 14.28–14.38
causation, 14.35–14.38
conduct, 14.29

Obtaining property by deception—*continued*
fact, deception as to, 14.30
intention, deception as to, 14.32
law, deception as to, 14.31
mens rea, 14.39–14.42
omission, deception by, 14.33
reckless, 14.40, 14.41
theft, and, 14.43–14.47
appropriation, and, 14.44, 14.45–14.47
Obtaining services by deception, 14.53–14.55
actus reus, 14.54
mens rea, 14.55
Offences against the person
non-fatal, 10.1–10.27
consent, and. *See* CONSENT
Offensive weapons, 18.85–18.90
actus reus, 18.86
ancillary offence, 18.89
mens rea, 18.87
"without lawful authority or reasonable
excuse", 18.88
Official secrets, 17.9–17.21
acts prejudicial to safety or interests of
state, 17.9, 17.10
authorised disclosure, 17.19
espionage, 17.9, 17.10
jurisdiction, 17.21
"prohibited place", 17.10
prosecution, 17.20
punishment, 17.20
trial, 17.20
unauthorised disclosure, 17.12–17.21
crime and special investigation powers,
17.16
defence, 17.14
information entrusted in confidence,
17.17, 17.18
information resulting from, 17.17
intelligence, 17.13
international relations, 17.15
security, 17.13
Omissions, 6.7–6.14
duty to act, and, 6.10
duty to save another from physical harm,
6.11
contract, under, 6.11
extent of, 6.13
parent and child, 6.11
public office, 6.11
voluntarily undertaking, 6.11
express offences, 6.8
mens rea, and, 6.14
special situations, 6.12
Outraging public decency, 19.23–19.27
actus reus, 19.24
mens rea, 19.25
overlap with other offences, 19.26
prosecution, 19.27
strict liability, 8.3

Participation, 23.1–23.46
consumer protection, and, 23.35
liability for unauthorised acts of another,
23.36–23.46

Perjury, 16.7–16.11
  false unsworn statement under evidence
    other jurisdictions, 16.9
  "lawfully sworn in judicial proceeding",
    16.8
  material statement, 16.8
  mens rea, 16.8
  offences under Act of 1911, 16.11
  subornation of, 16.10
Perpetrators, 23.1, 23.2
  innocent agency, 23.2
Police
  causing wasteful employment of, 16.6
  obstruction of. *See* OBSTRUCTING THE
    POLICE
Possession
  meaning, 19.31
Precedent, doctrine of, 3.6–3.11
  House of Lords, and, 3.8–3.10
  Judicial Committee of the Privy Council,
    3.11
  operation of, 3.7–3.11
Presumptions, 7.10–7.12
  fact, of, 7.12
  law, of, 7.11
Prohibition, 5.36
Proof, 7.1–7.33
  accident, and, 7.16
  general rule, 7.1
  ignorance, and, 7.17
  jury, and, 7.2
  mistake, and. *See* MISTAKE
  presumptions. *See* PRESUMPTIONS
  state of mind, of, 7.13, 7.14
  two burdens, 7.3–7.9. *See also* BURDEN OF
    PROOF
Proper scope of criminal law, 3.29
Prosecutions, 4.1–4.6
  discretion as to, 4.5
  interest of state in, 4.6
  leave to institute, 4.4
  private, 4.3
Provocation, 11.34–11.49
  abolition of reasonable relationship rule,
    11.46
  accused himself must have been provoked,
    11.40, 11.41
  "characteristics" of accused, 11.44
  conduct induced by accused, 11.38
  directed at accused, 11.37
  effect of words or conduct, 11.41–11.46
  judge and jury, function of, 11.47
  mistaken belief, and, 11.48
  need not come from victim, 11.36
  objective test, 11.41–11.46
  reasonable man test, 11.41–11.46
  reform of law, 11.49
  test of, 11.39
Public assemblies, 18.56–18.67
  meaning, 18.64
  offences, 18.65
Public morals, 19.1–19.35

Public nuisance
  strict liability, 8.3
Public order, 18.1–18.90
Public Order Act 1986
  intoxication, and, 9.79
Public or private defence, 22.1–22.15. *See also*
    SELF-DEFENCE
  draft Criminal Code, 22.15
  justification of force, 22.13
  operation of, 22.7–22.9
  reckless driving, and, 22.5
  resisting arrest or detention, 22.12
  wholly innocent person, and, 22.6
Public processions, 18.56–18.67
  advance notice, 18.58
  delegation of chief officer's powers, 18.66
  imposing conditions, 18.60
  meaning, 18.57
  offences, 18.59, 18.61, 18.63
  prohibition, 18.62

Racial hatred, 18.42–18.55
  common features of offences, 18.43
  corporations, offences by, 18.53
  court reports, 18.54
  intended or likely, 18.44
  Parliamentary reports, 18.54
  possession of racially inflammatory
    material, 18.50, 18.51
    mens rea, 18.51
  prosecution, 18.55
  "publishing or distributing", 18.48, 18.49
    mens rea, 18.49
  punishment, 18.55
  racial group, meaning, 18.43
  "threatening, abusive or insulting", 18.45
  trial, 18.55
  use of words or behaviour or display of
    written material, 18.46, 18.47
    mens rea, 18.47
Rape, 12.3–12.8
  actus reus, 12.4–12.6
  alternative verdicts, 12.8
  husband and wife, 12.6
  intoxication, and, 9.56
  mens rea, 12.7
  without consent of woman, 12.5
Recklessness, 6.43–6.53
  accused given thought, where, 6.52
  Caldwell-type, 6.45–6.47
    when sufficient, 6.53
  consequences, as to, 6.54–6.57
  degree of obvious risk, 6.51
  meaning, 6.43
  reason why accused gave no thought, 6.48
  risk obvious to whom, 6.49, 6.50
  subjective, 6.44, 6.46
Reward
  public advertisement of, 14.91
Riot, 18.2–18.11
  actus reus, 18.3–18.9
  conduct such as would cause fear, 18.9
  in pursuance of common purpose, 18.8

Riot—*continued*
mens rea, 18.10, 18.11
twelve or more persons, 18.6
unlawful violence, 18.5
use of unlawful violence, 18.4
"use or threaten unlawful violence", 18.7
Road traffic offences, 20.1–20.38
disqualification, 20.4
driving, 20.6
fixed penalties, 20.5
mechanically propelled vehicle, 20.7
motor vehicle, 20.7
punishment, 20.9
reporting of accidents, 20.3
road or other public place, 20.8
trial, 20.9
warning of prosecution, 20.2
Robbery, 14.2–14.5
force, 14.4, 14.5
theft, need for, 14.3

Sedition, 17.8
Self-defence, 22.1–22.15. *See also* PUBLIC OR
PRIVATE DEFENCE
circumstances, 22.8
conduct of accused, 22.9
draft Criminal Code, 22.15
excessive force, 22.11
intoxication, and, 9.59–9.61
mistake, and, 22.10
objective test, 22.8
prevention of crime, and, 22.3
reasonable force, 22.4, 22.8
Sentence
commital for, 5.21
Sexual intercourse
meaning, 12.2
unlawful. *See* UNLAWFUL SEXUAL INTER-
COURSE
Sexual offences, 12.1–12.36
Ships
offences on board, 6.79
Social morality, 3.22–3.29
acceptance, 3.23
authoritarian view, 3.27
libertarian view, 3.26, 3.28
proper scope of criminal law, and, 3.22–
3.29
rules not enforced by criminal law, 3.24
Sources of Criminal Law, 3.1–3.29
legislation, 3.14–3.21. *See also* LEGIS-
LATION
textwriters, 3.13
Sovereign immunity, 4.9
Specific intent, 6.41
intoxication, and, 9.52, 9.53
State, initiative of, 1.7
State of mind
proof of, 7.13, 7.14
Statutory offences, 3.14–3.18
Stolen goods
meaning, 14.78–14.80

Strict liability, 8.1–8.26
accomplices, and, 23.22
assisting enforcement of law, whether, 8.17
blasphemous libel, 8.3
"cause", 8.11
common law, 8.3
contempt of court, 8.3
criminal libel, 8.3
draft Criminal Code bill, 8.24–8.26
extent of strictness, 8.18
extrinsic factors, 8.13–8.16
justification for, 8.19
"knowingly", and, 8.4
maximum punishment, 8.16
mischief of crime, and, 8.15
"no-negligence" defences, 8.22
outraging public decency, 8.3
"permitting", 8.9
presumption that mens rea required, and,
8.5–8.7
rebutting, 8.7
Prince, 8.2
public nuisance, 8.3
statutory defences, 8.21–8.23
statutory offences, 8.4–8.26
subject-matter of enactment, and, 8.14
"suffering", 8.9
total absence of fault, 8.2
"wilfully", 8.10
wording of other offences in statute, 8.12
words of statute, 8.8–8.12
Subordinate legislation, 3.19
Suicide pacts, 11.32, 11.33
aiding and abetting suicide, 11.33
Summary trial, 5.16–5.21
committal for sentence, 5.21
insanity, and, 9.30
offence triable either way, 5.17
plea, 15.18
procedure, 5.19
sentences, 5.20
Summons, 4.13
Superior orders, 22.40–22.43
reasonable belief, and, 22.40
specific statutory defence, 22.42
unlawful, 22.40–22.43

Taking conveyances without authority, 14.18–
14.25
ancillary offence, 14.25
belief in lawful authority or consent, 14.24
conveyance, 14.19
for the accused or another's use, 14.21
taking, 14.20
without consent or other lawful authority,
14.22, 14.23
Temporary deprivation, 14.16–14.25
removal of article from place open to public, 14.17
taking conveyances without authority,
14.18–14.25. *See also* TAKING CON-
VEYANCES WITHOUT AUTHORITY
Terrorism, 17.6, 17.7

Theft, 13.1–13.66
  actus reus, 13.3–13.50
  appropriation, 13.3–13.19
    accused's state of mind, and, 13.16
    adverse interference with rights of owner, 13.8
    authority, and, 13.6
    bona fide purchaser, 13.17
    consent, and, 13.5, 13.7
    definition, 13.3–13.10
    examples, 13.11–13.13
    obtaining by deception, and, 13.15
    omission, by, 13.18
    person in possession, by, 13.14
    secret dishonest intention, 13.12
    specific property, 13.19
    time of, 13.3
  dishonesty, 13.52–13.59
    claim of right, 13.53
    honest finder, 13.53
    jury, role of, 13.54, 13.58
    statutory definition, 13.56–13.58
    willingness to pay, and, 13.59
  electricity, 13.22
  elements, 13.2
  handling, overlap with, 14.77
  intention of permanently depriving, 13.60–13.66
    borrowing, and, 13.60–13.61
    circumstances equivalent to outright taking or disposal, 13.63, 13.64
    conditional intention, 13.65
    conduct, and, 13.60
    intention to treat thing as own, 13.62
  land and things forming part of it, 13.23, 13.24
  mens rea, 13.51–13.66
  obtaining property by deception, and. *See* OBTAINING PROPERTY BY DECEPTION
  "other intangible property", 13.20
  property, 13.20–13.26
  property belonging to another, 13.27–13.37
    "control", 13.33
    corporation sole, 13.50
    mistake, and, 13.44–13.49
      civil law rule, and, 13.48
      equity, and, 13.44, 13.45
      legal obligation to make restoration, and, 13.46
    more than one person, 13.35
    ownership and possession, 13.28–13.32
    possession, 13.29
      bailee, 13.41
      obligation, 13.42
      trustee, 13.41
    property received under obligation to retain and deal in particular way, 13.39–13.43
    "proprietary right or interest", 13.34
    special cases, 13.37
    spouses, 13.36
    trusts, 13.38

Theft—*continued*
  "thing in action", 13.20
  wild creatures, 13.25, 13.26
Theft Act 1968
  overlap with Act of 1978, 14.68
Theft Act 1978
  overlap with Act of 1968, 14.68
Threatening, abusive, insulting or disorderly conduct, 18.20–18.41
  actus reus, 18.34–18.38
  defences, 18.40
  fear or provocation of violence, 18.21–18.31
    actus reus, 18.22–18.26
    causation, 18.30
    distribution or display of writing, 18.24
    mens rea, 18.27–18.29
    overlap of offences, 18.31
    public or private place, 18.26
    "threatening, abusive or insulting" 18.23
    towards another . . . or to another, 18.25
  harassment, alarm or distress, 18.32
    meaning, 18.36, 18.37
  mens rea, 18.39
  public or private places, 18.38
  "threatening, abusive, insulting or disorderly", 18.34
  victim, need for, 18.35
Tort law
  purpose of, 1.3
Treason, 17.1–17.5
  aid and comfort to enemy, 17.4
  "compassing the King's death", 17.2
  duress, and, 22.25
  levying war, 17.3
  who can commit, 17.5
Trespass. *See* ENTERING AND REMAINING ON PROPERTY
Trial, 5.1–5.22
  juveniles, of, *See* JUVENILES
  summary. *See* SUMMARY TRIAL
Trial on indictment, 5.1–5.15
  arraignment, 5.5–5.7
  conduct of case, 5.10, 5.11
  jury, 5.8, 5.9
  pre-trial review, 5.3
  summing up, 5.12
  time limits, 5.4
  verdict, 5.13–5.15
Trusts law
  purpose of, 1.3

Unfitness to be tried, 9.5–9.11
  magistrates' courts, 9.11
  persons committed to Crown Court, 9.5–9.10
  unfit to stand trial, 9.7–9.10
  urgent need for treatment: transfer direction by Home Secretary, 9.6
Unincorporated associations, 9.91
Unlawful sexual intercourse, 12.9–12.13
  defective, with, 12.12
  girls under 16, 12.13
  procuring, 12.10, 12.11

Venire de novo, 5.33
Verdict, 5.13–5.15
  insanity, and, 9.24–9.27
Vicarious liability, 23.36–23.46
  delegation, and, 23.39, 23.40
  exceptions to general rule, 23.37
  extensive construction of statutes, 23.38
  justification, 23.45
  liability of employee or delegate, 23.42
  statutory defences, 23.44
  "within scope of employment or authority", 23,41

Violent disorder, 18.12–18.14
  actus reus, 18.13
  mens rea, 18.14

Wounding, 10.18–10.27
  draft Criminal Code, 10.27
  section 18, 10.23–10.26
    actus reus, 10.24
    mens rea, 10.25, 10.26
  section 20, 10.19–10.22
    actus reus, 10.20, 10.21
    mens rea, 10.22